# THE BLACKWELL HANDBOOK OF STRATEGIC MANAGEMENT

## Handbooks in Management

Donald L. Sexton and Hans Landström
*The Blackwell Handbook of Entrepreneurship*

Edwin A. Locke
*The Blackwell Handbook of Principles of Organizational Behavior*

Martin J. Gannon and Karen L. Newman
*The Blackwell Handbook of Cross-Cultural Management*

Michael A. Hitt, R. Edward Freeman and Jeffrey S. Harrison
*The Blackwell Handbook of Strategic Management*

Mark Easterby-Smith and Marjorie A. Lyles
*The Blackwell Handbook of Organizational Learning and Knowledge Management*

Henry W. Lane, Martha L. Maznevski, Mark Mendenhall, and Jeanne McNett
*The Blackwell Handbook of Global Management*

Arne Evers, Neil Anderson and Olga Voskuijl
*The Blackwell Handbook of Personnel Selection*

# THE BLACKWELL HANDBOOK OF STRATEGIC MANAGEMENT

*Edited by*

MICHAEL A. HITT
*Arizona State University*

R. EDWARD FREEMAN
*University of Virginia*

JEFFREY S. HARRISON
*University of Central Florida*

© 2001, 2005 by Blackwell Publishing Ltd
Editorial apparatus and arrangement © 2001, 2005 by Michael A. Hitt, R. Edward Freeman, and Jeffrey S. Harrison

BLACKWELL PUBLISHING
350 Main Street, Malden, MA 02148-5020, USA
9600 Garsington Road, Oxford OX4 2DQ, UK
550 Swanston Street, Carlton, Victoria 3053, Australia

First published 2001
First published in paperback 2005 by Blackwell Publishing Ltd

1   2005

*Library of Congress Cataloging-in-Publication Data*

The Blackwell handbook of strategic management / edited by Michael A. Hitt, R. Edward Freeman, and Jeffrey S. Harrison.
      p.  cm. — (Handbooks in management)
Includes bibliographical references and index.
ISBN 0-631-21860-2 (hbk : alk. paper) — ISBN-10: 0-631-21861-0 (pbk : alk. paper)
     1. Teams in the workplace.  I. Hitt, Michael A.  II. Freeman, R. Edward, 1915–.
III. Harrison, Jeffrey S.  IV. Series.
  HD30.28 .B592  2001
  658.4'012—dc21

                2001000957

ISBN-13: 978-0-631-21860-9 (hbk : alk. paper) — ISBN-13: 978-0-631-21861-6 (pbk : alk. paper)

A catalogue record for this title is available from the British Library.

Set in 10 on 12 pt Baskerville
by Ace Filmsetting Ltd, Frome, Somerset
Printed and bound in the United Kingdom
by TJ International, Padstow, Cornwall

The publisher's policy is to use permanent paper from mills that operate a sustainable forestry policy, and which has been manufactured from pulp processed using acid-free and elementary chlorine-free practices. Furthermore, the publisher ensures that the text paper and cover board used have met acceptable environmental accreditation standards.

For further information on
Blackwell Publishing, visit our website:
www.blackwellpublishing.com

# Contents

# Figures

# Tables

# Contributors and Editors

**Asli M. Arikan**
*Ohio State University*

**Jay B. Barney**
*Ohio State University*

**Donald D. Bergh**
*Pennsylvania State University*

**Philip Bromiley**
*University of Minnesota*

**Sayan Chatterjee**
*Case Western Reserve University*

**Cynthia S. Cycyota**
*University of Texas*

**Gregory G. Dess**
*University of Kentucky*

**Walter J. Ferrier**
*University of Kentucky*

**Charles J. Fombrun**
*New York University*

**R. Edward Freeman**
*University of Virginia*

**Daniel R. Gilbert, Jr.**
*Gettysburg College*

**Kathryn R. Harrigan**
*Columbia University*

**Jeffrey S. Harrison**
*University of Central Florida*

**Michael A. Hitt**
*Arizona State University*

**Robert E. Hoskisson**
*University of Oklahoma*

**Lawrence G. Hrebiniak**
*University of Pennsylvania*

**Andrew C. Inkpen**
*American Graduate School of International Management*

**R. Duane Ireland**
*University of Richmond*

**Richard A. Johnson**
*University of Missouri-Columbia*

**Gareth R. Jones**
*Texas A & M University*

**William F. Joyce**
*Dartmouth College*

**Barbara Keats**
*Arizona State University*

**Gerald Keim**
*Arizona State University*

**Idalene F. Kesner**
*Indiana University*

**Peter J. Lane,**
*Arizona State University*

**Jeanne M. Liedtka**
*University of Virginia*

**Michael H. Lubatkin**
*University of Connecticut*

**G. T. Lumpkin**
*University of Illinois at Chicago*

**John McVea**
*University of Virginia*

**Kent D. Miller**
*Purdue University*

**Hermann Ndofor**
*University of Maryland*

**Paul Nutt**
*Ohio State University*

**Hugh M. O'Neill**
*University of North Carolina*

**Richard L. Priem**
*University of Wisconsin – Milwaukee*

**Devaki Rau**
*University of Minnesota*

**Saras D. Sarasvathy**
*University of Washington*

**William S. Schulze**
*Case Western Reserve University*

**Mark A. Shadur**
*Pennsylvania State University*

**Ken G. Smith**
*University of Maryland*

**Scott A. Snell**
*Pennsylvania State University*

**Stephen Tallman**
*University of Utah*

**S. Venkataraman**
*University of Virginia*

**William P. Wan**
*American Graduate School of International Management*

**Patrick M. Wright**
*Cornell University*

**Daphne Yiu**
*University of Oklahoma*

# Acknowledgments

Every attempt has been made to trace copyright holders. The editors and publishers would like to apologize in advance for any inadvertent use of copyright material. Acknowledgments are presented in entry order.

Table 1.4 reprinted from *Beyond Productivity: How Leading Companies Achieve Superior Performance by Leveraging their Human Capital*. Copyright © 1999 Gregory G. Dess and Joseph C. Picken. Used with permission of the publisher, AMACOM, a division of the American Management Association International, New York, NY. All rights reserved. http://www.amacombooks.org

Figure 1.1 reprinted from *Beyond Productivity: How Leading Companies Achieve Superior Performance by Leveraging their Human Capital*. Copyright © 1999 Gregory G. Dess and Joseph C. Picken. Used with permission of the publisher, AMACOM, a division of the American Management Association International, New York, NY. All rights reserved. http://www.amacombooks.org

Table 2.2 from Nutt, P. C. and Backoff, R. W., 1992, *The Strategic Management of Public and Third Sector Organizations*, © 1992 Jossey-Bass, San Francisco, California. Reprinted by permission of Jossey-Bass Inc., a subsidiary of John Wiley & Sons, Inc.

Figure 6.2 reprinted from *Academy of Management Executive*, Volume 10, Second Edition by Harrison and St. John. Copyright © 1996 by ACAD of MGMT. Reproduced with permission of ACAD of MGMT via Copyright Clearance Center.

Table 6.1 adapted from *Academy of Management Executive*, Volume 10, Second Edition by Harrison and St. John. Copyright © 1996 by ACAD of MGMT. Reproduced with permission of ACAD of MGMT via Copyright Clearance Center.

Figure 21.1 from Baron, D. *Business and its Environment*, Third Edition, © 2000. Upper

Saddle River, NJ: Prentice Hall. Adapted by permission of Pearson Education, Upper Saddle River, New Jersey.

Figure 22.2 from Hrebiniak, L. G. and Joyce, W. F., *Implementing Strategy*, © 1984. New York: Macmillan. Reprinted by permission of Pearson Education, Upper Saddle River, New Jersey.

Figure 22.3 adapted from Joyce, W., Slocum, J. and von Glinow, M. A. (1982). Models of fit in person-situation interaction. *Journal of Occupational Behaviour*, Volume 12. Reprinted by permission of John Wiley & Sons, Inc.

Figure 23.2 reprinted from *Academy of Management Review*, Volume 24, First Edition by Lepak and Snell. Copyright © 1999 by ACAD of MGMT. Reproduced with permission of ACAD of MGMT via Copyright Clearance Center.

# Introduction

A few years ago, Ed Freeman began a dialogue with Blackwell Publishers regarding the creation of a handbook on strategic management to complement Blackwell's impressive Handbook series. These early discussions led to the formation of our editorial team. Shortly after signing a contract, we began soliciting original chapters from the top scholars in the field. Our primary criterion was "If we were creating the ultimate Ph.D. seminar on strategic management as a series of guest speakers, whom would we invite?" However, there are a number of outstanding candidates and thus we had to make difficult decisions regarding whom to invite to participate. Authors were invited to write chapters on their own particular specialties and encouraged to express their own opinions. We did not want to make the *Handbook* a "plain vanilla," objective review of research. Rather, we wanted to tap some of the brightest minds in the field and allow them the freedom to approach their topics in their own way.

These fine authors surpassed our expectations. They wrote chapters that provide an excellent background on their topics, explained from their own unique perspectives. However, these chapters also contain new ideas that have the potential to guide research for many years to come. We believe that this volume will be attractive for Ph.D. programs and students in strategic management as well as related disciplines in management, marketing, finance, economics, and business and society. Advanced Master's degree students will also find it to be a highly useful resource. Researchers will find value in reading the *Handbook*, because it contains many new ideas, and will also serve as a ready reference over the long term. Finally, we believe that this volume will appeal to "thinking" managers who are interested in achieving a higher level of understanding of managing their organizations strategically.

The *Handbook of Strategic Management* is divided into five parts: Origin and Process, Theoretical Foundations, Strategy Types, Human Factors, and Teaching Methods. The Origin and Process part includes three chapters that deal with the strategic management process. In "Emerging Issues in Strategy Process Research," Gregory G. Dess and G. T. Lumpkin focus on how understanding the multidimensional nature of strategy-making processes can advance both normative and descriptive theory. Given the normative orientation of the strategic management field, they propose variables such as strategy, environment and stage of organizational development that moderate the relationship between the strategy-making process and performance. They discuss how strategy processes can help managers to combine and leverage resources for competitive advantage, especially in the knowledge economy. In "Strategic Decision Making," Paul Nutt explores research and develops propositions dealing with how decisions are made in organizations, what causes failure, and how to improve the prospects of success. Paul divides his analysis into developmental and non-developmental categories, which he argues is critical to determining the factors that lead to successful decisions. Finally, Jeanne M. Liedtka, in her chapter entitled, "Strategy Formulation: The Roles of Conversation and Design," defends the centrality of strategic thinking to successful strategic management, highlights the relationship of strategy to change and describes the role of planning in the process of strategy formulation. As she addresses these three often intersecting themes, she introduces the roles of strategic conversations and design.

The second part provides a theoretical groundwork for the field of strategic management. In the first chapter, "Strategic Flexibility in the Old and New Economies," Kathryn R. Harrigan reviews research on strategic flexibility, which is concerned with managing the uncertainty of suboptimal strategic postures. In old economy settings, she argues, mismatches typically developed between competitive success requirements and asset configurations – particularly involving tangible assets within capital-intensive industries. In new economy settings, intangible assets are increasingly germane, due to the differing success requirements of industry settings that value competition based on speed, specialization, and customization. In "The Resource-Based View: Origins and Implications," Jay B. Barney and Asli M. Arikan begin with a thorough summary of the theoretical origins of the resource-based view (RBV). They describe how the RBV differs from other explanations of persistent firm performance, summarize major empirical tests of the RBV and discuss unresolved issues and practical implications. The third chapter in this section, "A Stakeholder Approach to Strategic Management" by R. Edward Freeman and John McVea, provides a historical perspective on how the stakeholder view developed and why it is important to understanding strategic management. They conclude that a stakeholder orientation is essential to understanding how organizations behave and why some are more successful than others.

Two theoretical perspectives that have received significant attention in the strategic management literature are transaction cost theory and agency theory. Gareth R. Jones, in "Towards a Positive Interpretation of Transaction Cost Theory: The Central Roles of Entrepreneurship and Trust," offers a critique of transaction cost theory (TCT) that reappraises the theory's basic assumptions. Arguing for a positive, humanistic interpretation of the human factors in the model, the paper argues that the postulates of opportunism and bounded rationality should be replaced with those of trust and entrepreneurship. Based on this critique, a positive interpretation of TCT and of the emergence of organizational hierarchies is offered and a model of the value creation process is described. In "A Strategic Management Model of Agency Relationships in Firm Governance," Michael H. Lubatkin, Peter J. Lane and William S. Schulze concisely review assumptions underlying the agency model and question its relevance in four broad contexts. Based on these four domain-specific critiques, they present suggestions for developing a more general agency model, one that is consistent with the theory's foundation assumptions and those that ground the field of strategic management.

The Theoretical Foundations part ends with "Risk in Strategic Management Research" by Philip Bromiley, Kent D. Miller and Devaki Rau and "Corporate Reputations as Economic Assets," by Charles J. Fombrun. Bromiley, Miller and Rau provide an overview of the relevant research on risk, with particular emphasis on the concept and measurement of risk, and studies of risk-return relationships. Fombrun examines diverse points of view on corporate reputations, suggests a definition of corporate reputation that recognizes its roots in the perceptions and interpretations of resource-holders, and explores the socio-cognitive processes through which resource providers judge companies by interpreting cues and signals that emanate either directly from companies themselves or indirectly from institutional intermediaries.

Part 3 of the *Handbook* deals with various types of strategy. Ken G. Smith, Walter J. Ferrier, and Hermann Ndofor in "Competitive Dynamics Research: Critique and Future Directions," critically review the competitive dynamics literature in terms of underlying theory, methods and results. Their review reveals that the strongest and most consistent empirical relationships include the negative relationship between action/reaction timing and firm performance and the positive relationship between action/reaction aggressiveness and performance. In "Diversification Strategy Research at a Crossroads: Established, Emerging and Anticipated Paths," Donald D. Bergh argues that diversification strategy is one of the oldest, broadest and most consequential to the field of strategic management. He believes that the literature on diversification strategy has arrived at an important crossroads, and that researchers can contribute to this research through any of a variety of paths. Extending the diversification literature into tactics that are used to achieve diversification, Michael A. Hitt, R. Duane Ireland and Jeffrey S. Harrison, in "Mergers and Acquisitions: A Value Creating or Value Destroying Strategy," point out that although mergers and acquisitions continue to grow in volume and size, many of them fail. They describe several factors that can lead to success or failure in the M&A process. Andrew C. Inkpen, in "Strategic Alliances," provides a thorough review of the recently popular idea of competing through alliances. He considers the strategic alliance literature and the rationale for alliances, alliance performance and instability, alliance learning, issues of trust, control, and evolution.

While mergers and acquisitions and strategic alliances can lead firms into new businesses, many firms are now restructuring to reduce the scope of their operations, especially in the US and other developed economies. According to Robert E. Hoskisson, Richard A. Johnson, Daphne Yiu, and William P. Wan, in "Restructuring Strategies of Diversified Business Groups: Differences Associated with Country Institutional Environments," this downscoping is a result of poor performance of highly diversified firms. However, in developing economies, highly diversified firms may perform important functions that substitute for what might be called a "soft infrastructure" (i.e., laws, regulatory bodies, and financial intermediaries that facilitate the transactional environment) that exists in more developed economies. The international theme continues as the third part ends with "Global Strategic Management" by Stephen Tallman. Through a review of the global strategy literature, Tallman helps readers understand how international business and strategy support each other and where they differ. He examines the roots of international strategy in international economics and follows its development as different theoretical concepts have taken primacy in explaining the multinational firm and its strategic actions.

The fourth part deals with human factors in strategic management. Richard L. Priem and Cynthia S. Cycyota discuss leadership from an interesting perspective in "On Strategic Judgement." They note that strategic choice has been identified as the defining attribute of strategic management and that executive judgments – good or bad – must be formed before strategic choices can be made. Understanding the judgments of strategic leaders is essential to determining how mental processes are manifest in the strategies they develop and how these processes and strategies affect firm performance. In the second chapter of the section, "Organizational Structure: Looking Through a Strategy Lens," Barbara Keats and Hugh M. O'Neill examine the research in organization theory that informs strategic management research. They carefully trace the evolution of ideas about strategy, structure and performance from Weber to the present. In "Corporate Governance," Sayan Chatterjee and Jeffrey S. Harrison provide a foundation of understanding of corporate governance and then use that foundation to argue that the influence of governance is particularly important during periods of organizational crisis. This idea is developed in the context of a failed takeover attempt.

Part 4 continues with two chapters that apply the business and society literature to strategic management. Daniel R. Gilbert, Jr., in "Corporate Strategy and Ethics, as Corporate Strategy Comes of Age," surveys contemporary thinking about corporate strategy and ethics as a useful pairing. He also traces the development of ethical criticism of the concept of corporate strategy. Gerald Keim, in "Business and Public Policy: Competing in the Political Marketplace," envisions a marketplace for political power that largely mirrors the market for goods and services. The chapter argues that political strategy should be an active part of the firm's enterprise strategy, its strategy for attempting to influence the uncontrollable aspects of its environment.

In the sixth chapter of the human factors section, Lawrence G. Hrebiniak and William F. Joyce argue that, in spite of much discussion about the importance of strategy implementation, it is still a neglected area in the literature of strategic management. In "Implementing Strategy: An Appraisal and Agenda for Future Research," they note that, as a result of difficulties in doing research on implementation, even a cursory review of published research reveals the clear emphasis on strategy formulation issues. They provide guidance to researchers regarding how to develop meaningful theory on the topic. In the next chapter "Human Resources Strategy: The Era of Our Ways," Scott A. Snell, Mark A. Shadur and Patrick M. Wright discuss human resources in the context of history by examining the primary competitive challenges faced by firms in the past and how those influenced the concept of human resources. They also look at the accepted concepts and models that define human resources strategy and discuss their connection to the extant literature on strategic management. They point out that a key objective of HR strategy is to guide the process by which organizations develop and deploy human, social, and organizational capital to enhance their competitiveness. The final chapter in the human factors section is "Strategy and Entrepreneurship: Outlines of an Untold Story" by S. Venkataraman and Saras D. Sarasvathy. They describe entrepreneurship and strategy as fields that together seek to describe, explain, predict, and prescribe how value is discovered, created, captured, and perhaps destroyed. Consequently, these fields have much to learn from each other and are, in a sense, two sides of the same coin: the coin of value creation and capture.

Many scholars in the field not only conduct research in strategic management, but also teach it. Idalene F. Kesner at Indiana University has a reputation as an excellent teacher. Consequently, we invited her to share with us the secrets of her success. She did so in a chapter entitled, "The Strategic Management Course: Tools and Techniques for Successful Teaching." Much of the chapter focuses on effective use of cases in the classroom, but other tools and techniques are described as well.

We are indebted to the many people who helped make this project possible. First, we are grateful to the authors for doing such excellent work. Their work published in this volume shows why they are well known and widely respected. We thank all of them for their outstanding work. We thank the following doctoral students, Anke Arnaud, Jie Guo, Linda Isenhour, Mike McCardle and Nacef Mouri, for providing input on early drafts of many of the chapters. We are grateful to our wives and our children for their support and patience as we spent many hours away from them working on this *Handbook*. Finally, we would like to thank our Blackwell friends who helped bring this work to completion.

Michael A. Hitt
R. Edward Freeman
Jeffrey S. Harrison

# Part I

## ORIGIN AND PROCESS

# 1

# Emerging Issues in Strategy Process Research

## Gregory G. Dess and G. T. Lumpkin

Strategy-making processes (SMP) are organizational-level phenomena involving key decisions made on behalf of the entire organization. Strategic processes encompass a wide range of topics including analysis, planning, decision making and many aspects of an organization's culture, vision and value system (Hart, 1992). These diverse interests have contributed to a broad array of strategy process research. Over two decades ago, Bourgeois (1980) articulated the distinction between strategy process and strategy content. He suggested that strategy processes represent a unique domain that addresses the question of "how" strategy is enacted, in contrast to strategy content that addresses the question of "what strategy."

Despite the vast body of literature that has emerged since Bourgeois' (1980) article, there is still a lack of coherence to the theoretical and empirical contributions. For example, Rajagopalan, Rasheed, and Datta (1993) note that "the absence of such integrative models has resulted in process research remaining fragmented, characterized by limited theory building and empirical testing" (p. 350). Similarly, Pettigrew laments that "Strategic process research has been narrow in focus and its undoubted contribution has been obscured by the lack of explicit discourse about its analytical foundations" (1992: 5). Such a lack of integration, however, is viewed by many as a major strength and attraction of the strategic management field because its multidisciplinary nature draws on disciplines such as economics, sociology, behavioral sciences, marketing, finance, and so on. This certainly adds to the richness of both theory construction and research methodologies.

Given the broad and diverse nature of strategy process research, our goal is not to review and integrate multiple streams of literature. Instead, after briefly reviewing several key research contributions in two important areas of strategic process research, we focus on a third stream of the strategy-making process literature. We show how prior SMP scholarship is often cumulative and leads to the creation of new knowledge about strategy making. In our examples, we demonstrate how this growth in new knowledge is the result of relating insights gained from different areas of the field of management and evaluating them in a contingency framework. We also examine how such processes may be related to organizational performance and influence and are influenced by a broad array of internal and external organizational factors. In this way, our hope is to provide an in-depth analysis of the multidimensional nature of strategy making by illustrating how such elements combine to form a given strategic decision process.

The remainder of this chapter consists of five sections. In the next section we review three different ways in which the topic of strategic processes has been addressed in prior research. The first two of these include strategic decision making and strategic change. We briefly describe the historical roots of these views and several of the key scholarly contributions in these important areas. Then, we introduce a third area of strategic process research which is developed in depth in the succeeding sections.

In the second section, we outline the stream of strategy-making process (SMP) literature that led to our development of the entrepreneurial orientation (EO) construct. In addition to our initial paper that endeavored to integrate concepts and suggest possible hypotheses (Lumpkin and Dess, 1996), we also discuss empirical research that explored factors (e.g., environment, strategy) that moderate the EO–performance relationship. These include entrepreneurial orientation as a unidimensional construct (Dess, Lumpkin, and Covin, 1997) and as a multidimensional construct (Lumpkin and Dess, 2001) in which two subdimensions of EO – proactiveness and competitive aggressiveness – are hypothesized to vary independently rather than covary. We also include a discussion of the role of contingency and configurational models in more accurately predicting firm performance.

In the third section, we direct our attention to the conceptual development of the simplicity construct. Simplicity in strategy making refers to a single-minded focus on a narrow range of activity or a preoccupation with a single strategic goal or method. Here, we discuss how the work of scholars such as Hart (1991, 1992), Miller (1993), and Miller and Chen (1993) were salient in clarifying the simplicity construct. We also explore the role of stage of organizational development and environment in the strategy-making process by testing them as moderators of the simplicity–performance relationship (Lumpkin and Dess, 1995).

The fourth section addresses the role of strategic decision processes in improving organizational performance in the knowledge economy. We draw on the first author's work with Joseph Picken (Dess and Picken, 1999) and suggest how, among other things, strategy processes can play a key role in combining and leveraging resources, including human and social capital. As noted often in the strategic process literature, we find that it is important for organizations to look beyond their boundaries to all factors of production that may enhance supplier, customer, and alliance partner capital.

In the final section, we briefly summarize the chapter.


## STRATEGY MAKING, DECISION MAKING, AND CHANGE

Strategy making is a process that involves the range of activities that firms engage in to formulate and enact their strategic missions and goals. Strategic processes refer to the methods and practices organizations use to interpret opportunities and threats and make decisions about the effective use of skills and resources (Shrivastava, 1983). As these broad descriptions suggest, the study of strategy making includes a wide range of literature covering nearly half a century of scholarly inquiry. Numerous themes are evident in this literature, in part because the subject draws on knowledge from several fields of study including economics, sociology, and the behavioral sciences. As applied to the field of management, a review of the strategic process literature indicates that three prominent "streams" of research are evident. In this section, we will very briefly introduce two of these streams.

The first of these streams emphasizes the role of decision making in strategic processes. A key impetus for much of this research is a discussion from studies of management that first began to appear in the 1950s about the comprehensiveness of decision-making processes versus the problem of bounded rationality. Although a rational, linear, and comprehensive approach to strategy making has been considered by some to be "ideal" (e.g., Andrews, 1971; Hofer and Schendel, 1978), it has been challenged by others who consider it to be unattainable. Simon (1957) and Cyert and March (1963) were among the early theorists to argue that there are simply too many alternatives with incalculable possible outcomes to engage in purely rational decision making; rationality is, by necessity, "bounded" by the decision makers' cognitive limitations. This view was generally supported by authors such as Bower (1970) and Allison (1971) whose study of the Cuban missile crisis found that, in practice, outcomes typically diverge from the rational ideal because of organizational constraints and bureaucratic politics. Subsequently, other theorists suggested more realistic approaches such as Quinn's (1980) logical incrementalism and Mintzberg's adaptive model (1973, 1978), both of which suggest that decisions are best made in small steps that take into consideration ever-changing events.

From this starting point, some of the decision-making literature branched into the type of strategy making described above, but another branch was concerned with group decision-making processes and how different techniques and the characteristics of group members affected outcomes. Three key techniques have been explored extensively: devil's advocacy, dialectical inquiry, and consensus (e.g., Dess, 1987; Schwenk, 1984; Schweiger, Sandberg, and Ragan, 1986). Other aspects of this research have involved the characteristics of senior managers engaged in strategic decisions (e.g., Hitt and Tyler, 1991) and the speed of decision making (e.g., Eisenhardt, 1989), but most of this literature stream examines decision making as an organizational behavior issue, that is, how the group decision process interfaces with strategic outcomes.

The second stream of research that addresses strategic process issues refers to the role of strategic decision-making in bringing about change. The emphasis here is on change processes and the focus of many studies is on change management, organizational development and, in the context of entrepreneurship, the process of emergence. One of the champions of this perspective is Van de Ven who writes that this approach to strategic processes "takes an historical developmental perspective, and focuses on the sequences of incidents, activities, and stages that unfold over the duration of a central subject's existence" (1992: 170). This approach has been investigated by authors such as Scott (1971) and Greiner (1972) whose analysis of stages of organizational growth includes processes for resolving difficulties at each crisis point in the development of a firm. Strategic change often involves recognition, search, and evaluation processes that occur in an "unstructured" fashion and lead to unanticipated decisions (Mintzberg, Raisinghani, and Theoret, 1976). In the field of entrepreneurship, the emphasis on change processes can be found in research aimed at understanding the emergence of new firms (e.g., Katz and Gartner, 1988) and also in the processes whereby internally generated new ventures develop into new strategic initiatives in the context of corporate entrepreneurship (e.g., Burgelman, 1983).

Clearly, concepts from these two streams of literature are relevant to strategic processes and such research makes important contributions to the development of both descriptive and normative theory. An emphasis on effective decision making and ongoing change processes in strategic management may be critical for firms to succeed in today's fast-paced, global environment. Although these streams of literature are not central to our paper, many other scholars draw on this important work.

To understand the basis of the decisions and actions of managers, a third stream of research has addressed strategy making in terms of patterns of action or gestalts that can be identified and characterized across organizations. These gestalts are often described as "dimensions" or "modes" that reflect coherent approaches to strategy making at the organization level (Hart, 1992; Miller and Friesen, 1978; Mintzberg, 1973). Additionally, a central aim of these strategy-making processes is to obtain congruency or fit with key variables in order to achieve desired outcomes and strong performance. Thus, such processes are impacted by a wide array of contingencies both within and outside an organization's boundaries. In the two sections that follow, we develop these concepts in greater depth and endeavor to show that we have relied on a coherent stream of strategy-making process research in the development of both the simplicity SMP construct and the EO framework.

## Developing the Entrepreneurial Orientation Concept

The purpose of strategy-making processes is to enact the organization's purposes, sustain its vision and generate wealth. It consists of the organization mindset, decision-making processes and action steps that guide firms toward their desired outcomes. To understand the basis of these decisions and actions, scholars have often addressed strategy making in terms of patterns of action or gestalts that can be observed across many organizations (e.g., Rajagopalan, Rasheed, and Datta, 1993). To investigate these gestalts, many researchers have sought to delineate the elements or components of strategy making. These elements are typically labeled the *dimensions* of strategy making. For example, in his analysis of the effect of organizational structure on strategic decision processes, Fredrickson (1986) identified strategy-making dimensions such as comprehensiveness, proactiveness, rationality, and risk taking. Miller and Friesen (1978) identified eleven different dimensions of strategy making including adaptiveness, analysis, consciousness of strategies, expertise, futurity, integration, innovation, multiplexity (of decisions), proactiveness, risk taking, and attachment to traditions. The purpose of their 1978 study was to identify the "complexes of attributes and relationships" in strategy making associated with organizational success and failure. The strategy-making components identified by Miller and Friesen included various aspects of the planning, decision-making style and organizational mindset that goes into the strategy-making process. In subsequent research, three of the strategy-making dimensions identified in their 1978 study were found to be common among entrepreneurial firms – innovativeness, proactiveness, and risk taking (Miller, 1983; Miller and Friesen, 1982). These insights contributed significantly to the development of the entrepreneurial orientation construct.

The concept of strategy-making dimensions provides a useful framework for discussing an organization's various ongoing efforts to scan, analyze, plan and act in ways that will keep the organization aimed at its goals and correctly positioned in the marketplace. Some researchers have chosen to break down the dimensions of SMP even further by investigating subdimensions (c.f. Ibarra, 1993). But earlier efforts by writers of SMP scholarship tended to combine the dimensions into strategy-making *modes*. The notion of modes perhaps more clearly distinguishes the concept of SMP as an organization gestalt that consists of several elements working together. Mintzberg (1973), who was one of the earliest management scholars to address strategy making in terms of "modes," suggested an *entrepreneurial* strategy-making mode, consisting of decisiveness, opportunity seeking and risk taking, that was especially useful in developing the EO construct. He also suggested three other modes: an *adaptive* mode, in which strategic decisions are driven by stakeholder concerns; a *planning* mode characterized by formal analysis; and a *bargaining* mode for which the aim is to resolve the conflicting goals of key decision makers (Mintzberg, 1973, 1978; Mintzberg, Raisinghani, and Theoret, 1976).

Several other authors have developed typologies of strategy making by relying on multidimensional modes. Hart (1992: 327) proposed an "integrative framework for strategy-making processes composed of five modes: command, symbolic, rational, transactive and generative." Hart's framework is integrative because it highlights the many elements that go into SMP including the role of a firm's top managers, the involvement of organizational members and the interaction of these elements with the firm's vision and existing systems and strategies. Briefly, the *command* mode involves strategy making that is driven by strong leadership and enacted by organizational members who are good followers. The *symbolic* mode also tends to be directed primarily from the top, but the directing force for strategy making is the firm's vision; management's role is to coach and inspire organizational members to attain shared goals. The *rational* mode involves planning and analysis; the role of organizational members is to implement the plan – the role of top management is to maintain control and monitor results. With the *transactive* mode, strategy making is based on learning from an ongoing interactive dialogue with internal and external stakeholders; organizational members are part of the learning process – top management empowers the process. Finally, in the *generative* mode, strategy making occurs because of initiative, experimentation and "intrapreneuring" by organizational members at all levels.

Although none of the modes proposed by Hart is purely entrepreneurial, Hart suggests that his modes are not mutually exclusive and can be combined into distinct SMPs. Consistent with this insight, our prior research has suggested that both the command mode and the generative mode include aspects of entrepreneurial strategy making (Dess, Lumpkin, and Covin, 1997). The command mode represents the opportunity seeking and assertiveness suggested by Mintzberg's (1973) entrepreneurial strategy-making mode. The generative mode emphasizes the kind of autonomy, risk taking and experimentation often associated with internal corporate venturing (Burgelman, 1983). Thus, Hart's (1992) multidimensional approach to strategy-making processes provides a useful model that was especially valuable in developing the EO framework.

Venkatraman's (1989) concept of strategic orientation draws together the idea of strategic modes with the notion of strategy-making dimensions. His study explores the dimensionality of strategic processes and takes "a more holistic or interconnected perspective" consistent with the idea of multidimensional modes of strategy making. Although the primary purpose of his 1989 study was to investigate the operationalization and measurement of strategic orientations, he also identified *a priori* six different strategic orientations that represent the "means" and "patterns" that are evident in the strategic orientation of most firms. These include *aggressiveness*, a combative posture aimed at growing market share; *analysis*, a problem-solving orientation directed at finding the best solution among alternatives; *defensiveness*, a self-protective stance designed to preserve core domain; *futurity*, a long-term perspective emphasizing research and trend forecasting; *proactiveness*, an opportunity-seeking outlook focused on acting ahead of the competition; and *riskiness*, a tendency to make bold resource allocations in the face of uncertainty.

Venkatraman's emphasis on the gestalt of an "orientation" was useful in our development of the entrepreneurial orientation framework. Additionally, Venkatraman's research empirically supported an important difference between the dimensions of proactiveness and aggressiveness that was vital in our theoretical development of the relationship between these dimensions of EO. Unlike most prior research, we suggested that the dimensions of EO would vary independently under certain conditions rather than covary (Lumpkin and Dess, 1996 – see below). In a study comparing proactiveness and competitive aggressiveness, we found that (1) the two dimensions were negatively related to each other, and (2) proactiveness was positively related to performance, whereas, competitive aggressiveness had no significant relationship to performance (Lumpkin and Dess, 2001). Both of these findings corroborated Venkatraman's 1989 results.

Drawing on these sources of prior SMP research, in Lumpkin and Dess (1996) we developed the entrepreneurial orientation framework, including definitions of the dimensions of EO, and made several theoretical propositions regarding: (1) the relationship between these dimensions, and (2) the relationship of EO to performance. An entrepreneurial orientation refers to the processes, practices and decision-making activities that lead to new entry. It involves the intentions and actions of key players in the generative process of new venture creation. Such new entry may be undertaken by start-ups or established firms and is accomplished by entering new or established markets with new or existing goods or services. An EO consists of five dimensions defined as follows: *innovativeness* refers to a willingness to support creativity and experimentation in introducing new products/services, and novelty, technological leadership and RandD in developing new processes; *risk taking* involves a tendency to take bold actions by venturing into the unknown, borrowing heavily, and/or committing a large portion of resources to ventures with uncertain outcomes; *proactiveness* occurs when a firm has an opportunity-seeking, forward-looking perspective characterized by introducing new products or services ahead of the competition and acting in anticipation of future demand; *competitive aggressiveness* is the intensity of a firm's effort to outperform industry rivals, characterized by a strong offensive posture or aggressive responses to competitor actions; *autonomy* refers to independent action taken by entrepreneurial founders or teams aimed at bringing forth a new venture and carrying it through to completion.

Our analysis also suggested that the dimensions of EO are likely to vary independently rather than covary under certain conditions. This perspective is different from prior scholars such as Covin and Slevin (1989) who referred to EO (which they labeled "entrepreneurial strategic posture") as a "basic unidimensional strategic orientation" (1989: 79). By contrast, we argued that the dimensions of EO might occur in different combinations. For example, a high degree of innovativeness might benefit the first movers in an industry group by enhancing their efforts to introduce novel new products or make technological advances. But later entrants may achieve competitive advantages by taking high risks such as investing heavily in plant and equipment to make large-scale quantities of a product that is primarily imitative (i.e., low in innovativeness). A recent study of 865 healthcare executives that used structural equation modeling to test the proposition that the dimensions of EO tend to vary independently rather than covary found that, as a predictor of firm growth, "the entrepreneurial orientation construct was more robust" than the unidimensional entrepreneurial posture construct (Stetz, et al., 2000). Thus, unique combinations of the subdimensions of EO may provide more precise explanations of the EO–performance relationship. Understanding how the dimensions of EO are related to each other, however, provides only a partial explanation. To more fully specify the EO–performance relationship we now turn to the role of contingency and configuration models that combine the dimensions of EO with other key variables such as environmental and organizational conditions.

## *Entrepreneurial orientation: contingencies and configurations*

A central purpose for studying strategy-making processes is to understand how they contribute to or detract from firm performance. Such processes are rarely predictive of performance in isolation – they occur in the context of both organizational (internal) and environmental (external) forces. Thus, to gain a valid understanding of the SMP–performance relationship, it is important to address these issues in a contingency framework. Rosenberg (1968) suggests that the introduction of a third variable into the analysis of a two-variable relationship (e.g., SMP–performance) helps reduce the potential for misleading inferences and permits a "more *precise* and *specific* understanding" (1968: 100, emphasis in original) of the original two-variable relationship. Numerous studies have investigated the role of strategy making in terms of contingent factors such as organizational structure (e.g., Miller, 1987), environment (e.g., Fredrickson and Mitchell, 1984), decision-making approach (e.g., Schweiger, Sandberg, and Ragan, 1986) and political behavior (e.g., Eisenhardt and Bourgeois, 1988). In fact, evaluating strategy making in terms of the organizational and environmental factors that influence various SMPs and/or the performance outcomes of SMPs is a central issue in several articles that either propose comprehensive models of strategy making (e.g., Hart, 1992) and/or conduct extensive reviews of the SMP literature (e.g., Rajagopalan, Rasheed, and Datta, 1993).

To address such conditions, we proposed a multivariate contingency framework to investigate the EO–performance relationship. In Lumpkin and Dess (1996) we developed a contingency model of the EO–performance relationship that included sets of environmental and organizational conditions that might impact performance. We also provided examples of four different methods for investigating the effects of situational variables on the EO–performance relationship – moderating effects, mediating effects, independent effects, and interaction effects – based on Boal and Bryson (1987). In a later article that analyzed the role of EO in corporate entrepreneurship, we argued that valuable insights can be gleaned by exploring how three separate conceptual domains – strategy, structure, and process – may be combined or uniquely configured with elements of corporate entrepreneurship to affect firm performance (Dess, Lumpkin, and McGee, 1999). Thus, contingency modeling is a vital technique for understanding how an EO functions and contributes to performance.

In some instances, understanding the SMP–performance relationship may involve more elaborate modeling. Beyond the three-variable examples suggested in Lumpkin and Dess (1996) (e.g., EO–environment–performance), prior research suggests that configurational approaches may be needed to understand complex relationships between multiple variables and performance (e.g., Doty, Glick, and Huber, 1993). Organizational configurations or gestalts represent an elaboration of contingency approaches into multivariate combinations that represent complex interrelations that may have more predictive power than bivariate contingencies (Dess, Newport, and Rasheed, 1993). For example, Miller (1988) investigated configurations by examining multiple interactions among key strategy variables and found the highest performance among organizations whose alignment of strategy, structure, and environment were consistent with the normative contingency literature. High performance among firms exhibiting simple bivariate relationships were not supported in Miller's study, but configurations of multiple variables were positively related to performance. In a study of the relationship between entrepreneurial strategy making and performance, we conducted tests of contingency and configuration models involving key strategy and environmental variables (Dess, Lumpkin, and Covin, 1997). Consistent with Miller (1988), we found that high performance among firms exhibiting simple bivariate relationships was not supported. However, multivariate configurations using *both* strategic and environmental variables with entrepreneurial strategy making were stronger predictors of firm performance. Thus, configurations of the dimensions of EO with environmental conditions and organizational factors may provide the strongest indicators of how key variables combine to contribute to or detract from firm performance.

A third area addressed by our previous research considered how configurations of entrepreneurial orientation might relate to the operationalization and measurement of the EO construct (Lyon, Lumpkin, and Dess, 2000). To determine such issues as how the dimensions of EO relate to each other and the conditions under which various dimensions will contribute to strong performance, it is critical to consider the role of effective and accurate measurement. Drawing on prior research into EO and related constructs, we identified three approaches to measurement that seemed most common and useful in the literature. These included *managerial perceptions*, which are gathered via survey and interview data; *firm behavior* which relies on headlines and abstracts to obtain observations; and *resource allocations* which involve archival records such as financial reports and other firm statistics. By considering the specific research question, and depending on issues of practicality such as cost and access, the optimal methods for operationalizing and measuring elements of an entrepreneurial orientation can be determined and implemented. Additionally, by using these techniques in combination, an empirical study can triangulate on key issues to achieve more robust research results.

Table 1.1 summarizes key issues, important findings, and conclusions from several research analyses and empirical studies conducted by the authors.

TABLE 1.1 Entrepreneurial orientation research

| Title/authors | Type | Key topics | Key conclusions/findings |
|---|---|---|---|
| "Clarifying the entrepreneurial orientation construct and linking it to performance" Lumpkin and Dess (1996) | Conceptual | – Definitions<br>– EO dimensions<br>– Contingency framework | The EO construct consists of five dimensions; the dimensions of EO may vary independently rather than co-vary to understand the EO-performance relationship it is necessary to investigate it in a contingency framework. |
| "Entrepreneurial strategy making and firm performance: Tests of contingency and configurational models" Dess, Lumpkin, and Covin (1997) | Empirical: 96 executives from 32 firms | – Measurement of the entrepreneurial strategy-making mode<br>– Moderator hypotheses<br>– Bivariate vs. multivariate approaches | Multivariate configurations of entrepreneurial strategy-making, strategy content and environment were needed to explain the relationship of EO to performance. |
| "Linking corpporate entrepreneurship to strategy, structure and process: Suggested research directions" Dess, Lumpkin, and McGee (1999) | Conceptual | – Contingency framework for CE<br>– Key contingencies<br>– Applying EO to new and traditional strategic patterns | Applying the dimensions of EO to the study of corporate entrepreneurship may reveal patterns of strategy, structure and process that are most likely to contribute to strong performance. |
| "Linking two dimensions of entrepreneurial orientation to firm performance: The moderating role of environment and industry life cycle" Lumpkin and Dess (2001) | Empirical: 124 executives from 94 firms | – Uniqueness of EO dimensions<br>– Relationship of independent dimensions of EO to performance<br>– Role of contingencies in understanding EO–performance relationship | The EO dimensions of proactiveness and competitive aggressiveness (a) are conceptually distinct, (b) do not co-vary and, (c) are differentially related to performance. |
| "Enhancing research into a key strategic decision process: Three approaches to measuring entrepreneurial orientation" Lyon, Lumpkin, and Dess (2000) | Conceptual | – Operationalization and measurement of the EO construct<br>– Measurement issues<br>– Contingency modeling<br>– Triangulation | Three different approaches to measuring EO – managerial perceptions, firm behaviors, and resource allocations – may provide different insights depending on the context and/or may be used together to triangulate in research. |

## *Future research directions*

Future research into the entrepreneurial orientation construct may involve several areas of exploration and empirical testing. First, the role of additional contingencies on the EO–performance relationship is an important area that promises to contribute to a more complete understanding of how EO functions in various settings. In addition to the areas proposed in our original framework such as industry conditions, technological trends, the role of top management and stage of organizational development, later sections of this chapter address "new economy" and knowledge management issues that are affecting the wealth creation process. These conditions provide new contingencies to be evaluated in an EO framework. Such research may also lead to additional construct development, that is, the refinement of the EO construct as a result of new insights from business and contemporary scholarship.

Second, some authors have identified subdimensions of EO that may be investigated to analyze the EO–performance relationship with more precision. For example, Ibarra (1993) distinguished between two types of innovativeness – administrative and techno-logical. Furthermore, in the context of Porter's (1985) value-chain framework, innovation may occur within any of the primary or support activities. When viewing a focal firm as part of an expanded value chain, innovation can also take place in the inter-firm or supply chain activities between the firm and its customers, suppliers or alliance partners. Thus, the degree and type of innovativeness needs to be carefully specified depending on the research context.

Similarly, there can be a variety of perspectives on the dimension of risk taking. These could include, for example, managerial perceptions (Miller and Friesen, 1982; Miller, 1993); financial leverage, that is, the firm's debt-to-equity ratio (Hall and Weiss, 1967; Gale, 1972); income stream variability (Miller and Bromily, 1990); and the level of diversification (Jensen, 1989). The indicators that researchers select to operationalize risk-taking subdimensions can affect both the strength and the directionality of relationships with performance measures. Thus, in research designs that include EO and other strategy-making process dimensions, care must be taken in both developing theory to determine what concepts are to be included and also in the choice of indicator(s) used to measure the concepts in question.

This last point involves another issue that may affect the use of EO subdimensions as well as entrepreneurial orientation research generally. According to Weick, it is not possible for a research framework "to be simultaneously general, accurate, and simple" (1979: 35). The tradeoffs involved in conducting a study generally require that one of these three elements – generalizability, accuracy or simplicity – be sacrificed in the interest of obtaining more conclusive and non-trivial results. The study of EO will inevitably involve such tradeoffs. These issues lead to key questions that may affect EO–performance research in the future: Can specific conclusions about the role of risk taking (or any EO dimension) be made without this level of specificity? Does the additional accuracy that might be achieved by incorporating such subdimensions more than offset the loss of parsimony?

Although such issues may prove problematic, they may, on a positive note, suggest more specific research questions. For example, our study of proactiveness versus competi-tive aggressiveness (Lumpkin and Dess, 2001) was such a study in that it focused on the role of just two dimensions of EO and addressed the question of whether the dimensions tended to covary or vary independently. These and other questions provide a broad array of topics to be considered when investigating the EO framework in the future.

## SIMPLICITY AS A STRATEGY-MAKING PROCESS

Many theorists who study strategy-making processes have argued that SMPs can be identified across organizations (e.g., Mintzberg, 1973, 1978). Thus, for example, an SMP such as "analysis," which refers to an emphasis on research and systematic thought in strategy formulation, can be seen across most of the models discussed above with only slight differences in emphasis – strategy making that Venkatraman (1989) and Miller and Friesen (1978) label "analysis" is referred to as "rational" by Hart (1992) and Fredrickson (1986) and as "planning" by Mintzberg (1973). Some researchers have suggested that the set of organizational processes from which most strategic decisions emerge may be limited (Rajagopalan, Rasheed, and Datta, 1993). Hart (1992) suggests that his framework represents a comprehensive set of "pure" modes of strategy making, but also states that: (1) "organizations may combine two or more modes into distinctive combinations of strategy-making processes" (p. 335), and (2) "firms usually develop competence in several modes" (p. 328). Although not all scholars agree about the nature of strategy-making processes and it is an empirical question whether or not there is a finite set of processes that determine an organization's strategy making, it is clear that unique strategy-making modes continue to emerge under certain organizational and environmental conditions.

Such seemed to be the case when Danny Miller introduced the idea of "simplicity" in a book entitled *The Icarus Paradox* (1990) and an *Academy of Management Review* (*AMR*) article entitled "The architecture of simplicity" (1993). Miller's concept of simplicity can be thought of as a frame of mind or perspective that can negatively affect organizations that become highly successful and overconfident by virtue of pursuing a single strategic objective. In fact, the title *The Icarus Paradox* refers to this problem: when the fabled Icarus of Greek mythology overextends himself by flying too close to the sun, his artificial wax wings melt and he plunges to his death in the Aegean Sea. The paradox is that strong ambition based on a single-minded pursuit can lead to a precipitous fall. According to Miller, this is common among successful organizations as well: an excessive emphasis on the factors that have provided a competitive edge and led to a firm's initial success, such as a specific product-market offering or a highly focused skill set, prompts a firm to use increasingly simplified processes and a narrower repertoire of competitive actions (Miller and Chen, 1993). Such an orientation may affect an organization's strategy-making processes. Thus, the organization develops an "overwhelming preoccupation with a single goal, strategic activity, department or worldview" (Miller, 1993: 117) leading to decisions, values and strategy-making processes that are simplistic. Miller argues that this trend toward simplicity in strategy making can eventually lead to declining performance because of incomplete decision making, failure to evaluate alternatives, and an inability to adapt to changing circumstance or new opportunities. Even though the "problem" of simplicity is the primary thrust of Miller's argument, he also explains that simplicity can be a strong unifying force as well by focusing an organization in a way that consolidates its efforts and can contribute to initial success. Simplicity in strategy making, then, suggests a perspective that may restrict a firm's progress by diminishing its capabilities, or contribute to a firm's success by keeping it focused on specific niches, technologies or product-market relationships.

After carefully reading Miller (1993), we noted that there were many parallels between Miller's concept of simplicity and some of the strategy-making process issues addressed by Hart (1991, 1992). We observed that many aspects of simplicity were suggestive of a particular strategy-making style and surmised that Hart's (1991) strategy-making process scale might capture the major elements of a simplistic approach. Further, we noted that simplicity seemed to be a combination of two of the modes described by Hart (see above). Thus, consistent with Hart and other theorists who have argued that SMPs may be combined (e.g., Shrivastava and Grant, 1985), we began to analyze simplicity as a strategy-making process.

Table 1.2 describes the set of arguments that were developed, first by interpreting simplistic strategy making as a combination of two modes described by Hart, then by linking the simplicity arguments from Miller (1990, 1993) to Hart's 1991 scale. Finally, to test Miller's claim that simplistic strategy making might affect performance differently depending on the circumstances, we developed hypotheses based on a model in which stage of development and environment were moderators (refer to table 1.3). In addition to Miller's *AMR* study, we used an empirical test of the effect of simplicity on competi-tiveness in the airline industry (Miller and Chen, 1993) to develop our hypotheses.

As phase 1 in table 1.2 indicates, we reasoned that simplicity as a strategy-making process combines features of Hart's command and symbolic modes. A command mode often features single-minded focus in the form of steady and clear directives that are articulated by a dominant figure or management group, but that can "mire managers in a single way of seeing and doing things" (Miller, 1993: 122). A symbolic mode relies on a consistent vision to foster "an implicit control system, based on shared values" (Hart, 1991: 109). This vision helps align the efforts of organizational members, but may also create a sort of "one best way" approach that "can bring about oppressive conformity" (Miller, 1993: 122). In combination, these strategy-making modes may create a simplistic SMP.

At the time, we were working with a slightly modified version of Hart's (1991) 25-item instrument. The items that appeared to be related to simplicity in strategy making included the following:

V1. There is a clear blueprint for this organization's strategy that was set some time ago and has changed very little.

V2. There is a clear and consistent set of values in this organization that governs the way we do business.

V3. This organization has a characteristic "management style" and a common set of management practices.

V4. The way we do things in this organization is well suited to the business we are in.

As reported in phase 2 of table 1.2, in the next step of our research, we compared Miller's (1993) descriptions of simplicity with Hart's scale items. Our primary focus was on the process issues related to simplicity but, as is often the case with any organizational gestalt, other variables seemed to support our interpretation. For example, the culture of

TABLE 1.2 Theoretical development of simplicity as a strategy-making process – part 1: construct development

| *Phase 1 – Interpretation of simplistic SMP as a combination of command and symbolic modes* | | |
| --- | --- | --- |
| *Page* | *Hart (1992) cites/quotes* | *Interpretation* |
| 335 | "The five modes are not seen as mutually exclusive. In practice, organizations may combine two or more modes into distinctive combinations . . ." <br><br> "firms usually develop competence in several modes" | Hart consistently suggests that an organization's strategy-making process may result from the combining of his "pure" modes. This is the case with simplicity as an SMP. It can be argued that the simplistic mode is a combination of the symbolic mode and the command mode. |
| 335–6 | In the command mode a central leader or small management group succeeds in imposing their view on the whole organization. "In such a mode, strategies are deliberate, fully formed, and ready to be implemented" | The command mode suggests a highly focused approach in which stratregic decisions are handed down with little debate. As such the pet policies or dominant methods supported by strong leadership become the primary focus of the organization and thus it tends toward simplicity. |
| 340 | "With both the command and generative modes, particular organizational skills and capabilities go underutilized." | Just as the command mode is a less-than-optimal, underutilizing approach, a simplistic SMP is so narrow and focused that organizational resources and talents may be underutilized. |
| 341 | stated again: in the command mode, "skills go underutilized" | |
| 342 | "The command mode should, therefore, function well only in relatively simple situations – a task environment low in complexity." | In terms of key contingencies related to simplicity, a simplistic SMP appears to be more closely aligned with the low complexity, simple situation approach of the command mode rather than the flexible, dynamic approach suggested by the symbolic mode. This suggests further that the simplistic approach, while it may use the symbolic technique of persuading organizational members to closely adhere to the organization's mission, typically applies better in the low variety context suggested by the command mode. |
| 343 | "In a dynamic, high velocity environment, the symbolic mode may hold the key to the speed and flexibility necessary for competitive success." | |

*Phase 1 – continued.*

| Page | Hart (1992) cites/quotes | Interpretation |
|------|--------------------------|----------------|
| 334 | With the symbolic mode of strategy making, "leaders attend primarily to articulating a mission and creating a vision and common perspective that helps guide the actions of organizational members toward a common goal." | The symbolic mode relates to simplicity in that a prevailing culture and established set of values causes organizational members to develop an emotional commitment to an organization. It becomes simplistic, however, when "the culture of the organization comes to focus more narrowly and passionately on one or two pervasive and dominant goals" (Miller, 1993: 122). |
| 337 | "In this way the symbolic mode creates an implicit control system, which is based on shared values. It hinges on the nurturing of a shared perspective for all organizational members, that is, a clear mission, shared values, and an emotionally appealing corporate vision or dream." | There is an emphasis on motivating organizational members to adopt the vision and make the organization's mission a model for their own individual behavior. This creates a sort of "one best way" approach that "can bring about oppressive conformity" (Miller, 1993: 122). |
| 345–6 | "configurations of similar modes should be associated with lower performance. More specifically, proximal modes (those with more similar roles for top managers and organizational members such as the transactive and generative modes) should tend to occur together in lower performing firms." | In Hart's framework, the command and symbolic modes are proximal modes that may lead to lower performance when, in combination, they manifest as simplistic. |

*Phase 2 – Interpretation/analysis of Hart's (1991) scale*

| Page | Miller (1993) cites/quotes | Interpretation |
|------|----------------------------|----------------|
| 121 | Success gives executives "too much confidence in a single way of conducting business or in one dominant element of strategy." | Supports V3 – common set of management practices and V1 – strategy set some time ago and changed very little. |
| 119 | "experienced managers form quite definite opinions of what works and why." | Also supports V4 – the way we do things is well suited to the business we are in. |

122     "the culture of the organization comes to focus more narrowly and passionately on one or two pervasive and dominant goals. Such strong cultures can make work meaningful, can galvanize employees to take action, and can generate tremendous enthusiasm. But they also mire managers in a single way of seeing and doing things. They can bring about oppressive conformity, blindness and intolerance."

Support for V2 – consistent set of values in this organization that governs the way we do business.

Also supports V1 – blueprint set some time ago and changed very little and V4 – the way we do things is well suited to the business we are in.

123–4     Proposition 4: In successful organizations, *values will become more homogeneous*, reducing sub-unit differentiation; *a single department or elite will become more dominant*; and the skill set of the organization will narrow. These changes will contribute to the formation of monolithic cultures and strategies (emphasis added).

Support for V1, V2 and V4 as described above. Also support for V3 – characteristic management style and common set of practices.

124     Section on Structural Factors suggests that routines and established programs make strategies narrower and resistant to change.

Support for V1 – there is a clear blueprint for this organization's strategy that was set some time ago and has changed very little.

127     Section on Process Factors suggests that when decision-making is preprogrammed, "most activities do not take place in response to problems, but rather because policies, strategies, and programs *automatically* generate particular actions" (emphasis in original).

Also suppoort for V3 – a common set of management practices.

129–30     "Organizational configurations are highly thematic. Eventually all aspects of an organization reflect the core set of values, goals and interests . . . They can be likened to dynamic systems whose initial themes establish a characteristic momentum."

Support for V2 – clear and consistent set of values that govern and V3 – characteristic management style and practices.

an organization experiencing simplicity affects many aspects of its strategy-making processes. Overall, we determined that there were strong parallels between Miller's concept of simplicity and simplicity in strategy making as represented by Hart's scale.

Our next task was to relate simplicity to performance. Along with the information described in table 1.2, we interpreted other passages from Miller (1993) as well as an empirical study by Miller and Chen (1993) that suggested how a simplistic SMP might relate to performance and what conditions might impact that relationship. These interpretations are reported in table 1.3. Two key contingencies seemed to be most likely to affect performance. The first was the stage of organizational development. A key point in Miller's research was that simplicity might benefit firms in their early stages of development. The argument was that the kind of single-mindedness and targeted effort characteristic of simplicity might actually benefit either a young firm that needed to focus its efforts or a company with a simple structure (Mintzberg, 1979) that had to leverage a narrow resource base. But as the firm grew and faced more complex situations, it would need to evolve more complex systems as well, consistent with Ashby's (1956) "law of requisite variety." Thus, we hypothesized that firms in their early stages of development would benefit from a simplistic SMP whereas firms in later stages would suffer if they were overly simplistic.

A similar set of arguments and, in particular, the findings of Miller and Chen (1993), led us to two hypotheses about the role of simplicity in dynamic and heterogeneous environments. Miller and Chen had hypothesized that the complexity of heterogeneous environments was a poor match for firms with simple strategies. They found that firms with simple competitive repertoires were poorer performers in environments that were more heterogeneous. In Miller (1993), turbulent environments were also predicted to be problematic for simple firms. In the end, we hypothesized that both heterogenous and dynamic environments would be associated with lower performance in firms with a simple SMP.

Briefly, we conducted our study of simplistic strategy making in two phases (Lumpkin and Dess, 1995). In phase 1, we found that the four items we had identified above from Hart's 25-item scale did load on a single factor based on a factor analysis of the responses of 96 executives from firms competing in 13 different industries. (Three other factors also emerged in the study including participative SMP, innovative SMP, and adaptive SMP). The 96 executives represented 32 firms and, in phase 2, we conducted firm-level analysis using moderated hierarchical regression analysis. The findings supported our hypotheses about the effect of a simplistic SMP on performance in early stages of development: firms in early stages of organizational development benefited from simplicity in strategy making whereas the more established firms that had high levels of simplicity in strategy making had relatively poorer performance. With regard to the environment hypotheses, firms in heterogeneous environments that had relatively higher levels of simplicity in strategy making were found to have lower performance as predicted. The dynamism hypothesis was not statistically significant.

From this review, it is apparent that any given strategy-making process involves an earnest effort to make informed strategic decisions that coalesce the best strategic thinking around a well-researched action plan. It involves a keen awareness of the environment and knowledge of the status of numerous organization factors such as stage of development. From a practitioner's standpoint, it is also apparent that companies have choices in

TABLE 1.3 Theoretical development of simplicity as a strategy-making process –
part 2: hypothesis development

*Phase 1 – Stage of development hypothesis*

| Page | Miller (1993) cites/quotes | Interpretation |
|------|---------------------------|----------------|
| 118 | "Simplicity can initially bring great rewards when it marshals the strengths of an organization to accomplish what it does best." | Miller makes numerous references to the role of simplicity in the "initial" success of an organization. |
| 131 | "Proposition 8: *At first*, increases in all varieties of simplicity will lead to an increase in organizational performance" (emphasis added). | |
| 119 | "this article will present three classes of reasons for this encroaching and dangerous simplicity. First, . . . Third, a troublesome paradox exists: The sources of simplicity may underlie initial success and, thus, be doubly difficult to combat. Indeed, it is very hard to distinguish between the concentration and passionate dedication so necessary for success and competitive advantage and the simplistic fixations and extremes that lead to failure." | The first two classes of simplicity identified by Miller are encroaching simplicity – the simplicity that *results from* success. Our paper, however, primarily addresses the third type – dangerous simplicity – in which simplicity *leads to* success. Although most of Miller's discussion revolves around the simplicity that may encroach on a successful organization, he also addresses the paradox of simplicity whereby simplicity that leads to success may be a danger. |
| 130 | The Icarus paradox for outstanding companies – "the focus and simplicity that ultimately get them into trouble may once have been responsible for their initial successes." | Thus, simplicity may lead to the kind of "concentration and dedication" that makes for success in the early stages of organization development, but later leads to poor performance. |
| 117 | "simplicity implies little variety at a point in time." | Our study suggests that in the early stages of development, variety is low and therefore correctly matched with a simplistic SMP. This is consistent with Ashby's (1956) "law of requisite variety." |

*Phase 1 – continued*

| Page | *Miller and Chen (1993) cites/quotes* | *Interpretation* |
|---|---|---|
| 32 | "Sometimes simplicity will be a cause as well as a product of success." | Whereas Miller and Chen focused on investigating whether "competitive simplicity would develop *from* success" (p. 36 – emphasis added), our study investigated whether simplicity would *lead to* success, that is, be associated with success when used in the initial stages of organizational development. |
| 35 | Referring to Hypothesis 6, the authors investigated the proposition that "as simplicity increases, performance first rises and then declines." | We investigated how simplicity related to performance as a function of stage of organizational development. Our hypothesis was that simplicity would lead initially (in the initial stages) to success but be associated with declining performance in later stages. |

*Phase 2 – Environment hypotheses*

| Page | *Miller (1993) cites/quotes* | *Interpretation* |
|---|---|---|
| 118 | "if an organization were too simple to manage the complexity of its environment, its very survival might be threatened." | Simplicity is portrayed as the "opposite" of complexity. Miller suggests that simplicity in the face of a complex (or heterogeneous) environment not only inhibits performance but may affect a firm's survival. |
| 117 | The "objective" form of simplicity may include "dominance of a single goal or subunit" or the diminishment of a skill set. "But simplicity may also be reflected subjectively, by the narrowing, increasingly homogeneous managerial 'lenses' or world views that often underlie the more objective forms of simplicity." | Drawing on Ashby's (1956) "law of requisite variety," one of Miller's key arguments is that an organization's internal systems must have the same level of variety or heterogeneity as the external environment it faces. If managers become too homogeneous in their outlook, they may be unable to compete in a complex world, leading to poor firm performance. |

132     Proposition 10: Simplicity will be less          If it were to occur at all, a simplistic
        prevalent, even under conditions of              SMP would not likely be associated
        success, where . . . the environment             with successful outcomes under
        is turbulent."                                   conditions of environmental
                                                         dynamism and turbulence. Strategy
                                                         making that is characterized by norms
                                                         and routines is poorly suited for
                                                         environments that require flexibility
                                                         and quick response.

134     "Simplicity might be quite viable in
        stable environments, but it could
        lead to serious mismatches when
        external turbulence occasions the
        need for organizational reorientation."

*Phase 2 – continued*

| Page | Miller and Chen (1993) cites/quotes | Interpretation |
| --- | --- | --- |
| 32 | "In short, simplicity, which serves initially as a powerful competitive tool, may hurt performance in heterogeneous settings or when taken to extremes." | Miller and Chen (1993) found an inverse-U relationship between simplicity and performance: "as simplicity increases, performance first rises and then declines." However, when the interaction of simplicity and heteropgeneity was tested for its relationship to performance, it was found that simplicity was nearly always associated with poor performance. |
| 33 | "simplicity is especially harmful to performance in heterogeneous markets." | |
| 35 | "Diverse markets elicit a broad array of competitive tactics and discourage concentration on a few types of activities." | Even though Miller and Chen's study focused on the simplicity of competitive repertoires rather than simplicity in strategy making, their study provides several insights that may apply to a simplistic SMP. This includes the role of market diversity in contributing to environmental dynamism. Their findings suggest that a simplistic approach would be a poor match for a dynamic environment. |

how they engage in strategic processes. Although cultures, like personalities, are not easily changed, practices can be modified and new processes can be employed to achieve better outcomes as organizational and environmental conditions evolve. Rapid change, the emergence of new markets, intensified levels of innovation, and new applications of information technologies are among the factors that are affecting strategy-making processes in the emerging knowledge economy. It is this important topic that we turn to next.

## THE ROLE OF PROCESSES IN COMBINING AND LEVERAGING RESOURCES

For most of the twentieth century, the primary resources of concern to management were tangible resources such as land, natural resources, and money as well as intangibles including brands, image, reputation, and customer loyalty. (This discussion draws on Dess and Picken, 1999.) The major focus of managerial efforts was directed toward the more efficient allocation of labor and capital – the two key factors of production. However, today more than 50 percent of the Gross Domestic Product in developed economies is knowledge-based, that is, based on intellectual assets and intangible people skills. These include high-profile industries such as telecommunications, computers, software, pharmaceuticals, healthcare, education, and so on (*The Economist*, 1996; Hamel, 1997). As recently noted by Hamel and Prahalad:

> The machine age was a physical world. It consisted of things. Companies made and distributed things (physical products). Management allocated things (capital budgets); management measured things (the balance sheet); management invested in things (plant and equipment). In the machine age, people were ancillary, things were central. In the information age, things are ancillary, knowledge is central. A company's value derives not from things, but from knowledge, know-how, intellectual assets, competencies – all of it embodied in people (1996: 241).

In today's knowledge economy, wealth is increasingly generated through the management of knowledge workers instead of by the efficient control of physical and financial assets. Nowhere is this more evident that in the widening gap between the market capitalizations and book values of today's corporations whose keys to success lie in the effective leveraging of human capital. Consider, for example, the difference in the market value to book value ratios (as of November, 2000) for knowledge-intensive firms such as America Online (20.8), Amazon.com (47.4), Yahoo, Inc. (36.6), and Oracle (52.8) compared to traditional industrial firms with huge investments in physical assets such as General Motors (1.7), Alcoa (3.7) and Boeing (4.7).

As a result, leading-edge firms are recognizing the need to develop cultures, processes, structures, and effective organizational settings in order to combine and leverage individual competencies and talents. To be successful, it is not only the stock of resources that a firm possesses, but the extent to which they are profitably leveraged. Strategy-making processes are also evolving that reflect the heightened need to leverage knowledge assets. This evolution involves several elements including the more effective management and deployment of knowledge capital and networking techniques that enhance the creation of new knowledge. For example, in a 1992 interview, Paul Allaire, Xerox's newly appointed CEO, was asked how he intended to revitalize his firm. He articulated his intent to lead "a company that combined the best of both worlds – speed, flexibility, accountability and creativity that comes from being a part of a small, highly focused organization; and the economies of scale, access to resources, and strategic vision a large company can provide" (Howard, 1992: 109). He claimed his primary objective was to redesign and combine the three essential components of organizational architecture: *the hardware* – organizational structure and formal processes; *the people* – skills, personality and character; and *the software* – "the informal networks and practices linking people together, the value system, the culture" (Howard, 1992: 112). The notion that "informal networks and practices" are the "links" that bring organizations together is an idea that has also been articulated by Hamel and Prahalad. They argue that "the real sources of competitive advantage are to be found in management's ability to consolidate corporate-wide technologies and production skills into competencies that empower individual businesses to adapt quickly to changing opportunities" (Prahalad and Hamel, 1990: 82). Strategic processes, in this context, must enhance a firm's ability to capitalize on its collective strengths and constantly build new ones.

The potential sustainability of advantages created by combining and leveraging resources is also central to the resource-based view of the firm. Barney (1991) and Wernerfelt (1984) have argued that such advantages stem from *unique bundles* of resources that competitors cannot imitate. Typically, such imitation is difficult due to the scarcity, specialization, and tacit knowledge implicit in human assets (Lippman and Rumelt, 1982). By contrast, "physical technology, whether it takes the form of machine tools or robotics or complex information management systems, is by itself typically imitable" (Barney, 1991: 110). As noted by Bogner, Thomas, and McGee (1999), several authors have clarified the link between competitive resources and competitive advantage. For example, Amit and Schoemaker (1993) have distinguished between "resources" as assets that managers deploy and "capabilities," which include skills and competencies within the firm. These authors assert that a key role for managers is to develop (or leverage) the inherent value in these resources. To do so successfully, a fresh approach to strategy making that makes greater use of new knowledge technologies and simultaneously empowers managers to make vital strategic decisions is emerging. This view is reflected in new perspectives on the strategic processes by which competencies and capabilities are managed.

For example, Teece, Pisano, and Shuen (1997) have clarified the difference between "core competence" and "dynamic capabilities" by stressing the ongoing managerial processes involved in continually combining resources for advantage. In their view, dynamic capabilities refer to "firm specific capabilities that can be sources of advantages and . . . [that] combinations of competencies and resources can be developed, deployed and protected" (1997: 510). Spender has also argued that: "So long as we assume markets are reasonably efficient it follows that competitive advantage is more likely to arise from the intangible firm-specific knowledge which enables it to add value to the incoming factors of production in a relatively unique manner" (1996: 46). This emphasis on competencies, capabilities, and the dynamic aspects of strategic processes is central to successfully combining and leveraging the resources of a knowledge-based economy.

Leading companies are also realizing that hiring top-flight talent and creating work environments that support meaningful interactions is a critical step in attaining competitive advantages in an intensely competitive global economy. Beyond simply obtaining strong talent, however, successful strategy making requires that complementary skills and knowledge assets be effectively combined. Peteraf (1993) provides an interesting hypothetical example (embellished by the present authors) of the value inherent in such resource combinations. She discusses two contrasting scenarios in which a firm has hired a brilliant Nobel-prize winning scientist. In one case, the firm provides excellent facilities, financial resources, and so on, and then requires the scientist to essentially work alone. In the other case, the scientist is not only provided with such physical and financial resources, but also is expected to collaborate with other talented scientists. There is little question as to which scenario will lead to more favorable outcomes – clearly, it is in collaboration. Additionally, the collaborative approach would create an environment where the prize scientist would more likely develop firm-specific ties and be less likely to terminate his employment with the organization. Such ties are critical since, as noted by Miller and Shamsie (1996), knowledge-based resources are tacit in nature and cannot easily be protected against unauthorized transfer (as opposed to property-based resources). Capelli (2000) and others have argued that professionals tend to have more loyalty to their immediate workgroup than to their employing organization.

In addition to combining resources within the firm, the use of interorganizational network relationships with suppliers, customers, and alliance partners is also an increasingly common mechanism through which organizations combine and leverage resources (Dyer and Singh, 1998). A wide variety of industries are increasing their reliance on forms of network governance, a means of coordination characterized by informal social systems instead of bureaucratic structures within firms and formal contractual relationships (Powell, 1990; Ring and Van de Ven, 1994; Snow, Miles, and Coleman, 1992). Such governance structures not only serve to lower transaction costs but also are often essential to achieve a high level of coordination of products, services, and technologies in highly uncertain and competitive markets. These efforts take strategy making beyond the traditional corporate boundaries and into interorganizational fields where new rules are shaping the wealth creation process (Jones, Hesterly, and Borgatti, 1997).

## A suggested framework

As noted earlier, there has been a widening gap between the market value and book value of corporations of all sizes in industrialized economies of the world. This gap is more widely pronounced in firms and industries where the relative importance of human capital is high compared to physical and financial assets. Many authors (Stewart, 1997; Edvinsson and Malone, 1997) have used the term *intellectual capital* to characterize the sum of all of the intangible factors that contribute to the gap between market value and book value. This admittedly broad definition includes everything other than tangible assets that contribute to a firm's market value. This would include assets such as employee loyalty and commitment, company values, brand names, trademarks, customer loyalty, and the experience and skills of the employees. *Human capital*, on the other hand, is typically viewed as consisting of the individual skills, knowledge, and capabilities that are relevant to the task at hand, as well as the capacity to add to this base of knowledge. *Organizational knowledge* consists of the firm's legally protected information (e.g., patents

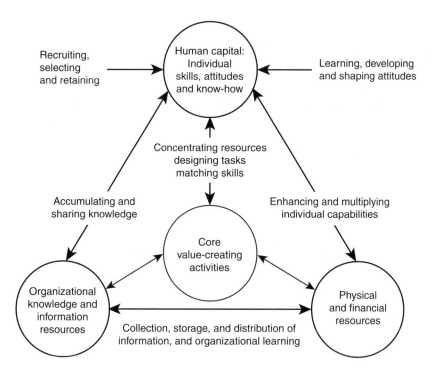

FIGURE 1.1  Opportunities for leveraging human capital
*Source*: Dess and Picken (1999: 19).

and copyrights), explicit knowledge and information (e.g., engineering drawings, sales collateral), and management processes, as well as industry know-how. Physical and financial resources consist of both physical assets (e.g., land, machinery, equipment) as well as financial assets (e.g., cash, accounts receivable). *Structural capital* may be described as "the embodiment, empowerment and supportive infrastructure of human capital – in a word, everything left at the office when the employees go home" (Edvinsson and Malone, 1997: 35). It includes core value-creating activities such as organization structure, systems, processes, and culture. The information and definitions in table 1.4 expand on these four key concepts.

Figure 1.1 illustrates the primary relationships among an organization's resources (human, information, physical, and financial), its core value-creating activities, and its organizational structure, systems, processes, and culture. The key role of structural capital is to link an organization's resources with the processes that create value for elements in a firm's expanded value chain (Porter, 1985) – customers, suppliers, and alliance partners – and advantages for the firm. The organization's core business activities – for example, order fulfillment, inbound logistics, sales and marketing – are essential elements of structural capital. However, equally important are a firm's information and communications structures, internal support functions, incentives and performance measurement systems, culture, leadership, and so forth. These elements are at the

TABLE 1.4 Leveraging human capital: key concepts

**Human capital**

Individual capabilities, knowledge, skill, and experience of the company's employees and managers, as they are relevant to the task at hand, as well as the capacity to add to this reservoir of knowledge, skills, and experience through individual learning.

**Organizational knowledge and information resources**

1)  The organization's documented and legally protected information, including patents, trademarks and propriety processes.
2)  Technical and financial data, engineering drawings and libraries, sales catalogs, customer lists, sales collateral, advertising copy, and so forth stored in files, databases, and other forms
3)  Management, process, and industry know-how.

**Physical and financial resources**

All of the organization's physical assets (land, buildings, equipment, inventories, leaseholds, etc.) and its financial resources (cash, accounts receivable, etc.)

**Structural capital**

Everything else – the organization's core value-creating activities, organizational knowledge, and information resources, and the organization's structure, systems processes, and culture. Following are the key components of structural capital:

**Core value-creating activities**
♦  Core busines processes
♦  External relationships with customers, suppliers, and alliance partners
♦  Reputation, brand loyalty, image, and legitimacy

**Organizational structure, systems, processes, and culture**
♦  Organizational and reporting structures
♦  Operating systems, processes, procedures, and task designs
♦  Information and communications infrastructures
♦  Resource acquisition, development, and allocation systems
♦  Decision processes and information flows
♦  Incentives, controls, and performance measurement systems
♦  Mechanisms to promote sharing, collaboration, and organizational learning
♦  Organizational culture, values, and leadership

*Source:* Adapted from Dess and Picken (1999).

heart of most strategy-making processes.

No one element or factor of structural capital by itself is likely to create a sustainable competitive advantage. Instead, sustainability typically requires complex interdependencies and interactions among multiple processes and resources as suggested above. Management's challenge is to structure, link, and combine human capital and other forms of capital into unique capabilities that not only maximize individual productivity but also the outcomes of collective efforts as well. The goal is to create sustainable advantages in the marketplace, that is, to be resistant to imitation (Barney, 1991). While a firm's physical and financial capital certainly cannot be ignored, effort must be directed at the continual development and leveraging of knowledge, skills and know-how from the organization's human capital. As noted by Hitt, et al. (2001: 9), "learning complex forms of knowledge requires face-to-face interactions (which) . . . can produce a combination of individual skills and knowledge that leads to novel and valuable outcomes." Successful implementation, in turn, will largely depend on how effectively the organization designs and implements the elements of its structural capital.

## Suggested research directions

We believe that the proposed framework for leveraging human capital (figure 1.1) has many implications for the conduct of future research into the role of strategy-making processes in the knowledge economy. The following examples form a large set of questions from which a strategy-making process research agenda could be derived.

First, Nahapiet and Ghoshal (1998) have eloquently argued that social capital facilitates the development and creation of intellectual capital. They refer to intellectual capital as "the knowledge and knowing capability of a social collectivity, such as an organization, intellectual community, or professional practice" (p. 245). Social capital is referred to as "the sum of actual and potential resources embedded within, available through, and developed from the network of relationships possessed by an individual or social unit" (p. 243). Thus, our framework could provide a means for assessing the role of social relations at many points of leverage such as in aiding in the accumulating and sharing of knowledge throughout the organization, enabling organizational learning, and concentrating resources through employees' identification with an organizational mission. In effect, it would provide insights into both "how" social capital facilitates the formation of intellectual capital, as well as "why" individuals are motivated to contribute to firm-specific knowledge which may have limited application beyond the organizational boundaries (Becker, 1964). The latter, of course, strengthens employees' firm-specific ties and decreases the mobility of human assets (Coff, 1997). Thus, future research might link personal motivation with issues of strategy-making processes and social capital, or investigate how social capital impacts the effectiveness of different strategy-making modes.

Second, drawing on our discussion earlier in this chapter, the framework could also provide insights as to how dimensions of a firm's entrepreneurial orientation (EO) can enhance a firm's efforts to achieve and sustain competitive advantages. For example, a strong culture and information system could enhance the diffusion of innovative activities throughout an organization's value-creating activities. This, in turn, might increase the likelihood that tacit knowledge would become codified (Polanyi, 1967) and applied to innovative initiatives by more organizational members. As noted by Nonaka and Takeuchi, "Knowledge is created and expanded through social interaction between tacit knowledge and explicit knowledge" (1995: 61). Quinn, Anderson, and Finkelstein (1996) have articulated how knowledge accumulates through information sharing. That is, as an individual shares knowledge with others, those individuals obtain the benefits from the information, that is, linear growth. However, when additional people share it with others and feed back questions, amplifications, and modifications that add further value for the original sender, such accumulation of knowledge creates exponential growth. Thus, the study of a firm's elements of structural capital could provide insights into the processes and social interaction's through which a firm's human capital (i.e., individual level) could be leveraged and combined more effectively – through reward systems, culture, leadership, and so on. The result might be a shift in strategy-making processes aimed at internal corporate development.

Third, researchers should implicitly recognize the need for alternate perspectives on the concept of risk taking in the knowledge economy. What may initially appear to be a risky endeavor may prove to be less risky when one considers the increasing salience of social, human, and intellectual capital as well as the implications of options theory. Many intangible resources lend themselves readily to new resource combinations (McGrath, 1999). For example, through entrepreneurial efforts, firms that develop dynamic capabilities, that is, knowledge and skills that can be readily redeployed, can more effectively compete in new markets or with new products and technologies (Teece, Pisano, and Shuen, 1997). Similarly, consistent with the real options literature, the "platform" from which organization learning may occur may also create new options (Grenadier and Weiss, 1997). Such learning adds to their resource stocks of "combinative capability" (Kogut and Zander, 1992). Thus, from the perspective of performance outcomes, efforts directed at strategy-making processes may result in longer-term economic payoffs than traditional efficiency and effectiveness measures would capture. In addition to the need to incorporate lag effects, therefore, researchers must strive to incorporate the increasing criticality of resource combinations and the creation of learning platforms as desirable – but more longer-term – outcomes in strategy-making processes.

Fourth, research could explore the extent to which each of the primary types of capital – that is, human capital, organizational knowledge, physical and financial – contribute to sustainability of advantages. Several research questions might be pursued. For example, are strategy-making processes, and cultural and structural conditions necessary to effectively overcome the limited physical and financial resource base inherent in many entrepreneurial ventures? Are all such conditions necessary, or is some subset of resources sufficient? Another issue to consider is: How can elements of structural capital (e.g., reputation) act as substitutes for other types of capital (e.g., financial) and enhance a firm's competitive advantages and sustainability?

Fifth, research may address the question of what factors in an organization inhibit the leveraging of human capital. Can an otherwise strong culture and structure lead to core rigidities (Hamel and Prahalad, 1996) that detract from innovation and creative activities? For example, should accepted behaviors and belief systems become institutionalized, innovation will become stifled because tacit social pressures may inhibit individuals from diverging from established procedures and practices (DiMaggio and Powell, 1983). If such a condition occurs, what structural and systems components can encourage the free flow of information throughout the organization and enhance a firm's knowledge base? Similar to the point above, how can other elements of structural capital "offset" a culture that has potentially dysfunctional outcomes? With regard to all of these issues, what are the implications in terms of implementing strategic processes that can overcome limitations and build on existing capabilities?

Sixth, work should also be directed toward exploring the "best practices" of leading-edge firms to explore how they are combining and leveraging resources. Such development of normative theory could inductively lead to more interesting research questions worthy of further inquiry. Additionally, a central question becomes the extent to which "best practices" may be generalized to other settings. Here, it may be useful to refer to Rosenberg's (1968) distinction between two types of generalization: descriptive and theoretical. Whereas descriptive generalizations involve generalizing "a finding based on a smaller number of cases to a broader population" (p. 222), theoretical generalizations occur when "variables are seen as *indicators* or *indices* of broader concepts" (p. 223, emphasis in original). Therefore, in the former case, one would need to exercise caution as to what conditions among cases in a study are sufficiently similar to generalize a "best practice," (e.g., in terms of size, industry, technology), at least in a normative sense. Further, one would have to carefully select industry settings at, for example, the four-digit SIC level given the high levels of intraindustry variation (Porter, 1980). This may be particularly true in rapidly changing, technologically intensive industries. The benefits first-movers would enjoy may vary significantly due to such factors as the level of technological intensity, entry and mobility barriers, stage of product life cycle, etc. Thus, the relationships between innovative and proactive decision processes may vary significantly within an industry.

With regard to theoretical generalizations, one must also exercise caution. As noted in table 1.4, the concept of structural capital has many subdimensions. Thus, one may be unwise to rely on just one or a small set of the subdimensions as indicators of the broader concept of structural capital. As an example, an innovative culture and dynamic leadership may be undercut by outdated information systems and a dysfunctional reward system. Thus, some positive elements of a firm's structural capital may be offset by relatively weaker elements.

## CONCLUSION

In this chapter we have addressed many theoretical and empirical issues associated with two strategy making process (SMP) constructs – entrepreneurial orientation (EO) and simplicity. We have summarized the research that helped to further clarify these constructs and have linked them to organizational performance. We investigated the role of several moderating variables in these relationships. In addition to advancing descriptive theory of strategy processes, we feel that these two constructs have important implications for normative theory as well. Given today's knowledge economy with its emphasis on innovation and creativity, we feel that it is important to identify factors that serve to augment (or suppress) such activities. Also, given that both the traditional factors of production and the managerial and knowledge resources that are so critical to success in today's economy are characterized by inherent scarcity, assessing the conditions under which a "simplicity" SMP is viable is also an important topic for future research. For example, when should a firm focus its efforts on a narrow range of strategic activities? And if a narrower strategy is pursued, does this also require simplicity in deploying knowledge resources, or would such a situation require more complexity in leveraging intellectual capital?

We have also addressed many research avenues concerning the relevance of strategy-making processes in successfully combining and leveraging resources. This is an especially salient topic in today's knowledge economy given the importance of "unique combinations of resources" as the basis for sustainable competitive advantages. The integrative model presented in figure 1.1 (Dess and Picken, 1999) provides a multidimensional framework that, we believe, can increase the rigor and relevance of both theory building and empirical research.

Research is a continual process of rediscovery. Our aim has been to provide a basis for some "interesting" (Davis, 1971) research endeavors. Also, given that there are numerous other perspectives and insights – some competing or conflicting – it is our hope that our efforts also spur additional dialogue and debate.

## ACKNOWLEDGMENTS

The authors wish to thank Tammy Ross, Bruce Skaggs, Wally Ferrier, and Doug Lyon for their helpful comments on an earlier draft of this manuscript.

## REFERENCES

Allison, G. T. (1971). *Essence of Decision*. Boston, MA: Little, Brown.

Amit, R., and Schoemaker, P. J. H. (1993). Strategic assets and organizational rent. *Strategic Management Journal*, 14: 33–46.

Andrews, K. R. (1971). *The Concept of Corporate Strategy*. Homewood, IL: Dow Jones-Irwin.

Ashby, W. R. (1956). *An Introduction to Cybernetics*. Englewood Cliffs, NJ: Prentice-Hall.

Barney, J. B. (1991). Firm resources and sustained competitive advantage. *Journal of Management*, 17: 99–120.

Becker, G. S. (1964). *Human Capital: A Theoretical and Empirical Analysis with Special Reference to Education*. Chicago: University of Chicago Press.

Boal, K., and Bryson, J. (1987). Representation, testing and policy implications of planning processes. *Strategic Management Journal*, 8: 211–31.

Bogner, W. C., Thomas, H., and McGee, J. (1999). Competence and competitive advantage: Towards a dynamic model. *British Journal of Management*, 10: 275–90.

Bourgeois, L. J. (1980). Strategy and environment: A conceptual integration. *Academy of Management Review*, 5: 25–39.

Bower, J. L. (1970). *Managing the Resource Allocation Process*. Cambridge, MA: Harvard University Press.

Burgelman, R. A. (1983). A process model of internal corporate venturing in the diversified major firm. *Administrative Science Quarterly*, 28: 223–44.

Capelli, P. (2000). A market-driven approach to retaining talent. *Harvard Business Review*, 78(1): 103–13.

Coff, R. W. (1997). Human assets and management dilemmas: Coping with hazards on the road to resource-based theory. *Academy of Management Review*, 22: 374–402.

Covin, J. G., and Slevin, D. P. (1989). Strategic management of small firms in hostile and benign environments. *Strategic Management Journal*, 10: 75–87.

Cyert, R. M., and March, J. G. (1963). *A Behavioral Theory of the Firm*. Englewood Cliffs, NJ: Prentice-Hall.

Davis, M. (1971). That's interesting! *Philosophy of Social Science*, 1: 309–44.

Dess, G. G. (1987). Consensus on strategy formulation and organizational performance: Competitors in a fragmented industry. *Strategic Management Journal*, 8: 259–77.

Dess, G. G., Lumpkin, G. T., and Covin, J. G. (1997). Entrepreneurial strategy making and firm performance: Tests of contingency and configuration models. *Strategic Management Journal*, 18(9): 677–95.

Dess, G. G., Lumpkin, G. T., and McGee, J. E. (1999). Linking corporate entrepreneurship to strategy, structure, and process: Suggested research directions. *Entrepreneurship Theory and Practice*, 23(3): 85–102.

Dess, G. G., Newport, S., and Rasheed, A. (1993). Configuration research in strategic management: Key issues and suggestions. *Journal of Management*, 19(4): 775–95.

Dess, G. G., and Picken, J. C. (1999). *Beyond Productivity: How Leading Companies Achieve Superior Performance by Leveraging their Human Capital*. New York: AMACOM.

DiMaggio, P. J., and Powell, W. W. (1983). The iron cage revisited: Institutional isomorphism and collective rationality in organizational fields. *American Sociological Review*, 48: 147–60.

Doty, D. H., Glick, W., and Huber, G. (1993). Fit, equifinality, and organizational effectiveness: A test of two configurational theories. *Academy of Management Journal*, 36(6): 1196–250.

Dyer, J. H., and Singh, H. (1998). The relational view: Cooperative strategy and sources of interorganizational competitive advantage. *Academy of Management Review*, 23: 660–79.

Edvinsson, L., and Malone, M. S. (1997). *Intellectual capital: Realizing your Company's True Value by Finding its Hidden Brainpower*. New York: HarperBusiness.

Eisenhardt, K. (1989). Making fast strategic decisions in high-velocity environments. *Academy of Management Journal*, 32: 543–76.

Eisenhardt, K., and Bourgeois, L. J. (1988). Politics of strategic decision making in high-velocity environments: Toward a mid-range theory. *Academy of Management Journal*, 31: 737–70.

Fredrickson, J. W. (1986). The strategic decision process and organizational structure. *Academy of Management Journal*, 11(2): 280–97.

Fredrickson, J., and Mitchell, T. (1984). Strategic decision processes: Comprehensiveness and performance in an industry with an unstable environment. *Academy of Management Journal*, 27: 399–423.

Gale, B. (1972). Market share and rate of return. *The Review of Economics and Statistics*, 54: 412–23.

Greiner, L. (1972). Evolution and revolution as organizations grow. *Harvard Business Review*, 60(4): 37–46.

Grenadier, S. R., and Weiss, A. M. (1997). Investment in technological innovations: An option pricing approach. *Journal of Financial Economics*, 44: 397–416.

Hall, M., and Weiss, L. (1967). Firm size and profitability. *The Review of Economics and Statistics*, 54: 319–31.

Hamel, G. (1997). Killer strategies that make shareholders rich. *Fortune*, June 23: 70–84.

Hamel, G., and Prahalad, C. K. (1996). Competing in the new economy: Managing out of bounds. *Strategic Management Journal*, 17: 232–42.

Hart, S. (1991). Intentionality and autonomy in strategy-making process: Modes, archetypes, and firm performance. In P. Shrivastava, A. Huff, and J. Dutton (eds.), *Advances in strategic management*, 7: 97–127. Greenwich, CT: JAI Press.

Hart, S. (1992). An integrative framework for strategy-making processes. *Academy of Management Review*, 17: 327–51.

Hitt, M. A., Bierman, L., Shimizu, K., and Kochhar, R. (2001). Direct and moderating effects of human capital on strategy and performance in professional service firms: A resource-based perspective. *Academy of Management Journal*, 44(1): 13–28.

Hitt, M. A., and Tyler, B. B. (1991). Strategic decision models: Integrating different perspectives. *Strategic Management Journal*, 12: 327–51.

Hofer, C. W., and Schendel, D. (1978). *Strategy Formulation: Analytical Concepts*. St Paul, MN: West Publishing.

Howard, R. (1992). The CEO as organizational architect: An interview with Xerox's Paul Allaire. *Harvard Business Review*, 70(5): 107–21.

Ibarra, H. (1993). Network centrality, power, and innovation involvement: Determinants of technical and administrative roles. *Academy of Management Journal*, 36: 471–501.

Jensen, M. C. (1989). Eclipse of the public corporation. *Harvard Business Review*, 67(5): 61–74.

Jones, C., Hesterly, W. S., and Borgatti, S. P. (1997). A general theory of network governance: Exchange conditions and social mechanisms. *Academy of Management Review*, 22: 911–45.

Katz, J., and Gartner, W. B. (1988). Properties of emerging organizations. *Academy of Management Review*, 13(3): 429–41.

Kogut, B., and Zander, U. (1992). Knowledge of the firm, combinative capabilities, and the replication of technology. *Organization Science*, 3: 383–97.

Lippman, S. A., and Rumelt, R. P. (1982). Uncertain imitability: An analysis of interfirm differences in efficiency under competition. *The Bell Journal of Economics*, 13: 418–38.

Lumpkin, G. T., and Dess, G. G. (1995). Simplicity as a strategy-making process: The effects of stage of organizational development and environment on performance. *Academy of Management Journal*, 38(5): 1386–407.

Lumpkin, G. T., and Dess, G. G. (1996). Clarifying the entrepreneurial orientation construct and linking it to performance. *Academy of Management Review*, 21: 135–72.

Lumpkin, G. T., and Dess, G. G. (2001). Linking two dimensions of entrepreneurial orientation to firm performance: The moderating role of environment and industry life cycle. *Journal of Business Venturing*.

Lyon, D., Lumpkin, G. T., and Dess, G. G. (2000). Enhancing entrepreneurial orientation research: operationalizing and measuring a key strategic decision making process. *Journal of Management*, 26(5): 1055–85.

McGrath, R. G. (1999). Falling forward: Real options reasoning and entrepreneurial failure. *Academy of Management Review*, 24: 13–30.

Miller, D. (1983). The correlates of entrepreneurship in three types of firms. *Management Science*, 29: 770–91.

Miller, D. (1987). Strategy making and structure: Analysis and implications for performance. *Academy of Management Journal*, 30: 7–32.

Miller, D. (1988). Relating Porter's business strategies to environment and structure: Analysis and performance implications. *Academy of Management Journal*, 31: 280–308.

Miller, D. (1990). *The Icarus Paradox*. New York: HarperCollins.

Miller, D. (1993). The architecture of simplicity. *Academy of Management Review*, 18: 116–38.

Miller, D., and Chen, M. (1993). The simplicity of competitive repertoires: An empirical analysis. Paper presented at the annual meeting of the Academy of Management (*Proceedings*, pp. 32–6).

Miller, D, and Friesen, P. (1978). Archetypes of strategy formulation. *Management Science*, 24: 921–33.

Miller, D., and Friesen, P. (1982). Innovation in conservative and entrepreneurial firms: Two models of strategic momentum. *Strategic Management Journal*, 3: 1–25.

Miller, D., and Friesen, P. (1983). Strategy-making and environment: The third link. *Strategic*

*Management Journal*, 4: 221–35.

Miller, D., and Shamsie, J. (1996). The resource-based view of the firm in two environments: The Hollywood film studios from 1936 to 1965. *Academy of Management Journal*, 39: 519–36.

Miller, K., and Bromily, P. (1990). Strategic risk and corporate performance: An analysis of alternative risk measures. *Academy of Management Journal*, 35: 759–79.

Mintzberg, H. (1973). Strategy making in three modes. *California Management Review*, 16(2): 44–53.

Mintzberg, H. (1978). Patterns in strategy formation. *Management Science*, 24: 934–49.

Mintzberg, H. (1979). *The Structuring of Organizations*. Englewood Cliffs, NJ: Prentice-Hall.

Mintzberg, H. (1983). *Power In and Around Organizations*. Englewood Cliffs, NJ: Prentice-Hall.

Mintzberg, H., Raisinghani, D., and Theoret, A. (1976). The structure of "unstructured" decision processes. *Administrative Science Quarterly*, 21(2): 246–75.

Nahapiet, J., and Ghoshal, S. (1998). Social capital, intellectual capital, and the organizational advantage. *Academy of Management Review*, 23: 242–66.

Nonaka, I., and Takeuchi, H. (1995). *The Knowledge-creating Company*. New York: Oxford University Press.

Peteraf, M. (1993). The cornerstones of competitive advantage: A resource-based view. *Strategic Management Journal*, 14: 179–91.

Pettigrew, A. M. (ed.) (1992). Strategy process research. (Special Issue). *Strategic Management Journal*, Winter.

Polanyi, M. (1967). *The Tacit Dimension*. Garden City, NY: Anchor Publishing.

Porter, M. E. (1980). *Competitive Strategy*. New York: Free Press.

Porter, M. E. (1985). *Competitive Advantage*. New York: Free Press.

Powell, W. W. (1990). Neither market nor hierarchy: Network forms of organization. In B. M. Staw and L. L. Cummings (eds.), *Research in Organizational Behavior*, vol. 12: 295–336. Greenwich, CT: JAI Press.

Prahalad, C. K., and Hamel, G. (1990). The core competence of the corporation. *Harvard Business Review*, 68(3): 79–91.

Quinn, J. B. (1980). *Strategies for Change: Logical Incrementalism*. Homewood, IL: Irwin.

Quinn, J. B., Anderson, P., and Finkelstein, S. (1996). Leveraging intellect. *Academy of Management Executive*, 10(3): 7–27.

Rajagopalan, N., Rasheed, A., and Datta, D. (1993). Strategic decision processes: Critical review and future directions. *Journal of Management*, 19: 349–84.

Ring, P. S., and Van de Ven, A. H. (1994). Structuring cooperative relationships between organizations. *Strategic Management Journal*, 13: 483–98.

Rosenberg, M. (1968). *The Logic of Survey Analysis*. New York: Basic Books.

Schweiger, D. M., Sandberg, W. R., and Ragan, J. W. (1986). Group approaches for improving strategic decision making: A comparative analysis of dialectical inquiry, devil's advocacy and consensus. *Academy of Management Journal*, 29: 51–71.

Schwenk, C. R. (1984). Effects of planning aids and representation media on performance and affective responses in strategic decision making. *Management Science*, 30: 263–71.

Scott, B. R. (1971). Stages of corporate development. Harvard University, Intercollegiate Case Clearing House Report No. 9-371-294 BP 998, Boston, MA.

Shrivastava, P. (1983). Variations in strategic decision-making processes. In R. Lamb (ed.), *Advances in Strategic Management*, Vol. 2: 177–89. Greenwich, CT: JAI Press.

Shrivastava, P., and Grant, J. H. (1985). Empirically derived models of strategic decision-making processes. *Strategic Management Journal*, 6: 97–113.

Simon, H. A. (1957). *Administrative Behavior*. New York: Free Press.

Snow, C. C., Miles, R. E., and Coleman, H. J., Jr. (1992). Managing 21st century network organizations. *Organizational Dynamics*, 20: 5–20.

Spender, J.-C. (1996). Making knowledge the basis of a dynamic theory of the firm. *Strategic*

*Management Journal*, 17: 45–62.

Stetz, P. E., Howell, R., Stewart, A., Blair, J. D., and Fottler, M. D. (2000). *Multidimensionality of Entrepreneurial Firm-level Processes: Do the Dimensions Covary?* Paper presented at the 2000 Babson-Kauffman Entrepreneurship Research Conference, Wellesley, MA.

Stewart, T. A. (1997). *Intellectual Capital: The New Wealth of Organizations.* New York: Doubleday/Currency.

Teece, D., Pisano, G., and Shuen, A. (1997). Dynamic capabilities and strategic management. *Strategic Management Journal*, 18: 509–34.

*The Economist* (1996). An acknowledged trend: The world economy survey. September 28: 25–28.

Van de Ven, A. H. (1992). Suggestions for studying strategy process: A research note. *Strategic Management Journal*, 13: 169–88.

Venkatraman, N. (1989). Strategic orientation of business enterprises: The construct, dimensionality, and measurement. *Management Science*, 35(8): 942–62.

Weick, K. E. (1979). *The Social Psychology of Organizing.* Reading, MA: Addison-Wesley.

Wernerfelt, B. (1984). A resource-based view of the firm. *Strategic Management Journal*, 5: 171–80.

# 2

# Strategic Decision-Making

## PAUL C. NUTT

Research into decision-making studies the expensive, risky, hard-to-alter choices with long-term consequences that can have a significant influence on the future success of contemporary organizations. Such choices often call for decisions that cut across many departments and geographically dispersed divisions involving many people with important stakes in what is decided. Organizational leaders must be concerned with the effects these decisions produce and people's perceptions of how they are made and the organizational commitments and values suggested by the choices that are made. Ignoring these considerations can lead to a decision debacle – the failed decision with significant negative consequences that becomes public (Snyder and Page, 1958; McKie, 1973; Nutt, 1999, 2001a).

Decision-making research is carried out to determine how decisions are made in organizations, what causes failure, and how to improve the prospects of success. Research efforts into these questions have been widely reported in the literature for at least four decades. This literature has taken many turns over this period. Behaviorism and description have competed with prescription and theory-driven efforts have displaced exploratory work, at least in some management journals. Such journals contend that there is a management theory to test, when this claim is debatable and likely misguided. Studies with these and still other perspectives have made a synthesis of the decision-making literature difficult. Capturing the diversity of work into decision-making and its many insights in a single chapter is not possible. Instead, it is better to concentrate on trying to show some of what has been done and what remains to be done from a single and homogeneous perspective. In this chapter, I will offer one such view. This view stresses field study, investigating real decisions made by real people in real organizations in which the consequences of the decisions are potentially measurable. The purpose of such an effort is to identify prescriptions for managers and management that concentrate on the steps taken to make decisions that work and do not work, called tactics, and conditions under which success can be improved.

## THEORETICAL BACKDROP

Decision-making takes place in an organization when managers who are facing important issues carry out a decision process to make choices that produce outcomes with
consequences. The issues that produce the decision situation can create surprise, confusion, or threat suggesting the speed of a response. The context of decision identifies
domains of action (top management or departmental), type of decision, such as whether
it is strategic or not, complexity, urgency, importance, uncertainty, resistance, etc. The
decision-maker has attributes such as the propensity to take risks, tolerance for certainty
and ambiguity, creativity, decision style, skill, need for control, power, experience,
education, and values. Organizations in which the decision is made have characteristics
that can be summed up in macro features, such as public/private differences, or in
internal features such as communication, control, and power. Process usually deals with
how decisions are made – the methods and procedures that are applied consciously or
unconsciously. Activities, such as coalition formation and social process control (i.e.,
bargaining) can be treated as part of the tactics applied by a decision-maker that respond
to needs to manage stakeholders as the process unfolds. The decision-maker uses
improvisation or customized, pre-established, rules to cope. Consequences capture the
effects of a decision, such as its benefits, and whether these benefits seem justified given
the cost, disruptions, and distractions to make it. Situation, context, decision-maker
attributes, organizational features, process, and process tactics have been found to
influence the choice that is made and its consequences (Nutt, 1984; Dean and Sharfman,
1992). As a result, research into decision-making must deal with many plausible causes
and many possible effects. Dealing with all of them in a single study is impractical so
researchers make simplifications.

Several notable research efforts have attempted to capture key questions about how
decisions are carried out by profiling actual decisions (e.g., Witte, 1972; Soelberg, 1967;
Cray et al., 1991). Studies of this type attempt to describe the process followed as
decisions are made. For example, Mintzberg et al. (1976) explored 24 cases and uncovered the phases and steps and routines within phases carried out by decision-makers and
interrupts that caused recycles, retracing earlier steps to make repairs. Phases included
identification, development, selection, and authorization. The identification phase initiates decision-making activity and has steps of recognition and diagnosis. During recognition, factual signals are examined by decision-makers to measure differences between an
actual situation and some standard, looking for a performance gap (Downs, 1967).
Diagnosis follows to uncover information that indicates whether the situation merits
attention. The development phase has search, design, and screen steps. Search and
screen steps provide a ready-made option and design a custom-made one. Selection
involves evaluation via bargaining, judgment, and analysis. Authorization deals with
implementation and installation issues. Mintzberg and his colleagues profiled decisions,
such as a major equipment purchase, showing how different decisions take different paths
through the framework they uncovered.

Quinn (1990) conducted studies of decision-making in ten major corporations, also
discovering activities and processes that were related to strategic decision-making. Managers were observed drawing on networks of people to get information depicting the need

for change. "Screens" that use subjective information depicting proliferation, exposure, overlap, lack of focus, low motivation, inconsistencies, and anomalies to compare a current position and a perception of future needs were observed (Fiske and Taylor, 1991). This differs from findings uncovered by Mintzberg et al. (1976), by calling for informal information sources and subjective measures to identify performance gaps formed by the difference between a performance measure (market share) and some norm or expectation for the performance (the hoped-for market share). In some instances, stringent norms were applied to make performance shortfalls seem worthy of attention. Search for optional ways to proceed was not directed by opportunities in these studies. Instead, search was carried out as a rational process in which the ends sought were made clear by stating a goal.

Related research finds decision-makers to be buffeted by streams of loosely coupled problems, solutions, stakeholders, and choice situations that flow at different rates in an organization (Cohen et al., 1976; March and Olsen, 1986; Mausch and LaPotin, 1989). March (1994) claims that these streams meet and couple due to accidents of timing, not any causal logic. Solutions seek problems, problems and solutions are looking for choice situations, and decision-makers respond by making choices according to their work load and how decisions bunch up, not by interpreting signals to set directions. The choice situation becomes a garbage can in which problems and solutions are dumped. Performance gaps are recognized (or problems rationalized) after an action is identified that seems useful. After the fact rationalizations, such as carefully crafted problem descriptions, are used to defend the "opportunity." Here an opportunity to act accompanied by justifications that can be expressed as performance shortfalls, dictates the decision.

In what has become known as the Bradford studies (Hickson et al., 1986; Hickson, 1987; and Cray et al., 1991), Hickson and his colleagues provide detailed accounts of 150 decisions (five episodes carried out in 30 organizations). They developed the notion of interests for various process types, such as vortex-sporadic and fluid. The process types were linked to the nature of the interests that arose. In a vortex-sporadic type a weighty and controversial decision drew in many players, making the decision politically volatile. Fluid decisions were more controllable but their novelty and diffusion through the organization drew in many players who wanted a voice in the outcome. The Bradford studies also collected perceptions of the decision and its outcome, but did not correlate outcome with context or process factors.

Dean and Sharfman (1992, 1996) studied decision-making in 25 firms using interviews with top managers. These studies concentrated on the act of making a choice to uncover its antecedents. Controlling for implementation steps taken and their quality, procedural rationality and political behavior were examined, finding rationality to be correlated with more effective decisions. Politics was correlated with less effective decisions. This stream of work has also examined contextual factors such as flexibility, the amount of slack resources, and recursive decisions. They find that process has a greater influence on the outcomes realized than does context (Sharfman and Dean, 1998).

In some recent work, Mintzberg (Mintzberg and Westley, 2001) identifies three different ways that people can approach a decision: *think first*, *see first*, and *do first*. Decision-makers who rely upon logic ("think first") are seen as following steps of defining, diagnosing, designing, and then deciding what to do. This is often called the rational approach, after Simon (1977). Such an approach is believed to work when choices can be counter-intuitive, calling for analysis to sort things out. A "think first" approach can be irrational because people's interests and ambitions are considered only indirectly. "Seeing first" draws on people's insight to see what is at issue and how to attack the issue. This can be essential for novel situations and for situations that demand creativity. There is a need to break away from the conventional and engage the heart, not the head, when such a decision must be made. Visioning in this way can be creative but such an approach can get lost when the incubation step fails to produce an illumination. When a manager is unable to think a decision through or to get a flash of insight, the "do first" approach is recommended. To "do" one engages in small-scale experimentation. A small move (best guess) is made and improvisation follows. The steps are enactment, selection, retention, and learning as one does. The downside here is going adrift. Not knowing where to start, the first "do" move can be wildly off target. The next move may be not much better, taking small steps into oblivion.

Note how these research efforts are both descriptive and somewhat anecdotal. Descriptive findings have been used to create prescriptions in much of this work. A connection between what people do and the consequences of their actions is required to draw a prescription, but this connection is rarely made. This prompts questions about prescriptions that have been drawn from descriptive research of decision-making. For example, Mintzberg finds that judgment is the preferred means of making a choice, that bargaining is ignored unless people are forced to compromise, and that analysis is seldom useful. These descriptive findings are used to argue against the use of analysis and to call for judgment thereby offering a prescription. Also, context is viewed as more important than what the decision-maker does. Contingency models that call for selecting what is to be done according to the situation being faced all make this claim (e.g., Lippitt and Mackenzie, 1976; Vroom and Jago, 1978). These models call for managers to select unilateral action when decisions are urgent and avoid participation because it is not timely. The empirical justification of this is lacking.

One way to bridge this gap is to draw behavioral studies into the prescriptive realm by including measures of success. This can be done by being clear about the actions that managers take and by including measures of key contextual factors, such as importance and urgency, as well as a measure of decision consequences. This has led me to concentrate on "tactics" that indicate how decision-makers carry out each phase of a decision-making process, linking tactics and their context to success. To make this task manageable, process has been broken down into the stages (or phases) of activity called for by researchers (e.g., Bryson et al., 1990; Harrison and Phillips, 1992; Eisenhardt and Zbaracki, 1992), so a research effort can be concentrated on a single stage. These stages call for decision-makers to employ tactics to gather intelligence, set directions, uncover alternatives, evaluate options, and implement a favored option. My work shows how decision-makers go about these tasks and the outcomes that were realized, controlling for context, identifying the successful and the unsuccessful tactics.

A variety of approaches can be used to carry out such an effort, such as role-playing, simulations, and laboratory experiments. Many find such efforts unconvincing and call for investigations that stay close to the phenomena being studied. This requires real decisions in real organizations made by real people and fieldwork to collect the required data. Such an approach gets the researcher close to the action so decision-making practices could be identified and connected to the consequences of a decision in which responsible people bore burdens or reaped benefits. Linking these outcomes to decision-making practices, both good and bad, provides a telling appraisal of the effectiveness of each practice. Such research must have a large database of decisions indicating how each decision is made, accounting for the situation being confronted, and measuring the decision's success. The decisions must involve the sort of things that managers deal with regularly – new products, equipment purchases, staffing, pricing, marketing, locating operations, etc. The decision database must also provide a rich description of events that allow one to probe for why some practices work and others do not, looking for ways to improve the chance of success. From this appraisal, conclusions can be drawn about what to do, what to avoid, and other things to do to improve the chance of being successful. In this chapter, the results of two long-term research efforts into decision-making are presented, discussing key findings about the tactics that work and those to avoid. The emphasis is on prescription, offering propositions that capture key findings and conclusions about what works and why.

## Types of Decisions

Strategic decisions can be *developmental* or non-developmental. A *developmental* decision requires a vision of how to alter the core businesses of an organization or its key business practices. The vision identifies changes in products/services, customers/clients, markets, service or distribution channels, alliances, sources of revenue, collaborative or competitive advantage, skills, ways to organize, and persona or image to be integrated with core competencies of the organization (Porter, 1985; Hamel and Prahalad, 1994; Nutt and Backoff, 1997a; Nutt, 2001a). Such decisions call for finding new businesses and/or business practices that lack precedent. To be successful, strategic decision-making in such situations departs from bounded rationality (March and Simon, 1958; Simon, 1969), partisan mutual adjustment (Lindblom, 1965), goal setting (Locke et al., 1991), and other time-honored approaches tailored for the non-developmental decision, or uses them differently.

A developmental decision stems from tensions that pull an organization in opposite directions (Nutt and Backoff, 1993, 1995). Consider a public school system that faces retrenchment due to levy failure and the demand to install costly new programs, mandated by a legislature, believed to increase graduation rates. Also consider automotive companies in the past decade that simultaneously faced the need to cut cost and increase quality (Pascale, 1990; Nutt and Backoff, 1997b). Such tensions pull an organization in opposite directions at the same time as key people attempt to reposition. To reposition, developmental decisions are made that change the company's core business and/or key business practices in response to critical tensions. Tensions that pull organizations in opposite directions at the same time are managed as the firm's leaders attempt to reposition the company by making developmental decisions that change aspects of its core business or key business practices.

*Non-developmental* decisions have less ambiguity. The organization's strategy is not in flux and can be used to provide premises that frame what needs to be done to make a decision. Decision premises can be inferred from the current products/services, customers/clients, markets, service or distribution channels, alliances, sources of revenue, collaborative or competitive advantage, skills, ways to organize, and persona or image. Such decisions are non-developmental because many of the expectations about products and the other strategy components are known and can be used to identify the ends to be sought that guide the search for a means. Many non-developmental decisions are complex and many are important, but they are not inherently developmental in their make-up. Consider an airline that is making choices about ways to better use its fleet of aircraft and sites in airports (gates) by simulating the system with various hub and route configurations. Such choices can be complex but have known or knowable ends and discoverable means that make them non-developmental. Such decisions also arise when dealing with cutting edge technology. The novel decision need not be developmental, even if the novelty calls for innovation (new to the organization) or radical innovation (new to the industry), which can tax a decision-maker's intuition and creativity.

Typologies that identify decision types do not deal with this distinction. For example, exporting Thompson (1967) "inspirational" decisions to developmental ones is tempting because both ends and means must be discovered. Because both purpose and action must be identified before such a decision can be made such a decision becomes complex, but not inherently developmental. Ackoff (1981) finds that a decision can be prompted by "wicked problems" that have complex interconnections that cause unexpected feedback with surprising consequences. The resulting situation becomes "unstructured" or a "mess" (Mitroff and Emshoff, 1979). The lack of clues in where to begin and the complexity of the situation present considerable ambiguity and a real challenge to sort out, but such decisions are not developmental unless changes in core businesses are to be made.

The practices called for to make non-developmental decisions are often extended to strategic ones. The reverse is true as well – researchers often treat decision-making as a generic task that extends to all types of decisions (Langley, 1989; Langley et al., 1995). Approaches that work for one type of decision often distort, misdirect, or mislead when applied to the other. For instance, Dutton's (Dutton and Jackson, 1987; Dutton and Duncan, 1987) work on strategic issues in which threats are given more weight than opportunity, implying that the opportunity can be lost, can mislead a non-developmental decision. For the non-developmental decision an undefined need (threat coupled with a concern) has more success than an opportunity in the face of a threat (Nutt, 2000). Here the opportunity prompts premature commitments that often lead to poor decisions (Nutt, 1999). An opportunity in an urgent situation gives temporary relief but increases the chance of downstream failure. Mintzberg's work on "emergent ideas" in which a decision-maker positions to look for ideas, hoping to engage his/her intuition to find something innovative ("see first"), increases the chance of failure as well. Thus, vastly different prescriptions capture best practice for the developmental and the non-developmental decision.

This confusion stems, in part, from some sloppy distinctions that were made in this field of study early on. For some time, researchers following the lead of Mintzberg et al. (1976) and Hickson et al. (1986) have referred to important decisions with long-term implications as strategic. Calling such decisions strategic requires them to be developmental; that is, a decision undertaken to change the company's strategy. Calling all decisions that seem important and have long-term implications strategic implies that all such decisions are developmental, which is not the case. To be developmental, a decision must be directed toward devising new businesses that change one or more aspects of a company's strategy. Such decisions can also become conflict ridden due to their tensions, and ambiguous and uncertain if the key tensions have many complex interconnections. Consider the decisions called strategic (developmental) in past work, such as the purchase of an aircraft in the Mintzberg study or a CT scanner in the Hickson study. Because neither calls for changes in products, customers, or the other aspects of strategy they are non-developmental. A decision is developmental when a vision about what is wanted is missing and must be created.

Managers moving from a technical area, such as accounting or engineering, to responsibilities in upper management are often confronted with developmental decisions for the first time. Not surprisingly, there is a big temptation to export what they have learned to a developmental decision. Such an approach should be avoided – for several reasons. In this chapter, we will discuss why such an adaptation is unwise, what can and can not be exported to the developmental decision, and offer some guidance in how to make a developmental decision. We will also consider how to successfully make the non-developmental decision by dodging pitfalls that are often encountered.

It is important to note that managers making non-developmental decisions have less than a sterling track record. More than half of these decisions fail: hardly a basis to continue, let alone export, these practices (Nutt, 1999). Even if one is exporting best practice, many of these practices have little relevance to the developmental decision or they play a very different role in developmental decision-making. Here we will set out some key distinctions that frame what is known about decision-making – both the non-developmental and the developmental. First, content (what is done) and process (how this is decided) distinctions will be considered. Content will be used to identify the nature of decisions called non-developmental and how these decisions differ from decisions that have a developmental intent. Process captures differences in the best practices that are recommended to make both the developmental and the non-developmental decision. To make these recommendations we will draw on information taken from studies of the outcomes produced by decisions and decision-makers.

One of the key findings of my work is that the actions taken by a manager, his/her process and tactics, are more important than the situation being faced (Nutt, 1999). Factors such as importance, resources, and urgency have less impact on success than does the kind of practices (process and tactics) followed by the manager. There is one exception to this – the type of decision. Non-developmental decisions require a different approach than does the developmental one.

*Proposition 1*: The prospect of success improves when both the tactics and the decision-making process (the sequence of these tactics) are tailored to the type of decision, given by whether it is developmental or non-developmental.

## Non-Developmental Decisions

Considerable research has been carried out that identifies what is required to be successful when making the non-developmental decision. As a result, much is known about best practice that considers both content and process. Content presents a startling finding. More than half of the decisions made in American companies fail (Nutt, 1999).

The expected benefits are not realized or, even worse, many are discarded without ever being tried.

The startling rate of failure prompts questions. Why is failure so prevalent? What are its causes? What can be done to reduce it? Answers to these questions have come in uncovering the blunders that decision-makers are prone to make (Nutt, 2001a). They are:

1. making premature commitments;
2. investing in the wrong things;
3. using failure-prone decision-making practices.

A rush to judgment, poor allocation, and bad practice blunders crop up again and again in studies of organizational decisions and decision-makers. The chain of events that leads to failure starts with one or more of these blunders. The blunders create traps that ensnare the unsuspecting decision-maker. To improve the chance of success one must avoid the blunders and dodge the traps. Let's consider the blunders and then ways to avoid the traps.

## Premature commitments

Managers blunder when they make premature commitments. Decision-makers frequently jump on the first idea that they spot and then spend literally years trying to make it work. This rush to judgment creates a commitment that is hard to back away from. Misguided pragmatism and artificial time pressure are the primary motivations for making a premature commitment. Decision-makers who grab the first idea that turns up justify this by homilies such as, "why rediscover the wheel when someone has done it for you" and create artificial urgency by admonishing others to "get on with it." This makes the first idea that comes up seem timely and pragmatic. Unanticipated delays will crop up as attempts are made to convince stakeholders that the company's interests, not the decision-maker's, are being served and retrofits are made.

## Poor investments

Managers fail to use decision-making resources wisely. Analytic evaluations capture much of their time and money. Little is spend on anything else. Analytic evaluations are often defensive in nature; carried out to defend an idea that a manager has become wedded to, giving the appearance that the analysis has little purpose beyond defending what the manager wants to do. People suspecting hidden motives become suspicious. The suggestion of a vested interest, even if there is none, prompts questions. More analysis is required to answer them. This persists even when the defensive evaluation is avoided. Managers spend vast sums on uncovering the benefits of a proposed action, but little on anything else such as searching for a new idea.

## Failure-prone practices

Managers use failure-prone practices over and over again and seem oblivious to their poor track record. This stems from misleading associations of past decisions and their outcomes with the steps taken to make them. Good decision-making practice does not guarantee success due to chance events. Bad luck, due to unexpected increases in fuel prices or bad weather, can be mistaken for bad practices. Good luck, such as windfall profits due to a favorable turn on the supply of raw materials that drives down prices, can cover up bad practice. Lacking information on this, managers make misleading associations between a decision-making practice and its results. This prompts the manager to discard perfectly good ways of making decisions and to continue to use others that have a poor track record.

The blunders of rushing to judgment, misusing available resources, and using poor decision-making practices can lead to five process-related traps that can ambush the unsuspecting manager. They occur when a manager fails to explore claims, ignores the barriers to taking action, gives ambiguous directions, becomes distracted by a quick fix, and misuses analysis. Managers that get caught in one or more of these traps are apt to make a bad call that can lead to a debacle. Lets see how one navigates around these traps by reserving judgment, allocating funds wisely, and using best practices. The order in which these tactics are applied is also important (Nutt, 1984, 2001a). Those who have the most influence on success (claim making, implementation, and direction setting) precede those with less influence on success. It is not the outcome of this, the idea or plan, as Mintzberg (1994) would have you believe, but the voyage that counts.

*Proposition 2*: The chance of success improves when decision-makers begin with claim reconciliation followed by implementation considerations, direction setting, uncovering options, and option evaluation.

## Avoiding the blunders and traps

The key to reducing failure and the possibility of a debacle, should the failure become public, can be found in the decision-making practices that are used. Decision-makers are admonished to apply practices that have a good track record and to avoid those that are failure-prone. The traps that lead to failure – failing to uncover concerns behind the claims, ignoring barriers to making changes, ambiguous directions, limited search, and inappropriate analysis can be avoided. Best practice calls for taking charge by reconciling claims, managing the social and political forces at work, picturing the results wanted and using them as directions, broadening search, and using analysis to measure risk as well as benefits. Proposition 2 suggests what to do and how to order these actions to avoid failure. Let us consider each in the order that is recommended showing what things should be avoided and what to do to increase the chance of success.

*Claim reconciliation.* People inside and outside of an organization reacting to warning signs and signals, note concerns and considerations that seem to be important, and make claims (Toulmin, 1979). Falling market share, for example, may alarm a board member. The observer notes this concern and makes a claim about the market share decline, such as calling for improved quality in existing products. As this example demonstrates, there can be a questionable inference that connects the concern and the claim. Such a connection may seems off base to key players. Decision-makers get trapped when they prematurely buy into a claim that has little or no connection with the concerns of informed people.

Disagreements arise as claims are made if claimants fail to share the concerns that prompted their claims (Nutt, 1998b, 2000). Many see this as a signal to choose among the claims and claimants by adopting the interpretation of events that seems to be logical, consistent with their views, and supported by powerful people they must cater to (Cyert and March, 1963). This can prompt concerned insiders, skeptics, and people who have something to lose to take defensive action (Nutt, 2001a). Opponents look for what appears to be an error or a misrepresentation in the claim and use it to question the need for action or argue against the legitimacy of the claim. Probing is required to reveal hidden concerns that prompt this behavior. Managers can get trapped when they fail to take the time or use available funds to identify the concerns of other significant stakeholders such as alliance partners, customers, suppliers, informed insiders, communities in which they operate, and the general public. A decision can be hindered, if not derailed, when decision-makers assume that key people understand and agree with their interpretation of the concerns that are motivating them to take action.

Managers can avoid this trap by asking people who make up stakeholder groups that matter to voice their claims, and the concerns behind them, using tactics like appreciative inquiry (Copperrider and Srivastra, 1987). Investing a few hours to poll each group of stakeholders, using a structured group process like the Nominal Group Technique (Delbecq et al., 1986) will pay big dividends. These groups are asked to silently list both the claims that they believe to be warranted and the concerns or considerations that prompt them. Both claims and concerns/considerations are then recorded on separate sheets one at a time to de-couple them. Discussion follows to explore, elaborate, and explain. The group members then select the most important concerns/considerations and link them to the claims that they support. Comparisons of claims and their motivating concerns/considerations across the stakeholder groups opens up the arena of action implied by the claims. The manager looks for an arena that will be acceptable to most, if not all, stakeholders. This allows the manager to champion action by taking charge to legitimize the effort, showing that they are aware of people's concerns/ considerations. People who can be shown that the proposed decision-making effort has taken into account what they believe to be important are more likely to be supportive. With this information, significant players are more apt to buy into the arguments for taking action. When supportive, such people will spread the word to others, making momentum easier to maintain.

*Proposition 3*: The prospects of success improve when the concerns of stakeholders are uncovered and used to fashion a claim that will be used as a call for action.

*Implementation considerations.*   Decisions are valueless unless put to use. Successful imple-mentation calls for an appreciation and careful management of social and political forces that are set in motion by a decision. Taking steps to uncover the interests and commit-ments of key people pays dividends. Left unmanaged, social and political concerns of key people can take on a life of their own. Ignoring this is a common trap that often leads to failure.

Two practices are widely used. Both are cheap and fast but are also failure-prone (Nutt, 1986, 1987). Many spend little time on implementation until a preferred course of action has been uncovered. Managers then apply power by using an edict. To tell people what to do a memo is written. Someone is hired, or training is begun. Edicts are apt to fail for two reasons. First, people who believe they can be disadvantaged are flushed out and enticed to fight back. If the disadvantaged lack the power to openly oppose they resort to passive tactics of tokenism, tacit resistance, or obstruction (Bardack, 1977). Second, people that have no interest in a decision are prompted to resist because they fear that yielding to force will set a bad precedent. Edicts are apt to prompt a power struggle in which the best outcome one can hope for is indifference in which people do not care enough to resist (DePree, 1992).

If the edict fails, decision-makers often resort to persuasion (Churchman, 1979) – now trying to explain why an action is needed. Persuasion is fouled by the previous power play, which often dooms it to failure. Selling an idea with a demonstration of its value or with the logic of its proposed action is limited by the extent to which people are indifferent to what the manager wants to do. It has little effect on people with something to lose. Nevertheless, edicts and persuasion, used singly or in tandem, are carried out in two of every three non-developmental decisions.

There are better ways to get a decision adopted than push implementation to the front of the decision-making process. If power must be shared, teams can be created and given the prerogative to make the decision (Fisher and Brown, 1988; Fisher and Torbert, 1991). People are more apt to disclose their interests in such an arrangement. Even when disclosure is limited, the act of negotiating a solution promotes ownership in the agreed upon plan that makes success likely (Stogdill, 1974; Hackman, 1990). Savvy managers who are not required to share their power also use participation because it increases their chance of success. To do this, managers create a task force with key individuals as members and delegate important aspects of a decision-making effort to the task force. Participation is used in less than one of five decisions, but it is very effective (Nutt, 1998c). Managers say they are aware of the effectiveness of participation but find it difficult to use because of its time requirements and the seeming loss of control that results. An explanation can be found in the "paradox of control." Managers that give up control through participation actually get more control. People are more apt to ask for help when they need it and more apt to be candid about barriers to action when asked to participate in the decision-making effort. Unilateral action closes off this type of information.

Participation effectiveness varies with the degree of involvement and the role of the participants. Token participation results when a few people affected by the decision are given limited involvement (Nutt, 1986, 1998c). In theory, all affected parties can be asked to identify and select among proposals, but there appear to be concerns about cost and unpredictability when decisions are delegated to this extent. Managers seem to be unaware that token participation has a lower rate of success. When task force members are given an important assignment, success is more likely, but wide involvement is more important than a meaningful task. Participation failures can be linked to low involvement. As the proportion of participants to all affected parties falls, the failure rate for participation increases. The power of co-optation, enticing people who participate to go along, is difficult to export. A few enthusiastic participants are unable to sway people who have vested interests or are suspicious about the manager's motives.

Another approach open to the decision-maker in such a situation is to network with stakeholders with the claim and its logic to demonstrate the necessity of acting, which is called intervention (Nutt, 1986, 1998c). This is done by showing key people information about current performance and performance norms to indicate the importance of taking action, collecting and managing interests as they go. People are more likely to be supportive when this networking makes them aware of performance shortfalls and what level of performance is possible. This rarely occurs but is very successful, no matter what the manager's organizational level. Intervention creates the need for change in the minds of key people by identifying and justifying new performance norms. Showing how a comparable organization is able to operate, for example, with lower cost creates new cost expectations, suggesting a real opportunity to make a positive change. After a solution is found, the manager intervenes again by showing how performance is improved.

The success of intervention and the success of participation hold no matter what the decision situation, even for crisis situations in which immediate action is needed (Nutt, 1987, 2001a).

> *Proposition 4*: The chance of success improves when intervention and participation are used to install a decision and declines when edicts and persuasion are applied, no matter what decision context or situation is being confronted.

*Direction setting.* Decision-makers are often unwilling to acknowledge a concern without having an immediate solution (Weick, 1979; March, 1981; Starbuck, 1983; March, 1994). Such managers close off surprise and learning about possibilities. The need for control makes them unwilling to admit doubt. Doubt can be a powerful force pushing the manager to think more deeply. Rapid action is universally preferred over this, prompting a rush to judgment and the trap of ambiguous directions. As a result, two-thirds of all organizational decisions establish a direction with an idea. A seemingly useful idea in the claims motivating action is fashioned into a ready-made solution. Managers see the idea as a pragmatic way to take decisive action, and make no effort to find another one. Speedy action is always favored, even in situations that have no real time pressure. However, managers using an idea direction often struggle to verify the virtues of their idea, to coax support from others, and have to repeatedly modify the idea to make it workable. Commitment becomes a trap that often produces failure. Indeed, solutions derived in this way are seldom successful. Managers become trapped by perceptions of sunk cost, perceived threats in admitting failure, and by the reluctance people have to starting over (Nutt, 1999).

This urge to start with a concrete action creates a trap that makes formal direction setting difficult (Nutt, 1993a). As a result, expected results are either misleading, assumed but never agreed to, or unknown. Managers who feel compelled to have an answer before they begin lack a clear picture of expected results (Nadler and Hibino, 1990). The answer displaces thinking about the results that one hopes to produce. Without clarity about the reasons for taking action people form different impressions about what is wanted. Disputes arise when these individuals develop a course of action to deal with their idiosyncratic notions of what is wanted, prompting conflict. The recommended action is discussed but not the hoped-for results that prompted it. People who argue about their preferred course of action often fail to tell others what results they were trying to achieve. Being clear about what is wanted by setting an objective clears away ambiguity and conflict and helps the decision-maker find an appropriate course of action.

Managers can overcome the ambiguous direction trap by identifying an objective to guide decision-making. The objective indicates the results that a manager wants to realize, such as lower cost or increased market share. This gives considerable freedom to search for solution ideas making one open to anything that would provide the desired result. Setting objectives is much more successful than using a ready-made solution or identifying problem to be overcome, boosting the rate of success by 50 percent (Nutt, 1993a) .Objectives are commonly known, but uncommonly practiced because managers have a bias for action. Action-oriented managers see objectives as an academic exercise. Identifying desired results seems obvious. Devoting time to something thought to be obvious is irritating to the action-oriented manager. Managers who stress the need to get on with it have little patience with objective-setting sessions. Also, many managers fear being seen as indecisive. To be seen as decisive managers creates artificial pressure for action. This pressure takes several forms. Higher-ups require managers to put their wake in front of their boat, making guarantees that promise a fix the moment a claim emerges. Saying what will be done as soon as a claim materializes makes one seem to be on top of things. The press and many others in an oversight role sneer at authorizing a study with objectives. This makes it difficult to champion an orderly process that clearly articulates desired results (an objective) and waits for solutions. Managers who would prefer to follow such a path are pressured by higher-ups or people in an oversight role to grab the first idea that pops up. The pressure for a quick fix wins out even when managers know that making decisions in this way is foolhardy.

> *Proposition 5*: The chance of success improves when an objective is set and declines when directions stem from an opportunity or a problem, no matter what decision context or situation is being confronted.

*Uncovering options.*    Search and innovation is often waylaid by traps found in the desire for a quick fix and the lure of current business practices (Nutt, 1993b). Being caught in these traps often leads to a failed decision. The pressure to act rapidly draws decision-makers to the conspicuous solutions found in people's set ideas (Cyert and March, 1963). The quick fix that results is hard to back away from. Also, many people don't know what they want until they see what they can get (Wildavsky, 1979). Having an answer eliminates this ambiguity but also keeps a decision-maker from finding other, as yet undiscovered ideas, that could be better. A quick fix mentality makes it difficult for decision-makers to find innovative options or even an additional option when innovation and multiple options are universally recommended.

Decision-makers who avoid a quick fix were confronted with a new challenge: the lure of current practices. It is difficult to move away from the tangible to the unknown when fast action and low cost are stressed and solution quality made to seem unimportant. In the failures that I have studied, many of the proposed actions are variations of current practices. Managers also duck the question of search by going on a site visit to find out what others are doing. A sister organization is visited and their business practices are copied to provide a workable, if not an ideal solution. This is done because people believe that the equivalent of a field test has been conducted by the other organization so the practice must have value. Adopting the business practices of others is thought to reduce decision-making time and cost and provide a workable, if not innovative, solution.

This can work when the other company's circumstances are similar. When the companies lack compatibility a retrofit is needed and costs will quickly escalate. These costs are almost always underestimated, as is the time to do the required tailoring. Decision-makers drawn to seeing "how others do it" are also pulled away from innovation and search. Using good search tactics and designing custom-made plans avoids the traps prompted by the quick fix and the lure of current practices (Nutt, 1993b).

Managers are said to use a "single benchmark" when they copy the practices of a *single* organization or work unit and tailor these practices to fit their needs. Managers who use single benchmarks often spend considerable time trying to make the idea work, as they did when a solution is imposed at the outset. The solution is often selected in haste, with little reflection, and then requires considerable tailoring later on to get it to work. Resources are then mobilized to justify the solution, which keeps the people from looking into other possibilities. A more sophisticated approach, called "integrated benchmarking" has better results. To use integrated benchmarking the practices of several organizations or work groups are examined, identifying the best features from each. An amalgamation of these practices produces the solution.

Search aids, such as a request for proposal (RFP), to find prepackaged solutions from vendors or consultants can be effective. Search efforts can be either single or multiple. Managers who feel that they are aware of standards by which to judge a proposed option carry out a *single search*. For a *multiple search*, the manager searches repeatedly to learn about what is available that can be put to use. Several competing proposals are accumulated and compared to discern their features and capabilities. With this knowledge, a new RFP is prepared that calls for a system with features known to be available *and* needed by the organization. In a multiple search, each new RFP is written with these new insights so choosing is deferred until learning is completed. This type of search is quite effective. Single searches open up the search process but allow less opportunity for learning. The investment in a multiple search pays dividends. Time is saved because fewer repairs are necessary to fix solutions gone awry.

Managers apply innovation to find custom-made options hoping for a new idea that has the potential to prompt a breakthrough. Innovation is controversial. Some argue that it should be used more often, which would increase the number of innovation attempts in organizations (Nadler, 1981; Morgan, 1986, 1993). Others view innovation as high risk (March, 1981) and dispute its use. My studies suggest this confusion has arisen, in part, from a failure to recognize conditions under which innovation has been successful. Innovation produces good results under certain conditions, such as for important decisions, when people's creativity is tapped, when multiple alternatives are sought, and most importantly when an objective is set (Nutt, 2001a). Innovation never reaches the success level of a multiple search and integrated benchmarking, unless these conditions are met. When they are, innovation can produce breakthroughs that can eclipse any other approach. To improve the prospects of success one must follow practices that stimulate people's creativity when developing ideas. Multiple options allow managers in a decision-making role to combine the best features of options to make a superior one, but they are seldom sought for a non-developmental decision. Objectives focus the effort indicating the results expected from an innovation attempt, such as increased revenue or more market share.

*Proposition 6*: The prospects of success will improve when integrated benchmarking or a multiple search is used to uncover ready-made options.

*Proposition 7*: The prospects of success for custom-made options improve when objectives are clear, multiple options are uncovered, and good practice that encourages people's creativity is followed for decisions considered to be important.

*Option evaluation.*    Once a conspicuous solution is found, analysis soon follows. Decision-makers often feel they must take a defensive posture at this point, attempting to justify a favored course of action. After all is said and done, more time and money is spent doing this type of analysis than any of the other steps discussed thus far (Nutt, 1998a, 2001a). Analysis without being clear about expected results is misleading or, even worse, meaningless. Analysis is meaningless when it concentrates on things like costs when the decision should have had other expectations, as in major infrastructure projects such as the Denver International Airport (Nutt, 2001a) and BART, San Francisco's rapid transit system (Nutt, 1989). Cost-driven analysis is misleading and tends to find what one expects to find, offering shallow and predictable results (Rasmusson and Batstone, 1991).

When the expected results are clear, analysis can be made useful by exploring risk and comparing options. Assumptions can be tested. This can help strip away some of the uncertainty and help to cope with conflict. Best and worst case assumptions about hotel occupancy and ticket sales could have been analyzed to determine risk in the location decision for EuroDisney (Nutt, 2001a). This would have exposed factors that would limit overnight stays (the park is a day trip from Paris) and ticket sales (it was less costly at the time for many Europeans to go to Orlando), lowering revenue projections and the likelihood of turning a profit. Factors that drive revenues upward and downward are frequently ignored so the decision's risk is never explored.

Little is spent in comparing options because there is seldom but one option considered. Even in this case, analysis can be useful. The benefits of the single option can be assessed by comparing it to a norm, such as how other, successful, organizations have done. Such a comparison gives insight into the merits of a possible action before commitments are made. When multiple options are considered, analysis can be used to validate a choice by documenting the benefits that show which option seems best (Nutt, 1998a).

*Proposition 8*: The prospects for success improve when an analytical evaluation is used to compare the benefits of options and not to defend a preferred choice.

*Proposition 9*: Analysis will increase the chance of success if objectives are clear and the analysis is directed toward measuring the extent to which options can meet the objective.

*Proposition 10*: Bargaining to find a course of action has a good chance of success.

## Developmental Decisions

There has been very little empirical research to uncover practices that increase the chance of success for a developmental decision. On those rare occasions in which there have been systematic studies developmental decisions have been mixed with non-developmental ones, so little can be said about them (e.g., Hickson et al., 1986). To fill this void, recommendations are based on the key tasks used for related processes, such as strategic management and strategic leadership (e.g., Schendel and Hofer, 1979; Ansoff, 1984; Bennis and Nanus, 1985; Pettigrew, 1985; Delbecq, 1989; Conger, 1991; El-Namaki, 1992; Coulson-Thomas, 1992; Larwood et al., 1993, 1995). This literature was examined to find the required tasks, the recommended sequence of these tasks, and ways to carry out these tasks, seeking a synthesis of the key ideas. The approach offered here presents the synthesis that was uncovered. Key ideas call for dealing with the obstacles encountered when undertaking a developmental decision – finding and then implementing a vision. The literature suggests that these moves that are made to walk the vision must also "walk the talk" with stakeholders (Meindl et al., 1985; Meindl, 1990; Nutt and Backoff, 1996a). The strategic decision-making process offered here embraces these two key ideas. Several of the tasks shifted in importance and emphasis, as well as their sequence, compared with those called for in a non-developmental decision. Others remained much the same. Table 2.1 compares these tasks and their sequence for developmental and non-developmental decisions. The recommended process calls for vision creation and implementation. A developmental decision carries out this implementation by following steps that call for co-creating a vision, exploring barriers to action, framing the vision for public consumption, blurring leader and follower distinctions, and pushing the action forward.

*Proposition 11*: The prospect of success improves when developmental decisions follow a process that begins with vision co-creation and is followed by exploring barriers, re-framing the vision for consumption, blurring leader–follower distinctions, and pushing the action forward to implement the vision.

TABLE 2.1 Contrasting the process for developmental and non-developmental decisions

| *Non-developmental decisions* | *Developmental decisions* |
| --- | --- |
| 1. Reconcile claims | 1. Co-create a vision |
| 2. Uncover social and political forces to manage key interests | 2. Explore barriers to action with stakeholder and resource assessments |
| 3. Set direction | 3. Re-frame vision for public consumption |
| 4. Uncover ideas |    a. Enlarge space |
| 5. Explore ideas with analysis to identify a preferred course of action |    b. Switch filters and context |
| | 4. Blur leader–follower differences |
| |    a. Give away information |
| |    b. Empower followers |
| | 5. Push forward the action |
| |    a. Position in a stream of action |
| |    b. Promote via networking |
| |    c. Create positive energy |
| |    d. Path clear for empowered followers |

Let us explore the steps called for by a developmental decision and their similarities and differences, compared to the non-developmental decision. The primary difference in the two processes is found in the treatment of idea creation. Here it leads ("see first") and for the non-developmental decision it follows ("think first"). Managers making developmental decisions that will change their business or business practices are called on to begin by making sense of possibilities (Weick, 1989, 1994; Van de Ven and Poole, 1995). They envision these possibilities as a place to start and infer purpose from the idea and its implications. The idea and its purpose are uncovered together (Nutt and Backoff, 1996b). This reverses several steps that were called for in the non-developmental decision. The role of the manager also changes from one of directing to one of leading. Calling for managers to become leaders when addressing developmental decisions signifies this. Here the leader has the more weighty tasks of coaching and facilitating, placing much less emphasis on directing and choosing (Fisher and Torbert, 1991).

The importance of vision in developmental decisions is stressed by every source that was reviewed. Little is said about vision creation. To address this, additional material was reviewed to find some clues. The remainder of the chapter is organized around these two core ideas. First, some key aspects of vision creation are presented followed by a discussion of the developmental decision-making process that has been fashioned to implement it.

## *Vision creation*

Sources from the social sciences, organizational development, leadership, and systems theory literatures were used to identify the key features of a vision and how to create one. The creation of focus (Nanus, 1989), an ideal image of future (Kouzes and Posner, 1987), a conceptual road map (Bryman, 1992), future organizational purpose (Land and Jarman, 1992; Kotter, 1996), a new order (Kelley, 1992), and principles and values that direct (Gardner, 1990; Nadler et al., 1992) suggest some key properties of a vision. A vision provides a vivid and reachable target that beckons (Watzawick et al., 1974). The picture has fresh ideas that inspire and build a commitment to change in the minds of key people. Many visions resemble slogans such as John F. Kennedy's "military strength with moral purpose" or Gorbachev's "Glasnost and Perestroika" (Nutt and Backoff, 1997b). Value-based principles also seem important. When McConnell at Worthington Industries used the "golden rule" to state personnel and customer policies he identified an enduring set of values that became Worthington's guide to conduct its business. During this period, it was printed on the back of every employee's business card.

A vision offers ways to alter a company's strategy – that is, new ideas for products/ services, customers, markets, channels, capabilities, sources of revenue, ways to organize, and image. For example, leaders in the LL Bean Company engaged in countless acts to implement its vision of treating customers like human beings. SAS president Carlzon (1987) used the notion of "50,000 daily moments of truth" to depict the emphasis to be placed on customer service quality by airline employees. People working for Scandinavian Airlines had to take steps to ensure that each "moment of truth" that was encountered would be a positive experience for its customers (Land and Jarman, 1992). This suggests that vision mobilizes and leadership is required to realize a vision's aims. Distinctions are needed that show what vision is and how it differs from other ways of articulating an enduring organizational purpose.

*Proposition 12*: The prospects of success improve when the vision has sufficient clarity to mobilize by showing when is intended.

*What distinguishes vision.* Vision has similarities with mission, aim, goal, target, and objective, as well as important differences. Like mission, aim, goal, target, and objective, vision can provide direction, create focus, produce clarity about what is wanted, and direct human action. An examination of the definitions of vision found in the literature suggests four properties that seem to distinguish vision from other forms of direction setting. A vision has clear and compelling imagery that offers an innovative way to improve, which recognizes and draws on traditions, and connects to actions that people can take to realize change. Vision taps people's emotion and energy. Properly articulated, a vision creates the enthusiasm that people have for sporting events and other leisure time activities, bringing this energy and commitment to the workplace. Other means of directing human action seem to lack these qualities.

Traditional ways to establish direction lack an innovative idea that embraces values and enrolls people using clear and compelling imagery. Goals and objectives do not contain an innovative solution. Nor do they embrace organizational values to show the way with a clear and compelling picture of the future. Goals and objectives are typically "solution free" and rarely consider values. They point to a desired result (better morale), not actions to take to realize the desired result (the golden rule at Worthington Industries). Missions and aims, by tradition and practice, may have a value component but often lack the compelling imagery of a good vision (Wheatley, 1992; Thompson and Strickland, 1995). According to Wall et al. (1992), mission is used to clarify purpose and prevent misunderstanding by elaborating on the key ideas in a vision. This suggests that vision is inspirational and mission tends to be instrumental.

Vision provides a prescription that goes beyond current business practices (Jantsch, 1975) to suggest future business opportunities. Vision provides a way to picture innovative ideas that suggest how to rethink an organization's strategy. The vision suggests changes in products/services, customers, distribution channels, competencies, sources of margin, bases of competitive advantage, ways to organize, or image and persona that can offer an organization distinction (Hamel and Prahalad, 1994; Nutt and Backoff, 1995). In the public sector, services/service channels and collaborative advantage replace products/services and competitive advantage. Vision calls for developmental change closely aligned to that found in strategic management (e.g., Schendel and Hofer, 1979; Porter, 1985; Daft, 1995).

A vision has fresh ideas suggesting a new order that offers a road map to the future. It is expected to offer new ways to be competitive in the marketplace via creative products, positioning in the market, or in other moves that alter the company's strategy in a major way to deal with future conditions that are believed to be emerging. It is often important for these ideas to be radically innovative – that is, new to the industry. This future orientation that anticipates markets and what the market wants requires an innovative response. Getting new ideas out before the competition has been a key competitive advantage of companies such as Disney, Intel, 3M company, and Hewlett-Packard.

*Proposition 13*: The prospects of success improve when the vision is innovative and improves even more when the vision is radically innovative.

*Criteria for vision creation.*   A vision has inspirational possibilities that are value centered, realizable, with superior imagery and articulation that can be called possibility, desirability, actionability, and articulation (Nutt and Backoff, 1997b). Each offers a design criterion for vision creation. A crucial feature is a "possibility set" that offers a mental model of an idealistic future or future perfect state, which sets standards of excellence and clarifies purpose. The desired possibility set is one that expands horizons and ambitions. To meet such a standard, a vision must fit the organization's traditions and values as well as the times, characterized by current trends and events. Visions are realized by aligning people's energies in productive directions and helping people to focus on what's important. Another feature stems from what constitutes a good illustration of a vision: a superior articulation that can be easily understood (Conger, 1991). People are drawn to a vision with powerful imagery that clarifies purpose, such as Paley at CBS who called radio "broadcasting," Monnet's "economic union for Europe" that became the rallying cry for the common market, or Burr's "no frills air travel" that gave purpose to People Express.

Vision should be able to create possibilities that are inspirational (Nutt and Backoff, 1997a), creative (El-Namaki, 1992), unique (Kouzes and Posner, 1993), vibrant (Land and Jarman, 1992), and offer a new order (Kelley, 1992) that can produce organizational distinction (Wheatley, 1992). Block (1988) sums this up as a deep expression of what is wanted: a dream that indicates what we want for the organization. For example, when leaders at Burroughs decided to "ship only what works," people realized that quality must be emphasized, even if costs increase (Tichy and Devanna, 1986, 1990). When this innovative possibility was used to direct action, performance improvements were realized at Burroughs.

Vision possibilities are similar to a scenario that captures social and technological trends and finds convergent and connective themes suggesting possible futures (El Sawy, 1985; Schwartz, 1991). The time horizon of these futures are constrained only by the arena in which speculation can be fruitful, such as tracking the exponential growth rate in the miniaturization and power of transistors. Vision is built in this manner, reaching into the future far enough to reveal opportunities with potentially important consequences that can be understood and appreciated (McGrath, 1988). Like a scenario, a vision walks down a path to discover what value is produced by an outcome with particular qualities. Thus, a vision suggests both means and ends, as in the Burroughs example.

Desirable visions draw on an organization's values and culture (e.g. Linstone, 1984; Quinn, 1988; Gardner, 1990; El-Namaki, 1992; Bryman, 1992; Shamir et al., 1993; Kirkpatrick and Locke, 1996). According to Meyer and Rowan (1977) and Torbert (1989), people in organizations come to accept a shared definition of social processes that specify the "way things are" and "the way things are done." Organizations use rewards, such as resources and legitimacy, as well as persuasion and role modeling to get people to conform to these expectations. The resulting behavioral norms create an institutional culture in which certain values are emphasized (DiMaggio, 1988; Quinn, 1988). Churchman (1979) and Ackoff (1981) note how values, such as morality and aesthetics, influence effectiveness and efficiency. For example, the last Australian labor prime minister, Cahill, offered his vision for a modern Australia in the late 1940s with a symbol: the Sydney Opera House (Nutt, 1989). Aesthetic value was allowed to dominate over matters of cost.

Cahill thought that such a symbol was needed to mark Australia as an emerging world power. In this case, an uplifting landmark was called for that could alter Australia's image and vault it into the mainstream of Western society. Note how Cahill's vision drew on values that denoted the emerging economic power and potential of his country. All visions must have this feature. A vision must connect the possibilities that are contained in a vision to organizational values, and make these values clear (Coulson-Thomas and Coe, 1991; Nadler et al., 1992; Oakley and Krug, 1993). Assuming people see it as ethical, a vision that contains such a feature helps people let go of the past and opens them up to acting on the new possibilities that are contained in a vision (Shamir et al., 1993). For instance, DePree (1992) showed how the value of interdependence was essential to his vision of empowerment for people at Herman Miller, and Hass illustrated the notion of "interconnectedness" to promote his vision of mutual commitment at Levi-Strauss (Wheatley, 1992). The tradition of customer satisfaction was used to promote the LL Bean's vision of always treating customers as human beings (Galbraeth and Lawler, 1992). In each of these examples, a leader drew on values in organizational norms to make the vision seem desirable.

Actionability is also important because people called on to carry out a vision must see a role for them to play (Boal and Bryson, 1988; Gardner, 1990; Ruvolu and Marcus, 1992; El-Namaki, 1992; Coulson-Thomas, 1992; Shamir et al., 1993). The possibilities and norms drawn on to articulate the vision mobilize people when they are understood and seen as challenging, but doable. An actionable vision points to activities that people can undertake that move toward a desirable future (Bryman, 1992). Bennis and Nanus (1989) and Bennis (1989a, b), call this "a target that beckons," Land and Jarman (1992) refer to it as "future-pull," and Oakley and Krug (1993) call it a mental image that embodies people's aspirations. Gardner (1990) contends that people are moved to action when they see how their acts fit into the larger action plan, which meets the reality test of El-Namaki (1992). People who see what they can do and how these acts can aid the vision are more apt to help make the vision a reality. For example, Sparks changed Whirlpool from an engineering company with a few marketing skills to a marketing company with engineering and manufacturing skills (Tichy and Devanna, 1990). Employees were encouraged to think about the company's markets and what each person could do to help Whirlpool be successful in a particular market segment.

The best visions have an uncanny ability to communicate. Note how the visions used as exemplars so far have qualities of superior articulation and powerful imagery that crystallizes what is wanted in people's mind. A vision with these qualities creates a picture that can be carried around in an individual's head, indicating how to foster change. People are drawn to a vision with superior imagery because it clarifies what they must do.

*Proposition 14*: A vision with clear and compelling imagery is more apt to be successful.

Commitment and enrollment are required to realize a vision (Senge, 1990; Shamir et al., 1993). Commitment stems from an attraction that pulls people toward the vision. To be enrolled, a person drawn to the vision embraces its inherent values by taking action, both requested and self-initiated, to realize its aims. The intent is to motivate people to do whatever can be done, within reason, to help to implement such a vision. Commitment and enrollment prospects improve when a vision has clear articulation and compelling imagery. A vision's articulation and imagery moves people between stages of non-compliance (resistance) to genuine compliance that requires both commitment and enrollment (El-Namaki, 1992). A vision with these features can also move people who offer grudging compliance (fails to see value, just does what's expected) and formal compliance (sees value, not inspired to take extraordinary steps) to the higher levels of energy produced by a vision with powerful imagery.

> *Proposition 15*: A vision that is value centered, realizable, with superior articulation containing a radically innovative possibility that is desirable and actionable with superior articulation is more apt to be successful.

## *Vision implementation and the developmental decision*

The steps called for to implement a developmental decision parallel those for vision implementation found in the literature. Next, each of these steps is considered in the order suggested to carry them out.

*Co-create a vision.* Developmental change can be quite a challenge for companies in which stakeholders have divided loyalties, there is poor leadership, and pervasive implied control that stems from many quarters. When such conditions are present, stakeholders may obstruct a developmental decision designed to implement a vision. Others resist radical innovation because they are very reluctant to take risks and radical innovation seems very risky. Such stakeholders are reluctant to experiment and this resistance poses a formidable barrier to developmental action (Fisher and Ury, 1981; Bass, 1985; Oakley and Krug, 1993). But those that resist experimentation can be swept along when involved in the process of change (Burns, 1978; Shamir et al., 1993). A leader can attempt to win such people over or involve them to create active supporters. The latter is more effective.

Leaders are called on to invent the future with the help of key exemplary followers (El-Namaki, 1992, and others such as Wheatley, 1992; Land and Jarman, 1993; Kouzes and Posner, 1993). Covey (1989, 1990) and Delbecq (1989) have shown that a radically innovative vision that integrates the best ideas of the key exemplary followers with those of the leader is an essential ingredient in a successful developmental decision. To do this the developmental decision-making process begins with the leader delegating aspects of vision development to "exemplary followers" (Kelley, 1992), knowledgeable people with high volition. Because the exemplary follower is responsible for 80 percent of the successful changes in organizations empowering such people, is both pragmatic and beneficial. To do so, the leader forms a strategic development group (SDG) made up of the company's exemplary followers. The leader takes on the role of a facilitator and chairs the SDG's efforts. The leader coaches the group and seeks to invent the future by seeking synergy that integrates the ideas of the group members with the leader's ideas. The SDG's membership must also include key line managers, representing important interests in the organization. Important stakeholders from outside the organization should be added whenever feasible. For example, an SDG for a historical society was made up of key volunteers, donors, exemplary staff, and line managers and would be chaired by the society director. Such a group can build commitment among key interests

TABLE 2.2 Stakeholder and resource assessments

| Traps to be avoided | Best practice | Steps required |
| --- | --- | --- |
| Failing to take charge by reconciling claims | Network with stakeholders | Involve stakeholders to uncover and reconcile concerns and formulate a claim |
| Ignoring barriers to action | Intervention or participation | Demonstrate the need to act and ways to consider the interests and commitment of stakeholders |
| Ambiguous directions | Set objectives | Create clear picture of expected results |
| Limited search | Innovation or search | Increase the number of options considered and those with potential first mover advantages |
| Misusing analysis | Explore risk and compare the benefits of the options | Expose options with unacceptable risk and validate the choice |
| Overlooking ethical questions | Look for important values and offer mediation | Uncover and confront the ethical questions of internal and external stakeholders |
| Failing to learn | Create win–win situations for all stakeholders | Look for and remove perverse incentives and encourage honest appraisal of company actions |

*Source*: Adapted from Nutt and Backoff (1992).

groups and provides a way to communicate when actions are questioned (Nutt and Backoff, 1992; Walton, 1985). Participants help to sell the results, as in the non-developmental decision guided by participation.

*Proposition 16*: The prospect of success improves when a vision is co-created with a team made up of exemplary followers and key organization leaders and outsiders.

*Explore barriers with stakeholder and resource assessments.*    Obstacles that block a vision and the changes it will bring arise from the limitations imposed by stakeholders and resources.

People who could affect a developmental decision or be influenced by it can materialize and become stakeholders (Mason and Mitroff, 1981; Freeman, 1984). Determining the positions or interests of those not included in vision development is essential. To be successful the positions and importance of interest groups such as customers, suppliers, oversight bodies, service providers, cooperating units, alliance partners, the communities in which the company will operate, and the public must be determined and managed. To do this a grid is used, as shown in table 2.1 (Nutt and Backoff, 1992). Having the SDG members and other knowledgeable people locate such stakeholders on the grid suggests who to target and some tactics to use, such as using supporters to try to win over the problematic and then mounting campaigns to manage antagonists. The number and nature of the stakeholders in each of the grid categories suggests the amount of effort that will be required.

Resources go beyond financial considerations to include political, legal, managerial, and professional staff resources, as well as people who will make reallocation decisions. The resources required to make the vision a reality are identified and then assessed in terms of their criticality (importance) and potential availability (ease of mobilizing) using the lower grid in table 2.2. The grid classifies an organization's resources as one of four key types. This assessment allows the leader to identify internal reallocations that seem feasible and external support that will be needed to insure success. A county library was able to pass a levy to support its developmental decision to expand service after such an assessment. State departments of natural resources were able to charge user fees to support their developmental plan (Wechsler and Backoff, 1986).

*Proposition 17*: Leaders that determine stakeholder support and required resources before taking action increase their chance of making a successful developmental decision.

*Frame the vision for public consumption.*   The attention focused on an organization attempting a developmental decision calls for special care when introducing the vision. If influential insiders or outsiders feel threatened, political influence can be mobilized and snuff out a good idea before it can be shaped to fit the situation. The images evoked by a vision must be carefully managed. The vision is presented to allay fears and to create a sense of purpose. It is not enough to paint a picture that entices, suggesting something that seems useful for the company using compelling imagery. In addition to enlisting others in a quest, the leader must demonstrate feasibility and provide reasons to change, as in the intervention tactic. The leader must also prepare for scrutiny that can misrepresent what is being purposed to serve selfish interests.

To deal with this situation, the leader re-frames the vision for each key interest group by considering what preferences and values are apt to be important to these individuals and groups. The primary message contained in a vision cannot be changed because of its public nature. Instead, aspects of the vision that serve an interest group are identified and then stressed in communications with this body. Two types of tactics are used. First, the leader attempts to expand the vision to create a bigger space, one that has more variety. For example, the leader of the historical society identified some common elements in preserving historical buildings and conducting historical plays, which appealed to the values of the interest groups that push each type of activity. A synthetic vision that draws on the best features of each is sought. To do this the vision is enlarged to incorporate the interests of key people.

   *Proposition 18*: A vision that is enlarged to incorporate the interests of key stakeholders is more apt to lead to a successful developmental decision.

Second, leaders describe the vision by switching filters and using context. By switching filters the leader casts light on aspects of the vision that deal with the needs and problems of key interest groups. For example, the historical society talked about cost containment aspects of the developmental vision to the state legislature, possible preservation programs to potential donors committed to saving historical landmarks, and new opportunities for activism to influential volunteers. Also, context can be switched to make the vision saleable. A public library can show the need for a developmental decision that alters its programs by describing the proposed cut in county funding that prompted them. People who understand the context of a proposed decision, such as the proposed cut, are more apt to support it. Developmental actions described through filters selected according to the preferences of the interest groups that take into account its context are more apt to be supported.

   *Proposition 19*: A developmental decision that is described through the filters selected according to the preferences of each interest group that takes into account context is more apt to be successful.

*Blur leader–follower differences.*   The differences between leaders and followers are becoming less clear-cut in well-run organizations (Kelley, 1992). People in key positions know they can often wait out leaders that they distrust or disagree with. Organizations have professional staff, such as accountants and engineers, who require autonomy and demand independence. Thus, control-oriented leaders have less power than they imagine. More importantly, to build ownership the leader must empower exemplary followers and other key players to initiate developmental thinking. Blurring leader–follower differences is both pragmatic, given the real power limitations of many leaders, and essential to get the needed commitments.

   Leaders can reduce hierarchy in several ways. First, leaders can give away information that depicts the company's status and important relationships in the authority network, such as strategic alliances and alliance partners. To illustrate, the leader of a workers' compensation bureau in a state government was coping with a crisis of shrinking reserves, caused by rate limits imposed by the state legislature, and pressure to approve all compensation settlements regardless of their merit. Reports by consultants describing the crisis, sequestered by the previous agency head, were distributed and the crisis described in detail to trusted exemplary followers. These individuals were asked to provide liaison to key members of the state legislature and other groups, a role that agency heads usually keep for themselves. This step got the organization closer to its customer – the legislature – and empowered followers to help in the quest. It also built trust and encourage reciprocity in relationships throughout the organization.

   As these actions are taken, the leader stresses the key values sought by the developmental decision. The leader in the workers' compensation bureau stressed, inside and outside the organization, the need for sound fiscal management in which rates are fair to employers and claims are fairly settled, for appropriate amounts, for the injured worker. Because ownership had been built in key insiders many were repeating the same message at the same time, increasing its chance of being acted on. Thus, empowered followers increase the chance that a developmental decision will be successfully implemented.

*Proposition 20*: Empowered followers increase the chance that a developmental decision will be successful.


*Push the action forward.*  When empowered exemplary followers are prepared to spread the word, the leader pushes the action forward. The leader positions in a stream of action, monitoring key transactions and networking. The leader creates attention and pays attention (Covey, 1989). Following Covey's prescription to first understand and then be understood does this. To understand, the leader listens to objections. When objections are fully appreciated, the leader positions to argue for the developmental decision.

To spread the word, the leader draws on the positive energy of learned optimism (Seiglman, 1991). Every threat is re-framed to create an opportunity. A public library passed the first ever levy in the face of opposition by community leaders by getting its message out. To push the action forward, its leader stressed the benefits that the levy would provide whenever threats by opponents were made in the local press. Such threats were treated as an opportunity that gave him a forum to respond. Instead of answering the criticism the leader pounded away at his message about the levy's benefits. Such an approach encourages learned optimism in which people routinely re-frame problems as opportunities.

*Proposition 21*: Leaders that create positive energy as they carry out a developmental decision are more apt to be successful.

The leader seeking to implement a developmental decision must carry on, often in the face of frustration with unfair and unwarranted attacks and the disenchantment such attacks bring. The leader copes with these challenges by helping people become more productive. Help is created by path clearing. The leader gets needed resources and removes barriers that limit what the exemplary follower can do. This calls for leaders to allow all such individuals to have self-management and peer-review of their actions, which cuts down on the fear of failure. The leader of the workers' compensation bureau visited field offices and helped to push along long-delayed requests for computer software that limited their effectiveness. The field staff was given the discretion to aggressively seek ways out of the bureau's claims gridlock. To reduce the fear of failure, the field staff was told that any progress in speeding up claim handling would be welcomed. When progress was noted, recognition was provided in the form of resources to make further improvements (Kouzes and Posner, 1987). Leaders that path-clear like this are more apt to realize their developmental decisions.

*Proposition 22*: Leaders who accept the role of path clearing for key people instrumental in implementing a developmental decision are more apt to be successful.

To push the decision forward, the leader gets out the message. One's net is cast widely, as in the intervention tactic, by walking the vision with all players, first to understand and then to be understood (Covey, 1989). This is done by walking the talk – a friendly one-on-one discussion in which the interests of each key player are addressed. To walk the talk, the leader describes what is expected to happen and gets feedback. The hallmark of such an effort is patience. Leaders must be willing to move slowly and build trust and to recycle when blocking occurs. Such a commitment puts the organization's interests on hold when key people believe they have been disadvantaged by changes that a developmental decision will bring. To be responsive, the leader waits for opportunities. Changes in the vision are sought that create a win-win action that overcomes objections and maintains or improves on the key features of a developmental decision.

## RESEARCHING DEVELOPMENTAL DECISIONS

Little is known empirically about developmental decisions. This puts a premium on such studies. There are, however, many complications and difficulties in conducting empirical research into developmental decisions. Some will be addressed here discussing the type of outcomes that can be realized, some study approaches, and suggestions for sources of data.

The content of a development identifies the type of change that is sought. The intent of a developmental decision is a transformation – a radical change in the strategy of an organization (Prigogine and Stengers, 1984). To study such decisions one must be clear about whether this occurred (Popper, 1959). The criteria offered here, a radical change in one aspect of a firm's strategy, is one approach. Whatever approach is used, there must be clarity on what kind of outcomes are required to qualify as a developmental decision.

Studies of content could sort developmental decisions by what has been added on. Counts of the number of attempts to change products, markets, etc. compared to the number of successes in each strategy category could be enlightening. Conventional wisdom suggests that a transformation is more likely with new products. Empirical evidence could test this view. Such a study could identify which aspects of a firm's strategy are targeted most often for change and which strategic moves have the greatest chance of leading to a transformation.

Prescriptions about process can be studied by sorting developmental decisions into those that prompted a transformation and those that did not. This would allow comparisons of the actions taken by leaders that produced a transformation with those that failed to do so. Such a study could be even more useful by documenting the impact of the transformation on the company's financial performance, comparing the before and after state of these indicators.

A radical change could have a de-developmental result as well in which a firm strips out organizational complexity to downsize (Nutt, 2001b). To de-develop, one goes beyond downsizing (Weitzel and Jonsson, 1987; Swoboda, 1995). A radical change is required that strips out organizational complexity dropping products, channels, etc. that are not working. Thus, a transformation adds on and de-development takes out components of an organization's strategy, being mindful of the synergy that binds the strategy components together. The study of de-development could be carried out as before. First, de-developmental efforts would be classified into successful and unsuccessful categories. This is followed by an evaluation of the before and after financial impact of each, connecting each of these decisions to the actions taken to produce these results.

Developmental decisions, whether transformational or de-developmental, can be investigated using retrospective and prospective approaches. Retrospective methods compare exemplars that display characteristics of interest. Prospective methods try out some of the process ideas and report on results.

Retrospective studies could be carried out with strategic management cases, case studies reported in the literature (e.g., Meyer and Zucker, 1981), or by developing a database of decisions as I have done for non-developmental decisions (e.g., Nutt, 1999). To use strategic management cases, the company and the case's author would be interviewed to uncover the steps taken to make the developmental decision and other factors of interest using qualitative methods (e.g., Lincoln and Guba, 1985; Patton, 1990; Denzin, 1989; Yin, 1993). To conduct such a study, a measurement scheme must be devised that classifies the cases according to type (i.e., transformational or de-development) and to measure the consequences that can be attributed to the decision. Better outcomes are predicted when a process like the one offered here is used. Alternately, the researcher can devise an approach to make developmental decisions and test it against what is actually done in organizations to make such a decision.

Relying upon cases in texts or the literature is limited by what has been written. Case write-ups are not likely to have all of the information needed to identify what was done to attempt to transform or to de-develop the organization. In addition, many such cases may fail to meet the criterion for a radical change. The change may fail to add on or take out products, customers, markets, etc. If cases with the required features can be found, the process called for in the propositions to realize a developmental decision could be tested. Such a test would compare the results realized when a change approach like that in the propositions is used with developmental decisions that used a different approach. The results could be quite revealing, making a powerful statement about the key ingredients to make a transformational or de-developmental change.

Retrospective studies can also be used to examine the nature of transformation and de-development. Cases that describe an organization at two points in time can be compared to determine how its strategy has changed. Radical changes that add on are predicted to improve financial performance. Radical changes that let go are predicted to have the same effect. Comparisons of radical changes that successfully add on organized complexity in this way to those that take it out could be revealing. This type of study would be limited by the availability of cases that describe radical change according to accepted definitions. If key participants can be interviewed to explore the aftermath of radical changes additional insight about the aftermath of such change can be sought.

Prospective studies could use action theory or simulation to test the propositions. Action theory (Harmon, 1981; Argyris et al., 1987; Copperrider and Srivastva, 1987) calls on the researcher to go into the world and make changes, drawing insight from the creation of action. It has the same motivations as participant observation, which positions the researcher to observe (e.g., Burrell and Morgan, 1979; Lincoln and Guba, 1985; Spradley, 1980; Denzin, 1989; Patton, 1990). To determine how meaning is created, the researcher is called on to make sense of what occurs as a development decision is made (Weick, 1979; Denzin, 1989; Patton, 1990). This follows the hermeneutic tradition of observing and then reflecting, seeking to understand (Shapiro and Sica, 1984).

Action theory seeks the same information as participant observation. Differences arise when the researcher becomes a facilitator and leads the effort to make a developmental decision for an organization. The researcher as a facilitator would work with a top management team (TMT), or form such a group, to devise such a decision. The researcher then reflects on the developmental process that was used, the decision that results, aspects of dialog, and the decision's consequences to probe the nature of the developmental decision-making process (Bakhtin, 1981). Sessions can be recorded to allow for later analysis. The researcher reflects on what transpired to clarify what happened and to uncover what seems to make a difference in crafting a developmental decision. Opportunities for this type of research stem from consulting engagements. The scope of such opportunities often limits the range of organizations that can be investigated, which is a key limitation for this type of research.

Action theory calls for the researcher to devise a way to make a development decision. The propositions indicate the key steps recommended here. In addition, the procedure to be followed must be crafted. To illustrate how this could be done, some key features of a post-modern logic of inquiry will be used. Post modernism or deconstruction (Ichazo, 1982; Rosenau, 1992; Hassard and Parker, 1993) applied to carry out a developmental decision-making effort would attempt to discredit current strategic practices with key people, such as the TMT. The facilitator would disassemble these practices, with each piece examined for its relevance before being reassembled. The facilitator helps the TMT closely examine with the intent to dismiss current practices, no matter how well accepted. By making everything subject to a "crossout," the outmoded and redundant can be swept away to uncover new truths about what the organization can become.

Post modernism encourages radical thinking to create a new vision for the organization. Each strategic component (e.g. products, markets, etc.) is examined by testing its value, importance, and future certainty (Mason and Mitroff, 1981; Nutt and Backoff, 1997a). This encourages participants to be wary of their attachments to components of a strategy, such as a venerated product, and to be willing to let go of them or to change them in a major way. Deconstruction for vision creation asserts that leaders can get new ideas to "re-vision" when an openness to question and explore current strategic practices is fostered. Such a posture moves people from being fixated on a present reality to considering future possibilities. To form a new vision using postmodern thinking, a team would be called upon to examine, dissemble, and then re-assemble the current strategy of an organization. The goal is not to discover how the strategy works, but to destroy any aspect of it that contains weak or unfounded assumptions. This is similar to a devil's advocate posture, with the dialectic focused on a retain-discard tension for each component.

The next steps would connect these components to find ancillary components (e.g. market channels for products) that make a retained component or the new one (e.g. product) viable. These connections add to the list of crucial pieces. The residual products, customers, markets, etc. would be slated for termination in de-development or new ones identified for a transformation. The group then considers how this new emphasis would change the organization so it responds to its new challenges listing key trends and events and directions (moving from, moving toward) for each (Nutt and Backoff, 1992). A match of strategic components to be let go or added on with these directions is made to test the extent to which outside challenges and realities have been met. Next, the group identifies moves needed to discard or to add on the products, etc.

Using deconstruction as an action theory could provide a number of prospectively devised developmental decision cases. The exemplars could be documented to create case narratives and other kinds of pictures that depict developmental decision-making practices (Lincoln and Guba, 1985). Following the suggestions of Yin (1981, 1989), various explanations can be compared with each case to determine how each explanation fits with the procedures used to make the developmental decisions. Contrasting particularly useful decisions with failed attempts may reveal patterns that can be linked to success and failure.

Simulations require a protocol and a setting. The protocol described for action theory could be applied in a setting such as an executive training to test the developmental decision-making process propositions. The facilitator (teacher-researcher) would guide participants through the required process steps using a stock set of cases. Such an approach can go beyond action theory because the practices of a comparison approach could also be included. This allows for a comparison of a proposed process with others (e.g., table 2.1). Comparing suggestions with what was done in the case, and its outcome, could be used to measure success. Alternatively, experts could evaluate the workshop proposals that result.

Although broader in its scope, the artificiality of the setting in a simulation puts limits on generalizability. The advantages of an action theory approach stems from its unambiguous connection to the phenomena of interest, developmental decisions and their consequences. Real organizations with real issues are used, avoiding the difficulties that can stem from workshops in which participants may lack motivation or skill. Misleading surrogates for success is also avoided. However, action theory sacrifices rigor in control and outcome measurement for this increased relevance. The outcome of an action theory research project is usually evaluated with before and after performance indicators. Superior performance could be an illusion. Improvements in performance could be due to uncontrolled and uncontrollable factors that can arise as the facilitator helps key people devise a developmental decision for their organization. Each of these uncontrolled factors, such as changes in participation or environmental shifts, provides a plausible explanation of the observed performance changes that cannot be ruled out. Also, without a control group, there is no way to tell if the organization would have done just as well with another approach.

## CONCLUSION

The strengths and weaknesses of retrospective and prospective approaches are complementary (Burrell and Morgan, 1979; Habermas, 1970). Each highlights different aspects of developmental decisions. Also, each approach views the effects of a developmental decision somewhat differently, and provides different interpretations of success. As a result, an accumulation of insights drawn from research using both approaches seems needed to investigate developmental decisions. This is similar to a multi-method research approach, called for by Lincoln and Guba (1985), Morgan (1984), and Woodman (1989).

REFERENCES

Ackoff, R. (1981). *Creating the Corporate Future*. New York: Wiley.

Ansoff, H. I. (1984). *Implanting Strategic Management*. Englewood Cliffs, NJ: Prentice-Hall.

Argyris, C., Putnam, R., and Smith, D. M. (1987). *Action Science*. San Francisco, CA: Jossey Bass.

Bakhtin, M. (1981). *The Dialogic Imagination*. Austin, TX: University of Texas Press.

Bardack, E. (1977). *The Implementation Game*. Cambridge, MA: MIT Press.

Bass, B. M. (1985). *Leadership and Performance Beyond Expectations*. New York: Free Press.

Bennis, W. (1989a). *On Becoming a Leader*. New York: Addison-Wesley.

Bennis, W. (1989b). *Why Leaders Can't Lead*. San Francisco, CA: Jossey Bass.

Bennis, W., and Nanus, B. (1989). *Leaders*. New York: Harper & Row.

Block, P. (1988). *The Empowered Manager*. San Francisco, CA: Jossey Bass.

Boal, K., and Bryson, J. (1988). Charismatic Leadership: A Phenomenological and Structural Approach, in J. Hunt, B. Baliga, H. Dachler, and C. Schriesheim (eds.), *Emerging Leadership Vistas*. Lexington, MA: Lexington Books, 11–28.

Bryman, A. (1992). *Charisma and Leadership*. London: Sage.

Bryson, J., Bromley, P. and Jung, V. (1990). The Influence of Context and Process on Project Planning Success. *Journal of Planning Education*, 9(3), 183–95.

Burns, J. M. (1978). *Leadership*. New York: Harper & Row.

Burrell, G. and Morgan, G. (1979). *Sociological Paradigms and Organizational Analysis*. London: Heinemann.

Carlzon, J. (1987). *Moments of Truth*. New York: Ballinger.

Churchman, C. W. (1979). *The Systems Approach and Its Enemies*. New York: Basic Books.

Cohen, M. D., March, J. P., and Olsen, J. P. (1976). A Garbage Can Model of Organizational Choice. *Administrative Science Quarterly*, 17, 1–25.

Conger, J. (1991). Inspiring Others: The Language of Leadership. *Academy of Management Executive*, 5(1), 31–45.

Copperrider, D., and Srivastra, R. (1987). Appreciative Inquiry in Organizational Life, in *Research in Organizational Change and Development*, 1.

Coulson-Thomas, C. (1992). Strategic Vision or Strategic Con: Rhetoric or Reality. *Long Range Planning*, 25(1), 81–9.

Coulson-Thomas, C., and Coe, T. (1991). *Managing the Flat Organization*. New York: BIM.

Covey, S. (1989). *The Seven Habits of Highly Effective Leaders*. New York: Simon and Schuster.

Covey, S. R. (1990). *Principled Central Leadership*. New York: Summit.

Cray, D., Mallory, G., Butler, R., Hickson, D., and Wilson, D. (1991). Explaining Decision Processes. *Journal of Management Science*, 28(3), 227–51.

Cyert, R. M., and March, J. G. (1963). *A Behavioral Theory of the Firm*. Englewood Cliffs, NJ: Prentice-Hall.

Daft, R. (1995). *Organization Theory and Design*. St. Paul, MN: West Publishing Co.

Dean, J., and Sharfman, M. (1992). Procedural Rationality in the Strategic Decision-making Process. *Journal of Management Studies*, 30, 587–611.

Dean, J., and Sharfman, M. (1996). Does Decision-making Matter? A Study of Strategic Decision-making Effectiveness. *Academy of management Journal*, 39(2), 368–96.

Delbecq, A. (1989). Sustaining Innovation as an American Competitive Advantage. Institute for Urban Studies, University of Maryland, College Park.

Delbecq, A., Van de Ven, A., and Gustafson, D. (1986). *Group Techniques for Program Planning*. Middletown, WI: Greenbrier.

Denzin, N. K. (1989). *The Research Act*. Englewood Cliffs, NJ: Prentice-Hall.

DePree, M. (1992). *Leadership Jazz*. New York: Doubleday.

DiMaggio, P. (1988). Interest and Agency in Institutional Theory, in L. G. Zucker (ed.), *Institutional*

*Patterns and Organizations.* Cambridge, MA: Ballinger, pp. 3–21.

Downs, A. (1967). *Inside Bureaucracy.* Boston, MA: Little, Brown.

Dutton, J. E. and Jackson, S. E. (1987). Categorizing Strategic Issues: Links to Organizational Action. *Academy of Management Review*, 12, 76–90.

Dutton, J. E., and Duncan, R. B. (1987). The Creation of Momentum for Change Through the Process of Strategic Issue Diagnosis. *Strategic Management Journal*, 8, 279–95.

Eisenhardt, K., and Zbaracki, M. (1992). Strategic Decision-Making. *Strategic Management Journal*, 13, 17–37.

El-Namaki, M. (1992). Creating a Corporate Vision. *Long Range Planning*, 25(6), 25–9.

El Sawy, O. A. (1985). Exploring Temporal Perspectives as a Bias to Managerial Attention. Center for Futures Research, Graduate School of Business Administration, University of Southern California, May.

Fisher, D., and Torbert, W. (1991). Transforming Management Practice: Beyond the Achiever Stage in L. L. Cummings and B. M. Staw (eds.), *Research in Organizational Development*, Greenwich, CT: JAI Press, Vol. 5, 143–73.

Fisher, R., and Brown S. (1988). *Getting Together: Building a Relationship that Gets to Yes.* Boston: Houghton Mifflin.

Fisher, R. and Ury, W. (1981). *Getting to Yes.* New York: Houghton Mifflin.

Fiske, S., and Taylor, S. (1991). *Social Cognition.* New York: McGraw-Hill.

Freeman, R. (1984). *Strategic Management: A Stakeholder Approach.* Boston: Pitman Press.

Galbraeth, J. R., Lawler, E. E. III, and Associates (1992). *Organizing for the Future.* San Francisco, CA: Jossey Bass.

Gardner, J. W. (1990). *On Leadership.* New York: Free Press.

Habermas, J. (1970). *Toward a Rational Society.* Boston: Beacon Press.

Hackman, R. (1990). *Groups that Work and Groups that Dont.* San Francisco, CA: Jossey Bass.

Hamel, G., and Prahalad, C. (1994). Competing for the Future. *Harvard Business Review*, July–Aug., 122–8.

Harmon, M. M. (1981). *Action Theory for Public Administration.* New York: Longman.

Harrison, M., and Phillips, B. (1992). Strategic Decision-making: An Integrative Explanation. *Research in the Sociology of Organizations*, 9, 319–58. Greenwich, CT: JAI Press.

Hassard, J., and Parker, M. (1993). *Postmodernism and Organizations.* London: Sage.

Hickson, D. A. (1987), Decisions Made at the Top of Organizations, *Annual Review of Sociology*, 9, 319–58.

Hickson, D., Butler, R., Gray, D., Mallory, G., and Wilson, D. (1986). *Top Decisions: Strategic Decision-making in Organizations.* San Francisco, CA: Jossey Bass.

Ichazo, O. (1982). *Between Meta Physics and Protoanalysis.* New York: Arica Institute Press.

Janis, I. (1989). *Crucial Decisions.* New York: Free Press.

Jantsch, E. (1975). *Design for Evolution: Self Organization and Planning in the Life of Systems.* New York: Brasilia.

Kelley, R. (1992). *The Power of Followership.* New York: Doubleday.

Kirkpatrick, S., and Locke, E. (1996). Direct and Indirect Effects of Three Core Charismatic Leadership Component on Performance and Attitudes. *Journal of Applied Psychology*, 84(1), 36–51.

Kotter, J. (1996). *Leading Change.* Cambridge, MA: HBS Press.

Kouzes, J. M., and Posner, B. Z. (1993). *Credibility.* San Francisco, CA: Jossey Bass.

Kouzes, J. M., and. Posner, B. Z. (1987). *The Leadership Challenge.* San Francisco, CA: Jossey Bass.

Land, G., and Jarman, B. (1992). *Breakpoint and Beyond: Mastering the Future Today.* New York: Harper Collins.

Langley, A. (1989). In Search of Rationality: The Purpose Behind the Use of Formal Analysis in Organizations. *Administrative Science Quarterly*, 34, 598–631.

Langley, A., Mintzberg, H., Pitcher, P., Posada, E., and Macary, J. (1995). Opening Up Decision-making: the View from the Back Stool. *Organization Science*, 6(3), 260–79.

Larwood, L., Falbe, C., Kriger, M., and Miesing, P. (1995). Structure and Meaning of Organizational Vision. *Academy of Management Journal*, 38(3), 740–69.

Larwood, L., Falbe, C., Kriger, M. (1993). Organizational Vision: An Investigation of the Vision Construct in Use of AACSB Business School Deans. *Group and Organizational Management*, 18(2), 214–36.

Lincoln, Y., and Guba, E. (1985). *Naturalistic Inquiry*. Beverly Hills, CA: Sage.

Lindblom, C. (1965). *The Intelligence of Democracy: Decision Process through Adjustment*. New York: Free Press.

Linstone, H. (1984). *Multiple Perspectives for Decision Making: Bridging the Gap Between Analysis and Action*. New York: North Holland.

Lippitt, M., and Mackenzie, K. (1976). Authority Task Problems. *Administrative Science Quarterly*, 21(4), 643–60.

Locke, E., Kirkpatrick, S., Wheeler, J., Schneider, J., Niles, K., Goldstein, H., Welsh, K., and Chah, D. (1991). *The Essence of Leadership*. New York: Lexington Books.

March, J. G. (1981). Footnotes to Organizational Change. *Administrative Science Quarterly*, 26(4), 563–77.

March, J. (1994). *A Primer on Decision-making: How Decisions Happen*. New York: Free Press.

March, J. G., and Olsen, J. P. (1986). Garbage Cans of Decision-making in Organizations, in J. G. March and R. Weissinger-Baylon (eds.), *Ambiguity and Command*. Marshfield, MA: Pitman.

March, J. G., and Simon, H. A. (1958). *Organizations*. New York: McGraw-Hill.

Mason, R. O., and Mitroff, I. I. (1981). *Challenging Strategic Planning Assumptions*. New York: Wiley-Interscience.

Mausch, M., and LaPotin, P. (1989). Beyond Garbage Can: An AI Model of Organizational Choice. *Administrative Science Quarterly*, 34, 38–67.

McGrath, J. E. (1988). *The Social Sociology of Time: New Perspectives*. Beverly Hills, CA: Sage.

McKie, D. (1973). *A Sadly Mismanaged Affair: The Political History of the Third London Airport*. London: Croom Helm.

Meindl, J. (1990). On Leadership: An Alternative to the Conventional Wisdom, in B. Staw and L. Cummings (eds.), *Research in Organizational Behavior*, Vol. 12, 159–203. Greenwich, CT: JAI Press.

Meindl, J., Ehrich, S., and Dukerich, J. (1985). The Romance of Leadership. *Administrative Science Quarterly*, 30, 78–102.

Meyer, J., and Rowan, B. (1977). Institutional Organizations: Formal Structure as Myth and Ceremony. *American Journal of Sociology*, 83, 340–63.

Meyer, M., and Zucker, L. (1981). *Permanently Failing Organizations*. Newbury Park, CA: Sage.

Mintzberg. H. (1978). Patterns in Strategy Formation. *Management Science*, 24, 934–48.

Mintzberg, H. (1994). *The Rise and the Fall of Strategic Planning*. New York: Free Press.

Mintzberg, H., Raisinghani, D., and Theoret, A. (1976). The Structure of Unstructured Decisions. *Administrative Science Quarterly*, 21(2), 246–75.

Mintzberg, H., and Westley, F. (2001). Decision-making: It's Not What You Think. *Sloan Management Review*, 42(3), 89–94.

Mitroff, I. I., and Emshoff, J. R. (1979). On Strategic Assumption-Making: A Dialectical Approach to Policy and Planning. *Academy of Management Review*, 4(1), 1–12.

Mohr, L. (1985). *Explaining Organizational Behavior*. San Francisco, CA: Jossey Bass.

Morgan, G. (1984). Opportunities Arising from Paradigms Diversity. *Administration and Society*, 16(3), 306–27.

Morgan, G. (1986). *Images of Organizations*. Beverly Hills, CA: Sage.

Morgan, G. (1993). *Imaginization*. Newbury Park, CA: Sage.

Nadler, D. A., Gerstein, M. S., Shaw, R. B., and Associates (1992). *Organizational Architecture*. San Francisco, CA: Jossey Bass.

Nadler, G. (1981). *The Planning and Design Approach*. New York: Wiley.

Nadler, G., and Hibino, S. (1990). *Breakthrough Thinking*. Rocklin, CA: Prima.

Nanus, B. (1989). *The Leader's Edge*. Chicago: Contemporary Books.

Nutt, P. C. (1984). Types of Organizational Decision Procession. *Administrative Science Quarterly*, 29(3), 414–50.

Nutt, P. C. (1986). The Tactics of Implementation. *Academy of Management Journal*, 29(2), 230–61.

Nutt, P. C. (1987). Identifying and Appraising How Managers Install Strategy. *Strategic Management Journal*, 8, 1–14.

Nutt, P. C. (1989). *Making Tough Decisions*. San Francisco, CA: Jossey Bass.

Nutt, P. C. (1990). Preventing Decision Debacles. *Technological Forecasting and Social Change*, 38, 159–74.

Nutt, P. C. (1993a). Formulation Processes and Tactics Used in Organizational Decision Making. *Organizational Science*, 4(2), 226–51.

Nutt, P. C. (1993b). The Identification of Solution Ideas During Organizational Decision Making. *Management Science*, 39(9), 1071–85.

Nutt, P. C. (1998a). Evaluating Complex Strategic Choices. *Management Science*, 44(8), 1148–6.

Nutt, P. C. (1998b). Framing Strategic Decisions. *Organization Science*, 9(2), 195–206.

Nutt, P. C. (1998c). Leverage, Resistance, and the Success of Implementation Approaches. *Journal of Management Studies*, 35(2), 213–40.

Nutt, P. C. (1999). Surprising but True: Half of Organizational Decisions Fail. *Academy of Management Executive*, 13(4), 75–90.

Nutt, P. C. (2000). Intelligence Gathering for Decision-Making, *DSI Proceedings*. Orlando, FL.

Nutt, P. C. (2001a). *Why Decisions Fail: The Blunders and Traps that Lead to Decision Debacles*. San Francisco, CA: Barrett-Koehler.

Nutt, P. C., (2001b). The De-development of Contemporary Organizations. *Research in Organizational Development and Change*, Vol 14. Greenwich, CT: JAI Press.

Nutt, P. C., and Backoff, R. W. (1992). *The Strategic Management of Public and Third Sector Organizations*. San Francisco, CA: Jossey Bass.

Nutt, P. C., and Backoff, R. W. (1993). Strategic Issues as Tensions. *Journal of Management Inquiry*, 2(1), 28–43.

Nutt, P. C., and Backoff, R. W. (1995). Strategy for Public and Third Sector Organizations. *Journal of Public Administration and Theory*, 5(2), 189–211.

Nutt, P. C., and Backoff, R. W. (1996a). Walking the Vision and Walking the Talk. *Public Productivity and Management Review*, 19(4), 455–86.

Nutt, P. C., and Backoff, R. W. (1996b). Fashioning and Sustaining Strategic Change. *Public Productivity and Management Review*, 19(3), 313–37.

Nutt, P. C., and Backoff, R. W. (1997a). Facilitating Transformational Change. *Journal of Applied Behavioral Science*, 33(4), 488–506.

Nutt, P. C., and Backoff, R. W. (1997b). Crafting Vision. *Journal of Management Inquiry*, 6(4), 308–28.

Nutt, P. C., and Backoff, R. W. (1997c). Organizational Transformation. *Journal of Management Inquiry*, 6(3), 235–5.

Oakley, E., and Krug, D. (1993). *Enlightened Leadership*. New York: Simon & Schuster.

Pascale, T. T. (1990). *Managing on the Edge*. New York: Simon & Schuster.

Patton, M. E. (1990). *Qualitative Evaluation and Research Methods*. Beverly Hills, CA: Sage.

Pettigrew, A. (1985). Context and Action in the Transformation of a Firm. *Journal of Management Studies*, 11(2), 31–48.

Popper, K. P. (1959). *The Logic of Scientific Discovery*. New York: Basic Books.

Porter, M. (1985). *Competitive Advantage*. New York: Free Press.

Prigogine, I., and Stengers, I. (1984). *Order Out of Chaos*. New York: Bantam.

Quinn, J. B. (1990). Managing Strategic Change, in A. A. Thompson, Jr., W. E. Fulmer, A. J. Strikland, III (eds.), *Strategic Management*, pp. 10–32. Homewood, IL: Irwin.

Quinn, R. E. (1988). *Beyond Rational Management: Mastering the Paradoxes and Competing Demands of High Performance*. San Francisco, CA: Jossey Bass.

Rasmusson, J., and Batstone, R. (1991). *Toward Improving Safety and Risk Management*. Washington, DC: World Bank.

Rosenau, P. (1992). *Post-Modernism and the Social Sciences*. Princeton, NJ: Princeton University Press.

Rothenburg, A. (1979). *The Emerging Goddess*. Chicago: University of Chicago Press.

Ruvolu, A., and Marsus, H. (1992). Possible Selves and Performance: The Power of Self-Relevant Imagery. *Social Cognition*, 10(1), 95–124.

Schendel, D., and Hofer, C. (1979). *Strategic Management*. Boston: Little, Brown.

Schwartz, P. (1991). *The Art of the Long View*. New York: Doubleday.

Seiglman, M. (1991). *Learned Optimism*. New York: Knopf.

Senge, P. (1990). *The Fifth Discipline: The Art and Management of the Learning Organization*. New York: Doubleday.

Shamir, B., House, R., and Arthur, M. (1993). The Motivational Effects of Charismatic Leadership: A Self-Concept Theory. *Organizational Science*, 4(4), 577–94.

Shapiro, G., and Sica, A. (1984). *Hermeneutics: Questions and Prospects*. Amherst, MA: University of Massachusetts Press.

Sharfman, M., and Dean, J. (1998). The Effects of Context on Strategic Management Process and Outcome, in V. Papadakis, and P. Barwise, (eds.), *Strategic Decisions*. Dordrecht, Holland: Kluwer.

Simon, H. A. (1969). *The Sciences of the Artificial*. Cambridge, MA: MIT Press.

Simon, H. A. (1977). *The New Science of Management Decision*. Englewood Cliffs, NJ: Prentice-Hall (revised edition).

Snyder, R. C., and Page, G. D. (1958). The United States Decision to Resist Aggression in Korea: The Application of an Analytical Scheme. *Administrative Science Quarterly*, 3, 341–78.

Soelberg, P. O. (1967). Unprogrammed Decision-making. *Industrial Management Review*, Spring, 19–29.

Spradley, J. P. (1980). *Participant Observation*. New York: Holt, Rinehart & Winston.

Starbuck, W. (1983). Organizations as Action Generators. *American Sociological Review*, 48, 91–102.

Staw, B., Sandelands, L., and Dutton, J. (1981). Threat-Rigidity Effects on Organization Behavior. *Administrative Science Quarterly*, 26, 501–24.

Stogdill, R. M. (1974). *Handbook of Leadership: A Survey of Theory and Research*. New York: Free Press.

Swoboda, F. (1995). Corporate Downsizing Goes Global. Washington News Service, April 11, A8.

Thompson, J. D. (1967). *Organizations in Action*. New York: McGraw-Hill.

Thompson, A., and Strickland, A. (1995). *Strategy Formulation and Implementation*. Homewood, IL: Irwin (sixth edition).

Tichy, N., and Devanna, M. (1986). *The Transformational Leader*. New York: Wiley.

Tichy, N., and Devanna, M. (1990). *Revisiting The Transformational Leader*. New York: Wiley.

Torbert, W. R. (1989). Leading Organizational Transformation in L. L. Cummings and B. M. Staw (eds.), *Research in Organizational Change and Development*, Vol. 3, 83–116. Greenwich, CT: JAI Press.

Toulmin, S. (1979). *Knowing and Acting: An Invitation to Philosophy*. New York: Macmillan.

Van de Ven, A., and Poole, M. S. (1995). Explaining Development and Change in Organizations. *Academy of Management Review*, 20(3), 510–40.

Vroom, V., and Jago, A. (1978). *The New Leadership: Managing Participation in Organizations*. Englewood Cliffs, NJ: Prentice-Hall.

Wall, B., Solum, R., and Sobol, M. (1992). *The Visionary Leader*. Rocklin, CA: Prima.

Walton, R. E. (1985). From Control to Commitment in the Workplace. *Harvard Business Review*, March–April, 77–94.

Watzawick, P., Weakland, J., and Frisch, R. (1974). *Change*. New York: Norton.

Wechsler, B., and Backoff, R. (1986). Policy Making and Administration in State Agencies: Strategic Management Approaches. *Public Administration Review*, July–Aug., 321–7.

Weick, K. (1979). *The Social Psychology of Organizing*. Reading, MA: Addison-Wesley.

Weick, K. (1989). Cognitive Processes in Organizations, in B. Staw (ed.), *Research in Organizational Behavior*, Vol. 1, 41–74. Greenwich, CT: JAI Press.

Weick, K. (1994). The Collapse of Sense-Making in Organizations: The Manngulch Disaster. *Administrative Science Quarterly*, 38(4–5), 628–52.

Weitzel, W., and Jonsson, E. (1987). Decline in Organizations: A Literature Integration and Extension. *Administrative Science Quarterly*, 34(1), 91–109.

Wheatley, M. J. (1992). *Leadership and the New Science*. New York: Berrett-Kohler.

Wildavsky, A. (1979). *Speaking Truth to Power: The Art and Craft of Policy Analysis*. Boston, MA: Little, Brown.

Witte, E. (1972). Field Research on Complex Decision-making Process – The Phase Theory. *International Studies of Management and Organization*, 56, 156–82.

Woodman, R. W. (1989). Evaluation Research and Organizational Change: Arguments for a Combined Paradigm Approach, in R. W. Woodman and W. A. Pasmore (eds.), *Research in Organizational Change and Development*, Vol. 3, 161–80. Greenwich, CT: JAI Press.

Yin, R. K. (1981). The Case Study Crisis: Some Answers. *Administrative Science Quarterly*, 26(10), 58–65.

Yin, R. K. (1989). *Case Study Research*. Hollywood, CA: Sage (second edition).

Yin, R. K. (1993). *Applications of Case Study Research*. Newbury Park, CA: Sage.

# 3

# Strategy Formulation: The Roles of Conversation and Design

## JEANNE M. LIEDTKA

In setting out to review the field of strategy formulation, Mintzberg, Ahlstrand, and Lampel (1998) find a vast literature on what they describe as "the strategic management beast," noting that, as strategy theoreticians:

> We are the blind people and strategy formation is our elephant. Since no one has had the vision to see the entire beast, everyone has grabbed hold of some part or other and railed on in utter ignorance about the rest (p. 3).

Their claim is a difficult one to dispute. The mainstream of the literature in the field has not offered an integrated view that seeks to synthesize the multiple perspectives offered. Instead, it has been dominated by a focus on the creation of typologies of different approaches to strategy formulation. Hart (1992), in a comprehensive review of the major works on the subject, noted the "model proliferation" that has characterized research on strategy making processes, and argued that "little cumulative knowledge has resulted."

Beginning with the publication in 1973 of his influential article on "Strategy-making in Three Modes," Mintzberg was the first to focus on delineating the alternative approaches taken by both academics and practitioners to the strategy-making process. Twenty-six years later, in an exhaustive review of the field, Mintzberg and co-authors (1998) catalog the sources, dimensions, champions, and messages of each of ten distinct "schools of thought" that characterize strategy making.[1]

Hart, himself, maps these multiple models into five, rather than ten, modes of strategy making.[2] Both Mintzberg and Hart make clear that they do not see the modes as mutually exclusive – in fact, the attractiveness of combining elements of different modes (the vision of the symbolic mode with the intrapreneurship of the generative mode, for example) is obvious. In field-testing his theory, Hart and Banbury (1994) demonstrate that this simultaneous use of multiple modes is often reflected in real practice behaviors. Furthermore, they found that firms who moved beyond individual modes and utilized multiple modes outperformed single-mode organizations. They conclude:

> To achieve high performance, top managers must provide a strong sense of strategic direction and organizational members must be active players in the strategy-making process.

In fact, firms which combine high levels of competence in multiple modes of strategy-making appear to be the highest performers (p. 266).

I will not attempt here to revisit these discussions of alternative processes. While theoretically interesting and perhaps empirically valid as descriptions, these typologies have not had much to say about how to improve strategy formulation, in my view. Instead, I will focus on a set of larger themes that underlie these particular typologies and pervade the strategy formulation literature, in general. These are:

1. The centrality of strategic thinking to successful strategic management – here I offer a hypothesized model of the attributes of the strategic thinking process.
2. The relationship of strategy to change – in this section, my focus is on extending the set of questions at the core of strategy making.
3. The role of planning in the process of strategy formulation management – I envision here a reformulation of the role and process of planning.

Addressing these three often intersecting themes, in turn, will lead me to introduce the topics of both strategic conversations and design – hence, the title of this chapter.

## THE RISE OF STRATEGIC THINKING

The term "strategic thinking" is often used so widely and generically today within the field of strategy that it risks becoming almost meaningless. Rarely do those who use the term define it. Most often, it appears that the term "strategic thinking" is used to denote all thinking *about strategy*, rather than to denote a particular mode of thinking, with specific characteristics. Within this broad usage, authors have used the term almost interchangeably with other concepts such as strategic planning or strategic management. Ian Wilson (1994) for example, in describing the evolution of strategic planning processes, observes:

> The need for strategic thinking has never been greater . . . This continuing improvement (in strategic planning) has profoundly changed the character of strategic planning so that it is now more appropriate to refer to it as *strategic management* or *strategic thinking*.

Those who have devoted attention to defining the term "strategic thinking" have often used broad, seemingly all-inclusive definitions, such as the one offered below by Nasi (1991):

> Strategic thinking extends both to the formulation and execution of strategies by business leaders and to the strategic performance of the total enterprise. It includes strategic analysis, strategic planning, organization and control and even strategic leadership. Therefore, strategic thinking basically covers all those attributes, which can be labeled "strategic."

Though these broad uses of the term may be pervasive, they are not consistent with the sense in which early proponents of the concept of strategic thinking use the term. For Mintzberg (1994), recognized as one of the foremost advocates of strategic thinking, the term is not merely alternative nomenclature for everything falling under the umbrella of strategic management; rather, it is a particular *way* of thinking, with specific characteristics. Mintzberg has devoted much of his attention to articulating the difference between strategic thinking and strategic planning. Strategic planning, he argues, is an analytical process aimed at programming already identified strategies. Its outcome is a plan. Strategic thinking, on the other hand, is a synthesizing process, utilizing intuition and creativity, whose outcome is "an integrated perspective of the enterprise." Rather than occurring hand-in-hand, traditional planning processes tend to drive out strategic thinking, Mintzberg argues, and as a result, impair rather than support successful organizational adaptation.

Hamel and Prahalad (1994), two other highly influential strategy theorists, join Mintzberg in indicting traditional approaches to planning which they describe as "strategy as form filling." Though they utilize the term, "crafting strategic architecture" rather than "strategic thinking," the same themes of creativity, exploration, and understanding discontinuities are prevalent as elements of the approach to strategy making that they advocate.

Ralph Stacey (1992), approaching strategy through a different lens – that of the discoveries of the "new sciences" of quantum physics and complexity theory – reaches much the same conclusions as the authors already cited. Though he is skeptical of according a major role to future vision as a driver of strategy, he sees strategy-making processes as successful when they are based on "designing actions on the basis of new learning," rather than following "pre-programmed rules." Strategic thinking, he asserts, is not "an intellectual exercise in exploring what is likely to happen . . . strategic thinking is using analogies and qualitative similarities to develop creative new ideas."

This dichotomy between the analytic and creative aspects of strategy making constitutes a pervasive theme in more detailed treatments on the subject of strategic thinking as well. Raimond (1996) divides strategic thinking into two modes: "strategy as intelligent machine" (a data-driven, information processing approach) and "strategy as creative imagination." Nasi (1991) differentiates between the "hard line" analytical approach, with its traditional focus on competition, and the "soft line" approach emphasizing values and culture.

These more specific discussions, taken together, still leave the practicing strategist interested in translating the concept of strategic thinking into actual business practice with several challenges. First, this literature focuses more on what strategic thinking is *not*, than on what it is. Though this is helpful in distinguishing strategic thinking from other concepts within the strategy field, it stops far short of the kind of careful delineation of the characteristics of strategic thinking needed to facilitate its exploration by research, its implementation by managers, and its development by educators. Second, the literature draws a sharp dichotomy between the creative and analytic aspects of strategy making, when both are clearly needed in any thoughtful strategy-making process. Finally, the literature leaves one with a strong sense that strategic thinking is clearly incompatible with strategic planning as we know it. Yet, we know that putting processes in place to ensure that managers attend to strategic issues, amidst the day-to-day crises that so capture their focus, is essential.

## THE ELEMENTS OF STRATEGIC THINKING

Drawing on a broad base of literature both within and outside of the strategy field, it is possible to bring greater clarity to the definition of strategic thinking. Following the views of Mintzberg, I define strategic thinking as a particular *way* of thinking, with five specific elements, each of which the following section will address, in turn.

## A systems perspective

Strategic thinking is built on the foundation of a systems perspective. A strategic thinker has a mental model of the complete end-to-end system of value creation, and understands the interdependencies within it. Senge (1992), in his work on learning organizations, has described the power of mental models in influencing our behavior:

> New insights fail to get put into practice because they conflict with deeply held internal images of how the world works, images that limit us to familiar ways of thinking and acting. That is why the discipline of managing mental models – surfacing, testing, and improving our internal pictures of how the world works – promises to be a major breakthrough . . .

In order to think strategically, this mental model of "how the world works" must incorporate an understanding of both the external and internal context of the organization. The dimension of the external context that has dominated strategy for many years has been industry-based (Porter, 1980). New writers in the field of strategy, Moore (1993) among them, have argued that a perspective beyond that of industry is fundamental to the ability to innovate:

> I suggest that a company be viewed not as a member of a single industry but as part of a *business ecosystem* that crosses a variety of industries. In a business ecosystem, companies co-evolve capabilities around a new innovation: they work cooperatively and competitively to support new products, satisfy customer needs, and eventually incorporate the next round of innovations.

In a similar vein, strategy theorizing about the impact of the "new economy" and interest in topics such as disintermediation has placed great emphasis on value chain relationships (Evans and Wurster, 1998). Thus, the ability to manage in these converging arenas requires that organizations think strategically about which of these competing networks of suppliers they join and how they position themselves within that ecosystem.

In addition to understanding the external business ecosystem in which the firm operates, strategic thinkers must also appreciate the inter-relationships among the internal pieces that, taken together, comprise the whole. Such a perspective locates, for each individual, his or her role within that larger system and clarifies for them the effects of their behavior on other parts of the system, as well as on its final outcome. The strategy literature has talked much about the importance of fit between the corporate, business, and functional levels of strategy. Fit with the fourth level – the personal – may be the most critical level of all. It is impossible to optimize the outcome of the system for the end customer without such understanding. The potential for damage wrought by well-intentioned but parochial managers optimizing their part of the system at the expense of the whole is substantial.

Thus, the strategic thinker sees vertical linkages within the system from multiple perspectives. He or she sees the relationship between corporate, business level, and functional strategies to each other, to the external context, and to the personal choices he or she makes on a daily basis. In addition, on a horizontal basis, he or she sees the connection across departments and functions, and between communities of suppliers and buyers.

## Intent-focused

Strategic thinking is intent-driven. Hamel and Prahalad (1994) have repeated this point for nearly ten years and have revolutionized the thinking about strategy in the process:

> Strategic intent is our term for such an animating dream . . . It also implies a particular point of view about the long-term market or competitive position that a firm hopes to build over the coming decade or so. Hence, it conveys a *sense of direction*. A strategic intent is differentiated; it implies a competitively unique point of view about the future. It holds out to employees the promise of exploring new competitive territory. Hence, it conveys a *sense of discovery*. Strategic intent has an emotional edge to it; it is a goal that employees perceive as inherently worthwhile. Hence, it implies a *sense of destiny*. Direction, discovery, and destiny. These are the attributes of strategic intent (pp. 129–30).

Evidence for the power of a clear intent comes from the world of social psychology, as well. Writing about how individuals attain the state of effortless outstanding performance that he calls "flow," Csikszentmihalyi (1990) draws our attention to what he calls the primacy of "psychic energy." We can focus attention, he argues, "like a beam of energy" or diffuse it in "desultory random movements . . . we create ourselves by how we invest this energy." Strategic intent provides the focus that allows individuals within an organization to marshal and leverage their energy, to focus attention, to resist distraction, and to concentrate for as long as it takes to achieve a goal. In the disorienting swirl of change, such psychic energy may well be the most scarce resource an organization has, and only those who utilize it most efficiently will succeed. Thus, strategic thinking inevitably is fundamentally concerned with, and driven by, the shaping and re-shaping of intent.

## Intelligent opportunism

Within this intent-driven focus, there must be room for intelligent opportunism – the capacity for managers throughout an organization to recognize and seize unanticipated opportunities that present themselves – that not only furthers intended strategy but that also leaves open the possibility of new strategies emerging. In writing about the role of "strategic dissonance" in the strategy-making process at Intel, Burgelman (1991) has highlighted the dilemma involved in using a well-articulated strategy to channel organizational efforts effectively and efficiently, against the risks of losing sight of alternative strategies better suited to a changing environment. This requires that an organization be capable of practicing "intelligent opportunism" at lower levels. He concludes that "One important manifestation of corporate capability is a company ability to adapt without having to rely on extraordinary top management foresight" (p. 208).

The opponents of intention-based planning systems, Ralph Stacey (1992) most prominent among them, argue that the definition of intention must be broad and flexible:

> Instead of intention to secure something relatively known and fixed, it becomes intention to discover what, why, and how to achieve. Such intention arises not from what managers foresee but from what they have experienced and now understand . . . The dynamic systems

perspective thus leads managers to think in terms, not of the prior intention represented by objectives and visions, but of continuously developing agendas of issues, aspirations, challenges, and individual intentions (p. 146).

## Thinking in time

As Stacey notes, strategy is not driven by future intent alone. Hamel and Prahalad agree, and argue that it is the *gap* between today's reality and that intent for the future that is critical:

> Strategic intent implies a sizable stretch for an organization. Current capabilities and resources will not suffice. This forces the organization to be more inventive, to make the most of limited resources. Whereas the traditional view of strategy focuses on the degree of fit between existing resources and current opportunities, strategic intent creates an extreme misfit between resources and ambitions (1994: 67).

Strategic thinking, then, is always "thinking in time" to borrow a phrase from historians Richard Neustadt and Ernest May (1986). Strategic thinking connects past, present, and future. As Neustadt and May argue:

> Thinking in time (has) three components. One is recognition that the future has no place to come from but the past, hence the past has predictive value. Another element is recognition that what matters for the future in the present is departures from the past, alterations, changes, which prospectively or actually divert familiar flows from accustomed channels . . . A third component is continuous comparison, an almost constant oscillation from the present to future to past and back, heedful of prospective change, concerned to expedite, limit, guide, counter, or accept it as the fruits of such comparison suggest (p. 251).

Thinking in time, in this view, uses both an institution's memory and its broad historical context to think well about creating its future. This requires a capability both for choosing and using appropriate analogies from its own and other's histories, and for recognizing patterns in these events.

This oscillation between the past, present, and future is essential for the execution of strategy as well as its formulation. Charles Handy (1994) has described the "rudderlessness" that can result when organizations disconnect from their past. He argues that institutions and individuals need both a sense of continuity with their past *and* a sense of direction for their future to maintain a feeling of control in the midst of change. Thus, the strategic question is not only "what does the future that we want to create look like?," it is "having seen the future that we want to create, what must we keep from our past, lose from that past, and create in our present, to get there?"

## Hypothesis-driven

The final element of strategic thinking recognizes it as an hypothesis-driven process. It mirrors the "scientific method," in that it deals with hypothesis generating and testing as central activities. In an environment of ever-increasing information availability and decreasing time to think, the ability to develop good hypotheses and to test them efficiently is critical.

Because it is hypothesis-driven, strategic thinking avoids the analytic-intuitive dichotomy that has characterized much of the debate on the value of formal planning. Strategic thinking is *both* creative and critical in nature. Figuring out how to accomplish both types of thinking simultaneously has long troubled cognitive psychologists, since it is necessary to *suspend* critical judgment in order to think more creatively (Paul, 1987).

The scientific method accommodates both creative and analytical thinking sequentially in its use of iterative cycles of hypothesis generating and testing. Hypothesis generation asks the creative question "what if . . . ?" Hypothesis testing follows with the critical question "If . . . , then . . . ?" and brings relevant data to bear on the analysis, including an analysis of a hypothetical set of financial flows associated with the idea. Taken together, and repeated over time, this sequence allows us to pose ever-improving hypotheses, without forfeiting the ability to explore new ideas. Such experimentation allows an organization to move beyond simplistic notions of cause and effect to provide on-going learning.

Joining these five elements, I propose that a strategic thinker be defined as someone with a broad field of view that sees the whole and the connections between its pieces, both across the four vertical levels of strategy (corporate, business, functional, and personal) and across the horizontal elements of the end-to-end value system. This view includes a sense of the future that drives the institution, including a sense of both where that future connects and disconnects with the past and demands anew in the present. The process toward which an institution moves into that future is an experimental one, that makes use of creative thinking to design options, and critical thinking to test them. Finally, the strategic thinker remains ever open to emerging opportunities, both in service to the defined intent and also in question as to the continuing appropriateness of that intent.

Clearly, more empirical work is needed in this area both to test the relevance of these hypothesized elements and to relate these to diversions of organizational performance.

Having noted this gap, we now turn to a different question: what has driven this emphasis on strategic thinking as central to management success? It is the increasing attention to the need for change – the topic to which we will now turn.

## LINKING STRATEGY WITH CHANGE

The field of strategy, since its inception, has been primarily concerned with the search for sustainable competitive advantage (Rumelt, Schendel, and Teece, 1994; Teece, Pisano, and Shuen, 1997). As the pace of change in the business environment has accelerated, this focus on sustaining advantage has increasingly translated into a strategy-making process fundamentally concerned with equipping organizations with the capability to deal successfully with a changing environment. What implications does this emphasis on change have for the adequacy of our traditional ways of thinking about strategy? Let us begin by examining a well-established view of the strategy-making process, first published by Ken Andrews (1971), that has been one of the cornerstones of the strategy field. In this model, strategy emerges from a top manager's consideration of factors both external and internal to the organization, and in response to four questions: (1) What *might* an institution do?; (2) What *can* an institution do?; (3) What do people within an institution *want* to do?; and (4) What *ought* an institution do, from the perspective of society?

## Closing the gap: strategy's traditional emphasis

One way to characterize Andrews' four questions is around their shared focus on *closing the gaps* between external demands and internal capabilities, on creating alignment. Strategy, then, in the traditional view, has been about closing gaps. Achieving significant change, on the other hand, is about disrupting alignment, opening gaps – cognitive gaps in the minds of change recipients between current reality and some future vision (Fritz, 1989). This is the logic behind Hamel and Prahalad's view of the articulation of strategic intent as the catalyst of strategy making processes. It is also the existence of the creative tension caused by the desire to close the gap that drives learning (Senge, 1990). This argues for a new set of questions that seek to open new gaps, as well as close old ones.

Closing the gap, correcting the lack of alignment, is necessary for increasing stability and efficiency and fostering high performance. Yet we know that disequilibrium is the driver of learning and innovation. When we reduce variation, we increase the performance of the system in the short-term. In the long-term, we risk depriving the system of the new information that it needs to move forward (Burgelman, 1991). This is the "adaptation paradox" – or as Karl Weick (1969) explains it, the observation that "adaptation precludes adaptability."

## Intended and emergent strategy

This also raises the relationship between the strategic intent perspective and Mintzberg's (1987) notions of emergent and intended strategies. Intended, or planned, strategy inhibits learning, Mintzberg argues. Emergent strategy, where "action drives thinking," fosters it. Yet others have noted the loss of focus and dilution of limited resources that autonomous or "grassroots" strategy formulation risks (Burgelman, 1991). Strategic intent, Hamel and Prahalad (1993) argue, incorporates both strategy as designed and strategy as incremental. But must opportunism always be incremental? Strategic intent argues for a vision of strategy as providing "stretch" rather than constraint, yet the stretch relates to means rather than ends. It would not appear to accommodate the kind of autonomous experiments that fall outside of the umbrella of corporate intent; experiments that Burgelman describes as central to Intel's culture. In the call for "entrepreneurial behaviors," the question arises as to what extent top management chooses to bound the entrepreneurial instincts of their employees.

Burgelman makes a convincing argument that successful firms adapt through "renewal," where major strategic change is preceded by internal experimentation that leverages learning, rather than through "reorientation," in which significant strategic shifts undo cumulative learning in a way that "bets the organization."

In this view, strategy making is ideally a process of continuous adaptation that straddles the tension between offering too much or too little direction, between relying too heavily on or disrupting too precipitously the status quo, between collaborating to create new value systems and competing for a larger piece of the system's profits, and between reaping the benefits of autonomy and losing the benefits of scale and scope.

In order to reflect these new realities, a new set of questions is called for – questions that bring with them an emphasis on *shaping* and *participating*, that move beyond Andrews' emphasis on fitting and implementing. These new questions collapse the boundaries between the industry environment and other stakeholders, on one hand, and the boundaries between capabilities and values, on the other.

The first question reframes and combines Andrews' previously separate external questions (questions 3 and 4): *How can we shape tomorrow's value system to create new possibilities, in partnership with other stakeholders?*

As boundaries collapse, the old industry categories of competitor, supplier, and customer are increasingly indistinguishable from each other. Is Intel a supplier or a competitor of Compaq these days? Though Compaq is the largest single purchaser of Intel's microprocessors and Intel does not produce a branded box that competes against Compaq at the retail level, the story unfolding as they jockey to control the value system that they share is instructive of the new complexities of managing these relationships. Regardless of what we label them in relation to each other, both are making investments in some vision of a future, and the uncertainty in their environment increases the urgency to create and coordinate complementary investments (Jordan and Teece, 1989). The important question is less in what category we place the firm and more the extent to which their interests align, or can be brought into alignment, in the future.

Because firms co-create the future with all of their stakeholders, the critical focus for attention becomes not just an individual firm's strategic intent, but how that intent aligns with the intent of other powerful players, and what that aligned intent makes possible for all stakeholders (Moore, 1996).

The second question brings together Andrews' separate categories of capabilities and values (questions 1 and 2), believing the issues of mindsets and skill sets to be inseparable: *What new capabilities are we committed to developing and to learning to care about?*

In an environment of change, we ask people to learn new skills and to care about different things, and the interaction of making strategy and managing its execution becomes critical. As Senge (1990) has pointed out, we learn about what we care about – what matters to us, out of a personal vision that we hold. Learning and caring about new things become possible when something new becomes personally important.

Senge's observation highlights why the traditional formulation/implementation dichotomy has been so problematic. Renewal at the organizational level begins with opening up a gap between today's reality and tomorrow's intent; change at the individual level begins with dissatisfaction with the status quo, coupled with a sense of a better way for the future. The two are inseparable because corporate intent, in the absence of individual behavioral change, is meaningless. Yet, for the individual to change willingly, the gain must be significant enough that it makes up for losing the comfort of familiar ways of doing things. Like all learning, this gap is more powerfully self-discovered than pronounced from on high. Participation in the making of strategy, then, invites individuals into a learning process in which they come to discover a new set of possibilities that they can shape in a way that creates personal commitments worth investing in.

As with the hypothesized elements of strategic thinking, these new questions require empirical testing.

## The Role of Planning

Against this backdrop, the debate about the specific value of strategic planning has raged on for years, with influential scholars like Mintzberg (1994) arguing that formal strategic planning is incapable of dealing intelligently with uncertain environments, and other scholars asserting that planning processes are most effective in turbulent environments (Hart and Banbury, 1994; Miller and Cardinal, 1994). The question that remains unanswered, despite the wealth of scholarly attention devoted to both evaluating the success or failure of historic approaches to planning and to describing alternative non-plan based approaches to strategy formulation, is whether there exists an approach to strategic planning that is consistent with and supportive of the central role that successful accomplishment of strategic change plays in sustaining competitive advantage.

### The planning literature

The seminal early works on formal planning processes (e.g., Ansoff, 1965; Anthony, 1965; Lorange, 1980; Steiner, 1979) link the value of strategic planning explicitly to the management of change. Lorange, writing in 1980, argues that "the purpose of strategic planning is thus to accomplish a sufficient process of innovation and change in the firm . . . if a formal system for strategic planning does not support innovation and change, it is a failure."

Steiner (1979) concurs:

> Strategic planning is not a simple aggregation of functional plans or an extrapolation of current budgets. It is truly a systems approach to maneuvering an enterprise over time through the uncertain waters of its changing environment to achieve prescribed aims (p. 16).

In moving beyond discussions of the purpose of planning to the specifics of the processes advocated, strategic planning processes, as Lorange and Steiner describe them, are oriented towards the selection of objectives and product/market choices by senior management, that a firm's lower level managers were then responsible for programming and implementing. Planning, in this view, provides a mechanism for setting and reviewing objectives, focusing on choices of long term significance, identifying strategic options, allocating resources among them, and achieving corporate-wide coordination, monitoring, and control. Thus, despite the avowed centrality of change to strategic planning, the specific processes advocated appear to be better suited to the coordination and control function, than to the facilitation of change, especially if that change requires speed in responsiveness, local knowledge, or radical changes in strategy.

On the other hand, Anthony's (1965) original conception of planning processes bear little evidence of the bureaucratized processes that strategic planning has often, in the minds of its critics at least, evolved into. Anthony distinguished between strategic and operational planning, at length. Strategic planning, he argued, is a process that is both creative and analytical, is issue rather than calendar-driven, and is primarily concerned with external data, usually not financial in nature. Systematizing an approach to strategic planning is inadvisable, he argued, in that it is likely to dampen the creativity so essential to the process. He also cautions against confusing strategic planning and long-range planning processes:

> In some companies, the so-called five year plan is nothing more than a mechanical extrapolation of current data, with no reflection of management decisions and judgment; such an exercise is totally worthless (p. 58).

In his exhaustive review of the planning literature, Mintzberg (1994) concurs, making an argument that many have found compelling, that these traditional planning approaches are more likely to impede, rather than facilitate, successful change under conditions of uncertainty.

Mintzberg's concerns about the deficiencies of formal planning, with its strong roots in the premise of rationality, is supported by emerging theories that have gained prominence in the broader context of the strategy and change literatures in the intervening decades since the above models of strategic planning processes were developed. In the strategy field, the concept of the resource-based view of competition has emerged prominently in the literature (Wernerfelt, 1984; Montgomery and Hariharan, 1991; Teece, Pisano, and Shuen, 1997). It has been argued to represent new views of the source of competitive advantage itself, with its focus on each individual firm's unique bundle of capabilities and assets, and their appropriateness for achieving the firm's specific strategy and meeting the needs of its marketplace.

This increased focus on the selection and development of capabilities, rather than the selection of products and markets as the central preoccupation of strategists, compliments Hamel and Prahalad's concept of "strategic intent." Taken together, these new views of the sources of competitive advantage would appear to call for planning processes capable of greater creativity, flexibility, opportunism, and more rapid implementation.

The literature in the area of strategic change has seen the increasing prominence of new theoretical approaches, as well. Najagopalan and Spreitzer (1997) describe the evolution of the strategic change literature from one focused primarily on content issues and the premise of rationality to one that recognizes the complexity of the "black box" of human processes of learning and cognition which underlie change. Whereas the rational lens has viewed strategic change as a process concerned with "the deliberate analysis of strategic alternatives" in a linear fashion, with "little scope for experimentation and learning," as Najagopalan and Spreitzer note, much recent work has focused on two alternative lens – the learning and the cognitive. The learning lens, these authors argue, sees change as an iterative and evolutionary process that is not linear, in which managerial actions play a central role. Similarly, the cognitive lens takes as central an enacted view of the environment where the interpretive process of individual managers is key and is shaped by belief structures. These authors offer an integrative view that pulls together the three perspectives, and acknowledges the contribution of each:

> The rational lens perspective reflects a crucial aspect of the reality facing managers, namely, that changes in strategies must match the requirements of a firm's environmental and organizational contexts in order to be successful . . . The cognitive lens perspective indicates that gaps between "objective reality" and managerial cognitions can result in firms not choosing to change their strategies and/or making inappropriate choices that may ultimately lead to organizational decline. The learning lens perspective is used to identify the crucial role played by managerial actions in creating an organizational and environmental context, which is more conducive to the context of the firm's new strategies and thus maximizes the likelihood that implementation of the strategic change is effective (pp. 70–1).

These same theories of learning and cognition have also influenced the strategy-making process literature. Challenges to the rationality premise are longstanding (Cyert and March, 1963) and are reflected in work on the significance of limited search (March and Simon, 1958; Lindblom, 1959), the use of schema (Weick, 1969; Dutton and Jackson, 1987), and the influence of organizational assumptions (Mason and Mitroff, 1981), among others.

## LINKING STRATEGIC PLANNING WITH STRATEGIC CHANGE

In reference to our final topic, I now set out to synthesize work across these various literatures, and offer a view of planning that I believe better fosters adaptability and change. This model distinguishes between two distinct but inter-related aspects of the process – one cognitive and one behavioral. At the cognitive level, the strategic planning process utilizes strategic thinking in a conversational process to design a future, working in a virtual world. At a behavioral level, these designs become reality as the organization "programs" them into the development of new routines and capabilities aimed at achieving the kinds of outcomes that the ideal future envisions. The learning that emerges from this process is then channeled back into the creation of a new, or refined, intent. Taken together, this cycle, which I have termed "generative strategic planning," pictured in figure 3.1, comprises a "reformed" strategic planning process.

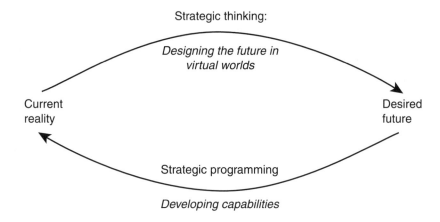

FIGURE 3.1 A model of generative strategic planning

As conceived by this model, the process is continuously in motion, as the gap between today's reality and tomorrow's intent is broadened, and subsequently narrowed, through the interaction of the new possibilities that the organization envisions in its virtual world and the new capabilities that it develops in its actual world.

## The cognitive loop: designing the future in virtual worlds

In this model, strategic change begins within a cognitive framework, in the minds of managers, with the creation of a gap between their view of the current reality and an image of a future to which they aspire. In the absence of such a gap, and the cognitive dissonance that it creates, there exists no internal motivation to change, as change theorists have long pointed out (Hendry, 1996). The opening of the gap – the creation of the intent for the future – is a process that is, ideally, both creative and analytic. The creation of a compelling intent, with the sense of "discovery, direction, and destiny" of which Hamel and Prahalad (1994) speak, relies heavily on the skill of alternative generation. As Simon (1993) has noted, alternative generation has received far less attention in the strategic decision-making literature than has alternative evaluation, but is more important in an environment of change. Levinthal and March (1993), in addition, note the tendency of organizations to favor exploitation of existing competencies over exploration of new ones. Thus, success in the cognitive loop begins with what cognitive psychologists have called "lateral" or "generative" thinking (DeBono, 1970). Such generative thinking, in the strategic planning context, begins with the generation of hypotheses about a set of possible alternative futures. Such hypothesis generation asks the creative "what if . . ." question. The creation of a *viable* intent, however, requires that the generative "what if" question be followed by the more analytical, hypothesis-testing question: "if, then" that the rational perspective utilizes to ascertain fit with the external realities or potential realities of the marketplace. These "what if . . .," "if, then . . ." thought experiments form the basis of the strategic thinking process so central to this cognitive loop of the cycle. Since all aspects of the external environment cannot be proactively shaped to an organization's wishes, the likely constraints that the future holds must be anticipated and factored into the rational analysis, as well.

As several strategy theorists have noted (Simon, 1993; Liedtka and Rosenblum, 1996), the above process is one of *design*. Though the term design has sometimes been used in the strategy literature to describe a process that is overly deliberate, simple, and detached (Mintzberg, 1994), this is not the view of design implied here. This design process is emergent, complex, and involved.

The iterative nature of design invokes the learning lens. Donald Schon (1983) defines design as a "shaping process," a "reflective conversation with a situation" in which "each move is a local experiment which contributes to the global experiment of reframing the problem," and which takes place in a "virtual," rather than physical, world. Planning's ability to foster the exploration of new strategies in virtual worlds is one of the sources of its value to organizations. To do *all* experimenting only in the marketplace and never in the minds of managers, as anti-planners advocate, would surely be as inefficient, painful, and misguided as its opposite – to believe that strategies are immutably set in the minds of executives, transferred to paper, and altered only in five-year cycles. Thus, the cognitive loop utilizes strategic thinking that is both creative and analytical, in an iterative way, to design a strategic intent.

## The behavioral loop: developing new capabilities

In order to accomplish change in the physical world, however, the behavioral dynamics within the organization must realign to support the new intent. Having envisioned a different future, organizational members must begin to act in new ways in the present. It is these new actions, culminating in the learning of new routines and, hence, capabilities, that will allow the organization to close the gap between today's reality and tomorrow's vision. The difficulty of learning new routines, however, cannot be underestimated, as many scholars have argued. Routines developed over time become parts of coherent self-sustaining systems. Achieving change usually requires re-aligning at the systems level (Teece et al., 1997), and cannot be accomplished on a piecemeal basis. Thus, closing the gap requires many of the detailed coordinating and integrating activities central to the "strategic programming" stage of traditional planning processes – determining new benchmarks and measurements, redesigning incentive and information systems, budget-ing for new capital investments and training programs, and so on. The new possibilities (or constraints) discovered in this behavioral loop are then channeled back to inform the re-creation, or refinement, of the evolving intent. The sequential nature of this iterative learning process is key, though the full cycle may be completed so quickly, at times, that it may appear simultaneous.

In essence, the cognitive loop is primarily concerned with learning in a double-loop fashion (Argyris, 1985), through its exploration of alternative virtual worlds; the behavioral loop operates in a single loop learning fashion, accepting as given the intent produced in the cognitive loop. In the absence of attention to the cognitive loop, the planning process deteriorates into the kind of incremental stability-favoring process that Mintzberg equates with the totality of planning, and which he describes as "strategic programming," but which I argue represents only part of the cycle.

This generative strategic planning process, with its simultaneous consideration of multiple alternatives, along with the elaboration of both strategies and their implementa-tion implications, mirrors the kind of processes that Eisenhardt (1989) describes as characterizing the best performers among the firms that she studied in high-velocity environments. Similarly, Grove's (1996) description of strategy making at Intel, where alternating periods of seeming chaos as multiple alternatives are pursued in mind, have been followed by periods of "intense and single-minded pursuit" of the course of action ultimately chosen, comes to mind.

An irreconcilable tension exists at the core of successful strategy-making processes, as Burgelman (1991) has noted. It is the tension between strategic change that is too fast and that which is too slow – the tension between aligning to exploit current capabilities and disrupting alignment in pursuit of new possibilities outside of a firm's current competency base. On-going thoughtful reflection on this tension can be one of the most significant contributions of the strategic planning process. Maintaining the iterative cycle of envision-ing multiple possibilities and acting on the most attractive of these requires both the kind of strategic thinking that traditional planning processes are seen as lacking *and* the strategic programming activities that they already possess. Such a process uses as its foundation contributions from the rational, cognitive, and learning lenses and exhibits what Simon (1993) has described as the three essential skills for successful strategic decision-making:

> The most important skills required for survival and success in the kind of uncertain, rapidly evolving world in which we live are (1) skill in anticipating the shape of an uncertain future, (2) skill in generating alternatives for operating effectively in changed environments, and (3) skill in implementing new plans rapidly and efficiently. These skills have to take a central place in the strategic planning process (p. 134).

TABLE 3.1 Traditional versus generative planning model

|  | *Traditional* | *Generative* |
|---|---|---|
| Primary purpose of planning | ◆ Coordination and control<br>◆ Creation of plan | ◆ Strategic change<br>◆ Development of strategic thinking |
| Level of involvement | ◆ Limited primarily to senior and division managers | ◆ Broadly inclusive of diverse members at all levels |
| Nature of involvement | ◆ Through written communication directed upward<br>◆ Advocacy mode | ◆ Dialogue-based<br>◆ Advocacy and inquiry mode<br>◆ Hypothesis-driven |
| Timing | ◆ Periodic<br>◆ Calendar-driven | ◆ Episodic<br>◆ Issue-driven |
| Competencies required | ◆ Analytic | ◆ Alternative generation and evaluation<br>◆ Conflict resolution |
| Leadership role | ◆ Strategic thinker<br>◆ Decision originator | ◆ Process enabler<br>◆ Synthesizer |
| Contextual elements | ◆ Clarity in providing objectives and planning guidelines | ◆ Clarity of purpose organizational<br>◆ Sense of urgency<br>◆ Psychological safety |

Table 3.1 suggests more specifically what an actual planning process modeled on this theoretical view of planning might look like, and compares the proposed generative model to the traditional model, along a number of dimensions often used to describe planning processes – level and nature of involvement, timing, skill sets required, and the role of leadership and context.

The elements of this model are not new. A distinguished set of scholars have previously advocated aspects of this generative model, including Mintzberg (1994), Burgelman (1991), Bourgeois and Brodwin (1984), Mason and Mitroff (1981), Chakravarthy and Doz (1992), and Hart (1992). What this most recent model emphasizes is the importance of *conversations* and of *design*.

## The metaphor of strategic conversation

The metaphor of conversation offers a way of thinking about how organizations can address both the gap opening and closing questions described earlier as well as the hypothesis generating and testing seen earlier as fundamental to strategic thinking. It conveys an inclusive "give and take" image and allows us to look at the different players and processes important to strategy making. The conversations occur at multiple levels – *within* the heads of single individuals, between them and their local environments, and throughout the organization *across* individuals, on an on-going basis.

These individual conversations with unique circumstances must somehow be aggregated at the institutional level; that is, we must organize the conversation that these distributed individuals have with each other if a coherent pattern is to emerge. The existence of such a pattern has been argued to constitute the test of whether a "strategy" really exists at all (Hayes and Wheelwright, 1984). This institutional level conversation acts to reshape and redefine corporate intent, based on the knowledge gained in the local conversation. It also serves to build coherence and commitment at the level of the whole. Together, these two kinds of conversations – one occurring with local environments across the organization and the other occurring centrally with each other within the organization – constitute the strategy-making process. These individual and organizational conversations are neither sequential nor independent of each other. Each shapes the other and like the functioning of a brain, they flow back and forth in iterative and unpredictable ways as they respond to stimuli and activate motor mechanisms. These "strategic conversations" are the interactions through which choices at all levels get made, tested, and the rationales behind them developed.

Frances Westley (1990) has argued that we have paid far too much attention to "strategic choices" in the strategy field, and too little attention to these strategic conversations, and that the tradition in strategy formulation has been to exclude all but senior managers from these conversations. Because it is through conversation that individuals co-create the shared meaning behind the strategy, managers deprived of these conversations lack the context in which to understand the strategic choices made and are confused and "de-energized." Implementing new strategies requires enormous amounts of Csikszentmihalyi's (1990) psychic energy. Confusion disrupts and dissipates the flow of energy needed to accomplish change.

It is not enough to merely be *told* of the rationale, because different groups of managers have different cognitive frames that process what they are told through the filters of their past experiences and current expectations. Senior managers, research has shown, consistently underestimate the difficulty of change because they overestimate the extent to which subordinates share their view of the world (Bartunek, Lacey and Wood, 1992). Managers must be able to sort through the paradoxes raised by interpreting decisions through their frames, rather than those of senior managers. This frame adjustment process works far more smoothly when they are included in the conversation. The result of such inclusion – being both talked with and listened to – is energizing.

Wider participation also potentially enhances the quality of the strategic choices themselves, not just their execution. Managers who do not share the same frames are more likely to question the assumptions underlying others' frames – assumptions which are often invisible to their holders. This questioning of assumptions is a critical step in the kind of dialogue processes that are seen as essential to generating better, more innovative solutions. Innovation is enhanced when participants who are skilled at managing conversations bring diverse perspectives and backgrounds to bear on shared challenges (Leonard-Barton, 1995). Thus, the strategy that is co-invented within a more inclusive conversation reflects a more complex and multi-faceted view of reality. As Burgelman (1991) notes:

> An atmosphere in which strategic ideas can be freely championed and fully contested by anyone with relevant information or insight may be a key factor in developing internal selection processes that maximize the probability of generating viable organizational strategies. Such processes generate strategic change that is neither too slow nor too fast.

The argument against such inclusion rests with the fear that individuals who bring narrow parochial views into strategic conversations are far more likely to retard, rather than enhance, the process, and that groups unskilled at talking across differences will polarize and sub-optimize, rather than produce better solutions. This recognition reinforces the premium placed on producing a high quality of strategic thinking at all levels in the organization. Thus, building a widely distributed strategy-making process requires strategic thinking at the individual level as well as the ability to use this as input into a larger conversation whose outcome is coherent at the organizational level. Strategy-making that operates at these two levels creates a kind of "meta-capability" that enhances the ability of a business to remain competitive over time. Meta-capabilities, as the term is used here, facilitate the on-going creation of particular business-specific capabilities by contributing the kinds of skills and knowledge that underlie the process of capability-building itself (Liedtka, 1996).

## *Developing "meta-capabilities"*

Many strategy researchers believe that strategically valuable capabilities create value for customers, are rare, and are hard for competitors to imitate (Barney, 1991). Day (1994) argues that they also make the organization more adaptable to change. The first three qualities – value creation, uniqueness, and inimitability – have been well recognized in the strategy literature. Yet, any particular set of skills that are valuable and hard to imitate will also be at great risk for being difficult to change, once alignment has been reached. This has been called the "adaptability paradox" and the "failure of success," and in stories from IBM to General Motors we have seen how the drivers of past success can lead to complacency and failure to adapt in the face of environmental change. The third quality of continuous adaptation requires the creation of a set of meta-capabilities. These meta-capabilities are comprised of a set of distinct, yet inter-related, skills. Learning is one. In fact, the ability to learn new sets of skills on an on-going basis has been argued by some to represent the *only* sustainable source of advantage for the future. Collaboration is another contributor to the meta-capability cluster. Collaboration allows organizations to converse, learn, and work *across* the silos that have characterized organizational structures, to "link and leverage across entrepreneurial units" in Ghoshal and Bartlett's (1995) terms. The ability to redesign processes is yet a third. The recent interest in total quality management, learning, and teamwork suggests an increasing recognition of the inherent value of these underlying process capabilities, across very different organizational contexts and strategies. A widely distributed capacity for strategy making constitutes another dimension of the meta-capability cluster. Only by coupling the meta-capabilities with a particular set of business-specific capabilities, can all four conditions – value creation, uniqueness, inimitability, adaptability – be satisfied.

Though the ability to learn, to collaborate, to redesign processes, and to facilitate strategic conversations are each theoretically differentiable, we believe them to be largely inseparable in practice. Each relies, at a fundamental level, on the ability of individuals throughout the organization to think at a systems level, to see their role as embedded within a larger system, and to be willing to experiment, to search for better solutions through a process of trial and error. Unfortunately, a hierarchical approach to strategy making, with grand strategy envisioned by senior management alone and controlled through planning and budgeting systems, is more likely to encourage managers to crave clarity and certainty in an ambiguous world and to think narrowly and parochially within complex systems.

The meta-capabilities for learning, collaborating, re-designing, and strategy-making rely on a widely distributed capacity for strategic thinking, as well as an inclusive set of strategic conversations at all levels in the organization, aimed at both furthering the intended strategy and at recognizing opportunities for emergent strategies.

These conversations are of a particular nature, however – they are conversations about *design*, the topic to which we now turn.

## *The metaphor of design*

The centrality of design skills to the practice of management has long been recognized. In 1969, Herbert Simon noted:

> Engineering, medicine, business, architecture, and painting are concerned not with the necessary but with the contingent – not with how things are but with how they might be – in short, with design . . . Everyone designs who devises courses of action aimed at changing existing situations into preferred ones . . . Design, so construed, is the core of all professional training.

The concept of design, however, has taken on a largely negative meaning in the field of strategic management, since Mintzberg (1990) issued his influential indictment of the approach to strategy-making that he labeled the "Design School." The Design School, as he defined it, represented a hierarchical, top-down approach that was ill suited for the realities of changing environments. With this important work, the term "design," in particular, and the concept of planning, in general, fell into disfavor. I use the term quite differently. The metaphor of design offers rich possibilities for helping us to think more deeply about the formation of business strategy, and it is time to liberate the idea of design from its association with outmoded approaches to strategy.

## *Characteristics of design thinking*

A detailed study of the design field literature (Liedtka, 2000) suggests that design thinking can be seen as having a specific set of characteristics. These help in clarifying the kind of strategic conversations that organizations need to create.

First, design thinking is *synthetic*. Out of the often-disparate demands presented by sub-units' requirements, a coherent overall design must be made to emerge. The process through which and the order in which the overall design and its sub-unit designs unfold remains a source of debate. What is clear is that the order in which they are given attention matters, as it determines the "givens" of subsequent designs, but ultimately successful designs can be expected to exhibit considerable diversity in their specifics. Strategic thinking is also *synthetic*. It seeks internal alignment and understands interdependencies. It is systemic in its focus. It requires the ability to understand and integrate across levels and elements, both horizontal and vertical, and to align strategies across those levels. Strategic thinking, as we have already noted, is built on the foundation of a systems perspective. A strategic thinker has a mental model of the complete end-to-end system of value creation, and understands the interdependencies within it.

The synthesizing process creates value not only in aligning the components, but also in creatively rearranging them. The creative solutions produced by many of today's entrepreneurs often rest more with the redesign of aspects of traditional strategies in ways that create added value for customers, rather than with dramatic breakthroughs (Petzinger, 1999).

Secondly, design thinking is *abductive* in nature, rather than deductive or inductive. Abductive thinking focuses on what is *possible* rather than provable. It is primarily concerned with the process of visualizing what might be, some desired future state, and creating a blueprint for realizing that intention. A design hypothesis, therefore, differs from a scientific hypothesis in that it cannot be demonstrated to be true. Any preferred competitive strategy, because it is an invention rather than a truth, must tell a compelling story to those who must implement it.

Design thinking is also *hypothesis-driven*. As such, it is both analytic, in its use of data for hypothesis testing, and creative, in the generation of hypotheses to be tested. The hypotheses are of two types. Primary is the design hypothesis, already discussed. The design hypothesis is conjectural and, as such, cannot be tested directly. Embedded in the selection of a particular promising design hypotheses, however, are a series of assumptions about a set of cause–effect relationships in today's environment that will support a set of actions aimed at transforming a situation from its current reality to its desired future state. These explanatory hypotheses must be identified and tested directly.

Cycles of hypothesis generation and testing are iterative. As successive loops of "what if" and "if then" questions are explored, the hypotheses become more sophisticated and the design unfolds. Strategic thinking is also *hypothesis-driven*. In an environment of ever-increasing information availability and decreasing time to think, the ability to develop good hypotheses and to test them efficiently is critical. Strategic thinking accommodates both creative and analytical thinking sequentially in its use of iterative cycles of hypothesis generating and testing. Taken together, and repeated over time, this sequence allows us to pose ever-improving hypotheses, without forfeiting the ability to explore new ideas. Such experimentation allows an organization to move beyond simplistic notions of cause and effect to provide ongoing learning.

Design thinking is *opportunistic*. As the above cycles iterate, the designer seeks new and emergent possibilities. The power of the design lies in the particular. Thus, it is in the translation from the abstract/global to the particular/local that unforeseen opportunities are most likely to emerge. Strategic thinking is *opportunistic*. Within this intent-driven focus, there must be room for opportunism that not only furthers intended strategy but that also leaves open the possibility of new strategies emerging.

Design thinking is *dialectical*. The designer lives at the intersection of often conflicting demands of possibilities, constraints, and uncertainty – recognizing the constraints of today's materials and the uncertainties that cannot be defined away, while envisioning tomorrow's possibilities. Innovative designs both satisfy and transcend today's constraints to realize new possibilities. Strategic thinking is *dialectical*, as well. In the process of inventing the image of the future, the strategist must mediate the tension between constraint, contingency, and possibility. The underlying emphasis of strategic intent is stretch – to reach explicitly for potentially unattainable goals. At the same time, all elements of the firm's environment are not shapeable and those constraints that are real must be acknowledged in designing strategy. Similarly, the "unknowables" must be recognized and the flexibility to deal with the range of outcomes that they represent must be designed in.

Finally, design thinking is *inquiring* and *value-driven* – open to scrutiny, welcoming of inquiry, willing to make its reasoning explicit to a broader audience, and cognizant of the values embedded within the conversation. It recognizes the primacy of the *Weltanschauung* of its audience. The architect imbues the design with his or her own values. Successful designs, in practice, educate and persuade by connecting with the values of the audience, as well. Strategic thinking is *inquiring* and, inevitably, *value-driven*. Because any particular strategy is invented, rather than discovered – chosen from among a larger set of plausible alternatives – it is contestable and reflective of the values of those making the choice. Its acceptance requires both connection with and movement beyond the existing mindset and value system of the rest of the organization. Such movement relies on inviting the broader community into the argumentation process – the strategic conversation. It is through participation in this dialogue that the strategy itself unfolds, both in the mind of the strategist and in that of the larger community that must come together to make the strategy happen. The conversation is what allows the strategist to pull his or her colleagues "through the keyhole" into a new *Weltanschauung*.

Taken together, these characteristics – synthetic, abductive, dialectical, hypothesis-driven, opportunistic, inquiring, and value-driven – all borrowed from the field of design, describe the strategic conversation.

## Leveraging the design metaphor

The metaphors of design and conversation offer windows into a deeper understanding of the process of strategy making. They do this by calling attention to the process of creating a purposeful space. Such spaces "work" because of much more than the structures visible to the eye. They work because they create an environment that fuses form and function; that builds relationships and capabilities and targets specific outcomes; that inspires, at an emotional and aesthetic level, those who work towards a shared purpose. Values play a vital role here, as do hypothesis generating and testing, and the ability to conjure a vivid picture of a set of possibilities that do not yet exist.

What would we do differently in organizations today, if we took seriously the design metaphor? A lot, I believe. It would call for significant changes in the way that strategic planning is approached, especially in large organizations. The problems with traditional approaches to planning have long been recognized. They include: the attempt to make a science of planning with its subsequent loss of creativity; the excessive emphasis on numbers; the drive for administrative efficiency that standardized inputs and formats at the expense of substance; and the dominance of single techniques, inappropriately applied. Yet, decades later, strategists continue to struggle to propose clear alternatives to traditional processes. Design offers a different approach and would suggest processes that are more widely participative, more dialogue-based, issue rather than calendar-driven, conflict using rather than conflict avoiding, all aimed at invention and learning, rather than control. In short, I hypothesize that organizations should involve more members of the organization in two-way strategic conversations, viewing the process as one of iteration and experimentation, and paying sequential attention to idea generation and evaluation in a way that attends first to possibilities before moving onto constraints. Finally, and perhaps most importantly, we would recognize the primary role that leadership and rhetoric play in strategy making, acknowledging that good designs succeed by persuading, and great designs by inspiring.

## CONCLUSION

What if we, as scholars, designed our research agendas around meeting the criteria for strategic conversations that I have laid out here? What would change? We would, I argue, pay much more attention to *synthesizing;* rather than focusing primarily on delineating theoretical alternative models we would seek integrative ones. We would utilize abductive reasoning – using our learning around strategic management to argue for what *might* be, rather than our current emphasis on proving what is or is not today. We would be as attuned to the *creative* endeavor of generating good hypotheses – especially design hypotheses, even if these are not testable in a traditional sense – as we are now to the analytic endeavor of hypothesis testing. We would adopt a willingness to live in the messy intersection of possibility, constraint, and uncertainty, rather than seeking the order and control attainable only through simplifying assumptions. We would respond more quickly to the emergent and, finally, be willing to advocate from a position that does not pretend to be value neutral.

   If we succeeded in doing so, we might expect to produce more good research that persuades our ultimate audience of practicing managers – and perhaps even some great research that inspires them.

## NOTES

1 These ten schools are the Design School, the Planning School, the Positioning School, the Entrepreneurial School, the Cognitive School, the Learning School, the Power School, the Cultural School, the Environmental School, and the Configuration School. See Mintzberg, Ahlstrand, and Lampel (1998: Table 12.1, pp. 354–9), for a detailed discussion of each.
2 These are the "transactive" mode (learning as central, with a broad set of stakeholders engaged in an interactive dialogue); the "symbolic" mode (a more cognitive perspective, according

transformative vision a central role); the "rational" mode (whose goal is comprehensiveness); the "commander" mode (a single entrepreneur, or small group of managers, control strategy formulation); and the "generative mode" (a different use of the term than the one that I will later employ) that focuses on intrapreneurship.

## REFERENCES

Andrews, K. (1971). *The Concept of Corporate Strategy*. New York: Irwin.

Ansoff, H. (1965). *Business Strategy and Policy: An Analytic Approach to Business Policy for Growth and Expansion*. New York: McGraw-Hill.

Anthony, R. (1965). *Planning and Control Systems: A Framework for Analysis*. Boston: Division of Research, Graduate School of Business Administration, Harvard University.

Argyris, C. (1985). *Strategy, Change, and Defensive Routines*. Marshfield, MA: Pitman Publishing.

Barney, J. (1991). Firm Resources and Sustained Competitive Advantage. *Journal of Management*, 17, 99–120

Bartunek, J., Lacey, C., and Wood D. (1992). Social Cognition in Change. *Journal of Applied Behavioral Science*, 18(2), 204–23.

Bourgeois, L., and Brodwin, D. (1984). Strategic Implementation: Five Approaches to an Elusive Phenomenon. *Strategic Management Journal*, 5, 241–64.

Burgelman, R. (1991). Intraorganizational Ecology of Strategy Making and Organizational Adaptation: Theory and Field Research. *Organizational Science*, 2(3), 239–62.

Chakravarthy, B., and Doz, D. (1992). Strategy Process Research: Focusing on Corporate Self-Renewal. *Strategic Management Journal*, 13, 5–14.

Csikszentmihalyi, M. (1990). *Flow*. New York: Harper & Row.

Cyert, R., and March, J. (1963). *A Behavioral Theory of the Firm*. New York: Prentice-Hall.

Day, G. (1994). The Capabilities of Market-Driven Organizations. *Journal of Marketing*, 58 (October), 37–52.

DeBono, E. (1970). *Lateral Thinking*. New York: Harper & Row.

Dutton, J., and Jackson, S. (1987). Categorizing Strategic Issues: Links to Organizational Action. *Academy of Management Review*, 12, 76–90.

Eisenhardt, K. (1989). Making Fast Strategic Decisions in High Velocity Environments. *Academy of Management Journal*, 32(3), 543–76.

Evans, P., and Wurster, T. (1998). *Blown to Bits*. New York: Free Press.

Fritz, R. (1989). *The Path of Least Resistance*. New York: Fawcett Columbine.

Ghoshal, S., and Bartlett, C. (1995). Changing the Role of Top Management: Beyond Structure to Process. *Harvard Business Review*, (January/February), 86–96.

Grove, A. (1996). *Only the Paranoid Survive*. New York: Doubleday.

Hamel, G., and Prahalad, C. (1989). Strategic Intent. *Harvard Business Review*, May/June, 63–76.

Hamel, G., and Prahalad, C. K. (1993). Strategy as Stretch and Leverage. *Harvard Business Review* (March/April), 75–84.

Hamel, G., and Prahalad, C. (1994). *Competing for the Future*. Boston: Harvard Business School Press.

Handy, C. (1994). *The Age of Paradox*. Boston: Harvard Business School Press.

Hart, S. (1992). An Integrative framework for Strategy-Making Processes. *Academy of Management Review*, 17(2), 327–51.

Hart, S., and Banbury, C. (1994). How Strategy-Making Processes Can Make a Difference. *Strategic Management Journal*, 15, 251–69.

Hayes, R., and Wheelwright, S. (1984). *Restoring Our Competitive Edge: Competing Through Manufacturing*. New York: Wiley.

Jordan, T., and Teece, D. (1989). Competition and Cooperation: Striking the Right Balance. *California Management Review*, (Spring), 25–37.

Lenz, R. (1987) Managing the Evolution of the Strategic Planning Process. *Business Horizons*, Jan./Feb., 34–9.

Leonard-Barton, D. (1995). *Well-Springs of Knowledge*. Boston: Harvard Business School Press.

Levinthal, D., and March, J. (1993). The Myopia of Learning. *Strategic Management Journal*, 14, 95–112.

Liedtka, J. (1996). Collaborating Across Lines of Business for Competitive Advantage. *Academy of Management Executive*, 10(2), 20–34.

Liedtka, J. (2000). In Defense of Strategy as Design. *California Management Review*, (Spring).

Liedtka, J., and Rosenblum, J. (1996). Shaping Conversations: Making Strategy, Managing Change. *California Management Review*, 39(1): 141–57.

Lindblom, C. (1959). The Science of Muddling Through. *Public Administration Review*, 19(2), 70–88.

Lorange, P. (1980). *Corporate Planning: An Executive Viewpoint*. Englewood Cliffs, NJ: Prentice-Hall.

March, J., and Simon, H. (1958). *Organizations*. New York: Wiley.

Mason, R., and Mitroff, I. (1981). *Challenging Strategic Planning Assumptions*. New York: Wiley.

Miller, C., and Cardinal, L. (1994). Strategic Planning and Firm Performance: A Synthesis of More than Two Decades of Research. *Academy of Management Journal*, 37(6), 1649–65.

Mintzberg, H. (1973). Strategy-making in Three Modes, *California Management Review*, (Winter).

Mintzberg, H. (1987). Crafting Strategy. *Harvard Business Review*, (July/August), 66–75.

Mintzberg, H. (1990). The Design School: Reconsideration of the Basic Premises of Strategic Management. *Strategic Management Journal*.

Mintzberg, H. (1994). *The Rise and Fall of Strategic Planning*. New York: Prentice-Hall.

Mintzberg, H., Ahlstrand, B., and Lampel, J. (1998). *Strategy Safari*. New York: Free Press.

Montgomery, C., and Hariharan, S. (1991). Diversified Expansion by Large Established Firms. *Journal of Economic Behavior*, 71–89.

Moore, J. (1993). Predators and Prey: A New Ecology of Competition. *Harvard Business Review* (May/June).

Moore, J. (1996). *The Death of Competition*. New York: Harper Business.

Najagopalan, N., and Spreitzer, G. (1997). Toward a Theory of Strategic Change: A Multi-lens Perspective and Integrative Framework. *Academy of Management Review*, 22: 48–79.

Nasi, J. (1991). *Arenas of Strategic Thinking*. Helsinki, Finland: Foundation for Economic Education.

Neustadt, R., and May, E. (1986). *Thinking in Time: The Uses of History for Decision-Makers*. New York: Free Press.

Paul, R. (1987). Dialogical Thinking: Critical Thought Essential to the Acquisition of Rational Knowledge and Passions, in J. B. Baron and R. J. Sternberg (eds.), *Teaching Thinking Skills: Theory and Practice*. New York: Freeman and Company.

Petzinger, T. (1999). *The New Pioneers*. New York: Simon and Schuster.

Porter, M. (1980). *Competitive Strategy*. New York: Free Press.

Raimond, R. (1996). Two Styles of Foresight. *Long Range Planning*, (April), 208–14.

Rumelt, R., Schendel, D., and Teece, D. (1994). *Fundamental Issues in Strategy*. Cambridge, MA: Harvard Business School Press.

Schon, D. (1983) *The Reflective Practitioner: How Professionals Think in Action*. New York: Basic Books.

Senge, P. (1990). *The Fifth Discipline*. New York: Doubleday.

Senge, P. (1992). Mental Models. *Planning Review*, (March/April), 4–10, 44.

Simon, H. (1969). *The Sciences of the Artificial*. Cambridge, MA: MIT Press.

Simon, H. (1993). Strategy and Organizational Evolution. *Strategic Management Journal*, 14, 131–42.

Stacey, R. (1992). *Managing the Unknowable*. San Francisco, CA: Jossey-Bass.

Steiner, G. (1979). *Strategic Planning*. New York: Free Press.

Teece, D., Pisano, G., and Shuen, A. (1997). Dynamic Capabilities and Strategic Management.

*Strategic Management Journal*, 18(7), 509–33.

Weick, K. (1969). *The Social Psychology of Organizing*. Reading, MA: Addison-Wesley.

Wernerfelt, B. (1984). A Resource-Based View of the Firm. *Strategic Management Journal*, 5, 171–80.

Westley, F. (1990). Middle Managers and Strategy: Micro dynamics of Inclusion. *Strategic Management Journal*, 11, 337–51.

Wilson, I. (1994). Strategic Planning Isn't Dead – It Changed. *Long Range Planning*, 27(4).

# Part II

## THEORETICAL FOUNDATIONS

# 4

# Strategic Flexibility in the Old and New Economies

## KATHRYN RUDIE HARRIGAN

Advances in computing and communications technologies epitomized by the internet revolution have hastened a schism between the success requirements of the smokestack, low-technology industries comprising the "old economy" and the high technology, knowledge-based industries of the "new economy." In the 21st century, there is an increasing urgency for strategic flexibility in both types of industries – particularly where internet time collapses the horizon during which the value of strategic investments can be recouped. How firms attain such flexibility will differ across the contexts of these two types of environment.

## DEFINITIONS

Strategic flexibility is about coping with uncertainty to earn (1) high returns while managing (2) accompanying risks (Harrigan, 1985b). It deals with the dark side of *timing* issues in strategy (rather than choices that determine the content of firms' strategies) because flexibility is rarely of interest until there is a need for change. In the past, choosing the wrong resource posture often put the firm at a relative disadvantage for ongoing competition, and substantial risks ensued – especially where entry (or mobility) barriers were high while customers' switching cost barriers were low (Caves and Porter, 1977; Caves and Ghemawat, 1992). Entry barriers became exit barriers as competition evolved (Porter, 1980).

### Exit barriers

Exit barriers are circumstances within an industry that discourage the exit (or mobility) of competitors whose performance in that particular business may be marginal. The timely extrication of a firm's resources from a business (or strategic posture) that is failing can be a delicate maneuver. A thin resale market may exist for assets that are blatantly inappropriate for effective competition, making divestiture (or re-positioning) difficult to achieve. Empirical evidence of exit barrier heights has largely been taken from old economy industries involving manufacturing, not the provision of low technology services (Harrigan, 1981, 1982, 1983).

Flexibility issues arise from the irreversibility of some firms' strategic postures – assets that have been amassed, resources configured (Sanchez, 1995), capabilities entrenched (Stalk et al., 1992), and relationships atrophied. When the high mobility barriers previously erected (as entry barriers) to protect a coveted market position proved too tedious to modify, exit barriers arising from such tangible (and other) assets exacerbated entrenched firms' propensities to fight (since flight is exceedingly difficult from an inflexible strategic posture). Competitors cornered by such barriers were judged to be highly committed, hence dangerous, until their overhanging productive capacity was rationalized – through endgame strategies involving salvage markets, turnarounds, and leveraged buy outs (LBO) privatizations (Harrigan and Porter, 1983). Highly committed competitors used price to vie for market share as well as to limit entry (Ghemawat, 1991; Ghemawat and del Sol, 1998). Their irreversible posture made firms more willing to fight price wars.

## Economic exit barriers

Economic exit barriers represent those factors that will influence firms to operate their physical assets, even if they earn subnormal rates of return on them. Such barriers can be the costs associated with eliminating a plant – such as the cost of dismantling a chemical plant and treating the land beneath the plant – or the deterrent effect created by the lack of a resale market for the plant and assets (Caves and Porter, 1978). Their effect is to keep excess capacity in operation that should have been retired.

When firms expand capacity in anticipation of demand, there is always a risk that the demand needed to absorb capacity may never materialize. While industry competitions evolved slowly, this capacity imbalance was not too damaging. Although overall unit shipments were increasing – albeit slowly – the price-cost pressures created by optimistic expansions were eventually ameliorated by overall market growth. But when it became apparent to all that some firms' capacities would be underutilized, customers exploited this weakness by demanding price cuts of all vendors. Falling over each other in a stampede to fill their respective plants beyond break-even levels of capacity, firms ignited vicious rounds of price cuts to capture market share. Once lowered, prices are very difficult to raise – unless there are capacity shortages.

Physical assets, such as plant, machinery, and inventory that must be written off on disposal, comprise the major types of economic assets that could act as exit barriers. A plant that is shared with another business could also constitute such a barrier because this factor could keep a facility in operation that should have been retired. The factors influencing the height of economic exit barriers are predominantly characteristics relating to the product's manufacturing technology (Porter, 1976b): (1) capital intensity, (2) asset specificity, (3) age of the assets (the extent to which their value has been depreciated), and (4) technological or operating reinvestment requirements. If the expenditures for other types of investments (advertising, R&D, or intangible plant improvements) are not expensed – if they are capitalized and undepreciated when exit must occur – they too can constitute economic exit barriers, in the sense that they might become an undesirable reported loss upon disposal when firms retire a facility that is no longer needed. (If accounting systems are included as economic barriers – as was the case in some countries during their economic development – all assets that have been capitalized could act as exit barriers by virtue of the reporting loss they would create if firms exited before depreciating them fully. This analysis assumes, of course, that recognition of reporting losses would injure the reputation of the ongoing firm – in the capital markets, with lenders, when recruiting employees, with potential merger partners, or in other salient forums.)

## Strategic exit barriers

Exit barriers could also emanate from firms' reluctance to sacrifice the benefits of cumulative, intangible assets that they have created through previous investments. Strategic exit barriers such as these could be created by image-maintenance goals, customer-service obligations, potential loss of customers or distribution channels, synergies between related businesses, shared facilities, or even a highly successful market position. Some forms of vertical integration may act as strategic exit barriers, as do favorable expectations regarding future demand.[1] Downstream linkages are easier to disentangle than upstream ones when dismantling vertical strategies (Harrigan, 1985a).

In summary, strategic flexibility is concerned with managing the uncertainty of suboptimal strategic postures. Evidence suggests that the risk is great that a firm's asset investments will prove to be irreversible in competitive battles where its strategic posture – the way in which it configures its assets to serve target markets – becomes weak in comparison with industry success requirements. Strategic flexibility issues address questions of commitment, asset specificity, and re-positioning options, and firms in all types of industries face the possibility of becoming stuck in a disadvantageous posture – especially within environments of rapid change.

## STRATEGIC FLEXIBILITY IN OLD ECONOMY INDUSTRIES

To illustrate how new economy approaches to competing on speed, specialization, and customization differ from old economy perspectives concerning flexibility, the evolution of concepts pertaining to strategic flexibility will be traced. Old economy issues concerning strategic repositioning will be compared with the apparent lack of re-positioning issues that are associated with virtual firm arrangements, and the nature of new economy exit barriers will be posited. Because the internet's impact on industry structure is most dramatically observable in value-chain relationships, comparisons between vertical strategies involving varying degrees of ownership will weigh heavily in contrasting flexibility differences within the old and new economies.

In the burgeoning industries of the new economy, where R&D-to-sales ratios are highest, and the workforce is heavily populated by scientists and engineers, entrepreneurs are exhorted to move quickly to capture coveted e-spaces – without regard for potential flexibility traps that such strategies may create. Getting to market first dominates concerns for quality and other higher-level bases for competition (Harrigan, 1994). Where patents are not defensible, critical resource battles focus on acquiring knowledge workers, brand equity, and reputation within value-chain relationships. Exit barriers do not rank highly among the issues that entrants worry about as they surge into glamorous, rapidly-growing industries.

In the lower-technology, old economy industries now facing maturing (if not declining) demand, flexibility has been an expedient afterthought, too – secondary to building infrastructures and investing in vertical processing stages far in excess of those activities where firms were later found to possess competencies (Harrigan, 1984). In such older industries, where unskilled and blue-collar workers comprised the majority of employees and entrants' investments were more likely to be in tangible (typically capital-intensive) assets (even if the product provided were a service), mismatches occurred over time between competitive success requirements and the assets that firms acquired or developed in-house to create competitive advantage. As the characteristics defining customers' preferred vendors evolved to reflect the changing bases for marketplace success and firms were caught having the wrong asset posture, their re-positionings were subsequently hampered where exit barriers were high.

## Business risks and competition

In both economic contexts, flexibility issues pertain to repositioning irreversible assets (that have created past competitive advantage) as industry and customer requirements evolve. Inflexibility is one of several risks that firms manage as uncertainties concerning entry by competitors, technological obsolescence, customer preferences, regulatory constraints, competitor investments, business models, and other matters are resolved. Inappropriate strategy choices jeopardize profitability due to several sources of inflexibility.

*Timing of entry risk.*   Early entrants face the risk that new resources will trump the basis for old entry barriers – leaving first movers in a disadvantaged position (Barney, 1991; Collis and Montgomery, 1998; Conner, 1991; Peteraf, 1993; Wernerfelt, 1984). Unless early entrants can reconfigure their strategic postures when the basis for competition changes, loss of market share is likely. Early entrants seeking first-mover advantages must weigh the benefits of setting product standards and shaping customer expectations concerning transactions against the risk of being supplanted by adroit late entrants that learn from pioneers' mistakes.

*Technological obsolescence risk.*   As technological standards evolve, risks of obsolescence increase for firms that cannot assimilate the new knowledge and other success requirements (D'Aveni, 1994). When the old recipes for success change, core competencies risk becoming core rigidities, or unleveragable within prevailing, new organizational forms (Leonard-Barton, 1992). The value of old technological platforms is shattered by customers' bias in favor of novelty and newer technologies.

*Re-engineering risk.*   Exit barriers can be organizational in nature, as well as being tangible or intangible assets (Porter, 1976b). Starting with a "clean sheet" in rethinking priorities repudiates the path by which organizations have acquired and enhanced their capabilities (Champy, 1996; Collis, 1994; Hammer and Champy, 1994). If an organization cannot make a clean break with old ideas when re-engineering because it is trapped by its dominant logic, fears of self-cannibalization, channel conflicts, or other baggage

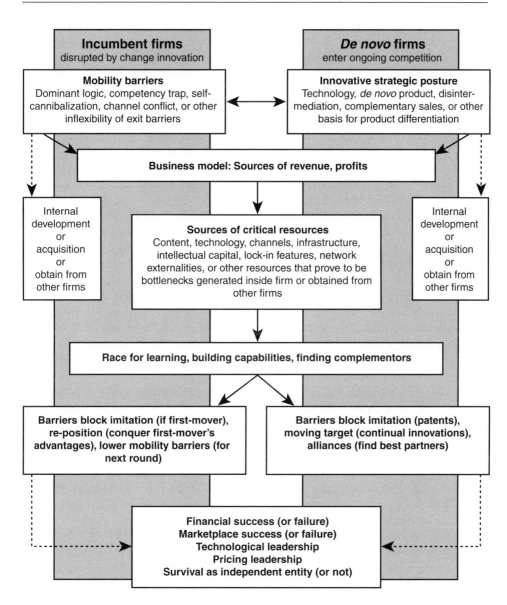

FIGURE 4.1 Competition between incumbent firms and *de novo* entrants

that explained early successes, it is hamstrung from executing timely repositionings, as figure 4.1 illustrates.

## Strategic choice and barriers

In formulating their strategies, firms seek unique market niches to serve effectively and protect their positions of historical advantage by building barriers to imitation. Because the entry barriers they erect can evolve into mobility (or exit) barriers, their competitive strategies must address flexibility issues as well as those of pre-emption. Inflexibility is closely identified with irreversible assets because each firm funds its asset configuration with the intent of pre-empting another firm from making identical asset investments (Coase, 1937). Entry by a competitor is deterred until customer demand grows enough to absorb the capacities of both firms' outputs. With entry barriers that have been massive, old economy firms have tended to face fewer challenges for their market space from potential entrants than do new economy firms operating in the egalitarian internet environment of low barriers and easy entry. Another difference: the speed with which flexibility issues become salient in old economy industries is slower than will be the case within new economy settings where competing on speed is of paramount importance (Stalk, 1988; Stalk and Hout, 1990).

The more highly specialized the asset configuration, the better suited the firm is to satisfy customers' idiosyncratic wants and needs. If changeover costs are high, a highly specialized strategic posture is appropriate to serve a critical mass of customers (so long as enough demand exists to absorb the fixed costs of that specialized posture). When the market's demands evolve (or another technology supplants extant asset configurations), highly specialized, but irreversible assets limit a firm's ability to serve customers effectively in a different way using the same specialized resources. The result is a competitive arena where firms have invested in unique asset configurations that could be potentially advantageous when used to serve customers that value most highly what the specialized (but irreversible) assets are best at providing.

*Asymmetrical strategic postures.* A firm's *de novo* posture when it first enters an industry is highly risky because much uncertainty exists concerning which posture will prove to offer the greatest, ultimate advantages. Because entry occurs at varying times during an industry's evolution (and customers' needs become better articulated with improved market information), the strategic postures by which newer firms enter are quite likely to differ technologically and in features offered from those of early entrants and extant competitors (Penrose, 1959). At a minimum, the entry barriers erected by early entrants have raised the stakes for admission by subsequent competitors by making the resources committed to market penetration more scarce and costly than those of pioneering firms (Bain, 1956). Second, the postures characterizing late entrants frequently differ on several salient dimensions from those of established firms because new competitors initially target under-served pockets of customers to gain a toehold market position without inciting violent retaliations (Reed and DeFillippi, 1990). Presumably, specialized resources needed to serve outlier customers effectively will differ significantly from those used to serve mainstream customers, else extant resources would have been effective in serving outliers and opportunities to gain a "toehold entry" would not exist (Conner, 1991; Wernerfelt, 1984). Third, technological innovations allow later entrants to embrace problem-solving methodologies for serving customers superior to those of first movers (Christensen, 1997).

Over time, the natural tensions of diverse firms' growth objectives (coupled with slowing demand growth due to market saturation) bring the resource differences existing among competitors into sharp focus as the re-positioning process begins. Industry consolidations that have been the outcome of technological upgrades force firms to replace older resource configurations, due to increasing returns to scale (Arthur, 1996).

Organizational change barriers as well as thin resale markets for unwanted assets exacerbate retrenchment difficulties (Caves and Porter, 1978; Harrigan, 1981). Some firms try to satisfy new demands using older asset configurations and these diverse strategic postures inevitably clash when competing for the same customers.

*Converging strategic groups.*    In old economy industries that faced slow growth, no growth, or declining growth in demand, firms embracing diverse strategic postures were forced into confrontation as they fought to serve a shrinking market for their outputs (Harrigan, 1980). Asymmetrical asset configurations – using assets placed into production long ago by early entrants that were of suboptimal scale or obsolete technologies – did not matter as long as demand was growing and outstripped capacity because vendors specialized in serving particular customers. Little turnover among customers occurred as long as capacity was constrained and fulfillment was on allocation. Even as excess capacity developed, customers' switching cost barriers may have permitted replacement of vendors only in a lumpy process (instead of incrementally). Moreover, contractual supplier obligations acted as exit barriers that threw old-fashioned assets headlong into competition with newer approaches to creating value for customers until barriers were reduced (Harrigan, 1980).

A fine balance exists between user stickiness being a blessing or curse, and industry evolution exacerbates propensities towards one or the other of these extremes at a particular point in time (Harrigan, 1980). Once trapped by inflexibility, ongoing firms' subsequent resource investments sometimes err by being too flexible – favoring generalized assets using multi-purpose software to make a wide range of products for a variety of customer tastes, but sacrificing some distinctiveness in the process (Harrigan, 1982). Although some managers diversify their firms away from confronting inflexibility problems, revitalization of remaining firms' stagnant strategic postures requires a re-thinking of competitive strategies and the logic underlying various strategic trade-offs to preserve profitability potential for surviving firms (Hayes and Abernathy, 1980).

*Value chains and activity maps.*    An alternative to investing in generalized assets that may lose their distinct advantage in serving particular customers is the choice of dis-investing from performing certain activities within, or steps of, the firm's value-creating system. Outsourcing tasks where a firm has little advantage may improve flexibility at the cost of unraveling a closely integrated gestalt of interdependent and mutually reinforcing business unit activities (Ghemawat and Pisano, 1999; Porter, 1996). Synergies enjoyed from leveraging core competencies may also be sacrificed by uncoupling closely coordinated business units (Prahalad and Hamel, 1990) and learning routines may be endangered. Because so many intangible assets arise from business unit interdependencies, vertical integration strategies frequently contribute to inflexibility problems – unless the organizational barriers to outsourcing can be overcome (Harrigan, 1985a).

When choosing which activities to outsource, activity map analysis may suggest which assets will be most valuable to retain (or develop) as competition evolves (Porter, 1996), and which activities may be entrusted to third-party affiliates. Because value creation frequently requires several, interdependent processing activities, firms often enter by investing in (or soon take on) vertically related businesses as part of their *de novo* entry postures. As firms rationalize their subsequent asset investments to modify their strategic postures (and lower exit barriers), a make-or-buy triage occurs concerning their vertical integration strategies.

## Vertical strategies and outsourcing

An effective vertical strategy involves the continuous process of re-designing task responsibilities (in collaboration with suppliers and customers) to create greater value-added internally in ways that leverage a firm's unique capabilities (Harrigan, 1983). At a particular time in its organizational evolution, the number of vertically-related processing stages within a firm's organizational span could encompass a large number of internal transactions – from ultra-raw materials to the ultimate consumer (Collis, 1986; Harrigan, 1985e). For example, Ford Motor once (1) mined the ore to make the (2) steel used to (3) fabricate the bodies of the automobiles it (4) assembled and (5) sold through wholly-owned distribution channels that culminated in (6) new car showrooms and (7) after-sale service salons. Shell Oil once (1) explored for and (2) produced crude oil that was (3) transported in (4) owned oil tankers, (5) polymerized in-house from (6) monomers (after the initial (7) cracking stage was performed within its own refinery), and (8) synthesized into various hydrocarbon compounds – such as plastics or resins – for ultimate sale as its (9) branded trash bags or paints.

In a well-designed vertical integration strategy – regardless of how many steps the firm performed in-house, and regardless of the form of business enterprise used to execute each step – the objective would be to capture high profits from each task comprising its value chain (Harrigan, 1984). Vertically related steps with lower profitability potential (or decreasing contributions to the firm's core competencies) would be outsourced (Harrigan, 1985c). A continual triage process would question which core knowledge the firm should build upon. Activities that have become less critical to competitive success would be outsourced to specialists as competition evolved; as an industry's success requirements evolve, so too does the mix of value adding activities emphasized by the firm (Harrigan, 1986).

*Ethical pharmaceuticals.*   Some pharmaceutical companies have recently been outsourcing research activities in the path to creating new molecules. For a company like Merck, research was its most important activity and the most critical asset it controlled was technological prowess – as evidenced by patents over its substances. As the pharmaceutical industry changed dramatically during the last 50 years, however, technology became less critical to success than being prescribed within managed healthcare centers – being pushed through a hospital's (or other healthcare delivery outlet's) portal for delivery to patients.

In a world with constant pressures for improved financial performance, companies must use their first mover advantages to exploit whatever advantages they possess quickly – for example, to become the standard medication recommended in hospital formularies for a specific indication. Physicians prescribe the first-mover substance primarily until the next innovator substance comes along and makes the previous standard obsolete. Having a seventeen-year-old patent means nothing in a hypercompetitive environment like the pharmaceutical industry where innovations are launched frequently (D'Aveni, 1994). There is too little breathing space between innovations to go it alone. The only breathing space between cannibalizing innovations is the time it takes the new substance to attain formulary approval in the healthcare delivery system. Perhaps that is why Merck used precious research dollars to acquire Medco, although it cannot merge databases until 2006.

*Contract research organizations (CROs) and contract manufacturing organizations (CMOs).*  Merck may still largely do its own research and development in-house, but many pharmaceutical companies contract with partner organizations for value-chain tasks – fundamental research, applied research, testing prior to Federal Drug Administration (FDA) approval, or manufacturing of one (or all) of the active ingredients – to accelerate the innovation process, especially in the face of the human genomics project. Such pharmaceutical companies use their distribution systems to market the ultimate substance – regardless of where the substance was created. Having their brand name on innovative substances preserves their image as a leading pharmaceutical company, when in actuality, their research prowess was enhanced by access to their virtual network of outsourcing partners. Such arrangements allow pharmaceutical firms to use other firms' skills, substances, and patents under licensing arrangements whereby all partners ultimately benefit from the pharmaceutical firm's success in the marketplace.

In the pharmaceutical industry examples, each outsourcing partner contributes a plank or two for the pharmaceutical firm's platform and the resulting virtual network thrives (or fails) depending upon how well a drug platform floats and how many prescribing physicians climb onboard it. Similarly, within contract manufacturing organizations, like Cambrex, productive capacity is prepared for manufacturing pharmaceutical active ingredients well in advance of FDA approval of new drugs. Pharmaceutical firms that outsource active ingredients share a platform with supplying partners and their respective successes are closely linked.

## *Synthesis: strategic flexibility issues and value-chain strategies*

In old economy industries, pioneering firms had a greater need to integrate forward (to legitimize their concept) than did technological followers. With this exception, less vertical integration was appropriate early (and late) in an industry's evolution. Multinational firms were engaged in more vertically related processing steps than were firms with little geographic diversification. Where outsourcing partners were readily available, firms performed tasks in-house that reinforced their core competencies, for which product scarcities existed, and where vertical synergies could not be otherwise exploited (Harrigan, 1983). Technological leaders often engaged in longer vertical processing chains to increase secrecy concerning the process innovations underlying technological milestones that were punctuated by patents, copyrights, and other forms of protecting intellectual capital (Harrigan, 1985e).

The competitive partnering practices necessitated by the bioengineering revolution in life sciences parallel many strategic posture choices made possible by the data-communications capabilities of the internet (used in developing the new economy scenario, below). The old economy meaning of strategic flexibility has been closely associated with ownership strategies and the difficulties created by irreversibility (Harrigan, 1985a). The new economy is concerned with speed of implementation (Stalk, 1988; Stalk and Hout, 1990; Tichy and Charan, 1989).

In many ways, the old economy verticality lessons have set the stage for strategic flexibility practices in the new economy world of virtuality. The risk of entering an industry with the wrong strategic posture endures, but different retrenchment problems arise due to the virtual nature of many assets deployed and the timing associated with modifying their mix.

In the past, vertically integrated companies have generally been assumed to give preference to vertically related sister business units when transacting business (so long as their transfer prices passed the "market test" for competitiveness) and inflexibility arose when changing vertical arrangements (Harrigan, 1985a). In this schema, the danger of preferring to sister business units arose when those business units did not keep up with competitive demands and became inadequate as suppliers. At that point, de-integration was warranted and some vertically integrated firms faced substantial exit barriers when executing this strategic repositioning due to relationships and other factors that reinforced regimens of internal transactions. The time required to de-integrate (due to exit barriers on asset disposal) and change business unit relationships (e.g., ending requirements contracts even where a business unit remained part of a corporate family) was less critical in old economy settings than it is in the new economy. The old ways of exiting take too long to implement in the new economy.

## Strategic Flexibility in New Economy Industries

The popular press lauds as being "new economy" those high technology industries with high knowledge worker-to-capital ratios where most employees perform high value-added work, and "knowledge workers" are largely scientists, engineers, and others with advanced degrees. Some older industries (e.g., telecommunications, ethical pharmaceuticals, and aerospace) possess traits from each of the groupings: (1) the "old economy's" capital intensity, blue-collar workforce, and regulatory interference, as well as (2) the "new economy's" intangible capital assets (patents, brand equity, programming-content libraries, reputation, and customer-preference databases), highly educated intellectual resources, and propensity to outsource. (Although post-industrial economies are employing increasing numbers of workers in service jobs, such as hamburger flipping, house cleaning, and entertaining guests at Disney World, the popular press accords no cachet to activities that do not create knowledge and have few value-chain affiliations with high technology.)

In the new economy, Net-centric industrial environment, transactions are made with different dancing partners as time passes. Strategic flexibility in the new economy parlance is associated with the freedom and ease to collaborate with any firms in any way by using any kind of business arrangement that may be expedient for the case at hand. Although the lack of asset ownership (including vertically related alliance partners) reduces some forms of mobility barriers (and exit barriers), new economy supplier-promiscuity carries other types of exit barriers. These barriers are not yet recognized because too little time has yet elapsed and the entrepreneurial firms staking out their initial industry positions in new economy settings have not yet confronted strategic flexibility disadvantages associated with virtual arrangements.

## Virtual firms and value nets

The new economy is a world where journalists adulate the virtual firm – a company that sits in the middle of a network of electronically linked alliances, but owns few physical assets. It is an extremely opportunistic model, in which alliance partners change frequently and rapidly. In this ideal world of virtuality, a concept company can sit in the middle of a spider's web of alliances, working its magic and its power over many smaller, partner companies that are easily replaced (Kaplan and Sawhney, 2000).

Many value-adding tasks within a virtual firm's value chain can be outsourced while still maintaining overall control of the project (Hagel and Singer, 1999). For example, a motion picture can be produced for a media firm by contracting for the performance of most tasks.[2] Once the motion picture has been completed, the media firm may exploit its film property through a variety of distribution outlets – including movie house screenings, videotape rentals, and television airings, among others – that may be owned by other firms.) In new economy parlance, the media firm's partners in this exploitation comprise members of its "value net" or "econet" (Bovet and Martha, 2000; Brandenburger and Nalebuff, 1996; Heng, 2000). The media firm need not own its value net's assets to produce the motion picture (nor distribute it to audiences once the film is produced).

*From "hollow corporation" to virtual firm.*   When *Business Week* noticed the virtual firm phenomenon in 1985, it called them "hollow corporations" and decried the loss of US competitiveness. Fifteen years later, virtual firms are the popular press's Net-centric champions of wily value exploitation and they are making strategic flexibility choices similar to old economy decision forks.

*Opportunism in e-space.*   The new virtual firm is extremely good at making matches between vertically related parties, finding logical dancing partners, forming temporary teams of outsourcers, and being an effective systems integrator. To accomplish this, necessarily, virtual firms use transactions that are very loosely coupled (Granovetter, 1985). In order to do so, virtual firms have networks of non-binding relationships from which they can choose partners for a particular transaction (Ahuja and Carley, 1999). For example, hospitals have memberships in several different pharmaceutical-buying plans to choose from, depending on which vendor offers the best prices for a specific product during a bidding round. In such loose alliances, firms leverage the power of being part of a team that uses its market power to get members a better price, but each firm remains an individual, non-linked entity that can claim membership opportunistically to get desired price breaks or other benefits. Participation is by mutual agreement and the virtual firm that manages the buying group must keep membership attractive. Promiscuity within new economy industries is condoned due to a prevalent "built-to-flip" mind set (Collins, 2000).

In the new economy industries, supported by new media start-ups, vast technology options, and turnkey internet consulting firms, the virtual firm is the ideal business model. A virtual firm enjoys the freedom and flexibility of a relationship of networked, temporary alliances to implement its strategy. Although alliances and outsourcing existed in the old economy, vertically integrated firms – large corporations that owned (or controlled) all aspects of their operations – dominated the old economy business arena and thinking about vertical strategies (Blois, 1972; Williamson, 1971). The similarities (and differences) among old and new economy firms may be observed in the speed with which they implement changes in strategic intent, and figure 4.1 depicts this competitive race. Differences in the vertical and virtual business models are next described to suggest how flexibility issues differ therein.

*Competitive iterations.*    In figure 4.1, *de novo* firms enter a market space served by incumbent firms. Their entry is possible because of an innovation they have applied to serve customers differently than incumbents. Perhaps they have syndicated valuable content to customize product offerings for diverse users by leveraging an idea (or platform) across related settings. *De novo* firms may have disintermediated traditional supplier–buyer relationships (replacing them with their own network of value-adding partners) while they leveraged market power in one setting to gain entrée into other value-net constellations.

The *de novo* firms applying these innovations are assumed to use virtual strategic postures and rely on virtual business models. Since their arrangements are informal (i.e., they own few assets that could become exit barriers), the *de novo* firms are assumed to have the greatest ease when re-positioning themselves in the face of turbulent competition.

In the race depicted in figure 4.1 to obtain resources that are critical to competitive success, virtual firms are expected to use other firms' resources while incumbent firms may have to develop critical resources in-house (or through acquisition). Similarly, the race to learn and develop new organizational capabilities relies heavily on finding complementors that can perform critical outsourced tasks so firms can focus their energies on areas of activity where they are effective.

While incumbent firms work to reduce barriers to flexibility by dismantling strategic postures that have served them well in the past, *de novo* firms struggle to survive into the next round of competition. Since few advantages provide *de novo* firms with Ricardian rents (e.g., enforceable patents), it is assumed that they strive to reinvent themselves through their own efforts or with the help of their network. Since product life cycles are shorter in hypercompetition, strategic flexibility issues become germane faster because strategic postures must be modified more frequently. Finally, figure 4.1 retains the old economy assumption that asymmetrical strategic groups can coexist because incumbents and *de novo* firms with differing time horizons will define success differently and invest accordingly. (This assumption may arise from the presence of different types of ownership groups with differing payback horizons.)

## VERTICAL AND VIRTUAL MODELS OF STRATEGIC FLEXIBILITY

In an old economy, vertical business model, the firm amasses its own resources and extracts rents from them (Backaitis, 1992). A firm's objective in formulating competitive strategy would be to develop a platform that could constitute a bottleneck for extracting rents. Once it had developed an insurmountable source of competitive advantage, the firm would leverage that advantage (which may constitute the firm's core competency and may comprise its growth path for realizing synergies). In the 1980s, when strategic alliances were a novelty, American companies were faced with the notion that they could not fund everything attractive under their own roof, and might find it necessary to work through other companies to accomplish their strategic objectives (Harrigan, 1985d).[3] As firms worked through the details of exploiting knowledge and other valuable resources in light of their need for partners, dynamics in their business models changed (Balakrishnan and Koza, 1993).

In the new economy, virtual companies have a very different approach to capturing vertical profits. Because they own few assets, they are interested in speedy turnovers (Ghosh, 1998). As virtual firms, internet companies seek ways to control an industry network by placing themselves centrally in a value chain and coordinating the activities of buyers and suppliers while leveraging the velocity of transactions (Rayport and Sviokla, 1995). Meanwhile each of the firm's network partners makes reciprocal outsourcing agreements with other partners that comprise nodes of their respective networks and many nodes of diverse value nets are overlapping in the identities of one or more of their members (Gulati, 1998). Their promiscuous pattern of partnering actually enhances the bargaining power of some virtual firms.

## Power in the network: competing business models

Venture capitalists heavily weight business models – ways in which firms can extract rents from their nets of activities – in their funding decisions, and the structure of a firm's business model ultimately determines its potential for overall profitability because it assesses the pervasiveness of the standard (Amit and Zott, 2000). In a new economy, virtual business model, hypercompetitive concerns may force firms to act opportunistically in the interest of expediency (D'Aveni, 1994). In such situations, there would not be enough time nor advantage in integrating partners with ongoing business units. Relationships with value net partners will be performance based.

In old economy business models, outsourcing was most prevalent when an industry's structure became well established and suppliers could be qualified to undertake tasks formerly done in-house (Harrigan, 1983). In the new economy, internet-enabled industries, new entrants can be virtual and enter market space through alliances. No time exists to develop brand equity, social capital, and numerous other stabilizing factors that cement supplier–buyer relationships within old economy industries because of the embryonic condition of most parts of the new internet-enabled industries.

*A negotiating quid pro quo.* As virtual firms face their own questions of make or buy – own or outsource – they eventually find that some resources must be owned. Virtual firms still need a bargaining chip in *e*-space that will pull customers to their portal rather than to a competitor's portal (Grant and Baden-Fuller, 1995). That chip can be strong brand equity, the standard-setting first-mover's advantage, platform strengths from getting partners to join the virtual firm's systems bandwagon, or other anchoring advantages. The strength of brand equity could be based upon an installed base of millions of satisfied customers. The bargaining chip could be a legal monopoly – such as a valuable patent – or a path of knowledge that comprises a trade secret (Hagedoorn, 1993). The resource's value may be its scarcity, such as for example, knowledge workers with a high degree of talent or specialized skills that are difficult to recruit (Ring and Van de Ven, 1992). Whatever the bargaining chip, virtual firms need a *quid pro quo* to recruit the most desirable partners into their networks (Harrigan, 1988).

*Syndication.*   The vertical nature of *e*-commerce requires virtual firms to solve a problem for one application by specializing in several vertical steps used in creating a total service offering for a narrow group of customers, for example, business-to-business (B2B) applications for morticians. They can build their infrastructure solution quickly, using the best software modules available from outsiders at that time. As service provider, they may (or may not) have created *de novo* one of the modules integrated into the turnkey service offering. After devising an infrastructure to serve those particular B2B customers well, the virtual firm grows by solving the same problem for similar, horizontally related customers – again relying upon its vertical expertise to amass a winning suite of solutions. By applying the vertical applications and relationships created to serve the first industry group's needs to other, similar industries, the virtual firm leverages its investment in a turnkey solution in many different, but specialized markets – hoping to become a platform that many systems providers will adopt (Werbach, 2000).

*Leveraging standard solutions.*   Once the virtual firm has created a platform package of standard systems, it can apply that package of systems (or relationships with substitute vendors offering comparable applications for its package) to similar types of products as well as to types of customers. That is essentially what Amazon.com has done – by applying their retailing platform to sell many similar kinds of products – books, CDs, toys, electronic items, drugstore items, hardware, flowers and so on. By outsourcing partner firms' turnkey software for applications that it did not create in-house – for transaction processing, inventorying, logistics, customer satisfaction, mail, reverse auction, or other applications – virtual firms like Amazon.com create bundled packages for specialized customers. The virtual firm manages customers' use of the package by serving as an application service provider (ASP) and updates the modules comprising its package, as better infrastructure platforms become available. By subcontracting its proprietary infrastructure for use by others that are developing total service offerings for other vertical markets, the virtual firm leverages itself into the constellations of firms in other value nets in reciprocal networks (Child and Faulkner, 1998). Proprietary solutions are valuable – even if the software has been outsourced to other application service providers – because they have become standards for solving a genre of problems and because of network externalities (Goldman Sachs, 1999). Value can be extracted through collection of royalties or by leveraging a success into inclusion in subsequent opportunities within the reciprocal networks where firms operate.

*Entrée into other constellations.*   While bundling these pieces in customized packaging for each respective vertical market it serves (and outsourcing its own ASP offerings to other value nets), the virtual company coordinates its own partner network while becoming a player in the outsourcing landscape of other companies' constellations of partners (Bear Stearns, 1999). Once the software is proven, virtual firms use the backbone of their systems to leverage that platform repeatedly to enter additional networks as the outsourcer of the proprietary function they built in-house. The more users that join the virtual firm's platform, the more valuable it becomes, due to network externalities (Jarillo, 1988). The larger the user base, the greater the usage tolls that are extracted as transactions rise.

  Inflexibility, in the form of switching cost barriers, occurs as more users adopt a virtual firm's platform. But lower entry barriers (hence smaller capital outlays to recover) and the relentless pursuit of newer technological solutions (even at the cost of self-cannibalization) ease the transition of platform users from one syndicated bundle of standard solutions to another, making it difficult to extract rents for a piece of the platform without its complements. Moreover, syndication practices reduce the power of recognizable brand equity among application providers (giving power to the system consolidator, e.g., a website built by Razorfish creates cachet, rather than to the subcontractors that Razorfish employs). Thus, the very expansion modes embraced to accelerate market entry and meet deadlines for customer deliverables reduce both corporate brand identity and strategic inflexibility. The virtual business model creates new types of inflexibility as it eliminates old forms of power.

### Informal partnering: a two-edged razor

In the perfect world of virtuality, everything should be fluid, thereby permitting concept firms to move easily from one alliance to another. Since the firm can link up with any partner, anywhere, in any position desired, there is no need to own what can be used without obligation. This is the business model of motion picture companies. Movie deals are sold with a great concept. Everything else in making the motion picture is a temporary arrangement of people coming together to work on the movie and then go on their separate ways. The fashion industry, also, juxtaposes contract labor, brand equity, and a concept; the product's success depends upon an alliance between the designer, brand name, and manufacturer.

The virtual business model also describes the internet consulting business whereby firms own nothing and employ few people, drawing instead on the talents of many affiliates. Like Razorfish (a consulting firm offering internet solutions), the project integrator uses a favorite dancing partner for doing graphics and another for building the technical backbone and yet another for providing the artwork. A fourth partner writes custom code. Identities of favored dancing partners may change as time goes by – particularly if the previous partners failed to satisfy the consulting firm adequately or if technology changes while the alliance partners lag behind. Since partnership is based on performance, it can be easily reconstituted in new economy settings.

*Disintermediation.*   At the intermediate level of an extended industry structure are many enterprises that once acted as middlemen to the vertically integrated firms. They have been pushed aside by the new virtual companies that have formed their own networks by re-intermediating with other companies that previously had no contractual linkages. The logic of the network is similar to the visible hand of management in vertically integrated enterprises – one company in the center of the virtual network controls all aspects of a system of transactions (Chandler, 1977); that firm aligns all functional contributions made by its army of outsourcers. What is different in this new structure is that the nodes of one firm's virtual network intersect with nodes in the networks of countless other firms, and the firm itself may play dual roles. As an application service provider to other firms chasing the same *e*-space, an internet firm will be both competing and cooperating in other firms' virtual networks.

*Use-based advantage.*   Within the network, an integrating concept serves as anchor; the virtual firm owns a brand name, a trademark, or other salient resource to leverage. Like a franchising arrangement, control issues must be balanced with entrepreneurial ones. The franchiser wishes to exploit a concept while still protecting that concept's integrity through standardization and controls over how the concept is used (Bradach, 1998). If the virtual firm can observe how its brand is used, measure user traffic, and have contractual safeguards that will be enforceable, the firm can develop systems for translating its concept to serve customers in many different arenas. Without such methods of verification, over-exposure of the firm's anchor assets could diminish the value of such resources.

In summary, strategies that work through the adoptions of network partners are a two-edged sword. Capital intensity (an important source of mobility barriers) is reduced through virtuality, but market power is based on persuading partners to use the firm's anchor assets in ways that reinforce their future value. Opportunistic partners rush to deplete an anchor asset's value quickly since such firms may not be included in subsequent rounds of partnerships. To protect their anchor assets, the integrating firm may voluntarily engage in greater formality within network relationships (e.g., jointly-owned companies) than is typically demanded.

## *Pressures to formalize linkages*

Network partners often have bilateral power (Gulati, 1995). Similar to partnership imbalances within strategic alliances, the nature of critical resources (that create temporary bargaining power) changes over time. Centrally located firms may have assembled the platform package, but the local partner (e.g., the franchisee) may provide the geographic access through its distribution systems and understand local market needs more precisely. Local partners may have provided valuable services that translate into loyalties based on relationships forged with customers. Because the partners controlling customer access inevitably renegotiate the value net's business model to improve their share from transactions, concept firms invest in activities to create countervailing power – such as advertising to create strong brand equity (Porter, 1976a). Since customers expect a seamless total service offering and will associate service quality with the brand's attributes, virtual firms are pressed towards exerting stronger controls over their network when distribution activities – such as order fulfillment, returns, repairs, and other service activities become critical to differentiation among competing value nets' offerings. That is why many franchisers prefer to acquire the outlets of successful franchisees once market acceptance of their concept has been established. Franchisers must persuade franchise owners to adopt innovations that the franchiser is championing (while company-owned outlets can be told to accept the new or modified products and policies by fiat).

*Pressures to formalize linkages.*   The freedom to end Net-centric alliances cuts both ways and competitive asymmetry may accelerate the switch to a different vertical posture (Singh and Mitchell, 1996). For example, Amazon.com – which began as a purely virtual company – spread its wholesaling purchases among three vendors and built its own warehouses when bn.com (Barnes & Noble's online-retailing venture) linked up with their former major wholesaler (Ingram Book Group). The alliance gave bn.com intelligence to build customer profiles and make inventorying adjustments (e.g., Merck and Medco). Suddenly Amazon.com's arrangement with its inventory-holding partner had lost its unique and advantageous aspect and Amazon.com accelerated its efforts to play a different game by becoming a retailing portal. When Barnes & Noble's dual distribution posture ("clicks and bricks") forced Amazon.com to invest in own warehousing operations, the formerly virtual firm learned that owning and operating order-picking warehouses was risky and dragged down earnings unless the investment was scaleable to an increasing base of activity. Amazon.com's warehouses changed the economics of its business model because diversification into many small items to be shipped in a similar order fulfillment system gives increasing bargaining power to order fulfillment firms (like Fingerhut). It also changed the timing and point where Amazon.com collected its rents from success.

*Increasing needs for control.* Where responsiveness becomes important to building relationships with customers, virtual firms that operate websites (but outsource all fulfillment tasks) have explored ways of allowing viewers to give them feedback to improve their website's competitiveness. In some cases, a virtual company offering a toll-free number – for capturing customer comments – has been perceived to be more service oriented towards customers. However, employing customer service representatives to collect customer suggestions means employing real people with real payroll expenses (and reduced flexibility). Having employees increases the virtual firm's riskiness, but contracting out to call centers is a less-controllable way of influencing loyalty relationships, and customer loyalty trumps most other new economy advantages in competition.

In summary, informal, virtual business models have limitations that are overcome by moving towards formal, vertical models involving greater control over (or ownership of) complementary assets. Each step towards realizing market (or network) power carries greater potential for raising firms' flexibility barriers by entrenching them in unique solutions that utilize their owned (or controlled) resources (thereby increasing asset specificity and decreasing flexibility).

## IMPLICATIONS FOR COMPETITIVE STRATEGY IN THE NEW ECONOMY

In old economy studies of exit barriers, increasing returns to scale increased strategic inflexibility, as did the attainment of significant product differentiation (through brand equity and other loyalty-enhancing forces). Involvement in long chains of vertically related activities increased exit-barrier heights, as did policies of high proportions of internal transfers between vertically related stages (Harrigan, 1985a). Synergies among business units that were realized by sharing flexible assets – such as scientific personnel, general-purpose laboratories, or inexpensive tools – did not raise exit barriers. Vertical integration achieved through shared ownership arrangements or strategic alliances created greater flexibility than policies of control through ownership. This section proposes implications for competitive strategies in settings of virtual ownership. Competitive evolution is expected to affect the use of vertical arrangements between network partners.

*Unconsolidated, embryonic industry structures.* In new economy settings, the rules regarding vertical relationships will be heavily influenced by the success requirements of the young industries where they are employed. In the past – when industries were so embryonic that expectations concerning customer (and organizational capabilities) had not yet been defined – product standards were unclear and competitors used unorthodox, expedient solutions to commercialize their products. When customer needs are fragmented and competition is chaotic, pressures for rapid exploitation of perishable advantages encourage the pursuit of multiple modes of distribution – under both branded and private labeling schemes – and the outsourcing of non-core parts of a product, including the provision of after-sale services. New economy firms are themselves so young that arrangements to realize synergies among sister business units scarcely have time to atrophy into core rigidities before hypercompetition nullifies the advantage of their Schumpeterian rents.

*Virtuality as core rigidity.* Early virtual firms within embryonic industries have invested heavily in the missionary work necessary to legitimize outsourcing. Virtuality has become a dogma to these early entrants because, in order for a virtual company to undertake what it has outsourced, the firm must create better information systems, better technology, and better organization designs than the specialists it has entrusted those tasks to must do. Virtual companies must move in ways that old economy companies cannot imagine – because the assets that old economy companies own limit their imaginations (hence, their strategic flexibility). Virtual firms have their own myopia concerning the timing of rent collection and risk insolvency when they postpone revenue gratification to build market share. Their business model is not enduring, and they are not receptive to managing under alternative organizational models.

## Pioneers' platforms and cannibalization

New economy industries face competition based on short cycle times, and competition on time is highly concerned with first-mover advantages. The first mover must create demand for a product's functionality while facing the risk that a nimble second mover can capture most of the pioneering benefits, while establishing its own brand's equity and own technology as the industry standard (D'Aveni, 1994). Advantage is won when an early design locks out acceptance of subsequent alternatives (thereby creating switching-cost barriers). Acceptance comes after (1) customers have gained comfort in using a particular arrangement, (2) complementary products have been configured to encompass the unique characteristics of the prototype's platform, and (3) the cumulative power of branding expenditures has elevated the equity of the first version to unassailable heights, among other conditions. The sunk costs implicit in switching-cost barriers, mobility barriers, and exit barriers explain an industry's sudden (albeit temporary) inflexibility in the face of innovation (Christensen, 1997); value-chain partners coalesce around platform standards that serve their respective economic interests. To reap such benefits, a firm must defend its product configuration standards against the inexorable onslaught of copycat competitors – even if such mercenary behavior violates the egalitarian norms of web culture.

What would be the implications of a fragmentation scenario where platform standards did not coalesce and industry structures evolved slowly? In old economy industries, slow change rates incubated fragmented industry structures for decades before consolidations occurred. In new economy industries – where financial pockets are deep enough and managers' wills are strong enough to assail extant barriers – hungry competitors will follow pioneering firms' successes in serving profitable customers. It should not be surprising, in that context, that underdog competitors will undermine the status quo bases for competition by adopting very different strategic postures, just as occurred in the old economy. Doing so is the only way that late entrants can drive a wedge of entry into evolving industry structures where standards are solidifying and constellations of supporting industries are energetically supporting the early entrant's platform. In most industry evolutions, détente among converging business models will be difficult to maintain when growth slows and economic pies become finite because all publicly traded firms seek to scale the heights of rising stock prices and many private firms willingly forego profits in their quest for market share advantages. While industry structures are still malleable and investors seek rapid gains, however, competing coalitions will each try to shape the industry's economics to favor their strategic postures by building bandwagons. Consolidations of built-to-flip firms will ensure that technological novelties outlive their inventors; the open wallets of venture capital firms will ensure that industry structures remain mutable for those willing to buy the market.

*Chaotic and embryonic industry structures.* Until an industry's structure coalesces around enduring standards and victorious coalitions, new resources can trump old entry barriers. The basis for competition can keep on changing until industry evolution finally occurs. While the industry structure is in chaos, early entrants' investments risk being disadvantaged (relative to late entrants) if first movers are unwilling to cannibalize their toehold investments repeatedly until conditions change (Schumpeter, 1934). Until providers of capital hold virtual firms to performance standards comparable to other high technology firms, industries facilitated by internet technologies (and venture capitalists) will not adopt irreversible standards (nor is technological progress well served by doing so).

*Resource endowments immaterial.* One implication of the internet industry's embryonic and stunted structure may be that the differing resource endowments of early entrants (versus later entrants) will not matter because each innovation will be a separate industry cycle that passes with alarming speed. If that were the case in figure 4.1, there would be no second-round iteration of adaptation and competition between incumbent and *de novo* firm. Independent firms – with different resource postures – would clash in each iteration of innovation and no carryover learning about competing against each other would occur (since no firms have previous experience in competition against each other). Alternatively, the internet industry's structure may not evolve from its embryonic state because no learning occurs where firms clash repeatedly – each time with different partners. Competitive learning may not occur where – in a manner similar to "born-again" firms coming out of bankruptcy protection – consolidation does not occur because losing coalitions continue to receive tranches of new venture capital funding from an overheated investor market.

*No synergies, no learning.* A second implication of the internet industry's embryonic and stunted structure may be that synergies become unleveragable in the new organizational forms that the virtual firm embraces. For example, the benefits of applying a vertical solution to horizontally related applications require making trade offs between the increasing returns of standardization versus local responsiveness. Operating synergies frequently require a centralization of activities that must be coordinated closely to realize scale, or scope, economies (Chandler, 1990). Facilities must be shared to realize vertical integration economies from technology transfers, cross-fertilization, and cross-organizational learning. Partnerships must be enduring to realize experience curve economies (Hamel, 1991).

Virtual firms thrive on the freedom of decentralization and operating autonomy. Potential synergies cannot be captured easily in regimes of duplicated facilities, overlapping turf, and incompatible products, processes, facilities, and so on. Arm's-length in-house technology transfers – for the sake of easier accountability and entrepreneurial spirit in buyer–vendor relationships – defeat the camaraderie needed for vertical synergies. Little organizational learning occurs when outsourcing is substituted for in-house capability development.

*Promiscuity penalties.*   A third implication of the internet industry's embryonic and stunted structure may be that virtual firms will face a backlash tantamount to inflexibility barriers. Virtual firms need partners that will support the technological platforms used to reduce customer uncertainty and accelerate the adoptions of new products. If an industry remains chaotic through wave after wave of new products, however, the identities of a firm's dancing partners will very likely change with each round of innovation.

The virtual firm approach is especially tempting in volatile, embryonic industries like *e*-commerce where strategic flexibility is desirable but demand- and technological-uncertainty is high. A network of alternatives is desirable in settings where several competing technological platforms exist and the winning technology cannot yet be predicted. The conceptual difference between the old approach to flexibility and the new approach may be seen in the exit barriers implicit in severing relationships. Old economy firms may pause before burning bridges when breaking with outsourcing or alliance partners that could be useful again in the future; new economy virtual firms terminate their affiliations abruptly and opportunistically.

## Synthesis: new to old

All vertical integration strategies assume control over assets – without necessarily owning them. Outright ownership of vertical partners is the most formal type of strategic posture. In the webs of strategic alliances underlying the virtual world, firms will have less and less control over deploying resources owned by outsourcing partners when rent extraction begins – especially if suppliers (or distributors) can find a better deal. Within effective strategic alliances, all partners must benefit if the partners wish to work together over time. Within virtual firms, the viability of a particular alliance has been of secondary concern to the opportunistic needs of the sponsoring company in its quest to build a market position. The concept firm has dominated outsourcing partners that have easily been replaced by a ready queue of willing suitors, and this regimen of musical chairs will persist until the industry structure consolidates, thereby forcing mutually beneficial partnerships to evolve to greater formality.

Alliances are just a temporary step enroute to a firm's ultimate evolution; they are not a long-lived organizational form because change forces make them too volatile to sustain – especially in hypercompetition (Harrigan, 1985d). The benefits of outsourced innovations obtained through alliances must be buttressed with knowledge-sharing mechanisms to ensure participation in improvements created by outsiders. To continue using alliances to improve its competitive position, the firm needs something valuable to trade; the virtual firm loses attractiveness as a partner if it does not keep inventing fresh approaches to serving customers in an industry with ample conduits for reaching customers. Because concept firms treat their partners opportunistically, virtual firms must keep the attraction of cooperation alive or risk becoming a one-time stepping stone – a complementary step in another firm's chain of partnerships and corpses.

## Flexibility and Evolutionary Advantage

An important difference between outsourcing in the capital-intensive, old economy context and the time-driven, new economy virtuality is how profitable the affiliation has been for outsourcing partners. When a technology was new and uncertain in the automobile industry, for example, assemblers like Ford or General Motors let supply contracts for new components to outside firms. After the component has been developed by suppliers and proves to be successful with car buyers, the automotive companies extracted the component's profits for themselves by creating their own component companies to compete in parallel with outsource partners (or withdrew intellectual property rights altogether). While it is needed by the automotive assembler, the in-house component company is awarded larger and larger proportions of the assembler's total requirements for the component until the outside vendors have been starved out of contention. When it is not as attractive to support vertical integration, suppliers like Delphi Automotive (or parts of DaimlerChrysler's in-house supplier family) are spun off opportunistically without any guarantees of future commerce.

In spite of repeated incidences of such opportunistic backward integration by their customers, supplier firms continue to develop prototype technologies for automotive assemblers because pricing during the early years as an outsource partner indemnifies them well for start up costs. Money still heals the wound for being shut out in later years of a technology's life cycle in the automotive industry.

Many companies that are now suppliers to the automotive industry were once members of vertically integrated companies, like DaimlerChrysler. Whenever automotive companies have adopted components offering valuable aftermarkets (or a bridge into important competencies), they have used outside companies to develop them. Assemblers have made components in-house when profitability was high and technological standards were established. Theirs is an opportunistic business model that can be pursued because of the power of automotive assemblers to reach ultimate customers. In order for such opportunism to work, all parties must be reconciled to the notion that, if necessary, outside suppliers are paid to be available at the last minute as a last resort. The risk of imbalance can be passed to outsiders.

## *The need for experiential evolution*

Virtuality works as long as there are outsourcing partners that are not vertically integrated to absorb imbalances in fluctuating demand (Harrigan, 1983). It is only possible where partners are capable of fulfilling their responsibilities competently. Outsourcing arrangements are always worthy of exploration – to create a competitive jolt when comparing cost structures as well as to increase strategic flexibility. Vertically-integrated firms should always evaluate whether formerly core activities should be spun out to partners. Rarely does outsourcing give firms people-embodied skills that can be built upon, however. If a firm constantly outsources, it does not learn what comprises suppliers' core competencies. If the firm never experiences the misery of giving birth, it misses the experiential learning needed for innovation. It is very difficult for firms to develop competencies if they constantly use outsourcing to leapfrog competitors' innovations. As their industry consolidates, firms will need to control their own knowledge development to develop that necessary *quid pro quo* bargaining chip.

In the new economy, companies have opportunities to exploit their knowledge faster by working with outside partners. If virtual companies focus on what they do better than others, they will know others in the same situation so they can bring together the complementary pieces needed to bring products to the market fast and uncouple easily when market demands change direction. While their industry structure is chaotic, virtual firms do not want to own pieces of the value chain that are not interesting to them or that they are not particularly good at – unless they must do so. As their industry's structure evolves, the trap will be that such firms may rationalize their ownership decisions retroactively and try to become good at activities where they are outclassed by competitors.

Virtual companies are players that can push the evolution of their industry's structure with great advantage. Their leaders visualize what could be possible if old economy traditions were trashed and new performance expectations were embraced. Ultimately, however, all virtual companies need a means of collecting their rents – by creating something valuable – or the new virtual players will look just like the old "hollow companies" that eviscerated the economy 15 years ago. The virtual company must build upon its own competencies, find its own version of knowledge workers, and experience the same apotheosis as any other learning organization.

## *Competency in virtuality*

The older virtual companies that are still thriving a decade later are the ones that used organizational flexibility to exploit the possibilities epitomized by the production of motion pictures or management of other temporary projects. They have learned how to come together as temporary organizations to make things happen and then part company after partners collect their respective rents. These survivors foster a faster feedback loop between identifying what customers want, getting a prototype to market, and developing ways to mass customize the prototype so that its appeal is never lost. They have internalized the challenge of shorter cycle times for competition.

If there are competencies in virtual companies that own few assets, the most critical knowledge a virtual company must master is the inter-organizational expertise of networking effectively. Because the virtual firm must change from one partner to the next as competition demands, it needs the flexibility to exit as easily and charmingly as it entered its alliances. It must master entrée into the vertical network of potential suppliers, distributors, and complementors – even if they are competitors or customers – as well as the traditional transaction partners.

The virtual company develops and packages concepts using other firms as its building blocks. Its turnkey systems legitimize technologies that the market is not ready to accept in an unbundled state. While its outsourcing partners are riding on the coat-tails of the virtual firm's concept, their ideas gain currency for the initial public offerings (IPOs) that repay their respective innovative efforts, as well as those of the virtual integrator. During this window of opportunity – while industry structure is embryonic and before customers are sophisticated enough to break the system into pieces and cherry pick each piece on its own merits – the *built-to-flip* mystique will dominate the older *built-to-last* phenomenon (Collins and Porras, 1994). Opportunism will be valued more highly than integrating virtual relationships.

## Limits to virtuality

The essential issues of vertical integration that old economy firms coped with will be the same problems that virtual companies must eventually face. Because they do not offer competencies deeper than their integrating concept, most virtual firms do not fare well in iterative revisions of vertical relationships. Because they have burned their bridges opportunistically instead of mending them, virtual firms do not negotiate effectively or coordinate well with partners that they burned in the past. Because they lack an effective way of integrating what they have learned, virtual firms will miss out on potential opportunities to realize vertical integration economies when their industry's structure ultimately evolves. Because they have been so preoccupied with extracting rents, many virtual integrators have no basis for survival when their industry consolidates and resources become scarce (instead of plentiful and fungible). The virtual firm's churning behaviors create negative synergies and many of the rigidities that have been associated with old economy dinosaurs will again become salient when switching-cost barriers rise among customers. Although virtual firms need the flexibility to use opportunistic coupling to implement their concepts in an embryonic industry, they also need long-term cooperation skills if they are to endure.

Until the structure of internet industries evolves, however, the trick will be in balancing the two approaches to vertical integration intelligently. Virtual firms must learn how to manage longer-lived relationships so they can adjust ownership to market vicissitudes. If the virtual firm truly deserves to sit at the hub of the network, it must assume statesmanlike responsibilities to ensure that there will be non-integrated players to take up slack. A good vertical integration strategy combines knowing when to buy and when to outsource, embracing the right partners while divorcing the losers gracefully and modifying its strategic posture frictionlessly.

Ultimately, the virtual firm will discover that their best dancing partner for a particular function dominates all others and they will long to create a more formal, quasi-integrated relationship to retain participation in relationships that they have built successfully. Without a means of harvesting their relationship investments, such as brand equity or other means of capturing customer loyalty, virtual firms will fail to exploit the full range of benefits available from their innovative approach to opportunities afforded by the technologies of the internet. As they add these means of collecting rents, they will also raise their mobility (and exit) barriers because they become wed to leveraging specific resources to reap the rewards of their successes.

## CONCLUSION

The suggestion that new economy industries will face challenges to their strategic flexibility where virtual firm arrangements are rampant is unexpected. By their virtual nature, requirements for asset specificity and commitment should be reduced. Ease of re-positioning should be high, and the impact of exit barriers should be minimal.

Strategic flexibility in the new economy will be more dependent on vertical relationships and permissions to leverage resources that other firms own or control than was the case in many old economy industries where the value of vertical integration has faded. Although implementation speeds can be greater when critical resources are licensed (rather than developed in-house), dependence on another firm's anchor assets can act much like old economy mobility barriers. The virtual relationships lauded for accelerating firms' entry into new market spaces will later impede their abilities to respond to change effectively.

Because they are tied to the success of the network's platform, strategic inflexibility is exacerbated if the network fails in competition – similar to the risks created by vertical integration strategies. Without their own valuable assets to leverage in virtual networks, firms will be perceived as complementors of an anchor firm's strategy. To evolve independently of the networks where firms leverage their assets, new economy firms must develop their own *quid pro quo* assets for use in reciprocal networks instead of becoming dependent on others' assets. If firms possess their own bargaining chips to leverage in competitions, they will face vertical integration risks that are very similar in nature to the traditional issues of strategic flexibility.

## NOTES

1 The exit barrier literature also posited that organizational inflexibility (e.g., resistance to change) could be an exit barrier (Porter, 1976b). Tests of the impact of organization change variables are beyond the scope of this paper.
2 A motion picture firm is elevated from its "service industry" status by its association with new economy technologies like the internet, which service firms often acquire in a vertical, quasi-integrated maneuver to improve their stock's perceived sizzle.
3 There are several partnering arrangements that involve degrees of shared decision-making (if not shared ownership). Cooperating with horizontally related competitors in post-industrial markets was a controversial idea in the 1980s.

## REFERENCES

Ahuja, M. K., and Carley, K. M. (1999). Network structure in virtual organizations. *Organization Science*, 10(6), 741–57.

Amit, R., and Zott, C. (2000). Value drivers of e-commerce business models. Unpublished manuscript, University of Pennsylvania, February 7.

Arthur, W. B. (1996). Increasing returns to scale. *Harvard Business Review*, July–August, 100–9.

Backaitis, N. T. (1992). Rethinking the relationship between customer and supplier: Some microorganizational considerations. Unpublished PhD dissertation. Columbia University.

Bain, J. S. (1956). *Barriers to New Competition*. Cambridge, MA: Harvard University Press.

Balakrishnan, S., and Koza, M. P. (1993). Information asymmetry, adverse selection and joint ventures: Theory and evidence. *Journal of Economic Behavior and Organization*, 20, 99–117.

Barney, J. B. (1991). Firm resources and sustained competitive advantage. *Journal of Management*, March, 99–120.

Bear Stearns Equity Research (1999). The internet business-to-business report. Analysts' report. September.

Blois, K. J. (1972). Vertical quasi-integration. *Journal of Industrial Economics*, 20, 253–72.

Bovet, D., and Martha, J. (2000). *Value Nets: Breaking the Supply Chain to Unlock Hidden Profits*. New York: John Wiley and Sons.

Bradach, J. L. (1998). *Franchise Organizations*. Boston: Harvard Business School Press.

Brandenburger, A., and Nalebuff, B. (1996). *Co-opetition*. New York: Currency Doubleday.

Caves, R. E., and Ghemawat, P. (1992). Identifying mobility barriers. *Strategic Management Journal*, 13, 1–12.

Caves, R. E., and Porter, M. E. (1977). From entry barriers to mobility barriers: Conjectural decisions and contrived deterrence to new competition. *Quarterly Journal of Economics*, November, 667–75.

Caves, R. E., and Porter, M. E. (1978). Barriers to exit. In R. T. Masson, and P. Qualls (eds.), *Essays on industrial organization in honor of Joe S. Bain*, Chapter 3. Cambridge, MA: Ballinger.

Champy, J. (1996). *Re-engineering management: A Mandate for New Leadership*. New York: Harper-Books.

Chandler, A. D. (1977). *The Visible Hand: The Managerial Revolution in American Business*. Cambridge, MA: Harvard University Press.

Chandler, A. D. (1990). *Scale and Scope: The Dynamics of Industrial Capitalism*. Cambridge, MA: Harvard University Press.

Child, J., and Faulkner, D. (1998). *Strategies of Cooperation: Managing Alliances, Networks, and Joint Ventures*. New York: Oxford University Press.

Christensen, C. R. (1997). *The Innovator's Dilemma*. Boston: Harvard Business School Press.

Coase, R. H. (1937). The nature of the firm. *Economica N.S.*, 4, 386–405.

Collins, J. (2000). Built to flip. *Fast Company*, March, 131–62.

Collins, J. and Porras, J. (1994). *Built to Last: Successful Habits of Visionary Companies*. HarperCollins.

Collis, D. J. (1986). The value added structure and competition within industries. Unpublished PhD dissertation. Harvard University.

Collis, D. J. (1994). How valuable are organizational capabilities? *Strategic Management Journal*, Winter, 143–52.

Collis, D. J., and Montgomery, C. A. (1995). Competing on resources: Strategy on the 1990s. *Harvard Business Review*, 73(4), 118–28.

Collis, D. J. and Montgomery, C. A. (1998). *Corporate Strategy: A Resource-based Approach*. New York: Irwin/McGraw-Hill.

Conner, K. R. (1991). A historical comparison of resource-based theory and five schools of thought within industrial organization economics: Do we have a new theory of the firm? *Journal of Management*, 1, 121–54.

D'Aveni, R. A. (1994). *Hypercompetition: Managing the Dynamics of Strategic Maneuvering*. New York: Free Press.

Ghemawat, P. (1991). *Commitment: The dynamic of strategy*. New York: Free Press.

Ghemawat, P., and del Sol, P. (1998). Commitment versus flexibility? *California Management Review*, Summer, 40, 26–42.

Ghemawat, P., and Pisano, G. P. (1999). Building and sustaining success. In P. Ghemawat (ed.), *Strategy and the Business Landscape: Text and Cases*, 111–34. Reading, MA: Addison-Wesley Longman.

Ghosh, S. (1998). Making business sense of the internet. *Harvard Business Review*, March–April, 126–35.

Goldman Sachs Investment Research. (1999). B2B: 2B or not 2B? Analysts' report, September 14.

Granovetter, M. (1985). Economic action and social structure: A theory of embeddedness. *American Journal of Sociology*, 91, 481–510.

Grant, R. M., and Baden-Fuller, C. (1995). A knowledge-based theory of interfirm collaboration. *Academy of Management Journal*, 38, 17–21.

Gulati, R. (1995). Social structure and alliance formation patterns: A longitudinal analysis. *Administrative Science Quarterly*, 40, 619–52.

Gulati, R. (1998). Alliances and networks. *Strategic Management Journal*, 19(4), 293–317.

Hagedoorn, J. (1993). Understanding the rationale of strategic technology partnering: Interorganizational modes of cooperation and sectoral differences. *Strategic Management Journal*, 14, 371–85.

Hagel, J., III, and Singer, M. (1999). Unbundling the corporation. *Harvard Business Review*, March–April, 133–41.

Hamel, G. (1991). Competition for competence and inter-partner learning within international strategic alliances. *Strategic Management Journal*, 12, 83–103.

Hammer, M., and Champy, J. (1994). *Re-engineering the Corporation: A Manifesto for Business*. New York: HarperBooks.

Harrigan, K. R. (1980). *Strategies for Declining Businesses*. Lexington, MA: Lexington Books.

Harrigan, K. R. (1981). Deterrents to divestiture. *Academy of Management Journal*, 24(2), 306–23.

Harrigan, K. R. (1982). Exit decisions in mature industries. *Academy of Management Journal*, 25(4), 707–32.

Harrigan, K. R. (1983). *Strategies for Vertical Integration*. Lexington, MA: Lexington Books.

Harrigan, K. R. (1984). Formulating vertical integration strategies. *Academy of Management Review*, 9(4), 638–52.

Harrigan, K. R. (1985a). Exit barriers and vertical integration. *Academy of Management Journal*, 28(3), 686–97.

Harrigan, K. R. (1985b). *Strategic Flexibility: A Management Guide for Changing Times*. Lexington, MA: Lexington Books.

Harrigan, K. R. (1985c). Strategies for intrafirm transfers and outside sourcing. *Academy of Management Journal*, 28(4), 914–25.

Harrigan, K. R. (1985d). *Strategies for Joint Ventures*. Lexington, MA: Lexington Books.

Harrigan, K. R. (1985e). Vertical integration and corporate strategy. *Academy of Management Journal*, 28(2), 397–425.

Harrigan, K. R. (1986). Matching vertical integration strategies to competitive conditions. *Strategic Management Journal*, 7, 535–55.

Harrigan, K. R. (1988). Joint ventures and competitive strategy. *Strategic Management Journal*, 9, 361–74.

Harrigan, K. R. (1994). Management concepts for turnarounds: Creating and nurturing competencies. *Technologie & Management*. Universitat Kaiserlauten, Kaiserlauten, Germany: Verband Deutscher

Wirtschaftsingenieure.

Harrigan, K. R., and Porter, M. E. (1983). Endgame strategies for declining industries. *Harvard Business Review*, 61(4), 111–20.

Hayes, R. H., and Abernathy, W. J. (1980). Managing our way to economic decline. *Harvard Business Review*, July–August, 67–77.

Heng, P. D. (2000). And now, econets. *Red Herring*, February, 75.

Jarillo, J. C. (1988). On strategic networks. *Strategic Management Journal*, 9, 31–41.

Kaplan, S., and Sawhney, M. (2000). E-hubs: The new B2B marketplaces. *Harvard Business Review*, May–June, 97–103.

Leonard-Barton, D. (1992). Core capabilities and core rigidities: A paradox in managing new product development. *Strategic Management Journal*, 13, 111–25.

Penrose, E. T. (1959). *The Theory of the Growth of the Firm*. Oxford: Basil Blackwell.

Peteraf, M. A. (1993). The cornerstones of competitive advantage: A resource-based view. *Strategic Management Journal*, 179–91.

Porter, M. E. (1976a). *Interbrand Choice, Strategy, and Bilateral Market Power*. Cambridge, MA: Harvard University Press.

Porter, M. E. (1976b). Please note location of nearest exit: Exit barriers and strategic and organizational planning. *California Management Review*, Winter, 21–33.

Porter, M. E. (1980). *Competitive Strategy: Techniques for Analyzing Industries and Competitors*. New York: Free Press.

Porter, M. E. (1996). What is strategy? *Harvard Business Review*, 74(6), 61–78.

Prahalad, C. K., and Hamel, G. (1990). The core competence of the corporation. *Harvard Business Review*, 68(3), 79–91.

Rayport, J. F., and Sviokla, J. J. (1995). Exploiting the virtual value chain. *Harvard Business Review*, November–December, 72, 141–150.

Reed, R., and DeFillippi, R. J. (1990). Causal ambiguity, barriers to imitation, and sustainable competitive advantage. *Academy of Management Review*, 15(1), 90–8.

Ring, P. S., and Van de Ven, A. (1992). Structuring cooperative relationships between organizations. *Strategic Management Journal*, 13(7), 483–97.

Sanchez, R. (1995). Strategic flexibility in product competition. *Strategic Management Journal*, 16, 135–59.

Schumpeter, J. A. (1934). *The Theory of Economic Development*. Cambridge, MA: Harvard University Press.

Singh, K., and Mitchell, W. (1996). Precarious collaboration: Business survival after partners shut down or form new partnerships. *Strategic Management Journal*, 17, 99–115.

Stalk, G. (1988). Time – The next source of competitive advantage. *Harvard Business Review*, July–August, 66(4).

Stalk, G., Evans, P., and Shulman, L. E. (1992). Competing on capabilities: The new rules of corporate strategy. *Harvard Business Review*, March–April, 70(2), 57–69.

Stalk, G., and Hout, T. M. (1990). *Competing against Time*. New York: Free Press.

Tichy, N., and Charan, R. (1989). Speed, simplicity, self-confidence. *Harvard Business Review*, September–October, 67(5), 112–20.

Werbach, K. (2000). Syndication: The emerging model for business in the internet era. *Harvard Business Review*, May–June, 85–93.

Wernerfelt, B. (1984). A resource-based view of the firm. *Strategic Management Journal*, 5, 171–80.

Williamson, O. E. (1971). The vertical integration of production: Market failure considerations. *American Economic Review*, 61, 112–23.

# 5

# The Resource-based View: Origins and Implications

## Jay B. Barney and Asli M. Arikan

The field of strategic management, like other social science disciplines, is organized around a central research question. That question is: "Why do some firms persistently outperform others?" This question does not presume that there will always be persistent performance differences between firms. Rather, it presumes only that it may be the case that, in some situations, persistent performance differences will exist between firms, and that those differences cannot be explained by traditional economic theories of firm performance. These traditional economic theories suggest, in general, that performance differences between firms should be unusual, will almost certainly not be persistent, and if they exist, are most likely a manifestation of anti-competitive collusive or monopolistic actions on the part of firms.[1]

The resource-based view (RBV) has emerged as one of several important explanations of persistent firm performance differences in the field of strategic management. After passing through an intense period of theoretical development and proliferation in the early 1990s, basic RBV logic was established and began to have an impact on empirical research in the field. At the same time, resource-based logic began to influence theoretical and empirical work in other non-strategic management disciplines including human resource management, marketing, management information systems, operations research, and so forth.

The purpose of this paper is to describe the theoretical history of the RBV, its major theoretical tenants and how they differ from other explanations of persistent firm performance differences, some of the empirical tests – both within the field of strategic management and in other disciplines – of the RBV, the managerial implications of the RBV, and finally, to discuss some unresolved issues about the RBV and its empirical and practical implications. We begin by discussing the theoretical history of the RBV.

## THE THEORETICAL HISTORY OF THE RBV

The resource-based view, like any theory, draws on prior theoretical work in developing its predictions and prescriptions. In the case of the RBV, important prior theoretical work comes from at least four sources: (1) the traditional study of distinctive competencies; (2) Ricardian economics; (3) Penrosian economics; and (4) the study of the anti-trust implications of economics. Each of these prior theories will be briefly discussed in turn.

## Traditional work on distinctive competencies

Since at least 1911, scholars have tried to answer the question, "Why do some firms persistently outperform others?" Before economic approaches to answering this question began to dominate this discussion (beginning with Porter, 1979 and continuing with Porter, 1980, 1981, 1985), this effort focused on what were known as a firm's distinctive competencies. Distinctive competencies are those attributes of a firm that enable it to pursue a strategy more efficiently and effectively than other firms (Hrebiniak and Snow, 1982; Hitt and Ireland, 1985, 1986; Learned et al., 1969).

Among the first distinctive competencies identified by those trying to understand persistent performance differences between firms was general management capability. General managers are managers in firms who have multiple functional managers reporting to them. Typically, general managers have full profit and loss responsibility in a firm, and when they do not have profit and loss responsibility, general managers are likely to lead cost centers. Whether profit center or cost center managers, general managers can have a significant impact on the strategies a firm decides to pursue and on the ability of a firm to implement the strategies it develops.

Given the impact that general managers can have on a firm's strategy, it naturally follows that firms that have "high quality" general managers will usually outperform firms that have "low quality" general managers. In this context, choosing high quality general managers is the most important strategic choice that can be made by a firm, and training high quality general managers is the most important mission of business schools (Pierson, 1959; Gordon and Howell, 1959).

The emphasis on general managers as distinctive competencies was important not only in the field of strategic management, but in closely related fields as well. For example, through the early 1950s, the study of business history was confined largely to the study of individual business people and firms. Traditionally, business historians were reluctant to generalize beyond individual biographies and firm histories to discuss broader trends in the economy that may have led to different forms of business organization, let alone the efficiency characteristics of these different organizational forms. For business history, like strategic management, explanations of the growth and success of firms was no more than the biographies of those who created and managed those firms (Chandler, 1984).

Indeed, there is little doubt that general managers can have a very significant impact on firm performance. There continues to be a tradition of leadership research that examines the skills and abilities of leaders and documents their impact on the performance of firms. Some of the best of this work focuses on general managers as change agents and emphasizes the impact that these "transformational leaders" can have on a firm's performance (Tichy and Devanna, 1986). Most observers can point to specific general managers that have been instrumental in improving the performance of the firms within which they work. These general managers include Lee Iaccoca at Chrysler, Jack Welch at General Electric, and Lou Gerstner at IBM (Labich and Ballen, 1988). The continuing popularity of books, articles, and seminars (e.g., Bennis, 1989; Covey, 1989) that describe the attributes of individuals that enable them to become leaders in their firms is a testament to the popularity of the belief that leaders, and in particular, general managers, are the most important determinant of a firm's performance.

Unfortunately, there are some very important limitations of this general management approach to explaining persistent performance differences among firms. First, even if one accepts the notion that general management decisions are the most important determinants of firm performance, the qualities and characteristics that make up a "high-quality" general manager are ambiguous and difficult to specify. In fact, the qualities of a "good" general manager are just as ambiguous as the qualities of "good" leaders (Yukl, 1989). In the case literature, general managers with widely different styles are shown to be quite effective. For example, John Connelly, former president of Crown Cork & Seal, was intensely involved in every aspect of his organization (Hamermesh and Rosenbloom, 1989). Other successful CEOs tend to delegate much of the day-to-day management of their firms (Stodgill, 1974). Yet both types of general managers can be very effective.

Second, general managers are an important possible distinctive competence for an organization, but they are not the only such competence. An exclusive emphasis on general managers as an explanation of superior performance ignores a wide variety of firm attributes that may be important for understanding firm performance. For example, it may be the case that a firm possesses very highly skilled general managers but lacks the other resources it needs to gain performance advantages. Or it may be the case that a firm has other resources that enable it to gain performance advantages, even though it does not have unusual managerial talent. In the end, general managers in organizations are probably similar to baseball managers: they receive too much credit when things go well and too much blame when things go poorly.

A sociologist named Phillip Selznick was among the first scholars to recognize that general management skill was only one of several distinctive competencies that a firm might control. In a series of articles and books, culminating in his book *Leadership in Administration* (Selznick, 1957), Selznick examined the relationship between what he called institutional leadership and distinctive competence.

According to Selznick, institutional leaders in organizations do more than carry out the classic general management functions of decision-making and administration. In addition, they create and define an organization's purpose or mission (Selznick, 1957). In more contemporary terms, institutional leaders help create a vision for an organization around which its members can rally (Collins and Porras, 1997; Finkelstein and Hambrick, 1996). Institutional leaders also organize and structure a firm so that it reflects this fundamental purpose and vision. With this organization in place, Selznick suggests, institutional leaders then focus their attention on safeguarding a firm's distinctive values and identity – the distinctive vision of a firm – from internal and external threats. This organizational vision, in combination with organizational structure, helps define a firm's distinctive competencies – those activities that a particular firm does better than any competing firms.

Selznick did not go on to analyze the competitive or performance implications of institutional leadership as a distinctive competence in any detail. However, it is not difficult to see that firms with distinctive competencies have strengths that may enable them to obtain superior performance, and that leaders as visionaries and institution builders, rather than just as decision makers and administrators, may be an important source of this performance advantage (Selznick, 1957).

Selznick's analysis of distinctive competence has much to recommend it, but it has limitations as well. Most important of these is that Selznick's analysis focuses only on senior managers (his institutional leaders) as the ultimate source of competitive advantage for a firm and on a single tool (the development of an organizational vision) that senior managers can use to create distinctive competencies. Although these are important possible explanations of performance differences across firms, they are not the only possible such explanations.

## Ricardian economics

Research on general managers and institutional leaders as possible explanations of differences in firm performance focuses exclusively on top managers, but the next major influence on the evolution of the RBV – Ricardian Economics – traditionally included little or no role for managers as possible sources of superior performance. Instead, David Ricardo was interested in the economic consequences of the "original, unaugmentable, and indestructible gifts of Nature" (Ricardo, 1817). Much of this early work focused on the economic consequences of owning land.

Unlike many factors of production, the total supply of land is relatively fixed and cannot be significantly increased in response to higher demand and prices. Such factors of production are perfectly inelastic, since their quantity of supply is fixed and does not respond to price changes. In these settings, it is possible for those that own higher-quality factors of production with inelastic supply to earn an economic rent. An economic rent is a payment to an owner of a factor of production in excess of the minimum required to induce that factor into employment (Hirshleifer, 1980).

Ricardo's argument concerning land as a factor of production is summarized in figure 5.1. Imagine that there are many parcels of land suitable for growing wheat. Also, suppose that the fertility of these different parcels of land varies from high fertility (low costs of production) to low fertility (high costs of production). The long-run supply curve for wheat in this market can be derived as follows: at low prices, only the most fertile land will be cultivated; as prices rise, production continues on the very fertile land and additional crops are planted on less fertile land; at still higher prices, even less fertile land will be cultivated. This analysis leads to the simple market supply curve presented in panel A of figure 5.1. Given market demand, $P^*$ is the market-determined price of wheat in this market.

Now consider the situation facing two different kinds of firms. Both of these firms follow traditional profit-maximizing logic by producing a quantity $(q)$ such that marginal cost equals marginal revenue. However, this profit- maximizing decision for the firm with less fertile land (in panel B of figure 5.1) generates zero economic profit. On the other hand, the firm with more fertile land (in panel C of figure 5.1) has average total costs less than the market-determined price and thus is able to earn an economic rent.

In traditional economic analysis, the economic rent earned by the firm with more fertile land should lead other firms to enter into this market, to obtain some land and begin production of wheat. However, all the land that can be used to produce wheat in a way that generates at least zero economic profits given the market price $P^*$ is already in production. In particular, there is no more very fertile land left, and fertile land (by assumption) cannot be created. This is what is meant by land being inelastic in supply.

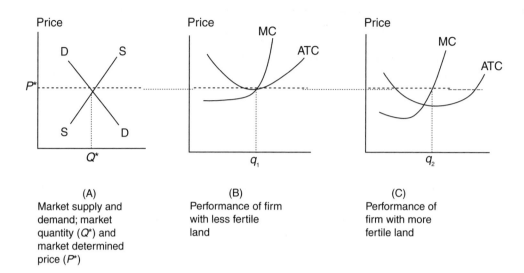

FIGURE 5.1 Ricardian rents and the economics of land with different levels of fertility

Thus the firm with more fertile land and lower production costs has a higher level of performance than farms with less fertile land, and this performance difference will persist, since fertile land is inelastic in supply.

Of course, at least two events can threaten this sustained performance advantage. First, market demand may shift down and to the left. This would force firms with less fertile land to cease production, and it would also reduce the economic rent of the firm with more fertile land. If demand shifted far enough, this economic rent may disappear altogether.

Second, firms with less fertile land may discover low-cost ways of increasing their land's fertility, thereby reducing the performance advantage of the firm with more fertile land. For example, firms with less fertile land may be able to use inexpensive fertilizers to increase their land's fertility, and they may be able to reduce their production costs to be closer to the costs of the firm that had the more fertile land initially. The existence of such low-cost fertilizers suggests that although *land* may be in fixed supply, *fertility* may not be. If enough firms can increase the fertility of their land, then the rent originally earned by the firm with the more fertile land will disappear, and firms competing in this market can expect to earn only zero economic rents.

Traditionally, most economists have implicitly assumed that relatively few factors of production have inelastic supply (Hirshleifer, 1980). Most economic models presume that if prices for a factor rise, more of that factor will be produced, increasing supply and ensuring that suppliers will earn only normal economic rents. However, the RBV suggests that numerous resources used by firms are inelastic in supply and are possible sources of economic rents. Thus although labor *per se* is probably not inelastic in supply, highly skilled and creative laborers may be. Although individual managers are probably not inelastic in supply, managers who can work effectively in teams may be. And although top managers may not be inelastic in supply, top managers who are also institutional leaders (as suggested by Selznick and others) may be. Firms that own (or control) these kinds of resources may be able to earn economic rents by exploiting them.

One issue that Ricardo did not examine, but which becomes very important in RBV logic is: "How did farms with more fertile land end up with that land?" Or, more precisely, "What price did farms with more fertile land pay for that land?" Resource-based logic suggests that if the price that farmers pay to gain access to more fertile land anticipates the economic rents that that land can create, then the value of those rents will be reflected in that price, and even though it may appear that farms with more fertile land are outperforming farms with less fertile land, this is not the case. This argument, originally developed in Barney (1986a) and extended by Dierickx and Cool (1989), is discussed in more detail below.

### Penrosian economics

In 1959 Edith Penrose published a book entitled *The Theory of the Growth of the Firm*. Penrose's objective was to understand the process through which firms grow and the limits of growth. Traditional economic models had analyzed firm growth using the assumptions and tools of neoclassical microeconomics (Penrose, 1959). Most important of these, for Penrose, was the assumption that firms could be appropriately modeled as if they were relatively simple production functions. In other words, traditional economic models assumed that firms simply observed supply and demand conditions in the market and translated these conditions into levels of production that maximized firm profits (Nelson and Winter, 1982).

This abstract notion of what a firm is, had and continues to have utility in some circumstances. However, in attempting to understand constraints on the growth of firms, Penrose (1959) concluded that this abstraction was not helpful. Instead, she argued that firms should be understood, first, as an administrative framework that links and coordi-nates activities of numerous individuals and groups, and second, as a bundle of produc-tive resources. The task facing managers was to exploit the bundle of productive resources controlled by a firm through the use of the administrative framework that had been created in a firm. According to Penrose, the growth of a firm is limited (1) by the productive opportunities that exist as a function of the bundle of productive resources controlled by a firm, and (2) the administrative framework used to coordinate the use of these resources.

Besides looking inside a firm to analyze the ability of firms to grow, Penrose made several other contributions to what became the RBV. First, she observed that the bundles of productive resources controlled by firms can vary significantly by firm – that firms, in this sense, are fundamentally heterogeneous even if they are in the same industry. Second, Penrose adopted a very broad definition of what might be considered a productive resource. Where traditional economists (including Ricardo) focused on just a few resources that might be inelastic in supply (such as land), Penrose began to study the competitive implications of such inelastic productive resources as managerial teams, top management groups, and entrepreneurial skills. Finally, Penrose recognized that, even within this extended typology of productive resources, there might still be additional sources of firm heterogeneity. Thus in her analysis of entrepreneurial skills as a possible productive resource, Penrose observed that some entrepreneurs are more versatile than others, that some are more ingenious in fund raising, that some are more ambitious, and that some exercise better judgment.

## The anti-trust implications of economics

As a field of study, economics has always been interested in the social policy implications of the theories it develops. One of the most important ways that economics has been used to guide social policy is in the area of anti-trust regulation. Based on the conclusion that social welfare is maximized when markets are perfectly competitive, economists have developed various techniques for describing when an industry is less than perfectly competitive, what the social welfare implications of this imperfect competition are, and what remedies, if any, are available to enhance competitiveness and restore social welfare (Scherer, 1980).

One of the most obvious ways that an industry may be less than perfectly competitive is if that industry is dominated by only a single firm (the condition of monopoly) or by a small number of cooperating firms (the condition of oligopoly). In both these settings, according to traditional economic analyses, prices will be higher than what would exist in a competitive market, and thus social welfare will be less than what would be the case in a more competitive market.

This approach to analyzing social welfare and anti-trust has developed into what is called the "structure-conduct-performance" (or SCP) paradigm (Bain, 1956). The SCP paradigm suggests that the structure of a firm's industry defines the range of activities that a firm can engage in – so-called "conduct" – and, in turn, the performance of firms in that industry. Firms that operate in industries with structures that are different than the perfectly competitive ideal in important ways may have conduct options that will enable them to obtain levels of performance that reduce social welfare in significant ways. In the extreme, this view of the determinants of firm performance suggests that any persistent superior performance enjoyed by a firm must, by definition, reflect non-competitive firm conduct that is antithetical to social welfare.

In developing his theory of why some firms persistently outperform other firms, Porter (1979, 1980) turned SCP theory "on its head" by suggesting that firms seeking persistent superior performance should choose to enter and operate only in industries that are imperfectly competitive. Thus, in Porter's theory of persistent superior firm performance, choosing the industries in which to operate is the most important strategic choice a firm can make.

Beginning in the early 1970s, a small group of anti-trust scholars began to question this SCP, and related, approaches to anti-trust regulation. Among the first of these was Harold Demsetz. In 1973, Demsetz published an article in the *Journal of Law and Economics* that argued that industry structure was not the only determinant of a firm's performance. Even more fundamentally, Demsetz (1973) argued that a firm earning persistent superior performance cannot be taken as *prima facie* evidence that that firm was engaging in anti-competitive activities. Indeed, anticipating the RBV, Demsetz argued that some firms may enjoy persistent performance advantages either because they are lucky, or because they are more competent in addressing customer needs than other firms. Demsetz (1973: 3) argues:

Superior performance can be attributed to the combination of great uncertainty plus luck or atypical insight by the management of a firm . . . Even though the profits that arise from a firm's activities may be eroded by competitive imitation, since information is costly to obtain and techniques are difficult to duplicate, the firm may enjoy growth and a superior rate of return for some time . . .

Superior ability also may be interpreted as a competitive basis for acquiring a measure of monopoly power. In a world in which information is costly and the future is uncertain, a firm that seizes an opportunity to better serve customers does so because it expects to enjoy some protection from its rivals because of their ignorance of this opportunity or because of their inability to imitate quickly.

While developed in the context of discussions of anti-trust regulation, Demsetz clearly anticipates some important tenets of resource-based logic. As interesting, Demsetz develops his arguments as an alternative to SCP-based theories of anti-trust. And since Porter (1979, 1980) traces the theoretical roots of his work back to the SCP paradigm, in an important sense, Demsetz also anticipates the theoretical debates that have emerged between the RBV and the Porter framework.

Thus we see that the RBV, far from emerging out of nowhere to become an important explanation of persistent superior firm performance in the field of strategic management, has deep theoretical roots in both economics and sociology. These theoretical streams have been united and modified to develop what has become the resource-based view.

## THE DEVELOPMENT OF RESOURCE-BASED THEORY

### Early resource-based contributions[2]

Perhaps the first resource-based publication in the field of strategic management identified as such was by Wernerfelt (1984). Ironically, Wernerfelt's resource-based arguments did not grow out of any of the four theoretical traditions identified above. Rather, Wernerfelt's argument is an example of dualistic reasoning common in economics. Such reasoning suggests that it is possible to restate a theory originally developed from one perspective with concepts and ideas developed in a complementary (or dual) perspective. For example, in microeconomics, it is possible to develop economic theories of decision making using either utility theory, revealed preference theory, or state preference theory; in finance, it is possible to estimate the value of an investment using the Capital Asset Pricing Model or Arbitrage Pricing Theory. Wernerfelt (1984) attempted to develop a theory of competitive advantage based on the resources a firm develops or acquires to implement product market strategy as a complement or dual of Porter's (1980) theory of competitive advantage based on a firm's product market position.

This approach to developing a theory of competitive advantage supposes that the portfolio of product market positions that a firm takes is reflected in the portfolio of resources it controls. Competition among product market positions held by firms can thus also be understood as competition among resource positions held by firms. In principle, for every concept that enables the analysis of the competitiveness of a firm's product market (e.g., barriers to entry), there should exist a complementary concept that enables the analysis of the level of competition among resources controlled by different firms (e.g., barriers to imitation).

One of Wernerfelt's (1984) primary contributions was recognizing that competition for resources and among firms based on their resource profiles can have important implications for the ability of firms to gain advantages in implementing product market strategies. In this way, Wernerfelt anticipated some of the critical elements of the RBV as it developed in the 1990s.

In the same year that Wernerfelt (1984) published his paper, Rumelt (1984) published a second resource-based paper in a book of readings coming out of a conference on strategic management. While these papers addressed similar kinds of issues, they did not refer to each other. Where Wernerfelt (1984) focused on establishing the possibility that a theory of firm performance differences could be developed in terms of the resources that a firm controls, Rumelt began describing a strategic theory of the firm, that is, a theory explaining why firms exist, that focused on the ability of firms to generate economic rents. At its most general level, such a theory would suggest the conditions under which firms, as an example of hierarchical governance (Williamson, 1975, 1985), would be a more efficient way to create and appropriate economic rents than other forms of governance, including markets. Rather than firms existing as efficient ways to minimize the threat of opportunism in transactions – as suggested by the transactions cost theorists (Williamson, 1975) – Rumelt (1984) was exploring the rent generating and appropriating characteristics of firms.

This theme of linking rent generation, transactions costs, and governance emerges much later, in the work of Conner and Prahalad (1996), Grant (1996), Liebeskind (1996), and Spender (1996), in efforts to develop a resource-based or knowledge-based theory of the firm. It also anticipates a very important issue that may ultimately serve as a theoretical link between resource-based theories of firm performance and transactions cost theories of governance. In particular, both theories point to the importance of transaction specific investments as independent variables that explain their different dependent variables. For resource-based theorists, transaction specific or firm specific investments can be thought of as resources that are most likely to have the ability to generate economic rents (see Barney, 2001: chapter 12). For transactions cost theorists, transactions-specific investments create problems of opportunism that must be resolved through governance choices. Teece (1980) brings these two ideas together explicitly by arguing that the kinds of relations among businesses that are most likely to be a source of economic profits for firms pursuing a corporate diversification strategy are also the kinds of relations that will be difficult to manage through non-hierarchical forms of governance. Thus, for Teece, resource-based theories and transactions cost theories, together, constitute a theory of corporate diversification.

The strategic theory of the firm that Rumelt (1984) develops has many of the attributes that will later be associated with the resource-based view. For example, Rumelt defines firms as a bundle of productive resources and he suggests that the economic value of these resources will vary, depending on the context within which they are applied. He also suggests that the imitability of these resources depends on the extent to which they are protected by an "isolating mechanism." He even develops a list of these isolating mechanisms and begins to discuss the attributes of resources that can enhance their inimitability.

The third resource-based article published in the field of strategic management is Barney (1986a). Similar to Wernerfelt (1984), Barney (1986a) suggests that it is possible to develop a theory of persistent superior firm performance based on the attributes of the resources a firm controls. However, Barney (1986a) moves beyond Wernerfelt (1984) by arguing that such a theory can have very different implications than theories of competitive advantage based on the product market positions of firms.

Barney (1986a) introduces the concept of strategic factor markets as the market where firms acquire or develop the resources they need to implement their product market strategies.[3] He shows that if strategic factor markets are perfectly competitive, the acquisition of resources in those markets will anticipate the performance those resources will create when used to implement product market strategies. This suggests that, if strategic factor markets are perfectly competitive, even if firms are successful in implementing strategies that create imperfectly competitive product markets, those strategies will not be a source of economic rents. Put differently, the fact that strategic factor markets can be perfectly competitive implies that theories of imperfect product market competition are not sufficient for the development of a theory of economic rents. This, of course, contradicts one of the central tenets of Porter's theory of industry attractiveness – that the ability of firms to enter and operate in attractive product markets is an explanation of persistent superior firm performance. In the extreme, Barney's argument suggests that if strategic factor markets are always perfectly competitive, that it is not possible for firms to earn economic rents.

Of course, strategic factor markets are not always perfectly competitive. Barney (1986a) suggests two ways that such markets can be imperfectly competitive and thus two ways that firms can acquire or develop the resources they need to implement product market strategies in ways that generate economic rents. First, following Demsetz (1973), in the face of uncertainty, firms can be lucky. That is, if all the firms competing in a particular strategic factor market expect that resources acquired there will generate $v$ levels of value in product markets, the price for those resources will quickly rise to $v$. However, if the actual value these resources can generate is $v + x$, where $x$ is some positive number, then firms that acquire this resource for $v$ will earn an economic rent.

Second, also following Demsetz (1973), it may be the case that a particular firm has unusual insights about the future value of the resources it is acquiring or developing in a strategic factor market. Firms with these special insights will generally not overpay for a resource (when the market determined price for that resource is greater than its actual value in implementing a product market strategy) and will generally be able to acquire or develop undervalued resources (when the market-determined price for that resource is less than its actual value in implementing a product market strategy). By avoiding errors and taking advantage of opportunities, firms with special insights can earn economic rents. Barney then shows that many other apparent competitive imperfections in strategic factor markets are actually special cases of these other two competitive imperfections.

Barney (1986a) concludes his paper by suggesting that the resources a firm already controls are more likely to be sources of economic rents for firms than resources that it acquires from external sources. This is because the resources a firm already controls were acquired or developed in a previous strategic factor market where their price was a function of the expected value of those resources in that market. However, if a firm can find new ways to use a resource to implement product market strategies, this new resource use would not have been anticipated in the original factor market and thus can be a source of economic rents.

Dierickx and Cool (1989) extended Barney's (1986a) argument by describing what it is about the resources a firm already controls that may make it possible for that resource to generate economic rents. Following Rumelt's (1984) discussion of isolating mechanisms, Dierickx and Cool (1989) suggest that resources that are subject to time compression diseconomies, that are causally ambiguous, that are characterized by interconnected asset stocks, or that are characterized by asset mass efficiencies are less likely to be subject to strategic factor market competition than other kinds of resources. Many of the attributes of a firm's resources that make them not subject to strategic factor market competition identified by Dierickx and Cool (1989) are later discussed and applied by Barney (1991a).

Together, these three papers – Wernerfelt (1984), Rumelt (1984), and Barney (1986a) as extended by Dierickx and Cool (1989) – outline some of the basic principles of resource-based logic. These papers suggest that it is possible to develop a theory of persistent superior firm performance using a firm's resources as a unit of analysis. Barney (1986a) goes furthest by suggesting that a theory of persistent superior firm performance must include some discussion of the conditions under which a firm's resources are acquired or developed and that a theory of product market competitive imperfections is insufficient to develop a theory of rents. These three papers suggest some of the attributes that resources must possess if they are to be a source of sustained superior firm performance – Rumelt's (1984) concepts of value and "isolating mechanisms" and Barney's (1986a) notion that resources already controlled by a firm are more likely to be a source of economic rents than other kinds of resources. They also suggest that it is the bundle of unique resources possessed by a firm that may enable a firm to gain and sustain superior performance.

That these papers have much in common does not suggest that they have no important differences. Indeed, one of the differences manifested in these papers has been a characteristic of virtually all succeeding resource-based work. Barney (1986a) focuses on the processes by which a firm's resources are developed or acquired and the implications of these processes for a firm's performance. Because this paper examines the conditions under which the use of resources to implement product market strategies can generate more value than generally anticipated when they are acquired or developed, Barney (1986a) can be thought of as a theory of economic rents. Wernerfelt (1984) and Rumelt (1984), on the other hand, do not examine the conditions under which a firm's resources are acquired or developed, but rather, following Ricardo (1817), take the heterogeneous distribution of resources across firms as given and then explore the competitive implications of this distribution. In this sense, these two articles can be thought of as theories of competitive advantage.[4]

Resource-based work subsequent to these first three papers tends to focus either on developing/testing a theory of economic rents, or developing/testing a theory of competitive advantage. Examples of papers that focus on economic rents include Conner (1991), Peteraf (1993), and Barney (1988). Examples of papers that focus on competitive advantage include Barney (1991a), Grant (1991), and Hendersen and Cockburn (1994). Clearly, both these types of work are important in developing a complete resource-based theory of persistent superior firm performance. However, there are differences between these traditions that are sometimes not fully appreciated.

For example, it can sometimes be the case that a firm can simultaneously enjoy a competitive advantage and earn an economic rent. Indeed, to the extent that a firm's ability to uniquely implement a value-creating strategy enables it to use resources in ways that were not anticipated in the strategic factor market where it was acquired or developed, a firm's competitive advantages can be a source of its economic rents.

On the other hand, it will not always be the case that a firm with a competitive advantage will also earn an economic rent. For example, if resources come in discrete bundles (e.g., as firms or as technologies) and if the number of these resources in a strategic factor market is limited, then only a small number of firms will be able to develop or acquire these resources, and product market strategies that firms pursue will likely be a source of competitive advantage. However, if those factor markets are perfectly competitive, then the price that a firm must pay to acquire or develop these resources will reflect their value in implementing a product market strategy. In this sense, a firm may enjoy a competitive advantage by being one of a small number of firms implementing a particular product market strategy, but not earn an economic rent, because the price paid to acquire or develop the resources needed to implement this strategy fully anticipates its value in the product market.

The conclusion that firms that enjoy a competitive advantage may not always earn economic rents is also consistent with the analysis of Ricardian rents presented in figure 5.1. Suppose that in this industry the market determined price ($P^*$) is below the average total costs (ATC) of the lowest cost firm in the industry. In this setting, this low cost firm has a competitive advantage – because it is uniquely implementing a valuable strategy in its market place. This strategy's value is reflected in the fact that this firm loses less money when it produces than its competitors. However, given the market determined price, this firm cannot earn an economic rent. Casual reading of the resource-based literature can lead to some confusion if the distinction between resource-based theories of economic rents and resource-based theories of competitive advantage is not appreciated.

## *Other early resource-based contributions*

The three papers cited above – Wernerfelt (1984), Rumelt (1984), and Barney (1986a) – set the stage for the development of what came to be known as resource-based theory. However, several other early contributions were important in the development of this set of ideas. For example, Barney (1986b) developed a resource-based explanation of why an organization's culture can be a source of sustained competitive advantage, and Barney (1988) applied the logic developed in Barney (1986a) to mergers and acquisitions to show that strategic relatedness, *per se*, was not sufficient for bidding firms to earn economic rents from acquiring target firms. Rather, strategic relatedness had to be either unique and private or unique and costly to imitate in order to generate such returns. Conner (1991) explored the relationship between the resource-based view and other traditions in microeconomics. Building on Rumelt (1984), she also began to explore some of the theory of the firm implications of resource-based logic. Castanias and Helfat (1991) showed how the creation and appropriation of economic rents aligned the interests of a firm's managers and equity holders and thus how resource-based logic helped to address in-centives problems identified in agency theory (see Alchian and Demsetz, 1972; Jensen and Meckling, 1976). Barney (1991a) published a paper that outlined the basic assumptions of resource-based logic and how those assumptions could be used to develop testable assertions about the relationship between a firm's resources and its competitive advantages.[5] Rumelt (1991) published an empirical paper that showed that firm level effects explained more variance in firm performance than either corporate or industry level effects, a result consistent with resource-based logic and a result that contradicted earlier published work that showed that industry effects were a more important determinant of firm performance than firm effects (Schmalensee, 1985; Wernerfelt and Montgomery, 1986). Hansen and Wernerfelt (1989) published a paper that demonstrated that the characteristics of a firm's organizational culture had a more significant impact on its performance than the attributes of the industry within which it operated – results that were also consistent with resource-based expectations. Peteraf (1993) published a paper that thoroughly grounded resource-based logic in microeconomics, and Mahoney (1993) published an article that compared and contrasted resource-based logic with other theories of competitive advantage. Grant (1996) published an article that, among other things, began to explore the managerial implications of resource-based logic.

Together, these and many other papers, created the foundation of what has become known as the resource-based view. The major assumptions, assertions, and predictions of this body of theory are examined in a subsequent section of this paper.

## Parallel streams of "resource-based" work

As this resource-based theory was developing, scholars in other research traditions were developing theories of competitive advantage that had numerous similarities to resource-based logic but were developed largely independent of the work cited earlier. Two of the most important of these parallel streams were the theory of invisible assets (Itami, 1987) and work on competence-based theories of corporate diversification (e.g., Prahalad and Bettis, 1986; Prahalad and Hamel, 1990).

*Accumulating and managing invisible assets.*   As described by Itami (1987: 12), invisible assets are information-based resources such as technology, customer trust, brand image, and control of distribution, corporate culture, and management skills. For Itami, physical (visible) assets must be present for business operations to take place but invisible assets are necessary for competitive success. Invisible assets are the real sources of competitive power and adaptability because they are hard and time-consuming to accumulate, can be used in multiple ways simultaneously, and are both inputs and outputs of business activity. People are both accumulators and producers of invisible assets.

Itami classifies information as being environmental, corporate, and internal. Environmental information flows from environment to the firm, creating invisible assets related to the environment, such as production skills and customer information. Corporate information, such as corporate reputation, brand image, corporate image, and marketing know-how, flows from the firm to its environment. Internal information, such as corporate culture, morale of workers, and management capability, originates and terminates within the firm. In each category, the amount of information gathered, its nature, as well as the channels through which it is gathered, are all invisible assets.

Invisible assets are accumulated either directly – where a firm takes explicit actions such as choosing a technology for research and development – or indirectly – where assets are accumulated as by-products of daily operations. According to Itami (1987), the accumulation and maintenance of invisible assets indirectly through operations can take more time than direct efforts, but the results of this process are more reliable. For example, word-of-mouth customer appreciation is much more effective than a television advertisement in convincing potential customers to buy a firm's products. However, this is not to suggest that the direct route has to be completely abandoned but rather that a balance between these two methods of invisible asset accumulation is necessary.

Given the role of both visible and invisible assets of the firm, firms should choose projects that are within the firm's area of expertise and appropriate to its skills (Itami, 1987: 159). However, firms intending to grow have to create deviations from this ideal fit to accumulate new invisible assets. Firms that choose to accumulate new invisible assets need to understand that they usually will not be able to compete in a new business as effectively as they have competed in their original market. However, this temporary loss of effectiveness may be necessary if a firm is to continually develop new invisible assets it can use to grow and prosper.

*Competence theories of corporate diversification.*   With respect to competence-based theories of corporate diversification, it has already been suggested that Teece (1980) was among the first scholars to begin to apply resource-based logic to the problem of corporate diversification. In an effort that paralleled Teece's work, Prahalad and his colleagues (Prahalad and Bettis, 1986; Prahalad and Hamel, 1990) also began developing an approach to understanding corporate diversification that, while never explicitly labeled as a "resource-based approach" had a great deal in common with resource-based logic as it was developing through the 1990s. Where most previous corporate strategy work had focused on the importance of shared tangible assets across the multiple businesses a diversified firm had begun operating in (see, for example, Rumelt, 1974; Montgomery, 1979), Prahalad began emphasizing the potential importance of sharing less tangible assets across businesses and the role that this sharing could play in creating value through diversification.

In Prahalad and Bettis (1986: 491), these shared intangible assets were called a firm's dominant logic. They define a firm's dominant logic as "a mind set or a world view or conceptualization of the business and the administrative tools to accomplish goals and make decisions in that business." Clearly, dominant logic, as an economic justification for corporate diversification, emphasizes intangible, even cognitive, bases for diversification. Certainly, one of the advantages of such bases of diversification, compared to more tangible bases is that competing corporations would have more difficulty imitating these intangible bases of diversification.

Prahalad and Hamel (1990) extended the concept of dominant logic in a very influential paper that defined the notion of a corporation's "core competence." Prahalad and Hamel (1990: 82) defined a corporation's core competence as "the collective learning in the organization, especially how to coordinate diverse production skills and integrate multiple streams of technologies." Here again, Prahalad and his co-authors focus on intangible rather than tangible assets as a basis for competitive advantage in choosing and implementing corporate strategy.

While developed independently of resource-based logic, this emphasis on the economic value of the intangible is common to both Prahalad's work and the resource-based view as it was developing in the 1990s. Indeed, since these early contributions by Prahalad, Bettis, and Hamel, most scholars that have either further developed the ideas of a firm's "dominant logic" (Grant, 1988) or "core competence" or tested the empirical implications of these ideas have approached this work in ways that are consistent with resource-based logic (e.g., Wernerfelt and Montgomery, 1988; Robins and Wiersema, 1995). Indeed, resource-based theories of corporate diversification, as will be shown below, have been one of the most popular ways to empirically test resource-based logic.[6]

## RESOURCE-BASED THEORY

Beginning in the 1980s, and continuing through the 1990s, resource-based theory has been developed through the publication of numerous papers in a wide variety of journals. Some of the key definitions, assumptions, assertions, and predictions of this body of literature are presented here.[7]

### Definitions

Because resource-based theory is a theory, it is important to begin by defining some of its critical terms. First among these is the term *resources*. While this term has been defined elsewhere (e.g., Wernerfelt, 1984; Rumelt, 1984; Barney, 1991b; 2001a) current use of the term suggests the following definition:

> *Resources* are the tangible and intangible assets firms use to conceive of and implement their strategies.

As was suggested earlier, firms develop or acquire resources in *strategic factor markets*. These markets may or may not be perfectly competitive.

As defined here, the concept of resources is closely related to the concept of routines first introduced in Nelson and Winter (1982). For Nelson and Winter (1982: 14), organizational routines are "all regular and predictable behavioral patterns of firms. They are a persistent feature of the organism and determine its possible behavior . . . they are heritable . . . and they are selectable . . ." Indeed, this common emphasis on intangible assets within the boundaries of a firm as a primary determinant of firm behavior/strategy has suggested to some authors an important link between resource-based theory and evolutionary theories of the firm (Barney, 2001b).

The economic and strategic value of these tangible and intangible resources also varies. In general, resources are valuable when they enable a firm to develop and implement strategies that have the effect of lowering a firm's net costs and/or increasing a firm's net revenues beyond what would have been the case if these resources had not been used to develop and implement these strategies. The value of resources can also be determined by their ability to enable firms to conceive of and implement strategies that are appropriate to the market within which a firm operates.

Notice that a firm that possesses valuable resources does not always gain superior performance, persistent or otherwise. For example, if competing firms in an industry possess the same resources and use them to conceive of and implement the same strategies, these resources will not be a source of superior performance, even if the costs of all these firms are lower and revenues higher than what would have been the case if these resources had not been used to conceive of and implement these strategies. In this sense, setting aside the role of luck, possessing valuable resources is a necessary, but not sufficient, condition for firms to obtain superior performance.

Of course, the tangibility of firm resources is a matter of degree. Resources that are typically more tangible include, but are not limited to, a firm's financial capital (e.g., equity capital, debt capital, retained earnings, leverage potential) and physical capital (e.g., the machines and buildings it owns). Resources that are typically less tangible include, but are not limited to, a firm's human capital (e.g., the training, experience, judgment, intelligence, relationships, and insights of individual managers and workers in a firm) and organizational capital (e.g., attributes of collections of individuals associated with a firm, including a firm's culture, its formal reporting structure, its reputation in the market place, and so forth).

Through the 1990s, various authors have tried to develop typologies of these tangible and intangible assets in an effort to suggest that different types of assets can have different competitive effects for firms. For example, Wernerfelt (1984) and Barney (1991a) simply called these assets "resources" and made no effort to divide them into any finer categories. Prahalad and Hamel (1990) developed the concept of "core competencies" and, building on Selznick (1957) and others, added the term "competence" to the resource-based lexicon. Stalk, Evans, and Shulman (1992) argued that there was a difference between competencies and capabilities, and thus this term (capabilities) was added to the terminological fray. Teece, Pisano, and Shuen (1997) emphasized the importance of the ability of firms to develop new capabilities, a perspective emphasized by their choice of the term "dynamic capabilities." Most recently, several authors have suggested that knowledge is the most important resource that can be controlled by a firm and have developed what they call a "knowledge based theory" of sustained superior firm performance (see, for example, Grant, 1996; Liebeskind, 1996; and Spender, 1996).

In principle, distinctions among terms like "resources," "competencies," "capabilities," "dynamic capabilities,"and "knowledge" can be drawn. For example, in their textbooks, Hill and Jones (1992) and Hitt, Ireland, and Hoskisson (1999), distinguish between resources and capabilities by suggesting that resources are a firm's "fundamental" financial, physical, individual, and organizational capital attributes, while capabilities are those attributes of a firm that enable it to exploit its resources in implementing strategies. Teece et al.'s (1997) concept of dynamic capabilities tends to focus on the ability of firms to learn and evolve (Lei, Hitt, and Bettis, 1996). General practice suggests that the concept of competencies is most often applied in the context of a firm's corporate diversification strategy. Knowledge is clearly a special case – albeit an important one – of some of these other terms.

However, while these distinctions among types of resources can be drawn and can be helpful in understanding the full range of resources a firm may possess, the effort to make these distinctions has had at least one unfortunate side effect: those who have developed new ways to describe a firm's resources have often labeled their work as a "new" theory of persistent superior performance. Thus, the strategic management literature currently has proponents of "resource based theories of superior performance," "capability theories of superior firm performance," "dynamic capability theories of superior performance," "competence theories of superior performance," and "knowledge-based theories of superior performance."

While each of these "theories" have slightly different ways of characterizing firm attributes, they share the same underlying theoretical structure. All focus on similar kinds of firm attributes as critical independent variables, specify about the same conditions under which these firm attributes will generate persistent superior performance, and lead to largely interchangeable empirically testable assertions. Battles over the label of this common theoretical framework are an extreme example of a classic academic "tempest in a tea pot" – "full of sound and fury but signifying nothing."[8]

What the label of this framework should be is actually not very important. In this paper, the first label, developed by Wernerfelt (1984), has been adopted. However, the content of this paper would not change at all if it had focused on "the capabilities view," the "dynamic capabilities view," the "competence view," or the "knowledge-based view." While work should continue expanding our understanding of the different kinds of firm attributes that can have an impact on firm performance, labeling each of these insights as a "new theory" of firm performance is very counterproductive.

There are terms in the definition of resources presented above that deserve further clarification. For example, the term strategy has been defined in numerous ways in the literature (see, Barney, 1986c). Following Drucker (1994), the definition of *strategy* adopted in this paper is

> *Strategy* is a firm's theory of how it can gain superior performance in the markets within which it operates.

This definition of strategy has several attractive properties (Barney, 2001a). For example, this definition includes both emergent and intended strategies (Mintzberg, 1990), it can be applied at both the business and corporate level, it introduces firm performance explicitly into the discussion, and it suggests that, before a strategy is actually implemented, it represents a "prediction" made by a firm about the economic processes that exist in a particular market or markets and how those processes can be used to gain superior performance. This definition can even be applied to firms that have no strategy – at least as defined in a traditional way. In this setting, a firm's theory of how to gain superior performance in the markets within which it operates is to not make explicit predictions about how that market operates.

In the definition of the term strategy, there are, once again, some additional terms that require definition. In particular, *superior performance* requires careful definition. It has already been suggested that resource-based logic can be used to understand the sources of a firm's economic rents and its competitive advantages. *Economic rents* exist when firms generate more value with the resources they have acquired or developed than was expected by the owners of those resources; *competitive advantages* exist when a firm is implementing value creating strategies not currently being implemented by competing firms.

These ways of characterizing a firm's performance can also be temporary or persistent. Economic rents are *temporary* when expectations of owners adjust to incorporate the higher than expected level of value created by a firm. Economic rents are *persistent* when a firm is able to consistently generate higher than expected value from the resources it controls. Competitive advantages are *temporary* when they are duplicated by competing firms. Competitive advantages are *persistent* when competing firms have ceased efforts to duplicate the advantages of a particular firm.

Taken together, these concepts – resources, strategic factor markets, strategy, superior performance, temporary and sustained economic rents, and – are fundamental in resource-based theory.

## Assumptions

Resource-based theory, like all theories, adopts several assumptions. Many of these assumptions are consistent with other theories of persistent superior firm performance, and thus will not receive particular attention here. For example, resource-based logic adopts the assumption that firms are profit-maximizing entities[9] and that managers in firms are boundedly rational. Over and above these basic assumptions, resource-based logic makes two additional assumptions that distinguish it from other strategic management theories: the assumption of *resource heterogeneity* and the assumption of *resource immobility* (Barney, 1991a). These assumptions are:

*Resource heterogeneity*: competing firms may possess different bundles of resources.

*Resource immobility*: these resource differences may persist.

Note that these two assumptions suggest that resource heterogeneity and immobility *may* exist. These assumptions do not suggest that all firms will always be unique in ways that are strategically relevant. Rather, these assumptions suggest that some firms, some of the time, may possess resources that enable them to more effectively develop and implement strategies than other firms, and that these resource differences can last.

The concept of heterogeneity incorporates two attributes of firm resources: scarcity and non-substitutability (Barney, 1991a). A firm's resource is *scarce* when the demand for that resource is greater than its supply. A resource is *non-substitutable* when no other resources can enable a firm to conceive of and implement the same strategies as efficiently or effectively as the original resource. The concept of immobility suggests that some resources, some of the time, may be *inelastic in supply*, that is, more of a particular resource is not forthcoming even though demand for that resource is greater than its supply. Firm resources may vary in the extent to which they are scarce, non-substitutable, and inelastic in supply.

## Propositions

Armed with these definitions and assumptions, resource-based theory develops a series of propositions. While numerous propositions have been developed, four are particularly important to resource-based logic (Peteraf, 1993). Each of these propositions is discussed below.

*Factor market competition and temporary rents.*   Proposition 1 focuses on the relationship of the competitiveness of the market within which a firm acquires or develops a resource and the ability of that resource to generate at least a temporary economic rent.

*Proposition 1*: Firms that acquire or develop valuable resources in imperfectly competitive strategic factor markets can gain at least temporary economic rents by using them to develop and implement strategies.

As suggested in Barney (1986a), when strategic factor markets are perfectly competitive, the cost of acquiring or developing a resource will equal the value of that resource in enabling a firm to conceive of and implement a strategy. Since the cost of acquiring or developing a resource equals its value in conceiving of or implementing a strategy, these resources will not be a source of economic rent. However, to the extent that these factor markets are imperfectly competitive, a rent can be generated by acquiring or developing a resource and implementing a strategy. This rent will only be temporary, since expectations about a firm's performance will adjust upward, and any unanticipated value creation will be anticipated whenever a firm acquires or develops additional resources to implement the same strategies in the future.

*Resource heterogeneity and temporary competitive advantages.*  Proposition 2 focuses on the relationship between heterogeneous firm resources and temporary competitive advantages:

> *Proposition 2*: Firms that control valuable, scarce and non-substitutable resources can gain at least temporary competitive advantages by using them to develop and implement strategies.

This proposition is a straightforward application of the Ricardian economic logic presented earlier.

*Resource heterogeneity and immobility and persistent competitive advantages.*  Proposition 3 is a temporal extension of Proposition 2:

> *Proposition 3*: Firms that control valuable, scarce, and non-substitutable resources that are inelastic in supply can gain persistent competitive advantages by using them to develop and implement strategies.

When resources that are a source of temporary competitive advantage (i.e., resources that are scarce and non-substitutable) are also inelastic in supply, the superior performance they generate does not lead to competitive duplication, since firms without the resources necessary to conceive of and implement a strategy efficiently and effectively will find it costly to acquire or develop them.

*Factor market competition and sustained economic rents.* In general, expectations about the value of a resource to enable a firm to develop and implement strategies will adjust to reflect previously unanticipated levels of value. However, to the extent that a firm can continue to find ways of generating value with the resources it controls that were not anticipated, based on previous levels of performance, a firm can continue to generate economic rents.

> *Proposition 4*: Firms that continue to use valuable resources to develop and implement strategies in ways others cannot anticipate can gain sustained economic rents.

## Parameterizing resource-based propositions

These four propositions are suggestive. However, empirical tests require that the concepts and relationships in them be parameterized. How each of these propositions has been parameterized in the literature is discussed below.

*Parameterizing the competitiveness of strategic factor markets.* Barney (1986a) suggests that strategic factor markets can be imperfectly competitive when (1) commonly held expectations about the future value of resources in enabling a firm to develop and implement a strategy underestimate the actual value of those resources in choosing and implementing product market strategies or (2) when some firms have more accurate expectations about the future value of those resources than other firms.

In order for the first form of imperfect competition to exist in a strategic factor market, there must be significant uncertainty about the actual future value of a resource. In this sense, the level of uncertainty that exists in a strategic factor market can be an indicator of the extent to which that market is imperfectly competitive.

In order for the second form of imperfect competition to exist in a strategic factor market, different firms must possess different expectations about the future value of a resource. Barney (1991a) and Dierickx and Cool (1989) suggest that different expectations about the future value of a resource reflect the other resources that a firm already controls. Thus, for example, the value of an acquisition, as a resource a firm needs to conceive of and implement a corporate diversification strategy, depends on the resources that a firm already possesses and the relationship between those resources and the firm it is going to acquire (Barney, 1988).

Because heterogeneous expectations in strategic factor markets are derived from prior heterogeneously distributed firm resources, the parameterization of this form of imperfect competition in a strategic factor market is actually a special case of parameterizing the concept of firm resource heterogeneity – through the parameterization of scarcity and non-substitutability – discussed later in this chapter.

*Parameterizing the value of firm attributes.* Not all the attributes of firms are strategically relevant. In fact, firm attributes, whether they are tangible or intangible, are only strategically relevant if they enable a firm to efficiently and effectively develop and implement a strategy that, in turn, generates superior performance. Firm attributes that do not enable such actions are not valuable resources. In this context, an important question becomes: when will a firm's attributes be valuable resources and when will those attributes not be valuable?

There are several different ways that the strategic value of a firm's attributes can be evaluated. For example, to the extent that a firm's attributes enable it to develop and implement strategies that have the effect of reducing a firm's net costs or increasing its net revenues compared to what would have been the case if those attributes had not been used to develop and implement those strategies, those attributes can be thought of as strategic resources. By examining the impact of using a firm's resources to conceive of and implement a strategy on a firm's net costs or net revenues, which attributes of a firm actually constitute strategically valuable resources can be determined.

Also, it is possible to describe the market structure within which a firm operates, the kinds of strategies that are likely to be sources of superior performance in that market, and the kinds of resources that enable firms to conceive of and implement these strategies. For example, in monopolistically competitive markets (Chamberlain, 1933), product differentiation can be a source of superior performance, and the creativity and innovativeness of a firm in developing new products can have an important impact on the ability of firms to conceive of and implement product differentiation strategies. To the extent that product differentiation is a source of superior performance in a monopolistically competitive market, and to the extent that creativity and innovativeness around new products enable a firm to conceive of and implement product differentiation strategies, then a firm's creativity and innovativeness can be understood as resources.

Notice that creativity and innovativeness focusing on the development of new products may not be equally valuable resources in all market settings. In markets with limited product differentiation opportunities, the ability to conceive of and implement strategies that reduce costs may be more appropriate. In this setting, relevant resources may include a firm's volume of production (to exploit economies of scope), its cumulative volume of production (to exploit learning curve economies), and so forth. In a very uncertain market setting, the ability of a firm to remain flexible and rapidly change strategies may be valuable firm attributes (Kogut, 1991; Trigeorgis, 1995, 1996).

In general, the extent to which a firm's attributes enable it to develop and implement strategies that lead to superior performance cannot be evaluated independently of the market context within which a firm is operating. Such firm attributes are intrinsically neither good nor bad, neither valuable nor non-valuable. Rather, their value depends entirely on their ability to enable firms to conceive of and implement strategies that generate superior performance. These observations suggest that resource-based explanations of superior performance cannot be developed independently of understanding the market and competitive context within which a firm operates. While some authors have suggested that models of opportunities and threats in a firm's competitive environment are theoretically very different than resource-based models of organizational strengths and weaknesses, it is nevertheless the case that resource-based logic requires some way of characterizing the market context with which resources are used to conceive of and implement strategies.

*Parameterizing scarcity.*    Resources are scarce to the extent that demand for them outstrips supply. One simple way of characterizing the scarcity of resources is simply to count them. When only one competing firm possesses a resource, that resource is scarce. More generally, as long as the number of firms that possess a resource is less than the number required to generate perfect competition around the strategies whose choice and implementation is facilitated by a resource, that resource is scarce.

*Parameterizing non-substitutability.*    Resources are non-substitutable to the extent that they can be uniquely used to help conceive of and implement a strategy. To the extent that such a one-to-one correspondence exists between a resource and a strategy, that strategy is non-substitutable.

The one-to-one correspondence approach to parameterizing non-substitutability can be complicated by two factors. First, it may not be single resources that enable a firm to develop and implement a strategy, but rather bundles of such resources. Isolating bundles of resources, and characterizing the extent to which they uniquely enable a firm to develop and implement a strategy can complicate this parameterization effort.

Second, it may be that different firms can use different resources to help develop and implement the same strategy. In this context, the task of parameterizing non-substitutability is to isolate all those resources that, separately or in combination, can enable a firm to develop and implement a strategy. These resources then constitute at least partial substitutes for each other. If the number of firms that possess these substitute resources is large, then the strategies that are associated with them are not rare, and thus not a source of superior performance. If the number of firms that possess these substitutes is small, they can still have competitive advantage implications.

*Parameterizing supply inelasticity.*    Several authors have parameterized the concept of supply inelasticity. For example, Dierickx and Cool (1989) suggest that resources are inelastic in supply when they are subject to time compression diseconomies, are causally ambiguous, are characterized by high interconnectedness among asset stocks, or subject to asset mass efficiencies or asset erosion. Barney (1991a) suggests that resources are inelastic in supply when they are path dependent, causally ambiguous, or socially complex. Itami (1987) suggests they are inelastic in supply when they are invisible.

   While these different ways of parameterizing the extent to which resources are inelastic in supply vary somewhat in detail, they also overlap. Clearly, resource-based logic suggests that resources that are developed or acquired over long periods of time, that link numerous individuals and technologies, and that are based on often taken-for-granted intangible relationships within a firm and between a firm and its stakeholders are more likely to be inelastic in supply than resources without these attributes. Barney (2001a) applies these concepts in evaluating when different sources of cost leadership, product differentiation, vertical integration, corporate diversification, and other strategies are more or less likely to be sources of persistent superior performance.

## *Deriving testable hypotheses*

Given the parameterization of the resource-based variables outlined here, it is possible to develop a series of testable hypotheses from resource-based logic. Examples of these hypotheses include[10]:

   *Hypothesis 1*: Firms that acquire or develop valuable resources under conditions of high uncertainty can gain temporary economic rents.

   *Hypothesis 2*: Firms that acquire or develop valuable resources in ways that exploit rare and non-substitutable resources they already control will gain temporary economic rents.

   *Hypothesis 3*: Firms that exploit valuable, rare, and non-substitutable resources in choosing and implementing strategies will gain temporary competitive advantages.

   *Hypothesis 4*: Firms that exploit valuable, rare, and non-substitutable resources in choosing and implementing strategies, where those resources are also path dependent, causally ambiguous, or socially complex will gain persistent competitive advantages.

   *Hypothesis 5*: Firms that continue to acquire or develop valuable resources in consistently uncertain settings can gain persistent economic rents.

   *Hypothesis 6*: Firms that continue to acquire or develop valuable resources in ways that exploit rare and non-substitutable resources they already control, where those resources are also path dependent, causally ambiguous, or socially complex will gain persistent economic rents.

## EMPIRICAL TESTS OF RESOURCE-BASED LOGIC

These, and other hypotheses, have been examined in the strategic management and other literatures. A partial list of this research, organized by discipline and major topic area, is presented in table 5.1. In the next several sections, the major trends and findings in each of these areas of work will be briefly described.

### Strategic management research

Not surprisingly, strategic management scholars have conducted the most empirical tests of resource-based logic. These tests examine several important assertions derived from the theory, including: (1) that firm effects should be more important than industry effects in determining firm performance; (2) that valuable, rare, and costly-to-imitate resources should have a more positive impact on firm performance than other kinds of resources; (3) that corporate strategies (including mergers, acquisitions, and diversification) that exploit valuable, rare, and costly-to-imitate resources should generate greater returns than corporate strategies that exploit other kinds of resources; (4) that international strategies that exploit valuable, rare, and costly-to-imitate resources will outperform international strategies that exploit other kinds of resources; (5) that strategic alliances that exploit valuable, rare, and costly-to-imitate resources will outperform other kinds of alliances; and (6) that there cannot be a "rule for riches" derived from strategic management theory.

*Industry versus firm effects on firm performance.*   Initial work done by Schmalansee (1985) and Wernerfelt and Montgomery (1988) on industry versus firm effects in explaining variance in firm performance was inconsistent with resource-based expectations. In particular, this work suggested that industry effects were more important than firm effects. However, in 1991, Rumelt published an article that contradicted these earlier findings. Rumelt (1991) argued that previous work had applied the wrong methods or had used inadequate data to evaluate the relative impact of industry and firm effects on firm performance. After solving these problems, Rumelt's results were consistent with resource-based expectations. Several authors have replicated Rumelt's results (e.g., Brush and Bromiley, 1997; McGahan and Porter, 1997; Mauri and Michaels, 1998). Some of these are critical of Rumelt's findings, but primarily in terms of the small corporate effect that Rumelt (1991) identified (Brush and Bromiley, 1997). However, all these replications continue to document that firm effects are a more important determinant of firm performance than industry effects, although the relative size of these effects can vary by industry.

*Resources and firm performance.*   The bulk of empirical resource-based work in the field of strategic management has focused on identifying resources that have the attributes that resource-based theory predicts will be important for firm performance and then examining whether or not the predicted performance effects exist. The performance effects of a wide variety of different types of firm resources have been examined, including a firm's

TABLE 5.1 Empirical tests of the RBV
Those articles marked with an asterisk generate results that are at least partially inconsistent with resource-based logic.

| Area of Research: Specific Topic: | **STRATEGIC MANAGEMENT**<br>**1. Firm vs. Industry Effects** – The RBV suggests that firm effects should have a larger impact on firm performance than industry effects. This research examines the relative impact of industry attributes and firm attributes on firm performance. |
| --- | --- |
| Schmalensee, 1985* | Industry-specific factors explain more variance in firm performance than firm specification. |
| Wernerfelt and Montgomery, 1988 | Industry attractiveness is not a universal dimension; instead what is attractive depends on a firm's relative advantage. |
| Hansen and Wernerfelt, 1989 | Inter-firm variance in profit rates is regressed against industry and firm variables. Both sets of factors are roughly independent and firm factors explain about twice as much variance in profit rates as economic factors. |
| Rumelt, 1991 | Business-specific factors explain more variance in firm performance than does industry membership, and industry membership explains more than corporate parentage. |
| Collis and Montgomery, 1995 | Where a company chooses to play will determine its profitability as much as its resources. |
| Swaminathan, 1996 | A study of US brewery and Argentine newspaper firms reveals that firms founded in adverse environments have higher mortality rates. However, among those that survive, beyond a certain age, firms founded in adverse environments have lower mortality rates than firms that are founded in less adverse environments. |
| Brush and Bromiley, 1997 | Business-specific factors explain more variance in firm performance than does industry membership, and industry membership explains more than corporate parentage. |
| Ingram and Baum, 1997 | A study of US hotel chains finds that (a) firms benefit from experiences initially but are harmed in the long run, (b) specialist firms are more strongly affected by their own experiences than generalist firms, (c) firms benefit from their operating experience in an industry, accumulated both before and after the firm's entry to the market, and (d) an industry's competitive experiences influence the firm only after its entry to the industry. |

| Area of Research: Specific Topic | **STRATEGIC MANAGEMENT**<br>**1. Firm vs. Industry Effects** – *continued* |
|---|---|
| McGahan and Porter, 1997 | An examination of the importance of year, industry, corporate-parent, and business-specific effects on the profitability of US public corporations within four-digit SIC categories show that industry, corporate-parent, and business-specific effects account for 19%, 4%, and 32%, respectively, of the aggregate variance in profitability. Industry effects account for a smaller portion of profit variance in manufacturing but a larger portion in lodging/entertainment, services, wholesale/retail trade, and transportation. |
| Mauri and Michaels, 1998 | A variance component analysis of 264 single-business companies from 69 industries suggest that firm effects are more important than industry effects on firm performance, but not on core strategies such as technology and marketing. |
| Marcus and Geffen, 1998 | Societal forces such as governments and markets influence a firm's capacity to search for talent, technology, and ideas, and to harmonize what it learns internally. These then contribute significantly to the acquisition and creation of new competencies. |
| Nickerson and Silverman, 1998 | High profitability buffers firms in the for-hire trucking industry from density-driven competitive pressures and this effect is moderated by the firm's strategic positioning choice. |
| Sharma and Vredenburg, 1998 | Strategies of proactive environmental responsiveness to deal with the uncertain environmental complications were associated with unique organizational capabilities that affect firm competitiveness. |
| Makadok, 1998 | First-movers and early-movers in money market mutual fund industry enjoy both highly sustainable pricing advantage and a moderately sustainable market share advantage although the industry can de described as having low barriers to entry/imitation. |
| Karagozoglu and Lindell, 1998 | Motives behind internationalization of small and medium-sized technology based firms can be explained more with firm-specific characteristics rather than uniform patterns. |
| Deephouse, 1999 | Firms should be as different as legitimately possible, and follow intermediate levels of strategic similarity that balance the pressure of competition and legitimation. |

| Area of Research:<br>Specific Topic: | **STRATEGIC MANAGEMENT**<br>**2. The Impact of Resources and Capabilities** – RBV suggests that valuable, rare, and costly-to-imitate resources can be sources of sustained competitive advantages. This research examines a variety of different resources that have these attributes to varying degrees, and examines their impact on performance. |
| --- | --- |
| Collis, 1991 | Firm specific administrative heritage, core competencies, and implementation capabilities determine product market position and global competition in bearing industry. |
| Hall, 1992 | Based on a survey in the UK, executives verified that intangible resources (i.e. patents, licenses, reputation, and employee know-how of operations) lead to a firm's sustainable competitive advantage and create capability differentials. |
| Hall, 1993 | The intangible resources most commonly identified as being a source of sustainable competitive advantage are: (1) company reputation, (2) product reputation, (3) employee know-how, (4) perception of quality standards, and (5) the ability to manage change. |
| Barnett, Greve, and Park, 1994 | Banks in Illinois that are single units and were able to survive difficult competitive conditions in their history, on average, are able to enjoy higher levels of performance in their current competitive situation. |
| Rao, 1994 | Firms' reputation is a socially constructed phenomenon that evolves over time. In the US auto industry, some firms were able to win "legitimacy contests" and were able to obtain a "head start" in building reputational advantage, which improved their chances of survival. |
| Henderson and Cockburn, 1994 | The research productivity in different pharmaceutical firms depends mostly on differences in research strategy, in firm and program-specific resources, and in organizational capability. Moreover, the "right" bundle allows firms to explore product development strategies that are not available to their competitors. |
| Pisano, 1994 | Among pharmaceutical companies involved in either chemical-based or biotechnology-based processes, there is no one best approach (learning-by-doing vs. learning-before-doing), but that it depends on the firm-specific knowledge environment. |

| Area of Research:<br>Specific Topic: | **STRATEGIC MANAGEMENT**<br>**2. The Impact of Resources and Capabilities** – *continued* |
| --- | --- |
| McGrath, MacMillan, and Venkataraman, 1995 | Empirical results from 160 new initiatives in 40 organizations from 16 countries suggest that there are two important antecedents of competence and competitive advantage: the comprehension of the management team working on developing a competence and the deftness of their task execution. Findings support the idea that firms deploy characteristic patterns of process (or routines) which over time, might lead to enduring heterogeneity. |
| Zander and Kogut, 1995 | The ease of codifying and communicating a manufacturing capability affect not only the time to its transfer, but also the time to imitation of the new product. The determinants of the time to imitation are found to be the extent to which knowledge of the manufacturing processes are common among competitors and the degree of continuous recombination of capabilities leading to improvements of the product or the manufacturing process. |
| Bates and Flynn, 1995 | Innovation capability rests on accumulated expertise and skills. Findings suggest that there is a strategy of building resources through manufacturing innovation over an extended period of time. |
| Poppo and Zenger, 1995* | No significant relationship between firm-specificity and the performance of internally governed activities is found. Also firms are more likely to outsource activities which require extensive skill sets. Moreover as skill sets become more extensive, firms benefit more from outsourcing rather than internally controlled activities. |
| Miller and Shamsie, 1996 | Among major US film studios, property-based resources (in the form of long-term exclusive contracts with stars and theaters) helped performance in stable environments during 1930–50. In contrast, knowledge-based resources (production and coordinative talent and budgets) improved performance after the 1950s. |
| Reed, Lemak, and Montgomery, 1996 | TQM programs that do not focus on the right firm-specific content issues but only emphasize a firm's environmental conditions will be unlikely to provide a positive return on investment and may in fact create losses. |
| Maijoor and Witteloostuijn, 1996 | In the Dutch audit industry, the largest firms and their partners appropriated rents from human capital. The sustainability of these rents requires both product and factor markets to be imperfect. |

|  |  |
|---|---|
| McGrath, Tsui, Venkataraman, and MacMillan, 1996 | The antecedents of achieving rent generating innovations are causal understanding, innovative proficiency, emergence and mobilization of new competencies, and creation of competitive advantage. |
| Dougherty and Hardy, 1996 | The inability to connect new products with firm resources, processes, and strategy impeded innovation in large and mature firms, mostly due to the innovators' lack of power. |
| Haunschild and Miner, 1997 | Distinct modes of selective interorganizational imitation are frequency, trait, and outcome. Results show that all three imitation modes occur independently in the context of an important decision: which investment banker to use as an adviser of an acquisition. However, only highly salient outcomes react to imitation. |
| Schoenecker and Cooper, 1998 | Technological and marketing resources are found to be associated with early entry. Also, early entry is predicted by organizational attributes such as commitment to a threatened market and firm size. |
| Glunk and Wilderom, 1998 | Top management capital (inspiration, competence, and communication) and organizational capital (external, professional, employee orientation and networking, financial management, market focus) are the major predictors of organizational performance. |
| Maskell, 1998 | In a low-tech furniture manufacturing industry in Denmark the firms are agglomerated to have access to intangible, localized, capabilities, which increases their survival probability and sustained competitiveness. |
| Ruiz-Navarro, 1998 | A case study of a shipyard illustrates the successful identification and acquisition of complementary capabilities for a firm that used to compete in the military and related mature industries. |
| Judge and Douglas, 1998 | The level of integration of environmental management concerns in the strategic planning process affects financial and environmental performance. Concern for environmental issues may yield positively competitive advantage in the marketplace. |
| Moingeon, Ramanantsoa, Metais, and Orton, 1998 | A case study of Salomon, sports company, reveals that the firm has unique project management techniques, tacit knowledge of outdoor sports, and a culture that supports manufacturing of sports equipment. |

| Area of Research:<br>Specific Topic: | **STRATEGIC MANAGEMENT**<br>**2. The Impact of Resources and Capabilities** – *continued* |
|---|---|
| Sherer, Rogovsky, and<br>Wright, 1998* | In a taxicab firm, hourly employment gave the organization the capability to provide a reliable service under environmental uncertainty. Older organizations used significantly more employees. Employees ensured quality. Owner-drivers cooperate with one another in response to external competition, but turn rivalrous once their organization captured the market. To ensure internal cooperation, such organizations require revenue as well as cost sharing. |
| Baum and Berta, 1999 | For interorganizational learning, firms target others that are high-status, socially proximate, and strategically similar, as well as those outside their local population but within their industry. |
| DeCarolis and Deeds,<br>1999 | Knowledge generation, accumulation, and application may be the source of superior performance. Location, products in the pipeline, and firm citations are significant predictors of firm performance in the biotechnology industry. |
| Greve, 1999 | Non-local learning in firms related by branch affiliations exists in the radio broadcasting industry and is harmful for the performance of such firms. |
| Hoopes and Postrel,<br>1999 | Gaps in shared knowledge due to lack of integration generate significant excess costs in product development efforts of a software company. |
| McEvily and Zaheer,<br>1999 | A firm's embeddedness in a network of ties is an important source of variation in the acquisition of competitive capabilities. |
| Stevens and Bagby,<br>1999 | Since economic and contractual imperatives of business may not conform to traditional research, instructional, and service roles of universities, there may be conflict in the transfer of intellectual property from universities to companies that seek to develop sustainable competitive advantage. |
| Lorenzoni and<br>Lipparini, 1999 | Relational capability (the ability to interact with other companies) accelerates a firm's knowledge access and transfer. This affects company growth and innovativeness in the packaging machine industry. Results show that managers can deliberately shape and design the interfirm network (supplier relationships) to develop the capability to integrate knowledge residing both internal and external to the firm's boundaries. |
| Maskell and Malmberg,<br>1999 | Proximity between firms plays an important role in the interactive learning processes. Knowledge creation is supported by the institutional embodiment of tacit knowledge. |

| | |
|---|---|
| Henderson, 1999 | Technology strategy has two important influences on the impacts of firm age: (a) standards-based strategies exhibited a liability of adolescence in their failure rates, while proprietary strategies exhibited a liability of obsolescence, (b) rates of sales growth increased with age for proprietary strategies, yet so did their risks of failure. Overall, multiple patterns of age dependence may simultaneously exist within a single population. |
| Brush and Artz, 1999 | Contingent combinations of firm-specific resources determine the performance of veterinary practices. |
| Gimeno, 1999 | Evidence from the airline industry suggests that airlines utilize their location in rivals' hub markets as a resource to reduce the competitive pressure from those rivals in their own hubs and thus to be able to sustain their dominant position in those markets. |
| Afuah, 2000 | Post-technological change performance decreases with the extent to which the technological change renders a competitor's capabilities (suppliers, customers, and complementers) obsolete. |
| McGuire, 2000 | Firms with higher growth potential make greater use of managerial equity ownership and long term incentives and have higher proportions of insiders on their boards of directors. |
| Oktemgil, Greenley, and Broderick, 2000 | Isolating mechanisms, which are idiosyncratic features of a firm's management that create barriers to competitive imitation, contribute to competitive advantage and company performance, and are intellectual constructs that explain competitive barriers at the individual firm level. |
| Area of Research: Specific Topic: | **STRATEGIC MANAGEMENT** <br> **3. Corporate Strategies** – This research examines resources and capabilities as a source of advantage in implementing corporate diversification strategies, including merger and acquisition strategies. Resource-based logic suggests that both tangible and intangible resources can be important in these strategies, but that only valuable, rare, costly-to-imitate, and non-substitutable resources can be a source of sustained competitive advantage for firms implementing merger, acquisition, and diversification corporate strategy. |
| Harrison, Hitt, Hoskisson, and Ireland, 1991 | Differences not similarities in resource allocations between targets and acquirers led to higher post-merger performance. |

| Area of Research:<br>Specific Topic: | **STRATEGIC MANAGEMENT**<br>**3. Corporate Strategies** – *continued* |
|---|---|
| Tallman, 1991 | Strategic grouping in the auto industry significantly explained the structural decisions of host country production subsidiaries. Firm-specific factors in a particular host environment were more powerful in explaining performance than the measures of worldwide, broad skills of the parent company. |
| Harrison, Hall, and Nargundkar, 1993 | Consistency (measured as similarities in financial resource allocation) across businesses in the emphasis given to R&D is positively related to the performance. But there was no support for capital intensity as a source of superior performance for diversified firms. |
| Ingham and Thompson, 1995 | Diversification in service industries is not an entirely random process (or a reflection of executive idiosyncracies) but follows a firm-specific and product-specific characteristics as well as firm size. |
| Robins and Wiersema, 1995 | Resource-based measure of "portfolio relatedness" in terms of shared strategic assets such as know-how or capabilities significantly accounts for the differences in performance of large diversified firms. |
| Markides and Williamson, 1996 | Related diversification enhances performance only when it allows a business to obtain preferential access to strategic assets that are rare, valuable, and highly inimitable. To sustain these supernormal profits, a firm has to build new strategic assets more quickly and efficiently than the competitors. But inter-unit transfer and sharing of these competencies are a necessary condition. |
| Anand and Singh, 1997 | Based on resource-based view, paper examines the performance differences between diversification-oriented and consolidation-oriented acquisitions in the defense sector – a sector that has experienced significant declines. Results show that consolidation-oriented acquisitions outperform diversification moves. There is also a positive relationship between Tobin's $q$ and corporate focus. Assets from declining industries are better redeployed through market mechanisms rather than within the firm. |
| Birkinshaw, Hood, and Jonsson, 1998 | A multinational subsidiary can help create firm-specific advantage through combining their resources with initiative and an entrepreneurial subsidiary culture. This process is enabled by subsidiary autonomy and a lower level of local competition. |
| Capron, Dussauge, and Mitchell, 1998 | The magnitude of redeployment of resources that are subject to market failure in horizontal acquisitions between the European and North American firms increases with the asymmetry of the merging companies' relative strength on the resource dimensions (R&D, manufacturing, marketing, managerial, and financial). |

| Farjoun, 1998 | A multidimensional definition based on skill and physical bases of relatedness improves the explanatory power of relatedness in diversified companies and their performance. Skill and physical bases, alone, had no significant effects on financial performance but the interaction of the two has a significant positive effect on most indicators of financial performance. |
| --- | --- |
| Capron, 1999 | The study examines the effects of post-acquisition divestiture and resource deployment on the long-term performance of horizontal acquisitions. Results show that both asset divestiture and redeployment can contribute to acquisition performance with, however, a significant risk of damaging acquisition performance when divested assets and redeployed resources are those of the target. |
| Chatterjee and Singh, 1999 | Firms on average emphasize the optimal way resources can be deployed in a market (type decision) and only secondarily decide on how to expand into such markets (mode decision). The trade-off between these two types of decisions, enabled by the availability of internal capital funds, occurs in the form of optimizing the type decision while subordinating the mode decision. However, the resources that are highly specific to the type or mode decision are not affected by this trade-off. |
| Coff, 1999 | Firms that seek acquisitions of targets in knowledge-intensive industries coped with the information dilemmas associated with knowledge-based assets by (a) offering lower bid premiums, (b) using contingent payment, (c) increasing information both through lengthy negotiations and by avoiding tender offers. |
| Silverman, 1999 | A firm's technological resource base (patent portfolio) significantly influences its diversification decision. Moreover firms prioritize their diversification options according to the *relative* applicability of their resources across these options. |
| Gupta and Govindarajan, 2000 | Study documents the positive effects of (i) the subsidiary's knowledge stock, its motivational disposition, and the richness of its transmission channels on the knowledge outflow from a subsidiary, and (ii) the richness of transmission channels, and the absorptive capacity of a division on the knowledge inflows to the subsidiary. |

| Area of Research: Specific Topic: | **STRATEGIC MANAGEMENT** **4. International Strategies** – This research examines the role of resources in an international context and is a theoretical extension of diversification research. This work also examines the impact of national differences on firm capabilities. |
|---|---|
| Kogut and Zander, 1993 | Firms specialize in the transfer of knowledge that is difficult to understand and codify. Results show that firms are able to transfer these technologies at a lower cost to wholly owned subsidiaries than to third parties. The advantage of a firm is its relative efficiency in transferring idiosyncratic technologies. |
| Karnoe, 1995 | The competence-building Danish firms and US firms in the wind energy industry are culturally shaped and embedded in a firm's routines and behavioral norms of engineers and workers. |
| Kotha and Nair, 1995* | Both firm strategies and the environment in the Japanese machine tool industry are significantly related to firm profitability, but only environmental variables are associated with firm growth. In contrast to results from US-based studies, capital expenditures and technological change are not negatively associated with firm profitability. Rather technological change is positively associated with firm growth. |
| Arora and Gambardella, 1997 | Theory of imperfect competition implies that market size has a more imprtant role when the performance is based on narrow, product-specific competencies, rather than generic competencies. The study tests this assertion by comparing the service industries that supplies engineering, and construction contracting to oil-refining and petrochemical plants in the US (larger market)  and Western Europe and Japan (smaller and fragmented markets). Results suggest that market size is important even if there are no economies of scale. If the firms have heterogeneous competencies that persist over time then the larger markets will have more efficient firms. This effect is more pronounced for firms with narrow, product-specific competencies. |
| Hitt, Hoskisson and Kim, 1997 | Early effects of international diversification on performance are found to be positive. However, increased international diversification at some point will become highly complex and hard to manage, which would hurt performance. Also product diversification moderates the curvilinear relationship between international diversification and performance. Single-business firms because they have not built the capability to manage multi-product firms are less likely to cope with the complexity of managing international diversification. |

| Mutinelli and Piscitello, 1998 | Study of Italian firms in 1986–93 reveals that joint venture is the best mode of entry of the MNEs seeking to enhance/utilize tacit skills and technological opportunities. The probability of establishing wholly-owned subsidiaries increases with the accumulated internationalization experience. |
| --- | --- |
| Appleyard, 1996 | Public sources of technical data play a larger role in knowledge diffusion in Japan than in the United States and in semiconductors relative to steel. |
| Athanassiou and Nigh, 1999 | A firm's extent of internationalization and linkages across its host countries are positively related to the top management team's IB advice network density. This density is measured as the team members demand for IB expertise and propensity to contribute to that expertise. There is idiosyncratic knowledge embedded in the TMT that is related to the internationalization process. |
| Delios and Beamish, 1999 | The geographic scope of Japanese firms was positively associated with firms' profitability, even when the competing effect of proprietary assets on firm performance was considered. Also, performance was not related to the extent of product diversification, although investment in rent-generating, proprietary assets was related to the extent of product diversification. |
| Jarvenpaa and Leidner, 1999 | A local Mexican company's dynamic capabilities of strategic foresight and flexibility as well as the core competency of trustworthiness are found to be critical in affecting internal and external change in the unstable environment of the local information industry. |
| Luo and Peng, 1999 | Intensity and diversity of host country experience is an important predictor of subunit performance in China. However the effect of intensity of host country experience diminishes over time, while diversity effect is constant. If the environment can be described as dynamic, complex, and hostile the positive effects of experience on performance increases. |
| Nachum and Rolle, 1999 | The findings from a sample of advertising agencies from the UK, France, and US suggest that above and beyond home country characteristics, firm-specific characteristics also play a role in determining a firm's competitive position in the international market. |
| Geringer, Tallman, and Olsen, 2000 | While diversification strategies of Japanese companies between 1977–93 vary between keiretsu and non-keiretsu firms, performance is not much different. International diversification has negative profitability and positive growth consequences in some periods. Product diversity has weak effects on firm performance only in one time period. |

| Area of Research: Specific Topic: | **STRATEGIC MANAGEMENT** **4. International Strategies** – *continued* |
|---|---|
| Zou and Ozsomer, 1999 | Coordination of R&D, which is influenced by global emphasis and human resource flexibility, is a key determinant of the firm's global strategic positioning. |
| Baldauf, Cravens, and Wagner, 2000 | Firm size, management's motives to internationalize, and the use of a differentiation strategy positively affect export performance of companies operating in small open economies, specifically in Austria. |
| Daily, Certo, and Dalton, 2000 | International experience of CEOs interacts with the degree of internationalization as well as the CEO succession, and significantly explains the corporate financial performance. |
| Area of Research: Specific Topic: | **STRATEGIC MANAGEMENT** **5. Strategic Alliance** – Role of resources in determining the performance of strategic alliances. Research on both domestic and international alliances are summarized here. |
| McGee, Dowling, and Megginson, 1995 | New high-tech ventures that have management teams with more functional expertise in the area that is most closely related to their choice of competitive strategy (e.g., marketing, R&D) were most successful in their cooperative agreements. |
| Sakakibara, 1997 | Skill-sharing R&D cooperation can be competition-enhancing, but cost-sharing R&D can be competition-suppressing. Also, the skill-sharing motive of partners increases R&D investment. |
| Mowery, Oxley, and Silverman, 1998 | An overlap of firm-specific technological capabilities predicts alliance formation. Once the alliance is formed, it affects the firms' technological portfolios. |
| Lane and Lubatkin, 1998 | The similarity of the partners' basic knowledge, lower management formalization, research centralization, compensation practices, and research communities were positively related to interorganizational learning. |
| Tyler and Steensma, 1998 | Top executives with a technical education, as well as executives from firms that emphasize technology and firms with successful past alliance experience, tend to focus more on the opportunities rather than the riskiness of the potential collaboration. |

| | |
|---|---|
| Combs and Ketchen, 1999 | Publicly-held restaurant chains emphasize resource-based concerns over considerations of cost-minimizing when deciding whether to engage in interfirm cooperation. However, some firms suffer loss of performance due to this emphasis. |
| Gulati, 1999 | Accumulated network resources arising from firm participation in the network of prior alliances (embeddedness) are influential in firms' decisions to enter into new alliances. |
| Luo, 1999 | After controlling for international strategic alliances' distinctive resources and discretionary managerial decision variables, industry structure is an important source of explaining the variations in International Strategic Alliance performance in the transitional economy of China. |
| Shenkar and Li, 1999 | Absorptive capacity is the principal mechanism governing the relationship between knowledge possession and knowledge search among prospective partners. The possession of complementary knowledge is a prerequisite for knowledge search. Furthermore, equity joint ventures are the vehicle of choice for firms seeking transfer of tacit, embedded knowledge. |
| Hitt, Dacin, Levitas, Arregle, and Borza, 2000 | This study looks at the international strategic alliance partner selection with a focus on the differences in partner selection criteria between emerging and developed market firms. The emergent market firms more strongly emphasized partners' financial assets, technical capabilities, intangible assets, and willingness to share expertise than did the developed market firms. On the other hand, developed market firms emphasized the partners' unique competencies and market knowledge and access than did the emergent market firms. |
| Dussauge, Garrette, and Mitchell, 2000 | Partners are more likely to reorganize or take over the link alliances (different capabilities); scale alliances (similar capabilities) are more likely to continue without material change. Link alliances lead to greater levels of learning than do scale alliances, but there is no difference in the length of duration between the two types. |
| McGaughey, Liesch, and Poulson, 2000 | Although a particular Australian manufacturing firm engaged in a joint venture with a firm in Hong Kong did not formally safeguard its intellectual property, it could still prevent the dissipation of intellectual property rights due to its novel bundles of firm-specific resources and capabilities. |

| Area of Research:<br>Specific Topic: | **STRATEGIC MANAGEMENT** |
|---|---|
| | **6. Rules for Riches** – RBV logic suggests that there can be no rule for generating persistent superior performance, that such performance depends instead on valuable, rare, and costly-to-imitate resources. |
| Mansfield, Schwartz, and Wagner, 1981 | Imitation costs are as high as the innovation costs when the innovator has a technological "know-how" edge over its rivals. Such technological "know-how" usually is not divulged in patents and is relatively inaccessible to potential imitators. |
| Lieberman, 1982, 1987 | Learning can be duplicated rapidly in most industries as firms increase their cumulative output and move down the learning curve. |
| Mansfield, 1985 | Decisions to introduce new products leak out within 12 to 18 months. The rivals know the detailed nature and operation of a new product/process within a year. Overall, differences in the rate of diffusion of technological information across industries do not have any explanatory power regarding the interindustry differences in the ease with which innovations can be imitated. |
| Tripsas, 1997 | The balance and interaction of three factors were shown to drive commercial performance of incumbents vs. new entrants in the typesetter industry in 1886–1990: investment, technical capabilities, and appropriability through specialized complementary assets. An analysis that examined investment or technical capabilities in isolation would have led to misleading results. |
| Schankerman, 1998 | Patent protection across different technology fields is a significant but not a major source of private returns to R&D. These characteristics vary across technology fields and nationalities (Japan, France, US, Germany, UK). |
| Miller and Toulouse, 1998 | Environmental uncertainty and environmental scanning are both negatively related to the simplicity of strategies (the focus on a few competencies). Paradoxically, scanning is likely to reduce simplicity if the environment is stable, and uncertainty is especially likely to reduce simplicity in the absence of scanning. Thus, it is not possible to deduce a fixed strategy based solely on environmental variables. |
| Segev, Raveh, and Farjoun, 1999 | Between the 25 leading business schools' MBA programs, the structure content (the particular mix of core and concentration areas) is, in itself, not a source of superior performance as measured in the 1994 rankings. |

| Makadok, 1999 | Money market mutual fund families with larger marginal returns to increasing their scale subsequently do gain market share at the expense of their competitors, but this effect diminishes over time, perhaps due to imitation. |
| Brews and Hunt, 1999 | Both formal planning and incrementalism form part of "good" strategic planning, especially in unstable environments where planning capabilities are far better developed. |
| Walston, Burns, and Kimberly, 2000 | Re-engineering alone was not found to improve a cost-competitive position; in fact, without integrative and coordinative efforts re-engineering may damage an organization's cost position. |

## HUMAN RESOURCES

| Area of Research: | |
|---|---|
| Gupta and Govindarajan, 1984 | There are no consistent managerial characteristics, such as tolerance for ambiguity and willingness to take risks, that would guarantee effective strategy implementation by SBUs. |
| Schuler and MacMillan, 1984 | Companies can create competitive advantage by aligning HRM practices to formulated strategy and helping their suppliers and distributors with their HRM practices. |
| Womack, Jones, and Roos, 1990 | An extensive study of over 70 plants in the global automotive industry revealed that only 6 of those plants had, simultaneously, cost leadership and very high quality. All of these 6 plants had the best manufacturing technology hardware available, in addition to policies and procedures that implemented a range of highly participative, group-oriented management techniques. |
| Huselid, 1995 | Investments in high performance work practices (HPWP) are associated with lower employee turnover and greater productivity and corporate financial performance. However, despite the strong theoretical expectation that better fit between HPWP with competitive strategy would be reflected in better financial performance, the results did not support the contention that fit has any incremental value over the main effects associated with the use of high performance work practices. |
| MacDuffie, 1995 | Innovative human resource practices (HR) affect performance not individually but as interrelated elements in an internally consistent HR "bundle" or system, and that these HR bundles contribute most to assembly plant productivity and quality when they are integrated with manufacturing policies under the "organizational logic" of a flexible production system. |

| Area of Research: | **HUMAN RESOURCES** *–continued* |
|---|---|
| Delery and Doty, 1996 | Findings suggest relatively strong support for a universalistic perspective (profit sharing, results-oriented appraisals, and employment security) and some support for both the contingency (participation, results-oriented appraisals, and internal career opportunities) and configurational perspectives (market-type employment). |
| Delaney and Huselid, 1996 | There is a positive relationship between HRM practices, e.g., training and staffing selectivity, and perceptual firm performance. |
| Koch and McGrath, 1996 | Positive and significant effects on labor productivity are found, especially in capital intensive firms that utilize more sophisticated human resource planning, recruitment, and selection strategies. |
| Youndt, Snell, Dean, and Lepak, 1996 | An HR system focused on human capital enhancement was directly related to multiple dimensions of operational performance (i.e., employee productivity, machine efficiency, and customer alignment). However this main effect was due to the linking of human-capital enhancing HR systems with a quality manufacturing strategy as well as other manufacturing strategies. |
| Welbourne and Andrews, 1996 | The results indicate that HR value and organization-based rewards predict initial investor reaction and long-term survival. The rewards variable negatively affects initial performance but positively affects survival. |
| Huselid, Jackson, and Schuler, 1997 | HR management effectiveness was associated with capabilities and attributes of the HR staff. Also, HR management's effectiveness had a positive effect on productivity, cash flow, and market value. |
| Truss, Gratton, Hope-Hailey, McGovern, and Stiles, 1997 | The two most widely adopted models of HRM are hard and soft versions reflecting opposing views of human nature and managerial control strategies based on theory X and theory Y respectively. In-depth case studies of 8 firms revealed that there was no pure example of either case. |
| Huselid and Becker, 1997 | The impact of the presence of high performance work systems (a skilled, motivated, and able workforce), and its effectiveness and fit with a firm's competitive strategy, has a positive effect on shareholder wealth. |
| Bennett, Ketchen, and Schultz, 1998 | The integration of the HR function with strategic decision making were found to be associated with strategic type and whether or not top management views employees as strategic resources, but labor market munificence and organizational growth were not. Paradoxically, integration is associated with a lower evaluation of the HRM function by top management. |

|  |  |
|---|---|
| Wright, MacMahan, McCormick, and Sherman, 1998 | Higher involvement of HR in firm strategy was strongly associated with the perception of HR effectiveness. This relationship was strongest when refineries pursued a product innovation strategy and viewed skilled employees as their core competence. HR involvement was unrelated to refinery performance, but it was negatively related when refineries emphasized efficient production as their core competence. |
| Pennings, Lee, and Witteloostuijn, 1998 | The effects of human capital (firm tenure, industry experience, and graduate education) and social capital (professionals' ties to potential clients) on dissolution reveal that the absolute value of firm-level human and social capital has a negative effect on survival of Dutch accounting firms in the period between 1880 and 1990. The relative value (determined by uniqueness and non-appropriability) of firm-level human and social capital has a positive effect on firm survival. |
| Boxall and Steeneveld, 1999 | Engineering consultancy firms in New Zealand adopted similar structural, competitive, operational, and HR responses associated with their evolving "industry recipe." The study could not establish an HR practice that would lead to superior performance but commented on the possibility of it. |
| Harel and Tzafrir, 1999 | The HRM practices of firms in Israel have a significant impact on both the perceived organizational performance (training has the most explanatory power) and market performance (training and employee selection practices had explanatory power). |
| Klaas, McClendon, and Gainey, 1999 | The relationship between the degree of outsourcing and perceived benefits generated is moderated by reliance on idiosyncratic HR practices, uncertainty, firm size, and cost pressures. |
| Lee and Miller, 1999 | Porter's strategies (1980) of cost leadership, marketing differentiation, and innovative differentiation are found to be executed more effectively where organizations exhibit a high level of commitment to their employees in Korea. Also in an organization where one of Porter's strategies is employed, strong employee commitment has a direct effect on ROA. |
| Fey, Bjorkman, and Pavlovskaya, 2000 | Based on 101 firms operating in Russia, the study tested the model of HR outcomes (motivation, retention, and development) as mediators between HR practices and firm performance. Non-technical training and high salaries will have a positive impact on managers, whereas job security is the most important predictor of HR outcomes for non-managerial employees. There is also a direct positive relationship between managerial promotions based on merit and firm performance for managers and job security and performance for non-managers. |

| Area of Research: | **HUMAN RESOURCES** *–continued* |
| --- | --- |
| Field, Chan, and Akhtar, 2000 | Greater reliance on internal development and promotion tends to increase uncertainty above having an adequate supply of managers, and greater competition tends to reduce training investments. Both of these findings might explain the high mobility of managers in the Hong Kong labor market. |
| Harmsen, Grunert, and Declerck, 2000 | R&D skills and market skills were not found to be the explanatory factors in the food processing industry with a low R&D expenditure; however, product development is important. |
| Khatri, 2000 | The findings of a study of 200 industrial firms in Singapore suggest that firm strategy affects HR practices, and the strategy-HR interaction accounts for more variation in firm performance than the main effect of HR. |
| Richard, 2000 | Racial diversity interacted with business strategy in determining firm performance measured in three different ways: productivity, return on equity, and market performance. The results demonstrate that cultural diversity does, in fact, add value and, within the proper context, contributes to firm competitive advantage. |

| Area of Research: | **MARKETING** |
| --- | --- |
| Hooley, Cox, Shipley, Fahy, Beracs, and Kolos, 1996 | This paper examines the impact of foreign direct investment of firms in Hungary. Hungarian firms seek marketing resources and capabilities from their investors that can then be deployed to create competitive advantage over rivals in the domestic market. |
| Ghingold and Johnson, 1997 | Higher levels of technical knowledge are linked to more desirable decision styles and decision outcomes, suggesting that managers' technical knowledge is an important asset for firms with manufacturing or process operations that allow those firms to offer "bundled" products to gain competitive advantage. |
| Gatignon, Robertson, and Fein, 1997 | This study finds that faster reactions to a new entrant have a positive impact on the perceived success of an incumbent's defense strategy. However, the greater the breadth of reaction (number of marketing mix instruments used), the less successful is the defense. The ability of an incumbent to maintain its market position is also significantly affected by industry characteristics and the degree of competitive threat posed by the new product entry. |

| | |
|---|---|
| Li and Calantone, 1998 | Market knowledge competence (processes that generate and integrate market knowledge) is positively related to product market performance. Also, the perceived importance of market knowledge by top management has the largest impact on the processes of market knowledge competence. |
| Johnson, 1999 | Dependence, flexibility, continuity expectations, and relationship age encouraged the industrial equipment distributors' strategic integration in industrial distribution channels, which enhanced distributor financial performance. Uncertainty did not play any role. |
| Menon, Bharadwaj, Adidam, and Edison, 1999 | Innovative culture is the fundamental antecedent to an effective marketing strategy-making process (components of which are situation analysis, comprehensiveness, emphasis on marketing assets and capabilities, cross-functional integration, communication quality, consensus, and resource commitment). Furthermore, individual components of a marketing strategy-making process may not be valuable by themselves but the combination of these elements contributes a firm-specific capability. |
| Maignan, Ferrell, and Hult, 1999 | Both market-oriented and humanistic cultures lead to proactive corporate citizenship, which in turn is associated with improved levels of employee commitment, business performance, and customer loyalty. Corporate citizenship can be a source of competitive advantage in internal and external marketing. |
| Capron and Hulland, 1999 | RBV is used to determine the extent to which three marketing resources (brands, sales force, and general marketing management) are redeployed after horizontal acquisitions. Highly immobile resources are more likely to be asymmetrically redeployed from the acquirer to the target rather than vice versa. The effects of redeployment on performance measures of product costs, product quality, product line breath, geographic coverage, market share, and profitability are tested. There is no evidence of cost-based synergies, but there is support for revenue-based synergies. |
| **Area of Research:** | **ENTREPRENEURSHIP** |
| Dean, Turner, and Bamford, 1997 | Availability of niches, high sunk costs, high levels of unionization, and high industry concentration appear to assist the post-entry new firm across multiple industries. |
| Michael and Robbins, 1998 | Retrenchment, as a common but not universal response to recession, can enhance the recovery of small-medium sized firms from declining performance if it focuses on factors that are easily tradable in the market (i.e., not firm-specific assets). |

| Area of Research: | **ENTREPRENEURSHIP** –continued |
|---|---|
| Brush and Chaganti, 1999 | In small service and retail businesses, resources, in particular human and organizational resources, may play a greater role in explaining performance than strategy. Also, the combination of these resources will vary across age and size. Although separately each resource (owner commitment, planning, systems, and staff skills) had positive effects on cash flow, when combined they had negative effects. |
| Rangone, 1999 | Three basic capabilities of small and entrepreneurial firms are innovativeness, production, and market management (marketing). |
| Borch, Huse, and Senneseth, 1999 | Firm-specific resources in small and entrepreneurial firms are human resources (experience, education), structure (governance structure), social resources (networks), and technology (proxy for non-imitable resources, operationalized as patents). Education and technology are positively related to employing product and growth strategies. Firms that have a formal structure and use social network pursue market and product strategies. |
| Chrisman, 1999 | Depending upon how start-up is defined significantly higher percentage of individuals who indicated entrepreneurial intent and received outside assistance started a business when compared to the individuals who indicated intent yet did not receive outsider assistance. Significant regional differences were observed in start-up propensities (measured as properties of boundary, resources, and exchange). |
| Deeds, DeCarolis, and Coombs, 2000 | Location is an important choice variable affecting the availability and quality of technical personnel. This study shows that non-saturated locations, such as San Diego, are preferable to Silicon Valley for biotech start-ups. The quality of scientific personnel, measured as past research citations, has a strong effect on a firm's productivity. Prior experience of a CEO in managing a commercial research facility enhances a firm's product development capability. However, having the scientific team as management detracts focus from product development. |

| Area of Research: | **MANAGEMENT INFORMATION SYSTEMS** |
|---|---|
| Dent-Micallef and Powell, 1998 | IT investment in and of itself has no effect on performance in the retail service industry. However, retail firms have gained a competitive advantage when combined with intangible, difficult-to-imitate complementary resources, such as a flexible culture, strategic planning, IT-integration, and supplier relationships. |

| | |
|---|---|
| Li and Ye, 1999 | IT investment appears to have a stronger positive effect on financial performance when there are greater environmental changes, more proactive company strategy, and stronger CEO/CIO ties. |
| Broadbent, Weill, and Neo, 1999 | More extensive IT infrastructure capability was found in firms where: (a) products changed quickly, (b) synergies across business units were aimed, (c) there was greater planned integration of information and IT needs, and (d) there was greater emphasis on tracking the implementation of long-term strategies. |
| Ray, 2000 | Service climate and managerial IT knowledge have a significant impact on customer service performance, after controlling for investments in IT and customer service, and firm size. Only firm specific managerial IT knowledge can be a source of sustainable competitive advantage. |
| **Area of Research:** | **OPERATIONS MANAGEMENT** |
| Powell, 1995 | Most TQM tools and techniques such as quality training, process improvement, and benchmarking do not generally produce competitive advantage, but certain tacit, behavioral, imperfectly-imitable features such as an open culture, employee empowerment, and executive commitment can be a source of competitive advantage. |
| Knights and McCabe, 1997 | A conformance-to-requirements approach towards TQM cannot fully address quality because (a) there can never be a precise conformance, and (b) it neglects customers and employees. |
| Morita and Flynn, 1997 | If manufacturing strategy is a source of competitive advantage, then the choices of manufacturing processes and other related characteristics are contingent on one another, and there is a positive relationship between "best practices" and performance. |
| Klassen and Whybark, 1999 | An environment technology portfolio – the pattern of investments in environmental technologies of a plant over time – is developed based on RBV and manufacturing strategy in the furniture industry. A significantly better manufacturing performance was observed in cases where management invested in the environmental technology portfolio and allocated resources toward pollution prevention technologies. Performance worsened as the proportion of pollution control technologies increased. |

| Area of Research: | **TECHNOLOGY AND INNOVATION MANAGEMENT** |
| --- | --- |
| Chang, 1995 | Optimal patent policy would extend broad protection to those inventions that have very little value (standing alone) relative to the improvements that others may subsequently invent. |
| Stuart and Podolny, 1996 | Evolution of firms' technological positions is derived from firm-specific ability to innovate in particular technological subfields that partly shapes their competitive success. The authors propose relational constructions of technological positions such that firms that have developed portfolios consisting of similar technologies are located near to one another. Firms' search behavior is locally bounded, and enables firms to be positioned and grouped according to the similarities in their innovative capabilities. |
| Helfat, 1997 | In response to rising oil prices, firms with larger amounts of complementary technological knowledge and physical assets also undertook larger amounts of R&D on coal conversion (a synthetic fuels process). Dynamic capabilities enable firms to stay competitive through changing market conditions. |
| Morris, 1997 | Pollution is negatively related to firm's cost advantage, suggesting that firms that pollute, on average, suffer from absence of modern manufacturing capabilities that would have reduced other manufacturing costs through enhanced productivity. |
| Irwin, Hoffman, and Lamont, 1998 | There is a positive and significant relationship between acquisition of medical technological innovation and hospital financial performance; the relationship is strongest when these technological innovations are simultaneously valuable, imperfectly imitable, and rare. |
| Del Canto and Gonzales, 1999 | Of the firm's resources and capabilities (financial, physical, and intangible), a study of 100 Spanish firms reveals that intangible factors are the main determinants of the probability of a firm carrying out internal R&D. |
| Albino, Garavelli, and Schiuma, 1999 | Knowledge transfer between customers and suppliers in industrial districts is a strategic issue for firms. This case study revealed that when the knowledge transfer has to be fast and reliable between customer and supplier, it has to be codified, but as the codification level increases, knowledge can be easily shared with other district suppliers. |

| Area of Research: | **OTHER DISCIPLINES** |
| --- | --- |
| Russo and Fouts, 1997 | Environmental performance and economic performance are positively related and this relationship is strengthened in high-growth industries. |
| Smart and Wolfe, 2000 | An exploratory study of Pennsylvania State University's football program led to the conclusion that the resources responsible for its sustained competitive advantage are the history, relationships, trust, and organizational culture that have developed within the coaching staff. |
| Bourke, 2000 | This case study involving medical education aims to determine the factors of the international service trade in higher education. Information about the foreign institution is the most influential variable in determining the student's choice of the foreign country and the school for higher education. |

history (e.g., Collis, 1991; Barnett, Greve, and Park, 1994; Rao, 1994), employee know-how (e.g., Hall, 1992, 1993; Glunk and Wilderom, 1998), its integrative capability (e.g., Henderson and Cockburn, 1994), its innovativeness (e.g., Bates and Flynn, 1995; McGrath et al., 1996), its culture (e.g., Moingeon et al., 1998), and its network position (e.g., McEvily and Zaheer, 1999; Baum and Berta, 1999), to name just a few. A wide variety of different methods have been used to examine the performance effects of firm resources including large sample surveys, small sample surveys, case studies, and simulations. Overall, results are consistent with resource-based expectations.

There are, however, a few studies that generate results that are inconsistent with resource-based expectations. For example, Poppo and Zenger's (1995) analysis of vertical integration is more consistent with transactions cost economics than resource-based theory. Also, Sherer, Rogovsky, and Wright (1998) do suggest that compensation policy can have an effect on cooperation among a firm's employees, but that environmental conditions are a more important determinant of this cooperation. These and similar results suggest that the conditions under which different resources are and are not valuable requires further development in resource-based theory (Priem and Butler, 2001).

*Resources and corporate strategy.* The impact of resources on corporate strategies has also been examined empirically. One of the most important findings in this area is that SIC-code based measures of strategic relatedness must be augmented by resource-based measures to capture the full performance effects of diversification strategies (e.g., Robins and Wiersema, 1995; Farjoun, 1998). Moreover, only when the basis of a diversification strategy is valuable, rare, and costly to imitate can firms expect such a strategy to generate superior firm performance (Markides and Williamson, 1996). Moreover, while finance scholars have identified an important discount in the value of firms when they begin to diversify (Lang and Stulz, 1994), resource-based theorists have shown that this discount either does not exist or is consistent with shareholder's interests when the characteristics of the resources on which a firm's diversification strategies are based are accounted for (Miller, 2000). Similar results have been found in studies on the return to mergers and acquisitions (e.g., Coff, 1999).

*International strategies.* Resource-based work on international strategies is a logical extension of the work on diversification strategies cited earlier. However, some attributes of resource-based arguments are highlighted in an international context. For example, this work shows that a firm's resources reflect its country of origin, and that these country differences are long lasting (e.g., Karnoe, 1995; Jarvenpaa and Leidner, 1999). This work also examines the role of different forms of governance in realizing cross-border economies of scope and suggests that the tacitness of the resources used to realize these economies is an important determinant of governance choices ( e.g., Zou and Ozsomer, 1999).

*Resources and strategic alliances.* Closely related to resource-based international research is work that focuses on the impact of resources of strategic alliances. In particular, this work focuses on how firms can use alliances to either exploit their pre-existing resources or to develop new resources. This latter work integrates insights from research on learning with resource-based logic (e.g., Shenkar and Li, 1999; Dussauge, Garrette, and Mitchell, 2000).

*Rules for riches.*    Finally, resource-based logic suggests that it is not possible to deduce "rules for riches" from strategic management theories. "Rules for riches" are rules that any firm can apply to gain sustained competitive advantages and economic rents. The implications of this assertion for managerial practice are discussed later in this paper. However, in the empirical work listed in table 5.1, the impossibility of deriving "rules from riches" from strategic management theory is examined in the context of the difficulty of sustaining competitive advantages through the application of well-known, widely understood, managerial practices. These include the use of re-engineering, learning curve logic, the structure of training programs, formal long range planning, and patenting procedures (Mansfield, 1985; Schankerman, 1998).

## Human resource management research

While the bulk of empirical research on the resource-based view of the firm focuses on strategic management implications of the theory, the theory has had implications in related fields as well. Among the most important of these is human resource management. Resource-based logic suggests that socially complex resources and capabilities should be among the most important sources of sustained competitive advantages for firms. Human resources are examples of socially complex resources and thus it is not surprising that human resource theorists have drawn heavily on resource-based logic to examine the impact of human resources and human resource policies on firm performance (Wright and McMahan, 1992; Wright, McMahan, and McWilliams, 1994; Barney and Wright, 1998).

Some of the earliest work in this area focused on the impact of human resources on cost and quality in manufacturing (Womack, Jones, and Roos, 1990; MacDuffie, 1995). More recently, this work has focused on various bundles of human resource practices that can have the effect of creating significant firm-specific human capital investments (e.g., Huselid and Becker, 1997; Harel and Tzafrir, 1999). While some of this work has been criticized (Becker and Gerhart, 1996), there is little doubt that resource-based logic has had an important impact on human resources research.

## Other disciplines

Several other disciplines have begun to explore the empirical implications of resource-based logic. These include marketing, entrepreneurship, management information systems, operations management, and technology and innovation management. While research approaches vary by discipline, in all these different settings, research examines how various kinds of functional resources affect firm performance in ways that are consistent with resource-based logic.

## Research exemplars

A few of the articles cited in table 5.1 can be seen as exemplars of how resource-based research can be done. Consider, for example, Henderson and Cockburn's (1994) examination of the impact of "component competence" and "architectural competence" on the research productivity of pharmaceutical firms. Henderson and Cockburn measure the value of these competencies by estimating their impact on the research productivity of pharmaceutical firms, under the assumption that pharmaceutical firms with more productive research efforts will outperform pharmaceutical firms with less productive research efforts. They measure the rarity of these competencies by showing that their level varies across competing pharmaceutical firms. And they measure the imitability of these competencies by showing that firm differences in the level of these competencies remain very stable over time. To the extent that high levels of research productivity are valuable in the pharmaceutical industry, Henderson and Cockburn's results are consistent with the RBV.

Makadok (1999) wrote another paper that rigorously tests the RBV. Makadok examines the impact of differential levels of economies of scale on the ability of money market mutual funds to increase their market share. Makadok measures the value of these economies of scale by first estimating the impact of the size of a family of funds on both its weighted-average risk-adjusted gross yield and its weighted-average expense ratio, and then shows that these yields and expenses affect the market share of a family of funds. He measures the rarity of economies of scale by showing that they vary across families of funds. And he examines the imitability of these scale differences by examining their impact on the market shares of families of funds over time. Consistent with the RBV, because economies of scale are not path dependent, causally ambiguous, or socially complex, Makadok does not expect these capability differences to be a source of sustained competitive advantage. And, in fact, the impact of scale differences on market share becomes smaller over time – results that are again consistent with the RBV.

## MANAGERIAL IMPLICATIONS OF THE RESOURCE-BASED VIEW

The resource-based view has generated empirically testable hypotheses. Many of these hypotheses have, in fact, been tested. However, consistent with the tradition of strategic management as a field, resource-based logic can also have important implications for management practice (Mosakowski, 1998).

For example, this logic can be used to help managers in firms that are experiencing strategic disadvantages to gain strategic parity by identifying those valuable and rare resources their firm currently does not possess and pointing out that the value of these resources can be duplicated either through imitation or substitution. In this sense, resource-based logic can be used to provide a theoretical underpinning to the process of benchmarking in which many firms engage (Fuld, 1995; Bisp, Sorenson, and Grunert, 1998).

Resource-based logic can also be used to help managers in firms that have the potential for gaining sustained competitive advantages, but where that potential is not being fully realized, to more fully realize this potential. This is done by helping managers more completely understand the kinds of resources that can generate sustained competitive advantages, using this understanding to evaluate the full range of resources a firm may possess, and then exploiting those resources a firm possesses that have the potential to generate sustained competitive advantage more completely. Resource-based logic can help identify what the most critical resources controlled by a firm are and thereby increase the likelihood that they will be used to gain sustained competitive advantages.

Resource-based logic can also be used by managers to ensure that they nurture and maintain those resources that are sources of a firm's current competitive advantages. Competitive advantages for firms are often based on bundles of related resources. Some of these resources are likely to be valuable, but either not rare, or not imperfectly imitable, or not non-substitutable. Others of these resources are likely to have these competitively important attributes. Nurturing and protecting this second class of resources is important if a firm is to maintain its sustained competitive advantage.

For example, suppose a firm possesses a nurturing organizational culture. In some settings, such a culture may be valuable (Barney, 1986b). If only one competing firm possesses this culture, it is rare, and thus perfect competition dynamics around this culture are not likely to develop. Moreover, because an organizational culture develops over long periods of time (the role of history) and is socially complex, it is likely to be inelastic in supply. Finally, there are few obvious close strategic substitutes for an organizational culture. In this situation, it is likely that a firm's culture will be a source of sustained competitive advantage. However, even if it takes many decades for an organizational culture with these specific attributes to develop, that culture can be destroyed very quickly by senior managers in a firm making decisions that are inconsistent with that culture. Resource-based logic identifies this kind of culture as a potentially important source of sustained competitive advantage. Armed with this understanding, managers in an organization may be less inclined to make decisions that have the effect of destroying the very resource that is generating a sustained competitive advantage for their firm.

However, while it is clear that resource-based logic can have very important managerial implications, this logic also suggests that there are important prescriptive limits associated with resource-based theories of competitive advantage. First, to the extent that a firm's competitive advantage is based on causally ambiguous resources, managers in that firm cannot know, with certainty, which of their resources actually generates that competitive advantage. This can significantly limit prescriptions derived from the theory.

Second, no theories of sustained competitive advantage can be used by managers in firms without the potential for generating sustained competitive advantages to create sustained competitive advantages. That is, resource-based logic cannot be used to create sustained competitive advantages when the potential for these advantages does not already exist. Any theory that purports to be able to accomplish this is proposing a "rule for riches."

As is well known, there cannot be a "rule for riches." If the application of a theory to a firm without any special resources can be used to create competitive advantages for that firm, then it could be used to create competitive advantages for any firm, and the actions undertaken by any one of these firms would not be a source of sustained competitive advantage. Even if a "rule for riches" created economic value, that value would be fully appropriated by those that invented and marketed this rule.

Thus, while the resources identified by resource-based logic as being most likely to generate sustained competitive advantages are frequently not amenable to managerial manipulation, it certainly does not follow that there are no prescriptive implications of that resource-based logic. Indeed, that resource-based logic is consistent with causal ambiguity and "rules for riches" constraints on theory-derived prescription provides an important external validity check on this logic.

## REMAINING ISSUES IN THE DEVELOPMENT AND TESTING OF THE RBV

While the RBV has emerged as an important and influential theory of persistent superior performance in the strategic management literature, there remain issues at the heart of this theory that have not yet been fully resolved. Three of the most important of these areas discussed here.

### *Generating strategic alternatives*

Resource-based theory has a very simple view about how resources are connected to the strategies that a firm pursues. It is almost as if once a firm becomes aware of the valuable, rare, costly to imitate, and non-substitutable resources it controls, that the actions it should take to exploit these resources will be self-evident. That certainly may be true some of the time. For example, if a firm possesses valuable, rare, costly-to-imitate, and non-substitutable economies of scale, learning curve economies, access to low-cost factors of production, and technological resources, it seems clear that it should pursue a cost leadership strategy (Barney, 2001a: Chapter 7). However, it may often be the case that the link between resources and the strategies a firm should pursue will not be so obvious.

For example, sometimes it might be the case that a firm's resources will be consistent with several different strategies, all with the ability to create the same level of competitive advantage. In this situation, how should a firm decide which of these several different strategies it should pursue?

Even more importantly, there may be times when choosing a strategy consistent with the resources a firm controls is a creative and even entrepreneurial act. This could occur, for example, when a firm possesses valuable, rare, costly-to-imitate, and non-substitutable resources which most agree are consistent with one strategy, and the firm is able to conceive of and implement a very different strategy that exploits these same resources, but in very different ways.

To the extent that developing strategic alternatives that a firm can use to exploit the resources it controls is a creative and entrepreneurial process, resource-based models of competitive advantage may need to be augmented by theories of the creative and entrepreneurial process. The application of these theories could then be used to understand the strategic alternatives a firm might be able to pursue, given the resources it controls. While we are currently unaware of such a highly developed theory, these observations suggest a very close relationship between theories of competitive advantage and theories of creativity and entrepreneurship.[11]

We recently taught a class where six groups analyzed the rent generating potential of an acquisition. Five of the groups accepted the assignment as given and applied the resource-based view and financial theory to estimate how much value this acquisition would create and how this value would be distributed between the bidding and target firm. One group concluded that this was the wrong question and developed an analysis that suggested that the bidding firm, in fact, should liquidate itself and distribute its value among its shareholders. Most of us who listened to these group presentations became convinced that the last group had the best analysis. After class, several class members asked, "Why was this one group able to consider a strategic alternative – liquidation – that the other groups had not even thought of?" Currently, strategic management theory does not provide a satisfactory answer to that question.

## Rent appropriation

As has already been suggested, resource-based theory can be used to evaluate the competitive potential of different strategic alternatives facing firms. However, this logic, as it was developed in the Barney (1991a) article, and as it has evolved since, does not address how the economic rents that a strategy might create are appropriated by a firm's stakeholders. It might be the case, for example, that implementing a particular strategy generates real economic rents for a firm, but that those rents are fully appropriated by a firm's employees, its customers, or even its suppliers. Some work has begun to examine this rent appropriation process (e.g., Coff, 1999). This work focuses on the relative bargaining power of a firm's stakeholders and the role of team production (Alchian and Demsetz, 1972) in determining how rents are distributed among a firm's stakeholders. And while this work is promising, it still does not constitute a complete theory of the rent appropriation process. For example, how do different stakeholders come to enjoy different bargaining positions? Why isn't the value of a stakeholder's bargaining position reflected in the cost of the investments necessary to create that position? Under what conditions will team production reduce the ability of employees to appropriate rents created by a firm's strategies? Why would employees agree to employment conditions that significantly reduce their ability to appropriate the rents that are created when a firm implements its strategies?

## Strategy implementation

Finally, in the 1991a paper, issues of strategy implementation do not receive sufficient attention. The paper seems to adopt the remarkably naive view that once a firm understands how to use its resources to implement strategies that can be sources of sustained competitive advantage, that implementation follows, almost automatically. This view is inconsistent both with agency theory arguments taken from organizational economics (Jensen and Meckling, 1976) and a huge organizational behavior literature on motivation, cooperation, and managerial decision-making.

Of course, that issues of strategy implementation are not emphasized in the 1991a paper does not imply that these issues are unimportant. It only implies that other issues received more attention in that paper than implementation issues. However, more work is needed before the full range of strategy implementation issues not included in the 1991a paper are integrated with a resource-based theory of competitive advantage.

## CONCLUSION

In general, there have been two approaches to addressing strategy implementation issues in the context of resource-based theory. First, some have suggested that the ability to implement strategies is, itself, a resource that can be a source of sustained competitive advantage. Work on the role of "cooperative capabilities" in implementing strategic alliance strategies (e.g., Hansen, Hoskisson, and Barney, 2000) and the impact of "trustworthiness" on exchange opportunities for a firm (Barney and Hansen, 1994) is consistent with this first approach.

Second, it has also been suggested that implementation depends on resources that are not themselves sources of sustained advantage, but rather are strategic complements to the other valuable, rare, costly-to-imitate, and non-substitutable resources controlled by a firm (Barney, 1995, 2001a).

Which of these approaches ultimately is most fruitful in bringing the analysis of strategy implementation into resource-based logic is an open question. However, it is clear that additional work is required here.

## NOTES

1 See Scherer (1980) and Nelson and Winter (1982) for reviews of this traditional economics literature. Scherer's review is largely sympathetic to this traditional literature, while Nelson and Winter, in the process of developing an evolutionary theory of the firm, are not at all sympathetic. Nelson and Winter's critiques are similar to those developed in this paper.

2 The contributions of, and relationships among, these early resource-based papers are subject to significant personal interpretation. The history described here is one interpretation, but certainly not the only interpretation, of those contributions and relationships. It is also the case that the history described here is not meant to emphasize some contributions over others. Our view is that, collectively, authors like Barney, Cool, Dierickx, Hamel, Montgomery, Prahalad, Rumelt, Teece, and Wernerfelt were all very important in the creation and development of the resource-based view, broadly interpreted.

3 Barney (1986a) was inspired by a not very well-known paper by Rumelt and Wensly (1981) published only in the *Proceedings of the Academy of Management*. In that paper, Rumelt and Wensly suggest the existence of the "market for market share" and argue that if the market for market share is perfectly competitive, increases in market share will not lead to increases in firm performance. Rumelt and Wensly also provide some rigorous empirical support for this assertion. If pressed to describe the "very first" resource-based paper published, a good argument could be made for Rumelt and Wensly (1981).

4 A firm has a competitive advantage when it is implementing valuable product market strategies not currently being implemented by several other competing firms. A firm has a sustained competitive advantage when it is implementing valuable product market strategies not currently being implemented by several other competing firms and where efforts to imitate those strategies have ceased.

5 Conner (1991), Castanias and Helfat (1991), and Barney (1991a) were all published in a special theory forum in the *Journal of Management* edited by Barney. See Barney (1991b). Interestingly, Peteraf (1993) and Teece, Pisano, and Shuen (1997) were both originally submitted to this special theory forum. Later, they were each published in the *Strategic Management Journal*.

6 This said, conversations with Prahalad suggest that he does not see this work as an example of resource-based logic. Some other of Prahalad's work, however, is explicitly cast in resource-based terms, e.g., Conner and Prahalad (1996).

7 It is necessarily the case that the state of the theory summarized in this section will reflect the tastes and biases of the current authors. Thus, there may be some scholars who label themselves as resource-based who will disagree with this characterization. We have made an effort to incorporate as many different perspectives as possible but acknowledge that there may still be some disagreements with the way the theory is summarized.

8  Imagine, for example, if every application of the law of gravity was labeled as a "new" theory, e.g., the theory of the earth's rotation around the sun, the theory of the moon's rotation around the earth, the theory of the solar system's rotation around the galaxy. While each of these "theories" would vary with respect to details in calculation and application, they would all be applying the same underlying theoretical framework. Such "theoretical proliferation" currently exists in the field of strategic management.

9  This assumption sets aside important agency problems that are discussed later in the paper.

10  For expositional convenience, these hypotheses temporarily set aside issues about the effectiveness with which firms implement their strategies. These organizational issues are discussed later in the paper.

11  Recent work on real options (McGrath and MacMillan, 2000) and innovation management (Brown and Eisenhardt, 1998; Christensen, 1997, 1999; McGrath, MacMillan, and Venkataraman, 1995).

## REFERENCES

Afuah, A. (2000). How much do your competitors' capabilities matter in the face of technological change? *Strategic Management Journal*, 21(3), 387–404.

Albino, V., Garavelli, A. C., and Schiuma, G. (1999). Knowledge transfer and inter-firm relationships in industrial districts: The role of the leader firm. *Technovation*, 19(1), 53–63 .

Alchian, A., and Demsetz, H. (1972). Production, information costs, and economic organization. *American Economic Review*, 62, 777–95.

Anand, J., and Singh, H. (1997). Asset redeployment, acquisitions and corporate strategy in declining industries. *Strategic Management Journal*, 18 (Summer Special Issue), 99–118 .

Appleyard, M. M. (1996). How does knowledge flow? Interfirm patterns in the semiconductor industry. *Strategic Management Journal*, Special Issue, 17, 137–154.

Arora, A., and Gambardella, A. (1997). Domestic markets and international competitiveness: Generic and product-specific competencies in the engineering sector. *Strategic Management Journal*, 18, Special Summer Issue, 53–74.

Athanassiou, N., and Nigh, D. (1999). The impact of U.S. company internationalization on top management team advice networks: A tacit knowledge perspective. *Strategic Management Journal*, 20(1), 83–92.

Bain, J. S. (1956). *Barriers to New Competition*. Cambridge, MA: Harvard University Press.

Baldauf, A., Cravens, D. W., and Wagner, U. (2000). Examining determinants of export performance in small open economies. *Journal of World Business*, 35(1), 61–79.

Barnett, W. P., Greve, H. R., and Park, D. Y. (1994). An evolutionary model of organizational performance. *Strategic Management Journal*, 15 (Winter Special Issue), 11–28.

Barney, J. B. (1986a). Strategic factor markets: Expectations, luck and business strategy. *Management Science*, 32, 1512–14.

Barney, J. B. (1986b). Organizational culture: Can it be a source of sustained competitive advantage? *Academy of Management Review*, 11, 656–65.

Barney, J. B. (1986c). Types of competition and the theory of strategy: Toward an integrative framework. *Academy of Management Review*, 11, 791–800.

Barney, J. B. (1988). Returns to bidding firms in mergers and acquisitions: Reconsidering the relatedness hypothesis. *Strategic Management Journal*, 9, 71–8.

Barney, J. B. (1991a). Firm resources and sustained competitive advantage. *Journal of Management*, 17, 99–120.

Barney, J. B. (1991b). The resource based view of strategy: Origins, implications, and prospects. Editor of Special Theory Forum in *Journal of Management*, 17, 97–211.

Barney, J. B. (1995). Looking inside for competitive advantage. *Academy of Management Executive*, 9(4), 49–61.

Barney, J. B. (2001a). *Gaining and Sustaining Competitive Advantage*. Second edition. Reading, MA: Addison-Wesley.

Barney, J. B. (2001b). Is the Resource-Based 'View' a Useful Perspective for Strategic Management Research? Yes. *Academy of Management Review*, forthcoming.

Barney, J. B., and Hansen, M. (1994). Trustworthiness as a source of competitive advantage. *Strategic Management Journal*, 15, 175–90.

Barney, J. B., and Wright, P. (1998). On becoming a strategic partner: The role of human resources in gaining competitive advantage. *Human Resource Management*, 37, 31–46.

Bates, K. A., and Flynn, E. J. (1995). Innovation history and competitive advantage: A resource-based view analysis of manufacturing technology innovations. *Academy of Management Journal*, 235–9.

Baum, J., and Berta, W. B. (1999). Sources, dynamics, and speed: A longitudinal behavioral simulation of interorganizational and population-level learning. *Advances in Strategic Management*, 16, 155–84.

Becker, B., and Gerhart, B. (1996). The impact of human resource management on organizational performance: Progress and prospects. *Academy of Management Journal*, 39(4), 779–801.

Bennett, N., Ketchen, D. J., and Schultz, E. B. (1998). An examination of factors associated with the integration of human resource management and strategic decision making. *Human Resource Management*, 37(1), 3–16.

Bennis, W. G. (1989). *On Becoming a Leader*. Reading, MA: Addison-Wesley Publishing Co.

Birkinshaw, J., Hood, N., and Jonsson, S. (1998). Building firm-specific advantages in multinational corporations: The role of subsidiary initiative. *Strategic Management Journal*, 19(3), 221–41.

Bisp, S., Sorenson, E., and Grunert, K. (1998). Using the key success factor concept in competitor intelligence and benchmarking. *Competitor Intelligence Review*, 9(3), 55–67.

Borch, O. J., Huse, M., and Senneseth, K. (1999). Resource configuration, competitive strategies, and corporate entrepreneurship: An empirical examination of small firms. *Entrepreneurship Theory and Practice*, 24(1), Fall, 49–70.

Bourke, A. (2000). A model of the determinants of international trade in higher Education. *Service Industries Journal*, 20(1), 110 38.

Boxall, P., and Steeneveld, M. (1999). Human resource strategy and competitive advantage: A longitudinal study of engineering consultancies. *Journal of Management Studies*, 36(4), 443–63.

Brews, P. J., and Hunt, M. R. (1999). Learning to plan and planning to learn: Resolving the planning school/learning school debate. *Strategic Management Journal*, 20(10), 889– 913.

Broadbent, M., Weill, P., and Neo, B. S. (1999). Strategic context and patterns of IT infrastructure capability. *Journal of Strategic Information Systems*, 8(2), 157–87.

Brown, S. L., and Eisenhardt, K. M. (1998). *Competing on the Edge: Strategy as Structured Chaos*. Boston: Harvard Business School Press.

Brush, C. G., and Chaganti, R. (1999). Businesses without glamour? An analysis of resources on performance by size and age in small service and retail firms. *Journal of Business Venturing*, 14(3), 233–57.

Brush, T. H., and Artz, K. W. (1999). Toward a contingent resource-based theory: The impact of information asymmetry on the value of capabilities in veterinary medicine. *Strategic Management Journal*, 20(3), 223–50.

Brush, T. H., and Bromiley, P. (1997). What does a small corporate effect mean? A variance components simulation of corporate and business effects. *Strategic Management Journal*, 18, 325–35.

Capron, L. (1999). The long-term performance of horizontal acquisitions. *Strategic Management Journal*, 20(11), 987–1018.

Capron, L., Dussauge, P., and Mitchell, W. (1998). Resource redeployment following horizontal acquisitions in Europe and North America, 1988–1992. *Strategic Management Journal*, 19(7), 631–61.

Capron, L., and Hulland, J. (1999). Redeployment of brands, sales forces, and general marketing management expertise following horizontal acquisitions: A resource-based view. *Journal of Marketing*, 63(2), 41–54.

Castanias, R. P., and Helfat, C. E. (1991). Managerial resources and rents. *Journal of Management*, 17(1), 155–71.

Chamberlain, E. H. (1933). *The Theory of Monopolistic Competition*. Cambridge, MA: Harvard University Press.

Chandler, A. (1984). Comparative business history. In D. C. Coleman and P. Mathias (eds.), *Enterprise and History: Essays in Honour of Charles Wilson*. Cambridge: Cambridge University Press, 3–26.

Chang, H. F. (1995). Patent scope, antitrust policy, and cumulative innovation. *The Rand Journal of Economics*, 26(1), Spring, 34–57.

Chatterjee, S., and Singh, J. (1999). Are tradeoffs inherent in diversification moves? A simultaneous model for type of diversification and mode of expansion decisions. *Management Science*, 45(1), 25–41.

Chrisman, J. J. (1999). The influence of outsider-generated knowledge resources on venture creation. *Journal of Small Business Management*, 37(4), 42–58.

Christensen, C. M. (1997). *The Innovator's Dilemma: When New Technologies Cause Great Firms to Fail*. Boston: Harvard Business School Press.

Christensen, C. M. (1999). *Title Innovation and the General Manager*. Boston: Irwin/McGraw-Hill.

Christensen, C. M., and Overdorf, M. (2000). Meeting the challenge of disruptive change. *Harvard Business Review*, March–April, 66–76.

Coff, R. (1999). How buyers cope with uncertainty when acquiring firms in knowledge-intensive industries: Caveat emptor. *Organization Science*, 10(2), March–April, 144–61.

Collins, J. C., and Porras, J. I. (1997). *Built to Last: Successful Habits of Visionary Companies*. New York: HarperCollins Publishers.

Collis, D. J. (1991). A resource-based analysis of global competition: The case of the bearings industry. *Strategic Management Journal*, 12, Summer, 49–68.

Collis, D. J., and Montgomery, C. A. (1995). Competing on resources: Strategy in the 1990s. *Harvard Business Review*, 73(4), 118–28.

Combs, J. G., and Ketchen, D. J., Jr. (1999). Explaining interfirm cooperation and performance: Toward a reconciliation of predictions from the resource-based view and organizational economics. *Strategic Management Journal*, 20(9), 867–88.

Conner, K. R. (1991). A historical comparison of resource based theory and five schools of thought within industrial organization economics: Do we have a new theory of the firm? *Journal of Management*, 17(1), 121–54.

Conner, K. R., and Prahalad, C. K. (1996). A resource based theory of the firm: Knowledge versus opportunism. *Organization Science*, 7(5), 477–501.

Covey, S. R. (1989). Basic principles of total quality. *Executive Excellence*, 6(5), May, 17–19.

Daily, C. M., Certo, S. T., and Dalton, D. R. (2000). International experience in the executive suite: The path to prosperity? *Strategic Management Journal*, 21(4), 515–23.

Dean, T. J., Turner, C. A., and Bamford, C. E. (1997). Impediments to Imitation and Rates of New Firm Failure. *Academy of Management Proceedings 1997*, 103–7.

DeCarolis, D. M., and Deeds, D. L. (1999). The impact of stocks and flows of organizational knowledge on firm performance: An empirical investigation of the biotechnology industry. *Strategic Management Journal*, 20(10), 953–68.

Deeds, D. L., DeCarolis, D., and Coombs, J. (2000). Dynamic capabilities and new product development in high technology ventures: An empirical analysis of new biotechnology firms.

*Journal of Business Venturing,* 15(3), 211–29.

Deephouse, D. L. (1999). To be different, or to be the same? It's a question (and theory) of strategic balance. *Strategic Management Journal,* 20(2), 147–66.

Delaney, J. T., and Huselid, M. A. (1996). The impact of human resource management practices on perceptions of organizational performance. *Academy of Management Journal,* 39(4), 949–69.

Del Canto, J. G., and Gonzalez, I. S. (1999). A resource-based analysis of the factors determining a firm's R&D activities. *Research Policy,* 28(8), 891–905.

Delery, J. E., and Doty, D. H. (1996). Modes of theorizing in strategic human resource management: Tests of universalistic, contingency, and configurational performance predictions. *Academy of Management Journal,* 39(4), 802–35.

Delios, A., and Beamish, P. W. (1999). Geographic scope, product diversification, and the corporate performance of Japanese firms. *Strategic Management Journal,* 20(8), 711–27.

Demsetz, H. (1973). Industry Structure, Market Rivalry, and Public Policy. *Journal of Law and Economics,* 16, 1–9.

Dent-Micallef, A., and Powell, T. (1998). Information technology: Strategic necessity of source of competitive advantage? An empirical study on the retail sector of the United States. *Canadian Journal of Administrative Sciences-Revue Canadienne des Sciences de L'Administration,* 15(1), 39–64.

Dierickx, J., and Cool, K. (1989). Asset stock accumulation and sustainability of competitive advantage. *Management Science,* 35, 1504–11.

Dougherty, D., and Hardy, C. (1996). Sustained product innovation in large, mature organizations: Overcoming innovation-to-organization problems. *Academy of Management Journal,* 39(5), 1120–53.

Drucker, P. (1994). The theory of business. *Harvard Business Review,* 75, Sept./Oct. 95–105.

Dussauge, P., Garrette, B., and Mitchell, W. (2000). Learning from competing partners: Outcomes and durations of scale and link alliances in Europe, North America and Asia. *Strategic Management Journal,* 21(2), 99–126.

Farjoun, M. (1998). The independent and joint effects of the skill and physical bases of relatedness in diversification. *Strategic Management Journal,* 19(7), 611–30.

Fey, C. F., Bjorkman, I., and Pavlovskaya, A. (2000). The effect of human resource management practices on firm performance in Russia. *International Journal of Human Resource Management,* 11(1), 1–18.

Field, D., Chan, A., and Akhtar, S. (2000). Organizational contest and human resource management strategy: A structural equation analysis of Hong Kong firms. *International Journal of Human Resource Management,* 11(2), 264–77.

Finkelstein, S., and Hambrick, D. (1996). *Strategic Leadership: Top Executives and their Effects on Organizations.* Minneapolis/St. Paul: West Publishing Company.

Fuld, L. M. (1995). *The New Competitor Intelligence: The Complete Resource for Finding, Analyzing, and Using Information about Your Competitors.* New York: John Wiley.

Gatignon, H., Robertson, T. S., and Fein, A. J. (1997). Incumbent defense strategies against new product entry. *International Journal Of Research In Marketing,* 14(2), 163–76.

Geringer, J. M., Tallman, S., and Olsen, D. M. (2000). Product and international diversification among Japanese multinational firms. *Strategic Management Journal,* 21(1), 51–80.

Ghingold, M., and Johnson, B. (1997). Technical knowledge as value added in business markets. *Industrial Marketing Management,* 26(3). 271–80.

Gimeno, J. (1999). Reciprocal threats in multimarket rivalry: Staking out 'spheres of influence' in the U.S. airline industry. *Strategic Management Journal.* 20(2), 101–28.

Glunk, U., and Wilderom, C. P. M. (1998). Predictors of organizational performance in small and medium-sized professional service firms. *International Journal of Technology Management,* 16(1–3), 23–36.

Gordon, R. A., and Howell, J. E. (1959). *Higher Education for Business.* New York: Columbia

University Press.

Grant, R. M. (1988). On "dominant logic" relatedness and the link between diversity and performance. *Strategic Management Journal*, 9, 639–42.

Grant, R. M. (1991). The resource-based theory of competitive advantage: Implications for strategy formulation. *California Management Review*, Spring, 114–35.

Grant, R. M. (1996). Toward a knowledge-based theory of the firm. *Strategic Management Journal*, 17, Winter Special Issue, 109–22.

Greve, H. R. (1999). Branch systems and nonlocal learning in populations. *Advances in Strategic Management*, 16, 57–80.

Gulati, R. (1999). Network location and learning: The influence of network resources and firm capabilities on alliance formation. *Strategic Management Journal*, 20(5), 97–420.

Gupta, A., and Govindarajan, V. (1984). Business unit strategy, managerial characteristics, and business unit effectiveness at strategy implementation. *Academy of Management Journal*, 27, 25–41.

Gupta, A. K., and Govindarajan, V. (2000). Knowledge flows within multinational corporations. *Strategic Management Journal*, 21(4), 473–96.

Hall, R. (1992). The strategic analysis of intangible resources. *Strategic Management Journal*, 13(2), 35–144.

Hall, R. (1993). A framework linking intangible resources and capabilities to sustainable competitive advantage. *Strategic Management Journal*, 14(8), 607–18.

Hamermesh, R., Gordon, K. D., and Reed, J. P. (1977). *Crown Cork & Seal, Inc.* Harvard Business School, case number 378–024.

Hamermesh, R. G., and Rosenbloom, R. S. (1989). *Crown Cork and Seal Co., Inc.* Harvard Business School, case number 9-388-096.

Hansen, G. S., and Wernerfelt, B. (1989). Determinants of firm performance: The relative importance of economic and organizational factors. *Strategic Management Journal*, 10, 399–411.

Hanson, M., Hoskisson, R., and Barney, J. B. (2000). Resolving the opportunism minimization-opportunity maximization paradox. Presented at the Academy of Management, 1999.

Harel, G. H., and Tzafrir, S. S. (1999). The effect of human resource management practices on the perceptions of organizational and market performance of the firm. *Human Resource Management*, 38(3), Fall, 85–199.

Harmsen, H., Grunert, K. G., and Declerck, F. (2000). Why did we make that cheese? An empirically based framework for understanding what drives innovation activity. *R&D Management*, 30(2), 151–66.

Harrison, J. S., Hall, E. H., Jr., and Nargundkar, R. (1993). Resource allocation as an outcropping of strategic consistency: Performance implications. *Academy of Management Journal*, 36(5), 1026–51.

Harrison, J. S., Hitt, M. A., Hoskisson, R. E., and Ireland, R. D. (1991). Synergies and postacquisition performance – Differences versus similarities in resource allocations. *Journal of Management*, 17(1), 173–90.

Haunschild, P. R., and Miner, A. S. (1997). Modes of interorganizational imitation: The effects of outcome salience and uncertainty. *Administrative Science Quarterly*, 42(3), 472–500.

Helfat, C. E. (1997). Know-how and asset complementarity and dynamic capability accumulation: The case of R&D. *Strategic Management Journal*, 18(5), 339–60.

Henderson, A. D. (1999). Firm strategy and age dependence: A contingent view of the liabilities of newness, adolescence, and obsolescence. *Administrative Science Quarterly*, 44(2), 281–314.

Henderson, R., and Cockburn, I. (1994). Measuring competence? Exploring firm effects in pharmaceutical research. *Strategic Management Journal*, 15, 63–84.

Hill, C. W. L., and Jones, G. R. (1992). *Strategic Management Theory: An Integrated Approach*. Boston: Houghton Mifflin.

Hillman, A., and Hitt, M. A. (1999). Corporate political strategy formulation: A model of approach, participation, and strategy decisions. *Academy of Management Review*, 24(4), 825–42.

Hirshleifer, J. (1980). *Price Theory and Applications*. Englewood Cliffs, NJ: Prentice-Hall.

Hitt, M. A., Dacin, M. T., Levitas, E., Arregle, J-L., and Borza, A. (2000). Partner selection in emerging and developed market contexts: Resource-based and organizational learning perspectives. *Academy of Management Journal*, 43(3), 449–67.

Hitt, M. A., Hoskisson, R. E., Ireland, R. D., and Harrison, J. S. (1991). Effects of acquisitions on R&D inputs and outputs. *Academy of Management Journal*, 34(3), 693–706.

Hitt, M. A., Hoskisson, R. E., and Kim, H. (1997). International diversification: Effects on innovation and firm performance in product-diversified firms. *Academy of Management Journal*, 40(4), 767–98.

Hitt, M. A., and Ireland, R. D. (1985). Corporate Distinctive Competence, Strategy, Industry and Performance. *Strategic Management Journal*, 6(3), 273–93.

Hitt, M. A., and Ireland, R. D. (1985). Strategy, Contextual factors, and performance. *Human Relations*, 38(8), 79–812.

Hitt, M. A., Ireland, R. D., and Hoskisson, R. E. (1999). *Strategic Management: Competitiveness and Globalization*. Cincinnati: South-Western College Publishing.

Hooley, G., Cox, T., Shipley, D., Fahy, J., Beracs, J., and Kolos, K. (1996). Foreign direct investment in Hungary: Resource acquisition and domestic competitive advantage. *Journal of International Business Studies*, 27(4), Fourth Quarter, 683–709.

Hoopes, D. G., and Postrel, S. (1999). Shared knowledge, 'glitches,' and product development performance. *Strategic Management Journal*, 20(9), 837–65.

Hrebiniak, L. G., and Snow. C. C. (1982). Top-management agreement and organizational performance. *Human Relations*, 35(12), 1139–57.

Huselid, M. (1995). The impact of human resource management practices on turnover, productivity, and corporate financial performance. *Academy of Management Journal*, 38, 635–72.

Huselid, M. A., and Becker, B. E. (1997). The impact of high performance work systems, implementation effectiveness, and alignment with strategy on shareholder wealth. *Academy of Management Proceedings '97*, 144–8.

Huselid, M. A., Jackson, S. E., and Schuler, R. S. (1997). Technical and strategic human resource management effectiveness as determinants of firm performance. *Academy of Management Journal*, 40(1), 171–88.

Ingham, H., and Thompson, S. (1995). Deregulation, firm capabilities and diversifying entry decisions: The case of financial services. *The Review of Economics and Statistics*, 77(1), 177–83.

Ingram, P., and Baum, J. A. C. (1997). Opportunity and constraint: Organizations' learning from the operating and competitive experience of industries. *Strategic Management Journal*, 18 (Summer Special Issue), 75–98.

Irwin, J. G., Hoffman, J. J., and Lamont, B. T. (1998). The effect of the acquisition of technological innovations on organizational performance: A resource-based view. *Journal of Engineering and Technology Management*, 15(1), 25–54.

Itami, H. (1987). *Mobilizing Invisible Assets*. Cambridge, MA: Harvard University Press.

Jarvenpaa, S. L., and Leidner, D. E. (1999). An information company in Mexico: Extending the resource-based view of the firm to a developing country context. *Information Systems Research*, 9(4), 342–61.

Jensen, M. C., and Meckling, W. H. (1976). Theory of the firm: Managerial behavior, agency costs, and ownership structure. *Journal of Financial Economics*, 3, 305–60.

Johnson, J. L. (1999). Strategic integration in industrial distribution channels: Managing the interfirm relationship as a strategic asset. *Journal of the Academy of Marketing Science*, 27(1), Winter, 4–18.

Judge, W. Q., and Douglas, T. J. (1998). Performance implications of incorporating natural environmental issues into the strategic planning process: An empirical assessment. *Journal Of Management Studies*, 35(2), 241–62.

Karagozoglu, N., and Lindell, M. (1998). Internationalization of small and medium-sized technology-based firms: An exploratory study. *Journal of Small Business Management*, 36(1), 44–59.

Karnoe, P. (1995). Competence as process and the social embeddedness of competence building. *Academy of Management Journal*, 1995, 427–31.

Khatri N. (2000). Managing human resource for competitive advantage: A study of companies in Singapore. *International Journal of Human Resource Management*, 11(2), 336–65.

Klaas, B. S., McClendon, J., and Gainey, T. W. (1999). HR outsourcing and its impact: The role of transaction costs. *Personnel Psychology*, 52(1), Spring, 113–36.

Klassen, R. D., and Whybark, D. C. (1999). The impact of environmental technologies on manufacturing performance. *Academy of Management Journal*, 42(6), 599–615.

Knights, D., and McCabe, D. (1997). How would you measure something like that?: Quality in a retail bank. *Journal of Management Studies*, 34(3), 371–88.

Koch, M. J., and McGrath, R. G. (1996). Improving labor productivity: *Human Resource Management* policies do matter. *Strategic Management Journal*, 17(5), 335–54.

Kogut, B. (1991). Joint ventures and the option to expand and acquire. *Management Science*, 37(1), 19–33.

Kogut, B., and Zander, U. (1993). Knowledge of the firm and the evolutionary theory of the multinational corporation. *Journal of International Business Studies*, 24(4), 625–45.

Kotha, S., and Nair, A. (1995). Strategy and environment as determinants of performance: Evidence from the Japanese machine tool industry. *Strategic Management Journal*, 16(7), 497–518.

Labich, K., and Ballen, K. (1988). The Seven Keys to Business Leadership. *Fortune*, 1198(9), Oct. 24.

Lane, P. J., and Lubatkin, M. (1998). Relative absorptive capacity and interorganizational learning. *Strategic Management Journal*, 19(5), 461–77.

Lang, L. H. P., and Stulz, R. M. (1994). Tobin's $q$, corporate diversification, and firm performance. *Journal of Political Economy*, 102(6), 1248–80.

Learned, E. P., Christensen, C. R., Andrew, K. R., and Guth, W. (1969). *Business Policy*. Homewood, IL: Irwin.

Lee, J., and Miller, D. (1999). People matter: Commitment to employees, strategy and performance in Korean firms. *Strategic Management Journal*, 20(6), 579–93.

Lei, D., Hitt, M. A., and Bettis, R. A. (1996). Dynamic core competences through meta-learning and strategic context. *Journal of Management*, 22, 549–69.

Li, T., and Calantone, R. J. (1998). The impact of market knowledge competence on new product advantage: Conceptualization and empirical examination. *Journal of Marketing*, 62(4), 3–29.

Li, M., and Ye, L. R. (1999). Information technology and firm performance: Linking with environmental, strategic and managerial contexts. *Information and Management*, 35(1), 3–51.

Lieberman, M. B. (1982). The learning curve, pricing and market structure in the chemical processing industries. Unpublished doctoral dissertation, Harvard University.

Lieberman, M. B. (1987). The learning curve, diffusion, and competitive strategy. *Strategic Management Journal*, 8, 441–52.

Liebeskind, J. P. (1996). Knowledge, strategy, and the theory of the firm. *Strategic Management Journal*, Winter Special Issue, 17, 93–107.

Lorenzoni, G., and Lipparini, A. (1999). The leveraging of interfirm relationships as a distinctive organizational capability: A longitudinal study. *Strategic Management Journal*, 20(4), 317–38.

Luo, Y. D. (1999). The structure-performance relationship in a transitional economy: An empirical study of multinational alliances in China. *Journal of Business Research*, 46(1), 15–30.

Luo, Y., and Peng, M. W. (1999). Learning to compete in a transition economy: Experience, environment, and performance. *Journal of International Business Studies*, 30(2), 269–96.

MacDuffie, J. (1995). Human resource bundles and manufacturing performance: Organizational logic and flexible production systems in the world auto industry. *Industrial and Labor Relations Review*, 49, 197–221.

Mahoney, J. T. (1993). Strategic management and determinism: Sustaining the conversation. *The Journal of Management Studies*, 30(1), 173–91.

Mahoney, J. T., and Pandian, J. R. (1992). The resource-based view within the conversation of strategic management. *Strategic Management Journal*, 13, 363–80.

Maignan, I., Ferrell, O. C., and Hult, G. T. M. (1999). Corporate citizenship: Cultural antecedents and business benefits. *Journal of the Academy of Marketing Science*, 27(4), Fall, 455–69.

Maijoor, S., and van Witteloostuijn, A. (1996). An empirical test of the resource-based theory: Strategic regulation in the Dutch audit industry. *Strategic Management Journal*, 17(7), 549–69.

Makadok, R. (1998). Can first-mover and early-mover advantages be sustained in an industry with low barriers to entry/imitation? *Strategic Management Journal*, 19(7), 683–96.

Makadok, R. (1999). Interfirm differences in scale economies and the evolution of market shares. *Strategic Management Journal*, 20(10), 935–52.

Mansfield, E. (1985). How rapidly does new industrial technology leak out? *Journal of Industrial Economics*, 34(2), 217–23.

Mansfield, E. (1986). Patents and innovation: An empirical study. *Management Science*, 32(2), 173–81.

Mansfield, E., Schwartz, M., and Wagner, S. (1981). Imitation costs and patents: An empirical study. *Economic Journal*, 91, 907–18.

Marcus, A., and effen, D. (1998). The dialectics of competency acquisition: Pollution prevention in electric generation. *Strategic Management Journal*, 19(12), 1145–68.

Markides, C. C., and Williamson, P. J. (1996). Corporate diversification and organizational structure: A resource-based view. *Academy of Management Journal*, 39(2), 340–67.

Maskell, P. (1998). Low-tech competitive advantages and the role of proximity: The Danish wooden furniture industry. *European Urban and Regional Studies*, 5(2), 99–118.

Maskell, P., and Malmberg, A. (1999). Localised learning and industrial competitiveness. *Cambridge Journal of Economics*, 23(2), 167–85.

Mauri, A. J., and Michaels, M. P. (1998). Firm and industry effects within strategic management: An empirical examination. *Strategic Management Journal*, 19(3), 211–19.

McEvily, B., and Zaheer, A. (1999). Bridging ties: A source of firm heterogeneity in competitive capabilities. *Strategic Management Journal*, 20(12), 1133–56.

McGahan, A. M., and Porter, M. E. (1997). How much does industry matter, really? *Strategic Management Journal*, 18 (Special Issue), Summer, 15–30.

McGaughey, S.L., Liesch, P. W., and Poulson, D. (2000). An unconventional approach to intellectual property protection: The case of an Australian firm transferring shipbuilding technologies to China. *Journal of World Business*, 35(1), Spring, 1–20.

McGee, J. E., Dowling, M. J., and Megginson, W. L. (1995). Cooperative strategy and new venture performance – The role of business strategy and management experience. *Strategic Management Journal*, 16(7), 565–80.

McGrath, R. G., and MacMillan, I. C. (2000). *The Entrepreneurial Mindset: Strategies for Continuously Creating Opportunity in an Age of Uncertainty*. Boston: Harvard Business School Press.

McGrath, R. G., MacMillan, I. C., and Venkataraman, S. (1995). Defining and developing a competence: A strategic process paradigm. *Strategic Management Journal*, 16(4), 251–75.

McGrath, R. G., Tsui, M-H., Venkataraman, S., and MacMillan, I. C. (1996). Innovation, competitive advantage and rent: A model and test. *Management Science*, 42(3), 389–403.

McGuire, J. (2000). Corporate Governance and Growth Potential: an empirical analysis. *Corporate Governance – An International Review*, 8(1), 32–42.

Menon, A., Bharadwaj, S. G., Adidam, P. T., and Edison, S. W. (1999). Antecedents and consequences of marketing strategy making: A model and a test. *Journal of Marketing*, 63(2), 8–40.

Michael, S. C., and Robbins, D. K. (1998). Retrenchment among small manufacturing firms during recession. *Journal of Small Business Management*, 36(3), 5–45.

Miller, D. J. (2000). Corporate Diversification, Relatedness, and Performance. Unpublished dissertation, Ohio State University.

Miller, D., and Shamsie, J. (1996). The resource-based view of the firm in two environments: The Hollywood film studios from 1936 to 1965. *Academy of Management Journal*, 39(3), 519–43.

Miller, D., and Toulouse, J.-M. (1998). Quasi-rational organizational responses: Functional and cognitive sources of strategic simplicity. *Revue Canadienne des Sciences de l'Administration*, 15(3), 230–44.

Mintzberg, H. (1990). The Design School: Reconsidering the basic premises of strategic management. *Strategic Management Journal*, March–April, 113, 171–95.

Moingeon, B., Ramanantsoa, B., Metais, E., and Orton, J. D. (1998). Another look at strategy-structure relationships: The resource-based view. *European Management Journal*, 16(3), 297–305 .

Montgomery, C. A. (1979). Diversification, Market Structure and Firm Performance: An Extension of Rumelt's Model. Unpublished dissertation, Purdue University.

Morita, M., and Flynn, E. J. (1997). The linkage among management systems, practices and behaviour [sic.] in successful manufacturing strategy. *International Journal of Operations & Production Management*, 17(10), 967–93.

Morris, S. A. (1997). Environmental pollution and competitive advantage: An exploratory study of U.S. industrial-goods manufacturers. *Academy of Management Proceedings '97*, 411–15.

Mosakowski, E. (1998). Managerial prescriptions under the resource-based view of strategy: The example of motivational techniques. *Strategic Management Journal*, 19(12), 1169–82.

Mowery, D. C., Oxley, J. E., and Silverman, B. S. (1998). Technological overlap and interfirm cooperation: Implications for the resource-based view of the firm. *Research Policy*, 27(5), 507–23.

Mutinelli, M., and Piscitello, L. (1998). The entry mode choice of MNEs: An evolutionary approach. *Research Policy*, 27(5), 491–506.

Nachum, L., and Rolle, J. D. (1999). The national origin of the ownership advantages of firms. *Service Industries Journal*, 19(4), 17–48.

Nelson, R., and Winter, S. (1982). *An Evolutionary Theory of Economic Change*. Cambridge, MA: Belknap Press.

Nickerson, J. A., and Silverman, B. S. (1998). Economic performance, strategic position, and vulnerability to ecological pressures among US interstate motor carriers. *Advances in Strategic Management*, 15, 37–61.

Oktemgil, M., Greenley, G. E., and Broderick, A. J. (2000). An empirical study of isolating mechanisms in UK companies. *European Journal of Operational Research*, 122(3), 638–55.

Pennings, J. M., Lee, K., and van Witteloostuijn, A. (1998). Human capital, social capital, and firm Dissolution. *Academy of Management Journal*, 41(4), 425–40.

Penrose, E. T. (1959). *The Theory of the Growth of the Firm*. New York: Wiley.

Peteraf, M. A. (1993). The cornerstones of competitive advantage: A resource-based view. *Strategic Management Journal*, 14, 179–91.

Pierson, F. C. (1959). *The Education of American Businessmen: A Study of University-College Programs in Business Administration*. New York: McGraw-Hill.

Pil, F. K., and MacDuffie, J. P. (2000). The effects of total quality management on corporate performance: an empirical investigation (paper first presented in 1995). In C. Ichniowski (ed.), *The American Workplace: Skills, Compensation, and Employee Involvement*, New York: Cambridge University Press.

Pisano, G. P. (1994). Knowledge, integration, and the locus of learning: An empirical analysis of process development. *Strategic Management Journal*, 15 Winter Special Issue, 85–100.

Poppo, L., and Zenger, T. (1995). Opportunism, routines, and boundary choices: A comparative test of transaction cost and resource-based explanations for make-or-buy decisions. *Academy of Management Journal*, 38(1), 42–6.

Porter, M. E. (1979). How competitive forces shape strategy. *Harvard Business Review*, March–April, 137–56.

Porter, M. E. (1980). *Competitive Strategy*. New York: Free Press.

Porter, M. E. (1981). The contribution of industrial organization to strategic management. *Academy of Management Review*, 6, 609–20.

Porter, M. E. (1985). *Competitive Advantage*: New York: Free Press.

Powell, T. C. (1995). Total quality management as competitive advantage: A review and empirical study. *Strategic Management Journal*, 16(1), 15–37.

Prahalad, C. K., and Bettis, R. A. (1986). The dominant logic: A new linkage between diversity and performance. *Strategic Management Journal*, 7, 485–501.

Prahalad, C. K., and Hamel, G. (1990). The Core Competence of the Corporation. *Harvard Business Review*, June, 79–91.

Priem, R. L., and Butler, J. E. (2001). Is the resource-based 'view' a useful perspective for strategic management research? *Academy of Management Review*, in press.

Rangone, A. (1999). A resource-based approach to strategy analysis in small-medium sized enterprises. *Small Business Economics*, 12(3), 233–48.

Rao, H. (1994). The social construction of reputation – certification contests, legitimation, and the survival of organizations in the American automobile-industry – 1895–1912. *Strategic Management Journal*, 15 (Special Winter Issue), 29–44.

Ray, G. (2000). *Information Systems and Competitive Advantage: A Process-Oriented Theory*. Unpublished dissertation, Ohio State University.

Reed, R., Lemak, D. J., and Montgomery, J. C. (1996). Beyond process: TQM content and firm performance. *The Academy of Management Review*, 21(1), 173–202.

Ricardo, D. (1817). *Principles of Political Economy and Taxation*. London: J. Murray.

Richard, O. C. (2000). Racial diversity, business strategy, and firm performance: A resource-based view. *Academy of Management Journal*, 43(2), 164–77.

Robins, J., and Wiersema, M. F. (1995). A resource-based approach to the multibusiness firm: Empirical analysis of portfolio interrelationships and corporate financial performance. *Strategic Management Journal*, 16, 277–99.

Ruiz-Navarro, J. (1998). Turnaround and renewal in a Spanish shipyard. *Long Range Planning*, 31(1), 51–9.

Rumelt, R. (1974). *Strategy, Structure, and Economic Performance*. Cambridge, MA: Harvard University Press.

Rumelt, R. (1984). Toward a strategic theory of the firm. In R. Lamb (ed.), *Competitive Strategic Management*. Englewood Cliffs, NJ: Prentice-Hall.

Rumelt, R. (1991). How much does industry matter? *Strategic Management Journal*, 12, 167–85.

Rumelt, R. P., and Wensley, R. (1981). In search of the market share effect. *Proceedings of the Academy of Management Meeting '81*, 2–6.

Russo, M. V., and Fouts, P. A. (1997). A resource-based perspective on corporate environmental performance and profitability. *Academy of Management Journal*, 40(3), 534–59.

Sakakibara, M. (1997). Heterogeneity of firm capabilities and cooperative research and development: An empirical examination of motives. *Strategic Management Journal*, 18 (Special Summer Issue), 143–64.

Schankerman, M. (1998). How valuable is patent protection? Estimates by technology field. *The Rand Journal of Economics*, 29(1), 77–107.

Scherer, F. M. (1980). *Industrial Market Structure and Economic Performance*. Boston: Houghton Mifflin.

Schmalensee, R. (1985). Do Markets Differ Much? *American Economic Review*, 75, 341–51.

Schoenecker, T. S., and Cooper, A. C. (1998). The role of firm resources and organizational attributes in determining entry timing: A cross-industry study. *Strategic Management Journal*, 19(12), 1127–43.

Schuler, R. S., and MacMillan, I. (1984). Gaining competitive advantage through human resource practices. *Human Resource Management*, 23, 241–56.

Segev, E., Raveh, A., and Farjoun, M. (1999). Conceptual maps of the leading MBA programs in the United States: Core courses, concentration areas, and the ranking of the school. *Strategic Management Journal*, 20(6), 549–65.

Selznick, P. (1957). *Leadership in Administration*. New York: Harper and Row.

Sharma, S., and Vredenburg, H. (1998). Proactive corporate environmental strategy and the development of competitively valuable organizational capabilities. *Strategic Management Journal*, 19(8), 729–53.

Shenkar, O., and Li, J. T. (1999). Knowledge search in international cooperative ventures. *Organizational Science*, 10(2), 134–43.

Sherer, P. D., Rogovsky, N., and Wright, N. (1998). What drives employment relationships in taxicab organizations? Linking agency to firm capabilities and strategic opportunities. *Organization Science*, 9(1), 34–48.

Silverman, B. S. (1999). Technological resources and the direction of corporate diversification: Toward an integration of the resource-based view and transaction cost economics. *Management Science*, 45(8), 1109–24.

Smart, D. L., and Wolfe, R. A. (2000). Examining sustainable competitive advantage in intercollegiate athletics: A resource-based view. *Journal of Sport Management*, 14(2), 133–53.

Spender, J. C. (1996). Making knowledge the basis of a dynamic theory of the firm. *Strategic Management Journal*, 17, Winter Special Issue, 109–22.

Stalk, G., Evans, P., and Shulman, L. (1992). Competing on capabilities: The new rules of corporate strategy. *Harvard Business Review*, March–April, 57–69.

Stevens, J. M., and Bagby, J. W. (1999). Intellectual property transfer from universities to business: requisite for sustained competitive advantage? *International Journal of Technology Management*, 18(5–8), 688–704.

Stogdill, R. M. (1974). *Handbook of Leadership: A Survey of Theory and Research*. New York: Free Press.

Stuart, T. E., and Podolny. J. M. (1996). Local search and the evolution of technological capabilities. *Strategic Management Journal*, 17 (Special Summer Issue), 21–38.

Swaminathan, A. (1996). Environmental conditions at founding and organizational mortality: A trial-by-fire model. *Academy of Management Journal*, 39(5), 1350–77.

Tallman, S. B. (1991). Strategic management models and resource-based strategies among MNEs in a host market. *Strategic Management Journal*, 12, Special Summer Issue, 69–82.

Teece, D. (1980). Economy of scope and the scope of the enterprise. *Journal of Economic Behavior and Organization*, 1, 223–45.

Teece, D. J., Pisano, G., and Shuen, A. (1997). Dynamic capabilities and strategic management. *Strategic Management Journal*, 18(7), 509–33.

Tichy, N. M., and Devanna, M. A. (1986). *The Transformational Leader*. New York: Wiley.

Trigeorgis, L. (1996). *Real Options: Managerial Flexibility and Strategy in Resource Allocation*. Cambridge, MA: MIT Press.

Trigeorgis, L. (ed.) (1995). *Real Options in Capital Investment: Models, Strategies, and Applications*. Westport, CT: Praeger.

Tripsas, M. (1997). Unraveling the process of creative destruction: Complementary assets and incumbent survival in the typesetter industry. *Strategic Management Journal*, 18 (Special Summer Issue), 119–42.

Truss, C., Gratton, L., Hope-Hailey, V., McGovern, P., and Stiles, P. (1997). Soft and hard models of human resource management: A reappraisal. *The Journal of Management Studies*, 34(1), 53–73.

Tyler, B. B., and Steensma, H. K. (1998). The effects of executives' experiences and perceptions on their assessment of potential technological alliances. *Strategic Management Journal*, 19(10), 939–65.

Walston, S. L., Burns, L. R., and Kimberly, J. R. (2000). Does reengineering really work? An examination of the context and outcomes of hospital reengineering initiatives. *Health Services Research*, 34(6), 1363–88.

Welbourne, T. M., and Andrews, A. O. (1996). Predicting the performance of initial public offerings: Should human resource management be in the equation? *Academy of Management Journal*, 39(4), 891–919.

Wernerfelt, B. (1984). A resource-based view of the firm. *Strategic Management Journal*, 5, 171–80.

Wernerfelt, B., and Montgomery, C. A. (1986). What is an attractive industry? *Management Science*, 32(10), 1223–30.

Wernerfelt, B., and Montgomery, C. A. (1988). Tobin's $q$ and the importance of focus in firm performance. *American Economic Review*, 78, 246–50.

Williamson, O. E. (1975). *Markets and Hierarchies: Analysis and Antitrust Implication*. New York: Free Press.

Williamson, O. E. (1985). *The Economic Institutions of Capitalism*. New York: Free Press.

Womack, J. P., Jones, D. I., and Roos, D. (1990). *The Machine That Changed the World*. New York: Rawson.

Wright, P. M., and McMahan, G. C. (1992). Alternative theoretical perspectives for strategic human resource management. *Journal of Management*, 18, 295–320.

Wright P. M., McMahan, G. C., and McWilliams, A. (1994). Human resources as a source of sustained competitive advantage. *International Journal of Human Resource Management*, 5, 299–324.

Wright, P. M., McMahan, G. C., McCormick, B., and Sherman, W. S. (1998). Strategy, core competence, and HR involvement as determinants of HR effectiveness and refinery performance. *Human Resource Management*, 37(1), 17–29.

Youndt, M. A., Snell, S. A., Dean, J. W., Jr., and Lepak, D. P. (1996). Human resource management, manufacturing strategy, and firm performance. *Academy of Management Journal*, 39(4), 836–66.

Yukl, G. (1989). Managerial leadership: A review of theory and research. *Journal of Management*, 15(2), 251–89.

Zander, U., and Kogut, B. (1995). Knowledge and the speed of the transfer and imitation of organizational capabilities: An empirical test. *Organization Science*, 6(1), 76–92.

Zou, S., and Ozsomer, A. (1999). Global product R&D and the firm's strategic position. *Journal of International Marketing*, 7(1), 57–76.

# 6

# A Stakeholder Approach to Strategic Management

## R. Edward Freeman and John McVea

The purpose of this chapter is to outline the development of the idea of "stakeholder management" as it has come to be applied in strategic management. We begin by developing a brief history of the concept. We then suggest that traditionally the stakeholder approach to strategic management has several related characteristics that serve as distinguishing features. We review recent work on stakeholder theory and suggest how stakeholder management has affected the practice of management. We end by suggesting further research questions.

## History of the Stakeholder Approach to Strategic Management

A stakeholder approach to strategy emerged in the mid-1980s. One focal point in this movement was the publication of R. Edward Freeman's *Strategic Management: A Stakeholder Approach* in 1984. Building on the process work of Ian Mitroff, Richard Mason, and James Emshoff (for statements of these views see Mason and Mitroff, 1982; and Emshoff, 1978), the impetus behind stakeholder management was to try and build a framework that was responsive to the concerns of managers who were being buffeted by unprecedented levels of environmental turbulence and change. Traditional strategy frameworks were neither helping managers to develop new strategic directions nor were they helping them to understand how to create new opportunities in the midst of so much change. As Freeman observed "[O]ur current theories are inconsistent with both the quantity and kinds of change that are occurring in the business environment of the 1980's . . . A new conceptual framework is needed" (Freeman, 1984: 5). A stakeholder approach was a response to this challenge. An obvious play on the word "stockholder," the approach sought to broaden the concept of strategic management beyond its traditional economic roots, by defining stakeholders as "any group or individual who is affected by or can affect the achievement of an organization's objectives." The purpose of stakeholder management was to devise methods to manage the myriad groups and relationships that resulted in a strategic fashion. While the stakeholder framework had roots in a number of academic fields, its heart lay in the clinical studies of management practitioners that were carried out over ten years through the Busch Center, the Wharton Applied Research Center, and the Managerial and Behavioral Science Center, all at The Wharton School, University of Pennsylvania, by a host of researchers.

While the 1980s provided an environment that demonstrated the power of a stakeholder approach, the idea was not entirely new. The use of the term stakeholder grew out of the pioneering work at Stanford Research Institute (now SRI International) in the 1960s. SRI's work, in turn, was heavily influenced by concepts that were developed in the planning department of Lockheed and these ideas were further developed through the work of Igor Ansoff and Robert Stewart. From the start the stakeholder approach grew out of management practice.[1]

SRI argued that managers needed to understand the concerns of shareholders, employees, customers, suppliers, lenders and society, in order to develop objectives that stakeholders would support. This support was necessary for long-term success. Therefore, management should actively explore its relationships with all stakeholders in order to develop business strategies.

For the most part these developments had a relatively small impact on the management theories of the time. However, fragments of the stakeholder concept survived and developed within four distinct management research streams over the next twenty years. Indeed, it was by pulling together these related stakeholder concepts from the corporate planning, systems theory, corporate social responsibility and organizational theory that the stakeholder approach crystallized as a framework for strategic management in the 1980s. What follows is a brief summary of these building blocks of stakeholder theory.

## The corporate planning literature

The corporate planning literature incorporated a limited role for stakeholders in the development of corporate strategy. Ansoff's classic book *Corporate Strategy* (1965) illustrated the importance of identifying critical stakeholders. However, stakeholders were viewed as constraints on the main objective of the firm and Ansoff actually rejects the usefulness of the idea. Here there is a fundamental difference between the SRI approach and corporate planning. Corporate planning simply recognized that stakeholders might place limits on the action of the firm. Thus, management should understand the needs of stakeholders in order to set the bounds of operation. However, within these bounds management should develop strategies that maximize the benefits to a single stakeholder group, the shareholders. In contrast SRI saw the support of all stakeholders as central to the sucess of the firm. Therefore, successful strategies are those that integrate the interests of all stakeholders, rather than maximize the position of one group within limitations provided by the others.

The *process* of strategy development is also entirely different under these two approaches. Corporate planning has two main elements: prediction and adaptation. First, management carries out an environmental scan to identify trends that help predict the future business environment. Second, management identifies the best way for the firm to adapt to the future environment in order to maximize its position. Within corporate planning stakeholder analysis is carried out as part of the environmental scan. As such stakeholders can be defined by their roles rather than as complex and multifaceted individuals. Therefore, corporate planners could carry out stakeholder analysis at a generic level, without having to develop a detailed knowledge of the actual stakeholders in the specific firm under question. This level of abstraction led to many analytical breakthroughs in strategy formulation. Both Mason and Mitroff (1982) and Emshoff (1978) produced a method called "strategic assumptions analysis" to address these issues.

The progress that was made in strategy formulation by the corporate planning approach did, however, have some drawbacks. First, the generic level of analysis tended to lead to generic strategies that could be applied regardless of industry or circumstances. Second, the use of particular analytical techniques put an emphasis on measurement in purely economic terms. Strategists measured what could be measured. Thus, aspects of strategy formulation that are difficult to quantify, such as the nature of specific stakeholder relationships or tacit skills and knowledge, tend to be neglected.

## Systems theory and organization theory

Systems theory has complex roots, but the strand that is relevant to stakeholder theory was pioneered by Russell Ackoff and C. West Churchman (1947). These ideas were applied to organizational systems in the early 1970s (Ackoff, 1970, 1974). Systems theory emphasizes the external links that are part of every organization. Thus, organizations described as 'open systems' are part of a much larger network rather than as independent self-standing entities. Identification of both the stakeholders and the interconnections between them is a critical step in this approach. From a systems perspective, problems can only be solved with the support of all the members, or stakeholders, in the network. Systems theory emphasizes the development of collective strategies that optimize the network. Individual optimization strategies are not the focus of analysis for this type of approach. Individual strategies would simply result in sub-optimal network solutions.

Traditionally organizational theory comes from the same roots as systems theory. In the 1960s Katz and Kahn (1966) began to develop organizational frameworks that defined the organization relative to the system that surrounded it. Thompson (1967) introduced the concept of "clientele" to take into account groups outside the traditional boundary of the firm. These approaches foreshadowed attempts to emphasize the external environment as a significant explanatory factor of the organization of the firm (Pfeffer and Salancik, 1978). The intention behind these organizational theories was to describe and explain the existence and nature of the organization. However, there was little attempt to deal with the choices and decisions that managers make, nor with prescriptive attempts to set new directions for the organization. Nevertheless, the discovery that it is difficult to describe the firm without full recognition of the relationships on which it depends, has helped underline the fundamental importance of the stakeholder concept itself.

Systems theory and organization theory suffer some limitations in their application in the world of business. First, the collectivist nature of the approach makes it difficult to incorporate the autonomy of the firm. If firms have no autonomy then it is difficult to understand either the meaning of corporate strategy or the role of management. Second, once problems have been formulated there is no obvious starting or ending point for the analysis. Thus, the value of these approaches to business strategies seems limited to monopolistic markets, such as utilities, where the objectives of the firm and the objectives of the network come into alignment. However, despite the inherent problems in applying these ideas, the approaches have been helpful in emphasizing the importance of expanding analysis of strategic problems to include all stakeholders.

## *The corporate social responsibility literature*

This area of academic research represents a collection of approaches rather than a coherent theoretical grouping. A broad range of business and social agendas falls under this banner. However, what most of these approaches share is the inclusion of stakeholder groups that have traditionally been omitted from analysis. Indeed, many of these groups have been ignored because they were assumed to have an adversarial relationship with the firm. Thus, a major contribution of the social responsibility literature was to broaden the scope of stakeholder analysis and to impress on management the importance of building relationships with previously estranged groups. The social activist movement has demonstrated the dangers of developing strategies that ignore the influence of antagonistic groups.

Most of this stakeholder analysis has been carried out at a generic level, independent of the strategies of individual firms. However, because of the influence of several high profile cases of catastrophic damage to corporate reputations, some attempts have been made to incorporate these findings into general strategic business objectives. Many of these corporate social responsibility initiatives have simply ended up characterizing stakeholder relationships as constraints, much in the same way as the corporate planning literature. This separation effectively isolates certain (societal and environmental) stakeholder relationships from the other (business focused) stakeholder relationships. This has resulted in corporate social responsibility being seen as either an "add-on" luxury that can be only afforded by the most successful businesses, or as damage limitation insurance, rather than as a core input to corporate strategy. Additionally, there has been some confusion in the corporate responsibility literature around the priorities of stakeholders. There is one point of view that all stakeholders are equally important, simply because all have moral standing. It is difficult to document this position in the writings of stakeholder theorists, for instance in Freeman (1984), yet this idea that all stakeholders, defined widely, are equally important has been a barrier to further development of this theory.

## THE DISTINGUISHING CHARACTERISTICS OF A STAKEHOLDER APPROACH

The idea of stakeholders, or stakeholder management, or a stakeholder approach to strategic management, suggests that managers must formulate and implement processes which satisfy all and only those groups who have a stake in the business. The central task in this process is to manage and integrate the relationships and interests of shareholders, employees, customers, suppliers, communities and other groups in a way that ensures the long-term success of the firm. A stakeholder approach emphasizes *active* management of the business environment, relationships and the promotion of shared interests.

A stakeholder approach suggests that we redraw our picture of the firm, along the lines

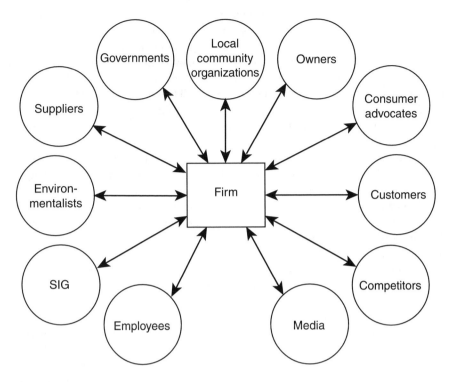

FIGURE 6.1 A typical stakeholder map
*Source*: Freeman (1984: 25). Used with permission.

of figure 6.1. For good or ill, there are myriad groups who have a stake in the success of the firm. Many traditional views of strategy have ignored some stakeholders, marginalized others and consistently traded-off the interests of others against favored stakeholder groups. Such an approach may well be appropriate in relatively stable environments. However, in a world of turbulence and accelerating change the limitations of traditional approaches to strategic management become increasingly apparent. The interests of key stakeholders must be integrated into the very purpose of the firm, and stakeholder relationships must be managed in a coherent and strategic fashion. The *stakeholder approach* that was developed from this work has several distinct characteristics:

First of all, a stakeholder approach is intended to provide a *single strategic framework*, flexible enough to deal with environmental shifts without requiring managers to regularly adopt new strategic paradigms. The intention is to break the confusing circle of "environmental shift → new strategic problem → development of new strategic framework → adoption of new strategic practices → new environmental shift → new problem."

Second, a stakeholder approach is a *strategic management* process rather than a strategic planning process. Strategic planning focuses on trying to predict the future environment and then independently developing plans for the firm to exploit its position. In contrast, strategic management actively plots a new direction for the firm and considers how the firm can affect the environment as well as how the environment may affect the firm.

Third, the central concern of a stakeholder approach is the *survival* of the firm, seen in Freeman's words as "the achievement of an organization's objectives." To survive in a turbulent environment management must *direct a course* for the firm, not merely optimize current output. To successfully change course, management must have the *support* of those who can affect the firm and understand how the firm will affect others (as in the long run they may make a reactive response). Therefore, understanding *stakeholder relationships* is, at least, a matter of achieving the organization's objectives which is in turn a matter of survival. The stakeholder framework does not rely on a single over-riding management objective for all decisions. As such it provides no rival to the traditional aim of "maximizing shareholder wealth." To the contrary, a stakeholder approach rejects the very idea of maximizing a single objective function as a useful way of thinking about management strategy. Rather, stakeholder management is a never-ending task of balancing and integrating multiple relationships and multiple objectives.

Fourth, a stakeholder approach encourages management to develop strategies by looking out from the firm and identifying, and investing in, all the relationships that will ensure long-term success. From this perspective it becomes clear that there is a critical role for values and "values-based management" within business strategy. Diverse collections of stakeholders can only cooperate over the long run if, despite their differences, they share a set of core values. Thus, for a stakeholder approach to be successful it must incorporate values as a key element of the strategic management process.

This characteristic helps explain the success and influence of the stakeholder concept within the fields of "business ethics" and "business and society." Scholars in these fields have added greatly to our understanding of how morality and ethics should play a role in the world of business, and stakeholder theory has played a very significant role in this progress. However, despite its association with business ethics as a separate discipline, a stakeholder approach remains a powerful and under-exploited theory of business strategy. Good stakeholder management develops integrated business strategies that are viable for stakeholders over the long run. While individual stakeholders may lose out on some individual decisions, all stakeholders remain supporters of the firm.

More so than in the early 1980s, when such an approach was being invented by a number of scholars, a stakeholder approach is even more appropriate to today's fast changing business environment. We propose that as the business world becomes ever more turbulent, interconnected and as the boundaries between firms, industries and our public and private lives become blurred, a stakeholder approach has more and more to tell us about both values and value creation.

Fifth, the stakeholder approach is both a *prescriptive* and *descriptive* approach, rather than purely empirical and descriptive. It calls for an approach to strategic management, which integrates economic, political, and moral analysis. Such an approach has implications for research in the discipline as well as practical results for managers. The purpose of a stakeholder approach to strategic management is to actively plan a new direction for the firm. It builds on concrete facts and analysis, and thus is descriptive, but it has to go beyond such description to recommend a direction for the firm, given its stakeholder environment. Stakeholder management suggests that stakeholder relationships can be created and influenced, not just taken as given. This is not merely a process of adapting the firm to management's best guess of the future environment. Strategic management is a process where management imaginatively plans how its actions might affect stakeholders and thus help to *create* the future environment. Stakeholder management is used to enrich management's understanding of the strategic options they can create.

Sixth, the stakeholder approach is about concrete "names and faces" for stakeholders rather than merely analyzing particular stakeholder roles. As such what is important is developing an understanding of the real, *concrete* stakeholders who are specific to the firm, and the circumstances in which it finds itself. It is only through this level of understanding that management can create options and strategies that have the support of all stakeholders. And it is only with this support that management can ensure the long-term survival of the firm. It matters less that management understands the reaction of "customers-in-general" to a price rise. It matters much more that they understand how *our actual* customers react, bearing in mind that the priority they were given during last winter's snowstorm, bearing in mind that they have 'tuned' their machinery to our product's specification and bearing in mind that the industry annual trade show is next month. It matters less that management understands that "shareholders-in-general" expect steady dividend growth. It matters more that we understand that our shareholders expect us to increase internal investment as fast as possible because they invested expecting us to be "first to market" with the next generation product. Good strategic management, according to this approach, emerges from the specifics rather than descending from the general and theoretical.

Finally stakeholder management calls for an *integrated* approach to strategic decision making. Rather than set strategy stakeholder by stakeholder, managers must find ways to satisfy multiple stakeholders simultaneously. Successful strategies integrate the perspectives of all stakeholders rather than offsetting one against another. This approach does not naively suggest that, by delving into the details, management can turn all constraints and trade-offs into a series of win-win situations. All stakeholders will not benefit all the time. Obviously, even with a detailed understanding of concrete stakeholder relationships, most strategies will distribute both benefits and harms between different groups of stakeholders. Win-win situations are not guaranteed. Indeed, it is just as important for management to develop strategies that distribute harms in a way that ensures the long-term support of all the stakeholders. Yet, over time, stakeholder interests must be managed in the same direction.

## RECENT WORK ON STAKEHOLDER MANAGEMENT

Since 1984 academic interest in a stakeholder approach has both grown and broadened. Indeed the number of citations using the word stakeholder has increased enormously as suggested by Donaldson and Preston (1995). Most of the research on the stakeholder concept has taken place in four sub-fields: normative theories of business; corporate governance and organizational theory; corporate social responsibility and performance; and, strategic management.

### A stakeholder approach to normative theories of business

A stakeholder approach emphasizes the importance of investing in the relationships with those who have a stake in the firm. The stability of these relationships depends on the sharing of, at least, a core of principles or values. Thus, stakeholder theory allows managers to incorporate personal values into the formulation and implementation of strategic plans. An example of this is the concept of an enterprise strategy. An enterprise strategy (Schendel and Hofer, 1979) describes the relationship between the firm and society by answering the question "What do we stand for?" In its original form a stakeholder approach emphasized the importance of developing an enterprise strategy, while leaving open the question of which type of values are the most appropriate. "It is very easy to misinterpret the foregoing analysis as yet another call for corporate social responsibility or business ethics. While these issues are important in their own right, enterprise level strategy is a different concept. We need to worry about the enterprise level strategy for the simple fact that corporate survival depends in part on there being some "fit" between the values of the corporation and its managers, the expectations of stakeholders in the firm and the societal issues which will determine the ability of the firm to sell its products" (Freeman, 1984: 107). However, the illustration that values are an essential ingredient to strategic management has, indeed, set in motion an inquiry into the normative roots of stakeholder theory.

Donaldson and Preston (1995) argued that stakeholder theories could be categorized from descriptive, instrumental or normative points of view. A descriptive theory would simply illustrate that firms have stakeholders; an instrumental theory would show that firms who consider their stakeholders devise successful strategies; a normative theory would describe why firms *should* give consideration to their stakeholders. Thus, the search for a normative justification for stakeholders takes the theory beyond strategic issues and into the realm of philosophical foundations.

The question this research stream is trying to answer is "above and beyond the consequences of stakeholder management, is there a fundamental moral requirement to adopt this style of management?" Various attempts have been made to ground stakeholder management in a broad range of philosophical foundations. Evan and Freeman (1993) developed a justification of a stakeholder approach based on Kantian principles. In its simplest form this approach argued that we are required to treat people "as ends unto themselves." Thus, managers should make corporate decisions respecting stakeholders' well being rather than treating them as *means to a corporate end*. This framework has been further developed by Norman Bowie (1999) into a fully fledged ethical theory of business. From a different perspective Phillips (1997) has grounded a stakeholder approach in the principle of fairness. When groups of individuals enter voluntarily into cooperative agreements they create an obligation to act fairly. As such, normal business transactions create a moral obligation for firms to treat stakeholders fairly and thus to consider their interests when making strategic decisions. Others (Wicks, Freeman, and Gilbert, 1994; Burton and Dunn, 1996) have tried to justify a stakeholder approach through the ethics of care. Contrasting the traditional emphasis on an individual rights-based approach to business, an ethics of care emphasizes the primacy of the network of relationships that create the business enterprise. This approach advocates the use of a stakeholder approach because of the need to formulate strategy in the context of the relationships that surround it, rather than with the firm as a lone actor. Finally, Donaldson and Dunfee (1999) have developed a justification for a stakeholder approach that is based on social contract theory.

Recently, Kochan (2000) has developed a normative stakeholder theory based on an extensive study of the Saturn automotive manufacturer. In this study he tries to answer the question "Why should stakeholder models be given serious consideration at this moment in history?" For Kochan this is both a normative and positive inquiry "and one that requires research that both explicates the normative issues and poses the theoretical questions in ways that promote tractable empirical research." He concludes that stakeholder firms will emerge when the stakeholders hold critical assets, expose these assets to risk and have both influence and voice. However, stakeholder firms will only be sustainable when leaders' incentives encourage responsiveness to stakeholders and when stakeholder legitimacy can overcome society's skeptical ideological legacy towards stakeholder management.

## A stakeholder approach to corporate governance and organizational theory

This stream of stakeholder research has grown out of the contrast between the traditional view that it is the fiduciary duty of management to protect the interests of the shareholder and the stakeholder view that management should make decisions for the benefit of all stakeholders. Williamson (1984) used a transaction cost framework to show that shareholders deserved special consideration over other stakeholders because of "asset specificity." He argued that a shareholder's stake was uniquely tied to the success of the firm and would have no residual value should the firm fail, unlike, for example, the labor of a worker. Freeman and Evan (1990) have argued, to the contrary, that Williamson's approach to corporate governance can indeed be used to explain all stakeholders' relationships. Many other stakeholders have stakes that are, to a degree, firm specific. Furthermore, shareholders have a more liquid market (the stock market) for exit than most other stakeholders. Thus, asset specificity alone does not grant a prime responsibility towards stockholders at the expense of all others.

Goodpaster (1991) outlined an apparent paradox that accompanies the stakeholder approach. Management appears to have a contractual duty to manage the firm in the interests of the stockholders and at the same time management seems to have a moral duty to take other stakeholders into account. This stakeholder paradox has been attacked by Boatright (1994) and Marens and Wicks (1999) and defended by Goodpaster and Holloran (1994). Others have explored the legal standing of the fiduciary duty of management towards stockholders (Blair, 1995; Orts, 1997). Many of these debates are on-going, with some advocating fundamental changes to corporate governance and with others rejecting the relevance of the whole debate to a stakeholder approach.

There have also been a number of attempts to expand stakeholder theory into what Jones (1995) has referred to as a "central paradigm" that links together theories such as agency theory, transactions costs and contracts theory into a coherent whole (Jones, 1995; Clarkson, 1995). From this perspective, stakeholder theory can be used as a counterpoint to traditional shareholder-based theory. While it is generally accepted that stakeholder theory could constitute good management practice, its main value for these theorists is to expose the traditional model as being morally untenable or at least too accommodating to immoral behaviour. This literature has historically consisted of a fractured collection of viewpoints that share an opposition to the dominant neoclassical positive approach to business. Because of its accommodating framework, the stakeholder concept provided an opportunity to develop an overarching theory that could link together such concepts as agency theory, transactions costs, human relationships, ethics and even the environment. More recently Jones and Wicks (1999) have explicitly tried to pull together diverging research streams in their paper "Convergent Stakeholder Theory."

## A stakeholder approach to social responsibility and social performance

A significant area of interest for theorists of social responsibility has been the definition of legitimate stakeholders. It has been stated that "one glaring shortcoming is the problem of stakeholder identity. That is, that the theory is often unable to distinguish those individuals and groups that are stakeholders from those that are not" (Phillips and Reichart, 1998). Mitchell, Agle, and Wood (1997) addressed this issue by developing a framework for stakeholder identification. Using qualitative criteria of *power, legitimacy and urgency*, they develop what they refer to as "the principle of who and what really counts." This line of research is particularly relevant in areas such as the environment and grassroots political activism. The critical question is whether there is such a thing as an illegitimate stakeholder, and if so how legitimacy should be defined. Bradley et al. (1999) have taken an opposite approach. Rather than try and theoretically define stakeholder legitimacy, they have conducted an empirical study to identify which stakeholders managers actually consider to be legitimate.

A large body of research has been carried out in order to test the "instrumental" claim that managing for stakeholders is just good management practice. This claim infers that firms practicing stakeholder management would out-perform firms that do not practice stakeholder management. Wood (1995) pointed out that causality is complex, the relationship between corporate social performance (CSP) and financial performance is ambiguous, there is no comprehensive measure of CSP and that the most that can be demonstrated with current data is that "bad social performance hurts a company financially."

It has often been hypothesized that firms who invest in stakeholder management and improve their social performance will be penalized by investors who are only interested in financial returns. This has been referred to as "the myopic institutions theory." Graves and Waddock (1990) have demonstrated the growth in importance of institutional stakeholders over the last twenty years. On further investigation they found that firms that demonstrated a high level of corporate social performance (CSP) tends to lead to an increase in the number of institutions that invest in the stock (Graves and Waddock, 1994). This result is "consistent with a steadily accumulating body of evidence that provides little support for the myopic institutions theory" (Graves and Waddock, 1994).

A range of recent studies have been carried out using new data and techniques to try shedding light on the links between stakeholder management and social and financial performance (Berman et al., 1999; Harrison and Fiet, 1999; Luoma and Goodstein, 1999). At a more practitioner level Ogden and Watson (1999) have carried out a detailed case study into corporate and stakeholder management in the UK water industry. At present most conclusions in this area are somewhat tentative as the precision of techniques and data sources continue to be developed.

## A stakeholder approach to strategic management

Harrison and St. John (1996, 1998) have provided leadership in developing an integrated approach with many of the conceptual frameworks of mainstream strategy theory. They argue that a stakeholder approach to strategic management allows the integration of perspectives from a variety of other traditional models, such as industrial organization economics, resource-based view, cognitive theory, and the institutional view of the firm. They distinguish between *stakeholder analysis* and *stakeholder management*. Stakeholder management is built on a partnering mentality that involves communicating, negotiating, contracting, managing relationships and motivating. These different aspects of stakeholder management are held together by the *enterprise strategy* which defines what the firm stands for. Ethics are a part of these processes, first, because unethical behaviour can have high costs and second, because codes of ethics provide the consistency and trust required for profitable cooperation.

Harrison and St. John (1996, 1998) are able to combine traditional and stakeholder approaches because they use the stakeholder approach as an overarching framework within which traditional approaches can operate as strategic tools. For example, they divide the environment into the *operating environment* and the *broader environment*. Within the *operating environment*, the "resource based view of the firm" is a useful framework to study the relationships of internal stakeholders such as management and employees. Equally, Porter's five-forces model (Porter, 1980) can be used to shed light on the relationships of many external stakeholders such as competitors and suppliers. However, strategic management does not stop at this analytical/ descriptive phase. Prioritizing stakeholders is more than a complex task of assessing the strength of their stake on the basis of economic or political power. "Priority is also a matter of strategic choice." (Harrison and St. John, 1998: 61). The values and the enterprise strategy of a firm may dictate priorities for particular partnerships and discourage others. Thus, a stakeholder approach allows management to infuse traditional strategic analysis with the values and direction that are unique to that organization.

Stakeholders must not only be understood in the present; they must also be managed over the long run. Harrison and St. John (1996, 1998) distinguish between two basic postures for managing stakeholders: *buffering* and *bridging* (Daft, 1992). *Buffering* is the traditional approach for most external stakeholder groups and it is aimed at containing the effects of stakeholders on the firm. It includes activities such as market research, public relations, and planning. Buffering raises the barriers between the firm and its external stakeholders. In contrast, *bridging* involves forming a strategic partnership (Barringer and Harrison, 2000). This approach requires recognizing common goals and lowering the barriers around the organization. Partnering is proactive and builds on interdependence. It is about creating and enlarging common goals rather than just adapting to stakeholder initiatives. They propose a framework for determining the importance of developing partnering tactics and when it is appropriate to rely on more traditional methods (see figure 6.2).

With this framework as a guide they have been able to identify a wide range of partnering tactics that can be used by management to manage their critical stakeholders and develop critical strategies (see table 6.1).

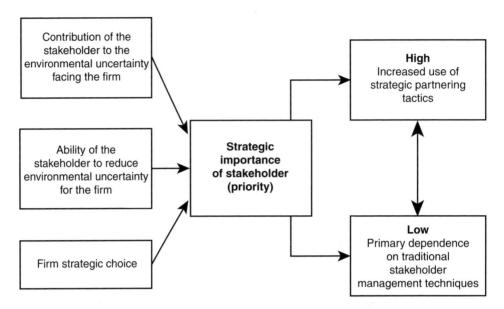

FIGURE 6.2 Factors influencing the strategic importance of external stakeholders and the basic approach to managing them
*Source*: Harrison and St. John (1996: 51).

TABLE 6.1 Tactics for managing and partnering with external stakeholders

| *Stakeholder* | *Stakeholder management tactics* | *Stakeholder partnering tactics* |
| --- | --- | --- |
| Customer | Customer services departments | Customer involvement on design teams |
| | Marketing research | Customer involvement in product testing |
| | Advertising | Joint planning sessions |
| | On-site visits | Enhanced communication linkages |
| | 800 Numbers | Joint training/service programs |
| | Long-term contracts | Sharing of facilities |
| | Product/service development | Financial investments in customer |
| | Market development | Appointment to board of directors |
| Suppliers | Purchasing departments | Supplier involvement on design teams |
| | Encourage competition among | Integration of ordering system with |
| | suppliers | manufacturing (i.e., just-in-time inventory) |
| | Sponsor new suppliers | Joint Information systems |
| | Threat of vertical integration | Jointly developing new products and |
| | Long-term contracts | applications |
| Competitors | Product and service differentiation | Kieretsu* |
| | Technological advances | Joint ventures for research and development |
| | Innovation | Joint venture for market development |

|  |  |  |
| --- | --- | --- |
|  | Speed | Collective lobbying efforts |
|  | Price cutting | Informal price leadership or collusion* |
|  | Market segmentation | Industry panels to deal with labor and |
|  | Intelligence systems | other problems |
|  | Corporate espionage* | Mergers (horizontal integration) |
| Government agencies/ administrators | Legal departments | Consortia on international trade and |
|  | Tax departments | competitiveness |
|  | Government relations departments | Jointly or government-sponsored research |
|  | Individual firm lobbying efforts | Joint ventures to work on social problems |
|  | Campaign contributions | such as crime and pollution |
|  | Individual firm political action committees | Joint foreign development projects |
|  | | Panels on product safety |
|  | Self-regulation | Appointment of retired government officials |
|  | Personal gifts to politicians* | to the board of directors |
|  | | Participation in government-sponsored initiatives |
| Local communities/ governments | Community relations offices | Task forces to solve skilled-labor shortages |
|  | Public relations advertising | Joint urban renewal programs |
|  | Involvement in community service/politics | Cooperative training programs |
|  | | Development committees/boards |
|  | Local purchases of supplies | Employment programs for workers with |
|  | Employment of local workers | special needs such as the handicapped |
|  | Donations to local government organizations | Joint education programs |
|  | Donations to local charities | |
|  | Gifts to local government officials* | |
| Activist groups | Internal programs to satsify demands | Consultation with members on sensitive issues |
|  | Public/political relations efforts to offset or protect from negative publicity | Joint ventures for research/research consortia |
|  | | Appointment of group representatives to |
|  | Financial donations | board of directors |
|  | | Jointly sponsored public relations efforts |
| Unions | Avoid unions through high levels of employee satisfaction | Mutually satisfactory (win-win) labor contracts |
|  | Avoid unions by thwarting attempts to organize* | Contract clauses that link pay to performance (i.e., profit sharing) |
|  | Hiring of professional negotiators | Joint committees on safety and other issues |
|  | Public relations advertising | of concern to employees |
|  | Chapter XI protection | Employee development programs |
|  | | Joint industry/labor panels |
|  | | Labor leaders appointed to board of directors included in major decisions |

---

* These tactics are of questionable ethical acceptability to some internal and external stakeholders in the US and elsewhere.
*Source*: Harrison and St. John (1996: 53). Used with permission.

## A STAKEHOLDER APPROACH AND MANAGEMENT PRACTICE

The impact of a stakeholder approach on management practice is difficult to establish. Much of contemporary debate and commentary is trapped in the rhetoric of a "stakeholder versus shareholder" debate. Once strategic management is divided into this false dichotomy, stakeholder theory can be mischaracterized as anti-capitalist, anti-profit and anti-business efficiency. For this reason the words "stakeholder management" have mostly been relegated to descriptions of a small number of radical businesses that are run very differently from mainstream corporations, for example Body Shop and Ben and Jerry's. However, the premise of the stakeholder approach that it is necessary for *all firms* would suggest that we should find many firms, rather than a radical few, using a stakeholder approach. Indeed that is what we find when we examine three recent books on the practice of management.

In *Built to Last* (Collins and Porras, 1994), Jim Collins and Jerry Porras put the "shareholder versus stockholder" debate in a new light. Collins and Porras attempted to explain the sustained success of firms across many industries by contrasting them with less successful peers. They proposed that a necessary condition of long-term financial success is *a strong set of core values* that permeates the organization. "Core values are like an ether that permeates an organization ... you can think of it as analogous to the philosophy of life that an individual might have. Core values are analogous to a biological organism's genetic code" (p. 29). The authors confirmed this hypothesis with a rigorous financial analysis of successful and unsuccessful firms over the last century. Not only does *Built to Last* provide strong support for the importance of an *enterprise strategy* as proposed in a stakeholder approach, many of the *core values* identified in the research confirm the importance of basing strategy on *collaborative stakeholder relationships*. For example 3M's core values include "a respect for individual initiative and personal growth"; Merck's core values include "profits, but profit from work that benefits humanity"; Hewlett-Packard's core values include "respect and opportunity for HP people" and "affordable quality for HP customers" and "profit and growth as a means to make all else possible"; Marriott's core values include "people are #1 – treat them well, expect a lot, and the rest will follow"; and Walt Disney's core values include "to bring happiness to millions, and to celebrate, nurture and promulgate wholesome American values."

*Built to Last* tells a story of the widespread use of a stakeholder approach by dozens of successful firms that include many elite multinationals. More importantly the authors found that the stakeholder approach in practice predates the formal articulation of stakeholder theory in academia. Thus, Collins and Porras provide both empirical support for the success of a stakeholder approach and they confirm that the academic theory grew out of management practice rather than vice versa.

In *The Stakeholder Strategy* (Svendsen, 1998), Svendsen investigates firms who are building a *collaborative stakeholder relationship* as part of their business strategy. From Wal-Mart, Marks and Spencer, Saturn, BankBoston and British Telecom to BC Hydro, Motoman Inc., Stillwater Technologies, and Van City Credit Union, she demonstrates how managements across the world are continuing to develop and implement their strategies by developing collaborative relationships with the stakeholders in their firms. Svendsen concludes that in an increasingly volatile world "the ability to balance the interests of all stakeholders will be a defining characteristic of successful companies in the next decade. This is not to say that companies will be able to satisfy everyone's interests all the time. However, companies that have a strong set of values and that can communicate their business goals clearly will maintain stakeholders' support when the results are not in their favor" (p. 188).

Wheeler and Sillanpaa (1997) trace the use of a stakeholder approach from Robert Owen, William Morris, Thomas Watson of IBM to The Body Shop. Their research illustrates the history, the rationale and the practical implementation of stakeholder ideas. They develop, and illustrate the use of, positively reinforcing *cycles of inclusion* that help build stronger and more cooperative stakeholder relationships. They also emphasize the need to *redescribe the world of business* in ways beyond, but not necessarily in contradiction to, the profit maximization view. As Anita Roddick points out in the foreword to the book, "Some of our best companies still retreat into 'shareholder value' justification for excellent community outreach programs when they should simply celebrate and say 'this is what business should be about'" (p. vii).

## AN AGENDA FOR FUTURE RESEARCH

So what are the critical issues facing a stakeholder approach to strategic management today? There are two main theoretical issues that stand out from the rest. First of all theorists must deal with what Freeman (1994) and Marens (1999) have called "The Separation Thesis." The Separation Thesis states that we cannot usefully analyze the world of business as if it is separate from the world of ethics or politics. Our personal values are embedded in all our actions; therefore unless our theories take this into account, they will do a poor job of explaining our world. The separation thesis was formulated because of the widespread adoption of a stakeholder approach within business ethics and because of the continued neglect of a stakeholder approach in the area of strategic management. This distortion has resulted in stakeholder theory being seen as an ethical rather than a business theory. This categorization serves to isolate ethical issues from the mainstream business theories and to isolate a stakeholder approach from mainstream business strategy.

Second, Wicks and Freeman (1998) have recently called for a pragmatist perspective to the study of management. A stakeholder approach grew out of a practical study of management problems. A pragmatic approach to strategic management would focus academic research on the detailed study of concrete business situations. Over time general theories might emerge, but not through abstract theory development.

Those who have called for a pragmatic approach to stakeholder theory have been seeking to combine a post-modern anti-foundationalist approach to theorizing with a Rortian desire to reform and redescribe the human enterprise (Wicks and Freeman, 1998). The post-modernist seeks to abandon the quest for Truth that began in the Enlightenment. These theorists argue that there is no truth about the world of business to be found. There are no irrefutable foundations for business theory or economics. The frameworks and laws that we use to describe business are simply ideas that have achieved a broad level of agreement among informed practitioners. To search for higher levels of abstraction, that would provide a foundation for these laws as Truth is a distraction to the progress of business strategy. To the contrary, the priority for business theorist should be to study the world of business and develop new ways to describe value creation and trade. New descriptions of bad or harmful business practices will inspire us to challenge existing practices, norms and attitudes. New ways of describing excellent ways of creating value will provide hope and stimulate change and innovation.

This approach to business research would challenge the idea that there is a separate world where "business is business" and where the fundamental principles, self-interest, unfettered competition and the maximizing of shareholder wealth have already been discovered. This approach would encourage researchers to challenge the language and metaphors of existing theories of business and economics. It would challenge the accepted laws and truths about business and to abandon the search for an overarching "true" paradigm of business. Rather, researchers should expect a multitude of theories and frameworks that describe different approaches and different aspects of business. There will still be good and bad theories of business strategy, but the value of the theory will depend on its ability to help managers make sense of their world, rather on the basis of theoretical elegance.

## CONCLUSION

The idea of stakeholders, or stakeholder management, or a stakeholder approach to strategic management, suggests that managers must formulate and implement processes which satisfy all and only those groups who have a stake in the business. The stakeholder approach grew out of clinical studies of management practice and integrated concepts from several streams of management theory. Over the last twenty years much progress has been made in theoretical and philosophical aspect aspects of stakeholder theory. The authors suggest that the time is right to switch attention to a more pragmatic approach that reconnects a stakeholder approach to management practice.

What would pragmatism mean for a stakeholder theory? First, it would mean the end of separate streams of business ethics and business strategy research. Second, it would mean an end to the search for normative or foundational roots for stakeholder theory. Third, it would mean abandoning the search for absolute object definitions of such things such as stakeholder legitimacy. These issues would depend on the question at hand and on the circumstances under consideration. A stakeholder approach might consist of a collection of interacting, reinforcing and contradicting theories of business strategy. Each theory would be based on concrete studies of real business case studies. This is not to say that we need to abandon the idea of general principles for the sake of contingent theories. At any point in time there will always be theories, based on specific examples, whose message holds true for a great many businesses and managers. These will still be general principles of business; indeed the idea that businesses should be managed in the interests of stakeholders is one of those ideas. However these principles will, over time, be continuously under review and will eventually be replaced by a description that is more useful. The work of Kochan and Rubenstein (2000) is, in many ways, at the vanguard of this approach. As outlined above there are theoretical, epistemological and research challenges for a stakeholder approach to strategic management. We believe that these challenges should be met by turning our faces towards practitioners and the development of a set of narratives that illustrate the myriad ways of creating value for stakeholders.

## NOTE

1 Recently, Mr Giles Slinger has revisited the early history of the idea of stakeholders. Through more extensive interviews, and the examination of a number of historical documents, Slinger rewrites the history as told in Freeman (1984). The essential difference is that the early use of the stakeholder idea was not particularly oriented towards the survival of the firm. Slinger's argument can be found in his doctoral dissertation, *Stakeholding and Takeovers: Three Essays*, University of Cambridge, forthcoming in 2001. An abridged version is in "Spanning the Gap: The Theoretical Principles Connecting Stakeholder Policies to Business Performance," Centre for Business Research, Department of Applied Economics, Working Paper, University of Cambridge, 1998.

## REFERENCES

Ackoff, R. (1970). *A concept of corporate Planning*. New York: Wiley.

Ackoff, R. (1974). *Redesigning the Future*. New York: Wiley.

Ackoff., R., and Churchman, C. (1947). An experimental definition of personality. *Philosophy of Science*, 14: 304–32.

Ansoff, I. (1965). *Corporate Strategy*. New York: McGraw-Hill.

Barringer, B. R., and Harrison, J. S. (2000). Walking a tightrope: Creating value through inter-organizational relationships. *Journal of Management*, 26: 367–403.

Berman, S., Wicks, A., Kotha, S., and Jones, T. (1999). Does stakeholder orientation matter: The relationship between stakeholder management models and firm financial performance. *Academy of Management Journal*, 42: 488–506.

Blair, M. (1995). Whose interests should be served? In *Ownership and Control: Rethinking Corporate Governance for the Twenty-first century*. Washington, DC: The Brookings Institution, 202–24.

Boatright, J. (1994). Fiduciary duties and the shareholder-management relation: Or, what's so special about shareholders? *Business Ethics Quarterly*, 393–407.

Bowie, N. (1999). *Business Ethics: A Kantian Perspective*. Oxford: Blackwell.

Bradley. R., Agle, B., Mitchell, R., and Sonnenfeld, J. (1999). Who matters to CEOs? An investigation of stakeholder attributes and salience, corporate performance, and CEO values. *Academy of Management Journal*, 42: 507–25.

Burton, B., and Dunn, C. (1996). Collaborative control and the commons: Safeguarding employee rights. *Business Ethics Quarterly*, 6: 277–88.

Clarkson, M. (1995). A stakeholder framework for analyzing and evaluating corporate social performance. *Academy of Management Review*, 20: 92–117.

Collins, J., and Porras, J. (1994). *Built to Last*. New York: Harper.

Daft, R. L. (1992). *Organization Theory and Design*, 4th Edn. St Paul, MN: West Publishing Company.

Donaldson, T., and Dunfee, T. (1999). *Ties that Bind: A Social Contracts Approach to Business Ethics*. Boston: Harvard Business School Press.

Donaldson, T., and Preston, L. (1995). The stakeholder theory of the corporation: Concepts, evidence, and implications. *Academy of Management Review*, 20: 65–91.

Emshoff, J. (1978). *Managerial Breakthroughs*. New York: AMACOM.

Evan, W., and Freeman, E. (1993). A stakeholder theory of the modern corporation: Kantian capitalism. In T. Beauchamp, and N. Bowie, *Ethical Theory and Business*, 5th edn. Englewood Cliffs: Prentice-Hall.

Freeman, R. E. (1984). *Strategic Management: A Stakeholder Approach*. Boston: Pitman.

Freeman, R. E., and Evan, W. (1990). Corporate goverance: A stakeholder interpretation, *Journal of Behavioral Economics*, 19(4): 337–59.

Goodpaster, K. (1991). Business ethics and stakeholder analysis. *Business Ethics Quarterly*, 1: 53–73.

Goodpaster, K., and Holloran, T. (1994). In defense of a paradox. *Business Ethics Quarterly*, 4: 423–30.

Graves, S. B., and Waddock, S.A. (1990). Institutional ownership and control: Implications for long-term corporate performance. *Academy of Management Executive*, 37: 1034–46.

Graves, S. B., and Waddock, S. A. (1994). Institutional owners and corporate social performance. *Academy of Management Journal*, 37: 1034–46.

Harrison, J. S., and Fiet, J. (1999). New CEOs pursue their own self-interests by sacrificing stakeholder values. *Journal of Business Ethics*, 19: 301–308.

Harrison, J. S. and St. John, C. H. (1996). Managing and partnering with external stakeholders. *Academy of Management Executive*, 10(2): 46–59.

Harrison, J. S. and St. John, C. H. (1998). *Strategic Management of Organizations and Stakeholders: Concepts and Cases*, 2nd Edn. Cincinnati, OH: South-Western Publishing.

Jones, T. (1995). Instrumental stakeholder theory: A synthesis of ethics and economics. *Academy of Management Review*, 20: 92–117.

Jones, T., and Wicks, A. (1999). Convergent stakeholder theory. *Academy of Management Review*, 24: 206–21.

Katz, D., and Kahn, R. (1966). *The Social Psychology of Organizations*. New York: Wiley.

Kochan, T. (2000). Towards a stakeholder theory of the firm: The Saturn partnership. *Organizational Science*, 11(4): 367–86

Luoma, P., and Goodstein, J. (1999). Stakeholders and corporate boards: Institutional influences on board composition and structure. *Academy of Management Journal*, 42: 553–63.

Marens, R. (1999). Getting real: Stakeholder theory, managerial practice, and the general irrelevance of fiduciary duties owed to shareholders. *Business Ethics Quarterly*, 9(2): 273–93.

Mason, R., and Mitroff, I. (1982). *Challenging Strategic Assumption*. New York: Wiley.

Mitchell, R., Agle, B., and Wood D. (1997). Toward a theory of stakeholder identification and salience: Defining the principle of who and what really counts. *Academy of Management Review*, 22: 853–86.

Ogden, S., and Watson, R. (1999). Corporate performance and stakeholder management: Balancing shareholder and customer interests in the UK privatized water industry. *Academy of Management Journal*, 42: 526–38.

Orts, E. (1997). A north American legal perspective on stakeholder management theory. In F. Patfield (ed.), *Perspectives on Company Law*, 2: 165–79.

Pfeffer, J., and Salancik, G. (1978). *The External Control of Organizations*. New York: Harper.

Phillips, R. (1997). Stakeholder theory and a principle of fairness. *Business Ethics Quarterly*, 7: 50–66.

Phillips, R., and Reichart, J. (1998). The environment as a stakeholder: A fairness-based approach. *Journal of Business Ethics*, 23(2): 185–97.

Porter, M. (1980). *Competitive Strategy: Techniques for Analyzing Industries and Competitors*. New York: Free Press.

Schendel, D., and Hofer, C. (eds.) (1979). *Strategic Management: A New View of Business Policy and Planning*. Boston: Little, Brown.

Slinger, G. (1998). Spanning the Gap: The theoretical principles connecting stakeholder policies to business performance. Centre for Business Research, Department of Applied Economics, Working Paper, University of Cambridge.

Slinger, G. (2001). *Stakeholding and Takeovers: Three Essays.* University of Cambridge doctoral thesis, Department of Applied Economics, forthcoming.

Svendsen, A. (1998). *The Stakeholder Strategy.* San Francisco: Berrett-Koehler Inc.

Thompson, J. (1967). *Organizations in action.* New York: McGraw-Hill.

Wheeler, D., and Sillanpaa, M. (1997). *The Stakeholder Corporation.* London: Pitman Publishing.

Wicks, A., and Freeman, E. (1998). Organization studies and the new pragmatism: Positivism, anti-positivism, and the search for ethics. *Organization Science,* 9(2): 123–40.

Wicks, A., Freeman, E. and Gilbert, D. (1994). A feminist reinterpretation of the stakeholder concept. *Business Ethics Quarterly,* 4: 475–97.

Williamson, O. (1984). *The Economic Institutions of Capitalism.* New York: Free Press.

Wood, D. J. (1995). The *Fortune* database as a CSP measure. *Business and Society,* 24(2): 1997–9.

# 7

# Towards a Positive Interpretation of Transaction Cost Theory: The Central Roles of Entrepreneurship and Trust

GARETH R. JONES

For several years, there has been a rising tide of articles that have been critical of some of the central assumptions of transaction cost theory (e.g., Dow, 1987; Granovetter, 1985; Perrow, 1986; Robins, 1987; Donaldson, 1990; Noorderhaven, 1995; Ghoshal and Moran, 1996). Criticism of any theory is central to academic debate because it can lead to further refinement or modification of a theory. Conversely, given that a theory can never be proven, only falsified (Popper, 1958), criticism can also lead to a theory being discarded when it cannot adequately explain observed facts. The nature of the criticism that has recently been directed at transaction cost theory is clearly of the "falsification kind." For example, Ghoshal and Moran recently attempted to debunk the theoretical foundation of transaction cost economics by attacking Williamson's assumption of opportunism. An attack that is necessary, Ghoshal and Moran (1996: 14) believe, because acceptance of the assumptions of transaction cost theory will lead to "debilitating consequences for organizations whose managers knowingly or unknowingly adopt its prescriptions."

Such strong criticism of a theoretical perspective is relatively rare in organizational theory. Williamson's (1975) postulate of opportunism, in particular, seems to raise a considerable degree of ire. His assumption that some people may be inclined to act in a "self-interest seeking way with guile" not only threatens firmly held humanistic values (Perrow, 1986), it also seems to several researchers to be theoretically ill-defined and conceptually unsatisfactory (e.g., Dow, 1987; Noorderhaven, 1995). Indeed, some have argued that the concept of opportunism has been used for analytical convenience to allow transaction cost theory to predict the movement to internalize transactions in a hierarchy (Granovetter, 1985; Perrow, 1986). The price of this, however, has been an ontologically inaccurate description of human nature (Donaldson, 1990; Ghoshal and Moran, 1996), one that distorts the real rationale for the emergence of social and economic organization. Indeed, recent interest in the "knowledge based view of the firm" has centered, in large part, on the relative merits of opportunism versus knowledge coordination as the appropriate theoretical basis for a theory of the firm (e.g., Conner and Prahalad, 1996; Foss, 1996a, b; Grant, 1996; Kogut and Zander, 1996; Madhok, 1996).

For those researchers who embrace the transaction cost approach and see considerable utility in the theory's ability to explain observed facts (e.g., Joskow, 1988; Masten, 1994; Schelanski and Klein, 1995), the ever increasing criticisms that have been directed against transaction cost theory because of the assumption of opportunism are distressing. It would seem that to use transaction cost theory one has to buy into Williamson's "unattractive view of human nature," one which "makes little provision for attributes such as kindness, sympathy, solidarity, and the like" (Williamson, 1985: 391–2).

The purpose of this paper is to offer a critique of transaction cost theory (TCT) that offers a reappraisal of the theory's basic assumptions and postulates in order to reveal its previously neglected positive and humanistic side. In so doing, this paper seeks to reorient TCT and demonstrate that (1) it is possible to embrace the central tenets of the theory and thus preserve the predictive ability of TCT while (2) weakening and even dispensing with the negative and emotive connotations or implications of terms such as opportunism and asset specificity and, thus, Williamson's "grim" view of human behavior.

First, a brief account of the history of TCT is given. Second, Williamson's (1975, 1985) postulates are critically examined and an alternative account of the human and environmental factors that give rise to transaction costs is presented. Then, based on this critique and analysis, a positive interpretation of TCT and of the emergence of organizational hierarchies is offered and a model of the value creation process based on the process of specialization and the development of specific assets is described. In essence, this analysis demonstrates that a strong assumption of opportunism is neither a necessary nor a sufficient condition for transaction cost theory to be able to generate refutable propositions and hypotheses. The real problem associated with the development of asset specificity is the measurement problems that arise when entrepreneurs take advantage of new ways to create value, not the potential for opportunism that comes into being when parties make specific investments in each other. Thus, TCT is not a flawed transplant from economics but a valuable addition and refinement to organizational theory that has taken the analysis of organizational issues and the theory of the firm to a new level of sophistication.

## A Brief History of Transaction Cost Theory

Typically, in TCT, transaction costs are conceptualized as the costs of negotiating, monitoring, and enforcing exchanges between parties. Transaction costs are often regarded as the friction of exchange (Powell, 1990), costs that must be borne for an exchange to take place but which nevertheless reduce the potential value that could be realized by a transaction. Hence, efficiency is increased whenever the parties to a transaction can find a governance structure that economizes on transaction costs. It is important to recognize, however, that efficiency in TCT is not conceptualized as some ratio of inputs to outputs, but as pareto efficiency where governance modes are compared according to their ability to facilitate transactions until the point at which it is impossible to make one party better off without making the other party worse off. Failure to recognize the value-optimizing, rather than cost-minimizing emphasis implicit in TCT, and in neoclassical economics in general, has led to many of the misunderstandings that have arisen about the theory, as discussed below.

The seminal idea behind TCT was expressed in Coase's (1937) paper in which he suggested that the operation of a market costs something and by forming an organization and allowing an entrepreneur to control and direct resources, the costs of making transactions in the market or transaction costs are avoided. If, for example, the parties to a transaction are exchanging non-specialized, freely-obtainable goods or services, the market price mechanism can be used to manage the transaction and parties do not have to enter into complicated forms of agreement to allow exchange to take place. If, however, the parties become involved in a specialized, embedded, exchange relationship, problems arise in determining what the appropriate prices are, and if it becomes too expensive to operate in the market (transaction costs increase) there will be a movement to internalize the transaction by bringing it inside the boundaries of one organization where one party has the authority to dictate and oversee the terms of the transaction and reduce the risks associated with it (Coase, 1937).

By replacing market transacting with transacting through a hierarchy, however, the transaction costs of managing exchanges are not eliminated (Coase, 1937). Managers also have to negotiate, monitor, and enforce the terms of the contracts among parties inside the organization. This, too, can result in risk since once the transaction is internalized, the parties or employees charged to carry out the transaction may have less incentive or desire to perform efficiently or effectively because they may prefer to pursue their own goals and objectives. Thus, Coase's central insight and theorem, and the reason why he was awarded the Nobel prize for economics, is that decision makers are situated at a boundary where, using a pareto efficiency approach, they have to constantly trade off the transaction costs of using the market against the costs of managing exchanges through a hierarchy.

The trade-off between the transaction costs associated with managing transactions in the market or in a hierarchy defines the efficient boundary of the firm; the pareto efficiency calculation determines which transactions firms prefer to leave in the market and which they bring into the hierarchy. However, as Coase (1988) notes, economists simultaneously embraced his theorem but then ignored it because, while interesting, it had little predictive power. The theorem had little predictive power because Coase did not provide a full or clear account of the factors that affect the level of transaction costs or organization costs and that, therefore, lead to the decision to internalize transactions inside a firm. For example, although the concept of asset specificity was integral to the development of his theorem, it was nevertheless only implicit in his writings (Coase, 1991b: 54–5). Klein, Crawford, and Alchian (1978) and Williamson (1985) formally develop asset specificity as the major factor leading to transaction difficulties, and therefore costs, and the decision to internalize transactions inside a hierarchy. Without some comprehensive analysis of the factors that could predict why and how transactions would move from market to hierarchy or back again, Coase's theorem was tautological because it could not be operationalized.

Perhaps the most important of Williamson's (1975, 1985) many substantive contributions to TCT was to provide the formal postulates that theoretically articulated the origin of transaction costs in the market – in essence, he provided the tools necessary to operationalize the theory and give it predictive power. In his view, the factors that produce equivocality and ambiguity in the contracting process and give rise to transaction costs are the result of the combination of certain human and environmental factors (Williamson, 1975: 40). The two human factors in the model are bounded rationality and opportunism. Bounded rationality means that the rationality of human behavior is limited by the ability of actors to process information; agents are intendedly rational, but only limitedly so. Opportunism, as noted earlier, means self-interest seeking with guile.

There are three main environmental factors in the model. The first is uncertainty and complexity which, given bounded rationality, increase one party's difficulty in monitoring the performance of the other and raises transaction costs. The second is the existence of a small numbers trading condition which limits the availability of other potential trans-action partners and thus raises the possibility of opportunism. That is, in some markets a small number of viable trading partners may exist so that market prices can become distorted from opportunistic bargaining. The third factor is asset-specificity which refers to investments in assets or value-creating resources that parties make in specific exchange relationships that are not transferable to other relationships, or which are of less value in their next best use.[1] For example, asset specificity arises from an investment in assets such as skilled labor, dedicated machines, or custom-designed computer software or hardware that are specific or dedicated to a particular exchange relationship.

As evident in Williamson's writings over time, asset specificity is the principal factor that gives rise to transaction costs, "Asset specificity is the big locomotive to which transaction cost economics owes much of its predictive content" (Williamson, 1985: 86). The central problem facing the individual or firm that has to decide about whether or not to make a specific investment on behalf of another individual or firm concerns the possibility that the other party may subsequently act opportunistically and attempt to turn the terms of the exchange in their favor by cheating or defrauding the other in some way once the investment has been made (*ex post* opportunism) because one party becomes dependent on the other as a small numbers trading condition or "bilateral monopoly" emerges. Opportunism becomes all the more likely if one party finds it more difficult to evaluate the performance of the other as the transaction extends over time so that uncertainty increases, which given bounded rationality only adds to the transaction difficulty (Williamson, 1975).

## THE JANUS-FACED NATURE OF TCT ASSUMPTIONS

What is noticeable in Williamson's approach is that, although he includes human factors in his model – bounded rationality and opportunism, he accords these a *passive* role and treats them as rational axioms about behavior or as postulates about human beings similar to intelligence or personality. In Williamson's model, opportunism or bounded rationality may differ from person to person much as personality or intelligence do (which is why only some people are assumed to be prone to act opportunistically Williamson, 1993a, b) but when transaction costs change, they do so because of changes in the environment, not in the person. For example, transaction costs rise when a change in the environment increases uncertainty, which given bounded rationality, increases negotiating and monitoring problems; when asset specificity increases, the number of trading partners falls, and given opportunism, problems of negotiating and monitoring the other party will increase. Thus, although he claims it is the combination of human factors and environmental factors that give rise to transaction costs, in his model, transaction costs are determined exogenously by changes in the environment. In other words, opportunistic inclinations will be actualized and lead to opportunistic behavior whenever conditions in the environment allow it (or an external governance structure does not prevent it).

In this paper, however, transaction costs are seen as being endogenously determined by person × situation interactions. This theoretical difference helps to explain the debate between Williamson and his critics over the way human postulates should be conceptualized in his model and in transaction cost theory in general (Noorderhaven, 1995). Below we first examine how opportunism is determined endogenously and then look at bounded rationality.

## Opportunism or trust?

Although the level of transaction costs depends on the extent to which people are inclined to act opportunistically, it is important to differentiate between two ways of viewing opportunism. The first view, Williamson's view, is that opportunism is an enduring disposition. That is, he views opportunism as a stable human propensity to act in a self-seeking way with guile: a propensity which gives rise to transaction costs because parties must spend time and invest in information to monitor the other's potential opportunistic behavior to detect whether or not the other party is behaving opportunistically. Since the development of asset specificity increases the risk or possibility of being subject to such opportunistic actions, in Williamson's model, one party prospectively, or *ex ante*, calculates the prospective risk, and then decides what governance structure should be created to avoid the potential losses that would be incurred as the result of the other's opportunism (Williamson, 1993a).

This paper adopts a very different view of opportunism that is drawn from an interactionist perspective rather than from a dispositional view. From an interactionist perspective, opportunism can be seen as both a disposition and a psychological state produced by the interaction of person and situational factors. In other words, the state of opportunism is not only the result of an enduring tendency to act in an opportunistic manner; it is also affected by many other personal and situational characteristics such as a person's attitudes, beliefs, and a person's past experience across many different social contexts, each characteristic of which may change, sometimes quickly, over time. Psychological states, such as opportunism, can change as a result of both changes in the environment and changes occurring inside a person over time – for example, as knowledge about a transaction partner changes or as increasing familiarity with a situation changes the way in which it is perceived.

Once the difference between opportunism as a trait and state is recognized, it becomes important to contrast it with propensity to trust others and the state of trust. In the literature, trust is commonly viewed as the converse of opportunism, as an expression of confidence between the parties in an exchange of some kind – confidence that they will not be harmed or put at risk by the actions of the other party (Axelrod, 1984; Bateson, 1988; Zucker, 1986). The need to trust also only arises because of uncertainty about future outcomes (Axelrod, 1984; Barber, 1983; Dasgupta, 1988). Conceptualized as states, people's inclinations can range the full behavioral spectrum from being opportunistic to being trusting or trustworthy. It is impossible to predict how a person will behave unless the interaction between person and current situation is considered because knowing only a person's trait is not sufficient to predict how they will behave in any particular situation. Other relevant personal and situational characteristics must be specified to predict behavior, particularly because opportunism and trust are dynamic psychological states that can change quickly over time (Axelrod, 1984; Barber, 1983; Gambetta, 1988). For example, a small business owner who discovers that a trusted employee has been embezzling funds may experience an immediate breakdown in the experience of trust.

The question that TCT fails to analyze and which Williamson assumes away because of his stable dispositional view of opportunism is what would cause exchange partners to adopt either an "opportunism" or a "trust" state or mindset to structure their interactions with one another. *A priori*, nothing can be assumed about the origins of a party's psychological state and his or her propensity to behave towards others except that they behave self-interestedly. However, note that it can be equally in one's self-interest to trust another person and to cooperate as it is to harm another person so the pursuit of self-interest has no inherent negative connotations (Axelrod, 1984; Bateson, 1988). Is there any reason to believe, therefore, that people would approach transactions with a propensity to behave one way or another?

There are several reasons to believe that it is psychologically more efficient for people to approach a transaction with a propensity to trust each other rather than a propensity to behave opportunistically. First, from a state point of view, the transactions that people are engaged in are embedded in time, and self-interested people know from their past experiences in many different social contexts that if they do act opportunistically this destroys any beliefs that they, and the other party, can trust each other – reputation does matter (Nooteboom, Berger, and Noorderhaven, 1997). Thus, if either party acts opportunistically, this immediately destroys any perceptions the other has that he or she can be trusted, destroys any reputation effect, and makes both parties' behaviors unreliable, making the future unpredictable (Axelrod, 1984). This paper argues that since people have learned from past experience that opportunism and trust are interrelated, and that the former destroys the latter, that when uncertainty and risk exists, it is more efficient to start from the state of trust rather than opportunism (unless one has reason to believe otherwise). Essentially, any particular transaction is embedded in one of many ongoing exchange relationships and people are able to extrapolate easily from one situation to the next, to make inferences about others, and to decide on the most efficient way to behave. Note that starting from a basic premise of trust rather than opportunism does not preclude the fact that opportunism may and can occur. Rather, what is being suggested here is that it is more efficient to assume the other is trustworthy until proven otherwise.

The goal of the parties to an exchange is to find a governance structure that economizes on the costs of exchange, or transaction costs, in order to maximize the joint value of what is exchanged. At the beginning of a social encounter, it is much more efficient for each party to suspend belief that the other party may not be trustworthy than it is to assume that they will be opportunistic, when uncertainty and risk is present. This does not mean that either party is gullible – a gullible person is one who, in the absence of any information of any kind, takes the other's trustworthiness on faith and assumes the risk of being exploited (e.g., Rotter, 1980). The actor in our model is not naïve, he or she just suspends belief that the other is anything but trustworthy and behaves as if the other can be trusted.

Beyond the argument that opportunism and trust are best viewed as states rather than traits in TCT, the literature on trust offers additional reasons to believe that in uncertain situations parties to an exchange are much more likely to approach the interaction with a trust mindset rather than an opportunism mindset. First, as Luhmann (1980: 72) suggests, the propensity to trust is more likely than the propensity to distrust another and assume possible opportunism because distrust "often absorb[s] the strength of the person who distrusts to an extent which leaves him[her] little energy to explore and adapt to his[her] environment . . . and hence allow him[her] fewer opportunities for learning." In other words, if you approach interactions with a distrust mindset you have to constantly spend time and effort to guard against being harmed by the other person since you are always on the lookout for the "shot in the dark." So, relatively, trust is the more efficient option because it economizes on time and information processing requirements; and for this reason, there is an incentive to begin a relationship with trust.

Second, consider the situation of a person attempting to decide if another person will behave opportunistically or behave in a trustworthy way. An enormous amount of time and energy would be taken up in discovering the true nature of the other's inclinations, leading to a major advantage associated with suspending belief that another person has sinister motives (Deutsch, 1958, 1960). Assuming the state of trust until proven otherwise economizes on transaction costs. Furthermore, as several authors have pointed out (Granovetter, 1985; Ghoshal and Moran, 1996; Hill, 1990; Nooteboom et al., 1997), the very fact that transactions are embedded in a social and cultural infrastructure promotes the development of trust between people and makes it, rather than opportunism, the "taken for granted rule" (Berger and Luckman, 1966) rather than the exception.

Chiles and McMackin (1996) also examine the relationship between risk and trust in TCT, arguing that trust allows managers to delay the point at which they internalize transactions. However, Chiles and McMackin (1996: 88) view trust as a mechanism for constraining opportunistic behavior and reducing bounded rationality, rather than a state or mindset that forms the foundation for the nature of the transaction itself. Put simply, with a trust mindset, there may be no opportunistic behavior to constrain, and if it does arise – one party acts opportunistically – trust will disappear quickly as one party becomes aware of the opportunistic inclinations of the other and no exchange will take place – unless there are few or no alternatives and the injured party is forced to acquiesce to the demands of the opportunistic partner.

There is another important reason for assuming that the state of trust rather than opportunism will be the mindset adopted by potential transaction partners: trust is a state that can change quickly over time, and as the experience of trust changes, the nature or quality of the transaction between people changes (Shapiro, Sheppard, and Cheraskin, 1992; Lewicki and Bunker, 1996). As noted above, at the beginning of an encounter, the parties simply assume the other is trustworthy until proven otherwise. However, over the course of repeated interactions, the parties exchange increasing amounts of information and knowledge. They come to know each other's attitudes and beliefs, and most importantly they may come to share similar guiding or orienting values, values which determine which types of behaviors, people, or situations are desirable and undesirable (Rokeach, 1973). When shared values structure exchanges, parties are more likely to invest in the relationship and look to the future rather than the present when deciding how to behave (Dasgupta, 1988). Parties are more likely to adopt broader role definitions, engage in help-seeking behaviors, and to set aside personal gains for the greater good, all of which enhance the cooperative experience between people.

The point at which parties share similar values is the crucial point at which a transaction transforms into a relationship. From this point on, the other's trustworthiness is taken as a given, based on confidence in the other's values backed up by empirical evidence derived from repeated behavioral interactions (Gulati, 1995; Zaheer, McEvily, and Perrone, 1998). The importance of this change in the experience of trust over time for TCT is that, when transactions become relationships, the form of cooperation between the parties becomes quite different and changes the quality or atmosphere of the exchange relationship (Nooteboom et al., 1997; Robinson, 1996). Thus, the changing nature of trust over time between people can confer greater and greater benefits on people individually and collectively.

Note that the changing nature of trust over time on transactions and cooperation has no place inside Williamson's analysis because his treatment of opportunism as a disposition and not a state does not allow for the experience of either trust or opportunism to modify or change significantly over the short run. In his model, opportunism is a given. There is no place for repeated interactions and for the effects of past experience to condition the transaction (or relationship) between them.

The differences that arise from using trust rather than opportunism to frame TCT has substantive implications for the way one analyzes the reasons for the emergence of hierarchies. When an initial state of trust in others rather than an assumption of human nature as opportunistic is posited as the first human factor in the model, a key concern is how changes in the environment increase the level of uncertainty and affect peoples' ability or desire to trust one another. Similarly, it is important to analyze how the development of asset-specificity in exchanges between people necessitates the existence of trust.

From a trust perspective, it is the need to promote, sustain, and strengthen the state of trust and prevent its dissolution in order to jointly optimize the benefits that will result from interactions that is key to the decision to internalize transactions and move from the market to the hierarchy. The issue from a positive TCT perspective is to uncover the characteristics of the trustor, trustee, and the situation that can threaten this expression of confidence (trust) and to analyze how the emergence of a hierarchy can be viewed positively as a governance structure adopted by the parties not just for contractual reasons, but to allow them to sustain and manage the experience of trust so that they can continue to cooperate with each other. However, before the relationship between trust and hierarchy can be addressed it is necessary to look at different possible approaches to understanding the transaction cost implications of bounded rationality.

## *Bounded rationality or entrepreneurship?*

As noted earlier, Williamson (1975) also argued that the need to economize on the transaction costs that result from the combination of bounded rationality with uncertainty and complexity gives rise to the use of a hierarchical governance mechanism. For example, the presence of hierarchical control and incentive systems allows managers to economize on the governance costs of transactions, especially when information impactedness increases due to the development of specific assets or a rapidly changing environment.

Williamson's (1993b: 459) focus on the need to "organize transactions so as to economize on bounded rationality" also has certain negative connotations attached to it. The negative connotations of his view arise from his treatment of bounded rationality and uncertainty. First, his treatment of bounded rationality essentially views people as being passive and defensive when confronted with the vagaries of an uncertain environment. As noted earlier, Williamson views bounded rationality as leading to transaction difficulties because people either cannot obtain or cannot process the amount of information needed to effectively deal with uncertainty; people are intentionally rational but only limitedly so. Thus, because of bounded rationality (an essential part of the human condition) the possibility of loss arises and people and organizations are put at risk (Chiles and McMackin, 1996; Shapira, 1995). Second, Williamson's view of uncertainty implicitly assumes that the environment is hostile, since uncertainty is treated as a threat that must be managed by finding a governance structure that allows managers to economize on transaction costs. The implication of this view is that people are always on the defensive because of the need to respond to threats that stem from an uncertain environment. Essentially, in his model the view is one of people trying to solve the transaction difficulties that result from their inability to control the environment.

Williamson's framing of the transaction difficulties that result from the combination of bounded rationality and complexity totally ignores the many positive, humanistic benefits that arise from the very existence of bounded rationality and uncertainty. As will be discussed below, both bounded rationality and uncertainty may be better conceptualized as opportunities, not as threats.

The point of departure for the positive perspective adopted in this paper is Knight's (1921) analysis of the relationship between uncertainty, risk, and entrepreneurship, and Coase's idea that what is important in TCT is not so much the problems associated with managing input–output transactions to economize on transaction costs, but to the issue of how to combine and manage transactions to *create value*. For example, a positive approach to transaction costs is embedded in the following quote from Coase (1988: 37–8):

> the way in which I presented my ideas has, I believe, led to or encouraged an undue emphasis on the role of the firm as a purchaser of the services of factors of production and on the choice of the contractual arrangements which it makes with them. As a consequence of this concentration on the firm as a purchaser of the inputs it uses, economists have tended to neglect the main activity of a firm, running a business.

By this quote, Coase puts the focus of attention on how to organize transactions to increase efficiency, which as noted earlier from a pareto efficiency view, means maximizing or optimizing the value that can be created from organizing transactions in various ways. It is here that a positive view of TCT takes off, for "running a business" means being an entrepreneur since in both Knight's work and relatedly in Austrian economics (Kirzner, 1973, 1986), entrepreneurship is viewed as the process of noticing opportunities to save on transaction costs and marshaling organizational resources and capabilities to capitalize on those opportunities to create value. Moreover, this noticing of opportunities occurs at all levels in the hierarchy, for as Coase (1991b: 59) notes, "What I meant by the entrepreneur is the hierarchy in business which directs resources and includes not only management but also foremen and many workmen . . . no single individual is responsible for the final control of the firm."

From this positive perspective, both bounded rationality and uncertainty are opportunities. As Knight (1921) notes, for example, while it is rational for people to wish to reduce uncertainty so that they can adapt and achieve their goals, "uncertainty is not abhorrent . . . we should not really prefer to live in a world where everything was 'cut and dried,' which is merely to say that we should not want our activity to be all perfectly rational" (p. 198). Why? Because with uncertainty absent, people's energies "are devoted altogether to doing things, it is doubtful whether intelligence itself would exist in such a situation; in a world, so built that perfect knowledge was theoretically possible, it would seem likely that all organic readjustments would become mechanical, all organisms automata" (p. 268). Complete certainty is monotonous; by contrast, uncertainty and bounded rationality create challenge; the entrepreneur is motivated by the possibility of gain that exists because the existence of uncertainty makes the results of innovative behavior unknown or unpredictable just as an artist is motivated by the desire to depict something new about the world. Essentially, the challenge is in the action itself; if there were no bounded rationality there would be no peak experiences or self-actualization. There would be no striving or desire to maximize the joint value than can be created through human interaction and cooperation.

The positive or entrepreneurial view is to recognize that, paradoxically, bounded rationality and uncertainty make it necessary for people to develop human qualities such as curiosity, imagination, and risk taking and, as discussed below, these human qualities provide a very different explanation for the emergence of hierarchy, and become the important human factors in a transaction cost model. That is, bounded rationality, far from being a threat, can be regarded as an opportunity. In a very real sense, only the existence of uncertainty gives rise to the desire to search for new solutions or leads to the actual experimenting during which serendipitous discoveries are often made. The issue is how should transactions best be structured – in the market or hierarchy – to maximize opportunities for people to behave entrepreneurially. Note that unlike Williamson's treatment of uncertainty and bounded rationality, there is no implication in a positive view that the hierarchy will always be the preferred way to organize transactions: the hierarchy will be chosen when it permits, leads, or promotes forms of entrepreneurship that cannot be achieved in the market.

In sum, it is only the presence or existence of uncertainty and bounded rationality that generates the need for entrepreneurial activity and unleashes the process of creative destruction and allows it to become a positive force in propelling firm and industry level innovation (Schumpeter, 1934). From a positive perspective, uncertainty and complexity are not problems to be managed and overcome, they are opportunities to be taken advantage of. When TCT is framed in this positive way criticisms such as those of Ghoshal and Moran (1996: 35) that TCT can only deal with "routine transactions" and that "Williamson ignored innovation-related activities that are efficient only in a dynamic sense" lose their force. As mentioned earlier, both Knight and Coase quite specifically noted that entrepreneurship also meant innovation in organizing transactions. It is unfortunate that TCT has come to be viewed from an input–output "cost minimization" perspective rather than the much more dynamic pareto efficiency "value optimization" approach which has always been implicit in the theory and advocated by its proponents.

The discussion below is framed in terms of the parties' attempts to structure transactions to jointly optimize the value of their exchanges rather than to minimize costs. From a positive perspective the firm or hierarchy can be recognized as a platform that promotes entrepreneurship and trust and allows mutually dependent people to cooperate to maximize the value of their transactions and relationships – value that cannot be actualized in the market because of measurement costs. Uncertainty causes entrepreneurs to develop and use new capabilities.


## A POSITIVE VIEW OF TRANSACTION COST THEORY

As the argument above suggests, the existence of uncertainty and risk simultaneously give rise to the need for trust and creates the possibility for entrepreneurial behavior. What kinds of transaction difficulties arise when the parties to an exchange seek to develop trusting relationships and to act entrepreneurially to take advantages of opportunities to create value? In particular, what kinds of transaction difficulties give rise to high levels of transaction costs that result in the need to internalize transactions within a hierarchy? To answer this question it is necessary to examine how trust and entrepreneurship interact with the most important factor that causes transaction difficulties in TCT, asset specificity. Building on the positive view of the postulates of TCT developed above, the argument that links uncertainty and risk, entrepreneurship, trust, and the development of specific assets is summarized in figure 7.1.

The problem facing the parties to an exchange when uncertainty and risk exists is to discover the best way to structure their transactions to maximize the value that can be obtained. The answer is to specialize because, as is well established in the literature, specialization can reduce uncertainty and is the source of many, if not most, of the value-creating benefits that derive from the division of labor (Alchian, 1984; Demsetz, 1991; Katz and Kahn, 1978; Smith, 1776; Stigler, 1961; Weber, 1947).[2] So, to reduce uncertainty, each party focuses on developing the skills and abilities necessary to perform specific tasks to give them a comparative advantage. However, the process of specialization cannot proceed very far unless certain preconditions exist. Specifically, the development of specialization depends on (1) people's willingness to bear the uncertainty associated with the process of becoming specialized (which is a form of entrepreneurship since an entrepreneur has been defined as someone who is the "bearer of uncertainty" (Knight, 1921; Kirzner, 1973) and (2) some measure of confidence in other people that if they do become specialized they can count on the other to enter into a quid pro quo trading relationship and to act reciprocally; that is, that they can *trust* the other so that they will not be put at risk if they do decide to specialize (Axelrod, 1984; Gouldner,

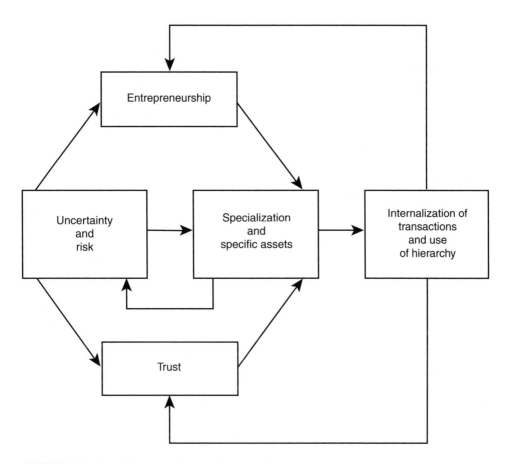

FIGURE 7.1 A positive view of transaction cost theory

1960). If these preconditions exist, then specialization will take place. While some kinds of specialization can be easily copied and imitated by other people who watch and learn from the entrepreneurs, other kinds of specialization, particularly those that involve cooperation between people cannot, and it is this latter kind of specialization that can result in the development of value-creating specific assets which in this paper are treated as forms of specialization that are unique or specific to an organization or between organizations. This argument is developed in detail below.

Specialization, following Smith (1776), is defined here as the process by which different individuals, functions, divisions, or organizations invest in different kinds of skills and assets so that, over time, each develops a comparative advantage over others in a specific kind of activity. As long as people are individually specialized, meaning that each performs a separate or clearly distinguishable task, they can often simply sell their output in the market to other people using the price mechanism or they can work for an organization, selling their specialized skills for an agreed upon price.

However, very often it becomes clear to people from "learning by doing" that if they cooperate and become jointly or collectively specialized, they can create more value from their exchanges. Joint specialization is defined here as the investment in assets to achieve economic benefits from the *product* of two or more individuals or groups. The key about joint specialization is that, to create value, the different individuals or groups have to adjust their actions and behaviors to meet the needs of other individuals or units on an ongoing basis. In essence, joint specialization produces the synergistic team relationships that emerge when individuals or groups cooperate during the production process (Alchian and Demsetz, 1972). The gains from joint specialization are multiplicative and non-separable (Alchian and Demsetz, 1972), they are the product of individuals' or groups' joint cooperation and are between-unit gains. As such, the development of joint speciali-zation creates specific assets when these assets are impossible or prohibitively expensive to transfer to other organizations.

There are important transaction difficulties associated with obtaining the value crea-tion opportunities from joint specialization that create significant measurement problems and give rise to transaction costs, however (Barzel, 1989; Cheung, 1983). As just discussed, joint specialization depends on embedded, interwoven production linkages between individuals, functions, divisions, or organizations which make it impossible or prohibitively expensive to evaluate the discrete contribution of each individual or subunit now and in the future (Alchian and Demsetz, 1972). As a result, no individual or subunit may be willing to bear the uncertainty and risk that its investment in specific assets will in fact lead to the gains that are anticipated and the benefits of joint specialization will not be obtained. Essentially, it becomes too dangerous to bear the uncertainty of increased specialization, even though this potentially can create much value, if there is no way to assure that others are able and willing to act reciprocally so as to jointly reap the rewards. For example, individual workers will have no incentive to invest in becoming more specialized and dependent on others if, because of uncertainty, they have no assurance that their increased specialization will payoff. The result is that sometimes the potential gains from specialization are too difficult to be realized in the market because asset specificity generates too much uncertainty and risk for any one person to bear and the level of entrepreneurship falls. Note that the need to avoid potential opportunistic behavior of others plays no part in this explanation; even when people trust one another and are motivated to cooperate, exchange is often impossible simply because of their inability to bear the uncertainty and risks of the venture (Madhok, 1996).

There is an even more crucial transaction difficulty that arises from joint specialization that causes measurement problems. This concerns the fact that in cooperating on joint tasks, it is very likely that entrepreneurs at all levels will notice new opportunities for combining factors of production in innovative ways; that is, they may recognize new product market possibilities or new ways of performing a task more efficiently. For example, by becoming involved with manufacturing on an ongoing basis, a research and development team may find new ways of reducing manufacturing costs that were not obvious before. However, securing the potential benefits to be derived from such coopera-tive activities on an ongoing basis may also not be realized because of uncertainty and risk.

When new opportunities arise in an ongoing manner, no amount of advance negotia-tions can decide how the fruits of such joint labor will be divided. Thus, with the best will in the world, people are likely to experience enormous problems in coming to an agreement about the best way to organize work simply because each person has a different utility preference schedule. For example, the different parties to an exchange may have different preferences concerning work and leisure, some may prefer to trade leisure for work while others may wish to work ever harder and harder to reach their goal and achieve a higher return. Moreover, people may have different preferences towards uncertainty and risk. Some people may choose to become entrepreneurs and accept the uncertain returns associated with bearing uncertainty while others may wish to become "workers" and accept the rewards that were guaranteed in their employment contracts (Knight, 1921). Resolving all these issues can be a major endeavor. Even more crucial is the problem in deciding what proportion of the surplus value created from their joint activities should be consumed now rather than invested for the future to maximize the long-run stream of value creation. For example, some workers might prefer to consume a larger share now, while others, the entrepreneurs, might be more concerned to forgo current consumption and to invest for the future. In a market, the prospective transaction or measurement costs (Barzel, 1989; Cheung, 1983) that must be borne to resolve the problems due to differences in preferences may be so high that such exchanges will simply not take place; the desire to trust *per se*, is not enough to bring a coordinated series of transactions into existence.

Once again, in a positive, entrepreneurial approach, these problems need not be reflective of the problem of opportunism but may arise simply out of the difficulty of sustaining cooperation to create new value in situations where uncertainty and risk is high. Uncertainty and risk is often the result of the cognitive complexity associated with the process of equitably distributing the rewards of value creation activities, rewards that accrue unpredictably over successive time periods. As Cheung (1983) notes, the problems involved in separating out each individual's contribution and negotiating over the equitable rewards of that contribution creates enormous measurement problems even when each individual is totally honest or trustworthy.

Hence, specialization, and the making of specific assets increases uncertainty and risk. Even though this uncertainty may generate potentially vast benefits, it produces transaction difficulties that give rise to major measurement problems. These problems can become so great that only some form of hierarchical governance mechanism can allow the benefits from joint specialization to be achieved. This is reflected in figure 7.1 by the two arrows leading from specialization and specific assets backward toward uncertainty and trust and forward towards internalization and the use of hierarchy.

In a hierarchy, for example, new ways of organizing factors of production can be found that are impossible to achieve in a market situation, and new opportunities for combining skills in innovative ways can be realized. That is, the adoption of a hierarchy is a form of entrepreneurship as important as new product innovation; and experimenting with different kinds of hierarchical governance structures is obviously impossible in the market – the market and hierarchy are not perfect substitutes. For example, assume that over time, different workers or functional groups come to recognize the comparative advantages of *other* workers or functions, it is very likely that a reshuffling of tasks will occur as tasks move to the workers and functions which can most efficiently perform the activity, giving the others the opportunity to develop new complementary skills and assets (Conner, 1991; Conner and Prahalad, 1996; Grant, 1996). At the same time, as this reshuffling of tasks occurs, it may become obvious that what before was one of a set of tasks is really a set of different specializations, so new areas of specialism or functions are created. Thus, as the level of joint specialization increases, the value embedded in a firm's specific assets or distinctive competences increases. In turn, new opportunities for firm growth become apparent as a firm's skills and competences develop and mature over time. Thus, increasing specialization can increase the level of specific assets inside an organization.

Note that this discussion shares with the knowledge-based view of the firm the assumption that a firm's distinctive competencies and capabilities are important sources of value creation over time (Amit and Schoemaker, 1993; Prahalad and Hamel, 1990). However, given the perspective taken in this paper these competences and capabilities are not seen as an alternative explanation for the development of hierarchy, one separate from a transaction cost approach. As Foss (1996b) notes, there is no *a priori* reason why many of these capabilities cannot be developed in the market, and there is no doubt that some capabilities do emerge between firms – witness the close synergistic linkages that exist between Japanese car companies and their network of embedded suppliers (Cusanamo, 1989; Womack, Jones, and Roos, 1990). Rather, the issue becomes one of explaining when and why specific assets (and organizational competences and capabilities, as firm-specific forms of specialization, *are* specific assets in terms of the theory developed in this paper) result in measurement problems, such as the ones discussed above. Then, to analyze how such measurement problems make it too expensive to operate in the market so that it becomes more effective for an entrepreneur, or team of entrepreneurs, to create a hierarchy and assume responsibility for creating and managing specific assets to maximize long-term value creation.

In essence, the positive TCT perspective developed here differs from the knowledge-based view of the firm because, unlike the latter, the explanation for the choice of hierarchy is not simply that organizations possess certain competences and capabilities for creating and sharing knowledge that are only possible to realize inside a hierarchy (Nahapiet and Ghoshal, 1998). On the contrary, given the postulate of trust, in theory, many forms of competences and capabilities can be realized in the market by actors who are motivated to cooperate. Rather the perspective taken in this paper is that the development of capabilities produces transaction difficulties that result in enormous measurement problems for reasons just outlined and it is the costs associated with resolving these measurement problems that are too expensive to bear in the market and that necessitate the movement to hierarchy. These are the real costs of the market that Coase was referring too.

The central issue is that in a hierarchy, managers don't need to resolve these measurement problems for exchange to take place since people are paid an agreed upon sum to resolve problems as they arise. Employees are not residual claimants who can claim a share of the profits that result from uncertain entrepreneurial ventures. In a hierarchy, transaction difficulties can be resolved incrementally, as the need arises, because all the surplus value created is the reward to the entrepreneur or residual claimant for bearing uncertainty and workers have little say in its distribution. Moreover, as is well understood, in a hierarchy, the monitoring and rewarding of individual and group activities is easier even when joint specialization is high because managers simply have more information and control – often by fiat (Williamson, 1975) – in a hierarchy than in a market to resolve measurement problems.

Over time, from a positive perspective, the firm or hierarchy can be recognized as a platform or springboard that promotes entrepreneurship and trust and allows mutually dependent people to manage the risk and uncertainty associated with organization-specific transactions and relationships. This is suggested by the feedback loops in figure 7.1. Thus, the use of a hierarchy (1) allows entrepreneurs to deal with *uncertainty* and promote innovation which leads to the evolution of new kinds of specialized skills which may generate specific assets and (2) allows workers' perceptions and experience of trust to build up and become stronger over time which reduces their perceptions of *risk*, promotes trust, as just discussed, which can also lead to the development of firm specific skills and competences.

For example, on the first issue, the creation of separate specialized divisions, each controlled by their own autonomous set of managers, provides a better platform for entrepreneurial behavior to emerge and helps develop specific assets. An increase in the level of specialization at the divisional level promotes the development of specific assets at the divisional, and therefore also at the corporate, level. The resources generated from these assets help to create the slack resources that successful entrepreneurial companies have at their disposal to invest in the individual divisions and create new resources. Thus, the hierarchy becomes more complex over time.

Similarly, the development of trust can also promote the development of specific assets. For example, when the hierarchy is chosen, it becomes possible to spread or share risk between workers (managers and employees) so that each individual worker bears less risk, and this, combined with the existence of an internal labor market, provides the signals or guarantees that promote trust and support and encourage the development of specialization and specific assets in the firm. Chiles and McMackin (1996), for example, argue that the presence of trust gives parties to an exchange the incentive to exchange information that is more accurate, comprehensive, and timely, and makes them more willing to listen to others and cooperate. This argument can be taken further because as discussed earlier, trust is a psychological state that can increase in potency over time. In particular, repeated behavioral interactions between jointly specialized people increases the likelihood that they will develop shared values and beliefs so that, as argued earlier, the willingness to suspend belief that the other is not trustworthy will transform into total confidence in the trustworthiness of the other and lead to the emergence of new forms of competences and capabilities. When exchanges become relationships, parties are more likely to subjugate their own needs and ego to pursue a common goal because shared values provide them with greater assurance that others will act in good faith and will be guided by the same shared prospective standards enhancing the development of specific assets. Indeed, the process of specialization provides a good testing ground for people to determine if values are shared, because as noted earlier, there are enormous measurement problems associated with apportioning future unknown benefits.

In sum, in a positive TCT perspective on internalization, the need to organize transactions to safeguard against opportunism or to economize on bounded rationality is seen far less important than the need to organize transactions so as to allow jointly specialized people to economize on the transaction costs associated with resolving the measurement problems associated with cooperative behavior. The real issue is that a hierarchy provides a platform or governance structure for managing uncertainty and risk efficiently; it (1) allows people to bear uncertainty and behave entrepreneurially and (2) allows people to share risk which sustains and promotes the experience of trust so that they can jointly produce more value or wealth. First, in team situations where individual outputs are indistinguishable, individuals can be more sure that their investments will pay off. Second, and most importantly, in situations where there are potential gains from specialization and the level and extent of these future gains cannot be anticipated, a hierarchy, and its associated control mechanisms such as internal labor markets and human relations procedures that ensure procedural and distributive justice gives people the security they need to make them want to trust and invest in an organization. Even when such control mechanisms are imperfect, as they probably most often are, they will still be a more efficient form of governance mechanism than market contracting.

## CONCLUSIONS

Probably because of its focus on transaction costs rather than transaction benefits, TCT has come to be seen as more concerned with the potential value-destroying, rather than the value-creating aspects of specialized exchange relationships. As the analysis in this paper has suggested, however, transaction costs are not just the friction of exchange that saps a system's energy but are a positive transformational force that allows a system to change itself and to generate new energy from the development of innovation and entrepreneurship. All the relationships in figure 7.1 are positive feedback loops suggesting that once started, the process of specialization and the development of specific assets both inside and between firms will be self-sustaining.

The main constraint on the level of firm specialization will be the problems surrounding an organization's ability to effectively govern hierarchical exchanges – in other words, on how fast the costs of managing the hierarchy increase as specialization proceeds (Masten, Meehan, and Synder, 1991). Once again the trade-off between the transaction costs of using the market and the hierarchy will determine this point, but as noted earlier, with a positive entreprencurial approach, managers will actively search for mechanisms to reduce transaction costs, such as when they spin off new ventures or use interorganizational mechanisms such as joint ventures or strategic alliances to further the process of specialization. What kind of mechanism will be chosen depends on the sources of uncertainty and risk present in the situation, and these will be a function of the particular characteristics of the transaction and of the transaction partners such as the complexity of the transaction, and the reputation of the parties involved.

Had TCT been framed from a trust and entrepreneurship point of view rather than an opportunism point of view, there may have been a very different kind of academic response to TCT. In particular, the vocal outcry against opportunism may have been avoided. However, it is important to note that, as far as can be determined by a review of the literature, in no empirical study of TCT has opportunism or bounded rationality or trust or entrepreneurship ever been directly measured. What has been measured in these empirical studies, using many different proxies, has been the way in which (1) the characteristics of the environment and changes in the environment and (2) the level of asset specificity, affect the choice of governance structure for managing the transaction. Thus, empirically, the available evidence can support either view of the linkages between the human and environmental factors in a transaction cost model and the decision about whether or not to internalize transactions in a hierarchy.

Finally, as the discussion above suggests, when viewed positively, transaction cost theory can incorporate many of the insights that have been developed by researchers interested in a knowledge-based view of the firm. The analysis in this paper suggests that it is not knowledge and knowledge embedded in capabilities *per se*, that is the reason for internalization and the development of hierarchy. Rather, the real source of the problem is the transaction difficulties, and consequent measurement problems, that derive from this specialized knowledge, knowledge that this paper views as being synonymous with organization-specific specialized assets that are the result of a continuous division of labor that takes place as entrepreneurs experiment with new ways of organizing transaction to create value. Thus, unlike Ghoshal and Moran (1996), this paper does not see any need for another "unestablished or undeveloped theory of the firm" to solve the problem of why hierarchies exist once the positive aspects of the firm are focused upon. As noted earlier, a positive view has been embedded in TCT from its beginnings, and in earlier work by Knight (1921) which, as Coase (1991) acknowledges, has many affinities to his own. This paper suggests that it is time to actualize this positive view of human nature and cooperation in future theorizing and research in TCT.

## NOTES

1 Technically, an asset is specific when the net value of the asset in its next best use is less than in its current use; the difference between these amounts is the asset's quasi rent. The difference in these amounts is also a measure of how specialized the asset is, for the more specialized an asset is, the higher will have to be the quasi rent to induce a supplier to bear the risks associated with making the specialized investment necessary to engage in the transaction. When risks and quasi rents become too great for one or both parties to bear, and no means can be found to reduce them, transactions are internalized and the hierarchy becomes the preferred choice of governance structure.

2 Note that the argument here is being framed from the perspective that specialization originally develops as a result of uncertainty and risk. It is framed this way because the paper assumes an "original position" where nobody is specialized, but they wish to be because they recognize that specialization reduces uncertainty and thus is the key to value creation. After people become specialized, however, this, in turn, increases risk and makes uncertainty important, and this is reflected in figure 7.1 by the feedback loop from specialization to uncertainty and risk, showing the reciprocal relationship between these variables. Any figure, by definition, can only be a static representation of a dynamic process, and the sequence of events is presented this way for analytical convenience.

## REFERENCES

Alchian, A. A. (1984). Specificity, specialization, and coalitions. *Journal of Institutional and Theoretical Economics*, 34.

Alchian, A. A., and Demsetz, H. (1972). Production, information costs, and economic performance. *American Economic Review*, 62: 777–795.

Amit, R., and Schoemaker, P. J. H. (1993). Strategic assets as organizational rent. *Strategic Management Journal*, 14: 33–46.

Arrow, K. (1970). *Essays in Risk Bearing*. Amsterdam: North Holland Publishing Company.

Axelrod, R. (1984). *The Evolution of Cooperation*. New York: Basic Books.

Barber, B. (1983). *The Logic and Limits of trust*. New Brunswick, NJ: Rutgers University Press.

Barzel, Y. (1989). *Economic Analysis of Property Rights*. Oxford: Oxford University Press.

Bateson, P. (1988). The biological evolution of cooperation and trust. In D. Gambetta (ed.), *Trust: Making and Breaking Cooperative Relations*: 14–30. New York: Basil Blackwell.

Becker, G. S. (1975), *Human Capital*. New York: National Bureau of Economic Research.

Berger, P. L., and Luckmann, T. (1966). *The Social Construction of Reality*. London: Penguin.

Cheung, S. N. S. (1983). The contractual nature of the firm. *Journal of Law and Economics*, 26: 1–21.

Chiles, T. H., and McMackin, J. F. (1996). Integrating variable risk preferences, trust, and transaction cost economics. *Academy of Management Review*, 21: 73–99.

Coase, R. H. (1937). The nature of the firm. *Economica*, 4 (New series), 386–405.

Coase, R. H. (1988). The nature of the firm: Influence. *Journal of Law, Economics, and Organizations*, 4: 33–47.

Coase, R. H. (1991a). The nature of the firm: Origin. In O. E. Williamson and S. G. Winter (eds.), *The Nature of the Firm: Origins, Evolution, and Development*, 34–47. New York: Oxford University Press.

Coase, R. H. (1991b). The nature of the firm: Meaning. In O. E. Williamson and S. G. Winter (eds.), *The Nature of the Firm: Origins, Evolution, and Development*: 48–60. New York: Oxford University Press.

Conner, K. R. (1991). A historical comparison of resource-based theory and five schools of thought within industrial economics: Do we have a new theory of the firm? *Journal of Management*, 17: 121–54.

Conner, K. R., and Prahalad, C. K. (1996). A resource-based theory of the firm: Knowledge versus opportunism. *Organization Science*, 7: 477–501.

Cusanamo, M. A. (1989). *The Japanese Automobile Industry*. Cambridge, MA: Harvard University Press.

Dasgupta, P. (1988). Trust as a commodity. In D. Gambetta (ed.), *Trust: Making and Breaking Cooperative Relations*: 49–72. New York: Basil Blackwell.

Demsetz, H. (1991). The theory of the firm revisited. In O. E. Williamson and S. G. Winter (eds.), *The Nature of the Firm: Origins, Evolution, and Development*, 159–78. New York: Oxford University Press.

Deutsch, M. (1958). Trust and suspicion. *Journal of Conflict Resolution*, 2: 265–79.

Deutsch, M. (1960). The effect of motivational orientation upon trust and suspicion. *Human Relations*, 13: 123–40.

Donaldson, L. (1990). The ethereal hand: Organizational economics and management theory. *Academy of Management Review*, 15: 369–81.

Dow, G. K. (1987). The function of authority in transaction cost economics. *Journal of Economic Behavior and Organization*, 8: 13–38.

Foss, N. J. (1996a). Knowledge-based approaches to the theory of the firm: Some critical comments. *Organization Science*, 7: 470–6.

Foss, N. J. (1996b). More critical comments on knowledge-based theories of the firm. *Organization Science*, 7: 519–23.

Gambetta, D. G. (1988). Can we trust trust? In D. G. Gambetta (ed.), *Trust: Making and Breaking Cooperative Relations*: 213–237. New York: Basil Blackwell.

Ghoshal, S., and Moran, P. (1996). Bad for practice: A critique of the transaction cost theory.

*Academy of Management Review*, 21: 13–47.

Gouldner, A. W. (1960). The norm of reciprocity: A preliminary statement. *American Sociological Review*, 25: 161–79.

Granovetter, M. (1985). Economic action and social structure: A theory of embeddedness. *American Journal of Sociology*, 91: 481–510.

Grant, R. M. (1996). Towards a knowledge based view of the firm. *Strategic Management Journal*, 17: 109–22.

Gulati, R. (1995). Does familiarity breed trust? The implications of repeated ties for contractual choice in alliances. *Academy of Management Journal*, 38: 85–112.

Hill, C. L. (1990). Cooperation, opportunism, and the invisible hand: Implications for transaction cost theory. *Academy of Management Review*, 15: 500–14.

Joskow, P. L. (1988). Asset-specificity and the structure of vertical relationships: Empirical evidence. *Journal of Law, Economics, and Organization*, 4: 95–117.

Katz, K., and Kahn, R. L. (1978). *The Social Psychology of Organizing*. New York: John Wiley and Sons.

Kirzner, I. M. (1973). Competition and entrepreneurship. Chicago: University of Chicago Press.

Kirzner, I. M. (1986). Another look at the subjectivism of costs. In I. M. Kirzner (ed.), *Subjectivism, Intelligibility and Economic Understanding*: 140–56. New York: New York University Press.

Klein, B. R., Crawford, R., and Alchian, A. A. (1978). Vertical integration, appropriable rents, and the competitive contracting process. *Journal of Law and Economics*, 21: 297–326.

Knight, F. H. (1921). *Risk, Uncertainty and Profit*. New York: Houghton Mifflin.

Kogut, B., and Zander, U. (1996). What firms do: Coordination, identity and learning. *Organization Science*, 7: 502–18.

Lewicki, R. J., and Bunker, B. B. (1996). Developing and maintaining trust in work relationships. In R. M. Kramer and T. R. Tyler (eds.), *Trust in Organizations*: 114–39. Thousand Oaks, CA: Sage.

Luhmann, N. (1980). *Trust and Power*. New York: John Wiley.

Madhok, A. (1996). The organization of economic activity: Transaction costs, firm capabilities, and the nature of governance. *Organization Science*, 7: 577–90.

Masten, S. E. (1994). *Empirical work in transaction cost economics: Challenges, progress, directions*. Working paper, School of Business Administration, University of Michigan.

Masten, S. E., Meehan, J. W., and Snyder, E. A. (1991). The costs of organization. *Journal of Law, Economics, and Organization*, 7: 125.

Mayer, R. C., Davis, J. H., and Schoorman, F. D. (1995). An integrative model of organizational trust. *Academy of Management Review*, 20: 709–34.

Nahapiet, J., and Ghoshal, S. (1998). Social capital, intellectual capital, and the organizational advantage. *Academy of Management Review*, 23: 242–66.

Noorderhaven, N. (1995). The argumentational texture of transaction cost economics. *Organization Studies*, 16: 605–23.

Nooteboom, B., Berger, H., and Noorderhaven, N. G. (1997). Effects of trust and governance on relational risk. *Academy of Management Journal*, 49: 308–38.

Panzar, J. C., and Willig, R. D. (1981). Economies of scope. *American Economic Review*, 71: 268–72.

Perrow, C. (1986). *Complex organizations: A Critical Essay*. 3rd edn. New York: Random House.

Popper, K. R. (1959). *The Logic of Scientific Discovery*. London: Routledge & Kegan Paul.

Powell, W. W. (1990). Neither market nor hierarchy: Network forms of organization. In B. M. Staw and L. L. Cummings (eds.), *Research in Organizational Behavior*, vol. 12: 295–336. Greenwich, CT: JAI Press.

Prahalad, C. K., and Hamel, G. (1990). The core competences of the corporation. *Harvard Business Review*, 90: 79–91.

Robins, J. A. (1987). Organizational economics: Notes on the use of transaction cost theory in the study of organizations. *Administrative Science Quarterly*, 32: 68–86.

Robinson, S. L. (1996). Trust and breach of the psychological contract. *Administrative Science Quarterly*, 41: 574–599

Rokeach, M. (1973). *The Nature of Human Values*. New York: Free Press.

Rotter, J. B. (1980). Interpersonal trust, trustworthiness, and gullibility. *American Psychologist*, 35: 1–7.

Schelanski, H. A., and Klein, P. G. (1995). Empirical research in transaction cost economics: A survey and assessment. *Journal of Law, Economics, and Organization*, 11: 335–61.

Schumpeter, J. A. (1934). *The Theory of Economic Development*. Cambridge, MA: Harvard University Press.

Shapira, Z. (1995). *Risk Taking: A Managerial Perspective*. New York: Russell Sage Foundation.

Shapiro, D. L., Sheppard, B. H., and Cheraskin, L. (1992). Business on a handshake. *Negotiation Journal*, October, 365–77.

Smith, A. (1776). *An Inquiry into the Nature and Causes of the Wealth of Nations*. London.

Stigler, G. J. (1961). The division of labor is limited by the extent of the market. *Journal of Political Economy*, 59: 185–93.

Weber, M. (1947). *The Theory of Social and Economic Organization*. New York: Oxford University Press.

Williamson, O. E. (1975). *Markets and Hierarchies*. New York: Free Press.

Williamson, O. E. (1985). *The Economic Institutions of Capitalism*. New York: Free Press.

Williamson, O. E. (1993a). Calculativeness, trust, and economic organization. *Journal of Law and Economics*, 36: 453–86.

Williamson, O. E. (1993b). Opportunism and its critics. *Managerial and Decision Economics*, 14: 97–107.

Womack, J. P., Jones, D. T., and Roos, D. (1990). *The Machine that Changed the World*. New York: Rawson and Associates.

Zaheer, A., McEvily, B., and Perrone, V. (1998). Does trust matter? *Organization Science*, 9: 141–59.

Zucker, L. G. (1986). Production of trust: Institutional sources of economic structure, 1840–920. In B. M. Staw and L. L. Cummings (eds.), *Research in Organizational Behavior*, vol. 8: 53–111. Greenwich, CT: JAI Press.

# 8

# A Strategic Management Model of Agency Relationships in Firm Governance

## Michael H. Lubatkin, Peter J. Lane and William S. Schulze

Based on the work of Berle and Means (1932), Coase (1937), Arrow (1971), and others, agency theory emerged in the 1970s to explain economic relationships under conditions of uncertainty and less-than-perfect information. It has become a widely used theoretical lens in strategic management research, with applications intended to inform research about corporate governance (Finkelstein and D'Aveni, 1994; Walsh and Kosnik, 1993), CEO compensation (Barkema and Gomez-Mehia, 1998), firm performance (Brush, Bromiley, and Hendrickx, 2000; Li and Simerly, 1998), firm risk (Bloom and Milkovich, 1998; Wiseman and Gomez-Mejia, 1998), and strategic decisions such as diversification (Kochhar, 1996; Markides and Singh, 1997) and mergers (Holl and Kyriazis, 1997; Reuer and Miller, 1997).

Despite its frequent use, the theory's relevance to the strategy field continues to be debated. For example, Walsh and Kosnik (1993) found little support for the disciplining role that the theory assumes is played by the market for corporate control. Finkelstein and D'Aveni (1994) found the theory lacking in its ability to explain why boards adopt CEO duality. Barkema and Gomez-Mejia (1998) found little support in the literature for the model to explain CEO pay. Lane, Cannella, and Lubatkin (1998) found no support for the agency theory predictions regarding firms' performance, risk, diversification and mergers; and, like Walsh and Kosnik, concluded that the theory's relevant domain may be much more circumscribed than its founders had envisioned.

In this chapter, we continue to explore the limits of the theory's domain by drawing upon some of our current research. Our intent is not to refute the theory, but rather to raise issues that might stimulate the development of a more general model of agency. We begin by briefly reviewing the assumptions underlying the foundation agency model, before turning our attention to the model most cited in strategy research, the Jensen and Meckling (1976) model, where we question its relevance in four broad contexts. First, we use a theoretical lens derived from a synthesis of a behavioral "transaction" cost theory of the firm and institutional economics to suggest why the current conceptualization of the J/M model may be too deeply rooted in the US experience to adequately explain governance issues in other national contexts. Second, we revisit our debate with Amihud and Lev (1981; 1999) and Denis, Denis, and Sarin (1999) to question the ability of the J/M model to explain governance issues in widely held (management-controlled) US firms. Third, we use a political-economic lens to identify limitations of the J/M model to accurately depict those agency problems that often arise at privately-owned firms. Finally, we use a household-economic lens to highlight reasons why the J/M model underestimates agency problems in family-owned and managed firms, the world's most common form of governance. Based on these four domain-specific critiques, we present suggestions for developing a more general agency model, one that is consistent with the theory's foundation assumptions and those that ground the field of strategic management.

## THE JENSEN–MECKLING MODEL

At its most base level, agency theory is concerned with problems that can arise in any cooperative exchange when one party (the "principal") contracts with another (the "agent") to make decisions on behalf of the principal (Alchain and Woodward, 1988; Fama and Jensen, 1983a, b). However, contracts tend to be incomplete and subject to hazard because of the nature of people (self-interest, bounded rationality, risk aversion), organizations (e.g., goal conflict among members), and the fact that information in organizations is typically distributed asymmetrically, making it costly for principals to know what agents actually accomplished. Agency problems therefore develop because agents can hide information and/or take actions that favor their own interests. This gives principals incentive to invest in monitoring and incentives, and agents reason to post performance bonds, as protection against potential losses. The costs of these protective measures, along with any residual loss as a result of the contracting, are referred to as *agency costs*. According to the theory, it is rational for the contracting parties to incur agency costs up to the point where the cost of fully eliminating conflicts of interest (i.e., agency problems) exceeds the benefits (Jensen and Smith, 1985).

Jensen and Meckling (1976) extended the foundation theory to those problems rooted in separation of ownership from control (Jensen, 1998). Building on Alchian and Demsetz (1972), they (1976: 310) viewed a firm as "a nexus for a set of contracting relationships" between factors of production in which one party (the firm's owners) is common to all the contracts (Fama, 1980). They further specified that a firm is "characterized by the existence of divisible claims on the assets and cash flows of the organization" that can be assigned or sold (Jensen and Meckling, 1976: 311). In its simplest case, the J/M model predicts that owner-managers will pursue a wealth-maximizing strategy by entering into contracts and allocating resources to other parties.

Jensen and Meckling (1976) then consider the case where owners employ other managers to oversee the firm's resource allocation decisions. Because outside-shareholding causes a *de facto* delegation of decision responsibility from some of the firm's principals (outside owners) to its agents (managers who may or may not be owners), a misalignment of incentives occurs because of different preferences for risk. Shareholders are indifferent to the specific (unsystematic) risk of any single firm, because they can diversify this source of earning variation away by spreading their investments across a diverse set of firms whose earnings are uncorrelated with each other. However, this will not reduce a shareholder's exposure to the variability in each firm's returns that is systematically tied to general economic uncertainties. Given two investment projects of equal systematic risk, therefore, shareholders will always prefer the project with the higher expected returns.

In contrast, managers are very concerned about firm-specific risk, for it exposes their personal (human) investment in a firm to uncertainty about the firm's survival and performance. This uncertainty is neither covered by their employment contract, nor can they not diversify away by holding employment contracts in a diverse set of firms. In other words, delegation and uncompensated risk caused by it, gives managers incentive to seek additional compensation through non-pecuniary means, such as shirking, free-riding, and perquisites (Jensen and Meckling, 1976). Delegation also creates information asymmetries between owners and managers that make it possible for agents to engage in these activities, which, if left unchecked, can threaten firm performance. These information asymmetries and the incentives to use them in an opportunistic and self-serving manner combine to pose a *moral hazard* to managers.

Jensen and Meckling (1976) discuss in detail two forms of monitoring: debt and stock analysts. Subsequent research has embellished the base J/M model by examining a range of other remedies, such as outside shareholders with large blocks of stock (Schleifer and Vishny, 1986; Walsh and Seward, 1990), boards of directors (Boyd, 1995; Hoskisson and Turk, 1990; Kosnik, 1987, 1990), and executive compensation (DeFusco, Zorn, and Johnson, 1991; Jensen and Murphy, 1990; Tosi and Gomez-Mejia, 1989). These remedies, combined with Jensen and Meckling's definitions of the firm and agency problems, constitute the current specification of the Jensen and Meckling agency model, which we summarize in figure 8.1.

While the Jensen–Meckling model is widely accepted among strategic management scholars, especially among those trained in the US, some have recently questioned the model's relevant domain, as we do in the next four sections of this chapter.[1]

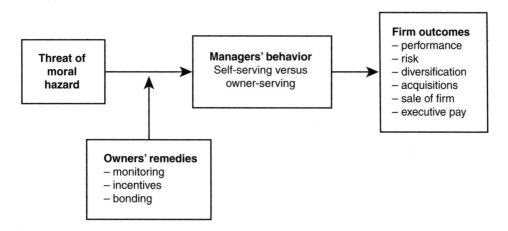

FIGURE 8.1  The Jensen and Meckling agency model of corporate governance

## Does the J/M Model Apply to Firms Outside the USA?

At the heart of the J/M model are three assumptions. First, agents are opportunistic by nature; that is, they will act in their own self-interest in the absence of restraints, even if their actions diminish shareholder's wealth. As such, this model of corporate governance, like other neoclassical organizational economic theories, makes no explicit distinction between opportunism as an attitude, or the propensity to act opportunistically, and opportunism as a behavior. Second, widely held firms are characterized by information asymmetry that engenders opportunistic behaviors. This asymmetry emanates from the fact that ownership at these firms are separated from their day-to-day control, and the fact that the principals (owners) are rationally bounded; that is, they have a limited ability to distinguish *a priori* between best behavior and self-serving behavior. Information asymmetry thus affords managers the opportunity to withhold, filter, and otherwise misrepresent information about their performance and hide actions for their personal gain. Consistent with these two assumptions is the presumption that managers require monitoring and incentives in order to minimize their ability to act opportunistically. Finally, the model assumes, albeit implicitly, that its behavioral views about opportunism and enforced compliance are not nationally bounded, but instead are universal truths.

In Lubatkin et al. (2001), we challenged this third assumption. We argued that its behavioral assumptions might be too rooted in the institutional structure of the US to explain the multiple strains of corporate governance that exists in nations with very different institutional structures. In brief, many of the institutions in the US perpetuate the general belief that acting in one's self interest is in many cases not only acceptable, but also necessary. The lone cowboy and the free agent professional athlete are but two of the many manifestations of "American self-reliance and independence" (see box 8.1 for more manifestations.) Our point is that the governance remedies at most US firms may have evolved into a form consistent with the J/M model's views of opportunism and enforced compliance, largely in the attempt to limit the self-interested tendencies of its agents. And since many of the primary contributors to the J/M model have come from US researchers as they attempted to explain the principal/agency problem at US organizations, it may be that the J/M model largely reflects the US experience, or what Doctor, Tung, and Von Glinow (1991), guest editors of a special issue of the *Academy of Management Review*, referred to as a "made in the USA" administrative theory. We support this speculation by noting the fact that some researchers have recently been uncovering evidence of national differences in corporate governance, which they claim cannot be adequately explained with the logic of this one strain of agency theory (Charkham, 1994; Bird and Wiersema, 1996: 176; Pedersen and Thompsen, 1997; Roe, 1993; Thomsen and Pedersen, 1996).

We then proposed how the Jensen–Meckling model could be adapted to accommodate national differences, by coupling its behavioral views about opportunism and enforced compliance with complimentary views coming from a behavioral "transaction cost" theory of the firm and institutional theory (see figure 8.2). Specifically, the behavioral "transaction cost" view of the firm, which was recently proposed by Ghoshal and Moran (1996) and Moran and Ghoshal (1996) (henceforth, G/M/G), makes the important distinction between the attitude (propensity) for behaving opportunistically and the actual behavior. Drawing upon the works of Simon (1985) and Fishbein and Ajzen (1977), they

---

BOX 8.1    THE INSTITUTIONAL MODEL OF CORPORATE GOVERNANCE IN THE US

Many of the US's background institutions, such as the family, the school systems, and the media, perpetuate positive attitudes of self-reliance, individual achievement, and the general belief that acting in one's self-interest is in many cases not only acceptable, but also necessary. This national bias is reinforced through the nation's primary and secondary schools, which rely on pedagogical methods that teach the values of pragmatism, an action-oriented way of thinking about cause and effect that encourage individuals to search for solutions outside the dominant paradigm (Lessem and Neubauer, 1994). This bias is also reinforced by the curriculum taught at the US schools and by the media, which together celebrate the nation's landmark events (e.g., independence day; abolition of slavery, the lunar landing, and defeat of the axis nations), and legendary figures (Washington, Lincoln, King; the early pioneers; entrepreneurs from Rockefeller to Gates; sports celebrities, etc.). This celebration includes not only the marketing of historical data, but more importantly, the meaning that the schools and media ascribe to them, which serve to shape the nation's social context by perpetuating key ethnocentric themes (Calori et al., 1997). Not surprisingly, US agents enter a US organizational situation predisposed to seizing opportunities as they happen to present themselves, for the individuals, and not their place of employment, are ultimately responsible for their own security, advancement, and wealth. This predisposition to acting opportunistically is reinforced, and even engendered by the ownership structure of publicly traded US firms, which expose agents at every level of the firm to a risk for which they are not fully compensated.

   In other words, the ongoing interactions between agents, given their prior socialization, and the organizational situation, given its ownership structure, may create a social context where opportunism becomes a fixed attribute, in the manner assumed by organizational economics in general, and the Jensen–Meckling (1976) agency model in specific. The US principles are sensitized to this behavioral tendency, having been socialized by the same background institutional influences as the agents, and aware of the firm's organizational situation and its social context through their own interactions with it. However, lacking the cognitive capability to detect the full scope of self-serving opportunistic behaviors by the agents, they feel compelled to incur agency costs (invest in monitoring and incentive structures) until the point that the cost equals the savings that they derive from limiting non-shareholder maximizing behaviors. The US formal institutions aid the principles in their attempt to curtail agent opportunistic behaviors, through its dense array of laws, regulations, and sanctions, intended to protect the principals' property rights. It seems plausible to conclude, without invoking a lot of historical data, that the Jensen and Meckling (1976) strain of agency theory, which is fundamentally a theory of self-interest and enforced compliance, may therefore be strongly rooted in the US experience.

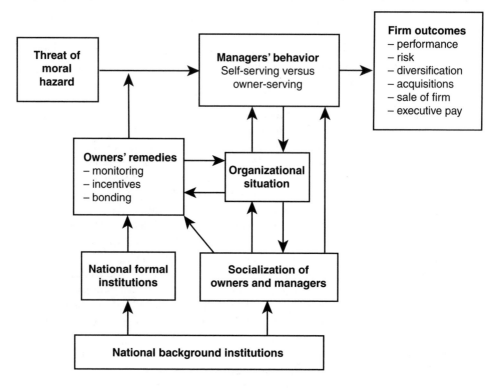

FIGURE 8.2 Accounting for national institutions in firm governance

argued that opportunism is not a fixed attribute of human behavior, but rather a variable, because individuals are capable of a full range of actions, varying from those that justify trust to those that are self-serving with guile. That is, the behaviors that agents choose at an organization are partly explained by agency theory; that is, the ability of corporate governance to restrain managers' opportunistic nature through imposing monitoring, incentives, and threatening legal sanctions. These mechanisms are deemed effective when each manager perceives that the cost of acting opportunistically exceeds the benefits of doing so. However, the behavior that agents choose at an organization is also explained by the organization's social context, which defines the prevalent attitudes (propensity) of its members towards behaving opportunistically.

Like G/M/G, we (Lubatkin et al., 2001) also viewed the agent's attitudes towards opportunism as being defined by the organization's social context, which depends upon three conditions. First, it depends on the agent's own pre-employment socialization; "all the attitudes and values formed through exposure to conscious as well as subliminal stimuli" (Krosnic et al., 1992) that transpired before being employed at the organization. Second, it depends on the organization's "situation," or the agent's favorable or unfavorable feelings, given their prior socialization, for the values, norms, routines, and hierarchical governance mechanisms that characterize the organization. Third, it depends on the interaction of the agent's priors and the situation.

The core insight that we drew from G/M/G (1996) is their notion of interaction, how it affects opportunism as both an attitude and a behavior, and why a theory of corporate governance cannot be fully specified without considering this interaction. For example, the organization exposes each agent to a new set of stimuli. Depending upon how the agent feels about this new situation, the mix of attitudes and values that he/she brought to the organization can be altered, as can his/her mode of behavior (opportunistic or trustworthy). At the same time, the organization, and the particular mix of behavioral stimuli that it signals to its agents, is itself altered by each agent, and more specifically, by the unique mix of attitudes and values that the agent brings to the organization due to his/her prior socialization. As such, the agent's socialization and the organizational situation "evolve interdependently in an iterative manner, each influencing and being influenced by the other" (Moran and Ghoshal, 1996: 60). Through this path-dependent evolutionary process of interaction, each organization develops its own unique "framework of attitudes" that defines an organization's social context and influences human behavior.

We proposed that G/M/G's notion of interaction as the process by which an organizational social context is formed is also useful in explaining how the principals who most closely monitor the firm develop their own unique social context. Vigilant principals, such as large block shareholders and outside directors, also come to an organization situation with attitudes about the behavioral nature of agents. These attitudes are products of the vigilant principals' own prior socialization experiences just as the agents' attitudes are products of their socialization. These perceptions serve as the initial cognitive lens by which principals sort through and try to make sense of the imperfect information that they have about managers' propensity to act opportunistically.

As it was with agents, the vigilant principals' priors need not be fixed. As owners interact with the organizational situation, they can develop a better framework of attitudes and perceptions (schemata or mental templates), which they can then impose on information to simplify its processing (Chase and Simon, 1973), while at the same time improve their analytical skills (Alba and Hutchinson, 1987). For example, the framework can provide them with insight for asking managers (agents) more perceptive questions, knowing what information is relevant, and knowing how to interpret that information (Fredrickson, 1985). Therefore, the framework of attitudes that develops from on-going interactions with the organizational situation reduces the principals' information disadvantages. While the vigilant principals' cognitive ability remains "bounded," their expert framework alters what information will be stored and how that information can be meaningfully linked. As such, the vigilant principals become more able to distinguish *a priori* between best behaviors and self-serving opportunistic behaviors, as well as the mix of governance mechanisms, or remedies that they rely on.

Drawing from the theory of relational governance (Dyer and Singh, 1998; Heide and John, 1990; MacNeil, 1980; Zaheer and Venkatraman, 1995), we also proposed that the notion of interactions not only improves the vigilant principals' cognitive understanding about the firm's management, it also improves their behavioral understanding. This literature is based on the premise that "social content" is embedded in all cooperative interactions, or what it refers to as "joint actions." Specifically, as the vigilant principals interact with the organizational situation, mostly through exchanges with the top management, information is conveyed about the values and norms of those managers. Over time and with repeated joint actions, the principals' framework of attitudes comes to include expectations about the managers' propensity to act either opportunistically or as good stewards. As with the cognitive understandings, these behavioral insights reduce the principals' information asymmetric disadvantages by simplifying the processing of information (efficiency), while at the same time improving their analytical skills (effectiveness). Like it was with the cognitive understandings, these behavioral insights improve the ability of the principals to distinguish, *a priori*, between best behaviors and self-serving opportunistic behaviors, as well as the mix of remedies that the principals will rely on.

Finally, we extended this behavioral theory about opportunism by considering theories about nations from institutional economics (e.g., North, 1986; 1990; Whitley, 1992) and sociology (e.g., Berger and Luckmann, 1967; Giddens, 1984). We posited that the institutions of a nation indirectly influence managers' *attitudes* toward opportunism, owners' *perceptions* of opportunism, and those formal governance mechanisms that were selected to limit opportunistic *behaviors*.

Specifically, the institutions in each nation shape the "rules of the game" by which individuals and organizations act and compete, and determine "what organizations come into existence and how they evolve" (North, 1990: 5). Hofstede (1984) referred to this nationally bounded framework as the "collective mental programming," which serves to legitimate certain ways of structuring economic exchange that sets the behaviors and governance practices in organizations from one nation apart from those of other nations. Put differently, national institutions collectively shape the "prior socialization" that agents and principals bring to their organizations, as well as determine the limit to which the organizational situation can alter those priors. We previously claimed that it is not possible to understand an agent's propensity to act opportunistically, a principals' attitudes about agent's trustworthiness, or the effectiveness of various governance structures to limit that behavior, without first considering a firm's social context. Based on two broad points, we will now extend this claim by arguing that it is not possible to understand a firm's social context without first understanding the social institutional context of the nation in which the firm resides.

Of course, it is important to note that not all institutions impart the same influence on a nation's social context. For example, North (1990) distinguishes between two types of national institutions: formal constraints ("rules") and informal constraints ("codes of behavior"). Whitley (1992) then provides a conceptualization of institutions which builds on North's concept of formal and informal constraints, but which we think better captures these different manners of influence. He distinguishes between formal ("proximate") institutions, such as a nation's political, legal, and financial systems, and "background" institutions, such as family, play, television and schools. According to his sociological view, formal institutions tend to have a coercive influence on human behavior in the sense that they define the legal bounds of acceptable behavior; that is, they establish a set of explicit rules and rational controls that govern economic exchanges within a nation, and then provide a set of enforcement mechanisms to identify, prosecute, and punish individuals who act outside of the established bounds. As such, formal institutions sanction certain types of governance mechanisms, such as contracts, that parties to economic exchanges can use to safeguard their interests, and/or protect themselves from opportunism. That is, formal institutions directly determine the governance mechanisms that are sanctioned by the nation state.

In practice, however, formal institutions may themselves turn out to be costly (inefficient) and even self-defeating mechanisms for governing exchanges. First, most legal enforcement mechanisms are time consuming, expensive, and imperfect (Arrow, 1974). Second, few rules and laws enacted by formal institutions are motivated purely for efficiency gains. Indeed, some government regulations may have the opposite effect (North, 1990). Finally, a society may perceive a legitimate need for "guarantees" against "the intrusion of unscreened and unpenalized opportunism" (Williamson, 1985: 65). The imposition of these formal safeguards, however, may also serve to initiate a self-fulfilling prophesy by encouraging the types of opportunistic behaviors that are more difficult to detect (Perrow, 1986).

On the other hand, background institutions are viewed as an effective and efficient mechanism for governing economic exchanges because their influence on human behavior is either mimetic (acquired, adopted or consciously imitated as best practices) or normative (imprinted or unconsciously incorporated through tacit beliefs) (DiMaggio and Powell, 1983; Scott, 1987; Whitley, 1992). First, background institutions provide a means for a society to disseminate explicit collective knowledge, or what Spender (1994) refers to as "science"; that is, an internalized understanding of cause and effect relationships that allows a society to repeat those practices which previously led to favorable outcomes. Second, background institutions "imprint" implicit collective knowledge, or what Spender (1994) refers to as "culture"; that is, a set of social norms, values, and routines tacit to a society, about "how things ought to be" and "how things ought to be done."

Finally, the background institutions of a nation play a major role in the socialization of its citizens, and thereby create a framework of attitudes that shape their behavior. According to Berger and Luckmann's (1967) theory of socialization, individuals develop a set of foundation cognitions (schema, belief structures, or mental templates) mostly through their primary socialization experiences with background institutions. Once this socially constructed view of reality is established, any new views that individuals are exposed to through secondary socialization experiences later in life are interpreted through these primary schemas and internalized only if they are consistent with, or extended from, their primary schemas.

It follows that background institutions, particularly those that influence primary socialization encounters, define a nation's general framework of attitudes. Put differently, background institutions nationally bound the priors of agents and principals. Note that where vigilant principals are also influenced by the organizational situation, the attitudes of passive principals are only influenced by background institutions. The prior of agents and principals, in turn, affects their feelings for any secondary socialization situations, such as the organization, and the potential for reconditioning (organizational socialization) that occurs from the accompanying interaction of the two. As such, a nation's background institutions indirectly affect the agents' propensity to act opportunistically at their place of employment, and the principals' perceptions of opportunism, and thus their ability to a priori distinguish between best behaviors and opportunistic behaviors. As such, background institutions have an indirect effect on the costs and benefits of opportunistic behaviors at the firm.

In summary, in Lubatkin et al. (2001), it was posited that the Jensen–Meckling model's behavioral views about opportunism and the agency cost of enforced compliance might suffer from a US bias, which would limit the theory's relevant domain to the US and nations with institutional structures similar to the US. Specifically, the model overlooks the fact that opportunism as a behavior is also constrained through the prior socialization and interaction of the agents and principals with the organizational situation. These constraints are themselves influenced by a nation's formal institutions, which delimits the opportunity set of governance mechanisms, and by its background institutions, which defines an individual's primary socialization (institutional theory). As such, we posit that it is not possible to fully understand the principal/agent problems at a firm without understanding the firm's social context, and it is not possible to understand a firm's social context without understanding of the social institutional context of the nation in which the firm resides.

Our proposition might represent one explanation for the dearth of international governance papers that have been published in the Anglo-American journals. Perhaps the US bias, which appears to characterize governance research, has placed the field into a paradigmatic straight-jacket. Perhaps the gatekeepers of our journals are too quick to reject international contributions because their "square" findings were not fitting into the "round" holes of the J/M model. Whatever the cause, we think there are as many opportunities to internationalize the field as there are institutional structures that differ from the US. Hopefully, our first critique of the J/M and our suggestions to break it out of its US bias will spark international governance research and provide the theoretical key to open the journal gates to it. We will now shift our attention to four questions having to do with the ability of the J/M model to adequately explain issues of governance in a US business setting.

## DOES THE J/M MODEL APPLY TO WIDELY HELD PUBLIC FIRMS?

Recall that in our opening remarks we noted that a core tenet of the Jensen and Meckling (1976) model is that delegation exposes agents at every level of the firm to a risk for which they are not fully compensated, while at the same time creating information asymmetries that make it possible for agents to engage in activities that, if left unchecked, would threaten firm performance and may ultimately harm the welfare of owners and agents alike. Information asymmetries and incentive combine and pose a moral hazard to agents. This post-contractual agency threat is therefore presumed by the J/M model to be a product of the ownership structure of the widely held firm (Alchian and Woodward, 1988; Jensen and Smith, 1985). "Widely held" are those firms where "stockholders are not required to have any other role in the organization, their residual claims are freely alienable, and the residual claims are rights in net cash flows for the life of the organization" (Jensen, 1998: 177).

In a paper widely cited in the economics, finance, accounting, and strategy literatures, Amihud and Lev (1981) relied on this insight to ground their two predictions about the non-shareholder maximizing behavioral tendencies of managers. Specifically, they presumed that when no single owner holds a large enough stake in the firm to have the incentive to carefully monitor managers' actions, managers have incentives to pursue strategies that are in their own best interests. And, since managers are typically over-invested in their firm in the sense that much of their wealth and status is derived from their employment, it is in their best interest to ensure the long-term survival of the firm (Coffee, 1986). That is, it is rational for them to pursue those strategies that reduce the overall variability (total risk) in their firm's returns, although those strategies are not necessarily in shareholders' best interests.

Using a strategic management lens, Lane, Cannella, and Lubatkin (1998) challenged the appropriateness of Amihud and Lev's agency theory based presumptions in this broad domain. First, we argued that: (1) both managers and shareholders are concerned about total risk; (2) managers will not act in self-serving and opportunistic ways unless their interests are clearly and directly at stake; (3) ownership structure will have little to no association with corporate diversification strategy; and (4) owner-controlled firms are not necessarily wealth maximizers. We then also questioned the measures of ownership structure, merger relatedness, and corporate diversification that Amihud and Lev used in their study as being imprecise. Finally, we developed hypotheses regarding the association between ownership structure, board vigilance, corporate strategy, and corporate performance, and then tested these hypotheses twice, once using Amihud and Lev's own data from the 1960s, and a second time using new data that we collected from the 1980s.

We found no evidence in either data set to support Amihud and Lev's widely cited findings that managers attempt to diversify their own risk through corporate diversification and unrelated mergers unless restrained by large block shareholders. We concluded that while the J/M agency model might explain managers' behavior during battles for corporate control (e.g., a hostile bid for a firm) and situations in which they are otherwise under siege (i.e., when there are sharp conflicts of interest, such as over pay), managers' strategic behaviors during times when they are not under siege may be beyond the theory's relevant domain (see figure 8.3). Indeed, our findings appeared to be more in keeping with the tenets of stewardship theory – a theory, which to date, is primarily a collection of negative assertions that defines itself largely as what agency theory is not.

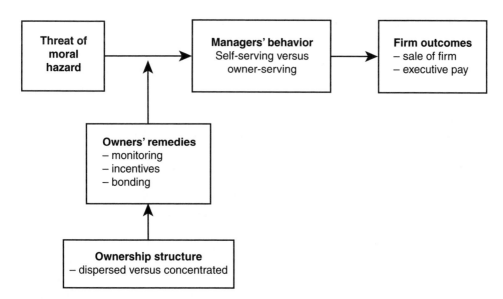

FIGURE 8.3 The limited domain of the J/M model for US public corporations

Amihud and Lev (1999) disagreed with our findings, claiming that the strategic management-based methods and measures were inappropriate. In a companion paper, Denis, Denis and Sarin (1999: 6) argued that the debate over which approach, agency theory or strategic management, is the more correct for describing management–shareholder relationships is ultimately an empirical issue. In our rejoinder to both of these papers, (Lane, Cannella, and Lubatkin, 1999) we discussed our reasons for disagreeing with both critiques and why we continued to stand behind our 1998 results.

In brief, we argued that researchers of strategic management and economics are socialized to accept different "world views," and that these differences can influence the meaning of shared concepts and methodological norms, and bias the interpretation of results. The field of strategic management tends to be less reductionist; its constructs, theories, and methods can involve multiple causes and different levels of analysis, some inspired from economics and others coming from an eclectic set of behavioral sciences like psychology, social psychology, and sociology. Indeed, strategic management's distinctive role among the social sciences is to integrate behavioral and economic theories with its own unique understanding of the purposeful management of complex organizations. We think that this allows strategy scholars the perspective potentially to develop a more enriched model of governance that can capture its subtleties.

Further, we think that the time is now right to develop such a model. Bear in mind that the study by Amihud and Lev (1981) discouraged research along one line of agency theory investigation for a number of years. Indeed, it is rare to find a paper about corporate governance in the strategy literature that doesn't cite the Amihud and Lev study at least once. The fact that we did not find support for their findings, even when using their data, suggests that the time may have come to reopen this line of investigation.

## Does the J/M Model Apply to Privately Owned and Owner-Managed Firms?

Jensen and Meckling (1976) presumed that the cost of reducing information asymmetries and the accompanying moral hazard is low when ownership is closely held, as is the case with privately owned firms. Consequently, these firms are presumed to have less of a need to incur agency costs because these firms face minimal agency threats (Hansmann, 1996; Jensen, 1998). We challenged this prediction (Schulze, Lubatkin, and Dino, 2000, 2001a, b; Schulze, Lubatkin, Dino, and Buchholtz, forthcoming). First, we argued that the J/M model overlooks the fact that the agency benefits that external governance mechanisms provide to publicly owned firms may not be available to privately owned firms. Second, we argued that the J/M model overestimates the ability of the private ownership to efficiently resolve their differences among the owners and align their interests. We therefore posit that this mainstream agency model does not extend to the domain of privately held companies because it underestimates the agency problems that can arise in these firms, and therefore, the need for them to incur agency costs (i.e., invest in owners' remedies).

Regarding our first argument, the J/M model recognizes the ability of the capital markets to reduce monitoring costs by tracking firm performance and making this

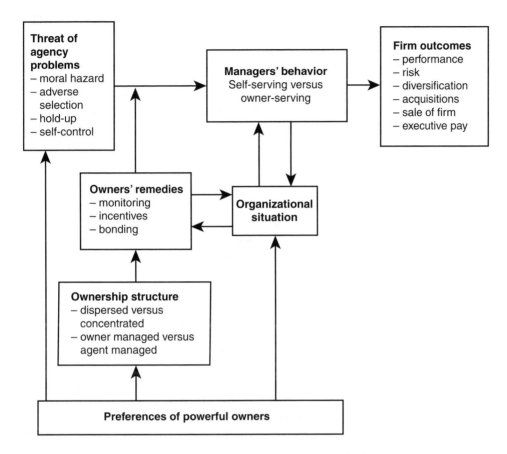

FIGURE 8.4 Accounting for private ownership and management in firm governance

information available to shareholders and potential investors in the form of share price. The model also recognizes: (1) the ability of the capital markets to reduce the detrimental effects of over-investment on the firm's decision makers by providing them with liquidity and distributing the firm's risk among a large number of shareholders (Fama and Jensen, 1983a; Reagan and Stulz, 1986); (2) the ability of product market competition and the market for corporate control for placing a variety of limits on managerial discretion (Jensen, 1993); and (3) the ability of competitive labor markets to reduce a firm's cost of recruiting qualified applicants, and thus, reduce the agency threat of pre-contractual opportunism or *adverse selection*. Adverse selection arises when applicants are able to hide information about themselves that a prospective employer needs to properly evaluate an applicant's quality and worth (Fama, 1980; Hansmann, 1996).

Private ownership, however, compromises the efficiency of the factor markets that serve these firms, and therefore, the external governance that these markets provide. For example, economists recognize that a self-selection, or *sorting* process, occurs in labor markets whenever the terms of the employment contract systematically influence the characteristics of the individuals whom firms can hire. Higher paying jobs, for example, attract more able workers and pay-for-performance contracts attract risk-takers (Besanko, Dranove, and Shanley, 1996). However, private firms cannot offer prospective employees the same terms of employment as public firms. Whereas public firms are able to entice prospective employees with stock options, private firms cannot, due to limited liquidity and the fact that majority shareholders are generally not willing to dilute their control of the firm (Lew and Kolodzeij, 1993; Morck, 1996). Public firms can also promise talented employees promotional opportunities while privately held firms typically cannot because important management positions are "chosen on the basis of wealth and willingness to bear risk, as well as for decision skills" (Fama and Jensen, 1983b: 332). As a consequence, important management positions in privately held firms tend to be held by shareholders.

These examples of factor market failures have five important implications for the cost of governing private firms. First, sorting increases the risk that these firms will inadvertently hire lower quality agents because it reduces the size, character, and quality of the labor pool which serves them. Second, they face an increased risk of hiring inferior and/ or opportunistic employees because reduced competition and the accompanying market inefficiencies make it more costly for firms to guard against adverse selection (Mohlo, 1997). Third, the owners' reluctance to dilute ownership hampers these firms' ability to post the bonds that public firms offer talented applicants to assure them that the firm will not take advantage of them (Rajan and Zingales, 1998). Private ownership thus weakens the institutional safeguards that help protect public firms from adverse selection and prospective agents from a form of owner opportunism known as *holdup* (Williamson, 1985). Fourth, private ownership increases monitoring cost since inferior compensation and limited promotion opportunities reduce these agents' incentive to monitor each others' conduct (Fama and Jensen, 1983a: 310) and to compete with one another in the tournament for advancement (Besanko, Dranove, and Shanley, 1996). Finally, private ownership increases the cost of monitoring firm performance because share price is not determined by the market. This shields owner-managers from the disciplinary pressure of the market for corporate control (Stulz, 1988). Jensen (1993: 847) notes that this can "make it extremely difficult for adjustment to take place until long after the problems have become severe, and in some cases, even unsolvable." We (Schulze et al., 2000, 2001a, b; Schulze et al., forthcoming) conclude that private ownership increases monitoring cost as well as the firms' exposure to pre-contractual agency threats rooted in "hidden information" and to post-contractual agency threats associated with "hidden actions."

Regarding our second argument having to do with the inability of private ownership to efficiently resolve differences among owners and align their interests, the J/M model presumes that conflicts of interest arise with fractional ownership of the firm because every owner's ability and/or willingness to bear risk varies with the relative size of their stake in the firm and their personal preference for risk (Fama and Jensen, 1983a, b; Reagan and Stulz, 1986; Wiseman and Gomez-Mejia, 1998). For example, owners who have a large portion of their wealth invested in the firm may prefer less risk than more diversified investors, and older owners are likely to be more risk averse than younger owners.

However, the J/M model also presumes that these conflicts do not generally engender agency threats because they are resolved efficiently by using one or more of the following mechanisms. First, the model assumes that because owners are economically rational (principally motivated by economic incentives), they have the incentive to develop rules and policies in an effort to minimize conflict and limit the cost of settling most disputes. Second, the model assumes that voting minimizes the economic cost of settling more divisive issues because votes are assumed to reflect the proportionate distribution of economic risks and rewards among the owners. Finally, the model assumes that liquid markets limit the agency cost of owner conflict by making it possible for conflicting parties to cut their losses by simply selling their shares (Alchian and Woodward, 1988; Jensen and Smith, 1985). This assures economic efficiency because it prevents any owner or group of owners from transferring a portion of their ownership costs onto others. In this light, agency theory presumes that owner-management minimizes but does not eliminate the agency cost of conflict among owners.

What happens if these assumptions are violated? Jensen (1993) notes that failures in the market for corporate control allows inside owners to advance their personal interests at the expense of outside owners. We posit that private ownership is also problematic because the absence of a liquid market for the firms' shares increases the threat of holdup. This agency threat arises whenever owners are able to use their voting rights or their control over a firm-specific resource to take the ownership interests of other owners "hostage." As long as the loss the hostaged owners might suffer from giving in to the hostage-taker is less than the cost they would incur from not giving in and/or selling their stake in the firm, the hostage-taker has incentive to force the firm to take actions that favor his or her interest. It follows that the ability to transfer ownership at low cost guards owners from this important agency threat (Williamson, 1985).

Further, the notion that the agency cost of conflict among the owners is negligible rests on contentious neoclassical economic assumption that all individuals are driven to maximize their welfare and behave in economically rational ways. A number of theories challenge this assumption, including the economic theory of the household (Becker, 1974), public choice (Buchanan, 1975), cooperation (Arthur, 1991; Margolis, 1982), and sociobiology (Krebs, 1987; Nowak and May, 1992). For example, economists like Arrow (1963), Buchanan (1975), Becker (1974; 1981) and Thaler and Shefrin (1981) have long recognized that individuals have preferences or tastes for non-economic, as well as economically motivated behaviors, and that people are naturally driven to maximize the utility they gain from each.

We posit that the presence of non-economic preferences poses two problems for the J/M model. First, agency theory presumes that owners share a common interest in their economic welfare. There is, however, little reason to presume that they have common non-economically motivated preferences. Further, the value of these preferences cannot be fully expressed or calibrated in terms of a common commodity, like money (Bergstrom, 1989). Consequently, ownership may be limited in its ability to reduce conflicts of interest among private owners because money (i.e., equity) alone is unlikely to align their attitudes toward growth opportunities and risk.

Second, agency costs can also arise because some non-economically motivated preferences can cause owners to take actions that threaten their own welfare as well as those around them. These "agency problems with oneself" (Jensen, 1998: 48) are rooted in each individual's utility that function and persist because the utility individuals gain from indulging a taste for drug consumption or the exercise of power (which can, as the saying goes, corrupt absolutely) is functionally indistinguishable from the utility that individuals gain from rationally motivated pursuits (Becker and Murphy, 1988; Thaler and Shefrin, 1981). Attempts to maximize one's welfare can, therefore, lead to a loss of self control and cause the individual to take actions that do not advance the common (economic) good. For example, a powerful owner might be tempted to veto a new venture because it threatens the status quo, entails too much effort, or is not in their personal financial interest (Jensen and Meckling, 1976). Interestingly, Jensen admits that he "failed for more than a decade to see the generality and importance of this self-control issue" (1994: 45). However, his subsequent publications, including the versions of Fama and Jensen (1983a, b) that appear in his 1998 book, make no mention of this agency problem when discussing private ownership.

We, therefore, posit that private ownership is not the kind of governance panacea that agency theorists make it out to be. Not only does this governance form fail to minimize the agency threat of ownership, but also it can engender agency costs of adverse selection and hold-up in these firms that are entirely overlooked in the J/M model. But what if the private firm is also owner-managed, as tends to be the case?

Recall that a core tenet of the J/M model is that shareholding causes a *de facto* delegation of managerial responsibility from the firm's principals to its agents, which creates the incentive (shirking and free riding) and the opportunity (information asymmetry) to pose a moral hazard to the agents. However, should managers hold an equity stake in a firm, the model presumes that they will naturally curtail their opportunistic behaviors, sparing associated expenses like formal monitoring systems and pay incentives. Management ownership also promotes communication, cooperation, and consensus (Jensen and Meckling, 1976).

In Schulze, Lubatkin, and Dino (2000, 2001a) and Schulze et al. (forthcoming) we question this tenet: Whenever a powerful CEO leads a firm, whether the base of the manager's power is socio-political (Cannella and Lubatkin, 1994) or ownership, the firm is vulnerable to the threat of self-control. This vulnerability is particularly nettlesome when the owner-managed firm is also private. In the next section, we argue that the agency problems of private ownership and owner-management can be even more pronounced when the privately owned and managed firm is owned and managed by a family.

## DOES THE J/M MODEL APPLY TO FAMILY-OWNED AND MANAGED FIRMS?

Fama and Jensen (1983a) contend that family management is an especially efficient form of owner-management because shares tend to be held by "agents whose special relations with other decision agents allow agency problems to be controlled without separation of the management and control decisions. For example, family members . . . therefore have advantages in monitoring and disciplining related decision agents." Further, "family members have many dimensions of exchange with one another over a long horizon, and therefore, have advantages in monitoring and disciplining related decision agents" (Fama and Jensen, 1983a: 306). Accordingly, family owned and managed firms (henceforth, family firms) should substitute for the costly control mechanisms that widely held, non-owner-managed firms use to limit agency problems.

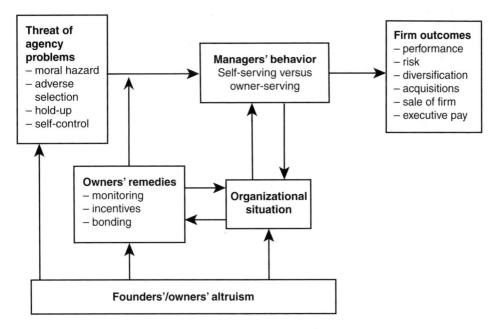

FIGURE 8.5 Accounting for family ownership and management in firm governance

We proposed (Schulze, Lubatkin, and Dino, 2000; 2001a) and tested (2001b; Schulze et al., forthcoming) the hypothesis that family relations can make agency problems associated with private ownership and owner-management even *more* difficult to resolve due to self-control and other problems engendered by altruism. Our hypothesis is largely drawn from the household economics literature, which discusses the influence that altruism has on family dynamics. We then extend these insights from the household to the family firm.

At the extreme, altruism is defined as a moral value that motivates individuals to undertake actions that benefit others without any expectation of external reward (Batson, 1990). However, researchers tend to view it as a trait or preference that is based, at least in part, on feelings, instincts, or sentiments (Lunati, 1997; Piliavin and Charng, 1990). A variety of fields, including economics (Bergstrom, 1995; Margolis, 1982), sociobiology (Krebs, 1987; Nowak and May, 1992), and sociology (Piliavin and Charng, 1990), thus subscribe to the view that altruistic actions necessarily involve a degree of self-interest. The economic literature thus models altruism as a trait that positively links the welfare (both intrinsic and extrinsic) of an individual to the welfare of others. As a consequence, altruism is motivated by both other-regarding and self-regarding preferences, inasmuch as other-regarding (altruistic) preferences are maximized along with individual self-regarding (egoistic) preferences (Lunati, 1997). It therefore compels parents to transfer resources to their children, since to refrain from doing so would harm the altruist's welfare.

Altruism brings a variety of benefits to the firm. For example, it creates a self-reinforcing system of incentives that encourages family members to be considerate of one another (Eshel, Samuelson, and Shaked, 1998) and promotes and sustains the family bond (Simon, 1993). This bond, in turn, should lend family firms a history, language, and identity, that make them special. Second, altruism makes each employed family member (henceforth, "family agent") a *de facto* owner of the firm, in the sense that each acts in the belief that they have a residual claim on the family's estate (Holtz-Eakin, Joulfian, and Rosen, 1993; Stark and Falk, 1998). Or, as Mancuso (1997: 9) states, "But none of the other kids had what my dad had. He owned his own business and we all felt like we owned it with him." Altruism therefore aligns interests among the family agents toward growth opportunities and risk, thereby reducing the cost of reaching, monitoring, and enforcing agreements. Altruism also increases communication and cooperation, thereby reducing information asymmetries among family agents and facilitating the use of informal agreements (Daily and Dollinger, 1992; Eshel et al., 1998; Simon, 1993). Altruism creates a heightened sense of interdependence among family agents since employment links their welfare directly to firm performance (Chami, 1997). Finally, altruism fosters loyalty to the firm, as well as a commitment among its leadership to the firm's long-run prosperity (Ward, 1987). Kang (2000), for example, concludes that family-managed firms are patient investors, capable of sticking with strategies through circumstances and over periods of time that non-family managed firms cannot.

The benefits of altruism, however, may be offset by agency costs since children can become spoiled (made selfish) by their parents' generosity (Buchanan, 1975). This complication occurs because the altruist's generosity is not contingent upon the receipt of any rewards from their children (Becker, 1981). Put differently, since altruism stems, at least in part, from the parents' desire to enhance their own personal welfare, they have incentive to continue to be generous even when their children are not grateful and/or view these transfers or gifts as "entitlements." However, because altruism links a parent's utility function with that of their children, and hence, to that which their children value, the risk that parents will spoil their children increases as their level of altruism rises.

Buchanan (1975) formalized this conundrum in his "Samaritan's Dilemma," which states that a positive relationship exists between a parent's level of altruism and their children's proclivity to shirk responsibilities (e.g., not do chores) and misrepresent their actions ("He did it!") – all in an attempt to either attain more resource transfers from the parent or increase the share received relative to that of their siblings ("Everyone gets more allowance than I do!"). Altruism can also bias the information that parents receive ("Junior would *never* do that!"). As such, Buchanan theorized that agency problems between parent and child increase as their respective levels of altruism become asymmetric.

We (Schulze et al., 2000, 2001a, b; and forthcoming) posit that because family agents depend on each other to take actions, asymmetric altruism engenders agency problems in family firms. The result is a complex web of entwined agency problems that adversely affects the performance of vertical (founder/family agent), horizontal (agent/agent), and inter-group (family/non-family) agency relationships in family firms.

For example, it follows from the Samaritan's dilemma that family agents will be threatened with moral hazard in family firms. That is, owner-control and altruism combine to give family agents incentive to promote their self-regarding interests as opposed to their other-regarding (altruistic) interests. As a consequence, there tends to be a positive relationship between the founders' altruism and their capacity to act altruistically, and the incentive family agents have to shirk. Put differently, the more generous the founder, the more likely it is that asymmetries will develop in altruism and information that reduces family agent productivity. Thus, while a conventional agency perspective suggests that family relationships eliminate the need to monitor or discipline family agents, our agency model suggests that altruism creates incentives that make it necessary for family firms to do both.

Paradoxically, higher levels of altruism also make it more difficult for founders to mitigate these agency threats with supervision, discipline and other remedies. This is because altruism tends to both bias their perceptions about family agent productivity (Chami, 1997) and make family agents reluctant to squeal on each other (Bergstrom, 1995: 61). The founder's ability to monitor family agent conduct is also compromised because family agents have a tendency to free-ride whenever the founder and the family agent's responsibilities overlap. Close supervision is thus rendered ineffective because it tends to foster increased dependence on the founder, just like it did in the household (Lindbeck and Weibull, 1988; Pollak, 1988). Lastly, the founder's ability to discipline family agents is compromised by the effects that disciplinary action might have on his or her own welfare, as well as the ramifications that disciplinary actions might have on familial relationships inside the firm and among the extended family outside the firm. As Levinson (1989) states, "Rare is the owner/manager who can fire a troublesome relative, and make it stick!"

It also follows that higher levels of altruism can exacerbate self-control problems that confound horizontal agency relationships in these firms. Selfish family agents, for example, have incentive to "free-ride" to the extent that the benefits they gain from taking advantage of the family's generosity are greater than losses they suffer from causing the family harm. At the extreme, some may, like the prodigal son in Bergstrom's (1989) interpretation of the parable, become so completely dependent on the founders generosity that they squander their wealth, knowing all too well that the altruist will come to their rescue. In contrast, an "industrious daughter" may have preferences that are more akin to those held by the founder. She might thus choose to labor in the family business, altruistically confident that she will inherit the fruits of her labor at a later date. The perverse consequence of such actions, however, is that her diligence makes free-riding even more lucrative for more selfishly inclined family agents. Her actions also place her future welfare at risk, since a change in circumstance can cause the altruistic founder to change transfer plans such that the deferred compensation she receives is less than what she is due. Asymmetries in the levels of altruism among family agents can therefore create incentives for some to take actions that adversely affect horizontal agency relationships.

Other agency problems arise because the self-control problems that altruism and owner-control exacerbate can make it difficult for the founder to choose between doing that which is best for themselves, best for their family, and because product markets place obvious demands on their firm, best for the firm as a going-concern. This limits the founder's ability to make impartial (that is, economically rational) business decisions. The problem is that if the founder remains untethered by internal governance mechanisms, self-control problems can cause their business decisions to lack consistency.

For example, self-control problems might cause founders to vacillate between distributing resources among family agents based on equity, which takes into account the agent's contribution or effort towards the attainment of the resources, or on equality, which ignores those contributions. Individuals are not indifferent to these rules of resource distribution (Gilliland, 1993). Those agents who define fairness in terms of equity will be offended if the rewards that they receive are suddenly not commensurate with their efforts. Alternatively, those agents who define fairness in terms of equality may find an equity-based reward system equally divisive and at odds with their sense of the family's values and beliefs. It follows from the distributive justice literature (Gilliland, 1993) that by vacillating between different rules of distribution, even altruistic founders can spark envy between family agents, and cause them to act opportunistically. We conclude that all family agents, and especially those with a significant portion of their wealth invested in the firm, have incentive to develop governance mechanisms that can prevent their own self-control problems from undermining the firm's viability, as well as those posed by others.

Finally, it follows that higher levels of altruism can confound vertical and horizontal inter-group (family/non-family) agency relationships. For example, altruism can cause the firm's non-family agents to experience feelings of "distributive injustice." Simply put, non-family agents are generally treated "less fairly" than family agents in family-controlled firms. As we discussed in the context of the sorting process that occurs in labor markets, family-controlled firms tend to withhold upper management positions for family agents, and thus, offer fewer promotional opportunities for non-family agents. Family-controlled firms also tend to offer perquisites and privileges to family agents, but not to non-family agents. Finally, non-family agents, due to their subordinate positions in the administrative hierarchy, may have to answer to the founder's selfish (rotten) kids. This may cause them to perceive a deep sense of inequity, and thereby threaten the family firm with *moral hazard*. That is, perceived inequities can give non-family agents added incentive to engage in shirking and other forms of opportunism (Baldridge and Schulze, 1999).

Oddly, treating non-family agents more like family agents can also create agency problems. High levels of altruism may tempt the founder to think generously of all the firm's employees in this way. However, it is problematic precisely because non-family agents are not family members. That is to say, since non-family agents respond to altruistic transfers differently than family agents, treating family and non-family agents alike can cause information asymmetries to develop. For example, the altruist's tendency to think generously of their employees makes it harder for them to monitor agent conduct and easier for non-family agents to capitalize on the inefficiencies that charac-terize these firm's internal labor markets. The inclination to treat non-family agents "like family members" is also risky because, as we noted earlier, altruism places constraints on the family agent's conduct but has no such effect on non-family agents. The altruistic founder's reluctance to implement and enforce formal control mechanisms therefore exacerbates the threat which opportunistic non-family agents might pose. Simply put, what is good for the goose in family firms may not be good for the gander.

In summary, the J/M model views the family-owned and managed firm as an especially efficient form of governance. We have proposed a very different, more complex view that is indirectly supported by field studies (Handler, 1990; Levinson, 1971; Meyer and Zucker, 1989) and folklore, which presents an ironic mandala where the expression from "rags to riches" ends with "and back to rags in three generations" (Ward, 1987).

We want to make it clear that we are not saying that altruism necessarily weakens leadership in family firms, nor are all family agents spoiled. Rather, we think that altruism adds to the self-control problems that accompany owner-control and owner-management in family firms. The resulting set of self-control problems, in turn, make it difficult for owner/managers to reliably represent their own best interests, or those of the firm and other family members. As such, altruism is both a blessing and a curse because it can make even well-intended founder/managers "bad agents" in the sense that it is their efforts to enhance family welfare that increase the threat of holdup and moral hazard to family members. Interestingly, while these actions are not selfish in the conventional sense – since they require that founder/managers sacrifice their own welfare for the benefit of others – our theory about family firms theory makes it possible to understand the insidious nature of the relationship between altruism and self-interest, and why it makes governance necessary. Further, our view points the way toward a fruitful research agenda about a governance domain that has been hampered by the absence of well-developed theory about this important segment of our economy (Wortman, 1994).

## DISCUSSION

The Jensen and Meckling model of agency theory is an area of applied microeconomics that views capital markets and capital management decisions from the perspective of investors. In keeping with its economics roots, the model makes a number of simplifying assumptions that reduce the complexity of what the discipline studies, as we illustrated in figure 8.1. For example, the model views firms to be little more than portfolios of investments, with performance impacted primarily by market forces. According to this world-view, managers represent potential impediments to investor interests, for they are rational economic actors who place self-interest above all else. As such, managers require monitoring, incentives, and bonding in order to minimize their propensity to act opportunistically. Indeed, many agency theorists wonder how the public corporation survives, given the unbridled self-interest of managers (e.g., Jensen and Meckling, 1976). Some, like Jensen (1989), viewed the problem of opportunism as so great that they predict the "eclipse" of the public corporation.

Strategic management is also rooted in applied microeconomics, but it places more emphasis on relevance to managerial practice and on capturing the complexities of real-world organizations and competition. Rather than viewing firms as little more than portfolios of investments, strategy scholars view firms as portfolios of resources and capabilities linked by the people who create and utilize them. The field also rejects economics-style reductionism and a dogmatic adherence to a single paradigm when it comes to explaining managerial motivations. Rather than assuming that self-interest is the primary motive behind managerial behavior, the field is willing to consider various manager-shareholder alignments that might induce value-enhancing entrepreneurship (Davis, Schoorman, and Donaldson, 1997; Finkelstein and Boyd, 1998).

Taking a broad view of managers, firms, their contexts, and the relevant levels of analysis, however, can leave the field of strategic management with a disorderliness that is at times disparaged by those in fields with one dominant paradigm (Mitchell, 1998).

Instead of viewing this as weakness, we take it as a sign of the field's intellectual vitality and ability to address the changing challenges firms face. Because the field of strategic management continues to reject a dominant paradigm, its distinctive role among the social sciences has been its ability to integrate behavioral and economic theories with our own unique understanding of the purposeful management of complex organizations. In the process of doing so, our field's research provides insights and guidance to the individuals who manage those complex organizations. And, as Bettis (1991) once noted, the objective of our field was never to do first class economics, but rather to use economics to help us do first class strategy research.

Consequently, our attempt to adapt and extend the J/M agency is in keeping with this integrative role for strategic management. Rather than clinging dogmatically to one theoretical hammer and viewing all firms as undifferentiated nails, we rummaged around in the social science toolbox to find other promising perspectives and used them to develop a more flexible tool. We drew from a theoretical lens derived from a synthesis of a behavioral "transaction" cost theory of the firm and institutional economics to suggest why the current conceptualization of the J/M model may be too rooted in the US experience to adequately explain governance issues in other national contexts. We then used a political-economic lens to identify limitations of the J/M model to accurately depict those agency problems that often arise at privately owned and owner-managed firms. Finally, we used a household-economic lens to highlight reasons why the J/M model underestimates agency problems in family-owned and managed firms, the world's most common governance form. Our search for new theoretical lenses to understand firm governance was driven primarily by pragmatic concerns: whatever helped to best explain observed patterns was added to our mix.

In figure 8.6, we present a first attempt to synthesize these many different theoretical lenses by combing elements from the previous five models into a single integrative model. Admittedly, our model may appear disorderly and does not represent an example for first-class economics, as does the Jensen and Meckling model. Nevertheless, we present it as a provisional starting point towards developing a general model of governance that is valid across nationalities and across ownership structures.

While many of the individual relationships in the model have already been discussed in previous sections, at least four additional insights emerge by viewing these relationships holistically. First, our model assumes that the set of preferences held by a firm's owners is more complex than that assumed by the J/M model; that is, in addition to financial preferences, our model recognizes that owners may also have non-pecuniary preferences, not only for themselves (self-regarding, or economically rational) but for others (e.g., altruism). We discussed the role "other-regarding" preferences in the context of family firms. However, the popular press makes numerous references to non-family firms like Southwest Airlines that value the well-being of their employees at least as much as they do that of their outside-shareholders.

Second, while agency theory depicts various aspects about a firm's ownership structure as a governance mechanism (e.g., large block shareholders are more effective at monitoring management), our model posits that the remedial role played by ownership structure is itself dependent on the national institutions, which both shape what types of ownership structure are permitted (formal institutions) and what types are preferred (background institutions). The former influences ownership structure directly while the latter does so

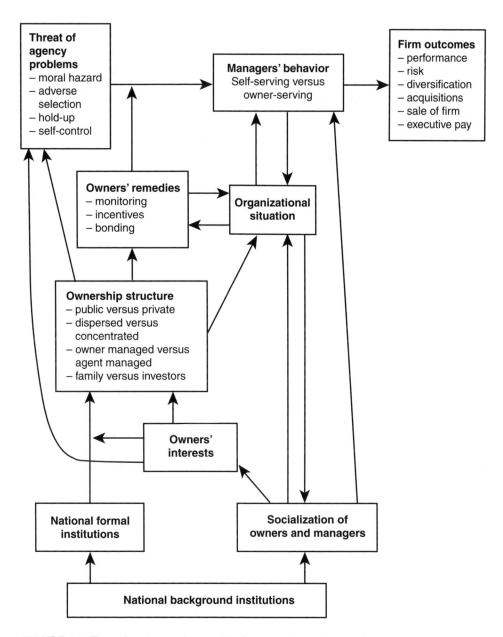

FIGURE 8.6 Toward an integrative model of agency relationships in firm governance

by shaping owners' interests. National institutions also influence managerial behaviors, and therefore, the likely types of agency problems that are likely to occur.

Third, the J/M model assumes capital and labor market efficiencies, and therefore focuses almost entirely on the moral hazard problem. We questioned the generalizability of this viewpoint to all but those firms with public and dispersed ownership structures, noting that other ownership forms may also experience problems of self-control, adverse selection, and hold-up, which, in turn, can have a direct impact on a firm's outcomes. However, even this viewpoint likely requires modification, when considered in the context of national institutions. For example, not all nations have external markets that operate as efficiently as they do in the US. Witness the recent "Asian flu," partly brought about by limited and selective disclosure of corporate earnings reports and hiring and contract practices based on "crony capitalism."

Fourth, our model only dealt with a few ownership structures. What about agency relationships in publicly traded firms that are controlled by a small group of owners, like Winnebago or Archer Daniels Midland? How do agency relationships in these firms differ from those found in publicly traded, professionally managed, family-controlled firms like Ford and Wal-Mart, where the founding family retains a sizeable ownership block? And, what are the implications of our theory for publicly traded firms such as Microsoft and other high-tech start-ups that were founded and continue to be led by a tightly knit group of friends? We think that these and other questions, coupled with our proposed integrative multi-disciplinary model, suggest a rich research agenda of theory building and testing, intended to promote a more general, contingent model of agency that would be relevant to a broad domain of firm contexts, all interesting to the field of strategic management.

## CONCLUSION

The model presented in figure 8.6 is a first step toward developing an integrative multi-disciplinary model of agency relationships in firm governance. It suggests that many of the factors considered fixed or exogenously determined by the J/M model may in fact be endogenous when viewed through a more diverse set of theoretical lenses. Clearly, much research needs to be done to refine these insights before a viable alternative to the J/M model can be defined. While our model of agency relationships in US public firms (figure 8.3) is supported by an empirical retest and extension of Amihud and Lev's (1981) study, and aspects of our model of family firms (figure 8.5) is supported by empirical field tests (Schulze et al., 2001b; and forthcoming), most of the relationships depicted in each of the component models and the integrative model have not been empirically explored. Figure 8.6 suggests caution in interpreting the findings from those studies that focus almost exclusively on moral hazard related agency problems, as has been the tradition in the strategy literature, while overlooking concomitant problems arising from adverse selection, holdup, and self-control. The figure also suggests caution when drawing generalizations from existing studies, since most are based on the US context. Systematic comparisons of the governance relationships of public, private, and family firms rooted in other institutional contexts are needed to evolve a more general strategic management theory of agency relationships in firm governance.

## Acknowledgments

The authors gratefully acknowledge the contributions of Albert Cannella (Texas A&M), Sven Collin (Lund University), and Philippe Very (EDHEC) towards the development of this paper.

## Note

1 More detailed discussions and reviews about the theory can be found in Barney and Ouchi, 1986; Eisenhardt, 1989; Jensen and Meckling, 1976; Perrow, 1986; and a 1990 special theory development forum in the *Academy of Management Review*, pages 367–499. Proponents of the Jensen–Meckling (J/M) model view it as revolutionary theory of the firm that provides a compelling, rigorous, and universal explanation for why various organization forms (hierarchies) persist apart from markets and its assertions about governance have been examined by strategists (e.g., Lane, Cannella and Lubatkin, 1998, 1999; Rediker and Seth, 1995), economists (e.g., Amihud and Lev, 1981, 1999; Denis, Denis and Sarin, 1999), and accountants (Baiman, 1990).

## References

Alba, J. W. and Hutchinson, J. W. (1987). Dimensions of consumer expertise. *Journal of Consumer Research*, 13: 411–54.

Alchian, A., and Demsetz, H. (1972). Production, information costs, and economic production. *American Economic Review*, 5: 777–95.

Alchian, A. A., and Woodward, S. (1988). The firm is dead: Long live the firm: A review of Oliver E. Williamson's, The Economic Institutions of Capitalism. *Journal of Economic Literature*, 26: 65–79.

Amihud, Y., and Lev, B. (1981). Risk reduction as a managerial motive for conglomerate mergers. *Bell Journal of Economics*, 12: 605–17.

Amihud, Y., and Lev, B. (1999). Does the corporate ownership structure affect its strategy toward diversification? *Strategic Management Journal*, 19(11): 1063–9.

Arrow, K. J. (1963). *Social Choice and Individual Values*. New York: Wiley.

Arrow, K. J. (1971). Essays in the Theory of Risk Bearing. Chicago: Markham.

Arrow, K. J. (1974). Limited knowledge and economic analysis. *American Economic Review*, 64(1): 1–10.

Arthur, W. B., (1991). Designing economic agents that act like human agents: a behavioral approach to bounded rationality. *American Economic Review*, 81(2): 353–9.

Baiman, S. (1990). Agency research in management accounting: A second look. *Accounting, Organizations and Society*, 15(4): 341–71.

Baldridge, D., and Schulze, W. S. (1999). Fairness in family firms. *1999 Best Paper Proceedings of the Academy of Management*.

Barkema, H. G., and Gomez-Mejia, L. R. (1998). Managerial compensation and firm performance: A general research framework. *Academy of Management Journal*, 41(2): 135–45.

Barney, J. B. and Ouchi, W. G. (1986). *Organizational Economics*. San Francisco: Jossey Bass.

Batson, C. D. (1990). How social is an animal? The Human Capacity for Caring. *American Psychologist*.

Becker, G. S. (1974). A theory of social interaction. *Journal of Political Economy*, 82: 1063–93.

Becker, G. S. (1981). *A Treatise on the Family*. Cambridge, MA: Harvard University Press.

Becker, G. S. and Murphy, K. M. (1988). A theory of rational addiction. *Journal of Political Economy*, 96(4): 675–700.

Berger, P. L., and Luckmann, T. (1967). *The Social Construction of Reality, A Treatise in the Sociology of Knowledge*. London: Penguin Books.

Bergstrom, T. C. (1989). A fresh look at the Rotten Kid theorem and other household mysteries. *Journal of Political Economy*, 97: 1138–59.

Bergstrom, T. C. (1995). On the evolution of altruistic rules for siblings. *American Economic Review*, 85(5): 58–81.

Berle, A. A., and Means, G. C. (1932). *The Modern Corporation and Private Property*. Chicago: Commerce Clearing House.

Besanko, D., Dranove, D., and Shanley, M. (1996). *Economics of Strategy*. New York: John Wiley and Sons.

Bettis, R. A. (1991). Strategic management and the straightjacket. *Organization Science*, 2(3): pp. 315–19.

Bird, A., and Wiersema, M. (1996). Underlying assumptions of agency theory and implications for non-US settings: The case of Japan. In *Research in the Sociology of Organizations*. Greenwich, CT: JAI Press, 14: 149–80.

Bloom, M., and Milkovich, G. T. (1998). Relationships among risk, incentive pay, and organizational performance. *Academy of Management Journal*, 41(3): 283–97.

Boyd, B. K. (1995). CEO duality and firm performance: A contingency model. *Strategic Management Journal*, 16(4): 301–12.

Brush, T. H., Bromiley, P., and Hendrickx, M. (2000). The free cash flow hypothesis for sales growth and firm performance. *Strategic Management Journal*, 21(4): 455–72.

Buchanan, J. M. (1975). The Samaritan's Dilemma. In E. S. Phelps (ed.), *Altruism, Morality and Economic Theory*. New York: Russell Sage Foundation.

Calori, R., Lubatkin, M., Very, P., and Veiga, J. (1997). Modeling the origins of nationally-bounded administrative heritage: A historical institutional analysis of French and British firms. *Organization Science*, 8(6): 681–96.

Cannella, B., and Lubatkin, M. (1994) Succession as a Sociopolitical Process: Internal Impediments to Outsider Selection. *Academy of Management Journal*, 36(4): 763–93.

Chami, R. (1997). What's different about family business? Social Science Research Network: Organizations and Markets Abstracts; Working Paper Series, file no. 98061505.

Chandler, A. D., Jr. (1990). *Scale and Scope: The Dynamics of Industrial Capitalism*, Cambridge, MA: Belknap Press.

Charkham, J. P. (1994). *Keeping Good Company: A Study of Corporate Governance in Five Countries*. Oxford: Clarendon Press.

Chase, W. G., and Simon, H. A. (1973). Perceptions in chess. *Cognitive Psychology*, 4: 55–81.

Coase, R. H. (1937). The nature of the firm. *Economica*, 4: 386–405.

Coffee, J. C., Jr. (1986). Shareholders versus managers: The strain in the corporate web. In J. C. Jr. Coffee, L. Lowenstein, and S. Rose-Ackerman (eds.), *Knights, Raiders and Targets: The Impact of Corporate Takeovers*: 77–134. New York: Oxford University Press.

Daily, C. M., and Dollinger, M. J. (1992). An empirical examination of ownership structure in family and professionally-managed firms. *Family Business Review*, 5(2): 117–36.

Davis, J. H., Schoorman, F. D., and Donaldson, L. (1997). Toward a stewardship theory of management. *Academy of Management Review*, 22(1), pp. 20–47.

DeFusco, R. A., Zorn, T. S. and Johnson, R. R. (1991). The association between executive stock option plan changes and managerial decision making. *Financial Management*, 20(1): 36–43.

Denis, D. J., Denis, D. K., and Sarin, A. (1999). Agency theory and the influence of equity ownership on corporate diversification strategies. *Strategic Management Journal*, 19(11): 1071–6.

Di Maggio, P. J., and Powell, W. W. (1983). The iron cage revisited: Institutional isomorphism and collective rationality in organizational fields. *American Sociological Review*, 48: 147–60.

Doctor, R., Tung, R. L., and Von Glinow, M. A. (1991). Future directions for management theory development. *Academy of Management Review*, 16(2): 362–5.

Dyer, J. H., and Singh, H. (1998). The relational view: Cooperative strategy and sources of interorganizational competitive advantage. *Academy of Management Review*, 23(4): 660–79.

Eisenhardt, K. M. (1989). Agency theory: An assessment and review. *Academy of Management Review*, 1: 57–74.

Eshel, I., Samuelson, L., and Shaked, A. (1998). Altruists, egoists, and holligans in a local interaction model. *American Economic Review*, 88(1): 157–79.

Fama, E. F. (1980). Agency problems and the theory of the firm. *Journal of Political Economy*, 88: 288–307.

Fama, E. F. and Jensen, M. C. (1983a). Separation of ownership and control. *Journal of Law and Economics*, 26: 301–25.

Fama, E. F. and Jensen, M. C. (1983b). Agency problems and residual claims. *Journal of Law and Economics*, 26: 325–44.

Finkelstein, S. and D'Aveni, R. A. (1994). CEO duality as a double-edged sword: How boards of directors balance entrenchment avoidance and unity of command. *Academy of Management Journal*, 37(5): 1079–108.

Finkelstein, S., and Boyd, B. K. (1998). How much does the CEO matter? The role of managerial discretion in the setting of CEO compensation. *Academy of Management Journal*, 41(2): 179–99.

Fishbein, M., and Ajzen, I. (1977). Attitude-behavior relations: A theoretical analysis and review of empirical research. *Psychological Bulletin*, 84: 888–918.

Ford, R. H. (1988). Outside directors and privately-held firms: Are they necessary? *Entrepreneurship Theory and Practice*, 13(1): 49–57.

Fredrickson, J. (1985). Effects of decision motives and organizational performance level on strategic decision processes. *Academy of Management Journal*, 28: 821–43.

Ghoshal, S., and Moran, P. (1996). Bad for practice: A critique of the transaction cost theory. *Academy of Management Review*, 21(1): 13–47.

Giddens, A. (1984). *The Constitution of Society : Outline of the Theory of Structuration*. Berkeley: University of California Press.

Gilliland, S. W. (1993). The perceived fairness of selection systems: An organizational justice perspective. *Academy of Management Review*, 18: 694–734.

Handler, W. C. (1990). Succession in owner-managed and family firms. A mutual role adjustment between the entrepreneur and the next generation. *Entrepreneurship Theory and Practice*, 15(19): 37–51.

Hansmann, H. (1996). *The Ownership of Enterprise*. Cambridge, MA: Harvard University Press.

Heide, J. B., and John, G. (1990). Alliances in industrial purchasing: The determinants of joint action in buyer-supplier relationships. *Journal of Marketing Research*, 27: 24–36.

Hofstede, G. (1994). *Cultures and Organizations, Software of the Mind*. London: McGraw-Hill.

Holl, P., and Kyriazis, D. (1997). Wealth creation and bid resistance in UK takeover bids. *Strategic Management Journal*, 18(6): 483–98.

Holtz-Eakin, D., Joulfian, D., and Rosen, H. S. (1993). The Carnagie conjecture: Some empirical evidence. *Quarterly Journal of Economics*, 108: 413–35.

Hoskisson, R., and Turk, T. (1990). Corporate restructuring and control limits of the internal capital markets. *Academy of Management Review*, 15(3): 459–77.

Jensen, M. C. (1989). Eclipse of the public corporation. *Harvard Business Review*, 67: 61–74.

Jensen, M. C. (1993). The modern industrial revolution, exit, and the failure of internal control systems. *The Journal of Finance*, 48(3): 831–80.

Jensen, M. C. (1994). Self-interest, altruism, incentives, and agency. *Journal of Applied Corporate Finance*.

Jensen, M. C. (1998). *Foundations of Organizational Strategy*, Cambridge, MA: Harvard University Press.

Jensen, M. C., and Meckling, W. F. (1976). Theory of the firm: Managerial behavior, agency costs, and ownership structure. *Journal of Financial Economics*, 3: 305–60.

Jensen, M. C., and Murphy, K. J. (1990). Performance pay and top-management incentives. *Journal of Political Economy*, 98(2): 225–64.

Jensen, M. C., and Smith, C. L. (1985). Stockholder, manager and creditor interests: Applications of agency theory, in E. I. Altman and M. G. Subrahmanyam (eds.), *Recent Advances in Corporate Finance*: 95–131. Homewood, IL: Irwin.

Kang, D. (2000). The impact of family ownership on performance in public organizations. A study of the US Fortune 500, 1982–1994. 2000 Academy of Management Meetings, Toronto CA.

Kochhar, R. (1996). Explaining firm capital structure: The role of agency theory vs. transaction cost economics. *Strategic Management Journal*, 17(9): 713–28.

Kosnik, R. (1987). Greenmail: A study in board performance in corporate governance. *Administrative Science Quarterly*, 32: 163–85.

Kosnik, R. (1990). Effects of board demography and directors incentives on corporate greenmail decisions. *Academy of Management Journal*, 33: 129–50.

Krebs, D. (1987). The challenge of altruism in biology and psychology. In C. Crawford, M. Smith, and D. Krebs (eds.), *Sociobiology and Psychology*. Hillsdale, NJ: Erlbaum.

Krosnic, J. A., Betz, A. L., Jussim, L. J., Lynn, A. R., and Stephens, L. (1992). Subliminal conditions of attitudes. *Personal Social Psychology Bulletin*, 18: 152–62.

Lane, P., Cannella, B., and Lubatkin, M. (1998). Agency problems and antecedents to unrelated mergers and diversification: Amihud and Lev reconsidered. *Strategic Management Journal*, 19(6): 455–578.

Lane, P. J., Cannella, A. A., and Lubatkin, M. H. (1999). Ownership structure and corporate strategy: One question viewed from two different worlds. *Strategic Management Journal*, 20(11): 1077–86.

Lessem, R., and Neubauer, F. (1994). *European Management Systems, Towards Unity Out of Cultural Diversity*. Maidenhead, UK: McGraw-Hill.

Levinson, H. (1971). Conflicts that plague family business. *Harvard Business Review*, March: 90–8.

Levinson, R. (1989). Problems in managing a family-owned business. Small Business Administration Publications, Item #MP3: 1–5.

Lew, M. I., and Kolodzeij, E. A. (1993). Compensation in a family-owned business. *Human Resources Professional*, 5(3): 55–7.

Li, M., and Simerly, R. L. (1998). The moderating effect of environmental dynamism on the ownership and performance relationship. *Strategic Management Journal*, 19(2): 169–79.

Lindbeck, A., and Weibull, J. W. (1988). Altruism and time consistency: The economics of a fait accompli. *Journal of Political Economy*, 96: 1165–82.

Lubatkin, M., Lane, P. J., Collin, S., and Very, P. (2001). A nationally-bounded theory of opportunism in corporate governance. University of Connecticut working paper.

Lunati, M. T. (1997). *Ethical Issues in Economics: From Altruism to Cooperation to Equity*. London: MacMillan Press.

MacNeil, I. R. (1980. *The New Social Contract*. New Haven, CT: Yale University Press.

Mancuso, R. (1997). Assuming the Position: A Family Business Survival Guide. Evanston: Houndstooth Press.

Margolis, H. (1982). *Selfishness, Altruism and Rationality*. Cambridge: Cambridge University Press.

Markides, C. and Singh, H. (1997). Corporate restructuring: A symptom of poor governance or a solution to past managerial mistakes? *European Management Journal*, 15(3): 212–19.

Meyer, M., and Zucker, L. G. (1989). *Permanently Failing Organizations*. Newbury Park, CA: Sage.

Mitchell, W. (1998). Commentary on 'Entry into new market segments in mature industries: Endogenous and exogenous segmentation in the U.S. brewing industry' by A. Swaminathan. *Strategic Management Journal*, 19: 405–11.

Mohlo, I. (1997). *The Economics of Information: Lying and Cheating in Markets and Organizations*. Oxford: Blackwell.

Moran, P., and Ghoshal, S. (1996). Theories of economic organization: The case for realism and balance. *Academy of Management Review*, 21(1): 58–72.

Morck, R. (1996). On the economics of concentrated ownership. *Canadian Business Law Journal*, 26: 63–85.

North, D. C. (1986). The new institutional economics. *Journal of Institutional and Theoretical Economics*, 142: 230–37.

North, D. C. (1990). *Institutions, Institutional Change and Economic Performance*. Cambridge: Cambridge University Press.

Nowak, M. A., and May, R. M. (1992). Evolutionary games and spatial chaos. *Nature*, 359: 826–29.

Pedersen, T., and Thomsen, S. (1997). TI: European patterns of corporate ownership: A twelve country study. *Journal of International Business Studies*, 28(4): 759–78.

Perrow, C. (1986). *Complex Organizations*. New York: Random House.

Piliavin, J. A., and Charng, H. (1990). Altruism: A review of recent theory and research. *Annual Review of Sociology*, 16: 27–65.

Pollak, R. A. (1988). Tied transfers and paternalistic preferences. *American Economic Review* (AEA Papers and Proceedings), 78: 372–7.

Rajan, R. G., and Zingales, L. (1998). Power in a theory of the firm. Social Science Research Network.

Reagan, P. B., and Stulz, R. M. (1986). Risk bearing, labor contracts, and capital markets. *Research in Finance*, 6: 217–232.

Rediker, K. J., and Seth, A. (1995). Boards of directors and substitution effects of alternative governance mechanisms. *Strategic Management Journal*, 16(2): 85–99

Reuer, J. J., and Miller, K. D. (1997). Agency costs and the performance implications of international joint venture internalization. *Strategic Management Journal*, 18(6): 425–38.

Roe, M. J. (1993). Some differences in corporate structure in Germany, Japan, and the United States. *Yale Law Journal*, 102(8): 1927–2003.

Schulze, W., Lubatkin, M., and Dino, R. (2000). Altruism and agency in family firms, Academy of Management's *Best Paper Proceedings*.

Schulze, B. , Lubatkin, M., and Dino, R. (2001a). Towards a theory of the family firm. University of Connecticut working paper.

Schulze, B., Lubatkin, M., and Dino, R (2001b). The organizational consequences of altruism in family-managed firms: Theory and evidence. University of Connecticut working paper.

Schulze, W., Lubatkin, M., Dino, R., and Buchholtz, A. (forthcoming). Agency relationships in family firms: Theory and evidence. *Organization Science*.

Scott, W. R. (1987). The adolescence of institutional theory. *Administrative Science Quarterly*, 32, 493–511.

Shleifer, A., and Vishny, R. (1986). Takeovers in the 60s and 80s: Evidence and Implications. *Strategic Management Journal*, 12 (Special Edition): 51–60.

Simon, H. A. (1985). Human nature and politics: The dialogue of psychology with political science. *American Political Science Review*, 79: 293–304.

Simon, H. A. (1993). Altruism and economics. *American Economic Review*, 83: 156–61.

Spender, J. C. (1994). Workplace knowledge: The individual and collective dimensions. Paper presented to the 2nd International Workshop on Managerial and Organizational Cognition, Brussels, EIASM, May.

Stark, O., and Falk, I. (1998). Transfers, empathy formation, and reverse transfers. *American Economic Review*, 88(2): 271–76.

Stulz, R. M. (1988). On takeover resistance, managerial discretion, and shareholder wealth. *Journal of Financial Economics*, 20: 25–54.

Thaler, R. H., and Shefrin, H. M. (1981). An economic theory of self-control. *Journal of Political Economy*, 89(2): 392–406.

Thomsen, S., and Pedersen, T. (1996). Nationality and ownership structures: The 100 largest companies in six European nations. *Management International Review*, 36(2): 149–66.

Tosi, H. L., and Gomez-Mejia, L. R. (1989). The decoupling of CEO pay and performance: An agency theory perspective. *Administrative Science Quarterly*, 34(2): 169–89.

Walsh, J. P., and Kosnik, R. D. (19930. Corporate raiders and their disciplinary role in the market for corporate control. *Academy of Management Journal*, 35: 671–700.

Walsh, J. P., and Seward, J. K. (1990). On the efficiency of internal and external control mechanisms. *Academy of Management Review*, 15(3): 421–58.

Ward, J. L. (1987). *Keeping the Family Business Healthy: How to Plan for Continuous Growth, Profitability, and Family Leadership*. San Francisco, CA: Jossey Bass.

Whitley, R. D. (1992). *Business Systems in East Asia: Firms, Markets and Societies*. London: Sage.

Williamson, O. E. (1985). *Economic Institutions of Capitalism*. New York: Free Press.

Wiseman R., and Gomez-Mejia, L. R. (1998). A behavioral agency model of managerial risk taking. *Academy of Management Review*, 23(1): 133–53.

Wortman, M. S., Jr. (1994). Theoretical foundations for family-owned business: A conceptual and research-based paradigm. *Family Business Review*, 7(1): 3–27.

Zaheer, A., and Venkatraman, N. (1995). Relational governance as an interorganizational strategy: An empirical test of the role of trust in economic exchange. *Strategic Management Journal*, 16(5): 373–92.

# 9

# Risk in Strategic Management Research

## Philip Bromiley, Kent D. Miller and Devaki Rau

Bowman's (1980) study has often been cited as the starting point for risk research within strategic management. Bowman credited work in finance and economics for motivating his interest in risk. Within industries, he found negative associations between corporate risk and return. He labeled this finding the "risk/return paradox" because it contradicted the positive risk-return relation of financial portfolio theory. Bowman explained how risk-return relations for organizations may differ from those in equity markets: "The firm with lower risks and higher returns (to the firm) can have its securities priced relatively higher by the securities marketplace, thus lowering its return to the securities buyer, which then eliminates the paradox at the level of the securities owner or buyer" (Bowman, 1980: 25).

Finance and strategic management have developed different theoretical perspectives on risk. Finance theory largely analyzes risk for efficient markets – the equity or debt market. Thus, in finance theory market forces determine risk-return relations. In contrast, corporate strategies largely cannot be purchased or sold. A strategic opportunity or innovation in one firm may have little value to other firms. Information about organizations and their strategies is often inaccessible. Whereas well-established markets exist for buying and selling small pieces of equity, organizations and the components of their strategies are often indivisible. Thus, risk analysis and risk phenomena within corporate strategy differ markedly from those within efficient capital markets.

Bowman (1980) called attention to the need for developing theory about risk within organizations, not just as a financial market phenomenon. He offered several possible explanations for the "risk/return paradox" including (1) differences in the quality of management enabled some firms to consistently achieve both lower risk and higher return than poorly managed firms, (2) the investment decisions of some firms reflect risk seeking rather than risk aversion, (3) less profitable firms take risks that more profitable firms avoid, and (4) market dominance may permit both higher profit and lower risk. These explanations focus on the roles of managers – their preferences and investment decisions – and firms' strategies within their industry contexts.

Since Bowman's (1980) study, an ongoing stream of research has continued to examine risk in strategic management. In many ways, this research reflects traits of Bowman's (1980) pioneering study. These researchers recognize risk as a core construct within management theory, although they often disagree about the construct's meaning and measurement. The theoretical perspectives they bring to risk vary and are often borrowed from other academic disciplines, including economics, finance, and psychology. Consistent with one of Bowman's (1980) own speculations, some researchers have attempted to explain risk-return relations as data artifacts and to dismiss interpretations in terms of substantive management or strategy phenomena.

Given the diversity of risk constructs and measures, and of theoretical perspectives on risk, it is difficult to assess the cumulative contribution of this research. After two decades of research activity, what do we know about risk within organizations? This chapter provides an overview of the relevant research with particular emphasis on the concept and measurement of risk, and studies of risk-return relations.[1] As strategic management research on risk enters its third decade of activity, we consider possible directions for advancing theory.

## Meaning and Measurement of Risk

### Definitions

Knight (1921) proposed the classic definitions of "uncertainty" and "risk" in economics. Following his definitions, "certainty" exists if the probabilities of decision outcomes are either zero or one. "Risk" is a state of accurate knowledge of the probability distribution of outcomes with probabilities taking values between zero and one. "Uncertainty" exists if the probability distribution of outcomes is unknown.

Despite wide use of Knight's definitions of "risk" and "uncertainty," his understandings of these terms have by no means met with universal acceptance. Scholars working on organizational issues have developed definitions of risk that differ markedly from those established by researchers in economics and psychology. Baird and Thomas (1990) and March and Shapira (1987) reported that managers' understandings of risk differ and generally conflict with Knight's definition. Related terms such as "uncertainty" and "ambiguity" complicate discussions of organizational risk.

Writing in the early 1980s, Bettis summarized the muddle surrounding risk and uncertainty:

> Technically, there is a distinction between risk and uncertainty . . . Almost all authors after noting this distinction ignore it and use risk and uncertainty interchangeably (Bettis, 1982: 22).

A few years later, Baird and Thomas offered a similar assessment:

> Eventually strategic management will need to refine its risk definition and develop a more complete classification system of risks that relates meaningfully to handling strategic problems (Baird and Thomas, 1985).

Baird and Thomas (1990) were among the first to address the problem they had identified. Drawing from the fields of psychology, management, finance, and marketing, they found numerous uses of the term "risk" including variability of returns, size and nature of outcomes (e.g., expected value and probabilities of possible outcomes), probability of loss, failure to attain targets, ruin, and lack of information. They found strategic management researchers most often defined risk as variability of accounting or stock returns, innovation, lack of information, entrepreneurship, and the threat of serious loss or bankruptcy.

What understandings of risk and uncertainty have gained prominence within strategic management? Strategic management researchers generally use the term risk to mean *unpredictability or down-side unpredictability of business outcome variables* such as revenues, costs, profit, market share, and so forth. They use empirical proxies such as the variance or semi-variance of business outcome variables. Downside measures of risk, such as semi-variance, conform to managers' frequent conceptualization of risk in terms of potential losses (Baird and Thomas, 1990; Mao, 1970; March and Shapira, 1987). This differs markedly from Knight's (1921) definition of risk which required knowledge of all of the possible outcomes and the probabilities assigned to each.

Uncertainty refers to the *perceived unpredictability of environmental and organizational contingencies*. Some of the most influential studies reflecting this view include Duncan (1972), Miles and Snow (1978), and Pfeffer and Salancik (1978). Milliken (1987) identified three types of perceived uncertainty about the environment: (1) *state uncertainty* – the inability to predict the future state of the environment; (2) *effect uncertainty* – the inability of managers to predict how environmental changes will impact on their organizations; and (3) *response uncertainty* – the inability of managers to identify potential organizational actions and their outcomes. Milliken's disaggregation of uncertainty concepts into three categories emphasizes both environmental and organizational factors, as well as organization–environment interactions.[2]

In summary, treatments of risk and uncertainty in strategic management often deviate from Knight's (1921) definitions, perhaps because Knight's definition of risk does not fit the context in which managers make strategic decisions. A few strategic decisions may have clear alternatives with known payoff probabilities; the immense majority of strategic choices involve uncertainty – in the multifaceted sense conveyed by Milliken (1987) rather than Knight's simpler portrayal.

## Risk measures

Strategic management researchers have used a variety of risk proxies in their empirical research. Most of these measures use accounting and stock returns data. Tables 9.1 and 9.2 summarize the risk measures used in previous research in strategic management.[3] The tables highlight studies focusing on risk and, as such, do not include studies focused on corporate diversification. Most often, researchers use variability in accounting returns (ROA or ROE) over time or the capital asset pricing model's (CAPM) systematic and unsystematic risk estimated using stock returns data. These choices appear to be driven by (1) data availability, (2) ease of computation, and (3) precedents in other fields.

The choice of risk measures has been a controversial topic among strategic management researchers since Bowman's (1980) influential study. Bowman used the variance in ROE (after-tax profit divided by stockholders' equity) from annual data over five- and nine-year periods. Subsequently, Bowman (1984) developed risk proxies by analyzing the contents of companies' annual reports. The majority of the studies since Bowman's (1980, 1982) work have used variance or standard deviation of ROE (Fiegenbaum and Thomas, 1986, 1988; Gooding, Goel, and Wiseman, 1996; Jegers, 1991), ROA (Jemison,

TABLE 9.1 Overview of studies using one or two risk measures

*Variance measures*

| | |
|---|---|
| Bowman (1980) | Variance of ROE |
| Marsh and Swanson (1984) | Adjusted variance of ROE |
| Fiegenbaum and Thomas (1986) | Variance of ROE |
| Jemison (1987) | Variance of ROA |
| Fiegenbaum and Thomas (1988) | Variance of ROE |
| Cool, Dierickx, and Jemison (1989) | Standard deviation of ROA and ROS |
| Fiegenbaum (1990) | Variance of ROA |
| Oviatt and Bauerschmidt (1991) | Variability of ROE around a time trend |
| Jegers (1991) | Variance of ROE |
| Balakrishnan and Fox (1993) | Standard deviation of annual percentage change in earnings |
| Baucus, Golec, and Cooper (1993) | Standard deviation of ROE and ROA |
| Gooding, Goel, and Wiseman (1996) | Standard deviation of ROE |

*CAPM measures*

| | |
|---|---|
| Aaker and Jacobson (1987) | Accounting beta using ROE |
| Amit and Wernerfelt (1990) | Unsystematic risk; Jensen's alpha |

*Other measures*

| | |
|---|---|
| Bowman (1984) | Annual report content analysis |
| Bromiley (1991b) | Standard deviation of EPS forecasts |
| D'Aveni and Ilinitch (1992) | Beta |
| | Altman's Z |
| Collins and Ruefli (1992) | Entropy measure based on shifting rank within an industry |
| Wiseman and Bromiley (1996) | Standard deviation of EPS forecasts |
| Palmer and Wiseman (1999) | Variance of ROA; Standard deviation of EPS forecasts |
| Deephouse and Wiseman (2000) | Standard deviation of EPS forecasts |

1987; Fiegenbaum, 1990; Cool, Dierickx, and Jemison, 1989), or ROS (Cool, Dierickx, and Jemison, 1989) as their risk proxies. Baucus, Golec, and Cooper (1993) drew attention to the distinctions between beginning-of-period and end-of-period measures of returns variability, using both ROE and ROA. Some researchers (e.g., Aaker and Jacobson, 1987; Fiegenbaum and Thomas, 1986; Fiegenbaum, 1990) justify using accounting returns variability by prior findings of positive correlations between accounting and market measures of risk (e.g., Beaver, Kettler, and Scholes, 1970; Beaver and Manegold, 1975; Bowman, 1979; Hill and Stone, 1980; Jacobson, 1987).

Other researchers have introduced idiosyncratic measures based on accounting returns. Their specifications come from concerns about the measurement properties of variance and standard deviation, or alternative conceptions of risk. Marsh and Swanson

TABLE 9.2 Overview of studies using more than two risk measures

| | |
|---|---|
| Woo (1987) | Sum of absolute deviation around average ROE |
| | Variability in market share around time trend |
| | Price-cost gap |
| Cool and Schendel (1987) | Standard deviation of market share |
| | Weighted segment share, and ROS |
| Fiegenbaum and Thomas (1990) | Absolute value of percentage change from average past ROE, ROA, current ratio, and sales to total assets |
| Miller and Bromiley (1990) | Standard deviation of ROA |
| | Standard deviation of ROE |
| | Standard deviation of analysts' EPS forecasts |
| | Coefficient of variation of analysts' EPS forecasts |
| | Beta |
| | Unsystematic risk |
| | Debt-to-equity ratio |
| | Capital intensity |
| | R&D intensity |
| Wiseman and Bromiley (1991) | Variance in ROE and ROA |
| | Variance in ROE and ROA around a time trend |
| Miller and Reuer (1996) | RLPM using stock returns |
| | RLPM using ROA and ROE |
| | Downside beta |
| | Probability of falling below industry average earnings to price ratio and ROA |
| | Standard deviation of ROA and ROE |
| | Beta |
| | Unsystematic risk |
| | Coefficient of variation of forecasted EPS |
| | Altman's Z |
| Miller and Leiblein (1996) | RLPM using ROA |
| | Standard deviation of ROA |
| | Standard deviation around ROA trend |
| Lehner (2000) | Absolute value of year-to-year change in ROE |
| | Mean of quadratic differences in ROE |
| | Variance of ROE around median |
| Reuer and Leiblein (2000) | RLPM using ROA and ROE |
| | Downside beta |

(1984) adjusted Bowman's (1980) risk measure for autocorrelation within firms over time, and market and industry factors across firms within periods. Rather than using the second-moment, Woo (1987) computed the sum of absolute deviations around each firm's average ROE over a four-year period.[4] Aaker and Jacobson (1987) fit accounting returns data (ROE) to a CAPM-type model to estimate accounting betas. Oviatt and Bauerschmidt (1991) and Wiseman and Bromiley (1991) measured risk as returns variability around a time trend. Balakrishnan and Fox (1993) used the standard deviation of annual percentage changes in earnings. Lehner (2000) used the mean quadratic differences over five-year periods, $d^2 = \Sigma(ROE_t - ROE_{t-1})^2/4$, and the variance in ROE around the median, rather than the mean.

Many studies use measures from the capital asset pricing model (Lintner, 1965; Sharpe, 1964). The CAPM model is specified as $r_{it} - r_{ft} = \beta(r_{mt} - r_{ft}) + \varepsilon_{it}$, where $r_{it}$, $r_{ft}$, and $r_{mt}$ are the stock $i$, risk-free, and market returns in period $t$. Researchers use time-series data to estimate the coefficient $\beta_i$. Unsystematic risk equals the standard deviation of the residuals from estimating the CAPM model. Amit and Wernerfelt (1990) focused on unsystematic risk, but also made use of Jensen's alpha (Jensen, 1969), computed as the intercept using the model, $r_{it} - r_{ft} = \alpha_i + \beta_i(r_{mt} - r_{ft}) + \varepsilon_{it}$. CAPM measures, particularly beta, have been the popular choice within corporate diversification research (Ruefli, Collins, and Lacugna, 1999). For their study of vertical integration, D'Aveni and Ilinitch (1992) chose both beta and Altman's $Z$, an inverse indicator of bankruptcy risk.[5]

For years, strategic management researchers have questioned the meaningfulness of CAPM risk measures and the CAPM's risk management implications. Bettis (1983) observed that, contrary to the assumptions of the CAPM, general managers are quite concerned about managing unsystematic risk. Bromiley (1990) challenged the relevance of beta for strategic management. Based on the lack of empirical support for the CAPM (see, for example, Fama and French, 1992) and contradictions with some fundamental assumptions of strategic management, Bromiley (1990), Ruefli, Collins, and Lacugna (1999), and Chatterjee, Lubatkin, and Schulze (1999) criticized the continued use of beta as a risk proxy in strategic management research.

Criticism has also been directed toward returns variability measures. Ruefli (1990; 1991) questioned the meaningfulness of estimating mean-variance relations. Ruefli and Wiggins (1994) extended this criticism to Oviatt and Bauerschmidt's (1991) measure using accounting returns variability around a time trend. Bromiley (1991a) and Miller and Leiblein (1996: Appendix B) tried to allay these concerns. Nevertheless, following Ruefli's critique the number of published studies employing risk measures has declined (Ruefli, Collins, and Lacugna, 1999), and researchers have shifted from contemporaneous to lagged relations between risk and performance or introduced novel risk measures.

Measures other than returns variability and CAPM (beta or alpha) have seen limited use in strategic management research. Despite the lack of attention from other researchers, these novel measures may reflect distinct conceptualizations of risk relevant to strategic management. For example, Bromiley (1991b) measured risk using the standard deviation of securities analysts' forecasts of earnings per share (EPS). This reflects a unique forward-looking (*ex ante*) perspective on risk. Wiseman and Bromiley (1996), Palmer and Wiseman (1999), and Deephouse and Wiseman (2000) also used this measure. Miller and Reuer (1996) advised using the coefficient of variation of forecasted EPS, rather than the standard deviation, to make comparisons across firms. The coefficient of variation is invariant to stock splits.

Several studies have proposed measures of risk that consider a firm's position relative to industry competitors. These measures indicate the volatility of market positions. Among her three measures of risk, Woo (1987) included a measure of business share instability, calculated from fluctuations around each firm's market share time trend. Cool and Schendel (1987) examined share instability using two different standard deviation measures. Collins and Ruefli (1992) proposed an ordinal measure of risk. Their measure reflects the intuitively appealing notion that managers care about their performance rankings relative to competitors.

Several key problems arise with risk measures formulated relative to industry competitors. First, these measures assume clear industry boundaries and may confuse risk with changes in the set of industry competitors (due, for example, to mergers and acquisitions or new entrants). Second, even with clear, stable industry composition, these measures only allow for intra-industry comparisons. Comparing the volatility of market shares or ranks across industries with fundamentally different structures (e.g., duopolies and fragmented markets) or numbers of competitors is problematic. Third, because these measures are based on relative position, they reflect the volatility of the industry, not just changes in firm-specific performance. A firm could have very stable returns and sales but high measured risk solely because of the volatility of its competitors. Fourth, these measures generally require aggregation over time, which requires the assumption of constant risk over time (an assumption rejected by Ruefli, 1990, 1991). The tie of this conceptualization of risk to specific theoretical perspectives on risk remains unclear.

Several studies have compared multiple risk measures.[6] Fiegenbaum and Thomas (1990) examined four financial ratios: ROE, ROA, current ratio, and sales to total assets (i.e., turnover). They measured risk as the absolute value of percentage deviations from the average ratio in the previous four years. Miller and Bromiley (1990) analyzed a broad set of risk proxies and found that they sorted into three categories: income stream risk (based on variance in accounting returns and EPS forecasts), stock returns risk (beta and unsystematic risk), and strategic risk (reflecting various accounting ratios associated with risk taking). This last category could be viewed as determinants of risk, rather than direct measures of risk. Both Fiegenbaum and Thomas (1990) and Miller and Bromiley (1990) argued that different risk measures reflect distinct stakeholder perspectives on firm risk and they cautioned against arbitrary selection of risk proxies.[7]

Miller and Reuer (1996) introduced three categories of measures based on downside, rather than variability, perspectives on risk. These categories included (1) lower partial moments (LPM), (2) beta from a downside version of the CAPM,[8] and (3) downside measures based on stock analysts' earnings forecasts. This study also provided comparisons with many measures used in previous strategic management research. Miller and Reuer (1996) identified five risk factors, which they labeled (1) unsystematic risk, (2) income stream risk, (3) systematic risk, (4) *ex ante* downside risk, and (5) bankruptcy risk. Miller and Leiblein (1996) used root lower partial moment (RLPM) measures based on ROA data over five-year periods. Comparison measures included the standard deviation of ROA and a measure of variability in ROA around a time trend. Reuer and Leiblein (2000) studied the risk characteristics of international joint ventures using a root lower partial moment measure based on ROA.

The variety of risk measures used in previous research makes comparisons across studies difficult. Beyond noting the diversity that characterizes strategic risk measurement, can we draw any conclusions from these studies?

This research indicates that strategic risk is a multidimensional construct. Measures based on a single performance indicator, such as variability in accounting returns, reflect only one aspect of strategic risk. Different theoretical perspectives call for different risk measures. In particular, the choice of risk measure should reflect the relevant stakeholder perspective for testing any particular theory. Variability in sales matters to employees and suppliers while variability in stock returns matters to stockholders. If theory does not indicate clearly the most appropriate category of risk measure, researchers should consider multiple measures. When borrowing measures from finance and accounting, researchers should provide theoretical arguments to demonstrate their relevance to a strategic management research topic, rather than simply invoking precedents in the literature.

In general, researchers should place greater emphasis on the validity and reliability of risk measures in strategic management. When specifying risk measures, researchers should consider several key questions. Are *ex ante* measures, such as those based on analysts' earnings forecasts, more appropriate than *ex post* measures derived from historical performance data? In changing firms and industries, *ex post* measures may not reflect the risk perceived when managers make decisions. Are downside or variability measures more appropriate? The answer to this question turns on the concept of risk relevant to the theory and stakeholder perspective under consideration. Should the risk measure reflect a reference level, such as the performance of other industry competitors? Finally, are the risk measures comparable across firms and time periods, and readily replicable by other researchers? These questions raise important research design considerations.

## Theoretical Perspectives and Empirical Findings on Organizational Risk

Most of the strategic management literature on risk attacks a single general question: what drives the riskiness of strategic choices? These studies generally assume managerial or organizational risk preferences influence strategic choices, that is, the risk characteristics of alternatives form a substantial factor in managerial evaluations of such alternatives.[9] As such, scholars refer to "risk taking" (e.g., MacCrimmon and Wehrung, 1986; March and Shapira, 1987; Shapira, 1994). They study the relations between antecedents associated with risk preferences and firm risk. With few exceptions (e.g., Greve, 1998; Palmer and Wiseman, 1999), these studies tie factors associated with managers' collective risk propensity directly to organizational risk with little attention given to the strategic choices that mediate the relation.

Other studies have examined environmental influences on organizational risk (e.g., Palmer and Wiseman, 1999; Lehner, 2000). Environmental factors may influence organizational risk in ways not entirely attributable to organizational or managerial risk preferences. For example, the organization's environment may become more turbulent, resulting in increased risk despite no change in managers' risk preferences or the firm's strategy. Sitkin and Weingart (1995) offered a model of risk-taking that distinguishes between risk perceptions and risk propensity. Their model has been supported in experiments, but we know of no field support.

Three theories dominate strategic management research on risk taking. Two primary theories shape behavioral work on risk-taking by organizations: Cyert and March's (1963) behavioral theory of the firm, and Kahneman and Tversky's prospect theory (Kahneman and Tversky, 1979; Tversky and Kahneman, 1992). As noted earlier, this

**Exogenous factors** → **Firm choices** → **Firm outcomes**
Business cycle          Capital structure        Financial performance
Aspirations             Asset allocations        Income stream uncertainty
Slack                   Lending decisions        Other risk measures
                        Diversification
                        R&D intensity
                        Other strategy changes

FIGURE 9.1 Key variables and relations in risk research

line of research implicitly assumes managerial or organizational risk preferences explain risk-taking strategies. The third line of theory development – agency theory – recognizes the moderating role of governance mechanisms on managers' expressions of risk preferences that may conflict with the interests of risk neutral shareholders. Figure 9.1 summarizes the key variables and relations in previous empirical risk research and some important studies are summarized in Appendix 9.

## Prospect theory

Bowman (1982) invoked Kahneman and Tversky's (1979) prospect theory to explain the risk/return paradox as risk taking by troubled firms. Kahneman and Tversky based their theory on experimental studies of individuals' risk preferences in which they found: (1) people measure outcomes relative to a reference point, typically the current wealth level; and (2) people evaluate probabilistic choices using a value function that is concave above the reference point (risk avoiding) and convex below (risk seeking).

Although Kahneman and Tversky (1979) offered a mathematical model, Bowman (1982) and those who followed in this line (Fiegenbaum, 1990; Fiegenbaum and Thomas, 1986, 1988, 1990; Jegers, 1991) have taken a qualitative approach to the theory. They argue that low performing firms will seek risk (because they define their current outcomes as undesirable) and high performing firms will avoid risk (because they define their current outcomes as above a reference point).

Researchers following this approach typically calculate the mean and standard deviation of return on assets or equity over some time period (often five years) for each firm. Using industry median return and median risk as cutoff values, they divide the firms within an industry into four groups. These groups can then be used to determine whether negative or positive risk-return relations predominate. These studies report: (1) for firms with performance below industry average or full sample average, returns and risk correlate negatively (Fiegenbaum and Thomas, 1988); (2) for firms with performance above industry average or full sample average, returns and risk correlate positively (Fiegenbaum and Thomas, 1988); (3) the patterns differ over time with greater environmental stability increasing the strength of positive risk-return associations for high-return industries, and greater instability strengthening negative risk-return associations for low-return industries (Fiegenbaum and Thomas, 1986).

Some criticisms have been raised of such work. Wiseman and Bromiley (1991) suggested non-stationarity of the return series might explain the phenomenon, but found removing trends from the series did not change the results. Lehner (2000) introduced alternative measures of risk and sought to estimate reference levels empirically. His results largely supported the Fiegenbaum and Thomas (1988) findings.

Ruefli (1990) claimed the mean-variance relation was inherently unidentified, but showed conventional assumptions identify the models (cf. Miller and Leiblein, 1996: Appendix B). If you want to look at relations between returns means and variances across firms (where firm-specific means and variances are calculated over some arbitrary time period such as five years), you must assume (1) the true mean for each firm is constant over the time period, (2) each firm's returns are normally distributed, and (3) the cross-sectional linear relation between risk and return must hold over the time period (allowing for stochastic error).

We have several concerns about the measure of risk and the theory in the prospect theory line of work. The use of historical returns and income stream uncertainty may mislead if *ex ante* risk differs systematically from *ex post*.[10] Researchers may be uncomfortable with the assumption that individual firms' risk and return levels do not change over an extended (e.g., five-year) interval (with the exception of stochastic noise). However, so far efforts to demonstrate these problems really influence the findings have failed (see, for instance, Bromiley, 1991b; Wiseman and Bromiley, 1991).

At a more fundamental level, we are uncomfortable with the prospect theory basis for these studies. Prospect theory attempted to explain individual behavior so its assumptions may not make sense for firms. Prospect theory researchers eliminate "extraneous" factors so that the effects they want to test dominate the situation within their experiments. In organizations, other completely different factors may dominate making the experimental results inapplicable (see, for instance, Bromiley (1987) on anchoring and adjustment and McNamara, Moon, and Bromiley (forthcoming), on escalation of commitment). Kahneman and Tversky (1979) presented individuals with choices framed either in the domain of losses or in the domain of gains. They wanted to know whether individuals prefer a sure loss to a probabilistic loss or a sure gain to a probabilistic gain (of comparable expected value). For the most part, the choices did not involve mixed (positive and negative possible outcome) choices.

Within prospect theory, the framing of alternatives explains the expressed risk preferences. This implies that to test prospect theory at the firm level, we would need to find a set of firms facing choices among alternative projects framed exclusively in either the domain of gains or the domain of losses. To derive from prospect theory the proposition driving the existing studies in strategic management, we must assume that because a firm has below median returns, all its options have negative expected values. The existing studies appear to modify prospect theory to make median returns on new projects the reference level, rather than using current wealth as the reference level. The theory also directly applies only to situations where decision makers face well-defined risky choices with clearly specified outcomes and probabilities, not the uncertain and amorphous set of possible actions that corporate management faces (cf. March, 1978; Milliken, 1987).

Most studies infer from prospect theory that risk seeking and risk aversion increase as the firm moves away from the reference point (Fiegenbaum and Thomas, 1986, 1988, 1990; Fiegenbaum, 1990; Lehner, 2000). However, Kahneman and Tversky (1979) simply asserted risk aversion in the domain of gains and risk seeking in the domain of losses, and not *increasing* risk aversion and risk seeking with distance from an expected payoff of zero. Most researchers ignore this issue and assume prospect theory predicts minimum risk aversion and risk seeking near the reference point. Prospect theory only asserts risk seeking in the domain of losses and risk aversion in the domain of gains and does not make comparative statements within domains.

## Behavioral theory of the firm

Studies by Bromiley (Bromiley, 1991b) and his students (Miller and Bromiley, 1990; Wiseman and Bromiley, 1991; Miller and Leiblein, 1996; Wiseman and Bromiley, 1996; McNamara and Bromiley, 1997; Wiseman and Catanach, 1997; McNamara and Bromiley, 1999) start from a different theoretical perspective – Cyert and March's (1963) behavioral theory of the firm (BTOF). The central BTOF themes of search and responses to uncertainty provide a basis for theorizing about organizational risk. March and Shapira (1987, 1992) and Shapira (1994) made explicit connections between the behavioral theory of the firm and risk taking, and introduced some modifications to the initial theory. The BTOF and related work offer two different models of risk-taking – one based on Cyert and March (1963) and the other on findings in March and Shapira (1987, 1992) and Shapira (1994). Let us begin with the original BTOF.

In the BTOF, firms have aspiration and performance levels. If performance exceeds aspirations, the firm continues to operate according to its established routines. If the firm does not perform up to its aspirations, it searches for ways to improve. Lant (1992) referred to the difference between aspirations and actual performance as attainment discrepancy. Bromiley (1991b) associated organizational search with increased risk. Finally, the BTOF raised the possibility that firms with extremely high levels of performance innovate because they have slack resources and such risk taking does not pose the threat of falling below aspirations.

The aspiration level depends on two kinds of comparisons: comparison to relevant others and to the firm's own past performance (Cyert and March, 1963; Lant, 1992). Bromiley (1991b) argued that firms with performance below industry norms will aspire to meeting industry norms while firms with performance above industry norms will aspire to slightly improve performance. This model results in a non-linear risk function that depends substantially on both the comparison to others and the firm's past performance. Risk taking increases as firms move further and further below industry average performance. For firms above industry average performance, risk taking will depend on the firm's performance relative to recent performance.

A variety of empirical work reflects this theoretical perspective. Singh (1986) used a small sample survey to find performance below target associated with risk taking. Bromiley (1991b) presented a BTOF model of risk taking and performance. Instead of using actual returns to measure risk, he used the standard deviation in analysts' forecasts of returns for a company as a proxy for the uncertainty of that company's income stream. Bromiley found low performance drove risk taking and risk taking lowered subsequent performance.

Wiseman and Bromiley (1996) applied the model from Bromiley (1991b) to a sample of declining firms and found risk taking by such firms reduced future performance. Wiseman and Catanach (1997) used risk measures directly related to savings and loan bank operations along with both BTOF and agency variables. They found that both performance relative to average performance and slack influenced risk, and the different risks related differently to the explanatory variables. Greve's (1998) study of radio broadcasters showed increased probability of changes in strategy (i.e., programming format) for below-aspiration firms relative to above-aspiration firms. Palmer and Wiseman (1999) examined a model where exogenous factors influence managerial risk taking (measured by R&D/ sales and diversification), and then these influence organizational risk (measured by variance in both ROA and price/earnings ratios). They find strong support for the mediating role of managerial risk taking, as well as strong support for the influence of attainment discrepancy on both managerial risk taking and income stream uncertainty.

March and Shapira (1987, 1992) offered a somewhat more complex model based on interviews with numerous managers. They proposed that managers judge their position relative to one of two reference points: a bankruptcy (disaster) level or an aspiration level. First, if a firm's managers expect to go bankrupt, they will take risks in an effort to avoid bankruptcy. Firms of higher performance but still low enough that bankruptcy constitutes their reference point, will avoid risk to reduce the possibility of bankruptcy. Second, most firms will focus on an aspiration level that constitutes satisfactory performance, perhaps industry average performance or past performance. For these firms, risk taking is low near the aspiration level and increases with distance from the aspiration level in either direction. Firms with performance below the reference point take risks trying to reach the reference point. Firms with extremely high resources (well above the reference point) may take risks because they can afford to gamble. Bromiley (1991b) found support for contention that performance below aspirations drives risk taking but little support for the "high performance allows risk taking" argument. Thus far, the implications of March and Shapira's (1987) findings have only been exhibited through their later (1992) simulation and not in organization-level empirical data.

Unlike prospect theory, the behavioral theory of the firm (Cyert and March, 1963) – including the variant offered by March and Shapira (1987, 1992) – is attractive because it offers an organization-level theory of risk taking. Nevertheless, it has some limitations when applied to risk research. The BTOF deals with problem-driven searches for alternative routines. As such, it seems more appropriate to apply the theory to incremental changes in strategy rather than broad shifts in strategy. The risk taking described in the BTOF applies to new initiatives launched in response to problems. Nevertheless, the empirical research has attempted to explain organization-wide risk taking. Data on strategic or project financing decisions over time may provide a more appropriate context for testing the theory. In addition, the BTOF is a theory of search that does not predict what kinds of strategies firms will adopt. If we are interested not only in the extent of search, but also the direction of search and likely search outcomes, we need to supplement the BTOF with additional theory.

## Agency theory and other perspectives

Agency theory (e.g., Demsetz, 1983; Fama, 1980; Jensen and Meckling, 1976) recognizes that managers may not have free reign to pursue their own risk preferences. It focuses on the problem of a principal (owner, shareholder, higher-level manager) trying to get an agent (employee, CEO, lower-level manager) to act in the principal's interest. Although the details vary somewhat, the models usually assume a risk-neutral principal and a risk-averse agent. The agent gains utility from income and some activities that are not in the principal's interest, for example, shirking and providing excess benefits to managers. The models assume the principal cannot observe the agent's actions directly and so must design incentive systems to control the agent's behavior. The models generally assume the principal can be trusted (e.g., pays all agreed-on amounts), the agent cannot (e.g., will overstate his or her effort), and there is a random component to the relation between effort and performance.

Although agency models have been widely applied in strategic management, their application in the organizational risk literature has been limited. Wiseman and Gomez-Mejia (1998) developed a behavioral model of agency and risk by incorporating prospect theory arguments into an agency framework. Palmer and Wiseman (1999) found that stock ownership (stock holdings of officers, directors, and top management) positively influences managerial risk taking. Wright et al. (1996) found insider stock ownership has a non-linear influence on risk that also depends on the firm's growth opportunities. Much of the agency work related to risk has been applied to diversification, a research stream that we have omitted due to space limitations.[11]

Other studies examine strategy, structure, and environmental relations with firm risk from diverse theoretical stances. Cool and Schendel (1987) found risk does not differ across strategic groups in the US pharmaceutical industry. Oviatt and Bauerschmidt (1991) estimated a simultaneous equation model that included return, risk (variance in returns), and debt as endogenous variables. They found that simultaneous estimation of the model eliminates direct risk-return relations; correlations between risk and return appear to be due to business strategy and industry factors influencing both variables.

## What Do We Know? How Should We Proceed?

Although much of the strategic management research on risk is hard to compare – using a variety of theories, measures, and databases – some general findings emerge from this stream of work.

First, and most fundamental, firm-level risk has multiple dimensions. If one wants to take a Cyert and March (1963) view of the firm as a coalition, or the related stakeholder view (Freeman, 1984), these differing risk dimensions reflect differing interests of the coalition members. Employees may concern themselves with variability that influences their employment prospects, whereas debt holders worry about bankruptcy.

Second, these risk dimensions influence performance. Miller and Bromiley (1990), Bromiley (1991b), and Wiseman and Bromiley (1996) found income stream uncertainty negatively influences performance. Miller and Leiblein (1996) found downside risk positively influences subsequent performance.

Third, some constructs from the BTOF influence risk taking. Performance below aspirations appears to increase risk taking (i.e., the greater the performance is below aspirations, the greater the risk taking). Slack generally reduces risk taking.

Fourth, consistent with agency theory, strong governance appears to mitigate managerial risk aversion. Stock ownership in particular seems to increase managerial risk taking (Wright et al., 1996; Palmer and Wiseman, 1999).

On the other hand, some substantial limitations remain. Much of the literature uses bivariate analyses opening issues of omitted variables bias. We have a wide set of risk measures whose construct validity and reliability need additional attention. For example, should the variance or the standard deviation be used for risk measurements? Linear relations under one measure become non-linear under the other, yet the reasons for our choices have not been clearly presented. In addition, possible correlations between risk measures constructed from accounting data and other accounting variables may be due to construction rather than substantive strategic behaviors. We also need to understand better the lag structure of risk-return relations.

Researchers should distinguish between the effects of environmental changes and managers' choices on firms' risk characteristics. At least some of the time, changes in firm risk derive from stable strategies in a changing environment. This differs drastically from managers consciously taking actions that increase risk. Our theories of risk and empirical research designs should allow for the possibility that managers may be surprised to find themselves in situations of greater or lesser risk than they anticipated when making earlier strategic decisions (see Harrison and March, 1984).

In addition, we need to connect work on managers' perceptions of environmental uncertainties with corporate responses. The relations between risk and uncertain environmental contingencies can be expressed in terms of the economic exposures of firms (Miller, 1998; Miller and Reuer, 1998a, b). To be of help to managers, researchers should examine specific responses to distinct kinds of uncertainties. For example, we would expect a firm facing technological uncertainty to respond very differently than a firm facing uncertainty regarding its relationships with key suppliers.

This leads to an interest in research on actual strategic decisions that reflect risk seeking and risk averse responses. Greve (1998) looked at risky format changes by radio stations. Palmer and Wiseman (1999) examined R&D/sales and levels of diversification. McNamara and Bromiley (1997, 1999) and McNamara, Moon, and Bromiley (forthcoming) studied risk-related lending decisions in commercial banking. Staw et al. (1997) looked at changes in top management and risk reduction at the corporate level in commercial loan portfolios. Wiseman and Catanach (1997) examined risk measures in the savings and loan industry where to some extent the risk levels reflect conscious managerial choices. As noted in the previous section, the BTOF may be more appropriately applied to on-going capital budgeting decisions than to broad strategic shifts.

Overall, we want to understand managerial strategic decisions, but lack research on actual decisions. Examining actual decisions poses many difficulties, even beyond the pragmatic concern of data access. It is often difficult to distinguish the riskiness of alternative courses of action, or even determine which decisions are risk seeking and which are risk averse. The time frame considered may be critical. Decisions that could be classified as risk seeking in the short-run, because they introduce innovation, may be risk averse in the long-run, because without innovation the firm faces inevitable demise. Scholars need to develop ways to categorize the extent of risk taking and risk aversion depending on firms' actions and the contexts they face. Understanding the existing exposures of a firm may provide insights into whether a particular strategic choice (e.g., an acquisition) will increase or decrease firm risk. Research on real options may inform which decisions reduce risk by enhancing flexibility.

Researchers may want to follow Singh's (1986) approach of measuring risk taking along multiple dimensions through questionnaires. Singh's risk measure included six items about reliance on innovation, debt financing, heavy R&D, and high risk-return investments.

Because our theories predict managers' choices based on their perceptions, research should address such perceptions. MacCrimmon and Wehrung's (1986) research provides an alternative basis for developing measures of risk taking. However, they also provide a strong warning that differing instruments measuring "risk" generate proxies that have almost zero correlation. As Palmer and Wiseman (1999) pointed out, risk taking and organizational risk are distinct constructs calling for distinct measures. The development of instruments to gather perceptual data on risk lags behind the work done on perceived environmental uncertainties (Duncan, 1972; Miller, 1993; Werner, Brouthers, and Brouthers, 1996).

Researchers need to consider the exact place of risk in their models. Although risk may influence performance, in many cases strategic choices influence both risk and performance simultaneously. It makes a substantial difference whether risk and performance associate because they both have the same antecedents, or whether risk directly influences performance.

Current theorizing has not given sufficient attention to the implications of risk for operating costs and revenues. A few researchers in finance have argued that variability in performance raises the cost of doing business and may discourage customers from doing business with the firm (e.g., Cornell and Shapiro, 1987; Shapiro and Titman, 1986). Although some strategic management researchers have recognized these arguments (e.g., Aaker and Jacobson, 1990; Amit and Wernerfelt, 1990; Miller, 1998; Deephouse and Wiseman, 2000), this plausible explanation for strategic and financial hedging has not been widely acknowledged, nor has it received the empirical attention it merits. The finding that risk negatively affects returns is consistent with this perspective, yet the causal explanation is quite different from the explanations most widely presented in strategic management research.

Finally, a prescriptive literature needs to assist managers in assessing and managing strategic risk. Two applications have been evident to date. Fiegenbaum, Hart, and Schendel (1996) began to examine aggregate risk-return conceptual frameworks and their ties to performance. Miller (1998) argued for sophisticated analyses of corporate exposures to different sources of risk, and the selective hedging of corporate risk through diversification and real option investments. Either or both approaches may prove productive in the future.

## CONCLUSION

Overall, strategic management work on risk has taken some important steps forward in the last two decades. From naïve analogies to stock market results, we have moved toward understanding the differing dimensions and consequences of strategic risk. However, there remain sufficient gaps in our understanding that others should be encouraged to pursue research in this area.

## NOTES

1 Fiegenbaum and Thomas (1988), Collins and Ruefli (1996: ch. 1), and Ruefli, Collins, and Lacugna (1999) provided earlier revies of risk research in strategic management. To keep the

scope of our review manageable, we do not consider the extensive research on corporate diversification that includes risk-related issues (see note 11). We also do not discuss the studies dealing with credit risk faced by banks.

2 Miller (1993) reviewed previous research on the measurement of perceived environmental uncertainty and proposed a measurement instrument based on strategic management and international business research (cf. Werner, Brouthers, and Brouthers, 1996).

3 Ruefli, Collins, and Lacugna (1999: Appendix 2) provide a similar table summarizing the risk measures used in research published in eight management journals over the period 1980–95. Their review included studies on corporate diversification. They identified 34 studies with "variance" measures, 57 with measures based on the CAPM, 11 with other measures, and 6 with more than one category of measure.

4 As noted in table 9.2, Woo (1987) also used a measure she referred to as the price-cost gap, essentially the mark-up on sales. She categorizes this as a measure of risk, but it probably would be better categorized as a measure of performance.

5 Altman's $Z$ is defined as $(1.2 \times LIQ) + (1.4 \times RE) + (3.3 \times ROA) + (0.6 \times MED) + (1.0 \times CAPINT)$, where $LIQ$ is working capital divided by total assets, $RE$ is retained earnings divided by total assets, $ROA$ is earnings before interest and taxes divided by total assets, $MED$ is the market value of equity divided by the book value of total liabilities, and $CAPINT$ is sales divided by total assets (Altman, 1983).

6 Vos (1992) discussed a variety of risk measures (CAPM beta, coefficient of variation using returns data, trend-adjusted measures, and accounting beta), but did not provide an empirical comparison.

7 Jemison (1987) also made this point.

8 The mean-lower partial moment CAPM uses the same model as the standard CAPM, however, beta is estimated only over those periods in which the market portfolio underperforms a target return. For details, see Harlow and Rao (1989) or Miller and Reuer (1996)

9 Although numerous examples could be cited, some prominent examples of strategic management studies approaching risk as a choice are Bowman (1982, 1984), Bromiley (1991b), Fiegenbaum and Thomas (1986, 1988, 1990), Sing (1986), and Wiseman and Bromiley (1996).

10 However, Miller and Bromiley (1990) and Miller and Reuer (1996) showed that the standard deviation of returns (either ROA or ROE) is highly correlated with the coefficient of variation of stock analysts' earnings per share forecasts.

11 Strategic management researchers have examined the relation between risk (measured in terms of systematic risk, beta, unsystematic risk, and total risk) and diversification. Many studies in this area find that related diversification is associated with lowered systematic risk (Chatterjee and Lubatkin, 1990; Lubatkin and Chatterjee, 1994; Lubatkin and O'Neill, 1987; Montgomery and Singh, 1984). However, other studies find little difference in systematic risk between unrelated and related diversification strategies (Bettis and Hall (1982). The level of unsystematic risk of acquiring firms seems to increase following mergers, regardless of the relatedness of the merging firms (Lubatkin and O'Neill, 1987). Some researchers have examined the relation between diversification and risk-adjusted performance. Bettis and Mahajan (1985) found that although related diversified firms outperform unrelated diversified firms on average, related diversification is no guarantee of a favorable risk/return performance. Different diversification strategies can result in a similar risk/return performance. Kim, Hwang, and Burgers (1993) found that the risk-adjusted performance of related diversifiers tends to be more favorable than that of unrelated diversifiers. Amit and Livnat (1988) classified firms into risk-return clusters and found that related diversification characterizes firms in the high risk–high return cluster, while low risk–low return firms were usually unrelated diversifiers.

APPENDIX

Appendix 9: A few selected studies on strategic risk

| Author(s) Article title | Risk construct and measure | Sample | Risk related findings |
|---|---|---|---|
| *Articles based on prospect theory* | | | |
| Bowman, E. H. (1980) A risk/return paradox for strategic management | Variability of profit | 85 industries covered by Value Line, including 1572 companies, in 1972–76 and 1968–76. A third study mixed 300 companies from 9 test industries arbitrarily chosen. | Study 1 (1972–76): In the majority of the industries studied, higher-average-profit companies tended to have lower risk, i.e., variance, over time. Study 2 (1968–76): 56 industries support the hypothesis of a negative risk/return correlation, 21 refute it, 8 are ties. The mixed companies showed no real relationship between corporate risk and return. There is a negative correlation within industries, which while apparently significant, is modest. |
| Bowman, E. H. (1984) Risk seeking by troubled firms | The president's report at the beginning of each annual report was coded for the word "new" which can be associated with risky and unknowable things. | 27 companies in the container industry as listed by Value Line in 1976. | Troubled companies take more risks. |
| Bowman, E. H. (1984) Content analysis of annual | Variability of returns. For the content analysis studies, three surrogate variables for risk were identified: (a) acquisition activity, (b) litigation involvement, (c) | 1. Content analysis of 26 annual reports for 1976 in the container industry using the | Negative correlation coefficient between risk and return for the three earlier series of studies. |

| Author(s) / Article title | Risk construct and measure | Sample | Risk related findings |
|---|---|---|---|
| reports for corporate strategy and risk. | new activities and ventures. For the study in this paper, four surrogate measures of risk were chosen corresponding roughly to managerial risk (the number of times the word "new" appears in the president's letter), legal risk (litigation), technological risk (%R&D compared to total sales), and financial risk (long-term debt/equity) | companies listed by Value Line. | This paper: companies with lower profits in the earlier period subsequently evidenced substantially risky behavior. |
| Fiegenbaum, A., and Thomas, H. (1986) Dynamic and risk measurement perspectives on Bowman's risk-return paradox for strategic management: An empirical study. | Variance of ROE | Data from COMPUSTAT database. Bowman type analyses performed for non-overlapping 5-year time periods 1960–64 (37 industries), 1965–69 (50 industries), 1970–74 (55 industries), 1975–79 (56 industries). | 1. The risk-return paradox appears to be dependent upon the time period adopted in the study. It appears more likely to hold in more uncertain, less predictable environments. 2. Better-performing industries tend to exhibit positive risk-return associations, whereas low-performing industries appear to be more prone to exhibit negative associations. This negative association tendency is more closely associated with the uncertain environments of the 1970s. 3. The use of market-based risk measures (betas) in calculating risk-return correlations tends to eliminate the risk/return paradox. |

| Study | Risk measure | Sample | Findings |
| --- | --- | --- | --- |
| Lehner, J. M. (2000) Shifts of reference points for framing strategic decisions and changing risk-return associations. | Risk was measured as mean of quadratic differences. $\Delta R_t = R_t - R_{t-1}$ $d^2 = \sum \Delta R_t^2 * 1/(T-1)$ | 876 firms in fourteen industries that contained at least 25 firms in the time period 1960–79. | 1. At least a minority of firms shift to individual reference points (as opposed to the industry median) 2. A firm's reference point, as it is estimated through the regression of returns on absolute differences in returns, is positively correlated with the firm's average return. 3. Risk-return relationships remain stable return as long as the relative position to the individual reference level is stable. |

*Studies based on the behavioral theory of the firm*

| Study | Risk measure | Sample | Findings |
| --- | --- | --- | --- |
| Gooding, R. Z., Goel, S., and Wiseman, R. W. (1996) Fixed versus variable reference points in the risk-return relationship | Standard deviation of the firm ROE around its mean ROE. | Data from COMPUSTAT industrial, full coverage, and research tapes; 29 industries with 1405 firms for 1970–74, 37 industries with 2403 firms for 1975–79, 41 industries with 3179 firms for 1980–84, and 45 industries with 5107 firms for 1985–89. | 1. Curvilinear risk-return relationship: firms above the reference point were risk averse and firms below it were risk seeking. 2. Gain-loss reference point across industries is greater than industry median performance. 3. The reference point varies across industries. 4. The location of the gain-loss reference point in relation to the industry median performance varies across time. |
| Jemison, D. B. (1987) Risk and relationship among strategy, | Variation in performance level. Standard deviation of its return on assets over the period 1975–79. | 20 banks from a population of 43 Indiana banks between $125 and $550 million in 1979 assets. | 1. Study examines relations among strategy, processes, and performance. 2. Banks with more focused strategies, and with greater efficiency, have less risk. 3. Decision centralization is greater in |

| Author(s) Article title | Risk construct and measure | Sample | Risk related findings |
|---|---|---|---|
| organizational processes, and performance | | | high return banks. 4. Lower risk is associated with more formalized planning systems. 5. Managers in low risk firms reported significantly more dependence on them by others than did managers in high risk firms. 6. In low risk and high return firms respectively, more influence over strategic decisions would be given to groups that interact with the environment than in high risk and low return firms. 7. Organizational processes associated with high and low return are different from those associated with high and low risk. 8. Perspective on return as performance level augmented by adding risk, variation in performance level. |
| Miller, K. D., and Bromiley, P. (1990) Strategic risk and corporate performance: | Nine measures of risk (systematic risk, unsystematic risk, debt-to-equity ratio, capital intensity, R&D intensity, standard deviation of ROA, ROE, stock analysts' earnings forecasts, coefficient of variation of stock analysts' earnings forecasts) | Data on nine risk variables for 526 firms during 1978–82, and data on 746 firms during 1983–87. | 1. Several distinct empirical risk factors exist and are stable over time. The factors identified were income stream uncertainty, stock returns risk, and strategic, or industry, risk. 2. Income stream risk reduces subsequent |

| Reference | Measures | Sample | Findings |
|---|---|---|---|
| An analysis of alternative risk measures | grouped into three categories: stock returns, financial ratios, and income stream uncertainty. | | performance. This influence exists across industries and performance levels. On the other hand, the influence of strategic risk on performance varies across industries and performance levels. 3. The influence of performance on income stream risk varies across performance levels. For high performers, performance reduces subsequent income stream risk, but for low performers, it increases income stream risk. Performance appears to reduce strategic risk for low-performing companies. |
| Miller, K. D., and Leiblein, M. J. (1996) Corporate risk-return relations: Returns variability versus downside risk. | Two measures used. 1. Downside risk: Measured as a function of the magnitude of performance shortfalls relative to an aspiration level. 2. Variability in returns. | All manufacturing firms in SIC codes 3000 to 3999 for which the necessary accounting data were available in the COMPUSTAT primary, secondary, and tertiary files during the years 1971 through 1991. | 1. Downside risk leads to strategic changes that improve, rather than diminish, subsequent firm performance. Firms with exceptionally high performance avoid downside risk in the subsequent period. Such downside risk avoidance drives down subsequent performance. 2. The primary role of slack is to facilitate organizational responses to downside risk, thus improving subsequent performance. Slack does not appear to play a role in determining organizational risk taking. 3. Mixed evidence regarding the relation between risk (measured by returns standard deviation) and returns. |

| Author(s) Article title | Risk construct and measure | Sample | Risk related findings |
|---|---|---|---|
| Palmer, T. B., and Wiseman, R. M. (1999) Decoupling risk taking from income stream uncertainty: A holistic model of risk. | Two types of risk: managerial risk taking (choices with high uncertainty) and organizational risk (firm performance uncertainty).<br><br>Managerial risk taking measured by (a) R&D expenses scaled by firm sales, (b) the five year average number of four digit industries that the sampled firms compete in, (c) entropy measure.<br><br>Organizational risk measured by variance in ROA, and five year variance in price earnings ratio. | 235 firms representing 64 manufacturing industries at the 3 digit SIC level from the Compustat database with a 2000–3999 SIC code. Period: 1984–91. | Risk taking and organizational risk are not isomorphic.<br>1. Dynamism and slack negatively influence managerial risk taking.<br>2. Attainment discrepancy and managerial ownership positively influence managerial risk taking.<br>3. Managerial risk taking exhibited a strong influence on organizational risk. |
| Reuer, J. J., and Leiblien, M. J. (2000) Downside risk implications of multinationality and international joint ventures. | Downside risk is a probability weighted function of below target performance outcomes.<br><br>Downside risk was specified as a function of a firm's annual ROA relative to a target level that changed over time. It was then measured as a second-order root lower partial moment. Also calculated using ROE data. | 357 US manufacturing firms in the SIC range 3000–3999 that had data available from COMPUSTAT, CRSP, and the Directory of International Affiliations. | 1. US manufacturing firms' investments in dispersed FDI and international joint ventures do not have a general, negative impact on organizational downside risk, as predicted by real options theory and international strategy research.<br>2. Corporate multinationality is not significantly related to downside risk, and firms that are more active in engaging in IJVs obtain higher, rather than lower, levels of downside risk. |

| Singh, J. V. (1986) Performance, slack, and risk taking in organizational decision making. | Risk taking was measured by a questionnaire measure using a 6-item scale. This scale asked top executives to rate how much their organizations were oriented towards risk taking and demonstrated by decisions such as reliance on innovation, debt-financing, heavy R&D, and high risk–high return investments as opposed to low risk–moderate return investments. | Multiple informants in top management groups from a cross sectional sample of 64 medium to large US and Canadian corporations. Period: 1973–75. | Performance has both direct and indirect relations with risk taking. 1. Poor performance is related to high risk taking in organizational decisions and good performance is related to low risk taking. 2. Good performance is also related to high absorbed and unabsorbed slack. Absorbed slack is related to increased risk taking as predicted, but unabsorbed slack does not have a relationship with risk taking. |
| Wiseman, R. M., and Bromiley, P. (1996) Toward a model of risk in declining organizations: An empirical examination of risk, performance, and decline. | Variance in security analysts' forecasts of a firm's income. | 344 low performing manufacturing companies in 1975–88. | 1. Risk: Reductions in slack and organization size increase risk among firms facing declining revenues. ◆ Attainment discrepancy appears to reduce not increase risk although the magnitude of the influence is very small. ◆ Two measures of slack, SG&A/sales (absorbed) and debt/equity (potential slack) decreased risk, while interest coverage (potential slack) and liquid slack (current assets/current debt) each had no effect. 2. Performance: Risk reduces performance. ◆ Recoverable slack in the form of SG&A/sales reduces performance. Other forms of slack (available slack and potential slack) positively contribute to subsequent performance. |

| Author(s) Article title | Risk construct and measure | Sample | Risk related findings |
|---|---|---|---|
| *Agency theory studies* | | | |
| Wright, P., Ferris, S. P., Sarin, A., and Awasthi, V. (1996) Impact of corporate insider, blockholder, and institutional equity ownership on firm risk taking. | Corporate risk taking was defined as the analysis and selection of projects that have varying uncertainties associated with their expected outcomes and corresponding cash flows. | 358 publicly traded firms for 1986 and 514 firms for 1992 (financial data available on COMPUSTAT tapes). | 1. When insiders possess a low degree of equity ownership, their ownership positively influences corporate risk taking. As insiders increase their investment in a firm, however, they tend to reduce risk taking. For firms without growth prospects, the impact of insider equity is statistically insignificant. 2. There is a significant and positive relation between the level of equity ownership by institutions and corporate risk taking by firms with growth opportunities. |
| Wiseman, R. M., and Catanach, A., Jr. (1997) A longitudinal disaggregation of operational risk under changing regulations: Evidence from the savings and loan industry. | Risk taking measured by outcome variables reflecting down-side risk in a lending institution: credit risk, interest-rate risk, and liquidity risk. | 23,159 firm-year observations on US Savings and Loan institutions in years 1979, 1980, 1986, 1987, and 1988. | 1. Both agency (ownership) and behavioral factors influence risk-taking. 2. Determinants of risk taking vary across differing measures of risk. 3. Risk significantly influenced performance. |

| Oviatt, B. M., and Bauerschmidt, A. D. (1991) Business risk and return: A test of simultaneous relationships | Variability of annual returns (measured deviations of annual returns around a trend line with an autoregressive time series model). Risk was also measured as the skewness of annual returns. | 141 single- and dominant-business firms in 8 industries for the decade of the 1970s. | Both business risk and business return are determined by a combination of industry and business effects, but after these are accounted for, risk and return have little influence on each other. |
| --- | --- | --- | --- |

# References

Aaker, D. A., and Jacobson, R. (1987). The role of risk in explaining differences in profitability. *Academy of Management Journal*, 30: 277–96.

Altman, E. I. (1983). *Corporate Distress: A Complete Guide to Predicting, Avoiding, and Dealing with Bankruptcy*. New York: Wiley.

Amit, R., and Livnat, J. (1988). Diversification and the risk-return trade off. *Academy of Management Journal*, 31: 154–66.

Amit, R., and Wernerfelt, B. (1990). Why do firms reduce business risk? *Academy of Management Journal*, 33, 520–33.

Baird, I. S., and Thomas, H. (1985). Toward a contingency model of strategic risk-taking. *Academy of Management Review*, 10: 230–44.

Baird, I. S., and Thomas, H. (1990). What is risk anyway?: Using and measuring risk in strategic management. In R. A. Bettis and H. Thomas (eds.), *Risk, Strategy, and Management*, Vol. 5: 21–54. Greenwich, CT: JAI Press.

Balakrishnan, S., and Fox, I. (1993). Asset specificity, firm heterogeneity and capital structure. *Strategic Management Journal*, 14: 3–16.

Baucus, D. A., Golec, J. H., and Cooper, J. R. (1993). Estimating risk-return relationships: An analysis of measures. *Strategic Management Journal*, 14: 387–96.

Beaver, W., Kettler, P., and Scholes, M. (1970). The association between market determined and accounting determined risk measures. *The Accounting Review*, 45: 654–82.

Beaver, W., and Manegold, J. (1975). The association between market-determined and accounting-determined measures of systematic risk: Some further evidence. *Journal of Financial and Quantitative Analysis*, 10(2): 231–84.

Bettis, R. A. (1982). Risk considerations in modeling corporate strategy. *Academy of Management Proceedings*: 22–5.

Bettis, R. A. (1983). Modern financial theory, corporate strategy and public policy: Three conundrums. *Academy of Management Review*, 8: 406–15.

Bettis, R. A., and Hall, W. K. (1982). Diversification strategy, accounting determined risk, and accounting determined return. *Academy of Management Journal*, 25: 254–64.

Bettis, R. A., and Mahajan, V. (1985). Risk/return performance of diversified firms. *Management Science*, 31 (7): 785–99.

Bowman, R. G. (1979. The theoretical relationship between systematic risk and financial (accounting) variables. *The Journal of Finance*, 34: 617–30.

Bowman, E. H. (1980). A risk/return paradox for strategic management. *Sloan Management Review*, 21: 17–31.

Bowman, E. H. (1982). Risk seeking by troubled firms. *Sloan Management Review*, 23: 33–42.

Bowman, E. H. (1984). Content analysis of annual reports for corporate strategy and risk. *Interfaces*, 14(1): 61–71.

Bromiley, P. (1987). Do forecasts produced by organizations reflect anchoring and adjustment? *Journal of Forecasting*, 6(3), 201–10.

Bromiley, P. (1990). On the use of finance theory in strategic management. In P. Shrivastava and R. Lamb (eds.), *Advances in Strategic Management*, Vol. 6: 71–98. Greenwich, CT: JAI Press.

Bromiley, P. (1991a). Paradox or at least variance found: A comment on "Mean-variance approaches to risk-return relationships in strategy: Paradox lost." *Management Science*, 37: 1206–15.

Bromiley, P. (1991b). Testing a causal model of corporate risk taking and performance. *Academy of Management Journal*, 34: 37–59.

Chatterjee, S., and Lubatkin, M. (1990). Corporate mergers, stockholder diversification, and changes in systematic risk. *Strategic Management Journal*, 11: 255–68.

Chatterjee, S., Lubatkin, M. H., and Schulze, W. S. (1999). Toward a strategic theory of risk premium: Moving beyond CAPM. *Academy of Management Review*, 24: 556–67.

Collins, J. M., and Ruefli, T. W. (1992). Strategic risk: An ordinal approach. *Management Science*, 38: 1707–31.

Collins, J. M., and Ruefli, T. W. (1996). *Strategic Risk: A State-Defined Approach*. Norwell, MA: Kluwer Academic Publishers.

Cool, K., Dierickx, I., and Jemison, D. (1989). Business strategy, market structure and risk-return relationships: A structural approach. *Strategic Management Journal*, 10: 507–22.

Cool, K. O., and Schendel, D. (1987). Strategic group formation and performance: The case of the U.S. pharmaceutical industry, 1963–1982. *Management Science*, 33: 1102–24.

Cornell, B., and Shapiro, A. C. (1987). Corporate stakeholders and corporate finance. *Financial Management*, 16(1): 5–14.

Cyert, R. M., and March, J. G. (1963). *A Behavioral Theory of the Firm*. Englewood Cliffs, NJ: Prentice-Hall.

D'Aveni, R. A., and Ilinitch, A. Y. (1992). Complex patterns of vertical integration in the forest products industry: Systematic and bankruptcy risks. *Academy of Management Journal*, 35: 596–625.

Deephouse, D. L., and Wiseman, R. M. (2000). Comparing alternative explanations for accounting risk-return relations. *Journal of Economic Behavior and Organization*, 42: 463–82.

Demsetz, H. (1983). The structure of ownership and the theory of the firm. *Journal of Law and Economics*, 26: 375–90.

Duncan, R. B. (1972). Characteristics of organizational environments and perceived environmental uncertainty. *Administrative Science Quarterly*, 17: 313–27.

Fama, E. (1980). Agency problems and the theory of the firm. *Journal of Political Economy*, 88: 288–307.

Fama, E. F., and French, K. R. (1992). The cross-section of expected stock returns. *Journal of Finance*, 67: 427–65.

Fiegenbaum, A. (1990). Prospect theory and the risk-return association: An empirical examination in 85 industries. *Journal of Economic Behavior and Organization*, 14: 187–203.

Fiegenbaum, A., Hart, S., and Schendel, D. (1996). Strategic reference point theory, *Strategic Management Journal*, 17(3): 216–36.

Fiegenbaum, A., and Thomas, H. (1986). Dynamic and risk measurement perspectives on Bowman's risk-return paradox for strategic management: An empirical study. *Strategic Management Journal*, 7: 395–407.

Fiegenbaum, A., and Thomas, H. (1988). Attitudes toward risk and the risk-return paradox: Prospect theory explanations. *Academy of Management Journal*, 31: 85–106.

Fiegenbaum, A., and Thomas, H. (1990). Stakeholder risks and Bowman's risk/return paradox: What risk measure is relevant for strategists? In R. A. Bettis and H. Thomas (eds.), *Risk, Strategy, and Management*, Vol. 5: 111–36. Greenwich, CT: JAI Press.

Freeman, R. E. (1984). *Strategic Management: A Stakeholder Approach*. Marshfield, MA: Pitman Publishing.

Gooding, R. Z., Goel, S., and Wiseman, R. M. (1996). Fixed versus variable reference points in the risk-return relationship. *Journal of Economic Behavior and Organization*, 29: 331–50.

Greve, H. R. (1998). Performance, aspirations, and risky organizational change. *Administrative Science Quarterly*, 43: 58–86.

Harlow, W. V., and Rao, R. K. S. (1989). Asset pricing in a generalized mean-lower partial moment framework. *Journal of Financial and Quantitative Analysis*, 24: 285–311.

Harrison, J. R., and March, J. G. (1984). Decision making and post-decision surprises. *Administrative Science Quarterly*, 29: 26–42.

Hill, N. C., and Stone, B. K. (1980). Accounting betas, systematic operating risk, and financial leverage: A risk-composition approach to the determination of systematic risk. *Journal of Financial and Quantitative Analysis*, 15: 595–638.

Jacobson, R. (1987). The validity of ROI as a measure of business performance. *The American Economic Review*, 77: 470–8.

Jegers, M. (1991). Prospect theory and the risk-return relation: Some Belgian evidence. *Academy of Management Journal*, 34: 215–25.

Jemison, D. B. (1987). Risk and the relationship among strategy, organizational processes, and performance. *Management Science*, 33: 1087–1101.

Jensen, M. C. (1969). Risk, the pricing of capital assets, and the evaluation of investment portfolios. *Journal of Business*, 42: 167–93.

Jensen, M., and Meckling, W. (1976). Theory of the firm: Managerial behavior, agency costs and ownership structure. *The Journal of Financial Economics*, 3: 305–60.

Kahneman, D., and Tversky, A. (1979). Prospect theory: An analysis of decision under risk. *Econometrica*, 47: 263–91.

Kim, W. C., Hwang, P., and Burgers, W. P. (1993). Multinationals' diversification and the risk-return trade-off. *Strategic Management Journal*, 14: 275–86.

Knight, F. H. (1921). *Risk, Uncertainty, and Profit*. Houghton Mifflin; reprint, Chicago: University of Chicago, 1971.

Lant, T. K. (1992). Aspiration Level Adaptation: An empirical exploration. *Management Science*, 38: 623–44.

Lehner, J. M. (2000). Shifts of reference points for framing of strategic decisions and changing risk-return associations. *Management Science*, 46: 63–76.

Lintner, J. (1965). The valuation of risk assets and the selection of risky investment in stock portfolios and capital budgets. *Review of Economics and Statistics*, 47: 13–37.

Lubatkin, M., and Chatterjee, S. (1994). Extending modern portfolio theory into the domain of corporate diversification: Does it apply? *Academy of Management Journal*, 37: 109–36.

Lubatkin, M., and O'Neill, H. M. (1987). Merger strategies and capital market risk. *Academy of Management Journal*, 30 (4): 665–84.

MacCrimmon, K. R., and Wehrung, D. A. (1986). *Taking risks: The Management of Uncertainty*. New York: Free Press.

Mao, J. C. T. (1970). Survey of capital budgeting: Theory and practice. *Journal of Finance*, 25: 349–60.

March, J. G. (1978). Bounded rationality, ambiguity, and the engineering of choice. *Bell Journal of Economics*, 9: 587–608.

March, J. G., and Shapira, Z. (1987). Managerial perspectives on risk and risk taking. *Management Science*, 33: 1404–18.

March, J. G., and Shapira, Z. (1992). Variable risk preferences and the focus of attention. *Psychological Review*, 99(1): 172–83.

Marsh, T. A., and Swanson, D. S. (1984). Risk-return tradeoffs for strategic management. *Sloan Management Review*, (Spring): 35–51.

McNamara, G., and Bromiley, P. (1997). Decision making in an organizational setting: Cognitive and organizational influences on risk assessment in commercial lending. *Academy of Management Journal*, 40: 1063–88.

McNamara, G., and Bromiley, P. (1999). Risk and return in organizational decision making. *Academy of Management Journal*, 42: 330–39.

McNamara, G., Moon, H., and Bromiley, P. (forthcoming). Banking on commitment: Intended and unintended consequences of an organization's attempt to minimize escalation of commitment. *Academy of Management Journal*.

Miles, R. E., and Snow, C. C. (1978). *Organizational Strategy, Structure, and Process*. New York: McGraw-Hill.

Miller, K. D. (1993). Industry and country effects on managers' perceptions of environmental uncertainties. *Journal of International Business Studies*, 24: 693–714.

Miller, K. D. (1998). Economic exposure and integrated risk management. *Strategic Management Journal*, 19: 497–514.

Miller, K. D., and Bromiley, P. (1990). Strategic risk and corporate performance: An analysis of alternative risk measures. *Academy of Management Journal*, 33: 756–79.

Miller, K. D., and Leiblein, M. J. (1996). Corporate risk-return relations: Returns variability versus downside risk. *Academy of Management Journal*, 39: 91–122.

Miller, K. D., and Reuer, J. J. (1996). Measuring organizational downside risk. *Strategic Management Journal*, 17: 671–91.

Miller, K. D., and Reuer, J. J. (1998a). Asymmetric corporate exposures to foreign exchange rate changes. *Strategic Management Journal*, 19: 1183–91.

Miller, K. D., and Reuer, J. J. (1998b). Firm strategy and economic exposure to foreign exchange rate movements. *Journal of International Business Studies*, 29: 493–513.

Milliken, F. J. (1987). Three types of perceived uncertainty about the environment: State, effect, and response uncertainty. *Academy of Management Review*, 12: 133–43.

Montgomery, C. A., and Singh, H. (1984). Diversification strategy and systematic risk. *Strategic Management Journal*, 5: 181–91.

Oviatt, B. M., and Bauerschmidt, A. D. (1991). Business risk and return: A test of simultaneous relationships. *Management Science*, 37: 1405–23.

Palmer, T. B., and Wiseman, R. M. (1999). Decoupling risk taking from income stream uncertainty: A holistic model of risk. *Strategic Management Journal*, 20: 1037–62.

Pfeffer, J., and Salancik, G. R. (1978). *The External Control of Organizations: A Resource Dependence Perspective*. New York: Harper and Row.

Reuer, J. J., and Leiblein, M. J. (2000). Downside risk implications of multinationality and international joint ventures. *Academy of Management Journal*, 43: 203–14.

Ruefli, T. W. (1990). Mean-variance approaches to risk-return relationships in strategy: Paradox lost. *Management Science*, 36, 368–80.

Ruefli, T. W. (1991). Reply to Bromiley's comment and further results: Paradox lost becomes dilemma found. *Management Science*, 37: 1210–15.

Ruefli, T. W., Collins, J. M., and Lacugna, J. R. (1999). Risk measures in strategic management research: Auld lang syne? *Strategic Management Journal*, 20: 167–94.

Ruefli, T. W., and Wiggins, R. R. (1994. When mean square error becomes variance: A comment on "Business risk and return: A test of simultaneous relationships." *Management Science*, 40: 750–59.

Shapira, Z. (1994). *Risk Taking: A Management Perspective*. New York: Russell Sage Foundation.

Shapiro, A. C., and Titman, S. (1986). An integrated approach to corporate risk management. In J. M. Stern, and D. H. Chew, Jr. (eds.), *The Revolution in Corporate Finance*: 215–229. Oxford: Blackwell.

Sharpe, W. F. (1964). Capital asset prices: A theory of market equilibrium under conditions of risk. *Journal of Finance*, 19: 425–42.

Singh, J. V. (1986). Performance, slack, and risk taking in organizational decision making. *Academy of Management Journal*, 29: 562–85.

Sitkin, S. B., and Weingart, L. R. (1995). Determinants of risky decision-making behavior: A test of the mediating role of risk perceptions and propensity. *Academy of Management Journal*, 38: 1573–92.

Staw, B. M., Barsade, S. G., Sigal, G., and Koput, K. W. (1997). Escalation at the credit window: A longitudinal study of bank executives' recognition and write-off of problem loans. *Journal of Applied Psychology*, 82(1): 130–42.

Tversky, A., and Kahneman, D. (1992). Advances in prospect theory: Cumulative representation of uncertainty. *Journal of Risk and Uncertainty*, 5: 297–323.

Vos, E. (1992). A conceptual framework for practical risk measurement in small businesses. *Journal of Small Business Management*, 30(3): 47–56.

Werner, S., Brouthers, L. E., and Brouthers, K. D. (1996). International risk and perceived environmental uncertainty: The dimensionality and internal consistency of Miller's measure. *Journal of International Business Studies*, 27: 571–87.

Wiseman, R. M., and Bromiley, P. (1991). Risk-return associations: Paradox or artefact? An empirically tested explanation. *Strategic Management Journal*, 12: 231–41.

Wiseman, R. M., and Bromiley, P. (1996). Toward a model of risk in declining organizations: An empirical examination of risk, performance and decline. *Organization Science*, 7: 524–43.

Wiseman, R. M., and Catanach, A., Jr. (1997). A longitudinal disaggregation of operational risk under changing regulations: Evidence from the savings and loan industry. *Academy of Management Journal*, 40: 799–830.

Woo, C. Y. (1987). Path analysis of the relationship between market share, business-level conduct and risk. *Strategic Management Journal*, 8: 149–68.

Wright, P., Ferris, S. P., Sarin, A., and Awasthi, V. (1996). Impact of corporate insider, blockholder, and institutional equity ownership on firm risk taking. *Academy of Management Journal*, 39: 441–63.

# 10

# Corporate Reputations as Economic Assets

## CHARLES J. FOMBRUN

Companies operate in competitive markets in which attracting financial and human resources is a constant challenge (Penrose, 1959; Barney, 1991; Peteraf, 1993). Survival and profitability depend on a company's relative ability to gain greater attention and support than competitors from four key resource providers: employees, customers, investors, and communities. Employees must be convinced to join and produce for the company; customers must be induced to buy the company's product and service offerings; investors must be persuaded to provide credit and equity financing; and communities must welcome the company to the neighborhood. Securing attractive *perceptions* of the company by these four resource providers is therefore crucial if a company is to build and sustain a competitive advantage in the marketplace (Rindova and Fombrun, 1999).

In turn, perceptions of companies as "better" or "best" energize bandwagon processes from which better-regarded companies derive a disproportionate share of attention and visibility in the marketplace (Abrahamson and Rosenberg, 1994). Under these conditions, companies with only marginally better performance records can develop outsized reputations, and contribute to producing a noticeably skewed aggregate distribution of reputations. Reputational markets can therefore be characterized as "winner-take-all" environments in which exaggerated rewards accrue to companies that develop even marginally better reputations than their rivals (Frank and Cook, 1996).

I begin this chapter by examining diverse points of view on corporate reputations. I then suggest a definition of corporate reputation that recognizes its roots in the perceptions and interpretations of resource-holders. The bottom-line effects of corporate reputations justify considering reputations as intangible economic assets that contribute to competitive advantage. I therefore explore the socio-cognitive processes through which resource providers judge companies by interpreting cues and signals that emanate either directly from companies themselves or indirectly from institutional intermediaries such as media reporters and financial analysts. The chapter concludes by suggesting three areas likely to dominate reputational research in the coming years: questions of measurement, valuation, and causality.

## WHAT ARE CORPORATE REPUTATIONS

Corporate reputations are viewed in different but complementary ways by economists, strategists, sociologists, marketers, and organization theorists (Fombrun and Van Riel, 1997). In this section, I examine some of these disciplinary contributions to the study of corporate reputations with a view to building a definition of the construct and proposing an integrative model.

### The economic view

Economists view corporate reputations as either traits or signals. In their review of game theory applications, Weigelt and Camerer (1988: 443) point out that "in game theory the reputation of a player is the perception others have of the player's values . . . which determine his/her choice of strategies." Information asymmetry forces external observers to rely on proxies to describe the preferences of rivals and their likely courses of action. Consumers rely on firms' reputations because they have less information than managers do about firms' commitment to delivering desirable product features like quality or reliability (Grossman and Stiglitz, 1980; Stiglitz, 1989). Similarly, since outside investors in firms' securities are less informed than managers about firms' future actions, corporate reputations increase investor confidence that managers will act in ways that are reputation-consistent. For game theorists, then, reputations are *functional*: they generate perceptions among employees, customers, investors, competitors, and the general public about what a company is, what it does, and what it stands for. These perceptions stabilize interactions between a firm and its publics.

Signalling theorists concur: reputations derive from prior resource allocations managers make to first-order activities likely to create a perception of reliability and predictability to outside observers (Myers and Majluf, 1984; Ross, 1977; Stigler, 1962). Since many features of a company and its products are hidden from view, companies build reputation to signal the company's hidden quality and increase an observer's confidence in the firm's products and services. In this view, advertising campaigns, charitable contributions, conference calls with analysts, campus receptions, all constitute "strategic projections" (Rindova and Fombrun, 1999) that companies use to signal their attractive features to potential customers, investors, and employees and through which they build reputation.

### The strategic view

Strategy scholars see reputations as assets and as mobility barriers (Caves and Porter, 1977). On one hand, a reputation is an asset that derives from the unique internal features of a company. It describes the history of the firm's interactions with its constituents, and so suggests to observers what the company stands for (Dutton and Dukerich, 1991).

At the same time, reputations are *externally* perceived, and so are largely outside the direct control of firms' managers (Barney, 1986). Rivals have difficulty duplicating the results of better-regarded firms because, other things being equal, constituents favor the products and services of better-reputed firms. It takes time for a reputation to coalesce in observers' minds, and empirical studies show that even when confronted with negative information, observers resist changing their reputational assessments (Wartick, 1992).

In turn, established reputations impede mobility and produce returns to firms because they are difficult to imitate (Barney, 1991). By limiting firms' actions and rivals' reactions, reputations are therefore features of industry structure (Abrahamson and Fombrun, 1994; Fombrun and Zajac, 1987). Like economists, then, strategists call attention to the competitive benefits of acquiring favorable reputations, and so implicitly support a focus on the longitudinal resource allocations firms must make to erect reputational barriers to the mobility of rivals.

Although strategists dwell on the economic and competitive aspects of managerial decision-making, scholars of business and society call attention to the social aspects of these decisions (Carroll, 1979). Social responsibility theorists traditionally take the moral high-ground to suggest principles and practices that managers should adhere to in order to induce ethically sound strategic decisions (Carroll, 1979; Wartick and Cochran, 1985). Students of business and society often take a teleological stance in emphasizing that firms have diverse constituents with valid claims on the strategies that firms pursue. They advise managers to pursue "enterprise strategies" that address social concerns in order to secure external support (Sethi, 1979; Freeman, 1984; Wartick, 1988; Jones, 1995). They imply that corporate reputations gauge the legitimacy of firms" actions in an institutional field (Elsbach, 1994; Suchman, 1995).

## The sociological view

Economists and strategists typically ignore the socio-cognitive processes that actually generate reputational rankings (Granovetter, 1985; White, 1981). In contrast, sociologists point out that rankings are social constructions that come into being through the relationships that a firm establishes with its constituents in a shared institutional environment (Goode, 1978; Rao, 1994). Firms have multiple evaluators, each of which applies different criteria in assessing firms. Reputational rankings therefore represent aggregated assessments of firms' institutional prestige and describe the stratification of the social system surrounding firms and industries (Shapiro, 1987).

Faced with incomplete information about firms' actions, observers not only interpret the signals that firms routinely broadcast, but also rely on the evaluative signals refracted by key intermediaries such as market analysts, professional investors, and reporters (Abrahamson and Fombrun, 1994; Fombrun and Rindova, 2001). Intermediaries are key nodes in an interfirm network that transmits and refracts information among firms and their constituents (Abrahamson and Fombrun, 1992). An empirical study of firms involved in nuclear-waste disposal and photovoltaic cell development demonstrated how in both these industries reputational status depended, not only on structural factors like company size and economic performance, but also on a firm's position in the interaction networks linking firms to the institutional field (Shrum and Wuthnow, 1988).

## The marketing view

Students of marketing and branding regard corporate reputations as an outcome of firms' efforts to induce customer purchases and build customer loyalty (Aaker, 1998;

Keller, 1999). Reputations are valuable insofar as they induce repeat purchases and stabilize corporate revenue streams. Corporate communications are elements of the marketing mix: They are strategic informational signals designed to familiarize customers and other constituents with the company's offerings, activities, and prospects, and thereby induce support (Van Riel, 1995). To strengthen customer identification, companies regularly develop attractive messages and images that they then communicate in their advertising and public relations campaigns. Often these messages and images are leveraged into communications targeted to other constituencies.

Economists suggest that companies invest in reputation-building to communicate their attractiveness when the quality of a company's products and services is not directly observable. High-quality producers do so to signal their quality to consumers who would not otherwise know (Shapiro, 1983). When successful, these investments in building reputation allow them to charge premium prices and earn rents from the repeat purchases that their reputations generate. In contrast, economists suggest that low-quality producers avoid investing in reputation-building because they do not expect repeat purchases (Allen, 1984; Bagwell, 1992; Milgrom and Roberts, 1986).

Similar dynamics may operate in the capital and labor markets. For instance, managers routinely try to communicate to investors about their economic performance. Since investors are more favorably disposed to companies that demonstrate high and stable earnings, managers often try to smooth quarterly earnings and keep dividend pay-out ratios high and fixed, despite earnings fluctuations (Brealy and Myers, 1988). Often companies will pay a premium price to hire high-reputation auditors and outside counsel. They rent the reputations of these agents in order to convey to investors, regulators, and other publics about their firm's probity and credibility (Wilson, 1983).

## *The organizational/ethical view*

Students of organization contend that reputations are emergent features of companies that are rooted in the shared understandings of employees and managers – their cultures and identities (Albert and Whetten, 1985). In this view, companies develop reputations from their "self-expressions" – most visibly in a company's logos and brands, but less visibly in the company's statements of beliefs and cultural practices (Schultz, Hatch, and Larsen, 2000).

From an organizational viewpoint, reputations are therefore "social facts" that crystallize the identity-consistent expressions that companies make – an emergent collective feature of companies that is central, distinctive, and enduring (Albert and Whetten, 1985). Schultz, Hatch, and Larsen (2000) describe how a strong reputation is built from *authentic* representations of a company's inner being – its identity. The book's counsel is consistent with Collins and Porras's (1996) findings that enduring companies have strong core ideologies. Both books assert that a company's reputation sits on the bedrock of its corporate identity – the core values that shape its actions, its communications, its culture and its decisions, and with which a company expresses itself to its constituents. Their prescriptions are consistent with those of business and society scholars who regard a company's ethical posture as the set of behavioral rules to which it adheres and which affect the decisions managers make (Jones, 1995).

Stronger, more favorable reputations are thought to develop from more *authentic* expressions of corporate cultures and identities, whereas weaker reputations result from impression management strategies that are unconnected to the company's core values and shared ideology (Collins and Porras, 1996). Fombrun and Rindova (2001) highlight Royal Dutch/Shell's efforts to build an expressive platform for its strategic initiatives and corporate communications. It began in 1996 when Shell embarked on an ambitious effort to rebuild a corporate reputation that was left in tatters following the company's mishandling of two major public crises in 1995. The program the company developed was rooted in a soul-searching process that required identifying the company's business principles and "core purpose" – the authentic values it supports, and the behaviors it is willing to endorse. Unearthed through the conduct of focus groups around the world, Shell's core purpose was defined as "Helping to Make the Future a Better Place" and has since become an anchor for the company's initiatives and communications.

## An integrative view

These diverse perspectives suggest that reputations are subjective, collective assessments of firms, with the following characteristics:

- reputations are *economic assets*: they signal observers about the attractiveness of a company's offerings and initiatives;
- reputations are *derivative, second-order* characteristics of a social system that crystallize the emergent status of firms in an institutional field of resource providers and institutional intermediaries;
- reputations develop from firms' prior resource allocations and histories and *constitute mobility barriers* that constrain both firms' actions and rivals' reactions;
- reputations are *assessments of past performance* by diverse evaluators who assess firms" ability and potential to satisfy their own economic and social, selfish and altruistic criteria;
- reputations reconcile the multiple external images of firms, and signal their *overall attractiveness* to employees, consumers, investors, and local communities;
- reputations embody multiple *judgments of firms' effectiveness* at delivering value to key resource providers;
- reputations crystallize the *strategic* and *expressive* efforts companies make to communicate their core purpose and identity to their resource providers.

Consistent with these characteristics, I therefore propose the following definition:

A corporate reputation is a collective representation of a company's past actions and future prospects that describes how key resource providers interpret a company's initiatives and assess its ability to deliver valued outcomes.

## WHY ARE REPUTATIONS IMPORTANT?

Reputations matter because they create value: they attract more and better resources to better-regarded companies (Fombrun, 1996). Companies therefore compete, not only in product, capital, and labor markets, but also in reputational markets. Their success at building competitive advantage in each of these markets has economic consequences for the company and its stakeholders (Rindova and Fombrun, 1999).

In a seminal paper on the "Economics of Superstars," Rosen (1981) identified the skewed distribution of rewards that accrue to performers in different sectors, including sports and the arts. He argued that disproportionate returns occur because of the human tendency to exaggerate small differences and to reward on the basis of relative performance rather than absolute performance. Differences are further exacerbated by intensified communications that converge on the few who are most noticeable (the "headliners") and largely ignore the rest.

The market for corporate reputation shares similar characteristics. Reputational markets are in fact "winner-take-all" environments in which a few companies come out on top, and most others lose (Frank and Cook, 1996). Disproportionate visibility and attention accrue to winners because of bandwagon processes that exaggerate minor differences in performance and fuel imitation (Abrahamson and Rosenberg, 1994). Bandwagons develop as slight differences between companies induce companies to advertise their superiority, increase familiarity, build reputation, and in turn fuel the company's attractiveness to resource holders, as well as imitation by rivals. So that Rosen's observation appears to hold in many areas, from sports (where differences in performance are typically measured in one tenth of a percent) to retail stores – where if you're only slightly better or cheaper than the competition, you can quickly dominate the market. Frank and Cook (1996) noted that across a variety of markets, the number one player regularly leaves its rivals in the dust, and reaps outsized market valuations, often giving it the means to consolidate its position further through acquisitions. Cisco Systems trounced Bay Networks, General Electric did the same to both United Technologies and CBS/Westinghouse. Consultants at Mercer Management Consulting have called it "the plight of the silver medalist."

## How do reputations create economic value?

Bandwagon processes are characteristics of complex systems in which small differences in performance create enlarged perceptions of value, and fuel "reinforcing loops" (Senge, 1995). These enlarged perceptions occur as each resource provider observes companies in an institutional field, and makes decisions about which companies to supply with scarce resources and which not. In figure 10.1, I illustrate the "value cycle" that fuels the "winner-take-all" process in reputational markets.

The logic of the "value cycle" that I propose can be explained in the following terms. A good reputation:

+ improves a company's ability to recruit top people to its jobs, making it an "employer of choice";
+ draws customers to the company's products and enhances repeat purchases, making it a "supplier of choice";
+ makes the company a "neighbor of choice" (Burke, 1996), and so makes it a better candidate for favorable treatment by the media and by local authorities;
+ helps a company become an "investment of choice," enhancing its ability to attract capital at a lower cost than rivals, thereby generating a price premium for the company's shares.

FIGURE 10.1  The value cycle

*Note*: The value cycle suggests that a company's financial value derives from perceptions of the company's future prospects. These perceptions develop from observations of supportive behaviors by resource providers towards the company, e.g. product sales, strong new hires, or favorable press. Growth itself demonstrates approval of the company's strategic initiatives, and is made possible by more attractive financial valuations.

The intrinsic economic value of a corporate reputation therefore lies in a company's ability to launch strategic initiatives that induce "supportive behaviors" from key resource-holders such as employees, customers, communities, and investors. The greater availability of resources to a better-regarded company improves its perceived prospects for the future, which encourages resource holders to bid up the financial value of the company.

Evidence for the validity of the value cycle can be deduced from various studies published in the inaugural issue of the *Corporate Reputation Review* (1997). For instance, a study of financial analysts found that the one-year earnings forecasts they made of 303 companies were heavily determined by financial variables, but were also influenced by the *non-financial* component of their corporate reputation. A comparison of 10 portfolios of companies demonstrated that investors were willing to pay more for companies with higher reputation but comparable risk and return, thereby lowering their cost of capital. Finally, a study of 200 business undergraduate students found them more attracted to jobs in companies whose workplaces were featured among the "100 Best Companies to Work For." All of these studies try to establish a causal relationship between a pair of variables subsumed under the value cycle. As I discuss later in the chapter, these causal analyses fall short of recognizing the full complexity of the cyclical process through which actions and perceptions mutually affect each other.

## WHERE DO REPUTATIONS COME FROM?

Corporate reputations are socially constructed from companies' interactions within an institutional field. They develop from three social processes that link companies and

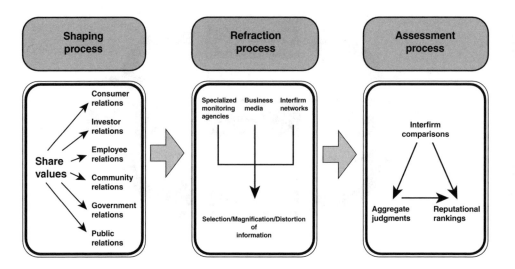

FIGURE 10.2 How reputations develop
*Note*: Reputations develop through three social processes: a shaping process, a refraction process and an assessment process (adapted from Fombrun and Rindova, 2001)

intermediaries to key resource providers (Fombrun and Rindova, 2001): (1) a *shaping process* that is rooted in a company's strategic efforts to influence key resource providers; (2) a *refraction process* that is anchored around the interpretations of institutional intermediaries such as media reporters and financial analysts and the communications they make; and (3) an *assessment process* that aggregates judgments of firms, and compares them to one another. Figure 10.2 suggests that reputational rankings crystallize from the intersection of these three processes.

## The shaping process

Various strategic initiatives contribute to reputation-building, including advertising, philanthropy, and community outreach (Pfeffer, 1981; Salancik and Meindl, 1984; Dowling, 1986; Alvesson, 1990). By targeting a particular constituent group, each of these programs creates images of a company that are more or less consistent. They constitute a corporate-level analog to impression management by individuals. Each strategic deployment calls attention to certain attributes of firms and de-emphasizes others, providing frameworks that guide the interpretations made by external evaluators (Tedeschi, 1981). Companies increasingly recognize the *indirect* benefits of their strategic initiatives, including cause-related marketing, corporate citizenship, and strategic philanthropy (Fombrun, Gardberg, and Barnett, 2000).

To develop favorable impressions with constituents, firms engage in self-presentations that appear in a wide range of activities, including image advertising, logo development, links to non-profit groups, press releases, and pro-bono work (Salancik and Meindl, 1984; Altheide and Johnson, 1980; McCaffrey, 1982). Variously described as "public relations" or "identity management," these presentations communicate analytical and symbolic information to emphasize aspects of corporate performance that each constituent group expects from firms. To understand and respond better to the expectations and concerns of these constituent groups and signal their commitment, managers often create internal departments to manage their relationships with each of these groups. Four relationships are among the more prominent ones that firms attend to:

1. *Customer relations*: shaping strategies intended to influence consumers include product and image advertising, the creation of customers service centers, the provision of warranties, and investments in building brand equity to market firms' goods and services. Managers try to generate favorable consumer appraisals by signalling their concern with meeting consumers' expectations of quality and service (Nelson, 1974; Milgrom and Roberts, 1986; Yoon, Guffey, and Kijewski, 1993).

2. *Investor relations*: firms target investors by hiring credible auditors, issuing carefully worded financial statements, and making presentations to investment analysts and institutional shareholders (Kaplan and Roll, 1972; Kaplan and Urwitz, 1979). Through investor relations firms disseminate information about their intended strategies, thus reducing investors' perceptions of risk and firms' cost of capital (Brealey and Myers, 1988).

3. *Employee relations:* managers try to shape favorable employee assessments of their firms by designing human resource practices for recruitment, compensation, and development that signal fairness, commitment, and concern for employees (Fombrun, Tichy, and Devanna, 1984). The nature of a company's human resource practices signal to prospective employees the merits of working there (Spence, 1974).

4. *Community relations*: firms signal their benevolence, corporate citizenship, and social responsiveness by engaging in pro-bono activities and making charitable contributions (Fry, Keim, and Meiners, 1982). By forming relationships with artistic, educational, and cultural institutions, firms integrate themselves into their local communities and shape favorable attitudes to their activities (Useem, 1988; Galaskiewicz and Burt, 1991).

Additionally, companies also actively manage relationships with two other indirect resource providers: government regulators and the general public.

5. *Government relations*: managers regularly signal their support for political issues by funding the political campaigns of elected officials. They distribute position papers, testify before committees, and lobby regulators. By forming close ties with the regulatory community, managers ingratiate themselves with powerful monitors and participate in shaping environments that support their activities (McCaffrey, 1982; Kingdon, 1984).

6. *Public/media relations*: finally, firms routinely rely on public relations professionals to shape public opinion (Cheney and Vibbert, 1987; Crable and Vibbert, 1985). Expert staffs manage relationships with the media: they create identity programs, issue press releases, stage public appearances of corporate executives, and, broadly speaking, attempt to specify the strategic issue set and frames of reference that govern the conversations of outside audiences (Boorstin, 1964).

Jointly, these six relationships describe managers' strategic efforts to shape more or less coherent images with resource providers. In each case, firms aggressively expend financial, social, and informational resources to build external support and reputational capital (Fombrun, 1996; Abrahamson and Fombrun, 1992). Managers demonstrate active involvement in these self-expressions and presentations when they budget more funds, pursue closer relationships, and disseminate more extensive propaganda.

## The refraction process

Various intermediaries actively monitor, evaluate, and diffuse judgments about firms' actions and results into the reputational marketplace (DiMaggio and Powell, 1983). These intermediaries make sense of a company's initiatives by noticing and attending to particular performance signals. As they communicate their assessments, they influence other observers' judgments of a company's future prospects (Daft and Weick, 1984). Figure 10.1 suggests that intermediaries like specialized monitors, the business media, and interfirm networks, mediate the relationships between companies and resource-holders by summarizing, coloring, reflecting, and refracting a company's self-presentations, with more or less favorable consequences: A company's market values fluctuate, as does its visibility in the media, and in local communities.

*Specialized monitors.* Resource-holders often rely on signals broadcast by specialized intermediaries, be they *government agencies* that assess firms' compliance with regulatory standards; *financial ratings agencies* that monitor firms' economic performance; *corporate conscience agencies* that evaluate firms" social performance; or *consumer agencies* that watch the quality of firms' products. Individual investors, prospective employees, potential consumers, and the general public often agree with the judgments of these intermediaries because they ascribe to them greater analytic resources and access to better information.

Specialized agencies usually develop unique skill at articulating and defending the interests of a particular constituent group. For instance, various government agencies devote public resources to assessing a company's compliance with health and environmental standards. A small community of financial analysts like Moody's, Dun & Bradstreet, and Standard & Poor's monitor and assess firms whose securities are publicly traded. A number of consumer advocates collect, summarize, and verify information about firms' products. In recent years, assorted agencies have gained visibility as watchdogs of ethical conduct (Lydenberg, Marlin, and Strub, 1986). Although the rankings that these specialized actors produce draw attention to particular performance dimensions, they contribute their share of information to the process of assessing companies.

*The business media.* The business media also magnify some corporate initiatives and signal a company's future prospects. They play an important role in creating an ambient informational context within which corporate images form. In general, reporters like to highlight the unusual: innovative, unexpected, and deviant practices and products receive more attention. Larger and better performing firms also get a disproportionate share of media coverage (Fombrun and Shanley, 1990; Wartick, 1992). The media therefore help to structure the evaluations that different resource-holders make of particular companies.

*Interfirm networks.* Additionally, information about firms' actions and performance outcomes propagates outward through interfirm networks, be they personnel exchanges between firms, board interlocks, or informal social ties among managers (Baker and Iyer, 1990). Like media reporters, network contacts selectively magnify, interpret, and distort firms' actions. Various studies suggest that information about firms such as rumors, managerial innovations, and know-how, may diffuse via indirect networks through a combination of blind imitation, persuasion, and self-serving interpretations (Abrahamson, 1991). The form and structure of these interfirm relationships can help shape the corporate images that propagate.

In such an anarchic network environment, a company's strategic efforts at directly shaping favorable images are unlikely to be entirely successful in determining the judgments that external groups make of firms' activities (Abrahamson and Fombrun, 1992). Not only are these external groups only loosely coupled to firms, they also rely on other sources of information and apply criteria that may be at odds with managers' goals. That's why, for instance, utilities that commit to nuclear power often find themselves the unwitting targets of public groups, media exposés, or community boycotts, no matter how extensively they invest in managing impressions. Chance events also occur that sometimes attract negative publicity and depress a company's perceived performance in the eyes of key constituent groups, with potentially damaging reputational effects (Shrivastava, 1986; Mitchell, 1989). A company's success at influencing the evaluations of resource providers depends on the form and strength of its relationships with the media, with specialized agencies, and on the density and connectedness of its interfirm network.

## The assessment process

A company's self-expressions and presentations combine with the evaluations of institutional intermediaries to proliferate multiple images of the company into the reputational marketplace. In this information-rich environment, individually held images and opinions aggregate into a wider representation of a company's success at fulfilling the diverse expectations of its resource providers, from which a *reputational ordering* crystallizes. Processes of convergence and processes of divergence shape the aggregation of fragmentary images into overall reputations.

A company's shaping strategy fosters a homogenization of external perceptions. So do the efforts by intermediaries to create and institutionalize formal practices for systematically disseminating standardized information (for instance, newsletters). Jointly these actions can contribute to a process of convergence that *strengthens* corporate images and produces singular and consistent reputations.

Despite managers' best efforts, however, resource providers will not necessarily concur with a company's self-presentations or with the evaluations of specialized agencies, the media, or the rumor-mill. The assessment process in figure 10.3 is only loosely coupled to managers' shaping strategies and to assessments by intermediaries. Ultimately, individual decision-makers are the ones who evaluate firms, who form expectations, and who make choices about their future exchanges with firms based on their own past experience and on institutionally transmitted information.

Moreover, both within and across stakeholder groups individual opinions can vary. Some individuals and groups actively monitor firms and try to shape opinions about them, others deliberately filter out the messages with which firms and institutional intermediaries bombard them. Some investors are socially responsible, and some are not,

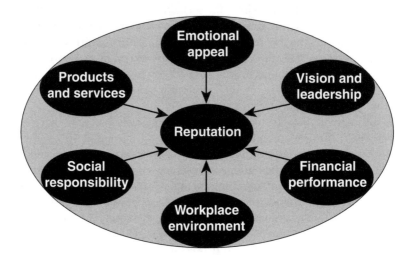

FIGURE 10.3 The building blocks of corporate reputation
*Note*: Research shows that people rate companies on 20 attributes that can be classified into six dimensions (Fombrun, Gardberg, and Sever, 1999).

some customers are "green," and some are "price-shoppers," and some employees consider pro-bono activities a job characteristic, while some only look to personal benefit. Diversity among evaluators fosters a divergence of opinions and images, and so *weakens* reputations.

Despite significant diversity among resource providers, their demands on companies are not so contradictory as to make an overall evaluation of firms' effectiveness or attractiveness impossible (Steers, 1975). In the short run, the expectations of some constituents can run counter to the expectations of others. For instance, investors welcome high earnings. However, consumers' demands for quality and service require resource allocations that drain earnings, as do employee petitions for higher wages and benefits, and community expectations of corporate responsiveness and citizenship.

In the end, the performance assessment process constructs the reputational market from individually held perceptions and images much like a jigsaw puzzle paints an identifiable picture out of interlocking pieces. Firms develop more or less consistent images among their multiple constituents. A reputation crystallizes the degree to which a firm has developed convergent and overlapping external images and evaluations. The greater the number of constituent groups whose demands a firm satisfies, and the more convergent the images a firm presents to those different groups, the stronger its ascribed reputation is likely to be.

Ultimately, figure 10.3 suggests that reputations congeal from the individual judgments made by all of a company's key constituent groups as they make interfirm comparisons and evaluate the behaviors of a firm. When juxtaposed against their assessments of rivals in an industry, the resulting rankings specify the prestige ordering of the industry. *The ordering reflects firms' relative success in meeting the expectations of the industry's constituents.*

## KEY ISSUES IN REPUTATION RESEARCH

The study of corporate reputations is now in its infancy and numerous questions must be addressed as research programs unfold in the coming years. I suggest here three salient issues that appear to dominate current discussions of corporate reputation: They involve: (1) measurement, (2) valuation, and (3) causality.

### Issue 1: measuring reputations

The reputational order derives from individual perceptions and interpretations. It means that the ontological status of "corporate reputations" remains problematic. Do singular reputations exist? And more importantly, are they meaningful? Carter and Deephouse (1999) contrasted the different dimensions of Wal-Mart's corporate reputation, and suggested that decomposing reputations into distinct components can help improve our understanding of corporate reputations. In contrast, Fombrun (1996) argues that the reputation construct can be meaningfully measured by combining perceptions of re-source providers on a common set of dimensions.

Whether singular or not, accurately measuring corporate reputations is crucial if they are to be better understood and managed. Unfortunately, measures of corporate reputation now proliferate, encouraging chaos and confusion about a company's reputational assets (Fombrun, 1996). Internally, many companies create their own proprietary performance indicators for use in benchmarking improvements. Externally, companies get rated by numerous groups, including non-governmental groups like the Council on Economic Priorities, private advisory groups like Kinder, Lydenberg and Domini, and in numerous surveys published in the media.

By far the most visible instrument is the one used to produce *Fortune*'s annual list of "America's Most Admired Companies." Since 1983, the magazine has described how executives rate companies in their own industries on eight attributes of performance: (1) the quality of the company's products and services, (2) the company's innovativeness; (3) value as a long-term investment, (4) financial soundness, (5) ability to attract, develop, and retain talent; (6) community responsibility, (7) use of corporate assets, and (8) quality of management. The list has spawned a host of imitators and spinoffs.

Close scrutiny of these measures, however, indicates methodological deficiencies that inhibit systematic analysis. Some are arbitrarily performed by expert panels, and so are not replicable. Some are carried out with private information, and so are unverifiable. All rely on their own idiosyncratic attributes, and are devoid of theoretical rationale. The result is a veritable cacophony of ratings, few of which are directly comparable.

*Fortune*'s popular measure is a case in point. On what basis are the eight attributes selected? Since executives and analysts are the only constituency invited to rate the listed companies, and they do so only in their own industry, won't those ratings be biased to financial performance? Fombrun and Shanley (1990) showed just that in a statistical analysis of *Fortune*'s ratings. Since then, discussions of the "financial halo" of *Fortune*'s ratings have proliferated, and sophisticated statistical methods have been developed to "remove" the financial halo from the data (Brown and Dacin, 1997). Far more important, however, is the profound limitation of those ratings: That they are obtained solely from a financial audience, and *not from a representative set of resource-holders*. Surely no one doubts that employees, customers, and communities are likely to rate the same companies differently than executives and analysts?

Research on "public opinion" has tangled with a similar problem, and now largely relies on an aggregation of individual opinions as a way to crystallize the public's point of view (Price, 1992). Anchored in a pluralistic worldview, this "micro" perspective adheres to the democratic principle of "one person, one vote" (Gallup and Rae, 1940; Childs, 1939). It advocates systematic random polling as a way to unearth the opinions of a diverse polity (Gallup and Rae, 1940; Lake, 1987). The critical concern is to create samples that are "representative" of the population at large. As Roll and Cantril (1972: 77) put it: "Respondents . . . are *not* selected because of their typicality or of their representativeness. Rather, each sampling area and each individual falls into the sample by chance and thus contributes a certain uniqueness to the whole. It is only when these unrepresentative elements are added together that the sample should become representative."

Much as opinion polls are used to construct a profile of "public opinion" on a particular topic, so too can corporate reputations be uncovered from systematically polling a company's publics. If fully representative, reputational polls could surface the covert cognitive field within which reputations develop, and so replicate the chaotic and cloudy aggregation that takes place as part of the assessment process.

To address these issues, in 1998 I joined forces with the market research firm of Harris Interactive to build a standardized but versatile instrument that could be used to measure perceptions of companies across industries and with multiple stakeholder segments. As part of that research, we conducted focus groups in the US. We began by asking people to name companies they liked and respected, as well as companies they didn't like or respect. We then asked them why they felt this way. When we analyzed the data from different groups and industries, the findings demonstrated that people justify their feelings about companies on one of 20 attributes that we grouped into 6 dimensions (see figure 10.3):

- *Emotional appeal*: how much the company is liked, admired, and respected.
- *Products and services*: perceptions of the quality, innovation, value, and reliability of the company's products and services.
- *Financial performance*: perceptions of the company's profitability, prospects, and risk.
- *Vision and leadership*: how much the company demonstrates a clear vision and strong leadership.
- *Workplace environment*: perceptions of how well the company is managed, how it is to work for, and the quality of its employees.
- *Social responsibility*: perceptions of the company as a good citizen in its dealings with communities, employees, and the environment.

We created an index that sums people's perceptions of companies on these 20 attributes, and called it the "reputation quotient" (RQ). We then conducted various empirical studies to benchmark the reputations of companies as seen by different stakeholder segments. The results indicate that the RQ is a valid instrument for measuring corporate reputations and can be used to benchmark companies across industries (Fombrun, Gardberg, and Sever, 2000).

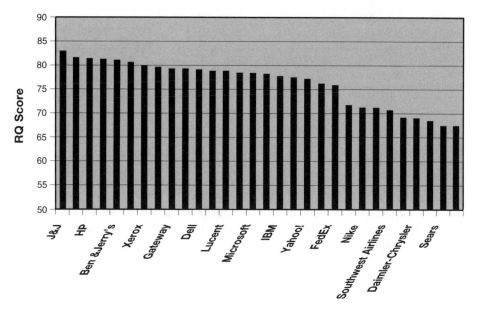

FIGURE 10.4 The best corporate reputations in America

*Note*: A study of the "Best Corporate Reputations in America" was conducted by the Reputation Institute with the market research firm Harris Interactive during August 25–31, 1999 (a description of the study appeared in Alsop, 1999). In the first part of the study, 4,500 people were polled online and by phone and asked to nominate the companies they believed had the best and worst reputations. In the second part of the study, another 10,830 respondents provided detailed ratings of the most visible companies. The figure shows the 30 best-regarded companies. Reputational ratings were weighted to be representative of the US population.

Figure 10.4 presents the reputation scores of a set of companies obtained from polling over 10,000 people to rate the best corporate reputations in the US in August 1999. The findings were featured in *The Wall Street Journal* (Alsop, 1999). Some surprises included the high ratings ascribed by the public to relatively small, unadvertised companies like Ben & Jerry's, and the lower ratings ascribed to companies that often top the *Fortune* ratings like General Electric.

Further study is needed to validate the 20-item RQ measure of corporate reputation cross-culturally. Research on the empirical correlates of the RQ will also help to establish the measure, and to strengthen its underpinnings.

## Issue 2: valuing reputations

No one doubts that a corporate reputation has economic value (Hall, 1993). Unfortunately, efforts to document these values invariably run up against the fact that a company's reputation is closely intertwined with other intangible assets. Isolating a corporate reputation's *unique* contribution to the value of the company is therefore difficult. Nonetheless, I review two pieces of evidence below: crisis effects and financial analyses.

*Crisis effects.*   An Exxon oil tanker hits a reef in Prudhoe Bay on a moonless night. A terrorist bomb rips open the belly of a Pan Am jet over Lockerbie, Scotland. A lethal gas cloud seeps from a Union Carbide plant in Bhopal, India. The flames from a Phillips Petroleum refinery fire engulf block after block in Pasadena, California.

The value of a corporate reputation is magnified at such times, because of the tragic loss of physical assets and human lives that occurred, and the expected clean-up and legal costs associated with the crisis. Comparable market losses occur, however, even when no physical assets are actually lost, and the crisis can be attributed solely to changed perceptions of the company by key resource-holders.

Consider what happened to the actual market values of the following companies listed in a one week window after they were plunged into unnatural crises that made headlines around the world:

- ◆ Johnson & Johnson dropped $1 billion in market value, or 14 percent, after some of its Tylenol bottles were laced with cyanide in 1982. J&J took another $1 billion hit when malicious tamperers struck again in 1985.
- ◆ The discovery that Intel Corp.'s new Pentium chip could not handle some simple math calculations knocked $3 billion, or 12 percent, off Intel's market value in 1985.
- ◆ Exxon Corp.'s stock was devalued by $3 billion, or 5 percent, in the first week after the oil gushing from the *Exxon Valdez* fouled Alaska's Prince William Sound in 1989.
- ◆ Salomon Brothers watched the bears take $1.3 billion or 30 percent of its value after one of its own traders was caught trying to corner the bond market in 1991.
- ◆ Motorola saw its capitalization fall by $6 billion or 16 percent after scientists hinted at a link between cell phones and brain cancer in 1995.

These losses are due to the changed expectations of resource-holders about the company's future profitability. The market losses are equally staggering, whether they involve material losses of physical capital, or whether they consist purely of changes in how the company is perceived in the marketplace. Exxon's subsequent clean-up and legal costs were of the order of $2.5 billion. But in 1995, Motorola's $6 billion losses from the brain tumor scare were purely intangible, as were most of Intel's from the Pentium chip.

Over time, some companies recover dissipated value quickly and the crisis fizzles. Others experience more extended damage. Research suggests that the difference may well lie in how the crisis is handled, and what the reputation of the company was beforehand.

Knight and Pretty (1999) conducted event studies to chart the impact of man-made catastrophes on the market values of 15 companies. They ranged from the first Tylenol tampering in 1982 to Source Perrier's recall of its gassy, green-bottled water because of benzene contamination in 1990, to a Heineken recall due to rumors of broken glass in its beer bottles in 1993. As the authors put it, catastrophes "provide a unique opportunity to evaluate how financial markets respond when major risks become reality." On average, all 15 stocks they studied took an initial hit of 8 percent of their market value. However, the companies quickly sorted themselves into two distinct groups that the Oxford professors called the "recoverers and non-recoverers."

The recoverers' stock sagged only 5 percent in the first weeks while the non-recoverers' stock lost 11 percent. After 10 weeks, the recoverers' stock actually rose 5 percent and stayed comfortably in positive territory for the balance of the year. In contrast, the non-recoverers' stock stayed down and finished the year off by a sobering 15 percent. The conclusion: all catastrophes have an initial negative impact on price, but paradoxically "they offer an opportunity for management to demonstrate their talent in dealing with difficult circumstances."

Event studies like these support the thesis that reputations have considerable hidden value as a form of insurance – they act like a "reservoir of goodwill." The insurance value derives from an ability to buffer better-regarded companies from taking as large a fall as companies with lesser reputations. Gregory (1998) examined the stock prices of companies on the New York Stock Exchange following the market crash of 1997. Consistent with the "reservoir hypothesis," he argued that better-regarded companies would be cushioned from the crisis. Their results confirmed that the market values of high-reputation companies were less affected by the market crash than those of a comparable sample of companies with weaker reputations.

Firestone and Ford are a case in point. A media fest occurred in 2000 as information was uncovered suggesting that Firestone's tires were to blame for numerous deadly accidents around the world involving the Ford Motor Company's Explorer sports utility vehicles. Ford took aggressive action, including a massive recall and a media campaign that featured its CEO, Jack Nasser. Ford's strategy was largely to place blame squarely on Firestone. In contrast, Firestone's communications were very guarded and contradictory, and failed to convey either responsibility or understanding of the situation. Time will tell, but it is probably not a coincidence that Ford appears to have weathered the storm while Firestone's reputation is at an all time low – and the survival of the corporate brand is in doubt.

*Financial analyses.*   Efforts to make direct estimates of the financial value of corporate reputations are also under way. To do so, it proves useful to decompose the market value (MV) of a public company into four components:

- physical capital (PC): the liquidation value of the company's tangible assets;
- market capital (MC): the net financial assets of the company;
- intellectual capital (IC): the value of the company's knowhow;
- reputational capital (RC): the value of the company's brands and stakeholder relationships.

Both physical capital and market capital can be estimated. However, accurate estimates of reputational capital require knowledge of the company's stock of intellectual capital – something that is as difficult to estimate as reputation itself. Failing that, it is possible to assess the company's pool of "intangible assets" as the joint value of its reputational and intellectual capital.

Comparing the book values of firms with market valuations suggests that the intangible assets of public companies in the US and the UK constitute on average some 55 percent of the total market valuations of those companies.

Another estimate of reputational capital results from asking: how much would a third party be willing to pay to *lease* a corporate name? In fact, licensing arrangements are actually royalty rates for corporate names. The more a licensee is prepared to pay to rent a corporate name, the greater must be the drawing power of the company's reputation, particularly to customers. Royalty percentages on corporate licenses generally range between 8 percent and 14 percent of projected sales. One estimate of the value of the company's reputation is therefore the present value of expected royalty payments over an arbitrary life of, say, 20 years.

Consider consumer goods giant Gillette. In 1993, the consulting firm Interbrand suggested that an 8 percent royalty rate might be expected from licensing the Gillette name. Applied to Gillette's $4.7 billion in sales, it meant potential royalty revenue of $375 million in the first year. Assuming sales growth of 5 percent a year over 20 years (an arbitrary life ascribed to use of the Gillette name), and discounting the royalty revenues back to the present at Gillette's own cost of capital of 10.12 percent, produces a financial estimate for Gillette's corporate name of about $4.5 billion in 1993, a significant proportion of Gillette's total market value (Fombrun, 1996).

Various academic efforts to quantify the value of reputation also find significant economic premiums associated with corporate reputations, although the exact size of the estimate is still in question. Shrivastava et al. (1997) compared ten groups of companies with similar levels of risk and return, but different average reputation scores. They found that a 60 percent difference in reputation score was associated with a 7 percent difference in market value. Since an average company in the study was valued at $3 billion, that means a 1-point difference in reputation score from 6 to 7 on a 10-point scale would be worth an additional $52.5 million in market value. Black, Carnes, and Richardson (2000) examined the relationship between market value, book value, profitability and reputation for all the firms rated in *Fortune*'s "most admired companies" survey between 1983 and 1997. They report that a 1-point change in reputation is associated with an average of $500 million in market value.

The good news is that research confirms that reputations are valuable intangible assets. The bad news is that the size of the effect is still in question. It is a safe bet from these studies, however, that reputations are worth a lot more than companies are now spending to manage them.

## Issue 3: causality

Causality is at the heart of much debate about corporate reputations. Are reputations central or are they purely epiphenomal? The value cycle of figure 10.1 helps explain the debate. On one hand, reputations derive from the first-order initiatives that companies make to directly improve corporate performance – their strategic initiatives. At the same time, good performance itself induces favorable interpretations by resource-holders and enables funding those initiatives. It is therefore difficult to untangle the causal ordering between a company's strategic initiatives, its financial performance, and the reputation ascribed to the company by observers: all three are mutually determined (McGuire, Sundgren, and Schneeweiss, 1988; Chakravarthy, 1986).

Nonetheless, efforts to identify the causes and consequences of corporate reputation are bound to dominate research debates in the coming years. I suggest four key correlates of corporate reputation that will be the subject of ongoing research in the area.

*Performance/profitability/risk.*   By far the most important question to the practitioner is the relationship between reputation and financial performance. Yet few studies reliably and consistently demonstrate the size of that effect. What is the impact of receiving a good reputational rating on a company's profitability and risk? Conversely, what do favorable or unfavorable earnings announcements and analyst estimates do to a company's reputation?

*Identity.* A company's culture and identity govern how managers interpret their roles and so influence the kinds of relationships that they establish with key resource providers like consumers, investors, employees, and local communities (Schultz, Hatch, and Larsen, 2000; Dutton and Dukerich, 1991). Through these relationships, managers seek to project attractive images of their firms and shape corporate assessments (Dowling, 1986; Winfrey, 1989). What is the relationship between a company's internal beliefs, sense of self, cultural practices, and the way it is perceived by resource-holders?

*Communications.* Obviously firms vary in the degree and coherence with which they actively try to shape constituent assessments. The effort and resources that firms expend to manage an exchange with a particular constituent depend on the value they place on a particular constituent. Therefore, the leading predictors of managers' efforts to shape favorable environments are likely to be a firm's core values, embodied in its culture and identity. What is the relationship between corporate reputation and the communications and self-presentations that a company elects to make? Are a company's efforts to manipulate external images through advertising and public relations bound to fail when they are disconnected from a company's identity?

*Citizenship.* Companies regularly expend time and money in pro-bono activities, philanthropic programs, and community-based initiatives. Such citizenship programs are often poorly understood and defended under corporate umbrellas. Fombrun, Gardberg, and Barnett (1999) argued that they are in fact mechanisms to manage upside and downside risks firms face from resource-holders. What effects do these programs have on a company's visibility and favor with key groups? How do they dovetail with one another?

## CONCLUSION

Corporate reputations are aggregate perceptions that resource-holders have of a company. A reputation can therefore be good or bad, strong or weak: it crystallizes how people *feel* about a company based on whatever information (or mis-information) they have about the company, its activities, workplace, past performance, and future prospects.

In time, favorable perceptions of a company by these key resource-holders crystallize into intangible assets that we call "corporate reputations." I suggest that these reputations have intrinsic economic value because they affect a company's bottom-line performance.

If competition is the motor of the market economy, I have suggested here that reputation is the fuel that makes it run. As Alan Greenspan, Chairman of the US Federal Reserve, put it in a commencement speech at Harvard University on June 10, 2000:

In today's world, where ideas are increasingly displacing the physical in the production of economic value, competition for reputation becomes a significant driving force, propelling our economy forward. Manufactured goods often can be evaluated before the completion of a transaction. Service providers, on the other hand, usually can offer only their reputations.

I have sketched out here the general contours of an emerging cross-disciplinary paradigm that views corporate reputations as strategic assets and as a source of economic value. Increasing commitments of theory and research are needed to crystallize the tangible behavioral and financial benefits associated with higher reputational standing.

"Reputation management" is the pragmatic counterpart of reputation research. Its central tenet is that strong reputations result from the development of initiatives and messages that convey the genuine and distinctive values and personality of a company. It suggests that the essence of reputation-building lies, not in posturing, spin doctoring, wordsmithing, or puffery – the characteristics that gave old line corporate communications a bad name. Rather, it proposes that reputation management is a source of competitive advantage – which makes it nothing less than enlightened self-interest. Future developments will benefit from a continuing dialogue between research and practice that can shed light on the ways in which companies build winning positions in reputational markets.

## REFERENCES

Aaker, D. (1998). *Strong Brands*. Englewood Cliffs, NJ: Prentice-Hall.

Abrahamson, E. (1991). Managerial fads and fashions: The diffusion and rejection of innovations. *Academy of Management Review*, 16: 586–612.

Abrahamson, E., and Fombrun, C. J. (1992). Forging the iron cage: Interorganizational networks and the production of macro-culture. *Journal of Management Studies*, 29: 175–94.

Abrahamson, E., and Fombrun, C. J. (1994). Macro-cultures: Determinants and consequences. *Academy of Management Review*, 19: 728–55.

Abrahamson and Rosenberg, (1994) *Academy of Management Journal*.

Albert, S., and Whetten, D. (1985). Organizational identity. In L. L. Cummings and B. M. Staw (eds.), *Research in Organizational Behavior*, 7: 263–95. Greenwich, CT: JAI Press.

Allen, F. (1984). Reputation and product quality. *Rand Journal of Economics*, 15: 311–27.

Alsop, R. (1999). The best corporate reputations in America. *The Wall Street Journal*, September 25.

Altheide, D. L., and Johnson, J. M. (1980). *Bureaucratic Propaganda*. Boston, MA: Allyn and Bacon.

Alvesson, M. (1990). Organization: From substance to image. *Organizational Studies*, 11: 373–94.

Bagwell, K. (1992). Pricing to signal product line quality. *Journal of Economics and Management Strategy*, 1: 151–74.

Baker, W. E., and Iyer, A. V. (1990). Information networks and market behavior. University of Chicago, Working paper.

Barney, J. (1991). Firm resources and sustained competitive advantage. *Journal of Management*, 17: 99–120.

Barney, J. B. (1986). Organizational culture: Can it be a source of sustained competitive advantage? *Academy of Management Review*, 11: 656–65.

Black, E., Carnes, T., and Richardson, V. (2000). The market value of corporate reputation. *Corporate Reputation Review*, 1: 31–42.

Boorstin, D. J. (1964). *The Image: A Guide to Pseudo-events in America*. New York: Harper & Row.

Brealy, R., and Myers, S. (1988). *Principles of Corporate Finance*. New York: McGraw-Hill.

Brown, T. J. and Dacin, P. A. (1997). The company and the product: Corporate associations and consumer product responses, *Journal of Marketing*, 61 (January): 421–36.

Carroll, A. B. (1979). A three-dimensional conceptual model of corporate social performance. *Academy of Management Review*, 4: 497–505.

Carter, S., and Deephouse, D. (1999). 'Tough Talk' and 'Soothing Speech': Managing Reputations of Being Tough and Being Good. *Corporate Reputation Review*, 2: 69–87.

Caves, R. E., and Porter, M. E. (1977). From entry barriers to mobility barriers. *Quarterly Journal of Economics*, 91: 421–34.

Chakravarthy, B. (1986). Measuring strategic performance. *Strategic Management Journal*, 7: 437–58.

Cheney, G., and Vibbert, S. (1987). Corporate discourse: Public relations and issue management. In F. Jablin, L. Putnam, K. Roberts, and L. Porter (eds.), *A Handbook of Organizational Communication: An Interdisciplinary Perspective*. Beverly Hills, CA: Sage Publications.

Childs, H. L. (1939). By public opinion I mean . . . *Public Opinion Quarterly*, 4: 53–69.

Collins, J., and Porras, J. (1996). *Built to Last*. New York: Free Press.

Crable, R., and Vibbert, S. (1985). Managing issues and influencing public policy. *Public Relations Review*, 11: 3–16.

Daft, R., and Weick, K. (1984). Toward a model of organizations as interpretation systems. *Academy of Management Review*, 9: 284–95.

DiMaggio, P., and Powell, W. (1983). The iron cage revisited: Institutional isomorphism and collective rationality in organizational fields. *American Sociological Review*, 48: 147–60.

Dowling, G. R. (1986). Managing your corporate images. *Industrial Marketing Management*, 15: 109–15.

Dutton, J. E., and Dukerich, J. M. (1991). Keeping an eye on the mirror: Image and identity in organizational adaptation. *Academy of Management Journal*, 34: 517–54.

Elsbach, K. (1994). Managing organizational legitimacy in the California cattle industry: The construction and effectiveness of verbal accounts. *Administrative Science Quarterly*, 39: 57–88.

Fombrun, C. J. (1996). *Reputation: Realizing Value from the Corporate Image*. Cambridge, MA: Harvard Business School Press.

Fombrun, C. J., Gardberg, N., and Barnett, M. (2000). Opportunity platforms and safety nets: Corporate citizenship and reputational risk. *Business and Society*, 105(1): 85–106.

Fombrun, C. J., Gardberg, N., and Sever, J. (2000). The reputation quotient: A multi-stakeholder measure of corporate reputation. *Journal of Brand Management*, 7(4): 241–55.

Fombrun, C. J., and Rindova, V. (2001). Fanning the flame: Corporate reputations as social constructions of performance. In J. Porac and M. Ventresca (eds.), *Constructing Markets and Industries*. New York: Oxford University Press, forthcoming.

Fombrun, C. J., and Shanley, M. (1990). What's in a name? Reputation-building and corporate strategy. *Academy of Management Journal*, 33: 233–58.

Fombrun, C., Tichy, N., and Devanna, M. A. (1984). *Strategic Human Resource Management*. New York: John Wiley.

Fombrun, C. J., and Van Riel, C. (1997). The reputational landscape. *Corporate Reputation Review*, 1: 5–13.

Fombrun, C. J., and Zajac, E. J. (1987). Structural and perceptual influences on intraindustry stratification. *Academy of Management Journal*, 30: 33–50.

Frank, R., and Cook, P. (1996). *The Winner Take All Society*. Englewood Cliffs, NJ: Prentice-Hall.

Freeman, R. E. (1984). *Strategic Management: A Stakeholder Approach*. Boston, MA: Pitman.

Fry, L. W., Keim, G. D., and Meiners, R. E. (1982). Corporate contributions: Altruistic or for-profit? *Academy of Management Journal*, 25: 94–106.

Galaskiewicz, J., and Burt, R. (1991). Interorganizational contagion in corporate philanthropy. *Administrative Science Quarterly*, 36(1): 88–105.

Gallup, G., and Rae, S. (1940). *The Pulse of Democracy*. New York: Simon & Schuster.

Gioia, D. (1986). The state of the art in organizational and social cognition: A personal view. In H. Sims and D. Gioia (eds.), *The Thinking Organization*. San Francisco, CA: Jossey Bass: 336–57.

Goode, W. (1978). *The Celebration of Heroes: Prestige as a Social Control System*. Berkeley, CA: University of California Press.

Granovetter, M. (1985). Economic action and social structure: The problem of embeddedness. *American Journal of Sociology*, 91: 481–510.

Gregory, J. R. (1998). Does corporate reputation provide a cushion to companies facing market volatility? Some supportive evidence, *Corporate Reputation Review*, 1: 288–90.

Grossman, S., and Stiglitz, J. (1980). On the impossibility of informationally efficient markets. *American Economic Review*, 70: 393–408.

Hall, R. (1992). The strategic analysis of intangible resources. *Strategic Management Journal*, 13: 135–44.

Hall, R. (1993). A framework linking intangible resources and capabilities. *Strategic Management Journal*, 14: 607–19.

Harris, M. A., Bock, G., Field, A., and Lewis, G. (1986). How IBM is fighting back. *Business Week*, November 17: 152.

Hatch, M. J. (1993). The dynamics of organizational culture. *Academy of Management Review*, 18(4): 657–93.

Hill, C., and Jones, T. (1992). Stakeholder-agency theory. *Journal of Management Studies*, 29: 131–54.

Huff, A. (1982). Industry influence on strategy reformulation. *Strategic Management Journal*, 3: 119–31.

Jones, T. (1995). Instrumental stakeholder theory: A synthesis of ethics and economics. *Academy of Management Review*, 20: 404–37.

Kaplan, R. S., and Roll, R. (1972). Investor evaluation of accounting information: Some empirical evidence. *Journal of Business*, 45: 225–57.

Kaplan, R. S., and Urwitz, G. (1979). Statistical models of bond ratings: A methodological inquiry. *Journal of Business*, 52: 231–61.

Keller, K. L. (1999). *Strategic Brand Management*. Irwin.

Kingdon, J. W. (1984). *Agendas, Alternatives, and Public Policies*. Boston, MA: Little, Brown.

Knight, R. and Pretty, D. (1999). Top of Mind: Corporate Catastrophes, Stock Returns and Trading Volume. *Corporate Reputation Review*, 2: 363–78.

Lake, C. C. (1987). *Public Opinion Polling*. Washington, DC: Island Press.

Lydenberg, S. D., Marlin, A. T., and Strub, S. O. (1986). *Rating America's Corporate Conscience*. Reading, MA: Addison-Wesley.

McCaffrey, D. P. (1982). Corporate resources and regulatory pressures: Toward explaining a discrepancy. *Administrative Science Quarterly*, 27(3): 398–419.

McGuire, J. B., Sundgren, A., and Schneeweis, T. (1988). Corporate social responsibility and firm financial performance. *Academy of Management Journal*, 31(4): 854–72.

Milgrom, P., and Roberts, J. (1986). Relying on the information of interested parties. *Rand Journal of Economics*, 17: 18–32.

Mitchell, M. L. (1989). The impact of external parties on brand-name capital: the 1982 Tylenol poisonings and subsequent cases. *Economic Inquiry*, 27: 601–18.

Myers, S., and Majluf, N. (1984). Corporate financing and investment decisions when firms have information investors do not have. *Journal of Financial Economics*, 13: 187–221.

Nelson, P. (1974). Advertising as information. *Journal of Political Economy*, 78: 311–29.

Penrose, E. T. (1959). *The Theory of the Growth of the Firm*. New York: John Wiley.

Peteraf, M. (1993). The cornerstones of competitive advantage: A resource-based view. *Strategic Management Journal*, 14: 179–91.

Pfeffer, J. (1981). *Power in Organizations*. Marshfield, MA: Pitman.

Pfeffer, J., and Salancik, G. (1978). *External Control of Organizations*. New York: Harper & Row.

Price, V. (1992). *Communication Concepts 4: Public Opinion*. Newbury Park, CA: Sage.

Rao, H. (1994). The social construction of reputation: Certification contests, legitimation, and the survival of organizations in the American automobile industry: 1895–1912. *Strategic Management Journal*, 15: 75–93.

Rindova, V. (1997). The image cascade and the formation of corporate reputations. *Corporate Reputation Review*, 1: 189–94.

Rindova, V. (1998). *Competing for the mind: Corporate communications and observers' interpretations of specialty coffee chains*. Unpublished doctoral dissertation. The Leonard Stern School of Business, New York University.

Rindova, V., and Fombrun, C.J. (1999). Constructing competitive advantage. *Strategic Management Journal*, 20: 111–27.

Rindova, V., and Schultz, M. (1998). Identity within and identity without: Lessons from corporate and organizational identity. In D. Whetten and P. Godfrey (eds.), *Identity in Organizations*. Thousand Oaks, CA: Sage Publications: 46–51.

Roll, C. W., and Cantril, A. H. (1972). *Polls: Their Use and Misuse in Politics*. New York: Basic Books.

Rosen, S. (1981). The economics of superstars. *American Economic Review*, 71: 845–57.

Ross, S. A. (1977). The determination of financial structure: The incentive-signalling approach. *Bell Journal of Economics*, 8(1): 23–40.

Salancik, G., and Meindl, J. (1984). Corporate attributions as strategic illusions of management control. *Administrative Science Quarterly*, 29: 238–54.

Schlenker, B. R. (1980). *Impression Management*. Monterey, CA: Brooks/Cole Publishing Company.

Schultz, M., Hatch, M. J., and Larsen, M. (2000). *The Expressive Organization*. London: Oxford University Press.

Senge, P. (1995). *The Fifth Dimension*. Englewood-Cliffs, NJ: Prentice-Hall.

Sethi, S. P. (1979). A conceptual framework for environmental analysis of social issues and evaluation of business response patterns. *Academy of Management Review*, 4: 63–74.

Shapiro, C. (1983). Premiums for high-quality products as returns to reputations. *Quarterly Journal of Economics*, 98: 659–81.

Shapiro, S. P. (1987). The social control of impersonal trust. *American Journal of Sociology*, 93: 623–58.

Shrivastava, P. (1986). *Bhopal: Anatomy of a Crisis*. Boston, MA: Ballinger.

Shrivastava, R. K., McInish, T. H., Wood, R. A., and Capraro, A. J. (1997). *Corporate Reputation Review*, 1: 62–8.

Shrum, W., and Wuthnow, R. (1988). Reputational status of organizations in technical systems. *American Journal of Sociology*, 93: 882–912.

Spence, A. M. (1974). *Market Signalling: Informational Transfer in Hiring and Related Screening Processes*. Cambridge, MA: Harvard University Press.

Steers, R. M. (1975). Problems in measurement of organizational effectiveness. *Administrative Science Quarterly*, 20: 546–58.

Stigler, G. J. (1962). Information in the labor market. *Journal of Political Economy*, 70: 49–73.

Stiglitz, J. E. (1989). Imperfect information in the product market. In R. Schmalensee and R. Willig (eds.), *Handbook of Industrial Organization*, Chapter 13: 769–847. Amsterdam, Holland: North Holland Press.

Suchman, M. (1995). Managing legitimacy: Strategic and institutional approaches. *Academy of Management Review*, 20(3): 571–611.

Tedeschi, J. T. (ed.) (1981). *Impression Management Theory and Social Psychological Research*. New York: Academic Press.

Useem, M. (1988). Market and institutional factors in corporate contributions. *California Management Review*, 30(2): 77–88.

Van Riel, C. (1995). *Principles of Corporate Communications*. Englewood Cliffs, NJ: Prentice-Hall.

Wartick, S. L. (1988). How issues management contributes to corporate performance. *Business Forum*, 13(2): 16–22.

Wartick, S. L. (1992). The relationship between intense media exposure and change in corporate reputation. *Business and Society*, 31: 33–49.

Wartick, S. L., and Cochran, P. L. (1985). The evolution of the corporate social performance model. *Academy of Management Review*, 10: 758–69.

Weigelt, K., and Camerer, C. (1988). Reputation and corporate strategy: A review of recent theory and applications. *Strategic Management Journal*, 9: 443–54.

White, H. C. (1981). Where do markets come from? *American Journal of Sociology*, 87: 517–47.

Wilson, R. (1983). Auditing: Perspectives from multi-person decision theory. *The Accounting Review*, 58: 305–18.

Winfrey, F. L. (1989). *Firm reputation and corporate social responsibility: A tale of two constructs*. Paper presented at the annual meeting of the Academy of Management, Social Issues in Management Division.

Yoon, E., Guffey, H., and Kijewski, V. (1993). The effects of information and company reputation on intentions to buy a business service. *Journal of Business Research*, 27: 215–28.

# Part III

## Strategy Types

# 11

# Competitive Dynamics Research: Critique and Future Directions

KEN G. SMITH, WALTER J. FERRIER AND
HERMANN NDOFOR

A series of actions (moves) and reactions (countermoves) among firms in an industry create competitive dynamics. These action/reaction dynamics reflect the normal and innovative movement of firms in pursuit of profits. Firms act creatively (introduce a new product, a new promotion, or a new marketing agreement) to enhance or improve profits, competitive advantage, and industry position; successful actions (actions which generate new customers and profits) promote competitive reaction as rivals attempt to block or imitate the action. The study of competitive dynamics is thus the study of how firm action (moves) affects competitors, competitive advantage, and performance. Sometimes these actions and reactions can escalate among firms so that the industry performance is adversely affected; at other times, the pattern of behavior can be more gentlemanly and profitable.

The importance of the competitive dynamics was highlighted in Schumpeter's (1934) theory of creative destruction. Schumpeter described the creative destruction process as a "perennial gale." The gale of competition was generated by the extraordinary profits earned by the movements or actions of the first moving firm. Indeed, in this dynamic gale, the gains obtained from leaders motivate other competitors to undertake actions or reactions in an attempt to overtake the leader and enjoy the same profits. Importantly, Schumpeter emphasized that as a result of this creative destruction process, no firm was safe from the market process of competition. Thus, Schumpeter argued that to truly understand profits and competition, one must examine the interplay and consequences of action and reaction. Over time, the creative actions of challengers whittle away at the leader's position, prompting an eventual leader dethronement and the beginning of a new battle.

Empirical research on competitive dynamics began in the 1980s with MacMillan, McCaffrey and Van Wijk's (1985) study of competitor response times to easily imitated new products in the banking industry. Bettis and Weeks (1987) followed by examining stock market reactions to product moves and countermoves between Polaroid and Kodak in instant photography. Smith, Grimm, Chen, and Gannon (1989) identified the characteristics of competitive actions that evoked speedy response in a sample of high technology firms.

During the early 1990s, a series of papers examining the antecedents and consequences of competitive action and reaction in the US Airline industry were published (Chen, Smith, and Grimm, 1992; Chen and MacMillan, 1992; Chen and Miller, 1994; Chen and Hambrick, 1995; Miller and Chen, 1994; Smith et al., 1991; Smith, Grimm, and Gannon, 1992). Moreover, new action data sets have emerged. For example, in a study of software producers, Young, Smith, and Grimm (1996) found that aggressive firms, those that engaged rivals with a greater number of actions, obtained the highest performance. In addition, Ferrier, Smith, and Grimm (1999) found that industry leaders were dethroned by the aggressive speedy moves of the number two challengers in a study of leader/challenger competition in 41 different industries. Most recently, in a study of new product rivalry in the brewing, telecommunications and personal computer industries, Lee et al. (2000) found that stock market returns to first movers and early imitators were greater than for late imitators.

Given all the recent research on dynamics, it is an appropriate time to take stock of the scientific developments in this new area of research and evaluate the progress. Accordingly, in this chapter we review and critique the theories, research studies and findings of competitive dynamics research. We conclude by setting a research agenda for the future that includes a proposal for new theory and connections of competitive dynamics research to the resource based view and industrial organization economics.

Our review of the competitive dynamics research will be concerned with the empirical study of *actions* and *reactions* of firms within the strategic management literature.[1] We take the position that markets are always in a state of flux; in some cases, markets are moving toward equilibrium, in other cases they are moving away from equilibrium (D'Aveni, 1994; Grimm and Smith, 1997). The root cause of this market flux and movement is the specific actions or jockeying of firms in a desire to improve industry position and profits (Kirzner, 1973). Figure 11.1, from Smith, Grimm, and Gannon (1992), highlights the relationship between actors and action, and reactors and reaction examined in this chapter. We use this figure as an organizing device and present it now to guide the reader in our review of the literature.

Overall, we analyzed over 30 published articles that focused on competitive dynamics. These included both conceptual and empirical contributions published primarily in management journals. To qualify for analysis, the articles had to focus on explaining or predicting competitive action or reaction, which was defined as a market-based move designed to build or defend competitive advantage and performance. The authors of this chapter read the various articles and classified them according to independent variables identified in figure 11.1.

## BACKGROUND

Much of the competitive dynamics research has been framed and motivated from Schumpeter's theory of creative destruction (e.g., Smith et al., 1991; Smith, Grimm and Gannon, 1992). Many years ago, Joseph Schumpeter (1934) developed the concept of "creative destruction" to explain the dynamic market process by which firms act and react in the pursuit of market opportunities. Creative destruction is defined as the inevitable and eventual market decline of leading firms through the process of competitive

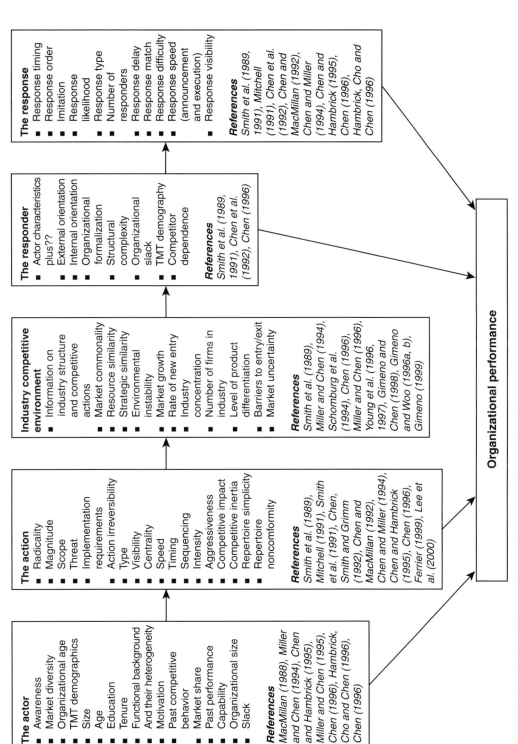

FIGURE 11.1 Studies of the predictors of action, reaction, and performance

action and reaction (Schumpeter, 1934, 1950). In this dynamic context, the creative actions of leaders in pursuit of new opportunities elicit reactions from rivals in an attempt to destroy the advantages sought by the leaders. Indeed, according to Schumpeter, the manner or process by which leaders and challengers act and react determine their long-term performance and survival. According to this theory, innovative first moving firms enjoy transient monopoly advantages and abnormal profits by virtue of the lag in response by rivals (Nelson and Winter, 1982; Porter, 1980). Consequently, competitive dynamics researchers have attempted to empirically identify strategic actions that will benefit from a delay in retaliation, or making the moves as to maximize the delay (Chen, 1988; Smith et al., 1991). Figure 11.1 is consistent with Schumpeter's ideas on action and reaction: firms act, and rivals react!

Young, Smith, and Grimm (1996) and Ferrier, Smith, and Grimm (1999) advanced the Schumpeterian ideas by integrating Austrian economics into the competitive dynamics stream. The Austrians believe, as Schumpeter did, that competition is a dynamic market process rather than a static market outcome, as neoclassical economists believe (Scherer and Ross, 1990). More specifically, market equilibrium (i.e., the lack of movement in prices, production quantities, different quality levels, etc.) occurs only in the absence of competition. As such, the Austrians focus their attention on the processes by which markets move toward and away from equilibrium. But they argue that markets never reach equilibrium because the profit forces for action will disrupt the stable state or status quo. To explain this disruption, the Austrians focus on the role of "entrepreneurial discovery." This is defined as the action of successfully directing the flow of resources toward fulfillment of consumer needs when market opportunities arise (Jacobsen, 1992; Mises, 1949; Schumpeter, 1934). From a competitive dynamics perspective, entrepreneurial discovery has led researchers to focus attention on the market and profit effects of innovative actions, such as radical actions or first movement behavior that disrupt the status quo.

Other key issues of competition from the Austrian perspective include strategic flexibility and resource heterogeneity (Jacobsen, 1992). First, successful firms possess the resources and flexibility to engage a variety of actions. Thus, the basis for creative destruction is as much the lack of strategic range in action by complacent firms as it is the inability or unwillingness to continually innovate. In addition, through the process of entrepreneurial discovery, successful firms are able to accumulate, combine, and direct resources differently than other firms. That is, their range and scope of strategic actions are, at least for the short run, superior to that of rival firms. However, this strategic advantage will eventually be eroded through imitation. Indeed, a major focus of competitive dynamic research has been on the process of competition examined through competitive reaction (Smith, Grimm, and Gannon, 1992) and imitation (Smith et al., 1991; Lee et al., 2000). Comparatively less work has been done on the accumulation of resources (Grimm and Smith, 1997).

Schumpeter (1934, 1950) and Austrian literature has played a critical role in helping competitive dynamic researchers identify key concepts. For example, the emphasis on action and reaction in competitive dynamics research comes directly from Schumpeter (1934) and Austrian economics, where action is the central unit of analysis (Mises, 1949). The concept of action and response timing is also fundamental in Austrian economics as it the first mover who often benefits from initial action or the laggard who frequently loses from late action (Kirzner, 1973). Industry structure or the market process of competition is also prominent and fundamental in Austrian economics as it provides the context and motivation for action.

From this grounding in Schumpeter and Austrian economics, competitive dynamics researchers have focused their attention on the role of competitive action and reaction. There are three distinguishing characteristics of competitive dynamics research. The first attribute is the focus on the specific and real behaviors or actions of firms in the marketplace. It has been argued that actions are the vehicle by which firms position themselves in the industry (Porter, 1980) and build resource advantages (Barney, 1991; Grimm and Smith, 1997). Actions are unique in that they occur at a particular time and place. For example, a firm can introduce a new product, offer a free product service contract, start a new promotional campaign, or lower its prices dramatically all in a desire to increase market share and profits. Each of these actions is distinctive with regard to the time they occur (day/month/year) and where (the market) they take place. With this action orientation, timing of actions and reactions has become a pivotal variable with substantial explanatory power (Smith et al., 1991; Lee et al., 2000). In addition, researchers have also examined the scope of action in terms of number of markets or customers affected (Chen, Smith, and Grimm, 1992), and the influence of multimarket competition on rivalry (Gimeno and Woo, 1996, 1999; Young et al., 2001).

The second characteristic of competitive dynamics research is its focus on competitive interdependence. Following Schumpeter (1934), research in competitive dynamics began with the conviction that the performance effects of a firm's strategy (action) depend upon the competitive context in which the strategy is carried out. In other words, firms are not independent, they feel the moves of one another, and for whatever the reason, are prone to interact. In this dynamic action/reaction context, firm performance is not simply a function of the strategies and actions a firm undertakes but it must be understood relative to the strategies and actions of rivals, or as Schumpeter (1934) described, the circular flow of competition. This is referred to as the competitive context. Thus, an important aspect of competitive dynamics research has been the construction of samples of firms that are interacting with one another. For example, Smith et al. (1991) examined all the competitive actions of US domestic airlines to one another over a six-year period, and Young, Smith, and Grimm (1996) studied the actions of all software producers to one another over a ten-year period. With a focus on the competitive context, competitive dynamics researchers center directly on the concept of rivalry, which is a fundamental aspect of all models of competitive advantage.

Finally, competitive dynamic research has broadly attempted to explain both the causes and consequences of action and reaction with particular emphasis on the perform-ance consequences of these dynamics. For example, Lee et al. (2000) examined the performance effects of new product introductions and specifically how competitive imitation cut into the profits of first movers, and Schomburg, Grimm, and Smith (1994) studied how industry structure impacted the order and timing of new product introduc-tions.

We next review the competitive dynamics theory, samples and empirical findings. We begin the review by defining and explaining the variables, concepts and connections outlined in figure 11.1.

## THE BASIC MODEL AND THEORY UNDERLYING COMPETITIVE DYNAMICS RESEARCH

Figure 11.1 provides an overview of the components of the model and the associated relationships as conceived by Smith, Grimm, and Gannon (1992), which includes the actor (the firm that takes a competitive action), the competitive action (the type or magnitude of action), the responder (the firm that reacts), and the response to the action. The final two components include the industry context of competitive activity and the performance outcomes of competitive interaction.

### *The actor*

The actor represents the firm carrying out a competitive action (Smith, Grimm, and Gannon, 1992). In competitive dynamics research, the actor is important to the extent that it is the originator of an action and the beneficiary (both positive and negative) from the action outcome. One important element of competitive dynamics research has focused on how characteristics of the actor affect the actions the firm chooses to implement. Drawing from diverse streams of research, there are three implicit, yet essential organizational characteristics that influence strategic action (Chen, 1996). These are organizational factors that influence the *awareness* of the context and challenges stemming from competitive interdependence, factors which induce or impede the *motivation* of firms to take action, and the resource-based factors, which influence the firm's *ability* to take action.[2]

Organizational characteristics that predict the characteristics of action can be broadly classified as a function of these three characteristics. For instance, *awareness* refers to how cognizant a focal firm is of its competitors, the drivers of competition within the industry, and the general competitive environment. The level of awareness is important because it affects the extent to which a firm understands and comprehends the consequences of its actions within the competitive landscape (Chen, 1996). In prior research, organizational characteristics such as the age of the firm, the diversity of markets in which it competes, and top management team (TMT) demographics have been used to reflect the level of awareness.

A firm might be aware of its rivals and the competitive environment without necessarily being motivated to act. *Motivation* accounts for the incentives that drive a firm to undertake action. Motivation relates to perceived gains or losses, which stem from its belief of whether it stands to gain advantages from action or stands to lose if no action is carried out. Within competitive dynamics research, organizational characteristics such as past performance or market dependence have been used to reflect the motivation to act.

Action is the outcome of not only the deployment of resources, but also the firm's decision-making processes (Grimm and Smith, 1997). Within the competitive dynamics research, both impact the firm's *ability* to act. Indeed, organizational resources such as unabsorbed slack (i.e., liquid financial resources) are required to undertake actions. Further, TMT demographics are also linked with the speed with which actions (and responses) are conceived of and implemented. Thus, despite being both aware and motivated to carry out action, these organizational characteristics underscore the importance of the ability to carry out action.

## Competitive action

Research in competitive dynamics has developed theory and empirical methods centering on a fine-grained conceptualization of firm strategy as *competitive action*, the principal vehicle by which firms position themselves in the competitive environment (Grimm and Smith, 1997; Smith, Grimm, and Gannon, 1992). Accordingly, the definition of competitive action serves as the conceptual foundation for this research stream. Competitive action (and response) is defined as *externally directed, specific, and observable competitive move initiated by a firm to enhance its relative competitive position* (e.g., Chen et al., 1992; Ferrier et al., 1999; Smith et al., 1991, 1992; Young et al., 1996). As discussed above, the research has explored the antecedents and consequences of competitive actions across several different industries. Hence, each particular industry is likely to differ with respect to the particular types of actions carried out. However, the vast majority of actions are represented by the following general categories: pricing actions, marketing actions, new product actions, capacity- and scale-related actions, service and operations actions, signaling actions, etc. Moreover, the most important contributions of this research stream have examined the characteristics of action developed at several distinct levels of analysis and aggregation. Appendix 11A provides a comprehensive list of action characteristics and their definitions at different levels of analysis and aggregation.

First, the early view of competitive dynamics focused attention on the characteristics of *individual actions, reactions*, and the relationship between *action-reaction dyads*. This research has shown, for example, that the characteristics of an action (i.e., *radicality, scope, magnitude, irreversibility*, etc.) are important predictors of competitive response (i.e., *likelihood, speed,* etc.) (e.g., Chen et al., 1992; Smith et al., 1991, 1992). Other researchers focused on the *order of moves*, that is, whether the firm was first to act, second, and so on (Lee et al., 2000; Smith et al., 1992). MacMillan, McCaffrey, and Van Wijk (1985), Smith et al. (1989) and Chen and MacMillan (1992) studied the *radicality* of action, defined as the extent to which the action departs from existing action norms. Radical actions will be difficult for rivals to interpret and as such will lead to fewer and slower actions. The *magnitude* of action concerns the amount of resources that are necessary to implement the action, whereas the *scope* of the action has been measured in terms of the number of competitors that are potentially affected by the action (Chen, et al., 1992). The degree of *threat* associated with an action has been measured in terms of the number of rivals'customers that are at risk to the action (Chen et al., 1992). It has been argued that as the magnitude of action increases, rivals will find it increasingly difficult to respond. However, as the scope and threat of an action increase, so will the likelihood and speed of response (Smith et al., 1992).

Second, this stream of research has aggregated the characteristics and frequency of specific actions and responses carried out by firms over a finite time period – the *firm-year* (Ferrier et al., 1999; Young et al., 1996). Research at this level of aggregation has, for example, shown that the more *total actions* a firm carries out and with greater *average speed* (i.e., *aggressiveness*), the better its profitability or market share.

Third, this research stream has also viewed the firm's entire set of competitive actions carried out in a given year as a *competitive repertoire* and has developed several important constructs related to repertoire structure (Ferrier et al., 1999; Miller and Chen, 1994, 1995, 1996). For instance, competitive repertoire *simplicity* is defined as "an overwhelming preoccupation with a single type of action – one that increasingly precludes the consideration of any others" (Miller and Chen, 1996). Competitive repertoire *nonconformity* refers to the tendency of a firm's competitive repertoire to depart from the norms of industry. This includes sets of action types that are atypical in the industry. Nonconforming repertoires consist of types of actions that are rarely being used by competitors or are void of those types of actions commonly used in the competitive arena (Miller and Chen, 1995). Competitive repertoire *inertia* refers to the level of activity that a firm exhibits when altering its competitive stance in terms of the number of market oriented changes it makes in trying to attract customers and outmaneuver competitors (Miller and Chen, 1994).

Finally, recent research has examined the characteristics of an uninterrupted *sequence* of competitive actions carried out over time. This view is consistent with prior research that conceptualized strategy as a logically unified sequence of actions (Kirzner, 1973), patterns or consistencies in streams of behaviors (Mintzberg and Waters, 1985), a coordinated series of actions (MacCrimmon, 1993), or sequential set of many actions (D'Aveni, 1994). For instance, a sequence of competitive actions exhibits the following structural dimensions: the number or *volume* of action that comprise the sequence, the average *duration* of an uninterrupted series of actions, the extent to which all possible types of action events are represented in the sequence (*complexity*), as well as the within-firm variability (*unpredictability*) and the between-firm variability (*heterogeneity*) of a firm's sequence of competitive actions carried out over time (Ferrier, 2000; Ferrier and Lee, 2000).

## *The reactor*

While all firms can take action, they are also capable of responding to the actions of rivals. Thus, the conceptual counterpart to a competitive action is a competitive response (Smith et al., 1991). This implies, of course, that responders possess all the organizational characteristics and attributes that pertain to actors (i.e., size, TMT demographics, etc.). The information processing perspective on competitor analysis proposed by Smith et al. (1992) provides a useful framework for understanding a firm as a reactor. Each competitive action carries a message, be it in terms of intent of the action or a signal relating to the strategy of the actor. To successfully compete, a firm should be able to decode the message embodied in an action (Smith et al., 1991). How a firm perceives and interprets an action will determine the nature of its response. As such, perceiving (via sensory capabilities) and interpreting the message embedded in the action represent crucial capabilities of the reacting firm.

A firm cannot conceive of and implement a competitive response without first realizing that a competitor has carried out an action (Smith et al., 1991). A firm's sensory systems represent its environmental scanning capability. Rich and timely information on competitor actions is useless to a firm if it cannot process this information. A firm's information processing and analytical mechanisms provide it with a means of interpreting the actions of rivals. This capacity to process information and analytical mechanisms are largely determined by an organization's internal structure (Huber and Daft, 1987).

For example, when an organization has a complex structure, the potential for information transmission failure increases.

## Competitive response

When a firm undertakes an action that generates abnormal profits or an action that affects a rival's position, competitors will be motivated to respond (Schumpeter, 1950). Porter (1980) defines a competitive response as a clear-cut, discernable counteraction carried out by the firm to defend or improve its position with regard to one or more competitors'initiated actions. One group of researchers measured *response likelihood, response type, response lag,* and *response order* (Lee et al., 2000; Smith et al., 1991). Other researchers developed measures such as *response noteworthiness, response scope,* and *response generation speed* (Chen and Hambrick, 1995; Hambrick, Cho, and Chen, 1996).

Response likelihood represents the extent to which a rival is likely to respond to a firm's action (Smith et al., 1991). It has been measured as the historical proportion of times a firm reacts to a rival's action in a given time period from the total number of times the firm had the opportunity to respond. Thus, a firm that has responded to nine out of ten of a rival's actions is more likely to respond in the future than a firm that has responded one out of ten times.

In deciding to respond to a move, competitors have a wide variety of response options available at their disposal. One key dimension of responses is to imitate the initiated action. Response imitation is defined as the extent to which a response mimics or is identical in type and form to the action (Smith et al., 1991). A response that duplicates or matches a competitor's move provides a powerful signal to the acting firm that the rival is committed to defending its market position (Chen and MacMillan, 1992).

Porter (1980: 98) argued, "Finding strategic moves that will benefit from a delay in retaliation, or making moves so as to maximize the delay, are key principles of competitive interaction." Response lag or response delay represents the amount of time that elapses between a competitive action and the initiation of a response. During this time lapse, the actor gains economic rents from the action, provided it is a "successful" action (Smith et al., 1989), whereas non- or slow-responding rivals often experience market share losses or missed profit opportunities (Lee et al., 2000; Smith, Ferrier, and Grimm, 2001). The longer the response delay, the less obvious is the connection between the action and the response, thus reducing the power of the response as a signaling device (Chen and MacMillan, 1992).

Another dimension of competitive response is the *response order.* This is "the position in a temporal series of responses a firm occupies" (Smith et al., 1991: 62). Since actions generally affect multiple competitors, there is usually more than one potential reactor to a competitive action. Response order represents the firm's ranking in the order of responses (among multiple responding rivals) to a competitive action. Thus, a firm could be the first to respond, second to respond or a late responder. The concept of *response order* is distinct from *response delay* in that the former represents a firm's ranking in the series of responses, whereas the latter represents the elapsed time between the action and the response (Lee et al., 2000; Smith et al., 1991).

## Industry competitive environment[3]

Competitive interaction occurs within the context of a given industry structure or environment. As with the effect of organizational characteristics on action, the characteristics of the competitive environment or industry are thought to influence the firm's awareness, motivation, and ability to carry out action (Smith et al., 1992). Competitive dynamics researchers have relied on traditional measures of industry structure, including industry growth rates, concentration and barriers to entry (Scherer and Ross, 1990). With regard to theory, researchers have borrowed from the structure-conduct-performance paradigm to predict relationships between industry structure and competitive action and reaction (Scherer and Ross, 1990). For example, it is argued that when industry growth rates and concentration are high, the level of competitive activity or rivalry will be low or that when barriers to entry are high, competitive response will be low (Schomburg et al., 1994).

Researchers have also examined the relationship between stage industry evolution and action and reaction (Porter, 1980; Smith et al., 1992). The argument has been that actions and reaction in emerging high growth industries will be less predictable and of greater scale and scope than in more mature industries. In new and emerging industries, firms will be less aware of one another, and because of this, they will be able to undertake action without immediate reaction. In contrast, in mature industries, characterized by slower rates of growth, firms will be more aware of the competition and also motivated to block the gains of rivals in a zero sum game.

## The consequences of action

Competitive interaction is not an end in and of itself. Firms engage each other (i.e., undertake actions and responses) to achieve certain competitive outcomes (Grimm and Smith, 1997). Competitive dynamics has generally used common measures of performance as the dependent variable, including: changes in market share (Chen and MacMillan, 1992; Ferrier et al., 1999), cumulative abnormal returns to shareholders (Lee et al., 2000), sales growth (Ferrier, 2000) and accounting measures of profitability and profit growth, such as return on investment (Hambrick et al., 1996; Smith et al., 1991; Young et al., 1996). Moreover, several studies of the effects of action on performance in the airline industry use an industry-specific measure of performance – operating revenue per available seat-mile – that accounts for efficiency, aircraft load factors, and revenue (Chen and Hambrick, 1995; Miller and Chen, 1994, 1995, 1996).

With regard to predicting the performance effects of action, researchers have used both aggregated year-end measures of action and reaction (Young et al., 1996; Ferrier et al., 1999) as well as characteristics of single action or reaction (Lee et al., 2000). For example, it has been argued that firms that undertake strategic, frequent, and complex *sets* of action will be high performers. Similarly, it has been contended that fast, early and unpredictable reactors will achieve superior performance. For the most part, scholars have used game theory to explain relationships between action/reaction and performance (e.g., Smith et al., 1992; Grimm and Smith, 1997). For example, via extended games (Grimm and Smith, 1997) or prisoner dilemma models (Smith et al., 1992), it has been argued that payoffs are greater to the first mover when reaction is delayed or that payoffs to fast reactors is greater than that of slow reactors.

In this section, we have provided an overview of the competitive dynamics model that has often been utilized to study and predict relationships between actors, actions, reactors, reactions, industry context, and performance. In the next section, we begin our review of the competitive dynamics empirical research.

## SAMPLES IN COMPETITIVE DYNAMICS RESEARCH

Competitive dynamics researchers have employed two basic methodologies. First, field studies in which researchers gathered primary data on action and reactions were prominent in early days of competitive dynamics research. These studies involved intensive examination of small samples of firms in order to identify actions and reactions and to test relationships between organizational characteristics and action (MacMillan et al., 1985; Smith et al., 1989). During the 1990s, field studies gave way to secondary data studies where researchers gathered data on firm action and reaction from published records. These archival studies allowed researchers to develop large samples of firm action and reaction and to study this behavior over time. We will review each of the methodologies in turn. The alternative studies are detailed in Appendix 11B.

### Field studies

Field studies or primary data gathering techniques require the researcher to go out in the field to make observations on firm action and reaction. The first step in the data collection process has been to interview executives to identify actions and responses that their firm has taken. In the second stage, questionnaires have been developed to measure characteristics of actions and reactions and also to gather data on other organizational characteristics. In some cases questionnaire and interview data were supplemented with secondary data obtained from corporate records. These methodologies have been confined to small samples in single industries and involved cross-sectional analyses of self-reported data.

Overall, there have been two field studies of competition among high technology firms, a study of competitive responses in the computer retailing industry and a study of responses to new product introductions in the banking industry. The first high tech study focused on 22 electrical manufacturers, the second examined 25 high technology firms. The computer retailing study examined the competitive responses of 25 retailers and the banking study focused on 22 bank innovations.

### Archival studies

Structured content analysis was developed in the late 1980s as a way of developing a larger longitudinal data set that would not be biased by self-reporting (Chen, 1988; Smith et al., 1991). Structured content analysis is based on a formal coding analysis that is applied to secondary data, such as newspapers, magazines and other published material. The contents of events are extracted according to predefined codes. With this methodology a series of competitive actions and reactions can be identified overtime and linked to other organizational and industry data that is also obtained from secondary sources. There have been five different archival studies.

*Airlines.*   Perhaps the most significant competitive dynamics research has involved the study of the US domestic airline industry (Chen, 1988). The airlines industry is one of the most competitive industries with a well-defined and known set of competitors. There is also an abundance of publicly available information that facilitates research (Smith et al, 1992). In addition, the airline industry has clearly defined boundaries and markets (routes) are easily identifiable facilitating the study of actions in specific markets (Chen et al., 1992). The airline studies involved 32 different carriers over an eight-year period. *Aviation Daily* was the primary source of information on airline actions and responses. By using predefined key words such as "reacting to," "following," "under pressure of" etc., researchers were able to identify 191 competitive actions and 418 competitive responses over the eight-year period. Organizational and industry data supplemented the action data to provide examination of the relationship between actors, action, reactors and reaction (see figure 11.1). Examples of research using this data set include Chen (1988) and Smith et al. (1992).

*Airlines, Part II.*   Gimeno and Woo (1996a, b, 1999) and Baum and Korn (1996) have also published a series of papers focusing on the relationship between the alternative markets a firm participates in with common rivals and the level of rivalry in those markets. These studies have been conducted with samples of domestic US airlines with the goal of testing relationships between multi-market contact and the level of competition. Gimeno and Woo (1996a, b, 1999) have focused on price/cost margins to infer rivalry, whereas Baum and Korn examined the degree of exit and entry into markets. The unit of analysis in much of this work concerns a firm's pricing or entry/exit behavior in a specific market or city pair route. The data can best be described as panel data comprised of multiple observations from each airline, market and period.

*Brewing, personal computers and telecommunication.*   This study focused on the effects of new product interactions in the brewing, personal computers and telecommunications industries. Structured content analysis was used to identify new product introductions and respective imitations from the period of 1975 to 1990 in each of these industries. The researchers focused only on new categories of products, those that began with the introduction of a new category of products (e.g., the introduction of lite beer). The Predicasts F & S index was used to identify 82 new product introductions categories and the 632 subsequent imitations. By studying new product categories (those that did not exist in prior time), the researchers could be certain who was the first mover. Also, by examining the imitations of products in the same category, the researchers could more clearly discern a competitive response and the timing of this response. The authors also gathered data on the structure of the personal computer, telecommunications and brewing industry to study the effects of industry structure on competition (Schomburg et al., 1994). In addition, the researchers used an event methodology to test the shareholder wealth effects of these new product introductions and the imitative responses (Lee et al., 2000). This was done by computing the cumulative abnormal returns emanating from a competitive actions or responses for a five-day trading period window (two days before and two days after).

*Software.*   The sample used in this study consisted of all public single-business computer software firms (SIC codes 7371, 7372, 7372 or 7373), identified by both Standard and

Poor's corporate directory and the disclosure database of SIC filings for the years 1983–91. These years were chosen because they were the formative years of the industry. The final sample consisted of 345 firm-year observations involving nearly 2,300 competitive actions and reactions. The Predicast F & S index was used to identify actions and reactions and corporate records were screened to assess firm resources and industry structure. Because the data set contained the actions of nearly all firms in the industry and because these actions studied were within certain markets (e.g., word processing), the authors could distinguish between actions and reactions and study the effects of action and reaction on performance and the effects of firm resources and industry structure on action (see Young et al., 1996).

*Industry study of leaders and challengers.*    This study was focused on the competitive interaction between market share leaders and the number one challenger across 41 different industries. To identify leaders and challengers, a sample of US firms with 1993 sales exceeding $500 million was selected and only firms identified to be single or dominant business firms were retained. Industries that did not contain at least two large non-diversified industry leaders and challengers during 1987–93 were dropped. Predicast F & S was used to identify competitive actions and reactions. The procedure was similar to the software and new product introduction studies. In all, nearly 5,000 headlines and articles from over 700 publications (newspapers, magazines etc) were content analyzed. This sample yielded a total of 4,876 competitive actions and reactions. In each industry it was assumed that leader and challenger actions were taken with regard to one another. The authors studied the effects of characteristics of action and reaction on the likelihood of market share dethronement and market share erosion (Ferrier et al., 1999).

## Empirical Findings

As we argued above, several important organizational level characteristics may influence the firm's awareness, motivation, and/or ability to carry out action. We first review the empirical studies that have studied and used characteristics of *actors* as an independent variable.

### Actor characteristics

*Organizational size.*    Within competitive dynamics research, organizational size has been conceived in different ways but the arguments have been consistent. The contention has been that large firms are better able to influence their environment and buffer themselves from competitors. As such, it has been argued that large organizations are better disposed to be able to carry out more effective and timely competitive actions. Smaller firms, on the other hand, are nimble, flexible and inconspicuous, thus possessing speed and stealth in their competitive actions (Chen and Hambrick, 1995).

The studies have provided some consistent findings pertaining to the effect of organizational size on competitive action. For instance, Chen and Hambrick (1995) found that relative to large firms, small firms are more likely to initiate competitive actions (*action propensity*) and do so more quickly (*action execution speed*). Other studies found that large firms are more likely to carry out more *total competitive moves* in a given time period (Young, Smith, and Grimm 1996) and carry out actions that are strategic in nature (action *significance)* and *visible* (Chen and Hambrick, 1995). Further, Miller and Chen (1994) report that large firms are less prone to *competitive inertia* (conceptualized as the number of market-oriented changes the firm carries out to outmaneuver rivals in the marketplace), whereas another study by these authors (Miller and Chen, 1996) found that large firms are more likely to employ a *simple competitive repertoire* (conceptualized as the firm's set of competitive actions consisting of only a few different types, as opposed to many different types).

The studies also produce some consistent findings with respect to the key dimensions of competitive response. For instance, large firms are more likely to respond to rivals' competitive challenges *(response likelihood, response propensity)* than small firms (Chen and Hambrick, 1995). Yet, the responses by large firms were found to be subtler and less *visible* (Chen and Hambrick, 1995). Also, with respect to the effect of firm size on the speed of competitive response, large firms were found to more quickly conceive of and announce responses to their rivals' actions *(response generation speed)* than small firms (Hambrick et al., 1996). Large firms were slower than smaller firms, however, in terms of the time elapsed between the announcement of their response and the actual implementation of the response *(response execution speed)* (Chen and Hambrick, 1995).

Research by Smith et al. (1992) found that firms with a reputation as a market leader, measured in terms of market share, were more likely to attract responses and more likely to have their actions imitated. However, no support was shown for market leaders attracting faster responses to their competitive actions.

*Structural complexity.*   Bureaucracy and standard operating procedures hamper structurally complex firms, thereby diminishing decision-making speed and, consequently, the firm's ability to act and respond to competitive challenges. Indeed, Smith et al. (1991) found that the higher the firm's structural complexity, the less likely it responds to competitive challenges *(response likelihood)*. Further, these authors also found that structurally complex firms responded *after* other responding firms *(response order)*. This study found no relationship between structural complexity and *response speed* or *response imitation*.

*Organizational age.*   As organizations get older, they repeat strategies and actions that have proven successful in the past (Lant, Milliken, and Batra, 1992; Miller and Chen, 1995). This "routinization" of action is based on the idea that firms seek to reduce search costs associated with environmental scanning. As such, older firms become less aware of the competitive environment and more predictable in action.

Younger firms, on the other hand, suffer from the *liability of newness* stemming from institutional forces and resource constraints associated with youth (Miller and Chen, 1996; Singh, Tucker, and House, 1986). Also, gaining familiarity with the industry's history of past successful actions is time-dependent, thereby putting younger firms at a disadvantage. In addition, younger firms will face an uphill battle to gain resources and institutional recognition from older firms and customers. This forces and motivates younger firms to continually scan their environment and track competitors for threats and opportunities that may arise.

Research that explored the effect of firm age on the characteristics of *individual* actions and responses has yielded little results. One possible explanation for the limited support of the effect of organizational age is its high correlation with market diversity and the size of the firm. Older firms are generally larger and compete in more diverse markets. This suggests that organizational size measures perhaps pick up some of the variance in action characteristics due to age. In these empirical studies, organizational age has been measured simply as the duration between the founding of a firm and the period a competitive action was taken.

Nonetheless, the research has found significant effects for firm action when aggregated to year-end measures. For instance, Young et al. (1996) found that older firms carry out fewer total competitive actions than younger firms. However, older firms carry out patterns of actions that exhibit less competitive inertia (Miller and Chen, 1994), conform to industry norms (Miller and Chen, 1995) and are less competitive simple (Miller and Chen, 1996).

*Multi-market competition.*    Most industries are composed of multiple markets, which are related in terms of resource characteristics, such as technologies, skills and competencies. Firms then can compete across multiple markets within an industry (broad scope) or they can compete more directly (narrow scope) in a single segment. A consequence of variation in firm scope across multiple market is that firms vary in the rivals they face in different markets, which has been referred to as multimarket contact (Edwards, 1955). When firms compete with other firms in multiple markets there is the potential for multiple point competition or "a situation when firms compete against each other simultaneously in several markets" (Karnani and Wernerfelt, 1985: 87). Multiple point competition theory suggests that when firms compete in multiple markets they have the potential to retaliate not only in the market where a move occurs, but also in other markets that may be more important to the rival. This ability to retaliate in each other's markets should lead to mutual forbearance or a circumstance limiting rivalry. By contrast, a lack of multimarket contact may lead a firm to be more rivalrous with actions. Such a firm cannot retaliate in other markets and therefore must be a more aggressive competitor in the markets it is in.

There have been three studies in strategic management that have examined the multiple point competition theory. Gimeno and Woo (1996a, b) found a positive relationship between multiple market overlap and price/cost margins in their study of airline competition, suggesting that the greater the multi-market contact, the lower the rivalry. With a more dynamic measure of rivalry, Baum and Korn (1996) found that California commuter airlines decreased the rate of market entry and exit as their multi-market contact increased. Young et al. (2001) examined the effects of software firms competing in multiple markets with the same competitors. They found that as multi-market contact increased between pairs of firms operating in the same markets, the frequency of firm action decreased, supporting the forbearance hypothesis.

In a related study, Smith et al. (1997) examined whether the level of rivalry (action and reaction) was greater within or between strategic groups with a sample of domestic airlines. Overall, the results suggest that responses to competitive actions can occur both between and within groups. That is, airlines appear just as likely to respond to the actions of rivals from different groups as they are to respond to firms in their own group. The authors conclude that in the airline industry there are few barriers or impediments to firms in responding to the competitive actions of airlines in other strategic groups.

*Market dependence.* Market dependence, strategic importance, and/or market salience, represent the extent to which a firm's revenues or profits are derived from a given segment of the market (Chen and MacMillan, 1992; Gimeno, 1999; Karnani and Wernerfelt, 1985). Thus, firms that are highly dependent on a given market (or customer segment) are more likely to vigorously defend their market positions.

Consistent with theory, the studies found that firms were more likely to respond (*response likelihood*) to competitive challenges in markets that they considered very important (*market dependence*) with actions that were large and substantial (*irreversible actions*) and often *matched* the attacking firm's actions (Chen and MacMillan, 1992). Interestingly, while market dependence may indeed relate to an aggressive response once the firm is provoked, it nevertheless reduces the likelihood of a quick response. However, as mentioned earlier, this strong and consistent support could also be as a result of market diversity accounting for the effects of organizational size and age, characteristics with which it is highly correlated.

*Past performance.* Research in strategic management has traditionally considered elements of financial feedback (e.g., profitability, sales growth, stock prices, etc.) as a dependent or outcome variable of firm performance (Chakravarthy, 1986). Yet, another important issue is how financial feedback influences the firm's future action (Thompson, 1967).

Theory within organizational learning explains how discrepancies between organizational goals and actual performance influences the likelihood of action, aggressiveness, predictable behavior, and strategic change (Heiner, 1983; Lant, Milliken, and Batra, 1992; Starbuck, 1983). For instance, success gives rise to complacency and a persistent reliance on well-learned organizational routines, thus inhibiting new competitive action and strategic change (Lant, Milliken, and Batra, 1992; Miller and Chen, 1994). Indeed, managers attribute (oftentimes erroneously) good past performance to their actions. This "superstitious learning" reinforces current mental models and reduces motivation for action and change (Barr, Stimpert, and Huff, 1992; Hambrick and D'Aveni, 1988; Lant, Milliken, and Batra, 1992). Poor past performance, however, provides motivation for the re-evaluation of current mental models and provides motivation to try new approaches to competing (Miller and Chen, 1995).

The empirical research suggests that successful firms are less likely to respond to competitive challenges (Hambrick et al., 1996). Moreover, when responses are carried out, successful firms do so more slowly (Hambrick et al., 1996; MacFhionnlaoich et al., 1996). Further, good past performance induces firms to carry out competitive repertoires characterized as having higher levels of inertia (Miller and Chen, 1994), simple action repertoires (Miller and Chen, 1996), and repertoires that conform to industry norms (Miller and Chen, 1995). Also, successful firms are more likely to carry out a simple (as opposed to complex) sequence of competitive moves over time (Ferrier, 2000).

Contrary to predictions, good past performance was positively related to the total number of competitive moves the firm carries out (Young et al., 1996). Recent studies, however, explored the possibility of a curvilinear relationship between past performance and total action carried out. For instance, MacFhionnlaoich et al. (1996) found a U-shaped relationship between past performance and total competitive moves tallied at year-end. This might occur because very successful, dominant firms realize that in order to maintain their market-leading position, they must carry out aggressive, deterrent behaviors such as: predatory pricing, product proliferation, advertising, and increasing scale or capacity (Scherer and Ross, 1990). By the same token, poor performing firms are likely to compete aggressively in an effort to improve their competitive positions (e.g., Fiegenbaum, 1990).

*Slack resources.* Organizational slack is defined as the buffer or cushion of actual or potential resources that may or may not be currently in use (Bourgeois, 1981). Prior research generally recognizes two types of slack: unabsorbed and absorbed. Indeed, both varieties are related to the firm's actions and responses.

*Unabsorbed slack* represents liquid resources that may be deployed wherever needed, it gives the firm leeway in managing responses to competitive pressures and a changing environment. It also permits the firm to experiment with innovation, take greater risks, and be more aggressive (Cyert and March, 1963). Hambrick et al. (1996) found that high levels of unabsorbed slack were negatively related to the likelihood that firms will initiate a competitive attack, but when attacks are initiated, slack allows for faster execution. A high level of unabsorbed slack was also related to a lower response likelihood (Hambrick et al., 1996; Smith et al., 1991) and response imitation (Smith et al., 1991). Yet, high levels of unabsorbed slack resulted in firms carrying out more total competitive moves (Young, Smith, and Grimm, 1996) and carrying out a competitive attack of longer duration that also consist of a more complex sequence of competitive moves (Ferrier, 2000).

*Absorbed slack* represents resource investments in firm activities, such as the costs of production and selling costs. High levels of absorbed slack reduces the firm's ability to respond (and respond quickly) to competitive attack (Smith et al., 1991). Absorbed slack was not related to the total number of competitive moves, competitive repertoire conformity, inertia and simplicity (Miller and Chen, 1994, 1995, 1996).

## Managerial characteristics

*Top management team.* The link between dynamic competitive interaction and the top management team (TMT) represents a synthesis of the core ideas from two important areas of research: the upper echelons view and strategic decision-making. Indeed, theory and prior research suggests that the composition of the TMT affects both the collective cognitive resources of the team and social relations among team members (Finkelstein and Hambrick, 1996; Hambrick and Mason, 1984). These, in turn, influence important organizational processes and outcomes such as: (a) problem sensing facilitated by greater awareness, (b) interpretation and enactment of environmental cues and signals, and (c) decision-making process that matches perceived problems with strategic solutions (Amason, 1996; Barr, Stimpert, and Huff, 1992; Smith et al., 1994).

The research has generally provided a strong link between the composition of the TMT and competitive actions and reactions. Competitive dynamics researchers have, in particular, examined the effect of TMT size, experience, and cognitive and experiential heterogeneity on action.

The overall size of the TMT has two oftentimes-countervailing effects on decision-making and strategy. On one hand, large TMTs possess greater cognitive and experiential resources that can be used in decision-making activities (Hambrick and D'Aveni, 1992; Haleblian and Finkelstein, 1993). On the other hand, large TMTs are prone to coordination and communication problems, which may limit group cohesion and social integration (Wagner, 1995; Shaw, 1981) oftentimes necessary for the development of strategic consensus (Smith et al., 1994; Shull, Delbecq, and Cummings, 1970).

Empirical research on the effect of TMT size on competitive activity generally supports the latter view. More specifically, large TMTs tend to carry out competitive actions that were less visible and of a tactical (as opposed to strategic) nature (Hambrick et al., 1996). Furthermore, Hambrick et al. (1996) found that large TMTs were less likely to respond to competitive challenges than smaller TMTs. These findings suggest that large TMTs were likely to carry out only incremental changes in strategy, and do so more slowly than smaller TMTs.

The TMT's level of experience and education are related to its collective knowledge and skills (Hambrick and Mason, 1984). In particular, managers with more experience are less likely to employ exhaustive information search and decision-making procedures related to strategy. Experienced TMTs will have likely developed explicit and well-defined mental models, which limit strategic flexibility (Hitt and Barr, 1989). However, formal education is linked to cognitive ability, which facilitates greater awareness, comprehensiveness, open-mindedness, and a greater receptivity toward strategic innovation (Kimberly and Evanisko, 1981).

The empirical findings that relate TMT experience and education levels with competitive strategy are generally supportive of theory. For instance, experienced TMTs are less likely to respond to competitive challenges carried out by rivals, and do so after other players in the industry have responded (*response order*) (Smith et al., 1991). Experienced TMTs, however, are more likely to carry out a complex competitive repertoire (Miller and Chen, 1996). Also, highly educated TMTs are more likely to carry out significant (i.e., strategic in nature), yet focused (i.e., limited in market scope) competitive attacks against rivals (Hambrick et al., 1996). Consequently, such actions garner much less industry attention (action visibility, noteworthiness) than highly visible strategic actions, thus provoking fewer total responses. Highly educated TMTs are more likely to respond to competitive challenges (Hambrick et al., 1996) by matching the attacker's action (Smith et al., 1991). Moreover, longer tenured TMTs appear less likely to initiate competitive actions, but are more likely and are better able to quickly respond to competitive challenges (Hambrick et al., 1996).

Effective response to a rival's competitive move requires the ability to detect and analyze the impact of the move. However, firms may differ greatly in this information-processing capability. Indeed, some firms are oriented internally, focusing on the efficiency of their internal operations. By contrast, other firms are oriented externally, giving primacy on their ability to relate to environmental changes by way of boundary-spanning activities (Miles and Snow, 1978). Accordingly, management teams that consider marketing and R&D activities and departments to be relatively more important than finance-accounting and production activities are believed to exhibit an *external orientation* with regard to the company's strategy (Miles and Snow, 1978; Smith et al., 1992). Interestingly, while TMTs having such an external orientation reduced the overall likelihood of responding to competitive challenges, they nevertheless generated faster responses (Smith et al., 1991, 1992).

The research linking TMT heterogeneity to action and reaction is interesting. Top management team heterogeneity is widely viewed as a proxy for cognitive and experiential heterogeneity (Finkelstein and Hambrick, 1996). The composition of the TMT shapes the lens-like cognitive structure that defines their collective field of vision (Hambrick and Mason, 1984; Miller, 1993). By way of greater *awareness* in sensing strategic problems, heterogeneous TMTs can match complex competitive challenges and uncertain contexts with a requisite level of cognitive and experiential variety. Aside from being more aware, heterogeneous TMTs also possess greater *ability* to generate a more complex and unpredictable mix of alternatives for strategic action by way of comprehensive decision making techniques characterized by debate, devil's advocacy, and dialectical inquiry (Mitroff and Emshoff, 1979; Simons, Pelled, and Smith, 2000). By contrast, TMT homogeneity is a key source of strategic simplicity (Miller, 1993; Miller and Chen, 1996; Milliken and Lant, 1991) and inertia (Hambrick, Geletkanycz, and Fredrickson, 1993; Miller and Chen, 1994).

With respect to empirical research, heterogeneous TMTs were found more likely to initiate significant (*action propensity*, *strategic actions*) actions affecting many competitors across a broad range of customer markets (*action scope*) (Hambrick et al., 1996). However, heterogeneous TMTs were less likely to respond to rivals'actions. Yet, when responses were executed, heterogeneous TMTs were also more likely to carry out responding actions that were *visible*, and affected many competitors and customers (*action scope*) (Hambrick et al., 1996).

## Reputational and strategic characteristics

*Reputation.* Although the study of organizational and managerial characteristics may indeed provide insight as to a company's future actions, an examination of the firm's past behavior may arguably be the most important indicator of future behavior. When a firm's historical actions are consistent and predictable, other firms ascribe certain tendencies or reputational characteristics to the firm. This reputation reflects information on the credibility of the firm as a competitor. For example, firms that constantly cut prices to gain/maintain market share are often viewed as predators (Smith et al., 1992). Reputation as used in competitive dynamics research has been defined as the positive or negative attribute ascribed by one rival to another based on past competitive behavior (Wilson, 1985; Smith et al., 1992).

Smith et al. (1992) measured a firm's reputation by the number of competitive actions it carried out in the previous year. More specifically, the number of *strategic actions* carried out in the previous year were summed up to operationalize the firm's reputation as a *strategic player* and the number of *pricing actions* were summed up to represent the firm's proclivity to be a *price predator* (Smith et al., 1992). With respect to the studies, firms with greater reputations as *strategic players* elicited slower responses to their competitive actions and a lower likelihood that rivals imitated their actions. Firms with a reputation as *price predators* generated faster responses to their competitive actions. However, contrary to expectation, price predators had less imitation of their competitive actions. The results also showed no relation between a firm's past competitive reputation and the number of responses to its actions.

*Generic strategy.*   Only one study that we know of examined the relationship between the firm's overall strategy or strategic position and action. Based on Porter's (1980) generic business-level strategies, Smith et al. (1997) classified airlines into three strategic categories: *large-scale, low-cost players; marketing-focused differentiated players;* and *smaller niche players.* These authors predicted that each firm's strategy type would influence its competitive activity. Firms following a low-cost strategy carried out more total actions (mostly price cutting actions) and were more likely to instigate or initiate rivalrous contact (Smith et al., 1997). Differentiated airlines were also prone to instigate rivalry; however, they typically do so, for example, with marketing-related actions or offering new first-class services, etc. By contrast, niche players were less likely to instigate rivalry and carried out fewer total actions. With respect to competitive response, low-cost players were more likely to match competitive challenges with imitative responses, whereas differentiated players were less likely to carry out matching responses.

## Industry characteristics

According to the structure-conduct-performance view within industrial economics, high levels of industry growth, barriers to entry, and industry concentration each buffer industry participants from intense competition (Scherer and Ross, 1990). Therefore, taken together, these important industry characteristics influence the firm's *motivation* to compete aggressively. We discuss each in turn.

*Industry growth.*   Industry growth is a basic indicator of industry demand (Schomburg et al., 1994). Under conditions of high demand, rivalry is generally lower than under conditions of low demand. Thus, slow growth frequently gives rise to more intense competition and lower profitability, which motivates strategic aggressiveness (Fombrun and Ginsberg, 1990; Smith et al., 1992). Several studies found strong support for the idea that industry growth influenced competitive behavior. For instance, firms competing in high growth industries respond to competitive challenges more slowly (Smith et al., 1989; Schomburg et al., 1994). Further, high industry growth was associated with more *simple competitive repertoires* (Miller and Chen, 1996), predictable patterns of competitive actions (*sequence predictability*), and reduces motivation to carry out a sequence of competitive actions of significant *duration* (Ferrier, 2000).

*Industry concentration.*   Due to potential for oligopolistic coordination, a high level of industry concentration should reduce the firm's *motivation* to compete aggressively (see Scherer and Ross, 1990). In support of this, Young, Smith, and Grimm (1996) found that higher levels of industry concentration resulted in fewer competitive moves carried out among incumbent firms. Also, industry concentration exhibited a negative relationship with action sequence complexity and differentiation (Ferrier, 2000). In addition, Schomburg et al. (1994) found that as the number of firms in the industry increased, response times and the radicality of action decreased.

*Barriers to entry.*   The barriers to entry literature also suggest that industries characterized by high levels of capital intensity, innovation, and advertising, for example, experience less competitive pressure from potential entrants. Barriers to entry were found to have a positive impact on industry performance principally because the intensity of competition among incumbents does not increase due to entry (Caves, Fortunato, and Ghemawat, 1984; Scherer and Ross, 1990). Therefore, firms competing in industries characterized as having high barriers to entry are less *motivated* to compete aggressively.

In support of this, firms competing in industries characterized as having high barriers to entry carried out a less complex and more predictable sequence of competitive moves (Ferrier, 2000). Schomburg et al. (1994) found that as barriers to entry decreased, the perceived threat of competitive actions increased and the radicality of action decreased.

*Other industry characteristics.*   One study developed a composite measure of *favorable industry structure* consisting of factors relating to the number of competitors, industry growth, and industry concentration (Smith et al., 1996). Findings suggest that when competing in such competition-favorable industries, firms were *slow to respond* to competitive challenges.

## The interdependence of actions and competitive response

A distinguishing characteristic of competitive dynamics research has been its focus on competitive interdependence. Indeed, Schumpeter (1950) highlighted this importance with his theory of creative destruction whereby the successful first moving firm evokes competitive imitation or competitive response. In this section we examine the relationship between action and reaction.

*Predicting response frequency.*   As noted above, actions may exhibit multiple characteristics. For example, actions that are more *strategic* in nature (as opposed to tactical) are more likely to have significant *implementation requirements*. Moreover, strategic actions with significant implementation requirements are also *difficult to reverse*. It is expected that these, and other, important characteristics will affect the likelihood, frequency, and timing of competitive responses in the marketplace.

Indeed, studies suggest that the characteristics of action do have an impact on response. For example, actions that are strategic, have greater implementation requirements, and are irreversible, elicit fewer total competitive responses (Chen and MacMillan, 1992; Chen et al., 1992). Also, actions that strongly and significantly threaten a large number of competitors (*competitive impact, action scope*) were more likely to elicit a larger number of *competitive responses* (Chen et al., 1992; Smith et al., 1992). Similarly, actions that targeted more and more of rivals'customers (*action threat, attack intensity, action centrality*) were also met with a high number of competitive responses (Chen and Miller, 1992; Chen et al., 1992; Smith et al., 1992).

Furthermore, strategic actions and those that affect multiple competitors and customers are less subtle and draw significant attention. Thus, highly visible, noteworthy actions also elicit a large number of competitive responses (Chen and Miller, 1994).

*Predicting response lag.*   Another basic characteristic of a particular competitive action is its type (e.g., pricing, product, marketing, etc.). A key argument of competitive dynamics researchers is that the speed of competitive response will be a function of the initial action's type. Indeed, Smith et al. (1992) found that in a sample of firms competing in a wide variety of high-tech industries (e.g., long-distance data transmission equipment, integrated circuits, medical testing systems, etc.) that actions such as *price cuts* and *new advertising campaigns* elicited faster responses overall (i.e., averaging about 7 months) than actions such as *new product introductions* (average response time about 22 months).

Moreover, other studies suggest that strategic actions that require significant efforts to implement and are difficult to reverse cause a delay in competitive response (Chen and Miller, 1992; Chen, Smith, and Grimm, 1992; Smith et al., 1992). However, actions that significant, deviated from the industry norm in terms of their radicality elicited faster responses (Smith et al., 1992).

The research also suggests that rivals responded slowly to actions that affected a large number of competitors (*action scope*) (Chen et al., 1992). However, the results relating to the extent to which an action threatens a competitor's key markets produced mixed results. On one hand, actions carried out to steal customers away from rivals (*action threat*) was met with quick response (Chen et al., 1992). On the other hand, threatening actions (*attack intensity*) elicited slower competitive responses (Chen et al., 1992).

## The consequences of competitive action and response

Our general model depicted in figure 11.1 suggests that action characteristics predicts competitive response, which, in turn, impacts on performance. Overall, the research has identified a great variety of relationships between action, reaction and organizational performance.

*Individual actions type.*   Initial studies that explored how a particular *type* of action influenced performance produced only marginal results. For instance, in their study of high tech firms, Smith et al. (1992) found that *new product actions* were associated with mildly better performance than *pricing* or *advertising* actions. Moreover, even the classification of actions as strategic versus tactical was not related to performance (Smith et al., 1992).

Recent studies in a wider range of industries produced somewhat better results with regard to action type. In a study of competitive actions carried out among leader-challenger pairs, Ferrier (1997) found that market share leaders experience a erosion of their market share and profitability leads held over challengers by carrying out *marketing* and *capacity-related* actions, whereas *pricing* actions hastened market share and profitability erosion. Moreover, the market share and profitability lead held by market share leaders was significantly eroded when challengers carried out *overt signaling actions* (i.e., non-behavioral actions defined as publicly made announcements, threats, bluffs, etc.).

*Individual responses.*   Consistent with theory, firms that carry out actions that elicited fewer *total responses* experienced better performance (Chen and Miller, 1994). Several studies explored the effect of *response speed* on performance. For example, in the airline studies, a negative relationship was found between response speed and performance (Smith et al., 1991, 1992, 1996). Relatedly, Chen and Hambrick (1995) found that when small firms deviate from the industry norm in terms of their response speed, they experience poor performance.

Nonetheless, when the studies also accounted for *response order* (i.e., the rank order in which competitors respond), response speed exhibits a stable positive relationship with performance across most industries studied (Lee et al., 2000; Smith et al., 1991, 1992).

This suggests that other factors may influence the relationship between response speed and performance. Further, *response order* may also play an important role in its own right.

*Competitive aggressiveness and repertoires of action.* Consistent with the hypercompetition and Austrian views of competitive interaction, the competitive dynamics research suggest that firms that compete aggressively will be exploiting more new profit and market opportunities and preempt rivals'own efforts to improve competitive position. Indeed, firms that carry out a greater number of *total actions* over a given time period relative to rivals experience better profitability (Smith et al., 1996; Young et al., 1996), market share gains, and are less likely to be dethroned by challengers (Ferrier et al., 1999).

In addition, firms that carry out more *complex repertoires* of competitive actions experience better performance than firms that implement simple repertoires (Ferrier et al., 1999; Miller and Chen, 1996). However, firms that execute few changes among the major strategic actions in their competitive repertoires (*inertia*) experience better performance (Miller and Chen, 1994). Moreover, Miller and Chen (1995) found a significant negative direct effect in the relationship between *action repertoire non-conformity* and performance. However, these authors also found that firm size and market diversity moderated this effect. In particular, large firms, and those that compete against many and different rivals and target diverse types of customers, experience better performance when they carry out a set of competitive actions that deviate significantly from the industry norm.

*Sequence of actions.* Multiple competitive actions carried out over time can also be conceptualized as a unified sequence or series of actions, which is also linked to performance (Ferrier, 2000; Kirzner, 1973; MacCrimmon, 1993). Firms that carry out a complex sequence of actions consisting of a wide range of action types, for example, are more aggressive by attacking rivals on multiple fronts, thereby causing a delay in competitive response (D'Aveni, 1994). Also, aggressive firms surprise rivals by making changes in strategy to avoid being predictable (D'Aveni, 1994; MacCrimmon, 1993). Therefore, firms that carry out an unpredictable sequence of competitive moves also disrupt the pattern of competition among rivals, thereby causing a delay in competitive response (D'Aveni, 1994).

For instance, Ferrier (2000) found that firms experience higher profits and revenue growth when they carry out a sequence of moves that is more *complex, unpredictable*, and *differentiated* relative to rivals'action sequences. This study also suggests that firms experience better performance when they are able to sustain a competitive attack that consists of many actions for significant *duration*. Another study found that positive stock market returns was also related to sequence unpredictability and complexity (Ferrier and Lee, 2000).

## CRITIQUE OF COMPETITIVE DYNAMICS RESEARCH

As revealed in the foregoing sections, the competitive dynamics stream of research has provided a number of important contributions to business-level strategic management. Indeed, because the studies have shown strong support for the model depicted in figure 11.1, this stream's focus on strategy as action, competitive interdependence, and explanations regarding the important antecedents and consequences of competitive action advances our understanding of competitive behavior and the relationship between these behaviors and performance.

More specifically, we believe that the general research model outlined in figure 11.1 has been robustly supported across a wide variety of industries in which competitors carried out thousands of competitive actions and responses. Consistent findings include the following. First, there is consistent support for the hypothesis that firm level characteristics are related to action. For example, we see that large firms and firms with significant levels of slack resources act and react differently from smaller firms and firms with limited resources. These findings highlight the importance of resources to action. Future research should examine "why" large firms behave differently than small firms and there is a need to link the behavior of large and small firms to organizational performance.

Second, consistent with Schumpeter (1950), there is a clear relationship between action and reaction. For example, in a variety of industries we find that tactical actions or non-radical actions, are responded to faster than strategic actions or actions that are more radical in nature. We also observe that firms that can undertake a long sequence of uninterrupted action can delay the reactions of rivals. One conclusion from these studies is that resources that serve as a basis of action are the reason why reaction is delayed. For example, radical and strategic actions will likely require more resources to carry out than will tactical or non-radical actions. Rivals may be delayed in responding until they cannot generate the same level of resources. Future research should explore the role of resources and action and the link between resources, action and reaction.

Another consistent finding is that measures of industry structure are related to action and reaction. For example, we observe that the frequency of action and reaction are lower under conditions of high barriers to entry and under high levels of concentration. Of course, this is the fundamental argument of the structure-conduct-performance paradigm (see Scherer and Ross, 1990). However, competitive dynamics researchers need to go one step further in examining the entire link between structure, conduct (action and reaction), and performance. Such an examination, to the extent it supported the structure-conduct-performance paradigm, would provide content validity to the study of action and reaction (see Young et al. (1996) for an example).

Finally, there is steady support for the relationship between action and reaction and performance. For example, there is a consistent relationship between action/reaction timing and performance. Namely, the faster a firm acts and the more it can delay reaction, the greater its performance. Moreover, we observe positive relationships between action aggressiveness and performance across a great variety of settings. These findings support the idea that aggressive firms outperform less aggressive competitors. We also observe relationships between repertoires of action and performance. For example, firms undertaking complex sets of actions perform better than firms that undertake more simple sets of actions.

We believe that the current research in competitive dynamics has provided a strong foundation for future research. However, we also contend that the current state of the science in competitive dynamics research has reached an important inflection point. We believe two types of research are necessary if the potential of competitive dynamics research is to be more fully realized. First, we recognize that despite its contributions, there are indeed some limitations in the overall research model outlined in figure 11.1. Thus, as we discuss more fully in the remainder of this section, future research could "fine tune" this model by exploring action, competitive interdependence, and important antecedents and consequences in new industry samples, applying new methods and research designs, or other organizational and industry influences.

We also believe, however, that competitive dynamics researchers need to broaden the theoretical roots of their models and propositions. Thus, we believe that there is a great opportunity to reach beyond the current model (e.g., figure 11.1) by developing and integrating entirely *new* theoretical perspectives. We offer our ideas for new theory integration in the next major section entitled "Toward a New Theory of Action."

## *Samples*

From the initial field studies that involved small samples, retrospective reporting, single respondents, poor statistical power and inadequate attention to construct validity, competitive dynamics research has dramatically improved their methods. These improvements were possible with the invention of the structured content analysis. The structured content analysis led to the development of large longitudinal databases composed of secondary data from a variety of firms and industries. The strengths of these newer methodologies which depend on archival data include: (1) the variety of firms and industries studied (nearly 300 firms, 50 different industries); (2) the development of large samples of firms (averaging approximately 300 firm years per study); and (3) the study of competitive dynamics over time where causality can be more safely be inferred.

Despite the range of industries studied thus far, however, this still represents a relatively small sample of industries, given the scope and complexity of the industrial landscape. Also, the studies have largely been limited to exploring the general research model with respect to publicly held domestic firms operating as single businesses. Given that the global economy consists of many closely held private firms, as well as powerful overseas competitors, future research could indeed explore the general model on new samples of firms, including global players, firms that have multiple lines of business, and firms that are structured to specifically engage in multi-market competition. In addition, research is needed to explore the relationship between the dynamics of industry change and the specific actions and reactions of firms within the industry, including the role of technological actions.

Finally, because the "costs" associated with collecting and measuring the characteristics of competitive actions are high (see below), there appears to be a discernable trade-off between the strengths and weaknesses relating to both the "depth" of understanding that single-industry studies provide versus the "breadth" of understanding that multi-industry studies provide. More specifically, the former type of study explores competitive interaction among all firms in a given industry (e.g., Chen, 1988, Young et al., 1996), whereas the latter includes only the largest few firms across multiple industries (e.g., Ferrier et al., 1999). Future research could explore the general research model with samples and methods that combine both breadth and depth.

## *Methods*

As noted above, one of this research stream's most significant contributions is the definition and measure of firm strategy as *competitive action* using structured content analysis of news articles and headlines. Across all studies, thousands of news articles, headlines and abstracts were systematically and painstakingly coded into individual competitive actions and responses. Importantly, this approach has yielded consistent findings across multiple industry contexts and levels of analysis. Research at the level of individual actions and responses, as well as the relationships among action-response dyads offers a fine-grained view of competitive interaction. Research at the repertoire or firm-year levels of analysis adds comprehensiveness to the overall research model by exploring the structural characteristics of the firm's entire set of competitive actions. Studies that view strategy as a sequence of competitive actions add the notion of "process' to the research stream, whereby the temporal orderliness of competitive action also explains performance outcomes.

Most measures of competitive action, however, are drawn from archival sources. Further, this methodology (structured content analysis) for collecting and measuring competitive action is critically dependent on the newsworthiness of the firms and their competitive actions. Future research could fruitfully explore ways to establish new measures, perhaps by gleaning action data directly from managers who are responsible for implementing such actions. Therefore, future researchers could use interview and observational techniques to more directly measure the TMTs decision-making and cognitive processes and their links to competitive actions.

Given the definition of competitive action, the studies excluded the firm's *internal* actions (such as using new information systems, reorganizing, or the shift to lean manufacturing, etc.). Nevertheless, some writers argue that competitive behavior is a function of the firm's resource profile, whereby resources and actions may be two sides of the same coin (e.g., Grimm and Smith, 1997; Wernerfelt, 1984). Future research could examine the link between internal actions and resources, competitive behavior, and external performance outcomes.

The vast majority of studies explore only the direct effects and linear relationships among the drivers and consequences of competitive action. Future research could possibly flesh out more moderated and curvilinear effects. For instance, Miller and Chen (1996) found a direct, linear relationship between competitive repertoire simplicity and performance. However, more recent research found that when firms carry out a simple competitive repertoire, those with heterogeneous TMTs actually experience better performance (Ferrier and Lyon, 1998).

## TOWARD A NEW THEORY OF ACTION

Our review of the competitive dynamics research reveals that scholars of competitive dynamics have closely aligned themselves to the all-knowing assumption consistent with early decision theory (Simon, 1955). Indeed, beyond the framing of papers based on Schumpeter and Austrian economics, most hypotheses are drawn from information theory or game theory. Information theory provides a completely rational explanation for competitive action: those who have the information will be most aware, motivated and capable of responding. Game theory is also generally based on the rational information processing capabilities of decision makers.

In this section we consider alternative theories of action that are based on different sets of assumptions. We believe these alternative theories may provide a broader and richer explanation of the actions and reactions than exists in the current research. In particular, to guide future research, we offer a preliminary set of propositions from institutional theory, evolutionary theory, organizational ecology, and network theory. Our goal is not to develop a new theory of action but instead to promote the development of more theory and research based on alternative assumptions about decision makers and their goals. The review is not exhaustive but meant to suggest new opportunities for theory building and testing.

Beginning with Simon's work (1955), there have been significant efforts to revise theory to more adequately reflect the observation that organizational action is often disjointed, incomplete and less than optimal. For example, there has been the argument that the selection of possible alternatives is not knowable and has to be discovered through action (Kirzner, 1973). Moreover, there is the contention that values that decision makers assign to outcomes will be variable, unstable and inconsistent across individuals (Simon, 1955; Weick, 1980).

Refined theory has emphasized action as rules and institutionalized behavior, action as routines formed through path historical dependencies and through environmental selection. In these more recent conceptualizations, the role of actors in selecting action alternatives is restricted by cognitive limitations and there are strong inertia pressures in organizations against change, despite the motives of decision makers.

## Institutional theory

The principle of explaining actions based on rules and social considerations has a long history in sociology (see Weber, 1946, 1964). From this viewpoint, action is not the result of estimation of alternative choices to maximize some individual utility function, but instead based on an attempt to gain legitimacy among peers and important constituencies. In other words, actions are selected based on social importance. Organizations do not simply respond to stimuli, they instead interpret the stimuli and then shape their actions in response (Weber, 1946, 1964). Labeled institutional theory, this viewpoint argues that choice of action is based on requirements of socialization, institutional norms, and pressures to conform.

Scott defines institutions as "cognitive, normative and regulative structures and activities that provide stability and meaning to social behavior" (1995: 33). From a competitive dynamics perspective, institutional pressures, conceived as regulative, normative and cognitive forces, may shape the firm's actions in a number of ways. Regulatory forces include the pressure to make actions conform to formal rules, the evaluation of actions in order to be certain they conform to these rules and the levying of sanctions in an attempt to maintain conformance. For example, an industry leader may directly engage a rival with price-cutting actions in an attempt to regulate the rival for deviating from accepted industry behaviors, or a group of firms may work to influence government regulations in order to formally define industry operating standards – as occurred in the US domestic airline industry with regard to setting standards for on-time arrival, baggage claims, etc.

Normative forces include the "prescriptive, evaluative and obligatory dimensions of social life" (Scott, 1995: 37). Norms define what types of actions are perceived as legitimate and acceptable to the larger industry group. From a competitive dynamics perspective, it is likely that every industry has its own unique norms of competition. These norms are established over time by the behavior of participants. These customs and norms may be observed in the consistency by which firms in an industry introduce new products (e.g., timing), how they test their new products in markets and how they promote these products after they are introduced. Over time, these norms become entrenched and define what most industry participants view as acceptable competitive behavior. In some industries, acceptable competitive behavior may involve cut-throat price-cutting, in other industries price-cutting may be frowned upon. When firms violate the accepted norms of the industry, sanctions may result. Firms that conform to these norms will be seen as legitimate and supported, firms that deviate will fail to achieve support.

Cognitive forces emphasize the extent to which belief systems and cultural forces are imposed on or adopted by individuals or organizations. The mechanism that is most prominent within the institutional literature is isomorphic process of imitation. From a competitive dynamics perspective, the cognitive force would suggest that firms behave in a consistent manner, in ways that will not cause them to stand out as deviant.

These three forces are obviously inter-related but suggest some important competitive dynamic propositions:

> *Proposition 1.* A firm's decision on the type, time and place of actions will be the result of their attempts to obey rules of competition, conform to normative beliefs of what is acceptable, and behave in conventional ways.
>
> *Proposition 2.* Over time, the patterns of action and reaction in an industry will converge on a few institutionally accepted behaviors.
>
> *Proposition 3.* Industry leaders will enforce normative types of actions by undertaking sanctions (reactions) against deviants.
>
> *Proposition 4.* New, young firms will tend to deviate from normatively accepted actions because they will be less aware of customs and norms.
>
> *Proposition 5.* The presence of industry associations or cooperative research groups will tend to regulate actions making them more similar.
>
> *Proposition 6.* Norms of competitive behavior will be clearer and more enforceable when there are cooperative research groups and industry associations.
>
> *Proposition 7.* New industries will experience heterogeneity in competitive behavior.
>
> *Proposition 8.* The greater the similarity of firms in an industry, the greater the likelihood of strong norms and regulatory pressures for conformance in types of action.

### Evolutionary theory

Evolutionary theory focuses on explaining how action, or sets of actions, change over time as a function of the dynamic change process (Nelson, 1995). For example, evolutionary theory would be interested in explaining how and why a firm can change from being a laggard to a first mover, from being a weak competitor to that of a predator. Evolutionary theory contends that a firm's action, or set of actions, is subject to random variation but that there are also some mechanisms that systemically narrow the variation in firm action over time. Thus, evolutionary theory realizes that there are strong forces for inertia (for old actions to be repeated and institutionalized), as well as processes that continually introduce new variation in action.

According to evolutionary theory, firms undertake action and learn from the results of action, which shapes future action. More specifically, new action is tentative because managers do not know the implications of their first moves or how to completely achieve the desired result (high profits). Initial new action then is preliminary and taken without commitment. As these new actions are undertaken, the manager learns about the effectiveness of these moves (actions that yielded high profits) and where actions need to be redesigned.

At the industry level and in early stages of industry development, there will be great variation in action among firms. When some actions become successful, rivals will attempt to imitate. The industry will gradually develop a structure in which only the firms that follow these actions or close variants thereof will survive.

Nelson (1995: 56) argues that the learning process associated with action can be "modeled in terms of the change in the probability distribution of possible actions that an organization might take at any time, coming about as a result of feedback from what has been tried, and the consequences." Nelson and Winter (1982) use the term "routines" to define behavior or actions that are taken without much explicit prior thinking. Such routines develop because they are deemed appropriate and effective in achieving desired outcomes. Routines develop through profit-oriented processes of learning (Nelson, 1995). Nelson describes three types of routine action. There are actions or routines that determine how much a firm produces – these would be actions designed to exploit existing resource configurations at a given point in time (e.g., to set a certain price, or advertising campaign). Second, there are the actions designed to affect the configuration of resources as a function of its profits (e.g., an action to hire a new scientist, train employees to improve their skills, or the action of building a new plant and equipment). Such actions influence the configuration of resources. Finally there are the deliberate actions of firms designed to search out new opportunities (e.g., these could be actions of introducing a new product, of entering a new market). Nelson (1995) notes that these search or entrepreneurial actions provide "differential fitness." Drawing from Schumpeter, firms that undertake actions that turn up better products, markets and resource combinations will earn profits and grow relative to their competitors. However, these search actions will also bind firms together as a community because they are partly based on what the competition is doing and other firms will imitate profitable actions.

Evolutionary theory suggests the following propositions:

*Proposition 9.* Competitive actions over time reflect the habits and customs of the firm; in other words, successful action will be repeated.

*Proposition 10.* Actions that exploit existing resource positions can be distinguished from actions that configure resources or search for opportunities.

*Proposition 11.* Exploitation of existing resources positions will be the most routinized (repeated) in terms of habits and customs.

*Proposition 12.* Search actions will involve innovation and new behaviors. Search actions that yield profits will be routinized and imitated.

*Proposition 13.* Profitable search actions will lead the firm to undertake new actions to reconfigure resource positions and hence new actions to exploit resource configurations.

*Proposition14.* There will be an evolutionary progression to action: from search, to resource configuration, to exploitation.

*Proposition 15.* Prior actions (path dependencies) to exploit and configure resources will constrain future search actions.

## Organizational ecology

Organizational ecology is the study of organizational diversity. The focus of the theory is on the processes that influence variety (Singh and Lumsden, 1990). Although organizational ecology broadly examines the rates of organizational creation, demise, and change, our focus will be primarily on diversity in organizational action.

The principal argument of organizational ecology is that firms are subject to strong inertial pressures due to the processes by which they were founded and dissolved. A major assumption of ecology is that processes of birth, demise and change in organizations parallels those in biology. As such, organizational ecology uses biological metaphors to predict diversity.

Consistent with organizational ecology researchers, we focus on how social and environmental conditions influence how new actions are created, why certain actions die out and why organizations change their actions. D'Aveni (1994) has proposed a life cycle to each action beginning with introduction, exploitation and escalating competitive reaction until a new action is required.

Concerning how new actions come about, organizational ecology suggests that as prior actions are given up, new resources will be released for new action. For example, as a firm gives up a long-standing advertising campaign that was initially successful, funds will be released for a new campaign. However, a new type of advertising campaign will encourage rivals to imitate the same actions by signaling a fertile area. As the imitation process continues, so many new advertising actions will be created that it will increase the competition for advertising resources and further discourage advertising actions. Thus, the ecology density argument suggests that the early types of new actions encourages and legitimizes further action of the same type (Singh and Lumsden, 1990). However, as the density of a certain type of new action increases, the legitimizing process will be overcome by the competitive process leading to a decrease in the rate of new action in a certain category.

Organizational ecology with regard to mortality is more complex. One particular theory concerns the liability of newness (Stinchcombe, 1965). When applied to action, the theory suggests that when firms undertake a *new* action, this new action will have to compete with existing proven actions in the marketplace. A firm that offers a new promotional campaign, or a new product, will have to contend with firms that already have existing campaigns or products in place. The fact that these other actions exists, suggests that they already receive customer support. Managers will have to devote more attention and resources to new actions in order to effectively compete with existing firms that have loyal customers. Thus, the odds are stacked against new actions being success-ful relative to existing actions leading to the liability to action newness.

Related to the argument about newness, is the liability of smallness. As it pertains to action, we might think of actions that are large, involving significant commitments of resources, versus actions that are relatively minor in nature. Hannan and Freeman (1984) contend that the level of organizational inertia increases with size. Moreover, the action selection processes in the market favor those with greater inertia; those actions that do not change and are stable. Thus, we might imagine that small actions that carry less resource commitment will be less likely to succeed relative to actions that are larger requiring greater commitment.

The organizational ecology literature also addresses the change process. With regard to action, it suggests that actions with inert features, such as long-term contracts, or actions that require significant commitments of physical capital, are more likely to survive in the long term and as they age, they become more inert. The implications are twofold. First, firms that deploy actions involving greater commitments of resources, are less likely to change these actions if proven successful. And as these actions age, the likelihood of their being changed decreases (Singh and Lumsden, 1990). Moreover, older firms are less likely to change actions than younger firms because they become embedded in their surrounding environment and develop relationships that limit their ability to be autonomous (Singh and Lumsden, 1990). Older firms will be more likely to stick with actions that have worked well in the past.

In summary, organizational ecology suggests the following propositions:

*Proposition 16.* As past actions are given up, resources will become available for new action. The greater the resources available, the greater the likelihood of new action.

*Proposition 17.* New actions of a certain type will signal fertile ground leading to increased imitations by rivals.

*Proposition 18.* Increased imitation in action will eventually lead to increased competition resulting in a decline in further action in the category.

*Proposition 19.* New actions suffer from a liability of newness and will not receive the customer support of existing actions.

*Proposition 20.* Smaller actions or actions requiring a smaller commitment of resources will not receive the same level of support as will larger actions requiring more resources.

*Proposition 21.* Actions that require a greater commitment of resources will be more enduring and more difficult to change or stop than will actions requiring less resources.

## Network theory

Recent theory on organizations as networks also offers to advance our understanding of action and reaction. For example, network theory suggests that firms are not free to undertake any competitive action (Burt, 1982; Granovetter, 1985). Instead, firms must act and react within the constraints of the social networks.

Gulati, Nohria, and Zaheer (2000) contend that as networks become increasingly more important for firms, we must understand them if we are to fully understand their actions or behaviors. Gnyawali and Madhavan (2000) treat the firm network positions as a *resource* which the firm can draw upon to deploy its actions. According to Gnyawali and Madhavan (2000), the likelihood of a firm undertaking an action or response will be influenced by its position in a network. Four important characteristics are identified: centrality, structural holes or autonomy, structural equivalence, and density. Drawing from Gnyawali and Madhavan (2000), we briefly outline the logic for these relationships below.

Centrality is defined as the extent to which a firm occupies a key position with strong ties with other network members (Wasserman and Faust, 1994). Firms that are located centrally in the network will have greater access to information and resources, which will allow the firm to be more competitively aware and motivated.

Structural holes may provide power and information to a firm as a result of its ability to hold important information within the network structure (Burt, 1992). If firm X is connected to firm Y and Z, but firm Y and Z are not connected to one another, then firm Y and Z can only reach each other through firm X. Firm X in this context has the power to exploit firm X and Y because of its network position and structural hole between X and Y. Structural holes will affect the awareness and motivation of network participants allowing for less redundancy and higher quality of information within the network. In addition, structural holes may allow faster access to information, and the potential to be included in many more information interactions (Burt, 1998). Finally, an actor that can fill a structural hole has the potential to control information between otherwise independent actors. As Gnyawali and Madhavan (2000) note, firms that fill a structural hole will have a different level of competitive awareness, motivation and resources capability than those that do not fill a hole.

Structurally equivalent concerns the extent to which network members have similar structure of relationships (Rice and Aydin, 1991). Network theory suggests that actors with equivalent networks will tend to be similar in their awareness, motivation and resource capabilities, and as a result, they will tend to act and react in similar ways. It is also possible that structurally equivalent firms will tend to behave in similar ways in a desire to achieve legitimacy.

Density refers to the extent to which members or firms in a network are intertwined in their relationships (Coleman, 1990). The greater the connectedness of members or firms in a network, the greater the density. Information in a dense network will move faster and more efficiently because of the many connections and potential lines of allocation (Coleman, 1990). In addition, to the extent that dense systems act as closed self-sufficient systems, participants will develop norms of trust and cooperation. Thus, firms in a dense network are more likely to be aware and motivated of the behavior of rivals within the network, which will affect the way they act and react. The following propositions are suggested from above.

*Proposition 22.* Firms that are central in a network and/or that fill structural holes will be more likely to take first moves and be more likely to be aggressive reactors. Alternatively, firms that are non-central or that do not fill structural holes in a network will be laggards and slow reactors.

*Proposition 23.* When network structures of firms are similar, they will act and react in a similar manner. When network structures are similar, firms will be less frequent actors, but react quickly when engaged.

*Proposition 24.* Firms that are centrally located, with large networks of relationship, and firms that fill structural holes, will seek to set and enforce industry standards for competition.

*Proposition 25.* Firms in dense networks of relationships will be reluctant to act (for fear of raising the level of rivalry) but will react quickly once action begins.

It should be clear that the domains of institutional theory, evolutionary theory, organizational ecology and network theory overlap and that the theories have been simplified for the purpose of this review. Moreover, we view the propositions we have offered as rudimentary. Our goal is to encourage researchers to explore these alternative theoretical viewpoints so that a richer set of propositions can be developed and tested. We believe by employing alternative theories, with their accompanying sets of assumptions, a more complete and comprehensive understanding of action and reaction can be achieved.

## DISCUSSION

Distinguishing characteristics of competitive dynamics research include a focus on the real behaviors or actions of firms which are time and place specific, an emphasis on competitive interdependence, which recognizes that the success of a firm's action (s) is dependent upon the competitive context where it takes place, and an attempt to predict both the causes and performance and competitive consequences of action. The research that we have reviewed in this chapter reflects this unique focus.

We have reviewed the theory, methods and empirical findings carried out by competitive dynamic researchers. We conclude that the most progress has been achieved in terms of research methods and samples and that more theoretical development is necessary if competitive dynamics research is to have enduring value. In this regard, we have suggested a set of alternative theories, which are based on different sets of decision-making assumptions and we offer some preliminary propositions from each theoretical domain. Our ultimate goal in offering these propositions is to inspire more conceptual work.

Overall, we note that most aspects of the model outlined in figure 11.1 have been tested. Moreover, these tests have been conducted in a good variety of industries and with large samples of firms. Some key findings from the research include the importance of action timing, action aggressiveness and action repertoires (being different) for firm performance. However, there are also inconsistent relationships and contradictory findings across the samples and future research is necessary to sort out the discrepancies. It is unclear whether these inconsistencies are related to the idiosyncratic nature of samples, or the research method.

It is our contention that competitive dynamics research has great potential to advance our understanding of business level strategy and competition. We see this evolving along three paths. First, study of actions and reactions can advance our understanding of rivalry, which is a fundamental aspect of all models of competitive advantage. For example, the level of rivalry or the ease with which firms act and duplicate advantages

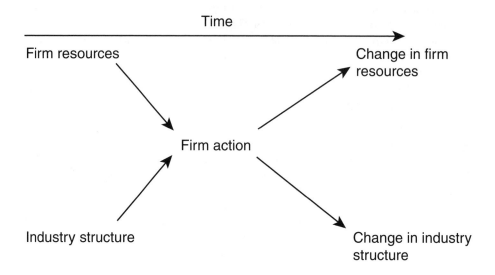

FIGURE 11.2 The relationship between resources, industry structure and action over time

is a key variable in the resource-based view of competitive advantage (Barney, 1991) and it is one of Porter's five forces affecting a firm's decision on industry positioning (Porter, 1980). Yet, rarely have strategy researchers directly measured the extent of rivalry in testing different aspects of these strategy/performance models. However, by directly examining rivalrous actions of firms, competitive dynamic researchers can make more realistic and more accurate predictions on competitive behavior and its links to competitive advantage and performance. As such they can contribute to an improved theory of competitor analysis (Chen, 1996; Porter, 1980).

Second, the competitive dynamics perspective can improve our understanding of the two key models of competitive advantage: the resource-based view and the industrial organization viewpoints on strategy and advantage. Figure 11.2 captures *our* theorized relationship between resources, the environment or industry structure, and firm action. In this model we see action as the vehicle by which firms change resource configuration and industry positioning. For example, with the empirical study of firm action, researchers can examine how certain configurations of resources affect action and delay reaction (how different resources might be valuable), or how certain industry structural conditions, such as barrier to entry, affect the actions/reactions of firms (the level of rivalry). Moreover, researchers can also study how action impacts future (changes) resource configuration and future (changes) in industry structure. In this regard, competitive dynamics research can inform and perhaps make these models of advantage more complete, dynamic, and valuable.

Finally, competitive dynamics research can improve our understanding of strategic choice and decision-making. Almost thirty years ago, John Child (1972) introduced the notion of strategic choice to distinguish the purposeful action of firms. Indeed, the concept of strategic choice stands as an *assumption* behind most strategic management research. Yet, researchers often must make inferences about the strategic decisions from coarse-grained annual reports, or from retrospective reporting by executives. An organization's actions do not occur without some executive deciding to undertake a move. Thus the study of action connects the researcher more closely with the central concept of strategy: strategic choice. Moreover, the aggregation of actions according to patterns, routines, and sequences provides a literal definition of strategy (Andrews, 1980; Mintzberg and Waters, 1985).

## CONCLUSION

We have covered a great deal of material in this chapter. Indeed, the extent of the review is perhaps suggestive of the progress of competitive dynamics research over the last decade. Yet, the review also has identified a number of important issues that must be resolved if competitive dynamics research is to fulfill its potential. We remain excited by the possibilities and optimistic for the future of competitive dynamics research.

## NOTES

1 Of course, there has been much research in economics that has focused on the concept of rivalry or competition (for a review see Scherer and Ross, 1990). However, much of this work makes inferences about rivalry by studying aggregated pricing or performance data. Because this research does not focus directly on firm actions or reactions, we have excluded it from our review. We have also excluded the literature on game theory that has not involved empirical observation of firm actions and reactions.
2 We note that researchers have not studied the actual cognitive awareness and motivation of decision makers. Instead, they have made inferences about these cognitions from organizational factors such as organizational size and structural complexity, which are expected to affect management cognition and motivation.
3 Although there is some empirical work linking the competitive environment to action and reaction, competitive dynamic researchers have mostly used industry variables as controls in their research and/or they have focused on single industry for investigation, and as such, there is no variation in industry. We focus on those studies that have explicitly hypothesized industry environmental effects.

APPENDIX 11A Conceptual and operational definitions of action by level of analysis

| Concepts studied | Operational definition | Empirical works |
| --- | --- | --- |
| Action characteristics: | Competitive Action: *An externally directed, observable competitive move carried out to improve the firm's relative competitive position.* | |
| Type, category | General functional or operational category of a particular action; pricing, marketing, product, service, R&D, overt signals, etc. | Smith, Grimm, Gannon and Chen, 1991; Chen and MacMillan, 1992; Smith, Grimm, and Gannon, 1992; Ferrier, 1997 |
| Magnitude, strategic type, strategic significance | The extent to which a particular action reflects a significant invest ment or reconfiguration in fixed and/or human assets; actions significant departed from industry norms; strategic versus tactical. | Chen, Smith, and Grimm, 1992; Smith et al., 1992; Hambrick, Cho, and Chen, 1996 |
| Threat, intensity, centrality | The degree to which an action threatens specific markets/customers of a given competitor; how strongly a given competitor is affected by an action. | Chen et al., 1992; Smith et al., 1992; Chen and Miller, 1994 |
| Scope (a), competitive impact | The total number of competitors affected by an action. | Chen et al., 1992; Smith et al., 1992 |
| Radicality | The extent to which an action significantly deviates from the industry norm. | Smith et al., 1992 |

| | | |
|---|---|---|
| Implementation requirement | The degree of effort required to execute an action in terms of resource allocations, interdepartmental coordination, coordination with external stakeholders, etc. | Chen et al., 1992 Smith et al., 1992 |
| Difficulty of response | Perceptual attribute of a particular action that accounts for the estimated financial expense of making a responding move, the need for complex coordination, the allocation of staff and/or equipment, etc. | Chen and Miller, 1994 |
| Irreversibility | The extent to which an action requires significant expenditures, legal and contractual relationships with other parties; requires significant interdepartmental coordination; disruption of systems and procedures. | Chen and MacMillan, 1992 |
| Noteworthiness, visibility | The amount of industry attention associated with a particular move; extent to which actions are non-subtle, etc. | Chen and Hambrick, 1995 Hambrick et al., 1996 |
| Scope (b) | The extent to which an action affects or requires the coordination among the full breadth of the firm's operations. | Hambrick et al., 1996 |
| Execution speed | The amount of time required to implement an announced action. | Chen and Hambrick, 1995 Hambrick et al., 1996 |
| Response characteristics: | Competitive Response: *An observable counter move carried out "in response to" or "in reaction to" an initiated action.* | |
| Number of responses | The total number of responses elicited by a given action. | Smith et al., 1991 Chen and MacMillan, 1992 Chen and Miller, 1994 |

| Concept | Description | References |
| --- | --- | --- |
| Imitation, matching response, tit-for-tat | The degree to which a firm's initiated action is imitated or matched in kind by a rival's competitive response. | Smith et al., 1991<br>Chen and MacMillan, 1992<br>Smith et al., 1992<br>Smith, Grimm, Young, and Wally, 1997 |
| Lag, delay, speed, move timing | The time elapsed between the focal firm's initiated competitive action and a rival's competitive response. | Smith et al., 1991<br>Chen and MacMillan, 1992<br>Smith et al., 1992<br>Smith et al., 1997<br>Lee, Smith, Grimm, and Schomburg, 2000 |
| Order | The firm's chronological rank position (among all responders) in terms of carrying out a competitive response to a rival's initiated action (i.e., 1st, 2nd, 3rd, etc.). | Smith et al., 1991<br>Smith et al., 1992<br>Lee et al., 2000 |
| Generation speed, announcement speed | The amount of time elapsed between the announcement of a firm's initiated action and the focal firm's announcement of a competitive response. | Chen and Hambrick, 1995<br>Hambrick et al., 1996 |
| Execution speed | The time elapsed between a firm's announcement of its competitive response to an action and the day the response was implemented. | Chen and Hambrick, 1995<br>Hambrick et al., 1996 |
| Scope | The extent to which a response affects or requires the coordination among the full breadth of the firm's operations. | Hambrick et al., 1996 |

| Firm-year aggregations, repertoire characteristics: | Action Repertoire: *A coherent set of competitive actions carried out by a firm over the course of a year* | |
| --- | --- | --- |
| Action propensity, total activity, move frequency | Total number of competitive actions carried out by a firm in a given year. | Chen and Hambrick, 1995<br>Hambrick et al., 1996<br>Young, Smith and Grimm, 1996<br>Smith et al., 1997<br>Ferrier, Smith and Grimm, 1999<br>Young, Smith, Grimm, and Simon, 2001 |
| Response propensity, responsiveness, likelihood, number of responses | The extent to which a firm actually responded to initiated competitive actions, given the total number of initiated actions carried out. | Smith et al., 1991<br>Chen and MacMillan, 1992<br>Smith et al., 1992<br>Chen and Hambrick, 1995<br>Hambrick et al., 1996 |
| Rivalry instigation | The number of first moves a firm carried out in a given year. | Smith et al., 1997 |
| Price cutting proclivity | The proportion of pricing moves relative to total moves carried out by a firm in a given year. | Smith et al., 1997 |
| Repertoire inertia | The number of market-oriented changes a company makes in the set of actions carried out in a given year to outmaneuver rivals in the marketplace. | Miller and Chen, 1994 |
| Repertoire non-conformity | The extent to which a firm's entire set of competitive actions carried out in a given year deviates from the industry norm. | Miller and Chen, 1995 |

| | | |
|---|---|---|
| Repertoire simplicity | The extent to which a firm's set of competitive actions carried out in a given year consists of a narrow (versus broad) range of actions of different types or categories; the tendency to concentrate on fewer types of competitive actions. | Miller and Chen, 1996<br>Ferrier and Lyon, 1998<br>Ferrier et al., 1999 |
| Repertoire heterogeneity | The extent to which a firm's set of competitive actions carried out in a given year deviates from rivals or the industry norm. | Ferrier et al., 1999 |
| Action timing, move timing | The average time elapsed between a set of actions carried out by a firm and the set of actions carried out by a rival. | Ferrier et al., 1999<br>Young et al., 2001 |
| Sequence characteristics: | *Action Sequence: A coherent, uninterrupted, and ordered series of competitive moves carried out in time.* | |
| Volume | The number of actions that comprise given uninterrupted series of competitive action carried out by a firm. | |
| Duration | The time elapsed from the first action to the last action in an uninterrupted series of competitive action carried out by a firm. | Ferrier, 2000 |
| Complexity | The extent to which a given uninterrupted series of competitive action carried out by a firm is comprised of a wide (versus narrow) range of actions of different types. | Ferrier, 2000<br>Ferrier and Lee, 2000 |
| Heterogeneity | The extent to which a given uninterrupted series of competitive action carried out by a firm deviates from that of a matched rival. | Ferrier, 2000<br>Ferrier and Lee, 2000 |

| | | |
|---|---|---|
| Intensity | The extent to which a firm's uninterrupted series of competitive actions consists of more and more actions within increasingly shorter timer periods; furious bursts of competitive activity versus sporadic activity. | Ferrier and Lee, 2000 |
| Unpredictability | The extent to which a given uninterrupted series of competitive action carried out by a firm changes from one time period to the next. | Ferrier, 2000<br>Ferrier and Lee, 2000 |

APPENDIX 11B  Samples of competitive dynamics research

| Industry | Time frame | Kind and number of actions/reactions | Key (new) variables of interest | Method |
|---|---|---|---|---|
| 1. Banking industry | 1980 | Responses to banking innovations | Firm characteristics and characteristics of action | Field/case study |
| 2. Photography | 1975–1980 | Actions and responses | Stock market reactions | Case study |
| 3. High Tech | 1985–1986 | 47 actions and reactions of all types | Action characteristics, response time, type, and firm performance | Field interviews and questionnaires |
| 4. Computer retailing | 1988 | 25 competitive reactions | Organizational resources | Field interviews and questionnaires |
| 5. US airlines | 1978–1986 | 191 actions and 418 responses | Response order, number of responders | Archival study of aviation daily |
| 6. Brewing, telecommunications, and personal computers | 1975–1990 | 82 new product introductions and 632 imitative responses | Industry structure and performance, stock market reactions | Archival study of F&S Predicast – 700 newspapers and business magazines, trade associations |
| 7. Software | 1980–1990 | 2,347 actions and reactions | Competition, cooperation and performance | Archival study of F&S Predicast |
| 8. Leader/challenger pairs – 41 different industries | 1986–1993 | 4,876 actions and reactions | Action repertoires, industry dethronement | Archival study of F&S Predicast |

# References

Amason, A. (1996). Distinguishing the effects of functional and dysfunctional conflict on strategic decision making: Resolving the paradox for top management teams. *Academy of Management Journal*, 39: 123–48.

Andrews, J. (1980). *The concept of corporate strategy* (2nd edition), Homewood, IL: Irwin.

Barney, J. (1991). Firm resources and sustained competitive advantage. *Journal of Management*, 17: 9–121.

Barr, P., Stimpert, L., and Huff, A. (1992). Cognitive change, strategic action, and organizational renewal. *Strategic Management Journal*, 13: 15–36.

Baum, J., and Korn, H. (1996). Competitive dynamics of interfirm rivalry. *Academy of Management Journal*, 392: 255–91.

Bettis, R., and Weeks, D. (1987). Financial returns and strategic interaction: The case of instant photography. *Strategic Management Journal*, 8: 549–63.

Bourgeois. L. (1981). On the measurement of organizational slack. *Academy of Management Review*, 6: 29–39.

Burt, R. (1982). *Toward a Structural Theory of Action*. New York: Academic Press.

Caves, R., Fortunato, M., and Ghemawat, P. (1984). The decline of dominant firms: 1905–29. *The Quarterly Journal of Economics*, August: 523–46.

Chakravarthy, B. (1986). Measuring strategic performance. *Strategic Management Journal*, 7: 437–59.

Chen, M. (1988. *Competitive Srategic Interaction: A study of Competitive Actions and Responses*. Doctoral dissertation, University of Maryland, College Park.

Chen, M. J. (1996). Competitor analysis and interfirm rivalry: Toward a theoretical integration. *Academy of Management Review*, 21: 100–34.

Chen, M., and Hambrick, D. (1995). Speed, stealth and selective attack: How small firms differ from large firms in competitive behavior. *Academy of Management Journal*, 38: 453–82.

Chen, M., and MacMillan, I. (1992). Nonresponse and delayed response to competitive moves. *Academy of Management Journal*, 35: 539–70.

Chen, M., and Miller, D. (1994). Competitive attack, retaliation and performance: An expectancy-valence framework. *Strategic Management Journal*, 15: 85–102.

Chen, M., Smith, K., and Grimm, C. (1992). Action characteristics as predictors of competitive responses. *Management Science*, 38: 439–55.

Child, J. (1972). Organization Structure, Environment and Performance: The role of strategic choice. *Sociology*, Vol. 6.

Coleman, J. (1990). *Foundations of Social Theory*. Cambridge, MA: Harvard University Press.

Cyert, R., and March, J. (1963). *A Behavioral Theory of the Firm*. Englewood Cliffs: Prentice-Hall.

D'Aveni, R. (1994). *Hypercompetition: Managing the Dynamics of Strategic Maneuvering*. New York: Freedom Press.

Duhaime, I., and Schwenk, C. (1985). Conjectures on cognitive simplification in acquisition and divestment decision making. *The Academy of Management Review*, 10: 287–96.

Edwards, C. D. (1955). Conglomerate business as a source of power. In National Bureau of Economics Research conference report. *Business Concentration and Price Policy*: 331–52. Princeton, NJ: Princeton University Press.

Ferrier, W. (1997). "Tough talk" and market leaders: The role of overt signaling and reputation-building behaviors in sustaining industry dominance. *Corporate Reputation Review*, Summer: 98–102.

Ferrier, W. (2000). Playing to win: The role of competitive disruption and aggressiveness. In M. Hitt, R. Bresser, D. Heuskel, and R. Nixon (eds.), *Winning Strategies in a Deconstructing World*. New York: John Wiley and Sons.

Ferrier, W. (2001) Navigating the competitive landscape: The drivers and consequences of competitive aggressiveness. *Academy of Management Journal*, forthcoming.

Ferrier, W., and Lyon, D. (1998). *Competitive repertoire simplicity and firm performance: The moderating role of TMT heterogeneity.* Presented at the Academy of Management Meeting, San Diego, CA.

Ferrier, W., and Lee, H. (2000). *Strategic aggressiveness, adaptation, and surprise: How the sequential pattern of competitive rivalry influences stock market returns.* Paper presented at the Strategic Management Society Annual International Conference, Vancouver, British Columbia, Canada.

Ferrier, W., Smith, K., and Grimm, C. (1999). The role of competition in market share erosion and dethronement: A study of industry leaders and challengers. *Academy of Management Journal*, 43(4): 372–88.

Fiegenbaum, A., and Thomas, H. (1990). Strategic groups and performance: The US insurance industry. *Strategic Management Journal*, 11(3): 197–216.

Finkelstein, S., and Hambrick, D. (1990). Top management team tenure and organizational outcomes: The moderating role of managerial discretion. *Administrative Science Quarterly*, 35: 484–503.

Finkelstein, S., and Hambrick, D. (1996). *Strategic Leadership: Top Executives and their Effects on Organizations.* Minneapolis/St Paul, MN: West Publishing Company.

Fombrun, C., and Ginsberg, A. (1990). Shifting gears: Enabling change in corporate aggressiveness. *Strategic Management Journal*, 11: 297–308.

Gannon, M., Smith, K., and Grimm, C. (1992). An organizational-information processing profile of first-movers. *Journal of Business Research*, 253: 231–42.

Gimeno, J. (1999). Reciprocal threats in multimarket rivalry: Staking out "spheres of influence" in the US airline industry. *Strategic Management Journal*, 20: 101–28.

Gimeno, J., and Chen, M. (1998). *The dynamics of competitive positioning: A pair-wise perspective.* Paper presented to the Academy of Management, San Diego, CA.

Gimeno, J., and Woo, C. (1996a). Do similar firms really compete less? Strategic distance and multimarket contact as predictors of rivalry among heterogeneous firms. *Organization Science*, 72: 323–41.

Gimeno, J., and Woo, C. (1996b). Hypercompetition in a multimarket environment: The role of strategic similarity and multimarket contact in competitive de-escalation. *Organization Science*, 73: 322–40.

Gimeno, J., and Woo, C. (1999). Multimarket contact, economies of scope, and firm performance. *Academy of Management Journal*, 42: 239–59.

Gnyawali, D. R., and Madhavan, R. (2000). *Network structure and competitive dynamics: A structural embeddedness perspective.* Working Paper. Virginia Tech University.

Granovetter, M. (1985). Economic action and social structure: The problem of embeddedness. *American Journal of Sociology*, 91(3).

Grimm, C., and Smith, K. (1997). *Strategy as Action: Industry Rivalry and Coordination.* Cincinnati, OH: South-Western College Publishing.

Gulati, R., Nohria, N., and Zaheer, A. (2000). Strategic networks. *Strategic Management Journal*, 21(3), 203–15.

Haleblian, J., and Finkelstein, S. (1993). Top management team size, CEO dominance, and firm performance: The moderating role of environmental turbulence and discretion. *Academy of Management Journal*, 36: 844–63.

Hambrick, D., Cho, T., and Chen, M. (1996). The influence of Top Management Team heterogeneity on firm's competitive moves. *Administrative Science Quarterly*, 414: 659–88.

Hambrick, D., and D'Aveni, R A. (1988). Large corporate failures as downward spirals. *Administrative Science Quarterly*, 33: 1–24.

Hambrick, D., and D'Aveni, R. (1992). Top team deterioration as a part of the downward spiral of large corporate bankruptcies. *Management Science*, 38: 1445–66.

Hambrick, D., Geletkanycz, M., and Fredrickson, J. (1993). Top executive commitment to the status quo: Some tests of its determinants. *Strategic Management Journal*, 14: 401–18.

Hambrick, D., and Mason, P. (1984). Upper echelon: The organization as a reflection of its top managers. *Academy of Management Review*, 9: 193–206.

Hannan, J. T., and Freeman, J. (1984). Structural inertia and organizational change. *American Sociological Review*, 49: 149–64.

Heiner, R. (1983). The origin of predictable behavior. *American Economic Review*, 73: 560–89.

Hitt, M., and Barr, S. (1989). Managerial selection decision models. *Journal of Applied Psychology*, 1: 53–62.

Huber, G., and Daft, R. (1987). The information environment of organizations. In F. Jablin, L. Putman, K. Roberts, and L. Porter (eds.), *Handbook of Organizational Communication*, 130–64. Newbury Park, CA: Sage.

Jacobson, R. (1992). The "Austrian" school of strategy. *Academy of Management Review*, 17: 782–807.

Karnani, A., and Wernerfelt, B. (1985). Research note and communication: Multiple point competition. *Strategic Management Journal*, 6: 87–97.

Kimberly, J., and Evanisko, M. (1981). Organizational innovation: The influence of individual, organizational, and contextual factors on hospital adoption of technological and administrative innovations. *Academy of Management Journal*, 24: 689–713.

Kirzner, I. (1973). *Competition and Entrepreneurship*. Chicago: University of Chicago Press.

Lant, T. K., Milliken, F. J., and Batra, B. (1992). The role of managerial learning and interpretation in strategic persistence: An empirical exploration. *Strategic Management Journal*, 13: 585–608.

Lee, H., Smith, K., and Grimm, C. (1995). *Shareholder wealth effects of new product rivalry: First movers, second movers and laggards*. Presented at Academy of Management Annual Meetings, Vancouver, B.C.

Lee, H., Smith, K., Grimm, C., and Schomburg, A. (2000). Timing, order and durability of new product advantages with imitation. *Strategic Management Journal*, 21: 23–30.

MacCrimmon, K. (1993). Do firm strategies exist? *Strategic Management Journal*, 14: 113–30.

MacFhionnlaoich, C., and Ferrier, W. (1996). *Holding their own: The rivalrous conduct of financially distressed firms*. Presented at the Strategic Management Society Annual International Conference, Phoenix, Arizona.

MacFhionnlaoich, C., Ferrier, W., Smith, K., and Grimm, C. (1996). *The impact of financial condition on competitive behavior: Towards a reconciliation of competing views*. Presented at the Academy of Management Meeting, San Diego, CA.

MacMillan, I. (1988). Controlling competitive dynamics by taking strategic initiative. *Academy of Management Executive*, 2(2): 111–18.

MacMillan, I., McCaffrey, M., and Van Wijk, G. (1985). Competitor's responses to easily imitated new products: Exploring commercial banking product introductions. *Strategic Management Journal*, 6: 75–86.

Miles, R. E., and Snow, J. G. (1978). *Organization Strategy, Structure, and Process*. New York: McGraw-Hill.

Miller, D. (1993). The architecture of simplicity. *Academy of Management Review*, 18: 116–38.

Miller, D. (1994). What happens after success: The perils of excellence. *Journal of Management Studies*, 31: 325–58.

Miller, D., and Chen, M. (1994). Sources and consequences of competitive inertia. *Administrative Science Quarterly*, 39: 1–23.

Miller, D., and Chen, M. (1995). Nonconformity in competitive repertoires. *Academy of Management Proceedings*.

Miller, D., and Chen, M. J. (1996). The simplicity of competitive repertoires: An empirical analysis. *Strategic Management Journal*, 17: 419–40.

Milliken, F., and Lant, T. (1991). The impact of an organization's recent performance history on strategic persistence and change. In P. Shrivastava, A. Huff, and J. Dutton (eds.), *Advances in Strategic Management*, 7: 129–56. Greenwich, CT: JAI Press.

Mintzberg, H., and Waters, J. (1985). Of strategies, deliberate and emergent. *Strategic Management Journal*, 6: 257–72.

Mises, L. Von (1949). *Human Action: A Treatise on Economics*. New Haven: Yale University Press.

Mitchell, W. (1991). Dual clocks: Entry order influences on incumbent and newcomer market share and survival when specialized assets retain their value. *Strategic Management Journal*, 12: 25–100

Mitroff, I., and Emshoff, J. (1979). On strategic assumption-making: A dialectical approach to policy and planning. *Academy of Management Review*, 4.

Nelson, R. (1995). Co-evolution of industry structure, technology and supporting institutions, and the making of comparative advantage. *International Journal of the Economics of Business*, 2: 171–84.

Nelson, R. and Winter, S. (1982). *An Evolutionary Theory of Economic Change*. Cambridge, MA: Harvard University Press.

Porter, M. (1980). *Competitive Strategy: Techniques for Analyzing Industries and Competitors*. New York: Free Press.

Prahalad, C., and Bettis, R. (1986). The dominant logic: A new linkage between diversity and performance. *Strategic Management Journal*, 7: 485–502.

Rice, R., and Aydin, C. (1991). Attitudes toward new organizational technology: Network proximity as a mechanism for social information processing. *Administrative Science Quarterly*, 36: 219–45.

Scherer, F., and Ross, D. (1990). *Industrial Market Structure and Economic Performance*. Boston: Houghton Mifflin Co.

Schomburg, A., Grimm, C., and Smith, K. (1994). Avoiding new product warfare: The role of industry structure. In P. Shrivastava, A. Huff and J. Dutton (eds), *Advances in Strategic Management*, vol. 10, Part B. Greenwich, CT: JAI Press.

Schumpeter, J. (1934). *The Theory of Economic Development*. Cambridge, MA: Harvard University Press.

Schumpeter, J. (1950). *Capitalism, Socialism and Democracy*. New York: Harper.

Scott, W. (1995). *Institutions and Organizations*. Thousand Oaks, CA: Sage.

Shaw, M. (1981). *Group Dynamics*. New York: McGraw-Hill.

Shull, F., Delbecq, A., and Cummings, L. (1970). *Organizational Decision Making*. New York: McGraw-Hill.

Simon, H. A. (1955). A behavioral model of rational choice. *Quarterly Journal of Economics*, 69: 99–118.

Simons, T., Pelled, L., and Smith, K. A. (2000). Making use of difference: Diversity, debate, and decision comprehensiveness in top management teams. *Academy of Management Journal*, 42: 662–73.

Singh, J., and Lumsden, C. (1990). Theory and research in organizational psychology. *Annual Review of Sociology*, 16: 161–95.

Singh, J., Tucker, D., and House, R. (1986). Organizational legitimacy and the liability of newness. *Administrative Science Quarterly*, 31: 171–93.

Smith, K., Ferrier, W., and Grimm, C. (2001). King of the hill: Dethroning the industry leader. *Academy of Management Executive*.

Smith, K., Gannon, M., Grimm, C., and Mitchell, T. (1988). Decision making behavior in smaller entrepreneurial and larger professionally managed firms. *Journal of Business Venturing*. New York.

Smith, K. G., and Grimm, C. (1991). A communication-information model of competitive response time. *Journal of Management*, 171: 5–34.

Smith, K. G., Grimm, C., and Chen, M., and Gannon, M. (1989). Predictors of response time to competitive strategic actions: Preliminary theory and evidence. *Journal of Business Research*, 183: 245–59.

Smith, K. G., Grimm, C., and Gannon, M. (1992). *Dynamics of Competitive Strategy*. London: Sage Publications.

Smith, K. G., Grimm, C., Gannon, M., and Chen, M. J. (1991). Organizational information processing, competitive responses and performance in the U.S. domestic airline industry. *Academy of Management Journal*, 34: 60–85.

Smith, K. G., Grimm, C., Young., G., and Wally, S. (1997). Strategic groups and rivalrous firm behavior. Towards a reconciliation. *Strategic Management Journal*, 18: 149–57.

Smith, K. G., Guthrie, J., and Chen, M. (1989). Strategy, size and performance. *Organizational Studies*, 10: 63–81.

Smith, K. G., Smith, K. A., Olian, J., Sims, H., O'Bannon, D., and Scully, J. (1994). Top management team demography and process: The role of social integration and communication. *Administrative Science Quarterly*, 39: 412–38.

Smith, K. G., Young, G., Becerra, M., and Grimm, C. (1996). An assessment of the validity of competitive dynamic research. *The Best Paper Proceedings of the Academy of Management*. Cincinnati, OH: 61–5.

Starbuck. W. (1983). Organizations as action generators. *American Sociological Review*, 48: 91–102.

Stinchcombe, A. (1965). Social structure and organizations. In J. March (ed.), *Handbook of Organizations*. Chicago: Rand McNally.

Thompson, J. D. (1967). *Organizations in Action*. New York: McGraw-Hill.

Wagner, J. (1995. Studies of individualism-collectivism: Effects on cooperation in groups. *Academy of Management Journal*, 3: 152–72.

Wasserman, S., and Faust, K. (1994). *Social Network Analysis: Methods and Applications*. New York: Cambridge University Press.

Weber, M. (1946). *Essays in Sociology*. New York: Oxford University Press.

Weber, M. (1964). *The Theory of Social and Economic Organizations*. New York: Free Press.

Weick, K. (1969). *The Social Psychology of Organizations*. Reading, MA: Addison-Wesley.

Weick, K. (1980). The Management of eloquence. *Executive*, 6: 18–22.

Wiersema, M., and Bantel, K. (1992). Top management yeam demography and corporate strategic change. *Academy of Management Journal*, 35: 91–122.

Wernerfelt, B. (1984). A resource-based view of the firm. *Strategic Management Journal*, 5: 171–81.

Wilson, R. (1985). Reputation in games and markets. In A. E. Roth (ed.). *Game-theoretic Models of Bargaining*, 27–62. Cambridge, UK: Cambridge University Press.

Young, G., Smith, K. G., and Grimm, C. (1996). "Austrian' and industrial organization perspectives on firm-level competitive activity and performance. *Organization Science*, 73: 243–54.

Young, G., Smith, K. G., and Grimm, C. (1997). Multimarket contact, resource heterogeneity, and rivalrous firm behavior. *Academy of Management Best Paper Proceedings*.

Young, G., Smith, K. G., Grimm, C., and Simon, D. (2001) Multimarket contact, resource heterogeneity, and rivalrous firm behavior. *The Journal of Management*.

# 12

# Diversification Strategy Research at a Crossroads: Established, Emerging and Anticipated Paths

## Donald D. Bergh

One of the most important strategic decisions facing top executives is forming and managing the product lines of their companies. Known more formally as diversification strategy, managers develop plans that concern which businesses to be in, which to avoid and how to manage the aggregate holdings afterwards. These are highly significant considerations, as they can have long-lasting effects on the composition and prosperity of organizations. In addition, the main tools of diversification strategy implementation – namely acquisitions, internal developments and restructuring – have been a common feature of the corporate landscape for well over 100 years now (Gaughan, 1999). Diversification strategy is one of the most popular and central topics within the field of strategic management.

Efforts to understand diversification strategy have played an instrumental role in the development of the field of strategic management. For example, some of the earliest studies in the field were examinations into diversification strategy (e.g., Chandler, 1962; Rumelt, 1974). Moreover, since those days, research on diversification strategy has literally exploded, as studies into motives, direction, entry mode, diversity status, management of diversity structure, development of control systems, synergies, effects of environments and resources, and of course, overall impact on financial performance have been conducted (Ramanujam and Varadarajan, 1989; see Datta, Rajagopalan, and Rasheed, 1991; Dess et al., 1995, for additional reviews). Further, research on diversification strategy may represent some of the more significant advances in the field of strategic management research, as it has provided an arena for the development of each of the major theoretical perspectives in the field, beginning with the early work on contingency views (Ansoff, 1965; Chandler, 1962) and including the application of industrial organization economics (Porter, 1980), organizational economics (Williamson, 1975), the introduction of the resource-based view (Wernerfelt, 1984) and applications of the upper echelons perspective (Hambrick and Mason, 1984).

When considered collectively, the literature on diversification strategy is one of the oldest, broadest and most consequential to the field of strategic management. This extensive literature provides fascinating questions for further investigation. New perspectives and research designs are emerging, different answers are being provided to old problems, and new questions are being raised that are extending and pushing traditional explanations. Researchers are re-defining and deconstructing central concepts in the literature so to provide a more complete understanding of diversification strategy.

In my view, the literature on diversification strategy has arrived at an important crossroads, and many research paths can be followed. The purpose of this chapter is to discuss these different paths and provide arguments as to what each one holds for advancing theory development. I offer thoughts and ideas on where the literature has come from, where it is currently at, where it may be going and how researchers can contribute to any one of these paths. The chapter starts with a review of the conceptual and theoretical development of diversification strategy. This first path seeks to provide some insights on where the literature has been and how it has evolved. The next two paths build upon that review, providing a discussion of how some current thinking is emerging. With these paths, I focus on topics and theories that represent a rather significant departure from those that are more traditional in the field. Finally, the last path provides some sketches for where fruitful contributions may exist in future research. My overall goal in this chapter is to introduce the reader to the literature on diversification strategy and provide a research agenda that challenges convention and compels new thinking that will enrich our understanding of this critical strategic topic.

## PATH 1: ESTABLISHED PERSPECTIVES ON DIVERSIFICATION STRATEGY

### Development of the diversification strategy concept

Diversification strategy is a complex concept. First, it involves the management of multiple business lines. Pitts and Hopkins observe that "diversification has at its root the word 'diverse,' which means literally 'different; unlike; distinct; separate' " (1982: 620). They indicate that diversification strategy involves the management of business operations in several different businesses simultaneously. Second, it includes diversification moves, or entries into product-market activities that extend an organization into new business activities. Note that simple product line extensions that are not accompanied by changes in administrative mechanisms do not fall under the conceptualization of diversification (Ramanujam and Varadarajan, 1989; Rumelt, 1974). Viewed from this light, diversification strategy pertains to the scope of the firm in terms of the industries and markets in which it competes (Grant, 1998), and how managers buy, create and sell different businesses to match skills and strengths with opportunities presented to the firm (see Ramanujam and Varadarajan (1989), for a review of popular definitions of diversification).

Development of the diversification strategy concept has produced one of the main pillars of strategic management research. Management scholars began serious study of diversification strategy in the late 1950s and early 1960s, with Ansoff (1957, 1958) and Chandler (1962), the historian, leading the way. Wrigley (1970) built from these early works, providing an initial framework for describing and defining diversification strategy. He suggested that there were two critical factors that combine to determine diversification strategy. First, the unit of analysis is discrete product-market activities, a logic that refers to strategic relationships within the diversified organization. This focus was different than the conventional industrial organizational (IO) economic approach that focused upon the spread of a company's activities across SIC industries (Keats, 1990), where strategy would refer to the count of industries in which a firm owned businesses.

Second, Wrigley applied the term *specialization ratio* (SR) to represent the proportion of a firm's annual revenues that were attributable to its largest product-market activity. He used this term as a measure of the "firm's commitment to diversity," enabling discrimination between different companies that operate in the same industies yet receive varying amounts of revenues from those industries. Applying these factors, Wrigley identified four different types of diversification strategies: (1) the single product firm has an SR of between 0.95 and 1.0; (2) the dominant product firm has an SR between 0.70 and 0.95; (3) the related product firm has an SR less than 0.70 which has diversified by adding activities that have a tangible relationship with the collective skills and strengths of the diversifying firm; (4) the unrelated product firm is one whose business activities are not related to the original skills and strengths – other than financial – of the firm.

Rumelt (1974) noted several limitations in Wrigley's categories, and he developed his own classification system to overcome them. In essence, he combined Wrigley's specialization ratio with two other ratios, the *related ratio* (RR) – was the proportion of a firm's revenues attributable to its largest group of related businesses – and the *vertical ratio* (VR) – proportion of a firm's revenues that arise from all products of a vertically integrated sequence of processing activities. These concepts were used to identify ten different strategy types, most of which are refinements of Wrigley's original categories (Rumelt, 1974; see Grant and Jammine, 1988, for a comparison of the Rumelt and Wrigley approaches).

In short, Rumelt's categorization scheme defined the single business or single vertical organization that has a SR of 95 percent or more. Four different dominant business types (vertical, constrained, linked, unrelated) were identified. The dominant-vertical business received 70 percent or more of its sales from vertically related product markets. Each of the other three dominant business types had an SR of 70–95 percent, and the differences between each depended on relationships among the businesses within the overall organization. There were two related business types (constrained, linked). The related-constrained business had an SR less than 70 percent and 70 percent and higher of the businesses were related to each other. The related-linked business types have SRs less than 70 percent and RRs greater than 70 percent. The distinctions between these two types depend on relationships of the other businesses to each other. Finally, the multibusiness and unrelated business types have SRs and RRs of less than 70 percent each (see Rumelt, 1974: 11–32; Montgomery, 1982: 301). Considered collectively, Rumelt's categorization system characterizes the extent and types of diversification strategies (Varadarajan and Ramanujam, 1987), and helped capture the strategy guiding diversification.

The main ingredients of the diversification strategy concept have not changed much since Rumelt's work. Although many measures of diversification strategy exist, most of which are continuous in nature (i.e., the number of industries a firm has diversified into) rather than categorical like Rumelt's, the view of diversification strategy offered by Rumelt seems to have persevered as something of a gold standard of sorts, leading some to observe that it has "dominated subsequent diversification research in the strategic management literature" (Keats, 1990: 62). However, there are three areas of developing inquiry that may extend the current description of diversification strategy.

First, researchers are re-thinking the meaning of relatedness. Such research is potentially very important because relatedness is the cornerstone of the definition and measurement of diversification strategy (see Robins and Wiersema, 1995). To date, that research has begun to unpack the relatedness concept, suggesting that traditional depictions are overly general and may be incomplete because they do not account for assets and resource differences of related businesses (see Farjoun, 1998; Harrison, Hall, and Nargundkar, 1993; Markides and Williamson, 1994, 1996; Stimpert and Duhaime, 1997). These arguments direct attention to the unit of analysis in Rumelt's conception of diversification strategy; the strategic relationship may be more specific than presented and may take different forms depending on the type of relatedness within that relationship (e.g., product relatedness, market relatedness, R&D relatedness, strategic relatedness, etc.). By recognizing that relatedness can vary, then how we conceive strategic relationships may also vary, leading to different types of diversification strategy, some of which may fall outside the boundaries of the Rumelt approach. It would appear that a new conception of diversification strategy is going to emerge sometime in the near future, at least one that focuses on interrelationships using a revised depiction of relatedness (Robins and Wiersema, 1995).

Second, research into international diversification strategy may add a new dimension to the diversification strategy concept. International diversification strategy includes the traditional product markets, but also entails the number and relative importance of the different markets in which a diversified firm operates (Hitt, Hoskisson, and Kim, 1997). International diversification is treated as different than product diversification (Geringer, Beamish, and daCosta, 1989; Hoskisson and Hitt, 1994), but combinations of the two are frequently considered simultaneously (Hitt, Hoskisson, and Ireland, 1994; Kim, Hwang, and Burgers, 1988; Tallman and Li, 1996). However, this union provides a potential extension to diversification when it involves different product lines than those in the domestic markets. Consequently, to the degree that international diversification falls outside the pillars of the specialization ratio, relatedness ratio and vertical ratio, it may represent a new dimension of diversification strategy, and as a result, require a broadening of the concept and measurement schemes.

Finally, researchers are testing the ways in which diversification strategy is measured. This line of research contrasts different measures of diversification with each other, usually with the intention of demonstrating construct validation. These efforts have a long history (Montgomery, 1982; Varadarajan and Ramanujam, 1987) and feature a variety of validation techniques, ranging from comparisons and univariate tests of differences in diversification approaches (Hall and St. John, 1994; Lubatkin, Merchant, and Srinivasan, 1993) to more sophisticated analytical approaches which test for multivariate relationships among those measures (Hoskisson et al., 1993). In general, these studies find some overlap in the alternative measures, but that those measures still explain some unique parts as well. Such results suggest that the concept of diversification strategy is more expansive than earlier conceived. Put more simply, efforts to validate the measurement of diversification strategy suggest that it may be more multi-faceted than Rumelt proposed. Future work that integrates the dimensions of diversification strategy that are represented by the alternative measures would represent an extension of our current depiction of the diversification strategy concept.

Regardless of how these three newer streams of inquiry evolve, the prior development of the diversification strategy concept has occurred in parallel with advancements in explanations of its antecedents and outcomes (see Hoskisson and Hitt, 1990; Dess et al., 1995, and Montgomery, 1994, for reviews). Indeed, efforts to create and develop theoretical explanations of diversification strategy have been a predominant feature of the strategic management literature (Hoskisson et al., 1999; Ramanujam and Varadarajan, 1989).

## Theoretical development of diversification strategy

Perhaps the most enduring theme in diversification strategy research is the effort to explain the effects of diversification strategy on financial performance. This theme seems to have emerged as the centerpiece of the literature on diversification strategy (see Datta, Rajagopalon, and Rasheed, 1991; Palich, Cardinal, and Miller, 2000, for reviews), and it provides a fertile source of theories that apply to diversification strategy. Indeed, some of the more popular theoretical perspectives in the literature can be traced to the diversification strategy-performance studies.

Historically, three theoretical perspectives in particular appear to represent the most application to diversification strategy.[1] First, during the late 1970s through the 1980s, the structure-conduct-performance paradigm of IO economics was very popular in strategic management research. It is not surprising, then, that some of the initial explanations of diversification strategy borrowed from the IO economics literature. One of the more early of such applications can be traced to Cynthia Montgomery's (1979) dissertation, where she tested whether industry structure and performance influenced Rumelt's empirical findings. Shortly thereafter, Bettis and Hall (1982) observed that Rumelt's findings of the superiority of one strategy type (related-constrained business types) could be attributed to an over-representation of a particularly profitable industry within Rumelt's sample. Christensen and Montgomery (1981) suggested that differences in market structures across the firms in the different diversification strategy categories, rather than the categories themselves, may have been responsible for the performance differences reported by Rumelt (Varadarajan and Ramanujam, 1987: 381).

Continuing with this line of inquiry, Montgomery (1985) controlled for industry structure facets (market share and industry profitability) and found that diversification did not have an effect on financial performance. More recently, evidence suggests that industry performance may actually precede diversification strategy, than vice versa, as suggested by some. Stimpert and Duhaime (1997) observed that low industry profitability would lead to extensive diversification. Considered collectively, these findings provide rather consistent evidence that industry structure and profitability have an influence on diversification strategy (note that the evidence on the diversification strategy-performance relationship is much less clear). The bottom line is that the guiding predictions from IO economics played a strong role in the early developments of theoretical explanations of diversification strategy (see Hoskisson and Hitt, 1990, for additional review).

Second, the resource-based perspective (RBV) of the firm has also been used to explain diversification strategy. This approach directs attention away from product-market actors, such as competitors, buyers, suppliers and so forth, to resource factors, such as land, labor, capital, technology and entrepreneuship. The RBV perspective was developed by Penrose (1959) and introduced to the strategic management literature by Wernerfelt (1984). It has been applied to diversification strategy in six general ways (Mahoney and Pandian, 1992, address the first four in depth).

First, the RBV provides an explanation of limits to the growth of the firm, suggesting that resources of the firm may bound the markets entered and limit the ability to produce and fund production and investments, and that managerial capabilities to manage growth effectively are constrained (Wernerfelt, 1989). Second, the RBV explains motivations for diversification, such as utilizing excess capacity and unused productive services to fuel growth (Penrose, 1959). Third, the RBV provides a rationale for predicting the direction of diversification. The types of resources available to the firm have been shown to influence whether the firm pursues related or unrelated diversification (Chatterjee and Wernerfelt, 1991; Montgomery and Hariharan, 1991). Fourth, the RBV provides an explanation of the diversification strategy and performance relationship, namely that the resources associated with particular strategy types will be related to financial performance, and that firm-specific resources will lead to higher performance than general resources, and that resources lose value when transferred across dissimilar markets (Montgomery and Wernerfelt, 1988; Wernerfelt and Montgomery, 1988).

Fifth, the RBV offers insights into interrelationships at the portfolio level, and how such linkages can be used to explain financial performance. Robins and Wiersema (1995) show how the RBV overcomes problems inherent in the IO view both conceptually and empirically for explaining the relationship between diversification strategy and performance. Finally, the RBV may provide insights into the efficient management of diversification strategy. A recent study by Markides and Williamson (1996) provides a compelling argument for how resources and strategic relatedness affects the strategy-organization structure relationship.

Finally, transaction cost economics provides an explanation of the internal management of diversification strategy. In essence, this perspective suggests that in order for diversified firms to survive, then they need to organize and run themselves in such ways that reduce their overall organization costs to points below the costs of using alternative methods of conducting business transactions (Dundas and Richardson, 1980, 1982; Teece, 1982; Williamson, 1975, 1985). Such logic builds from Chandler's (1962) observations that strategy and structure need to be aligned closely for the diversified firm to operate efficiently. Such structures can take several different forms, providing alternatives for each of the different types of diversification strategies. These structures generally operate with the intention of realizing efficiency through one of three general control systems: strategic, financial or hybrid (Hill, Hitt, and Hoskisson, 1992; see also Hoskisson, Hill, and Kim, 1993).

The strategic form of control emphasizes cooperation, coordination, cohesion and close working relationships. We find such control systems in vertically related businesses, and those with very little, if any, product diversification. These systems are very expensive to manage, yet provide the closest and most detailed assessment of control (Hill and Hoskisson, 1987). The financial form of control offers a stark contrast to that of the strategic form, as this mode focuses on competition to realize efficiency. This approach, which has Williamson's M-form system at its roots (Williamson, 1975), organizes business lines into profit centers, each of which is accountable for its own performance. These profit centers provide the headquarters of the diversified firm with their total revenues (no pre-emptive claims are permitted). The performance of each center is evaluated using strict financial measures (such as return on assets, market share, etc.), and resources are redistributed back to the centers on the basis of relative performance of each. These methods are not expensive to manage, as all assessments are based on simple monitoring of financial statements, and measures are commonly known to all parties and can be used to compare unrelated business lines (such as market share, return on assets, etc.). We find such systems being used in the more highly diversified business organizations.

The hybrid system combines features of the strategic and financial control types, and conceivably could integrate parts of each system, such as the detailed understanding and cooperation of the strategic system with the internal cost discipline of the financial one.[2]

Theoretically, these hybrid systems would seem to best match firms having moderate levels of diversification. In principle, the strategic controls could be used for managing the business lines that share resources or common assets and are known by the managers of the headquarters. The financial controls would be applied to those lines that are unrelated to the other business lines and unknown by the HQ's managers. However, although such logic seems sensible, it is difficult to apply, as the strategic and financial systems are believed to be mutually incompatible with each other. The benefits of each system are offset by the benefits of the other; the advantages of the strategic system – sharing and cooperation – are canceled by the competitive pressures of the financial system, and vice versa, creating inefficient control of diversification strategy. Thus, it is not surprising that the firms most likely to employ hybrid systems tend to restructure (Hoskisson and Johnson, 1992), especially when faced with environmental uncertainty (Bergh and Lawless, 1998). The interested reader should see Hill, Hitt, and Hoskisson (1992) for more development of these arguments.

In sum, these three perspectives – IO economics, the RBV of the firm and transaction cost economics – represent only three frameworks that have been applied to diversification strategy. They are discussed here because they tend to represent some of the more dominant viewpoints and because they are comparatively well developed within the literature. But, at the same time, research into diversification strategy continues and new topics and explanations are receiving attention. This research can be considered in our second path.

## Path 2: Emerging Topics of Research Developments

Recent investigation into diversification strategy has, of course, developed along several fronts. We see research continuing into the founding subjects of the field, such as diversification and performance, as well as into relatively new topics. For example, a perusal of the *Strategic Management Journal* shows that research into areas such as mode of entry, configurations, cognitive maps, strategic groups and dominant logic is increasing. However, while those research subjects are emerging as important ones in the field, there are two subjects – multi-market competition and limits to growth – which may become increasingly important because they represent some of the consequences of the increase in diversification activities over the last ten years. Specifically, diversification actions, particularly mergers and acquisitions, have been at record levels since about the mid-1990s with each successive year producing yet higher volume and gross dollar value. This evidence suggests that managers will have to address new problems, particularly how to compete with other diversified firms and whether there are limits in growth.

## Multi-market competition

With the ever-increasing number of acquisitions, and a sustained level of diversification (Montgomery, 1994), companies may find themselves competing against common rivals in multiple product lines simultaneously. Now, more than ever, the level of strategic competition is expanding from the single-business/single-industry level to the multi-business/multi-industry level. This broader level becomes an important consideration for diversification strategy, as shared rivals across multiple markets stand to influence the motives and outcomes of diversification strategies.

Such issues lie at the heart of what has become known as multi-market competition, which refers to competition among the same firms operating in multiple common markets. When firms share markets, then they may develop an interdependence with each other (Areeda and Turner, 1979). The managers recognize these linkages, assess the potential of competitive interactions and tailor strategies accordingly. It is important to recognize that these interdependencies can be conceived at several different levels, ranging from market to market, firm to firm, and relationship to relationship (Barnett, 1993; Baum and Korn, 1996; Chen, 1996).

This point on competitive interactions has been a point of interest to academics, managers and anti-trust courts. In particular, some managers may hesitate to contest a particular market vigorously because the prospect of an advantage in one market may prompt responses in other markets by other competitors (Baum and Korn, 1996; Edwards, 1955). This phenomenon, known as the mutual forbearance hypothesis, occurs because "competitors interacting in multiple markets would be less motivated to compete aggressively in a market because of their awareness of the possibility of retaliation across various markets" (Chen, 1996: 112). Researchers have modeled such practices, formally showing that multiple contact across markets plays a role in determining competitiveness in a particular industry and that firms may cooperate and collude, which lowers rivalry and pressures for competitive equilibrium, and tacit coordination becomes possible (Bernheim and Whinston, 1990).

The theoretical developments on multi-market contact have direct application to diversification strategy. For example, the motives for diversification strategy might be influenced by mutual forbearance. Entering a market or new industry might represent a threat to incumbents, who in response, may present a countering move in an industry the new entrant presently occupies. Such threats serve to shape diversification strategies, as companies might enter industries whose competitors are likely to pose the least amount of resistance to their base industries. These dynamics suggest that the motives for entering markets might be influenced by rivals that share common markets.

Once companies have entered industries and/or multiple markets and now have common rivals, multi-point competition provides explanations for how they are likely to interact with each other. Chen's (1996) model of market commonality and resource similarity provides a framework for considering how diversified firms might attack and defend against each other. Companies that have higher degrees of market commonality and resource similarity are less likely to initiate attacks against each other, as the attacker is likely to respond very vigorously. This logic suggests that diversified companies may be directed (and limited) to specific segments of their markets by the potential responses of their shared competitors. Diversification strategies are likely to reflect these competitive pressures.

It also follows that the outcomes of diversification strategies are affected by multi-market competition. With competitors staking out "spheres of influence" within their industries and posing threats of retaliation in markets of overlap (Gimeno, 1999), the profitability potential of a company's diversification strategy would be limited to the economics of the segments in which it resides. Although economies of scope may offset some pressures due to mutual forbearance (Gimeno and Woo, 1999), the likelihood of dynamic relationships among shared rivals is likely to constrain where firms are able to go within their markets and, as such, what revenues they can compete for (Baum and Korn, 1996).

In summary, the advances in multi-market competition have received little application to diversification strategy. Frankly, we know very little about how multi-market competition influences the formulation, implementation and outcomes of diversification strategy. Although our understanding of multi-market competition is expanding rapidly, and our knowledge of diversification strategy is approaching a more mature level, researchers have not put these two literatures together. By applying multi-market competition to diversification strategy, several new research avenues can be suggested.

## *Limits to growth*

During the 1960s and 1970s, many firms diversified into unrelated businesses by making conglomerate acquisitions. These firms became unusually large, and in the case of some, owned over 500 different business lines. Shortly afterwards, during the 1980s and early 1990s, many of those highly diversified businesses were reorganized, using refocusing actions to reduce diversification and size and return them to a more focused strategy type (see Johnson, 1996, for a review of this literature; see evidence in Williams, Paez, and Sanders, 1988, and in Montgomery, 1994).

Explanations for this reversal of firm growth tend to rely mostly on efficiency arguments, as it is commonly argued that the diversification actions in the 1960s and 1970s had made firms so unwieldy that they could not be managed economically. Whether by mistake, poor strategy and/or breakdowns in governance (Hoskisson and Hitt, 1994; Hoskisson and Turk, 1990), it is argued that managers had diversified their firms beyond the managers' abilities to manage them efficiently. This logic builds from Williamson (1985), who argues that firms and markets are governance alternatives to each other, and that when firms grow too large, then they lose their comparative efficiency advantages and transactions are transferred into the more efficient market mode of governance. Jones and Hill (1988) place these arguments in the context of comparing internal costs and benefits of diversification, showing that the costs and benefits of internalizing additional business lines have an equilibrium point, beyond which the firm cannot manage additional lines and size efficiently. This equilibrium point represents an upper threshold to a firm's efficiency relative to the market.

Ollinger (1994) extends this logic to show that the transferability of firm-specific skills and the efficiency of internal governance systems limit firm growth (in terms of scope). Moreover, highly diversified firms that are subsequently refocused tend to receive short-term financial gains from the stock market; Markides (1992) shows that investors react positively when managers of highly diversified companies trim unrelated businesses, suggesting that reducing diversification and firm size in such firms creates economic value. Finally, this upper boundary to growth appears to be influenced by environmental uncertainty. Increases in environmental uncertainty raise the demands and difficulties of managing a diversified firm, and in essence, create internal costs that in turn lower the ceiling of how large a firm can become (Jones and Hill, 1988). Decreases in uncertainty lower the demands and complexities of managing the firm, lower the internal costs of managing diversification and thereby raise the ceiling of firm growth (Bergh, 1998; Bergh and Lawless, 1998).

This efficiency-oriented logic represents the dominant explanation of limits to firm growth. However, there are some compelling observations that raise questions about the application of its arguments. First, the historical trends of refocusing in the 1980s and early 1990s have been reversed in some cases and in other instances, companies have began growing again by acquiring suppliers, competitors and organizations that extend them into new markets. Indeed, some companies have achieved even larger growth more by acquiring competitors than they ever had by acquiring unrelated businesses.

Second, the argument that highly diversified firms in the 1980s were inefficient due to internal cost diseconomies is inconsistent with current acquisition strategies. Specifically, the type of control systems needed to manage the current predominant related-type acquisitions – strategic controls – are actually more expensive to manage internally than the control systems used to manage the relationships of the highly diversified firms in the 1980s. As noted above, the costs of managing a financial relationship, which is the primary exchange in a financial system, are substantially lower than the costs of managing a strategic relationship, which is the predominant relationship in the strategic system of control (Hill, Hitt, and Hoskisson, 1992; Hill and Hoskisson, 1987). When combined, these observations suggest that the internal costs and respective benefits of managing diversified firms may not have driven the refocusing. If internal costs and control problems led to a limit in size and were responsible for the restructuring of the firms in the 1980s, then why have so many of those same firms added so significantly to their internal costs by making new acquisitions and by implementing strategic control systems?

It appears that additional research is needed to explain limits to firm growth. Inquiry into factors that moderate or mediate the economic explanations is needed. For example, building on Bergh and Lawless's (1998) findings that environmental uncertainty moderates firm growth, then what other factors are relevant? One possibility for other explanations may come from non-efficiency driven perspectives. For example, Davis, Diekmann, and Tinsley (1994) found that restructuring in the 1980s was correlated with institutional pressures to downsize. They suggest that reversals of firm growth may be associated with an effort by managers to imitate what they see as trends in their environments. This type of research, especially when combined or tested against the predominant efficiency perspectives, may yield a comprehensive treatment of limits to firm growth. Regardless of form, it is important that we investigate firm growth boundaries more fully, as the binge acquiring raises questions about how long such strategies can continue.

## PATH 3: EMERGING PERSPECTIVES ON DIVERSIFICATION STRATEGY

Our explanations of diversification strategy have tended to focus on efficiency and economic factors (see Dess et al., 1995; Hoskisson and Hitt, 1990; Montgomery, 1994). However, some non-economic views are beginning to receive application to diversification strategy. Two in particular offer great promise for future research, namely the organizational learning and upper echelons perspectives. These viewpoints raise new questions for diversification strategy and offer insights into long-standing questions and problems that have evaded the traditional economic perspectives which have guided most prior theoretical work. Of course, there are other theoretical perspectives that could be applied here too; however, these two seem to be gaining momentum in their application and as such, warrant especially close attention.

### Organization learning

The organizational learning perspective (OLP) suggests that an organization and its actions reflect prior decisions and experiences (Fiol and Lyles, 1985; Huber, 1991). The underlying premise is that experience influences learning, which in turn, affects future actions. Experience plays a central element in the organizational learning perspective, and attention focuses on how organizations learn and the impediments to and applications of learning (cf. Herriot, Leventhal, and March, 1985). The OLP is predicated on the assumption that organizations evolve as they accumulate experience, adjust reactions to similar problems and absorb feedback about past decisions (Pennings, Barkema, and Douma, 1994). The learning aspect of this progression is linked to the cumulative experiences of the organizations (Chang, 1995). Learning takes place as organizations engage in actions, and occurs in a discontinuous and nonlinear manner (March, 1988; March, Sproull, and Tamuz, 1991).

The quality of the learning is contingent upon several key dimensions. First, the degree of environmental diversity affects an organization's background of experiences. Organizations that operate "in diverse environments increase the variety of events and ideas to which a firm is exposed, leading to a more extensive knowledge base and stronger technological capabilities" (Barkema and Vermeulen, 1998: 7). Conversely, organizations that stay within one industry have a limited range of challenges and, as a consequence, learn less and are more likely to experience blind spots and holes in knowledge structures (Walsh, 1995). In other words, diversity improves opportunities to learn, creating alternative opportunities for learning and capability building. Second, the frequency of actions influences familiarity with the antecedents, processes and outcomes of the acquisitions. Such familiarity affects how managers understand the actions and whether they can leverage past and current experiences for future actions. Finally, learning is bounded, as constraints exist to information sharing within an organization (Barkema and Vermeulen, 1998). Limits to managerial and corporate dispositions affect the interpretation of experiences and the type of actions available and conceivable to managers (Pennings, Barkema, and Douma, 1994).

Considered collectively, the organizational learning perspective provides a basis for predicting outcomes. Learning from prior exposures provides a foundation for success. Successful ventures are those most likely to draw upon prior experiences (competencies) while less successful ventures are those that stray from prior experiences.

This logic applies well for understanding diversification strategy. Prior and ongoing diversification actions will shape the organization's overall knowledge and experience base. Organizations that have engaged in more broader diversification strategies, such as those encompassing multinational and multi-product actions, will have a richer knowledge base for future strategies than those that remained focused within a particular industry or product genre (Hitt, Hoskisson, and Kim, 1997). With more diverse prior experiences, the multinational and multi-product organization learns more about how to manage the diversification process effectively. Feedback from prior ventures, especially those that are different from prior efforts, contribute the most to learning. In addition, organizations that have diversified with higher frequency will develop a cumulative skill-base that can be applied to future diversification strategies. Viewed from this light, prior experience with diversification would increase the odds of success at a later point in time, as the learning from prior endeavors could be stored and applied in the future. Of course, such learning would be constrained by the willingness and capabilities of managers to share information with each other and to learn from past strategies.

This logic helps explain the outcomes of diversification strategy. If managers learn from prior ventures in the diversification process, then prior experience with diversification should create a knowledge basis they can use for future decisions. Firms that expand along avenues already known should perform better than firms that expand into areas they do not know as well. Organizations that expand along avenues (industries, product lines) in which their managers already have experience will have a better idea of the key success factors and competencies that are needed to compete effectively than when they expand into unknown venues or products. Expansions, whether by acquisition or internal development, should be most beneficial if they are relatively proximate to a firm's skill base, derived from its past experiences. In general, then, diversification outcome success can be viewed as the degree to which new expansions (either by acquisition or by innovation) relate to the content of a firm's core skills; the more remote the expansion, the more shallow the firm's experience basis from which to draw. (This logic draws from Barkema and Vermeulen, 1999; Chang, 1995; and Pennings, Barkema, and Douma, 1994. Note that Haleblian and Finkelstein, 1998, use similar arguments for explaining acquisition performance, a different level of analysis than our current focus on diversification strategy.)

The foregoing reasoning provides insights into long-standing questions as well as raises new hypotheses. First, it suggests a new perspective for understanding why related types of acquisitions – such as those involving competitors and suppliers – tend to have higher performance outcomes than unrelated types (those involving businesses having only a financial relationship with the diversifying firm). Second, it provides a foundation for new research questions that promise to challenge current thinking on and about diversification strategy. Drawing from Barkema and Vermeulen (1998) and Pennings, Barkema, and Douma (1994) we see these questions arising: what are the comparative advantages of domestic versus foreign expansions? When is it better to acquire existing firms or start from scratch? Is majority or minority ownership more profitable? How do track records of prior diversification strategy influence later strategies? How does the contextual effects of multinational diversity, product diversity and relatedness matter? Finally, the similar findings of the learning perspective for diversification and acquisition strategy suggest that learning may provide a broad template for explaining corporate strategy and key strategic processes and interrelationships. Such a template would provide a powerful contribution to our developing explanations of diversification strategy and its effects on performance. In addition, it provides an accessible, logical and intuitive theoretical counterpart to the other explanations that exist within the field.

## Upper echelons perspective

Hambrick and Mason's (1984) conception of the upper echelons perspective (UEP) links top executives to corporate actions. It suggests that organizations are a reflection of powerful actors in the organization; that is, leaders make decisions that reflect their own perspectives, which in turn, shape organizations in ways that resemble their views on risk, strategy, culture and so on. An underlying premise is that managers "matter" and that a linkage exists between the upper echelon of an organization and its ultimate form and performance.

The UEP is based on the logic that the backgrounds and experiences of executives in the top management team are believed to affect interactions and decision making within the team and how they approach the management and outcomes of their companies. This relationship is based on the premise that the biases, information filters and managerial processes that influence executive decisions are unobserveable, but can be understood through executives' demographic characteristics (Pfeffer, 1983). Those traits reflect dispositional and situational factors that affect executives' behaviors (cf. Finkelstein and Hambrick, 1990; Hambrick and Mason, 1984). In essence, it is argued that factors such as age, education, functional background, tenure and size of top management teams provide proxies for strategic behaviors. Researchers have focused on both the average and heterogeneity of these factors, linking them to such behaviors as risk, competitive interactions and innovation (see Finkelstein and Hambrick, 1996, for a thorough review of this literature). For example, it is argued that executive teams having longer relative tenure within the organization and industry are more likely to experience a commitment to the status quo than executive teams having shorter relative tenure (Hambrick, Geletkanycz, and Fredrickson, 1993). The longer tenured teams are more likely to remain fixed to a course of action and less likely to change strategies than their shorter tenured counterparts.

These arguments have been used to explain diversification strategy. For instance, Michel and Hambrick (1992) related demographic features of top management teams to four of Rumelt's diversification strategy categories. They argued that the interdependencies of the businesses in a firm's diversification strategy place demands upon the social cohesion and knowledge base among members of the top management team. Some strategy types have low interdependencies, such as unrelated businesses, and require little social cohesion or knowledge base among top management teams. However, other strategy types have higher interdependencies, such as vertically integrated businesses, and demand high cohesion and knowledge base of the top management team. Wiersema and Bantel (1992) argued that demographic characteristics reflect diversity of information sources and creativity in decision making, both of which will influence corporate strategic change. Finkelstein and Hambrick (1996) build on these two studies, offering several propositions linking top management team heterogeneity and size with interdependence of diversification posture (strategy type). Considered collectively, these studies suggest an association between the top management team and diversification strategy.

These foregoing arguments present several interesting avenues for further research. It has long been implied that managers "matter" when it comes to diversification – several theories for diversification focus on the self-interests of the managers – so it seems quite apparent that the top management team will have an association of some sort with diversification strategy. Three such avenues seem most apparent for investigation.

First, research into the relationship between top management teams and performance of diversification strategy needs more study. This research may want to start with the enduring argument in strategic management and finance that higher risk usually merits higher performance. If top management teams, on the basis of their composition, have a proclivity toward or away from risks, then predictions about the performance of their diversification strategies can be made. In particular, it would seem that top management teams with low average organizational tenure would be more likely to break from the strategic status quo and follow a risky strategy. Such teams would more likely have higher performing diversification strategy than those teams that have high average organizational tenure and are more wedded to an unchanging strategy, and one that avoids risky strategic actions.

Second, inquiry into the dynamics of the team decision-making process and strategic implementation is sorely needed. Such research appears to build closely upon recent theoretical developments. Prior research has linked the heterogeneity of the top management team with the degree of consensus and conflict the team realizes during decision making; more diverse teams are believed to challenge convention and arrive at better decisions than less diverse ones (see Finkelstein and Hambrick, 1996; Hambrick, Cho, and Chen, 1996). This finding provides a basis for linking the top management team with the implementation of the diversification strategy. Diverse teams would have more successful implementation efforts than non-diverse teams because they are more willing to challenge each other, push for creative solutions and innovate, each of which are needed when implementing diversification strategy.

A final avenue for future research into diversification strategy research arises, ironically, by way of recent criticisms of the UEP's focus on demographic factors. For instance, the focus on demographic characteristics fails to provide a direct measurement of cognitive and social processes of and within top management teams. However, the rationale supporting the demographic proxies has recently come under attack; methodological and data availability problems no longer make demographic characteristics the only or preferable ways to measure cognitions and processes of the team (Reger, 1997). Indeed, Smith et al. (1994: 432) observed that "relationships between team demography, team process, and organizational performance are not as straightforward or as simple as scholars have previously believed." These criticisms of the demographic positions suggest that future research into direct measures of cognitive diversity and interrelationships within teams may provide new insights into the UEP. Such developments may revise prior explanations of, as well as suggest new questions for, the relationship between the top management team and diversification strategy.

## PATH 4: ANTICIPATED PERSPECTIVES ON DIVERSIFICATION STRATEGY

Throughout this chapter, it has been observed that research into established and emerging topics and perspectives offer ways for enhancing our understanding of diversification strategy. In this last path, I provide some thoughts on how future research may develop. In essence, I propose that future research will continue along four different avenues. Some have been discussed above and will be expanded upon here; others are new. Each offers promise.

First, evaluations of how diversification strategy has been conducted, such as meta-analyses, will likely continue, as researchers attempt to untangle conflicting results that characterize much prior research (see Palich, Cardinal, and Miller, 2000). Included in this research are likely to be evaluations of how decisions on research designs, construct validations and analytical strategies may influence results. For example, variability in research designs and analytical decisions can lead to variation in empirical results and lead to different conclusions for theory development (Bergh, 1995; Bergh and Holbein, 1997). Bergh (1995) found that the relationship between diversification strategy and performance depended on whether the study design was cross-sectional (data were collected for one time period only) or longitudinal (data gathered over multiple time periods), and whether the empirical relationship was viewed as static or changeable. Such research may help reconcile conflicting and controversial results in the field, focusing attention to whether designs were cross-sectional or longitudinal, and how aspects of the study were measured. In addition, the application of more sophisticated analytical techniques may allow subjects to be examined with more power or differently, raising potentially new insights into diversification strategy (Hitt, Gimeno, and Hoskisson, 1998).

This research may also continue to challenge conventional arguments and premises, so to see if and when they may hold. Lubatkin and Chatterjee (1994), who tested the link between risk, diversification strategy and performance conducted an example of such research. They challenged the "three legged stool" argument that risk is best minimized through acquiring companies whose revenue fluctuations appear to offset each other (i.e., the adage, "do not have your eggs in the same basket, but have them in different baskets"). The argument of diversifying risk through having portfolios of unrelated businesses was found not to produce the lowest risk. Lubatkin and Chatterjee (1994) uncovered evidence that risk is best minimized through a mid-range level of diversification, as opposed to a high level. They concluded that having all of one's eggs in similar baskets – not in the same or different ones – is the best way to lower risk. Such a conclusion challenged the conventional wisdom.

Second, another way to extend our knowledge is by applying traditional theoretical perspectives to relatively new topics. Several examples of this particular approach are evident in the above reviews. Consider the work by Gimeno and Woo (1999) who applied the concept of economies of scope to help explain multi-market contact. Similarly, Hitt, Hoskisson, and Kim (1997) use the resource-based view of the firm to help explain international diversification strategy. They also adapt a traditional measure of diversification strategy – the entropy measure – to account for international diversification. This research provides the opportunity for building and further developing theoretical explanations. For example, by applying transaction cost economics to such subjects as vertical integration, internal organization and limits to firm growth, we are able to explain these topics from an efficiency basis, that at least to some degree, managers appear to be motivated by efficiency when growing, organizing and managing the boundaries of their firms. By expanding traditional theoretical perspectives into new topics, we advance explanations in an incremental way that serves as the foundation for strengthening current views as well as opening up new research vistas.

A third opportunity is opposite the second: to apply emerging perspectives to established topics. This type of research provides two very interesting ways for researchers to expand understanding of diversification strategy.

On one front, investigators raise and answer new questions about relatively well-researched topics, while on the other, they can offer new insights into the subject itself. Consider, for example, an application of the upper echelon perspective to the relationship between diversification strategy and risk. The upper echelon perspective suggests that a firm's strategy is a reflection of its top executive team. This would suggest that variations in diversification strategy would be associated with variation in top executive teams. We might argue that less risky diversification strategies, such as those with moderate levels of diversity (Lubatkin and Chatterjee, 1994) would be associated with top executives teams that prefer lower rather than higher risk levels. From a demographic perspective, such executive teams would likely be those with high average ages, as age is generally related negatively to risk and innovation (the older we are, the less risky we become in our decisions). This argument highlights two potential contributions: first we see the introduction of new questions in the relationship (does diversification strategy and risk depend on top executive perspectives toward risk?), questions which represent extensions to theory development. The second contribution is new insights into the topic: executives make decisions that drive diversification strategy and as such, represent important actors in the research stream.

In addition, a variant of this third approach is possible through combining emerging topics and established research questions. For instance, the application of multi-point competition or limits to firm growth to diversification strategy raises several new questions, each of which represent extensions to the topics and research on diversification strategy.

Finally, and perhaps most fascinating, is the application of emerging perspectives to emerging topics. These combinations unite the latest theorizing with the most recent subjects, the product of which raises potentially new extensions for the explanation and for the topic itself. For instance, does the upper echelon perspective offer new insights into multi-market competition? Most depictions of multi-market competition focus on efficiency and equilibrium; however, it is conceivable that the types of reactions, provocations and the arenas of competition would be influenced by predispositions of the top executives.

Indeed, it is hard to imagine that the risk propensities of the top executives would not influence how the firm interacts competitively with others; decisions on how far to push, where and when are probably not all influenced by considerations of efficiency and equilibrium, and may instead be affected by psychological filters, biases and preferences. It would seem that a research effort that uses the upper echelons perspective to explain multi-market competition would have the potential for making a significant contribution, both to the perspective and the topic itself.

The same expectations can be levied against applications of the organizational learning perspective with multi-market competition or limits to firm growth. It seems likely that the downsizing and downscoping of the 1980s (Hoskisson and Hitt, 1994) would produce lessons that would influence diversification strategies in the 1990s and beyond. Considering the alternative – that managers did not learn from those times – seems strained and suggests that firms will repeat the same mistakes is not persuasive for the majority of healthy and successful companies. The bottom line is that by combining new perspectives, such as the upper echelon perspective or organizational learning, with new research subjects, such as multi-market competition or limits to growth, presents the opportunities for making new and interesting insights for theoretical development of diversification strategy.

In summary, I anticipate that future research will continue along at least four avenues. Of course, each of these avenues can be supplemented with different topics or perspectives than those suggested here. Indeed, my suggestions are meant to provide a structure for considering anticipated research and that other combinations of topics and perspectives may raise even more interesting and provocative insights and explanations than those proposed herein. My suggestions are made to inspire such creativity. I leave it to you to develop this work.

## CONCLUSION

Diversification strategy represents one of the most important strategic challenges facing top executives. It is not surprising, then, to see that it is a popular and well-researched area within the field of strategic management. However, despite the attention paid to explaining diversification strategy, much remains unknown. In particular, issues such as foreign entry, international diversification and limits to firm size pose new questions that need to be resolved to better understand diversification strategy in the 21st century. Researchers are also borrowing from other areas and fields to help explain diversification strategy, as perspectives from organizational learning and evolutionary economics are beginning to appear in the literature. Moreover, researchers are working to refine and validate the basic building blocks of the literature, such as the meaning of relatedness, measuring diversification strategy. Hence, when we consider the literature on diversification strategy, we find, in some ways, a literature that is very much at a crossroads, one whereby researchers can pursue any number of fruitful and interesting avenues. It is, indeed, a very exciting time filled with many interesting prospects.

It must also be recognized that many topics were not reviewed here, simply because when one looks at any map, certain roads are taken while others are left unexplored. Conspicuously absent has been a discussion of cognition, planning, and processes. The interested reader will find those topics in need of much attention, as significant contribution awaits scholars grounded in psychology who can help explain the decision processes and schematics involved in the formulation and implementation of diversification strategy. I hope that future researchers will pick up where I left off, and provide insights and directions for understanding such topics which typically evade the traditional economic-based explanations so popular in diversification research. At this crossroads, many paths await.

## NOTES

1 These frameworks reflect the predominant deductive orientations at their time. Note that each is economic in orientation and that other frameworks exist that are non-economic in nature.
2 Note that the hybrid system is also known as the CM-form, or centralized multi-divisional organization structure. In these forms, the corporate center of a diversified firm exercises centralized control over, and intervenes in, the decision making of its divisions (Markides and Williamson, 1996). Such control combines strategic and financial systems.

## REFERENCES

Ansoff, H. I. (1957). Strategies for diversification. *Harvard Business Review*, 35(5): 113–24.
Ansoff, H. I. (1958). A model of diversification. *Management Science*, 4: 392–414.
Ansoff, H. I. 1965). *Corporate Strategy*. New York: McGraw-Hill.
Areeda, P., and Turner, D. (1979). Conglomerate mergers: Extended interdependence and effects on interindustry competition as grounds for condemnation. *University of Pennsylvania Law Review*, 127: 1082–103.
Barkema, H. G., and Vermeulen, F. (1998). International expansion through start-up or acquisition: A learning perspective. *Academy of Management Journal*, 41: 7–26.
Barnett, W. P. (1993). Strategic deterrence among multi-point competitors. *Industrial and Corporate Change*, 2: 249–78.
Baum, J. A. C., and Korn, H. J. (1996). Competitive dynamics and interfirm rivalry. *Academy of Management Journal*, 39: 255–91.
Bergh, D. D. (1995). Problems with repeated measures analysis: Demonstration with a study of the diversification strategy and performance relationship. *Academy of Management Journal*, 38: 1692–1708.
Bergh, D. D. (1998). Product-market uncertainty, portfolio restructuring, and performance: An information-processing and resource-based view. *Journal of Management*, 24: 135–55.
Bergh, D. D., and Holbein, G. F. (1997). Assessment and redirection of longitudinal analysis: Demonstration with a study of the diversification and divestiture relationship. *Strategic Management Journal*, 18: 557–71.
Bergh, D. D., and Lawless, M. W. (1998). Portfolio restructuring and limits to hierarchical governance: Effects of environmental uncertainty and diversification strategy. *Organization Science*, 9: 87–102.
Bernheim, D., and Whinston, M. D. (1990). Multimarket contact and collusive behavior. *RAND Journal of Economics*, 21: 1–26.
Bettis, R. A., and Hall, W. K. (1982). Diversification strategy, accounting determined risk, and accounting determined returns. *Academy of Management Journal*, 25: 254–64.
Chandler, A. (1962). *Strategy and Structure: Chapters in the History of American Industrial Enterprise*. Cambridge, MA: MIT Press.

Chang, S. J. (1995). International expansion strategy of Japanese firms: Capability building through sequential entry. *Academy of Management Journal*, 38: 383–407.

Chatterjee, S., and Wernerfelt, B. (1991). The link between resources and types of diversification: Theory and evidence. *Strategic Management Journal*, 12: 33–48.

Chen, M-J. (1996). Competitor analysis and inter-firm rivalry: Toward a theoretical integration. *Academy of Management Review*, 21: 100–34.

Christensen, H. K., and Montgomery, C. A. (1981). Corporate economic performance: Diversification strategy versus market structure. *Strategic Management Journal*, 2: 327–43.

Datta, D. K., Rajagopalan, N., and Rasheed, A. (1991). Diversification and performance: Critical review and future directions. *Journal of Management Studies*, 28: 529–58.

Davis, G. F., Diekman, K. A., and Tinsley, C. H. (1994). The decline and fall of the conglomerate firm in the 1980s: The deinstitutionalization of an organizational form. *American Sociological Review*, 59: 547–70.

Dess, G. G., Gupta, A., Hennart, J-F., and Hill, C. W. L. (1995). Conducting and integrating strategy research at the international, corporate and business levels: Issues and directions. *Journal of Management*, 21: 357–93.

Dundas, K. M., and Richardson, P. R. (1980). Corporate strategy and the concept of market failure. *Strategic Management Journal*, 1: 177–88.

Dundas, K. M., and Richardson, P. R. (1982). Implementing the unrelated product strategy. *Strategic Management Journal*, 3: 287–301.

Edwards, C. D. (1955). Conglomerate bigness as a source of power. *Business concentration and price policy*. National Bureau of Economic Research conference report: 331–52. Princeton, NJ: Princeton University Press.

Farjoun, M. (1998). The independent and joint effects of the skill and physical bases of relatedness in diversification. *Strategic Management Journal*, 19: 611–30.

Finkelstein, S., and Hambrick, D. C. (1990). Top management team tenure and organizational outcomes: The moderating role of managerial discretion. *Administrative Science Quarterly*, 35: 484–503.

Finkelstein, S., and Hambrick, D. C. (1996). Strategic Leadership: *Top Executives and their Effects on Organizations*. Minneapolis/St. Paul: West Publishing Company.

Fiol, C. M., and Lyles, M. A. (1985). Organizational learning. *Academy of Management Review*, 10: 803–13.

Gaughan, P. A. (1999). *Mergers, Acquisitions, and Corporate Restructurings* (2nd ed.). New York: Wiley.

Geringer, J., Beamish, P., and daCosta, R. (1989). Diversification strategy and internationalization: Implications for MNE performance. *Strategic Management Journal*, 10: 109–19.

Gimeno, J. (1999). Reciprocal threats in multimarket rivalry: Staking out "spheres of influence" in the US airline industry. *Strategic Management Journal*, 20: 101–28.

Gimeno, J., and Woo, C. Y. (1999). Multimarket contact, economies of scope, and firm performance. *Academy of Management Journal*, 42: 239–59.

Grant, R. M. (1998). *Contemporary Strategy Analysis*, 3rd edn. Oxford: Blackwell.

Grant, R., and Jammine, A. (1988). Performance differences between the Wrigley/Rumelt strategic categories. *Strategic Management Journal*, 9: 333–46.

Haleblian, J., and Finkelstein, S. (1998). The influence of organization acquisition experience on acquisition performance: A behavioral learning perspective. *Administrative Science Quarterly*, 44: 29–56.

Hall, E. H., Jr., and St. John, C. H. (1994). A methodological note on diversity measurement. *Strategic Management Journal*, 15: 153–68.

Hambrick, D. C., Cho, T., and Chen, M-J. (1996). The influence of top management team heterogeneity on firms' competitive moves. *Administrative Science Quarterly*, 41: 659–84.

Hambrick, D. C., Geletkanycz, M., and Fredrickson, J. W. (1993). Top executive commitment to the status quo: Some tests of its determinants. *Strategic Management Journal*, 14: 401–18.

Hambrick, D. C., and Mason, O. (1984). Upper echelons: The organization as a reflection of its top managers. *Academy of Management Review*, 9: 193–206.

Harrison, J. S., Hall, E. H., Jr., and Nargundkar, R. (1993). Resource allocation as an outcropping of strategic consistency: Performance implications. *Academy of Management Journal*, 36: 1026–52.

Herriot, S. R., Leventhal, D., and March, J. (1985). Learning from experience in organizations. *American Economic Review*, 75: 298–302.

Hill, C. W. L., Hitt, M. A., and Hoskisson, R. E. (1992). Cooperative versus competitive structures in related and unrelated diversified firms. *Organization Science*, 3: 501–21.

Hill, C. W. L., and Hoskisson, R. E. (1987). Strategy and structure in the multiproduct firm. *Academy of Management Review*, 12: 331–41.

Hitt, M. A., Gimeno, J., and Hoskisson, R. E. (1998). Current and future research methods in strategic management. *Organizational Research Methods*, 1: 6–44.

Hitt, M. A., Hoskisson, R. E., and Ireland, R. D. (1994). A mid-range theory of the interactive effects of international and product diversification on innovation and performance. *Journal of Management*, 20: 297–326.

Hitt, M. A., Hoskisson, R. E., and Kim, H. (1997). International diversification: Effects of innovation and firm performance in product-diversified firms. *Academy of Management Journal*, 40: 767–98.

Hoskisson, R. E., Hill, C. W. L., and Kim, H. (1993). Multidivisional structure: Organizational fossil or source of value? *Journal of Management*, 19: 269–98.

Hoskisson, R. E., and Hitt, M. A. (1990). Antecedents and performance outcomes of diversification: A review and critique of theoretical perspectives. *Journal of Management*, 16: 461–509.

Hoskisson, R. E., and Hitt, M. A. (1994). *Downscoping: How to tame a diversified firm*. New York: Oxford University Press.

Hoskisson, R. E., Hitt, M. A., Johnson, R. A., and Moesel, D. D. (1993). Construct validity of an objective (entropy) categorical measure of diversification strategy. *Strategic Management Journal*, 14: 215–35.

Hoskisson, R. E., Hitt, M. A., Wan, W. and Yiu, D. (1999). Theory and research in strategic management research: Swings of a pendulum. *Journal of Management*, 25: 417–56.

Hoskisson, R. E., and Johnson, R. A. (1992). Corporate restructuring and strategic change: The effect on diversification strategy and R&D intensity. *Strategic Management Journal*, 13: 625–34.

Hoskisson, R. E., and Turk, T. A. (1990). Corporate restructuring: governance and control limits of the internal capital market. *Academy of Management Review*, 15: 459–77.

Huber, G. P. (1991). Organizational learning: The contributing processes and literatures. *Organization Science*, 2 (special issue): 88–115.

Jayachandran, S., Gimeno, J., and Varadarajan, P. (1999). The theory of multimarket competition: A synthesis and implications for marketing strategy. *Journal of Marketing*, 63(3).

Johnson, R. A. (1996). Antecedents and outcomes of corporate refocusing. *Journal of Management*, 22: 439–483.

Jones, G. R., and Hill, C. W. L. (1988). Transaction cost analysis of strategy-structure choice. *Strategic Management Journal*, 9: 159–72.

Keats, B. (1990). Diversification and business economic performance revisited: Issues of measurement and causality. *Journal of Management*, 16: 61–72.

Kim, W., Hwang, P., and Burgers, W. (1988). Global diversification strategy and corporate profit performance. *Strategic Management Journal*, 10: 45–57.

Lubatkin, M. H., and Chatterjee, S. (1994). Extending modern portfolio theory into the domain of corporate diversification: Does it apply? *Academy of Management Journal*, 37: 109–36.

Lubatkin, M. H., Merchant, H., and Srinivasan, N. (1993). Construct validity of some unweighted product-count measures. *Strategic Management Journal*, 14: 433–49.

Mahoney, J. T., and Pandian, J. R. (1992). The resource-based view within the conversation of strategic management. *Strategic Management Journal*, 13: 363–80.

March, J. G. (1988). *Decisions and organizations*. Oxford: Blackwell.

March, J. G., Sproull, L. S., and Tamuz, M. (1991). Learning from samples of one or fewer. *Organization science*, 2: 1–13.

Markides, C. C. (1992). Consequences of corporate refocusing: Ex ante evidence. *Academy of Management Journal*, 35: 398–412.

Markides, C. C., and Williamson, P. J. (1994). Related diversification, core competencies and corporate performance. *Strategic Management Journal*, 15 (Special Issue): 149–65.

Markides, C. C., and Williamson, P. J. (1996). Corporate diversification and organizational structure: A resource-based view. *Academy of Management Journal*, 39: 340–67.

Michel, J. G., and Hambrick, D. C. (1992). Diversification posture and top management team characteristics. *Academy of Management Journal*, 35: 9–37.

Montgomery, C. A. (1979). *Diversification, market structure, and firm performance: An extension of Rumelt's work*. Doctoral dissertation, Purdue University.

Montgomery, C. A. (1982). The measurement of firm diversification: Some new empirical evidence. *Academy of Management Journal*, 25: 299–307.

Montgomery, C. A. (1985). Product-market diversification and market power. *Academy of Management Journal*, 28: 789–98.

Montgomery, C. A. (1994). Corporate diversification. *Journal of Economic Perspectives*, 8: 163–78.

Montgomery, C. A., and Hariharan, S. (1991). Diversified entry by established firms. *Journal of Economic Behavior and Organizations*, 15: 71–89.

Montgomery, C. A., and Wernerfelt, B. (1988). Diversification, Ricardian rents, and Tobin's Q. *RAND Journal of Economics*, 19: 623–32.

Ollinger, M. (1994). The limits of growth of the multidivisional firm: A case study of the US Oil industry from 1930–1990. *Strategic Management Journal*, 15: 503–20.

Palich, L. E., Cardinal, L. B., and Miller, C. C. (2000). Curvilinearity in the diversification-performance linkage: An examination of over three decades of research. *Strategic Management Journal*, 21: 155–74.

Pennings, J. M., Barkema, H., and Douma, S. (1994). Organizational learning and diversification. *Academy of Management Journal*, 37: 608–40.

Penrose, E. (1959). *The Theory of the Growth of the Firm*. New York: Wiley.

Pfeffer, J. (1983). Organizational demography. In L. L. Cummings and B. M. Staw (eds.), *Research in Organizational Behaviour*, vol. 5: 299–357. Greenwich, CT: JAI Press.

Pitts, R. A., and Hopkins, H. D. (1982). Firm diversity: Conceptualization and measurement. *Academy of Management Review*, 7: 620–29.

Porter, M. E. (1980). *Competitive Strategy*. New York: Free Press.

Ramanujam, V., and Varadarajan, P. (1989). Research on corporate diversification: A synthesis. *Strategic Management Journal*, 7: 485–502.

Reger, R. K. (1997). Review of Finkelstein and Hambrick's Strategic leadership: Top executives and their effects on organizations. *Academy of Management Review*, 22: 802–4.

Robins, J., and Wiersema, M. (1995). A resource-based approach to the multibusiness firm: Empirical analysis of portfolio interrelationships and corporate financial performance. *Strategic Management Journal*, 16: 277–300.

Rumelt, R .P. (1974). *Strategy, Structure and Economic Performance*. Cambridge, MA: Harvard University Press.

Smith, K .G., Smith, K. A., Olian, J. D., Simrs, Jr., H. P., O'Bannon, D. P., and Scully, J. A. (1994). Top management team demography and process: The role of social integration and communication. *Administrative Science Quarterly*, 39: 412–38.

Stimpert, L., and Duhaime, I. (1997). Seeing the big picture: The influence of industry, diversification and business strategy on performance. *Academy of Management Journal*, 40: 560–83.

Tallman, S., and Li, J. (1996). Effects of international diversity and product diversity on the performance of multinational firms. *Academy of Management Journal*, 39: 179–96.

Teece, D. J. (1982). Towards an economic theory of the multi-product firm. *Journal of Economic Behavior and Organization*, 3: 39–63.

Varadarajan, P. and Ramanujam, V. (1987). Diversfication and performance: A re-examination using a new two-dimensional conceptualization of diversity in firms. *Academy of Management Review*, 30: 380–93.

Walsh, J. P. (1995) Managerial and organizational cognition: Notes from a trip down memory lane. *Organization Science*, 6: 280–321.

Wernerfelt, B. (1984). A resource-based view of the firm. *Strategic Management Journal*, 5: 171–80.

Wernerfelt, B. (1989). From critical resources to corporate strategy. *Journal of General Management*, 14: 4–12.

Wernerfelt, B., and Montgomery, C. A. (1988). Tobin's $q$ and the importance of focus in firm performance. *American Economic Review*, 78: 246–50.

Wiersema, M. F., and Bantel, K. A. (1992). Top management team demography and corporate strategic change. *Academy of Management Journal*, 35: 91:121.

Williams, J. R., Paez, B., and Sanders, L. (1988). Conglomerates revisited. *Strategic Management Journal*, 9: 403–14.

Williamson, O. E. (1975). *Markets and Hierarchies: Analysis and Antitrust Implications*. New York: Free Press.

Williamson, O. E. (1985). *The Economic Institutions of Capitalism*. New York: Free Press.

Wrigley, L. (1970)). *Divisional Autonomy and Diversification*. Unpublished doctoral dissertation. Harvard Business School.

# 13

# Mergers and Acquisitions: A Value Creating or Value Destroying Strategy?

## Michael A. Hitt, R. Duane Ireland and Jeffrey S. Harrison

The volume and magnitude of mergers and acquisitions continue to grow on a global basis (Hitt, Harrison, and Ireland, 2001). Although the decade of the 1980s, produced 55,000 merger and acquisition transactions at a total value of $1.3 trillion, known as "merger mania," the 1990s produced more than twice that number, at a value of approximately $11 trillion. One observer suggested that the merger wave of the 1980s was a tidal wave during the 1990s, becoming CEOs' favorite growth strategy in the process (Sirower, 1998b).

As the new millennium unfolds, there is no evidence that merger and acquisition activity is doing anything other than increasing (Bennett, 1998; Hitt, Harrison, and Ireland, 2001). Many recent acquisitions have been undertaken to achieve economies (e.g., of scale and scope) and market power with the purpose of increasing competitiveness in global markets. In addition, global companies want to be viewed as "fast-growth" and to lead or dominate the markets in which they participate. An active merger and acquisition strategy facilitates efforts to reach these growth-oriented objectives (Lucenko, 2000). Evidence indicates that merger and acquisition-related actions such as these are not limited to a few countries (Very, Lubatkin, Calorit, and Veiga, 1997). Rather, they are common in many regions of the world (e.g., Asia, Europe, North America). Increasingly, mergers and acquisitions are a strategy being used in emerging economies as well. For example, Poland, with an economy that was growing faster than any other in the European Union during the late 1990s, is experiencing rapid infusions of foreign direct investment partially as a result of the nation's growth rate. Because of this, analysts predict that foreign multinational firms will use acquisitions as a means of entering this expanding and maturing economy (Schoenberg, 1998). In addition, in some instances, firms are attempting to prepare for dramatic changes in their industries, often due to technological developments (e.g., telecommunications industry). At an industry level, mergers and acquisitions may have a significant effect on the nature of the set of competitive actions and reactions (i.e., competitive dynamics) occurring among competitors.

Despite their popularity, many acquisitions do not produce the financial benefits expected or desired by acquiring firms (Carper, 1990; Datta, Pinches, and Narayanan, 1992; Glassman, 1998; Loderer and Martin, 1992; Porter, 1987; Ravenscraft and Sherer, 1987). In fact, evidence suggests that as much as 70 percent of merger and acquisition activity fails to improve a firm's performance as measured by the value of its stock (Barfield, 1998). A study by McKinsey & Co. revealed that only 37 percent of US acquirers outperform their peers in shareholder returns (Haigh, 1999). Jensen (1988a) showed that although acquired firm shareholders often earn above-average returns, shareholders of acquiring firms earn returns, on average, close to zero. Findings such as those reported by Jensen (1988a) lead to the observation that mergers and acquisitions "are notorious for not creating value for shareholders – unless one is fortunate enough to hold shares in the acquired company" (Barfield, 1998). Thus, some have concluded that creating value through an active merger and acquisition strategy is often in the minds of CEOs, but is less obvious to the world's stock markets (Anand, 2000). Contributing to merger and acquisition failure is a host of factors, including illusory synergies, managerial hubris, and sluggish integration of the acquiring and acquired firms (Barfield, 1998).

However, not all mergers and acquisitions produce negative results. In a study of high- and low-performing outlier acquisitions, Hitt et al. (1998) found that while there were many more low-performing than high-performing acquisitions, some of the positive acquisitions produced very high returns for the acquiring firm. Taken further, Federal Reserve Chairman, Alan Greenspan, said that the national wave of mega mergers produces no sign of economic danger and strongly recommended that the government respect the dynamism of modern free markets (Gordon, 1998).

Consequently, based on previous research we can conclude that mergers and acquisitions have the potential to produce positive outcomes, but they remain a high-risk strategy. Many studies demonstrate that mergers and acquisitions are complex and challenging strategies for top executives to implement and manage. One management problem concerns integrating two large and complex firms that often have diverse cultures, structures and operating systems (Haspeslagh and Jemison, 1991). Some argue strongly that most acquirers still lack the skills required to effectively integrate additional acquisitions into the then-current form of their company (Lucenko, 2000). Managerial hubris may also be a problem in mergers and acquisitions as it often stifles and sometimes precludes an adequate analysis of the target firm or leads to the payment of substantial premiums for firms that are acquired (Roll, 1986). If a suitor fails to adequately evaluate a target before acquiring it, unexpected difficulties may be encountered during post-merger integration processes. In turn, integration-related difficulties reduce the likelihood that the newly created firm will achieve intended outcomes (e.g., greater market power, economies of scale or scope, and so on).

In addition, an unintended consequence of mergers and acquisitions is reduced innovation (Hitt, Hoskisson, and Ireland, 1990; Hitt et al., 1991a; Hitt et al., 1996). Firms engaged in multiple acquisitions over time are likely to introduce fewer new products to the market because they often over-emphasize financial controls leading managers to become increasingly risk averse. When this occurs, firms try to acquire others to supplement their innovations. As they acquire firms with new products, they are integrated into a system that discourages innovation, and thus the acquirers must continue to buy additional firms with innovative new products to remain competitive

(Hitt et al., 1996). This is important because increasingly firms are seeking to introduce new and innovative products rapidly as a means of competing successfully in fast changing and unpredictable markets (Eisenhardt and Brown, 1998; Ireland et al., 2001).

Regardless of the potential pitfalls, mergers and acquisitions represent a popular and commonly used strategy (Barfield, 1998). Technically, a merger occurs any time companies combine to form one legal entity. However, the term merger has come to be understood as a transaction between two firms that agree to integrate their operations on a relatively coequal basis. The resulting firm has a new identity and name that is different from either of the pre-merger firms. These types of transactions are rare. Our focus in this chapter is primarily on acquisitions, a form of merger in which one firm buys a controlling interest (up to 100 percent) in another firm, thereby making the acquired businesses a part of its own portfolio (Hitt, Ireland, and Hoskisson, 2001).

In this chapter we discuss what we, as a field, think we know about how to create value through mergers and acquisitions. The current research literature is the source of the field's compiled knowledge. Our emphasis is on how executives should pursue acquisitions (and mergers to the extent they occur) so as to maximize positive benefits and minimize risks. Factors that seem to greatly influence merger and acquisition outcomes include due diligence, type of financing, the ability to learn from experience with acquisitions, the existence or absence of complementary resources, the degree of integration and the synergy created, and the level of cooperation between the acquiring and target firm managers. The bulk of this chapter is organized around these topics. We also discuss several ethical and governance issues and explore the increasingly popular cross-border acquisitions. Finally, we provide direction concerning fruitful avenues for future research. We begin the discussion with due diligence.

## DUE DILIGENCE

Effective acquisitions begin with a strategic vision (Sirower, 1998a). Acquiring firm decision makers must have a clear vision of how synergy will be created in the combined firm and how positive financial outcomes will be obtained (Sirower and O'Byrne, 1998). Such a vision is worked out through careful due diligence on the part of acquiring firm executives before a decision is made to proceed with the acquisition. Effective visions do not result from transactions that are completed quickly and without careful analyses (*The Economist*, 2000b). A thorough due diligence process includes careful examination of multiple areas in the target firm such as balance of equity and debt capital, sale of assets, transfer of shares, environmental issues, financial resources and performance, customer and marketing-related issues, tax issues, operations and many other business aspects (Hitt, Harrison, and Ireland, 2001). However, effective due diligence goes beyond financial numbers and inventories to include such critical attributes as organizational culture and human capital. Research has shown that human capital is important to the success of firms in general but especially to mergers and acquisitions (Hitt et al., 2001; Ireland and Hitt, 1999).

The due diligence process involves both ethical and legal obligations for corporations and its agents (e.g., investment bankers). Ineffective, unethical and illegal practices must be identified and disclosed, although it is often difficult to do this. One reason for this

difficulty is that ethical abuses can occur anywhere in an organization – in all departments among all levels of employees, in a multitude of corporate practice areas. Price
fixing, discriminatory hiring practices, bribery and false advertising are just a few
examples of ethical abuses that an effective due diligence process might uncover.
Moreover, acquirers face an added layer of complexity when trying to identify unethical
practices, if any, in acquisitions of companies in countries outside their own nation.
Understanding the ethical implications of practices in different cultures is challenging
(Harrison, 1999). In general, then, the due diligence process must be not only thorough,
but conducted with integrity (Laufer, 1996).

The due diligence process is generally performed by a team of experts that may
include accountants, investment bankers, lawyers, internal specialists and consultants.
Typically, a due diligence process has two primary objectives. The first is to identify and
clarify what is being acquired. By placing a meaningful value on a target's assets,
including its human capital, the acquiring firm increases its understanding of the capabilities that it is purchasing. The second objective is to anticipate and mitigate the risks
of undesirable post-acquisition realities such as market share losses (Weiss, 1998). Thus,
due diligence is a highly complex process (Byczek, 1997; Lepak, 1998). The most
effective due diligence processes begin in the early stages of the acquisition process. For
example, the due diligence process should help a firm select a target for acquisition. It
should help choose the target that will facilitate the firm obtaining a long-term competitive advantage and thereby increase shareholder wealth. Thus, one critical outcome of
effective due diligence is the assessment of the viability of the post-merger integration of
the two firms.

Due diligence is further complicated by cross-border acquisitions because of the
differences in legal structure, tax rates, accounting practices, environmental laws, etc.,
that often exist in the separate countries. For example, firms must carefully analyze the
potential to transfer money easily across country borders. Some countries, such as China
and Russia, do not allow free movement of currency across their border (Allweiss, 1998).

## Potential due diligence problems

There are at least two potential major problems that reduce the effectiveness of due
diligence: managerial hubris and an inadequate process. Managerial hubris may lead
firms to do an inadequate job of due diligence or to ignore information received from the
due diligence process. Research suggests that hubris is a major cause of high premiums
paid for acquisitions. Hayward and Hambrick (1997) found that premiums were higher
when the acquiring firm had experienced more recent success in its financial performance, when the media had recently praised the CEO and when CEOs rated their own
self-importance highly. Thus, their research supported the potential problems of managerial hubris. Furthermore, they found that larger premiums were paid when corporate
governance was weak (e.g., more inside directors or when the CEO was also the chair of
the board of directors).

With regard to ineffective process, sometimes firms conduct effective financial due
diligence but do not consider other factors that are related to organizational, cultural or
possible human capital conditions in the process. For example, acquiring firms should
carefully examine the list of major customers and the length of time that customers have

been buying products from the target firm. Additionally, the costs and revenues for continued operation or provision of the services should be forecasted. The target firm's culture should also be examined. Often, potential synergies may seem significant but existing organizational and cultural barriers may prevent achievement of those synergies. Investment bankers can help overcome some of these potential problems by sharing their knowledge of the target firms.

## The role of investment bankers

The role of investment bankers in mergers and acquisitions has increased in recent years because of large cross-border deals and the growing number of mergers and acquisitions in European countries such as Germany (Gray, 1998; Shearlock, 1995; Tully, 1998). Investment bankers can add value to an acquisition by helping to identify acquisition targets that are likely to produce economies and other forms of synergy and by helping to value the acquisition (Bowers and Miller, 1990). Research has shown that these institutions produce higher value for their acquiring firm clients, relative to the fees paid. However, studies also show that there is variance in the quality of advice provided by prominent investment banking institutions (Michel, Shaked, and Lee, 1991). Furthermore, Perlmurth (1996) reported research showing that firms conducting the due diligence process internally, compared to those using investment banks, achieve higher returns from the acquisitions.

Research has shown a positive relationship between the premium paid for a target firm and the compensation paid to investment bankers. Consequently, one criticism of investment bankers is that the fees they charge are often contingent on the price paid for the target by the acquiring firm. This fee arrangement provides the wrong set of incentives for the investment banking firm and may lead to a conflict of interest (Kesner, Shapiro, and Sharma, 1994). The conflict of interest problem applies only from the perspective of the acquiring firm, since it is in the best interests of acquired firm shareholders to obtain a high price. Other research found that the average investment banker advisory fee was 1.29 percent of the value of the completed acquisition, which does not appear to be unreasonable. However, most fees are largely contingent on the outcome of the acquisition negotiations, thereby providing investment bankers significant incentives to ensure that the acquisition is completed (McLaughlin, 1990). This pressure may result in completion of transactions that, based on information discovered during deal negotiations, were not as attractive to the acquiring firm as thought originally. Even if due diligence leads to a positive recommendation regarding an acquisition, effective financing is essential to making the deal a success.

## FINANCING ACQUISITIONS

Acquisitions may be financed through cash purchase, an exchange of stock or a combination of cash and stock. Cash became the most popular financing medium for acquisitions during the 1970s (Carleton et al., 1983). Although in the past several years many huge and highly visible multi-billion dollar deals have been financed with stock, across the group of all acquisitions cash transactions have continued to dominate the other two methods over the past decade. Even in large deals (over $100 million), pure cash transactions still account for nearly 50 percent of the total (*Mergers and Acquisitions*, 1998). When engaged in cross-border acquisitions, firms often find it quite challenging to offer a price for the target that maximizes the opportunity of completing the transaction yet does not provide a premium that reduces the firm's ability to generate future expected returns on that investment (de Castillo et al., 1998). While this can be a problem in most acquisitions, it is especially salient in cross-border transactions because of heightened information asymmetries. Higher prices require greater capital to finance the acquisition and because of the uncertainties, cross-border acquisitions may be more difficult to finance.

## *Factors influencing selection of financing*

In the United States, the country with the most acquisitions, if at least 50 percent of a target's shares are exchanged for stock, the Internal Revenue Code has traditionally classified the acquisition as a "continuity of interests," which means that the transaction is non-taxable (tax deferred) to the target firm shareholders (Brown and Ryngaert, 1991). While this is advantageous to the target firm, the acquiring firm may favor a taxable transaction, because ownership rights are considered sold and the acquiring firm is allowed to increase the depreciation basis of the assets acquired. On the other hand, target firm shareholders are likely to expect a larger premium if their gains are taxed. Brown and Ryngaert (1991: 665) argue that, all things considered, "stock is at worst tax neutral and at best an advantage" in an acquisition. Consequently, the popularity of cash transactions is probably not the result of tax treatment.

The medium of exchange also influences the way an acquisition is treated for accounting purposes. Research suggests that there is not one superior type of accounting convention (Carleton et al., 1983; Hong, Kaplan, and Mandelker, 1978). However, in the past, stock transactions have allowed accountants to create a more favorable picture of future performance. Until recently, they could be accounted for as a pooling of interests (the assets of the two firms are combined at book value), but this ruling has changed. Pooling interests eliminated goodwill charges, thus boosting future earnings. On the other hand, cash deals must be treated as a purchase, requiring that premiums paid (purchase price over the book value) be reported as goodwill in financial statements. Unfortunately, goodwill is not tax deductible.

If target firm managers value control in the combined company, they will prefer to receive stock, especially in targets with high levels of management ownership. In support of this idea, Ghosh and Ruland (1998) demonstrated that the managers of target firms were more likely to keep their jobs after acquisition when stock was the medium of exchange. In addition, they found that stock exchanges were common when managerial ownership of the target company was high.

Managers of acquiring firms often favor stock financing when they have greater investment opportunities (Martin, 1996). They desire to conserve cash and borrowing potential to finance future growth. Also, according to Hansen (1987), if a target firm knows its own value better than the acquiring firm, managers will prefer a stock transaction. This is a result of the contingent pricing characteristics associated with a stock exchange. If the transaction is overpriced, the stock price of the acquiring firm will eventually (if not immediately) decline and the value of the deal to target firm shareholders will be reduced. This phenomenon shifts some of the risk associated with the value of the transaction to the target firm shareholders; however, they may resist taking this risk.

In spite of the influence of taxes, accounting convention, management control, investment opportunities and contingent pricing, cash is still the most popular form of payment for an acquisition. The psychology of market participants partially explains the popularity of cash transactions. Wansley, Lane, and Yang (1987) found that the choice of financing sends signals to the market. When management of the bidding firm believes that its own stock is overvalued, securities are the preferred form of payment. Acquiring firm managers may be reluctant to send this sort of signal to the market. Also, since stock-financed acquisitions lead to increased risk for target firm shareholders, they may insist on a cash deal. As long as reliable information is available on the target, there is no strong reason for an acquiring firm to resist a cash transaction. However, the most important reason for the popularity of cash deals is probably that they provide more attractive immediate returns to both acquiring and target companies.

Much research on mergers and acquisitions has demonstrated that higher than normal stock returns for acquiring firms are unlikely. However, stock transactions perform even worse than cash transactions (Agarwall, Jaffe, and Mandelker, 1992; Datta, Pinches, and Narayanan, 1992; Servaes, 1991). Target firm stock returns are also higher in cash transactions. Target firms experience positive abnormal stock returns of almost 34 percent in cash acquisitions, compared to approximately 17 percent in stock deals (Wansley, Lane, and Yang, 1987).

The literature on financial slack suggests that acquirers with higher cash balances should prefer cash-financed acquisitions. In general, this idea is supported in the empirical literature (Crawford, 1987; Martin, 1996); however, some evidence exists to the contrary (Chaney, Lovata, and Philipich, 1991). Jensen (1988b) argues that managers often engage in unprofitable or hasty acquisitions to spend available cash. Jensen's argument has found some support from researchers who study acquisitions (Lang, Stulz, and Walkling, 1991). However, alternative arguments exist. The existence of slack, whether in the form of large amounts of cash or excess borrowing capacity, may cause managers to seek an acquisition, but it also can facilitate the acquisition process, making an acquisition easier to integrate and reduce the costs of doing so. Bourgeois (1981) argued that slack allows a firm to adapt successfully to internal and external changes such as those required by an acquisition. Hitt et al. (1998) discovered substantial financial slack, either in low debt or borrowing capacity, in nearly half of the most successful acquisitions they identified.

## The importance of debt

Hitt et al.'s (1998) study of highly successful and highly unsuccessful acquisitions (based on accounting returns and innovations produced three years after the acquisition) found that debt was the only factor important to both groups. Eighty-three percent of the successful acquisitions had low to moderate debt while 92 percent of the unsuccessful acquisitions had large or extraordinary debt. The successful acquisitions with slack also had low to moderate debt levels. Other acquisitions kept debt levels low through the use of stock. Some acquiring firms used high levels of debt financing for the acquisition, but then paid the debt down quickly.

Debt plays an important role in acquisition success because acquisitions are often very expensive. Target company stock price premiums vary from year to year, but historically they are generally over 30 percent. While premiums are supposed to estimate the value added from the synergy of integrating the two firms, research findings do not support this perspective (Datta, Pinches, and Narayanan, 1992; Jensen and Rubach, 1983). Barney (1988) argued that without the rare presence of a unique synergistic opportunity between the buyer and seller that is unavailable to other potential buyers, the acquiring firm will bid up the price to a value equal to or greater than the value of the target firm. Other costs include consultant fees, investment banker fees, legal fees and post-acquisition costs associated with plant closings, relocations, layoff of redundant employees and integration of information and accounting systems.

The expenses described above have an indirect effect on debt; they reduce slack and create the need to assume more debt. These costs are especially detrimental because they are unproductive – they do not lead to the manufacture and distribution of goods and services. Acquisitions also have a direct effect on debt. Obviously, a cash transaction can result in higher debt levels, as an organization borrows money to make the purchase. Acquisitions also frequently involve the assumption of a significant amount of debt that had been accumulated by the acquired firm. Additionally, even stock financing does not eliminate the use of debt. The acquiring firm in a stock deal must absorb transaction and integration costs. Also, the assumption of large amounts of debt is common in stock transactions. Hitt et al. (1991b) found an average increase in debt to equity of over 25 percent by the acquirer, including stock, cash and combination deals. The debt did not return to normal levels in the combined firms for three years after the acquisition.

Debt servicing costs can reduce earnings performance directly. Thus, high debt makes it difficult to make acquisitions profitable. High debt levels also increase the likelihood of bankruptcy that can lead rating agencies such as Standard & Poor's or Moody's to downgrade the firm's credit rating. This makes future debt more difficult to obtain and more costly (i.e., at higher interest rates). Servicing debt from acquisitions may divert resources from other important areas. Activities with short-term costs but long-term payoffs such as human resource training and research and development often are among the first to be reduced. Advertising and quality control may also be cut. In addition, the need to reduce payrolls to cover debt payments can lead to layoffs.

In contrast to the negative effects associated with high levels of debt – low levels of debt, a form of slack – can mitigate the negative effects from an acquisition. Some scholars (e.g., Jensen, 1988b) have argued that debt is necessary as a disciplinary force for managers (i.e., keeps them from making inappropriate investments that are not in the best interests of the shareholders). We do not accept this view as it relates to mergers and acquisitions. For example, some recent research found that too little slack, in general, discouraged experimentation in multinational corporations (Nohria and Gulati, 1996). While these two researchers also found that too much slack fostered complacency with regard to innovation, firms involved in an acquisition are unlikely to have too much slack. Low to moderate debt levels may also allow managers more strategic flexibility, which is necessary for success in a dynamic and hypercompetitive environment (D'Aveni, 1994).

In summary, acquiring firms have a number of issues to consider when deciding how to finance an acquisition. A clear recommendation with regard to the use of cash, stock or a combination of both does not emerge from the literature; however, the stock market responds more positively to cash transactions. It is also evident that manageable debt levels increase the likelihood of success.

Learning from prior acquisitions is another important factor to acquisition success.

## LEARNING FROM ACQUISITIONS

Knowledge creation can be a source of organizational renewal and sustainable competitive advantage (Quinn, 1992). Certainly, acquisitions are one area in which organizations should be able to benefit from learning. Specialized skills associated with deal negotiation, financing, integration and assimilation hold the potential for substantial success or significant problems. Acquiring firms also must develop systems to communicate with newly acquired companies. In addition, human resources and other management systems must be integrated. Mastering these skills may lead to a core competency, which Prahalad and Hamel (1990: 85) define as "collective learning in the organization, especially how to coordinate diverse production skills and integrate multiple teams of technologies." Cisco Systems appears to have a core competence when it comes to integrating acquisitions. Observing this company's success with an active acquisition strategy, an analyst suggested that Cisco "has turned acquisitions, a notoriously high-risk activity, into a normal 30-day business process" (Donlon, 2000).

Some of the skills associated with acquisitions may be difficult to master if a firm makes acquisitions infrequently. This difficulty is partially explained by the manner in which organizational knowledge is discovered. Much of the knowledge found in organizations is based on the discovery of patterns over time. For example, managerial autonomy is important to performance in unrelated, but not related acquisitions (Datta and Grant, 1990). Organizations that engage in a small number of acquisitions would be unlikely to discern patterns such as this one.

Therefore, organizations that are highly active in the acquisition market should be better able to master the necessary skills associated with acquisition success (Hitt et al., 1998). Nevertheless, as some researchers have discovered, a relatively high frequency of acquisitions does not, by itself, ensure that an organization will obtain higher acquisition-based performance (Fowler and Schmidt, 1989; Kusewitt, 1985; Pennings, Barkema, and Douma, 1994). The relationship between acquisition frequency and performance may be curvilinear, with the most successful companies either engaging in many acquisitions, thus taking advantage of learning effects, or on a very small scale, thus limiting organizational disruption and other costs and allowing the acquiring firm to be much more selective (Haleblian and Finkelstein, 1999; Hitt, Harrison, and Ireland, 2001).

Learning is facilitated if companies make the same type of acquisition repeatedly because they can learn from patterns of what does or does not work (Amburgey and Miner, 1992). Also, researchers have discovered that higher performing acquisitions occur when the acquiring firm has a pattern of acquiring targets in its industry (Haleblian and Finkelstein, 1999). Apparently, industry familiarity facilitates learning from acquisitions. Companies involved in an acquisition program may also learn from the experiences of competitors and other companies pursuing similar types of deals, thus reducing the need to learn from mistakes.

One of many challenges associated with learning from acquisitions is that often knowledge is divided into pieces and spread throughout the organization (Huber, 1991). An important part of the learning process involves discovering where relevant information is, combining it and then making sense out of it. Many organizations create special acquisition units that are involved in each and every acquisition. Such broad and deep involvements are necessary because these units are responsible for ensuring that the organization learns from prior acquisitions. The creation of acquisitions units is a luxury that may be too expensive for an infrequent acquirer, which reinforces the idea that frequent acquirers enjoy a potential competitive advantage in the acquisitions market.

An interesting management paradox exists with regard to learning from acquisitions. Experience with acquisitions can be used to enhance the performance of future acquisitions. However, acquisitions may stifle other types of learning associated with R&D and innovation (Hitt et al., 1991a). They create conditions within the organization that make outsourcing organizational skills more attractive than building those skills internally (Lei and Hitt, 1995). They also provide executives with the option of "buying" the skills they need instead of developing them "in house."

We have concluded thus far that rigorous due diligence, appropriate financing and debt levels, and learning from acquisitions appear to be important to acquisition success. However, these are process issues that apply across any type of acquisition. The more specific issues that drive acquisitions deal with the resources of the two firms and how they will be integrated to produce synergy and competitive advantage. We discuss resource issues, synergy and integration in the following sections.

## COMPLEMENTARY RESOURCES

*Complementary resources* exist when the resources of the acquiring and target firms differ, yet are mutually supportive. In contrast, *resource similarity* suggests a significant overlap between the resources of the acquiring and the acquired firms. Research shows that integrating *complementary* rather than *highly similar* resources through an acquisition increases the probability that the newly formed firm will be able to create economic value through its operations (Harrison et al., 1991).

Firms with highly similar resources also have highly similar strategic capabilities and vulnerabilities in the marketplace (Chen, 1996). Thus, an acquisition that integrates highly similar resources does not change the environmental opportunities and threats that the firms faced as independent entities. Given this evidence, it is economically rational (within the constraints of limited information, cognitive biases and causal ambiguity) for firms pursuing competitive advantages in the marketplace to seek complementary instead of highly similar or even identical resources in a target firm (Oliver, 1997).

### Value of complementary resources

Barney (1988) argued that without the opportunity for synergy between the acquirer and target firm that cannot be captured by other potential buyers, the acquiring firm will be forced to bid up the price to a value equal to or greater than the value of the target firm. Complementary resources can be especially valuable when they result in private synergy.

In essence, private synergy exists when the acquiring firm has knowledge about the complementarity of its resources with those of the target firm that is unknown to others. The most valuable of all types of synergy, private synergy exists when it is possible for two firms to combine their complementary resources in a way that creates more value than would any other combination of their resources (Harrison et al., 1991).

In addition, integration of complementary resources between an acquiring firm and a target may be difficult if not impossible for competitors to imitate (Teece, Pisano, and Shuen, 1997). More specifically, this desirable outcome is achieved when integration of two firms' resources makes it more difficult for competitors to compete against the merged businesses than to compete against them as individual entities. Consequently, when considering an acquisition, firms should focus on resource complementarities rather than relatedness among the product offerings of the acquiring and target firm. Hitt et al. (1998) found that even conglomerate firms were able to gain a competitive advantage if the target firm had resources that were complementary to at least some of those in the acquiring firm.

## Synergy

Competitive benefits through the use of complementary resources are gained when synergy has been created. Synergy exists when the combined firm creates more value than the summed value created by the companies when they acted as independent entities (Goold and Campbell, 1998). For shareholders, synergy exists when they acquire gains they could not obtain through their own portfolio diversification decisions. This is difficult for firms to achieve in that shareholders can diversify their ownership positions more cheaply than can firms, simply by grouping stakes in a set of companies (Sirower, 1997).

Typically, synergy yields gains to the acquiring firm through two sources: (1) improved operating efficiency based on economies of scale or scope; and (2) the sharing of one or more skills (Harrison et al., 1991). Synergy is difficult to achieve, and thus gaining sufficient value from it is not likely even in the relatively unusual instance when the acquiring firm does not pay a substantial premium. However, when a premium is paid, the challenge is more significant because greater synergy is required to generate incremental economic value. As we discuss next, effective integration of the acquiring firm with its target is one of the keys to creating intended levels of synergy.

## Integration Processes

Synergy creation requires proper integration of the acquired firm into an acquiring firm's current operations. One of the objectives of integration processes is to uncover potential problems that could prevent the newly formed firm from creating competitive advantage and to determine actions that will prevent integration-related difficulties from surfacing (Altier, 1997). The integration process begins when involved parties begin to work out an agreement for the acquisition and continues through assimilation of the acquired firm into the acquiring firm. The probability of achieving integration success is improved when actions are taken quickly. Success is also a result of strategic and organizational fit.

## Strategic fit

Strategic fit "refers to the effective matching of strategic organizational capabilities" (Harrison and St. John, 1998: 180). Generally speaking, the opportunity to create synergy that produces a competitive advantage and enhances shareholder wealth is reduced when an acquisition combines firms or business units that are both strong and/ or weak in the same business activities. In such instances, the newly created firm exhibits the same capabilities (or lack of capabilities) although the magnitude of either a strength or weakness is greater.

Strategic fit can lead to the creation of synergy through integration of value-enhancing activities between two or more units or businesses. For example, operations synergy results from economies of scale and/or scope or shared R&D/technology programs that lead to advantages that are not generally available to competitors. Also, marketing synergy is possible when the firm successfully links various marketing-related activities including those related to the sharing of brand names, distribution channels, advertising and promotion campaigns and even sales forces. In addition, management synergies are typically gained when competitively relevant skills possessed by upper- and lower-level managers in the formerly independent companies or business units are transferred successfully between units within the newly formed firm.

## Organizational fit

Organizational fit "occurs when two organizations or business units have similar management processes, cultures, systems and structures" (Harrison and St. John, 1998: 180). As a foundation to synergy creation, organizational fit suggests that firms have a reasonably high degree of compatibility. From an operational perspective, the existence of compatibility facilitates the integration processes used to meld the firms' or business units' operations and helps to produce desired results quickly, effectively and efficiently. Thus, organizational compatibility facilitates resource sharing, enhances the effectiveness of communication patterns and improves the company's capability to transfer knowledge and skills. The *absence* of organizational fit stifles and sometimes prevents integration of an acquired unit.

## Managerial actions

Even if both strategic and organizational fit exists, synergy does not just happen. Managerial actions must be initiated to effectively match strategic capabilities to gain the competitive benefits that are permitted by the complementary managerial process, cultures, systems and structures. According to Marks and Mirvis (1998), the probability of synergy creation and eventual acquisition success are increased when managers engage in the following actions: (1) dedicating their time and energy to helping others in the firm create intended synergies, (2) forming a leadership team that is responsible for the facilitation of actions linked with synergy creation, (3) creating and stating a sense of purpose and direction for the firm with each acquisition so all can understand how individual actions will help produce synergy and enhance performance, and (4) modeling the behaviors that are expected of others in order to create synergy. Achieving integration and synergy is also much easier if managers have formed a cooperative acquisition climate.

## COOPERATIVE ACQUISITIONS

Mergers and acquisitions can challenge even the most adept managers. Thoughtful selection, diligent planning and appropriate financing of acquisitions are important, but these actions are not enough. Success also requires cooperation. Some of the best combinations require enormous amounts of goodwill, cooperation, and planning. Hitt et al. (1998) found cooperation between acquiring and target firm executives in every one of the successful acquisitions they studied. A key resource that target firm executives bring to the newly created company is their institutional memory. This memory helps acquiring firm executives understand the acquired firm's culture, historical conditions and strategic logic that have driven business decisions across time. Knowledge of this institutional memory also serves as protection against the making of short-run ineffective decisions (*The Economist*, 2000a). Because the cooperation and expertise of an acquired firm's management team is vital to long-term success, appropriate incentives, in the form of performance-based compensation packages, should be offered to the members of that team (Peterson, 1998). Merging two companies is so complicated and requires so much work by so many people that an uncooperative spirit in the target can lead to disastrous results. Friendliness can help potential merger partners overcome a multitude of obstacles that might otherwise lead to problems during negotiations and post-merger integration.

### Building cooperation

Creating an appropriate climate for acquisition negotiations requires understanding the mindset of the acquiring and target firm managers. According to Marks and Mirvis (1998: 29), "The acquirer often will have a 'victor' attitude and will tend to dominate the action. The target, the 'vanquished,' often feels powerless to defend its interests or control its fate. Target management may respond with hostility, or withdraw in defeatism." Marks and Mirvis (1998) suggest that some target firm managers in hostile takeovers refer to the process as "rape" and their buyers as "barbarians." Even in friendly deals, acquired firm managers talk of being "seduced" by promises.

Negative or derogatory attitudes obviously are counterproductive during the negotiation process; however, they can produce longer-term disadvantages as well. For example, executive turnover is much higher than normal in acquired firms (Walsh, 1988; Walsh and Ellwood, 1991). One of the great mysteries associated with the popularity of acquisitions is that the executives of acquiring companies pay a premium for the assets of a target, yet they understand that some of the most valuable of those assets, human talent, will be gone within the first few years. The level of turnover in the acquiring firm is influenced by the nature of merger negotiations (Walsh, 1989). More hostile negotiations produce greater turnover in the acquired firm after completion of the acquisition. One of the keys to a successful acquisition, then, is to avoid a win–lose climate that may eventually lead to high levels of turnover among the most valuable managers and employees.

Acquiring firm executives should be sensitive to the culture of the target and the strength of that culture (Nahavandi and Malekzadeh, 1988). Firms that have been successful are likely to have strong cultures, which requires greater adjustments and sensitivity on the part of acquiring firm executives. Other actions that can help include jointly creating goals and a business plan for the combined firm, beginning transition planning before the deal is completed, announcing a transition team and allowing transition team members to be present and participate in the final stages of the negotiation process (Heitner, 1998). These actions can help create shared purpose and greatly reduce integration problems after the acquisition is completed.

Another critical aspect of creating a friendly and cooperative climate is effective communication. Direct communication with customers and employees is essential to retaining them through the merger process (Heitner, 1998). Managerial communication with employees about the anticipated effects of the change helps to reduce their anxiety. Realistic merger previews also reduce dysfunctional outcomes after the acquisition is complete. For example, Schweiger and DeNisi (1991) conducted a study in two plants owned by *Fortune* 500 companies that were involved in mergers. The employees of one plant were given a realistic preview of the expected changes, while employees in the other facility were not. The employees of the plant in which the preview was given experienced less stress, less uncertainty and significantly higher job satisfaction, commitment and performance. In addition, they perceived that the company was more trustworthy, honest and caring.

Potential merger partners may also find it easier to achieve a friendly and productive relationship during the acquisition process if they have previously worked together. Hitt et al. (1998) found that several of the highly successful acquisitions were natural extensions of earlier ventures together. Adequate time together also is a critical factor for a friendly deal, even if the time is not spent in a formal business venture. As mentioned in our earlier discussion of due diligence, executives should avoid rushing into deals. Taking time to study a potential acquisition allows the principals from both firms to learn about each other. The best possible scenario is one in which the companies privately work together, either as partners in a venture or during a careful due diligence process.

"White knight" transactions, in which an acquiring firm rescues a target from an unwanted suitor, are friendly, but they do not enjoy all of the benefits of a privately negotiated deal. They enjoy many cooperation benefits, but not necessarily financial benefits, because "white knight" transactions involve a bidding war with another suitor that may drive up the premium. Bidding wars occur when there is resistance to a takeover.

## Resistance

From the perspective of the acquiring firm, target firm resistance typically has a negative impact on acquisition success. However, the effect on the target firm depends on the nature of the resistance. There are two general types of target firm resistance: auction-inducing resistance and competition-reducing resistance (Davis, 1991; Kosnik, 1987; Turk, 1992). Auction inducing resistance has as its ultimate goal the achievement of a higher sales price. Typically this type of resistance is considered to be in the best interests of target firm shareholders. Auction-inducing resistance includes such tactics as public opposition, litigation and bidder solicitation. Resisting a bid provides other potential suitors time to evaluate the effect an acquisition might have on the industry and their own companies. Competitors, in particular, will evaluate a potential acquisition with great interest. If top executives of a competing firm perceive the acquisition as a threat to their firm's market position or if the target, after analysis, might be a good fit with their own company, they may enter a competing bid or file a legal action to block the acquisition or delay action in order to complete a more thorough evaluation (Turk, 1992). There is potential advantage here for the target firm, but increased risk as well. A competing bid can increase the price received, but a legal suit could delay or block the acquisition.

Competition-reducing resistance is intended to make a target less attractive in the market, thereby discouraging auctions and reducing gains to target firm shareholders (Turk, 1992). So called "poison pills" can take many forms, but they all have a common goal of making the firm more costly to a potential suitor (Davis, 1991). "Shark repellants" are a special class of poison pills that typically require approval by the shareholders (Davis, 1991; Pound, 1987; Sundaramurthy, 1996). One form of shark repellents is the classified board provision, which divides directors into distinct classes (typically three), with only one class up for election each year. Consequently, a successful takeover does not ensure that the new owner can immediately assume control of the board of directors. Therefore, such a provision prevents the acquiring firm from firing top managers upon acquisition. The majority of large US corporations have instituted some form of shark repellent; such measures are also common in other countries (Davis, 1991).

From the perspective of the acquiring firm, all types of resistance can be costly. The existence of multiple bidders leads to lower returns for the acquiring firm and poison pills often are prohibitively expensive. Tender offers, which are considered hostile, are most often associated with higher final bid prices, probably because so many of them are resisted (Datta, Pinches, and Narayanan, 1992). Hostile takeovers are associated with higher levels of management turnover and lower post-acquisition performance for the acquirer (Fowler and Schmidt, 1989; Walsh, 1989). Also, hostility adversely affects post-merger integration (Jemison and Sitkin, 1986). Perhaps most importantly, unexpected tender offers deprive acquiring firm executives of the advantages of working effectively with target firm executives, thus eliminating many of the advantages of a friendly acquisition. When acquiring firm executives negotiate a friendly deal with target firm executives, the ill effects of competition-reducing resistance can be eliminated and the costs associated with auction-inducing resistance are likely to be minimized.

There is a potential agency problem associated with competition-reducing resistance, as managers act to protect their own jobs and/or organizational autonomy at the expense of shareholder interests (Amihud and Lev, 1981). They reduce the frequency of takeover bids. Also, the adoption of an anti-takeover charter amendment often leads investors to devalue a firm's stock (Mahoney and Mahoney, 1993).

There has been debate on why managers are allowed to pursue actions that are not in shareholders' best interests. One view is that entrenched managers, acting in their own self-interests, are able to pursue strategies that offer protection to their own positions at the expense of the shareholders because: (1) ownership is widely distributed; (2) shareholders are rarely well organized; (3) some shareholders may not be aware of the negative implications of such provisions; and (4) boards of directors are tightly linked to managers through both formal and informal (social) ties and therefore are more likely to support managers in such cases. The entrenchment hypothesis is supported by some research findings (e.g., Davis, 1991; Herman, 1981; Kosnik, 1987; Singh and Harianto, 1989).

An alternative view is that anti-takeover amendments are in the best interest of shareholders because they strengthen the ability of managers to fend off hostile suitors who want to acquire the firm at an unreasonably low price (Mahoney and Mahoney, 1993). Poison pills provide strong motivation for acquiring firm executives to negotiate directly with target firm executives, as opposed to offering to buy shares directly from shareholders in a tender offer. Most poison pills become void if the target firm's top executives approve the acquisition.

Poison pills are not the only aspects of mergers and acquisitions that have ethical implications. We now address a few of the more important ethical implications of mergers and acquisitions.

## ETHICAL IMPLICATIONS

There are ethical implications associated with mergers and acquisitions that differ from the occurrence of unethical actions that an effective due diligence process can identify. As we discussed previously, due diligence is conducted in part to recognize any unethical practices that may have taken place in a target. But there are ethical implications from the perspective of the acquiring firm as well. In this context, many of the potential ethical issues related to mergers and acquisitions, such as the adoption of "shark repellants," stem from managerial conflicts of interest (agency problems). Agency problems exist any time managers pursue their own interests at the expense of shareholders. Consequently, mergers and acquisitions offer great potential for agency problems. First, engaging in mergers and acquisitions may be designed to provide managers with more discretion in their jobs as well as reducing risk to their careers. If a manager's self-interest is the primary reason for engaging in a merger or acquisition, as opposed to maximizing shareholder value and satisfying other constituencies' needs, decisions to engage in this activity could be considered unethical (Achampong and Zemedkun, 1995).

Some research results show that acquisitions perform poorly when managers act in their own self-interest (Morck, Shleifer, and Vishny, 1990). Often these firms were performing poorly prior to making the acquisition, suggesting that managers were failing to effectively manage the company. The acquisition only exacerbated the problems. Because of the poor performance, such acquisitions often require the use of risky debt to finance them (because of a lack of capital and/or appropriate financial slack in the poorly performing firm prior to the acquisition). The use of risky debt, in turn, may lead to underinvestment in the newly merged firm, which creates the conditions for continuing poor performance (Teresa, 1986, 1991).

One outcome of mergers and acquisitions based on managerial self-interest is targeting unrelated businesses to acquire. There is less potential synergy in the acquisition of an unrelated business and therefore a lower potential to enhance shareholder value. However, managers sometimes favor acquiring unrelated businesses because doing so reduces their career risks (Lane, Cannella, and Lubatkin, 1998). Buying an unrelated business should balance the risk of loss of demand in the firm's current businesses resulting from economic recessions or competitors' actions. Studies show that unrelated acquisitions often fail and are divested within a few years (Blanchard, Lopez-de-Silanes, and Shleifer, 1994).

There are several issues related to the negotiation and implementation of mergers and acquisitions in which a potential exists for the surfacing of ethical issues. These issues include lies and deception in negotiations, coercion, maximization of value without consideration of other parties' needs and termination of employees. Problems such as these can impede the integration process and also result in the unintentional loss of valuable human capital (Hitt, Harrison, and Ireland, 2001; Ireland and Hitt, 1999). As discussed earlier, an effective due diligence process can identify these issues quickly, allowing more time for their resolution.

Ethical problems have led to the creation of governance mechanisms to ensure the protection of shareholders' interests.

## GOVERNANCE

The board of directors is intended to operate as a governance mechanism overseeing managerial actions and ensuring that they are in shareholders' best interests. Unfortunately, in companies where top managers have engaged in unethical activities, board members are prominently visible largely by their absent voice. Governance in these cases may be more problematic when the CEO engages in such activities and also serves as chair of the board of directors. Because of close personal relationships with the executives and a lack of time and/or interest, members of boards of directors may cede too much power to the firm's top executives (Evans, Noe, and Thornton, 1997).

Ownership in a company may contribute to effective governance and/or prevent inappropriate managerial actions. For example, some studies have shown that where the ownership in a particular company is concentrated and when outside members of the board of directors own equity in the company, firms are more likely to sell unrelated businesses in order to enhance firm performance (Bergh, 1995). Evidence also shows that the more equity owned by managers of target firms, the more they act in the best interest of the shareholders in situations where their firm is acquired (Hubbard and Palia, 1995). For example, when managers of the firm targeted for takeover have greater equity in the firm, there tend to be fewer anti-takeover provisions that discourage or prevent takeovers (Petry and Settle, 1991). When managers own equity in their firm, it may also strengthen the relationship within the top management team and between the managers and major shareholders, which would tend to reduce internal corporate politics and improve the effectiveness of decision-making processes in the firm (Green, 1992).

Hostile takeovers are assumed to be a governance mechanism in the market for corporate control. They are designed to target firms' assets that are undervalued by the market and the management of the firm is either unable or unwilling to make the changes necessary to ensure that the market properly values them (Almeder and Carey, 1991). However, evidence shows that not all hostile takeover bids are designed to accomplish these purposes. For example, in some cases, after the hostile takeover is completed, managers of the acquired firm continue to operate the firm as they did previously. In these cases, the hostile takeover does not discipline poorly performing managers. Also, in some instances, hostile takeover bids have been made for firms that were performing well above their industry counterparts. The managers of these firms likely do not need disciplining (Franks and Mayer, 1996).

We have now discussed some of the most important factors that influence the success of mergers and acquisitions, as well as significant ethical and governance issues. However, before offering our suggestions for future research, we discuss one of the most pervasive trends in the field of strategic management today. Increasingly, organizations around the world are engaging in cross-border acquisitions.

## CROSS-BORDER ACQUISITIONS

The number of cross-border mergers and acquisitions is growing quickly. At least five reasons may account for this. Through merger and acquisition transactions completed with companies outside their home nation, firms may be able to increase their market power, overcome market entry barriers, reduce the cost and length of time to develop new products, increase their speed to market and become more diversified (Hitt, Hoskisson, and Ireland, 1994; Hitt et al., 1996; Hitt, Hoskisson, and Kim, 1997; McCardle and Viswanathan, 1994). Evidence suggests that most cross-border acquisitions are motivated by a combination of several of these reasons (Hitt, Harrison, and Ireland, 2001).

In 1999, cross-border acquisitions totaled approximately $1.4 trillion. This represented about 40 percent of the total value of all acquisitions during this year. Furthermore, this figure was double the 1998 percentage. In the first half of 2000, the percentage of cross-border mergers and acquisitions increased to one-half of total acquisition value (Hansen, 2000). Stimulating this increased activity were several conditions, including the worldwide phenomenon of industry consolidations and movement towards a common currency in Europe (Lebis, 1999). Additionally, the privatization and liberalization of global power markets continued to spur cross-border transactions.

The continuing rapid growth of cross-border acquisitions, some of which are completed with companies resident in countries with relatively unstable financial economies, may suggest a caution to firms to avoid completing ill-advised transactions during what may have become a corporate "frenzy" to achieve global growth (*Global Finance*, 2000). This caution notwithstanding, cross-border mergers and acquisitions have become a major strategic tool for corporate growth, especially for multinational corporations (Morosini, Shane, and Singh, 1998). They provide potential to increase the efficiency and effectiveness of whole industries in addition to affecting individual companies' competitive ability. This is so because these transactions help to consolidate an industry on a global level. Without consolidation (and the synergistic benefits that can accrue from it), overcapacity and the cost pressures and competitive pricing tactics that accompany it harm industry participants. Cross-border acquisitions also have the potential to influence whole economies, as companies in developing nations build permanent ownership relationships with companies in industrialized economies, thus gaining knowledge and much-needed resources (Zahra, Ireland, and Hitt, 2000; Zahra, Ireland, Guiterrez, and Hitt, 2000).

Organizations that are particularly effective in completing cross-border transactions use a set of valuable, firm-specific resources and capabilities that cannot be imitated easily or substituted (Rouse and Daellenbach, 1999). Developed across time and through repeated use, these resources and capabilities are the foundation for successful cross-border acquisitions. For example, a global mindset affects the success of cross-border acquisitions. This mindset has several distinct components, including "multicultural values, basing status on merit rather than nationality, being open to ideas from other cultures, being excited rather than fearful in new cultural settings, and being sensitive to cultural differences without being intimidated by them" (Dutton, 1999). Operationally, especially regarding actions taken to integrate firms into a single new entity, thinking globally means "taking the best [that] other cultures have to offer and blending that into a third culture" (Dutton, 1999).

As researchers, we know little about the causes of cross-border acquisition success. One of the difficult issues that need to be addressed is whether cross-border acquisitions are fundamentally different from domestic ones. In many studies of mergers and acquisitions, cross-border acquisitions are grouped together with domestic ones. In other studies, cross-border acquisitions are excluded completely. Relatively few studies have investigated cross-border acquisitions as a group. One possibility is that cross-border acquisitions do not differ fundamentally from domestic acquisitions. If this is the case, then theory regarding mergers and acquisitions can be applied to cross-border acquisitions as well. The opposite case would be that almost nothing that applies to domestic acquisitions applies to cross-border acquisitions. The truth obviously lies between these two extremes, and determining what applies and what does not suggests an interesting set of questions warranting scholarly inquiry.

## RECOMMENDATIONS FOR FUTURE RESEARCH

There are no simple formulas for success in mergers and acquisitions. Business is complicated and constantly changing, making success difficult to obtain and even more difficult to sustain. This is especially true with regard to mergers and acquisitions. The research literature on mergers and acquisitions seems to suggest that financial success requires careful combination of complementary or otherwise related resources, coupled with appropriate financing, a friendly negotiation climate, organizational fit and managerial actions that help the combined firm realize potential synergies. Opportunism or other ethical problems (e.g., high debt, target firm resistance or straying from the core business) can erase potential financial gains. If these latter attributes exist, a merger or acquisition is often unwarranted.

Many of these conclusions are tentative and require further testing. For example, although governance issues have been explored in some depth, other ethical issues associated with acquisition activities are only beginning to be addressed. In particular, researchers could examine the influence of acquisitions on a much wider range of stakeholders (e.g., employees, communities, suppliers, etc.). The influence of debt on merger and acquisition outcomes is another fruitful avenue requiring substantially more research. The importance (or lack thereof) of slack in motivating acquisitions and influencing their performance is still an issue of debate. Also, as mentioned previously, much of the theory on mergers and acquisitions is probably applicable to cross-border acquisitions as well; however, only more research will determine how much of what we think we know really applies when borders are crossed. There is ample room for new theory development related to cross-border acquisitions.

Researchers should also consider the influence of combinations of attributes as opposed to individual factors. Some of the ingredients of successful acquisitions combine in interesting ways. Specifically, particular attributes may need to be present for other attributes to be effective. For example, if merging firms enjoy resource complementarity, but the transaction is unfriendly, synergy is unlikely because synergy creation requires managers from the merging firms to work together. Cooperation is unlikely in a hostile acquisition. Another important relationship is between debt and innovation. Low-to-moderate debt levels increase the probability that innovation activity will continue after the merger. Hitt et al. (1998) found both low debt levels and an emphasis on innovation in many successful mergers and acquisitions. Unfortunately, high debt can divert resources away from R&D and cause managers to be more risk averse, which reduces the likelihood that they will promote research projects considered to be higher in risk.

Other combinations of attributes are also likely to influence merger and acquisition outcomes. For example, due diligence is likely to have an impact on many other attributes of successful acquisitions. Complete and probing due diligence may reduce the probability that ethical problems will surface either during or after the transaction. Furthermore, the information gained during due diligence would probably help a potential acquirer uncover uniquely valuable synergistic opportunities and determine an appropriate bid price for the target. Organizational learning likewise should influence all of the other attributes we have mentioned. In addition, high premiums may lead to higher debt, which could be significant in firms that lack financial slack.

## CONCLUSION

As a field, we have much to learn. At present, the unexplained variance in the performance of mergers and acquisitions is greater than what we have been able to explain. Furthermore, the global environment in which mergers and acquisitions take place is changing constantly. Consequently, researchers should have plenty to investigate as they attempt to confirm existing ideas, test current theories in cross-border settings, develop new factors and combine currently identified factors in new ways.

## REFERENCES

Achampong, F. K., and Zemedkun, W. (1995). An empirical and ethical analysis of factors motivating managers' merger decision. *Journal of Business Ethics*, 14: 855–65.

Agarwall, J. F., Jaffe, J. F., and Mandelker, G. N. (1992). The post-merger performance of acquiring firms: A re-examination of an anomaly. *Journal of Finance*, 47: 1605–21.

Allweiss, A. (1998). The perils and pitfalls of expanding to Europe. *Commercial Lending Review*, 13: 23–8.

Almeder, R., and Carey, D. (1991). In defense of sharks: Moral issues in hostile liquidating takeovers. *Journal of Business Ethics*, 10: 471–84.

Altier, W. J. (1997). A method for unearthing likely post-deal snags. *Mergers and Acquisitions*, January/February: 33–5.

Amburgey, T. L., and Miner, A. S. (1992). Strategic momentum: The effects of repetitive, positional and contextual momentum on merger activity. *Strategic Management Journal*, 13: 335–48.

Amihud, Y., and Lev, B. (1981). Risk reduction as a managerial motive for conglomerate mergers. *Bell Journal of Economics*, 12: 650–7.

Anand, J. (2000). A match made in heaven? *Ivey Business Journal*, July/August: 68–73.

Barfield, R. (1998). Creating value through mergers. *The Banker*, July: 24–5.

Barney, J. (1988). Returns to bidding firms in mergers and acquisitions: Reconsidering the relatedness hypothesis. *Strategic Management Journal*, 9 (special issue): 71–8.

Bennett, J. (1998). Merger tally hits $626B – But nothing lasts forever. *Wall Street Journal Interactive Edition*, May 11, interactive.wsj.com/archive.

Bergh, D. D. (1995). Size and relatedness of units sold: An agency theory and resource-based perspective. *Strategic Management Journal*, 16: 221–39.

Blanchard, O. J., Lopez-de-Silanes, F., and Shleifer, A. (1994). What do firms do with cash windfalls? *Journal of Financial Economics*, 36: 337–60.

Bourgeois, L. J. (1981). On the measurement of organizational slack. *Academy of Management Review*, 26: 29–39.

Bowers, H. M. and Miller, R. E. (1990). Choice of investment banker and shareholder's wealth of firms involved in acquisitions. *Financial Management*, Winter: 34–44.

Brown, D. T., and Ryngaert, M. D. (1991). The mode of acquisition in takeovers: Taxes and asymmetric information. *Journal of Finance*, 46: 653–69.

Byczek, R. C. (1997). Are you getting what you pay for in an acquisition? *Mergers and Acquisitions*, July/August: 20–3.

Carleton, W. T., Guilkey, D. K., Harris, R. S., and Stewart, J. F. (1983). An empirical analysis of the role of the medium of exchange in mergers. *Journal of Finance*, 38: 813–26.

Carper, W. B. (1990). Corporate acquisitions and shareholder wealth: A review and explanatory analysis. *Journal of Management*, 16: 807–23.

Chaney, P. K., Lovata, L. M. and Philipich, K. L. (1991). Acquiring firm characteristics and the medium of exchange. *Quarterly Journal of Business and Economics*, 30: 55–69.

Chen, M. J. (1996). Competitor analysis and interfirm rivalry: Toward a theoretical integration. *Academy of Management Review*, 21: 100–34.

Crawford, D. (1987). *The Structure of Corporate Mergers: Accounting, Tax and Form-of-payment Choices*. Unpublished dissertation, University of Rochester, New York.

D'Aveni, R. A. (1994). *Hypercompetition*. New York: Free Press.

Datta, D. K., and Grant, J. H. (1990). Relationships between type of acquisition, the autonomy given to the acquired firm and acquisition success: An empirical analysis. *Journal of Management*, 16: 29–44.

Datta, D. K., Pinches, G. E., and Narayanan, V. K. (1992). Factors influencing wealth creation from mergers and acquisitions: A meta-analysis. *Strategic Management Journal*, 13: 67–84.

Davis, G. F. (1991). Agents without principles? The spread of the poison pill through the intercorporate network. *Administrative Science Quarterly*, 36: 583–613.

de Castillo, N., Lopez, A., Mullerat, R., and Solano, M. (1998). Tax strategies for acquirers in Latin America. *Corporate Finance*, February: 40–5.

Donlon, J. P. (2000). Why John Chambers is the CEO of the future. *Chief Executive*, July: 26–36.

Dutton, G. (1999). Building a global brain. *Management Review*, May: 23–30.

Eisenhardt, K. M., and Brown, S. L. (1998). Time pacing: Competing in markets that won't stand still. *Harvard Business Review*, 76(2): 59–69.

Evans, J., Noe, T. H., and Thornton, J. H. Jr., 1997. Regulatory distortion of management compensation: The case of golden parachutes for bank managers. *Journal of Banking and Finance*, 21: 825–48.

Fowler, K. L., and Schmidt, D. R. (1989). Determinants of tender offer post-acquisition financial performance. *Strategic Management Journal*, 10: 339–50.

Franks, J., and Mayer, C. (1996). Hostile takeovers and the direction of managerial failure. *Journal of Financial Economics*, 40: 163–81.

Ghosh, A., and Ruland, W. (1998). Managerial ownership, the method of payment for acquisitions and executive job retention. *Journal of Finance*, 53: 785–98.

Glassman, J. K. (1998). Selecting profitable stocks from mergers no slam dunk. *Houston Chronicle*, May 18: 4D.

*Global Finance* (2000). UK tops US in cross border M&A. June: 80.

Goold, M., and Campbell, A. (1998). Desperately seeking synergy. *Harvard Business Review*, 76 (5): 131–43.

Gordon, M. (1998). Merger wave no threat, Greenspan tells senators. *Bryan-College Station Eagle*, June 17: 6C.

Gray, J. (1998). M&A takes off with a bang. *The Banker*, March: 31–4.

Green, S. (1992). Managerial motivation and strategy in management buyouts: A cultural analysis. *Journal of Management Studies*, 29: 513–35.

Haigh, D. (1999). Mergers will fail unless the focus is on marketing. *Marketing*, February 11: 20.

Haleblian, J., and Finkelstein, S. (1999). The influence of organizational acquisition experience on acquisition performance: A behavioral perspective. *Administrative Science Quarterly*, 44: 29–56.

Hansen, F. (2000). Global mergers and acquisitions explode. *Business Credit*, June: 21–5.

Hansen, R. G. (1987). A theory for the choice of exchange medium in mergers and acquisitions. *Journal of Business*, 60: 75–95.

Harrison, J. (1999). Finding the ethics soft spots of a target. *Mergers and Acquisitions*, September/October: 8–11.

Harrison, J. E., and St. John, C. (1998). *Strategic management of organizations and stakeholders*, 2nd edn. Cincinnati: SouthWestern College Publishing.

Harrison, J. S., Hitt, M. A., Hoskisson, R. E., and Ireland, R. D. (1991). Synergies and post-acquisition performance: Differences versus similarities in resource allocations. *Journal of Management*, 17: 173–90.

Haspeslagh, P., and Jemison, D. B. (1991). *Managing acquisitions*. New York: Free Press.

Hayward, M. L. A., and Hambrick, D. C. (1997). Explaining the premiums paid for large acquisitions: Evidence of CEO hubris. *Administrative Science Quarterly*, 42: 103–27.

Heitner, M. (1998. The thorny business of merging rival firms. *Mergers and Acquisitions*, January/February: 18–22.

Herman, E. S. (1981). *Corporate Control, Corporate Power*. New York: Cambridge University Press.

Hitt, M. A., Bierman, L., Shimizu, K., and Kochhar, R. (2001). Direct and moderating effects of human capital and strategy on performance in professional service firms: A resource based perspective. *Academy of Management Journal*, in press.

Hitt, M. A., Harrison, J. R., and Ireland, R. D. (2001). *Mergers and Acquisitions: A Guide to Creating Value for Stakeholders*. New York: Oxford University Press.

Hitt, M. A., Harrison, J. R., Ireland, R. D., and Best, A. (1998). Attributes of successful and unsuccessful acquisitions of US firms. *British Journal of Management*, 9: 91–114.

Hitt, M. A., Hoskisson, R. E., and Ireland, R. D. (1990). Mergers and acquisitions and managerial commitment to innovation in M-form firms. *Strategic Management Journal*, 11(special issue): 29–47.

Hitt, M. A., Hoskisson, R. E., and Ireland, R. D. (1994). A mid-range theory of the interactive effects of international and product diversification on innovation and performance. *Journal of Management*, 20: 297–326.

Hitt, M. A., Hoskisson, R. E., Ireland, R. D., and Harrison, J. S. (1991a). Effects of acquisitions on R&D inputs and outputs. *Academy of Management Journal*, 34: 693–706.

Hitt, M. A., Hoskisson, R. E., Ireland, R. D., and Harrison, J. S. (1991b). Are acquisitions a poison pill for innovation? *Academy of Management Executive*, 5(4): 22–34.

Hitt, M. A., Hoskisson, R. E., Johnson, R. A., and Moesel, D. D. (1996). The market for corporate control and firm innovation. *Academy of Management Journal*, 39: 1084–119.

Hitt, M. A., Hoskisson, R. E., and Kim, H. (1997). International diversification: Effects on innovation and firm performance in product-diversified firms. *Academy of Management Journal*, 40: 767–98.

Hitt, M. A., Ireland, R. D., and Hoskisson, R. E. (2001). *Strategic management: Competitiveness and globalization*, 4th edn. Cincinnati, OH: SouthWestern Publishing Company.

Hong, H., Kaplan, R. S., and Mandelker, G. (1978). Pooling vs. purchase: The effects of accounting for mergers on stock prices. *The Accounting Review*, 53: 31–47.

Hubbard, R. G., and Palia, D. (1995). Benefits of control, managerial ownership, and the stock returns of acquiring firms. *Rand Journal of Economics*, 26: 781–92.

Huber, G. P. (1991). Organizational learning: The contributing processes and the literatures. *Organization Science*, 2: 88–115.

Ireland, R. D., and Hitt, M. A. (1999). Achieving and maintaining strategic competitiveness in the 21st century: The role of strategic leadership. *Academy of Management Executive*, 12(1): 43–57.

Ireland, R. D., Hitt, M. A., Camp, S. M., and Sexton, D. L. (2001). Integrating entrepreneurship and strategic management thinking to create firm wealth. *Academy of Management Executive*, 13(1): in press.

Jemison, D. B., and Sitkin, S. B. (1986). Corporate acquisitions: A process perspective. *Academy of Management Review*, 11: 145–63.

Jensen, M. C., and Rubach, R. S. (1983). The market for corporate control: The scientific evidence. *Journal of Financial Economics*, 11: 305–60.

Jensen, M. C. (1988a). Takeovers: Their causes and consequences. *Journal of Economic Perspectives*, 1: 21–48).

Jensen, M. C. (1988b. Agency costs of free cash flow, corporate finance and the market for takeovers. *American Economic Review*, 76: 323–29.

Kesner, I. F., Shapiro, D. L., and Sharma, A. (1994). Brokering mergers: An agency theory perspective on the role of representatives. *Academy of Management Journal*, 37: 703–21.

Kosnik, R. D. (1987). Greenmail: A study of board performance in corporate governance. *Administrative Science Quarterly*, 32: 163–85.

Kusewitt, J. B., Jr. (1985). An exploratory study of strategic acquisition factors relating to performance. *Strategic Management Journal*, 6: 151–69.

Lane, P. J., Cannella, A. A., Jr., and Lubatkin, M. H. (1998). Agency problems as antecedents to unrelated mergers and diversification: Amihud and Lev reconsidered. *Strategic Management Journal*, 19: 555–78.

Lang, L. H. P., Stulz, R. M., and Walkling, R. A. (1991). A test of the free cash flow hypothesis: The case of bidder returns. *Journal of Financial Economics*, 29: 315–35.

Laufer, W. S. (1996). Integrity, diligence and the limits of good corporate citizenship. *American Business Law Journal*, 34: 157–81.

Lebis, A. (1999). Foremost on cross-border dealmakers' list of concerns? Integrating cultures. *Securities Data Publishing*, May 31.

Lepak, S. (1998). How to sabotage a multicultural merger? "Ignore it." *Computer World*, 32: I1S7.

Lei, D., and Hitt, M. A. (1995). Strategic restructuring and outsourcing: The effect of mergers and acquisitions and LBOs on building firm skills and capabilities. *Journal of Management*, 21: 835–59.

Loderer, C., and Martin, K. (1992). Post acquisition performance of acquiring firms. *Financial Management*, 21: 69–77.

Lucenko, K. (2000). Strategies for growth. *Across the Board*, September: 63.

Mahoney, J. M., and Mahoney, J. T. (1993). An empirical investigation of the effect of corporate charter antitakeover amendments on stockholder wealth. *Strategic Management Journal*, 14: 17–31.

Marks, M. L., and Mirvis, P. H. (1998). How mind-set clashes get merger partners off to a bad start. *Mergers and Acquisitions*, September/October: 29.

Martin, K. J. (1996). The method of payment in corporate acquisitions, investment opportunities and management ownership. *Journal of Finance*, 51: 1227–46.

McCardle, K. F., and Viswanathan, S. (1994). The direct entry versus takeover decision and stock price performance around takeovers. *Journal of Business*, 67: 1–43.

McLaughlin, R. M. (1990). Investment-banking contracts in tender offers. *Journal of Financial Economics*, 28: 209–32.

*Mergers and Acquisitions* (1998). Form of payment in M&A deals by price range. April/May: 47.

Michel, A., Shaked, I., and Lee, Y.T. (1991). An evaluation of investment banker acquisition advice: The shareholder's perspective. *Financial Management*, Summer: 40–9.

Morck, R., Shleifer, A., and Vishny, R. W. (1990). Do managerial objectives drive bad acquisitions? *Journal of Finance*, 45: 31–48.

Morosini, P., Shane, S., and Singh, H. (1998). National cultural distance and cross-border acquisition performance. *Journal of International Business Studies*, 29(1): 137–58.

Nahavandi, A., and Malekzadeh, A. R. (1988). Acculturation in mergers and acquisitions. *Academy of Management Review*, 13: 79–90.

Nohria, N., and Gulati, R. (1996). Is slack good or bad for innovation? *Academy of Management Journal*, 39: 1234–64.

Oliver, C. (1997). Sustainable competitive advantage: Combining institutional and resource-based views. *Strategic Management Journal*, 18: 697–713.

Pennings, J. M., Barkema, H., and Douma, S. (1994). Organizational learning and diversification. *Academy of Management Journal*, 37: 608–40.

Perlmurth, L. (1996). Who needs M&A bankers? *Institutional Investor*, 30 (April): 32.

Peterson, P. A. (1998). Performance-based nonqualified retirement plans: Creating value in mergers and acquisitions. *Benefits Quarterly*, Third Quarter: 59–67.

Petry, G., and Settle, J. (1991). Relationship of takeover gains to the state of owners in the acquiring firms. *Journal of Economics and Business*, 43(2): 99–114.

Porter, M. E. (1987). From competitive advantage to corporate strategy. *Harvard Business Review*, 67(3): 43–59.

Pound, J. (1987). The effects of antitakeover amendments on takeover activity: Some direct evidence. *Journal of Law and Economics*, 30: 353–67.

Prahalad, C. K., and Hamel, G. (1990). The core competence of the corporation. *Harvard Business Review*, 68(3): 85.

Quinn, J. B. (1992). *The Intelligent Enterprise*. New York: Free Press.

Ravenscraft, D. J., and Scherer, R. M. (1987). *Mergers, sell-offs and economic efficiency*. Washington, DC: Brookings Institute.

Roll, R. (1986). The hubris hypothesis of corporate takeovers. *Journal of Business*, 59: 197–216.

Rouse, M. J., and Daellenbach, U. S. (1999). Rethinking research methods for the resource-based perspective: Isolating sources of sustainable competitive advantage. *Strategic Management Journal*, 20: 487–94.

Schoenberg, R. (1998). Acquisitions in Central Europe: Myths and realities. *European Business Journal*, 10: 34–8.

Schweiger, D. M., and Denisi, A. S. (1991). Communication with employees following a merger: A longitudinal field experiment. *Academy of Management Journal*, 34: 110–35.

Servaes, H. (1991). Tobin's $q$ and the gains from takeovers. *Journal of Finance*, 46: 409–19.

Shearlock, P. (1995). The investment picture is shaped by boom in cross-border deals and in U.S. mergers and acquisitions. *The Banker*, February: 16–19.

Singh, H., and Harianto, F. (1989). Management-board relationships, takeover risk and the adoption of golden parachutes. *Academy of Management Journal*, 32: 7–24.

Sirower, M. L. (1997). *The synergy trap*. New York: Free Press.

Sirower, M. L. (1998a). Constructing a synergistic base for premier deals. *Mergers and Acquisitions*, May/June: 41–9.

Sirower, M. L. (1998b). Imagined synergy: A prescription for a no-win deal. *Mergers and Acquisitions*, January/February: 23–9.

Sirower, M. L., and O'Byrne, S. F. (1998). The measurement of post-acquisition performance: Toward a value-based benchmarking methodology. *Journal of Applied Corporate Finance*, 11: 107–21.

Sundaramurthy, C. (1996). Corporate governance within the context of antitakeover provisions. *Strategic Management Journal*, 17: 377–94.

*The Economist*. (2000a). First among equals. August 26: 59–60.

*The Economist*. (2000b). A Bavarian botch-up. August 5: 65–6.

Teece, D. J., Pisano, G., and Shuen, A. (1997). Dynamic capabilities and strategic management. *Strategic Management Journal*, 18: 509–33.

Teresa, J. A. (1986). Mergers and investment incentives. *Journal of Financial and Quantitative Analysis*, 21: 393–413.

Teresa, J. A. (1991). Corporate restructuring and incentive effects of leverage and taxes. *Managerial & Decision Economics*, 12: 461–72.

Tully, S. (1998). Merrill Lynch takes over. *Fortune*, April 27: 138–44.

Turk, T. A. (1992). Takeover resistance, information leakage and target firm value. *Journal of Management*, 18: 503–22.

Very, T., Lubatkin, M., Calori, R., and Veiga, J. (1997). Relative standing and the performance of recently acquired European firms. *Strategic Management Journal*, 18: 593–614.

Walsh, J. P. (1988). Top management turnover following mergers and acquisitions. *Strategic Management Journal*, 9: 173–84.

Walsh, J. P. (1989). Doing a deal: Merger and acquisition negotiations and their impact upon target company top management turnover. *Strategic Management Journal*, 10: 307–22.

Walsh, J. P., and Ellwood, J. W. (1991). Mergers, acquisitions and the pruning of managerial deadwood. *Strategic Management Journal*, 12: 201–17.

Wansley, J. W., Lane, W. R., and Yang, H. C. (1987). Gains to bidder firms in cash and securities transactions. *The Financial Review*, 22: 403–14.

Weiss, B. D. (1998). Information-age acquisitions: Locking up assets, Part I. *Mergers and Acquisitions*, July/August: 19–26.

Zahra, S. A., Ireland, R. D., Gutierrez, I., and Hitt, M. A. (2000). Privatization and entrepreneurial transformation: Emerging issues and a future research agenda. *Academy of Management Review*, 25: 509–24.

Zahra, S. A., Ireland, R. D., and Hitt, M. A. (2000). International expansion by new venture firms: International diversity, mode of market entry, technological learning, and performance. *Academy of Management Journal*, 43: 925–50.

# 14

## Strategic Alliances

### ANDREW C. INKPEN

Strategic alliances have become well established as a viable organizational form and an important means of strategy implementation. In many industries, complexity and uncertainty have increased to the point that competing autonomously is no longer an option. Strategic alliances have the potential to create various benefits for the partner firms, such as access to new technologies and complementary skills, economies of scale, and the reduction of risk. This chapter provides an analysis of major issues and research questions involving strategic alliances. The chapter begins with a definition of alliances and then moves on to consider the rationale for alliances, learning as an alliance motive, alliance performance and instability, control issues, trust and alliances, and evolutionary processes. Within each section, key research areas and questions are identified and the major supporting research and associated findings are discussed. In the concluding section, several important directions for future research are identified.

## A DEFINITION OF STRATEGIC ALLIANCES

Strategic alliances are collaborative organizational arrangements that use resources and/ or governance structures from more than one existing organization. Strategic alliances have three important characteristics. First, the two (or more) firms partnering remain independent subsequent to the formation of the alliance. Second, alliances possess the feature of ongoing mutual interdependence, in which one party is vulnerable to the other (Parkhe, 1993). Mutual interdependence leads to shared control and management, which contributes to the complexity of alliance management and often creates significant administrative and coordination costs. Third, because the partners remain independent, there is uncertainty as to what one party expects the other party to do (Powell, 1996).

Based on the previous definition, a broad range of organizational forms can be classified as alliances, including equity joint ventures, licensing arrangements, shared product development projects, minority equity relationships, and shared purchasing and manufacturing. The two types of interfirm relationships excluded from the strategic alliance definition are market-based transactions undertaken by two firms and the merger of firms. Although some authors have treated mergers and acquisitions as a form of alliance, this is inconsistent with the concept of an alliance. The new organization that results from a merger or acquisition does not depend on two or more existing organizations for its survival, as does an alliance.

## Alliances and knowledge exchange

Until the late 1980s, the equity joint venture was viewed virtually synonymously with the term alliance. More recently, and concurrent with the vast number of new alliance formations, researchers have been investigating a much broader set of collaborative arrangements (e.g. Hagedoorn, 1993). In addition, because the alliance concept has become so widely used in practice, it is necessary to provide some additional boundary conditions to distinguish alliances from other forms of interorganizational relationships (IORs). Strategic alliances and the associated challenges of management do not exist when a relationship is based on an arms-length market-based transaction. More importantly, alliances create interesting managerial issues because they involve the exchange of knowledge between two or more firms. The knowledge may be associated with partner skills, technologies, future plans, etc. When knowledge is exchanged between firms, there is a risk that the knowledge may be appropriated or somehow misused. When knowledge is exchanged, firms have two options: they can try to protect themselves with contracts or they can resort to trust. Invariably, not every contingency can be anticipated at the outset of an alliance so trust will play a key role in alliance management. If trust between the partners is relatively unimportant because of the simplicity of the alliance or the comprehensiveness of the contract, the alliance management challenge and issues of interest to alliance researchers are minimized. Later in this chapter I examine trust in more detail.

## Alliance forms and alliance research

Because of the many alliance forms that exist (and new forms are emerging all the time), alliance researchers have three choices with respect to theory development. One is to focus on a specific form, such as equity joint ventures. The second is to incorporate variables that capture aspects of alliance form. For example, Dyer and Singh (1998) develop a framework for understanding how relational rents are earned and preserved. One of the constructs in the framework is effective governance, which allows the authors to introduce issues associated with different alliance forms. The third, and theoretically unsupportable, option is to focus on alliances as a single organizational form. Any general theory of alliances is destined to be limited in explanatory power unless the theory deals with differences in alliance form. The dynamics of creating value through equity joint ventures are very different than those associated with say, R&D collaborations or licensing agreements. For example, technology-based alliances are often formed with planned termination dates; equity joint ventures usually do not have a planned termination. Depending on the alliance form, the nature and type of resource allocations will be different, as will be competitive dynamics, bargaining power, and performance measurement.

## THE RATIONALE FOR STRATEGIC ALLIANCES

Strategic alliances are formed for a variety of reasons. These reasons are examined in this section by addressing two key questions: what are the collaborative objectives in forming an alliance and why is an alliance the preferred organizational form? Although the questions are addressed separately, in practice they are intertwined in a firm's decision to collaborate.

### *Collaborative objectives*

By definition, alliances are formed by two or more firms to perform a joint task. By pooling resources, the parents can create value in a way that could not be achieved by acting alone. Value creation refers to the process of combining the capabilities and resources of the partners to perform a joint task that has the potential to create monetary or other benefits for the partners. Although the perceived value to each of the partners need not be the same, and will rarely be the same, each alliance partner must gain some benefits for an alliance to be the preferred option (Porter and Fuller, 1986). Thus, selecting the appropriate partner is an important managerial decision (for research in this area, see Geringer, 1988; Hitt et al., 2000).

The collaborative objectives refer to the objectives that are achieved by working with one or more partners. These objectives are discussed extensively in the alliance literature (e.g., Contractor and Lorange, 1988; Gulati, 1998; Harrigan, 1986; Hennart, 1988, 1991; Inkpen, 1995a; Kogut, 1988; Osborn and Hagedoorn, 1997; Porter and Fuller, 1986). The objectives, or benefits of alliances, can be classified broadly in several categories. Although discussed individually, firms will usually have concurrent strategic objectives in forming alliances.

An increasingly important collaborative objective in today's fast moving competitive environment is speed. Given the choice between internal development and alliance, many firms choose alliances because they allow faster strategy implementation. For example, now that alliances are no longer legally required in China (for most industries), firms have the option of creating a wholly-owned subsidiary. However, entering the Chinese market alone is often slower than entering via alliances. As well, in a world moving at "internet speed," a go-it-alone strategy may not allow firms to capitalize on new opportunities. Because technology, market access, or complementary skills may be obtainable quickly via a partner, an alliance can be a more rapid means of establishing a competitive position than through replication or internal development. This implies that alliances may be more likely to occur in industries undergoing rapid structural change. The telecommunications industry of the 21st century is a good example of an industry with rapidly evolving technology and a multitude of alliances.

A second objective is to gain economies of scale by pooling economic activities such as raw materials supply, manufacturing, and marketing and distribution. The internet is making it easy for small firms to collaborate in order to gain scale economies in areas such as purchasing and distribution. A third objective is to reduce risk and promote stability. Alliances may be an attractive option for large, risky projects, such as oil and gas exploration, because neither partner bears the full cost of the venture activity. Alliances also may be used when there is a high degree of technological uncertainty and firms are unwilling to proceed on their own, such as with the SEMATECH alliance in semiconductors (Browning, Beyer, and Shetler, 1995). A fourth objective is legitimacy (Oliver, 1990). Firms may seek established partners to capitalize on the partner's reputation. This objective may be prevalent in cases where small firms seek cooperative relationships with larger firms. In the software industry, large firms such as Microsoft have established many relationships with small software developers. For the small firms, having a partner like Microsoft creates important industry legitimacy.

A fifth objective is to gain access to another firm's knowledge or ability to perform an activity where there are skill asymmetries between firms. Using alliances to enter foreign markets or to bring foreign products to local markets can give the firm access to resources that would not be available if the firm attempted the market entry alone. Firms may pool complementary resources in order to diversify into new product or geographic markets. Firms also may seek new technology in their core business area and therefore use an alliance to gain access to that knowledge. Sometimes alliances are used as a means of learning about a partner to identify potential synergies that could result if the partner firm were acquired. Hitt et al. (1998) found that such acquisitions were much more successful than others. Other alliance objectives could include co-opting or blocking competition, vertical quasi-integration, and overcoming government mandated investment guidelines that prevent wholly-owned subsidiaries (Contractor and Lorange, 1988).

## Alliances and organizational forms

The strategic benefits discussed above provide a strategic rationale as to why firms form alliances. However, strategic explanations alone are not sufficient to explain the formation of an alliance because for each of the objectives, alternative organizational forms or structures could, in many cases, be chosen to achieve the same objective (Buckley and Casson, 1996; Hennart, 1988). Therefore, the question of why an alliance is preferred to another form, such as an internally developed wholly-owned subsidiary, acquisition, or a market-based contract, must be addressed.

Transaction cost theory has been used to explain why a firm prefers an alliance over both arms-length transactions and over the options of internal development or mergers and acquisition. The transaction cost explanation for the formation of alliances is based on the approach proposed by Williamson (1975, 1981). Williamson's main argument was that hierarchically organized firms will replace the market for transactions in situations where the market for intermediate goods is inefficient. This inefficiency arises when there is uncertainty about the outcome or value of the transactions (i.e. a high degree of asset specificity) and when there is difficulty in creating the proper performance incentives for each party in the transaction. Williamson proposed that firms choose how to transact with the objective of minimizing transaction and production costs.

The majority of the work on transaction costs and alliances has been in international business/international management. Using transaction costs theory, persuasive arguments for the formation of alliances as an alternative to the multinational corporation (MNC) subsidiary can be made (e.g. Beamish and Banks, 1987; Contractor, 1990; Dunning, 1995; Hennart, 1988, 1991; Madhok, 1997). Transaction cost theory maintains that alliance arrangements develop under conditions of too many uncertainties for a complete contract to be written but when it is not effective to internalize (Hennart, 1988). Madhok (1997) argued that markets may be unable to adequately bundle together the relevant tacit resources and capabilities. Beamish and Banks (1987) and Contractor (1990) proposed that alliances are preferable to MNCs when the transactional difficulties of opportunism, bounded rationality, uncertainty, and small numbers condition can efficiently be dealt with in an alliance. As well, alliances reduce the transaction and coordinating costs of arms-length market transactions (Dunning, 1995).

Another situation where alliances may be preferable to acquisition occurs when acquiring the desired firm-specific assets also means acquiring other businesses that are foreign to the buyer (Chi, 1994; Hennart, 1988). Thus, an alliance can be more economically feasible and involve a less irreversible commitment than acquisition. Because there is no transfer of ownership rights, the relationship may be rescinded at a relatively low cost.

## Organizational Learning and Alliances

The previous section discussed the rationale for forming alliances and why alliances may be preferable to other organizational forms. In this and subsequent sections, key managerial issues associated with strategic alliances are examined. Because organizational learning through alliances is both a formation motive and an evolutionary process that occurs over the life of the alliance, learning will be the initial managerial issue discussed. The chapter then continues with an examination of alliance issues such as performance, control, and trust.

Value creation in an alliance occurs after the venture is formed. Much of the alliance research is concerned with how to manage the collaborative process to maximize joint value creation. In recent years, there has been much greater attention focused on individual firm value appropriation through monetary and long-term competitive gains. An organizational learning motive provides a viable theoretical rationale for alliance formation that is not necessarily linked to collaborative objectives. Alliances provide a platform for organizational learning, giving firms access to the knowledge of their partners. Through the shared execution of the alliance task, mutual interdependence and problem solving, and observation of alliance activities and outcomes, firms can learn from their partners (Inkpen, 1996). Two or more organizations are brought together because of their different skills, knowledge, and strategic complementarity. The differences in partner skills and knowledge provide the catalyst for learning by the alliance parents. As well, unlike other learning contexts, the formation of an alliance reduces the risk that the knowledge will dissipate quickly (Powell, 1987).

There is a significant body of theoretical research (Inkpen, 2000a; Kogut, 1988; Kumar and Nti, 1998; Larsson et al., 1998; Makhija and Ganesh, 1997; Mody, 1993; Parkhe, 1991; Pucik, 1991) and empirical studies (Dodgson, 1993; Hamel, 1991; Hitt et al., 2000; Inkpen and Crossan, 1995; Inkpen and Dinur, 1998; Lane and Lubatkin, 1998; Mowery, Oxley, and Silverman, 1996; Powell, Koput, and Smith-Doerr, 1996; Simonin, 1997, 1999) addressing the issue of alliances and learning. This stream of research addresses some of the important questions associated with the conditions under which organizations exploit alliance learning opportunities.

Various different learning perspectives have been examined in the alliance literature. Learning processes, as Doz (1996) argued, are central to the evolution of an alliance. From the alliance partner's point of view, learning can be examined from two perspectives: (1) learning about the alliance partner, which can be an antecedent to the development of interfirm trust and (2) learning from the alliance partner. Doz and Hamel (1998) emphasized that the motivations and effects of the two types of partner learning are very different. They referred to learning *about* the alliance partner as skill familiarity that supported the alliance partner's ability to jointly create value. Thus, this type of learning should not be viewed as an alliance motive but rather, as a factor that supports effective alliance management. Learning *from* an alliance partner is a very different type of alliance learning and is a key determinant of alliance bargaining power (Hamel, 1991; Inkpen and Beamish, 1997; Yan, 1998). In turn, partner learning influences the extent of control one firm can exert over its alliance. Firms that can learn quickly are able to acquire partner skills, reducing dependence and increasing bargaining power (discussed in more detail in a later section).

When a firm learns from its alliance partner, the knowledge generated can be used by parent firms to enhance strategy and operations in areas unrelated to the alliance activities. This knowledge constitutes the private benefits that a firm can earn unilaterally by picking up skills from its partner (Khanna, Gulati, and Nohria, 1998). When a firm learns from its partner, the knowledge has value to the firm outside the alliance agreement, which means that the knowledge can be internalized by the parent and applied to new geographic markets, products, and businesses. This potentially useful knowledge is knowledge the parent would not have had access to without forming the alliance. Note that a learning perspective should not be viewed as just a one-way static process. All alliance partners will have learning opportunities that may or may not be exploited. As well, as the alliance evolves, the learning opportunities will change as the partners interact and the relationship itself evolves. Firms that are involved in multiple alliances may also adjust their learning objectives and efforts depending on what is learned through other relationships.

Taking a different tack, Kogut (1991) suggested that alliances may be investments that provide firms with expansion opportunities. Faced with uncertainty and a desire to learn, firms may prefer an alliance to acquisition. If one partner has the option to purchase the other's equity in the venture, that partner can utilize the alliance as a means of acquiring complex knowledge about the business. Once the party with the option to buy has acquired (i.e. learned) the skills of the partner firm, further investment in the venture might not be warranted. At this point the buy option may be exercised and the alliance terminated. More recently, Chi (2000) provided a detailed examination of alliances as options.

Various other alliance studies have incorporated learning perspectives. For example, Makhija and Ganesh (1997) linked learning and control in a conceptual framework. Khanna, Gulati, and Nohria (1998) examined how the tension between cooperation and competition affects the dynamics of learning alliances. Using the concepts of private and common benefits to the alliance partners, they suggested that firms often fail to understand the magnitude of partner asymmetric differences. Lyles and Salk (1996) examined the factors that influenced knowledge acquisition by the joint venture organization from the foreign parent. The opposite of learning, which is the protection of proprietary knowledge, has received some attention (e.g. Kale, Singh, and Perlmutter, 2000; Lorange, 1997). Given the interest in learning theories in other business disciplines it is likely that learning will continue to be a focus for alliance researchers in years to come.

## Knowledge creation and knowledge management processes

Although many generalizations have been drawn about the merits of knowledge-based resources and the creation of knowledge, limited efforts have been made to establish systematically how firms acquire and manage new knowledge in an alliance context. In one of the few studies, using data from a longitudinal study of North American-based joint ventures between North American and Japanese firms, Inkpen and Dinur (1998) addressed three related research questions: (1) what processes do alliance partners use to gain access to alliance knowledge?; (2) what types of knowledge are associated with the different processes and how should that knowledge be classified?; and (3) what is the relationship between organizational levels, knowledge types, and the transfer of knowledge?

Inkpen and Dinur (1998) identified four critical processes: technology sharing, alliance-parent interaction, personnel transfers, and strategic integration. The four processes share a conceptual underpinning in that each represents a knowledge connection, which creates the potential for individuals to share their observations and experiences. Each of the four processes provided an avenue for managers to gain exposure to knowledge and ideas outside their traditional organizational boundaries and created a connection for individual managers to communicate their alliance experiences to others. In that sense, the four processes represent the locus of knowledge creation because it is through those processes that different types of knowledge converge and become accessible.

Using Spender's (1996) typology of knowledge, Inkpen and Dinur linked the knowledge management processes with types of knowledge. For example, the knowledge associated with technology sharing was classified as explicit, objectified knowledge because it was related primarily to product designs or specific manufacturing procedures. The processes and primary knowledge types were then linked to organizational levels in the parent firms. For example, strategic integration involved knowledge ranging from low to high in tacitness that penetrated mainly the group-organization levels. Strategic integration also generated some individual knowledge.

Inkpen and Dinur (1998) generated four broad conclusions. First, knowledge creation can be a significant payoff from alliances. Although not all knowledge creation efforts will have immediate performance payoffs, over the long term successful knowledge creation should strengthen and reinforce a firm's competitive strategy. Second, each alliance partner has knowledge that, at least in part, should be considered valuable by the other partner(s). Third, knowledge creation is a dynamic process involving interactions at various organizational levels and an expanding community of individuals that enlarge, amplify, and internalize the alliance knowledge. Finally, knowledge creation and the upward movement of knowledge through the different organizational levels can be responsive to managerial influence.

## *Alliances as a race to learn*

Alliances have also been described as a "race to learn," with the partner learning the fastest dominating the relationship (Hamel, 1991). In this scenario of inevitable instability there are clear winners and losers. The race to learn in alliances is an intriguing concept, as is the notion of learning alliances in which the primary objective of the partners is to learn. But, particularly in equity joint ventures, the race to learn is, in my view, largely unrealistic. I have no doubt that the reluctant loser scenario which Khanna, Gulati, and Nohria (1998) described is a reasonably common occurrence, as long as it is acknowledged that the loser was probably never aware that a race was happening. But, a real race to learn requires multiple participants that acknowledge being in a race (you cannot have a race with only one contestant). As well, based on empirical evidence to date, alliances that truly can be classified as learning alliances are quite rare. Firms that develop a reputation for aggressive learning will likely not find it easy to form new alliances. Learning is often an important alliance motive but will generally not be the primary one (Inkpen and Beamish, 1997). More typical are alliances in which the partners openly acknowledge both asymmetric alliance objectives and an expectation of learning via private benefits (Inkpen, 2000b). In this type of alliance, there are varying levels of performance outcomes and it is quite possible that all partners learn, albeit with different learning abilities and at different speeds.

## STRATEGIC ALLIANCE PERFORMANCE

Strategic alliances are often described, particularly in the business press, as inherently unstable organizational forms that are prone to failure. Porter (1990) suggested that competitive and coordination costs make many alliances transitional rather than stable arrangements and therefore, alliances are rarely a sustainable means for creating competitive advantage. Supporting this argument, several empirical studies of alliances have found instability rates of close to 50 percent (e.g. Kogut, 1988). Based on the finding that 24 of the 49 alliances they studied were considered failures by one or both partners, Bleeke and Ernst (1991) suggested that most alliances will terminate, even successful ones.

From a practitioner viewpoint, various factors have been identified to explain alliance failure: inflexibility in management of the alliance, breakdowns in trust, problems with information exchange, excessive partner conflict, a lack of management continuity, and different partner expectations. In the academic literature, however, linking these factors with empirical evidence of alliance performance problems has proven illusive. The reality is that alliance performance is complex and multidimesional and thus, the measurement of alliance performance has challenged alliance researchers for decades. The difficulties of measuring alliance performance are rooted in both theoretical and methodological challenges. Because alliances are formed for a variety of purposes and often in highly uncertain settings, performance evaluation becomes a very difficult task (Anderson, 1990). One perspective argues that alliance performance should be evaluated as a mutual outcome and take into account the perspectives of the multiple partners (Beamish, 1988). A different perspective suggests that performance should be viewed in terms of value creation by individual partners. Because each partner will have different cooperative objectives and abilities to appropriate alliance benefits, the focus should be on the individual monetary and competitive gains of each partner (Hamel, 1991). A further perspective is that alliances should be evaluated as stand-alone entities seeking to maximize their own performance, not the partners' (Anderson, 1990; Woodcock, Beamish, and Makino, 1994). Still another approach is to examine the effects of the alliances on parent firm survival (Singh and Mitchell, 1996). Finally, possibly because of the ease by which it can be measured, alliance longevity and survival has been viewed as a performance indicator (Barkema, Bell, and Pennings, 1996; Gomes-Casseres, 1989; Kogut, 1989; Park and Russo, 1996; Steensma and Lyles, 2000).

Empirical studies of alliance performance have mainly dealt with equity joint ventures. Geringer and Hebert (1991) identified the various performance measures used in international joint venture studies: profitability, growth and cost position; venture survival; duration; instability of ownership; renegotiation of the alliance contract. Geringer and Hebert's empirical work found that an objective measure of joint venture performance was correlated with a measure based on venture performance relative to initial objectives. More recently, authors have developed extensive surveys (e.g. Parkhe, 1993) with the objective of capturing partner asymmetries in perceptions of performance. This area should prove to be a fruitful avenue for future research.

## Alliances and shareholder value

A stream of research has attempted to link alliances with stock market effects (e.g., Koh and Venkatraman, 1991). Most of the studies have looked at domestic equity joint venture formation announcements. Both Merchant and Schendel (2000) and Gulati (1998) reported that the results from this research show mixed evidence as to the shareholder value implications of alliance announcements. Merchant and Schendel (2000: 725) concluded "it is notable just how mixed previous empirical findings really are – and how much these inconsistencies persist." Empirical research that has examined the shareholder value implications of international joint venture formation has also produced mixed results (Reuer, 2000). Reuer attempted to overcome some of the limitations of the earlier domestic and international work both by incorporating alliance life-cycle stages into his analysis. Reuer used an event study methodology to measure valuation outcomes from both joint venture formation and termination. He concluded that both alliance formation and termination provide opportunities for the parents to create shareholder value.

## Alliance instability

Because of the difficulty of measuring performance, a more tractable and operationalizable approach has been to focus on alliance stability, based on the underlying assumption that an unstable alliance is not successful. Inkpen and Beamish (1997) argued that instability in equity joint ventures should be linked with *unplanned* equity changes or major reorganizations. They defined instability as a major change in relationship status that was *unplanned* and *premature* from one or both partners' perspectives. Usually, instability will result in premature alliance termination, either when one partner acquires the alliance business or the venture is dissolved. Using this definition of instability provides a clear link with alliance performance.

Killing (1983) considered both a shift in alliance control and venture termination as evidence of instability. Other researchers have adopted a narrower view. For example, Kogut (1989) used venture termination as the sole indicator of instability. However, as Kogut indicated, an alliance cannot be considered unstable simply because its lifespan is short. All relationships between firms face challenges that threaten to change or terminate the basis for cooperation. Sometimes terminations are planned and anticipated by the parties involved. Ventures may also be terminated as a matter of policy when there is a change in parent ownership or management. In other cases, difficulties associated with ending a relationship may create a rationale for maintaining an existing alliance that would otherwise be terminated.

A complicating factor in examining instability is that alliance termination will not always be a mutual decision (Parkhe, 1991). Premature termination may be precipitated by the actions of one partner. For example, when one firm is trying to learn from its partner in order to reduce its dependency, the partner doing the learning may have very different longevity objectives than the partner that is the knowledge source. Yan (1998) extended these arguments by drawing on structural instability and structural inertia perspectives to trace the destabilizing forces in joint ventures. Yan suggested that alliance researchers should move away from the assumption that stability produces success whereas instability produces failure. More recently, Das and Teng (2000) provided a comprehensive review of the instability literature and developed a framework around the internal tensions of cooperation versus competition, rigidity versus flexibility, and short-term versus long-term orientation.

## Instability and bargaining power

A bargaining power perspective is particularly appropriate for the examination of alliance stability because all alliances involve a negotiated bargain between the partners. This perspective has its roots in work by Emerson (1962) and generalized to the organizational level in Pfeffer and Salancik's (1978) resource-dependence model. The essence of the model is that the possession or control of key resources by one entity may make other organizations dependent on that entity. A firm that has the option to contribute or withhold an important resource or input can use that option as leverage in bargaining with its partner (Pfeffer, 1981).

At a general level, bargaining power in alliances arises out of the relative urgency of cooperation, available resources, commitments, other alternatives, and the strengths and weaknesses of each partner (Schelling, 1956). Yan and Gray's (1994) inductive study, the most systematic exploration of the concept of bargaining power in alliances to date, identified both resource-based and context-based components of bargaining power. The resources and capabilities committed by the partners to the alliance were a major source of bargaining power. Local knowledge in areas such as sourcing, domestic distribution, and personnel management was the main resource contributed by the local partners (Yan and Gray, 1994). For the foreign partners, resource contributions included expertise and technology for production management and global support.

To link the partner resource contributions directly to bargaining power and to understand the process of bargaining power shifts, concepts of organizational knowledge management must be incorporated in the framework. The pace of knowledge acquisition by one alliance partner is an important process dimension because, as Hamel (1991) argued, this dimension is very much within the firm's control. Because of this controllability, Hamel identified learning as the most important element in determining relative bargaining power. Substantial knowledge acquisition by one partner over time can erode the value of the knowledge contributed by the other partner, breaking down the bargaining relationship between the partners and enabling one firm to eliminate its dependency on its partner.

Extending Hamel's (1991) arguments, Inkpen and Beamish (1997) examined the root causes of instability in international joint ventures and argued that once the venture is formed, if the foreign partner attaches a high value to the acquisition of local knowledge and has the ability to acquire the knowledge, the probability of instability increases. Once a foreign partner has acquired local knowledge, unless the local partner is contributing other valuable and non-imitable skills to the alliance, the rationale for cooperation will be eliminated. Instability may be the result, although relationship attributes between the partners may moderate the shifts in bargaining power. Thus, the acquisition of local knowledge is an enabling device for the foreign partner to operate autonomously.

## Partner compatibility and performance

Compatibility between the partners and congruency in partner cultural factors are often cited in the business press as critical to alliance success. But, as Osborn and Hagedoorn (1997) pointed out, the measurement of compatibility is more illusive than its definition. Compatibility can be viewed from multiple perspectives, including organizational fit, strategic symmetry, resource complementarities, and alliance task-based factors (e.g., see Barkema and Vermeulen, 1997). Not surprisingly, research linking partner compatibility with performance has yielded inconsistent results. One stream of predominantly international research argues that the more culturally distant two firms are, the greater the differences in their organizational and administrative practices, employee expectations, and accordingly, the less likely it is that the alliance will be successful. For example, Lane and Beamish (1990) posited that cultural compatibility between the partners is the most important factor in the endurance of an international alliance. The limited empirical research in this area, however, does not bear this out. In a study of Japanese–US joint ventures, Park and Ungson (1997) found that organizational measures of compatibility were not important in dissolution rates. Luo (1997) found that the link between partners' sociocultural distance and joint venture performance was not significant. Clearly, more research is needed in this area, particularly as alliances continue to bring together more and more firms that in the past would have opted for independence.

## CONTROL OF STRATEGIC ALLIANCES

The structure and design of alliances is critical to the implementation of a successful alliance strategy. From the perspective of the alliance partners, how the alliance is controlled is a key structural element. In the alliance context, control refers to the process by which partner firms influence an alliance entity, the alliance partners, and the alliance managers to behave in a manner that achieves partner objectives, which of course are rarely the same for all partners. The process of alliance control includes the use of power, authority, and a range of bureaucratic, cultural, and informal mechanisms (Geringer and Hebert, 1989).

In alliances, control issues are often at the heart of management conflict between the partners, especially in the case of equity joint ventures. As Killing (1982) pointed out, the primary problems in managing alliances stem from one cause: there is more than one parent. Thus, the ability of an alliance partner to exercise control over its alliance is a function not only of its influence over its alliance managers but also of the influence over the other partner (Child, Yan, and Lu, 1997). Alliance partners are often visible and powerful; they can and will disagree on just about anything. Given the potential for partner conflict, control issues are usually an important consideration for alliance partners (Geringer and Hebert, 1989; Killing, 1983; Yan and Gray, 1994). However, in comparison with wholly-owned subsidiaries, exercising effective control over alliances is often difficult for the parent firms, especially if they are unable to rely solely on their ownership position (Geringer and Hebert, 1989).

Various approaches have been employed to develop an understanding of alliance control. Geringer and Hebert (1989) made a significant contribution in analyzing the approaches and identifying three dimensions of control: (1) the mechanisms used by the parents to exercise control; (2) the extent of control achieved by the parents; and (3) the scope of activities over which parents exercise control. While Geringer and Hebert argued that the dimensions are complementary and interdependent, there is a paucity of empirical work to support their arguments. Child, Yan, and Lu (1997) made a distinction between contractual and non-contractual resource inputs as sources of bargaining power and, hence, control over alliance activities. Makhija and Ganesh (1997) identified formal and informal alliance controls. Formal controls were predictable, regular, and involved explicit information transfers. Informal controls were more uncertain, ambiguous, and organizationally embedded (Deakin and Wilkinson, 1998).

## Control and performance

A prominent, and controversial, research question in the literature on strategic alliances, and especially involving equity joint ventures, is the relationship between control and performance. Conceptualizing control in terms of the locus of decision making and the *extent* of control exercised by partner firms provides one way to examine performance and control. Killing (1982) identified three categories of alliances based on the extent of shared decision-making: dominant parent, shared management, and independent ventures. The primary determinant of the alliance type was the degree of parent involvement in the decision-making of the alliances and the extent to which both parents had active roles. In making the link between control and performance, Killing (1982) found that dominant partner alliances were more likely to be successful than shared partner ventures. Killing argued that when a single parent controlled the venture's activities, the risks associated with coordination and potential conflicts were reduced. Killing's argument is persuasive, especially when interpreted within a transaction cost framework. Coordination between partners entails significant costs that make many alliances transitional rather than stable arrangements. Reducing the risks associated with coordination can minimize transaction costs and stabilize the alliance. Following this logic, alliances in which a dominant partner has decision-making control should perform better than ventures where control is shared.

Beamish (1988) reviewed the literature on the control-performance link and concluded that the link between dominant control and good performance weakened when the study focus shifted from the developed countries to the less developed countries. Blodgett (1992), using ownership to measure control, and stability to measure performance, found that 50–50 shared management arrangements had a greater chance for long life than majority-owned ventures. Blodgett argued that when partners have equal ownership, there will be pressure on both sides to make accommodations to the alliance to protect their investments and therefore, both partners will be committed to making the venture successful. In a majority-owned venture, one partner may have the ability to configure the venture in a manner that is undesirable to the other partner(s). Bleeke and Ernst (1993) also found that 50–50 alliances performed the best.

Child, Yan, and Lu (1997) found no consistent link between the relative level of control over the joint ventures held by the parent companies and assessments of their performance. Mjoen and Tallman (1997) combined an ownership-focused control model with a resource input-based bargaining power model. Their results rejected an approach to joint venture governance based solely on ownership as the basis for control, arguing instead for a bargaining power-based model of control. Taking a different perspective, several studies have suggested that firms with different national backgrounds have different preferences in ownership (Erramilli, 1996; Pan, 1996), which might impact how they view alliance performance. In summary, the control–performance relationship remains a question of great interest to managers because of the implication for alliance structure and design. Perhaps the key to answering the question lies in a deeper understanding of linkages between alliances, parent firm strategy, inter-partner trust, and alliance resource commitments.

## TRUST AND STRATEGIC ALLIANCES

Although difficult to measure and subject to multiple conceptual treatments, trust has become a core alliance concept. Alliance research (e.g. Beamish and Banks, 1987; Buckley and Casson, 1988; Das and Teng, 1998; Inkpen and Beamish, 1997; Inkpen and Currall, 1998; Madhok, 1995; Yan and Gray, 1994) has repeatedly argued that mutual trust is essential for successful alliances. Ariño and de la Torre (1998), in their study of a failed joint venture, concluded that in the absence of a reserve of trust, alliances that encounter threats to stability will not be sustainable. Yan (1998: 786) wrote that "lack of trust between the partners at the international joint venture formation can be a major source of structural instability." As noted by Child and Faulkner (1998), trust is particularly fragile in international alliances because risk and uncertainty involved in a domestic alliance are heightened in the alliance context by cross-national differences between partner firms with respect to culture, law, politics, and trade policy.

Inkpen and Currall (1998) discussed alliance trust antecedents and consequences and argued that trust plays a crucial role in the overall nature of alliance processes. As well, alliance trust should be viewed as an evolving rather than static concept. Over time, as the partners and partner managers learn about each other and the alliance becomes an operating entity, the level of interpartner trust will change. Trust requires familiarity and mutual understanding and, hence, depends on time and context (Nooteboom, Berger, and Noorderhaven, 1997). As the relationship ages, previous successes, failures, and partner interactions will influence the level of trust in the alliance. Furthermore, unlike most economic commodities, trust may grow rather than wear out through use (Hirschman, 1984). Trust may also decrease over the life of the relationship. For example, when an alliance is formed, there is a subjective probability that a partner will cooperate. Experience will lead to adjustment of the probability, which in turn may lead to a shift in the level of trust.

Risk is a precondition for the existence of trust, and the trustor must be cognizant of risk (Mayer, Davis, and Schoorman, 1995; Sitkin and Pablo, 1992). The risk of negative outcomes must be present for trust to operate and the trustor must be willing to be vulnerable. In the absence of risk, trust is irrelevant because there is no vulnerability. The greater the risk, the higher the confidence threshold required to engage in trusting action. The nature of risk and its relationship with trust has received limited research attention in the alliance literature.

## Trust and performance

Although it has generally been argued that trust enhances alliance performance (e.g. Harrigan, 1986; Saxton, 1997), the argument that performance leads to trust has merit as well. Yan and Gray (1994) suggested that performance may have a feedback effect on trust. Poor performance may cause distrust between the partners, which in turn leads to poor long term alliance performance (Killing, 1983). A firm's review of past alliance results, in comparison with expectations, can lead to a firm's prediction of the extent to which the partner firm will follow through on its current promises (i.e. is trust in the partner warranted?). If alliance performance is worse than expected, alliance partners are likely to question the competence and capabilities of their partners. The level of trust in the relationship will therefore suffer accordingly. In turn, performance may suffer because the alliance managers become embroiled in conflict, resulting in a deviation-amplifying loop where a decrease in alliance performance leads to a decrease in trust, which continues to amplify the problem with performance.

The strongest empirical support for the trust-to-performance relationship in an inter-firm context can be found in the marketing literature on channel relationships (e.g. Aulakh, Kotabe, and Sahay, 1996; Mohr and Spekman, 1994, Robichaux and Coleman, 1994; Smith and Barclay, 1997). In the equity joint venture literature, despite numerous conceptual arguments, there is limited empirical support. Using perception of opportunistic behavior as a proxy for trust, Parkhe (1993) found a strong relationship between perception of opportunistic behavior and alliance performance. Inkpen and Currall (1997) found support for the argument that trust has an indirect effect on performance mediated by forbearance. In their qualitative study of United States–China joint ventures, Yan and Gray (1994) identified trust as a mechanism that moderated the relationship between formal management control and venture performance. Park and Ungson (1997) and Saxton (1997) found a positive relationship between antecedents of trust and alliance outcomes.

## Trust and organizational levels

In alliances, trust may exist at multiple organization levels (Currall and Inkpen, 2000). For example, trust may exist between the individual managers assigned to the alliance by the respective alliance partners. Or, trust may exist at an organizational level because of extensive inter-firm collaboration prior to the formation of the focal alliance. In some cases, alliance-based trust may be present at one level and absent at another. The question of how trust at one organizational level shapes and influences trust at other levels is an important and under-researched question. This question has important implications for the successful formation and implementation of strategic alliances. As Doz (1996) pointed out, negotiating and forming an alliance initiates a dynamic relationship that, to be successful, will have to go through a series of evolutionary transitions. The evolution of trust, as well as the movement of trust across levels, plays a central role in these transitions, which are discussed in the following section.

## Trust and control

An area that has received limited attention is the link between trust and control, two critical alliance concepts. As indicated earlier, work in the area of performance and control has been particularly ambiguous and suggests that deeper study into the role of trust should contribute valuable insights. Inter-firm trust should be viewed as determinant of the governance structures and control mechanisms that evolve in an alliance (Faulkner, 2000). Informal and non-contractual safeguards are more likely when there is a high level of trust between the partners. For example, in cases of high trust, the alliance agreement may be less detailed because of perceptions of a low probability of opportunism. Governance costs under conditions of distrust will be greater and procedures will be more formal, such as more detailed contract documentation, more frequent board meetings, closer scrutiny by lawyers, and more communication between partner headquarters and the alliance. These procedures will result in additional transaction costs to the alliance partners (Dyer, 1997). Parkhe (1993) found support for the hypothesis that elaborateness of safeguards and the perception of opportunistic behavior are strongly related.

However, because trust cannot be instantaneously created or destroyed, partner firms must balance the inevitable trade-off between trust and control. In newly formed alliances between firms without any common cultural background or without prior interactions, the basis for trust may be absent when the alliance is formed. In new alliances, partners are often suspicious of each other and unsure of the value of the collaborative opportunity (Doz and Hamel, 1998). In this case, the partners may have no choice but to exercise control through extensive reliance on contracts and monitoring.

The trust and control relationship should also be viewed as a reciprocal one. A lack of trust can lead to a desire for increased control. In turn, excessive control by one partner may lead to opportunistic behavior by the other partner (Provan and Skinner, 1989), which can lead to a further decrease in trust. As well, effective control in an alliance will require a certain level of trust between the partners (Goold and Quinn, 1990). In the absence of trust, it is unlikely that the partners will be able to agree on control mechanisms. This is a problem that confounds many new alliances. One of the challenging realities in alliance management is that partners must work closely together in the initial years of an alliance and yet, this is the time when the partners are least prepared to cooperate (Doz and Hamel, 1998). In a young alliance with little trust, both partners may want to implement control mechanisms. But, because the partners don't trust each other, they struggle to agree on the nature of controls, as well as the roles of managers.

## ALLIANCE DEVELOPMENT AND EVOLUTIONS

Over the course of their life, all alliances, both stable and unstable, will go through a series of transitions. One of the certainties that alliance managers must deal with is that alliances will evolve in ways that are difficult to predict at the outset. However, alliances must evolve if they are to survive and, according to Lorange (1997), can be seen as always in a temporal stage and always on the way to something else. Contractual agreements between alliance partners are often executed under conditions of high uncertainty and, therefore, it is highly unlikely that all future contingencies and environmental shifts can be anticipated at the outset. Consequently, the management of alliance evolutions and developmental patterns is an important skill in an alliance manager's arsenal.

The study of alliance evolutions is a research area with great promise and currently, limited output. As Yan (1998) stated, although the formation and termination events have been studied extensively, there has been limited attention given to the mid-life of alliances and the developmental dynamics of alliances. Some recent work provides important understanding in the area of strategic alliance evolution. Doz (1996) proposed that successful alliances go through an evolutionary process involving sequential interactive cycles of learning, re-evaluation, and readjustment. In contrast, failing projects were highly inertial and characterized by little learning or divergent learning. Focusing on the formation process, Doz, Olk, and Ring (2000) found that distinct pathways of formation processes were associated with R&D consortia, with initial conditions playing a key role in formation. Child and Faulkner (1998) considered the evolution of trust-based relationships and suggested that trust tends to develop gradually over time as the partners move from one stage to the next. Ariño and de la Torre (1998) examined the interaction between two partners in a failed international joint venture. They found that positive feedback loops were critical in the evolutionary process and that procedural issues were critical in fostering a climate for positive reinforcement and mutual trust and confidence in the relationship.

### Attachment between alliance partners

In addition to learning processes and structural developments, alliance dynamics are shaped by the evolving relationship between the partners and individual managers. Attachment is the concept that deals with interfirm relationships and understanding how attachment ebbs and flows is key to developing insights into alliance evolutions. Attachment is the binding of one party to another (Salancik, 1977). Attachment between partners develops through experience in the collaborative relationship and through investments the partners make in the relationship over time (Seabright, Leventhal, and

Fichman, 1992). When the partners have developed a strong attachment, there may be inertial forces that block the pressures for change in relationship status (Blau, 1964; Salancik, 1977). If firms have worked together in the past, they will have basic understandings about each other's skills and capabilities (Heide and Miner, 1992). According to Parkhe (1993: 803), "the older a relationship, the greater the likelihood it has passed through a critical shakeout period of conflict and influence attempts by both sides." Because of prior relationships, firms often form alliances with firms with whom they have transacted in the past. For example, in a study of 40 international joint ventures, Inkpen (1995b) found that in 24 cases, the partners had previously worked together, primarily in technology sharing relationships.

Attachments in collaborative relationships may be the result of individual or structural ties that reflect the prior history of the relationship (Seabright, Leventhal, and Fichman, 1992). Individual attachment reflects the socialization by individuals during their involvement in exchange activities. In alliances, individual attachment may be represented by personal relationships between partner managers. Continuing business relationships often become overlaid with social content that generates strong expectations of trust and forbearance (Granovetter, 1985). Thus, attachment can lead to alliances that begin their existence with an existing stock of "relationship assets" (Fichman and Leventhal, 1991) and a high degree of inter-partner trust (Gulati, 1995). Parkhe (1991) suggested that unplanned alliance termination is more likely when firms are working together for the first time. Kogut (1989) found that structural ties between alliance partners was negatively related to alliance dissolution. Kogut's variable for structured ties was a composite of three types of relationships: supply, other alliances, and licensing agreements.

## FUTURE ALLIANCE RESEARCH ISSUES

Although the alliance literature is rich and multi-disciplinary in nature, many exciting research opportunities remain. Three can be specifically singled out as warranting attention. The first major research opportunity is in the area of alliance evolutionary processes. There is a real need for greater understanding of what happens once the formation of an alliance begins. For example, what initial conditions between the partners play a role in alliance stability and bargaining power shifts? How does trust at one organizational level shape and influence trust at another level? How do contractual changes in the alliance influence interactions between managers? What are the evolutionary phases that characterize successful alliances versus unsuccessful alliances? If, as Madhok and Tallman (1998) suggested, refraining from opportunistic behavior may have little to do with the development of trust and more to do with good business, how do managers analyze the cost-benefits associated with the likelihood of opportunism and non-opportunism over the life of the alliance? These research questions and many others associated with evolutionary processes have the potential to generate a new chapter in strategic alliance research.

The second research opportunity involves the theoretical linkages between alliances and networks. The study of networks has become a field unto itself that until recently, had barely intersected the mainstream alliance literature. This field has developed specialized methodologies, well-developed theoretical frameworks, and some confusing terminology, such as organizational networks, industry networks, and constellations (Gomes-Casseres, 1996). From an alliance and collaborative perspective, networks can be defined as a set of organizations linked by a set of social and business relationships that create strategic interfirm opportunities for the organizations. Although strategy research in the domestic arena has begun examining the social context of networks within which firms are embedded (e.g., Lorenzoni and Lipparini, 1999), the alliance literature has not yet examined this in any detail. As well there are many other opportunities to examine how networks can be linked with strategic issues. Gulati, Nohria, and Zaheer (2000) provide an overview of key areas of strategy research in which there is a potential for incorporating strategic networks.

The third major research opportunity is expanded understanding of multiple alliance forms and in particular, internet and e-commerce-based alliances. Most of the empirical research in the alliance area has dealt with equity joint ventures. In comparison, we know far less about the management of alliances such as R&D consortia and minority equity relationships. New alliances forms with an internet orientation promise to challenge accepted wisdom and theories about how alliances are formed and managed. In the internet economy, alliances will become easier to create, and terminate, and location and firm size will become less critical variables. E-commerce business opportunities will result in new, complex, and highly uncertain collaborative relationships, often between competitors. New forms of open-ended collaboration will be quickly formed and dissolved. The classic market entry bricks and mortar equity joint venture will decline in relevance as firms discover that relationships can be easily and efficiently established electronically. In the international arena, alliances will provide firms with enormous reach and opportunities to partner anywhere in the world. Studying these new alliance forms will provide an exciting theoretical and empirical thrust to the field of strategic alliances.

## CONCLUSION

In this chapter I have discussed the primary alliance research questions and issues studied over the past few decades. Although the objective was to be as comprehensive as possible, the enormous output in alliance studies, especially in the 1990s, necessitated that various areas could be discussed only peripherally. For example, more specialized topics such as alliance manager selection and rewards (e.g., Schaan and Beamish, 1988); alliance negotiation strategies (e.g., Weiss, 1997); and alliance contract structures (e.g., Aulakh, Cavusgil and Sarkar, 1998) were dealt with only peripherally. As well, although I discussed international issues as they impacted specific areas, I did not provide a detailed examination of international alliance issues such as alliances versus wholly-owned subsidiaries for geographic market entry; cross-cultural management and alliance partner conflict; cross-cultural negotiation; country differences in alliance usage and performance; and developed versus emerging market influences on alliance performance. Although each of these issues is important, the theoretical underpinnings of alliance research do not change when the research context becomes international. What does change is the complexity of analysis and the importance of concepts such as local knowledge, regulatory issues, and cross-cultural management (e.g., see the earlier discussion on partner compatibility and performance).

Finally, I did not explicitly track the intersections and departures between the alliance literature and the IOR literature. The IOR concept is much broader than the alliance concept in that it includes all types of relationships between firms and the origins of IOR research are in non-market settings (Oliver, 1990). Nevertheless, the IOR literature has provided many important theoretical ideas that contribute to strategic alliance understanding, such as resource dependence, legitimacy, and power asymmetry between collaborating firms. For a comprehensive overview of the literature on IORs, see Barringer and Harrison (2000).

## REFERENCES

Anderson, E. (1990). Two firms, one frontier: On assessing joint venture performance. *Sloan Management Review*, 18 (Winter): 19–30.

Ariño, A., and de la Torre, J. (1998). Learning from failure: Towards an evolutionary model of collaborative ventures. *Organization Science*, 9: 306–25.

Aulakh, P., Cavusgil, S. T., and Sarkar, M. B. (1998). Compensation in international licensing agreements. *Journal of International Business Studies*, 29: 409–20.

Aulakh, P., Kotabe, M., and Sahay, A. (1996). Trust and performance in cross-border marketing partnerships: A behavioral approach. *Journal of International Business Studies*, 27: 1005–32.

Barkema, H. G., Bell, J. H., and Pennings, J. M. (1996). Foreign entry, cultural barriers, and learning. *Strategic Management Journal*, 17: 151–66.

Barkema, H. G., and Vermeulen, F. (1997). What differences in the cultural backgrounds of partners are detrimental for international joint ventures? *Journal of International Business Studies*, 28: 845–64.

Barringer, B. R., and Harrison, J. S. (2000). Walking a tightrope: Creating value through interorganizational relationships. *Journal of Management*, 26: 367–403.

Beamish, P. W. (1988). *Multinational Joint Ventures in Developing Countries*. London: Routledge.

Beamish, P. W., and Banks. J. C. (1987). Equity joint ventures and the theory of the multinational enterprise. *Journal of International Business Studies*, (Summer): 1–16.

Blau, P. M. (1964). *Exchange and power in social life*. New York: Wiley.

Bleeke, J., and Ernst, D. (1991). The way to win in cross-border alliances. *Harvard Business Review*, 69(6): 127–35.

Bleeke, J., and Ernst, D. (1993). *Collaborating to Compete: Using Strategic Alliances and Acquisitions in the Global Marketplace*. New York: Wiley.

Blodgett, L. L. (1992). Factors in the instability of international joint ventures: An event history analysis. *Strategic Management Journal*, 13: 475–81.

Browning, L., Beyer, J., and Shetler, J. (1995). Building cooperation in a competitive industry: SEMATECH and the semiconductor industry. *Academy of Management Journal*, 38: 113–51.

Buckley, P. J., and Casson, M. (1988). A theory of cooperation in international business. In F. Contractor and P. Lorange (eds.), *Cooperative Strategies in International Business*: 31–53. Lexington, MA: Lexington Books.

Buckley, P. J., and Casson, M. (1996). An economic model of international joint venture strategy. *Journal of International Business Studies*, 27: 849–76.

Chi, T. (1994). Trading in strategic resources: Necessary conditions, transaction cost problems, and choice of exchange structure. *Strategic Management Journal*, 15: 271–90.

Chi, T. (2000). Option to acquire or divest a joint venture. *Strategic Management Journal*, 21: 665–87.

Child, J., and Faulkner, D. (1998). *Strategies of Cooperation: Managing Alliances, Networks, and Joint Ventures.* New York: Oxford University Press.

Child, J., Yan, Y., and Lu, Y. (1997). Ownership and control in Sino-foreign joint ventures. In P. Beamish and J. Killing (eds.), *Cooperative Strategies: Asian Pacific Perspectives*: 181–225. San Francisco, CA: New Lexington.

Contractor, F. J. (1990). Contractual and cooperative forms of international business: towards a unified theory of modal choice. *Management International Review*, 30(1): 31–54.

Contractor, F. J., and Lorange, P. (1988). Why should firms cooperate: The strategy and economics basis for cooperative ventures. In F. Contractor and P. Lorange (eds.), *Cooperative Strategies in International Business*, 3–30. Lexington, MA: Lexington Books.

Currall, S. C., and Inkpen, C. (2000). Joint venture trust: Interpersonal, inter-group, and inter-firm levels. In D. Faulkner and M. de Rond (eds.), *Cooperative Strategy: Economic, Business, and Organizational Issues*: 324–340. Oxford, UK: Oxford University Press.

Das, T. K., and Teng, B. S. (2000). Instabilities of strategic alliances: An internal tensions perspective. *Organization Science*, 11: 77–101.

Das, T. K., and Teng, B. S. (1998). Between trust and control: Developing confidence in partner cooperation in alliances. *Academy of Management Review*, 23: 491–512.

Deakin, S., and Wilkinson, F. (1998). Contract law and the economics of interorganizational trust. In C. Lane and R. Bachmann (eds.), *Trust Within and Between Organizations*, 146–72. Oxford, UK: Oxford University Press.

Dodgson, M. (1993). Learning, trust, and technological collaboration. *Human Relations*, 46: 77–95.

Doz, Y. (1996). The evolution of cooperation in strategic alliances: Initial conditions or learning processes? *Strategic Management Journal*, 17 (Summer special issue): 55–84.

Doz, Y., and Hamel, G. (1998). *Alliance Advantage: The Art of Creating Value Through Partnering.* Boston, MA: Harvard Business School Press.

Doz, Y. L., Olk, P. M., and Ring, P. S. (2000). Formation processes of R&D consortia: Which path to take? Where does it lead? *Strategic Management Journal*, 21: 239–66.

Dunning, J. H. (1995). Reappraising the eclectic paradigm in an age of alliance capitalism. *Journal of International Business Studies*, 26: 461–92.

Dyer, J. H. (1997). Effective interfirm collaboration: How firms minimize transaction costs and maximize transaction value. *Strategic Management Journal*, 18: 535–56.

Dyer, J. H., and Singh, H. (1998). The relational view: Cooperative strategy and sources of interorganizational competitive advantage. *Academy of Management Review*, 23: 660–79

Emerson, R. M. (1962). Power dependence relationships. *American Sociological Review*, 27 (February): 31–41.

Erramilli, M. K. (1996). Nationality and subsidiary ownership patterns in multinational corporations. *Journal of International Business Studies*, 27: 225–48.

Faulkner, D. O. (2000). Trust and control: Opposing or complementary functions? In D. Faulkner and M. de Rond (eds.), *Cooperative Strategy: Economic, Business, and Organizational Issues*, 341–64. Oxford, UK: Oxford University Press.

Fichman, M., and Leventhal, D. A. (1991). Honeymoons and the liability of adolescence: A new perspective on duration dependence in social and organizational relationships. *Academy of Management Review*, 16: 442–68.

Geringer, J. M. (1988). *Joint Venture Partner Selection: Strategies for Developed Countries.* Westport, CT: Quorum Books.

Geringer, J. M., and Hebert, L. (1989). Control and performance of international joint ventures. *Journal of International Business Studies*, 20: 235–54.

Geringer, J. M., and Hebert, L. (1991). Measuring performance of international joint ventures. *Journal of International Business Studies*, 22(2): 253–67

Gomes-Casseres, B. (1989). Joint ventures in the face of global competition. *Sloan Management*

*Review*, 17 (Spring): 17–26.

Gomes-Casseres, B. (1996). *The Alliance Revolution: The New Shape of Business Rivalry*. Cambridge, MA: Harvard University Press.

Goold, M., and Quinn, J. J. (1990). The paradox of strategic controls. *Strategic Management Journal*, 11: 43–57.

Granovetter, M. (1985). Economic action and social structure: The problem of embeddedness. *American Journal of Sociology*, 78: 481–510.

Gulati, R. (1995). Does familiarity breed trust? The implications of repeated ties for contractual choice in alliances. *Academy of Management Journal*, 38: 85–112.

Gulati, R. (1998). Alliances and networks. *Strategic Management Journal*, 19: 293–318.

Gulati, R., Nohria, N., and Zaheer, A. (2000). Strategic networks. *Strategic Management Journal*, 21: 203–15.

Hagedoorn, J. (1993). Understanding the rationale of strategic technology partnering: international modes of cooperation and sectoral differences. *Strategic Management Journal*, 14: 371–85.

Hamel, G. (1991). Competition for competence and inter-partner learning within international strategic alliances. *Strategic Management Journal*, 12 (special issue): 83–104.

Harrigan, K. R. (1986). *Managing for Joint Venture Success*. Lexington, MA: Lexington Books.

Heide, J. B., and Miner, A. S. (1992). The shadow of the future: Effects of anticipated interaction and the frequency of contact on buyer-seller cooperation. *Academy of Management Journal*, 35: 265–91.

Hennart, J. F. (1988). A transactions costs theory of equity JVs. *Strategic Management Journal*, 9: 361–74.

Hennart, J. F. (1991). The transactions cost theory of joint ventures: An empirical study of Japanese subsidiaries in the United States. *Management Science*, 37: 483–97.

Hirschman, A. O. (1984). Against parsimony: Three easy ways of complicating some categories of economic discourse. *American Economic Review*, 74: 88–96.

Hitt, M. A., Dacin, M. T., Levitas, E., Arregle, J-L., and Borza, A. (2000). Partner selection in emerging and developed market contexts: Resource-based and organizational learning perspectives. *Academy of Management Journal*, 43: 449–67.

Hitt, M. A., Harrison, J. S., Ireland, R. D., and Best, A. (1998). Attributes of successful and unsuccessful acquisitions of US firms. *British Journal of Management*, 9: 91–114.

Inkpen, A. C. (1995a). *The Management of International Joint Ventures: An Organizational Learning Perspective*. London: Routledge Press.

Inkpen, A. C. (1995b). Organizational learning and international joint ventures. *Journal of International Management*, 1: 165–98.

Inkpen, A. C. (1996). Creating knowledge through collaboration. *California Management Review*, 39(1): 123–40.

Inkpen, A. C. (2000a). Learning through joint ventures: a framework of knowledge acquisition. *Journal of Management Studies*, 37: 1019–43.

Inkpen, A. C. (2000b). A note on the dynamics of learning alliances: Competition, cooperation and relative scope. *Strategic Management Journal*, 21: 775–9.

Inkpen, A. C., and Beamish, P. W. (1997). Knowledge, bargaining power and international joint venture stability. *Academy of Management Review*, 22: 177–202.

Inkpen, A. C., and Crossan, M. M. (1995). Believing is seeing: Joint ventures and organization learning. *Journal of Management Studies*, 32: 595–618.

Inkpen, A. C., and Currall, S. C. (1997). International joint venture trust: an empirical examination. In P. W. Beamish and J. P. Killing (eds.), *Cooperative Strategies: North American Perspectives*: 308–34. San Francisco, CA: New Lexington Press.

Inkpen, A. C., and Currall, S. C. (1998). The nature, antecedents and consequences of joint venture trust. *Journal of International Management*, 4: 1–20.

Inkpen, A. C., and Dinur, A. (1998). Knowledge management processes and international joint ventures. *Organization Science*, 9: 454–68.

Kale, P., Singh, H., and Perlmutter, H. (2000). Learning and protection of proprietary assets in strategic alliances: Building relational capital. *Strategic Management Journal*, 21: 217–37.

Khanna, T., Gulati, R., and Nohria, N. (1998). The dynamics of learning alliances: Competition, cooperation, and relative Scope. *Strategic Management Journal*, 19: 193–210.

Killing, J. P. (1982). How to make a global joint venture work. *Harvard Business Review*, 60(3): 120–7.

Killing, J. P. (1983). *Strategies for Joint Venture Success*. New York: Praeger.

Kogut, B. (1988). Joint ventures: Theoretical and empirical perspectives. *Strategic Management Journal*, 9: 319–22.

Kogut, B. (1989). The stability of joint ventures: Reciprocity and competitive rivalry. *The Journal of Industrial Economics*, 38: 183–98.

Kogut, B. (1991). Joint ventures and the option to expand and acquire. *Management Science*, 37(1): 19–33.

Koh, J., and Venkatraman, N. (1991). Joint venture formations and stock market reactions: An assessment in the information technology sector. *Academy of Management Journal*, 34: 869–92.

Kumar, R., and Nti, K. O. (1998). Differential learning and interaction in alliance dynamics. *Organization Science*, 9: 356–67

Lane, H. W., and Beamish, P. W. (1990). Cross-cultural cooperative behavior in joint ventures in LDCs. *Management International Review*, (special issue), 30: 87–102.

Lane, P. J., and Lubatkin, M. (1998). Relative absorptive capacity and interorganizational learning. *Strategic Management Journal*, 19: 461–77.

Larsson, R., Bengtsson, L., Henriksson, K., and Sparks, J. (1998). The interorganizational learning dilemma: Collective knowledge development in strategic alliances. *Organization Science*, 9: 285–305.

Lorange, P. (1997). Black-box protection of your core competencies in strategic alliances. In P. W. Beamish and J. P. Killing (eds.), *Cooperative Strategies: European Perspectives*, 59–73. San Francisco: New Lexington Press.

Lorenzoni, G., and Lipparini, A. (1999). The leveraging of interfirm relationships as a distinctive organizational capability: A longitudinal study. *Strategic Management Journal*, 20: 317–38.

Luo, Y. (1997). Partner selection and venturing success: The case of joint ventures with firms in the people's republic of China. *Organization Science*, 8: 648–62.

Lyles, M. A., and Salk, J. E. (1996). Knowledge acquisition from foreign parents in international joint ventures: An empirical examination in the Hungarian context. *Journal of International Business Studies*, 27: 877–903.

Madhok, A. (1995). Revisiting multinational firms' tolerance for joint ventures: A trust-based approach. *Journal of International Business Studies*, 26: 117–38.

Madhok, A. (1997). Cost, value, and foreign market entry mode: The transaction and the firm. *Strategic Management Journal*, 18: 39–61.

Madhok, A., and Tallman, S. B. (1998). Resources, transactions, and rents: Managing value through interfirm collaborative relationships. *Organization Science*, 9: 326–39.

Makhija, M. V., and Ganesh, U. (1997). The relationship between control and partner learning in learning-related joint ventures. *Organization Science*, 5: 508–20.

Mayer, R. C., Davis, J. H., and Schoorman, F. D. (1995). An integrative model of organizational trust. *Academy of Management Review*, 20: 709–34.

Merchant, H., and Schendel, D. (2000). How do international joint ventures create shareholder value? *Strategic Management Journal*, 21: 723–37.

Mjoen, H., and Tallman, S. (1997). Control and performance in international joint ventures. *Organization Science*, 8: 257–74.

Mody, A. (1993). Learning through alliances. *Journal of Economic Behavior and Organizations*, 20: 151–70.

Mohr, J., and Spekman, R. (1994). Characteristics of partnership success, partnership attributes, communication behavior, and conflict resolution techniques. *Strategic Management Journal*, 15: 135–52.

Mowery, D. C., Oxley, J. E., and Silverman, B. S. (1996). Strategic alliances and interfirm knowledge transfer. *Strategic Management Journal*, 17 (Special issue, Winter): 77–92.

Nooteboom, B., Berger, H., and Noorderhaven, N. G. (1997). Effects of trust and governance on relational risk. *Academy of Management Journal*, 40: 308–38.

Oliver, C. (1990). Determinants of interorganizational relationships: Integration and future directions. *Academy of Management Review*, 15(2): 241–65.

Osborn, R., and Hagedoorn, J. (1997). The institutionalization and evolutionary dynamics of interorganizational alliances and network. *Academy of Management Journal*, 40: 261–78.

Pan, Y. (1996). Influences on foreign equity ownership level in joint ventures in China. *Journal of International Business Studies*, 27: 1–26.

Park, S. H., and Russo, M. V. (1996). When competition eclipses cooperation: an event history of joint venture failure. *Management Science*, 42: 875–90.

Park, S. H., and Ungson, G. R. (1997). The effect of national culture, organizational complementarity, and economic motivation on joint venture dissolution. *Academy of Management Journal*, 40: 279–307.

Parkhe, A. (1991). Interfirm diversity, organizational learning and longevity in global strategic alliances. *Journal of International Business Studies*, 22: 579–602.

Parkhe, A. (1993). Strategic alliance structuring: A game theoretic and transaction cost examination of interfirm cooperation. *Academy of Management Journal*, 36: 794–829.

Pfeffer, J. (1981). *Power in Organizations*. New York: Pitman.

Pfeffer, J., and Salancik, G. R. (1978). *The External Control of Organizations: A Resource Dependence Perspective*. New York: Harper and Row.

Porter, M. E. (1990). *The Competitive Advantage of Nations*. New York: Free Press.

Porter, M. E., and Fuller, M. B. (1986). Coalitions and global strategy. In M. E. Porter (ed.), *Competition in Global Industries*, 315–43. Boston, MA: Harvard Business School Press.

Powell, W. W. (1987). Hybrid organizational forms. *California Management Review*, 30(1): 67–87.

Powell, W. W. (1996). Trust-based forms of governance. In R. M. Kramer and T. R. Tyler (eds.), *Trust in Organizations: Frontiers of Theory and Research*, 51–67. Thousand Oaks, CA: Sage.

Powell, W. W., Koput, K. W., and Smith-Doerr, L. (1996). Interorganizational collaboration and the locus of innovation: networks of learning in biotechnology. *Administrative Science Quarterly*, 41: 116–45.

Provan, K. G., and Skinner, S. J. (1989). Interorganizational dependence and control as predictors of opportunism in dealer-supplier relations. *Academy of Management Journal*, 32: 202–12.

Pucik, V. (1991). Technology transfer in strategic alliances: competitive collaboration and organizational learning. In T. Agmon and M. A. Von Glinow (eds.), *Technology Transfer in International Business*: 121–38. New York: Oxford University Press.

Reuer, J. J. (2000). Parent firm performance across international joint venture life-cycle stages. *Journal of International Business Studies*, 31: 1–20.

Robichaux, R. A., and Coleman, J. A. (1994). The structure of marketing channel relationships. *Journal of the Academy of Marketing Science*, 22(1): 38–51.

Salancik, G. R. (1977). Commitment and the control of organizational behavior and belief. In B. Staw and G. Salancik (eds.), *New Directions in Organizational Behavior*, 1–54. Chicago: St. Clair Press.

Saxton, T. (1997). The effects of partner and relationship characteristics on alliance outcomes. *Academy of Management Journal*, 40: 443–61.

Schaan , J-L., and Beamish, P. (1988). Joint venture general managers in developing countries. In F. Contractor and P. Lorange (eds.), *Cooperative Strategies in International Business*: 279–99. Lexington, MA: Lexington Books.

Schelling, T. C. (1956). An essay on bargaining. *American Economic Review*, 46: 281–306.

Seabright, M. A., Leventhal, D. A., and Fichman, M. (1992). Role of individual attachments in the dissolution of interorganizational relationships. *Academy of Management Journal*, 35: 122–60.

Singh, K., and Mitchell, W. (1996). Precarious collaboration: Business survival after partners shut down or form new partnerships. *Strategic Management Journal*, 17 (Summer Special Issue): 99–116.

Simonin, B. L. (1997). The importance of collaborative know-how: An empirical test of the learning organization. *Academy of Management Journal*, 40: 1150–74.

Simonin, B. L. (1999). Ambiguity and the process of knowledge transfer in strategic alliances. *Strategic Management Journal*, 20: 595–624.

Sitkin, S. B., and Pablo, A. L. (1992). Reconceptualizing the determinants of risk behavior. *Academy of Management Review*, 17: 9–38.

Smith, J. B., and Barclay, D. (1997). The effects of organizational differences and trust on the effectiveness of selling partner relationships. *Journal of Marketing*, 61 (January): 3–21.

Spender, J. C. (1996). Making knowledge the basis of a dynamic theory of the firm. *Strategic Management Journal* (special issue): 45–62.

Steensma, H. K., and Lyles, M. A. (2000). Explaining IJV survival in a transitional economy through social exchange and knowledge-based perspectives. *Strategic Management Journal*, 21: 831–51.

Weiss, S. E. (1997). Explaining outcomes of negotiation: toward a grounded model for negotiations between organizations. In R. J. Lewicki, R. J. Bies, and B. H. Sheppard (eds.), *Research on Negotiation in Organizations*, Volume 6, 247–333. Greenwich, CT: JAI Press.

Williamson, O. E. (1975). *Markets and Hierarchies: Analysis and Antitrust Implications*. New York: Free Press.

Williamson, O. E. (1981). The economics of organization: the transaction cost approach. *American Journal of Sociology*, 87(3): 548–77.

Woodcock, C. P., Beamish, P. W., and Makino, S. (1994). Ownership-based entry mode strategies and international performance. *Journal of International Business Studies*, 25: 253–73.

Yan, A. (1998). Structural stability and reconfiguration of international joint ventures. *Journal of International Business Studies*, 29: 773–96.

Yan, A., and Gray, B. (1994). Bargaining power, management control, and performance in United States–China joint ventures: A comparative case study. *Academy of Management Journal*, 37: 1478–517.

# 15

# Restructuring Strategies of Diversified Business Groups: Differences Associated with Country Institutional Environments

ROBERT E. HOSKISSON, RICHARD A. JOHNSON,
DAPHNE YIU AND WILLIAM P. WAN

Large firms with portfolios of unrelated businesses throughout the world's emerging economies, as well as many developed economies, are seeking to restructure their business portfolios to a set of core businesses. The intention of these strategic actions is often to improve performance. These large diversified business groups are actually quite typical of the capitalist countries that have industrialized since World War II. Many explanations have been given as to why these large firms dominate the economies of most countries (Amsden and Hikino, 1994; Granovetter, 1994; Khanna and Palepu, 1997; Leff, 1976, 1978; Strachan, 1976). Academics, owners of business groups and policy makers are debating the future of such large diversified business groups (Ghemawat, Kennedy, and Khanna, 1998; Sachs and Warner, 1994).

Many of these firms from Asia and Latin America are using a model of Western corporate strategies and are refocusing their diversified operations. But, at times, this refocusing may not be appropriate for emerging economy situations (Khanna and Palepu, 1999a). Nonetheless, many of these firms have followed the pattern in the United States and the United Kingdom, where high levels of diversified operations have been refocused. A large proportion of these refocused firms specialize in managing businesses with operations related to the firm's core operations so as to realize the benefits associated with related diversification (Johnson, 1996).

However, in emerging economies, and in many highly developed economies such as France, Germany, and Italy, these diversified business groups have dominated the competitive landscape and are highly diversified for rational reasons. For instance, extending the logic of transaction cost economics (Coase, 1937), Williamson (1975) provided an economic rationale for conglomerates that rapidly grew in the US during the 1960s. He attributed the emergence of conglomerates primarily to inefficiencies in external capital markets. Williamson (1975) contended that conglomerates – as internal capital markets – could overcome inefficiencies associated with external capital markets. He observed that headquarters in conglomerates performed roles analogous to those of investors in external capital markets.

Some have argued that the underlying reason for having these conglomerates have not changed that much, especially for emerging economies. Khanna and Palepu (1999a), accordingly, argued that the total restructuring of these diversified business groups is flawed because the reasons for diversification have not been altered that much in emerging economies.

The reason these diversified business groups evolved in many countries was not only due to underdeveloped capital markets, but also had to do with labor and management development opportunities as well. The main problem with capital markets is unequal (asymmetric) information and potential conflicts of interest between buyers and sellers in these markets. Where advance capital markets exist, there are effective intermediaries, sound regulations and contract laws that can minimize this unequal information and potential conflict between buyers and sellers. For instance, in the US financial market, investment bankers play an intermediary role in the allocation of capital between businesses. Furthermore, the Securities and Exchange Commission makes sure that investors can rely on corporate disclosure and thereby adequate information. In addition, well-developed contract law helps resolve conflicts between buyers and sellers. Also, hundreds of business schools provide graduates who possess the knowledge required to manage firms successfully through use of the strategic management process. However, in emerging economies, these institutional mechanisms are often missing, creating additional transaction costs between businesses (Newman, 2000; Spicer, McDermott, and Kogut, 2000). The existence of the "soft infrastructure" (laws, regulatory bodies, and financial intermediaries that facilitate the transactional environment) is as important as hard physical infrastructure such as roads, ports and telecommunications systems because this infrastructure reduces such transaction costs. China, for example, has invested heavily in physical infrastructure but has made little progress in creating strong institutional infrastructure. Instead, China has been fostering large diversified business groups, such as the Baoshan Iron and Steel Group Corporation in steel-making and the Haier Group in appliances (Chang, 1998). Although Western analysts have been disappointed with the formation of these large diversified corporations because they are viewed as inefficient in more developed economies, they may be necessary due to a lack of "soft infrastructure" mentioned above. As in other emerging economies, these large diversified business groups serve as internal capital markets for allocation of capital by a strong corporate headquarters. Furthermore, they function as a way to manage transactions, often through their own subsidiaries, without appropriate legal infrastructure. Transactions are effective because the corporation has a way of managing transactions equitably within the firm and through family members or closely affiliated partners. Furthermore, these diversified companies serve as training grounds for managers in the labor market system because the educational institutions lack distinct ways of training managers in the distinctive business programs such as those found in Western educational institutions.

This paper provides theory as to how these large diversified businesses might profitably restructure given their countries' stage of not only economic development (physical infrastructure), but also more particularly on their countries' social infrastructure that determines a firm's transaction environment. In the sections that follow, we first address the significance of why studying restructuring is important and also why focusing on differing institutional environments might suggest different diversification and restructuring approaches. We then address theoretical and practical approaches to restructuring that might be associated with emerging, partially developed and developed economic environments.

## SIGNIFICANCE OF RESTRUCTURING AND INSTITUTIONAL DIFFERENCES

Defined formally, restructuring is a strategy through which a firm changes its set of businesses and/or financial structure (Bethel and Liebeskind, 1993). Acquisitions and divestitures have been a popular strategy among US firms for many years. Some believe that acquisitions and divestitures strategies played a central role in an effective restructuring of US businesses during the 1980s and 1990s (*Mergers and Acquisitions*, 2000). The total value of these acquisitions exceeded $1.3 trillion (Hitt, Harrison, and Ireland, 2001). However, the merger and acquisition activity of the 1980s pales in comparison to what occurred in the 1990s. Increasingly, such strategies are becoming more popular with firms in other nations and economic regions including Europe. In fact, in the third quarter of 1999, for the first time the dollar volume of merger and acquisition transactions announced in Europe exceeded the value announced in the United States (Portanger, 2000).Evidence suggests, however, that at least for acquiring firms, acquisition strategies may not result in these desirable outcomes. Recently, for example, a survey by accounting and consulting firm KPMG estimated that 83 percent of mergers failed to increase shareholder value in acquiring firms; in 53 percent of the transactions, shareholder value in acquiring firms was actually reduced (Deener, 1999). These results are consistent with those obtained through studies by academic researchers who have found that *shareholders of acquired firms* often earn above-average returns from an acquisition while *shareholders of acquiring firms* are less likely to do so, typically earning returns from the transaction that are close to zero (Jensen, 1993). Apparently, investors anticipate these results as indicated by the fact that in approximately two-thirds of all acquisitions, the acquiring firm's stock price falls immediately after the intended transaction is announced. This negative response is viewed by some as an indication of "investors' skepticism about the likelihood that the acquirer will be able both to maintain the original values of the businesses in question and to achieve the synergies required to justify the premium" (Rappaport and Sirower, 1999).

Although there are many examples of successful acquisitions (Hitt, Harrison, and Ireland, 2001), the majority of acquisitions that were completed from roughly the 1970s through the 1990s did not enhance firms' value. In fact, some researchers observe that, "history shows that anywhere between one-third to more than half of all acquisitions are ultimately divested or spun-off" (Anand, 1999). Thus, firms often use restructuring strategies to correct for the failure of a merger or an acquisition. According to Peter Drucker, restructuring strategies are being used more frequently. To support his view, he observes that on a single, yet typical day in the business world, the *Wall Street Journal* reported that "Hewlett-Packard was spinning off its $8 billion business in test and measuring instruments, Procter & Gamble was selling its adult-incontinence business to a mid-sized company, and the Harris Co. was selling its entire semi-conductor business to a small company" (Drucker, 2000).

In the last two decades, especially in the US, and more recently throughout the world, many firms have restructured their operations because of changes in their external and internal environments. For example, in many nations the institutional environment is in flux. In such cases, restructuring may be appropriate in order to position the firm so that it can create more value for stakeholders, given these environmental changes. Although research on corporate diversification and restructuring has made important contributions to the field of strategic management (Hoskisson and Hitt, 1990, 1994; Johnson, 1996), the dominant conceptual approaches have largely been premised on the United States and United Kingdom contexts. Our knowledge about corporate diversification and restructuring in other countries throughout the world is thus limited. While diversified business conglomerates often dominate the competitive landscape in many countries outside the United States (Khanna and Palepu, 1997), this phenomenon seems to contradict the extant theoretical argument that high levels of product diversification are detrimental to firm performance (Montgomery, 1994; Rumelt, 1974).

Accordingly, contextual differences in which the diversification strategies are adopted are often ignored. Variations in production factor endowments have long been emphasized in economics or business studies in accounting for countries' economic fortunes. In comparison, countries' institutional infrastructures are rarely examined although its importance has increasingly been recognized (e.g., North, 1990). Institutional contexts have been studied by institutional economists, political scientists and sociologists (e.g., Coleman, 1990; Fukuyama, 1995; Knack and Keefer 1997; Putnam, 1993). Improvements in a countries' institution contexts facilitate economic exchange. The rest of the paper is divided into three sections each discussing different institutional or transaction environments which are likely to impact restructuring approaches and the underlying diversification strategies being sought by the restructuring firms.

## RESTRUCTURING IN EMERGING ECONOMIES

Research indicates that the conglomerate or unrelated strategy has not disappeared, especially in Europe where it has actually increased in number. Although many conglomerates have refocused in developed economies such as ITT and Hansen Trust, other unrelated diversified firms spring up in their place. The Achilles heel, or main problem, of the unrelated strategy in developed economies is that conglomerates have a fairly short life cycle because financial economies are more easily duplicated relative to sources of operational and corporate relatedness (Ruigrok et al., 1999). This is less of a problem in emerging economies where the lack of "soft infrastructure" (e.g., lack of effective financial intermediaries, sound regulations and contract laws) supports and encourages the diversified business groups following an unrelated strategy. We first describe why these diversified business groups fit in an emerging economy. This is to be followed by a section on restructuring through privatization in emerging economies.

## Emergence of diversified business groups

Foundational work on diversified business groups in emerging markets falls broadly into three streams. Most prominent is the work from transaction cost theory which conceptualizes groups as responses to market imperfections. This work is exemplified by Leff (1976, 1978a), who primarily emphasized imperfections in capital markets, and Chang and Choi's (1988) work on Korean chaebols. Khanna and Palepu (1997) and Amsden and Hikino (1994), however, argued that the existence of diversified business groups might also resolve market failures in product markets, labor markets, as well as the markets for cross-border flows of technology and capital.

Granovetter (1994), employing a sociological perspective, suggests that norms and codes of behavior that prevail in business groups come from the institutional setting in which the firm is embedded. These two streams of work, emanating from transaction cost economics and from sociology, generally see diversified business groups as value-enhancing organizational forms. In contrast, the third important stream, grounded in political economy, emphasizes a socially counter-productive "rent-seeking" view of business groups, under rents in the economy accrue disproportionately to the handful of families which control major groups to the detriment of the majority of the population (Ghemawat and Khanna, 1998). Much of this latter work is descriptive in nature, and details the patterns of interrelationships between groups and the power structure (Encarnation, 1989; Schwartz, 1992), though econometric work has begun to appear (Fisman, 1998). It is similar to work in developed economies regarding how the M-form was slow to be adopted in the US economy because it represented decentralization of financial control to division managers relative to traditional family or financial institutional control (Palmer, Jennings, and Zhou, 1993).

Research regarding diversified business groups has tended to ignore perspectives developed in disciplines outside of the dominant perspective associated with which research originates. The approach taken here, then, will tend to be broader than just the traditional transaction cost view which has tended to be emphasized in strategic management research regarding diversification and restructuring. In particular, we will attempt to explore the institutional context of emerging economies which facilitates transactions.

Although prominent economists have emphasized that institutions affect economic outcomes (North, 1990; Williamson, 1985), they have tended to view the institutional context primarily in terms of the extent to which it is characterized by the presence of specialized intermediaries (Spulber, 1996). A long tradition of economic theory has suggested how efficient intermediation reduces the costs of transacting in product (Akerlof, 1970), labor (Spence, 1973) and capital markets (Diamond, 1984). Transaction cost theories (Coase, 1937; Williamson, 1975, 1985) suggest that the optimal scope of the firm is a function of transaction costs, and hence of the extent of specialized intermediation in the economy. Khanna and Palepu (1997) draw upon this literature to arrive at the proposition that the institutional context is important in determining the extent to which diversified business groups create or destroy value.

In emerging markets there are a variety of market failures, caused by information and agency problems. For example, financial markets are characterized by a lack of adequate disclosure and weak corporate governance and control. Intermediaries such as mutual funds, investment bankers, venture capitalists, and associated financial analysts have not fully evolved. The financial press may not have either the access to relevant information or the authority to release sensitive information because of government restrictions or lack of sophistication. Securities regulations may be weak and lack disclosure and may create information asymmetries between potential owners, family members, and managers. Because external labor markets may not be fully developed, combined with the absence of good educational institutions and professional and skill certification, labor market failure is also likely. In this scenario employees with suitable backgrounds and skills may be unavailable. Information problems in product markets may also be problematic because product certification organizations (e.g., *Consumer Reports*) have not evolved, retail distribution channels may be poor or inadequate, and lower levels of literacy than in advanced economies may make it costlier to create trust with consumers and establish the value of products and services.

Missing institutional features (e.g., shortage of skilled labor, thin capital markets, infrastructure problems, political and economic instability, public suspicion of foreign firms) have deterred inward foreign direct investment (FDI) in emerging economies. A primary impediment appears to be the lack of well-defined property rights that convey exclusivity, transferability and quality of title (Devlin, Grafton, and Rowlands, 1998). Lack of a strong legal framework has allowed a large increase in opportunism, rent shifting, bribery, and corruption (Nelson, Tilley, and Walker, 1998). These problems have particularly affected the ability to *enforce* property rights even where legislation has been *enacted* (Estrin and Wright, 1999). As a result, institutional capacity building was, and continues to be, key for attracting inward FDI (Rondinelli, 1998). In summary, legal, product, labor, and capital markets are likely to be institutionally ineffectual.

Such institutional underdevelopment must be made up in other ways. Large diversified business groups therefore often act as brokers between individual entrepreneurs and imperfect capital, labor, and product markets. For example, groups diversified across unrelated business units may use their broad scope to ensure access to internal finance in an environment where external finance is difficult to obtain relatively more developed economies. Additionally, because much of the funding is bank debt, large diversified firms have more power to negotiate for better terms or obtain government financial backing. Internal labor markets associates with large business groups may facilitate training and allocation of managerial talent because external labor mobility is often stifled. In general, large diversified business groups substitute for a variety of institutional functions not supported by external markets in developed economies, often through the group headquarters.

However, these substitution effects of diversification in emerging markets may not be sufficient to offset the risks associated with diversification. Without strong internal or external governance, compensation schemes may be inefficient. Top managers may make poor decisions due to overdiversification (Hoskisson, Johnson, and Moesel, 1994). The typical agency and strategic problems of diversification can be made worse by family ownership structures that often tend toward paternalism and conflicts of interest between controlling family shareholders and minority shareholders. Economically inefficient decisions may also evolve because of weak regulatory and disclosure requirements and a poorly developed market for corporate control (La Porta, Lopez-de-Silanes, and Shleifer, 1999).

Also, in the early stage of a country's economic development, it was almost impossible to raise large amounts of funds through domestic sources because of the underdeveloped nature of capital markets in both size and efficiency. Only the government could borrow abroad and channel these funds into strategic or export-oriented sectors at below-market interest rates. Firms which diversified into strategic sectors in response to the government's initiative could readily secure funds, diversify their business portfolios, and grow into big business groups. In contrast, companies sticking to their core businesses at such a time may be very likely to atrophy or fail.

Once diversified business structures are in place, business groups could then multiply the use of internal capital. This occurred in Korea. When a new subsidiary was established in a Korean business group or chaebol, equity and working capital could be provided by subsidiaries. Given the backwardness of external capital markets in the Korean economy, such internal financing capabilities were often essential to funding the rapid growth of business groups.

Diversified business structures also help business groups raise funds from external markets. Due to the lack and ambiguity of company information, financial institutions tend to prefer large, diversified companies to specialized or small- and medium-sized ones. Also, the size and diversified business structure of business groups are helpful at securing high-quality human resources. Business groups generated many opportunities for promotions and career development by expanding into new promising areas continuously (Amsden, 1989). In the absence of well-developed external labor markets, the size and diversity of internal labor markets of business groups attracted high-quality human capital.

The absence of external labor markets in Korea made it difficult to hire junior and senior managers from the outside, which was a barrier to starting new businesses (Kim, Han, and Hoskisson, 2000). However, internal labor market capabilities enabled business groups to accumulate and utilize human capital in an efficient way. In the early stages of economic development, business groups compete at the low-end segments of global markets based on low priced goods that allowed market entry, given their cost structures at the time. As such, however, they did not require advanced technological and marketing skills. In Korea, competent entrepreneurs – with the availability of low cost capital (supported by the government) and human resources – were able to move into many sectors and pre-empt emerging market opportunities. Business groups' abilities to accumulate and share financial and human capital constituted a significant advantage.

In Korea, during the industrialization process, new business opportunities proliferated. By entering into the strategic sectors according to the government plan, business groups could obtain policy loans, which came at reduced cost of capital, and enjoy monopolistic profits, which became sources of capital for additional market entry. Thus, pre-emption of strategic market opportunities preceded development of competitive advantage and capability in priority. In pre-empting new business opportunities, relatedness and the associated capabilities were often not pursed because of the lack of incentive to create specialized strategic assets such as technological and marketing skills. Business groups could enter new markets rapidly and cost-efficiently by utilizing cheaply and readily available externally subsidized capital and internally accumulated capital and human resources. Diversification appeared attractive for two reasons. By diversification, business groups could pre-empt attractive business opportunities, reduce group risk, and build internal markets. Thus, business groups such as the South Korean chaebols have dominated many of the emerging economies of the world.

Given the above arguments, restructuring may not always be appropriate for emerging economies because large diversified business groups have a better fit with the conditions in emerging economies because of inadequate institutional evolution (Khanna and Palepu, 1999a). However, there still may exist the need to restructure due to the problems of poor governance and overdiversification as mentioned above. Still, restructuring might not occur because the governance system by internal players may be lax and external owners may not require it. It may take an external financial crisis such as the 1997 currency crisis to spur governments to force restructuring in Asia because of the general threat of bankruptcy and economic collapse.

Alternatively, in some emerging economies, providers of capital may also have different orientations regarding diversification. Bankers may prefer unrelated diversification because they receive business from large diversified business groups. However, mutual funds or foreign capital investors may require better disclosure as well as improved internal governance as a requirement before foreign direct investment is committed. Thus, some restructuring may take place due to differential requirements of shareholders.

## Privatization as a restructuring approach in emerging economies

Because most emerging economies have historically been dominated by government ownership, a number of approaches to facilitating economic transition have taken place through privatization programs. Because many of these emerging economies in Russia, Latin America and Asia (especially China) have been dominated by governance ownership of the economic enterprise, restructuring has primarily consisted of privatization programs. Accordingly, we will discuss such programs of restructuring in three emerging economies: Russia, China and Latin America (e.g., Argentina).

The privatization program of 1992 involved issuing vouchers to all Russian adults, which could then be exchanged for enterprise stock (Wright et al., 1998). This approach facilitated political acceptance of the privatization process. Accordingly, firms could achieve privatization three ways (termed *variants* in the legislation), which gave different degrees of insider ownership.

Variant 1 allowed employees to obtain 25 percent of the stock in an enterprise using their vouchers plus a further 10 percent purchased at a discount. In Variant 2, employees obtain 51 percent using their vouchers. In Variant 3 employees acquire 20 percent at face value if they agree to maintain output and a further 20 percent at a discount. Reflecting the problems of maintaining output in Russia during transition, only 4 percent surveyed chose this variant. Managers and employees could also purchase enterprises outside the formal voucher privatization program. After 1995, privatizations continued following the end of the central program, with resource-based or defense-related companies being variously auctioned openly or allocated to particular state-owned banks.

The nature of the Russian privatization program (as described above) meant that insiders generally became significant equity owners. As such they have an especially important role in restructuring. Because the voucher program did not by itself encourage capital infusions, significant restructuring was difficult to accomplish. Accordingly, their attitudes of managers and employees have important implications for the relative feasibility and governance of the various forms of market entry open to foreign investors, notably acquisitions versus strategic alliances and joint ventures. While there is a long-term need in Russia for "deep restructuring" involving enhanced management skills, extensive capital investment and new product development, this may be difficult to achieve if, in the short term, management pursues job protection and entrenchment. Misperceptions about the objectives of outsiders can lead to mistrust and further barriers to market entry. However, foreign investors who are both aware of these issues and equipped to deal with them are in a potentially strong position to exploit the opportunities offered by the Russian market.

Filatotchev, Buck, and Zhukov (2000) combine institutional theory and agency theory to examine the willingness and incentive to change of managers in privatized enterprises in Russia, Ukraine, and Belarus. They focused on downsizing and corporate restructuring as the most appropriate response in an environment of economic crisis where capital markets are undeveloped and where privatization did not inject capital to enterprises. In fact, they found that where insider managers dominated, restructuring was only cursory. When outside owners had significant positions, they were in a more favorable position to facilitate change. However, generally, because insiders dominate the power structure of these privatized firms, outside shareholding has largely failed to effectively counterbalance managerial opportunism. "Insider privatization has effectively moved the balance of power toward incumbents as opposed to outsider investors, a trend that may have negative implications for corporate restructuring" (Filatotchev, Buck, and Zhukov, 2000: 300).

Although the Russian approach created privatized enterprises, it did not lead to significant restructuring. Furthermore, because of the lack of significant restructuring, Russia has lagged behind other countries using different approaches to privatization. Opposite the approach in Russia, Grosse and Yanes (1998) describe the successful restructuring and privatization of the Argentine national oil company, Yacimentos Petroliferos Fiscales (YPF). The company's situation in the early 1990s was clearly ripe for a rationalization process. YPF demonstrated many of the characteristics of poorly managed state-owned firms at that time: YPF was overstaffed employing 39,000 direct employees and 13,000 contractees on a continuous, permanent basis and had an oil output of only 410,000 barrels per day (similar to current output of the properties retained after disengaging from its non-core reserves) and mainly concentrated in upstream and refining operations. Accordingly, YPF lost US$ 576 million for the fiscal year 1990. YPF also operated numerous unrelated activities such as hospitals, schools, housing, and utilities, and also many businesses of clearly low strategic value.

The first process to restructure YPF required government action to transform YPF into a corporation so that the restructuring process could proceed. This took place in 1990 through a decree of the Argentine government. Once this process was accomplished the Memem government brought in a manager with significant credibility to manage the process, Jose Estenssoro. The second step of the process of remaking YPF began in 1991. It involved both the massive downsizing of the firm and the reorganization of its human resources and operating structure. In fact, these two processes were largely unconnected with each other, because of the speed with which they were designed, implemented, and completed. The organization's grossly inflated levels of management had never been systematically evaluated, so Estenssoro and a team of external consultants decided to eliminate all positions and start from a clean slate while building the new organizational frame. Since YPF was a state-owned enterprise that underpaid its personnel and offered few challenges, it was assumed that those who would elect to stay in a new, demanding environment would be the exceptions. The plan was simple and transparent: everyone from top to bottom was offered a clear economic incentive to leave the company. This generous plan concluded with 50,000 employees, many political appointees, leaving the company.

Parallel to YPF's organizational rightsizing was the step of organizing the new structure. The Arthur D. Little consulting firm was called in and assigned the task of redesigning the new structure, following the most modern concepts of re-engineering. The resulting management structure was simple and compact: autonomous strategic business units that shared service/staff units. To fill key positions, an intensive executive selection process took place in which highly skilled, high-potential people were chosen, based on leadership, moral fortitude, intelligence and judgment, rather than only on the conventional qualities of education and experience.

As the new organization took shape, it became evident that new information technology was necessary for the implementation of the new organizational structure. A leaner YPF, with fewer middlemen in the decision ladder, was achievable only with a modern communication and information infrastructure. Andersen Consulting, with its proven skill in information technology, was brought in to assist with the task of formulating new work processes and designing and linking the new information network with the most modern technology and systems. Given the importance of information technology to competitive positioning, the information technology phase of YPF's modernization lasted over four years. During its peak the company was using some 200 international experts simultaneously, mostly Andersen consultants.

The third and final step of the privatization process as identified by Estenssoro was the domestic and international sale of shares in YPF through an initial public offering. Once conditions had been established for the sell-off, the government proceeded to orchestrate the initial public offering (IPO). It was at this point that the government actually authorized the privatization. Price Waterhouse was retained to carry out a valuation of the firm, with the end of setting a price on the shares to be issued. By transforming and restructuring the firm prior to the public offering, the value of the firm was more than doubled to $8 billion. The IPO was the largest to take place on the New York exchange in 1993.

Different from the outright privatization approach taken in Russia and Argentina and other countries, China has taken a more gradual approach in its privatization program. Zhou (1993) estimated that, assuming one state-owned enterprise (SOE) is auctioned per week and there are 4,000 large groups of SOEs in China, it would take 80 years to privatize unless significant capital comes from abroad. In applying the gradual approach, the State Enterprise Reform program started in 1978. Since then, the central planning regime has been gradually dismantled and the government has been relinquishing its role in policing economic exchanges and tolerating more private ownership of firms. This gradual approach has been implemented through decentralization of government control to provincial and local government entities. It fits China's cultural mentality and institutional environment. Murrell and Wang (1993) suggested that a gradual pace of privatization is more realistic given the undeveloped state of factor markets in transitional economies such as that of China.

Moreover, there are a number of barriers to the transfer of economic assets to private ownership in China, especially through a massive privatization program. There is a "three no change" policy imposed by the Chinese government in regard to ownership transfer. First, there should be no change in enterprise to government agency relationships. Second, there should be no change in the nature of ownership when acquisition or other transactions occur. Third, the change of ownership should cause no change in fiscal and tax remittance revenues (Wu, 1990). As a consequence, government agencies at all levels (state, provincial, county, and local) retain their bureaucratic control in privatized former SOEs. Finally, the residual socialist ideology of keeping everyone employed and the fear of social unrest resulting from massive layoffs have made the government hesitant to engage in large-scale privatization. The fact that Chinese SOEs are burdened with so many social welfare responsibilities suggests that there will be extraordinary difficulty in implementing a privatization program large enough to seriously undermine the role of the state in economic exchange (Lin, Cai, and Li, 1998). Furthermore, as mentioned above, to deal with the lack of soft infrastructure, many Chinese SOEs have been organized into business groups.

## RESTRUCTURING IN PARTIALLY DEVELOPED ECONOMIES

Partially developed countries, or hybrid economies, are situated between the developed economies which are more market-based and the emerging economies which are predominantly government-based (see figure 15.1). In general, the institutional infrastructures of the hybrid economies are not as well developed as the developed economies but stronger than those of the emerging economies. Of course, there are still a lot of variations among countries in terms of the degree of development in their institutional environments. Nonetheless, there is a common characteristic which can tie all these partial-developed countries together; that is, different institutional mechanisms evolved to fill in different institutional voids in the capital, labor, and product markets (Khanna and Palepu, 1997). These institutions include banks in Japan and Germany, and families in continental European countries such as Sweden, France, and Italy. In the following, we will examine these void-filling institutional mechanisms and discuss how they will have an impact on firms' restructuring strategies.

### Bank-centered economies: Japan and Germany

Deviating not so far from the market-centered system are countries such as Japan and Germany. Both Japan and Germany are economically advanced countries with well-developed infrastructures and business environments. They are ranked as the 14th and the 3rd respectively in the most recent *Global Competitiveness Report* (World Economic Forum, 2000). However, Japan and Germany do not have a strong capital market when compared to the Anglo-Saxon market-based systems in the US and UK. Banks and other financial institutions constitute the major players in their external capital markets and play an important role in firms' corporate governance systems. According to Patrick (1994), Japanese regulatory restrictions and economic incentives fostered by the Ministry of Finance inhibits corporate bond issues and the development of secondary debt markets. For example, only public utilities and long-term credit banks can issue bonds.

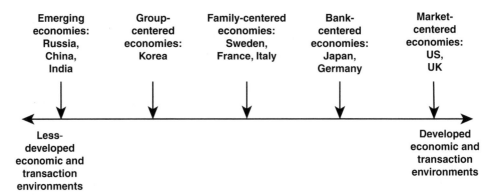

FIGURE 15.1 Institutional differences across countries

Equity issues are expensive for management-controlled firms, because dividends were paid out of after-tax profits while interests payments were a deductible expense.

Furthermore, the issuance of commercial paper for short-term finance was not allowed until 1987. Therefore, firms have no choice but to borrow from the banks. At the same time, Japanese banks can hold up to 5 percent of the total equity of a firm and a group of financial institutions can hold up to 40 percent (Aoki, 1990). Accordingly, banks can exercise control much more freely than their counterparts in developed countries (Sheard, 1994). In Germany, the importance of banks in corporate governance is reflected by their shareholdings in firms and holding proxy votes on the bearer shares deposited by private investors for safekeeping (Mayer, 1998). For instance, the Deutsche Bank, Dresdner Bank, and Commerz Bank together have 31.5 percent direct holdings in Daimler Benz, which provide them with 72.8 percent of the voting rights in the firm (Macey and Miller, 1997).

The bank-centered system substitutes for the development of markets for corporate control, thus saving the cost of expensive hostile takeovers found in market-centered governance systems (Hoshi, Kashyap, and Scharfstein, 1990). Firms have a lower bankruptcy risk for banks and other financial institutions, as a lender and a central risk-bearer, are willing to accept higher debt levels in order to help member firms overcome financial distress. However, banks take over underperforming firms in some cases. Under the provision of Japan's Commercial Code, any director can be replaced at any time by a two-thirds vote of the stockholder general meeting and the bank can initiate temporary takeover of a failing firm (Aoki, 1988).

Historically, in Germany, like Japan, there has not been an active market for corporate control. With banks interested in firm's liquidity and cash flows stability where they have substantial ownership and lending relationships, risky projects are discouraged. Such risk aversion is furthered increased by the Codetermination Act that requires both public and private firms with more than 2,000 employees to have a supervisory board with labor representatives, which in turn, monitor the management board. With the controlling interests of banks and labor, the risk of firm bankruptcy and the incentives for restructuring activities such as downsizing are lowered. The involvement of employees may have an impact on firm decision by fostering stability and discouraging changes. In declining industries, firms may be reluctant to take restructuring measures such as closures or layoffs (Clarke and Bostock, 1997). Similarly, it is not common to find layoffs in distressed firms in Japan due to the practice of lifetime employment. Employee transfer is not uncommon among business partners, particularly between banks and their client firms or between large firms and their suppliers (Lincoln, Gerlach, and Takahashi, 1992). At the industry level, restructuring may take a longer time because of the accumulation of firm-specific and industry-specific human capital through lifetime employment.

Although banks became the conduits of capital investment to supply loans to member firms to facilitate restructurings, they appear to have had significant problems with non-performing loans during the economic downturn (Kim and Hoskisson, 1997). Excessive diversification within keiretsu groups leads to overcapacity problems. Also, the practices of lifetime employment and seniority-based systems require continuous corporate expansion and diversification which contribute to the problem of overstaffing. All these problems became more serious when the Japanese economy experienced significant economic slowdown in the recent decade. With increasing competition in global product and capital markets, the financial sector of Japan is under the so-called "Big Bang" transformation that was first announced in 1996. The Big Bang will focus on three key areas: (1) cross-border capital flows, (2) securities brokerage business and financial product development, and (3) merging of commercial and investment banking and insurance (Ozawa, 2000). Subsequently regulatory changes were made to assist the financial reforms. For instance, with the revised Anti-Monopoly Law in 1997, we saw the first unification of three giant Japanese banks: Fuji Bank, Dai-Ichi Kangyo Bank, and Industrial Bank of Japan. Firms are also motivated to restructure their businesses in the non-financial sector. The revised corporate tax code under a more consolidated tax system will encourage firms to spin off their unprofitable businesses. The financial sector reforms and regulatory change may turn Japan's bank-centered system towards a more arm's-length system, which may induce more corporate restructuring activities in Japanese firms.

In Germany, bank influence in corporations has been reduced while institutional shareholdings that come primarily from non-financial enterprises and foreign investors is increasing. The calls for harmonization and greater transparency with the emergence of the European Union, together with increasing pressures from global competition, are driving firms to consolidate themselves in order to pursue a pan-European strategy. Most of these restructurings are intended to streamline the companies and to focus on a narrow set of businesses and short-term cost-cutting objectives.

### Family-centered economies: Sweden, France, and Italy

La Porta et al. (2000) argued that the nature of investor protection, and more generally of regulation of financial markets, is deeply rooted in the legal structure of each country and in the origin of its laws. Some evidence also indicates that French civil law countries, where neither credit markets nor stock markets are especially well developed, tend to have poor minority investor protection and are relatively more corrupted (La Porta et al., 1999). Levine, Loayza, and Beck (2000) find that creditor rights are correlated with financial intermediaries development across countries, while shareholder rights are correlated with stock market development. Drawing the relationship between corporate law and corporate governance, La Porta and his colleagues (1997) found that countries with poor investor protection tend to have higher ownership concentration by the families or the state.

The importance of families in control of large corporations is one of the central features distinguishing continental European systems from those of the Anglo-Saxon system (Berglof, 2000). For example, about 32 percent of the 200 largest French corporations are managed by their founders or the heirs of founders (Bauer and Bertin-Mourot, 1995). Shleifer and Vishny (1997) argued that the fundamental agency problem in the large corporations in most countries is not the Berle and Means conflict between outside investors and managers, but rather that between outside investors and controlling shareholders who have nearly full control over managers. Family control of firms is common, significant, and typically unchallenged by other equity holders (La Porta, Lopez-de-Silanes, and Shleifer, 1999). Usually, family control is gained through pyramidal structures. For example, in France, families gain control through a pyramidal ownership structure, or through the "multi-tier control network." At the lowest level, the parent company holds shares of its subsidiaries. At the second level, different parent companies are linked to a large financial corporation. At the upper level, the large financial institutions are linked to each other through capital networks and interlocking directorates (Windolf, 1998).

Pyramiding is important in countries where the capital market is underdeveloped and the protection of minority shareholders is rather weak (Bianco and Casavola, 1999). By spreading the voting rights of minority shareholders over a large number of firms and concentrating those of the ultimate owner at the top of the pyramid, it allows the ultimate controlling owner to minimize its capital stake without affecting the concentration of control. In this way, the pyramid structure fills the voids of the capital market by enabling controlling shareholders to finance new growth, diversifying the investment portfolios of the shareholders, and providing an internal monitoring device alternative to the discipline of the market (Berglof, 2000). Nevertheless, the growth of a more liquid capital market and corporate restructuring activities are severely hampered by concentrated ownership. Bergh (1995) found that firms with concentrated owners are more likely to divest unrelated and small units and pursue related and cooperative strategies. However, the opaque system of the pyramidal structure makes sell-offs difficult since it is hard to evaluate the overall value of the firms assets. Also, the market for corporate control is not very active. While many cross-border takeovers in continental Europe are related to control changes, to developing market power and consolidation (Hitt, Harrison, and Ireland, 2001) some takeovers in continental Europe are used as a mechanism to withdraw firms from the stock exchange rather than as a device to change control in firms (Berglof, 2000). Yet, with the emergence of the European Union and the increasing influence of foreign investors, continental countries such as France and Sweden are under rapid transitions in their financial and legal systems. The external capitalization of these two countries has been increased enormously since the 1980s (La Porta et al., 1997). More strict company disclosure and accounting standards, tax subsidies to attract smaller investors to stock exchange, and ownership restructuring through large-scale privatizations are leading France and Sweden towards the direction of the Anglo-Saxon market-centered financial system (Berglof, 2000).

Despite the ongoing market adjustments, corporate restructuring activities may still be hampered without corresponding changes in the legal environment. The major weakness of the family-controlled system is that the expropriation behaviors of insiders and the lack of minority investors' protection (Johnson et al., 2000). Italy is one of the typical countries with poor protection for minority investors. Controlling shareholders often have control rights in excess of their cash flow rights due to the deviation from one-share one-vote system. For instance, in an ownership survey conducted by La Porta et al. (1999), they found that Fiat, the third most valuable company in Italy, is also controlled by a voting trust, Ifi, which has 14.8 percent of the capital and 22.3 percent of the votes in Fiat. Giovanni Agnelli and his family, which together hold 49.95 percent of the capital and 100 percent of the votes in Ifi, control Ifi. Such deviations from the one-share one-vote principle will make if difficult for minority owners to monitor the firms. Therefore, one important concern to do with corporate restructuring is the legal reforms undertaken at the national level. The mandatory requirement of the one-share one-vote is necessary for improving minority shareholder rights.

In summary, in partially developed countries asset restructuring through takeovers are less common due to both economic factors (e.g., the lack of well-established financial sector and legal system) and cultural factors (e.g., avoidance of unfriendly behavior and maximizing social welfare). Financial restructuring is not common due to the complexity of bank domination and concentrated ownership, as well as the lack of a strong financial sector and investor protection rights. Therefore, little deep restructuring has been taking place relative to the developed economies. However, with the changes in both the global and regional competitive landscapes, partially developed countries are transforming themselves towards the market-centered systems as in the developed countries.

## RESTRUCTURING IN DEVELOPED ECONOMIES

In the United States and the United Kingdom, the institutional context is characterized by well functioning capital, labor, and product markets. These markets, and the evolution of intermediaries in these markets to address potential information and agency problems, permit individual entrepreneurs to raise capital, access management talent, earn customer acceptance and play by the rules of the game. They can be sure of the protection of the property rights that the legal environment confers upon the fruits of their entrepreneurial activity. Thus, for example, an entrepreneur need not rely on the internal capital markets that can be maintained by diversified groups or diversified corporations when she faces limited information and contracting problems in accessing a well-developed external market. In this context, it is less likely that the entrepreneur will benefit significantly by being associated with a corporate entity, which is diversified across unrelated industries (relative to the benefits that an entrepreneur would receive from such an association in an economy with more severe imperfections). Hence, the costs of unrelated business diversification are likely to exceed any potential benefits. Several recent reviews of the literature (Hoskisson and Hitt, 1990; Montgomery, 1994; Ramanujan and Varadarajan, 1989), while providing evidence of some of the benefits of diversification across related industries (Rumelt, 1974), support this assessment of the costs of unrelated diversification in the United States.

However, David, Kochhar, and Levitas (1998) found that different owners preferred different kinds of executive compensation. Hoskisson et al. (2000) found that different institutional investors (mutual fund versus pension fund managers) preferred external innovation (acquisition of access to new technology or markets) versus internal innovation through R&D commitments. Lane, Cannella, and Lubatkin (1998) also found that management controlled firms engage more in "related constrained" diversification, which is more in line with efficient risk and return than would be predicted by agency theory. This may suggest that different owners have different risk preferences, which allow different diversification strategies to exist including the unrelated strategy.

During the 1980s and 1990s, many highly diversified firms engaged in asset restructuring through sell-offs, split-ups, spin-offs, buyouts, and liquidations (Forest, 1995; Hoskisson and Hitt, 1994; Johnson, 1996). For example, over 18,000 divestitures worth over $940 billion took place between 1981 and the first half of 1995 (Sikora, 1995). Estimates of restructuring activity (Bowman and Singh, 1993) suggest that between 33 percent and 50 percent of *Fortune* 500 firms engaged in portfolio (asset) restructuring during the 1980s. In addition, divestiture activity shows no sign of slowing down in the latter half of the 1990s (Forest, 1995) and into the 21st century. For instance, as Bower (2001) notes a large percentage of acquisitions are from divestitures and restructuring due to over-capacity (such as the acquisition and restructuring of Chrysler by Daimler in the auto industry). Another category is due to a "multibusiness company" selling a division to a financial acquirer (such as LBO firm Kolberg Kravis and Roberts) or to a firm with a better fit. An example of this type of restructuring has been happening in chemical firms who have been spinning of many of their life science operations. For example, DuPont recently approved a plan to divest its pharmaceuticals unit and focus on its core chemicals business (Wee and Belton, 2001).

### Antecedents of restructuring activity in developed economies

One of the antecedents for restructuring that is uniquely found in developed economies relates to firm governance and the market for corporate control. Institutional investors have taken increased interest in not only the financial performance of their investor firms, but also interest and involvement in the specific strategies and activities of the firms in which they invest (Holderness and Sheehan, 1988; Pound, 1992; Smith, 1996). Another major antecedent is environmental factors. Researchers have offered several alternatives as triggers for the recent restructuring activity amongst highly diversified firms. Some have speculated that tax (Hoskisson and Hitt, 1990; Turk and Baysinger, 1989) and/or antitrust policy (Shleifer and Vishny, 1991) changes triggered the realignment of assets among diversified firms in the early 1980s. Others have argued that increases in global competition led to restructuring (Hoskisson and Hitt, 1994; Shleifer and Vishny, 1991). These changes in the business environment suggest that firms engage in restructuring to shed unwanted or under valued assets. The final antecedent for restructuring is poor strategy formulation or implementation. Firms may have diversified beyond optimal levels, causing performance to suffer, thus giving rise to the need to restructure. The following sections describe the aforementioned antecedents in greater detail.

## Firm governance and the market for corporate control

*Internal governance.*    Agency theorists argue that restructuring during the 1980s was a correction for overdiversification in the 1960s and 1970s. During this time period, managers increased firm size and diversified without increasing firm value (Jensen, 1986) because governance systems were inadequate to restrain diversification (Hoskisson and Turk, 1990). This view suggests that the board of directors, ownership concentration (equity held by blockholders), and managerial incentives were ineffective and resulted in the failure of internal governance as a system (Jensen, 1993). Inadequate governance may be related to diffusion of shareholdings among outside owners, characteristics of managers and board members, and board passivity.

As noted previously, institutional investor ownership has increased dramatically during the 1980s and has continued to increase throughout the 1990s. This has had several important impacts on firm governance. First, unlike individual stockholders, the large investments by institutional shareholders gives them less discretion to quickly move in and out of funds without affecting share price. Institutional investors, then, have the incentive to monitor management more closely and press for needed changes (exercise "voice") due to their inability to "exit" the firm by selling large blocks of stock (Pound, 1992). This exercise of voice may come in the form of proxy contests, shareholder amendments, floor resolutions during shareholder meetings and through direct communication with management (Smith, 1996; Silverstein, 1994).

Second, due to their power through equity ownership, institutional investors may select individuals to serve on the firm's board (Silverstein, 1994). These directors effectively represent the institutional investors. Perhaps in concert with the increase in institutional investor equity ownership, the percentage of outside directors has increased dramatically as has the use of stock options and increased equity ownership to re-align manager interests with those of shareholders. Despite the increase in institutional holdings, the impact of institutional ownership on firm performance has been mixed (Smith, 1996; Wahal, 1996).

Recent research in the area suggests that institutional investors may impact performance indirectly through firm strategies (Johnson and Greening, 1999). For example, Bethel and Liebeskind (1993) found that blockholder ownership (5 percent owners) was positively related to reductions in diversified scope but not to increases in specialization. Buy-ins by blockholders into diffusely held firms was also a significant determinant of downsizing, reductions in diversification, and increases in cash payouts in sample firms. Consistent with agency theory predictions, Bethel and Liebeskind's results suggest that blockholders have a disciplinary effect on managers. Bergh (1995) examined large-block shareholders and found that ownership concentration was positively related to the divestiture of unrelated and small units to pursue related and cooperative strategies. Hoskisson, Johnson, and Moesel (1994) examined the relationship between firm governance and divestment intensity. They found that blockholders influenced the level of divestiture activity but that the relationship was mediated by the level of product diversification. High levels of blockholder ownership coupled with high levels of unrelated diversification increased the level of divestment intensity. These findings suggest that blockholders in the latter half of 1980s may not have had a direct influence on amount of restructuring among highly diversified firms but served as a deterrent to excessive diversification. It should be noted that the aforementioned relationship was probably weaker in the early 1980s and especially in the 1960s and 1970s given the much lower levels of institutional ownership. Johnson, Hoskisson, and Hitt (1993) found that board involvement in restructuring was more likely as performance declined. Managerial equity holdings and strategic controls were negatively related to board involvement, suggesting that managers had sufficient incentives to initiate action prior to the board and institutional investors getting involved. Recent research has suggested that outside directors have inadequate incentives to monitor unless they have substantial equity stakes in the firm (Kosnik, 1990). This research supports the importance of outside director equity in that board involvement was higher when there were more outsiders on the board and they had substantial equity stakes.

*Market for corporate control.*    Much has been written concerning the effect of anti-trust regulation changes on the types of acquisitions that firms are allowed to make (Lee and Cooperman, 1989; Shleifer and Vishny, 1991). Prior to the 1980s, the Celler-Kefauver Act disallowed firms from acquiring companies in the same industry segment (Shleifer and Vishny, 1991). However, when the Reagan Administration took office, it instituted a change in anti-trust policy by redefining the point at which concentration began creating inappropriate monopoly power. The recent takeover wave of the 1980s may be partially attributed to this redefinition of industry concentration because it allowed horizontal mergers and related acquisitions. Thus, the increasing number of hostile takeovers has often been attributed to the new anti-trust policy (Shleifer and Vishny, 1991). Subsequent to hostile takeovers in the 1980s, the acquirer often separated the acquired firm's businesses and sold off the divisions to firms operating in the same industry as the target firm. Bhagat, Shleifer, and Vishny (1990) found that 70 percent of the assets acquired in hostile takeovers were sold to firms in the same line of business.

As a result of the aforementioned trends, management was faced with an increasingly active market for corporate control (Jensen, 1993) and the understanding that firm size was no longer a deterrent to takeover (Ambrose and Megginson, 1992). As such, many instances of corporate restructuring among highly diversified firms may have been initiated in response to the strategic uncertainty created by a perceived takeover threat or a rumor that the firm was in play (Loh, Bezjak, and Toms, 1995; Mitchell and Mulherin, 1996). Loh et al. (1995) report that 22 percent of firms in their sample engaged in divestitures after receiving takeover threats. Similarly, Blackwell, Marr, and Spivey (1990) found that roughly 13 percent of the plant closings in their sample took place after the firm received a tender offer. Rumors that a firm is a potential takeover target may pressure top management to improve firm performance to protect their positions within the firm.

One assumed characteristic of many takeover rumors and threats is that the target firm is performing poorly or is undervalued. However, this is not always the case; Walsh and Kosnik (1993) found that many takeovers were not the result of poor performance or undervalued assets. Nonetheless, firms engaged in a program of multiple divestitures (downscoping) often are performing poorly prior to the initiation of restructuring activities. For example, results reported by Hoskisson and Johnson (1992), Hoskisson, Johnson, and Moesel (1994), and Markides (1992b) all suggest that average divesting firm return on assets (ROA) was below industry averages in the pre-restructuring period. Based on structured interviews, John, Lang, and Netter (1992) concluded that managers in their sample of highly diversified firms used sell-offs 63 percent of the time, layoffs 43 percent, closed plants 26 percent, and reduced capacity 11 percent of the time when faced with declining performance. Thus, managers of poorly performing firms may be pressured into asset restructuring to improve performance and avoid a possible takeover. In these cases, asset restructuring by firm management may accomplish changes in the firm similar to those sought by corporate raiders; namely the sell-off of under-valued assets and a change in strategy.

## Environmental factors affecting restructuring

*Global and domestic competition.* The increase in international trade over the last few decades has increased foreign competition dramatically. Katics and Petersen (1994) document the growing vulnerability of many US industries to foreign competitors. Mitchell and Mulherin (1996) found that import penetration increased in many industries during the 1980s (up to 15 percent by 1987 in manufacturing industries) and that heightened foreign competition affects price-cost margins and other measures of efficiency. Hoskisson and Hitt (1994) provide evidence suggesting that US competitiveness declined in the 1980s and early 1990s. Hoskisson and Hitt (1994) further argue that many US firms have been highly diversified and inefficient in the internal development of new products. Highly diversified firms operate in multiple markets and may find it difficult to respond to competition in these markets due to their inability to allocate resources responsibly and efficiently. Thus, Prahalad and Hamel (1991) argue that these same firms may find it difficult to maintain a competitive advantage in the markets in which they compete.

In addition to global competition, domestic competition has increased as firms attempt to protect their market positions (Brahm, 1995). Trends in the level of competition coupled with increased penetration of US markets by foreign competitors have produced conditions of excess capacity and declines in performance (Katics and Petersen, 1994; Mitchell and Mulherin, 1996). In their study of declining firms, John, Lang, and Netter (1992) reported that managers blamed competition (57 percent), foreign competition (43 percent) and deregulation (13 percent) for performance declines and the need to restructure during the 1980s. Additionally, major changes in technology have also contributed to subnormal profits, severe price competition, and excess capacity in some markets (Brahm, 1995). Excess capacity may also result when multiple competitors simultaneously introduce highly productive technologies (Brahm, 1995) without considering the aggregate effects on demand for the final product (Jensen, 1993). Thus the interaction of globalization and new technological developments has produced significant changes in industry structure and competitive actions.

*Deregulation effects.* Major deregulation of the US economy (including trucking, rail, airlines, telecommunications, and banking and financial service industries) contributed to competition, excess capacity (Jensen, 1993), and greater uncertainty (Bergh and Lawless, 1998). For example, the Airline Deregulation Act of 1978 phased out governmental control of airline routes and pricing during the 1980s. Deregulation facilitated entry of new competitors and increased the level of competition (Mitchell and Mulherin, 1996).

Results from Bergh and Lawless (1998) suggest that firms encountering radical changes in their environment, such as those surrounding competition and deregulation, resort to restructuring to decrease problems in managing diverse businesses and to allow managerial time and energy to focus on the core competency within the firm.

Overall, deregulation and increased global and domestic competition created conditions of excess capacity, difficulty in managing the diverse operations of the firm, and a decline in performance in many industries. As noted by Bergh (1998), businesses can differ radically in how they respond to increased environmental uncertainty. For example, firms in the computer, telecommunications, higher education and defense industries have responded to increased environmental uncertainty by acquiring competitors (Bergh, 1998), while others have restructured by selling off unrelated business units in an attempt to focus on core businesses (Hoskisson and Johnson, 1992; Markides, 1992b). Most of these actions have the potential additional advantage of reducing diversified scope, thereby allowing managers to focus on core competencies (Hoskisson and Hitt, 1994; Johnson, 1996). Reductions in diversified scope through asset restructuring may also allow the implementation of strategic control systems (Hoskisson and Johnson, 1992) which, in turn, facilitate innovation activity (Hitt et al., 1996) that Franko (1989) has argued is critical for competitiveness in the global market.

*Tax incentives for restructuring.*    Restructuring may also be motivated by changes in the institutional environment associated with government action; such as tax code changes (Gilson, Scholes, and Wolfson, 1988; Hoskisson and Hitt, 1990). During the 1960s and 1970s, dividends were taxed more heavily than ordinary personal income (Turk and Baysinger, 1989). Therefore, shareholders may have preferred that companies retain these funds and invest them in the firm. This resultant increase in free cash flows (Jensen, 1986) coupled with antitrust laws led to an emphasis on unrelated diversification. However, in the 1980s, the top ordinary individual income tax rate decreased from 50 percent to 28 percent and the capital gains taxes were changed such that capital gains were treated as ordinary income (Hoskisson and Hitt, 1990). Turk and Baysinger (1989) further argued that the elimination of personal interest deductability and the lower attractiveness of retained earnings to shareholders have prompted the use of greater leverage by firms (interest expense is tax deductible). Therefore, changes in tax benefits have reduced the value that unrelated diversified firms provide shareholders. The end result has been an unraveling of much of the conglomerate diversification that took place during the 1960s and 1970s (Lee and Cooperman, 1989).

In addition to changes in the tax laws, the leverage ratios of many US firms have increased dramatically over the past decade, largely due to the tax advantages of debt over equity. Debt is a less expensive form of financing than equity because the interest expense is tax deductible while dividend payments are not. Leveraged recapitalizations such as leveraged stock repurchases and debt for equity swaps (securities swaps and leveraged cash-outs) increase a firm's intrinsic market value because debt shelters operating profits from being fully taxed. The aforementioned tax motivations may lead to increased use of various forms of financial restructuring such as leveraged recapitalizations (leveraged share repurchases, cash-outs and securities swaps), and employee stock option plans (ESOPs) which provides a tax benefit and increases firm value (Cornett and Travlos, 1989). The increase in debt associated with leveraged recapitalizations may force managers to restructure the firm (sell-off assets) to pay down debt if the firm becomes over-leveraged (Lee and Cooperman, 1989).

In the 1990s, however, equity has been emphasized to finance many acquisitions deals (Hitt, Harrison, and Ireland, 2001). This is due to tax, accounting and managerial control issues which now favor equity transactions, especially when the acquiring firm thinks that its stock is overvalued. But equity financing most often leads to overpayment, which can lead to higher debt and forced restructuring to pay down such associated debt.

Overdiversification, especially in developed economies, may lead to the need for restructuring. This often happens when a firm reaches beyond its capabilities to manage a diversified portfolio of business and does not provide "parental advantage."

## Parental advantage and restructuring

As mentioned above, developed economies do not suffer from the problems of inefficient resource allocation and information asymmetry with more well-functioning capital, labor, and product markets. Therefore, the opportunities of achieving advantages of substituting these market functions by diversified business groups are smaller in the developed economies than in the emerging economies. In the developed economies, the parent of a multibusiness firm "acts as an intermediary, influencing the decisions and strategies pursued by the businesses, and standing between the businesses and those who provide capital for their use" (Goold, Campbell, and Alexander, 1994: 12). "Parental advantages" result when a parent provides insights about opportunities to create value, possess distinctive characteristics to realize this value in a unique way, and identifies a set of competencies on which to focus its business portfolio. Parental advantages emphasize the fit between the characteristics of the parent and those of the businesses it owns. If the parent fails to achieve this fit, with the pressures from both product market competition and market for corporate control, a second and better parent may be able to pay a premium to gain corporate control. An alternative of being taken over by another parent is restructuring. Some businesses are worth less under the control of their parents than if they are stand-alone entities (Wright et al., 2000). By spinning off these misfit businesses, a firm can create value through restructuring. Accordingly, firms may decide to restructure and refocus themselves, but often this occurs under the threat of hostile takeover.

In the 1980s the optimal level of diversification decreased due to the factors described in the environment section. Also, without the need to fill the voids in the capital, labor, and product markets, it is easier for firms to overdiversify. Both Hoskisson, Hitt, and Hill (1991) and Ravenscraft and Scherer (1991) argue that excessive diversification may create control loss and misallocation of corporate resources. Over-diversification may lead to inefficiencies and subsequent performance loss (Hoskisson and Turk, 1990; Markides, 1992b). In fact, Berger and Ofek (1995) report an average value loss of 13–15 percent between 1986 and 1991 for unrelated diversifiers.

The loss of firm value resulting from overdiversification is due to several factors. First, overdiversification leads to high debt levels and lower product innovations. Baysinger and Hoskisson (1989) found that diversification was positively related to debt levels and that debt and diversified scope has a negative impact on R&D intensity. As firms using an unrelated diversified strategy acquire businesses they generally increase the level of corporate debt (Lee and Cooperman, 1989). This debt, which requires interest payments, can serve to limit funds ordinarily devoted to innovation activities. In effect, managers may be forced to rely more on external acquisition of new products and processes (Hitt et al., 1996).

In addition to debt concerns, Hitt, Hoskisson, and Ireland (1990) and Hoskisson and Hitt (1988) argue that as diversification increases, managers cannot process all the information necessary to use strategic controls and instead emphasize financial controls based on short-term quarterly results such as return on investment (ROI). Financial controls, which emphasize cash flows, ROI, and *ex-ante* budgets, do not present the same information processing problems that subjective evaluative criteria and both face-to-face informal and formal meetings between divisional and corporate managers do. They further argue that emphasis on financial controls leads to managerial risk aversion (in the form of lower R&D intensity). Markides (1992b) found that firms with high levels of R&D expenditures in their core business were less likely to sell off unrelated units. Ravenscraft and Scherer (1991) report that sell-offs were more likely the lower the market share, the lower the R&D/sales ratio, and in the aftermath of CEO change. In addition, Hill and Hoskisson (1987) argue that related-constrained firms focusing on synergistic economies require different control systems than firms focusing on financial economies such as unrelated diversified firms. They further suggest that these different control systems are incompatible and may contribute to managerial control loss and inefficiencies. Therefore, as managers emphasize financial controls, the mismatch between control systems and structure may nullify the opportunity to gain benefits from sharing resources (in the case of related units).

Several studies have examined the relationship between the level of diversification and corporate restructuring in diversified firms (Johnson, 1996). For example, Markides (1992b) found that firms with very high levels of diversification relative to industry counterparts were more likely to restructure than firms with less diversification. Hoskisson, Johnson, and Moesel (1994) found that restructuring firms on average exhibited higher levels of diversified scope than the industry average and that these high levels were positively related to divestment intensity (number of units sold, percentage of assets divested, and the time spent refocusing). Overall, results indicate that high levels of diversification result in inefficiencies that may lead to declines in performance and refocusing. Hoskisson and Johnson (1992) argued that many of the refocusing firms experienced control system inefficiencies due to a mixture of strategic and financial controls. They found that the majority of firms restructuring were related-linked (firms that include components of related and unrelated diversification). Most of the firms either downscoped to a related-constrained strategy emphasizing synergistic economies or divested related units to pursue an unrelated diversified strategy (though on a much smaller scale).

In summary, the strategic rationale for restructuring may vary considerably. In general, research in the area of restructuring has found that firms tend to sell off unrelated units due to managerial control loss and the inherent inefficiencies associated with managing diverse businesses under uncertainty (Johnson, 1996). Duhaime and Grant (1984) report that managers cited a lack of fit with other units as one of the primary reasons to divest. Similarly, Hoskisson and Johnson (1992) reported that many highly diversified firms announced they were refocusing on core operations for various reasons including competitiveness issues and financial performance. Markides (1992b) reported that managers found the current firm to be unmanageable or that they were choosing to emphasize core operations and that the divested units exhibited both lower relatedness and growth than retained units.

## Overall effects

Although unrelated diversification continues to exist in the US and UK (Lane, Cannella, and Lubatkin, 1998), the advantages appear to be fleeting (Ruigrok et al., 1999) because unrelated firms focus on advantages that are based on generalized rather than firm-specific assets. Based on the limitations of the unrelated diversified strategy and the aforementioned changes in the environment, the requirements for successful strategy implementation and a more active market for corporate control, it is not surprising that the use of unrelated diversified strategies has decreased dramatically in developed economies. The following discussion details the overall effects of restructuring on conglomerates and highly diversified firms in developed economies.

One of the most common stated goals of restructuring is to change firm strategy (Johnson, 1996). This change may serve to improve parental advantage, that is, the fit between firm parent and businesses, restore competitiveness, and improve efficiency in resource allocation within the multibusiness firm. Moreover, restructuring also improves the control relationships between parent and businesses. Given one of the goals of restructuring is to reduce diversified scope, then firms in R&D intensive industries might be expected to re-implement strategic controls to increase managerial risk taking through R&D expenditures (Hoskisson and Johnson, 1992). Hitt et al. (1996) examined the effect of participation in the market for corporate control (acquisitions and divestitures) and found that both acquisition and divestiture intensity lead to an emphasis on financial controls and a reduction in strategic control usage due to information-processing problems. Hitt and colleagues (1996) also found that an emphasis on financial controls has a negative impact on internal innovation (R&D and new product announcements). Strategic controls, the study found, increase internal innovation. Firms actively altering their portfolio were more likely to acquire new technology and products as opposed to developing them internally.

Hoskisson and Johnson (1992) found that once firms completed restructuring they have moved away from the related-linked strategy to either related-constrained or unrelated strategies that emphasize either strategic or financial controls (but not both). The majority of firms downscoped and focused on related businesses. Downscoping was positively related to R&D intensity, while divestiture of related units and an emphasis on unrelated units was negatively related to R&D intensity. These results suggest that downscoping firms solved their overdiversification problem and re-implemented strategic controls. Hitt et al. (1996) provide support for this assertion using a subset of firms that had completed refocusing. Hitt and colleagues found that once firms completed restructuring they re-implemented strategic controls and increased R&D intensity and new product introductions.

Sell-offs of business units generally earn positive abnormal returns (Hite, Owers, and Rogers, 1987; Jain, 1985), especially when the sell-offs are made as part of an integrated strategic plan (Montgomery, Thomas, and Kamath, 1984). While the aforementioned studies examined single divestiture events, the results are not dissimilar to research examining market responses to announcements of downscoping programs. Markides (1992a) examined returns to firms that announced a refocusing move in the *Wall Street Journal* and found that firms earned positive and significant returns of 1.73 percent during the two days surrounding the announcement. Similarly, Slovin, Sushka and Ferraro (1995) found that firms announcing a refocusing earned a 2-day CAR of 3.22 percent while industry rivals earned returns of 0.55 percent suggesting that announcements of refocusing lead to a positive information effect for the future prospects of the industry. Thus the evidence suggests that firms that reduce diversified scope realize short-term gains.

Research examining longer-term implications of restructuring have also found a positive association between restructuring and profitability. Comment and Jarrell (1995) examined the population of firms on the Compustat tapes and found that firms that refocused during the 1980s experienced an upward trend in net-of-market wealth while firms that decreased focus experienced a decline in net-of-market wealth. Similarly, John and Ofek (1995) report that earnings before interest, taxes, and depreciation (EBITD)/sales and ROA improved for each of the three years following asset sales. Hoskisson and Johnson (1992) examined firms that announced a refocusing in the *Wall Street Journal* and found that industry-adjusted ROA was significantly higher in the post-refocusing versus the pre-refocusing period. In summary, the preponderance of the evidence suggests that reductions in diversified scope does improve shareholder returns as well as operating profits.

Perhaps the most important change that may occur with a reduction in diversified scope is an increase in strategic flexibility. The dramatic increase in global and domestic competition coupled with shortening product life cycles has emphasized the need for flexibility in order for a firm to remain competitive. In this context, strategic flexibility denotes a firm's ability to thrive in the current economic conditions and the ability to respond to changing conditions. This ability to change is facilitated by flexible structures (Raynor, 2000). The primary issue is that firms in a highly diversified business may not exhibit obvious ways to share resources given current industry conditions even though these conditions may become apparent in the future due to technological, sociocultural or economic changes. As noted by Raynor (2000) strategic flexibility implies divisional managers operate within boundaries imposed by corporate management.

Interestingly, Raynor's position is that strategic flexibility is facilitated by higher levels of diversified scope. These hybrid or related-linked firms are composed of both related and unrelated units. While this line of reasoning is appealing, there are several pitfalls associated with the related-linked strategy. First, Hill and Hoskisson (1987) argue that to obtain synergistic economies, top management must oversee divisional managers' strategies through the use of strategic controls. The aforementioned control systems are difficult to implement with higher diversification levels. Second, Hoskisson, Hitt, and Hill (1991) found that unrelated diversified firms are characterized as having competitive relationships as opposed to the cooperative arrangements among related diversified firms. Competition between divisions may mitigate potential or identified synergies. Third, Hoskisson and Johnson (1992) report that the majority of restructuring in the 1980s was undertaken by related-linked or hybrid firms. They further argue that there may be a control system mismatch within these hybrid firms that leads to managerial risk aversion, lower R&D, less internal innovation as well as performance declines. This suggests a trade-off between the need for strategic flexibility and the need for appropriate control systems.

## CONCLUSION

This chapter provides theory about how these large diversified business groups might profitably restructure given their countries' stage of not only economic development (physical infrastructure), but more particularly on their countries' social infrastructure that facilitates a firm's transaction environment. In all, we posit that diversified business groups emerge as an intermediary to substitute the ineffectual legal, capital, labor, and capital markets in the emerging economies. However, with more developed physical and soft infrastructures as well as increasing penetration of foreign investment and competition, such substitution advantages are lessened in the partially developed economies and almost absent in the developed economies. In the developed economies, firms depend more on organizational advantages to maintain strategic competitiveness as well as to mitigate threats from the market for corporate control. Internal governance also influences the balance of diversification between managerial and ownership expectations. Beyond these, firms rely on making the right buy and sell of their businesses in the market to maintain the fit between the parent's capabilities and its businesses. Given the contextual differences, there is much more room for diversified business groups to realize the advantages of unrelated diversifications in emerging economies. On the other hand, firms in developed economies may more often experience problems of overdiversification where synergies are more illusory (Sirower, 1997) and no longer create value between the businesses. Therefore, restructuring activities are highly related to firm strategy in the developed economies (Hoskisson, Johnson, and Moesel, 1994), while corporate restructurings are, to a larger extent, forced by environmental crises or institutional changes in less developed and emerging economies.

## REFERENCES

Akerlof, G. (1970). The market for lemons. Quality uncertainty and the market mechanism. *Quarterly Journal of Economics*, 488–500.

Ambrose, B. W. and Megginson, W. L. (1992). The role of asset structure, ownership structure and takeover defenses in determining acquisition likelihood. *Journal of Financial and Quantitative Analysis*, 27: 575–89.

Amsden, A. (1989). *Asia's Next Giant: South Korea and Late Industrialization*. New York: Oxford University Press.

Amsden, A. H., and Hikino, T. (1994). Project execution capability, organizational know-how and conglomerate corporate growth in late industrialization. *Industrial and Corporate Change*, 3: 111–48.

Anand, J. (1999). How many matches are made in heaven. Mastering Strategy Part Five. *Financial Times*, October 25: 6–7.

Aoki, M. (1988). *Information, Incentives, and Bargaining in the Japanese Economy*. Cambridge, UK: Cambridge University Press.

Aoki, M, (1990). Toward and economic model of the Japanese firm. *Journal of Economic Literature*, 28: 1–27.

Bauer, M., and Bertin-Mourot, B. (1995). *L'accès au sommet des grandes entreprises françaises 1985–1994*. Paris: CNRS/Boyden.

Baysinger, B. D., and Hoskisson, R. E. (1989). Diversification strategy and R&D intensity in large multiproduct firms. *Academy of Management Journal*, 32: 310–32.

Berger, P. G., and Ofek, E. (1995). Diversification's effect on firm value. *Journal of Financial Economics*, 37: 39–65.

Bergh, D. D. (1995). Size and relatedness of units sold: An agency theory and resource-based perspective. *Strategic Management Journal*, 16: 221–39.

Bergh, D. D. (1998). Product-market uncertainty, portfolio restructuring, and performance: An information-processing and resource-based view. *Journal of Management*, 24: 135–55.

Bergh, D. D., and Lawless, M. W. (1998). Effects of product-market uncertainty and diversification strategy on portfolio restructuring: A transaction cost model. *Organization Science*, 9: 87–113.

Berglof, E. (2000). Reforming corporate governance: Redirecting the European agenda. In S. S. Cohen and G. Boyd (eds.), *Corporate Governance and Globalization*. Northampton, MA: Edward Elgar, 245–74.

Bethel, J. E. and Liebeskind, J. (1993). The effects of ownership structure on corporate restructuring. *Strategic Management Journal*, 14 Special Issue: 15–32.

Bhagat, S., Shleifer, A., and Vishny, R. W. (1990). Hostile takeovers in the 1980s: The return to corporate specialization. *Brookings Papers on Economic Activity, Microeconomics 1990*: 1–72.

Bianco, M., and Casavola, P. (1999). Italian corporate governance: Effects on financial structure and firm performance. *European Economic Review*, 43: 1057–69.

Blackwell, D. W., Marr, M. W., and Spivey, M. F. (1990). Plant-closing decisions and the market value of the firm. *Journal of Financial Economics*, 26: 277–88.

Bower, J. L. (2001). Not all M&As are alike – and that matters, *Harvard Business Review*, 73(3): 93–101.

Bowman, E. H., and Singh, H. (1993). Corporate restructuring: Reconfiguring the firm. *Strategic Management Journal*, 14 Special Issue: 5–14.

Brahm, R. (1995). National targeting policies, high technology industries, and excessive competition. *Strategic Management Journal*, 16 Special Issue: 71–91.

*Business Week* (1999). Japan: No room at the top. August 9.

Chang, L. (1998), Big is beautiful. *Wall Street Journal*, April 30: R9.

Chang, S., and Choi, U. (1988). Strategy, structure and performance of Korean business groups. *Journal of Industrial Economics*, 37: 141–58.

Chang, S., and Hong, J. (2000). Economic performance of group-affiliated companies in Korea: Intragroup resource sharing and internal business transactions. *Academy of Management Journal*, 43: 429–48.

Clarke, T., and Bostock, R. (1997). Governance in Germany: The foundations of corporate structure? In K. Keasy, S. Thompson, and M. Wright (eds.), *Corporate Governance: Economic and Financial Issues*: 233–51. New York: Oxford University Press.

Coase, R. H. (1937). The nature of the firm. *Economica*, 4: 386–405.

Coleman, J. S. (1990). *Foundations of Social Theory*. Cambridge, MA: Harvard University Press.

Comment, R., and Jarrell, G. A. (1995). Corporate focus and stock returns. *Journal of Financial Economics*, 37: 67–87.

Cornett, M. M. and Travlos, N. G. (1989). Information effects associated with debt-for-equity and equity-for-debt exchange offers. *Journal of Finance*, 44: 451–68.

David, P., Kochhar, R., and Levitas, E. (1998). The effect of institutional investors on the level and mix of CEO compensation. *Academy of Management Journal*, 41: 200–208.

Deener, B. (1999). Mega-deals stifle shares, survey implies. *Dallas Morning News*, November 30: D1, D6.

Devlin. R. A., Grafton, R. Q., and Rowlands, D. (1998). Rights and wrongs: A property rights perspective of Russia's market reforms. *Antitrust Bulletin*, 43: 275–96.

Diamond, D. W. (1984). Financial intermediation and delegated monitoring. *Review of Economic Studies*, 513: 99.393–414.

Drucker, P. F. 2000). The unrecognized boom. *Across the Board*, January: 15–16.

Duhaime, I. M., and Grant, J. H. (1984). Factors influencing divestment decision-making: Evidence from a field study. *Strategic Management Journal*, 5: 301–18.

*Economist*. (1998). South Korea restructuring: Cut to fit. December 12.

Encarnation, D. (1989). *Dislodging Multinationals: India's Comparative Perspective*. Ithaca, NY: Cornell University Press.

Estrin, S., and Wright, M. (1999). Corporate governance in the former Soviet Union: An overview of the issues. *Journal of Comparative Economics*, 27: 398–421.

*Financial Times* (1999). Germany: The monoliths stir, http://www.ft.com, September 29.

Filatotchev, I., Buck, T., and Zhukov, V. (2000). Downsizing in privatized firms in Russia, Ukraine, and Belarus. *Academy of Management Journal*, 43: 286–304.

Fisman, R. (1998). The incentives to rent seeking: Estimating the value of political connections. Manuscript, World Bank, Washington, DC.

Forest, S. (1995). The whirlwind breaking up companies. *Business Week*, August 14: 44.

Franko, L. G. (1989). Global corporate competition: Who's winning, who's losing and the R&D factor as one reason why. *Strategic Management Journal*, 10: 449–74.

Franks, J., and Mayer, C. (1996). Hostile takeovers and the correction of managerial failure. *Journal of Financial Economics*, 40: 163–81.

Fukuyama, F. (1995). *Trust: The Docial Virtues and the Creation of Prosperity*. New York: Free Press.

Ghemawat, P., Kennedy, R., and Khanna, T. (1998). Competitive policy shocks and strategic management. In M. Hitt, J. E. Ricart, and R. Nixon (eds.), *Managing Strategically in an Interconnected World*. New York: Wiley, 15–38.

Ghemawat, P. and Khanna, T. (1998). The nature of diversified groups: A research design and two case studies. *Journal of Industrial Economics*, 46: 35–62.

Gilson, R., Scholes, M., and Wolfson, M. (1988). Taxation and the dynamics of corporate control: The uncertain case for tax motivated acquisitions. In J. C. Coffee, L. Lowenstein, and S. Rose-Ackerman (eds.), *Knights, Raiders and Targets: The Impact of the Hostile Takeover*. New York: Oxford University Press, 279–99..

Goold, M., Campbell, A., and Alexander, M. (1994). *Corporate-level Strategy: Creating Value in the Multibusiness Company*. New York: John Wiley and Sons.

Granovetter, M. (1994). Business groups, chapter 18. In *Handbook of economic sociology*. Princeton, NJ: Princeton University Press, 453–75.

Grosse, R., and Yanes, J. (1998). Carrying out a successful privatization: The YPF case. *Academy of Management Executive*, 12(2): 51–63.

Guillen, M. (1997). Business groups in economic development. *Academy of Management Best Paper Proceedings*: 170–74.

Halpern, P. J. N. (2000). Systemic perspectives on corporate governance systems. In S. S. Cohen and G. Boyd (eds.), *Corporate Governance and Globalization*. Northampton, MA: Edward Elgar, 1–58.

Hill, C. W. L., and Hoskisson, R. E. (1987). Strategy and structure in the multiproduct firm. *Academy of Management Review*, 12: 331–41.

Hite, G. L., Owers, J. E., and Rogers, R. C. (1987). The market for interfirm asset sales: Partial sell-offs and total liquidations. *Journal of Financial Economics*, 18: 229–52.

Hitt, M. A., Harrison, J. S., and Ireland, R. D. (2001). *Creating Value through Mergers and Acquisitions: A Complete Guide to Successful M&As*. New York: Oxford University Press.

Hitt, M. A., Hoskisson, R. E., and Ireland, R. D. (1990). Mergers and acquisitions and managerial committment to innovation in M-form firms. *Strategic Management Journal*, 11, Special Issue: 29–47.

Hitt, M. A., Hoskisson, R. E., Johnson, R. A., and Moesel, D. D. (1996). The market for corporate control and firm innovation. *Academy of Management Journal*, 39: 1084–119.

Holderness, C. G., and Sheehan, D. P. (1988). The role of majority shareholders in publicly held corporations: An exploratory analysis. *Journal of Financial Economics*. 20: 317–46.

Hoshi, T., Kashyap, A., and Scharfstein, D. (1990. The role of banks in reducing the cost of financial distress in Japan. *Journal of Financial Economics*, 27: 67–88.

Hoskisson, R. E., and Hitt, M. A. (1988). Strategic control systems and relative R&D investment in large multi-product firms. *Strategic Management Journal*, 9: 605–21.

Hoskisson, R. E., and Hitt, M. A. (1990). Antecedents and performance outcomes of diversification: A review and critique of theoretical perspectives. *Journal of Management*, 16: 461–509.

Hoskisson, R. E. and Hitt, M. A. (1994). *Downscoping: How to Tame the Diversified Firm.* New York: Oxford University Press.

Hoskisson, R. E., Hitt, M. A., and Hill, C. W. L. (1991). Managerial risk taking in diversified firms: An evolutionary perspective. *Organization Science*, 2: 296–313.

Hoskisson, R. E., Hitt, M. A., Johnson, R. A., and Grossman. W. (2000) Conflicting voices: The effects of ownership heterogeneity and internal governance on corporate strategy. Paper presented at the 20th Annual Strategic Management Conference, Vancouver, Canada, October 15–18.

Hoskisson, R. E., and Johnson, R. A. (1992). Corporate restructuring and strategic change: The effect on diversification strategy and R&D intensity. *Strategic Management Journal*, 13: 625–34.

Hoskisson, R. E., Johnson, R. A., and Moesel, D. D. (1994). Divestment intensity of restructuring Firms: Effects of governance, strategy and performance. *Academy of Management Journal*, 37: 1207–51.

Hoskisson, R. E., and Turk, T. A. (1990). Corporate restructuring: Governance and control limits of the internal capital market. *Academy of Management Review*, 15: 459–77.

Jain, P. C. (1985). The effect of voluntary sell-off announcements on shareholder wealth. *Journal of Finance*, 40: 209–24.

Jensen, M. C. (1986). Agency costs of free cash flow, corporate finance and takeovers. *American Economic Review*, 76: 323–29.

Jensen, M. C. (1993). The modern industrial revolution, exit, and the failure of internal control systems. *Journal of Finance*, 48: 831–80.

John, K., and Ofek, E. (1995). Asset sales and increase in focus. *Journal of Financial Economics*, 37: 105–26.

John, K., Lang, L. H. P., and Netter, J. (1992). The voluntary restructuring of large firms in response to performance decline. *Journal of Finance*, 47: 891–917.

Johnson, R. A. (1996), Antecedents and outcomes of corporate refocusing. *Journal of Management*, 22: 437–81.

Johnson, R. A. and Greening, D. W. (1999). The effects of corporate governance and institutional ownership types on corporate social performance. *Academy of Management Journal*, 42: 564–76.

Johnson, R. A., Hoskisson, R. E., and Hitt, M. A. (1993). Board of director involvement in restructuring: The effects of board versus managerial controls and characteristics. *Strategic Management Journal*, 14, special issue: 33–50.

Johnson, S., Boone, P., Breach, A., and Friedman, E. (2000). Corporate governance in the Asian financial crisis. *Journal of Financial Economics*, 58: 241–86.

Katics, M. M., and Petersen, B. C. (1994). The effect of rising import competition on market power: A panel data study of US manufacturing. *Journal of Industrial Economics*, 42: 277–86.

Khanna, T., and Palepu, K. (1997). Why focused strategies may be wrong for emerging markets. *Harvard Business Review*, 75(4): 41–51.

Khanna, T., and Palepu, K. (1999a). The right way to restructure conglomerates in emerging markets. *Harvard Business Review*, 77(4): 125–34.

Khanna, T., and Palepu, K. (1999b). Is group membership profitable in emerging markets? An analysis of diversified Indian business groups. *Journal of Finance*, 55: 867–92.

Khanna, T., and Palepu, K. (2000). The future of business groups in emerging markets: Long-run evidence from Chile. *Academy of Management*, 43: 268–85.

Kim, H., Han, J. W., and Hoskisson, R. E. (2000). An evolution of Korean business groups: Resources, organizations, and business portfolios. In S. H. Jwa and I. K. Lee (eds.), *Korean Chaebol in Transition: Road Ahead and Agenda*. Seoul, Korea: Korea Economic Research Institute, 263–303.

Kim, H., and Hoskisson, R. E. (1997). Market United States versus managed Japanese governance. In K. Keasey, S. Thompson, and M. Wright (eds.), *Corporate Governance: Economic, Management, and Financial Issue*. New York: Oxford University Press, 174–99.

Knack, S., and Keefer, P. (1997). Does social capital have an economic payoff? A cross-country investigation. *Quarterly Journal of Economics*, 1251–88.

Kosnik, R. D. (1990). Effects of board demography and directors' incentives on corporate greenmail decisions. *Academy of Management Journal*, 33: 129–50.

La Porta, R., Lopez-de-Silanes, F., and Shleifer, A. (1999). Corporate ownership around the world. *Journal of Finance*, 54: 471–517.

La Porta, R., Lopez-de-Silanes, F., Shleifer, A., and Vishny, R. (1997). Legal determinants of external finance. *Journal of Finance*, 52: 1131–50.

La Porta, R., Lopez-de-Silanes, F., Shleifer, A., and Vishny, R. (1999). The quality of government. *Journal of Law, Economics and Organization*, 15: 222–79.

La Porta, R., Lopez-de-Silanes, F., Shleifer, A., and Vishny, R. (2000). Investor protection and corporate governance. *Journal of Financial Economics*, 58: 3–27.

Lane, P. J., Cannella, A. A., and Lubatkin, M. H. (1998). Agency problems as antecedents to unrelated mergers and diversification: Amihud and Lev reconsidered. *Strategic Management Journal*, 19: 555–78.

Lee, W. B., and Cooperman, E. S. (1989). Conglomerates in the 1980s: A performance appraisal. *Financial Management*, 18: 45–54.

Leff, N. (1976). Capital markets in the less developed countries: The group principle. In R. McKinnon (ed.), *Money and Finance in Economic Growth and Development*. New York: Marcel Dekker.

Leff, N. (1978a). Industrial organization and entrepreneurship in the developing countries: The economic groups. *Economic Development and Cultural Change*, 26: 661–75.

Levine, R., Loayza, N., and Beck, T., (2000). Financial intermediary development and economics growth: Causality and causes. *Journal of Monetary Economics*, 461: 31–77.

Lin, J. Y., Cai, F., and Li, Z. (1998). Competition, policy burdens, and state-owned enterprises. *American Economic Review*, 88: 422–7.

Lincoln, R., Gerlach, M. L., and Takahashi, P. (1992). Keiretsu networks in the Japanese economy: a dyad analysis of intercorporateties. *American Sociological Review*, 575: 561–85.

Loh, C., Bezjak, J. R., and Toms, H. (1995). Voluntary corporate divestitures as antitakeover mechanisms. *The Financial Review*, 30: 41–60.

Macey, J., and Miller, G. (1997). Universal banks are not the answer to America's corporate governance "Problem": A look at Germany, Japan, and the US. *Bank of America Journal of Applied Corporate Finance*, 57–73.

Markides, C. C. (1992a). Consequences of corporate refocusing: Ex ante evidence. *Academy of Management Journal*, 35: 398–412.

Markides, C. C. (1992b). The economic characteristics of de-diversifying firms. *British Journal of Management*, 3: 91–100.

Mayer, C. (1998). Financial systems and corporate governance: A review of the internal evidence.

*Journal of Institutional and Theoretical Economics*, 154: 144–65.

*Mergers and Acquisitions*. (2000). How M&A will navigate the turn into a new century. *Mergers and Acquisitions*, January: 29–35.

Mitchell, M. L., and Mulherin, J. H. (1996). The impact of industry shocks on takeover and restructuring activity. *Journal of Financial Economics*, 41: 193–230.

Montgomery, C. A. (1994). Corporate diversification. *Journal of Economic Perspective*, 8: 163–78.

Montgomery, C. A., Thomas, A. R., and Kamath, R. (1984). Divestiture, market valuation, and strategy. *Academy of Management Journal*, 27: 830–40.

Murrell, P., and Wang, Y. (1993). When privatization should be delayed? *Journal of Comparative Economics*, 17: 200–13.

Nelson, J. M., Tilley, C., and Walker, L. (eds.) (1998). *Transforming Post-Communist Political Economies: Task Force on Economies in Transition, National Research Council*. Washington, DC: National Academy Press.

Newman, K. L. (2000). Organizational transformation during institutional upheaval. *Academy of Management Review*, 25: 602–19.

North, D. (1990). *Institutions, Institutional Change and Economic Performance*. New York: Cambridge University Press.

Ozawa, T. (2000). Japanese firms in deepening integration: Evolving corporate governance. In S. S. Cohen and G. Boyd (eds.), *Corporate Governance and Globalization*, Northampton, MA: Edward Elgar, 216–44.

Palmer, D. A., Jennings, P. D., and Zhou, X. (1993). Late adoption of the multidivisional form by large US corporations: Institutional, political and economic accounts. *Administrative Science Quarterly*, 38: 100–32.

Patrick, H. T. (1994). The relevance of Japanese finance and its main bank system. In M. Aoki and H. Patrick (eds.), *The Japanese Main Bank System*. Oxford: Oxford University Press, 353–408.

Portanger, E. (2000). Europe sets the stage for more megamergers. *Wall Street Journal*, January 4: A17.

Pound, J. (1992). Beyond takeovers: Politics comes to corporate control. *Harvard Business Review*, 70(2): 83–93.

Prahalad, C. K., and Hamel, G. (1991). The core competence of the corporation. *Harvard Business Review*, May–June: 79–91.

Putnam, R. D. (1993). *Making democracy work: Civic traditions in modern Italy*. Princeton, NJ: Princeton University Press.

Ramanujam, V., and Varadarajan, P. (1989). Research on corporate diversification: A synthesis. *Strategic Management Journal*, 10: 523–51.

Rappaport, A., and Sirower, M. L. (1999). Stock or cash? *Harvard Business Review*, 776: 147–58.

Ravenscraft, D. J., and Scherer, F. M. (1991). Divisional sell-off: A hazard function analysis. *Managerial and Decision Economics*, 12: 429–38.

Raynor, M. (2000). Real organizations for real options: The dynamic of corporate strategy. Paper presented at the 20th annual Strategic Management Society meeting, October 14–18, Vancouver.

Rondinelli, D. (1998). Institutions and market development: Capacity building for economic and social transition. IPPRED Working Paper No. 14. Enterprise and Cooperative development Department. Geneva: International Labor Organization.

Ruigrok, W., Pettigrew, A., Peck, S., and Whittington, R. (1999), Corporate restructuring and new forms of organizing: Evidence from Europe. *Management International Review*, 39, Special Issue: 41–64.

Rumelt, R. P. (1974). *Strategy, structure, and economic performance*. Cambridge, MA: Harvard University Press.

Sachs, J., and Warner, A. (1995). Economic reform and the process of global integration. *Brookings*

*Papers on Economic Activity*, 25th Anniversary Issue.

Schuman, M., and Lee, J. L. (1999). Dismantling of Daewoo shows how radically Korea is changing. *Wall Street Journal*, August 17: A1, A10.

Schwartz, A. (1992). *A Nation in Waiting: Indonesia in the 1990s*. Sydney: Allen & Unwin.

Sheard, P. (1994). Interlocking shareholdings and corporate governance. In M. Aoki and R. Dore (eds.), *The Japanese Firm: Sources of Competitive Strength*. New York: Oxford University Press, 310–44.

Shleifer, A., and Vishny, R. W. (1991). Takeovers in the '60s and the '80s: Evidence and implications. *Strategic Management Journal*, 12, Special Issue: 51–60.

Shleifer, A., and Vishny, R. (1997). A survey of corporate governance. *Journal of Finance*, 52: 737–83.

Sikora, M. (1995). The winding trail: A 30-year profile of M&A dynamism. *Mergers and Acquisitions*, 302: 45–51.

Silverstein, K. (1994). Pension funds increase presence in boardrooms. *Pension World*, 305: 4.

Sirower, M. (1997). *The Synergy Trap: How Companies Lose the Acquisition Game*. New York: Free Press.

Slovin, M. B., Sushka, M. E., and Ferraro, S. R. (1995). A comparison of the information conveyed by equity carve-outs, spin-offs, and asset sell-offs. *Journal of Financial Economics*, 37: 89–104.

Smith, M. P. (1996), Shareholder activism by institutional investors: Evidence from CalPERS. *Journal of Finance*, 51: 227–52.

Spence, M. (1973). Job market signaling. *Quarterly Journal of Economics*, 87: 355–74.

Spicer, A., McDermott, G. A., and Kogut, B. (2000). Entrepreneurship and privatization in Central Europe: The tenuous balance between destruction and creation. *Academy of Management Review*, 25: 630–49.

Spulber, D. F. (1996). Market microstructure and intermediation. *Journal of Economic Perspective*, 10 3: 135–52.

Strachan, H. (1976). *Family and Other Business Groups in Economic Development: The case of Nicaragua*. New York: Praeger.

Turk, T. A., and Baysinger, B. (1989). The impact of public policy on corporate strategy: Taxes, antitrust policy, and diversification clienteles. Working paper, Texas A&M University.

Wahal, S. (1996). Pension fund activism and firm performance. *Journal of Financial and Quantitative Analysis*, 31: 1–23.

Walsh, J. P., and Kosnik, R. D. (1993). Corporate raiders and their disciplinary role in the market for corporate control. *Academy of Management Journal*, 36: 671–700.

Wee, H., and Belton, B. (2001). The missing synergy that's killing life sciences. *Business Week Online*, January 2, www.businessweek.com.

Williamson, O. E. (1975). *Markets and Hierarchies, Analysis and Antitrust Implications: A Study in the Economics of Internal Organization*. New York: Free Press.

Williamson, O. E. (1985). *The Economic Institutions of Capitalism: Firms, Markets, Relational Contracting*. New York: Free Press.

Windolf, P. (1998). The governance structure of large French corporations: A comparative perspective. Paper presented at the Sloan Project on Corporate Governance at Columbia Law School, May 1998.

World Economic Forum (2000). *The Global Competitiveness Report 2000*. New York: Oxford University Press.

Wright, M., Hoskisson, R. E., Busenitz, L. W., and Dial, J. (2000). Entrepreneurial rowth through rivatization: The upside of management buyouts. *Academy of Management Review*, 25: 591–601.

Wright, M., Hoskisson, R. E., Filatotchev, I., and Buck, T. (1998). Revitalizing privatized Russian enterprises. *Academy of Management Executive*, 12(2): 74–85.

Wu, C. (1990). Enterprise groups in China's industry. *Asia Pacific Journal of Management*, 7(2): 123–36.

Zhou, X. (1993). Privatization versus a minimum reform package. *China Economic Review*, 4(1): 65–74.

# 16

# Global Strategic Management

STEPHEN TALLMAN

Global strategic management is the application of strategic management in global markets, most often through the organizational form of multinational enterprises (MNEs). An effective global strategy is essential to a geographically widespread MNE facing equally multinational competitors in a globalizing industry. Globalization has become one of the identifying concepts of the post-industrial economy, describing the increasing integration of national and regional economies and the domination of the world economy by massive MNEs. The term also describes the convergence of individual tastes at the expense of local cultures, worldwide political domination by a small number of industrialized states and the international non-governmental organizations (NGOs) that are seen as their tools, the integration of capital markets, the increasing ubiquity of communication and information around the world, and the spread of technology to the farthest reaches of the globe. In such times, the global strategies of multinational enterprise naturally are of great concern to business and business academics, but also to governments, NGOs, and people who – individually and collectively – buy from, work for, fear, distrust, desire, court, sue, and otherwise interact with these companies. It seems that concern for global strategy is a particularly timely issue for management scholars, a chance to provide new insights on the principal actors in the global economy.

However, many management scholars see global strategy as simply the application of strategic management in a larger arena. This perspective says that multinational firms are really no different from other diversified companies, that global strategy is a straight-forward extension of domestic business and corporate strategies, that contextual differences force MNEs to adapt their strategies to the international marketplace, but do not alter the essential dimensions of strategic management itself. Other scholars point to the historical legacy of international economics and trade theory, to the powerful effects of cultural differences, to the role of exchange rate risk, and to the very different institutional conditions in different countries and see the strategic concerns of multinational firms to be intrinsically different from their domestic cousins. Both perspectives have some merit. Many of the theories and dicta of strategic management can be applied to the global strategies of MNEs to the benefit of theoretician and practitioner.

International business can learn much about the purposes of multinational companies by incorporating ideas from strategic management. As the study of international business has come to focus more on the firms conducting that business rather than the nations across which it is conducted, firm level concerns such as strategy have become critical to the study of the phenomenon.

At the same time, strategic management scholars can learn from global firms, markets, and competition. Greater variation in the background, capabilities, intentions, objectives, and organizations of firms from different countries working in even more different markets provides a much broader and more differentiated pool of subjects for study. Interactions of companies, markets, competition, alliances, and other factors of importance to business can occur in the context of global business that simply do not happen in smaller, more uniform domestic markets. Cross-border transactions, the key activity of MNEs and the basic units of multinational strategies, require considerations of tariff and other trade barriers, extremes in economic development and other location-tied characteristics of markets and production sites, cultural differences, currency exchange rate risks, political and legal differences, and a variety of other concerns that are not present in transactions in domestic markets. The external environment plays a much more visible part in the international context of strategy than it does in single markets. An important purpose of this chapter is to help its readers to understand where international business and strategy support each other and where they are at odds.

The next part of the chapter examines the roots of international strategy in international economics and follows its development as different theoretical concepts have taken primacy in explaining the multinational firm and its strategic actions. This is followed by more detailed discussion of current resource and capability-based and evolutionary models of the MNE and supporting empirical evidence. An important aspect of international, even global, strategies is the strategic role of the national subsidiary, and issues concerning subsidiary roles in global strategy will be covered in the final section.

## What Is Global Strategy?

This chapter refers to the strategies of globally integrated multinational enterprises as global strategies. However, this usage requires a bit of qualification and a definition. Traditionally (Bartlett and Ghoshal, 1989; Prahalad and Doz, 1987), a global strategy was aimed at maximizing global efficiency by integrating national markets and providing the same low cost goods around the world. This contrasts with a multinational or multi-domestic strategy that permits national subsidiaries to adapt completely to local conditions. The "new global strategy", similar to Bartlett and Ghoshal's (1989) transnational strategy, is one through which an MNE integrates a worldwide network of differentiated affiliates to exploit the best location for each value-adding activity in order to deliver superior world-class value for money and highly flexible customer responsiveness. Global strategic management in this model provides world-scale volume, world-class flexible processes, and access to world-best production locations to provide globally competitive prices. To this, it adds world-class product technology, quality, reliability, and design to generate products that can compete with the best from around the world. These products are marketed to worldwide customers through global brand identities, efficient distribution, and highly responsive customer service. Such a complex set of demands can only be met by an MNE with world-class organizational capabilities that can extend core competencies into multiple markets, coordinate the worldwide operations of highly differentiated networks of affiliates and subsidiaries, manage financial activities globally, and create political leverage in many countries and regions.

## The components of global strategy

Despite the many definitions provided by scholars of international or global strategy, most seem to ultimately arrive at two key aspects of the strategies of MNEs. These are (1) international expansion. – *internationalization*, or a strategy of increasing presence in international locations, and (2) global integration – *globalization*, or a strategy of consolidating international markets and operations into a single worldwide strategic entity.

*International expansion.* The process of building an expanding operational presence in foreign locations, or what Porter (1986) calls an international configuration, is the primary concern of traditional models of the MNE. With an efficient transmission mechanism, international expansion provides increasing economies of scope in applying the unique assets and capabilities of the firm (Caves, 1971). The international diversification literature (Grant, Jammine, and Thomas, 1988; Hitt, Hoskisson, and Kim, 1997; Tallman and Li, 1996) is built on the idea that the more MNEs can leverage their assets across national borders, the greater the benefits in the form of economies of scope and scale, access to new customers, entry into less competitive markets, market power, and other advantages of size and scope that will accrue to the MNE. Firms can also use asset-seeking investment to tap new assets and capabilities abroad, whether these are less expensive or more effective processes, less expensive labor, better technology, intangible capabilities arising from diverse markets, or superior management. These assets, when brought inside the firm, can make the company more competitive in many markets, including "back home".

*Global integration.* Global integration is the process of integrating worldwide activities into a single world strategy through a network of differentiated but integrated affiliates, alliances, and associations. Porter (1986) finds that global integration results from a decentralized configuration and high levels of coordination across units in exploiting the firm's capabilities across markets in response to industry demands. Likewise, Doz (1978) treats globalization of strategy as a response to industry pressures toward ever increasing efficiency through world wide economies of scale and scope. Leverage of the competencies of the MNE is assisted by coordinated activities in multiple markets (Hamel and Prahalad, 1985; Kogut, 1985). Global flexibility, arbitrage possibilities, and cost optimization are all improved if the firm has integrated its activities and its decision-making apparatus. From an asset-seeking perspective, global integration can help to spread new resources throughout the worldwide firm, to combine with existing capabilities, and to exploit these new competencies widely while they are still unique.

International scope and global integration are the essential components of global strategy for multinational firms. Early models of global strategy, flowing from macro-economic theory, focused on the reasons for seeking international markets and production, as we will see in the next section. More recently, as organizational economic models and sociological perspectives have been applied to multinationals, the focus has shifted to integration across borders rather than on the impact of multinational firms on a country-by-country basis. This shift is particularly evident in the application of strategic management theories such as resource-based or capabilities-based strategy to multinational firms, as we see in subsequent sections.

## THE ECONOMIC PURPOSES OF GLOBAL STRATEGIES[1]

Doing business in a company's home market seems much simpler in many ways than operating in international, much less global markets, yet businesses have looked abroad for millennia and appear to becoming only more dependent on international markets and global strategies. Why? What are the basic drivers of global strategy? These forces seem to come from sources both external and internal to the firm. Because the study of multinational firms evolved from the study of international trade, the usual focus has been on drivers of direct investment (Robock and Simmonds, 1989):

◆ the search for new markets
◆ the search for new resources
◆ production-efficiency seeking
◆ technology seeking
◆ the search for lower risk
◆ countering the competition.

Summarizing these arguments for international strategies, Ghoshal (1987) points first to the strategic focus on increased efficiency. Companies find that they gain efficiency and become more competitive by expanding into new markets and/or new product lines. Certain of these firms eventually discover that they still have latent efficiencies and competitive benefits when they have conquered their share of the home national market. Of course, the point at which this happens is very dependent on the size of the home market and on the industry. Firms from small countries often become multinationals while still quite small. In larger home markets, traditional industries can accommodate fairly large firms before companies begin to look abroad, while technology-intensive companies look for international customers when they are formed (McDougall and Oviatt, 2000) – consider the burgeoning Internet-based scene as an example. Whenever in their lives that companies begin to look to international markets, they can gain economies of scale by producing for regional or global markets, and economies of scope for fixed investments in technology, brands, or distribution by applying these resources to broader markets. When such economies are of particular relevance to an industry, firms are driven to integrate their operations across markets to take maximum advantage of efficiency benefits (Kobrin, 1991), although the degree of integration that provides maximum benefit varies from industry to industry and from activity to activity (Bartlett, 1985).

Overseas production is often tied to the search for new markets, as economic, social, and consumer demands make exports less competitive in foreign markets. MNEs can gain efficiencies through centralized international production, and can also benefit from lower factor costs and possibly from superior process technology. Market-based internationalization begins to improve efficiency in the home country, but becomes the basis for improved efficiency, superior technology, and improved quality through a global perspective on all phases of the value chain, not just sales. The organization can learn and innovate as it adapts to many environments (Ghoshal, 1987). Other companies have become multinational through seeking assets rather than markets. For centuries, companies in the natural resource extracting industries (mining, agriculture, wood products, and so forth) have looked to overseas sources of supply, not so much to enter foreign markets as to continue to service home customers.

Asset seeking investment, too, has been transformed in the modern era beyond the search for location-based comparative advantages tied to natural resources and conditions to a search for the best, most competitive worldwide source of new skills and knowledge as embodied, for instance, in Porter's model of created advantage in national clusters (Porter, 1990). The MNE becomes a mechanism for transmitting knowledge rather than intermediate goods. The diversity of environments in which the MNE operates provides greater opportunity to gain unique skills. The globalized MNEs of today's economy seek knowledge as much as hard assets, and are increasingly willing to develop their businesses around what they see as "sticky knowledge" (Dunning, 1997), maintaining and developing the knowledge base in its intellectual home ground and transmitting codified or embodied bits of knowledge rather than trying to transplant the underlying know-how.

Risk, or the variability of returns, is an unavoidable aspect of doing business. Firms diversify into new products and new markets to reduce their reliance on one set of customers for one line of goods or services for their entire revenue stream. Multinational strategies can figure prominently in strategies to reduce risks. From a macroeconomic perspective, different national and regional markets tend to show different cycles. The single-nation firm must work within the business cycle of its home market, while the multinational can offset weak demand in one location with strong in another. Other macro-, but non-economic, risks also can be reduced. The effects of political or social processes can be alleviated. For instance, we see companies with environmental pollution problems locating overseas in search of easier regulatory regimes for their production operations than they can find in the European Union or in the United States. And finally, basic business risks can also be reduced. The possibility of competitors lurking abroad to threaten home markets, the danger of relying on too small a customer base, the desire to find more reliable and less expensive sources of inputs – all are helped by the wider horizons of global strategy.

## The Development of the Theory of the MNE and Global Strategy

The pressures from the drivers described above move firms to engage in international and global strategies. However, strategy as a motivating force for companies was not really recognized by early models of international business. These models of the multinational firm focused on its economic activities – exports and foreign direct investment (FDI). Global strategies on the part of individual firms were not addressed, and the general focus was on internationalization, not integration. Trade theory based on the theory of comparative advantage dominated macroeconomic models of international exchange. In the purest approaches to neoclassical trade theory, factors of production are assumed to be fixed in specific locations, while goods can move freely around the world. In such models, import and export trade takes place between countries with different endowments of production factors such as land, labor, or capital, and goods are produced where the production factor(s) used most intensively in their production are the most abundant – and least expensive. The role of individual firms is essentially ignored in such models. Foreign direct investment became part of the equation by removing the immobility assumption for capital, which limited direct investment by multinationals to MNEs from capital-rich industrial countries investing in land and labor-rich developing countries. Capital could move to permit local production in place of the export of final goods. When the free movement of products further was recognized to be limited by shipping costs, tariffs, and other trade barriers, the macro-economic model of trade and direct investment appeared to be complete. The focus was on location, rather than management of investments (Kogut, 1989).

## Industrial organization models

However, this clean but abstract economic model was upset by Stephen Hymer, whose 1960 dissertation pointed out that most trade and investment actually took place between industrial countries, not between industrialized and developing countries. He hypothesized that trade and investment patterns actually reflected the extension of oligopolistic rivalry between large MNEs across borders (Kogut, 1989). Working from an industrial organization economics, or structure–conduct–performance perspective, Hymer (1960) and subsequent scholars (Kindleberger, 1969) suggested that market-based trade was the preferred mode of international exchange in efficient markets. However, monopolistic firms from advanced countries could use foreign direct investment to distort foreign markets through their market manipulations, or through their superior capacity to differentiate products (Caves, 1971). In industries with many competitors and strong competition, most exchange would be via exports or licensing, market means, and returns on investment would be limited to fair market rates. However, in parallel with contemporary thinking about domestic competition, this model suggested that in industries subject to economies of scale and other benefits to the size of firms, foreign direct investment by large MNEs would be used to extend domestic oligopoly practices abroad.

This approach to multinationals implied extensive use of "strategic maneuvering" to exploit the structural constraints of the industry and attain superior performance. "Follow-the-leader" investment patterns (Knickerbocker, 1973), market splitting arrangements (Graham, 1974), and international product lifecycles (Vernon, 1966) all supported the model of an international marketplace dominated by a few large MNEs with the power to challenge the sovereignty of nations, and the business ways of continents (Vernon, 1971). Caves (1971) said that vertical foreign direct investment is typically the result of efforts to provide advantage in an oligopolistic home market, and that horizontal direct investment amounts to entry by dominant established firms into new market segments that happen to be defined geographically.

Industry characteristics have continued to be proposed as the drivers of international and global strategies. Prahalad (1975) developed a model in which global integration and local responsiveness were characterized as orthogonal dimensions of MNE strategy. Industry pressures for efficiency drove MNEs to integrate manufacturing across borders, while local market pressures encouraged local production in response to differentiated demand. Successful strategies matched firm levels of these two characteristics with industry-specific levels of these two strategic drivers (Prahalad and Doz, 1987). Bartlett (1985) further proposed that this model could be applied to specify the strategies of individual firms or even of each separate value-adding activity, and Bartlett and Ghoshal (1989) added a dimension of organizational learning in their model of the transnational firm – still the most influential model of global strategy and structure. In a slightly different approach, Porter (1986) proposed two alternative dimensions, international configuration of activities and international coordination of activities, the importance of which was determined by industry and could define global strategies, but again the focus was on industry characteristics which would make a particular combination of these imperatives successful for MNEs competing in the industry.

Ghoshal (1987) says that competitive advantage in these models relies on (1) exploiting national differences in comparative advantage, (2) scale economies in production of individual products in quantities beyond what a single market can absorb, and (3) scope economies from sharing physical assets such as plants, external relations such as customer identification, and knowledge of products, technologies, or markets. Collis (1991) summarizes global strategy in the industrial organization model as requiring interdependencies across national boundaries that are based on identifiable and defensible factors, consideration of the configuration and coordination of activities, and an organization that balances integration and localization. George Yip (1992) proposes that multiple industry-determined globalization drivers prescribe what level of strategic integration will be applied by firms in any given circumstance. Johansson and Yip (1994) show that for Japanese and American MNEs, a model in which industry drivers predict strategic response which then determines firm structure was the most successful explanatory system for the relative performance of these MNEs. Key to all of these models is industry structure, such that performance success of a firm is driven by strategic fit of the firm to the predetermined characteristics of the industry.

Industrial organization, or "oligopoly power" models of the MNE have received considerable criticism for their reliance on oligopolistic industry structures to explain FDI and firm performance. Strategic power or industry-based competitive models of multinational strategy were challenged in the mid-1970s. Buckley and Casson (1976) rejected the general applicability of Hymer's and Kindleberger's models due to their focus on initial firm endowments without consideration of costs. Teece (1986) found that a focus on market power rather than efficiency limited the applicability of oligopoly models to special cases. Calvet (1981) rejected the market power approach for its reliance on static, technologically determined market structure imperfections. Empirical studies of FDI into the United States (McClain, 1982; Lall and Siddharthan, 1982), generally did not support the assumptions of the oligopoly power model, suggesting that this perspective may have been relevant only to the US MNEs of the 1960s tested in early models. Industrial organization models of international strategy developed at a time that US multinational firms were dominant, and at a time that industrial organization economics was first popularized as an explanation for differential performance levels across firms and industries. These models came from the Harvard Business School and nearby schools (Kogut, 1997). They had the advantage of displacing neoclassical economic models of business behavior, but were strongly influenced by their times and circumstances. Ray Vernon, originator of the "international product life cycle" (1966), later significantly modified his model to reflect a changing and more competitive international marketplace.

## Internalization models

In the 1970s, the emphasis of international business scholars began to switch from oligopolistic interaction to transactional efficiency, based on models derived from the much earlier writings of Ronald Coase (1937). This movement began with the publication of an article by McManus (1972) and a book, *The Future of the Multinational Enterprise*, in 1976 by Peter Buckley and Mark Casson.[2] Buckley and Casson described a model of the multinational enterprise in which final goods markets might be perfect or imperfect, but in which the decision to expand internationally was tied to market failure for intermediate goods. They proposed that export markets for goods, or license markets for know-how, would be the preferred means for conducting international commerce under perfect market conditions, but that such markets would tend to fail in the face of large transaction costs. If shipping costs or trade barriers were high, the risk of misappropriation of knowledge was high, information asymmetries between potential buyers and sellers were great, or other conditions existed that raised the costs of market transactions, then multinational firms would respond by internalizing markets for intermediate goods, including specialized know-how (Kogut, 1989). Such conditions tend to be found in the vertical supply chains of natural resource industries, where firms become specialized to single sources of supply which they will attempt to acquire and in technology-intensive industries where knowledge, especially tacit knowledge, is impossible to transmit via market mechanisms. This viewpoint was supported and developed by Rugman (1980) and Hennart (1982), among others, who concluded that firms would expand abroad through foreign direct investment when this was more efficient than servicing the same markets through trade or licensing.

Teece (1986) pointed out that these arguments were parallel to those of transaction cost economics (TCE) in organizational economics and that the internalization model of the MNE should be considered as a sub-set of this more general model. The TCE focus on the individual transaction provided a framework for determining when a transaction should be internalized, an issue closely connected to investment in specialized assets. Proponents of internalization theory accepted this, and rapidly developed the transaction cost economics view of the MNE into the "standard model" of the MNE (Hill and Kim, 1988). The multinational firm became seen as the product of efficiency considerations for transactions involving specialized investment and therefore a need to avoid potentially opportunistic partners rather than strategic maneuvering or conduct.

The final important model to emerge from this tradition of international economics was the eclectic model or OLI model of John Dunning (1981, 1988, 1993), a model supported by Teece (1986) and others. Dunning's model brought together aspects of industrial organization and location economics, but was particularly dependent on internalization economies to drive FDI. Dunning (1981) describes three essential factors for international expansion, all of which tie to possession of our search for firm-level competencies:

◆ *Ownership* factors (strategic advantage factors in Teece) are unique resources, skills, or capabilities, developed in the home market, that permit the firm to compete successfully in overseas markets. The current competitive advantage of the company is tied to these competencies in the core businesses of the firm and which, if considered alone, can be addressed through exports of the product, unless there are also:

◆ *Location* factors tied to the foreign locale which make production in the host country preferable. They could include cheaper labor, superior production processes, high shipping costs, local image, governmental trade barriers, or other factors. Usually, location factors act as complementary assets to the core competencies of the multinational firm, but at times may include investment into regional clusters in order to gain new competencies that can be exploited internationally through the complementary resources of the multinational – international distribution, financing, efficient production, etc. Location can be addressed by licensing to a local partner or negotiating a supplier contract unless there are also:

◆ *Internalization* factors (transaction cost factors in Teece), typically related to the industry, that make markets for this product subject to failure. If exports are limited by, for instance, high shipping costs and licensing is risky due to limited patent protections, the firm will use foreign direct investment to internalize overseas production, thus expanding its international operating scope and freeing itself to pursue a strategy without competing demands. Teece summarizes this by saying that "the multinational enterprise and foreign direct investment represent a response to high transactions costs by firms with unique assets/capabilities which have value when utilized in production facilities located in foreign markets" (1986: 27).

Dunning's model introduces explicit consideration of "ownership factors" which are very close to the ideas of resources, skills, and capabilities in resource-based models of strategy. His internalization factors are related to competencies in organizing across borders. If the firm has competencies in managing multiple units in various locations, then it will tend to internalize transactions in order to protect and most effectively exploit its ownership factors. He also includes location factors in the host market to determine where production should take place, focusing on factors that lower production costs. The eclectic model connects current models of multinational strategy with earlier economic models of the MNE. As the analysis of firm actions has moved from neoclassical microeconomic theory to industrial organization economics to transaction cost economics, so the analysis of foreign direct investment and MNEs has moved from neoclassical international trade theory to strategic behavior models to internalization models. As the study of strategy has come to focus on firm characteristics in resource-based and capability-based models of strategy, so the focus of multinational strategy has shifted to a model that is built around the concept of unique firm assets. The extension of this approach leads naturally to a resource-based or capability-based approach to multinational strategy in which the actions of firms in international markets, their strategies, are tied more to their "strategic advantage factors" than to their transaction cost structure (Fladmoe-Lindquist and Tallman, 1994).

## STRATEGIC MANAGEMENT MODELS OF GLOBAL STRATEGY

The great majority of conceptual and empirical studies of MNEs focus on the role of external forces in creating the conditions for more internationalized and integrated strategies, and on the reactions of MNEs to these forces. Thus, increasing internationalization – that is, geographical spread into more international locations – is treated as a response to the need to grow the firm into new markets in the face of cost pressures, and increasing global integration – tying international markets and operations more into a single worldwide strategic entity – as a response to increasing similarities of demand, competition, and technology across national markets (Johansson and Yip, 1994; Porter, 1990). At the same time, the focus of strategic management studies has moved to firm-level strategic resources and their role in determining strategy and performance (Barney, 1991). The resource-based view proposes that sustained competitive advantage and concomitant superior performance are driven by firm-specific resources, and particularly by socially complex, organizationally embedded, causally ambiguous, tacit sets of actions and propensities for action. These include simple routines for performing repetitive tasks, technical capabilities in the firm's business fields, and complex corporate capabilities or competences in organizing and directing the firm (Nelson and Winter, 1982; Sanchez, Heene, and Thomas, 1996; Teece, Pisano, and Shuen, 1997). As resource-based models have come to focus on ever more complex organizational resources, they have also added a dynamic, evolutionary aspect, recognizing that the capabilities of the firm must change with a changing environment in order to provide sustained advantage.

This section of the chapter applies a dynamic capabilities model of firm strategy to the analysis of international expansion and global integration strategies as an alternative perspective on multinational strategies to the traditional industry- and market-driven models. Teece (1986) observes that possession of unique assets by an MNE is given, and thus has no influence on the important issues of multinational strategy. A resource or capability-based view forces a re-evaluation of this idea. These unique firm-specific resources and capabilities vary from firm to firm and generate a wide range of strategies as firms attempt to exploit them in search of economic rents. The invisible, or tacit, assets of the firm become the focus of strategy (Itami, 1987). The transaction cost focus on efficient boundaries is subsumed as part of a larger rent-seeking, rather than cost-avoiding, set of activities. As Kogut and Zander (1993) would have it, the nature of the firm's advantage will influence the scope of its activities more surely than the unlikely failure of markets. Knowledge transfer has costs even when it occurs internal to the firm, and the development of capabilities for speeding internal transfer is the key to multinational performance.

### Resource-based models

Only a small number of concepts of the multinational firm have implicitly incorporated portions of the resource-based view (Fladmoe-Lindquist and Tallman, 1994), and even fewer have attempted a dynamic capability approach. Theory and example suggest that there are two key dimensions of capability strategy relevant to the study of the evolution of multinational strategies: *capability leverage* or exploitation (which provides rent generation) and *capability building* or creation (which provides future rent-generating capacity). Similar approaches are devised from a resource-based perspective by Dierickx and Cool (1989) with their market and resource strategy dichotomy and by Sanchez, Heene, and Thomas (1996) with their model of competence building and leverage. Collis (1991) introduced these concepts from resource-based theory (core competencies and firm capabilities in his terminology) to the study of the multinational firm in his study of the bearings industry, adding path dependency constraints on choice and the existence of complex capabilities as sources of unique advantage to the four rules described above. Kogut (1997) explicitly incorporates evolutionary considerations into a first attempt to describe a new model of the MNE, although more from an international business than a strategic perspective, and Hedlund and Ridderstrale (1993) use dynamic capabilities theory to address organizational issues in MNEs. They describe previous models of the MNE as focused on "the exploitation of givens, rather than the creation of novelty" (Hedlund and Ridderstrale, 1993: 5). They propose that both exploitation and creation are essential to a successful multinational strategy, yet they discuss them as diametrically opposed strategies. This section addresses how MNEs might pursue one or both of these imperatives of a capabilities-based, sustainable multinational strategy.

For the MNE developing and pursuing a strategy in the international arena, organizational capabilities present two major strategic imperatives. First, for the firm with existing unexploited or slack resources, expansion into international markets and integration across these markets provide new opportunities to derive additional rents from existing capabilities, that is, capability leverage. The process of building an operational presence in foreign locations is the primary concern of traditional internalization models (Buckley and Casson, 1976), the eclectic model of Dunning (1981), and of market power models of the multinational (Calvet, 1991). Resource-based or capability-based models see international expansion as providing a wide scope for the exploitation of existing assets and skills to increase rents to core technologies while reducing competitive risks, and to compete more successfully with local and international competitors. This vision of MNE strategy provides an interpretation of international activity that is compatible with traditional and industrial organization models, but with a micro-analytical focus. Global integration permits the MNE to exploit local comparative advantage efficiently, to leverage its bargaining power across markets, and to arbitrage cost differentials effectively (Kogut, 1985). Hitt, Hoskisson, and Kim (1997) and Cantwell and Piscitello (1997) provide some evidence that firms that have developed divisional structures for domestic product diversification can leverage these organizational competencies into multinational organization forms, suggesting that the key skill of transferring knowledge throughout a complex organization (Kogut and Zander, 1993) can be the basis for multinational expansion.

Second, international expansion and global integration provide capability building or creating opportunities through exposure to new markets, internalization of new concepts, ideas from new cultures, access to new resources, and exposure to new competitors and terms of competition which can turn the MNE into a pluralistic rather than nationalistic entity. Collis (1991) sees the availability of organizational capabilities for change and learning as a key to sustained success for multinational firms. International opportunities can result (intentionally or not) in organizational learning and in building new capabilities that may be applicable to both old and new locations, and thus to the evolution of the firm's strategic configuration. Kogut and Zander (1993) show that firms transfer less codifiable knowledge more often to wholly-owned subsidiaries. They find that the existence of skills in the transfer of knowledge explain the existence of the MNE better than market failure considerations. From a capability building perspective, firms can tap regional clusters (Porter, 1998; Dunning, 1997) in other countries either through acquisition of or alliance with a cluster member or through a start up in a highly advantaged region. Multinationals are no longer limited to competitive advantages developed back in the home market, but can uncover and incorporate new capabilities and resources abroad (Hedlund and Ridderstrale, 1993). These new and traditional approaches to the multinational firm suggest that existing assets and capabilities can be leveraged and enhanced through greater international presence.

### Capability leverage strategies and the multinational firm

The leverage of existing resources and capabilities suggests consequences for the multinational firm as it devises its strategy. First, leverage implies static sources of advantage. Thus, international markets represent opportunities to further leverage assets and capabilities which have exhausted the home market. Worldwide markets emphasize scale efficiency-focused capabilities while multi-domestic markets emphasize skills in flexible design, smaller scale production, sales, and marketing capabilities. Second, a preference for whole ownership is implied to protect these capabilities from prying partners and to permit the maximum strategic freedom to apply them in the "approved" manner. Third, big companies are generally implied, as they have the managerial assets and financial assets to build an organization of wholly-owned subsidiaries over time and the existing market power to move product on the basis of low price while fighting to counter imitative competition. Fourth, home-based new product development is also implied, as this provides the best protection for skills in research and design. Foreign subsidiaries engaged in a corporate leverage strategy may modify home market designs given new knowledge about their host markets, but learning is very much in the "exploitative learning" mode (March, 1991) – the subsidiaries are learning to do better what the MNE already does. The consequence of these strategic and structural characteristics of capability-leverage strategies is that they result primarily in internationalization and globalization of markets, not globalization of strategy. Firms expand their market access and their dependency on international markets. They may well move operations abroad. They may organize into global (worldwide) product divisions as their product lines supersede international boundaries. They may become large and powerful multinational firms, and may even sell similar product lines around the world, but in the absence of a competence-building, organizational learning-focused strategy, they will not be truly global. What we can see clearly is that leverage or exploitative strategies are in line with the expectations of both industrial organization and transaction cost-based models that MNEs primarily operate to extend home-based advantage into international markets. Whether looking to strategic maneuvering or to internalization to extend and protect competitive advantage, both concepts look to home markets as the sources of advantage and are largely concerned with exploiting and protecting existing sources of advantage in foreign markets.

*Capability leverage and internationalization.*   Most studies of international diversification look to leveraging capabilities across more national markets as the key to economic success. Resource-based theory suggests that the same benefits of shared capabilities should occur across national markets as across product markets (Fladmoe-Lindquist and Tallman, 1994) and transaction cost theory provides a strong argument for competitive advantage based on internal expansion by multinational firms (Teece, 1986). Firms with profit-making internal capabilities (ownership factors) will seek additional profits in international market locations, whether through exports or direct investment (Dunning, 1993). If these capabilities are such that they are embedded in the firm's structure, these international markets will be internalized by foreign direct investment, ensuring the best application of these capabilities while protecting them from compromise (Buckley, 1988). So long as the ownership factors can be applied profitably, greater international market presence should generate higher performance levels. Multinational firms that stay in their same product lines as they spread into new markets would seem able to leverage at least some of their unique capabilities in any national market, despite the need to adjust to local environmental factors (Bartlett and Ghoshal, 1989; Kim, Hwang, and Burgers, 1993). Hitt, Hoskisson, and Kim (1997) argue that multinational expansion is difficult and complex, which is undoubtedly the case, and that greater international dispersion should lead to the increased bureaucratic costs, limiting the scope of benefits to strategic resources internationally.

Empirical studies have produced a variety of results in this area, however. Collis (1991) found evidence of international strategic decisions that do not make sense except when made with a sense of path-dependent capabilities of the individual firm. Grant, Jammine, and Thomas (1989) found that increased multinationalism among British MNEs improved accounting performance. Kim, Hwang, and Burgers (1989) found an interaction of product and international diversification. Geringer, Beamish, and DaCosta (1988) suggested a weak curvilinear response of performance to increased international spread, as do Hitt, Hoskisson, and Kim (1997). However, when variables such as firm size, national identity, or industry characteristics are introduced as controls, the significance of the effect of international diversification on performance tends to be reduced (Tallman and Li, 1996). As with product diversification, results are not always positive (Lall and Siddharthan, 1982; Michel and Shaked, 1986), but the different measures used to describe geographical diversification also are not necessarily related to each other (Cosset and Nguyen, 1991), effects may vary across different dependent variables, direction of investment flow may represent very different strategic purposes, and contextual differences such as exchange rates or economic performance can have a profound impact on the result of diversification. For instance, Delios and Beamish (1999) and Geringer, Tallman, and Olsen (2000) found that increased international operations among Japanese multinationals led to increasing sales and lower profitability – but that these outcomes varied over time. So the negative effects of external conditions and of bureaucratic costs may well temper the rent-earning potential of international expansion.

*Capability leverage and globalization.*   Leverage is enhanced by the integration of markets. The ability to manage extensive networks of international subsidiaries at low transactional cost seems to be a key capability and source of sustainable competitive advantage for successful multinational firms (Kogut and Zander, 1993; Fladmoe-Lindquist and

Tallman, 1994). Not only are existing capabilities extended to foreign markets, they are applied to a world market. Given the need to adapt somewhat to local differences, as described by Ohmae (1989), core capabilities that can be targeted at global markets gain maximum benefits to size and market strength. The multi-plant problem applied globally permits each process technology to be pushed to its limit, global products provide the returns needed to push technology and quality as far as possible, brand names take on a larger-than-life aura. In addition to scope advantages, Kogut (1985) describes advantages of being able to arbitrage across markets, bargain more effectively in multiple markets, and leverage advantages from one market into others. Hamel and Prahalad (1985) focus on global brands, distribution capabilities, and leverage of financial resources across markets as hallmarks of global strategy.

Hitt, Hoskisson, and Kim (1997), among others, propose that managing a product-diversified firm can be leveraged into managing an internationally diversified firm. Management capabilities, as well as technical skills, can be brought from national to international to global competition through extension and exploitative, efficiency oriented learning. On the other hand, Tallman and Li (1996) investigate if, and Hitt et al. (1997) show that, excessive bureaucratic costs associated with extremes of multinational expansion (and possibly global integration – the two are not easily separated in studies) will cause the performance of MNEs to fall off as diversification exceeds some intermediate level. Exactly what degree of diversification will cause bureaucratic costs to outstrip the cost economies and revenue enhancements due to more extensive exploitation of core competencies and capabilities. In any case, global integration certainly adds to the bureaucratic costs of MNEs over an international holding company format. The outcome of improved capability leverage at a higher cost is an empirical question, and one that is likely to vary across environments, industries, and firms. As large sample studies observe only levels of diversity of activities and related performance, but cannot easily address issues of strategic intent or management control structure, the value of global integration has not been well supported. Johansson and Yip (1994) use interview data to compare small samples of Japanese and American firms in a structural equation model of industry drivers and globalization strategies, finding that global strategy (more multinationalization) and structure affect performance of US firms more than that of Japanese firms, but have positive impacts in both cases.

## Capability building strategies and the multinational firm

In addition to leveraging their existing capabilities, most long-term successful MNEs also are trying to build capabilities, an essential activity if the firm is to have assets and capabilities to leverage on a continuing basis (Hedlund and Ridderstrale, 1993; Tallman and Fladmoe-Lindquist, 2000). Kogut (1997) suggests that dynamic models of the MNE be grouped as evolutionary models, in that the process of internalizing or developing new capabilities is best described as a process of variation, selection, and retention among firm-level activities and routines, building on Nelson and Winter's evolutionary economics (1982). Other authors stay with the dynamic capabilities label, but propose an essentially similar process of interaction between firm-level initiatives and environmental pressures. As in the case of leverage strategies, certain consequences for the strategic configuration of the multinational firm can be drawn from the demands of competence-building. First, advantage becomes dynamic, based on ability to create, not to exploit, capabilities. This implies the extensive use of joint ventures, alliances, and acquisitions to explore for new knowledge rather than a focus on whole ownership to protect old knowledge. Second, as technical capabilities can best be developed where the local "diamond" (Porter, 1990) favors them, a global search for new products and processes suggests product divisions based around the world, not based in the home country. Third, capabilities must be shared, both inside and outside the firm, to make use of them before new learning makes them obsolete and to bring them together with other essential skills. This implies that internal networks are critical, providing a much more active role for the central headquarters and the need for active cooperation and routines to promote it. If differentiated networks (Nohria and Ghoshal, 1997) are indeed the organizational structure of the global firm, then building managerial capabilities for running complex organizations become sources of rents as well as drivers of internaliza-tion (Buckley, 1988). Thus, fourth, managing capabilities is as important to rent-earning as developing them, suggesting that central management functions may be value-enhanc-ing, not value-destroying. However, the dispersed and decentralized nature of value-creating activities suggests that central management is more a matter of facilitating cooperation among subsidiaries in a "heterarchy" than directing operations of a hierar-chy (Hedlund, 1986). Rather than finding such skills in international markets, the global MNE must generate them internally through processes of variation, identification, test-ing, and retention. To a large extent, the above suggests that the characteristics of successful leverage strategies create barriers to building innovative strategies, an implica-tion borne out in most of the globalization literature. Understanding the nature of this anomaly and its possible solutions is perhaps the major issue in global strategy at this time. The most interesting new models of the MNE, such as dynamic capabilities models and evolutionary models, are concerned in great part with resolving the building–exploiting conundrum of global strategy (Hedlund and Ridderstrale, 1993).

*Capability building and internationalization.* If capability leverage strategies seem most in-tensely related to international expansion, capability building among multinationals appears to be more closely tied to globalization efforts. However, internationalization certainly provides access to new products, processes, and technologies which can be incorporated into the firm's array of technical competencies. No one country or region has the secret to technology. Many firms have come to the US seeking technical skills to either out-source or incorporate in the search for international competitive advantage, and, indeed, US-based firms are discovering the same technological capacities in Euro-pean, East Asian, even former socialist countries – highly skilled Russian computer programmers have been used by Western industry for ten years. Global multinationals encourage major new businesses to develop in the most demanding foreign local markets where these technologies are most advanced. A good bit of this learning is likely to be exploitative, in the sense that the international firm is most likely to acquire capabilities and assets which are related to its existing resources. The role of the MNE in acquiring new skills and transmitting them to other units is challenged by the differences across markets. Even in relatively recent writings, home country-derived tacit knowledge is treated as the strength of the firm (Kogut, 1991; Porter, 1990). However, as the value of regional clusters of highly skilled firms to the development of knowledge has become more apparent, the possibilities for MNEs to learn significant new capabilities, not just locally exploitable know-how, has given international spread a much greater role in knowledge asset development. Such activities imply an openness to entirely new constructs which is not a part of traditional models, whether based on market power or internalization, of the multinational firm. Ultimately, they also require a level of integration of knowledge generating and knowledge using operations that is far beyond that necessary to traditional MNEs.

*Capability building and globalization.* It is through global integration that corporations appear to have the best chance to develop knowledge resources and build new capabilities in international markets. New models propose that the integrated global firm can find technical and managerial know-how in foreign locations which would otherwise not be available to the firm (Nohria and Ghoshal, 1997), and then bring them into the broader set of company skills to build new corporate capabilities. As Nohria and Ghoshal (1997: 208) have it, "a key advantage of the multinational arises from its ability to create new value through the accumulation, transfer, and integration of different kinds of knowledge, resources, and capabilities across its dispersed organizational units." Hitt, Hoskisson, and Kim (1997) point to organizational learning effects from complex domestic organizations that might be applicable to international organization. How much greater would the learning be from direct experiences in international markets? The existence of such learning is the basic assumption of Bartlett and Ghoshal's (1989) transnational firm and related models. Organizational learning and development of organizational capabilities among multinationals suggest that the negative effects of bureaucratic costs overcome the benefits of multinational strategies and organization only in the extreme. These studies and others show that global integration provides global scope for search and recombination opportunities in creating new technology, and that operating a global network organization develops new management capabilities that inexperienced MNEs or domestic firms simply do not possess. Building capabilities through globalization is as much a creative process as an accumulative process. Simply gathering knowledge from various locations provides some value, but real rent-generating capacity requires the combination of this knowledge with old firm level understandings on a much broader scale.

The empirical evidence of the advantages of capability building for organizational performance is limited and largely anecdotal. However, even the early Internationalization model of Johansson and Vahlne (1977) was based on observations of learning in international markets. Kogut and Zander (1993) show that the internal transfer of uncodifiable knowledge is typical of MNEs, inferring that the primary role of the MNE is this knowledge transfer. Collis (1991) finds that while a strong heritage of national characteristics is carried by MNEs, continuous improvement on all dimensions of strategy is essential to long-term competitive advantage. Hedlund (1986) bases his idea of the decentralized, differentiated heterarchy on observation of the actions of Scandinavian MNEs. The case observations of Bartlett and Ghoshal (1989) and the more detailed studies presented by Nohria and Ghoshal (1997) show MNEs building new capabilities for competing successfully on a global scale, albeit starting from a nationally based administrative heritage. Observation suggests a sea of change in global strategy over the last decade or so from a focus on exploitative strategy with ancillary learning to a conscious and clearly expressed strategy among top multinational firms of seeking new products, processes, and capabilities around the world and moving these throughout the many integrated operations of the firm as rapidly as possible.

Integrating capability exploitation and capability building both in individual foreign markets and in the wider global environment is the hallmark of modern global strategy. Bartlett and Ghoshal (1989) describe the integrated global firm as "transnational", but they offer this same focus on integrating capability-leveraging activities across subsidiaries and developing capabilities at managing the integrated global organization. In the transnational model, globalization leads to integrating strategic demands for worldwide efficiency, local market responsiveness, and the spread of world-class technology across all national markets. The transnational model also addresses the need for an organizational structure that is capable of controlling this integration without losing the unique qualities of the individual firm. From a structural perspective, the heterarchical multinational from Hedlund (1986) and the differentiated network of Nohria and Ghoshal (1997) both find that advantage comes to the global firm that is able to decentralize operational responsibilities to differentiated subsidiaries while supporting strong integration among all affiliates. These scholars have moved significantly away from industry as the determinant of multinational strategy and identified internal processes as critical to the development of transnational (global) advantage in many industries. We can see an evolution of thinking about multinational firms from an industry-driven set of similar organizations to a resource- or competence-type model in which unique heritage and idiosyncratic capabilities are reflected in firms facing similar market demands but meeting these with individual responses toward globalization.

As in any resource-based model, firm-level performance does interact with the environment of the firm, particularly the terms of competition in its industry, to drive performance. However, as multinational firms move toward superior processes, better technologies, and more efficient adaptation to local needs, they are driving their industries toward more global competition as much as they are reacting to the demands of the industry. In a world of information technology, multinational firms are finding that conservative, opportunism-avoiding, defensive strategies cannot win in the long term – in any industry. The future appears to be about radically decentralized resources integrated by central coordination, not headquarters control. Manufacturing has perhaps led the way toward the new global strategy, but services are rapidly adopting global market perspectives and strong learning ethics as information technologies provide new efficiencies. Firms still adapt to local environments, but do so within a flexible global strategy that emphasizes corporate level firm-specific capabilities. Industry characteristics still favor some competencies over others, but competitive advantage is more than ever a matter of unique firm-level skills rather than industry-standard practices. The next section provides insight on the interaction of the forces of corporate strategy and structure, local conditions, and industry as they combine to provide competitive advantage in individual markets.

# A Strategic Management Model of the MNE in a Host Market[3]

As analysis of the MNE as a corporate entity has moved from consideration of foreign direct investment in individual overseas markets to the titanic struggles of massive global networks, many in the field of global strategy have begun to ignore the role of the national subsidiary except as a trivial manifestation of the larger corporate entity. However, investment still takes place on a market-by-market basis, and national boundaries do still make a difference to entry in each market. The traditional role of the host-country subsidiary has been as a conduit for firm-specific advantages developed in the home country to local customers in the foreign market. Resource leverage was the operative strategic posture. As we have seen previously, various early models of the MNE offer such perspectives. This section develops the concepts proposed in the previous section by applying them to a specific case. Strategic management models tie success to a proper fit among resources and capabilities, strategy, structure, and the environment. This section shows how strategic fit works for an MNE competing in a single foreign market (Birkinshaw and Morrison, 1995).

From a strategic perspective, market entry should result from managerial analysis of the worldwide strategy of the MNE, knowledge of its available resources, and determination of its apparent sources of competitive advantage in a particular host country market. The host market resource strategy and the firm's competitive skills are considered in the context of the local market's unique demands to generate a best apparent resource governance structure or level of internalization with a primary goal of gaining long-term competitive advantage. In selecting both strategy and structure, managers make decisions with incomplete information under conditions of uncertainty. Thus, uncertainty reduction is a second, and equally relevant, goal of risk-averse managers. Uncertainty can be reduced by increased information gathering, which increases transaction costs, or by internalizing control, which increases governance costs. The MNE can also reduce its uncertainty by limiting its strategic options in a host country. Therefore, we can expect to encounter often a condition of inertia (the retention of a tried strategy for the sake of lowered uncertainty) in pursuing goals (Romanelli and Tushman, 1986).

The MNE responds directly to discretionary managerial decisions and only indirectly to pressures from the host country economic environment. However, various studies (Rosenzweig and Singh, 1991; Birkinshaw and Hood, 1998) show that the managers of subsidiary companies must consciously balance the demands of the MNE network and the demands of local interests. Kim and Hwang (1992) suggest that the greater the global synergies expected from a subsidiary, the higher the level of control the MNE will seek. Likewise, the greater the value and the greater the tacitness of the specific know-how to be transmitted to the subsidiary, the greater the desired level of control. Institutional pressures in a country tend to move all organizations, including subsidiaries, toward local practices, while organizational replication as the MNE enters new countries and the drive to control all parts of the firm tend to differentiate the subsidiaries of foreign MNEs. The host market manager, without market diversification options, will attempt simultaneously to increase performance levels and to reduce uncertainty levels.

## Internalization and resource structure

Since economic models of the MNE focus on the structural form chosen for host countries, the choice of structure is a key factor in the entry decision. Structural choices influence performance levels by determining how the market strategy will be applied and controlled, by controlling transaction costs, and by selecting which and how capabilities will be applied in the country market. For instance, maximum revenues from a brand-name based consumer product strategy may require close control of advertising, and therefore some form of FDI. However, if the firm does not have the capital resources to set up or buy a local advertising firm, it may be forced to save on resource costs by accepting a joint venture deal. Structural choice also affects uncertainty levels, and thus transaction costs. The uncertainty of that portion of the environment with which the firm interacts regularly is lessened due to more intense interaction levels. Therefore, one way of reducing the information costs of resource control is to extend the governance structure of the firm (see McManus, 1972). When the firm extends its structure, it both internalizes some previously external transactions and expands its region of reduced uncertainty. In the international realm, the MNE can reduce its uncertainty about a market through FDI, but must accept increased governance costs for its increased assets and increased opportunity costs from reduced flexibility for future strategic moves. Options models of joint ventures (Kogut and Zander, 1992) suggest that alliances may provide increased knowledge of a market without the capital investment and resulting risk of a wholly owned subsidiary. In TCE terms, the net costs of uncertainty risks and governance mechanisms are reduced by limiting transaction-specific investment.

The national firm about to enter an international market is made up of resources from its home country environment, structured in a fashion developed in the home country industry of which it is a part. Entry strategies at this point will be largely based on home market experiences. As the MNE gains international experience, it acquires resources and develops capabilities from interacting with the larger environment. Strategic options will expand to reflect this broadened resource structure. Resources and capabilities are only identified as sources of competitive advantage and economic rents when they have generated rents during the implementation of a strategy. Therefore, the set of unique or specialized capabilities that belong to an MNE at any given time is a function of the strategies that the MNE has used before that time. Dependency on past performance to identify capabilities produces an interactive relationship between strategy and capabilities. This dependency also encourages the natural conservatism, or risk-aversion, of strategic managers entering a new host country.

## Capabilities and business strategy in the host country

Strategy from one time period plays a key role in identifying the unique capabilities of the firm for subsequent time periods. For an MNE contemplating a new market, its existing capability stock limits the range of strategic possibilities considered for that country. The capabilities identified from previous strategic successes will suggest the most likely entry strategy(ies) for the new market. If resources with profit potential are identified through certain strategies in the past, uncertainty about the future will be allayed by applying the same resources and capabilities in support of strategies similar to past policies. Thus, a firm that has considerable experience with acquisition might be expected to prefer acquisition when another firm, with experience in using alliances, might choose a joint venture under the same circumstances. While the decision to enter a new market is entrepreneurial at its heart, we would most often expect to find essential strategic boldness tempered with some imitative caution. Of course, this approach is likely to reduce performance if (as is almost certain) the new context is different from the past. Maximizing profit performance and minimizing uncertainty are not always compatible objectives – and their differences will be emphasized in foreign markets.

However, its entire inventory of capabilities may not be appropriate for an MNE in a particular host location. Even to a manager entering a new market, some resources obviously will not fit the new environment. Skills developed in industrialized nations may be inappropriate or impossible to apply in less developed locations. Market strategies oriented toward only part of a market, such as an intent to skim a consumer product market by focusing on the local elite, will provide little opportunity to exploit resources related to size or capital availability. In other cases, local government requirements for licensing or cooperative ventures may limit the ability of the firm to apply resources relating to internal organizational systems. Only those resources and capabilities that are compatible with the characteristics of the market are likely to generate economic rents. Thus, strategies and capabilities interact with each other and with location effects to generate competitive advantage for the MNE in a particular market through the structural form chosen for that market. The cycle of activities in the new market may well develop new capabilities that can then be transmitted to the parent MNE or to other subsidiaries. The distinctive impacts of location effects on capabilities, strategies, and their interactions are unique to MNEs as compared to other similar size firms.

## Performance as feedback in an evolutionary model

After entry and a period of operation in any market, new capabilities will develop in the host market that were not among the original set of parent resources and which may not be available outside of that market – capability building takes place. These new market-specific capabilities, plus the experience of competition in the host market will force changes over time in the strategy and structure chosen at entry. Observation of performance levels provides the feedback that managers need to adjust their organization. This suggests a simple decision rule: *firms will try to generate relative improvements in net returns on investment while reducing uncertainty about future outcomes.* Imitative strategies and inherent uncertainties imply that goal success will be judged in comparison to competitors, since "real" potential maximum returns are unknowable. The strategy and the combination of capabilities and location factors determine the revenue potential for the product/market choice over any period. The internalization, or governance structure, decision determines how the unique firm resources will interact with environmental factors to determine the cost structure over the same time span and also can control the level of uncertainty that the firm must accept. Success, or the generation of positive economic rents, indicates that the combination of strategy and structure has generated a competitive advantage for the firm in a specific host market and will lead the firm toward efforts to retain its capabilities. Lower performance in a specific market suggests a lack of fit and will encourage the firm to develop new routines in that market, whether by positive efforts with specific goals or by openness to new variation. Note, too, that uncertainty reduction goals will have less explicit effect on strategies as firms become familiar with specific markets.

Internalization models of the MNE emphasize the importance of transaction costs to the exclusion of the other aspects of the cost/revenue function. In a strategic management model, transactions costs are limited to a role as part of the structural decision, "Should we use licensing, exports, or a form of FDI?", and can be determined precisely only after initial entry. As transaction costs are only measurable after an activity takes place, they can cause unforeseeable reductions in returns and therefore are important to defining the stochastic nature of the strategic feedback loop and to changes in structural form. While experience can give firms some feel for the transaction costs likely to be associated with an entry decision, uncertainty about the actual interaction of firm and environment suggests that these costs are no more predictable than are the expected returns to a set of resources and capabilities. Cost control does provide pressure toward structural efficiency. However, a high revenue strategy may support a high cost structure in a national market, if net benefits are higher than for alternative low-cost structural forms. Uncertainty about sources of competitive advantage and the limited rationality of decision-makers also obstruct the instantaneous adjustment of firms toward an optimal structure. In addition, competitive conditions may move firms to accept cost inefficiencies or risks in exchange for increased revenues. Ultimately, an MNE entering a new market or entering with a new product is forced to accept some uncertainty in its expectation of increased rents to its firm-specific assets. The entry decision requires assessment of the applicability and value of these assets, a more or less risky determination of the risks and gains to a specific location, and a judgment about the balance of uncertainty reduction and governance cost of the possible organization structures that might be chosen. However, a successful entry followed by competitive operations in a country can create significant benefits to the MNE.

## THE DEVELOPING STRATEGIC ROLE OF THE FOREIGN SUBSIDIARY

Early strategic behavior and internalization models of the MNE implied that relationships between headquarters and subsidiaries were determined by the demands of the industry interacting with the multinational firm, or by the "internalization factors" of the firm in the international marketplace. In either case, the character of individual transactions was determined by exogenous forces, suggesting that these relationships should be similar so long as the environment did not change. Models of the MNE tacitly assumed that subsidiaries would be more or less similar, except perhaps in size (a characteristic related to the size of the local market), as seen in the many text book typologies of MNE structures (Yip, 1992). Subsidiaries represented home office strategies, whether as (1) sales and marketing offices (in a global export strategy within an international division), (2) local "miniature replicas" of the parent with a complete set of operational responsibilities in the local market (in a multi-local strategy with country or area divisions), or (3) local or regional production centers with little autonomous scope (in an international technology-transfer strategy with worldwide product divisions). This presumption was carried through the integration-responsiveness models of Prahalad and Doz (1987).

Dunning's (1981, 1988) eclectic model suggested that specific location-based character-istics interact with the ownership and internalization factors of the MNE, implying that subsidiaries in different places might have different relationships to the parent firm. Gunnar Hedlund (1986) suggested that large Scandinavian firms, which had long conducted production, marketing, and sales outside their home countries, were beginning in the mid-1980s to shift traditional headquarters functions abroad to these same subsidiaries. These functions included research and development, finances, and executive management activities *for the corporation, not just for the local unit.* In addition, these subsidiaries were being told to coordinate directly with each other, avoiding passing information through the center where it would be slowed, corrupted, and politicized. Bartlett and Ghoshal (1989), besides recognizing the need for matrix or transnational network structures overall, also recognized that individual subsidiaries had very different roles to play. They and Nohria and Ghoshal (1997) called for explicit recognition that different subsidiaries would have different strategic roles in the transnational or differen-tiated network firm. In common with Hedlund (1986), these models saw that strategic leadership in some areas of endeavor was devolving onto certain exceptionally capable subsidiaries, while other affiliates remained dependent on the MNE network for direction and capabilities. Such an approach is compatible with capability-based models that would anticipate different path-dependent capabilities in all separated units of an MNE.

Bartlett and Ghoshal (1986), Birkinshaw and Morrison (1995), and others provide similar typologies of the roles played by subsidiaries of MNEs. Birkinshaw and Morrison summarize this train of research as suggesting subsidiary strategies of (1) local implemen-tation, (2) specialized contribution, and (3) world mandate. The local implementer has a single-country scope and a limited product mandate. These units previously were quite autonomous, but global integration has left them with little strategic independence and at most a responsibility for adapting products to the local scene. Specialized contributors are part of an interdependent network of subsidiaries, often in a global or regional production role. Subsidiaries with world mandates are responsible for an entire business, not just part of a value chain. Activities are integrated, but by the subsidiary, not the corporate head office. The various authors suggest slightly different constructs, but retain the key idea that the roles of the subsidiaries will vary with their competencies and opportunities.

In particular, innovation, the development of new competencies, capabilities, re-sources, and products, is rapidly becoming a focus of growing numbers of foreign subsidiaries (Nohria and Ghoshal, 1997). These decentralized activities, located in highly differentiated subsidiaries, are tied together through intensive and extensive use of electronic communication. Of great importance, though, is the condition that these communications are no longer primarily vertical, from headquarters to subsidiary and back, but horizontal, directly from subsidiary to subsidiary. The global center participates only in headquarters-relevant issues, such as financial reporting, key account manage-ment, executive level management development and the like. These firms require high levels of normative control, as the formal role of the center as an authoritarian controller is reduced. Use of standard, simple but meaningful formal reports is also a likely feature. Central control is neither feasible nor desirable. The subsidiary firm has become, in some cases, a headquarters site for a global product company, complete with research, financial, product development, and marketing responsibilities for the worldwide operations of a particular business within the MNE's corporate structure.

Birkinshaw and Hood (1998) propose that the strategic role of the subsidiary indeed is driven by head-office assignment of role, but also by choices made by subsidiary managers for their own purposes and by local environmental drivers. The head office role is much the same as that proposed in the product life cycle and internationalization process models. The impact of environmental factors and managerial responses to this impact on performance has been discussed above in relation to organizational capabilities models (Madhok, 1997). Of unique interest is the idea of autonomous action on the part of subsidiary behavior and its role in the evolution of subsidiary strategic roles. From a network perspective, the subsidiary is seen as part of a larger group of quasi-independent members of the MNE network, not just part of a dyadic headquarters-subsidiary relationship. This provides the means for subsidiaries with original visions to become world leaders with world product mandates. Researchers in Canada and Sweden find solid evidence of autonomous action by subsidiaries (Birkinshaw, 1995; Forsgren, Holm, and Johanson, 1995). In essence, they recognize the subsidiary as a semi-autonomous organization operating within a network of subsidiaries, similar in organizational level, but of considerably different capabilities. While addressing the issue from the perspective of the subsidiary, the conclusion for the MNE as a whole is quite similar to the transnational of Bartlett and Ghoshal and to Hedlund's heterarchy – the role of the erstwhile headquarters is shrinking and strategic leadership is migrating to the subsidiaries.

These new concepts of multinational corporate structuring suggest a fundamental change in the relationship between the center and the subsidiaries. Perhaps reflecting a developing organizational maturity, and certainly reflecting the impact of computers and communications technology, subsidiary companies are being given new independence from the central headquarters, not to "do their own things", but to become interdependent on each other. A key result of this networking is that subsidiaries must take on differentiated roles – the old model of a set of identical affiliate companies is no longer sufficient.

## Conclusions

This chapter has addressed a number of issues surrounding global strategy. In the first place, the view of the MNE as a simple extension of a multi-plant logistics problem across borders is presented as excessively naïve. The global firm is involved with many more analytical concerns than a simple economic choice of production location. It is also much more than a mechanism for transferring goods across boundaries into foreign markets. Strategic management suggests that the global MNE is much better described as a mechanism for transferring resources and capabilities, particularly those involving tacit knowledge, across borders when markets are inefficient to the purpose. At the same time, the MNE provides the local knowledge to adapt these system-wide capabilities to the local context, an essential step in most cases where increased sales are desired. Working in the same paradigm, the successful MNE is one that can develop (or evolve) capabilities for transferring such firm-specific knowledge and for seamlessly combining it with location-specific knowledge in a subsidiary or affiliate. The organization economics position that the characteristics of the transferred knowledge determine the strategic and structural decisions of the global firm appears to be as untenable as the international macroeconomic position that such outcomes were determined by local factor prices.

At the same time, MNEs are combining and recombining and subsidiary roles are changing, so that the rent-earning resources and capabilities may well be derived from another foreign subsidiary, not from the parent company – whatever that has become. Application of capabilities is a complex decision based on knowledge type, organizational capabilities, and local conditions, but so is the development of new capabilities. Such conditions appear to be ever more prevalent as knowledge-driven industries rise to primacy in post-industrial societies, making the vision of the global firm as a multinational network rather than a transnational hierarchy most appropriate. Global strategy for such a firm becomes a question of understanding the character of many very different places and many very different parts of the company in making determinations of where, how, and what to develop, to produce, to sell, and to service, even while understanding that the entire analytical process will be reconsidered as soon as it is in place.

## NOTES

1 The following section is adapted in large part from Tallman, 1999.
2 Similar ideas were developed from Coase's work at about the same time by Oliver Williamson (1975) and applied to a general transaction cost economics model of the firm, but Buckley and Casson's (1976) internalization model was developed independently from TCE.
3 The following section is adapted in large part from Tallman, 1992.

## REFERENCES

Barney, J. B. (1991). Firm resources and sustained competitive advantage. *Journal of Management*, 17 (1): 99–120.

Bartlett, C. A. (1985). *Global Competition and MNC Managers*. ICCH Note No. 0-385-287. Boston: Harvard Business School Press.

Bartlett, C. A., and Ghoshal, S. (1989). *Managing across Borders*. Boston: Harvard Business School Press.

Birkinshaw, J. M. (1995). Entrepreneurship in multinational corporations: The initiative process in Canadian subsidiaries. Unpublished doctoral dissertation, University of Western Ontario.

Birkinshaw, J. M., and Hood, N. (1998). Multinational subsidiary evolution: Capability and charter change in foreign-owned subsidiary companies. *Academy of Management Review*, 23(4): 773–95.

Birkinshaw, J. M., and Morrison, A. J. (1995). Configurations of strategy and structure in subsidiaries of multinational corporations. *Journal of International Business Studies*, 26(4): 729–54.

Buckley, P. J. (1988). The limits of explanation: Testing the internalization theory of the multinational enterprise. *Journal of International Business Studies*, 19(2): 181–94.

Buckley, P. and Casson, M. (1976). *The Future of the Multinational Enterprise*. London: Macmillan.

Calvet, A. L. (1981). A synthesis of foreign direct investment theories and theories of the multinational firm. *Journal of International Business Studies*, Spring/Summer 1: 43–59.

Cantwell, J. A., and Piscitello. L. (1997). Accumulating technological competence – its changing impact on corporate diversification and internationalization. Department of Economics Discussion Papers in International Investment and Management, University of Reading, UK.

Caves, R. E. (1971). International corporations: The industrial economics of foreign investment. *Economica*, 38: 1–27.

Coase, R. H. (1937). The nature of the firm. *Economica*, 386–495.

Collis, D. (1991). A resource-based analysis of global competition: The case of the bearings industry. *Strategic Management Journal*, 12, summer special issue: 49–68.

Cosset, J. C., and Nguyen, T. H. (1991). The measurement of the degree of foreign involvement. *University of South Carolina CIBER Working Paper Series*, D-91-01.

Delios, A., and Beamish, P. W. (1999). Geographic scope, product diversification and the corporate performance of Japanese firms. *Strategic Management Journal*, 20: 711–28.

Dierickx, I., and Cool, K. (1989). Asset stock accumulation and competitive advantage. *Management Science*, 12: 1504–11.

Doz, Y. L. (1978). Managing manufacturing rationalization within multinational companies. *Columbia Journal of World Business*, Fall: 82–94.

Dunning, J. H. (1981). *International Production and the Multinational Enterprise*. London: George Allen and Unwin.

Dunning, J. H. (1988). The eclectic paradigm of international production: a restatement and some possible extensions. *Journal of International Business Studies*, 19(1): 1–32.

Dunning, J. H. (1993). *The Globalisation of Strategy*. London: Routledge.

Dunning, J. H. (1997). Knowledge capitalism: Competitiveness reevaluated, a macro-organizational viewpoint. *Transcript of all academy symposium on knowledge capitalism: Competitiveness reevaluated*. Briarcliff Manor, NY: Academy of Management.

Fladmoe-Lindquist, K., and Tallman, S. (1994). Resource-based strategy and competitive advantage among multinationals. In P. Shrivastava, A. Huff, and J. Dutton (eds.), *Advances in Strategic Management*, Vol. 10: 45–72, Greenwich, CT: JAI Press.

Forsgren, M., Holm, U., and Johanson, J. (1995). Division headquarters go abroad – A step in the internationalization of the multinational corporation. *Journal of Management Studies*, 32: 475–91.

Geringer, J. M., Beamish, P. W., and daCosta, R. C. (1989). Diversification strategy and internationalization: Implications for MNE performance. *Strategic Management Journal*, 10: 109–19.

Geringer, J. M., Tallman, S., and Olsen, D. M. (2000). Product and international diversification among Japanese multinational firms. *Strategic Management Journal*, 21: 51–80.

Ghoshal, S. (1987). Global strategy: An organizing framework. *Strategic Management Journal*, 8: 425–40.

Graham, E. M. (1974). *Oligopolistic Imitation and European Direct Investment in the United States*, PhD Thesis, Harvard Business School.

Grant, R. M., Jammine, A. P., and Thomas, H. (1988). Diversity, diversification, and profitability among British manufacturing companies, 1972–84. *Academy of Management Journal*, 31(4): 771–801.

Hamel, G., and Prahalad, C. K. (1985). Do you really have a global strategy? *Harvard Business Review*, 63(4): 139–48.

Hedlund, G. (1986). The hypermodern MNC – a heterarchy? *Human Resource Management*, 25: 9–35.

Hedlund, G., and Ridderstrale, J. (1993). Toward the N-form corporation: Exploitation and creation in the MNC. Institute of International Business, Stockholm School of Economics RP 92/15.

Hennart, J.-F. (1982). *A Theory of the Multinational Enterprise*. Ann Arbor: University of Michigan Press.

Hill, C. W., and Kim, W. C. (1988) Searching for a dynamic theory of the multinational enterprise: A transaction cost model. *Strategic Management Journal*, 9, 93–104.

Hitt, M. A., Hoskisson, R. E., and Kim, H. (1997). International diversification: Effects on innovation and firm performance in product-diversified firms. *Academy of Management Journal*, 31: 771–801.

Hymer, S. (1960). The international operations of national firms: a study of direct foreign investment. Unpublished PhD dissertation, MIT (published by MIT Press, 1976).

Itami, H. (1987). *Mobilizing Invisible Assets*. Cambridge, MA: Harvard University Press.

Johansson, J. K., and Vahlne, J. E. (1977). The internationalization process of the firm: A model of knowledge development and increasing foreign market commitments. *Journal of International Business Studies*, 8 (Spring/Summer): 23–32.

Johansson, J. K., and Yip, G. S. (1994). Exploiting globalization potential: US and Japanese strategies. *Strategic Management Journal*, 15(8): 579–601.

Kim, W. C., and Hwang, P. (1992). Global strategy and multinationals' entry mode choices. *Journal of International Business Studies*, 23(1): 29–53.

Kim, W. C., Hwang, P., and Burgers, W. P. (1989). Global diversification strategy and corporate profit performance. *Strategic Management Journal*, 10(1): 45–57.

Kim, W .C., Hwang, P., and Burgers, W. P. (1993). Multinationals' diversification and the risk-return trade-off. *Strategic Management Journal*, 14: 275–86.

Kindelberger, C. P. (1969). *American Business Abroad: Six Lectures on Direct Investment*. New Haven: Yale University Press.

Knickerbocker, F. T. (1973). *Oligopolistic Reaction and Multinational Enterprise*. Cambridge: Harvard Business School Division of Research.

Kobrin, S. J. (1991). An empirical analysis of the determinants of global integration. *Strategic Management Journal*, 12: 17–31.

Kogut, B. (1985). Designing global strategies: profiting from operational flexibility. *Sloan Management Review*, Fall: 27–38.

Kogut, B. (1989). A note on global strategies. *Strategic Management Journal*, 10(4): 383–89.

Kogut, B. (1991). Country capabilities and the permeability of borders. *Strategic Management Journal*, 12, special issue: 33–48.

Kogut, B. (1997). The evolutionary theory of the multinational corporation: Within and across country options, in B. Toyne and D. Nigh (eds.), *International Business: An Emerging Vision*. Columbia, SC: University of South Carolina Press.

Kogut, B., and Zander, U. (1992). Knowledge of the firm, combinative capabilities, and the replication of technology. *Organization Science*, 3(3): 383–97.

Kogut, B., and Zander, U. (1993). Knowledge of the firm, and the evolutionary theory of the multinational corporation. *Journal of International Business Studies*, 24(4): 625–45.

Lall, S., and Siddharthan, N. S. (1982). The monopolistic advantages of multinationals: Lessons from foreign investment in the US. *The Economic Journal*, 92: 668–83.

Madhok, A. (1997). Cost, value, and foreign market entry mode: The transaction and the firm. *Strategic Management Journal*, 18: 39–61.

March, J. (1991). Exploration and exploitation in organizational learning. *Organization Science*, 2(1): 71–87.

McClain, D. (1982). FDI in the US: Old currents, "new waves", and the theory of direct investment. In C. P. Kindleberger and D. B. Andretsch (eds.), *The Multinational Corporation in the 1980s*. Cambridge, MA: MIT Press.

McDougall, P. P., and Oviatt, B. M. (2000). International entrepreneurship: The intersection of two research paths. *Academy of Management Journal*, 43(5): 902–6.

McManus, J. (1972). The theory of the international firm. In G. Paquet (ed.), *The Multinational Firm and the Nation State*. Ontario, Canada: Collier-Macmillan.

Michel, A., and Shaked, I. (1986). Multinational corporatins vs. domestic corporations: Financial performance and characteristics. *Journal of International Business Studies*, 16: 89–106.

Nelson, R. R., and Winter, S. G. (1982). *An Evolutionary Theory of Economic Change*. Cambridge, MA: Belknap Press of Harvard University Press.

Nohria, N., and Ghoshal, S. (1997). *The Differentiated Network*. San Francisco, CA: Jossey-Bass.

Ohmae, K. (1989). Managing in a borderless world, *Harvard Business Review*, May–June: 2–9.

Porter, M. E. (1986). Changing patterns of international competition. *California Management Review*, 28(2): 9–40.

Porter, M. E. (1990). *The Competitive Advantage of Nations*. New York: Free Press.

Porter, M. E. (1998). Clusters and the now economics of competition. *Harvard Business Review*, 76(6): 77–90.

Prahalad, C. K. (1975). *The Strategic Process in a Multinational Corporation*. Unpublished doctoral dissertation, Harvard Business School.

Prahalad, C. K., and Doz, Y. (1987). *The Multinational Mission: Balancing Local Demands and Global Vision*. New York: Free Press.

Robock, S., and Simmonds, K. (1989). *International Business and Multinational Enterprise*. Homewood, IL: Irwin.

Romanelli, E., and Tushman, M. L. (1986). Inertia, environments, and strategic choice: A quasi-experimental design for comparative-longitudinal research. *Management Science*, 32(5): 608–21.

Rosenzweig, P. M., and Singh, J. V. (1991). Organizational environments and the multinational enterprise. *Academy of Management Journal*, 16(2): 340–61.

Rugman, A. M. (1980). Internalization as a general theory of foreign direct investment: A re-appraisal of the literature. *Weltwirtschaftliches Archiv*, 116: 365–79.

Sanchez, R., Heene, A., and Thomas, H. (1996). Chapter 1. In R. Sanchez, A. Heene, H. Thomas (eds.), *Dynamics of Competence-based Competition*. Oxford: Elsevier Pergamon.

Tallman, S. B. (1992). A strategic management perspective on host country structure of multinational enterprises. *Journal of Management*, 18(3): 455–72.

Tallman, S. (1999). Strategy. In A. Plath (ed.), *MBA International Enterprise*. Milton Keynes, UK: The Open University.

Tallman, S., and Fladmoe-Lindquist, K. (2000). Resource and competence-driven global strategies. In R. Sanchez and A. Heene, *Advances in Applied Business Strategy*, 6A: 229–48. Stamford, CT: JAI Press.

Tallman, S., and Li, J. T. (1996). The effects of international diversity and product diversity on the performance of multinational firms. *Academy of Management Journal*, 39(1): 179–96.

Teece, D. J. (1986). Transactions cost economics and the multinational enterprise. *Journal of Economic Behavior and Organization*, 7:21–45.

Teece, D. J., Pisano, G., and Shuen, A. (1997). Dynamic capabilities and strategic management. *Strategic Management Journal*, 18: 509–33.

Vernon, R. (1966). International trade and international investment in the product life cycle. *Quarterly Journal of Economics*, May: 190–207.

Vernon, R. (1971). *Sovereignty at Bay: The Multinational Spread of US Enterprises*. New York: Basic Books.

Williamson, O. E. (1975). *Markets and Hierarchies: Analysis and Antitrust Implications*. New York: Free Press.

Yip, G. S. (1992). *Total Global Strategy: Managing for Worldwide Competitive Advantage*. Englewood Cliffs, NJ: Prentice-Hall.

# Part IV

## HUMAN FACTORS

# 17

# On Strategic Judgment

RICHARD L. PRIEM AND CYNTHIA S. CYCYOTA

True ease in writing comes from art,[1] not chance,
As those move easiest who have learn'd to dance.

(Alexander Pope, *Essay on Criticism*)

The dominant belief in Alexander Pope's time was that superior writing–seemingly natural, easily flowing, with just the right words in just the right places–meant that the writer had been visited by a muse.[2] Pope believed differently. He argued that good writing comes from study and experience, which together build writing skills and sound creative judgment.

Sound judgment also is cited as a characteristic of superior strategic leadership. *Industry Week*, for example, named Lou Gerstner of IBM their "CEO of the Year" for 1997 due to his "business skills, judgment, and tough-minded leadership" (Stevens, 1997). Steve Jobs of Apple Computer has been praised for his skill and vision in judging the commercial potential of new internet products (e.g., Schlender, 2000). And Henry Kissinger, in a comparison of statesmen's and CEOs' responsibilities, argued that CEO judgment is an essential skill for charting a course for the organization (Pellet, 1997).

Conversely, boards of directors, other stakeholders, and the business press sometimes question strategic leaders' judgments. Doug Ivester was slow in addressing the health crisis when schoolchildren in Belgium became ill after drinking Coke™. The board eventually dismissed him as CEO of Coca-Cola™, because he failed to anticipate the ensuing public outcry (Morris and Sellers, 2000). In the eyes of his board, Mr. Ivester did not properly judge the causal factors prompting the crisis, or their interrelationships. Similarly, Nucor Corporation recently replaced both its chairman and chief executive for their poorly received judgments regarding acquisitions and staffing (Foust, 1999). Together these examples – good and bad – indicate that attributions about judgment are made frequently in the business world.

Management scholars also seem to believe that sound judgment is an essential quality for strategic leadership. Barnard (1938) is an early example. He considered good judgment to "transcend the capacity of intellectual methods and techniques of discriminating the factors of the situation . . . a matter of art rather than science, aesthetic rather than logic, recognized rather than described, known by effect rather than by analysis" (1938: 235). Penrose (1959) similarly believed that sound judgment is required for top leaders to effectively gather information, recognize risks and uncertainties, and develop appropriate expectations for growth. Sir Geoffrey Vickers described skill in strategic judgment as "excellence in the capacity to comprehend and analyze complex situations . . . that produces apt solutions to problems set by surveys of reality" (1965: 88). He identified three elements of each strategic judgment: (1) determining how things are; (2) determining how things ought to be; (3) determining the best way to reduce the distance between the two. This comparison of a particularistic situation against the top manager's vision for the organization is the essence of strategic decision (Mintzberg, Ahlstrand, and Lampel, 1998). Strategic judgment therefore must be central to the study of strategic leadership.

More recently, some scholars have reinforced the primacy of strategic judgment, describing it as expert intuition (Simon, 1989), as an essential ingredient of effective decisions (Drucker, 1996), and as a part of the overall mental state of effective leaders (Mintzberg, Ahlstrand, and Lampel, 1998). Strategic choice has been identified as the defining attribute of strategic management (Child, 1997), and executive judgments – good or bad – must be formed before strategic choices can be made (Priem and Harrison, 1994). In short, understanding the judgments of strategic leaders is essential to determining (1) how mental processes are manifest in the strategies they develop, and (2) how these processes and strategies affect firm performance.

## DEFINING STRATEGIC JUDGMENT

Overall, judgment appears to be an important criterion for evaluating top managers. But, what exactly is meant when an executive is said to have "good" or "sound" strategic judgment? Judging as a process is "the forming of an opinion, estimate, notion, or conclusion, as from circumstances presented to the mind." Judgment *as a personal capacity* is "the ability to make a decision, or form an opinion objectively or wisely, especially in matters affecting action; good sense; discernment," or alternately as "sense tempered and refined by experience, training, and maturity."[3] Judgment *as an outcome* is simply "the opinion formed."

Analogy may help to clarify what we mean by "strategic judgment." An extensive academic literature on medical judgment has examined the diagnostic skills of medical doctors. When a medical doctor is presented with a complaining patient, for example, a judgment process ensues. The doctor first makes a judgment about what symptoms to look for, and then determines the presence or absence of those symptoms, or estimates their levels. Next, the particular combination of symptoms and their levels are processed, a diagnosis is reached, and a treatment is recommended. The doctor's skill in making diagnoses – based on training, experience, and personal qualities such as maturity and "good sense" – represents a personal capacity for sound diagnostic judgment.

Judgment, as we have defined it, can thus encompass the ability to identify, perceive, and attend to salient variables, to form objective opinions about the present quantities (or levels) of the variables, to identify the likely form and strength of simple bivariate relationships that may exist among these variables, and to estimate the effects that multivariate contingencies (i.e., configurations) of these variables would likely have on performance in the context of a particular firm (i.e., a specific though uncertain view of "how the world works"). Thus, executive strategic judgment is required to determine the "astutely-chosen configurations" of Eisenhardt and Martin (2000) or the "desired end states" of Vickers (1965). (See Priem and Harrison (1994) for an extended discussion, and Arkes and Hammond (1986) for the terminology used in the extensive micro literature on judgment and decision making.)

## THE NATURE OF STRATEGIC JUDGMENTS

Natural science theories are about objects that are relatively "solid," with object–to–object relationships that are relatively unchanging. These objects and relationships can be organized and verified – or, at least, not falsified – inductively, through hypothesis testing. Even the ephemeral tau neutrino now has been "seen" by the traces it left on a film-like emulsion.

Social science objects and relationships are more difficult to reduce to invariant laws (Berlin, 1996; McKelvey, 1997; Numagami, 1998). Strategic management theories can cause their objects to change their behaviors (however seldom that currently may occur), thereby affecting the efficacy of the initial theories (Drucker, 1999). Moreover, firms are heterogeneous (Barney, 1991) and strategic contexts are subject to continuous change (D'Aveni, 1995; Drucker, 1999; Eisenhardt and Martin, 2000), further complicating attempts at generalization.

Thus, the settings for strategic judgments are particularistic and unique. Each situation presents the decision-maker with a new combination of factors, some familiar and others unfamiliar. Each strategic manager also is unique, bringing different "tools" with which to evaluate her scenario. Some success-related regularities in judgment can surely be found across scenarios, sorted perhaps by decision type, via social science induction. These are the requisite *content* for strategic judgment. Still, a special capacity for sound judgment – the ability to integrate many and appropriate bits of information, to view objectively the totality of one's particular situation, and to creatively visualize alternative feasible futures – is also necessary. Strategists could never rely totally on specific rules for decision. Any rule, at its creation, might have left unconsidered the one, key item that makes the current strategic scenario unique and possibly not subject to the rule (e.g., Berlin, 1996). Strategists therefore must of necessity be "puzzle-masters," making complex strategic judgments based on personal experience, strategy expertise, and an astute understanding of the specific situation.

Thus, how best to study strategic judgment is a perplexing question. If we as strategy scholars limit ourselves to the study of only those rules that are discoverable through social science induction techniques, we isolate ourselves from that which is unique and creative in strategic judgment. If, on the other hand, we focus immediately on the more metaphysical aspects of strategic judgment, under a "great man" approach to leadership, we risk falling in league with the management gurus.

The social science approach – that is, the focused attempt to find regularities in successful strategic judgment processes, and in the content of successful strategic judgments regarding classes of issues–is necessary to establish the underpinnings that can lead to effective exploration of creative synthesis in strategic judgment. As we discuss in a later section, *both* approaches are necessary if we are to get to the heart of the matter.

## Leadership Research and Strategic Judgment

We have argued that executives and the business press pay considerable attention to strategic judgment, and that strategy theorists have expressed a continuing interest. For individual managers, judgment is at the "intersection" of information gathering and other factors such as experience, demographics, the external environment and the internal capabilities of firms (e.g. Sternberg et al., 1995). Moreover, critical judgments have been studied productively in other fields, such as medical diagnostics and consumer choice. One therefore might expect that the strategic judgments of practicing executives would be "center stage" in strategic management research. This is not the case.

The following, necessarily brief, "tour" of recent research focusing on top managers shows how inconsequential strategic judgment has become in strategic management research. This general research inattention may be understandable given the myriad challenges of operationalizing judgment and accessing top executives, which we address later. Yet by eschewing judgment-related research the strategy field might be avoiding the very subject with the greatest potential for further illuminating complex strategic issues.

### Strategy content research

Early strategy content research sought to establish regularities between firms' outcomes (e.g., strategies pursued, structures achieved, alignments with environmental factors) and their performance outcomes (see, e.g., Fahey and Christensen (1986) for a review). Top managers were then offered these regularities as prescriptions to be used when making future choices. This type of prescription may seem eminently reasonable – top managers *should* strive to arrange their firms in ways that have produced strong performances in other firms.

At least two key assumptions must be correct, however, for this type of prescription to be valid. First, one must assume that differences in the tangible firm outcomes measured in the content studies are the result of *choice itself*, and that they are not instead due to differences in executives' charisma, or their communication skills, or their delegation skills, and so on. Conceivably, for example, all the executives in a sample could have had the same intentions (i.e., made the same correct or incorrect choice), but could have achieved differing firm outcomes due to implementation anomalies. We cannot disentangle these plausible alternative influences in strategy content studies, because only the company outcomes were linked to performance.

Second, one must assume that the executives being prescribed to can actually influence each of the firm outcomes under examination. That is, the observed differences in firm outcomes are the result of executive volition rather than either luck or some deterministic evolutionary process. This assumption must also hold for valid prescription.

Yet, without examining judgment and choice, these assumptions remain unverified. In Mintzberg and Waters' (1985) terms, this approach is similar to asserting that a firm's "realized" strategies perfectly represent its executives' "intended" strategies, and then not bothering to measure the intentions. Because executive intentions remain unmeasured, an empirical link is not established between top managers' choices and firm outcomes.

Instead, the strategic outcome is *presumed* to be due to strategic choice (Priem and Harrison, 1994).

Content studies have provided much valuable information regarding which firm outcomes are associated with high performance. Still, although these studies identify effective resource alignments, they offer few solid insights into top managers' choices, processes or skills, or the potential links between these strategic leadership variables and firm outcomes and performance.

## The upper echelons perspective

Hambrick and Mason introduced the "upper echelons" perspective in 1984, arguing that executives make choices based upon their idiosyncratic experiences, values and dispositions. Following Pfeffer's (1983) suggestion that demographic characteristics – objective, accessible and easily measured – can represent executives' differences along important psychological constructs, Hambrick and Mason (1984) advocated viewing top managers as a team (i.e., the TMT), and examining team issues via demographic indicators. Their article offered an important redirection for strategy research by asserting that top managers can make a difference to firm outcomes, and thus to performance. They helped move the focus from achieved outcomes to the decision-making executives themselves. Even better, Hambrick and Mason offered a measurement method for evaluating top management's influence!

Subsequent to 1984, demographics-based research on top managers and TMTs flourished. The demographics approach generally has been successful in finding relationships between executive or TMT demographic indicators and firm outcomes, including firm performance (e.g., Bantel and Jackson, 1989; Eisenhardt and Schoonhoven, 1990; Finkelstein and Hambrick, 1990; Keck, 1997; Michel and Hambrick, 1992; Murray, 1989; Norburn, 1986; Norburn and Birley, 1988; Wiersema and Bantel, 1992). These studies show quite clearly that top managers do indeed "matter" to firm outcomes, as was originally argued by Hambrick and Mason (1984).

Critics have raised concerns, however, that demographics-based TMT research: (1) can be conducted without direct researcher contact with top managers (Pettigrew, 1992); (2) produces "research without emotion, drama or action" (Reger, 1997: 804); (3) assumes that demographic predictors are correlated with presumed intervening processes which remain in a "black box" (Lawrence, 1997); (4) uses demographic proxies that may be related to organization outcomes primarily through *other* variables (Smith et al., 1994); and (5) is limited at the group level of analysis by intrinsic trade-offs which sacrifice construct validity for measurement reliability, explanation for prediction, and prescription for description (Priem, Lyon, and Dess, 1999).

These criticisms are each highly pertinent. Demographics-based TMT research leans heavily upon assumed "congruence" among demographics, unmeasured mediators, and outcomes (Lawrence, 1997), and thus substitutes "a semantic connection between process and outcome for an empirical one" (Drazin and Sandelands, 1992: 231). This is why TMT demographic studies, although they can determine that top managers *do matter* to firm outcomes, cannot say *how* they matter. The unmeasured mediating factor *through which* TMTs actually influence performance could be their choices, or their charisma, or their implementation skills, or some other factor – we just can't know from these studies.

## The resource-based "view"

The resource-based "view" (RBV) of strategy (Barney, 1991; Wernerfelt, 1984) has provided another platform from which scholars could study top managers – as "resources" for the firm. Although early conceptual work in strategic management had generally given nearly equivalent attention to firm strengths and weaknesses versus the opportunities and threats in the competitive environment (e.g., Andrews, 1971; Ansoff, 1965; Learned et al., 1965), much research attention had shifted toward external, industry-based competitive issues (e.g., Porter, 1980). Wernerfelt (1984) directed strategy scholars back toward resources as important antecedents to products and, ultimately, firm performance. Wernerfelt's (1984) article served as a reminder that both strategy scholars and "managers often fail to recognize that a bundle of assets, rather than the particular product market combination chosen for its deployment, lies at the heart of their firm's competitive position" (Dierickx and Cool, 1989: 1504).

Barney (1991) then extended the RBV by providing an "organizing framework . . . that organizational resources that are valuable, rare, difficult to imitate and non-substitutable can yield sustained competitive advantage" (Meyer, 1991: 823). Thus, top managers' evaluations of internal firm resources and how they should be combined were recognized as important areas requiring careful managerial judgment – just as the importance of positioning relative to the external environment long had been recognized.

RBV-oriented theoretical work and, to a much lesser extent, empirical work has exploded over the last ten years. Some of this work has focused on top managers as resources for their firms (e.g., Castanius and Helfat, 1991; Daily, Certo, and Dalton, 2000; Harris and Helfat, 1997). Dailey et al. (2000), for example, examined the firm-level and individual career benefits of international experience by CEOs. They found that CEO international experience was associated with firm performance, particularly for heavily internationalized firms and for CEOs hired from outside the firm. Castanias and Helfat (1991) argued that CEOs (as firm resources) are likely to have superior or inferior management skills, but they offered no basis for discriminating among superior and inferior CEOs other than waiting for their firms' performance results. Harris and Helfat (1997) determined that external successor CEOs receive an initial compensation premium relative to internal successors. They hypothesized that this premium compensates for the risk taken by an external successor CEO in forgoing the firm-specific skills he or she had developed in the previous position.

The increased attention the RBV has brought to firm resources has been beneficial in helping to: (1) clarify the potential contributions of resources to competitive advantage; (2) introduce strategy scholars to a number of useful descriptive theories from industrial organization economics (e.g., Alchian and Demsetz (1972) on "teamwork" production, or DeVany and Saving (1983) on price as a signal of quality); and (3) alleviate any previous analytical *over*emphasis on the opportunities and threats that arise from the product side.

The RBV, however, has recently drawn critics who argue that its contributions have fallen well short of its original promise, particularly given the attention it has garnered to date. The RBV has been criticized as a deficient theoretical system (Bromiley and Fleming, 2001; Ryall, 1999), as making limited contributions to strategic management (McWilliams and Smart, 1993), or both (Priem and Butler, 2001a, b). For example, Priem and Butler's investigation concluded that:

... or as a potential theory: 1) the elemental RBV does not yet meet the requirements of a theoretical structure, 2) the RBV makes implicit assumptions about stability in product markets, and 3) the fundamental "value" variable is exogenous to the RBV. As a perspective for strategy research: 4) overly inclusive and imprecise definitions of resources hinder useful, RBV-based prescription, and 5) static approaches to RBV development and testing result in causal "hows and whys" remaining in a "black box" (2001a).

Such concerns indicate that one must be particularly careful when attempting to draw prescriptive implications for *strategic leadership* from descriptive insights developed under the view of top managers as resources for the firm. The "CEO resources" ideas developed by Castanias and Helfat (1991) provide one example – prescriptions to CEOs of poorly performing firms that they are the source of the problem and should think about voluntarily exiting clearly would be considered unhelpful by the CEOs. In this case viewing CEOs as resources would have more prescriptive implications for boards of directors than for the CEOs themselves. Similarly, viewing boards of directors as resources would have more prescriptive implications for the CEOs who appoint boards or the governments that regulate them than for the boards themselves. This suggests that some resources may be of less interest to strategy researchers than others, depending on the group – frequently CEOs – for whom prescriptions are desired. Thus, researchers must be clear concerning the practitioner level at which prescriptions can be made when examining CEOs as resources for their firms.

Yet two offshoots of the RBV deserve careful attention for their potential contribution to our understanding of strategic leadership. One is the "knowledge-based view" of the firm (Conner and Prahalad, 1996; Kogut and Zander, 1993, 1996), and the other is "resource-advantage" theory (Hunt, 1997, 2000). Each of these may be helpful in advancing the study of strategic managers' judgments.

The "knowledge-based view" (KBV) of the theory of the firm appears to argue essentially that the firm's existence and boundaries can be explained via its unique ability to obtain, build, combine, and retain knowledge (Conner and Prahalad, 1996; Kogut and Zander, 1993, 1996; see Eisenhardt and Santos, 2001, for a recent review). That is, hierarchical organization is particularly effective for building and combining knowledge, and thereby developing "path dependent" capabilities and knowledge assets.

These positions follow from earlier arguments of Penrose (1959), Alchian and Demsetz (1972), and Arrow (1962), among others. Penrose's (1959) well-known logic, for example, noted that a firm's possible directions for growth are limited by its available management resources, and by the knowledge and capabilities obtained in its previous activities. Alchian and Demsetz (1972) argued that well-known resources from inside the firm could be combined more effectively than could unfamiliar resources from the outside. "Efficient production with heterogeneous resources is a result not of having *better* resources but in *knowing more accurately* the relative productive performances of those resources" (1972: 793, italics in the original). Finally, Arrow (1992: 616) noted that "the central economic fact about the processes of invention and research is that they are devoted to the production of information. By the very definition of information, invention must be a risky process, in that the output (information obtained) can never be predicted perfectly from the inputs."

Foss (1996a, b, 1999) has argued that the current knowledge-based perspectives are insufficient explanations for the existence of the firm – the KBV cannot explain the scope or existence of the firm without support from contracts-based opportunism arguments (e.g., Williamson, 1979), and it lacks "clear microfoundations" (Foss, 1999: 737). Moreover, the current KBV appears to us to ignore important, information-focused work from more conventional transaction cost economics (TCE) research. Alston and Gillespie (1989), for example, evaluated the likely effects of within-firm and between-firm information transfer costs on firm boundaries. Their ideas might be useful in further developing the KBV. Attempts to compare and integrate Alston and Gillespie's (1989) TCE-based information transfer work with the ideas of Grant (1996) on knowledge coordination within the firm might be particularly promising. Similarly, empirical strategy literature that is more solidly grounded in economic theory, such as the recent TCE-KBV study by Poppo and Zenger (1998), could also help to develop the KBV in ways that would make it more useful to scholars interested in strategic leadership.

In spite of their current limitations, knowledge-based perspectives may provide a new and revitalized platform for examining strategic judgment because, at least for top executives, they direct attention specifically toward the *substantive knowledge* required for strategic decision making, how that knowledge is built and how it is retained. Eisenhardt and Martin (2000), for example, have redefined "dynamic capabilities" (e.g., Teece, Pisano, and Shuen, 1997) as "the specific organizational and strategic processes (e.g., product innovation, strategic decision making, alliancing) by which managers alter their resource base" (Eisenhardt and Martin, 2000). They argued further that the potential for long-term advantage from these processes (i.e., "dynamic capabilities") "lies in using dynamic capabilities sooner, more astutely, or more fortuitously than the competition to create resource configurations that have that advantage." Indeed, both good timing and astute, substantive choice that is appropriate to the particular context indicate the type of sound strategic judgment we are discussing. Luck is a different issue, although Isaiah Berlin (1996) has remarked that individuals with good judgment might tend to experience good fortune more often than most!

The other interesting offshoot of the RBV is the "resource advantage theory," offered by Hunt (1997, 2000) as an evolutionary theory of competitive advantage. Hunt has attempted to integrate the heterogeneous firm resources approach of the RBV with marketing's most prominent theory of heterogeneous market demand (Alderson, 1957, 1965). Wroe Alderson's general theory of marketing argues that the function of marketing is to take the heterogeneous raw materials found in nature and, through a series of sorts and transformations, convert them into the heterogeneous end products desired by consumers. The sorts are made to decrease or increase heterogeneity (e.g., by accumulating a raw material or offering a broad assortment of finished goods), and the transformations affect the physical form of a good or its location in time or space. The closer the match of the resulting assortment of heterogeneous end products with the heterogeneous wants of consumers, the more effective the marketing channel and its constituent firms. The lower the summed costs of the sequential sorts and transformations, the more efficient the marketing channel and its constituent firms.[4]

Hunt's (2000) work is particularly interesting for strategic leadership scholars because it combines the "strengths and weaknesses" focus of the RBV with the "opportunities and threats" focus of Alderson's marketing theory, thereby encompassing the major aspects of strategic judgment (Learned et al., 1965). Moreover, Hunt has taken a dynamic approach that incorporates temporal issues. Once again the emphasis is on developing the most effective resource configurations, but in this case those configurations are effective only if they support sorts and transformations that lead to the satisfaction of consumer wants.

## Managerial cognitions research

The managerial cognitions research area is in many ways the one that might have been expected to provide the greatest insight into the effectiveness of top managers' strategic judgments. It just might be, however, the most fragmented among those literatures we have considered thus far as potentially relating to strategic leadership, with the most widely dispersed antecedents (see Walsh, 1995, for a recent review).

Strategy-relevant, applied work on cognitions can be found in the literatures on medical decision-making (Hoffman, Slovic, and Rorer, 1968), consumer decision-making (e.g., Green and Wind, 1973), individual "lay person" versus expert cause-and-effect understandings (e.g., Bostrom, Fischhoff, and Morgan, 1992), and small group, strategic group, and industry level cause maps (e.g., Bougon, Weick, and Binkhorst, 1977; Reger and Huff, 1993; Spender, 1989). Unfortunately, different jargon tends to be used between and even *within* each of these literatures (e.g., schemas, cause maps, knowledge structures, mindsets, recipes, decision rules, judgment policies, cognitions, beliefs, perceptions, judgments, reasoning, thinking, mental models, and so on). These terminology differences have limited the information exchange between these literatures and the managerial cognitions work, and perhaps even within the managerial cognitions field itself. Even individuals whose specialty is managerial cognitions are often unfamiliar with the terminologies used in other fields!

The managerial cognitions "school" (Mintzberg, Ahlstrand, and Lampel, 1998) can be divided into at least two primary areas. The first of these is information processing and sensing-making, which examines how organizational members – including top managers – scan, interpret and extract meanings from the environment (Meindl, Stubbart, and Porac, 1996; Thomas, Gioia, and Ketchen, 1997). Studies from this perspective have included themes such as biases affecting decision making (Busenitz and Barney, 1997; Tversky and Kahnemann, 1974); information processing (Daft and Weick, 1984; Milliken, 1990); strategic issue diagnosis (Dutton, Fahey, and Narayanan, 1983; Dutton and Jackson, 1987); and the mental structures of managers and causal mapping (Barr, Stimpert, and Huff, 1992; Huff, 1990).

The second area of managerial cognitions research relates more to how groups, organizations, and industries act, as "cognitive communities," in constructing their own common views of the environment (Meindl, Stubbart, and Porac, 1996; Mintzberg, Ahlstrand, and Lampel, 1998; Walsh, 1995). This area has covered topics including organizational culture and shared meanings (Hofstede, 1980; Martin, 1992); industry influences on strategy formulation (Huff, 1982; Phillips, 1994; Spender, 1989); and organizational learning (Thomas, Gioia, and Ketchen, 1997).

Overall, the multiple views of managerial cognition provide a rich foundation for the study of top managers. This plurality also can be a weakness, however, making the conclusions drawn from cognition studies fragmented and difficult to build upon in a coherent way. This situation may be normal for a research area in such an early stage. Meindl, Stubbart, and Porac (1996) identified five key, unresolved issues in the study of managerial cognitions. These are: (1) lack of consistency in constructs; (2) difficulties with levels of analysis; (3) failure to establish consistent relations between cognitive structure and cognitive processes; (4) measurement of relationship between cognitive structure and organizational outcomes; and (5) problems in development of relevancy for practitioners. Although individual examples of advances can be noted in each of these areas, there appears to have been a general lack of consistent progress to date in theory building and research.

We see two additional issues in much of the existing managerial cognitions research that become limitations when the research is applied in the context of strategic leadership. The first of these limitations is that many of the inferences made concerning "managerial cognitions" have been drawn from research that didn't involve managers at all, let alone top managers of consequential business firms. The findings of much cognitions research that used lower-level employees or even students as subjects have been assumed rather uncritically to hold for top managers. This may at first seem reasonable because of the difficulty in accessing top managers for cognitions research, but it presents an important and unresolved generalizability issue. CEOs typically have survived an extensive and rigorous selection process, earning promotions in increasingly competitive arenas throughout their careers prior to their appointments as CEO. It is at least possible – if not highly probable – that their business judgments will be better, and less affected by biases, than that of lower level employees or university students. Indeed, Hitt and Tyler (1991) found little variance in cognitive complexity among CEOs in their sample, and concluded that they all likely had to be cognitively complex in order to reach their CEO positions. Yet much theory building on managerial cognitions has adopted Tversky and Kahnemann's (1974) general decision biases (e.g., Busenitz and Barney, 1997; Das and Teng, 1999; Schwenk, 1988). Unresolved questions are (1) to what extent will these biases apply to CEOs just as they do to others, (2) might CEOs tend to have their own, unique biases, and (3) what are or should be the *standards* (see, e.g., Simon, 1957) against which the existence of and magnitudes of possible biases can be evaluated? Until we begin to address these questions, it isn't surprising that cautionary tales of potential biases may go generally unheeded by practitioners (Meindl, Stubbart, and Porac, 1996).

Another potential limitation for the application of managerial cognition research in strategic leadership is the apparent focus on identification of homogeneous and universal *group-level* cognitions. The primary interest has been to establish commonalities in the way managers view the world and then to translate these commonalities into prescriptions for executives (Spender, 1989). This emphasis is seen in research examining "individual" cognitions as well as in the more overtly group-level research. Hitt and Tyler (1991), for example, used policy capturing to identify the causal beliefs of top managers when evaluating potential acquisitions for likelihood of acquisition success. They then aggregated the managers' cause maps to produce an overall model of causal beliefs. Similar aggregation can be seen in other early studies (e.g., De Sarbo, MacMillan, and Day, 1987; Reger and Huff, 1993).

Given a focus on, for example, strategic groups, such aggregation is appropriate and useful. The overriding interest in strategic leadership research, however, lies in identifying how *differences* in managers' judgments (i.e., cognitions) (Calori, Johnson, and Sarnin, 1994) may be differentially associated with firm performance. If all CEOs already hold a particular judgment that is effective, for example, and each has learned this judgment through her experience "on the way up," that judgment may have descriptive importance but it has little implication for prescription – all CEOs already hold that judgment from experiential learning. Instead, strategic leadership research is particularly concerned with those decision areas where there is *variance* in judgment among CEOs. For such areas, one may examine which judgments are most effective in which circumstances and begin to offer useful prescriptions to CEOs. Thus, variance in judgment, and even outliers' judgments examined qualitatively, might be useful for prescription whereas homogeneous judgment is not.

This is why linking CEOs' judgment differences, through organization design outcomes, to firm performance (Markóczy, 1997; Melone, 1994; Priem, 1994), and specifying relationships between individual and organizational level thinking (Swan and Newell, 1998), may be especially worthwhile. Applied work in managerial cognition must emphasize individual differences for maximum usefulness to strategic leadership. Stimpert (1999: 362) has insisted that the worthwhile questions in cognitive research relate to "how cognitive tools will allow managers to analyze and alter their beliefs to improve real time strategy making efforts." We agree, but what a long way remains before we even approach such a goal! Perhaps a good first step simply would be more effort toward directly measuring the causal beliefs of CEOs who lead consequential firms (e.g., Markóczy, 1997).

## The influence of strategic leadership research to date

So far we have detailed some alternative courses strategy researchers have taken to provide both descriptions of strategic outcomes and prescriptions for improved strategic leadership. The one area of apparently strong agreement among researchers is that executives have paid little attention to this work (e.g., Bettis, 1991; Daft and Lewin, 1990; Hambrick, 1994; Miner, 1997; Mowday, 1997; Slocum, 1997). In fact, the *Academy of Management Journal* solicited manuscripts for a special issue on "knowledge transfer between academics and practitioners" because "considerable evidence suggests that practitioners typically turn to sources of information other than academics or the scientific literature when designing organizational polices and innovations" (*AMJ*, 1998, 41: 746).

Yet, the unsubstantiated leadership "theories" touted by management gurus have flourished during this time, primarily by targeting practitioner-perceived needs for new methods for business success. Argyris (2000) has described four requirements for effective advice to practitioners. It must: (1) specify outcomes or objectives; (2) detail the sequence of actions required to produce intended consequences; (3) use concepts or skills employees have or can be taught; and (4) not be prevented by the organizational context. He argued further that the gurus' advice customarily falls short; it often is inconsistent and inactionable.

According to Eccles and Nohria (1992), however, correct content may not matter to the practitioner acceptance of gurus' prescriptions. Even if these prescriptions are without substantive operating value, they provide top managers with a means for communicating goals and visions of the future, and for developing a culture of shared meanings within their organizations (see also Martin, 1992). Thus, the rhetoric used in popular business prescriptions may have value for top managers, even if the substance of the new "theory" itself is ineffective or is just a repackaged version of an established business practice. Executives appear to understand very well that "the way people talk about the world has everything to do with *the way the world is ultimately understood and acted in*" (Eccles and Nohria, 1992: 29, emphasis added). Thus, the frequent turnover in fashionable management theories may have benefits for practitioners, independent of any particular theory's details or substantive effectiveness, as a renewable prod to organizational action (Abrahamson, 1991, 1996).

Neither academics nor executives, however, can afford to give up on the search for management theories with effective content. That would limit executives' scope simply to deciding when and how to most effectively introduce new, *in*effective theory in order to spur action in their organizations. We know through casual empiricism that executives make *many* decisions that are much more momentous than that for their firms. These decisions require effective judgment (i.e., "content"). Some have argued with impeccable logic that there can be no "rule for riches" – any theory with effective content will spread throughout the management community like an internet virus, thereby eliminating any relative advantage offered by that theory (see, e.g., Barney, 1986; Mosakowski, 1998; Rumelt, Schendel, and Teece, 1991). With the current level of practitioner acceptance of academic theories, however, this is unlikely to be a near-term issue. Moreover, casual empiricism shows also that firms and their leaders are quite heterogeneous, both in resource combinations and in ideas. The dynamics of strategic interaction (e.g., D'Aveni, 1995; Eisenhardt and Martin, 2000) suggest that this heterogeneity will be long lasting.[5]

Academics are most comfortable with precise, exact theory. By dint of training and personality, we tend to search for knowledge that may be easily reducible to universal rules (Berlin, 1996). But strategic judgment is messy. Perhaps to avoid the messiness, strategic leadership research has been creative in avoiding direct engagement with executives and their judgments. It is likely that we can find new research approaches that extend the creative avoidance policy.

Yet without confronting executive judgment directly, we cannot really hope to explain strategy. Executives have little use for, and less time to wait for, universal solutions. They must judge now, in imperfect and uncertain situations. Perhaps if we would expend more of our creative effort in finding empirical regularities in how the most successful executives fit information and situations together, and in their perceptions of their causal worlds, practitioners might pay more heed to our work. Moreover, these substantive issues are indispensable to progress in our field. This subject is addressed in the next section.

## STUDYING STRATEGIC JUDGMENT

The previous sections may have foreshadowed our belief that both quantitative and qualitative studies will be necessary to advance our understanding of strategic judgment. We can perhaps learn most by combining quantitative studies, which like textbooks report regularities identified via scientific induction, and qualitative studies, which like novels provide a sense of direct acquaintance with a particularistic situation. Lee (1991) has described the complementary nature of quantitative and qualitative research methods. He recommended that positivist and interpretive viewpoints be integrated into a research model with three levels of understanding – subjective meanings, interpretive understanding and positivist understanding. Through this approach the "everyday meanings" of research subjects can be understood by researchers and then tested empirically with other subjects.

Thomas, Gioia, and Ketchen (1997) have recommended a similar research strategy of *developing* theory using qualitative methods and then *testing* theory using quantitative methods. Qualitative research requires close contact with research subjects, and therefore can surface important issues that might otherwise remain unnoticed in "arms-length," quantitative research. Mintzberg's (1973) observational study of CEOs' work habits, for example, identified several previously unsuspected aspects of CEOs' behavior at work. And Eisenhardt's (1989) study of high technology firms indicated that, contrary to accepted thought at the time, the successful firms in "high-velocity" environments are those that are *more* comprehensive in their strategic decision making. Interpretive, interview-based studies such as these cannot test hypotheses adequately, because their extensive contact with subjects invariably results in small sample sizes. But such studies may generate insights and testable hypotheses, like those identified by Mintzberg (1973) and Eisenhardt (1989), that may then be used to design larger sample, quantitative evaluations.

Hitt and Barr (1989) provided a quantitative study example. They showed how specific, substantive managerial judgments concerning employee selection could be evaluated using employee characteristics previously identified as important in the human resources management literature. Managers individually were presented with a series of job applicants, each of whom had varying combinations (i.e., presence-absence or a particular level) of experience, education and demographic characteristics. Each manager's task was to form a favorability opinion and to recommend a starting salary for each applicant. Hitt and Barr (1989) found that the simultaneous presence of multiple characteristics greatly increased perceived favorability and the salary recommended. That is, they found interaction effects among the characteristics on both favorability and recommended salary, beyond their simple main effects. The researchers concluded that the managers exhibited configural (what we in strategy now would call "configurational") thinking in making their recommendations. Furthermore, after the study each manager's selection thinking (i.e., their individual mental model or "decision rules") could be evaluated against legal or normative standards for personnel selection (e.g., for non–discrimination based on race, age, or gender). The relative worth of quantitative work such as this depends in great measure on the salience of the characteristics selected *a priori* for inclusion in the decision model. These factors are generally determined by reviewing previous, often qualitative, research.

In the sections that follow we turn to strategic leadership examples and focus primarily on quantitative approaches, as that is our bent. But our discussion remains at the conceptual level. First, we briefly discuss the current state of applicable research methods. We then selectively suggest types of applied research questions that can be answered with existing methods, and discuss sample studies if they exist. Lastly, we address the practical issue of access to top executives.

## Quantitative methods

Gist, Hopper, and Daniels (1998) have argued that behavioral simulation approaches have noteworthy potential for management research. Indeed, the literature in management on these types of approaches is growing rapidly. Priem and Harrison (1994), for example, described decomposition methods and composition methods for analyzing strategic judgments. Decomposition methods focus on an executive's choices in responding to a series of decision scenarios (i.e., behavioral simulations). The variance in the executive's choices is evaluated against the factors of interest in the study, which had been manipulated across scenarios, using the error theory of analysis of variance. The resulting model shows the factors the executive considered in making choices. Similar to regression models, decomposition methods can show the directions and the strengths of both main effects and interactions in an executive's choice (judgment) policy. Decomposition methods include axiomatic conjoint analysis, non-metric conjoint analysis, metric conjoint analysis, and policy capturing. For these methods, an individual's judgment policy (or rule) is determined by "backing it out" from a series of decisions.

Composition methods focus on the process the executive goes through in forming a judgment. In these methods, an executive is presented with a behavioral scenario, and his or her thinking is tracked (via verbalizations, actions, or self-reports) as they move toward a decision concerning that scenario. Composition methods include verbal protocol analysis, information search, and cause mapping. For these methods, an individual's judgment process is determined by "following along" while the judgment is being made.

Mohammed, Klimoski, and Rentsch (2000) evaluated four additional techniques for measuring team mental models – pathfinder, multidimensional scaling, interactively elicited cognitive mapping, and text based cognitive mapping. Markóczy and Goldberg (1995) presented a conjoint-based technique for eliciting executives' beliefs. Gist, Hopper, and Daniels (1998) suggested steps for designing simulations, and criteria for effective simulation techniques. Furthermore, there are descriptions of apt techniques in the medical diagnostics, judgment and decision making, consumer behavior, and research methods literatures.[6] Thus, established quantitative techniques are available for the applied study of strategic judgment. These are not nearly as well known among macro organizational scholars, however, as are more fashionable and accepted data analysis techniques like moderated hierarchical regression, confirmatory modeling, or event history analysis.

In the next sections, we identify some exemplar studies and discuss, in turn, how quantitative techniques for measuring managerial cognitions can contribute to the strategic leadership literature by aiding classification, process evaluation, content evaluation, and some specific, leadership-related content areas.

*Classification.*   McKelvey (1982) has argued that effective classification is a necessary first step for theory building in the organizational sciences. Priem, Love, and Shaffer's (1999) research provides an example of a judgment-based classification study. They argued that the absence of recent, inductive research on how top executives perceive and classify environmental uncertainty might be hindering theory development in strategic leadership. They noted that recent research on perceived environmental uncertainty (PEU) has generally presented executives with groupings of the environment into pre-established sectors. Yet these sector classifications, based on inferences drawn from executive interviews conducted from 20 to 40 years ago (e.g., Dill, 1958; Miles and Snow, 1978), may no longer accurately reflect the usage and groupings of present-day executives.

Priem, Love, and Shaffer (1999), therefore, used object sorting techniques (Walsh, 1995) to determine how international executives (i.e., managing directors and senior vice presidents) would group sources of environmental uncertainty without the "prompting" of researcher-selected sector classifications. Top executives in Hong Kong were asked, first, individually to list all sources of uncertainty that were facing their firms. These lists then were condensed to eliminate duplication, and the listed sources of PEU were transferred to a set of index cards for each executive. Each executive next individually grouped the uncertainty sources, like with like. These data matrices were analyzed using multidimensional scaling to determine the underlying dimensions used by the executives in distinguishing among the uncertainty sources. The dimensions then were validated using a new sample of executives. Next, the original executives as a group labeled each dimension. Finally, cluster analysis grouped the PEU sources, because each possible category from the dimensions needn't necessarily contain an uncertainty source.

The results indicated that the Hong Kong executives distinguished uncertainty sources using three underlying dimensions: a staffing versus macro economy "resource costs" dimension; a macro politics versus competitive environment "industry competition" dimension; and a local social climate versus international location "comparative advantage" dimension. The executives used these dimensions to group uncertainty sources into six clusters. These were labeled: international comparative advantage, costs/industry competition, resource availability/product demand, business climate, trends/disequilibrium, and exchange rates.

The lack of convergence between these dimensions and uncertainty sectors and those identified in early literature (e.g., Duncan, 1972; Katz and Kahn, 1978; Miles and Snow, 1978) suggests that the PEU classifications of top executives warrant further qualitative and quantitative study. The Hong Kong executives were certainly facing a great deal of uncertainty at the time of this study – just prior to the handover to the PRC. This suggests that their taxonomy is likely quite comprehensive (McKelvey, 1982). Generalizability of the taxonomy to executives in other locations, however, must yet be determined. Nevertheless, this study shows how quantitative techniques can be applied to empirically derive more rigorous classifications, based directly on the "information processing and sense-making" aspects of executive judgment.

*Process evaluation.* Process evaluation also could benefit from additional study via managerial judgment. This area includes strategic issue diagnosis (Dutton, 1983, 1986; Dutton and Jackson, 1987; D'Aveni and MacMillan, 1990), information comprehensiveness in particular situations (Eisenhardt, 1989), and other process-related questions that emphasize the role of the individual decision makers (Rajagopalan, Rasheed, and Datta, 1993.)

Melone's 1994 study is a good example of process evaluation via verbal protocol analysis. She used a simulation experiment to evaluate the reasoning processes used by CFOs and corporate development VPs in evaluating potential acquisition candidates. She tape-recorded the executives' verbalizations as they "talked their way through" their decision processes. Melone determined that both shared corporate level expertise and experience/role-based differences contributed to the executives' evaluations.

Walters, Priem, and Shook (2001) employed a computer-based simulation to determine the degree to which business level strategy influences the order and the frequency with which manufacturing firm CEOs scan external environment sectors and internal firm capabilities. Each of 47 CEOs was presented in his office (all were men) with a differentiation scenario and with a cost leadership scenario, in random order, describing similar manufacturing firms. After each scenario was presented, the CEO was allowed total control over his information search on a laptop computer. The CEO could make selections from a menu to receive a "nugget" of information about the firm in the scenario from among four sectors of the external environment or from among six internal capability areas. When a sector/area was selected, the CEO could then select a type of information source (e.g., newspaper, face-to-face with employee, telephone with industry analyst, etc.) based on the common $2 \times 2$ "personal–impersonal and internal–external" matrix. A computer algorithm tracked, for each CEO, the order of sector/area selection, the frequency of sector/area selection, and the length of time spent in the each sector/area. Thus, a "trace" of each CEO's scanning process was obtained.

The results shed some light on a different version of the debate about the possible influence of functional experience on problem framing (e.g., Beyer et al., 1997; Chattopadhyay et al., 1999; Dearborn and Simon, 1958; Walsh, 1988). Walters, Priem, and Shook (2001) found that the business level strategy used by a CEO's firm (i.e., his experience with a particular strategy) influenced his scanning pattern, even if the scenario for which he was scanning described the *opposite* business level strategy. The larger influence, however, was that of the CEO himself. That is, the CEOs made significant, volitional changes in their scanning processes when the scenarios had them leading firms with different business level strategies.

*Content evaluation.*   A growing understanding of strategic leadership processes is likely to be enhanced by a growing understanding of the content knowledge that is applied by strategic leaders, and vice versa. The content-related judgment of managers remains important in interpreting environmental changes, and in developing strategies to achieve organizational goals (Sternberg et al., 1995). Moreover, the alignment and adjustment of these goals through manager judgment, to achieve an overall business vision, remains a primary concern (Mintzberg, Ahlstrand, and Lampel, 1998; Vickers, 1965).

Markóczy (1997) performed a multi-step study that evaluated the causal beliefs of 91 international managers in Hungary. She first identified 49 constructs important to success in Hungary by interviewing a separate sample of 30 Hungarian managers. The 91 participating managers then, via a grouping technique, individually selected the ten constructs that they believed were most important to the performance of their firms. Each manager then developed a cause map by a pair-wise comparison process wherein a causal direction was identified for each construct pair. The resulting causal maps were then compared across managers through a distance algorithm to identify "like-thinking" managers (i.e., managers whose judgments of "how the world works" were similar).

Priem and Rosenstein (2000) conducted a similar "content evaluation" study concerning perceived relationships between strategy-structure-environment "fit" and firm performance. This study built upon a previous study (Priem, 1994) that had found associations between 33 manufacturing firm CEOs' strategy-structure-environment "fit" judgment policies, their firms' realized fit, and their firms' performance. Priem and Rosenstein compared the judgment policies of those 33 CEOs to the judgment policies of graduating MBAs, to the judgment policies of a liberal arts graduate students (i.e., educated "lay persons"), and to the prescriptions of business level contingency theory (e.g., Miller, 1987).

This study found that the judgment policies of the graduating MBAs most closely followed the prescriptions of business level contingency theory. The judgment policies of the practicing CEOs and the liberal arts graduate students were much less consistent with the prescribed contingencies than were those of the graduating MBAs. Thus, Priem and Rosenstein (2000) showed that the prescriptions of at least one well-known organization theory are not already "obvious" to, or widely known by, practicing CEOs.

*Other promising areas for judgment research.* The studies that have been described in this section are only illustrative of the types of explorations that can be conducted via quantitative research involving strategic judgment. We now note some specific topic areas that might be particularly fruitful for study. Strategy scholars are currently pursuing some of these, while others remain "fertile fields." For example, Thomas, Gioia, and Ketchen (1997) have suggested organizational learning as a means to bridge the gap between managerial cognition and organizational action. Top managers' judgments in filtering information provided to them by organizational members, or in how best to incorporate feedback loops into their organizations' designs, could contribute to building this bridge.

Social and ethical issues also could benefit from study via managerial judgments and their influences on strategic decisions. Ethical judgment is a key aspect of strategic leadership (e.g., Andrews, 1971; Hosmer, 1994). Studies of strategic judgment could help us to better understand the antecedents and perceived consequences of illegal, unethical, or simply unpopular corporate actions (e.g., Baucus and Near, 1991; Daboub et al., 1995; Frooman, 1997; Worrell, Davidson, and Sharma, 1991).

Organizational structure and control are vital aspects of strategy implementation (Amburgey and Dacin, 1994; Chandler, 1962). Information about the judgments managers make concerning appropriate relationships among organizational levels and functions, and about the flexibility/control required in their organizations, could improve our understanding of the relationships between organizational structure and optimal performance.

The final area we suggest as being of particular interest for study via managerial judgment is the leadership of international firms. Judgment-related cognitions studies could improve our understanding of national cultures and biases (Hofstede, 1980; Kim and Nam, 1998), role conflicts facing top executives in international ventures (Shneker and Zeira, 1992), the tacit knowledge of international managers (Athanassiou and Nigh, 1999), and the relative importance of economic, political, social and cultural factors on "mode of entry" decisions for foreign investments (Tse, Pan, and Au, 1997).

This "laundry list" of promising research areas is not intended to be exhaustive. Instead, we hope it gives a sense of the range of important strategic leadership issues that could be studied effectively through judgment related cognitions research.

## Accessing executives

Top executives are the most knowledgeable sources of information about their firms and strategies (Norburn and Birley, 1988), and are "key informants" regarding the processes used to craft those strategies (Kumar, Stern, and Anderson, 1993). Some studies have attempted to infer CEO judgments through, for example, content analysis of the letters to shareholders that appear in annual reports (e.g., Barr, Stimpert, and Huff, 1992). Such approaches have potential shortcomings similar to those identified by critics of demographics-based studies (e.g., Pettigrew, 1992; Priem, Lyon, and Dess, 1999). "Arms length," artifact-based analyses are useful for validating other, more direct methods. Used alone, however, the risk of misinterpretation in such studies is high, particularly given the early stage of cognitions-based research on strategic leadership. We believe that primary data, gathered via direct contacts with executives, are far preferable for determining the cognitive processes of individual executives.

Organizational researchers face many obstacles, however, when contemplating the direct study of top managers. One is access. Executives, while extremely visible, are often assumed to be difficult to access due to the demands on their time (Mintzberg, 1973); the possible organizational "gatekeepers" whose job it is to guard the executives' time (Thomas, 1993); or a reluctance by executives to discuss proprietary operating strategies (D'Aveni, 1995).

Researchers have suggested ways to overcome barriers to access. These include: contact through industry, trade, or professional groups; university contact with visiting professors and alumnae (Thomas, 1993); and personal and professional contacts (Hirsch, 1995). Some researchers have found the salience of the research topic, particularly when framed to appeal to "hot topics" relevant to the executive, to be especially useful in gaining access to executives (Heberlein and Baumgartner, 1978; Yeager and Kram, 1990). And, anthropology researchers have provided considerable insight and "how to" information on the study of "elite" groups (Hertz and Imber, 1995).

Our experience is that a salient topic, an introductory letter promising results that will show how the executive's firm compares to similar firms on that topic, phone calls several days later to schedule a short meeting, aggressive follow-up phone calls to get through gatekeepers, a second letter to non-respondents, and a willingness to meet "anywhere, anytime," combine to produce success in accessing CEOs of medium-sized (i.e., $10 million to $1 billion annual sales) manufacturing firms. Response rates for the multiple studies of CEOs we have performed have all been between 30 percent and 40 percent. Over 50 percent of the CEOs actually reached by phone agreed to participate.[7]

A second set of obstacles is presented after the researcher gains access. How can the needed information be obtained? Executives often have an established rhetoric designed to craft answers to questions in a consistent manner (Eccles and Nohria, 1992; Useem, 1995), or offer politically acceptable answers that do not reflect the way things "really are" (Brunsson, 1989). In some cases, the desired information may reflect tacit knowledge (Polyani, 1961) of which the executives themselves may not be fully aware.

Behavioral simulation (Gis, Hopper, and Daniels, 1998) involving the decomposition methods of data analysis (Arkes and Hammond, 1986; Priem and Harrison, 1994) offers one solution. These techniques can "decompose" judgment policies from a series of choices even if the participants are not fully aware of their own rules for judgment.

Moreover, the consistency of an *individual* respondent's judgment policies can be evaluated statistically, so those who made random or inconsistent judgments can be identified. When composition methods or qualitative methods are used, however, direct contact with the executives, close questioning and a healthy dose of skepticism may be the best ways to identify possible misinformation.

## CONCLUSION

We have argued that – excluding simple good fortune – sound strategic judgment is an essential quality for effective business strategists. Yet our review of several areas of strategic management research has suggested that the strategic judgments of top managers have been studied infrequently. There are serious gaps in our understanding of how and what strategic judgments are made by executives (i.e., their process and content), and of the effects such judgments might have on the strategies and operations of the firm. These gaps may be hampering (1) our understanding of CEOs and other upper echelon managers, and (2) our ability to offer meaningful prescription. "Rely on good luck" is not substantive advice.

Yet, the gaps in current knowledge also highlight the potential for strategic judgment research to aid academics in building strategy theory and to aid practitioners in making strategic decisions. An improved academic understanding of effective strategy process and content judgments in particular contexts likely will produce highly salient and practicable prescriptions – a fundamental goal of strategic management (Meyer, 1991). And, the further we move toward establishing a research foundation on strategic judgment, the better prepared we will be to evaluate its more creative aspects.

Research methods are available that may be applied in a variety of strategic judgment arenas. With patience and creativity, executives can be accessed for research, and might even participate with gusto! Our knowledge of strategic judgment can be extended most effectively through direct contact with strategic managers. Proxy-based research has shown us that top managers *are* important to firm outcomes. We agree with Markóczy (1997), however, that strategic leadership scholars now must move beyond proxies and into judgment-based research.

We urge that strategic judgment receives additional research attention. Field research on judgment, with its unfamiliar issues and methods, is not likely to be as effortless or as "clean" as proxy research using established methods and secondary data. Mistakes will be made. Research designs addressing new questions in new ways will not be as elegant as are those for incremental research. Thus, some colleagues may not accept field research on judgment quite as easily as they would more proxy research. The payoff, however, could be a much better knowledge (1) of the strategist's "art" in Alexander Pope's sense of a learned skill, and (2) ultimately of the strategist's "art" in the modern sense of creativity or strategic "genius." The reward is worth the effort.

## NOTES

1  In the English of the sixteenth through the early eighteenth centuries, "'nature' meant that which is born in a man–that is, natural ability; art was that which came with study and training. 'Art' thus meant technical skill. Today the word 'artist' implies also a touch of genius, and is confined chiefly to experts in painting, sculpture, music, literature and acting. In Shakespeare's time an artist was a skilled craftsman" (Harrison, 1968: 1642). Effective strategic leaders in our time likely posses both technical skill and "a touch of genius."

2  The Muses were nine Greek goddesses, daughters of Zeus, who presided over the arts. This led to the idea of a metaphysical "muse" who provides "the inspiration that motivates a poet, artist, thinker, or the like" (*Random House-Webster's College Dictionary*, 1991; all subsequent definitions are from this dictionary edition unless otherwise indicated).

3  This definition is from the *Merriam–Webster Dictionary* 2000 at www.m–w.com. M–W lists the following words as *synonyms*, yet does a particularly good job showing how they relate *differently* to one another. "SENSE, COMMON SENSE, JUDGMENT, and WISDOM mean ability to reach intelligent conclusions. SENSE implies a reliable ability to judge and decide with soundness, prudence, and intelligence <a choice showing good sense>. COMMON SENSE suggests an average degree of such ability without sophistication or special knowledge <common sense tells me it's wrong>. JUDGMENT implies sense tempered and refined by experience, training, and maturity <they relied on her judgment for guidance>. WISDOM implies sense and judgment far above average <a leader of rare wisdom>.

4  For an accessible introduction to Alderson's theory, including a discussion of supportive empirical results from industrial organization economics, see Priem (1992). Priem, Rasheed, and Amirani (1997) compare Porter's "value chain" concept with Alderson's "transvection."

5  It is interesting that the "no rules for riches" discussion has taken place in part in the RBV literature, with its quite reasonable assumption of inter-firm *heterogeneity* of resources, skills and ideas. It might be that there can be no "forever rules" for sustainable riches – sooner or later, great innovations will be widely adopted (e.g., the "Fosbury flop" in high jumping). Yet at any point in time, the existence of rules for advantage seems assured.

6  We have found Louviere (1988) and Hair, Anderson, and Tatham (1987) particularly cogent and accessible regarding metric conjoint analysis and non-metric conjoint analysis, respectively.

7  Flexibility and persistence are paramount. I interviewed the CEO of a $500 million sorting equipment manufacturer on a Saturday morning, after his jog. I have found that many CEOs are generous with their time once a meeting is scheduled. You must complete the "business" part of the meeting right away, within the allocated 20 minutes or so, to show you are serious/organized. But then, as often as not, I have been given plant tours, been introduced to others, and been engaged in discussions that extended the interaction to 1–2 hours. These CEOs typically were quite interested in the research and the research process. On the less encouraging side, I was surprised to learn from the CEO of a very small ($30 million) manufacturer, that he receives three or four requests for participation in some type of research each month! His general policy is to participate in the one he likes best each month, and relegate the others to the circular file.

## REFERENCES

Abrahamson, E. (1991). Managerial fads and fashions: The diffusion and rejection of innovations. *Academy of Management Review*, 16(3): 586–612.

Abrahamson, E. (1996). Management fashion, academic fashion, and enduring truths. *Academy of*

*Management Review*, 21(3): 616–18.

Alderson, W. (1957). *Marketing Behavior and Executive Action*. Homewood, IL: Irwin.

Alderson, W. (1965). *Dynamic Marketing Behavior*. Homewood, IL: Irwin.

Alchian, A. A., and Demsetz, H. (1972). Production, information costs, and economic organization. *American Economic Review*, 62: 777–94.

Alston, L. J., and Gillespie, W. (1989). Resource coordination and transaction costs: A framework for analyzing the firm/market boundary. *Journal of Economic Behavior and Organization*, 11(2): 191–212.

Amburgey, T. L., and Dacin, T. (1994). As the left foot follows the right? The dynamics of strategic and structural change. *Academy of Management Journal*, 37(6): 1427–52.

Andrews, K. R. (1971). *The Concept of Corporate Strategy*. Homewood, IL: Dow Jones-Irwin.

Ansoff, H. I. (1965). *Corporate Strategy*. New York: McGraw-Hill.

Argyris, C. (2000). *Flawed Advice and the Management Trap: How Managers Can Know When They're Getting Good Advice and When They're Not*. New York: Oxford University Press.

Arkes, H. R., and Hammond K. R. (eds.) (1986). *Judgment and Decision Making: An Interdisciplinary Reader*. Cambridge, UK: Cambridge University Press.

Arrow, K. J. (1962). Economic welfare and the allocation of resources for invention. In *The Rate and Direction of Inventive Activity: Economic and Social Factors*, 609–25. Princeton, NJ: Princeton University Press.

Athanassiou, N., and Nigh, D. (1999). The impact of US company internationalization on top management team advice networks: A tacit knowledge perspective. *Strategic Management Journal*, 20(1): 83–92.

Bantel, K. A., and Jackson, S. E. (1989). Top management and innovations in banking: Does the composition of the top team make a difference? *Strategic Management Journal*, 10: 107–24.

Barnard, C. I. (1938). *The Functions of the Executive*. Cambridge, MA: Harvard University Press.

Barney, J. B. (1986). Strategic factor markets: Expectations, luck, and business strategy. *Management Science*, 32: 1231–41.

Barney, J. (1991). Firm resources and sustainable competitive advantage. *Journal of Management*, 17: 99–120.

Barr, P. S., Stimpert, J. L., and Huff, A. S. (1992). Cognitive change, strategic action, and organizational renewal. *Strategic Management Journal*, 13: 15–36.

Baucus, M. S., and Near, J. P. (1991). Can illegal corporate behavior be predicted? An event history analysis. *Academy of Management Journal*, 34(1): 9–36.

Berlin, I. (1996). On political judgment. *The New York Review*: 26–30.

Bettis, R. A. (1991). Strategic management and the straightjacket: An editorial essay. *Organization Science*, 2: 315–19.

Beyer, J., Chattopadhyay, P., George, E., Glick, W. H., Ogilvie, D., and Pugliese, D. (1997). The selective perception of managers revisited. *Academy of Management Journal*, 40: 716–37.

Bostrom, A., Fischhoff, B., and Morgan, M. G. (1992). Characterizing mental models of hazardous processes: A methodology and an application to radon. *Journal of Social Issues*, 48(4): 85–100.

Bougon, M. G., Weick, K. E., and Binkhorst, D. (1977). Cognition in organizations: An analysis of the Utrecht jazz orchestra. *Administrative Science Quarterly*, 22: 606–39.

Bromiley, P., and Fleming, L. (2001). The resource based view of strategy: An evolutionist's critique. In M. Augier, and J. G. March (eds.), *The Economics of Choice, Change, and Organizations: Essays in Memory of Richard M. Cyert*. Cheltenham, UK: Edward Elgar Publishing.

Brunsson, N. (1989). *The Organization of Hypocrisy: Talk, Decisions and Actions in Organizations*. New York: John Wiley.

Busenitz, L. W., and Barney, J. B. (1997). Differences between entrepreneurs and managers in large organizations: Biases and heuristics in strategic decision-making. *Journal of Business Venturing*, 12(1): 9–30.

Calori, R., Johnson, G., and Sarnin, P. (1994). CEO's cognitive maps and the scope of the organization. *Strategic Management Journal*, 15(6): 437–57.

Castanias, R. P. and Helfat, C. E. (1991). Managerial resources and rents. *Journal of Management*, 17: 155–71.

Chandler, A. D. (1962). *Strategy and Structure*. Cambridge, MA: MIT Press.

Chattopadhyay, P., Glick, W. H., Miller, C. C., and Huber, G. P. (1999). Determinants of executive beliefs: Comparing functional conditioning and social influence. *Strategic Management Journal*, 20: 763–89.

Child, J. (1997). Strategic choice in the analysis of action, structure, organizations and environment: Retrospect and prospect. *Organizational Studies*, 18(1): 43–76.

Conner, K. R., and Prahalad, C. K. (1996). A resource-based theory of the firm: Knowledge versus opportunism. *Organization Science*, 7(5): 477–501.

Cyert, R. M., and March, J. G. (1963). *A Behavioral Theory of the Firm*. Englewood Cliffs, NJ: Prentice-Hall.

Daboub, A. J., Rasheed, A. M. A., Priem, R. L., and Gray, D. A. (1995). Top management team characteristics and corporate illegal activity. *Academy of Management Review*, 20: 138–70.

Daft, R. L., and Lewin, A. Y. (1990). Can organization studies begin to break out of the normal science straightjacket? An editorial essay. *Organization Science*, 1: 1–9.

Daft, R. L., and Weick, K. E. (1984). Toward a model of organizations as interpretation systems. *Academy of Management Review*, 9: 284–95.

Daily, C. M., Certo, S. T., and Dalton, D. R. (2000). International experience in the executive suite: The path to prosperity? *Strategic Management Journal*, 21: 515–23.

Das, T. K., and Teng, B.-S. (1999). Cognitive biases and strategic decision processes: An integrative perspective. *Journal of Management Studies*, 36(6): 757–78.

D'Aveni, R. A. (1995). *Hypercompetitive rivalries*. New York: Free Press.

D'Aveni, R. A., and MacMillan, I. C. (1990). Crisis and the content of managerial communications: A study of the focus of attention of top managers in surviving and failing firms. *Administrative Science Quarterly*, 35(4): 634–57.

Dearborn, D. C., and Simon, H. A. (1958). Selective perceptions: a note on the departmental identifications of executives. *Sociometry*, 21: 140–4.

DeSarbo, W., MacMillan, I. C., and Day, D. L. (1987). Criteria for corporate venturing: importance assigned by managers. *Journal of Business Venturing*, 2(4): 329–50.

De Vany, A. S. and Saving, T. R. (1983). The economics of quality. *Journal of Political Economy*, 91: 979–1000.

Dierickx, I., Cool, K., and Barney, J. B. (1989). Asset stock accumulation and sustainability of competitive advantage; Comment; Reply. *Management Science*, 35(12): 1504–14.

Dill, W. R. (1958). Environment as an influence on managerial autonomy. *Administrative Science Quarterly*, 2: 409–43.

Drazin, R., and Sandelands, L. (1992). Autogenesis: A perspective on the process of organizing. *Organization Science*, 3: 230–49.

Drucker, P. F. (1996). *The Executive in Action*. New York: Harper Business.

Drucker, P. F. (1999). *Management Challenges for the 21st Century*. New York: HarperCollins.

Duncan, R. (1972). Characteristics of organizational environments and perceived environmental uncertainty. *Administrative Science Quarterly*, 17(3): 313–27.

Dutton, J. E. (1983). *The Process of Strategic Issue Resolution*. Chicago: Northwestern University.

Dutton, J. E. (1986). The processing of crisis and non-crisis strategic issues. *Journal of Management Studies*, 23(5): 501–17.

Dutton, J. E., and Duncan, R. B. (1987). The creation of momentum for change through the process of strategic issue diagnosis. *Strategic Management Journal*, 8(3): 279–95.

Dutton, J. E., Fahey, L., and Narayanan, V. K. (1983). Toward understanding strategic issues diagnosis. *Strategic Management Journal*, 4: 307–23.

Dutton, J. E., and Jackson, S. E. (1987). Categorizing strategic issues: Links to organizational action. *Academy of Management Review*, 12: 76–90.

Eccles, R. G., and Nohria, N. (1992). *Beyond the Hype: Rediscovering the Essence of Management*. Boston, MA: Harvard Business School Press.

Eisenhardt, K. M. (1989). Making fast strategic decisions in high-velocity environments. *Academy of Management Journal*, 32(3): 543–76.

Eisenhardt, K. M., and Martin, J. A. (2000). Dynamic capabilities: What are they? *Strategic Management Journal*, 21(10/11): 1105–21.

Eisenhardt, K. M., and Santos, F. M. (2001). Knowledge-based view: A new theory of strategy? In A. Pettigrew, H. Thomas, and R. Whittington (eds.), *Handbook of Strategy and Management*. Thousand Oaks, CA: Sage Publications.

Eisenhardt, K. M., and Schoonhoven, C. B. (1990). Organizational growth: linking founding team, strategy, environment, and growth among US semiconductor ventures, 1978–1988. *Administrative Science Quarterly*, 35(3): 504–29.

Fahey, L., and Christensen, H. K. (1986). Evaluating the research on strategy content. *Journal of Management*, 12(2): 167–83.

Finkelstein, S., and Hambrick, D. C. (1990). Top-management-team tenure and organizational outcomes: The moderating role of managerial discretion. *Administrative Science Quarterly*, 35(3): 484–503.

Foss, N. J. (1996a). Knowledge-based approaches to the theory of the firm: Some critical comments. *Organization Science*, 7: 470–6.

Foss, N. J. (1996b). More critical comments on knowledge-based theories of the firm. *Organization Science*, 7: 519–23.

Foss, N. J. (1999). Research in the strategic theory of the firm: "Isolationism" and "integrationism." *Journal of Management Studies*, 36(6): 725–55.

Foust, D. (1999). Nucor: Meltdown in the corner office. *Business Week*, June 21: 37.

Frooman, J. (1997). Socially irresponsible and illegal behavior and shareholder wealth. *Business and Society*, 36: 221–49.

Gist, M. E., Hopper, H., and Daniels D. (1998). Behavioral simulations: Application and potential in management research. *Organizational Research Methods*, 1(3): 251–95.

Grant, R. M. (1996). Toward a knowledge-based theory of the firm. *Strategic Management Journal*, 17 (Winter Special Issue): 109–22.

Green, P.E., and Wind, Y. (1973). *Multiattribute Decisions in Marketing: A Measurement Approach*. Hinsdale, IL: Dryden.

Hair, J. F., Jr., Anderson, R. E., and Tatham, R. I. (1987). *Multivariate Data Analysis*. New York: Macmillan.

Hambrick, D. C. (1994). What if the Academy actually mattered? *Academy of Management Review*, 19(1): 11–16.

Hambrick, D. C., and Mason, P. A. (1984). Upper echelons: The organization as a reflection of its top managers. *Academy of Management Review*, 9(2): 193–206.

Harris, D., and Helfat, C. (1997). Specificity of CEO human capital and compensation. *Strategic Management Journal*, 18: 895–920.

Harrison, G. B. (ed.) (1968). *Shakespeare: The Complete Works*. New York: Harcourt, Brace and World.

Heberlein, T. A., and Baumgartner, R. (1978). Factors affecting response rates to mailed questionnaires: A quantitative analysis of published literature. *American Sociological Review*, 43: 447–62.

Hertz, R., and Imber, J. B. (eds.) (1995). *Studying Elites using Qualitative Methods*, Thousand Oaks, CA: Sage Publications.

Hirsch, P. M. (1995). Tales from the field: Learning from researchers' accounts. In R. Hertz, and J. B. Imber (eds.), *Studying Elites Using Qualitative Methods*. Thousand Oaks, CA: Sage: 72–79.

Hitt, M. A., and Barr, S. H. (1989). Managerial selection decision models: Examination of configural cue processing. *Journal of Applied Psychology*, 74: 53–61.

Hitt, M. A., and Tyler, B. B. (1991). Strategic decision models: integrating different perspectives. *Strategic Management Journal*, 12(5): 327–51.

Hoffman, P. J., Slovic, P., and Rorer, L. G. (1968). An analysis of variance model for the assessment of configural cue utilization in clinical judgment. *Psychological Bulletin*, 69: 338–49.

Hofstede, G. (1980). *Culture's Consequences: International Differences in Work-related Values*. Beverly Hills, CA: Sage.

Hosmer, L. T. (1994). Strategic planning as if ethics mattered. *Strategic Management Journal*, 15: 17–34.

Huff, A. S. (1982). Industry influences on strategy reformulation. *Strategic Management Journal*, 3(2): 119–31.

Huff, A. S. (1990). *Mapping Strategic Thought*. New York: Wiley.

Hunt, S. D. (1997). Resource-advantage theory: An evolutionary theory of competitive behavior? *Journal of Economic Issues*, 31(1): 59–77.

Hunt, S. D. (1999). The strategic imperative and sustainable competitive advantage: Public policy implications of resource-advantage theory. *Journal of the Academy of Marketing Science*, 28(2): 133–59.

Hunt, S. D. (2000). *A General Theory of Competition: Resources, Competences, Productivity, Economic Growth (Marketing for a New Century)*. Thousand Oaks, CA: Sage Publications.

Katz, D., and Kahn, R. L. (1978). *The Social Psychology of Organizations*, 2nd edn. New York: Wiley.

Keck, S. L. (1997). Top management team structure: Differential effects by environmental context. *Organization Science*, 8(2): 143–56.

Kim, J. Y., and Nam, S. H. (1998). The concept and dynamics of face: Implications for organizational behavior in Asia. *Organization Science*, 9: 522–34.

Kogut, B., and Zander, U. (1993). Knowledge of the firm and the evolutionary theory of the multinational corporation. *Journal of International Business Studies*, 24(4): 625–45.

Kogut, B., and Zander, U. (1996). What firms do? Coordination, identity, and learning. *Organization Science*, 7(5): 502–18.

Kumar, N., Stern, L. W., and Anderson, J. C. (1993). Conducting interorganizational research using key informants. *Academy of Management Journal*, 36(6): 33–51.

Lawrence, B. S. (1997). The black box of organizational demography. *Organization Science*, 8(1): 1–22.

Learned, E. P., Christensen, C. R., Andrews, K. R., and Guth, W. P. (1965). *Business Policy: Text and Cases*. Homewood, IL: Irwin.

Lee, A. S. (1991). Integrating positivist and interpretive approaches to organizational research. *Organizational Science*, 2: 342–65.

Louviere, J. J. (1988). *Analyzing Decision Making: Metric Conjoint Analysis*. Sage University Paper Series on Quantitative Applications in the Social Sciences, 67. Beverly Hills, CA: Sage Publications.

Markóczy, L. (1997). Measuring beliefs: Accept no substitutes. *Academy of Management Journal*, 40: 1128–42.

Markóczy, L., and Goldberg, J. (1995). A method for eliciting and comparing causal maps. *Journal of Management*, 21(2): 305–33.

Martin, J. (1992). *Cultures in Organizations: Three Perspectives*. New York: Oxford University Press.

McKelvey, B. (1982). *Organization systematics: Taxonomy, Evolution, Classification*. Berkeley: University of California Press.

McKelvey, B. (1997). Quasi-natural organization science. *Organization Science*, 8: 352–80.

McWilliams, A., and Smart, D. L. (1993). Efficiency v. structure-conduct-performance: Implications for strategy research and practice. *Journal of Management*, 19(1): 63–78.

Meindl, J. R., Stubbart, C., and Porac, J. F. (1996). *Cognition within and between organizations*. Thousand Oaks, CA: Sage.

Melone, N .P. (1994). Reasoning in the executive suite: The influence of role/experience based expertise on decision processes of corporate executives. *Organization Science*, 5: 438–55.

Meyer, A. D. (1991). What is strategy's distinctive competence? *Journal of Management*, 17(4): 821–33.

Michel, J. G., and Hambrick, D. C. (1992). Diversification posture and top management team characteristics. *Academy of Management Journal*, 35(1): 9–37.

Miles, R. E., and Snow, C. C. (1978). *Organization Strategy, Structure, and Process*. New York: McGraw-Hill.

Miller, D. (1987). The genesis of configuration. *Academy of Management Review*, 12(4): 686–701.

Milliken, F. J. (1990). Perceiving and interpreting environmental changes: An examination of college administrators' interpretation of changing demographics. *Academy of Management Journal*, 33: 42–63.

Miner, J. B. (1997). Participating in profound change. *Academy of Management Journal*, 40: 1420–28.

Mintzberg, H. (1973). *The Nature of Managerial Work*. New York: Harper and Row.

Mintzberg, H., Ahlstrand, B., and Lampel, J. (1998). *Strategy Safari: A Guided Tour through the Wilds of Strategic Management*. New York: Free Press.

Mintzberg, H., and Waters, J. A. (1985). Of strategies, deliberate and emergent. *Strategic Management Journal*, 6: 257–72.

Mohammed, S., Klimoski, R., and Reutsch, J. R. (2000). The measurement of team mental models: We have no shared schema. *Organizational Research Methods*, 3(2): 123–65.

Morris, B., and Sellers, P. (2000). What really happened at Coke. *Fortune*, January 10:114.

Mosakowski, E. (1998). Managerial prescriptions under the resource-based view of strategy: The example of motivational techniques. *Strategic Management Journal*, 19(12): 1169–82.

Mowday, R. T. (1997). Celebrating 40 years of the *Academy of Management Journal*. *Academy of Management Journal*, 40: 1400–13.

Murray, A. I. (1989). Top management group heterogeneity and firm performance. *Strategic Management Journal*, 10: 125.

Norburn, D. (1986). GOGOs, YOYOs and DODOs: Company directors and industry performance. *Strategic Management Journal*, 7(2): 101–17.

Norburn, D., and Birley, S. (1988). The top management team and corporate performance. *Strategic Management Journal*, 9(3): 225–37.

Numagami, T. (1998). The infeasibility of invarient laws in management studies: A reflective dialogue in defense of case studies. *Organization Science*, 9: 2–15.

Pellet, J. (1997). Our dinner with Henry. *Chief Executive*, 120: 34–9.

Penrose, E. T. (1959). *The Theory of the Growth of the Firm*. New York: Wiley.

Pettigrew, A. M. (1992). On studying managerial elites. *Strategic Management Journal* (Winter Special Issue) 13: 163–82.

Pfeffer, J. (1983). Organizational Demography. In L. L. Cummings, and B. M. Staw (eds.), *Research in Organizational Behavior*, 299–357. Greenwich, CT: JAI Press.

Phillips, M. E. (1994). Industry mindsets: Exploring the cultures of two macro-organizational settings. *Organization Science*, 4(3): 384–402.

Polanyi, M. (1961). *The tacit dimension*. Garden City, NJ: Doubleday.

Poppo, L., and Zenger, T. (1998). Testing alternative theories of the firm: Transaction cost, knowledge-based, and measurement explanations for make-or-buy decisions in information services. *Strategic Management Journal*, 19: 853–877.

Porter, M. E. (1980). *Competitive strategy: Techniques for analyzing industries and competitors*. New York: Free Press.

Priem, R. L. (1992). Industrial organizational economics and Alderson's general theory of marketing. *Journal of the Academy of Marketing Science*, 20: 135–141.

Priem, R. L. (1994). Executive judgment, organizational congruence, and firm performance.

*Organization Science*, 5: 421–437.

Priem, R. L., and Butler, J. E. (2001a). Is the resource-based "view" a useful perspective for strategic management research? *Academy of Management Review*, 26(1): 22–24.

Priem, R. L., and Butler, J. E. (2001b). Tautology in the resource–based view and the implications of externally determined resource value: Further comments. *Academy of Management Review*, 26(1): 57–66.

Priem, R. L., and Harrison, D. A. (1994). Exploring strategic judgment: Methods for testing the assumptions of prescriptive contingency theories. *Strategic Management Journal*, 15: 311–24.

Priem, R. L., Love, L. G., and Shaffer, M. (1999). Executive perceptions of environmental uncertainty sources: A taxonomy and underlying dimensions. *Academy of Management Best Papers Proceedings*.

Priem, R. L., Lyon, D. W., and Dess, G. G. (1999). Inherent limitations of demographic proxies in top management team heterogeneity research. *Journal of Management*, 25: 935–53.

Priem, R. L., Rasheed, A. M. A., and Amirani, S. (1997). Alderson's transvection and Porter's value chain: A comparison of two independently developed theories. *Journal of Management History*, 3: 145–65.

Priem, R. L., and Rosenstein, J. (2000). Is organization theory obvious to practitioners? A test of one established theory. *Organization Science*, 11(5): 509–24.

Rajagopalan, N., Rasheed, M. A., and Datta, D.K. (1993). Strategic decision processes: Critical review and future directions. *Journal of Management*, 19: 349–84.

Reger, R. K. (1997). Strategic leadership: Top executives and their effects on organizations. *Academy of Management Review*, 22(3): 802–5.

Reger, R. K., and Huff, A. S. (1993). Strategic groups: A cognitive perspective. *Strategic Management Journal*, 14: 103–23.

Rumelt, R. P., Schendel, D., and Teece, D. J. (1991). Strategic management and economics. *Strategic Management Journal*, 12(3): 167–85.

Ryall, M. D. (1999). When competencies are not core: Self-confirming theories and the destruction of firm value. University of Rochester working paper, Version RO4G.

Schlender, B. (2000). Steve Jobs' Apple gets way cooler. *Fortune*, January 24: 66.

Schwenk, C. R. (1988). The cognitive perspective on strategic decision making. *Journal of Management Studies*, 25: 41–55.

Shneker, O., and Zeira, Y. (1992). Role conflict and role ambiguity of chief executive officers in international joint ventures. *Journal of International Business Studies*, 23(1): 55–75.

Simon, H. A. (1957). *Administrative behavior*. New York: Macmillan.

Simon, H. (1989). Making management decisions: The role of intuition and emotion. In W. Agor (ed.), *Intuition in Organizations: Leading and Managing Productively*, 23–39. Newbury Park, CA: Sage.

Slocum, J. W., Jr. (1997). Unlearning to learn. *Academy of Management Journal*, 40(6): 1429–31.

Smith, K. G., Smith, K. A., Olian, J. D., Sims, H. P., Jr., O'Bannon, D. P., and Scully, J. (1994). Top management team demography and process: The role of social integration and communication. *Administrative Science Quarterly*, 39(3): 412–38.

Spender, J. C. (1989). *Industry Recipes: An Enquiry into the Nature and Sources of Managerial Judgment*. Cambridge, MA: Basil Blackwell.

Sternberg, R. J., Wagner, R. K., Williams, W. M., and Horvath, J. A. (1995). Testing common sense. *American Psychologist*, 50(11): 912–27.

Stevens, T. (1997). Deja blue. *Industry Week*, 246(21): 82–8.

Stimpert, J .L. (1999). Review: Managerial and organizational cognition. *Academy of Management Review*, 24(2): 360–2.

Swan, J., and Newell, S. (1998). Making sense of technological innovation: The political and social dynamics of cognition. In C. Eden and J. C. Spender (eds.), *Managerial and Organizational Cognition: Theory, Methods, and Research*, 108–29. London: Sage.

Teece, D. J., Pisano, G., and Shuen, A. (1997). Dynamic capabilities and strategic management. *Strategic Management Journal*, 18(7): 509–33.

Thomas, R. J. (1993). Interviewing important people in big companies. *Journal of Contemporary Ethnography*, 22(1): 80–96.

Thomas, J. B., Gioia, D. A., and Ketchen, D. J., Jr. (1997). Strategic sense-making: Learning through scanning, interpretation, action, and performance. In J. P. Walsh and A. S. Huff (eds), *Advances in Strategic Management*, Volume 14, 299–329. Greenwich, CT: JAI Press.

Tse, D. K., Pan, Y., and Au, K. Y. (1997). How MNCs choose entry modes and form alliances: The China experience. *Journal of International Business Studies*, 28(4): 779–805.

Tversky, A., and Kahnemann, D. (1974). Judgement under uncertainty: Heuristics and biases. *Science*, 185: 1124–31.

Useem, M. (1995). Reaching corporate executives. In R. Hertz and J. B. Imber (eds.), *Studying Elites Using Qualitative Methods*. Thousand Oaks, CA: Sage: 18–39.

Vickers, G. (1965. *The Art of Judgment: A Study of Policy Making*. Thousand Oaks, CA: Sage.

Walsh, J. P. (1988). Selectivity and selective perception: An investigation of managers' belief structures and information processing. *Academy of Management Journal*, 31: 873–96.

Walsh, J. P. (1995). Managerial and organizational cognition: Notes from a trip down memory lane. *Organization Science*, 6(3): 280–321.

Walters, B. A., Priem, R. L., and Shook, C. (2001). Business strategy and chief executive scanning. Louisiana Tech University working paper.

Wernerfelt, B. (1984). A resource-based view of the firm. *Strategic Management Journal*, 5: 171–80.

Wiersema, M. F., and Bantel, K. (1992). Top management team demography and corporate strategic change. *Academy of Management Journal*, 35: 91–121.

Williamson, O. E. (1979). Transaction-cost economics: The governance of contractual relations. *Journal of Law and Economics*, 22: 233–61.

Worrell, D. L., Davidson, W. N., and Sharma, J. G. (1991). Layoff announcements and stockholder wealth. *Academy of Management Journal*, 34: 662–78.

Yeager, P. C., and Kram, K. E. (1990). Fielding hot topics in cool settings: The study of corporate elites. *Qualitative Sociology*, 13(2): 127–48.

# 18

# Organizational Structure: Looking Through a Strategy Lens

## BARBARA KEATS AND HUGH M. O'NEILL

At the beginning of the 21st century the world of commerce has provided glimpses of radically new concepts for organization, and begs the questions of critical factors for success for differing types of organization structures. These questions, and more importantly their answers, form the heart of the field of strategic management. Academic research in this field of investigation emerged only in the last quarter of the 20th century. Thus, the field is still quite young, and in search of a body of foundational knowledge.

Research in strategic management has its foundations in a number of disciplines. One of these is organization theory.[1] Both strategic management and organization theory seek to understand why some organizations thrive while others falter and fail. In organization theory, a primary construct is organizational effectiveness. Organization theory researchers worked to identify contingency factors (if-then statements) and "imperatives," suggesting that organizational effectiveness would be strongly affected by relationships among technology, environmental characteristics and organizational structure (the concept of "fit"). Similarly, the earliest critical questions in strategic management also reflected interest in finding "contingencies" and "imperatives" (i.e., are there strategic characteristics of high performance firms that distinguish them from low performance firms?) including the role of organization structure in producing profits (similar but somewhat different from "effectiveness"). In this chapter, we examine the research in organization theory that informs strategic management research, and the strategic management research that follows from it.[2]

## EARLY CONCEPTS IN STRUCTURE

Weber's promulgation of the concept of *bureaucracy* (written about 1910, see 1978 translation) provides one of the earliest articulations about the important role of organizational structure. Although the term "bureaucracy" has taken on a pejorative mantle in recent decades, Weber's notions of structure replaced the concept of position and privilege based on birthright and social power with the concept of position and privilege based on competence and professionalism. Weber's "ideal bureaucracy" became the model for professional organizations in the 20th century. The concept of bureaucracy borrowed from traditional roles and relationships defined in military organizations: line versus staff functions.

An organization formed on Weberian principles would exhibit stable job titles that existed independently of the incumbent, clear lines of authority and communication (centralization and hierarchy), authority commensurate with responsibility, division of labor and tenure (to avoid capricious hiring/firing). Those in "line" positions held the authority to take and implement decisions directly related to the organization's production, while staff functions were advisory in nature. The functional[3] organizational structure, which became the dominant organization structural form in most developed economies, emerged from Weber's theories.

Prior to World War I, most business organizations in developed countries were relatively small, often dominated by the founder (or his shadow) and were usually focused on one or two primary products. In the early 1900s, the concepts of scientific management dominated thoughts about structure. This meant that virtually all planning and decision making took place at the "top" of the hierarchy so that behavior and operations at lower levels was specified in detail in advance. Structures were designed based on rather simple rules, such as "keep the span of control to about six." This way of thinking yielded the notion that there was "one best way" to structure an organization regardless of context.

## *The emergence of contingency theory*

In the wake of increasing globalization in the aftermath of the two world wars, the relatively small, focused organization model began to give way to larger organizations with expanding product lines engaged in diverse markets. Additionally, the economies of developed nations became increasingly complex and interdependent. These factors led to the emergence of many new organizational forms. As strategies evolved and changed, so did the structures through which the strategies were realized.

Organization theory scholars took note when firms that participated in the same industries or markets had different performance records. Seeking explanations for these differences, researchers examined various organizational attributes.

The "orthodoxy consensus" (Atkinson, 1971) emerging at the time was grounded in functionalism and "normal science" (Kuhn, 1970). The former assumes that organizations are systems that are functionally effective to the extent they achieve specific goals through rational decision making. The latter asserts that a researcher's task is to collect objective data regarding the way the organization functions around this goal orientation using formal research designs and quantitative data models. Thus, all organizational attributes tended to be defined and measured in ways consistent with these assumptions.[4]

One of the attributes researchers began to examine was organizational structure (see table 18.1 for a summary). Burns and Stalker (1961) provided one means to classify structure. These researchers considered structure in terms of the degree to which the organization exhibited high or low levels of centralization of authority, formalized policy statements and ironclad patterns of communication and reporting relationship. Those that exhibited high levels of these characteristics were considered "mechanistic," while

TABLE 18.1 Summary of the structural imperatives

| Author | Imperative | Implication |
| --- | --- | --- |
| Burns and Stalker | Environment | Mechanistic or organic form, depending on turbulence in environment |
| Woodward | Technology | Structural form related to the technology: unit, batch or mass |
| Lawrence and Lorsch | Environment | Structural differentiation related to complexity of environment; integration as important as differentiation |
| Thompson | Encvironment and technology | Organizational core matched to requirement of technology; boundary spanning units matched to environment |
| Chandler | Strategy | Pattern of growth determines structural form |

those that exhibited lower levels were considered "organic," terminology that remains in use. This view of structure provided a means to study an important source of variation in effectiveness.

Joan Woodward (1965), based on measures of structural attributes such as span of control, number of levels in the hierarchy and ratio of direct to indirect labor, suggested that effective firms were those whose structure "fit" their technology. Within mass production (or "routine") type technologies, the most effective firms were those that also employed what Burns and Stalker called a mechanistic type of structure. Within customized (or "nonroutine") technologies, successful firms were those that employed an organic type of structure, because the types of tasks they had to manage were quite different. This led to the assertion of a "technological imperative" for organizational structure.

Woodward's research was limited to 100 firms in England, but it touched a nerve and inspired other researchers to examine the "fit" questions across a number of different organizational situations, including many who favored the search for "imperatives." Woodward and Burns and Stalker all speculated that inevitable impending technological change would force structural change. They sought to focus managers' attention on the nature of this relationship and stressed the potential for inefficiencies inherent in structural inertia.

Lawrence and Lorsch (1967) proposed an environmental imperative, and suggested two critical structural dimensions: differentiation and integration. Differentiation (differences across structural and/or functional subunits) reflected the organization's response to the complexity of its environment. Integration reflected the degree to which the organization coordinated all the various subunits. The most effective firms were those that differentiated to the extent required by the environment, and developed rational processes (such as hierarchy, rules, task forces, interdepartmental committees and teams) to integrate the differentiated functions.

James Thompson (1967) provides perhaps the single most enduring work on the issues of structure, technology and the environment. He suggested that managers have preferences about how the world should function. These preferences, based on managerial cognitions, influence decisions about how to structure organizations. For example, according to Thompson, managers tend to favor the "closed system" view of scientific management in which the elements of organizational activity are controllable and predictable. They may try to gain a sense of control by behaving as if the organization is, indeed, a closed system (e.g., in the measures they use to assess effectiveness). However, managers actually live in the context of an open system that interjects uncertainty and unpredictably into organizational activities. Thus, the "picture" of the organization we see is an amalgam of the impact of the uncertainty and unpredictability imposed by the environment and managers' attempts to create a predictable, controllable internal system.

The result of this amalgam is an organization formed with a technical core at the "center," and boundary-spanning managers protecting that core by absorbing uncertainty from the environment before it reaches the core. The internal structural complexity of an effective organization is, in Thompson's view, a function of both its technology and its environment, and the degree to which managers recognize and resist their inclination towards closed system thinking.

Thompson anticipated the interest in the increasing diversification of large firms by including some of the work of Alfred Chandler (1962, below) as a basis for proposing how a firm's product/market strategy impacts structure. Thompson argued that product/market domain selection, together with choice of technology, determined the points at which the organization would be dependent on others for its key resources. Those points in turn determine the power–dependence relationships between the focal organization and others in the domain. Firms manage these relationships by designing structures to exploit distinctive competencies and control critical dependencies. Hence, firms tend to grow by incorporating into their internal structure those elements of the external environment that represent critical contingencies for what Thompson calls "fitness for the future," or effectiveness. So, for example, in an environment where mass consumer marketing is a critical requirement for success, firms would include a strong marketing department, and may "coopt" market research or consulting firms into their structure. Similarly, in an environment where parts supply is critical to maintaining an efficient production line, firms would vertically integrate to increase their control. A source of tension for managers, then, is the impact of uncertainty on their intendedly rational structures. A difficulty for researchers is that managers, reacting in uncertain ways to partially perceived environments, create a gap between "messy" reality and the orderly assumptions of functionalism and normal science.

## Structure and strategic management

The domain of organization theory intersected with the emerging field of strategic management through the work of business historian Alfred Chandler (1962).[5] In his study

of several large American firms, Chandler formulated hypotheses that stimulated generations of subsequent strategic management research. He proposed that patterns in organizational structure follow the growth pattern of the organization. He observed that in the
postwar world of business expansion, firms tended to grow in somewhat predictable
stages: first by volume, then by geography, then integration (vertical, horizontal) and
finally through product/business diversification.

In general, firms appeared to attempt implementation of these new strategies while
continuing to employ traditional structural forms (the functional, primarily bureaucratic

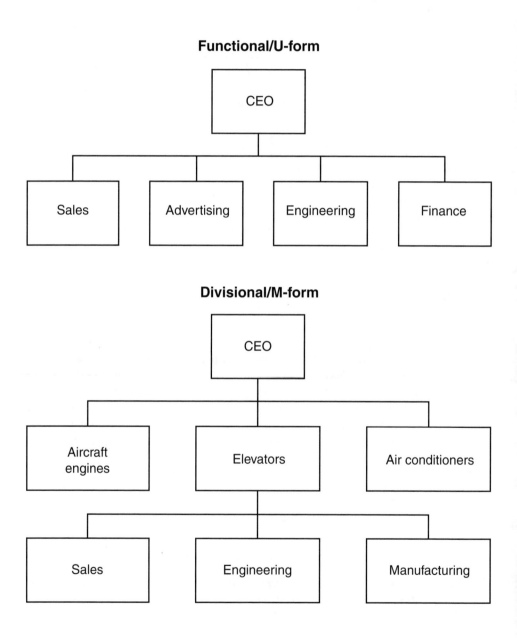

## Matrix form

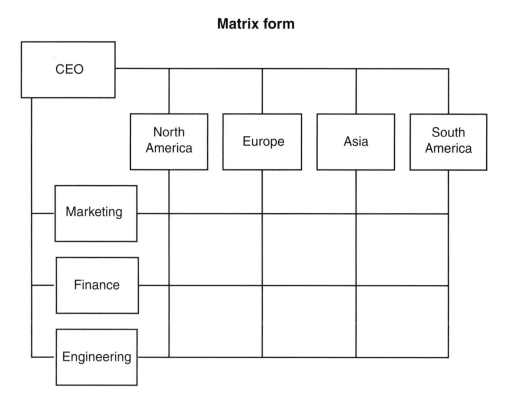

FIGURE 18.1 Structural forms

forms mentioned above). However, Chandler noted new structural forms emerging as diversification increased. He concluded that business expansion overtaxed the administrative capacity of functional organizational forms, resulting in negative financial outcomes. The administrative and financial pressures led to the development of new structural forms such as the multidivisional form (M-form, discussed below) that created several groupings (based on geography or product, for example) and SBUs (strategic business units, which were essentially collections of divisions related in some way). His conclusion was that structure follows strategy because organizations would not change their structures (the *status quo*) unless provoked by inefficiency to do so. In an "imperative" or contingency theory form, Chandler's thesis would read "strategy dictates structure" (if you want to be successful).

Williamson (1975) hypothesized an information imperative for organizational form. His M-form hypothesis suggests that large diversified enterprises are not efficiently served by organizing along functional lines (which he labeled as U-form). He proposed that due to limitations on rationality (Simon, 1961), information impactedness and individual opportunism, diversified product flows through functional divisions place heavy demands for control and coordination on functional units. The M-form substitutes quasi-autonomous operating divisions organized primarily along product, brand or geographic lines for the untenable U-form structure. Burton and Obel (1980) also concluded that the M-form is most appropriate when growth is accomplished through diversification.

Increases in the size and complexity of organizations spawned more complex structures. The matrix structure, a hybrid form that mixes U-form and M-form characteristics, was originally designed to manage large projects that required project teams drawn from a variety of functional areas. The distinctive characteristic of the matrix is its twin axis form, representing dual reporting relationships (see figure 18.1). The twin axes of the matrix could represent different business units and functions (an option popular with technology firms), or different geographic regions and functions (an option frequently adopted by multinationals). For example, a manufacturer of commercial aircraft might employ a different project team for each model of aircraft. Each team has members from various functional areas with reporting relationships to both the project director and their functional vice-president. In another setting, a European sales person might report both to the divisional head for Europe (the geographic axis) and the head of sales at world headquarters (the functional axis). In effect, then, the matrix provides the advantage of flexibility in response to regional or product differences, with the scale and professionalism of worldwide functional expertise. There are potential hazards in creating such dual-reporting relationships, particularly if lines of authority, accountability and responsibility are not clear.

Many large and complex organizations adopt multiple forms of structures. So, for example, one national office for a globalized firm might be organized within its region as a matrix, while at the same time serving as part of worldwide divisional structure. Similarly, organizations also customize general forms to their specific needs. So, an M-form organization in a firm following a conglomerate strategy (that is, a collection of unrelated business) might choose a different method for division-corporate reporting relationships than an M-form organization following a related strategy. Hoskisson, Hill, and Kim (1993) refer to the M-form for a conglomerate as a competitive M-form, and the M-form for a related diversifier as a cooperative M-form. There seemed to be a meaningful correspondence between strategy type and structural form.

*Strategy/structure: the empirical search.*   Wrigley (1970) conducted an initial investigation of Chandler's thesis. His survey of 1967's *Fortune* 500 companies built on Chandler's work by recognizing that diversification might occur in a variety of ways. He developed a system of four categories based on a firm's product-market scope and diversification rationale. These categories included: (1) single product (not diversified), (2) dominant product (primarily committed to a single product which accounted for more than 70 percent of sales but diversified to a small degree), (3) related product (a firm expanded into new areas that were related in some fashion to current activity), and (4) unrelated product (diversified without regard to maintaining such relationships). Wrigley's results indicated that diversification had become a widely accepted strategy by 1967, and the multidivisional structure appeared to have followed the choice of strategy, as diversified firms (related and unrelated) adopted M-form structures.

Rumelt's (1974) landmark study examined a number of issues related to Wrigley and Chandler's work. Rumelt did away with the "product" notion and turned instead to a consideration of the relationships among discrete businesses within the corporation. He subdivided the four main category headings (single, dominant, related and unrelated) into a nine category system: single business; dominant vertical, dominant constrained, dominant linked and dominant unrelated; related constrained, related linked; unrelated passive, unrelated conglomerate. Rumelt assigned firms to one of the four main categories (single, dominant, related, unrelated) on the basis of percentage of total sales attributable to one discrete business, and then to a subcategory based on the kinds of linkages among the businesses. The firm's linkages could be based on any of a number of possible related strengths, such as production skills, marketing skills, or channel dominance.

Rumelt's results supported both Chandler's and Wrigley's assertions about increasing diversification. However, the results did not provide clear evidence of a causal relationship between strategy and divisionalization of structure – in either direction. Rumelt concluded that while diversification and divisionalization were clearly linked in the 1950s, the link was less clear in the 1960s, although both trends continued unabated (1974: 77). Thus, it was difficult to make any assertions regarding strategic contingencies or imperatives.

Some economists thought perhaps the relationships between strategy and structure and performance might be moderated by competition. No clear evidence emerged to support this view. Williamson (1970, 1975) challenged many traditional economists' views of prices and markets (the "invisible hand" of competition) as the primary institutions through which efficient economic transactions could take place. He argued that under circumstances characterized by uncertainty, differentially distributed information and opportunism, the invisible hand does not function efficiently, and internal hierarchies function more efficiently than external markets. As firms become more diversified, and larger and more complex, and management becomes more separated from ownership, both the functional organization (U-form) and capital markets become increasingly inefficient. Williamson's point was that for large firms operating in diverse markets, a multi-divisional structure ("M-form") is a more efficient means of allocating resources than functional organizations or business units operating independently, regulated only by markets.

Chandler's point was that strategy would lead to M-form structures. Williamson's point was that complexity would lead to M-form structures. Chandler saw management as the chief architect of strategy, and therefore structure. Williamson described the environment as the source of strategic opportunity, increased complexity, and the M-form structure. Both theorists built on the work of organization theory scholars, and both continued to influence scholarship through the final decades of the 20th century.

In testing the ideas of Chandler and Williamson, Hoskisson (1987) found that adoption of the M-form of organization structure improved accounting based performance for firms pursing an unrelated diversification strategy. In contrast, the adoption of the M-form reduced the rate of return for firms adopting a vertical integration strategy, and did not change the performance of firms following a related diversification strategy. Hoskisson, Harrison and Dubofsky (1991), using capital market measures, found that adoption of the M-form led to improvements in performance. Like the accounting based study, the capital markets study found that the diversification strategy influenced M-form returns, in that investors viewed the M-form as more favorable for unrelated than related strategies. These studies support the arguments of Hoskisson (1987), who suggested that unrelated diversification strategies imposed simpler information and reporting requirements than related or vertical diversification strategies. Due to the complex information requirements of related diversification, related-linked diversifiers might use SBUs (strategic business units) to group linked firms together, while related constrained firms might use a cooperative M-form.

Keats and Hitt (1988) provide an interesting counterpoint to Chandler's view that strategy causes structure. These authors note that the causal flow may be in the opposite direction. The choice of a structure leads to a pattern of decision-making in an organization, which favors the continuance of that structural alternative. Structures, once chosen, exhibit inertial properties.

The Keats and Hitt counterpoint reflects, in part, the evolving nature of strategy and structure. Chandler's initial work focused on early adopters of new organization forms at the beginning of the 20th century. Keats and Hitt studied the forms after some decades of diffusion through the economy. Some firms may have adopted the wrong form for their strategy, or the wrong strategy. Other firms may have adopted the correct form initially, and then conditions may have changed. In both instances, either misguided adoptions or deterioration over time, a firm's will or ability to change a structural choice is hindered by inertial forces. An important question, then, is what are the forces that influence structural choices, structural persistence and structural change?

*Is there an imperative?*   Khandwalla (1973) and Child (1974, 1975) suggested that "congruence" among organizational structure, processes and systems might be more important for performance than "fit" with the environment. The work of Miles and Snow (1978) placed the concept of congruence squarely in the strategic management domain. These researchers categorized firms based on their approach to the marketplace: defenders, prospectors, analyzers and reactors.[6] Contrary to what many (especially economists) had thought, successful firms of each type could be found in each of the industries they studied (although not in equal numbers). If the industry did not dictate which sort of strategy would be successful, what did? According to Miles and Snow, it was the congruence of organizational structures and processes with the chosen strategy.

Thus, high performing prospectors exhibited flexible, organic types of structures, while effective defenders revealed more mechanistic structures. Analyzers required a mixed structural pattern and reactors (who have no clearly articulated strategy) had no clear structural pattern. Miles and Snow argued that the key to performance was a good internal "fit" among the elements of strategy and structure.

At least one other perspective would account for the patterns of organization choice and changes in those choices. Institutional theory (Selznick, 1957) suggests that, in addition to their role-defining function, formal structures also have symbolic properties. Structures serve as one means of securing social legitimacy. They do this by apparently reflecting core organizational values and demonstrating consistency between those core values and the values of the larger society.

If society values rational, efficient forms of organizing, risk-taking behavior, expansion or a "stick-to-the-knitting" approach, it will reward organizations whose structures reflect such values, whether or not they reflect actual behavior within the organization. Meyer and Rowan (1977) suggested that these external social forces were at least as powerful as internal production processes. The social legitimation value of observed structures (even dysfunctional ones) often supercedes observed performance outcomes. That is, resources may flow to organizations that become (or at least appear to be) isomorphic with the institutional environment even if they are inefficient (contrary to natural selection models, described below) or do not "match" the demands of their technology (contrary to contingency theory models). Public sector and not for profit organizations often develop acute sensitivity to this "rule."

*Another perspective.*     Aldrich (1979) and Hannan and Freeman (1977) offered a contrasting perspective to the managerialist theories proposed by Chandler and his Harvard-based colleagues and by Miles and Snow. For these sociologists, organizational effectiveness, performance and survival became a function of a "natural selection" process in the environment. Organizations are "judged" according to how they present themselves to the environment through a process of variation, selection, competition and retention. In the view of these scholars, questions about how internal structural variations arise (i.e., planned or unplanned, or based on internal social forces such as power/domination) are of little concern. When successful variations are known, managers can attempt to copy them. More often, they are not known. The behavior of consumers and competitors can be unpredictable. The probability of choosing a "correct variation" is low. Even when successful variations are known, it is difficult to identify the causes for that success, so attempts at copying successful firms are essentially experimental.

In this natural selection view, age has an important impact on performance. Young organizations have a higher rate of failure. This *liability of newness* (Stinchcomb, 1965) means that younger firms are vulnerable, even suspect, because they lack demonstrable reliability (Hannan and Freeman, 1984). Hannan and Freeman suggest there is also an effect for size, a *liability of smallness*. Large size tends to legitimate organizations. Thus, the selection process favors larger, older organizations. This selection in turn results in a tendency toward inertia among structural forms. The inertia constrains experimentation with strategies that require reconfiguration in existing structures, and hence, internal social relationships (Cascio, Young, and Morris, 1997).

Some have argued for a more nuanced view of liability (Barron, West, and Hannan, 1994; Baum, 1989; Bruderl and Schussler, 1990; Fichman and Leventhal, 1991). These writers suggest a *liability of adolescence* and a *liability of aging*. The former describes new organizations as starting out with a stock of resources. The larger the stock, the longer the organization is buffered in a honeymoon period, even if early outcomes seem negative (as is the case in .com firms obtaining high IPO evaluations in their early years). In their adolescence, these firms may find they have failed to develop and establish the resources and relationships necessary for continued survival. These theories offer a timely explanation for the bubble of excitement surrounding IPOs in internet companies which are followed by precipitous decline and "death" when the bubble bursts and the young founders discover the weaknesses in their business model.

The *liability of aging* suggests that organizations tend to reflect the conditions present at the time of their founding (the *inertial forces* mentioned above). As the environment changes, the "fit" erodes, and survival then depends on the degree to which the organization can overcome both the increasing limitations on their information processing and the influx of new organizations that reflect the current conditions.

The structure of established firms also defines the range of information about change options from which managers select. In response to change, an organization will typically limit its search to a comfort zone of options only incrementally different from its current positions (Zajac and Shortell, 1989). Penrose (1959) noted that rent-seeking managers want to find the optimally efficient form for under-performing functions, and the managers in these functions define a range of acceptable options based on the opportunities for that function. These options will be limited to extensions of existing functional areas.

A recent study of changes in organizational forms made in response to environmental change employed the Miles and Snow typology and studied organizations (hospitals) in unstable environmental conditions (Forte et al., 2000). The study found that the organizations generally recognized their lack of fit to the changed environment, and sought to change. Defenders seemed to have the most difficulty changing form, while some reactors seemed to do quite well. In fact, some of the defenders moved into the reactor category.

One possible reason for this finding might be the manner in which successful defender organizations are configured. In a well-configured defender organization, the structure and strategy are geared toward improvements and R&D within existing products/services and markets. The "comfort zone" is thus constrained to incremental change with little incentive for scanning of potentially disruptive environmental events. Analyzers have at least some experience in prospecting, and reactors have no entrenched commitment to a given form, so they are more apt to change structure quickly as the environment changes, perhaps finding a successful form. Somewhat ironically, this implies that organizations well suited for a specific environment may be at a disadvantage, compared to less well-suited competitors, if the environment becomes unstable. We might refer to this as the *liability of success*.

Christensen (1997), in using the term "innovator's dilemma" provides an illustration of the liabilities of success. A firm becomes successful by listening attentively to its customers. These voices often call for more and more development and extensions of current products and services. Because of this focus, emerging (and often low-end) competitive alternatives ("disruptive technologies") fail to attract the attention of decision makers in the firm. This failure is partially an artifact of the organization structure, because managers in the structure are rewarded based on marginal returns produced by their decisions, and marginal returns will always be higher for an established successful product in the early days of a competitor's emergence. If the new competitor succeeds, though, the incumbent's returns will start to decline, at a time when the new competitor will be so well entrenched that the once mighty incumbent cannot enter the new segment. In this way, Compaq and Dell successfully displaced an industry leader, in this case Digital Equipment Company.

## STRATEGY–STRUCTURE: A DYNAMIC VIEW

Early writers on the pairing of strategy–structure tended to take strong positions. Initial theorists argued that technology, environmental conditions, or strategy caused particular structural configurations. Later theorists (Miller, 1986) argued that understanding the congruence between strategy, structure and other systems was more important than identifying specific causal relationships between particular elements of strategy and structure, *per se*.

One popular version of the configuration model is the McKinsey 7-S model (Waterman, 1982). This model implies that managers need to balance strategy, structure, staff, style, skill, systems and subordinate goals. In providing some empirical support for these ideas, Hoskisson and Hitt (1988) found that firms adopting unrelated strategies used decentralized structures (M-form) and emphasized the use of financial control systems. In contrast, firms adopting related strategies used centralized structures and relied on strategic control systems.

The move from causal arguments about the relationship between strategy and structure to covariance and configuration arguments is an indirect indicator of the complex, dynamic nature of these relationships. Four issues, in particular, contribute to the dynamic relationship. First, strategy and structure have a reciprocal, but unequal, influence on each other. Second, the forces that lead to change in strategy and/or structure often move the organization from equilibrium to disequilibrium. Changes inducing disequilibrium are, by their nature, loosely linked and chaotic. Third, environments and organizations can have a reciprocal relationship. Finally, environments differ in their rate of turbulence and influence across industries and across time.

In explaining the reciprocal nature of the strategy–structure relationship, Mintzberg (1990) used the analogy of footsteps. At one step, the left foot leads the right. At the next step, the right foot leads the left. The analogy is a powerful one, and provides a picture of strategy leading to structure, which then influences the strategy. For example, managers engaged in a dominant-vertical strategy will be connected to one another, and their environment, in a centralized structure. This set of structural connections will limit managers' field of vision, and make them less likely to adopt an alternate strategy. Once an organization adopts a particular strategy–structure configuration, inertial forces will constrain that configuration until the organization experiences significant downturns in performance.

Amburgey and Dacin (1994) support the concept that strategy and structure are intertwined in a reciprocal manner, but note that the reciprocal influences are not equally balanced. Changes in strategy lead to quick changes in structure, while changes in structure influence strategy only slowly. Further, they note that strategy has a much more important influence on structure than the reverse. The disproportionate influence of strategy may be a direct result of the market for corporate control and the differences in material causal influences on each construct.[7]

Efficiency-oriented forces trigger changes in strategy. These forces demand visible and discrete responses to downshifts in performance. In contrast, "the link from structure to strategy is based on the evolution of managerial cognitions and skills" (Amburgey and Dacin, 1994: 1432). If firms change too slowly, perhaps because of the dominant logic of incumbent management (Prahalad and Bettis, 1986), markets for control often lead to a change in management, which then leads to a change in strategy and then to a change in structure. Put differently, the firm's strategy is subject to different and usually more immediate forces for change than the firm's structure.

Amburgey and Dacin build on Mintzberg's analogy, and assert that one foot follows the other – "but they do not have equal strides." The important question, then, is what happens when the strategy and structure are forced "off-stride." Following the Mintzberg analogy, we suggest that when the firm is forced off-stride, it enters a period of disequilibrium. Tushman and Romanelli (1985) refer to this process as "punctuated equilibrium." A punctuated equilibrium occurs when, affected by some form of environmental pressure, the organization's traditional patterns of behavior no longer work. The organization's traditional equilibrium is punctuated, and the organization enters a period of search for a new match with its environment.

As firms endure the period of a punctuated equilibrium, they search for new configurations of strategy, structure and systems. During periods of punctuated equilibrium, specific matches between strategy and structure are temporary. Because the causes of punctuated equilibrium reside primarily in the environment, the rate of turbulence in the environment then determines the relative endurance of particular strategy–structure pairings.

Thus, just as strategies and structures tend to change together, so do environments and organizations. The point is an important one because it implies that relationships within organizations are embedded in an economic and social context, and change as the economic and social (and hence, institutional) context changes.

Given this environmental sensitivity of organizational structures, one option that organizations might take to afford some chance of long-term vitality is the option of controlling as much of the environment as they can. As noted earlier, Pfeffer and Salancik (1978), and Thompson (1967) argued that firms will act to control the most critical environmental resources.

Yet actions do not guarantee success. D'Aveni (1994) has argued that some environments change quickly, and become hypercompetitive. D'Aveni's thesis about hypercompetition has direct structural implications. Hitt, Keats, and DeMarie (1998) describe the type of flexible organization structure that would allow organizations to navigate in the hypercompetitive environment. This organizational form would be horizontal, organized around processes, and willing to shift organizational assets from one task focus to another. Organizational flexibility demands a learning culture, where individuals change their behavioral repertoires over time, to match the demands of the new environment. The resilient organization, then, has a decentralized structure, simultaneously pursues different options, and forms and reforms relationships quickly.

D'Aveni's thesis, though, brings us back to earlier theory about organizational structure, in its assertion that the environment demands particular kinds of organizational forms. Hypercompetition demands organic organizational forms. If a relatively stable environment shifts to an unstable or hypercompetitive state, organizations must either change structural form or disappear. However, there are important differences between this assertion and the earlier notion of an environmental imperative, in that D'Aveni's theories imply that structures and imperatives change frequently.

Based on the study of organizational forms and structures, from Weber to D'Aveni, we conclude that there is no "one best" way to organize. The relationships between internal technological innovations or external, environmental changes and organizational structure are complex. In times of stability, organizations may exercise strong influence on their environments. The intrusion of hypercompetition reduces this influence and triggers searches for new forms. One possible outcome of this dynamic interaction between the environment and organizations is that surviving organizations create a new equilibrium, and regain some control over their environments. A second possible outcome is that the environment continues shifting, without reaching any specific point of equilibrium. In such circumstances, the concept of organizational learning suggests that organizations that become more flexible and agile, and capable of frequent substantive reforming to meet the demands of a constantly changing environment, will be more likely to endure (Fiol and Lyles, 1985). On the other hand, organizations that fail to perceive changes or to create sufficient organizational flexibility will be far less likely to endure.

Weick (1979) has long argued that the environment is not merely a set of objective variables "out there," but is in part a social construction, or enactment. Enactment is a term used to capture the reciprocity between organizations and their environments. Miles and Cameron (1982) argued that given a particular environmental shift, some organizations will choose a domain defense strategy, while other organizations will use a domain offense strategy. Each response will create a different kind of potential impact on the environment, which in turn becomes part of the environmental impact on other organizations. The net effect, then, is a dynamic interaction among current environments, organizational strategies, organizational structures, and evolving new environments.

### Strategy and structure – thresholds and management responses

To this point, we have not directly considered the specific role of management in the creation, maintenance and change of organizational structures. Though some organizational scholars (such as population ecologists) hold that management's role may be only symbolic, organization theory and strategic management both generally assert that managers act in intentional (though not always successful) ways to build and change organizational forms. To the extent that environments do permit choice, the roles and decisions of managers have a material impact on organizational strategies and forms of organizational structures. What, then, causes managers to change structures?

As noted above, Chandler (1962) suggested that managers take notice when confronted with salient information regarding organizational performance. (Information is salient if it affects the dominant logic of the organization.) Two forms of information appear capable of achieving this impact – the performance of the firm, or the behavior of referent actors in the environment.

Unexpected changes in performance prompt the search for explanations. Continued negative performance compounds the pressure on management to change *something*, whether some aspect of strategy or structure. Managers who fail to engage in credible change efforts may experience reductions in economic performance, and perhaps even the loss of their positions.

Astute managers understand that their role is not merely one of reaction to exogenous change. They are capable of anticipating change, and in fact are typically required to do so. Thus they frequently act to change strategies (and structures) in anticipation of environmental change, especially if that change might later be linked to performance shortfalls. Management's anticipation is likely to be at its highest point when other actors in the environment are changing their strategies.

DiMaggio and Powell (1983) suggested that under conditions of uncertainty, managers look to outside referents in order to institute change. They are especially likely to imitate organizations they perceive as more successful (and may or may not be aware they are doing so). Galaskiewicz and Wasserman (1989) added to DiMaggio and Powell's ideas by noting that managers initiate changes in structures based on their informal interpersonal and interorganizational contacts. Through mimetic pressures, then, managers across organizations often act in similar ways whether or not they are aware of doing so.

Thus, managers make strategic and structural changes as a result of both direct and indirect performance feedback (including potential outcomes of anticipated events). In this manner, then, the environment influences strategy, which in turn influences structure, which in turn influences other actors in the environment. In the context of these dynamic and complex relationships, we can observe increases and decreases in the incidence of particular kinds of strategies and organizational forms. We will illustrate some of these relationships by describing three types of strategies – restructuring strategies, turnaround strategies, and acquisition strategies.

For example, during the 1960s and 1970s, large numbers of business firms in the United States exhibited similar patterns of diversification of a conglomerate (or "unrelated business") form and its structural corollary, the M-form. Throughout the 1990s, large numbers of firms adopted restructuring strategies, also labeled as "stick to the knitting," re-engineering, downsizing, rightsizing, and so on. Occasionally *Business Week* even ran cover stories on what was "out" and what was "in" when it came to management fads, buzz words and forms of strategy and structure.

In the early 1980s, several forces combined to decrease the value of the diversification strategy and create pressures for restructuring. Global markets opened up, providing opportunity for increased horizontal extensions. American markets opened up to specialized global competitors, changing the competitive dynamics in many industries. Increased costs for energy and financing decreased the margins in most businesses.

In addition to the global changes affecting strategy in the 1980s, major political and financial changes took place. For example, the interpretation of anti-trust laws changed, increasing the attraction for related acquisitions. A very active market for corporate control created pressures on managers, who may have over-diversified in the 1960s and 1970s, given the institutional pressures for isomorphism that existed in that era. Internal and external environmental changes, then, triggered the movement toward restructuring among American companies. The restructuring firms frequently created new "spin-off" firms. So, AT&T restructured, creating Lucent Technologies; Hewlett Packard restructured, creating Agilent.

Markides (1992, 1995) showed that firms adopting restructuring replaced the "M" (market) form with the "CM" (centralized market) form. Markides found that, previous to the restructuring, these firms had over-diversified. Similarly, Hoskisson and Johnson (1992) found that most restructuring firms had diversified in an inconsistent manner, creating a misfit between strategy and structure. Newly restructuring firms, then, moved to a position of better fit between their strategy and structure.

Two important points emerge from these studies of restructuring. First, the inappropriate strategies existed for some period of time. This persistence of inappropriate strategies is consistent with Amburgey and Dacin's (1994) work which predicts that the longer the time span since the initial strategy was created, the slower the response to poor performance. Second, the initial reversals of strategic position by some organizations increased the pressure on other organizations to change. So, structural forces within the organization hold the firm on a single course of action until environmental forces cumulate to sufficient strength to render the structural forces less credible.

The study of turnaround strategies provides further illustration of the process. Hofer (1980) first proposed that managers experiencing performance declines would be hesitant to change their strategies, and would try to preserve the existing strategy and structure. Ford (1985) later argued that the reason for management's slow response to a perform-ance decline was due to systematic biases in attribution. Managers are slow to conclude that strategies are wrong, as the conclusion is an admission that previous management decisions were wrong. Only strong forces – either strong governance or dramatic declines that provide compelling evidence to counter self-serving attributions – trigger strategy changes in the firm. Hofer asserts that, usually, major strategic change requires a new management. More recent evidence provided by Barker and Duhaime (1997) shows that strategies do change more frequently than Hofer's thesis would imply, yet their evidence also shows that hesitancy to change the strategy (and structure) is a frequent response.

Finally, acquisition strategies provide an illustration of the process. For the acquired firm, an acquisition frequently means rather large-scale structural change. The acquired firm will experience new reporting relationships. The depth of the structural change is related to the type of strategy. The more "related" the acquisition, the more structural change necessary to gain value for the organization. The manager of the acquired firm, then, faces the classic agency conflict. While the acquisition may have value for the organization and its owners, realization of that value may require that the manager loses his/her job. It is not surprising, then, that managers in target firms frequently engage in forms of resistance affecting both strategy and structure issues that delay the completion of an acquisition and increase its cost (Harrison, O'Neill, and Hoskisson, 2000).

This brief review of three types of strategy demonstrates the important role that managers play in the interdependent relationships between the environment, strategy, and structure. In the contexts of various schools of thought, managers have been described as blind responders to a powerful environment, intendedly rational responders to a neutral environment, and Schumpertarian creators of their own environments. Each "school" holds some truth, for some types of environments and organizations. What is important for both practice and research, then, is a constant and dynamic search for the "truth" of the complexity of relationships among environment, strategy, and structure attributes.

## Emerging thoughts on structure and strategy

At the turn of the 21st century, we are discovering that strategy *is* structure. For example, an emerging organizational form is described as the *intelligent organization*. A design form common in knowledge-intensive industries, the intelligent organization "is a move from relationships of dominance and submission up and down the chain of command to horizontal relationships of peers across a network of voluntary cooperation and market-based exchanges" (Pinchot and Pinchot, 1994). The intelligent organization has a flat structure, a form uniquely geared to the task of delivering knowledge-based sources of value. Thompson's organizational model reflected a traditional production-based core buffered by structural hierarchies designed to absorb the impact of environmental uncertainty. The intelligent organization's structure provides opportunities for direct interaction with the environment in the creation, storage, retrieval, and sale of know-ledge. In this case, then, strategy and structure are tightly interwoven and deeply embedded within one another. Rather than a singular causal relationship (in either direction), they occur simultaneously. The organization's intellect *is* its strategy *and* its structure.

Quinn, Anderson, and Finkelstein (1996) describe four forms through which firms engage in "leveraging intellect." The *infinitely flat* organization leverages intellect from within the center. That is, it creates a central knowledge base that serves an ever-expanding set of nodes. Each node enjoys the properties of both small human scale and large, centralized support activities. The central base exerts control by standardization, commonality of norms, egalitarian communication and frequent sharing of information/data, usually enhanced by electronic technologies. Examples of infinitely flat organizations include some brokerage firms, such as Schwab's, some airlines, such as Southwest, and some retail organizations such as Wal-Mart.

The *inverted* organization leverages intellect at the points of contact with the environment through relatively independent nodes. These are typically professionals (e.g., medical, legal). A hierarchy provides the support systems and services to enhance the professionals' effectiveness with little control over their behavior. The two principal service functions performed by these hierarchies are record keeping and access to knowledge. Before the emergence of intranets and digitally enhanced forms of communication these services had limited ability to enjoy economies of scale, so inverted organizations tended to be small. To the extent that technology enables scale effects in these functions, inverted organizations may become larger.

With such growth comes the ability to combine the point-of-contact personalization at the node (like infinitely flat organizations) with large-scale investment in support services at the center (the difference being in the issue of control from the center). An example might be the Nationwide Vision Centers. They started as a small operation in Arizona, opening offices first in the Phoenix area and then in other areas of the state. Each office has an optometrist on site and a selection of eyeglass frames, and they advertise low cost package prices (exam plus eyeglasses). They encourage relationship building through incentives to customers for repeat visits. Clients are recognized and addressed by name and see the same optometrist each time. The company centralizes information services and record keeping, provides standard formats in electronic form for reporting from the nodes and provides a combination of customized and standardized advertising in the node's local area.

The *starburst* organization leverages intellect at both its center *and* its nodes. The interchange of information and roles between center and nodes is such that it often creates transformation of the organizational form. The starburst organization will spin off some nodes to become centers of new starbursts, which in turn spin off some of their own. In the context of a more traditional discussion of the strategy–structure relationship the starburst is similar in some ways to a related-diversified firm with a classic M-form structure, except that its relatedness is built around a specific form of intellectual competency as opposed to more traditional understandings of related "business." That is, the strategy *is* the structure.

Finally, the *spider web* organization leverages intellect by combining, deconstructing and recombining across nodes. Nodes typically operate independently, and combine to provide specialized attention to specific problems. The role of the center is to coordinate the needs of the nodes and match needs and capabilities of the nodes with problems to be solved. An example of a spider web might be Amgen, a research organization. At Amgen, research teams come together, disband and recombine according to their research interests, the encouragement of the lead scientists at the center, and the nature of problems to be solved.

These four forms of intelligent organizations share two characteristics: an emphasis on the care for and development of human resources and a need to maintain systems to codify and exchange knowledge in a way that enhances those human resources. The latter depends on electronic technologies, a dependence which, in some way, seems to take us back to the research of Woodward and her 100 manufacturing firms in England. To some extent, it appears that the myriad of new and emerging communication technologies facilitate the emergence of new organizational structures and forms. An important difference, however, is that they do not seem to pose an imperative, nor does any *single* force seem to have the power to serve as an imperative among the new forms.

## New Boundaries – Where are Thoughts about Structures Trending?

The evolution of thought about organizational structures closely mirrors the evolution of the modern economy. The mass production age spawned an organizational form that might be characterized by its level of specialization, standardization and control. The last years of the 20th century produced a new age, the information age. The norms, not yet fully formed, that characterize this age include speed, initiative and change. These newly emerging norms demand a different set of organizational routines than those favored in the mass production model. One model, though, will not fully replace the other. Some organizations will succeed by using forms that reflect characteristics of the mass production age (e.g., production lines, control sheets, standard reporting routines), while others will succeed by implementing forms that are more consistent with the demands of the information age (e.g., cubicles, playscapes, naturally forming teams and "virtual" everything). In the shorthand of the day, some will be "bricks" and some will be "clicks." Most, though, will combine some aspects of bricks and clicks.

In the 21st century, the best organizations will combine the design principles of both the mass production and the information organization. Amazon.com, a prime mover and exemplar of the information-driven organization, needs to build and manage production age-driven warehouses. General Motors, perhaps the prime exemplar of the production-driven organization, needs to manage information intensive tasks like car design more quickly and effectively.

Fortunately, some of our current leading organizations and organizational thinkers are focused on solving some of the challenges inherent in combining these two models. Three principles or concepts seem to guide these efforts. These include a new conceptualization of the term "boundary," a focus on cooperative relationships, and the "democratization" of strategy, and by extension, structure. We will consider each in order.

The term "boundary-less" organization was first used at General Electric to illustrate the principle that organizational boundaries should be more like short walls than fortified barriers, and that individuals should feel as comfortable crossing boundaries as they do staying within them. Intel uses the term "permeable boundaries" to illustrate the same principle. Internal boundary spanning enables and encourages the development of core competencies described by Prahalad and Hamel (1990).

The attention to boundary spanning is also external. Organizations appear to be developing cooperative arrangements more frequently than ever before. Where ownership and vertical integration once seemed to be the dominant form for managing important environmental contingencies, now cooperation and joint venture relationships appears to be gaining primacy. The "new" economic model also seems to thrive on the formation of "virtual" teams, departments, supply chain linkages, and so on. So, cooperative arrangements like alliances and networks now provide key strategic services, freeing the corporation to focus on its truly distinctive competence. Alliances permit the outsourcing of services like telecommunications, electronic data processing, purchasing, and personnel. The applications service provider (ASP) and the intranet form an important middle ground between the expensive corporate hierarchy and the chaotic, unorganized market. Reasons for the shift to these alliances and networks include the development of global standards for quality, the increasing ease of communications, and the coordination impact of open systems of information architecture.

Given the increased amount of both internal and external boundary spanning, the role of managers at the mid-level of the corporation is to be increasingly involved in the formation of strategy. Previous generations of organization structure built on strongly held assumptions that strategy was the exclusive purview of the executive office (sitting atop a rigid hierarchy). The assumption even guided the distribution of information, leading to conditions where executives had exclusive access to information that might guide the actions of associates several levels and miles from the executive suite. It appears, for example, that the individuals who could solve the Firestone/Ford Explore tire problems in a timely manner may have had neither the data nor the authority to do so.

The last point illustrates an important conclusion, and motivates a call for action. The mass production platform is a poor foundation for emerging business models. Fortunately, theory and practice are providing some early clues about how organizations can solve the paradoxical structural requirements of the mass production era and the information age in this emerging world in which firms are increasingly global, borderless entities. The clues point to a need to relax the constraints of organizational structure as defined by Weberian notions of bureaucracy, and to add more variety in, and fluidity among, role types. Organizations seem to be implementing variety in role types in three ways.

First, organization members often have multiple roles. McDonough and Leifer (1983) provided early evidence that organizations typically have more than one structural configuration. Across time, for different situations, parts of the organization temporarily shift from one structural form to another. The shifts help the organization solve problems more quickly. So, for example, the most successful attempts at total quality management included creation of role switches whereby line-workers could take on the role of managers. Victor, Boyton, and Stephens-Jahng (2000) describe the difficulties and benefits of switching role behavior in mass production organizations.

Second, organizations often adopt a wide variety in role types. As Reich (1991) noted, there are many temporary roles in the modern organization. Most members are subject to a form of "employment at will" contract, and as the environment shifts, the need for many of the firm's contractors shifts.

Third, organizations frequently redefine their boundaries. They use temporary employment relationships and temporary alliances. They engage in toe-hold investments and options taking. Permanence is bound by the performance of a specific product-service option. As specific options lose performance value, the organization exits that option, and redefines its structure.

## CONCLUSION

The emerging set of organizational structures, then, is quite different than the Weberian ideal bureaucracy. Weber studied stasis, but what appears to be more important in the 21st century is movement. Therefore, the study of structure in the 21st century is likely to emphasize polymorphism even more than isomorphism – the capacity to enact change in forms, including the creation of new forms, the disappearance of customary forms, and the change of existing forms into alternatives, in very short time frames. The tasks of describing, documenting and evaluating these changes present daunting challenges for research and practice. At a minimum, an increase in studies adopting multiple levels of analysis, the creation of new constructs to describe the emerging "semi-permanent" organizational arrangements and an increase in the use of dynamic, time series perspectives is called for.

Past work on structure has provided a strong foundation of informed inquiry and clever use of methods. The phenomena continues to change, though, and in that change lies the opportunity for improved foundations, better informed inquiry, and the creation of new research methods. Let the work begin.

## NOTES

1 The study of organizations as understood today within sociology is not much older than work in strategy, dating from the late 1940s and the work of Merton (e.g., 1948).

2 There are many, many studies in this domain, and this review must necessarily select a few of them to serve as examples. Readers are encouraged to acquaint themselves with the rich history in this domain.

3 A functional structure is one in which specializations are grouped together, such that all like activities are grouped together. Each department manager reports to the chief executive. In the context of bureaucracy, the patterns of relationship and communication among these functional groupings are firmly delineated, with little or no "cross level" or cross department interaction below the executive level.

4 As we will note, there were and are many organization theory scholars who held/hold quite different assumptions, and many organizations that do not fit neatly into the definitions used in such studies.

5 Certain characteristics of historical research ought to be noted. First, the facts may be seen by two historians differently. Second, the historical record is written by the victors, so it is often difficult to sort out what failed. Third, when groups succeed they perceive high levels of cohesiveness and effective leadership. The attribution is if we are doing well it must be because we are effectively supervised, communicating effectively, and so on (Pfeffer and Salancik, 1978).

6 Prospectors seek growth through leading edge developments in new products and new markets;

defenders through innovations in existing products and markets; analyzers try to have a combination of both; reactors have no clearly articulated strategy, and hence are at the mercy of external market variations.

7 Walsh and Kosnick (1993) provide an excellent discussion of markets for corporate control. The chapter on Agency Theory provides a explanation of how financial markets act to influence organization structures. A major implication of these discussions is that strategy–structure relationships are embedded in a market context characterized by diverse ownership varying in capability of unseating entrenched management.

## REFERENCES

Aldrich, H. E. (1979). *Organizations and Environments*. Englewood Cliffs, NJ: Prentice-Hall.

Amburgey, T. L., and Dacin, T. (1994). As the left foot follows the right?: The dynamics of strategic and structural change. *Academy of Management Journal*, 37: 1427–52.

Atkinson, M. (1971). *Orthodox Consensus and Radical Alternative: A Study in Sociological Theory*. London: Heinemann.

Barker, V., and Duhaime, I. (1997). Strategic change in the turnaround process: Theory and empirical evidence. *Strategic Management Journal*, 18: 13–38.

Barron, D. N., West, E. and Hannan, M. T. (1994). A time to grow and a time to die: Growth and mortality of credit unions in New York City, 1914–1990. *American Journal of Sociology*, 100: 381–421.

Baum, J. A. C. (1989). Liabilities of newness, adolescence and obsolescence: Exploring age dependence in the dissolution of organizational relationships and organizations. *Proceedings of the Administrative Sciences Association of Canada*, 10(5): 1–10.

Bruderl, J., and Schussler, R. (1990). Organizational mortality: The liabilities of newness and adolescence. *Administrative Science Quarterly*, 35: 530–47.

Burns, T., and Stalker, G. M. (1961). *The Management of Innovation*. London: Tavistok.

Burton, R. M., and Obel, B. (1980). A computer simulation test of the M-form hypothesis. *Administrative Science Quarterly*, 25: 457–76.

Cascio, W., Young, C., and Morris, J. (1997). Financial consequences of employment change decisions in major US corporations. *Academy of Management Journal*, 40: 1175–89.

Chandler, A. (1962). *Strategy and Structure*. Cambridge, MA: MIT Press.

Child, J. (1974). Managerial and organizational factors associated with company performance Part I: A contingency analysis. *Journal of Management Studies*, October, 11: 175–89.

Child, J. (1975). Managerial and organizational factors associated with company performance – Part II: A contingency analysis. *Journal of Management Studies*, February, 12: 12–27.

Christensen, C. M. (1997). *The Innovator's Dilemma: When New Technologies Cause Great Firms to Fail*. Boston, MA: Harvard University Press.

D'Aveni, R. D. (1994). *Hypercompetition*. New York: Free Press.

DiMaggio, P., and Powell, W. W. (1983). The iron cage revisited: Institutional isomorphism and collective rationality in organizational fields. *American Sociological Review*, 48: 147–60.

Fichman, M., and Leventhal, D. A. (1991). Honeymoons and the liability of adolescence: A new perspective on duration dependence in social and organizational relationships. *Academy of Management Review*, 16: 442–67.

Fiol. M. C., and Lyles, M. A. (1985). Organizational learning. *The Academy of Management Review*, 10: 803–13.

Ford, J. D. (1985). The effects of causal attributions on decision makers' responses to performance downturns. *Academy of Management Review*, 10: 770–86.

Forte, M., Hoffman, J. J., Lamont, B. T., and Brockman, E. N. (2000). Organizational form and environment: An analysis of between-form and within-form responses to environmental change. *Strategic Management Journal*, 21: 753–73.

Galaskiewicz, J., and Wasserman, S. (1989). Mimetic processes within an interorganizational field: An empirical test. *Administrative Science Quarterly*, 34: 454–79.

Hannan, M. T., and Freeman, J. (1977). The population ecology of organizations. *American Journal of Sociology*, 82: 929–63.

Harrison, J. S., O'Neill, H. M., and Hoskisson, R. E. (2000). Acquisition strategy and target resistance: A theory of countervailing effects of pre-merger bidding and post-merger integration. In C. Cooper and A. Gregory (eds.), *Advances in Mergers and Acquisitions*. Greenwich, CT: JAI Press.

Hitt, M. A., Keats, B. W., and DeMarie, S. M. (1998). Navigating in the new competitive landscape: Building strategic flexibility and competitive advantage in the 21st Century. *Academy of Management Executive*, 12(4): 22–42.

Hofer, C. (1980). Turnaround strategies. *Journal of Business Strategy*, 1: 19–31.

Hoskisson, R. E. (1987). Multidivisional structure and performance: The contingency of diversification strategy. *Academy of Management Journal*, 29: 625–44.

Hoskisson, R. E., Harrison, J. S., and Dubofsky, D. A. (1991). Capital market evaluation of M-form implementation and diversification strategy. *Strategic Management Journal*, 12: 271–9.

Hoskisson, R. E., Hill, C. W. L., and Kim, H. (1993). The multidivisional structure: Organizational fossil or source of value? *Journal of Management*, 19: 269–98.

Hoskisson, R. E., and Hitt, M. A. (1988). Strategic control systems and relative R&D investment in large multiproduct firms. *Strategic Management Journal*, 9: 650–721.

Hoskisson, R. E., and Johnson, R. (1992). Corporate restructuring and strategic change: The effect on diversification strategy and R&D intensity. *Strategic Management Journal*, 13: 625–34.

Keats, B. W., and Hitt, M. A. (1988). A causal model of linkages among environmental dimensions, macro organizational characteristics, and performance. *Academy of Management Journal*, 31: 570–98.

Khandwalla, P. (1973). Effect of competition on the structure of top management control. *Academy of Management Journal*, 16: 285–95.

Kuhn, T. S. (1970). *Structure of Scientific Revolutions*. Chicago: University of Chicago Press.

Lawrence, P. R., and Lorsch, J. W. (1967). *Organization and Environment*. Homewood, IL: Richard D. Irwin.

Markides, C. (1992). Consequences of corporate refocusing: Ex ante evidence. *Academy of Management Journal*, 35: 398–412.

Markides, C. (1995). Diversification, restructuring and economic performance. *Strategic Management Journal*, 16: 101–18.

McDonough, E. F., III, and Leifer, R. (1983). Using simultaneous structures to cope with uncertainty. *Academy of Management Journal*, 26: 727–35.

Merton, R. (1948). Manifest and latent functions. In R. Merton (ed.), *Social Theory and Social Structure*. Glencoe, IL: Free Press, 37–59.

Meyer, J. W., and Rowan B. (1977). Institutionalised Organisations: Formal structure as myth and ceremony. *American Journal of Sociology*, 83: 340–63

Miles, R. E., and Snow, C. C. (1978). *Organizational Strategy, Structure and Process*. New York: McGraw-Hill.

Miles, R. H., and Cameron, K. S. (1982). *Coffin Nails and Corporate Strategies*. Englewood Cliffs, NJ: Prentice-Hall.

Miller, D. (1986). Configurations of strategy and structure: Towards a synthesis. *Strategic Management Journal*, 7: 233–49.

Mintzberg, H. (1990). The design school: Reconsidering the basic premises of strategic management. *Strategic Management Journal*, 11: 171–95.

Penrose, E. (1959). *The Theory of the Growth of the Firm*. New York: Wiley.

Pfeffer, J., and Salancix, G. R. (1978). *The External Control of Organizations: A Resource Dependence Perspective*. New York: Harper and Row.

Pinchot, G., and Pinchot, E. (1994). *The Intelligent Organization*. San Francisco: Barrett-Koehler Publishers

Prahalad, C. K., and Bettis, R. A. (1986). The dominant logic: A new linkage between diversity and performance. *Strategic Management Journal*, 7(6): 485–502.

Prahalad, C. K., and Hamel, G. (1990). The core competence of the corporation. *Harvard Business Review*, 68(3): 79–91.

Quinn, J. B., Anderson, P., and Finkelstein, S. (1996). Leveraging Intellect. *The Academy of Management Executive*, 10(3): 7–27.

Reich, R. B. (1991). *The Work of Nations: Preparing Ourselves for 21st-Century Capitalism*. New York: A. A. Knopf.

Rumelt, R. (1974). *Strategy, Structure and Economic Performance*. Cambridge, MA: Harvard University Press.

Selznick, P. (1957). *Leadership in Administration: A Sociological Interpretation*. New York: Harper and Row.

Simon, H. (1960). *The New Science of Management Decision*. New York: Harper and Row.

Stinchcombe, A. L. (1965). Social structure and organizations. In J. G. March (ed.), *Handbook of Organizations*. Chicago, IL: Rand McNally.

Thompson, J. (1967). *Organizations in Action*. New York: McGraw-Hill.

Tushman, M., and Romanelli, E. (1985). Organizational evolution: A metamorphosis model of convergence and reorientation. *Research in organizational behavior*, 7: 171–222.

Victor, B., Boynton, A., and Stephens-Jahng, T. (2000). The effective design of work under total quality management. *Organization Science*, 11: 102–17.

Walsh, J. P., and Kosnick, R. P. (1993). Corporate raiders and their disciplinary role in the market. *Academy of Management Journal*, 36: 671–700.

Waterman, R. H., Jr. (1982). The seven elements of strategic fit. *Journal of Business Strategy*, 3 (Winter): 69–73.

Weber, M. (1978). *Economy and Society: An Outline of Interpretive Sociology*. Berkeley, CA: University of California Press.

Weick, K. (1979). *The Social Psychology of Organizing*. Reading, MA: Addison-Wesley.

Williamson, O. E. (1970). *Corporate Control and Business Behavior*. Englewood Cliffs, NJ: Prentice-Hall.

Williamson, O. E. (1975). *Markets and Hierarchies: Analysis and Anti-trust Implications*. New York: Free Press.

Woodward, J. (1965). *Industrial Organization: Theory and Practice*. London: Oxford University Press.

Wrigley, L. (1970). Divisional autonomy and diversification. Unpublished doctoral dissertation, Graduate School of Business Administration, Harvard University.

Zajac, E. J., and Shortell, S. M. (1989). Changing generic strategies: Likelihood, direction, and Performance implications. *Strategic Management Journal*, 10: 413–30.

# 19

# Corporate Governance

SAYAN CHATTERJEE AND JEFFREY S. HARRISON

The separation of ownership from control in modern corporations has led to some interesting questions and much debate among researchers and practicing managers (Baysinger and Hoskisson, 1990; Berle and Means, 1932; Johnson, Daily, and Ellstrand, 1996; Zahra and Pearce, 1989). Individual shareholders, unless they are also managers or hold a large block of stock, have very little influence on the company. Managers, as agents for the shareholders, make most important decisions with regard to corporate operations. Stewardship theory suggests that managers should be given maximum liberty to make decisions so that they are not encumbered by rules and influences that can jeopardize optimal performance (Davis, Schoorman, and Donaldson, 1997). However, many researchers and practitioners wonder whether managers can be relied upon to sacrifice their own self-interests and behave in a manner that is in the best interests of the shareholders.

When managers serve their own interests at the expense of the shareholders, an agency problem is said to exist (Williamson, 1984; Fama and Jensen, 1983). Agency problems have been identified in a variety of situations, including aggressive but unprofitable growth strategies (empire building), higher than warranted CEO salaries, executive perquisites and CEO duality – a situation in which the CEO also chairs the board of directors (Harrison and St. John, 1998). One of the important roles of boards of directors is to exercise oversight and control in an effort to reduce the potential for agency problems (Baysinger and Hoskisson, 1990; Pfeffer and Salancik, 1978; Walsh and Seward, 1990). In this role, boards select or fire the CEO, determine executive pay, and monitor the behavior of top managers. The effectiveness of boards in controlling the behavior of top executives seems to be dependent on social and organizational factors. For example, board reform advocates argue that many times directors are too passive because of special relationships with top managers that are a result of personal, social or business ties (Fredrickson, Hambrick, and Baumrin, 1988; Spencer, 1983; Walsh and Seward, 1990; Westphal, 1999). In the extreme case, CEOs may use their de facto power to select and compensate directors, thus packing their boards with supporters (Herman, 1981; Mace, 1986; Pfeffer, 1972; Wade, O'Reilly, and Chandratat, 1990).

Another equally important function of the board of directors is to provide advice and insight to managers (Baysinger and Butler, 1985; Gomez-Mejia and Wiseman, 1997; Johnson, Daily, and Ellstrand, 1996). Johnson et al. (1996) explain that this service role can vary from simply advising top executives on administrative matters to actually becoming involved in the formulation of strategies. However, the effectiveness with which boards of directors advise top managers may be dependent on factors such as personal relationships between directors and top managers, and compensation schemes that align the interests of shareholders and managers (Westphal, 1999).

External board members may also provide a link to the external environment (Pfeffer and Salancik, 1978). Consequently, they provide valuable information, including information leading to the acquisition of critical resources (Daily and Dalton, 1994). In this role, directors often represent specific institutions with which a firm conducts business; however, the appointment of outside directors may also serve to legitimize the organization (Selznick, 1949).

In the broad sense of the term, corporate governance deals with all of the factors and forces, both internal and external to the organization, that work to harmonize the interests of managers and shareholders (Baysinger and Hoskisson, 1990). For example, a consumer advisory panel is a governance mechanism, as is a works council. We do not accept unequivocally the view that the shareholder is the only legitimate stakeholder with rights that are worthy of protection. However, like much of the research on the topic, and in an effort to bring some focus to the subject, we will emphasize the role of boards of directors as a corporate governance mechanism. We will begin by examining the influence of boards of directors on organizational outcomes such as the behavior of top executives and organizational performance. In particular, we will focus on factors that influence whether the interests of shareholders are well served. It is not our intention to provide an exhaustive review of all studies on the topic. Good reviews of this literature are provided by Johnson, Daily, and Ellstrand (1996) and earlier, by Zahra and Pearce (1989). Instead, our intention is to provide a foundation in the area. We will use this foundation to argue that the influence of governance is particularly important during periods of organizational crisis. This idea will be developed in the context of a failed takeover attempt. Several propositions and their implications will round out the chapter.

## BOARDS OF DIRECTORS AND ORGANIZATIONAL OUTCOMES

A large literature exists on the role of the board of directors in creating (or not creating) organizational value. One of the important trends driving this research is that now over half of the stock in large corporations is held by large institutional investors (Useem, 1993, 1996). Furthermore, these investors are holding the board more accountable for organizational performance and other outcomes. For instance, TIAA-CREF, a major insurer and fund manager, has adopted a policy statement that focuses solely on the board of directors. Some large shareholders are even targeting individual directors for removal from the board if they do not measure up in terms of commitment, independence, involvement and ownership (Byrne, Brown, and Barnathan, 1997). Also, New York State Comptroller Edward V. Regan circulated a proposal to permit large shareholders access to information for evaluations of board performance.

Although there is no consensus with regard to how boards of directors can add value to the organization, much of the research centers on three important roles (Johnson, Daily, and Ellstrand, 1996). First, the largest part of the literature deals with the board's role in monitoring the behavior of managers, referred to as the control role. A second function is the service role of giving advice. Finally, the resource dependence role focuses on the use of directors to provide links to the external environment in an effort to acquire critical resources. This section will be organized around these three roles.

## *Control of managerial behavior*

State law requires corporations to create a board of directors (Bainbridge, 1993; Lowenstein, 1994). From a legal perspective, the primary responsibility of a board is to monitor managers, specifically top managers, for the benefit of the corporation (Bainbridge, 1993; Miller, 1993). The courts evaluate whether directors are fulfilling this fiduciary responsibility based on the business judgment rule, which presumes that directors make informed decisions, in good faith, with the best interests of the corporation in mind, and independently of personal interests or relationships (Block, Barton, and Radin, 1989; Manning, 1984; Miller, 1993). Directors have an obligation to exercise care in the execution of their duties and to exhibit loyalty, which means that they may not take advantage of situations that would provide personal benefits at the expense of the corporation (Bogart, 1994; Manning, 1984; Miller, 1993).

However, many factors can reduce the effectiveness of boards of directors in fulfilling their fiduciary duties. First, top executives have much of the control over board membership. This control is exerted through the proxy mechanism. Although shareholders elect directors, many of them do not take the time to become involved in the election process. They sign a proxy card granting voting rights to management. Also, state laws allow shareholders to elect, but not nominate, directors (Brudney, 1985; Goforth, 1994). This is similar to elections in many dictator-led countries. If top management, in essence, selects their own monitoring body, then the effectiveness of the monitoring is likely to be reduced. In addition to the proxy process, conflicts of interest can emerge when directors identify more strongly with the executives they are monitoring than with the shareholders. This often occurs due to social ties or because many outside directors are themselves CEOs or high level executives (Bainbridge, 1993; Manning, 1984).

Legal and financial community trends are leading to a more appropriate balance between manager influence and board independence. In the legal environment, the Securities and Exchange Commission Act, Section 14a, requires managers to include shareholder-initiated proposals in the proxy materials they send to shareholders (Barnard, 1991). Also, the Delaware courts have adopted a rule that shifts more of the responsibility to directors to prove that their decisions are reasonable and independent (Cieri, Sullivan, and Lennox, 1994). In the financial community institutional investors, which now own the majority of shares of large corporations, are becoming more vocal in influencing top managers both through boards and directly (Barnard, 1991). One group of institutional investors, public pension funds, are particularly active in governance. Private institutional investors, such as banks and insurance companies, may still have conflicts of interest because of current or future business dealings with particular corporations; however, public pension funds are free of such conflicts (Coffee, 1994).

Institutional investor activism has been directed at reforming boards to include more independent directors. Most of the research literature defines independent directors as non-managers (Cochran, Wood, and Jones, 1985; Daily and Dalton, 1992; Dalton and Kesner, 1987; Johnson, Daily, and Ellstrand, 1996). Because board decisions are usually made through majority rule, boards that consist largely of independent directors are expected to be better monitors of executive actions and performance (Bainbridge, 1993; Baysinger and Butler, 1985). For example, inside directors may be uncomfortable providing periodic reviews of the CEO or other top executives (Baysinger and Hoskisson, 1990; Weisbach, 1988). In addition, sometimes inside directors may be asked to make decisions that could personally affect them, such as the adoption of anti-takeover provisions, executive succession, or executive compensation (Johnson, Daily, and Ellstrand, 1996; Sundaramurthy, Rechner, and Wang, 1996). With regard to these types of provisions, Sundaramurthy, Mahoney, and Mahoney (1997) discovered that separation of the positions of CEO and chairperson of the board reduces the negative market reaction from adopting anti-takeover provisions, while the inclusion of more outsiders increases the negative market reaction. This is surprising because outsiders should be perceived by the market as protecting shareholder interests. On the other hand, Coles and Hesterly (2000) discovered an interaction effect that helps explain these findings. They demonstrated that the stock market reaction is positively related to outsider representation for firms that have an independent leadership structure (chairperson is not a former officer of the firm).

There is, however, a case for including at least a few inside directors (Fama and Jensen, 1983; Baysinger and Hoskisson, 1990). Internal directors know more about what top management actually does, whereas outside directors may be less able to monitor their actions due to information asymmetries. Outside directors may also rely too heavily on financial indicators of performance simply because these are the only indicators available to them (Baysinger and Hoskisson, 1990). Overdependence on financial performance indicators can result in executive behaviors that enhance performance in the short run at the expense of the long run. For example, Harrison and Fiet (1999) discovered that new CEOs of large US companies frequently reduce their company's relative investments in R&D and pension funding for the first few years after their appointments. They found empirical support that these reductions led to short-term performance increases, reasoning that new CEOs were trying to enhance their reputations with board members and other stakeholders.

While outside directors, due to their independence from the CEO and the firm, are thought to be better monitors of executive action, many researchers have begun to question whether directors really are independent (Bainbridge, 1993; Daily and Dalton, 1994). Outside directors that have personal or business relationships with the CEO or other organizational executives are unlikely to be completely objective in evaluating executive decisions and performance (Baysinger and Butler, 1985; Daily and Dalton, 1994; Johnson, Hoskisson, and Hitt, 1993; Weisbach, 1988). The Securities and Exchange Commission requires that information regarding personal and/or business relationships between directors and a corporation or its managers shall be reported in proxy materials.

Many researchers have investigated the influence of director independence on firm performance; however, the evidence is contradictory. While some have found a positive relationship between the proportion of inside directors and financial performance (Cochran, Wood, and Jones, 1985; Kesner, 1987; Vance, 1964), others have found no relationship (Daily and Johnson, 1997; Mallette and Fowler, 1992; Molz, 1988). Still others have found a positive relationship between the proportion of outside directors and performance (Hill and Snell, 1988; Pearce and Zahra, 1992; Schellenger, Wood, and Tashakori, 1989). In an extensive meta-analysis of board composition, leadership structure and financial performance, Dalton et al. (1998) conclude that there is little evidence of a systematic relationship between governance structure and performance.

The contradictory evidence on director independence and firm performance has led to some interesting ideas, including the proposition that there may be a reverse causal relationship between independence and performance. For example, Daily and Johnson (1997) discovered that prior firm financial success is related to a more dependent board structure. Furthermore, Hermalin and Weisbach (1988) and Pearce and Zahra (1992) found that corporations tend to add more outside directors following periods of poor performance. Consequently, one possible conclusion is that high firm performance gives CEOs more power to select directors that are less likely to oppose their ideas and strategies. On the other hand, low performance may ignite boards to action. If reverse causality exists, then some might argue that the current system of governance is working. They might ask why a board should interfere if the corporation is providing high returns to shareholders. However, history has taught that CEOs with unchecked power can lead a company to ruin. The case of Harding Lawrence, the CEO who led Braniff International Airlines to insolvency, is a well-known example. Lawrence led the company on a reckless route acquisition strategy, humiliating or eliminating anyone who stood in his path.

Another interesting perspective on the board independence/performance relationship is that, under normal circumstances, the board may not have a direct influence on firm performance (Kesner and Johnson, 1990). However, in extreme situations, such as a crisis, boards may become more important (Daily, 1996; Daily and Dalton, 1994, 1995; Lorsch and MacIver, 1989). This theme will receive further development later in this chapter.

Researchers have also studied the influence of board independence on executive turnover, social responsibility and CEO compensation. With regard to executive turnover, Weisbach (1988) found that boards dominated by outsiders were more likely to rely on performance indicators when deciding whether to terminate a CEO. Also, Boeker and Goodstein (1993) discovered that firms with more insiders were less likely to select an outsider as the new CEO. With regard to social responsibility, Johnson and Greening (1999) found that outside director representation was positively related to corporate social performance. This is a potentially important finding in that it suggests that even if outside representation does not play an important role in increasing shareholder value in normal times, outside directors may still perform an important function in protecting the interests of society as a whole.

Regarding board independence and CEO compensation, the results are mixed. Some researchers have been unable to establish a relationship between the proportion of outside directors and compensation (Mangel and Singh, 1993; Kerr and Kren, 1992), however, Westphal and Zajac (1995) found that powerful CEOs appointed demographically similar directors and that these types of boards were associated with higher levels of

CEO compensation. The results are also mixed with regard to the adoption of golden parachute contracts. While Cochran, Wood, and Jones (1985) and Singh and Harianto (1989) found a positive relationship between the proportion of outsider directors and golden parachutes, Wade, O'Reilly, and Chandratat (1990) found evidence to the contrary in firms that do not have a dominant stockholder. More recently, Conyon and Peck (1998) conclude that top management pay is more closely aligned with corporate performance in companies with remuneration committees and boards dominated by outsiders.

Other interesting research investigates the influence of factors such as the frequency of board meetings and the structure of board committees on the nature of controls used by boards in evaluating CEO performance. Beekun, Stedham, and Young (1998) discovered that boards that meet infrequently and lack a strategic planning committee are likely to emphasize outcome-based controls and that this emphasis tends to make the CEO more risk averse, especially with regard to capital investment. This sort of risk aversion is likely to have a long-term impact on an organization. Similarly, Hoskisson and Turk (1990) argued that ineffective governance and inappropriate controls can lead to poor management decisions and low performance, which then leads to restructuring of both the organization and the governance structure. Consequently, it is possible that to some extent, over the longer term, governance problems are self-correcting.

In summary, boards of directors are legally responsible for monitoring the actions of top executives. Nevertheless, the proxy machinery and special relationships between directors and the corporation or its top executives may reduce the ability of directors to govern in a responsible and unbiased fashion. As a response to such concerns, investor activism, especially among institutional investors such as public pension fund managers, is resulting in new governmental policies and a move towards independent boards consisting of more outside directors. However, in spite of the belief that independent boards are better suited to govern top manager behavior, the evidence with regard to the relationship between board independence and performance is mixed. One explanation that has received some empirical support is that board structure does not influence corporate performance, but rather corporate performance influences board structure. Another promising idea is that the composition of boards of directors is more important during periods of crisis than it is during less-turbulent times. We will now discuss the service function of boards of directors.

## Services provided to top management

Rosenstein et al. (1993) found that the CEOs of high technology startups valued the information and expertise gained from their outside board members, especially in the early stages of development. Lorsch and MacIver (1989) noted that a considerable amount of a director's time is spent advising the CEO. Organizations can draw from the knowledge of outside directors to monitor trends in the external environment (Kesner and Johnson, 1990). Also, active or retired CEOs are sometimes asked to serve on boards, which provides CEOs with a vast store of experience from which to draw (Lorsch and MacIver, 1989).

Interlocking directorates, in which CEOs serve on the boards of stakeholder companies, may provide opportunities to diffuse innovation. For example, Davis (1991) found that anti-takeover defenses were diffused through the system of interlocking directorates. Also, close relationships among boards were found to be related to similarities in contributions to political action committees by major corporations (Mizruchi, 1989). Conversely, Hill and Snell (1988) discovered that outsider representation on the board was negatively associated with the adoption of innovation. Consequently, the influence of boards of directors on innovation is still a subject of debate.

Although Tashakori and Boulton (1983) reported that most directors are not directly involved in strategy formulation, they noticed that board involvement in all phases of strategic planning was increasing. A decade later, Judge and Zeithaml (1992) found that board involvement in strategic decisions was positively related to financial performance. Coles and Hesterly (2000) argue that inside directors, in particular, provide critical information to guide board decision making. In addition, Judge and Dobbins (1995) noted that director awareness of major strategic issues was positively related to financial performance and negatively related to risk. Support for an active board was also found by Pearce and Zahra (1991), who discovered higher performance in corporations with powerful, participative boards (see also Beekun, Stedham, and Young, 1998). Also, Dalton et al. (1999), based on a meta-analysis of 131 samples, found evidence that in similar-sized organizations larger boards are associated with higher performance. Obviously, a larger board provides more options to a CEO when soliciting information and counsel.

Although social ties and other special relationships between top executives and outside directors are thought to reduce the effectiveness of the governance process, these relationships may actually facilitate the advising process (Westphal, 1999). For example, social ties with directors should increase the probability that a CEO will seek advice, as well as the tendency for directors to offer it. Westphal (1999) found that social ties did not reduce the level of monitoring by the board and, importantly, enhanced the level of advice and counsel from outside directors on strategic issues. He also discovered that CEO incentive alignment moderated the relationship, with higher levels of CEO ownership or long-term incentives strengthening the relationship between social ties and board advice.

Other factors are also capable of influencing board effectiveness. Forbes and Milliken (1999) propose a model that links factors such as board demography, the presence of knowledge and skills to processes such as effort norms, cognitive conflict and the use of knowledge of skills. These factors are then related to board-level outcomes such as task performance and cohesiveness and ultimately to firm performance. This line of inquiry has great potential for advancing our understanding of how the advisory role of a board of directors can influence organizational performance.

To summarize, evidence exists that directors are involved in providing advice and counsel to top executives and that this advice is appreciated. Westphal (1999) calls this the collaborative model. Furthermore, preliminary evidence seems to indicate that collaborative activities are positively linked to organizational performance. We believe that a more collaborative environment will also enhance the ability of organizations to deal with crisis situations, since these situations typically require novel solutions and a great deal of information gathering. Having discussed the control and service functions of boards of directors, we will now turn our attention to the role of directors in helping corporations acquire critical resources.

## *Acquisition of essential resources*

The acquisition and development of resources is a key element of strategic management and strategic advantage (Barney, 1991). Boards of directors are one mechanism that firms may use to enhance their abilities to acquire critical resources (Galaskiewicz, 1985; Johnson, Daily, and Ellstrand, 1996; Pfeffer and Salancik, 1978; Zahra and Pearce, 1989). For example, an organization that needs a scarce raw material or component to manufacture its own products may invite its supplier's CEO to sit on the board in order to enhance contract negotiations. An overlap frequently occurs between the service and resource roles of directors in the area of knowledge acquisition. For instance, a corporation may appoint as a director a top executive of a company that has state-of-the-art technology in an effort to obtain knowledge that will enhance its own operations. While the appointment is intended to help the organization obtain a knowledge resource, the method through which this knowledge is likely to be transferred is through counsel and advice.

Much of the research on the acquisition of resources through boards of directors has focused on capital. This research generally supports the idea that board membership by representatives of financial institutions can facilitate the acquisition of capital (Johnson, Daily, and Ellstrand, 1996). In fact, Stearns and Mizruchi (1993) studied large Japanese firms and discovered that the types and amounts of financing obtained by corporations was related to the types of financial institutions represented on their board. They also found that declining profits and contractions in the business cycle were related to the appointment of representatives from financial institutions. These results were supported by Kaplan and Minton (1994); however, Kaplan and Minton argued that it was the representatives of financial institutions themselves that sought board memberships in an effort to protect the interests of their organizations.

The resource role seems to be particularly important in two settings. First, entrepreneurial firms have far fewer resources than their larger industry counterparts and are thus much more dependent on the good will of resource providers (Pfeffer and Salancik, 1978). Furthermore, these firms lack historical legitimacy and therefore can benefit greatly from the appointment of a prestigious director (Johnson, Daily, and Ellstrand, 1996). Second, the resource role is especially important for firms in crisis situations such as those experiencing declining performance (Johnson, Daily and Ellstrand, 1996). Researchers have noticed declines in board memberships to be associated with bankruptcy (Daily, 1995; Gales and Kesner, 1994). During any type of crisis, maintaining exchange relationships with key constituencies is vitally important (Sutton and Callahan, 1987). One way to keep these relationships strong is through director representation.

In summary, the three most widely discussed roles of boards of directors are the monitoring or control role, the service or advisement role, and the resource acquisition role. A recurring theme throughout our discussion of each of these roles is that governance seems to be most important when an organization is in crisis. In the next section, we will develop this idea further.

## Boards of Directors and Organizational Crises

The central thesis of this chapter is that governance matters. However, under normal circumstances not all "independent" boards act as they are supposed to and neither do all large shareholders. In this chapter, we develop a set of contingencies under which most, if not all, independent boards and large shareholders can be theoretically expected to assert their independence (and power). The basic contingency that the chapter looks at is the aftermath of a *rejected* takeover offer. Takeover attempts are an event of such magnitude for the target firm that they send shockwaves throughout the entire organization. Consequently, we believe that they qualify as a crisis. However, unlike many other types of organizational crises that are likely to be firm specific, the basic nature of takeover attempts is similar across a variety of organizations and industries. Therefore, we believe that this particular type of crisis situation lends itself to systematic investigation.

In our brief review of the literature, we highlighted several factors and forces that lead to the conclusion that governance structure may be more important during a crisis than in less turbulent situations. First, we noted that the board composition literature is largely inconclusive with regard to performance and that this may be because board structure is not critical if the organization's environment and performance are stable. Second, preliminary evidence supports the notion that a more collaborative relationship between the CEO and the board leads to higher performance. Collaboration seems especially critical if the CEO is charting a course through unsailed waters, which is certainly the case during a crisis. Finally, the continuance of exchange relationships from which critical resources are acquired is vital to the continued success of the organization. As Pettigrew (1992) noted, most studies that have found evidence of board effectiveness have studied crisis situations.

We argue that during a crisis, specifically in the aftermath of a rejected takeover, most independent boards and large shareholders can be expected to assert their independence (and power). However, even in a crisis mode, not all boards and large shareholders will choose to assert their independence in the same manner. We also develop propositions that predict which firms are more likely to be subsequently acquired after rejecting an initial offer. One proposition is that boards that are independent on paper (consist primarily of non-managers) *and* were vigilant in the past support management in keeping the firm independent. We also propose that only if an "independent" board had *not* been vigilant in the past, are they most likely to agree to a subsequent sale. Further, firms without independent boards and large shareholders are also likely to reject future takeover attempts. The propositions have implications for addressing some of the inconsistencies in governance research.

### Foundational premises

Our basic proposition that governance matters is dominant in most governance research. However, unless we can acknowledge the real life problems in testing this proposition, it is unlikely that we will ever have a decisive answer. These problems can be stated in the form of the following premises:

1. Board independence and the presence of large shareholders are necessary but not sufficient for better governance.

   1(a) For effective governance independent boards and large shareholders have to be vigilant. 1 and 1(a) constitute the necessary and sufficient conditions for effective governance.

2. Not all boards and large shareholders are vigilant in normal times.
3. Not all large shareholders act uniformly in the pursuit of shareholder value.
4. Boards and large shareholders are likely to become more vigilant due to a crisis.
5. The market for corporate control (MCC) is not hubris free.

We treat the basic proposition that governance matters as axiomatic. To quote Ira Milstein as reported by Monks and Minow (1995: 450–1), "I'm always surprised when people debate the linkage between corporate governance and performance . . . Does the absence of conclusive empirical proof that participating in corporate governance improves the bottom line mean we ignore the obvious linkage?"

*Board independence and vigilance.*   Premises 1 and 1a suggest that independent directors are *potentially* more effective if and only if they are vigilant. This idea is by no means empirically established even though it is theoretically accepted quite widely (for the standard academic arguments see Zajac and Westphal, 1995: 512). In the introduction to this chapter, we have already cited the conflicting findings regarding the effect of board composition and performance. Monks and Minow (1995: 204) add, "Although there are much theory and some data to recommend outside directors, their impact is still difficult to quantify, and research on this subject remains limited."

We believe that a main contributory factor for the inconsistent findings is the second premise that not all boards and large shareholders are vigilant during normal times. We do not have irrefutable empirical evidence that some boards are not vigilant under normal circumstances. However, it seems to be a reasonable portrayal of reality and something that has to be explicitly built into any theoretical framework that is ultimately trying to prove that board independence leads to effective governance. Anecdotally, the fact that *Business Week* (Byrne, 2000) annually publishes *The Best and Worst Boards*, and the institutional shareholders' new found target is boards (rather than CEOs) suggest that some boards are not being accountable to the shareholders.

Also, consider the case of the Walt Disney Company, headed by CEO Michael D. Eisner. *Business Week* (Byrne, 2000), which considers Disney's board to be "packed with Eisner chums," classified it as the worst board in America. However, using proxy data we found that the majority of Disney directors are non-managers (even counting ex-Disney officials). By most academic standards this would be classified as an independent board. Yet this board had done little to guide management's strategies in the past, a classic illustration of "sometimes independence may mean indifference" (Monks and Minow, 1995: 205). On the other hand, there are independent boards such as Compaq's that are independent on paper *and* also seem to create shareholder value. The point here is simply that independence alone will not necessarily lead to the creation of value.

*Large shareholders.*   Part of the problem with the research on large shareholders may be similar to that of the research on board effectiveness. Large shareholders may not have a major role to play in normal times. As Useem (1995: 640) points out, "the main issue for many institutional investors remains actual company performance, not its oversight." However, apart from normal versus crisis modes, large shareholders are also not a monolithic block. Part of the inconsistency in research findings has been attributed to the fact that sometimes large shareholders would actually side with management depending on the type of the large shareholders. There exists empirical evidence that some categories of large shareholders are more apt to be involved in actively seeking to maximize shareholder value while others would go along with the board's recommendations (see Useem (1996) for some examples). For example, in the context of the *initial* takeover offer there is evidence that large shareholders can support, or oppose, the takeover offer depending on their type (corporations, individual, mutual funds or financial institutions) (Barklay and Holderness, 1991; Holderness and Sheehan, 1988; Shome and Singh, 1995; Useem, 1996). Specifically, if the board decides to reject the initial offer, then financial institutions like banks and insurance companies have been observed to support the board, while individuals and mutual fund managers may support the bidding entity and sale of the firm. Thus, to effectively verify the role of large shareholders, tests should be conducted in situations in which *all* the large shareholders can be theoretically expected to act consistently. To our knowledge, this has never been done in the literature, even though researchers have investigated actions taken by different categories of large shareholders.

*Normal versus crisis mode.* There is a fair amount of evidence regarding the fourth premise that large shareholders and boards become more vigilant in periods of crisis such as a takeover offer. During these situations, large shareholders may actively tender their shares to risk arbitrageurs (Peck, 1996) or take other forms of action to increase shareholder value (Denis and Serrano, 1996; Pound, 1992). In many cases, large block shareholders play a pivotal role in persuading management to agree to sell the firm to the initial or a subsequent bidder. For example, when Asyst Technologies missed its quarterly earning three quarters in a row, Paul Wick, a large investor, actively sought out PRI Automation as a possible acquirer of Asyst.

Takeovers may, in fact, be fueled by the desire for liquidity on the part of large block shareholders. Very simply, the immediate gains from a takeover premium are much more meaningful to many large block shareholders who may not fully comprehend, or are willing to live with, the uncertainties of a long-term strategy to increase shareholder value. Further, some large block shareholders may also reduce the effects of any management entrenchment by tendering their shares or supporting a dissident slate of directors in a proxy vote. Regarding boards, Pettigrew's (1992) observation illustrates the fact that boards have been proven to be active under crisis (takeovers and litigations) situations. Also, Johnson, Hoskisson, and Hitt (1993) suggest that boards become more involved in governance activities when there is a perception that managerial strategies may be inadequate in safeguarding shareholder interests. Apart from the well-known legal obligations of boards, there is also evidence that board composition can influence the probability of a takeover (Cotter, Shivdasani and Zenner, 1997).

*Hubris in takeovers.* The fifth premise is not an absolute necessity for our purposes, but there is clearly evidence in support of it (Franks and Mayer, 1996; Hitt, Harrison, and Ireland, 2001; Hitt et al., 1998; Roll, 1986; Walsh and Kosnik, 1993). Basically, takeover

offers seem equally likely to be targeted toward underperforming firms and over performing firms. Since we are focusing on firms targeted as takeovers we would like to
acknowledge the possibility of hubris in our theoretical framework.

In the rest of this chapter, we will develop testable propositions of the basic question
– does governance matter? – given the reality of all five of these premises. We submit
that if our basic arguments are correct then *all* of the following propositions should be
supportable through empirical research. It is fair to say that our theory has evolved partly
from unexpected findings from previous and concurrent research in similar areas.

## Propositions about governance during a crisis

Governance, if it matters, should be involved in monitoring the strategic direction of the
firm. We develop our propositions assuming that rejecting an initial takeover offer
provides a *prima facie* stimulus for reconsidering the strategic direction of the firm. Our
propositions predict how a firm is expected to react to this stimulus given its antecedent
governance characteristics. Before developing these propositions, we would like to introduce a few illustrative cases that demonstrate typical reactions to the market for corporate control.

ITT is one of the last relics of the 1960s style conglomerates. Hilton's initial offer to
buy ITT was a signal that ITT still has to undo some of its past conglomerations which
ITT's board (which is fairly independent according to governance guidelines) never
questioned. However, even though ITT rejected Hilton's bid, ITT's board subsequently
put the company up for sale to the highest bidder, which was Starwood Lodging. Part of
the persuasion to put the firm up for sale also came from a large institutional shareholder
called Michael Price and his ally Al "Chainsaw" Dunlap, the CEO of Sunbeam.

On the other hand, Gillette fought off a prolonged proxy fight from Coniston Partners
in 1986 and was saved by Warren Buffet, who sided with management. Gillette has
subsequently earned a generous return on equity for its shareholders. Recently, Dayton
Hudson fought off a hostile offer from J.C. Penny, and Chrysler once fought off Kirk
Kerkorian. However, neither firm has undertaken any significant strategic changes. Both
of these firms have been quite successful since the rejection of the initial takeover offers.

The point of these cases is that different firms will react differently to a takeover offer
and the signal from the market for corporate control does not always imply that a firm
has to follow through with the suggestions of strategic changes (or restructuring) implicit
in the offer. We now develop testable propositions regarding the role of the board and
large shareholders in determining the actions suggested by signals from the market for
corporate control.

## Testable implications for firms that are subsequently acquired

The time frame in which we are interested is the period within approximately four years
after the takeover attempt. We believe that any subsequent takeover beyond the four
years period is unlikely to be related to the original takeover offer.

*The role of the board.*   Can we predict the characteristics of the board of a firm that would
likely be acquired subsequently? If we assume that the stock price is an unbiased

estimator (i.e., ignoring the possibility of hubris, which we will incorporate later), then a takeover offer reflects the market for corporate control's sentiment that the firm's resources can be put to better use. The initial rejection suggests that the board, and management, had not considered the fact that their firm can be managed differently. However, once the takeover offer is public, the board has both fiscal and legal obligations to consider the ramifications of selling the firm – if the board believes in the validity of the market's signal. Unfortunately, even if the market's signal is correct on average (no hubris), a takeover offer may or may not lead to any changes unless the board has the independence to act on the signal from the market. This inaction by the board can happen if insiders dominate the board or if management is entrenched. The board independence premise would, therefore, suggest that boards dominated by outsiders are more likely to act on the signal, perhaps with a little persuasion from large shareholders as the second proposition (see below) suggests. In other words, a board that can act decisively and is not emotionally attached to the strategy of management is likely to be objective about the signal from the market and act on it (Byrd and Hickman, 1992). Formally stated:

> *Proposition 1*: In the aftermath of a failed takeover bid, target firms that have boards with independent governance characteristics are likely to be eventually acquired by another entity.

*The role of large shareholders.*   There is a large body of literature which suggests that the presence of large block shareholders leads to value-maximizing decisions (Johnson, Hoskisson, and Hitt, 1993). Anecdotally, large block shareholders (such as Michael Price) have coerced management (such as that of ITT) into value-maximizing decisions which may include selling the firm after the initial bid has failed (see Raad and Ryan (1995) for empirical evidence of similar actions). Mutual fund managers like Price are willing to support any takeovers to improve the value of their investments.

> *Proposition 1a*: In the aftermath of a failed takeover attempt, target firms that have investors with large blockholdings are likely to be acquired by another entity.

There is, however, an important caveat to Propositions 1 and 1a. It does not follow that all the firms that do not agree to be taken over have insider dominated boards or lack large shareholders. In the next section, we will argue that it is possible to predict the governance characteristics of firms that refuse to be subsequently taken over once we accept the proposition that not all independent boards are vigilant in normal times.

*The effect of prior performance.*   If a board is independent on paper but was not vigilant about a firm's strategy in the past, then, to the extent that governance matters (our first premise), it is likely that prior to the takeover offer such a firm would have underperformed the market. On the other hand, if an independent board had been vigilant then such a firm is likely to have outperformed the market prior to the takeover offer. We submit that subsequent to a takeover offer, the actions of independent boards (and large shareholders) for the group of firms that have underperformed in the past would be different from the group of firms that outperformed. Under the spotlight of the takeover offer, both groups of independent boards will assert their independence – but in different ways. The independent board that had been vigilant will assert independence by maintaining confidence in the firm's strategy – they will refuse to be taken over. Basically, the board that had been vigilant is more likely to conclude that the takeover offer was driven by hubris.

We do not want to be drawn into defending or attacking the hubris hypothesis of takeovers. The studies (Walsh and Kosnik, 1993; Franks and Mayer, 1996; Hitt et al., 1998, 2001) that demonstrate that takeover offers are not always targeted towards improving performance is not definitive proof of hubris in the sense that Hayward and Hambrick (1997) suggest. Our proposition incorporates the reality of the above findings and extends these by predicting that the firms that underperformed prior to the takeover offer are likely to have ineffective (not vigilant) governance – on average. A takeover offer may justifiably be made for a firm that had superior performance in the past, if the takeover can justify even better performance in the future. In this case an independent and vigilant board should agree to a subsequent takeover. Our proposition simply suggests that this latter situation is not likely to be a central tendency even if the market for corporate control is always correct (no hubris) because it is much less likely that a successful firm will admit to error and more likely to claim that the market is in error. The refusal of Computer Sciences to be acquired by Computer Associates, a firm that has been remarkably successful with past acquisitions, illustrates this point.

On the other hand, the board that had not been vigilant is more likely to acknowledge that the market for corporate control has exposed the shortcomings of the firm's strategy. If such a board has the independence to act on their realization then it will agree to sell the firm to a subsequent bidder. If propositions 1 and 1a are valid, then we assume that the firms that subsequently agree to be taken over have independent governance characteristics. The previous arguments suggest that it is more likely that in the past the boards and large shareholders for this group of firms (that were subsequently acquired) were not vigilant. If our central thesis that governance matters is correct, then we would expect this group of firms to underperform relative to the market and especially relative to the group of firms with vigilant governance that refused to be taken over later. Formally stated:

*Proposition 2*: In the aftermath of a failed takeover attempt, target firms that are subsequently acquired by another entity had low market performance prior to the initial takeover offer.

## Testable implications for firms that remain independent

*The role of the board and large shareholder vigilance.* We can reinforce proposition 2 by developing propositions regarding the prior performance of the group of firms that remain independent. Recall that firms that will remain independent are likely to fall into two categories. These are (a) firms whose independent boards had been vigilant in the past and (b) firms whose boards are not independent enough or management is entrenched enough to prevent a takeover. If our premise that vigilant governance will lead to improved performance is correct, then the next proposition is reasonable as well:

*Proposition 3*: In the aftermath of a failed takeover attempt, of the target firms that remain autonomous, firms with independent governance characteristics and large shareholders also had superior performance prior to the initial takeover offer.

Finally, we can reinforce proposition 3 by examining how the capital market should value the firms in the immediate proximity of the time when other firms are taken over (in our experience, if a subsequent acquisition takes place, it occurs 14 to 20 months after the initial rejected offer). For firms that are still autonomous in the 14 to 20-month period after rejecting the initial takeover bid, the market will make some judgment about their future prospects. Chatterjee (1992) and Bradley, Desai, and Kim (1983) demonstrated that firms that do not get taken over will subsequently trade at a higher premium than the market because of anticipated future takeovers or the possibility of future refocusing (Chatterjee, 1992). If our basic logic is correct, then amongst firms that remain autonomous, the firms with non-independent boards and few large shareholders are most likely to have the highest takeover/refocusing premium because they were the poorest performers prior to the takeover offer. The capital market is likely to conclude that of the firms that remained independent, the ones with poor governance had not "learned their lesson." Such firms are most likely to benefit from refocusing or being taken over at a yet future date (Chatterjee, 1992; Chatterjee and Kosnik, 1997). This logic is tightly linked to propositions 1 and 1a which suggest that independent internal governance and strong external governance will lead to quick action upon receipt of the signal from the capital market. Note, however, that if these firms do not get taken over in the long run then their market value should decline unless they refocus (Bradley, Desai, and Kim, 1983).

There is actually some prior evidence of this prediction – evidence that was thought to be counterintuitive, but in reality is easily explained by our logic. Chatterjee and Kosnik (1997) demonstrated that firms that had weak governance at the time of the initial takeover offer, traded at a higher premium because these firms were the worst performers prior to the offer and had the most to gain. This expectation is also supported by research done by Hoskisson, Johnson, and Moesel (1994), among others (see Johnson, 1996). The same story is true for firms without large external shareholders, which allows management to hold out for a larger takeover premium (Morck, Shleifer, and Vishny, 1988b; Stulz, 1988), at least in the intermediate term when the market still sees possibilities of a future takeover. Thus, we advance the following propositions:

*Proposition 4*: After the initial takeover offer is rejected, firms that have boards without independent governance characteristics or ones that are impeded from acting quickly will be trading at a higher market premium.

*Proposition 5*: After the initial takeover offer is rejected, firms that do not have large block shareholders will be trading at a higher market premium.

*Proposition 6*: After the initial takeover offer is rejected, firms that had low performance prior to the takeover will be trading at a higher market premium.

## DISCUSSION

Three specific roles of boards of directors are most often discussed in the governance literature. The most attention has been directed towards the control role, which describes the board's role in monitoring the behavior of managers. A board also serves a service role in giving advice to the CEO and other top executives and a resource dependence role, which focuses on the use of directors to provide links to the external environment in an effort to acquire critical resources. In our brief review of this literature, we pointed out that these three roles would all seem to be more important in times of crisis. Also, a great deal of research attention has been devoted to characteristics of boards and shareholders that lead to effective governance, such as the independence of directors and the existence of large shareholders. However, in spite of the large volume of research on these topics, the empirical support for the notion that effective governance matters is not overwhelming. In this chapter, we have developed theory to support the idea that governance is more important in a crisis, using independence and shareholder size variables to develop testable propositions.

In summary, we believe that independent boards, as measured by conventional academic constructs, and the existence of large shareholders, are not necessarily good predictors of the quality of governance under normal conditions. However, in times of crisis, when the governance mechanisms come under close scrutiny, independence and shareholder size are likely to influence governance powers to benefit shareholders. We used this belief to develop propositions that predict how firms are likely to react to a takeover offer that they initially reject. Firms with strong governance on paper as well as in action (as measured by past performance) are much more likely to ignore the takeover offer completely and not change their strategy. Firms with strong governance on paper but not in action (as measured by past performance) are much more likely to acquiesce to being acquired at a subsequent date. Firms with poor governance will try to remain independent but are most likely to be subject to other forms of corporate control or restructuring measures.

The propositions developed herein are consistent with studies that conclude that independent directors enhance target shareholder wealth during tender offers (Cotter, Shivdasani, and Zenner, 1997). ITT's refusal to be taken over by Hilton and subsequent sale to Starwood Lodging is a good illustration of our theory. According to *Business Week*'s (quantitative) governance guidance analysis, which is a composite measure of board independence, ITT's board scores high on independence and shareholder accountability (7/10), even though this board was ranked by *Business Week* as one of the worst boards (using qualitative measures) because investors felt that the board was blocking the initial takeover offer by Hilton. It is also interesting to note that immediately after the publication of the *Business Week* article, the board started talks to be acquired by Starwood Lodging. Finally, ITT also received considerable coercion from large investors such as Michael Price of Mutual Shares.

Like Hoskisson, Johnson, and Moesel (1994) and others (see Monks and Minow, 1995: 205), we believe that when outside directors hold equity in the firm, they are more likely to familiarize themselves with the strategy of the firm. Some practitioners take the extreme step in assuming that any director (insider or outsider) with a large enough equity stake in the company should be considered an insider. This brings us naturally to another research question that is closely related to the theory developed herein. Do equity holdings by outside director's make them behave more like inside directors who also hold equity, especially with regard to the strategic control of the firm? The findings of Morck, Shleifer and Vishny (1988a) regarding equity holding of *all* directors (insiders and outsiders) are consistent with an affirmative answer to this question.

The primary purpose of this chapter is to guide governance researchers in future research by demonstrating that mixed empirical support for the value of appropriate governance may be a function of organizational context (crisis versus non-crisis). However, the implications of the propositions developed herein, if supported, may also have implications to a firm's management. The basic recommendation to governance activists is that board independence can make a difference, but it is much more important to develop measures of board vigilance rather than simply counting the number of independent directors. To governance activists, we suggest that even if you believe that a board is not vigilant or is beholden to the CEO, if they appear to be independent on paper *and* the firm has been outperforming the market, then it is probably best to leave well enough alone. In such a case somebody – the board, management, or both – is doing the right thing for the shareholders. In other words, as long as Disney continues to perform well, don't worry too much about its board composition.

## CONCLUSION

As we begin a new century, there is considerable pressure from both institutional investors and governance activists on boards to be held accountable for the failure of managers. This does not mean that such pressures always work, and more importantly are always correct. However, we believe that by further investigation of how boards act in both normal times and times of crisis, we will be able to develop better normative frameworks to guide governance activists as well as help firms manage their relationship with their boards.

## REFERENCES

Bainbridge, S. M. (1993). Independent directors and the ALI corporate governance project. *George Washington Law Review*, 61: 1034–83.

Barklay, M. J., and Holderness, C. G. (1991). Negotiated block trades and corporate control. *Journal of Finance*, 46: 861–78.

Barnard, J. W. (1991). Institutional investors and the new corporate governance. *North Carolina Law Review*, 69: 1135–87.

Barney, J. (1991). Firm resources and sustained competitive advantage. *Journal of Management*, 17: 99–120.

Baysinger, B. D., and Butler, H. (1985). Corporate governance and the board of directors: Performance effects of changes in board composition. *Journal of Law, Economics and Organization*, 1: 101–34.

Baysinger, B. D., and Hoskisson, R. E. (1990). The composition of boards of directors and strategic control: Effects on corporate strategy. *Academy of Management Review*, 15: 72–87.

Beekun, R. I., Stedham, Y., and Young, G. J. (1998). Board characteristics, managerial controls and corporate strategy: A study of US hospitals. *Journal of Management*, 24: 3–19.

Berle, A. A., and Means, G. C. (1932). *The Modern Corporation and Private Property*. New York: Macmillan.

Block, D. Barton, N., and Radin, S. (1989). *The Business Judgment Rule: Fiduciary Duties of Corporate Directors* (3rd Edn.). Englewood Cliffs, NJ: Prentice-Hall Law and Business.

Boeker, W., and Goodstein, J. (1993). Performance and successor choice: The moderating effects of governance and ownership. *Academy of Management Journal*, 36: 172–86.

Bogart, D. B. (1994). Liability of directors of Chapter 11 debtors in possession: "Don't look back – something may be gaining on you." *American Bankruptcy Law Journal*, 68 (Winter): 155–267.

Bradley, M., Desai, A., and Kim, E. H. (1983). The rationale behind interfirm tender offers: Information or synergy? *Journal of Financial Economics*, 11: 183–206.

Brudney, V. (1983). Equal treatment of shareholders in corporate distributions and reorganizations. *California Law Review*, 71: 1403–44.

Byrd, J., and Hickman, K. (1992). Do outside directors monitor managers? Evidence from tender offer bids. *Journal of Financial Economics*, 32: 195–221.

Byrne, J. A., Brown, L., and Barnathan, J. (1997). Directors in the hot seat. *Business Week*, December 8: 100.

Byrne, J. A. (2000). The best and worst boards. *Business Week*, January 24: 142–52.

Cochran, P. L., Wood, R. A., and Jones, T. B. (1985). The composition of boards of directors and incidence of golden parachutes. *Academy of Management Journal*, 28: 664–71.

Chatterjee, S. (1992). Sources of value in takeovers: Synergy or restructuring – Implications for target and bidder firms. *Strategic Management Journal*, 13: 267–86.

Chatterjee S., and Kosnik, R. (1997). *Corporate Restructuring: The Result of Good or Bad Governance*. Presented at the annual meeting to the Strategic Management Society.

Cieri, R. M., Sullivan, P. F., and Lennox, H. (1994). The fiduciary duties of directors of financially troubled companies. *Journal of Bankruptcy Law and Practice*, 3: 405–22.

Cochran, P. L., Wood, R. A., and Jones, T. B. (1985). The composition of boards of directors and incidence of golden parachutes. *Academy of Management Journal*, 28: 644–71.

Coffee, J. C. (1994). The SEC and the institutional investor: A half-time report. *Cardozo Law Review*, 15: 837–907.

Coles, J. W., and Hesterley, W. S. (2000). Independence of the chairman and board composition: Firm choices and shareholder value. *Journal of Management*, 26: 195–214.

Conyon, M. J., and Peck, S. I. (1998). Board control, remuneration committees, and top management compensation. *Academy of Management Journal*, 41: 146–57.

Cotter, J. F., Shivdasani, A., and Zenner, M. (1997). Do independent directors enhance target sharehlder wealth during tender offers? *Journal of Financial Economics*, 43: 195–218.

Daily, C. M. (1995). The relationship between board composition and leadership structure and bankruptcy reorganization outcomes. *Journal of Management*, 21: 1041–56.

Daily, C. M. (1996). Governance patterns in bankruptcy reorganizations. *Strategic Management Journal*, 17: 355–75.

Daily, C. M., and Dalton, D. R. (1992). The relationship between governance structure and corporate performance in entrepreneurial firms. *Journal of Business Venturing*, 7: 375–86.

Daily, C. M., and Dalton, D. R. (1994). Corporate governance and the bankrupt firm: An empirical assessment. *Strategic Management Journal*, 15: 643–54.

Daily, C. M., and Dalton, D. R. (1995). CEO and director turnover in failing firms: An illusion of change? *Strategic Management Journal*, 16: 393–400.

Daily, C. M., and Johnson, J. L. (1997). Sources of CEO power and firm financial performance: A longitudinal assessment. *Journal of Management*, 23: 97–117.

Dalton, D. R., Daily, C. M., Ellstrand, A. E., and Johnson, J. L. (1998). Meta-analytic reviews of board composition, leadership structure and financial performance. *Strategic Management Journal*, 19: 269–90.

Dalton, D. R., Daily, C. M., Johnson, J. L., and Ellstrand, A. E. (1999). Number of directors and financial performance: A meta-analysis. *Academy of Management Journal*, 42: 674–86.

Dalton, D. R., and Kesner, I. F. (1987). Composition of CEO duality in board of directors: An international perspective. *Journal of International Business Studies*, 18: 33–42.

Davis, G. F. (1991). Agents without principles? The spread of the poison pill through the intercorporate network. *Administrative Science Quarterly*, 36: 583–613.

Davis, J. H., Schoorman, F. D., and Donaldson, L. (1997). Toward a stewardship theory of management. *Academy of Management Review*, 22: 20–47.

Denis, D. J., and Serrano, J. M. (1996). Active investors and management turnover following unsuccessful control contests. *Journal of Financial Economics*, 40: 239–66.

Fama, E. F., and Jensen, M. C. (1983). Separation of ownership and corporate control. *Journal of Law and Economics*, 26: 301–25.

Forbes, D. P., and Milliken, F. J. (1999). Cognition and corporate governance: Understanding boards of directors as strategic decision-making groups. *Academy of Management Review*, 24: 489–505.

Franks, J., and Mayer, C. (1996). Hostile takeovers and the correction of managerial failure. *Journal of Financial Economics*, 40: 163–81.

Fredrickson, J. W., Hambrick, D. C., and Baumrin, S. (1988). A model of CEO dismissal. *Academy of Management Review*, 13: 255–70.

Galaskiewicz, J. (1985). Interorganizational relations. *Annual Review of Sociology*, 11: 281–304.

Gales, L. M., and Kesner, I. F. (1994). An analysis of board of director size and composition in bankrupt organizations. *Journal of Business Research*, 30: 27–39.

Goforth, C. (1994). Proxy reform as a means of increasing shareholder participation in corporate governance: Too little, but not too late. *The American University Law Review*, 43: 379–465.

Gomez-Mejia, L., and Wiseman, R. M. (1997). Reframing executive compensations: An assessment and outlook. *Journal of Management*, 23: 291–374.

Harrison, J. S., and Fiet, J. O. (1999). New CEOs pursue their own interests by sacrificing stakeholder value. *Journal of Business Ethics*, 19: 301–8.

Harrison, J. S., and St. John, C. H. (1998). *Foundations of Strategic Management*. Cincinnati, OH: South-Western College Publishing.

Hayward, M., and Hambrick, D. (1997). Explaining the premium paid for large acquisitions: Evidence of CEO hubris. *Administrative Science Quarterly*, 42(1): 103–27.

Hermalin, B. E., and Weisbach, M. S. (1988). The determinants of board composition. *Rand Journal of Economics*, 19: 569–606.

Herman, E. S. (1981). *Corporate Control, Corporate Power*. New York: Cambridge University Press.

Hill, C. W. L., and Snell, S. A. (1988). External control, corporate strategy, and firm performance in research intensive industries. *Strategic Management Journal*, 32: 25–46.

Hitt, M. A., Harrison, J. S., and Ireland, R. D. (2001). Creating value through mergers and acquisitions. Oxford, UK: Oxford University Press.

Hitt, M. A., Harrison, J. S., Ireland, R. D., and Best, A. (1998). Attributes of successful and unsuccessful acquisitions of US firms. *British Journal of Management*, 9: 91–114.

Holderness, C. G., and Sheehan, D. P. (1988). The role of majority shareholders in publicly held corporations: An exploratory analysis. *Journal of Financial Economics*, 19: 569–606.

Hoskisson, R. E., Johnson, R. A., and Moesel, D. D. (1994). Corporate divestiture intensity in restructuring firms: Effects of governance, strategy, and performance. *Academy of Management Journal*, 37: 1207–51.

Hoskisson, R. E., and Turk, T. A. (1990). Corporate restructuring: Governance and control limits of the internal capital market. *Academy of Management Review*, 15: 459–77.

Johnson, J. L., Daily, C. M., and Ellstrand, A. E. (1996). Boards of directors: A review and research agenda. *Journal of Management*, 22: 409–38.

Johnson, R. A. (1996). Antecedents and outcomes of corporate refocusing. *Journal of Management*, 22: 439–83.

Johnson, R. A., and Greening, D. W. (1999). The effects of corporate governance and institutional ownership types on corporate social performance. *Academy of Management Journal*, 42: 564–76.

Johnson, R. A., Hoskisson, R. E., and Hitt, M. A. (1993). Board of director involvement in restructuring: The effects of board versus managerial controls and characteristics. *Strategic*

*Management Journal*, 14: 33–50.

Judge, W. Q., Jr., and Dobbins, G. H. (1995). Antecedents and effects of outside director's awareness of CEO decision style. *Journal of Management*, 21: 43–64.

Judge, W. Q., Jr,. and Zeithaml, C. P. (1992). Institutional and strategic choice perspectives on board involvement in the strategic decision process. *Academy of Management Journal*, 35: 766–94.

Kaplan, S. N., and Minton, B. A. (1994). Appointments of outsiders to Japanese boards: Determinants and implications for managers. *Journal of Financial Economics*, 36: 225–58.

Kerr, J. L., and Kren, L. (1992). Effect of relative decision monitoring on chief executive compensation. *Academy of Management Journal*, 35: 370–97.

Kesner, I. F. (1987). Directors' stock ownership and organizational performance: An investigation of *Fortune 500* companies. *Journal of Management*, 13: 499–507.

Kesner, I. F., and Johnson, R. B. (1990). An investigation of the relationship between board composition and stockholder suits. *Strategic Management Journal*, 11: 327–36.

Lorsch, J. W., and MacIver, E. (1989). *Pawns or Potentates: The Reality of America's Corporate Boards.* Boston, MA: Harvard Business School Press.

Lowenstein, M. J. (1994). The SEC and the future of corporate governance. *Alabama Law Review* 45: 783–815.

Mace, M. (1986). *Directors: Myth and Reality* (2nd Edn.). Boston: Harvard Business School Press.

Mallette, P., and Fowler, K. L. (1992). Effects of board composition and stock ownership on the adoption of "poison pills." *Academy of Management Journal*, 35: 1010–26.

Mangel, R., and Singh, H. (1993). Ownership structure, board relationships and CEO compensation in large US corporations. *Accounting and Business Research*, 23: 339–50.

Manning, B. A. (1984). The business judgment rule in overview. *Ohio State Law Journal*, 45: 615–27.

Miller, H. R. (1993). Corporate governance in Chapter 11: The fiduciary relationship between directors and stockholders of solvent and insolvent corporation. *Seton Hall Law Review*, 23: 1467–515.

Mizruchi, M. S. (1989). Similarity of political behavior among large American corporations. *American Journal of Sociology*, 95: 401–24.

Molz, R. (1988). Managerial domination of boards of directors and financial performance. *Journal of Business Research*, 16: 235–49.

Monks, R. A. G., and Minow, N. (1995). *Corporate Governance.* Cambridge, MA: Blackwell.

Morck, R. I., Schleifer, A., and Vishny, R. W. (1988a). Characteristics of targets of hostile and friendly takeovers. In A. J. Auerbach (ed.), *Takeovers: Causes and Consequences*, 101–36. Chicago: University of Chicago Press.

Morck, R. I., Shleifer, A., and Vishny, R. W. (1988b). Management ownership and market valuation: An empirical analysis. *Journal of Financial Economics*, 20: 293–315.

Pearce, J. A., and Zahra, S. A. (1991). The relative power of CEOs and boards of directors: Associations with corporate performance. *Strategic Management Journal*, 12: 135–53.

Pearce, J. A., and Zahra, S. A. (1992). Board composition from a strategic contingency perspective. *Journal of Management Studies*, 29: 411–38.

Peck, S. W. (1996). The influence of professional investors on the failure of management buyout attempts. *Journal of Financial Economics*, 40: 267–94.

Pettigrew, A. (1992). On studying managerial elites. *Strategic Management Journal*, 13: 163–82.

Pffefer, J. (1972). Size and composition of corporate boards of directors: The organization and its environment. *Administrative Science Quarterly*, 17: 218–28.

Pffefer, J., and Salancik, G. R. (1978). *The External Control of Organizations: A Resource Dependence Perspective.* New York: Harper and Row.

Pound, J. (1992). Beyond takeovers: Politics comes to corporate control. *Harvard Business Review*, 70(2): 83–93.

Raad, E., and Ryan, R. (1995). Capital structure and ownership distribution of tender offer targets:

An empirical study. *Financial Management*, 24(1): 46–56.

Roll, R. (1986). The hubris hypothesis of corporate takeovers. *Journal of Business*, 59: 197–216.

Rosenstein, S., Bruno, A. V., Bygrave, W. D., and Taylor, N. T. (1993). The CEO, venture capitalists, and the board. *Journal of Business Venturing*, 8: 99–113.

Schellenger, M. H., Wood, D. D., and Tashakori, A. (1989). Board of director composition, shareholder wealth and dividend policy. *Journal of Management*, 15: 457–67.

Selznick, A. (1949). *TVA and the Grass Roots*. Berkeley: University of California Press.

Shome, D. K., and Singh, S. (1995). Firm value and external blockholdings. *Financial Management*, 24(4): 3–15.

Singh, H., and Harianto, F. (1989). Management-board relationships, takeover risk, and the adoption of golden parachutes. *Academy of Management Journal*, 32: 7–24.

Spencer, A. (1983). *On the Edge of Organization: The Role of Outside Director*. New York: Wiley.

Stearns, L. B., and Mizruchi, M. S. (1993). Board composition and corporate financing: The impact of financial institution representation of borrowing. *Academy of Management Journal*, 36: 603–618.

Stulz, R. M. (1988). Managerial control of voting rights. *Journal of Financial Economics*, January/March: 25–54.

Sundaramurthy, C., Mahoney, J. M., and Mahoney, J. T. (1997). Board structure, antitakeover provisions, and stockholder wealth. *Strategic Management Journal*, 18: 231–45.

Sundaramurthy, C., Rechner, P., and Wang, W. (1996). Governance antecedents and board entrenchment: The case of classified board provisions. *Journal of Management*, 22: 783–99.

Sutton, R. I., and Callahan, A. L. (1987). The stigma of bankruptcy: Spoiled organizational image and its management. *Academy of Management Journal*, 30: 405–36.

Tashakori, A., and Boulton, W. R. (1983). A look at the board's role in planning. *Journal of Business Strategy*, 3(2): 64–70.

Useem, M. (1993). *Executive Defense: Shareholder Power and Corporate Reorganization*. Cambridge, MA: Harvard University Press.

Useem, M. (1996). *Investor Capitalism*. New York: Basic Books.

Vance, S. C. (1964). *Boards of Directors: Structure and Performance*. Eugene, OR: University of Oregon Press.

Wade, J., O'Reilly, C. A., and Chandratat, I. (1990). Golden parachutes: CEOs and the exercise of social influence. *Administrative Science Quarterly*, 35: 587–603.

Walsh, J. P., and Kosnik, R. D. (1993). Corporate raiders and their disciplinary role in the market for corporate control. *Academy of Management Journal*, 36: 671–700.

Walsh, J. P., and Seward, J. K. (1990). On the efficiency of internal and external corporate control mechanisms. *Academy of Management Review*, 15: 421–58.

Weisbach, M. C. (1988). Outside directors and CEO turnover. *Journal of Financial Economics*, 20: 431–60.

Westphal, J. D. (1999). Collaboration in the boardroom: Behavioral and performance consequences of CEO-board social ties. *Academy of Management Journal*, 42: 7–24.

Westphal, J. D., and Zajac, E. J. (1995). Who shall govern? CEO/board power, demographic similarity, and new director selection. *Administrative Science Quarterly*, 40: 60–83.

Williamson, O. E. (1984). Corporate governance. *Yale Law Journal*, 93: 1197–230.

Zahra, S. A., and Pearce, J. A., II (1989). Boards of directors and corporate financial performance: A review and integrative model. *Journal of Management*, 15: 291–334.

Zajac, E. J., and Westphal, J. D. (1995). Accounting for the explanations of CEO compensation: Substance and symbolism. *Administrative Science Quarterly*, 40: 283–308.

# 20

# Corporate Strategy and Ethics, as Corporate Strategy Comes of Age

### Daniel R. Gilbert, Jr.

Twenty years ago in *The Concept of Corporate Strategy*, Kenneth Andrews (1980: 10–11) linked corporate strategy and ethics by making three references to "worth":

> The prototype of the chief executive that we are developing is, in short, the able victory-seeking organizational leader who is making sure in what is done and the changes pioneered in purpose and practice that *the game is worth playing, the victory worth seeking, and life and career worth living.* (Emphasis added)

Subsequently, Andrews (1980: 11) designated "the chief executive as architect of purpose." Purposeful human participation in worthy pursuits is a subject in which corporate strategists and ethicists alike are keenly interested. According to LaRue Hosmer, this convergence of interests has a long history in American business thought. Hosmer (1994: 17) traces the link between corporate strategy and ethics to the writings of Chester Barnard in the early twentieth century. An argument can be made that Hosmer's genealogy is too abbreviated.

Spanning the 1868 publication of *Ragged Dick* and the 1890 publication of *Struggling Upward*, Horatio Alger (1985) explained variation in economic performance, the dependent variable that interests several generations of corporate strategists, in terms of ethics. Alger's successful businessmen, Greyson in *Ragged Dick* and Reed and Armstrong in *Struggling Upward*, possessed the virtues of purposefulness, honesty, and humility (Gilbert, 1996a: 152). A line linking corporate strategy and ethics connects the work of Alger with the work of novelists Frank Norris and Sloan Wilson. In *The Octopus*, Norris (1901) wrote of nineteenth-century California farmers who vainly sought competitive advantage – a foundational concept of corporate strategy – and justice every day in their dealings with managers of the railroad monopoly. The corporate strategists in Wilson's (1955) *The Man in the Gray Flannel Suit* search for worthy games, worthy victories, worthy lives, and worthy careers. Richard Wheeler (2000) writes *The Buffalo Commons* is a moving story about corporate strategists who try to preserve worthy ways of living and working on the American Great Plains, and who struggle with the incompatibility of their respective pursuits. Linking corporate strategy and ethics is an American literary tradition.

The first purpose of this chapter, then, is to survey contemporary thinking about corporate strategy and ethics as a useful pairing. What has become of the ethical proposition that Andrews expressed poetically a generation ago? At first glance, an affirmative answer to this question seems improbable. Contemporary conversations about the concept of corporate strategy are conducted in the languages of economics, social psychology, and biology, not ethics (Hosmer, 1994). Nonetheless, a number of American educators keep alive Andrews' proposition that corporate strategy and ethics can share a common vocabulary that is anchored by *"the game is worth playing, the victory worth seeking, and life and career worth living."* In this chapter, you will meet some of us and our work.

The central theme of this chapter is that corporate strategy and ethics are now customarily linked in three distinct ways. Two of these connections between corporate strategy and ethics involve the incorporation of ethical considerations into the strategic management process. The third connection between corporate strategy and ethics is an ethical criticism that drives a wedge between the strategic management process and the concept of corporate strategy. Strategic management and corporate strategy are not the same thing, in this critical view.

The second purpose of this chapter is to trace the development of ethical criticism of the concept of corporate strategy. One sure sign that the concepts of corporate strategy and strategic management have come of age is that they have attracted the attention of persistent critics. Critics do not waste their time on trivial matters. Critics call attention to crucial matters. From the standpoint of the critics who ask ethical questions about corporate strategy, the concept of corporate strategy is as important as it gets.

## The Strategic Management Process and Ethics

The link between the strategic management process and ethics has become acceptable in American management education. This acceptance is plain to see in a number of different strategic management textbooks. In these textbooks, the spirit of Andrews' stirring exhortation lives on in the form of a recurring proposition. By this proposition, *ethics is useful as a modifying influence on the strategic management process.*

The first place where we encounter ethics modifying the strategic management process is the editorial layout of strategic management textbooks. In their textbook *Strategic Management: Competitiveness and Globalization,* Hitt, Ireland, and Hoskisson (1999) conclude every one of the thirteen chapters with the same format. "Review Questions" precede "Application Discussion Questions." "Ethics Questions" follow "Application Discussion Chapters." A proper place for ethics is unmistakable in this format. There are important questions to review about the strategic management process. Then there are applications of the strategic management process. Then ethics is injected to modify these more important questions.

In nine of the twelve chapters in their textbook *Strategic Management: Building and Sustaining Competitive Advantage,* Pitts and Lei (2000) explain a strategic management concept. Then they modify that explanation with a concluding section entitled "Ethical Dimensions." Again, the logical relationship is clear. There are main lessons to learn about the strategic management process. Then ethics is welcomed as a complement to the main lessons.

In their textbook *Strategic Management: Concepts and Cases*, Thompson and Strickland (1999: 53–4) discuss "Three Strategy-Making Tasks." Then they move to identify "The Factors that *Shape* a Company's Strategy" (emphasis added). A discussion of ethics is contained in the latter section. First you make strategy; then you shape it with finishing touches from ideas such as ethics.

This editorial convention for linking corporate strategy and ethics is reinforced in the words that these textbook authors and their peers use to describe the strategic management process. According to Thompson and Strickland (1999: 58, 59, 343, respectively):

> Managerial values also *shape the ethical quality* of a firm's strategy. (Emphasis added)

> Strategy ought to be ethical. It should involve rightful actions, not wrongful ones; *otherwise it won't pass the test of moral scrutiny.* (Emphasis added)

> An ethical corporate culture *has a positive impact on a company's long-term strategic success*; an unethical culture can undermine it. (Emphasis added)

Hitt, Ireland, and Hoskisson (1999: 460) observe ethics modifying the strategic management process in this proposition:

> The effectiveness of strategy implementation processes *increases when they are based on ethical practices.* (Emphasis added)

Pitts and Lei (2000: 20, 51, 287, respectively) connect corporate strategy and ethics in these expressions:

> Ethical dilemmas *work to shape and sometimes constrain* a firm's ability to take certain actions. (Emphasis added)

> Careful positioning can enable [a firm] to charge higher prices and limit rivalry. *But are these objectives really proper?* (Emphasis added)

> The rise of strategic alliances should *encourage managers to think about the ethical problems likely to emerge* when undertaking such arrangements. (Emphasis added)

In their textbook *Strategic Management and Business Policy: Entering 21st Century Global Society*, Wheelen and Hunger (2000: 39) call attention to situations that "raise questions of the appropriateness of certain missions, objectives, and strategies of business corporations." They proceed to apply ethics as a modifier to the strategic management process (Wheelen and Hunger, 2000: 39):

> Managers must be able to deal with these conflicting interests *in an ethical manner to formulate a viable strategic plan.* (Emphasis added)

In their textbook *Strategic Management: Formulation, Implementation, and Control*, Pearce and Robinson (1997: 54) link ethics and the strategic management process through the corporate mission statement:

> [A mission statement] asserts the firm's *commitment to responsible action in symbiosis with* the preservation and protection of *the essential claims of insider stakeholders'* survival, growth, and profitability. (Emphasis added)

In their textbook *Strategic Management*, Miller and Dess (1993: 91, 265, respectively) propose that ethics can modify the strategic management process through "consideration."

We are reminded that there is an important place *for the consideration of ethics* in any decision to try influencing the business environment. (Emphasis added)

Because of the impact divestment can have on employees and the local community in general, corporate managers *should also consider their ethical and social responsibility* to manage divestments carefully. (Emphasis added)

## *The proposition evolves*

These affirmations that ethics can modify the strategic management process are indications that the link between corporate strategy and ethics has come of age. Still, it was not that long ago that this link looked questionable. Nearly two decades ago, George Steiner, John Miner, and Edmund Gray, in their *Management Policy and Strategy* (1982: 8) textbook, discussed the emerging emphasis on "organizational obligations to society." Steiner, Miner, and Gray (1982: 8) continued:

> This new emphasis is creating major policy and strategy problems for organizations. To begin with, *there is no clear theory or set of practices that managers can consult to tell them precisely what are the social responsibilities and ethical standards that they should incorporate in their policy/strategy decisions.* (Emphasis added)

Two decades ago, Steiner, Miner, and Gray expressed uncertainty about whether corporate strategy and ethics were at all compatible. In the years since, this uncertainty has been replaced with confidence. The strategic management textbooks have become repositories of the proposition that ethics is a useful modifier of the strategic management process.

## *Perspective*

This link between the strategic management process and ethics is a safe and orderly intellectual development for three reasons. First, it is safe and orderly because the strategic management process remains intact when ethics is applied as a modifier. A grammatical analogy is a useful way to explain this point. In grammatical terms, adjectives and adverbs are modifiers that complement, but do not challenge, the authority of the nouns and verbs with which sentences are structured. The same authority relationship between the strategic management process and ethics is true in the strategic management textbooks.

All these strategic management textbook authors acknowledge that ethical questions are profound. They acknowledge that ethics involves acts of introspection, humility, and forbearance. Yet, none of these authors lets ethics become too influential in their explanations of the strategic management process. Except for Wheelen and Hunger (2000), none of these authors does much to explain that theories about ethics actually exist. And, Wheelen and Hunger go no further than briefly identifying these theories.

The predominant view in these textbooks appears to be that strategic managers have already internalized ethics sufficiently to ask the sophisticated and responsible questions that need to be asked about the refinement of corporate strategies. In all these textbooks, it is strategy formulation, strategy implementation, strategic control, and the quest for competitive advantage that comprise the truth about the strategic management process.

As long as ethics can complement these accepted processes, the reasoning goes, then ethics is welcome as a modifier on what strategic managers are already doing. Twenty years after Andrews' statement, this kind of welcome mat has been unrolled for ethics.

Second, this link between strategic management process and ethics is a safe and orderly one because it can claim kinship with, and support from, scholarly work in the field of business and society (also commonly known as "social issues in management"). Business and society is the discipline in management education where ethics, social responsibility, and corporate social performance have long been the guiding concepts. The entire December 2000 issue of the *Business and Society* journal reaffirms that business and society educators claim these concepts as the signature of their franchise (Griffin, 2000; Rowley and Berman, 2000; Wood, 2000). Ethics as a modifier on the strategic management process is a safe and orderly conceptual pairing, in other words, because it travels in the good intellectual company of business and society.

Business and society is home to the twin premise that (a) business firms are social institutions and hence (b) that these institutions must earn their legitimacy from multiple sectors of society (Wood, 1991). Archie Carroll has long been active in shaping and applying these two premises. Carroll (1979: 500) argued that the responsibilities of a firm's senior management are economic, legal, ethical, and discretionary, in order of their "evolution of importance." This historical evolution of responsibilities further legitimizes the assumption that ethics usefully modifies the strategic management process, because it depicts economic responsibilities (fulfilled in large part through the strategic management process) being modified over time by emerging ethical responsibilities. Wheelen and Hunger (2000: 40–5) openly acknowledge their debt to Carroll's work, as they connect corporate strategy and ethics.

This intellectual support for the strategic management process has deepened as mainstream business and society educators have moved to create links between ethics and the strategic management process. In his *Business and Society: Ethics and Stakeholder Management*, Carroll (1993: 551) uses "corporate public policy" to apply ethics as a modifier to the strategic management process:

> Corporate public policy is seen as that part of the overall strategic management of the organization that focuses specifically on public or ethical issues embedded in the functioning and decision processes of the firm.

The very title, *Business and Society: Corporate Strategy, Public Policy, Ethics*, indicates that Post, Lawrence, and Weber assign to ethics a modifying role in relation to corporate strategy. They reaffirm this relationship when they identify two contributors to business legitimacy (Post, Lawrence, and Weber, 1999: 17):

> To maintain public support and credibility – that is, *business legitimacy* – businesses must find ways to balance and integrate these two social demands: high economic performance and high ethical standards. (Emphasis in the original)

In both these expressions, business and society textbook authors list ethics as a modifier to the priority matter of running a profitable business. This is music to the ears of strategic management theorists who seek a safe and orderly way to apply ethical modification of the strategic management process.

Third, ethical modification of the strategic management process is safe and orderly, because it reinforces managerial capitalism. The strategic management process is where the doctrine of managerial capitalism is put into action. Strategic managers are the experts who plan, motivate, and control in the name of fulfilling their fiduciary duties to the corporation's shareholders. Managerial capitalism is particularly marked by the discretion that managers enjoy as agents for their owner-principals (Drucker, 1954; Chandler, 1977; Andrews, 1980; Evan and Freeman, 1988). Putting something as vital as ethics in the service of the strategic management process provides managerial capitalists, who are already responsible for the strategic management process, that much more discretionary power. Wheelen and Hunger (2000: 45) make it very clear why ethics as a modifier offers safety and order for the interests of managerial capitalists. "For self interest, if for no other reason, managers should be more ethical in their decision making."

## However

For ethics to be used as a safe and orderly modifier of the strategic management process, the disciplined study of ethics must be kept at arm's length. Its entry into strategic management theory must be blocked. Otherwise, there is the potential that troubling and disorderly questions will be raised about the strategic management process.

In the strategic management textbooks, this entry is firmly blocked. This is one example of what Freeman (1994) has called "the separation thesis" in management thought and management practice.

In the years since Andrews linked corporate strategy and ethics, the barrier has begun to crumble. The safe and orderly place where ethics modifies the strategic management process has been infiltrated. It has been infiltrated by those who argue that the strategic management process and ethics are conceptual co-equals. Proceeding from the assumption that the strategic management process and ethics are intellectually compatible, these infiltrators have introduced a second kind of link between corporate strategy and ethics. In this linkage, ethics is called upon to perform more substantial work than merely modifying the strategic management process.

## THE STRATEGIC MANAGEMENT PROCESS AS APPLIED ETHICS

Two unusual papers appeared in the *Strategic Management Journal* in 1994. They were unusual because "ethics" and "moral philosophy," respectively, appeared in the paper titles. What made these papers even more unusual was the fact that the authors of these papers moved ethics far deeper into the strategic management process than is required if ethics is a modifier on that process. LaRue Hosmer (1994) and Alan Singer (1994), respectively, were not content with ethics modifying the strategic management process. They went further to argue that strategic management could be reconceived as an application of ethics. *Strategic management as an application of principled ethical reasoning* is a second kind of contemporary linkage between corporate strategy and ethics.

Hosmer (1994: 19–20) translates the strategic management process into a continuing problem of sorting through the harms and benefits that accompany any strategic decision. The strategic management process becomes an exercise in applied ethics, because harms and benefits are two building blocks in ethical theory. Hosmer (1994: 20–32) argues for a set of "known" ethical principles that are readily available for use by strategic managers. Through the application of these ethical principles, Hosmer (1994: 32) argues, the strategic management process is an attempt to build trust with the many stakeholders of a given corporation.

> ... the trust, commitment and effort on the part of all of the stake-holders of a firm are as essential to the success of that firm as are the competitive advantages and strategic positions of its planning process ...

Hosmer (1994: 32) concludes with this string of propositions:

> Stakeholders who develop trust in the direction of the firm will show commitment to its future. Commitment to the future of a firm will ensure efforts that are both cooperative and innovative. Cooperative, innovative, and directed efforts on the part of all of the stakeholder groups will lead to competitive and economic success, however measured, for that firm over time.

Singer (1994: 200) links ethics and the strategic management process on the grounds that both are rational decision-making processes:

> If strategy and rationality are both broadly concerned with problems of action, decision and behavior set in socioeconomic contexts, then so too are ethics and the broad discipline of moral philosophy.

Observing a "manifest symbiosis" between strategic management and moral philosophy, Singer (1994: 206–7) argues that students of strategic management should immerse themselves in the study of developments in moral philosophy. He concludes:

> In sum, Strategy as Moral Philosophy now offers major corporate players a quite sustainable theoretical justification for their steps toward lifting the spirit of the competitive game (Singer, 1994: 207).

Andrews' work is in Singer's list of references. The spirit of Andrews' work is reaffirmed in Singer's work.

## Perspective

These works by Hosmer and Singer, respectively, break from the tradition of assigning ethics a modifying role in the strategic management process. As Hosmer and Singer see it, ethics does not modify the strategic management process. *Rather, ethics infuses the strategic management process with meaning.* When the strategic management process becomes an application of principled ethical reasoning, the study of corporate strategy now requires the study of ethics. When ethics modifies the strategic management process, it is sufficient to assume that senior corporate management has already internalized ethics.

Hosmer and Singer are not the first to link corporate strategy and ethics by translating corporate strategy into the language of ethics. Nor are they the last ones to do so. Hosmer (1994: 18) acknowledges two prior translations of corporate strategy into applied ethics. One is Freeman's (1984) account of strategic management as a process of negotiating with stakeholders. The other translation is the subsequent (to Freeman's) argument that corporate strategy can be translated into a pattern of "personal projects" – an application of the ethical concept of personal autonomy – that stakeholders expect a corporate strategy will empower (Freeman and Gilbert, 1988: 158–75).

These works by Hosmer and Singer are bracketed in time by two other translations of corporate strategy into applied ethics. Evan and Freeman (1988) argue that management should be interpreted as an act of fulfilling fiduciary obligations to stakeholders who put their trust in the management of a corporate entity. This conception of management was extended nearly a decade later in the argument that a corporate strategy, as a statement about the act of searching for distinction through coexistence with others who also are acting in search of distinction, is nothing less than an ethical principle (Gilbert, 1996a).

At first, it might look like Hosmer and Singer have several allies in the project to reinterpret strategic management as an application of principled ethical reasoning. But, these other four arguments turn out not to be companions. They are instead harbingers of a third, radically different approach to linking corporate strategy and ethics.

The difference is this. Hosmer and Singer do not break with managerial capitalism. True, Hosmer and Singer move ethics from the background to the foreground of corporate strategy. Still, they leave untouched a fundamental foreground assumption of managerial capitalism: that corporate strategy is the domain of a select group of managerial specialists who are privileged to protect and perpetuate a single corporate entity (Drucker, 1954). Strategic management as an application of principled ethical reasoning is, in the accounts by Hosmer and Singer, successful when management has preserved the corporate entity that they are privileged to defend.

The argument by Freeman and Gilbert and the argument by Evan and Freeman signal the beginning of a break with this faith in managerial capitalism. On the other side of this break is a third approach to linking corporate strategy and ethics. *Ethical criticism of the concept of corporate strategy* is this approach.

## *Shorthand notation*

The remainder of this chapter is devoted to explaining what this critical approach to corporate strategy and ethics entails and how it has evolved in the United States. Throughout the sections that follow, I use "ethical criticism of corporate strategy" (or ECCS, for short) as a convenient way to refer to this line of inquiry. ECCS is not (yet, at least) a formal term used to distinguish this line of inquiry from mainstream corporate strategy research. Rather, ECCS is shorthand notation that is presently useful and that leaves room for different critical traditions to emerge over time.

## ETHICAL CRITICISM AND CORPORATE STRATEGY

Ethical criticism of corporate strategy (ECCS) is an act of affirmative, ethical criticism about the concept of corporate strategy and the related, subsidiary concept of the strategic management process. ECCS critics believe that corporate strategy is an under-developed, underachieving idea. By reinterpreting corporate strategy as a narrative about voluntary self-restrained action that shapes human communities, ECCS critics clear the way logically for corporate strategy to join other ideas in conversations about democratic and marketplace institutions. Hence, ECCS critics foresee the day when the corporate strategy concept is accorded a legitimate place in undergraduate liberal education curriculums and in public intellectual debates. This means that ethical criticism of corporate strategy departs from the conventional belief that business concepts, such as corporate strategy, are properly studied as preparation for managerial careers.

Criticism is an artistic act. Corporate strategy research is a social science. These are very different intellectual endeavors. The latter is much better known than the former in the field of corporate strategy. Thus, it is useful to explain briefly what the act of criticism entails.

## The act of criticism

Any critic is engaged in the intellectual act of translation. The critic literally takes the object of critique out of one context and puts it into another context. Working with a translation of the work in question, the critic makes sense of the object in ways that she could not interpret if the object had remained locked in its "home" territory. Based on this reinterpretation, a critic eventually commits an act of reasoned projection about what lies ahead for a particular object of criticism.

Film, music, and literary critics routinely act this way. Each takes a given work out of its context and relocates it in a new and larger group of works. Oftentimes, this involves locating that work in the artist's repertoire of accomplishments. This could also involve locating the work in a genre of performances, such as mystery novels and science fiction cinema. After translating the work into a new context, the critic overlays her critical criteria on this work. She might comment on the depth of the novel's characters, the pacing of a film, or the energy a musician puts into the remake of an old song.

Eventually, the critic concludes with reasoned projections about the work. Often, she will project why a certain group of listeners and viewers might find the performance stimulating. She might also project that, based on her translation and reinterpretation of this work, the artist's skills are in ascendance or in decline.

The test of a critic's work is how daringly she challenges herself and her readers to take an unconventional look at conventional ideas and practices. When translating, the critic must choose a context where the object of criticism can still be recognized, yet where some new questions can be asked about it. If the context is too "friendly" to the object of criticism, then the criticism is rigged in favor of the object. No intellectual progress occurs that way. If the new context does not hold a place for the object of criticism, then the critic is "setting up straw men." (See Gilbert, 1992: 3–54; Gilbert: 1996a: 3–17; and Gilbert, 1997a, for primers on criticism of business concepts.) No intellectual progress occurs that way either.

## The act of ethical criticism of corporate strategy, in three layers

Ethical criticism of corporate strategy is an artistic act that incorporates the practice of criticism, the study of ethics, and optimism that the corporate strategy concept can be used beyond the practice of business. Ethical criticism of corporate strategy is a layered act in which criticism sets the stage for ethics, and ethics sets the stage for an affirmative belief in the intellectual potential of the concept of corporate strategy. Here is how these layers combine into a plan for making intellectual progress.

First, ethical criticism of corporate strategy is criticism in the sense that ECCS critics closely study, as do their literary critic (Gilbert, 1997a), film critic, food critic, and architectural critic counterparts, the evolution of thoughtful human practices, in context and over time. ECCS critics are faithful to the central, canonical proposition of corporate strategy that Andrews (1980: 46) articulated twenty years ago:

> . . . a business enterprise guided by a clear sense of purpose rationally arrived at and emotionally ratified by commitment is more likely to have a successful outcome, in terms of profit and social good, than a company whose future is left to guesswork and chance.

ECCS critics demonstrate their faith in this central proposition when they interpret corporate strategy as the thoughtful human practice of locating a business enterprise in a marketplace and on a logical path into the future (Freeman, 1984; Gilbert, 1992). Hence, given the crucial part that thoughtful human practice plays in it, corporate strategy is clearly subject to criticism, by this sophisticated meaning of the act of criticism.

Second, ECCS is ethical criticism in the sense that ECCS critics proceed from the assumption that there is a logical relationship between (a) corporate strategy and (b) ethical theories about individual human conduct (see Freeman, 1984; Gilbert, 1986; Freeman, Gilbert, and Hartman, 1988; Gilbert, 1992; Wicks, Gilbert, and Freeman, 1994; Hosmer, 1994; Gilbert, 1996a). ECCS critics interpret corporate strategy as an act by which individual human beings (e.g., corporate CEOs) voluntarily and collaboratively embark on a self-restrained course of action in accordance with a guiding principle. This guiding principle is known as a corporate strategy (Andrews, 1980; Freeman, Gilbert, and Hartman, 1988).

This is precisely the territory of ethical theories about individual human conduct and the moral communities that result from such conduct. (See, for example, Rawls, 1971; Gauthier, 1986; Donaldson and Dunfee, 1999.) Ethical theory is the systematic study of human beings voluntarily reasoning about, and exercising self-restraint in, their conduct in one another's company. Ethical theory is a repository and crucible of many different guiding principles about human conduct in the company of other human beings. Common among such ethical principles are honesty, keeping promises, aiding those who are vulnerable, staying out of another's private domain, and seeking another person's consent (McMahon, 1981; Gilbert, 1986; Freeman and Gilbert, 1988). Hence, according to the ECCS critic, corporate strategy and ethical theories about individual human conduct converge on (a) matters of principle (Singer, 1994, stops here) and (b) voluntary, principled action in the company of other human beings.

Third, ethical criticism of corporate strategy is affirmative ethical criticism in the sense that ECCS critics proceed from the twin assumptions that the corporate strategy concept is (a) full of intellectual promise that (b) will not emerge as long as the central, canonical proposition of corporate strategy goes unchallenged. ECCS critics work to usher corporate strategy into conversations that reach far beyond the business circumstances in which the concept is customarily invoked.

Here is where ECCS critics rebel against the culture of corporate strategy, even as they remain true to the central proposition of corporate strategy. (See Mulligan, 1987, regarding the culture of business discourse.) In the culture of corporate strategy, as Hunt (2000: 135) and Oster (1990) have reaffirmed, corporate strategy is a business concept that is used to explain why some businesses outperform other businesses financially. Writing to his corporate strategy colleagues, Barney (1995) asserts that the "research question, 'why do some firms outperform other firms?' is ours alone." According to

ECCS critics, this use of corporate strategy isolates the concept from conversations in which its intellectual potential can blossom.

In particular, ECCS critics claim that corporate strategy, as a narrative about voluntary, purposeful, principled action in the company of others, is the pathway along which a truly integrated conception of business ethics can flourish. A particular manifestation of such affirmative ethical criticism is the idea that ethics runs "through and through" the concept of corporate strategy (Gilbert, 1996a). "Ethics through and through corporate strategy" means that any corporate strategy – that is, the principle that results from the strategic management process – is logically a statement of ethical principle about worthy human ambitions and about getting along with other human beings (Gilbert, 1996a: 87–106). This is an affirmation of what college students can learn about their personhood and about their places in the world when they study corporate strategy.

## THE CHALLENGES OF AFFIRMATIVE ETHICAL CRITICISM OF CORPORATE STRATEGY

Affirmative ethical criticism of corporate strategy faces two prominent challenges that are peculiar to the concept of corporate strategy. First, the customary language of corporate strategy is a blend of business vocabulary and social science vocabulary. With the exception of Andrews' (1980: 11–12) elegant exposition and the papers by Hosmer and Singer, discussions of ethical matters are rare in the corporate strategy literature. Hosmer (1994: 17) observes wryly:

> The *Strategic Management Journal* is certainly acknowledged as publishing the most advanced work in the discipline, yet over the past 3 years the term 'ethics' has never burdened the readers' understanding.

Much more common in the corporate strategy literature is what novelist George Lee Walker (1985: 48–9) observes in his *The Chronicles of Doodah*:

> A sanitized kind of language in which all emotion, all opinion, all the feel, taste, and smell of human experience has been removed.

One can read long stretches in strategic management textbooks and research papers without encountering human beings, much less their actions in one another's company and their striving for excellence. (See, for instance, the passage cited by Gilbert, 1992: 230, n. 9.)

Second, resistance to the connection between business and ethics runs deep in the business academy. Freeman (1994) calls attention to this resistance with the "separation thesis" idea. In corporate strategy circles, Barney's (1995) statement is one confirmation of the systematic separation between business and ethics. Nothing in Barney's claim gives any indication that the fundamental research question of corporate strategy has anything to do with voluntary, purposeful, principled, collaborative human pursuits. For all the distance that he moves from conventional thinking about corporate strategy, Hosmer (1994: 32) still separates business ends from ethical ends. His focus is on the former, not the latter. The bottom line for Hosmer (1994: 32) is the "competitive and economic success, however measured, for that firm over time."

In the wider business academy, Jennings (1997) has criticized the scholarly project of reconceiving the corporation and strategic management in terms of ethical treatment of stakeholders. She labels this project "trendy" and "a trite exercise devoid of virtue." In the contemporary business academy, her separation of business and ethics is an eminently safe position to take.

As a consequence of both challenges, translation of the corporate strategy concept into a vocabulary of ethics gets little assistance and encouragement from the mainstream business academy in which the corporate strategy community is anchored. This is why ECCS critics have employed a number of strategies for translating the concept of corporate strategy into ethical terms and ethical ends.

## ETHICAL CRITICISM OF CORPORATE STRATEGY EMERGES

Ethical criticism of corporate strategy emerged subtly in Freeman's (1984) *Strategic Management: A Stakeholder Approach*. Freeman portrayed the corporate strategist (the CEO) as someone who transacts and negotiates with a cast of diverse human beings who hold stakes in the future course that the strategist sets for his corporation. What Freeman did is to translate the roles of chief executive officer, suppliers, customers, corporate critics, and regulators alike into human beings whose projects are morally legitimate. These projects inevitably converge, and often collide, in the strategic management process. Thus arises what ethical theorists recognize as a problem of justice (Rawls, 1971). Hence, Freeman (1984: 249) concludes that strategic management is a practice that must address questions of distributive justice among competing claims that many moral agents make on the corporation.

Two sequels to this reinterpretation soon appeared. Freeman and Gilbert (1988: 158–75) extended this reinterpretation of corporate strategy as a problem of justice by arguing that a corporate strategy is justified if it advances the "personal projects" of persons whose interests are joined by a corporate strategy (Gilbert, 1987). Freeman, Gilbert, and Hartman (1988) then argued that something in the logic of corporate strategy blocks the logical step from Andrews' (1980: 74–85) proposition that CEOs set strategy based on their values to the proposition that *many other moral agents* set their respective strategies based on their respective values, too. This idiosyncrasy in corporate strategy was a key impetus for an affirmative, ethical criticism of corporate strategy.

### An unlikely impetus

Another key impetus for ethical criticism of corporate strategy came from an unlikely source. Michael Porter's writings about competitive strategy are widely read in corporate strategy circles. Porter's writings about competitive strategy are not routinely included in the business ethics literature. Yet Porter (1985: 228) gave ethical critics of corporate strategy a boost when he wrote, "A firm must compete aggressively but not indiscriminately." Here was a statement about voluntary, purposeful, principled action in the company of others. Ethical criticism of corporate strategy is radical enough to include Porter's writings in its set of guiding texts.

## A Stream of Ethical Criticisms of Corporate Strategy

In the years since these first acts of ethical criticism of corporate strategy, a stream of five criticism projects has been published. Each of these critical analyses of corporate strategy has been conducted as a search for answers to this ethical question: "If a human being faithfully practices the central, canonical proposition of corporate strategy, as Andrews articulated it, then how must that human being consistently treat other human beings?" This is an ethical question, because one person's treatment of other persons is the central issue. This question is based, in other words, on the assumption that the proper ends of the practice of corporate strategy are ethical ends, not economic ones. This is where the difference is crystal clear between ethical criticism of corporate strategy and the two other ways corporate strategy and ethics have been linked in the service of managerial capitalism.

This ethical question about corporate strategy is also replete with significant political ramifications. The practice of corporate strategy is a political act in the sense that it is a claim by corporate executives that a certain kind of "good life" can be institutionalized by and for a community of voluntary participants who are faithful to a given corporate strategy. In other words, corporate strategy is one manifestation, among many, of liberal democracy at work. It is a narrative about private citizens doing things together.

One example of this critical political interpretation of corporate strategy is found in James Moore's *The Death of Competition*. Faithful to the central, canonical proposition of corporate strategy, Moore (1997) coins the term "business ecosystem" to describe the strategic management process as a process of building and sustaining a political regime. Thus, Moore's argument provides one example of how the ethical question that guides these five critical projects also yields insights about the governance of human communities and about how the model, or paradigm, citizens should behave in those communities. Thus, too, corporate strategy has *prima facie* eligibility for a place in conversations about liberal democratic institutions.

### Five critical analyses

This stream of ethical criticism of corporate strategy begins with an interpretation of corporate strategy as a narrative about decision-making process, a narrative called "strategy through process" (Gilbert, 1992). In ethical terms, strategy through process requires every participant in a corporation to subordinate his and her values and aspirations to the values and aspirations that the CEO designates as appropriate for the enterprise. This is Andrews' (1980) conception of corporate strategy, a conception that honors the legacy of Carnegie, Barnard, and Sloan. Politically, strategy through process is a story of isolationism. In the world of corporate strategy, model citizens are either corporate elites or the obedient servants who work to institutionalize the preferences of the elites (CEO), thereby insulating the corporation from unwanted outside influences.

A second project in this stream of ethical criticism addressed the corporate strategy practice that Hammer and Champy (1993) called corporate re-engineering. Ethical criticism led to the conclusion that corporate re-engineering was ethically incoherent (Gilbert, 1995). This conclusion is particularly disappointing to ECCS critics because

Hammer and Champy (1993) introduced corporate re-engineering as a process of collaborative soul-searching about the very meaning of a business enterprise. When scrutinized in terms of the proper treatment of other human beings, corporate re-engineering was shown to contain four contradictory approaches to the proper treatment of other human beings. In political terms, this project of ethical criticism concluded that corporate re-engineering turns on a politics of tyranny and fear within the corporation (Gilbert, 1995).

The third project in this stream of ethical criticism of corporate strategy addresses the analytical device known as "the prisoner's dilemma." In brief terms (Gilbert, 1997b: 502):

> The Prisoner's Dilemma story-line involves two prisoners who are suspected of committing a single crime. The prisoners sit in separate prison cells awaiting interrogation. The prisoners are pure egoists who rationally prefer less jail time to more jail time. The story also includes, in the background, a district attorney who lacks sufficient evidence to obtain any conviction without a confession from at least one of the prisoners.

Throughout the 1980s, game theoretic analyses of corporate strategy hovered on the edges of mainstream corporate strategy research, and the prisoner's dilemma has long been a favorite of game theorists. (See, for example, Oster, 1990; Dixit and Nalebuff, 1991; and the review by Gilbert, 1993, of Dixit and Nalebuff's book.) Not surprisingly, applications of the prisoner's dilemma have appeared in the corporate strategy literature (for example, McMillan, 1992).

Ethical criticism of the prisoner's dilemma has led to the conclusion that its popularity is undeserved. When the prisoner's dilemma is subjected to ethical criticism from the standpoints of all three participants, two prisoners and an authority figure, what emerges is the conclusion that the prisoner's dilemma is logically unsuitable for meaningful discussions about the proper treatment of other human beings. This is because there are no voluntary human relationships anywhere in the prisoner's dilemma (Gilbert, 1996b; 1997b). Still further, this ethical criticism revealed that the most interesting part of the prisoner's dilemma, the relationship from which the interrogating officer draws his authority, is still missing from the analysis (Gilbert, 1996b). The prisoner's dilemma is, in fact, the *prisoners'* dilemma. All three parties are caught in a web of totalitarian politics.

The fourth in this stream of ethical criticisms of corporate strategy moved into the realm of marketplace competition. The attention here turned to the corporation as an entity that is inextricably linked to other participants in the marketplace (Gilbert, 1996a). This relational conception of corporate strategy is a dramatic departure from strategy through process. In this particular project of ethical criticism, the focus is relocated from inside the walls of the corporation to the way corporate strategy can be connected with a larger narrative about human interaction.

This line of ethical criticism focused on corporate strategy models that already incorporate assumptions about relationships with outsiders (Gilbert, 1996a). Porter's (1985) work is a case in point. This criticism showed that corporate strategy, as tradition-ally conceived, is ill-suited for a move beyond the boundaries of the corporation (Gilbert, 1996a). While these corporate strategy models did acknowledge relationships with outsid-ers, proper treatment of those others consisted, at best, of thoughtful efforts to live in "armed" truces with others by containing the strategic movements of those others (principally, competitors). The "stakeholder containment imperative" is an appropriate designation for this ethical and political approach to corporate strategy (Gilbert, 1996a). It is a politics in which the paradigm citizens are colonial governors and their colonial subjects (Gilbert, 1996a).

Most recently, this colonial approach to corporate strategy was detected as permeating the concept of co-opetition, an idea advanced by Adam Brandenburger and Barry Nalebuff (1996). The co-opetitive strategist treats others properly only when it is in his advantage to do so (Gilbert, 1998). True to its game theory lineage, "co-opetition" turns on the assumption that living harmoniously with other human beings can be profitably avoided.

### Summary of this stream of ethical criticism

In each of these analyses, the ethical criticism employed the twin ethical standards of (a) autonomous moral agent and (b) tolerance of others' pursuits. In number and in depth, these are minimal ethical standards of citizenship in a liberal democratic society. Nonetheless, the paradigm citizens of corporate strategy consistently struggle to satisfy even these standards. For this reason, a question can be raised about whether, in the name of preparing college undergraduates for lives of worthy citizenship, it is appropriate at all to teach corporate strategy to undergraduate college students (Gilbert, 1996a, 1996b).

An affirmative answer to this question is beginning to take shape.

## ETHICAL CRITICISIM OF CORPORATE STRATEGY ARRIVES AT TWO DESTINATIONS

Ethical criticism of corporate strategy has enabled critics to reach two kinds of preliminary conclusions about the intellectual promise of the corporate strategy concept.

First, corporate strategy is a concept laced with ethical and political contradictions. On the one hand, corporate strategy is a blueprint for building orderly and broadly prosperous human associations based on thoughtful adherence to a thoughtfully devised plan of action. In ethical and political terms, these emphases on aspiration, cooperation, civic-mindedness, and stewardship are encouraging. *They are emphases that qualify corporate strategy for a place in larger discussions about human striving, human connection, and democracy.*

On the other hand, corporate strategy is permeated by xenophobia about the legitimate pursuits of others who do not necessarily value what the CEO wants to accomplish at his corporation. A long-standing feature of the corporate strategy concept is silence about competitors. Scan any strategic management textbook, and you will read relatively little about competitors, other than their membership in an aggregation called "The Competition." This silence masks a deep antipathy toward competitors (Gilbert, 1992). Ironically, this silence has been broken in a book that is faithful to the central proposition of corporate strategy. In Richard D'Aveni's *Hypercompetition* (1994), the principal character trait of paradigm citizens is xenophobia. The model citizen of D'Aveni's narrative destroys competitors' efforts. In terms of the ethical and political potential of the corporate strategy concept, this kind of citizenship is a setback.

One consequence of this ethical and political tension within corporate strategy is that it opens corporate strategy to the following question: *In a world of globalization, a world increasingly shorn of literal and figurative walls, how well suited is the corporate strategy concept?* This research question is a clear manifestation of the "affirmative" in the practice of ethical criticism of corporate strategy. There is reason to doubt that a concept that is predicated on both dedicated human striving and xenophobia can endure logically in the world of globalization such as that described recently by Thomas Friedman in *The Lexus and the Olive Tree* (2000). Friedman writes of a world in which walls come down. Corporate strategy theorists write of a world in which smart strategists erect walls (in the name of protecting inimitable resources, for example).

As a second conclusion, ethical critics of corporate strategy can begin to point to a literature that is useful for teaching about corporate strategy as a means for human beings to live ethically and politically worthy lives. The texts in this new literature cut across a wide range of institutions in a liberal democratic society. This is one more place where ethical criticism of corporate strategy meets liberal education.

## A reading list

Some of these texts are about intercollegiate athletics. Among the most promising are the writings of sports journalist John Feinstein. In three recent accounts about intercollegiate athletics rivalries, Feinstein (1997, 1998, 2000) addresses many of the same assumptions and propositions that occupy students of corporate strategy. But Feinstein introduces us to strategists who are not gripped with xenophobia. The strategists who meet as competitors in Feinstein's narratives actually create stronger human connections as they compete.

Some of these texts are about politics. Wayne Johnston's (1998) *The Colony of Unrequited Dreams* is a historical novel about Joey Smallwood, the first Premier of the Canadian province of Newfoundland. Johnston's protagonists seek worthy lives, ethically and politically. They struggle to do so against a backdrop of historical anonymity, harsh climate, and crushing poverty in Newfoundland.

Some of these texts are about what Norris Hundley (1992) calls the "hydraulic society" that we know as modern California. Hundley's (1992) *The Great Thirst*, Joan Didion's (1979) *The White Album*, Mike Davis's (1992) *City of Quartz*, and Carey McWilliams's (1949) *California: The Great Exception* introduce us to the long line of power brokers who enacted their vision of establishing a thriving political economy in a desert. The complicated pursuits of worthy games, victories, lives, and careers unite these very different portrayals of Californians.

Some of these texts are about business. In *The Soul of a New Machine*, Tracy Kidder (1982) provides a penetrating look at the corporate strategists who were creating the American minicomputer industry. Likewise in *Hard Landing*, Thomas Petzinger (1996) introduces us to the pioneers of the American passenger airlines industry.

The point about all these texts is not that the corporate strategists all lead exemplary lives. Some do not. The point is that each of these authors makes it possible for us to meet corporate strategists as distinctive human beings who, through the very practice of corporate strategy, can aspire to create lives of ethical accomplishment. This aspiration is at the heart of liberal education. And, this link between corporate strategy and ethics is a complete reversal of the two other established relationships between corporate strategy and ethics.

## Conclusion

Ethical criticism of corporate strategy is driven by the restlessness that Kluge (1993: 250) urged on his colleagues as he concluded his book *Alma Mater*: "I can't stop imagining how much better we could be if we asked more of ourselves." There is no logical terminus to ethical criticism of corporate strategy, or for that matter any practice of criticism. There is only the practice of asking more of ourselves, as academics who share an interest in corporate strategy. We ask more of ourselves by "asking" corporate strategy to meet higher and higher intellectual standards. For the foreseeable future, ethical criticism of corporate strategy will be a campaign to defend expectations that the corporate strategy concept can deliver more to American college curriculums and to public debates about liberal democracy than can statements like "Corporation X outperformed Corporation Y due to corporate strategy approach S."

## Acknowledgments

This work has benefited immeasurably from conversations with R. Edward Freeman, Jeffrey Harrison, Edwin Hartman, Dawn Elm, Carol Jacobson, Andrew Wicks, Craig Dunn, Diane Swanson, Gordon Meyer, and Kathryn Rogers. Robert Pitts and Steven Samaras have generously shared their respective strategic management libraries with me. Library resources at Gettysburg College and Lancaster Bible College have been helpful, too. I am also grateful to Herbert Addison, my senior editor at Oxford University Press.

## References

Alger, H. (1985). *Ragged Dick and Struggling Upward*. New York: Penguin.
Andrews, K. (1980). *The Concept of Corporate Strategy* (rev. edn.). Homewood, IL: Irwin.
Barney, J. (1995). Letter to the members from the division chair Jay Barney. *Business Policy and Strategy Division, Academy of Management, Newsletter*, Fall: 3.
Brandenburger, A. M. and Nalebuff, B. J. (1996). *Co-opetition*. New York: Currency Doubleday.
Carroll, A. B. (1979). A three-dimension conceptual model of corporate performance. *Academy of Management Review*, 4: 497–505.
Carroll, A. B. (1993). *Business and society: Ethics and Stakeholder Management* (2nd edn.). Cincinnati: South-Western.
Chandler, A. D., Jr. (1977). *The Visible Hand: The Managerial Revolution in American Business*. Cambridge, MA: Belknap Press of Harvard University Press.
D'Aveni, R. A. (1994). *Hypercompetition: Managing the Dynamics of Strategic Maneuvering*. New York: Free Press.
Davis, M. (1992). *City of Quartz: Excavating the Future in Los Angeles*. New York: Vintage.
Didion, J. (1979). *The White Album*. New York: Simon and Schuster.
Dixit, A., and Nalebuff, B. J. (1991). *Thinking Strategically: The Competitive Edge in Business, Politics, and Everyday Life*. New York: W. W. Norton.
Donaldson, T. and Dunfee, T. (1999). *Ties that Bind: A Social Contracts Approach to Business Ethics*. Boston: Harvard Business School Press.

Drucker, P. F. (1954). *The Practice of Management*. New York: Harper and Row.

Evan W. M., and Freeman, R. E. (1988). A stakeholder theory of the modern corporation: Kantian capitalism. In T. L. Beauchamp and N. E. Bowie (eds.), *Ethical Theory and Business* (3rd edn.) (pp. 97–106). Englewood Cliffs, NJ: Prentice-Hall.

Feinstein, J. (1997). *A Civil War: Army vs. Navy*. Boston: Little, Brown.

Feinstein, J. (1998). *A March to Madness*. Boston: Little, Brown.

Feinstein, J. (2000). *The Last Amateurs*. Boston: Little, Brown.

Freeman, R. E. (1984). *Strategic Management: A Stakeholder Approach*. Boston: Pitman.

Freeman, R. E. (1994). The politics of stakeholder theory. *Business Ethics Quarterly*, 4: 409–22.

Freeman, R. E. and Gilbert, D. R., Jr. (1988). *Corporate Strategy and the Search for Ethics*. Englewood Cliffs, NJ: Prentice-Hall.

Freeman, R. E., Gilbert, D. R., Jr., and Hartman, E. (1988). Values and the foundations of strategic management. *Journal of Business Ethics*, 7: 821–34.

Friedman, T. (2000). *The Lexus and the Olive Tree*. New York: Anchor.

Gauthier, D. (1986). *Morals by Agreement*. Oxford: Clarendon Press.

Gilbert, D. R., Jr. (1986). Corporate strategy and ethics. *Journal of Business Ethics*, 5: 137–50.

Gilbert, D. R., Jr. (1987). *Strategy and Justice*. Doctoral dissertation. University of Minnesota.

Gilbert, D. R., Jr. (1992). *The Twilight of Corporate Strategy*. New York: Oxford University Press.

Gilbert, D. R., Jr. (1995). Management and four stakeholder politics: Corporate reengineering as a crossroads case. *Business and Society*, 34: 90–7.

Gilbert, D. R., Jr. (1996a). *Ethics through Corporate Strategy*. New York: Oxford University Press.

Gilbert, D. R., Jr. (1996b). The prisoner's dilemma and the prisoners of the prisoner's dilemma. *Business Ethics Quarterly*, 6: 165–78.

Gilbert, D. R., Jr. (1997a). A critique and a retrieval of management and the humanities. *Journal of Business Ethics*, 16: 23–35.

Gilbert, D. R., Jr. (1997b). Prisoner's dilemma. In P. H. Werhane and R. E. Freeman (eds.), *The Blackwell Encyclopedic Dictionary of Business Ethics* (pp. 502–04). Oxford: Blackwell.

Gilbert, D. R., Jr. (1998). *Co-opetition* by Adam Brandenburger and Barry Nalebuff. *Business and Society*, 37: 468–76.

Gilbert, D. R., Jr. (1993). A review of Dixit and Nalebuff, "Thinking strategically: The competitive edge in business, politics, and everyday life." *Journal of Business Ethics*, 12: 264, 274, 280, 322, 338–340.

Griffin, J. J. (2000). Corporate social performance: Research directions for the 21st century. *Business and Society*, 39: 479–91.

Hammer, M., and Champy, J. (1993). *Reengineering the Corporation: A Manifesto for Business Revolution*. New York: Harper Business.

Hitt, M. A., Ireland, R. D., and Hoskisson, R. E. (1999). *Strategic Management: Competitiveness and Globalization* (3rd edn.). Cincinnati: South-Western.

Hosmer, L. (1994). Strategic planning as if ethics mattered. *Strategic Management Journal*, 15 (Special Issue): 17–34.

Hundley, N., Jr. (1992). *The Great Thirst: Californians and Water, 1770s-1990s*. Berkeley, CA: University of California Press.

Hunt, S. D. (2000). *A General Theory of Competition: Resources, Competences, Productivity, and Economic Growth*. Thousand Oaks, CA: Sage Publications.

Jennings, M. (1997). Trendy causes are no substitute for ethics. *Wall Street Journal*, December 1: A22.

Johnston, W. (1998). *The Colony of Unrequited Dreams*. New York: Anchor.

Kidder, T. (1982). *The Soul of a New Machine*. New York: Avon.

Kluge, P. F. (1993). *Alma Mater*. Boston: Addison-Wesley.

McMahon, C. (1981). Morality and the invisible hand. *Philosophy and Public Affairs*, Summer: 247–77.

McMillan, J. (1992). *Games, Strategies, and Managers.* New York: Oxford University Press.

McWilliams, C. (1949). *California: The Great Exception.* Santa Barbara, CA: Peregrine Smith.

Miller, A. and Dess, G. G. (1993). *Strategic Management* (2nd edn.). New York: McGraw-Hill.

Moore, J. (1997). *The Death of Competition.* New York: Harper Business.

Mulligan, T. (1987). The two cultures in business education. *Academy of Management Review,* 12: 593–9.

Norris, F. (1901). *The Octopus.* New York: Doubleday, Page and Co.

Oster, S. M. (1990). *Modern Competitive Analysis.* New York: Oxford University Press.

Pearce, J. A. II and Robinson, R. B., Jr. (1997). *Strategic Management: Formulation, Implementation, and Control* (6th edn.). Burr Ridge, IL: Irwin.

Petzinger, T. Jr. (1996). *Hard Landing.* New York: Times Business.

Pitts, R. A. and Lei, D. (2000). *Strategic Management: Building and Sustaining Competitive Advantage* (2nd edn.). Cincinnati: South-Western.

Porter, M. E. (1985). *Competitive Advantage.* New York: Free Press.

Post, J. E., Lawrence, A. T., and Weber, J. (1999). *Business and Society: Corporate Strategy, Public Policy, Ethics* (9th edn.). Burr Ridge, IL: Irwin/McGraw-Hill.

Rawls, J. (1971). *A Theory of Justice.* Cambridge, MA: Harvard University Press.

Rowley, T., and Berman, S. (2000). A brand new brand of corporate social performance. *Business and Society,* 39: 397–418.

Singer, A. F. (1994). Strategy as moral philosophy. *Strategic Management Journal,* 15: 191–213.

Steiner, G. A., Miner, J. B., and Gray, E. R. (1982). *Management policy and strategy* (2nd edn.). New York: Macmillan.

Thompson, A. A., Jr., and Strickland, A. J. III (1999). *Strategic Management: Concepts and Cases* (11th edn.). Burr Ridge, IL: Irwin/McGraw-Hill.

Walker, G. L. (1985). *The Chronicles of Doodah.* Boston: Houghton Mifflin.

Wheelen, T. L. and Hunger, J. D. (2000). *Strategic Management and Business Policy: Entering 21st Century Global Society* (7th edn.). Upper Saddle River, NJ: Prentice-Hall.

Wheeler, R. S. (2000). *The Buffalo Commons.* New York: Forge.

Wicks, A. C., Gilbert, D. R., Jr., and Freeman, R. E. (1996). A feminist reinterpretation of the stakeholder concept. *Business Ethics Quarterly,* 4: 475–97.

Wilson, S. (1955). *The Man in the Gray Flannel Suit.* New York: Arbor.

Wood, D. J. (1991). Corporate social performance revisited. *Academy of Management Review,* 16: 691–718.

Wood, D. J. (2000). Theory and integrity in business and society. *Business and Society,* 39: 359–78.

# 21

# Business and Public Policy: Competing in the Political Marketplace

## Gerald Keim

Strategic management is about organizational efforts to discover and exploit value-creating opportunities. At any point in time opportunities differ across geographic space. In different locales organizations operate within environments comprised of what Nobel Laureate Douglas North has described as formal and informal institutions (North, 1994, 1990). Formal institutions include laws, rules, policies and their actual enforcement, while informal institutions are the norms, values and mental models of the constituents who make up a country or political region (North, 1994, 1990). For any particular organization, the activities of the other organizations, ranging from competitors and suppliers to political parties and interest groups, operating in the same environment also affect the existing opportunities. Numerous strategy researchers examine the fit between the organization and the external environment (Nohria and Ghoshal, 1994; Venkatraman, 1989). In rapidly changing environments, however, opportunities (and threats) are created on an ongoing basis. Thus the static concept of firm fit is not as useful as the dynamic concept of the firm's frequent actions to improve competitive position in anticipation and/or reaction to changes in the environment (Ferrier, Smith, and Grimm, 1999; Smith, Grimm, and Gannon, 1992). In dynamic environments, opportunities (and threats) evolve from the interaction of organizations with each other *and* with their institutional environment.

Because formal institutions are consciously created and informal institutions are not, formal institutions are easier to change. Organizations seeking to create new opportunities can and do exert influence in the process by which formal institutions are changed. In the United States during the 1970s, the newly formed MCI Corporation created new market opportunities by successfully lobbying for changes in US federal regulations to permit competition in the long distance telephone market (Yoffie and Bergstein, 1985). In the 1980s and 90s the policies to adopt a single currency and reduce internal barriers to trade in the European Union were actively pushed by large multinational corporations seeking to reduce transaction costs of trade and utilize their economies of scale to compete in numerous member state markets. Deliberations in the US Congress in 2000 to establish permanent normal trade relations with China were actively supported by various businesses like Starbucks and Avon Products desirous of creating new business opportunities (Maggs, 2000; Scrivo, 2000).

Seeking to change formal institutions in order to alter existing opportunities can be an important part of an organization's strategy. Likewise, firms may also actively resist change in formal institutions to protect existing business operations from new or foreign competitors as the steel industry (Schuler, 1996) as other industries (Marsh, 1998) have done in the US and in other countries. Some firms may actively resist alterations in formal institutions at one point in time and then encourage new policies or modification of existing policies later when organizational or other environmental circumstances have changed. British Telecom, for example, actively resisted deregulation sought by the Thatcher government during the 1980s. During this time it simultaneously sought to improve its marketing capabilities and reduce operating costs and then became an advocate for deregulation in the 1990s after it had improved its competitive capabilities and sought entry into other still regulated markets in Europe and the US (Bonardi, 1999).

Not all firms consider potential opportunities (or threats) that could be created by changing formal institutions when formulating their strategy. Managers can choose one of three approaches to considering the formal institutional environment in which they operate. They can simply react as laws or regulations are changed, they can seek to anticipate changes and incorporate the expected changes in their strategy formulation process, or they can actively seek changes in formal institutional arrangements as part of their strategy (Salmon and Seigfried, 1977; Weidenbaum, 1980).

This chapter will focus on the third option – incorporating political strategy as an *active* part of the firm's enterprise strategy. Schendel and Hofer (1979) describe enterprise strategy as efforts to "integrate the firm with its broader noncontrollable environment." While this use of the term "enterprise strategy" is an extension of the Schendel and Hofer concept, the perspective developed here is that some aspects of a firm's environment *are controllable* or at least subject to influence. Laws, regulations and policies – and their enforcement – that comprise the formal institutional environment of business do change over time and are affected by explicit advocacy efforts of businesses and other organizations. Baron (1995, 1997) includes such advocacy efforts by firms in the set of activities he labels "non-market strategies" and argues that firms can benefit from integrating their market and non-market strategies.

The next section will begin by considering why political strategies are often not included in the study of business strategy. This will be followed by a description of some research indicating why endeavors to affect public policy decisions should be part of firms' overall strategies. Next the role of firm capabilities to implement various political strategies will be discussed. The final section will conclude with a brief overview of how different institutional settings can affect opportunities for businesses to bring about change in laws, regulations or policies.

## Why Is Political Strategy Often not Included as Part of Business Strategy?

When government actors implement new, or alter existing, policies that pertain to taxes, property rights, trade restrictions, environmental controls, competition policy, human resource practices, product or workplace safety and standards, advertising, privacy, subsidies, or government contracts as well as many other issues, these decisions often affect individual firms' operations and opportunities. In Porter's discussion of the forces that shape an organization's strategy he makes specific reference to the importance of government policy, but when describing how firms can devise a strategy that takes the offensive he implies that these are "external factors" (1979: 9). All strategy researchers understand the importance of public policies but many mainstream strategy scholars still treat the process by which such policies are decided as if it were exogenous to the firm's environment. Why is this?

Perhaps it is because many strategy researchers have backgrounds in industrial organization economics and many economists also ignored the process by which public policies were decided for many years (some still do). Peruse most economics texts written before 1990 and look for explicit discussion of the political process by which public policies like competition policy or trade regulations, for example, are decided. While there may be extensive discussion of effects of various policy proposals ranging from minimum wage legislation to environmental regulations or trade subsidies, little is written about the process by which such policies are selected, enforced, or changed. Alternatively, one can examine many current business strategy texts and observe that there are still few with any substantive discussion of how firms can alter their opportunity sets by trying to affect public policy decisions.

A growing number of economists began to acknowledge the importance of the process by which economic policies are decided after James Buchanan won the Nobel Prize in economics in 1986. Buchanan's work explained how different decision-making rules affected the processes by which individuals make collective decisions (Buchanan and Tullock, 1962; Buchanan, 1968, 1975, 1986). Buchanan built on earlier work by political scientists, Arthur Bentley (1935) and David Truman (1951), that emphasized competition among organized interest groups as a primary driver of public policy outcomes in the United States.

The relevance of Buchanan's work to the study of corporate political strategy is straightforward. "To predict behavior, either in governmental bureaucracy or in privately organized . . . institutions, it is necessary to examine carefully the constraints and opportunities faced by individual decision makers" (1988: 7). That is, individual decision makers in government agencies, ministries, cabinets, or legislatures can be modeled as self-interested actors in the same way that managers, employees, suppliers, investors, creditors, or consumers are viewed by scholars studying management, marketing or finance. Empirical work by Stigler (1971), Peltzman (1976, 1987), Maloney, McCormick, and Tollison (1984), and Peltzman, Levine, and Noll (1989) were among the first to support this view of regulatory decision-makers. McCormick and Tollison (1978) and Crain and Tollison (1980) also found evidence to support this view of legislators in the US. Grier, McDonald, and Tollison (1995) extended the analysis to the executive veto.

Incentives and constraints matter to actors in the public policy process just as they matter to actors engaged in private sector activities.

Buchanan's work is at the core of a field of political economy known as "public choice" – the study of how individuals make collective choices – in contrast to "private choice" which refers to the private activities traditionally studied in economics and business (Mueller, 1989). An important methodological contribution of this work is the conceptualization of the political process as exchange between actors. It may be useful to elaborate on this point. Buchanan notes that:

> markets are institutions of exchange; persons enter markets to exchange one thing for another. They do not enter markets to further some supra-exchange or supra-individual result . . .
>
> The extension of this exchange conceptualization to politics counters the classical prejudice that persons participate in politics through some common search for the good, the true, and the beautiful, with these ideals being defined independently of the values of the participants as these might or might not be expressed by behavior . . . The relevant difference between markets and politics does not lie in the kinds of values/interests that persons pursue, but in the conditions under which they pursue their various interests. Politics is a structure of complex exchange among individuals, a structure within which persons seek to secure collectively their own privately defined objectives that cannot be efficiently secured through simple market exchanges. In the absence of individual interest, there is no interest. (1987: 246).

In the public choice framework, individual actors have demands for various public policy outcomes just as they have demands for Asian food, digital technology or local suppliers. Individuals' public policy demands are organized through various interest aggregation mechanisms such as interest groups, business or trade associations and/or other coalitions of organized groups. These interest aggregation mechanisms differ across institutional settings and this will be discussed in more detail later in the chapter. In democracies operating in most modern economies, there is competition among groups, associations and coalitions seeking to influence political decision-makers. This competition among various aggregations of individuals can be thought of as demand-side competition among potential buyers in the political marketplace.

There is also competition among individuals to become political decision-makers, that is, competition among those seeking to become suppliers of public policies. On the legislative supply side, the obvious competition is between those currently in elected offices and those who are currently the opposition or who want to be future members of legislatures or parliaments. Competition among political suppliers also exists in the executive branch of governments as agencies, bureaus or ministries compete for influence and jurisdiction on various policy issues as well as for budget and other resources (Niskanen, 1971, 1975).

## THE PUBLIC POLICY PROCESS AND BUSINESS STRATEGY

This modeling of the public policy process as a set of market-like interactions identifies a potential role for businesses as participants on the demand side of the public policy process. The rationale for incorporating consideration of public policy decision-making into the strategy formulation and implementation process is a direct implication of management research examining corporate political activities. Numerous scholars acknowledge the importance of corporate political activity, defined as all activities by firms designed to influence the decisions of government decision-makers, including both the means used in these activities and the targets toward whom these are directed (Salorio, 1993). Epstein argues that "political competition follows in the wake of economic competition" and that government may be viewed as a opportunity to create the environment most favorable to a firm's competitive position (1969: 242). Mitnick (1993) develops Epstein's conceptualization of government decision-making as a contestable process further. Keim (1981) cites evidence of the increasing formalization of corporate public affairs functions in large US companies. He contends that "successful managers must understand the public policy process, anticipate the potential consequences of emerging issues, and implement effective corporate political strategies" (1981: 41). In a study of the tobacco industry, Miles (1982) finds that the tobacco industry as a whole was able to defend its domain and profitability through political action and government co-optation. Boddewyn (1993) notes that US automobile companies sought government protection when they had difficulty competing with the products offered by Japanese producers in US markets. Boddewyn asserts that when a firm cannot be a cost, differentiation, or focus leader, the firm may still beat the competition in the political arena.

Operating on the demand side of the public policy market, firms can engage in political activities to try to protect, sustain or create competitive advantages domestically and internationally (Wood, 1986). Firm goals for political strategies may range from increasing market size or bargaining power relative to suppliers to reducing the threats of new entrants in existing markets (Gale and Buchholz, 1987). Another Nobel laureate, George Stigler, (1971) outlines four categories of benefits that firms may get from regulatory protection (or pursuing a "shelter" strategy as defined by Rugman and Verbeke, 1993): direct subsidies; control over entry into the market; power affecting substitutes and complements; and price fixing. Mitnick (1981) also offers numerous examples of opportunities for firms to behave strategically with regard to regulatory policy decisions. Moran (1985) calculates that seeking protection is one of the most lucrative activities a firm can undertake, producing by some estimates an average return of more than 200 percent on investment (legal fees) per year, with the US government picking up almost 90 percent of the costs, no matter what the outcome. Tollison (1982) shows that a firm might be willing to spend up to the present value of a rent produced by some form of government policy to prevent such a provision from being eliminated. Government relations may be more than defensive in that they could have real "earning" potential and deserve as much attention as other management functions within a firm (Boddewyn, 1975). Hillman, Zardkoohi, and Bierman (1999) show that firms whose executives or directors are appointed or elected to government positions are observed to earn abnormal market returns at the time of the appointment or election. This latter study is one of the first to show a positive relationship between corporate political action and shareholder value creation.

As noted earlier, Baron (1995) includes political strategy in the set of activities that comprise a firm's non-market strategy. He argues that firms should consider both market and non-market strategies in order to improve performance; market strategies emphasize economic performance whereas non-market strategies emphasize overall performance by taking into account social and political environmental factors. Non-market strategies have the potential to help realize competitive advantage and also help offset competitive disadvantage. Thus both market and non-market strategies should be considered in addressing and defending against market forces. Baron calls for integrated strategy formulation, which combines a market or competitive analysis and a non-market analysis into a comprehensive strategy. Indeed, a recent examination of the airline industry by Shaffer, Quasney, and Grimm (2000) finds evidence that the integration of market and non-market strategies has a positive and significant impact on firm performance.

The "non-market" classification for political strategies offered by Baron (1995) serves to distinguish political strategies from more traditional conceptualizations of business strategy. There is reason, however, for viewing the political arena as a market as well. Buchanan (1968) and other political economists have done so (Mueller, 1989). Keim and Baysinger (1988) and Hillman and Keim (1995) also model political competition in a market setting. The advantages of viewing the public policy process as a marketplace, at least in democracies, are several. One is to explicitly recognize the exchange nature of politics and to identify the demanders and suppliers. Another is to consider the interests of actors who are demanders and suppliers and understand the nature of what may be exchanged in the process. A third reason is to recognize explicitly the competitive nature of the political arena, particularly on the demand side.

Despite the differences in semantics, Baron (1995), like Boddewyn (1993), contends that the non-market environment should be treated as endogenous rather than exogenous. Firms can and do influence political agendas and the rules by which they operate, and new regulations and standards are passed frequently (Aharoni, 1993). By treating the government as endogenous, when a firm looks to the future, neither the market nor the institutional environment should be considered static. To the extent that individual firms are able to influence public policies, corporate political behavior should be viewed as strategic (Salorio, 1993).

Given the strategic implications of political behavior, Gale and Buchholz (1987) argue that competition in public policy is as fierce as competition in the market and that political behavior is an important part of overall competitive strategy. As we begin the 21st century, certainly this is the case for the tobacco industry in the United States and in other advanced democracies. It is also true for pharmaceutical companies as they deal with pressures to weaken their patent protection in the US and elsewhere in an effort to make healthcare more affordable for the poor. It is also the case for any industries producing genetically modified products, or those producing greenhouse gasses that may be affected by provisions of the Kyoto treaty. For these industries and others it is important for firms to develop political behavior and strategies as a part of their overall strategies (Oberman, 1993; Yoffie and Bergenstein, 1985). If the government is important to a firm's competitive future, political behavior must be a business priority (Yoffie, 1988). Boddewyn (1975, 1993) and Mahon (1993) argue that political advantages may also be a part of a firm's competitive advantage. Aharoni asserts that "the capabilities of the firm, to the extent they fit the environment (or when the firm can shape the environment), are the major means by which strategic advantage is won" (1993: 34). Firm political behavior is an attempt to shape the institutional environment in which firms compete.

At any point in time, numerous organizations may be trying to shape the institutional environment to their advantage. These organizations and groups compete to have their preferences translated into policy. On some issues, competitors in an industry may work toward a common goal, competing only against outside interests (e.g. a Canadian trade association lobbying for import restrictions against third world textile imports). In other cases, however, members of an industry may actually have different preferences and compete against one another to affect policy. For example, in the late 1990s energy companies took opposing positions on the use of fuel additives in reformulated gasoline to meet EPA standards in the US. Environmental groups like the Sierra Club and the Environmental Defense Fund were also advocating different positions on this issue (Baron, 2000). Keim and Baysinger (1988) contend that because of the competitive nature of the public policy process, businesses must seek ways to establish competitive advantage vis-à-vis other groups in the political arena.

## POLITICAL COMPETENCIES AND FIRM ADVANTAGES IN THE POLITICAL MARKETPLACE

The resource-based view of the firm (Barney, 1986, 1991; Penrose, 1959; Peteraf, 1993; Rumelt, 1984) holds that a firm's competencies that are rare, inimitable, non-substitutable, and create value for a firm may result in sustained competitive advantage in the marketplace. Boddewyn (1993) argues that political competencies, which are not commonly discussed by the resource-based view, may be important to competitive advantage. Political competencies may include better intelligence about the institutional environment; better access to decision and opinion makers; better bargaining and non-bargaining skills; money; and other tools such as reputation, coalition-building ability and political entrepreneurship (Boddewyn and Brewer, 1994). These may be viewed as assets and Baron asserts that "at any instant in time, these distinctive competencies and firm-specific nonmarket assets are fixed, but over time they can be developed or lost" (1995: 61).

Consider a firm's strategy for dealing with the physical environment as an example. While some firms have sought to resist public policy initiatives to hold organizations responsible for their use of the physical environment, other firms have purposefully tried to reduce the environmental impact of their operations beyond what is required by existing rules and regulations. These "green strategies" can lead to more profitable performance for some firms (Russo and Fouts, 1997). Aside from the appeal to green consumers, the reputation such firms develop may also be a political asset that may help them gain access to, and have increased credibility with, some of the legislators and regulators who will formulate future environmental protection policies and influence changes to existing policies. This, in turn, will enable such firms to better anticipate the direction of future polices and to play a role in shaping the details of such policies. Both capabilities can be sources of competitive advantage that will be difficult for other firms that did not pursue green strategies to duplicate. This is an example of the development of firm assets that will be helpful in the competition to influence policy decision-makers (suppliers) in the political marketplace.

In the US, a few public policy issues seem to be driven by broad-based interest among voters while many political issues are salient only to some well-organized groups. Unorganized voters are rationally ignorant of these issues and don't participate in process to influence such decisions (Keim and Zeithaml, 1986). Indeed in a recent presidential year election survey, less than a third of Americans knew the name of their member of Congress (Morin, 1996). One can reasonably infer that the same individuals who don't know who their legislator is would be unable to identify many issues on which their legislator had voted in Congress. Consequently the competition on many issues is among organized voters for whom the issue is salient (Keim and Zeithaml, 1986).

Keim and Baysinger (1988) contend that the competitive nature of this competition to exert influence in the political market place will encourage firms to develop capabilities that lead to competitive advantage in political market competition. Consistent with the RBV, firms will seek capabilities that create political value in unique ways and are difficult to imitate. While some political competencies such as money for contributions, information obtained or supplied by lobbying, and access to policy makers are a result of human resources that may be imitated or hired away from a particular firm, some political competencies may not be imitable. Attributes of a firm's reputation and long-term dealings with political decision-makers which establishes trust may not be so easily duplicated or substituted.

Some aspects of political competencies are embedded in past events, or are path dependent (Arthur, 1989; North, 1990). For example, a firm, or interest group may develop a relationship with a particular politician early in his/her career as when serving in a state legislature. Through time, the politician learns to depend on the firm for credible information, campaign support and other resources. Later, this politician may be elected to the US Congress and progress to a leadership position. Because this relation-ship was developed early on, this firm may enjoy access that a new firm attempting to build a relationship with the legislator could not. As far back as 1970, Kindleberger asserted that a firm's political power may be retained longer than economic power because political changes are less frequent than economic or market changes and political boundaries are more clearly defined than are markets. This creates the possibil-ity for a sustainable political advantage (Boddewyn, 1993), and potentially has an impact on the skills a firm and its managers need in order to succeed (Leone, 1979). This source of competitive advantage, however, is not infinitely sustainable in that the value of organizational strategies and capabilities such as political competencies is context de-pendent (Collis, 1994). At this point, a more detailed examination of the types of corporate political action studied to date may be useful.

## CORPORATE POLITICAL ACTION

Students of corporate political action have categorized these activities in a variety of ways. Most of the taxonomies in the literature may be classified into three implementa-tion levels as discussed by Schollhammer (1975): collective action, action by individual corporations, and action taken by individuals within the organization such as executives. Leone (1979) argued that political savvy was a necessary resource for managers to succeed in an increasingly regulated environment. Indeed, even recent surveys of key legislative assistants have identified lobbying by executives or direct contact by executives as one of the more effective political tactics (Lord, 2000). Therefore, political activities may be implemented at three different levels within and among firms.

Similar to these three levels of implementation are the three general approaches to corporate political strategy outlined by Oberman (1993). These approaches are delineated as: bottom-up approaches, which include efforts to use individual voter pressure such as grassroots building, or advocacy advertising; top-down approaches, such as Political Action Committee (PAC) contributions or lobbying efforts instigated by the top levels of an organization; and evolutionary approaches, which emphasize developing a pattern of behavior over time (Keim 2000).

Yoffie (1987) examines general political strategies at the collective and individual firm levels noting the different roles firms can play in collective efforts. Given the nature of the public policy process where many organized groups compete to influence policy decision-makers, it is rational for some of these groups, or organizations, to free ride or leave participation in politics to others (Lenway and Rehbein, 1991). Many aspects of public policies are collective in nature; that is, the benefits or costs of the policy affect many organizations including those who actively sought to influence the policy decision and those that did nothing. For example, if a group of domestic textile companies lobbies for trade restrictions against imported textiles and succeeds, these restrictions would benefit all firms in the domestic textile industry, not only the firms that participated in the lobbying effort. Thus, given the collective nature of the benefit, and the low marginal probability of being able to affect the policy, some firms may opt out of the effort to influence the political process.

The benefits of collective action, however, may accrue to firms on a differential basis. That is, some firms – often larger volume producers – may benefit more from a policy decision with collective benefits than other, smaller firms. Schuler's (1996) research on the US steel industry finds that the firms with the largest market share were the most politically active on trade issues. When firms are heterogeneous on some dimensions it is likely that the collective benefits (or costs) of a policy may affect these firms differentially as well. An example might be a sulfur emissions policy pertaining to gasses emitted from coal fired generators in the US. Firms that are using low sulfur Western coal may be affected less than firms burning dirtier coal from the eastern US. Yoffie contends that corporations will follow a free-rider strategy only if the political issue is of low salience or if resources for political action are limited.

Alternatively, firms may choose to be followers or leaders in collective political activity. Firms are likely to participate in collective political action, or be followers, as long as they perceive some strategic salience and they are not seriously constrained in terms of resources. However, for a firm to be a leader depends largely on the salience of the issue for the firm, as well as having sufficient resources for political action. In this case, the implicit assumption is that firm decision-makers have incentives that align their interests with owners' interests. If not, individual and organizational goal conflict might arise on the part of a CEO who has personal political ambitions and may result in a firm being a leader for reasons that are not in the best interest of the firm but may advance the CEO's political interests. Such agency problems are certainly possible but will not be explored here.

In some cases the benefits of a policy are largely concentrated on an individual firm. When collective action is difficult due to a lack of consensus, or monopoly rents are possible, firms may have the motivation to seek policies with largely private benefits.

Yoffie contends that the use of these types of political strategies depends upon two variables: issue salience and resources (financial, human, and relational). Another

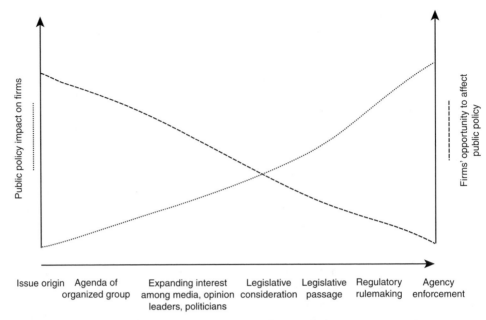

Source: Based on Baron's "Non-market Issue Life Cycle and Strategy" (Baron, 2000: 33)

FIGURE 21.1 Issue impact and opportunities to influence over the issue life cycle

consideration is timing. Political issues over-develop and follow a predictable life cycle (Buchholz, 1992; Baron, 2000).

Issues originate for reasons that are not always well understood. A few individuals may write letters to the editor of a newspaper, or create a website, or a small protest may develop at a location and attract some media attention. If this issue is to be sustained and grow either an interest group is formed to advance the issue or some existing group adds the issue to their agenda. If interest in the issue expands and/or if the issue attracts additional media attention, it may be considered by political decision-makers. If there is sufficient interest in the issue on the part of political decision-makers and among political constituents in a parliamentary system, a party may add the issue to their agenda. In the United States, legislation may be introduced at the state or federal level pertaining to the issue. Continued and growing interest and the lack of significant opposition may lead to passage of legislation related to the issue. This may in turn lead to new programs, rules or regulations to be implemented and enforced by various agencies or levels of government. The impact of an issue on a firm's plans or opportunities increases as the issue moves through the life cycle. The opportunities for a firm or group to influence a public policy issue decrease as the issue moves through the life cycle (see figure 21.1).

During different stages of an issue's life cycle, different types of political strategies will be effective. During early stages bottom-up approaches (Oberman, 1993) or tactics such as: advocacy advertising (Sethi, 1982) (public advertising of the company's position in the media); public image advertising (advertisements are not focused on the issue *per se* but on the overall image of the company, such as the environmentally friendly commercials Exxon used after the *Exxon Valdez* oil spill); economic education (attempts by the company to educate the public as to potential costs and/or benefits of certain issues); or other "communication strategies" may be used to help shape public opinion and influence the political agenda. While the issue is in the formation stage, however, Buchholz (1992) recommends that "participation strategies," or more top-down approaches (Oberman, 1993) be used. These include lobbying individually, lobbying as part of a trade association, making PAC contributions, or other constituency building techniques (Baysinger, Keim, and Zeithaml, 1985; Keim, 1981) such as grassroots mobilization by firm employees, suppliers, or retirees, or coalition building with other companies and interest groups on an ad hoc basis rather than through trade associations. Both communication strategies and participation strategies are primarily proactive in that they focus on affecting an issue before the policy is drafted. Buchholz recommends that compliance strategies, on the other hand, be used as a reactive response once a law has been passed and is in the implementation stage. Compliance strategies may include legal strategies through the court system, complying with the regulation, non-compliance, or perhaps, creating a new issue that changes the position of the first issue in the issue life cycle.

Aplin and Hegarty (1980) also develop a categorization of political strategies for the political influence process. Their categories of influence strategies include information, public exposure/appeal, direct pressure, and political. The information strategy includes activities such as serving as expert witnesses, making personal visits to policy makers, providing specific arguments or positions to decision-makers, and writing technical reports on issues. Public exposure/ appeal tactics, on the other hand, are focused not on the decision-makers but on the public, who in turn influence the policy-makers. These tactics include such activities as publishing politicians' voting records, using third-party influence, mounting letter-writing campaigns, and media campaigns such as the advertising and communication strategies discussed by Buchholz (1992). Direct pressure tactics include PAC contributions or other types of financial support. Finally, political tactics of influence consist of constituent contact and colleague contact.

Keim and Zeithaml (1986) use a similar logic in discussing the choice among these strategies, as did Yoffie (1987). They argue that a firm's political strategy is influenced in part by the salience of the political issue and by the re-election goals of legislators. They contend that the likelihood of political action by a firm is based upon the probability that action will lead to collective benefits, the value of the collective benefit, the expected value of the collective benefit to the individual firm, the value of any private or selective benefits, and the costs of the political action. Although the authors suggest that political strategies are a result of a cost/benefit analysis and rely on issue salience and the goals of legislators, no specific theory is developed on how cost/benefit analysis leads to the choice of a particular tactic. Rather, the calculation of cost and benefit leads to the decision of whether or not to take political action.

Getz's (1993) taxonomy of political tactics contains many of the tactics considered by other scholars: lobbying, reporting research results, reporting survey results, testifying at hearings, building constituencies, and taking legal action once a regulation is passed, but also includes a seventh type of tactic not mentioned in previous literature – personal service. Getz defines personal service as having a firm member serve in a political capacity. Examples of personal service include firm members running for local, state, or federal office or as a state or federal appointee. This is supported, as noted earlier by the event study of Hillman, Zardkoohi, and Bierman (1999). Hillman and her colleagues theorize that firm benefits may accrue from such a strategy through a possible increase in influence or access to political decision-makers. Although these authors do not contend that personal service is always a conscious strategy used by firms to influence the policy process, it nonetheless is a method for influence and/or access.

Based on this previous literature, Hillman and Hitt (1999) develop a comprehensive taxonomy of corporate political strategies that separates political action by approach – transactional or relational, by level of participation – individual or collective, and by tactics used. They consider three alternative strategies that each entail different sets of tactics: the provision of information to political decision-makers, the provision of financial incentives, and efforts to generate constituent pressure. Hillman and Hitt also identify firm variables such as related or unrelated diversification and financial resources, as well as institutional variables including features of the political system such as how interest group participation is organized, that are likely to affect firms' choices of political strategies. This is one of the few studies in the field to ask how institutional features in other countries will affect the choice of political strategies by firms operating there.

Corporate political action is certainly important for multinational enterprises (MNEs) operating across national borders (Boddewyn and Brewer, 1994; Doz, 1986). While Aharoni (1993) argues that a domestic firm that cannot catch up with MNEs can still command higher than average profits by generating rents through political action, the same potential for rents holds for any firm, foreign or domestic, that is successful in creating a political advantage (Boddewyn, 1993). In addition, crossing national borders generates additional strategic options that may be missing in national settings due to differences in institutional settings, and because international business activities offer leverage through the opportunity to play one government off another (Boddewyn, 1993).

Ricks, Toyne, and Martinez (1990) identify some political approaches used frequently by international businesses. These authors identify four approaches commonly used by international businesses: international political risk forecasting, lobbying for favorable host government treatment, lobbying for home government assistance, and attempting to protect local operations from host government intervention. While the two forms of lobbying clearly fit into other commonly discussed political strategies, risk forecasting is not a strategy used to influence public policy, but is rather a tool of country analysis. Similarly, the fourth approach of protecting operations from government intervention seems to be more of an objective than a political approach.

An explicit consideration of institutional setting in which firms may try to influence political decision-makers will be considered next.


## THE INSTITUTIONAL CONTEXT OF BUSINESS POLITICAL ACTION

North's (1994) three-part framework for understanding the institutional setting in which businesses operate was introduced at the beginning of this chapter. It is the interaction of organizations with their formal and informal institutions that determines the environment in which businesses operate at any point in time in different locales. This framework helps identify key features of the firm's environment that may affect the choices and the efficacy of different political strategies and tactics. Formal institutions and their enforcement, that is the laws, policies, and regulations that are implemented and enforced in a particular country or state, help define the opportunity set for businesses at a point in time. Businesses may engage in efforts to change, or resist changes in, formal institutions as a way of altering or protecting opportunities. Some formal institutions, particularly those of a constitutional nature that determine the decision-making rules have direct impact on the choice of political strategies by firms and other organizations seeking to influence public policy decision-makers. As Hillman and Keim (1995) point out, differences in the way parliamentary systems and the US presidential-congressional systems operate provide differing opportunities for organizations and groups seeking to influence policies.

Ministries in parliamentary systems often play a more important role in policy formulation than is the case for cabinet agencies in the US (Hillman and Keim, 1995). The use of public referenda in countries like Switzerland or states like California and Texas affects the choices of influence strategies that can be used by corporations or other groups. Advocacy advertising becomes much more important when trying to influence a referenda vote whereas this strategy is often viewed as ineffective with legislative issues (Lord, 2000). Hillman and Hitt (1999) describe distinctions between corporatist systems like Sweden and Austria where interest group aggregation, especially business and labor, is formally organized by law, and pluralist systems like the United States where the participation of interest groups is more informal and disaggregated.

The interaction between business and government is an interaction between *people*. When business strategists are considering political action to affect public policy decision-makers it is important to understand the institutional setting in which these decision-makers operate. Members of legislatures are more directly dependent on voters' concerns than are career civil servants that work in ministries, departments or agencies. The latter may be more concerned with evidence from respected researchers while the former may be more responsive to public opinion polls or the volume of constituent mail received pertaining to an issue. Furthermore, career officials will usually have longer time horizons when considering issues than will legislators worried about surviving the next election. In parliamentary systems with strong political parties like Germany or Canada, for example, the leadership of the party has significant influence over the party's agenda which in turn determines the policies proposed in the parliament and the position taken by party members. In political systems with weak political parties like the United States, even the President may have great difficulty controlling his own party as indicated by the refusal of many Democrats in Congress to support President Clinton's repeated proposals pertaining to expedited trade negotiations in his second term of office.

Informal institutions (North, 1994), that is, the norms, values and mental models of citizens, also affect business political action. In parliamentary systems it is often the case that individual businesses through the activities of their executives become associated with a particular political party, while this is uncommon in the United States as it is considered risky to side too closely with one party. Individual executives may be active in a party but they are usually careful not to appear to represent their firms in such activities. Informal institutions can also influence the substance of issues that may affect business operations or opportunities when these issues result in changes in laws or regulations or enforcement. Strongly held environmental or "green" concerns in states like Oregon and Washington or in countries like Austria lead to strong support for strict environmental statutes and regulations having to do with air and water pollution and recycling. Citizens in Texas, Louisiana and Russia on the other hand appear to be less concerned with environmental issues and the resulting formal rules and regulations are less strict.

Different institutional settings also have different organizational actors. As suggested above, organizations often drive the changes in public policy in democracies. In countries like Germany, for example, labor unions have organized a much larger percentage of the work force than in the United States (IMD, 1999) and can be more effective political adversaries for business as a result. Businesses, on the other hand, can benefit from formal umbrella associations like the Federation of German Industry that provide the means to organize broad business support for some issues. While the US Chamber of Commerce, the Business Roundtable, and the National Federation of Independent Business each represents different subsets of American business, there is no equivalent organization that can speak with one voice for business in the United States (Hillman and Keim, 1995).

The interaction of these three components on the business environment can be illustrated with an example. In a recent study of 47 national economies Canada and Austria ranked third and first, respectively, in terms of quality of life measured by surveys of inhabitants (IMD, 1999). Canada and Austria also have very similar levels of per capita income and rank tenth and eleventh in the same survey on this dimension. The percentage of their populations of working age is also very similar. In each country similar fractions of the workforce belong to labor unions. In terms of fewest working days lost to strikes in a year, however, Austria is at the top of the ranking while Canada is near the bottom. Why?

In Austria there is a unique emphasis on cooperation between labor and management known as the social partnership (AK, 1999). This cooperation seems to result from lessons learned after a bitter civil war in the 1930s. After World War II ended, Austria was a divided country with the Russian forces occupying land north of the Danube River and the Allies controlling the southern part of the country. Reunification of the country required extreme cooperation to ensure that the demands of both parties in the cold war could be met. To facilitate cooperation after the war, the government created mandatory membership in organizations that represented the interests of all workers and business people. These chambers, as they are called, are important organizations that represent their constituencies and seek to find common ground on important questions of economic policy in Austria. Finding cooperative solutions to what would otherwise be divisive problems is still seen as a virtue by many Austrians today.

In this example the important organizational players in the public policy process are the chambers organizations which resulted from the formal institutional requirement of mandatory membership organizations for workers and business owners. The important informal institution is the emphasis on cooperation as a social norm that developed after the Austrian civil war and World War II. This norm permeates the cultural setting and discourages labor and management strife. In Canada, since neither these organizations nor the norm of cooperation exists, business can expect labor organizations to be more combative adversaries on public policy issues.

## Conclusion

For any business organization, strategy formulation necessarily involves making choices on the basis of some analysis of the particular firm and the environment in which it operates or seeks to operate. The conclusion of this chapter is that the formal institutional part of the environment – the laws, policies, regulations and their enforcement – is subject to change as a result of the actions of organizational players operating in that environment. Tomorrow's opportunity set results in part from the actions that relevant organizations like competing firms, suppliers, environmental groups, labor unions, or other interest groups take today. Thus firms should think about how to create new opportunities by trying to alter the environment and should also be thinking about how other organizations may likewise try to alter the environment.

The analysis here suggests that the formal institutional environment of business is another marketplace in which various organizations use their resources in an exchange process to demand policy outcomes from suppliers who are the elected, appointed, and career public officials who make decisions about public policies. Depending on the informal institutional setting – norms, values, mental models of the individuals – and the formal institutional setting – parliament or congress for example – different organizational strategies to affect the suppliers will be more or less successful.

From a firm's perspective, executives and managers must view opportunities as being embedded in an environment that is dynamic. They must be able to understand the existing informal institutions in which the opportunities are or will be embedded and realize that these will usually change slowly. Firms operating in the new market economies of Central Europe see this in the pace of change in the attitudes of employees and customers. The older individuals, where the attitudes have been nested for many years, are particularly slow to change. The opportunities for more rapid change in opportunities come instead from the policies that create the formal institutions. Here, change often results from the actions of other organizations operating in the same environment as they try to change policies to their advantage. It seems likely that some organizations will be able to develop internal resources or capabilities that will enable them to be more effective competitors in the political marketplace than others and that this can be a source of competitive advantage.

From the perspective of management research, three intellectual streams have been combined here. First, the understanding of the institutional environment of business as developed by modern institutional economists like Douglas North was introduced. Next the public choice perspective of the political process as exchange in a competitive setting (as pioneered by James Buchanan and his followers) was elaborated. Finally, the work on business political activity and particularly that which emphasizes the importance of firm-specific political resources was reviewed. Combining these three perspectives, hopefully, will convince strategy researchers that the political environment of business is endogenous to the system in which business firms compete and should be an important part of strategy formulation and implementation research.

# References

Aharoni, Y. (1993). From Adam Smith to Shumpeterian global firms. In A. Rugman and A. Verbeke (eds.), *Research in Global Strategic Management*, 4: 231–62. Greenwich, CT: JAI Press.

AK (1999). *The Chamber of Labour – an Austrian Solution*. Vienna: Kammer für Arbeiter und Angestellte.

Aplin, J., and Hegarty, H. (1980). Political influence: Strategies employed by organizations to impact legislation in business and economic matters. *Academy of Management Journal*, 23: 438–50.

Arthur, W. (1989). Competing technologies, increasing returns and lock-in by historical events. *Economic Journal*, 99: 116–31.

Barney, J. (1986). Organizational culture: Can it be a source of sustained competitive advantage? *Academy of Management Review*, 11: 656–65.

Barney, J. (1991). Firm resources and sustained competitive advantage. *Journal of Management*, 17: 99–120.

Baron, D. (1995). Integrated strategy: Market and nonmarket components. *California Management Review*, 37: 47–65.

Baron, D. (1997). Integrated strategy, trade policy, and global competition. *California Management Review*, 39: 145–70.

Baron, D. (2000). *Business and Its Environment*. Upper Saddle River, NJ: Prentice-Hall.

Baysinger, B., Keim, G., and Zeithaml, C. (1985). An empirical evaluation of the potential for including shareholders in corporate constituency programs. *Academy of Management Journal*, 28: 180–200.

Bentley, A. (1935). *The Process of Government*. Bloomington, IN: Principia Press.

Boddewyn, J. (1975). Multinational business-government relations: Six principles for effectiveness. In P. Boarman and H. Schollhammer (eds.), *Multinational Corporations and Governments: Business-Government Relations in an International Context*, 1–23. New York: Praeger.

Boddewyn, J. (1993). Political resources and markets in international business: Beyond Porter's generic strategies. In A. Rugman and A. Verbeke (eds.), *Research in Global Strategic Management* 4: 162–84. Greenwich, CT: JAI Press.

Boddewyn, J. and Brewer, T. (1994). International business political behavior: New theoretical directions. *Academy of Management Review*, 19: 119–43.

Bonardi, J. (1999. Market and nonmarket strategies during deregulation: The case of British Telecom. *Business and Politics*, 1: 203–31.

Buchanan, J. (1968). *The Demand and Supply of Public Goods*. Chicago, IL: Rand McNally and Co.

Buchanan, J. (1975). *The Limits of Liberty*. Chicago, IL: University of Chicago Press.

Buchanan, J. (1986). *Liberty, Market and the State*. Brighton: Wheatsheaf.

Buchanan, J. (1987). The constitution of economic policy. *The American Economic Review*, 77: 243–50.

Buchanan, J. (1988). The economic theory of politics reborn. *Challenge*, March–April: 4–10.

Buchanan, J., and Tullock, G. (1962). *The Calculus of Consent: Logical Foundations of Constitutional Democracy*. Ann Arbor, MI: University of Michigan Press.

Buchholz, R. (1992). *Business Environments and Public Policy*. Englewood Cliffs, NJ: Prentice-Hall.

Collis, D. (1994). How valuable are organizational capabilities? *Strategic Management Journal*, 15: 143–52.

Crain, M., and Tollison, R. (1980). The size of majorities. *Southern Economic Journal*, 46: 726–34.

Doz, Y. (1986). *Strategic Management in Multinational Companies*. New York: Pergamon Press.

Epstein, E. (1969). *The Corporation in American Politics*. Englewood Cliffs, NJ: Prentice-Hall.

Ferrier, W., Smith, K., and Grimm, C. (1999). The role of competitive action in market share erosion and industry dethronement: A study of industry leaders and challengers. *Academy of Management Journal*, 42: 372–88.

Gale, J. and Buchholz, R. (1987). The political pursuit of competitive advantage: What business can gain from government. In A. Marcus, A. Kaufman, and D. Beam (eds.), *Business Strategy and Public Policy*, 231–52. New York: Quorum Books.

Getz, K. (1993). Selecting corporate political tactics. In B. Mitnick (ed.), *Corporate Political Agency*, 152–70. Newbury Park, CA: Sage Publications.

Grier, K., McDonald, M., and Tollison, R. (1995). Electioral politics and the executive veto: A predictive theory. *Economic Inquiry*, 33: 427–40.

Hillman, A., and Hitt, M. (1999). Corporate political strategy formulation: A model of approach, participation, and strategy decisions. *Academy of Management Review*, 24: 825–42.

Hillman, A., and Keim, G. (1995). International variation in the business-government interface: Institutional and organizational considerations. *Academy of Management Review*, 20: 193–214.

Hillman, A., Zardkoohi, A., and Bierman, L. (1999). Corporate political strategies and firm performance: Indications of firm-specific benefits from personal service in the US government. *Strategic Management Journal*, 20: 67–81.

IMD (1999). *The World Competitiveness Yearbook*. Lausanne, Switzerland: IMD Press.

Keim, G. (1981). Foundations of a political strategy for business. *California Management Review*, 23: 41–8.

Keim, G. (2000). Grassroots motivation via modern management techniques. In T. Kramer (ed.), *Winning at the Grassroots*, 89–91. The Public Affairs Council, Washington, DC.

Keim, G., and Baysinger, B. (1988). The efficacy of business political activity. *Journal of Management*, 14: 163–80.

Keim, G., and Zeithaml, C. (1986). Corporate political strategies and legislative decision making: A review and contingency approach. *Academy of Management Review*, 11: 828–43.

Kindleberger, C. (1970). *Power and Money*. New York: Basic Books.

Leone, R. (1979). The real costs of regulation. *Harvard Business Review*, 25: 134–42.

Lenway, S., and Rehbein, K. (1991). Leaders, followers, and free riders: An empirical test of variation in corporate political involvement. *Academy of Management Journal*, 34: 893–905.

Lord, M. 2000. Corporate political strategy and legislative decision making: The impact of orporate legislative influence activities. *Business and Society*, 39: 76–94.

Maggs, J. (2000). Art of the deal. *National Journal*, 21, May 20, 2000: 1586–92.

Mahon, J. (1993). Shaping issues/manufacturing agents: Corporate political sculpting. In B. Mitnick (ed.), *Corporate Political Agency*, 22–39. Newbury Park, CA: Sage Publications.

Maloney, M., McCormick, R., and Tollison, R. (1984). Economic regulation, competitive governments and specialized resources. *Journal of Law and Economics*, 27: 329–39.

Marsh, S. (1998). Creating barriers for foreign competitors: a study of the impact of anti-dumping actions on the performance of US firms. *Strategic Management Journal*, 19: 25–38.

McCormick, R., and Tollison, R. (1978). Legislatures as unions. *The Journal of Political Economy*, 86: 63–78.

Miles, R. (1982). *Coffin Nails and Corporate Strategies*. Englewood Cliffs, NJ: Prentice-Hall.

Mitnick, B. (1981).The strategic uses of regulation and deregulation. *Business Horizons*, 24: 71–83.

Mitnick, B. (1993). Political contestability in corporate political agency. In B. Mitnick (ed.), *Corporate Political Agency*, 40–66. Newbury Park, CA: Sage Publications.

Moran, T. (1985). *MNCs: The Political Economy of FDI*. Lexington, MA: Lexington Books.

Morin, R. (1996). Who's in control? Many don't know or care; knowledge gap affects attitudes and participation. *The Washington Post*, January 29.

Mueller, D. (1989). *Public Choice II*. Cambridge: Cambridge University Press.

Niskanen, W. (1971). *Bureaucracy and Representative Government*. Chicago, IL: Aldine.

Niskanen, W. (1975). Bureaucrats and politicians. *Journal of Law and Economics*, 18: 617–43.

Nohria, N., and Goshal, S. (1994). Differentiated fit and shared values: Alternatives for managing headquarters/subsidiary relations. *Strategic Management Journal*, 15: 491–502.

North, D. (1990). *Institutions, Institutional Change, and Economic Performance*. New York: Cambridge University Press.

North, D. (1994). Economic performance through time. *The American Economic Review*, 84: 359–68.

Oberman, W. (1993). Strategy and tactic choice in an institutional resource context. In B. Mitnick (ed.), *Corporate Political Agency*, 301–24. Newbury Park, CA: Sage Publications.

Peltzman, S. (1976). Toward a more general theory of regulation. *Journal of Law and Economics*, 19: 211–40.

Peltzman, S. (1987). The health effects of mandatory prescriptions. *Journal of Law and Economics*, 30: 207–39.

Peltzman, S., Levine, M., and Noll, R. (1989). The economic theory of regulation after a decade of deregulation. *Brookings Papers on Economic Activity*. Washington, DC: The Brookings Institute.

Penrose, E. (1959). *The Theory of Growth of the Firm*. Oxford, UK: Basil Blackwell.

Peteraf, M. (1993). The cornerstones of competitive advantage: A resource-based view. *Strategic Management Journal*, 6: 179–92.

Porter, M. (1979). How competitive forces shape strategy. *Harvard Business Review*, March–April: 1–10.

Ricks, D., Toyne, B., and Martinez, Z. (1990). Recent developments in international management. *Journal of Management*, 16: 219–53.

Rugman, A., and Verbeke, A. (1993). Generic strategies in global competition. In A. Rugman and A. Verbeke (eds.), *Research in Global Strategic Management*, 4: 1–18. Greenwich, CT: JAI Press.

Rumelt, R. (1984). Toward a strategic theory of the firm. In R. Lamb (ed.), *Competitive Strategic Management*, 62–81. Englewood Cliffs, NJ: Prentice-Hall.

Russo, M., and Fouts, P. (1997). A resource-based perspective on corporate environmental performance and profitability. *Academy of Management Journal*, 40: 534–59.

Salmon, L., and Seigfried, J. (1977). Economic power and political influence: The impact of industry structure on public policy. *American Political Science Review*, 71: 1026–43.

Salorio, E. (1993). Strategic use of import protection: Seeking shelter for competitive advantage. In A. Rugman and A. Verbeke (eds.), *Research in Global Strategic Management*, 4: 62–87. Greenwich, CT: JAI Press.

Schendel, D., and Hofer, C. (1979). *Strategic Management: A New View of Business Policy and Planning*. Boston: Little, Brown and Company.

Schollhammer, H. (1975). Business-government relations in an international context: An assessment. In P. Boarman and H. Schollhammer (eds.), *Multinational Corporations and Governments: Business-Government Relations in an International Context*, 32–51. New York: Praeger.

Schuler, D. (1996). Corporate political strategy and foreign competition: The case of the steel industry. *Academy of Management Journal*, 39: 720–37.

Scrivo, K. (2000). Door-to-door diplomacy. *National Journal*, 21, May 20: 1594.

Sethi, P. (1982). Corporate political activism. *California Management Review*, 24: 32–42.

Shaffer, B., Quasney, T., and Grimm, C. (2000). Firm level performance implications of nonmarket actions. *Business and Society*, 39: 126–43.

Smith, K., Grimm, C., and Gannon, M. (1992). *Dynamics of Competitive Strategy*. Newbury Park, CA: Sage Publications.

Stigler, G. (1971). The theory of economic regulation. *The Bell Journal of Economics and Management Science*, 2: 3–21.

Tollison, R. (1982). Rent-seeking: A survey. *Kyklos*, 35(4): 575–602.

Truman, D. (1951). *The Governmental Process: Political Interests and Public Opinion*. New York: Alfred Knopf.

Venkatraman, N. (1989). The concept of fit in strategy research: Toward verbal and statistical correspondence. *Academy of Management Review*, 14: 423–44.

Weidenbaum, M. (1980). Public policy: No longer a spectator sport for business. *Journal of Business Strategy*, 3: 46–53.

Wood, D. (1986). *Strategic Uses of Public Policy*. Marshfield, MA: Pitman Publishing.

Yoffie, D. (1987). Corporate strategy for political action: A rational model. In A. Marcus, A. Kaufman, and D. Beam (eds.), *Business Strategy and Public Policy*, 92–111. New York: Quorum Books.

Yoffie, D. (1988). How an industry builds political advantage. *Harvard Business Review*, 38: 80–9.

Yoffie, D., and Bergenstein, S. (1985). Creating political advantage: The rise of the corporate political entrepreneur. *California Management Review*, 28: 124–39.

# 22

# Implementing Strategy: An Appraisal and Agenda for Future Research

LAWRENCE G. HREBINIAK AND WILLIAM F. JOYCE

Over a decade ago, we published *Implementing Strategy* (Hrebiniak and Joyce, 1984), a work driven by a number of perceived shortcomings in the literature on strategy implementation in complex organizations. The book was important to us because we felt that the field of strategy desperately needed better models of implementation. Our feeling, relatedly, was that the topic of implementation was a sorely neglected or overlooked one in the strategic management literature. What, then, have time and research wrought in the area of strategy implementation since our efforts over a decade and a half ago? What conclusions can be drawn after careful assessment of the strategic management literature regarding the contribution of work on implementation to that body of knowledge?

The quick and somewhat disconcerting answer to these questions is that *strategy implementation is still a neglected area in the literature of strategic management*. Despite the volume of work published, implementation studies and theoretical frameworks have not received even a modest share of the literature on strategic management. Even a cursory review of published research reveals the clear emphasis on strategy formulation issues to the neglect of implementation research. Before proceeding to an appraisal of the work that has been done and a discussion of the major theoretical issues facing the field of implementation, we must first address an overriding issue that has been significant in retarding development of this important area of research.

## DISTINGUISHING FORMULATION AND IMPLEMENTATION

Formulation and implementation are clearly related activities, both of which must be accomplished in order to attain organizational objectives. However, recently an argument has emerged that formulation and implementation are essentially the same thing and that research concerning implementation *per se* is misplaced. While one could easily argue that a logically equivalent conclusion is that research concerning *formulation* is redundant and misplaced, we believe that such a conclusion is harmful to the development of the strategic management field.

Three separate arguments support this belief. First, strategy formulation and implementation are complementary and logically distinguishable areas of strategic management research. Second, because of this, calling everything the same thing is logically confusing and theoretically dysfunctional. Third, when we admit that strategic management is more than just strategy formulation, empirical research reveals that many implementation-related variables are vitally important in explaining firm performance. In fact, these variables may explain substantially more variance in firm performance than those related to formulation. Our conclusion is that research concerning both formulation and implementation is needed, there is little to be gained by separating them, and that the theoretically dysfunctional argument about redundancy should be discontinued and more research concerning implementation undertaken. We consider each of these three arguments in greater detail in the following paragraphs.

As noted above some have argued that implementation is simply part of the strategy formulation process and, accordingly, deserves little or no researchers' attention and efforts. The work on "emergent" strategies, for example, suggests that the adaptation, changes, or fine-tuning of strategies are simply part and parcel of strategy formulation (Mintzberg, 1985, 1987). While we agree that environmental surveillance and adaptation are vital to strategic management (Hrebiniak and Joyce, 1985), we feel that such a limited view of implementation activities is a mistake, and such thinking, if pervasive, clearly is detrimental to implementation research.

Strategy formulation and implementation are *separate, distinguishable parts of the strategic management process*. Each can be differentiated and discussed separately, conceptually and practically. Logically, implementation follows formulation; one cannot implement, carry out, or ensure fulfillment of something until that something exists. Making strategy work implies the existence of strategy. Of course, formulation and implementation are *interdependent*, part and parcel of an overall process of planning–executing–adapting. While any variable in the implementation process can be singled out and discussed separately and logically (e.g., structure, incentives plans, control systems), a focus on one part or variable only, without consideration of interdependence in the entire strategic management process, can lead to disastrous results.

Sound strategic management must recognize this symbiotic relationship between strategy formulation and implementation. It is silly to argue that each stands alone or that one or the other is more or less vital to company performance. Both are central to the attainment of desired results and competitive advantage, and top management attention is properly devoted to both in the strategic management process.

If formulation and implementation were synonymous, formulation, at the very minimum, would include a very wide range of activities. These would include activities and processes to analyze industries and competitors, manage decisional awareness, explore options, select from among these options, commit to a course of action, align resources to achieve options, assign responsibilities for executing these options, develop individual and group action plans to implement them, assess the success in attaining them, provide feedback to the actors assigned these responsibilities, and take actions to motivate their compliance and engagement with these objectives.

Many topics included in this list are studied by researchers from outside the field of strategic management, including those from organization theory, organizational behavior, and organizational development. Variables which they have studied include, *inter alia*, organizational structure and processes (OT); individual and group behavior, motivation, and job design (OB); and building shared goals, mobilizing commitment, and measuring and assessing the results of change processes (OD). Important research literatures have grown up around each of these topics within each of these disciplines. The very fact that these fields exist and thrive is evidence that they are addressing important problems. It is doubtful that researchers in these fields would believe that calling all of these diverse activities "strategy formulation" would encourage development of their fields or serve any other theoretical or practical purpose.

Using more specific theoretical terms than simply "formulation" directs attention to important literatures within each of these different fields and to more desirable variables for theory building. Dubin (1969) notes that summative variables such as "formulation" are not useful for theory building because they unnecessarily lump together variables that cannot be disentangled in subsequent research testing for their determinants and consequences, and thus for their theoretical importance. Combining all of these variables together and simply calling them formulation encourages researchers from within strategic management to ignore the important and complementary contributions of these other research areas, as well as the specific meaning of their theoretical terms.

Strategy implementation, unlike the argument claiming that implementation does not exist, does not take implementation as an exclusionary concept or as a summative variable, but rather as an area of research that draws selectively from various fields of research – including formulation – as described above. We will discuss the special issues derived from this perspective below, but it is important to note here that we are not proposing implementation as a *variable*, but rather as a related set of issues worthy of inquiry, eclectic in nature and fundamentally concerned with integration and not the exclusion of various theoretical perspectives. A parochial interest and a disciplinary allegiance to strategic management and its fundamental interest in strategy formulation (at least to the "formulation is everything" advocates), trivializes these contributions.

We believe that the field of management should be erected on an explicit recognition of its interdisciplinary nature, and the inclusion of *all* research that can help us more rigorously address the eclectic set of issues above. Indeed the failure to do so may be why so much of strategic management research has been less than satisfying. The issue is not whether all research can be subsumed under the name, formulation, but rather how research from multiple disciplines can be integrated without diluting the strength of their contributions. We believe that this is the fundamental objective of research in management.

Implementation research is eclectic, interdisciplinary and specifically concerned with such integration. It does not deny the importance of formulation and embraces complementary aspects of research concerning both implementation and formulation. As Kaplan (1968: 128) noted: "In research we need all that we can get." It draws selectively from all of the fields above and also undertakes to resolve issues that are unique to it. This integration of disciplinary perspectives and exploration of special issues is not encouraged by calling everything formulation. Implementation is not everything, but it is certainly "not nothing" as those who espouse the "formulation is everything" argument would have us believe.

If we allow for multiple areas for research in strategic management, including implementation, and abandon the "formulation is everything" argument, activities that are
easily classified as implementation activities are powerful in explaining organizational
performance. One of the authors has recently completed a study of a wide range of
factors potentially relevant in this regard. Joyce (2000a) studied 200 firms from four
major industry groups over a ten-year period from 1985 to 1995. Using a team of 15
coders, over 60,000 pages of text relevant to the performance of these firms were
analyzed using sequence comparison methodologies (McGee and Joyce, 2000) and nomic
analysis (Joyce, McGee, and Slocum, 1997). The results of these analyses indicated that
firms that were able to sustain unusually high performance, or who were able to turn
around poor performance and achieve subsequent high performance, relied upon four
key activities. These were developing a clear strategic direction, building a fast and
effective organization, establishing an adaptive culture, and executing against needs for
customer focus and cost reduction (Joyce, 2000a).

Of these four, only the first clearly falls within the realm of what is generally called
strategy formulation, while the latter comprise activities more related to implementation.
Calling all of them formulation unnecessarily focuses our research attention on variables
explaining only a minority component of the variation in firm performance. Clearly,
research concerning both formulation and implementation is needed and there is little to
be gained by unnecessarily subjugating either as an important area of inquiry.

The purpose of the remainder of this paper is to lay out a research agenda for future
work on strategy implementation. In so doing we will explore other causes for neglect in
this important research area. Our efforts are directed, in part, to logically justifying the
need for implementation research while, simultaneously, identifying areas needing further empirical investigation. To achieve this two-fold goal, the following discussion will
analyze and expand the following five themes:

1. Strategy implementation is important, but difficult.
2. Work on strategy implementation exists, but it is fragmented.
3. Achieving integration requires that models must meet six rigorous criteria of
   theoretical and practical usefulness.
4. Meeting the criteria of usefulness requires an improved understanding of "fit."
5. A focus on search and adaptation is central to theories and models of strategy
   implementation.

## STRATEGY IMPLEMENTATION IS IMPORTANT, BUT DIFFICULT

A great deal has been written in the past two decades about strategy formulation.
Managers at all levels or organization, in various industries, and in different functional
areas, have benefited from the insights provided by a host of analyses and empirical
examinations of the strategy formulation process.

Consider, for example, the attention devoted to competitive analysis, especially the
examination of industry forces that directly affect the intensity of competition and
profitability in an industry. The work of Michael Porter (1980) alone clearly has provided
valuable insights into the competitive arena, including the strategies companies can
employ to combat industry forces, anticipate and thwart competitors' actions, and gain

ground in an increasingly competitive global marketplace. Similarly, managers and researchers alike have become acutely aware of the importance of a company's capabilities or competencies and how they relate to new product and market opportunities (Barney, 1991; Prahalad and Hamel, 1990; Wernerfelt, 1984; Peteraf, 1993; Amit and Schoemaker, 1993). The picture of an organization as a collection of competencies or as a nourisher and user of distinctive skills or capabilities, while not a recent invention (Selznick, 1949), certainly has received renewed attention of late and has been instrumental in guiding top management's strategic choices. The mention of strategic choice suggests the importance of recent work that has examined the relationship between managerial choice and environmental determinism in the strategy formulation process (Hrebiniak and Joyce, 1985).

Where the research and practical advice are still weak is in the area of strategy implementation. Most managers know a great deal more about strategy formulation than they do about implementing their plans. Managers, of course, realize the importance of organizational capabilities and competencies. But having these resources is not sufficient; capabilities and competencies rely entirely on effective execution or implementation, and this is where organizations are weak. The knowledge of strategy execution and its performance consequences are woefully underemphasized in the literature on strategic management and decision making, and this research void exacerbates the implementation weaknesses in the applied world of corporate management. What accounts for the relatively greater attention to the knowledge of strategy formulation models and decisions? Why do practitioners and researchers alike know a great deal more about industry analysis, competitor surveillance, and generic strategies than they do about the successful implementation of those strategies?

The first and simplest answer to these questions is that strategy implementation is more difficult and challenging than strategy formulation. As problematical as the planning process is, the problems that must be overcome to implement strategy effectively are even more formidable. And it is logical to assume that the difficulty of implementation in the real world clearly translates into research-related problems and issues for the academic research and observer. To see this relationship, consider some of the factors that increase the difficulty of the strategy implementation process and conducting research on it.

## Time frames involved

Strategy implementation activities usually are played out over longer periods of time than the formulation of plans. Strategy formulation is usually more time bound and focused than implementation of the plans generated, the former lasting weeks or months but the latter often lasting years. The longer the time period, the more it is likely that competitors' actions and unforeseen factors ("noise") come into play and must be handled. Competitors' actions, for example, are occasionally contrary to those predicted during strategic planning, and company reactions must be developed or altered over time. Extended time frames also suggest the movement or turnover of key personnel, reallocations of resources, and other changes that increase the difficulty of focusing on implementation programs without distraction.

It is easy to see how these extended time frames affect not only implementation in organizations, but the research on strategy implementation as well. Clearly, some of the work in this area must be longitudinal in nature. Emphasis must be placed on controlling variables over time to ascertain the direct results of implementation activities. As in the real world, "noise" must be controlled to determine underlying or main effects in implementation research. Longitudinal research of this type, with adequate controls over key variables, is difficult and unpopular in a research world that stresses instead cross-sectional work with shorter time horizons and faster publication schedules.

## Number of people involved and task complexity

Generally, the number of people involved or affected is much greater during strategy implementation than strategy formulation. This raises a host of issues, including the control and management of diverse implementation activities with many participants or players. Large numbers increase the difficulties of managing diverse or conflicting motivations, as well as the need to coordinate the actions of players in different functions or organizations. Simply put, large numbers increase the complexity of the implementation process.

Research on strategy implementation also is made more difficult by large numbers. If implementation depends on interdependent people spread across various functions or departments in organizations, as well as across different vertical or hierarchical levels, the study of that phenomenon must also be made more problematical by that complexity.

Additional complexity is added to the research task when trying to rationalize and control implementation variables or actions. If implementation involves the analysis of multiple variables, including strategy, structure, interdependence, incentives, motivations, controls, coordination, and so on (Hrebiniak and Joyce, 1984), this adds even more complexity and difficulty to the implementation task. Complexity and a large number of variables make it extremely hard to determine the effects or influence of any given variable or of multiple forces, in interaction, on relevant implementation outcomes. This fact obviously presents major conceptual and statistical challenges for the implementation researcher.

## Need for sequential and simultaneous thinking

Researchers and managers involved in strategy implementation efforts must be able to think *sequentially* and *simultaneously* about key decisions. This need is a defining character-istic of strategy implementation, and it by no means is an easy task. On one hand, sequential thinking implies a logical process, an order between or among implementation decisions and actions (Hrebiniak and Joyce, 1984; Thompson, 1967). It involves the creation of a sequential causal chain, such as the following:

$$A \rightarrow B \rightarrow C \rightarrow D$$

Managers must first decide on A, or what comes first in the implementation process. Next, the question is, "what are the effects on B?" or, alternatively, "how must B be developed or changed to support A?" For example, if A represents business strategy and B, organizational structure, the issue is how strategy drives structure or how structure must be modified or developed to support the demands of strategy. Once the A–B relationship is determined, the logical sequence turns next to changes or requirements at C, which in turn can affect choices at D, E, F, and so on. The planned step-by-step analysis of this sequential logic is critical to the rational development of a coherent implementation process.

Sequential thinking, however, is not sufficient. What is also required is simultaneous thinking and analysis of the entire chain of events or consequences. While analyzing strategy and structure (A + B) rationally, the decision maker is looking at one piece of the implementation process. He or she is reducing a large problem to smaller, more manageable portions and handling each logically, focusing only on A and B in the causal chain. But despite the prime attention to A and B, the decision maker must also conceptualize the big picture, the overall implementation process. While thinking of the A–B relationship, one must also be thinking *concurrently* about C, D, E, and, indeed, X, Y, and Z.

Consider again analysis of strategy and structure. While emphasis is rightfully being placed on the costs and benefits of competing organizational designs, given the business strategy being pursued, a focus on only strategy and structure is not sufficient. Issues that come later in time or in the logical flow of implementation activities must also be on the decision makers' minds. For example, the strategy–structure nexus may hold implications for company control systems and management information systems (MIS) requirements due to the interdependencies and coordination needs inherent in the new structural configuration. Actual choices of information systems hardware, re-engineering require-ments, and coordination mechanisms will not be made for some time. Yet, analysis of strategy and structure must consider and be affected by these subsequent decisions.

Analysis, then, must be broad conceptually and not exclusively focused on A and B. What is needed is a simultaneous focus on X, Y, and Z, the later stages of the implementation sequence, to ensure coherence and consistency in the overall process. Early decisions or investments that create unanticipated demands, impossible require-ments, or excessive costs for the company at a latter point can scuttle the entire strategy implementation process. The problem confronting both the researcher and practitioner, of course, is that simultaneous thinking is difficult to operationalize in the decision-making or research process. Managers and researchers tend logically to focus on small manageable problems or short casual chains to control the number of variables and clarify cause–effect relationships. These actions or decisions militate against simultaneous thinking, detracting from the efficacy of implementation activities and research.

## WORK ON STRATEGY IMPLEMENTATION IS FRAGMENTED

As a starting point for this argument, it is important to note that we probably know more about strategy implementation than we think that we do. Figure 22.1 illustrates some of the many topics about which there are emerging theories, all of which have an important hearing on both the theory and practice of implementation. Although these emerging theories can be organized in a number of interesting ways, figure 22.1 has clustered them by discipline, and it is apparent that they are easily placed in these categories. It is seen that the set of activities which are central to the study of strategy implementation is divided among several academic fields of study. We are led to the conclusion that,

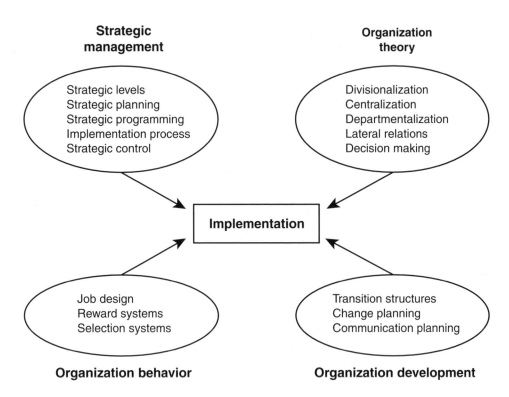

**FIGURE 22.1** Fields of organization and management theories performing implementation research
*Source*: Based on Baron's "Non-market Issue Life Cycle and Strategy" (Baron, 2000: 33).

although we know more than we think about strategy implementation, what we do know is fragmented, both theoretically and by the typical organization of academic departments in graduate schools. Conventional theory in organization design would suggest that this differentiation should result in problems in developing models concerning the integration of these areas, precisely the objective of theory building in strategy implementation.

There has been some consensus for a long time that, in fact, this is what has occurred. Galbraith noted that "the division of labor used by behavioral scientists does not reflect the nature of organization design choices . . . it has retarded the application of organization theory" (1977). Dubin similarly wrote that "Largely for imperialistic reasons, each social science discipline seeks to keep its theory from being "debased" to a different level of explanation . . . the ranting has contributed nothing to the issue of whether or not there is some linkage among the various levels of analysis" (1969: 14).

This threat of reductionism coupled with the natural consequences of division of labor has resulted in parochialism in addressing problems of strategy implementation. When we view the various theories and disciplines in figure 22.1 from an implementation perspective, there is a clear, logical relationship among them. At the risk of oversimplifying, strategic management is concerned with developing strategic goals and objectives and the necessary tactical actions to achieve them; organization theory with the creation and alignment of organizational structures and processes to facilitate these actions; and organizational behavior with managing human resources within these structures and processes.

This view is to be contrasted with that encouraged by reductionism and division of labor, in which each constituent discipline is concerned primarily with problems within its area and typically considers linkage issues only peripherally. For example, organizational behavior and industrial psychology have been criticized for taking structure and strategy as "givens," or only as boundary conditions in the development of their theories, as when Argyris complains "Where is the environment – the organization – in the models used by industrial psychologists who select, place, and train individuals for organizations? The answer is, I believe, in a *black box* between the predictor variables and the criterion variables" (1975: 10).

This implicit representation of organizations in the organizational behavior literature may be contrasted with the "partial" representation of strategy in organization theory. Hrebiniak and Joyce note that:

> although many design approaches take [contingency variables] as a "starting point" or reference point for further choices of organization design, these contingency variables are themselves products of previous strategic choices . . . Strategic analyses concerning stage of product/market evolution, market segmentation, and industry characteristics such as firm size and rivalry obviously bear on the characteristics of what organization designers have simply termed "environment" (1984: 155).

Of the major constituent disciplines, strategic management has been the most explicit about the inclusion of linkages to logically previous elements of the implementation chain, although there have been persistent arguments that the inclusion of goals as a decision element in strategy formulation is inappropriate (see Hofer and Schendel, 1977, for an interesting discussion of this debate). One consequence of this viewpoint is that the various disciplines bearing on a theory of implementation have been fragmented, and critical relationships among them have often been only partially or implicitly represented in theory development. This has retarded interest and work in the area of strategy implementation over time.

## ACHIEVING INTEGRATION REQUIRES USEFUL THEORY

In 1984 we published a model that focused on the eclectic and integrative nature of strategy implementation (Hrebiniak and Joyce, 1984) and attempted to overcome the fragmentation above. Figure 22.2 shows this model, which depicts a logical, serial progression of key implementation decisions deriving from the diverse literatures of strategic management, organization theory, and organizational behavior. The model suggests, in effect, that successful strategy implementation is a function of variables that have received separate, differentiated attention in management and organizational research, but which must be fully integrated and discussed in interaction in order to clarify and understand the total implementation process. Simply understanding this interactive

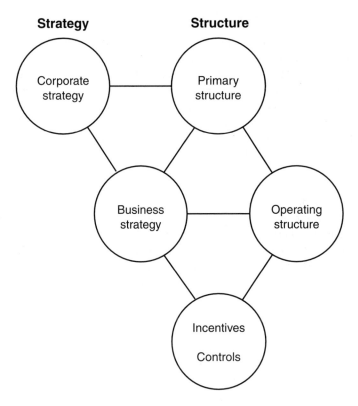

FIGURE 22.2  Hrebiniak and Joyce implementation model
*Source*: Adapted from Hrebiniak and Joyce (1984).

process is difficult enough; doing sound research that captures conceptually and statistically the nature of key interactions adds even more difficulty and challenge to the task,
a point that we will return to in the next section.

In developing this model we were guided by issues of both theoretical and practical
usefulness. Attempts at conceptual or theoretical integration that do not meet this test
simply will be ignored by the very people they purport to help, and will be irrelevant to
both theory and practice. In our opinion, useful models must meet six specific criteria of
usefulness. Four of these – logic, action, parsimony, and contingent prescription – are
general criteria for theory building in management. The remaining two – cognitive
manageability and efficiency – are specific to the complex nature of the implementation
process as developed above. Each of these criteria and their relationship to implementation activities is discussed below, leading to the next major section of the paper that
argues that meeting these criteria requires a more complete and rigorous understanding
of the concept of fit in models of implementation.

## General criteria of usefulness

*Logic.*   A useful model of strategy implementation requires the property of logic for at least three reasons. First, a logical model facilitates decision making by casting problems within a rational framework. Although there are clear and well-known limitations for rational decision making, it is true that rational models are more easy to apply and implement than those that require us to think in ways that are contrary to our basic cognitive style. Logical models are easier to "think about" than illogical or irrational ones.

A second reason why logic is important is that it facilitates prediction through its deductive properties. Hrebiniak and Joyce note that: "managers must anticipate the consequences of [their actions] . . . often with little experience to guide them. We can partially compensate for this need to be omniscient through the use of a logical model that allows us to deduce consequences of implementation activities" (1984: 22).

Finally, a logical model, to the extent that it has been carefully developed and reflects both theory and practice, allows the decision maker access to a pool of experience considerably larger than that which can be accumulated by a single individual, no matter how long or distinguished his career might be. Because the logical model is founded on the experience of managers and academics gained in many organizations and across many industries, this "collective wisdom" should facilitate informed choice and effective implementation research.

*Action.*   A useful model requires that it be capable of aiding managers in "producing solutions" (Argyris and Schon, 1982). This requirement implies a need for the model to facilitate purposive change. Purposive change relies on manipulable variables. Although hypothetical constructs are interesting and important, variables which can never be seen, heard, or touched are less accessible to change or managerial intervention. The criterion of action recognizes this problem and directs our attention to variables which are manipulable, or failing this, are at least more objective. As Argyris stated a long time ago, for a model "to be helpful for change, it must, in addition to being valid, be given in terms of directly observable behavior. The more concrete and operational . . . the more helpful it can be" (1975: 15).

*Parsimony.*   A useful model of implementation must also have the property of parsimony. Parsimony facilitates cognitive manageability. Many social science models are too complex to be implemented without reference to a large "external memory." The usefulness of any model would be increased to the extent that it accounts for significant amounts of criterion variance with a minimum number of predictors. Given an equivalent amount of explained variance in the outcomes of interest, the model accomplishing this with the fewer number of predictors would be judged the more useful. In building models, Homans' advice regarding the number of variables, though old, is still sage: "As few as you may, as many as you must" (1959: 18).

*Contingent prescription.*   Our last general requirement for a useful model is the criterion of contingent prescription. Over the years, contingency views of organization and strategic management have become common. These views correctly recognize the important distinction between *laws* (describing relatively stable relationships among variables, and exemplified by classical organization theory) and *theories* (which are bodies of laws logically connected, as in contingency views of organization design). But the development of contingency views has tended to obscure one of the significant strengths of traditional "models;" that is, that they told us what to do. In general, it is not enough to know that "it all depends;" managers need to know what it all depends on, how, and what they can do about it. Our position is that both contingency and prescription should be criteria for a useful model of implementation.

## Criteria specific to implementation

The criteria for useful models developed in the section above are general criteria in the sense that they apply to attempts to develop useful models regardless of the specific content of these models or the particular problems to which they are addressed. In addition, a useful model of strategy implementation must also deal with important problems arising from the implementation task itself. Two of the more important of these are achieving cognitive manageability and efficiency (Joyce, 2000a).

*Cognitive manageability.* In implementing strategy, managers are faced with an almost bewildering array of relevant variables, potential points of intervention, and sets of relationships. The problem becomes one of making sense of this complexity and operating within it to obtain the strategic objectives of the organization. To a certain extent, problems of strategy implementation are problems of decision-making in the face of complexity and uncertainty, a topic which has received considerable attention since the pioneering work of March and Simon (1958). Recognition of this fact suggests that models of implementation must account for some of the same limitations on decision capability that have been widely discussed in the organizational and strategic management literatures, in particular that they address the bounded but intended rationality of decision makers themselves.

This position is supported by important research concerning implementation. Lindblom, for example, writes that: "For complex problems, the (rational-comprehensive method) is, of course, impossible. Although such an approach can be described, it cannot be practiced, except for relatively simple problems, and even then, in a somewhat modified form. It assumes intellectual capacities and sources of information that men simply do not possess . . . (1979: 88). Quinn similarly comments: "Because so many uncertainties are involved, no manager or management team can predict the precise way in which any major subsystem will ultimately evolve, much less the way all will interact to create the enterprises overall strategic posture" (1980: 63).

*Efficiency.* In implementing strategy, managers must not only address problems arising from complexity, they must also do so in an efficient manner. Organizations and their managements operate within constraints that require the application of resources so as to obtain maximum benefit from these resources. The problem of efficiency recognizes the importance of the pursuit of economic rationality in organizations, but it also recognizes important cognitive and ethical constraints in implementation as well. At least three forms of efficiency are important, termed economic, cognitive, and ethical efficiency, respectively.

Economic efficiency is the most familiar of the three types of efficiency that we will discuss. Hrebiniak and Joyce argue that managers who are intendedly rational "attempt to implement strategy within the constraints of economic efficiency, choosing those courses of action that solve their problems with minimum costs to the organization" (1984: 8). In the strategy literature, Chandler (1962) found that organizations changed their organizational structures only when forced to do so by operating inefficiencies. The resulting adjustment represented the minimum action necessary to restore efficient operations and increase economic performance.

Similar arguments are prevalent in the organizational literature as well. In presenting different structures for achieving coordination in complex organizations, Galbraith states that "the forms are listed below in order of increasing cost ... as task uncertainty increases, the organization will sequentially adopt these mechanisms up through the matrix organization" (1977: 82). All of these positions recognize that implementation activities are themselves consumers of economic resources, and that activities that achieve desired outcomes at minimum cost are to be preferred.

The problem of cognitive efficiency is similar to the problem of complexity in the sense that they both arise due to limited information-processing capability. The problem of complexity arises due to the decision-maker's need to achieve some degree of control and predictability in the face of uncertainty and bounded rationality. The problem of cognitive efficiency arises because this same bounded rationality implies a scarce resource that must be carefully applied in order to produce solutions to problems before this critical resource is exhausted. As Cyert and March (1963), note, the search for acceptable solutions is itself a consumer of resources, and reasons of cognitive efficiency require that this process be managed within the constraints of limited information handling capacity. Whereas complexity implies that decision-makers cannot understand everything and recognizes limited decision capability, cognitive efficiency implies that even if complex problems could be understood, our limited decision capacity would prescribe the exhaustive search required to exploit this capability. Concerns with cognitive efficiency encourage incremental implementation activities, as when decision makers limit investigation to policies differing only slightly from present policies, a practice that "immediately reduces the number of alternatives to be investigated and also drastically simplifies the character of the investigation of each" (Lindblom, 1979: 55).

The final type of efficiency that is important is ethical efficiency. Ethical efficiency represents the decision maker's desire to intervene at the lowest possible level in order to prevent unanticipated and deleterious consequences for individuals. "As depth of intervention increases, so also do a number of concomitants of depth: [these are the] centrality of the individual and the risk of unintended consequences for individuals. These suggest a criterion for the depth of the intervention: to intervene at a level no deeper than that required to produce enduring solutions to the problems at hand" (Harrison, 1970: 280).

The point of these arguments is that when faced with a problem, the organization should respond so as to solve it, but not at unnecessary financial, cognitive, or human cost. Disregard for these considerations results in unnecessary change and potentially negative impact on individuals involved in the implementation process.

In sum, current work on strategy implementation is fragmented. Models of implementation, accordingly, must be eclectic or integrative in order to capture the complexity of the implementation task for practitioners and researchers alike. Besides being integrative, models of strategy implementation must be useful, satisfying the related criteria of logic, action, contingent prescription, parsimony, cognitive manageability, and efficiency.

## Strategy Implementation Models Require an Improved Understanding of "Fit"

Meeting the criteria set forth in the second section of this paper requires an improved understanding of the concept of fit. The critical nature of fit is explicit in the general model criterion of logic, for logical models can only be constructed by understanding the critical interactions among key implementation variables. A logical model is one that follows logical rules or prescribes logical relationships among its components. It offers a reasonable expectation of what will happen when model components are manipulated, and this requires knowledge of interactions or fit. Fit is obviously explicit in the criterion of contingent prescription because contingency and fit both signify a conditional relationship. And, it is implicit in the general criterion of parsimony, for only by understanding the relationships and effects of fit among implementation variables will we be able to choose that subset which produces the largest component of explained variance in desired outcomes while maintaining cognitive manageability.

Fit is also a critical aspect of addressing the two problems of complexity and efficiency. Complexity requires that we "take apart" the complex set of activities involved in implementing strategy and work on them within the constraints of manageable proportions. When something is taken apart, the relationships among its components are unchanged; that is, they must still be fit together to obtain the whole. Some pieces must fit with others, but every component does not have to fit with all others. Understanding the structure of these relationships, the fit, allows us to reconstruct the "whole."

Implementation models such as the McKinsey 7-S model which argues that everything depends on everything else therefore imply one of two mutually absurd arguments. Either, first, that we have taken apart the complex set of implementation activities but have learned nothing about the set of relationships among them, much like the careless person who disassembles his watch only to find that he can't put it together again. Or, second, that we have learned what the critical relationships among implementation variables are and that they are adequately portrayed by models in which all elements depend on all others. Although this is possible, it is not very likely, for it would argue that causal direction is irrelevant, that no variables dominate others, that it makes no difference where we begin implementation activities, and so on. We are left with the conclusion that the problem of complexity and fit are strongly connected.

A similar conclusion is reached with respect to the problem of efficiency. Reverting to our previous example, when we take something apart to fix it, it is not usually the case that everything is broken. Some parts may be repaired while others are still perfectly functional. This analogy implies that, when implementing strategy, everything does not always have to be changed. Efficiently addressing pertinent elements of the implementation model requires knowledge of the functions and fit among its components.

This argument is less obvious than it seems, given the popularity of the notion of fit in the strategic management and organizational literatures. While fit is often argued to be important, it is paradoxical that research continues to rely on primitive notions of the concept and to ignore a reasonable body of research that could be useful in improving research. While we give fit considerable lip service, it remains true that existing research specifically concerning fit rarely finds its way into studies testing contingency views. When one reviews this work, it is easy to conclude that although fit is important, we do in fact know very little about it. Such a conclusion is perhaps too pessimistic. Although we need to know more, we know more than we think.

## We know more about fit than we think

As an illustration of our assertion that we know more about fit than we think, consider the possibility that fit is not a single concept, but rather a set of related but distinct concepts. Research in all of the constituent disciplines relevant to strategy implementation has rarely paused to consider the possibility that when we casually use the term "fit," that it is possible that we are not all referring to the same empirical phenomenon. Instead, it has become customary to refer to the fit between strategy and structure, between organization and environment, or between persons and situations as if it was commonly understood and accepted that fit referred to a specific relationship among the variables of interest. It is our contention that we know more about fit than these simplistic statements admit and that theory would be advanced if we would begin to use what we know.

To illustrate this point consider the typology of competing models of fit developed by Joyce, Slocum, and von Glinow (1982) and presented in figure 22.3. Although a detailed discussion of the origins of these models is beyond the scope of this paper, a brief introduction to the competing concepts and the interesting distinctions among them can be made. This will then allow us to show how the strategic management literature employs these alternative notions indiscriminately leading to unnecessary conceptual confusion.

The differing concepts of fit may be distinguished as follows. *Effect congruency* is the type of fit that occurs when two variables are consistent in their main effects on criteria. For example, if both increased supervision and more complete job specification resulted in improved job performance, this definition would judge that there was a fit between these variables.

*General* or *theoretical congruency* occurs when variables are judged to be consistent with one another on the basis of previous theory but without reference to any specific outcome criteria. Such propositions have been common in psychology, as when individuals are hypothesized to fit with situations when their needs match the "press" of the particular setting (Lewin, 1936; Murray, 1950; Stern, 1972). For example, we might say that a motivated person fits his job when the job is seen to be challenging.

Finally, *functional congruency* represents the type of fit that is determined on the basis of the effects of interactions among variables on relevant criteria. Fit is whatever configuration of predictor variables that results in effects on the outcome variables of interest. In this case there are as many "fits" as there are outcome criteria, and fit is empirically rather than theoretically determined. This third type of fit allows for the interesting possibility that variables may substitute or compensate for one another, as in figure 22.3(c) where raising the level of one of the variables produces improvement

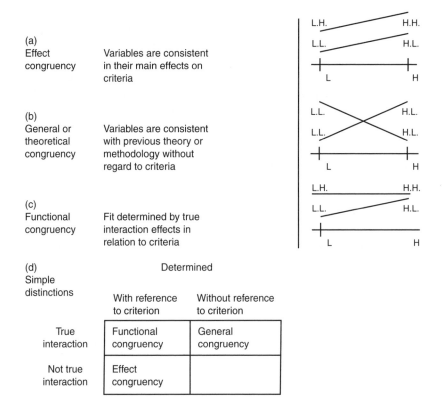

(a)
Effect
congruency        Variables are consistent
                  in their main effects on
                  criteria

(b)
General or        Variables are consistent
theoretical       with previous theory or
congruency        methodology without
                  regard to criteria

(c)
Functional        Fit determined by true
congruency        interaction effects in
                  relation to criteria

(d)
Simple
distinctions                        Determined

|  | With reference to criterion | Without reference to criterion |
|---|---|---|
| True interaction | Functional congruency | General congruency |
| Not true interaction | Effect congruency | |

FIGURE 22.3  Competing models of fit

*Source*: Adapted from Joyce, Slocum, and von Glinow (1982a: 45–63).

in outcomes, but raising both does not result in more improvement than that obtained through manipulating either one alone.

Figure 22.3(d) makes some distinctions among these competing concepts which helps to clarify these complex models. First, it can be seen that effect congruency, although a frequently employed concept of fit, is not really fit at all. Statistically, effect congruency represents a simple main effect model that does not involve true interaction effects. In fact, there are no joint effects due to these variables at all, and the fit between them is totally irrelevant as a predictor. This is to be contrasted with both theoretical and functional congruency which both represent true models of interaction or fit.

The latter two types of fit may be distinguished on the basis of whether fit is judged with or without reference to criteria. Theoretical congruence is judged without considering the effects on an explicit criterion as in the examples above, and involves consistency with previous theory. Functional congruency is judged with respect to specific criteria allowing the possibilities of substitute (Kerr and Jermier, 1982) and blocking (Joyce, Slocum, and von Glinow, 1982b).

In the next section we will show how these ideas have been confounded in the strategic management literature, leading to unnecessary confusion. We may summarize this section by noting that all of these models are important, but that each says something different about what constitutes fit. Effect congruency argues that "more is better," theoretical congruency that "less can be better, if appropriate" (as when the L.L. condition produces the same criterion levels as the H.H. case in fig. 22.3), and effect congruency that "more can be too much" as in the substitute effect illustrated in the figure. The next section provides examples from the strategic management literature showing how these concepts have been confounded with negative consequences for both our own research and that of others.

## IMPROVED KNOWLEDGE OF FIT CAN CLARIFY IMPLEMENTATION THEORY

Because the strategic management literature has generally not been very precise in defining and using the concept of fit, a number of confusions have resulted. These confusions have resulted from two main sources, either using the concept inconsistently or using it incorrectly. These problems are described and illustrated below under the headings "How we confuse others" and "How we confuse ourselves."

### How we confuse others

We believe that we often confuse other researchers when we use a term correctly but inconsistently. Even outstanding research is not immune from this problem. Consider, for example, the Harvard Organization and Environment Research Program (Lawrence and Lorsch, 1967; Lawrence, 1981). In this work we can discern all three types of fit discussed above but without any distinction being made among them. The following quotations from Lawrence and Lorsch (1967) illustrate our point:

> Effect Congruency: "We wondered if it would be at all possible for organizations simultaneously to achieve *both* the high degree of differentiation *and* the tight integration required for successful performance." (p. 56, emphasis ours)

This quotation indicates that both differentiation and integration contribute to performance and that outcomes are improved when both of these variables are consistent in their main effects on the criteria, clearly an effects additive model of fit. Now consider the next quotation:

> Theoretical Congruency: "The key question is: Were the organizations that achieved the *closest fit* between departmental differentiation and the attributes of their environments *also* the highest performers?" (p. 62, emphasis ours)

In this quotation it is clear that the authors are referring to fit as the relationship between structure and environment without regard to the outcome "performance." Since it is the relationship between the predictors and not their absolute levels themselves which was hypothesized to impact on performance, this is seen to be a model hypothesizing true interactions judged without reference to a criterion (for purposes of determining fit), or a model of theoretical congruency. Now, our final example:

> Functional Congruency: "We focused on *what fits were most effective* and not on the process by which these fits were achieved." (p. 88, emphasis ours)

This is obviously an example of what we termed functional congruency, completing our illustration of the fact that the term has been utilized inconsistently in *research that has been central to the development of the concept of fit itself*. It is not our intention to be critical of this research, but simply to point out in a formal way that even the very best work in this area has sometimes been inconsistent in its treatment of this important concept. It is more difficult not to be critical when we consider the next category of confusion.

## How we confuse ourselves

We believe that we confuse ourselves when we use the fit concept not only inconsistently but also incorrectly for our purposes. The following quotations from Lorange (1980) illustrate our point. In referring *to the same concept of fit* he makes the following two statements:

> the matching of each system elements design to the particular *needs of the situational setting* . . . automatically implies that internal consistency is ensured among the elements of the strategic system (p. 152, emphasis ours).

Shortly thereafter he writes:

> What might be the consequences of a lack of consistency among the elements of the strategic system? . . . Each element is *dependent on the others* . . . the strategic decision-making tool will not function unless there is a tight interrelationship (p. 163, emphasis ours).

In the first quotation Lorange is arguing that aligning elements of the strategic system with the needs of the setting automatically results in fit among them. This represents what we have called effect congruency in which fit is determined on the basis of relationship to an external criterion, in this case the "needs" of the setting. We have shown that this is not really a true interaction at all, and that relationships among predictor variables are irrelevant in this formulation of the concept. Yet he goes on to argue that it is these very interrelationships which account for the effectiveness of the strategic system, a position that he implicitly forbids in his initial arguments. It is easy to confuse others when we are confused ourselves. But lest we be too harsh it is appropriate to point out that it is easy to make such errors in the absence of rigorous thinking concerning key concepts in our theory. But it is still problematical because similar errors are often seen in practice, as the following quotations concerning the McKinsey 7–S model indicate:

> it is the "fittedness" *among* the S's that turn a good strategic idea into a lean, mean program for corporate success (Henderson, 1982, emphasis ours).

Speaking of the same model, he also writes:

> think of the 7-S diagram as a set of compasses . . . When the needles are aligned (with strategy) the company is organized; when they are not, the company has yet to be really organized even if its structure looks right.

Using the terminology developed above it is clear that the first quotation implies either theoretical or functional congruency, and thus a true interaction, whereas the second proposes effect congruency, and thus the irrelevancy of the "fittedness" desired by the first. When such an error is made in so prominent an approach the implications are of more than academic interest. We must have it one way or the other, and in the final analysis unclear thinking confuses not only theory but also practice.

The implications of this discussion are clear. Rigorous understanding of the several varieties of fit, coupled with statistical procedures for detecting and operationalizing them, must be used in future research. The methodology for accomplishing this already exists (Joyce, Slocum, and von Glinow, 1982b) but has not been widely utilized within the strategic management literature (perhaps because it was published in a psychology journal). It is time for us to use what is available to us and to continue to refine it. This failure may be due to a methodological parochialism, not unlike the theoretical parochialism above. Joyce, McGee, and Slocum (2000), in an empirical assessment of the diversification literature, showed that the most significant connections between the findings in diversification research were within single individual's programs of research. There were far weaker connections between different researcher's findings. This suggests an insular approach to both theory and methodology that is surely retarding further developments in strategic management.

## A FOCUS ON SEARCH IS CENTRAL TO THEORIES AND MODELS OF IMPLEMENTATION

A better understanding of fit coupled with a more rigorous application of statistical methodology is necessary for improved research concerning strategy implementation. However, we also need to pay more attention to the organizational processes responsible for achieving fit. Successful strategy implementation implies effective organization adaptation over time. Our implementation model, for example, discusses control capabilities that focus on environmental surveillance, feedback regarding organizational performance, and change processes that enable the organization to adapt successfully (Hrebiniak and Joyce, 1984). Indeed, one could argue pointedly that a critical component of strategy implementation efforts, if not its *raison d'être*, is that which deals with proactive change in complex, turbulent, and evolving environments. Successful implementation indicates that action has been taken, learning has occurred, that an organization has received feedback about its performance, evaluated it, and made the necessary adjustments in its competitive stance.

### Search and adaptation

The management literature has long focused on organizational change and adaptation, at both the macro or population level and at the level of individuals' receptivity or resistance to change. Explaining how organizations create strategies to adapt to environmental changes clearly is a central underlying aspect of the study of strategic management (Child, 1972; Hrebiniak and Joyce, 1985). Similarly, explaining why some organizations perform better than others in this process of adaptation is yet another critical question confronting students of organization (Barnett, Greve, and Park, 1994). To some, the answer to the latter question is found in a firm's positional advantage in an industry (Porter, 1980); for others, the answer lies in an organization's ability to create firm-specific capabilities or competencies that differentiate it from competitors (Selznick, 1949; Prahalad and Hamel, 1990; Wernerfelt, 1984). Both views have merit, and both have received attention in the literature of strategic management.

One important aspect of organizational adaptation, however, that has not received sufficient attention, despite its central importance, is the process of search in organizations. Search underlies and is central to organizational adaptation. In the strategy implementation process, search refers to activities aimed at producing information useful for achieving an effective fit among an organization's internal capabilities and resources, strategies, practices, and procedures. It refers to an organization's scanning capability, its ability to identify, observe, and codify its own behavior and that of competitors, customers, and relevant others, while also identifying opportunities and threats posed by competitors and other organizational stakeholders. The absence of effective search and surveillance techniques suggests that a company would not observe or react in a timely fashion to important industry or competitive changes, perhaps with dire consequences for organizational performance and viability. Simply stated, organizational search processes are central to any model of strategy implementation which, in turn, is vital to organizational adaptation and change over time.

Search, then, is an important aspect of strategic management. Whether it is viewed as a process or capability, organizations need to see, create, or react to environmental contingencies in order to formulate and implement strategy successfully. Research is sorely needed on this critical phenomenon. Future implementation research must study the determinants and correlates of search to improve our understanding of how organizations implement and change their plans in an overall process of adaptation.

What, then, affects search in complex organizations? Why are some companies better than others in their ability to observe, gather, and use knowledge effectively for competitive advantage? The following discussion highlights a number of points or propositions that may guide future efforts in this important research area.

## Search and organizational competencies

Research suggests that search will focus in areas in which the organization enjoys competitive advantage or in which it believes it has an "excess capacity" of crucial skills or abilities (Prahalad and Hamel, 1990). In similar terms, a resource-based view of the firm posits the existence of tangible and intangible firm-specific resources that allow a company to identify, develop, and implement new successful competitive strategies (Wernerfelt, 1984; Barney, 1991; Amit and Schoemaker, 1993; Peteraf, 1993; Collis and Montgomery, 1997). The logical inference here is that core competence or critical firm-specific resources drive the search process, allowing the organization to evaluate its own performance, analyze industry and competitive forces, and execute needed changes as part of the strategy implementation process.

If an organization's resources include boundary-spanning units and individuals charged with the task of search and surveillance, one could postulate an increased effectiveness of the strategy implementation process. Investments in control and feedback mechanisms that facilitate search and surveillance methods allow the organization to benchmark others more easily, observe competitors' actions, and develop contingency plans for change and adaptation. An absence of such capabilities can only hurt strategy implementation and an organization's ability to adapt to industry forces and competitive pressures.

## Past performance and search

Years ago, March (1981) argued that search varies with organizational performance, and more recent research suggests a similar argument. Poor performance motivates a search for ways to improve performance, while good performance motivates managers to seek ways to build upon their advantage, for example, build entry barriers to limit competitors' options (Porter 1980; Barnett , Greve, and Park, 1994; Marlin, Lamont, and Hoffman, 1994). March (1981) went so far as to categorize search as solution-driven, when organizational performance is poor, and slack search, when performance is good. The former search focuses on solving problems, finding ways to change or adapt strategies to eliminate the poor performance. The latter represents experimentation, R&D, or even informal "dabbling" not unlike the "skunk-works" findings of Peters and Waterman (1982).

One could hypothesize that an effective strategy implementation process requires both kinds of search, although both are quite distinct. Poor performance demands that organizations redress their problems before suffering irreparable competitive damage. Time is of the essence in this case, and the organization must quickly and accurately read its environment and adapt accordingly, often changing some or all of the key variables involved in the strategy implementation process, such as structure, incentives, or methods of integration or communication (Hrebiniak and Joyce, 1984; Cohen and Leventhal, 1990). When organizational performance is good, slack search is more decentralized and informal, leading to a more casual and experimental approach to problem solving.

The surveillance capabilities so vital to effective strategy implementation would benefit immensely by motivating both solution-driven and slack search. Creating boundary spanning roles, developing information and control systems that "embrace" rather than avoid error (Michael, 1973), emphasizing the "organic" aspect of organizational structures (Burns and Stalker, 1961), and facilitating the intra-organizational transfer of knowledge gathered from without (Cohen and Leventhal, 1990), represent just a few ways to structure the strategy implementation process to maximize the benefits of both types of search. Strategy implementation requires both effective surveillance or information gathering and effective information dissemination; the former facilitates organizational adaptation or change, while the latter aids the internal examination of fit among key implementation variables or decisions. Development of processes, structures, or methods aimed at the facilitation of solution-driven and slack search would appear to represent a wise organizational investment.

## Search and organizational learning

Learning is vital to organizational adaptation and performance. Learning can affect how organizations search and how effective the strategy implementation process will be.

Search is affected by learning. If past activities or decisions unmistakably and unequivocally are seen as producing positive outcomes, the tendency is to rely on those same activities or decisions in the future. Learning, that is, affects future search and strategy implementation efforts. An obvious danger of this influence on search is excessive inertia in the face of changing environmental conditions. Under conditions of excessive change, inertia and a blind reliance on past areas of success may affect search and implementation negatively, resulting in ineffective adaptation (Hrebiniak and Joyce, 1985). Similarly, responding to new problems with old routines and practices can seriously limit the search process, perhaps causing the organization to fall into a "competency trap" in which it performs poorly by doing what it has learned so well (Levitt and March, 1988; Leventhal and March, 1993; Simon, 1993; Barnett, Greve, and Park, 1994; Ingram and Baum, 1997). In these cases, learning and past experience negatively affect search, strategy implementation, and adaptation in organizations.

Additional research is needed on the effects of learning on search and strategy implementation effectiveness. This work must focus on both the collection of knowledge from without and the dissemination of knowledge within the organization, as organizations try to avoid inertia or competency traps. Research should include variables that directly affect this information gathering and usage, including incentives, organizational structures, and the ability of the organization to create "absorptive capacity" (Burns and Stalker, 1961; Hrebiniak and Joyce, 1984; Cohen and Leventhal, 1990). Simply put, learning affects search which, in turn, determines the effectiveness of the strategy implementation process. The more we learn about these causal linkages, the greater will be our ability to understand what affects implementation designs and outcomes.

## SUMMARY

This chapter presented several arguments with implications for future research concerning strategy implementation. In arguing for the need for improved models we suggested that what we know about implementation is fragmented among several fields or disciplines. Although we agree that there are important relationships among these areas, current models have not been as successful in providing the understanding of these interdependencies as is required to advance both theory and practice.

Models of implementation must meet both general and specific criteria if they are too useful for these purposes. General criteria are criteria relevant to all usable models, and include the criteria of logic, action, parsimony, and contingent prescription. Specific criteria are particular to the content of the model being developed. For implementation activities two important criteria are that the model addresses both the problem of complexity and the problem of efficiency.

Meeting these criteria requires an improved understanding of the concept of fit or contingency in models of implementation. Although we know more about fit than we think, the concept has been rather casually applied. Fit is more appropriately viewed as a family of competing concepts than as a single, unitary term. Lack of precision in specifying which of these concepts is being employed has resulted in confusion, not only for other researchers, but also in our own research. It is time that we become more rigorous in our thinking about fit. The idea of a contingency view of organization and management has been around for some time now, and academically can be traced at least as far back as Simon (1946). Some researchers called for more rigorous thinking in this area years ago (Hrebiniak, 1978; Joyce, Slocum, and von Glinow, 1982a), and we believe that more such research is desperately needed now.

Despite the rigor and elegance of the models of fit discussed this paper, they still fail to capture the complexity of the situations encountered in practice. "Real" situations rarely involve so few as three variables, raising what Dubin called the "paradox of precision" (1969: 37), that is, although we may have a reasonable understanding of fit, it may still not afford us much in the way of prediction. Yet avoiding the type of rigorous thinking that we call for will only ensure that we will never have it, and therein lies our dilemma: focusing on theory does not significantly aid practice, while focusing on practice ensures that we will never have the models we ultimately need to practice well! The dilemma can be resolved if we admit the possibility of introducing practice into theory and theory into practice. Managers do use "lay" models of fit implicitly or explicitly to address the critical interdependencies which we have highlighted in this paper. A promising direction for future research in strategic management is to explore and study these processes. Again, some pioneering work in this direction has begun; there are gains to be made if we begin to merge theory with practice and take this as a starting point for future inquiry.

Finally, we need to know more about search in complex organizations. Search processes or capabilities facilitate organizational adaptation. They allow the organization to focus on environmental surveillance and generate the information vital to strategy implementation activities and organizational change. Both solution-driven and slack search are integral aspects of this adaptation process; both, consequently, should be encouraged by organizational incentives, structures, and business processes. The latter would include processes and structures that facilitate the effective dissemination and usage of information within the organization, for only then can the fit among key implementation variables be analyzed and their effects ascertained.

## CONCLUSION

Search, then, and the information it provides, are vital to organizational adaptation, learning, and a more complete analysis of the strategy implementation process in organizations. It is through search that learning occurs and fit is achieved in implementation decisions and actions. Effective search helps the organization avoid competency traps, thereby maintaining the integrity and usefulness of the strategy implementation process. Search, in effect, represents an important competence that allows the organization to deal with change in complex, turbulent environments, evaluate the impact of strategy implementation activities, and enhance organizational performance in increasingly competitive environments.

## ACKNOWLEDGMENTS

Portions of this work were supported by grants from the Amos Tuck School of Business at Dartmouth College and The Wharton School, University of Pennsylvania.

# REFERENCES

Amit, R., and Schoemaker, P. J. H. (1993). Strategic assets and organizational rents. *Strategic Management Journal*, 14(1): 33–46.

Argyris, C. (1975). Personality and organization theory. *Administrative Science Quarterly*, 20: 8–23.

Argyris, C., and Schon, D. (1982). *Theories in Use*. San Francisco, CA: Jossey-Bass.

Barnett, W. P., Greve, H. R., and Park, D. Y. (1994). An evolutionary model of organizational performance. *Strategic Management Journal*, Winter Special Issue, 15: 11–28.

Barney, J. B. (1991). Firm resources and sustained competitive advantage. *Journal of Management*, 17: 99–120.

Burns, T., and Stalker, G. M. (1961). *The Management of Innovation*. London: Tavistock Publications.

Chandler, A. D. (1962). *Strategy and Structure: Chapters in the History of the American Industry Enterprise*. Cambridge, MA: MIT Press.

Child, J. (1972). Organization structure, environment and performance: the role of strategic choice. *Sociology*, 6: 1–22.

Cohen, W. M., and Leventhal, D. A. (1990). Absorptive capacity: A new perspective on learning and innovation. *Administrative Science Quarterly*, 35: 128–52.

Collis, D. J., and Montgomery, C. A. (1997). *Corporate Strategy: Resources and Scope of the Firm*. Chicago: McGraw-Hill.

Cyert, R. M., and March, J. G. (1963). *A Behavioral Theory of the Firm*. Englewood Cliffs, NJ: Prentice-Hall.

Dubin, R. (1969). *Theory Building*. New York: McGraw-Hill.

Galbrath, J. (1977). *Designing Complex Organizations*. Reading, MA: Addison-Wesley.

Harrison, R. (1970). Determining the depth of intervention, *Journal of Applied Behavioral Science*, 15: 273–85.

Henderson, B. (1982). Strategy implementation. *McKinsey Quarterly*.

Hofer, C., and Schendel, D. (1977). *Strategy Formulation*. St Paul, MN: West Publishing.

Homans, G. (1959). *The Human Group*. Boston, MA: Harvard University Publishing.

Hrebiniak, L. G. (1978). *Complex Organizations*. St Paul: West Publishing.

Hrebiniak, L. G., and Joyce, W. (1984). *Implementing Strategy*. New York: Macmillan.

Hrebiniak, L. G., and Joyce, W. F. (1985). Organizational adaptation: Strategic choice and environmental determinism. *Administrative Science Quarterly*, 30: 336–49.

Ingram, P., and Baum, J. A. (1997). Chain affiliation and the failure of Manhattan hotels, 1896–1980. *Administrative Science Quarterly*, 42: 68–102.

Joyce, W. (2000a). Instrumental contextualism and the limits of rigor in organizational science, *Amos Tuck School Working Paper Series*. Amos Tuck School, Dartmouth College, Hanover, p. 12.

Joyce, W. (2000b), Execution as a cause for organizational performance, *Amos Tuck School Working Paper Series*. Amos Tuck School, Dartmouth College, Hanover, NH.

Joyce, W., McGee, V., and Slocum, J. (1997). Argument, controversy, and evidence in research concerning diversification and firm performance, paper presented at the 15th Annual Meeting of the Strategic Management Society, Mexico City, Mexico.

Joyce. W., McGee, V., and Slocum, J. (2000). Argument, controversy and evidence in research concerning diversification and firm performance, *Amos Tuck School Working Paper Series*. Amos Tuck School, Dartmouth College, Hanover, NH.

Joyce, W., Slocum, J., and von Glinow, M. A. (1982a). Models of fit in person-situation interaction. *Journal of Occupational Behavior*, 12: 45–63.

Joyce, W., Slocum, J., and von Glinow, M. (1982b). Person-situation interaction: competing models of fit. *Journal of Occupational Behavior*, 3: 265–80.

Kaplan, A. (1968). *The Conduct of Inquiry*. New York: Simon and Schuster.

Kerr, S., and Jermier J. (1974). Substitutes for leadership: Their meaning and measurement. *Organizational Behavior and Human Performance*, 12: 62–82.

Lawrence, P. (1981). The Harvard organization and environment research program. In A. H. Van de Ven and William Joyce (eds.), *Perspectives on Organization Design and Behavior*. New York: Wiley-Interscience.

Lawrence, P., and Lorsch, J. (1967). *Organization and Environment*. Boston: Graduate School of Business Administration, Harvard University.

Leventhal, D. A., and March, J. G. (1993). The myopia of learning. *Strategic Management Journal*, Winter Special Issue, 14: 95–112.

Levitt, B., and March, J. G. (1988). Organizational Learning, *Annual Review of Sociology*, 14: 319–40.

Lewin, K. (1936). *Principles of Topological Psychology*. New York: Simon and Schuster.

Lindblom, C. E., and Cohen, D. K. (1979). *Usable Knowledge: Social Science and Social Problem Solving*. New Haven: Yale University Press.

Loraine, P. (1980). *Top Management Planning*. New York: McGraw-Hill.

March, J. G. (1981). Footnotes to organizational change. *Administrative Science Quarterly*, 26: 563–77.

March, J. G., and Simon, H. A. (with the collaboration of Harold Guetzkow) (1958). *Organizations*. New York: Wiley.

Marlin, D., Lamont, B. T., and Hoffman, J. J. (1994). Choice situation, strategy, and performance: A reexamination. *Strategic Management Journal*, 15: 229–39.

McGee, V., and Joyce, W. (2000). How similar are two strings?, *Amos Tuck School Working Paper Series*. Amos Tuck School, Dartmouth College, Hanover, NH.

Michael, D. N. (1973) *On Learning to Plan and Planning to Learn*. San Francisco: Jossey-Bass.

Mintzberg, H. (1985). Of strategies: Deliberate and emergent, *Strategic Management Journal*, 6: 257–72.

Mitzberg, H. (1987). Crafting Strategy. *Harvard Business Review*, 65, July–August.

Murray, H. A. (1938). *Explorations in Personality*. New York: Harper and Collins.

Peteraf, M. A. (1993). The cornerstone of competitive advantage: A resource-based view. *Strategic Management Journal*, 14(3): 179–92.

Peters, T. J., and Waterman, R. H. (1982). *In Search of Excellence*. New York: HarperCollins, 1982.

Porter, M. E. (1980). *Competitive Strategy*. New York: Free Press.

Prahalad, C. K., and Hamel, G. (1990). The core competence of the corporation. *Harvard Business Review*, 11: 183.

Quinn, J. B. (1980). *Strategies for Change: Logical Incrementalism*. New York: Irwin.

Selznick, P. (1949). *TVA and the Grass Roots*. Berkeley, CA: University of California Press.

Simon, H. A. (1946). *Administrative Behavior*. New York: McGraw-Hill.

Simon, H. A. (1993). Strategy and organizational evolution. *Strategic Management Journal*, Winter Special Issue, 14: 131–42.

Stern, R. (1972). *People in Context*. New Haven: Yale University Press.

Thompson, J. (1967). *Organizations in Action*. New York: McGraw-Hill.

Wernerfelt, B. (1984). A resource-based view of the firm. *Strategic Management Journal*, 5(2): 171–80.

# 23

## Human Resources Strategy: The Era of Our Ways

### SCOTT A. SNELL, MARK A. SHADUR AND PATRICK M. WRIGHT

The purpose of this chapter is to discuss some of the main features and trends in human resources (HR) strategy. Inasmuch as people are among the most important resources available to firms, one could argue that HR strategy should be central to any debate about how firms achieve competitive advantage. But this "people are our most important asset" argument is actually fairly hollow in light of the evidence. Far too many articles on HR start with this premise, but the reality is that organizations have historically not rested their fortunes on human resources. The HR function remains among the least influential in most organizations, and competitive strategies have not typically been based on the skills, capabilities, and behaviors of employees. In fact, as Snell, Youndt, and Wright (1996: 62) noted, in the past executives have typically tried to "take human resources out of the strategy equation – i.e., by substituting capital for labor where possible, and by designing hierarchical organizations that separate those who think from those who actually do the work."

So what is different now? Why are people more important today? What is it about HR issues that bring them into a discussion of strategic management? Part of the answer to these questions has to do with shifting priorities and perspectives about competition and firm advantage. As theories of strategic management turn inward toward resource-based and knowledge-based views of the firm, where competitive advantage increasingly resides in a firm's ability to learn, innovate, and change, the human element becomes increasingly important in generating economic value (e.g., Conner and Prahalad, 1996; Itami, 1987). As Quinn (1992: 241) noted, "with rare exceptions, the economic and producing power of the firm lies more in its intellectual and service capabilities than in its hard assets – land, plant and equipment . . . [V]irtually all public and private enterprises – including most successful corporations – are becoming dominantly repositories and coordinators of intellect."

Two things happen when we shift perspectives in this way. First, the distinctions between HR strategy and competitive strategy begin to blur. If the competitive potential of a firm rests in its intellectual and service activities, then what people know and how they behave are the *sine qua non* of strategic management. Neither the formation nor implementation of strategies can be separated from how people are managed.

But a second thing that happens when we shift perspectives this way, and it also increases the importance of HR strategy. When people are no longer viewed simply as "hands and feet" in a production function, but as key sources of strategic capability, our focus on organization and governance necessarily changes as well. A common tenet among economists is that, unlike other assets, organizations cannot own their human capital (Becker, 1964). Employees own it themselves, and this dramatically shifts the balance of power in organizations. Further, organizations cannot easily control the exchanges and relationships among employees with those in the external environment (i.e., the Barnard/Simon notion of partial inclusion). Those who conceptualize organizations as knowledge communities (Kogut and Zander, 1992) understand the difficulty of defining and managing the boundaries of organizations in this case. So in addition to managing the knowledge base of an organization, competitiveness depends on managing the relational bases of members of organizations as well. The cultures, attitudes, values and commitments of employees are perhaps more important to success than ever. And these elements differentiate between successful and unsuccessful firms (cf. O'Reilly and Pfeffer, 2000).

Each of these issues at once increases the importance of HR strategy for firm competitiveness, and makes it infinitely more difficult to manage. A key objective of HR strategy is to guide *the process by which organizations develop and deploy human, social, and organizational capital to enhance their competitiveness*. Although we can articulate this objective here at the front end of the chapter, we hope to clarify its meaning more fully as we go through the ideas and concepts that extend throughout the chapter. As we delve more deeply into these issues, we will summarize several of the key frameworks and research on HR strategy that shape our views. In addition, we hope to provide insights into where the field is likely to go.

To organize our discussion, we break the chapter down into three parts: First, we discuss HR in the context of history by examining the primary competitive challenges faced by firms in the past and show how those influenced our concept of HR. Second, we look at the accepted concepts and models that define HR strategy right now and discuss their connection to the extant literature on strategic management. Finally, we draw inferences from emerging work in the field of strategic management and HRM to identify the dimensions of a paradigm that is beginning to take shape.

## THE ERA OF PERSON–JOB FIT

Snow and Snell (1993) noted that although the concept of HR strategy *per se* is fairly new, its underlying logic and principles date back as far as the industrial revolution in the United States. Over time, the concept has evolved to reflect our changing views of strategic management and the arising challenges within HR. As summarized in table 23.1, each phase of this evolution represents a paradigm for research and practice in that they not only influence the way we conceptualize HR, they also orient our priorities for managing people.

At the height of the industrial revolution, in industries such as railroads, autos, and

TABLE 23.1 Three eras of human resource strategy

| HR strategy era/paradigm | Person–job fit | Systemic fit | Competitive potential |
|---|---|---|---|
| Strategic drivers | ◆ Vertical integration<br>◆ Economies of scale<br>◆ Efficiency/productivity | ◆ Globalization<br>◆ Diversification<br>◆ TQM/re-engineering | ◆ Knowledge-based competition<br>◆ Innovation and change<br>◆ Outsourcing, alliances<br>◆ Network organizations |
| Focus of HR strategy | ◆ Administrative<br>◆ Job-centric<br>◆ Tasks | ◆ Strategy implementation<br>◆ System (e.g., team)<br>◆ Behaviors/roles | ◆ Strategy formation<br>◆ Competencies<br>◆ Knowledge (learning) and culture (values) |
| Prevailing logic | ◆ Analysis (job analysis)<br>◆ Deductive | ◆ Synthesis (integration)<br>◆ Deductive | ◆ Generative<br>◆ Inductive |
| Key design parameters | ◆ Division of labor<br>◆ Work standardization<br>◆ Employment stability<br>◆ Efficiency (input/output)<br>◆ Ease of replacement<br>◆ Minimum investment | ◆ Internal (horizontal) fit<br>◆ External (vertical) fit<br>◆ Bundling<br>◆ High performance work systems<br>◆ Configurations<br>◆ Contingency models | ◆ Strategic value of capital<br>◆ Uniqueness (firm specific)<br>◆ Knowledge creation, transfer and integration<br>◆ Agility (flexibility and fit)<br>◆ Architectures of multiple HR systems |
| Measurement issues | ◆ Efficiency (cost per hire)<br>◆ Validity/utility<br>◆ Turnover, absenteeism<br>◆ Department size | ◆ Synergy among practices<br>◆ Rater agreement/reliability<br>◆ Strategy<br>◆ Firm performance | ◆ Intellectual capital<br>◆ Competencies<br>◆ Balanced scorecard |

steel, corporate strategies were marked by a focus on volume expansion and vertical integration. The overriding organizational challenge for many firms was maximizing efficiency. In that context, labor came to be viewed as one of the most costly and uncontrollable resources (Chandler, 1962). Organizations and work systems were influenced by the administrative principles of Weber, Fayol, and Taylor that emphasized rational, impersonal management authority. In large and complex organizations of the day, the administrative burden associated with hiring, work design, training, compensation, and employment relations, required that personnel management become its own functional specialty.

## The importance of person–job fit

The concept of HR strategy was certainly not explicit at the time, but the *de facto* strategy for managing people focused on *person–job fit*. Traditional employment models were oriented toward employment stability, efficiency, and productivity through division of labor, specialization, and work standardization (Becker, 1976; Capelli, 1995; Hirschhorn, 1984). Care was taken to ensure that jobs were designed so that most people could perform them with a minimum investment of time and/or money and that employees were replaceable should they leave. A preoccupation with analytic methods (as an outgrowth of scientific management) pervaded nearly all HR-related activities. Job analysis in particular – that is, the breakdown of tasks, duties and responsibilities as well as the accompanying skills, knowledge, and abilities required to perform them – became the foundation for virtually all HR decision-making. Selection testing, time-motion studies, job evaluation and the like were each based on job analysis and they collectively defined an implicit HR strategy of matching individuals to the requirements of jobs.

There are two things notable about this period. First, there is ample evidence indicating that the systematic analysis of jobs, individuals, and performance added logic and precision to what previously had been a fairly informal (if not haphazard) approach to personnel decision-making. Measurement systems were developed to assess the administrative efficiency of the HR function as well as its effectiveness in meeting business goals (e.g., costs per new hire, validity of selection systems, absenteeism, turnover). The rigor and precision evidenced in this approach has been the standard for excellence in HR for many decades. But even more noteworthy in the context of strategy is the consistency among all facets of HR as well as their complementarity to the needs of the business. We will discuss the importance of these two issues in the next section. For now it is important to note that HR activities built around the idea of person–job fit enabled organizations to establish a level of efficiency and stability necessary to meet the competitive requirements of organizations of that time.

## The beginnings of a paradigm shift

During this era there were several innovations in management thought and practice – with clear implications for organizational performance – that began to precipitate a paradigm shift in HRM. The human relations and sociotechnical schools, for example, emphasized the "human factors" underlying productivity issues (Roethlisberger and Dickson, 1939; Herzberg, 1957; McGregor, 1960; Trist, 1963). Analysts provided evidence to support the argument that enhancing work conditions could lead to improvements in work outputs. Jobs could be redesigned and enriched, and managers were urged to eschew autocratic leadership styles. These more humanistic approaches to HR policy and practice stood in contrast to the principles and assumptions of the scientific management. The sociotechnical systems approach in particular emphasized the importance of integrating human systems and work systems. This was a marked departure from a purely analytical model of HR strategy.

Even so, HR strategy remained essentially unchanged in light of these newer management models. The focus on person–job fit remained paramount – albeit modified in light of the research – for much of the 20th century. Nevertheless, the tension between philosophies during the 1960s and 1970s made it increasingly apparent that the old model was not a panacea for managers.

## The Era of Systemic Fit

During the 1980s, a new logic pervaded organizations, and its effect was seen in the broader agenda of HRM. As challenges associated with global competition, diversification, total quality management, and the like took center stage, observers such as Mason and Mitroff (1981: 15) noted that we needed to deal with organizational problems "in a holistic or synthetic way as well as in an analytic way." So in addition to subdividing HR into its analytic elements, researchers began to look at how the pieces fit together to establish a more comprehensive and integrated system for managing people. It was at this time that the concept of HR strategy appeared in the literature (Walker, 1980; Tichy, Fombrun, and DeVanna, 1982; Miles and Snow, 1984). Writers such as Wright and McMahan (1992: 298) described HR strategy as "the *pattern* of planned HR deployments and activities" in order to capture the ideas of continuity over time as well as consistency across various decisions and actions. Baird and Meshoulam (1988) wrote an influential piece on the principles and parameters that governed HR strategy and noted that two issues – internal and external fit – were paramount for research and practice. The concept of internal fit refers to how the components of HR support and complement each other inside the organization. For example, if the objective is to select high quality candidates, then HR practices regarding development, compensation, and appraisal need to support the retention of these key staff. External fit focuses on how the HR strategies and practices are congruent with the developmental stage and the strategic direction of the firm. In start up firms, HR practices focus on pay, staffing and record keeping with the founder making many decisions. But as the firm grows in complexity, then managers are less able to carry out the expanding HR roles and a personnel or HR department is formed to assist with hiring, training and compensating employees (Baird and Meshoulam, 1988).

### The importance of internal fit

The concept of internal fit (also referred to as *horizontal fit*) in HR strategy captured the importance of coherence among sets of practices in order to be mutually reinforcing. At times HR practices such as selection and training can be complementary, compensatory, or mutually reinforcing. At other times, HR practices can be "deadly combinations" that work against one another and send inconsistent or conflicting messages (Boxall and Purcell, 2000). Managing the system in this case, rather than the individual practices may be a key element of HR strategy. Beer et al. (1984) were among the first to propose a systems-based approach to HR strategy that exemplified the notion of internal fit. Arthur (1994), MacDuffie (1995), and others reinforced this idea by showing how "bundles" of HR practices tended to occur together in organizations and that the overall logic linking those practices was perhaps more important for understanding HR strategy than the practices themselves.

These studies all reflected a trend toward synergistic views of HR and drew a close parallel with the configurational approaches to organization strategy (Doty and Glick, 1994; Lado and Wilson, 1994). In order to identify and conceptualize HR strategies as meaningful ideal types, researchers developed – and borrowed – terminology such as behavior and output control (Snell, 1992), commitment-based HR (Arthur, 1994; MacDuffie, 1995), high performance work systems (Huselid, 1995), human capital enhancing systems (Youndt et al., 1996), and the transformed workplace (Kochan, Katz, and McKersie, 1986) to describe the overall pattern of employment practices. The important point is that rather than looking at the mechanics of individual HR practices in isolation, these frameworks reoriented our view toward the overarching employment relationships that organizations established with employees (cf. Baron and Kreps, 1999; Delery and Doty, 1996; Dyer and Holder, 1988; Osterman, 1987; Schuler and Jackson, 1987).

## The importance of external fit

In concert with the notion of internal fit, the idea of *external fit* (also referred to as *vertical fit*) captured the alignment of HR practices with the needs of the business. By acknowledging the various postures that firms establish *vis-à-vis* their environments, researchers began addressing the possibility of contingency perspectives in HR strategy. Much of the research on HR strategies during this period focused on matching HR practices with various generic business strategies (e.g., Delery and Doty, 1996; Jackson, Schuler, and Rivero, 1989; Olian and Rynes, 1984; Wright and Snell, 1991). Miles and Snow (1984), in particular, are notable in that they were among the first to develop a typology of competitive strategies and then extended this model to include HR strategies that were appropriate under each condition.

It is interesting to note that while a few studies have supported a contingency perspective (cf. Delery and Doty, 1996; Gomez-Mejia, 1992; Wright, Smart, and McMahan, 1995; Youndt et al., 1996) there is still compelling evidence that a universal approach (particularly one based on creating high-commitment work systems) is equally if not more strongly related to firm performance (cf. Huselid, 1995; MacDuffie, 1995). So while the idea of internal fit has become well established in the HR strategy literature, the debate about "best fit" versus "best practice" is ongoing (Boxall and Purcell, 2000).

Part of the controversy surrounding the issues of fit and strategic contingencies centers on debates about measurement (e.g., Boudreau and Ramstad, 1997; Ulrich, 1997). For instance, it is yet unclear whether firms should operationalize internal fit using additive scaling or attempt to capture its synergistic effects via multiplicative interactions (Huselid,

Jackson, and Schuler, 1997; Delery and Doty, 1996). Extending beyond this, there are also concerns regarding the appropriate measurement of business strategy and firm performance (Rogers and Wright, 1998). Although these issues pertain more to debates among researchers, they also have implications for managers who accept the underlying logic of strategic fit and need to develop metrics to assure its implementation. As researchers have expanded their views of HR strategy, they have also wrestled with the appropriate ways to operationalize the broader set of constructs (Guest, 1999).

Overall, this era of HR strategy helped us develop a much broader understanding of how administrative systems underlie strategy implementation, and in the process trans-formed the way we looked at the design of HR systems. Instead of focusing only on the technical characteristics of a particular HR practice, we began to look at how sets of practices worked in concert to elicit, reinforce, and support patterns of behavior that benefit the firm. As researchers expanded their view of HR strategy, they also developed a more integrative perspective of how policies and practices can and do work together to support the firm's strategic intentions. In the process, HR took its place alongside other organizational systems such as structure, culture and technology.

The proliferation of frameworks during this era to link HR systems and generic business strategies reflected the field's focus on concepts and logic, perhaps at the expense of empirical progress. But these efforts were important in several respects. Not only did they provide a platform for discussion and debate about ideas such as contingency, synergy, and best practice in HR, they became the means by which we could understand and communicate the logic of business strategy that was, until that time, largely foreign to many of us. While typologies such as Miles and Snow's (1978) or Porter's (1980) have their critics, their prominence during the 1980s epitomized the field's interest in logical connections among resources, and alignment of firms with the broader environment.

Considering the dramatic transitions in HR occurring during this era, terminology was destined to change as well. The word "personnel" evolved into "human resources," not only reflecting a reorientation away from viewing people as costs to viewing them as assets, but also indicating that both executives and academics had redefined the field to be something substantively different from what it had been. Guest (1987) argued that to be a meaningful transition from traditional personnel management, HRM needed to embrace policies to facilitate integration, commitment and flexibility. Writers such as Yeung, Brockbank, and Ulrich (1994) described how the roles and responsibilities of the HR function were changing and the competencies needed to execute those new roles. In addition to the technical and functional competencies that had been a mainstay in HR, staff specialists were being asked to step into the roles of business partners and change agents (Dyer, 1983; Barney and Wright, 1998). Likewise, line managers were assuming more responsibility for HR-related matters and working in close coordination with the HR staffs.

## The beginnings of a paradigm shift

As with the era of person–job fit, there were notable exceptions to the HR strategy paradigm based on systemic fit that began to loosen its foundation. For instance, much of the research during this period cast HR in the role of strategy implementation rather than strategy formation. As one of the last vestiges of the hierarchical model of organizations, strategy (at the top) was taken as given, and HR was seen as adapting itself to the resulting needs and requirements. While researchers such as Dyer (1983) and Buller (1988) found occasional instances where business planning and HR planning had reciprocal relationships, most often there was a one-way linkage from business strategy to HR. As Lengnick-Hall and Lengnick-Hall (1988) noted, "Rarely are human resources seen as a strategic capacity from which competitive choices should be derived." This severely limits the potential contribution of HR to firm competitiveness. In this context, HR is seen as an enabling factor at best, and a limiting factor at worst.

But by the end of the 1900s, it was clear that much is changing today. As traditional bases of competitive advantage, such as protected markets, access to capital, and the like are eroding, and as resources are more accessible to a wider range of firms, there are fewer unique ways to succeed except through people (Pfeffer, 1994; Pucik, 1988; Schuler and MacMillan, 1984). In high velocity environments that characterize business today, HR is now being viewed more as a catalyst for strategic capability. That is, HR is viewed as propelling strategy rather than the other way around.

## THE ERA OF COMPETITIVE POTENTIAL

Just as the strategic priorities of the 1980s changed the way we looked at HR back then, competitive challenges in today's organizations are reorienting HR strategy again. The new competitive equation places a premium on knowledge-based assets and the processes that underlie learning and innovation (cf. Leonard-Barton, 1992). In some ways, this evolving paradigm stands in contrast to the previous model(s) of HR strategy. Rather than viewing HR as a result of strategic planning, strategic planning is now increasingly built on the capabilities and potential available through a firm's human resources.

Employee skills, knowledge, and abilities are among the most distinctive and renewable resources upon which a company can draw. As the pace of change places a premium on innovation and learning, strategy formation increasingly resides in "people-embodied know-how." Because people can learn and adapt, they potentially are a self-renewing resource (Davenport and Prusak, 1998; Nonaka and Takeuchi, 1995). Further, in combination with broader organizational systems and technologies, people form the basis of a firm's core competencies (Prahalad and Hamel, 1990).

From this standpoint, HR strategy is seen as cultivating the competencies, cultures, and composition of workers that underlie a firm's competitive potential. There are three elements to the current paradigm shift in HR strategy: (1) knowledge-based perspectives complement behavioral perspectives of HR; (2) the concept of agility is used to reconcile simultaneous needs for flexibility and strategic fit; and (3) architectural models provide a more elaborate view of employment and HR. Each of these is discussed below.

### Incorporating knowledge-based perspectives

Several trends in strategic management – such as a shift toward resource-based and knowledge-based views of the firm, a focus on intangible assets, intellectual capital, knowledge management, and the like – have placed HR-related issues at center stage in organizations (cf., Barney, 1991; Davenport and Prusak, 1998; Kogut and Zander, 1992;

Nonaka and Takeuchi, 1995). And these theories have fundamentally altered the way we look at HR strategy.

In the past, our perspective has been focused on the requisite behaviors required to implement a given strategy. Porter's (1980) generic strategies, for example, had implications for HR strategy so that firms with low-cost strategies were seen as needing efficient behaviors, which implied an HR focus on routinized job design, incentives based on output targets, and relatively low levels of training. Differentiation strategies emphasized creativity and innovation, which suggested HR policies to attract and retain highly skilled employees, high employee participation, and extensive training (Schuler and Jackson, 1987). But these earlier strategic models did not explicitly incorporate an HR dimension within them. There were implications for HRM but human resources were not seen as a central contributor to strategy implementation. A break with this approach came from strategy analysts such as Prahalad and Hamel (1990) who argued that core competencies are derived from the collective learning with the corporation and that a central focus of top management must be to provide a strategic architecture to enhance competence building. Human resources were thus positioned as a pivotal component of competitive advantage. One interesting consequence of incorporating knowledge-based perspectives into strategic management, and the consequent elevation of HR strategy, was that the earlier exaggerated separation of strategy formulation and implementation was reduced. When knowledge assets are seen as a key success factor, then strategy making more closely draws upon internal competencies and capabilities for executing strategy (Hamel and Prahalad, 1994).

In retrospect, the omission of HR is to an extent understandable. Because HR has its roots in psychology and other social sciences, its focus has been on individual and/or group behavior. Given this heritage, it is not surprising that in the past we have made inferences about the kinds of behaviors needed from employees to execute a given strategy. However, researchers such as Barney (1991), Ulrich (1991), Snell and Dean (1992) and others have argued that competitive advantage rests in something that is more durable and fundamental than behaviors alone. Wright and Snell (1991) noted that while HR strategies were important for controlling and coordinating behavior, they also played a pivotal role in developing and coordinating competencies. Researchers began to blend a behavioral perspective of HR strategy with one based on resource-based views and, later, knowledge-based views of the firm.

Snell, Youndt, and Wright (1996) borrowed from Barney (1991) to discuss how employee skills and knowledge – that is, their *human capital* – can be valuable, rare, inimitable, and non-substitutable. The concept of human capital is powerful in that it blends traditional aspects of personnel management (e.g., employee skills, knowledge, abilities) with economic principles of capital accumulation, investment, deployment and value creation that underlie much of strategic management (cf. Dierickx and Cool, 1989).

Related to this, researchers in the areas of knowledge management and organizational learning also recognize that people are often the key to sustainable competitive advantage (Davenport and Prusak, 1998; Nonaka and Takeuchi, 1995). Because the process of creating, sharing, and integrating knowledge tends to be tacit, path dependent, and socially complex, it tends to be difficult to imitate and non-transferable to different contexts (cf., Dierickx and Cool, 1989; Peteraf, 1993). These relational elements of learning and competitive advantage extend beyond human capital and highlight the importance of *social capital* (Coleman, 1988; Edvinsson and Malone, 1997). While human capital represents the economic value of individual knowledge, social capital represents the value of "resources embedded within, available through, and derived from the network of relationships" (Nahapit and Ghoshal, 1998: 243).

In the context of social capital and learning, HR strategy transcends the development of knowledge, skills, and behaviors alone to also incorporate the development of relationships and exchanges inside and outside the organization. The boundaries between organizations were becoming increasingly blurred and Harrison and St. John (1996) explained that non-traditional management techniques that were being used within the firm could also be applied to relationships outside the firm. Instead of seeking relationships based on control and monitoring, more emphasis is placed on cooperation with stakeholders inside and outside the firm. When we consider that these relationships are based on norms of trust and reciprocity, we expand the purview of HR strategy further to include the values and principles that guide relational action. Leanna and VanBuren (1999), for example, laid out a model of social capital that explains how HR practices can elevate the levels of trust and associability (willingness and ability to interact) to encourage widespread cooperation and sharing of knowledge.

It may also be that emerging concepts of moral and/or ethical capital are likely to take their place within the domain of HR strategy as well. As O'Reilly and Pfeffer (2000) put it, when engaged with a common purpose and values, people energize organizations to create "hidden value" that is perhaps most difficult to imitate or duplicate in other firms. They represent a source of cultural vitality in organizations that mobilizes extraordinary performance.

Finally, in addition to knowledge contained in individuals and social networks, much of what an organization knows is contained in its systems and processes. As Daft and Weick (1984: 284) noted, "individuals come and go, but organizations preserve knowledge over time." Becker et al. (1997) followed Wright and McMahan (1992) in noting that HR practices, processes and systems institutionalize a firm's know-how about managing people and can therefore represent an important economic asset. Competitors can often acquire hardware and software similar to that of leading firms, but it is much more difficult to replicate the underlying capability and collective knowledge embedded in organizational practices, routines, and systems (Day, 1997, Oliveira, 1999). As a form of *organizational capital* the overall configuration of these systems – when intertwined in idiosyncratic ways – can be nearly impossible to imitate or duplicate in other firms.

The combination of human, social, and organizational capital represents the foundation of core competencies and the outcome of processes that facilitate knowledge management. Although a good deal of research needs to be done, it is clear that our orientation to HR strategy is moving away from a strictly behavioral focus to one that incorporates ideas about managing intellectual capital.

Part of the challenge in making this transition to a knowledge-based paradigm is the development of metrics that capture essential ideas and principles of intellectual capital. Since the mid 1990s, there has been increasing recognition that traditional measures of firm assets and performance (based substantially on financial indicators) are incomplete. To address this, Sveiby (1997) developed an "intangible assets monitor" that captured various aspects of intellectual capital including employee competence (e.g., efficiency, growth, and the value-adding role of professionals), internal structure (e.g., intellectual property rights, internal organization, support staff), and external structure (e.g., relationships with customers and suppliers). Similarly, in the broader area of strategic management, Kaplan and Norton's (1996) "balanced scorecard" tied four sets of metrics (financial, customer, internal business processes and learning) to broader assessments of market value and organizational effectiveness. Initiatives such as these are instrumental in establishing concrete methods for assessing intangible elements of firm competitiveness.

## Reconciling fit and flexibility

A second major thrust in HR strategy today relates to reconciling the notions of fit and flexibility (Milliman, von Glinow, and Nathan, 1991). Lengnick-Hall and Lengnick-Hall (1988), for example, pointed out that where adaptation and flexibility are paramount, tight fit between HR and strategy might be ill advised. "Fit can be counterproductive from a competitive perspective because it may inhibit innovativeness and constrain the firm's repertoire of skills" (1988: 457). Schneider (1987) raised a similar concern in his framework of organizational attraction-selection-attrition (ASA) cycles. If organizations attract and retain an increasingly homogeneous group of members, particularly with regard to their values and personalities, it can result in organizations that have unique structures, processes, and cultures. In the near term, this can be quite beneficial with a view toward strategic fit and inimitability. However, over time homogeneity may constrain the variety of interests and perspectives needed to generate new ideas. A tightly fitted ASA cycle may thereby work against the forces of change.

HR systems themselves (not the people, but the practices) may inhibit flexibility as well. Snell and Dean (1994) noted that, once in place, administrative systems such as HR practices tend to be notoriously intractable. Because they are held in place by numerous forces, such as written records, organizational traditions, corporate regulations, and employee expectations, they represent one of the major forces of organizational inertia that prevent change.

To address these issues, Wright and Snell (1998) developed a framework that balances the needs of fit and flexibility. Rather than viewing fit and flexibility as opposite ends of a continuum, these authors saw the two as complementary dimensions (cf. Milliman, von Glinow, and Nathan, 1991). Fit is conceptualized as a static element seen at a point in time, whereas flexibility is viewed as the capacity for change and adaptation over time. This distinction raises the possibility that HR systems as well as work force characteristics can be both flexible and fitted to the needs of the organization. Building on work by Sanchez (1995), Wright and Snell focused on two key elements: resource flexibility and coordination flexibility. *Resource flexibility* refers to the extent to which a resource can be applied to a larger range of alternative uses. For example, some HR practices are more flexible than others (e.g., management by objectives versus behaviorally-based appraisals) and can be used in multiple contexts. Likewise, some employees have more flexible skills sets (e.g., broader skill sets versus specialists) and behavioral repertoires (e.g., contextually altered versus tightly scripted routines) than others and can adapt more readily to new situations. *Coordination flexibility* extends these ideas by characterizing a firm's ability to reconfigure, reallocate, and redeploy the chain of resources. Similar terms such as organizational capability and strategic capability have been used in the literature to describe a firm's potential to simultaneously conceive and implement a wide range of strategies with minimal response time (cf. Lenz, 1980; Prahalad, 1983).

Dyer and Shafer (1999) provide perhaps the most comprehensive treatment of these ideas about flexibility in the context of HR strategy. Building on extant literatures in innovation and change, they view organizational adaptation not as a one-time or even periodic event, but as a continuous process termed *organizational agility* (cf. Brown and Eisenhardt, 1997). This is a subtle but important distinction and alters our viewpoint from a "change in strategy" to a "strategy of change." In agile organizations, the role of HR strategy is multifaceted. On the one hand, it is designed to forge a stable core of shared values, vision, and common performance metrics. But around this core, HR strategy plays an instrumental role in developing competencies and behaviors of an agile workforce that embraces change and learning. Supporting this, HR strategy also comprises an infrastructure that can be reconfigured rapidly to enable change and adaptation (e.g., through fluid assignments, empowerment).

The net result of these initiatives is an HR strategy that supports stability as well as change. To paraphrase Brown and Eisenhardt (1997), HR strategies in agile organizations combine limited structure (e.g., priorities, responsibilities) with extensive interaction and freedom to improvise. This combination is neither so rigid as to control the process nor so chaotic that the process falls apart. Successful managers explore the future by experimenting with a wide variety of low cost probes. They neither rely on a single plan for the future nor are they completely reactive. Through rhythmic transition processes from present to future ones, they create a relentless pace of change.

### Elaborating on the HR architecture

The third major thrust in HR strategy today is a focus on more complete architectures used to manage people. Recently, Lepak and Snell (1999) argued that in our previous efforts to view HR strategy more broadly, we perhaps cast it too simplistically. HR strategy researchers have tended to aggregate – both conceptually and empirically – all employees into one comprehensive "workforce" that is studied as though it were managed with a single (or at least dominant) HR configuration. While aggregation such as this adds parsimony, and helps us highlight organization-level phenomena, it is an analytical compromise that treats variation *within* firms as noise. Interestingly, earlier work in organizational theory on differentiation alerted us to notable differences between, for example, production, sales and research departments with respect to organizational structure and interpersonal relationships (Lawrence and Lorsch, 1967). But, with some notable exceptions (e.g. Baron, Davis-Blake, and Bielby, 1986; Osterman, 1987), a disaggregated analysis of the workforce did not occupy center stage in HR research.

An architectural perspective of HR begins with the assumption that different employees contribute in different ways to organizations. As a consequence, they are likely to be managed in different ways as well. As noted by Mangum, Mayall, and Nelson (1985: 599):

> Many employers carefully select a core group of employees, invest in them, and take elaborate measures to reduce their turnover and maintain their attachment to the firm. Many of these same employers, however, also maintain a peripheral group of employees from whom they prefer to remain relatively detached, even at the cost of high turnover, and to whom they make few commitments.

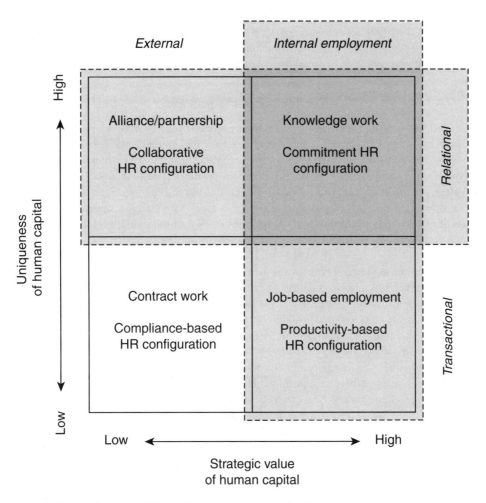

FIGURE 23.1 Human capital, employment modes, relationships, and HR configurations
*Source*: Adapted from Lepak and Snell (1999)

Lepak and Snell's architectural framework begins with a focus on the strategic value and uniqueness (firm-specificity) of human capital. As shown in figure 23.1, by juxtaposing these two dimensions, the model lays out four different cells in a matrix. Corresponding to these human capital differences, each cell differs in terms of the employment modes, psychological contracts, and HR configurations used to manage employees. The four configurations can be referred to as commitment-based, job-based, compliance-based, and collaborative (see figure 23.1).

This architectural perspective integrates a number of research streams to inform HR strategy. Baron, Davis-Blake, and Bielby (1986), for example, found that multiple internal labor markets (ILMs) exist within firms in response to differences in firm-specific skills, occupational differentiation, technology, and the like. Similarly, Osterman (1987) argued that industrial, salaried, craft, and secondary employment subsystems tend to co-exist within firms. More recently, researchers such as Matusik and Hill (1998), Rousseau (1995), and Tsui et al. (1995) have articulated a variety of employment relationships that simultaneously exist within firms ranging from long-term relationships with core employees to short-term exchanges with external guest workers and other forms of contract labor.

## The beginnings of a paradigm

It is a bit too soon to determine exactly how we might portray this era of HR strategy. What seems to be emerging is a more complex view that parallels the evolving nature of strategic management. As firms reorient themselves toward the development and deployment of core competencies while simultaneously entering into alliances with outside partners, the infrastructure of organizations and human resource management is at once more differentiated and purposefully integrated. Figure 23.2 shows three main dimensions of HR strategy in this context: (a) the composition of the workforce, (b) the cultures of the workforce, as well as (c) the competencies of the workforce.

*Composition of the workforce.*   One of the primary dimensions of HR strategy has always been workforce composition. Getting the right number and kinds of people in the right places at the right times doing things that benefit both them as individuals and the firm as a whole is an arduous and multifaceted process. Blending the facets of traditional manpower planning with strategic analysis is more difficult in today's environments of change and workforce fragmentation. The process hinges on an understanding of how various cohorts of individuals contribute to the firm.

At the core of workforce composition, HR strategy focuses on the development of a cadre of knowledge workers that are central to a firm's advantage. These "gold collar workers" (Huey, 1998) have substantial autonomy to pursue initiatives upon which the firm is likely to build its future strategies. At the same time, HR strategy is oriented toward preserving existing relationships with employees in more traditional work arrangements as well as making more use of a contingent workforce that includes part-timers, temporary workers, contractors and long-term partners.

In this context, the architectural perspective of HR strategy focuses on managing the complexities of employment in a network organization. Each cohort of workers is likely to vary in several ways: the types of human capital they bring, the expectations placed upon them by the firm, the investments made in their development, and the like. Each of these differences translates into a different configuration of HR practices.

But HR strategy necessarily moves beyond merely management of these pieces to the management of the whole. HR strategy must incorporate decisions about the balance and mix of different types of human capital within this matrix as well. Today, decisions about what work should be kept internally, what should be outsourced, with whom to partner, the nature, scope, and duration of those partnerships are as central to HR strategy as they are to business strategy in general. Because some of the most important work may be done externally, the myriad combinations create real questions about the boundaries of the firm and the nature of exchange (Matusik and Hill, 1999). Too often, decisions about internalization and externalization rest solely on cost considerations, but a more strategic view combines HR-related concerns with strategic concerns of competency development and exploitation.

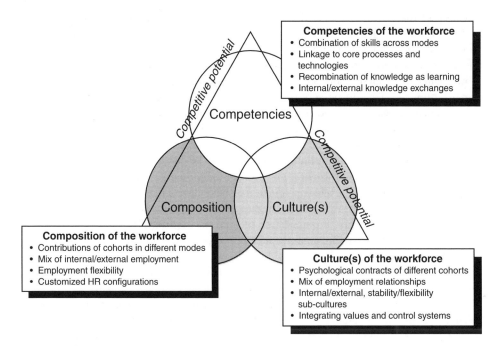

FIGURE 23.2 Dimensions of HR strategy in the era of competitive potential

Future research might focus more on decisions regarding the type of work that should be kept internal to a firm, what work should be externalized, and how the integration of those activities might be best achieved. Do firms do better when they hold all their assets internally, or is there an optimal mix of internal and external arrangements? If so, why do some firms bring a particular form of expertise into the organization, while others leave it outside? Is flexibility (through externalized employment) achieved at the expense of efficiency and competency development? Each of these research issues becomes important in an environment that explicitly views employment composition as an issue of portfolio management.

*Culture(s) of the workforce.* Hand in hand with issues of workforce composition, an architectural view of HR strategy also incorporates issues of culture and control. We have known (and sometimes ignored the fact) that individuals in different cohorts have different allegiances to firms, different values, and different attachments to their work (cf. Lawrence and Lorsch, 1967). Subcultures are embedded in the psychological contracts established with different cohorts and manifested in their various control systems and HR practices (Osterman, 1987).

For example, the work of individuals with unique and specialized human capital is likely to be difficult to specify or monitor (Conner and Prahalad, 1996). As a consequence control systems are likely to give discretion to these individuals and emphasize achievement of results (Kerr, 1985; Snell, 1992). Their employment relationships are likely to reflect a more relational connection that more fully includes them in the strategic direction of the firm (Rousseau, 1995; Tsui et al., 1995). This stands in contrast to the work of traditional job-based employees whose work tends to reflect the principles of behavior control and transactional employment. The HR practices and systems establish and reinforce different employment relationships with each group.

Emerging from these contrasting employment relationships, Rose (1988) noted that organizations are likely to be comprised of various subcultures. In contrast to the view that organization can or should be characterized by one culture, it seems that combinations may be necessary from a competitive standpoint. As Schein (1990) pointed out, culture is developed as an organization learns to cope with the dual problems of external adaptation and internal integration. Dennison and Mishra (1995) found that cultures overly oriented toward consistency and commitment tended to focus too much on internal adjustment to the exclusion of external flexibility. They pointed out the advantages of cultures that could mix internal and external perspectives with those that balance flexibility as well as stability. From an architectural perspective, HR strategy focuses our attention toward the creation, maintenance, coordination – and then integration – of these different subcultures.

The process of integrating or aggregating subcultures into a collective is an extraordinarily complicated endeavor of course. And we will not try to address the entire issue here. But in addition to creating a core set of values that unites a workforce and guides collective action, an architectural view of HR strategy would also draw our attention to the relational interactions among various subcultures in a firm. No longer is this simply a white collar/blue collar distinction; relational exchanges among different cohorts preserve the complexity and richness of perspectives within organizations while achieving a common strategic posture.

When we consider knowledge workers from a cultural perspective then several research issues emerge. Can different subcultures be detected among different cohorts, such as core knowledge workers and those in more traditional job-based employment? What dimensions should be used for assessing differences that might exist between knowledge workers and other subcultures? What are the HR implications for managing knowledge workers if subcultural differences exist? Do knowledge workers have greater affinity with other knowledge workers outside their organization than with other subcultures within their firm?

*Competencies of the workforce.*    As we combine issues of composition and culture, we begin to get a better perspective of the fabric underlying a firm's competencies. An architectural view of HR strategy addresses the integration and combination of talents, from different cohorts who have different attachments to the firm and different attachments with each other. Particularly in the context of core competencies, if we recognize that competitive potential does not reside in any one set of individuals, then strategy development requires explicit attention to the aggregation of skills across modes to create differentiated value. For example, if we identify the key business processes and technologies that establish the infrastructure of a core competency, then we can identify the individuals and teams who "plug into" those processes, thereby mapping the talent base of a firm's competency. In this context, a firm's core competency could be comprised not just from the skills of knowledge workers, but from some traditional employees, as well as some contract workers and strategic partners. It is their combination that is most essential for planning.

Too often HR researchers are quick to advocate placing all employees into the "knowledge worker" category (high value, high uniqueness) with one set of "best practice" tools for managing commitment and performance. However, this approach would be prohibitive from an investment standpoint, unproductive from an efficiency standpoint, and unlikely from an employment standpoint (many workers would not choose this option). Instead an architectural view of HR strategy focuses on establishing relationships across different cohorts to engender knowledge exchange, combination, and reconfiguration. Efforts to do so bring together HRM and strategic management as never before.

Initial efforts to map individuals to a given competency, identify their contributions, and articulate the nature of their exchanges with others are important first steps. However, it is important to note that as competencies develop, decay, and transform, the contribution of different individuals is likely to vary over time. Just as individuals adapt as they learn, the *combination* of individuals that contribute to a competency is likely to transform over time. This transformation reflects (or defines) organizational learning. The result is a renewed and/or transformed competency. Our earlier discussion of resource flexibility and allocation flexibility takes on a new importance in this context (Wright and Snell, 1999). As organizations establish new relationships both internally and externally – and combine the knowledge sets of contributing parties – they increase their chances of being able to develop a more flexible workforce with dynamic capabilities. The flexibility is derived not just from the combinations that can be reassembled and recombined over time, but through the rapid learning that occurs through knowledge exchange (Brown and Eisenhardt, 1997; Cohen and Leventhal, 1990; Matusik and Hill, 1999; Teece, Pisano, and Shuen, 1997).

HR researchers can therefore address important questions to illuminate how firms use competencies more effectively. For example, how do we adequately distinguish which skill groups contribute to a firm's core competencies? How do those individuals combine their talents in a way that is both value creating and inimitable? How can we best leverage those competencies throughout the organization – in effect transferring and integrating the knowledge to other workers? How do we ensure that knowledge outside the firm is acquired and assimilated, transferred and transformed, in order to create competitive potential that is renewable over time? If we can begin to answer some of these questions, HR researchers will contribute substantially to the development of theory and practice in strategic management.

## DISCUSSION

One of the chief purposes in writing this chapter was to summarize the key trends in HR strategy that have defined the field. We identified three eras in research and practice that were defined by particular sets of assumptions and perspectives about managing people for competitive advantage. Each of these eras of HR strategy had their parallels in strategic management.

During the era of person–job fit, HR activities were focused on establishing the levels of efficiency and employment stability required in firms pursuing strategies of expansion and vertical integration. During the era of systemic fit, HR strategies focused on the internal consistency among HR bundles and then linked them vertically with the requirements of strategy. Instead of focusing on the individual practices in isolation, this HR strategy paradigm placed a premium on developing synergies inherent in the overall system. Today's emerging HR paradigm reflects an era of strategic management that emphasizes knowledge-based competition. HR systems are being designed to develop and reinforce ideas of intellectual capital and knowledge management that propel strategy formation. Just as firms are establishing networks of alliances and partners to complement their core competencies, the architectural view of HR strategy addresses the combinations of employment modes and relationships that support knowledge management and organizational agility.

Beyond describing these elements of each HR strategy paradigm, another important purpose for this chapter was to show how the fields of HR and strategic management are converging. This trend can perhaps best be seen by reflecting on the origins of each field, their evolution over time, and the challenges that set their agendas today. Early strategy thinkers were strongly influenced by I/O economics (e.g., Porter, 1980). Since then, however, conceptualizations have generally refocused on internal aspects of the firm especially within a resource-based view of the firm (Wernerfelt, 1984; Teece, Pisano, and Shuen, 1997). This evolution has put people issues at the forefront of strategic management models, specifically focusing on managing intellectual capital as a valuable and rare firm resource as well as understanding how firms can develop dynamic capabilities.

On the other hand, early strategic HRM models were based in psychology (e.g., Schuler and MacMillan, 1984) but have consistently moved toward more macro approaches that integrate organization theory and economics into our understanding of HR strategy (Wright and McMahan, 1992). Most recently, emphases on exploring HR strategy as a means of managing the intellectual capital of a firm (Lepak and Snell, 1999) and managing the fit/flexibility dilemma have emerged as central issues in this literature.

As these two fields merge, we believe there are several ways that researchers can establish mutual gains. For example, strategy's emphasis on organization-wide (macro) issues provides context and perspective for HR researchers while HR's orientation toward more specific (micro) details adds precision to strategic analysis and practice. Related to this, theories of organization, competition, cooperation, and the like are important to HR researchers, particularly in light of criticisms that HR has traditionally been "theory-free." On the other hand, HR's focus on actual practices helps translate strategy theory into more firmly rooted tools and techniques that managers actually use. Prahalad and Hamel (1990), for example, noted that the ideas and concepts surrounding core competency development leaves off where HRM begins. Identifying exactly "how" firms develop and manage core competencies requires more elaboration of the staffing, training, compensation and performance management systems used in firms.

It is likely that research will continue to explore and specify in more detail the actual relationships between strategy and human resources and determine if the trend toward convergence and complementarity will persist. One area that is still clouded is the question of causality in the relationship between strategy formulation and implementation. Earlier research presupposed that strategy was formed largely on the basis of external analysis and internal management focused on implementation. However, an intellectual capital and resource-based view of the firm blurred this distinction. The internal capabilities were seen to give rise to strategic options and provide valuable and difficult to imitate advantages. So the focus for many researchers has shifted to inside the firm (Barney, 1995). But it seems likely that a complex inter-relation of external and internal factors is at work here and research is needed to explore how these factors interact. Further analysis of the interaction of internal and external factors will also help to inform us on how firms can successfully manage in turbulent environments. Complexity theorists (e.g., Brown and Eisenhardt, 1998) have begun this analysis and have assisted in identifying how firms cope with continuous change using strategic flexibility, co-adaptation, and experimentation. The pace and extent of change in the environment accentuates the focus on internal dynamic capabilities. HR research will need to focus on how firms create, transfer and integrate knowledge in order to cope with rapid change.

## CONCLUSION

In conclusion, we see a continuing convergence between the business strategy and HR strategy literatures that we believe will benefit both fields. This convergence should result in a deeper and broader understanding of how firms can effectively manage all of their resources to gain competitive advantage.

## REFERENCES

Arthur, J. B. (1994). Effects of human resource systems on manufacturing performance and turnover. *Academy of Management Journal*, 37(3): 670–87.

Baird, L., and Meshoulam, I. (1988). Managing two fits of strategic human resource management. *Academy of Management Review*, 13(1): 116–28.

Barney, J. (1991). Firm resources and sustained competitive advantage. *Journal of Management*, 17(1): 99–120.

Barney, J. B. (1995). Looking inside for competitive advantage. *Academy of Management Executive*, 9 (4): 49–61.

Barney, J. B., and Wright, P. M. (1998). On becoming a strategic partner: The role of human resources in gaining competitive advantage. *Human Resource Management*, 37(1): 31–46.

Baron, J. N., Davis-Blake, A., and Bielby, W. T. (1986). The structure of opportunity: How promotion ladders vary within and among organizations. *Administrative Science Quarterly*, 31: 248–73.

Baron, J. N., and Kreps, D. M. (1999). Consistent human resource practices. *California Management Review*, 41(3): 29–53.

Becker, B. E., Huselid, M. A., Pickus, P. S., and Spratt, M. F. (1997). HR as a source of shareholder value. *Human Resource Management*, 36(1): 39–47.

Becker, G. S. (1964). *Human Capital*. New York: Columbia University Press.

Beer, M., Spector, B., Lawrence, P. R., Mills, D. Q., and Walton, R. E. (1985). *Human Resource Management*. New York: Free Press.

Boudreau, J. W., and Ramstad, P. M. (1997). Measuring intellectual capital: Learning from financial history. *Human Resource Management*, 36: 343–56.

Boudreau, J. W., and Ramstad, P. M. (1999). Human resource metrics: can measures be strategic? In G. R. Ferris (ed.), *Research in Personnel and Human Resources Management*, 75–98, Supplement 4. London: JAI Press.

Boxall, P., and Purcell, J. (2000). Strategic human resource management: where have we come from and where should we be going? *International Journal of Management Reviews*, 2 (2): 183–203.

Brown, S. L., and Eisenhardt, K. M. (1997). The art of continuous change: Linking complexity theory and time-paced evolution in relentlessly shifting organizations. *Administrative Science Quarterly*, 42: 1–34.

Brown, S. L., and Eisenhardt, K. M. (1998). *Competing on the Edge: Strategy as Structured Chaos*. Boston: Harvard Business School Press.

Buller, P. F. (1988). Successful partnerships: HR and strategic planning at eight top firms. *Organizational Dynamics*, 17(2): 27–44.

Cappelli, P. (1995). Rethinking employment. *British Journal of Industrial Relations*, 33(4): 563–602.

Chandler, A. D. (1962). *Strategy and Structure*. Cambridge, MA: MIT Press.

Cohen, W. M., and Leventhal, D. A. (1990). Absorptive capacity: A new perspective on learning and innovation. *Administrative Science Quarterly*, 35: 128–52.

Coleman, J. S. (1988). Social capital in the creation of human capital. *American Journal of Sociology*, 94: S95–S120.

Conner, K. R., and Prahalad, C. K. (1996). A resource-based theory of the firm: Knowledge versus opportunism. *Organization Science*, 7(5): 477–501.

Daft, R. L., and Weick, K. E. (1984).Toward a model of organizations as interpretation systems. *Academy of Management Review*, 9: 284–96.

Davenport, T. H., and Prusak, L. (1998). *Working Knowledge: How Organizations Manage What They Know*. Boston, MA: Harvard Business School Press.

Day, G. S. (1997). Maintaining the competitive edge: creating and sustaining advantages in dynamic competitive environments. In G. S. Day and D. J. Reibstein (eds.), *Wharton on Dynamic Strategy*, 48–75. New York: Wiley.

Delery, J., and Doty, D. H. (1996). Modes of theorizing in strategic human resource management: Tests of universalistic, contingency and configurational performance predictions. *Academy of Management Journal*, 39(4): 802–35.

Dennison, D. R., and Mishra, A. K. (1995). Toward a theory of organizational culture and effectiveness. *Organization Science*, 6(2): 204–24.

Dierickx, I., and Cool, K. (1989). Asset stock accumulation and sustainability of competitive advantage. *Management Science*, 35(12): 1504–11.

Doty, H. D., and Glick, W. H. (1994). Typologies as a unique form of theory building: Toward improved understanding and modeling. *Academy of Management Review*, 19: 230–51.

Dyer, L. (1983). Bringing human resources into the strategy formulation process. *Human Resource Management*, 22: 257–71.

Dyer, L., and Holder, G. W. (1988). A strategic perspective of human resources management. In L. Dyer and G. W. Holder (eds.), *Human Resources Management: Evolving Roles and Responsibilities*. 1–45. Washington, DC: American Society for Personnel Administration.

Dyer, L., and Shafer, R. A. (1999). From human resource strategy to organizational effectiveness: Lessons from research on organizational agility. In G. R. Ferris (ed.), *Research in Personnel and Human Resources Management*, 145–74, Supplement 4. London: JAI Press.

Edvinsson, L., and Malone, M. S. (1997). *Intellectual Capital: Realizing your Company's True Value by Finding its Hidden Brainpower*. New York: Harper Business.

Gomez-Mejia, L. R. (1992). Structure and process of diversification, compensation strategy, and firm performance. *Strategic Management Journal*, 13: 381–97.

Guest, D. E. (1987). Human resource management and industrial relations. *Journal of Management Studies*, 24(5): 503–21.

Guest, D. E. (1999). Human resource management and performance: a review and research agenda. In R. S. Schuler and S. E. Jackson (eds.), *Strategic Human Resource Management*, 177–90. Oxford: Blackwell Business.

Hamel, G., and Prahalad, C. K. (1994). *Competing for the Future*. Boston: Harvard Business School.

Harrison, J. S., and St. John, C. H. (1996). Managing and partnering with external stakeholders.

*Academy of Management Executive*, 10(2): 46–60.

Herzberg, F. (1957). *Job Attitudes: Review of Research and Opinion*. Pittsburgh: Psychological Service of Pittsburgh.

Hirschhorn, L. (1984). *Beyond Mechanization: Work and Technology in a Postindustrial Age*. Cambridge, MA: MIT Press.

Huey, J. W., Jr. (1998). Organization man – not. *Fortune*, 137(5): 16.

Huselid, M. A. (1995). The impact of human resource management practices on turnover, productivity and corporate financial performance. *Academy of Management Journal*, 38: 635–70.

Huselid, M. A., Jackson, S. E., and Schuler, R. S. (1997). The significance of human resource management implementation effectiveness for corporate financial performance. *Academy of Management Journal*, 40(1): 173–88.

Itami, H. (1987). *Mobilizing Invisible Assets*. Cambridge, MA: Harvard University Press.

Jackson, S. E., Schuler, R., and Rivero, J. C. (1989). Organizational characteristics as predictors of personnel practices. *Personnel Psychology*, 42: 727–86.

Kaplan, R. S., and Norton, D. P. (1996). *The Balanced Scorecard: Translating Strategy into Action*, Boston: Harvard Business School Press.

Kerr, J. L. (1985). Diversification strategies and managerial rewards: An empirical study. *Academy of Management Journal*, 28: 155–79.

Kochan, T. A., Katz, H., and McKersie, R. (1986). *The Transformation of American Industrial Relations*, New York: Basic Books.

Kogut, B., and Zander, U. (1992). Knowledge of the firm, combinative capabilities, and the replication of technology. *Organization Science*, 3: 383–97.

Lado, A. A., and Wilson, M. C. (1994). Human resource systems and sustained competitive advantage: A competency-based perspective. *Academy of Management Review*, 19(4): 699–727.

Lawrence, P. R., and Lorsch, J. W. (1967). *Organization and Environment: Managing Differentiation and Integration*. Boston: Harvard Business School Press.

Leanna, C. R., and VanBuren, H. J., III. (1999). Organizational social capital and employment practices. *Academy of Management Review*, 24(3): 538–55.

Lengnick-Hall, C. A., and Lengnick-Hall, M. L. (1998). Strategic human resources management: A review of the literature and a proposed typology. *Academy of Management Review*, 13(3): 454–70.

Lenz, R. T. (1980). Strategic capability: A concept and framework for analysis. *Academy of Management Review*, 13: 454–70.

Leonard-Barton, D. (1992). The factory as a learning laboratory. *Sloan Management Review*, Fall: 23–38.

Lepak, D. P., and Snell, S. A. (1999). The human resource architecture: Toward a theory of human capital allocation and development. *Academy of Management Review*, 24: 31–48.

MacDuffie, J. P. (1995). Human resource bundles and manufacturing performance: Organizational logic and flexible production systems in the world auto industry. *Industrial and Labor Relations Review*, 48(2): 197–221.

Mangum, G., Mayall, D., and Nelson, K. (1985). The temporary help industry: A response to the dual internal labor market. *Industrial and Labor Relations Review*, 38: 599–612.

Mason, R. O., and Mitroff, I. I. Creating a Dialectical Social Science: Concepts, Methods and Models. Boston, MA: D. Reidel.

Matusik, S. F., and Hill, C. W. L. (1998). The utilization of contingent work, knowledge creation, and competitive advantage. *Academy of Management Review*, 23: 680–97.

McGregor, H. (1960). *The human Side of Enterprise*. New York: McGraw-Hill.

Miles, R. E., and Snow, C. C. (1978). *Organizational Strategy, Structure, and Process*. New York: McGraw-Hill.

Miles, R. E., and Snow, C. C. (1984). Designing strategic human resources systems. *Organizational Dynamics*, Summer: 36–52.

Milliman, J., von Glinow, M. A., and Nathan, M. (1991). Organizational life cycles and strategic international human resource management in multinational companies: Implications for congruence theory. *Academy of Management Review*, 16: 318–39.

Nahapiet, J., and Ghoshal, S. (1998). Social capital, intellectual capital, and the organizational advantage. *Academy of Management Review*, 23: 242–66.

Nonaka, I., and Takeuchi, H. (1995). *The Knowledge-Creating Company: How Japanese Companies Create the Dynamics of Innovation*. New York: Oxford University Press.

Olian, J. D., and Rynes, S. L. (1984). Organizational staffing: Integrating practice with strategy. *Industrial Relations*, 23: 170–81.

Oliveira, M. M. (1999). Core competencies and the knowledge of the firm. In M. A. Hitt, P. G. Clifford, R. D. Nixon, and K. P. Coyne (eds.), *Dynamic Strategic Processes: Development, Diffusion and Integration*, 17–41. New York: Wiley.

O'Reilly, C. A., and Pfeffer, J. (2000). *Hidden Value: How Great Companies Achieve Extraordinary Results with Ordinary People*. Boston: Harvard Business School Press.

Osterman, P. (1987). Choice of employment systems in internal labor markets. *Industrial Relations*, 26(1): 48–63.

Peteraf, M. A. (1993). The cornerstones of competitive advantage: A resource-based view. *Strategic Management Journal*, 14: 179–91.

Pfeffer, J. (1994). *Competitive Advantage through People: Unleashing the Power of the Workforce*. Boston: Harvard Business School Press.

Porter, M. E. (1980). *Competitive Strategy: Techniques for Analyzing Industries and Competitors*. New York: Free Press.

Prahalad, C. K. (1983). Developing strategic capability: An agenda for to management. *Human Resources Management*, 22: 237–54.

Prahalad, C. K., and Hamel, G. (1990). *The Core Competence of the Corporation*. Harvard Business Review, May–June, 68(3): 79–91.

Pucik, V. (1988). Strategic alliances, organizational learning, and competitive advantage: The HRD agenda. *Human Resource Management*, 27(1): 77–93.

Quinn, J. B. (1992). The intelligent enterprise: A new paradigm. *Academy of Management Executive*, 6(4): 48–63.

Roethlisberger, F. J., and Dickson, W. J. (1939). *Management and the Worker: An Account of a Research Program Conducted by the Western Electric Company, Hawthorne Works, Chicago*. Cambridge, MA: Harvard University Press.

Rogers, E. W., and Wright, P. M. (1998). Measuring organizational performance in strategic human resource management: Problems, prospects, and performance information markets. *Human Resource Management Review*, 8(3): 311–31.

Rose, R. A. (1988). Organizations as multiple cultures: A rules theory analysis. *Human Relations*, 41: 139–70.

Rousseau, D. M. (1995). *Psychological Contracts in Organizations: Understanding Written and Unwritten Agreements*. Thousand Oaks, CA: Sage Publications.

Sanchez, R. (1995). Strategic flexibility in product competition. *Strategic Management Journal*, 16: 135–59.

Schein, E. (1990). Organization culture. *American Psychologist*, 45(2): 109–19.

Schneider, B. (1987). The people make the place. *Personnel Psychology*, 40(3): 437–54.

Schuler, R. S., and Jackson, S. E. (1987). Linking competitive strategies with human resource practices. *Academy of Management Executive*, 1: 207–19.

Schuler, R. S., and MacMillan, I. (1984). Gaining competitive advantage through human resource practices. *Human Resource Management*, 23: 241–56.

Snell, S. A. (1992). Control theory in strategic human resource management: The mediating effect of administrative information. *Academy of Management Journal*, 35: 292–327.

Snell, S. A., and Dean, J. W. (1992). Integrated manufacturing and human resource management: A human capital perspective. *Academy of Management Journal*, 35(3): 467–504.

Snow, C. C., and Snell, S. A. (1993). Staffing as strategy. In N. Schmitt, W. C. Borman, and Associates (eds.), *Personnel Selection in Organizations*. San Francisco: Jossey-Bass.

Sveiby, K. E. (1997). *The New Organizational Wealth: Managing and Measuring Knowledge-based Assets*. San Francisco: Barrett-Koehler.

Teece, D., Pisano, G., and Shuen, A. (1997). Dynamic capabilities and strategic management. *Strategic Management Journal*, 18: 509–33.

Tichy, N. M., Fombrun, C. J., and DeVanna, M. A. (1982). Strategic human resource management. *Sloan Management Review*, 23: 47–61.

Trist, E. L. (1963). *Organizational Choice: Capabilities of Groups at the coal Face under Changing Technologies: The Loss, Re-discovery and Transformation of a Work Tradition*. London: Tavistock Publications.

Tsui, A. S., Pearce, J. L., Porter, L. W., and Hite, J. P. (1995). Choice of employee-organization relationship: Influence of external and internal organizational factors. In G. R. Ferris (ed.), *Research in Personnel and Human Resources Management*, 117–51. Greenwich, CT: JAI Press.

Ulrich, D. (1991). Using human resources for competitive advantage. In R. Kilmann, I. Kilmann, and Associates (eds.), *Making Organizations Competitive*. San Francisco: Jossey-Bass.

Ulrich, D. (1997). Measuring human resources: an overview of practice and a prescription for results. *Human Resource Management*, 36(3): 303–20.

Walker, J. W. (1980). *Human Resource Planning*. New York: McGraw-Hill.

Wernerfelt, B. (1984). A resource-based view of the firm. *Strategic Management Journal*, 5: 171–80.

Wright, P. M., and McMahan, G. C. (1992). Theoretical perspectives for strategic human resource management. *Journal of Management*, 18(2): 295–320.

Wright, P. M., Smart, D., and McMahan, G. C. (1995). On the integration of strategy and human resources: An investigation of the match between human resources and strategy among NCAA basketball teams. *Academy of Management Journal*, 38: 1052–74.

Wright, P. M., and Snell, S. A. (1991). Toward an integrative view of strategic human resource management. *Human Resource Management Review*, 1: 203–25.

Wright, P. M., and Snell, S. A. (1998). Toward a unifying framework for exploring fit and flexibility in strategic human resource management. *Academy of Management Review*, 23: 756–72.

Yeung, A. Brockbank, W., and Ulrich, D. (1994). Lower cost, higher value: Human resource function in transformation. *Human Resource Planning*, 17(3): 1–16.

Youndt, M. A., Snell, S. A. Dean, J. W., Jr., and Lepak, D. P. (1996). Human resource management, manufacturing strategy, and firm performance. *Academy of Management Journal*, Special Issue, 39(4): 836–66.

# 24

# Strategy and Entrepreneurship: Outlines of an Untold Story

## S. Venkataraman and Saras D. Sarasvathy

In his book "Invention," Professor Norbert Wiener (1993), commenting on the relative importance accorded to individuals and institutions in historical narratives of science and inventions, asks us to imagine Shakespeare's "Romeo and Juliet" without either Romeo or the balcony.[1] The story is just not the same. He likens much of the study of the economic history of science and accounts of inventions as "all balcony and no Romeo." The balcony for Norbert Wiener captures the context in which the story unfolds – the culture, the institutions, the constraints and the catalysts that move the plot forward and thicken it. Romeos, for Wiener, play the leading parts in the story, because there is a strong fortuitous element to inventions and there is no inevitability that a possible discovery will be made at a *given time and space*. Take away either one, Romeo or the balcony, and the whole story falls apart. In a similar vein, we would liken studies of strategic management to "all balcony and no Romeo." But if we accuse strategic management of being "all balcony and no Romeo," strategic management scholars could legitimately accuse entrepreneurship of being "all Romeo and no balcony."

In this chapter we wish to suggest a point of view from entrepreneurship that will allow strategic management scholars to accommodate more Romeos in their stories. Although these two fields have much to offer each other (trade in balconies and Romeos), they have developed largely independent of each other. We wish to suggest that entrepreneurship has a role to play in strategic management theory and that strategic management theory enriches our understanding of the entrepreneurial process, although this latter aspect will not be the focus of this chapter.

One useful way of thinking about entrepreneurship is that it is concerned with understanding how, in the absence of markets for future goods and services, these goods and services manage to come into existence (Venkataraman, 1997). To the extent that value is embodied in products and services, entrepreneurship is concerned with how the opportunity to create "value" in society is discovered and acted upon by some individuals. As Wiener has noted (Wiener, 1993: 7), at the beginning stages of a new idea, the effectiveness of the individual is enormous: "Before any new idea can arise in theory and practice, some person or persons must have introduced it in their own minds ... The absence of original mind, even though it might not have excluded a certain element of progress in the distant future, may well delay it for fifty years or a century."

The field of strategic management can be usefully described as having to do with the "methods" used to create this "value" and the ensuing struggle to capture a significant share of that "value" by individuals and firms. Thus, if we understand entrepreneurship and strategic management as the fields that together seek to describe, explain, predict and prescribe how value is discovered, created, captured, and perhaps destroyed, then there is not only much that we can learn from each other, but together we represent two sides of the same coin: the coin of value creation and capture.

One side of the coin, namely strategic management, has to do with the achievement of ends – obtaining market share, profit, and sustained competitive advantage. The other side of the coin, namely entrepreneurship, has to do with the achievement of beginnings – *creating* products, firms, and markets. But the clarity and complexity with which an author connects beginnings and ends is what makes a great story. We believe the really interesting story between strategic management and entrepreneurship has not yet been told. The main reason for this is that in general, creation calls for very different modes of thinking and behavior than capture and sustenance over time. Yet the creation process not only determines certain powerful tendencies for survival and growth, but some elements of it also persist over long periods of time, subtly and substantially influencing the selection and achievement of later ends. Carefully bearing in mind that large expanses of strategic management may have no overlap with entrepreneurship,[2] this chapter nevertheless focuses exclusively on where entrepreneurship and strategic management overlap.

In the preface to their 1994 book, Rumelt, Schendel, and Teece identify the subject matter of strategic management as "the purposeful direction and natural evolution of enterprises." They further identify four fundamental issues that comprise a research agenda in strategic management:

1. *Firm Behavior*[3]   How do firms behave? Or, do firms really behave like rational actors, and, if not, what models of their behavior should be used by researchers and policy makers?
2. *Firm Differentiation*   Why are firms different? Or, what sustains the heterogeneity in resources and performance among close competitors despite competition and imitative attempts?
3. *Firm Scope*   What is the function of or value added by the headquarters unit in a diversified firm? Or, what limits the scope of the firm?
4. *Firm Performance*   What determines success or failure in international competition? Or, what are the origins of success and what are their particular manifestations in international settings or global competition?

In answering the four questions stated above, economics and strategic management theories generally tend to focus on rational decision making (whether unbounded or bounded and linear or non-linear) based on causal reasoning and the logic of prediction. Our explication of entrepreneurship, however, rests upon creative action based on effectual reasoning and the logic of control.

We have elsewhere identified the subject matter of entrepreneurship as having to do with the exploitation of opportunities for creating hitherto non-existent economic artifacts (Venkataraman, 1997; Shane and Venkataraman, 2000; Sarasvathy and Simon, 2000; Sarasvathy, 2001). Depending upon the completeness and/or consistency of the larger environment, entrepreneurial opportunities may have to be recognized or discovered or created. In this chapter, we first examine these three types of action connected with entrepreneurial opportunities through a framework based on the preconditions for their existence. Thereafter, we explore the four fundamental issues of strategic management listed above from an "entrepreneurial opportunity" perspective.

## ENTREPRENEURIAL OPPORTUNITIES[4]

The *Oxford English Dictionary* defines opportunity as "a time, juncture, or condition of things favorable to an end or purpose, or admitting of something being done or effected." As is clear from this definition, at the minimum, an opportunity involves an end or purpose, and things favorable to the achievement of it. An entrepreneurial opportunity consists of the opportunity to create future economic artifacts and as such, involves a demand side, a supply side and the means to bring them together. Therefore, in the case of an entrepreneurial opportunity, the "things favorable" consist of two categories: (a) beliefs about the future; and (b) actions based on those beliefs. In sum, an entrepreneurial opportunity consists of:

1. Supply side: New or existing idea(s) or invention(s);
2. Demand side: One or more ends – may be subjective (endogenous) aspirations or objective (exogenous) goals or both;[5]
3. Beliefs about things favorable to the achievement of those ends; and,
4. Possible implementations of those ends through the creation of new economic artifacts.

At this point, it is important to note that entrepreneurial opportunities exist at all levels of the economy – individual, corporate, and macroeconomic. For example, the invention of the internet not only led to the identification and creation of entrepreneurial opportunities for individuals and firms, but also opportunities for the US economy as a whole in terms of more effective globalization. Similarly, Adam Smith's exposition of the "invisible hand" guided both economic policy at the government level as well as the decisions of individual economic agents and firms in the creation of "free market" institutions.

But entrepreneurial opportunities are extremely context specific. What might be an opportunity today in Ukraine may not be an opportunity at all in the US today or even in Ukraine tomorrow. This means that entrepreneurial opportunities do not necessarily lie around waiting to be discovered by the serendipitous entrepreneur who stumbles upon them or even to be "divined" by entrepreneurial geniuses, if any such geniuses exist. Instead, entrepreneurial opportunities are often residuals of human activities in non-economic spheres and emerge contingent upon conscious actions by entrepreneurs who continually strive to transform the outputs of those non-economic activities into new products and firms and in the process fulfil and transform human aspirations into new markets.

In other words, before there are products and firms, there is human imagination; and before there are markets, there are human aspirations. Creative outputs of the human imagination in every realm of human action be it the arts or the sciences, sports or philosophy, become inputs for the economic domain. It is an empirical fact that profits for the individual and the firm, and welfare for the economy come as much from Jerry Seinfeld's jokes and Michael Jordan's baskets, as from great technological inventions and the tearing down of the Berlin wall. Similarly, human aspirations may range from career goals and individual prosperity to freedom and justice and the good life for all and peace on earth. These aspirations have to be transformed into demand functions and markets for specific economic artifacts such as particular goods, services and firms. Entrepreneurship consists in matching up the products of human imagination with human aspirations to create markets for goods and services that did not exist before the entrepreneurial act.

In fact, most entrepreneurial opportunities, be they supply based or demand based, do not originate in the economic domain at all. For example, the internet was developed as a way to facilitate communication between defense scientists and remained out of the economic domain for several years. The mere existence of the internet did not guarantee the development of e-commerce. Rather, this artifact created to solve a political problem (namely, defense), had to be transformed through several intentional and unintentional activities to become a universe of entrepreneurial opportunities in the economic domain. To cite another example, entrepreneurs such as Robert Lucas transform literary and artistic endeavors into the Star Wars marketing empire by matching up creations of the human imagination with human aspirations such as the desire to participate in the triumph of good over evil. That is why if we are to understand entrepreneurial opportunities, we have to delve into the preconditions for their existence – that is, the preconditions for the existence of demand and supply combinations that constitute entrepreneurial opportunities. This leads us to a simple typology of entrepreneurial actions in relation to opportunities as follows:

1.  *Opportunity recognition.* If both sources of supply and demand exist rather obviously, the opportunity for bringing them together has to be "recognized" and then the match-up between supply and demand has to be implemented either through an existing firm or a new firm. Examples include arbitrage and franchises. For example, through its first successful coffee shop, Starbucks proved the existence of a demand for specialty coffees as also a viable and effective way to satisfy that demand. Thereafter, each Starbucks' franchisee only has to *recognize* potential geographic locations for extending that demand and supply combination. They do not have to invent sources of supply, or induce demand for a completely new product.

2.  *Opportunity discovery.* If only one side exists in an obvious manner and the other side either does not exist or is so latent as to be virtually non-existent for most people – that is, demand exists, but supply does not, and vice versa – then, the non-existent side has to be "discovered" before the match-up can be implemented. In other words, when demand exists; supply has to be discovered. An example of this is Ron Popeil and his inventions for more convenient and health-conscious kitchen devices. On the other side of the coin, supply might exist; then demand has to be discovered. The history of technology entrepreneurship is strewn with solutions in search of problems. Xerox had the technology for the Macintosh computer, but it took Jobs and Wozniak to discover and exploit its potential demand.

3.  *Opportunity creation.* If neither supply nor demand exist in an obvious manner, one or both have to be "created," and several economic inventions in marketing, financing, management etc. have to be made, for the opportunity to come into existence. Examples

include Wedgwood Pottery, Edison's General Electric, U-Haul, AES Corporation, Netscape, Beanie Babies, and the MIR space resort.

Historically, opportunities have been supposed to exist – and the entrepreneur either is alert to them (Kirzner, 1979) or somehow goes about "discovering" them (Hayek, 1945; Schumpeter, 1976). But the idea we will explore in this chapter is that entrepreneurial opportunities often have to be "created" by using the entrepreneurial imagination to *embody* human aspirations in concrete products and markets.

## THE CREATIVE ENTREPRENEURIAL ASPECTS OF FUNDAMENTAL ISSUES IN STRATEGIC MANAGEMENT

### *Firm behavior: emphasizing the creativity of human action*

*How do firms behave? Or, do firms really behave like rational actors, and, if not, what models of their behavior should be used by researchers and policy makers?*

*Rational action.* Economics has long rested on foundations of rational action; and it has long been criticized for it. For example, studies have shown that that there are severe limits – lack of knowledge, computational ability, and ability to consider more than a few factors simultaneously – that place an upper bound on human objective rationality (Simon, 1959; Bar-Hillel, 1980; Tversky and Kahneman, 1982; Payne, Bettman and Johnson, 1993). Although this does not imply that decision makers are irrational, it shows that they must usually use heuristics and approximate inductive logics – that nevertheless often lead to very effective decisions (Gigerenzer, Hell, and Blank, 1988). They seldom have the luxury of behaving like utility maximizers.

But most criticisms of the "rational" foundations of economics attack and try to relax assumptions of rationality rather than provide an overarching alternative framework. In 1991, however, Buchanan and Vanberg called for more drastic measures, particularly for our understanding of entrepreneurship (Buchanan and Vanberg, 1991). In that paper, they argue for the usefulness of a perceptual construct of the market as a *creative* process, rather than as a *discovery* process, or the more familiar *allocative* process. Their arguments are based on a fundamental assumption of the future that is not merely unknown, but essentially unknowable. Only speculations and conjectures are possible about the future because the future is *created* by the choices that human beings make: "Entrepreneurial activity, in particular, is not to be modeled as discovery of that which is "out there." Such activity, by contrast, *creates* a reality that will be different subsequent on differing choices. Hence, the reality of the future must be shaped by choices yet to be made, and this reality has no existence independent of these choices. With regard to a "yet to be created" reality, it is surely confusing to consider its emergence in terms of the discovery of "overlooked opportunities" (p. 178).

*Creative action.* Pursuant to the detailed arguments advanced by Buchanan and Vanberg, we propose the following answer to the first fundamental issue in strategic management: *firms behave creatively.* Firms not only use rational and analytical decision making, they also use creative action as a way to figure out both goals and strategies in an intrinsically dynamic process. If we are to build theories of strategic management and entrepreneur-ship based on *creative* rather than *rational* action,[6] we need to first examine what we know so far about creative action.

In a powerful theoretical exposition, Joas (1996) has argued in considerable detail for the fundamentally creative nature of all human action.

> All theories of action which proceed from a type of rational action – irrespective of whether they are based on a narrower or broader, a utilitarian or a normative concept of rationality – make at least three assumptions. They presuppose firstly that the actor is capable of purposive action, secondly that he has control over his own body, and thirdly that he is autonomous vis-à-vis his fellow human beings and environment . . . The proponents of such conceptions are well aware that the preconditions assumed by the model of rational action are frequently not to be found in empirically observable action. However, these writers are forced to claim that the limited degree to which these preconditions obtain is not a deficiency of their particular theory but a fault of the actors themselves . . . I am not in any way denying the empirical usefulness of rational models of action when it comes to analyzing certain social phenomena. What I do question, however, is the claim that because of its usefulness this model of rational action, with all its tacit assumptions, can be applied to an ever increasing number of fields of study without a thorough reflection of precisely those intrinsic presuppositions. (Joas, 1996: 147)

Joas then goes on to analyze *the intentional character, the specific corporeality and the primary sociality of all human capacity for action*, with a view to developing a theory of creative action that could form a basis for the social sciences.

*Creative action and endogenous goals.*    Both works cited above (Buchanan and Vanberg, 1991; Joas, 1996) explicitly question the pre-existence of goals. Both exhort the necessity for developing a theory of human intentionality in which human purposes emerge *within* the processes studied and are not given *a priori*. For example, economics imposes utility maximization as the sole purpose or *telos* on the individual; profit maximization on the firm; and, welfare maximization on the economy. But others, such as psychologists and historians have argued that individuals and firms and even economies may have a variety of purposes that are not given *a priori* and that are born, change, and die over time. While Buchanan and Vanberg decry the economist's imposition of an exogenous telos on the phenomena they study, Joas brings to bear a wide variety of authorities from the pragmatist philosophers to expressivist anthropologists to develop a theory of creative action in which telos is neither ignored, nor imposed externally, nor assumed as a precondition for action. Within management literature, March too has called for theories that do not assume pre-existent goals (March, 1982):

> To say that we make decisions now in terms of goals that will only be knowable later is nonsensical – as long as we accept the basic framework of the theory of choice and its presumptions of pre-existent goals. I do not know in detail what is required, but I think it will be substantial. As we challenge the dogma of pre-existent goals, we will be forced to reexamine some of our most precious prejudices . . . We should indeed be able to develop better techniques. Whatever those techniques may be, however, they will almost certainly undermine the superstructure of biases erected on purpose, consistency, and rationality. They will involve some way of thinking about action now as occurring in terms of a set of unknown future values.

The first step in building a strategic management based on creative action, therefore, would call for theories that explain the selection of goals as *endogenous* to the strategic management process. In strategic management, researchers such as Mintzberg have called for a research program to examine strategies that were intended as well as those that were realized despite intentions (Mintzberg, 1978). One such theory, the theory of effectual (as opposed to causal) reasoning has recently been developed in entrepreneurship and as will be seen in the following sections, will bring additional new answers to the other three fundamental questions in strategic management. While creativity in causal reasoning consists in generating alternative means for the achievement of pre-specified goals, creativity in effectual reasoning involves the generation of possible goals, given limited means and constraints within dynamic and interactive environments. The theory of effectuation suggests that the solution to goal ambiguity need not lie in random and equivocal efforts or in dumb luck.

### Firm differentiation: emphasizing effectuation rather than causation

*Why are firms different? Or, what sustains the heterogeneity in resources and performance among close competitors despite competition and imitative attempts?*

*Differentiating between generalized aspirations and specific goals.* The issue of differentiation is even an issue only if we assume homogeneity of goals, especially goals that are determined prior to choice. In reality, however, human beings do not begin with specific goals – only with vague and generalized aspirations, that are themselves contingent upon a host of situational and temporal factors. This intrinsically pluralizing role of contingent aspirations affects both demand-side and supply-side choices. For example, on the demand side, most hungry customers do not start with the "need" for a specific food such as hamburgers. Instead they start with a generalized hunger for something to eat. The entrepreneur induces the customer to transform that generalized aspiration into a concrete demand for a specific product such as the hamburgers manufactured by a particular company.

There are two types of choice here. The first one involves the transformation of a vague aspiration such as hunger into the specific desire for a hamburger. The second one involves the choice between possible hamburger joints, *given the desire for a hamburger*. As proponents of the resource-based theory of the firm have pointed out, in mainstream economics and management, we tend to model the latter type of choice (i.e., choice between means to achieve a particular goal) rather than the earlier one – that is, the choice between possible ends, given particular means and very generalized aspirations (Ulrich and Barney, 1984).

Similarly, on the supply side, most entrepreneurs do not set out to build a particular company for a particular product within a particular market (Ex: to create a profitable company for manufacturing and selling razor blades). Instead, when setting out, the entrepreneur only has some very general aim, such as the desire to make lots of money, or to create a lasting institution, or more commonly, just an interesting idea that seems worth pursuing. For example, Gillette started with the idea of making some product that would need to be repurchased repeatedly. Moving from that relatively vague starting point to actually designing and manufacturing the disposable razor involved a very different set of choices than after he had determined the particular product that he wanted to make and sell. The type of reasoning involved when specific goals have to be created from contingent aspirations is necessarily different from the type of reasoning involved in attaining that specific goal once it is finalized. Given a specific goal, selecting between alternative means involves causal reasoning. Transforming contingent aspirations into possible specific goals and choosing between them involves effectuation.

Effectuation finds its theoretical antecedents in researchers such as March who investigated exploration and exploitation in organizational learning. Organizational learning involves decisions that allocate scarce resources (including attention) between the exploration of new possibilities and the exploitation of old certainties. These decisions are complicated by the fact that their costs and benefits may be dispersed over time and space, and that they are subject to the effects of ecological interaction. Yet, balancing the allocation between exploration and exploitation is crucial to the survival and sustenance of the organization. March argues that understanding the relationship between these two horns of a continuing dilemma in organizational evolution leads us away from a linear approach to concepts such as "success" and "sustainable competitive advantage." For example, introducing a new technology such as computerized decision support systems, while improving the organization's chance of avoiding being the worst competitor, may reduce its chance to be the overall winner in the game (March 1991: 84).

But effectuation goes beyond the dichotomies of exploration and exploitation, or the distinction between linear and non-linear thinking. Effectuation is useful in domains where there is no pre-existent universe of possibilities to explore – instead, such a universe gets *created*, often unintentionally, by acts of human imagination. These acts of the imagination may occur in the normal course of human activity in a wide variety of domains, most of which may not be driven by any immediate economic goal. For example, the theory of effectuation would argue that no exploration of any relevant economic domains could have led to the "discovery" of the internet and its e-commerce possibilities. Instead, an artifact created to solve a particular problem in an unrelated domain (in the internet example, the communication problem for defense scientists) was eventually transformed into a universe of possible economic opportunities by internet entrepreneurs. This transformation did not happen overnight. The mere existence of the internet did not inevitably imply the creation of e-commerce. Instead, that creation had to await several fortuitous inventions (such as the web browser), serendipitous insights (such as Netscape's marketing strategy), and arduous institutional developments (such as security procedures, privacy laws, and so on, that continue even as this chapter is being written). It is this transformation process that involves entrepreneurial effectuation and is ignored in many economic and management theories of strategic management and so-called opportunity *recognition*.

*Causation and effectuation.* Just as exploration and exploitation are both essential to the continuing sustenance of firms, both causation and effectuation are important aspects of entrepreneurial and strategic decision making in individuals. To generalize the ideas illustrated in the Gillette example earlier into a theory of effectuation, we will use techniques in the received tradition of Edgeworth box economics – that is, we will present an oversimplified example to clarify the *theoretical* distinction between the two types of reasoning and then continue to introduce complications that bring the theory back to empirical reality. We will begin by imagining a chef assigned the task of cooking dinner. There are two ways the task could be organized. In the first case the chef starts with a predetermined menu, lists the ingredients needed, shops for them and then actually cooks the meal. This is a process of causation. In the second instance, the chef looks through the cupboards in the kitchen for possible ingredients and utensils, and fashions a meal using them. This is a process of effectuation.

A variety of such simple examples can be imagined: a carpenter who is asked to build a desk, versus one who is given a toolbox and some wood, and asked to build whatever he or she chooses to; an artist who is asked to paint a portrait of a particular person, versus one who is given a blank canvas and some paints, and required to paint anything he or she chooses to; a scientist who is involved in developing and commercializing a new technology versus one who is developing the principles of basic science; an entrepreneur who begins with a specific business plan to develop a specific company versus one who wishes to be his own boss and has to figure out what business to go into, and so on. As cited earlier, all King Gillette knew when he set out was that he would like to create a product that had to be re-purchased repeatedly. From that, to decide upon and develop the disposable razor involves a process of effectuation. Once an entrepreneur creates a product and establishes the existence of a market for it, others can use processes of causation to create similar products within the new marketplace brought into being by the effectuating entrepreneur.

These are obviously oversimplified examples *à la* the Edgeworth box. To bring the definitions closer to reality through, say, the dinner example, we would have to add elements of dynamism, and contingencies of various kinds including multiple interacting chefs and hosts and dinner guests. But the point here is that in each example, the *generalized* end goal or *aspiration* remains the same both in causation and effectuation – that is, to cook a meal, to build some wooden artifact, to create a painting, to make an invention, etc. In fact, an effect is the objectification of an abstract human aspiration. The distinguishing characteristic between causation and effectuation is in the set of choices: choosing between means to create a particular effect, versus choosing between many possible effects using a given set of means. While causation models consist of many-to-one mappings, effectuation models involve one-to-many mappings.

*Existence proof for effectuation.*   Both causation and effectuation are integral parts of human reasoning that can occur simultaneously, overlapping and intertwining over different contexts of decisions and actions. Yet almost all of the literature in economics and management focuses exclusively on models embodying causal reasoning. The existence of effectuation processes in entrepreneurial decision making has recently been empirically confirmed by a study by Sarasvathy (1998), gathering and analyzing think-aloud verbal protocols of 27 entrepreneurs who had founded and grown companies ranging in size from $200 million to $6.5 billion. The subjects consisted of founders with a wide variety of entrepreneurial expertise and the subject pool was drawn from a number of disparate industries including retail (such as teddy bears and razors), technology (such as semiconductors, telecommunications, and bio-tech), services (such as security), and old economy (such as steel and railroads). Each subject was presented with ten typical problems that arise in a startup (beginning with the exact same imaginary product – a computer game of entrepreneurship), and asked to think aloud continuously as they solved the problems.

The logic behind the study was to discover commonalties in the decision processes used by expert entrepreneurs with a diverse background and experiences, and cull together a baseline model of *entrepreneurial* expertise.

The data show that the subjects' decisions conform overwhelmingly to a model of effectuation rather than a causation process of choosing between means toward predetermined ends. More precisely, 74 percent of the participants in the study behaved in accordance with the effectuation model at least 63 percent of the time, and 44 percent of them, at least 85 percent of the time (Sarasvathy, 1999). To summarize briefly, causation processes are effect-dependent – focusing on expected returns, competitive analyses, pre-existent knowledge, and prediction; effectuation processes are actor-dependent – emphasizing affordable loss, strategic partnerships, contingent action, and control. For a detailed exposition of causation versus effectuation processes, see Sarasvathy (2001).

*Means for effectuation.*   Entrepreneurs begin with three categories of what we have called "means." They know who they are, what they know, and whom they know – their traits, tastes and abilities, the knowledge corridors they are in, and the social networks they are a part of. Their marketing efforts, for example, focus not so much on structural and competitive analysis of a pre-selected market, as on imagined combinations of their abilities, expertise, experience, resources, and social networks that would lead to stable resource-stakeholder-market configurations. In the process, they not only end up creating new firms, but often end up creating new products and even new market niches that emerge as the *residuals* of their decisions rather than as pre-existent goals to be achieved through their decisions. Effectuation is essentially a divergent process that increases the dimensionality of the commodity space. In a world where effectuation processes dominate, firm differentiation is not a phenomenon to be explained – it is the expected outcome.

There is a particularly interesting corollary to the above exposition of three categories of "means" in effectuation. These three categories occur not only at the individual level, they also have counterparts at the level of the firm and even at the level of the economy. At the level of the firm, the corresponding means are its physical resources, human resources, and organizational resources, *à la* the resource-based theory of the firm (Barney, 1991). At the level of the economy, these means become demographics, technological capabilities, and socio-political institutions (such as property rights). Newman, for example, explicates the role of institutional upheaval in creating ambiguous cause-effect relationships in economies such as the ones in Eastern Europe as they come out of communist systems (Newman, 2000). She further speculates that this ambiguity in turn requires a stock of entrepreneurial talent (within firms) to enable organizational learning leading to organizational transformation and successful adaptation. Our research supports that by implying that the use of effectuation is the key to managing such cause-effect ambiguities.

It turns out, therefore, that effectuation processes bring some important perspectives and issues to the table with regard to the resource-based theory of the firm. For example, effectuation suggests that what will make the resource based view of the firm powerful is not a focus on what the resources are and how they influence outcomes and value creation. Rather the more powerful contribution will be if we focus on the following questions: *Given* particular sets of resources, means, and capabilities, what is the process of creating and achieving a plurality of new and profitable ends? Under what circumstances do which type of reasoning processes (causal and effectual) get used? By whom? How? With what consequences? Through what routines, procedures, decisions, actions?

### *Firm scope: emphasizing the logic of control rather than the logic of prediction*

*What is the function of or value added by the headquarters unit in a diversified firm? Or, what limits the scope of the firm?*

*The tension between creativity and efficiency.*   By setting out to create a strategic management based on creative action, that is originative choice in the absence of pre-existent goals, we have moved to a world where effectuation is at least as valid an alternative as causation. But the mere existence of effectuation processes suggests at least one more answer to this third fundamental question in strategic management, namely, that firms have to manage a continual and/or iterative tension between creativity and efficiency. Furthermore, we posit that they manage this tension by differential uses of causal and effectual reasoning, and that that differential limits the scope of particular firms at least to a partial degree. The tension between creativity and efficiency has manifested itself in many forms both in theories and data in strategic management, as well as in management and economics. To cite but two examples: in a major historical synthesis of several bodies of economic literature, Galambos (1988), identifies the fundamental tension between the corporation's thrust towards market control and efficiency, on the one hand, and the necessity to continually innovate, on the other. Similarly, in a seminal article in management, March has highlighted the trade-offs between exploration and exploitation in organizational learning (March, 1991).

Several suggestions have been developed in the literature on how to deal with this tension. Chandler suggests the necessity (and the historical reality) of firms in more mature and complex industries using strategic and market control techniques while firms in more technologically turbulent environments resort to more entrepreneurial techniques (Chandler, 1962). But others prefer one or the other more. For example, Williamson advocates more of an efficiency perspective for the headquarters of a large business firm, eschewing a more proactive entrepreneurial strategizing (Williamson, 1975). Overall, the consensus seems to be towards some kind of a balanced portfolio or diversification approach to this particular strategic management question.

*The real options approach.*   Furthermore, in recent years, particular advances have come from the "real options approach" to evaluate projects in the portfolio for possible investment. For example, in a recent exposition Raynor discusses how hybrid diversification established real option for firms (Raynor, 2000). Real options allow a firm to deal with uncertainty by limiting the floor (possible loss) on an investment to the value of the option while allowing the ceiling to extend to the fullest extent the project could potentially attain (Trigeorgis, 1993; McGrath, 1997). The real options approach, unlike traditional NPV analyses, but very much like the effectuation approach may not lead to higher success rates, but it is more likely to reduce the *costs* of failure. This is because both the real options approach and the effectuation process tie up outlays to tighter feedback loops at lower levels of investment, and enable failures to occur early.

However, both the real options approach and the more traditional NPV analyses begin with a *given* portfolio of potential projects. In other words, in both these cases, the scope of the firm is limited by the portfolio that it actually considers for its investment decision. Effectuation brings another perspective to the table, a perspective that enables the firm to expand its portfolio beyond any current potential projects available to it. In other words, the portfolio metaphor for constructing and bounding firm scope is replaced by a new metaphor – that of the blank slate. The advantage of the blank slate approach is precisely that the firm is not limited to a focus on reduction of unpleasant surprises. Instead, the blank slate allows the firm to open itself to pleasant surprises that it cannot possibly forecast through any current prediction of future possibilities. The options that the firm does not know it has are precisely the ones that effectuation allows it to access and create.

*The logic of control.* This brings us to the interesting question: how does one pick an option that one does not know one has (or might have in the future)? To achieve this, we have to move our focus from using a logic of prediction to a logic of control. The logic of prediction states that *to the extent we predict the future, we can control it.* Therefore, the preferred strategies under this logic consist in analyzing the history and structure of the environment to make predictions about future trends, which then form the basis for strategic decisions. Effectuation, however, operates on a logic of control. The logic of control states that *to the extent that we can control the future, we do not need to predict it.* This logic accordingly emphasizes strategic alliances and pre-commitments as a way to control rather than predict future trends.

Again, a simple example would serve to illustrate the difference between the two. A classic example of Knightian uncertainty is that of predicting next year's fashions. Not only is the future in this example unknown, it is also unknowable. Yet fashion designers routinely succeed by actually controlling and molding people's tastes rather than by trying to predict them. By forming enduring relationships with movie stars and other taste leaders, fashion designers either *prescribe* tastes in their promotions ("This is what you *should* be wearing") and/or present them as *fait accompli* ("Animal prints are *in* this year").

We would like to emphasize here that we do not advocate the normative superiority of effectuation over causation or control over prediction in any overall or general fashion. In fact, causation processes have been studied and used successfully for a long time and are crucial under several circumstances of decision making. For example, when strategic outcomes are a result of maturing technologies or extensions of proven demand-supply combinations as in franchising, causation models undoubtedly work and have been proven effective. Effectuation, however, brings into existence a new decision domain that has been previously inaccessible to systematic understanding because it involves the absence of predictive rationality, pre-existent goals, and environmental selection. This is a space characterized by a *combination* of Knightian uncertainty, Marchian goal ambiguity, and Weickian enactment (Knight, 1921; Weick, 1979; March, 1982).

*The Knightian–Marchian–Weickian decision domain.* This new decision domain can be clearly explicated by extending the familiar metaphor of the statistical urn containing different colored balls that researchers studying decision making under uncertainty have used to model the future. Problems involving risk are akin to a speculative game with an urn containing five green balls and five red balls. The drawer of a red ball is awarded a prize of $50. For any given draw, we can precisely calculate the probability of getting a red ball, because we know the underlying distribution of balls inside the urn from which we are making the draw. Problems involving uncertainty involve the same award of $50 for the draw of a red ball – except this time we do not know how many balls are in the urn, of which colors, or even if there are any red balls at all in the distribution. In statistical terminology, decisions involving the first type of urn with the known distribution call for classical analytical techniques; and the decisions involving the second type of urn with the unknown distribution call for estimation techniques. Once the underlying distribution is discovered through estimation procedures, the urn with the unknown distribution is transformed, as it were, into the urn with the known distribution and becomes susceptible to analytical techniques. Both these urns exemplify the logic of prediction.

The process of effectuation, however, seems to suggest the following conjecture about the decision maker's logic, that is, the logic of control:

> I do not care what color balls are in the urn or their underlying distribution. If I am playing a game where drawing a red ball wins $50, I will go acquire red balls and put them in the urn. I will also look for other people who have red balls and induce them to put them in the urn and play the game as my partners. As time goes by, there would be so many red balls in the distribution as to make almost every draw a red ball. Furthermore, if neither I nor my acquaintances have red balls, only green ones, we will put enough of them in the urn so as to make the original game obsolete and create a new game where green balls win.

In managing the tension between creativity and efficiency, large corporations as well as individual entrepreneurs can use the logic of control to shape and create a future that cannot be predicted. To cite but a few scenarios, they need not always strive to articulate a clear strategic vision or specify ordered lading lists of outcomes to be pursued. Sometimes a series of tentative projects can be undertaken based exclusively on the enthusiastic engagement of committed stakeholders and strategic goals can be allowed to emerge as part of the process. For example, IBM took the big step of moving into computers not only because top management believed in the future of computers but particularly because IBM's scientists and engineers loved the new technology (Olegario, 1997: 362). Steve Wozniak similarly developed Apple as the machine he himself wanted to have – and Sant and Bakke set out to start a company *they* would want to work in (Waterman and Peters). As suggested earlier, effectuation works well in situations where predictive rationality, pre-existent goals, and environmental selection break down. Most entrepreneurs (individual or corporate) operate within such spaces; and most creative choices even in established businesses happen within such domains. Under these circumstances, effectuation, rather than causal reasoning, is called for.

### Firm performance: emphasizing locality and contingency

*What determines success or failure in international competition? Or, what are the origins of success and what are their particular manifestations in international settings or global competition.*[7]

*The diversified multinational corporation (DMNC) and the I–R framework.* Firm performance has been a holy grail both for strategic management theorists and entrepreneurship researchers. The quest for identifying both necessary and sufficient conditions for successful performance, performance being defined as profitability in the short run and survival and growth in the long run, has consumed considerable research resources. In this section, we suggest answers to the questions listed immediately above by applying the theory of effectuation to explain the performance of one particular type of "successful" firm, the DMNC.

Summarizing the efforts to explain firm performance especially as they pertain to the management of DMNCs, Doz and Prahalad (1994) argue that the emerging paradigm uses *the global integration–local responsiveness (I–R) framework*, with the basic unit of analysis being the individual manager, rather than an abstraction at a higher level of aggregation.

*Near-decomposability and the rapid evolution of systems that out-perform their competition.* How do we approach this suggested paradigm (the I–R framework) starting with effectuation processes preferred and used by entrepreneurs who end up building such DMNCs from scratch? A connection between effectuation processes and the I–R framework can be forged through the concept of near-decomposability. Near-decomposability refers to the property of complex systems that enables each of their components, by appropriate specialization, to carry on most of its activities, especially those activities that are innovative, with only moderate impact upon, and interaction with the other components (Simon, 1996). This idea of near-decomposability has been used before in the entrepreneurship literature to explain the ability of entrepreneurs to create intermediate stable forms as a precondition for longer-term survival of their new enterprises, and also for the ability of entrepreneurs to fulfill their evolving aspirations (Venkataraman, 1989, 1990). In a more recent essay, Sarasvathy and Simon (2000) have shown that near-decomposability is a necessary condition for quick response to opportunity – the opportunity provided by a new idea or discovery, or by a change in the environment (Simon, 1996) or through processes of effectuation (Sarasvathy, 2000).

Near-decomposability is a pervasive feature of the architecture of the complex systems that we find in the world, both inorganic and organic, ranging from elementary particles to social systems (Simon, 1969). A complex system is nearly decomposable if it is comprised of a number of interconnected subsystems in such a way that elements within any particular subsystem interact much more vigorously and rapidly with each other than do elements belonging to different subsystems. There may be a whole hierarchy of systems, subsystems, sub-subsystems, and so on, where this same property holds between any two levels. In such systems, (1) the short-term (high-frequency) behavior of each subsystem is approximately independent of the other subsystems at its level, and (2) in the long run, the (low-frequency) behavior of a subsystem depends on that of the other components only in an (approximately) aggregate way.

We may compare a nearly-decomposable system with a computer program using closed subroutines, so that the behavior of each routine depends only upon the inputs and outputs of its subroutines, without regard to the detailed processes these subroutines use to produce their outputs from their inputs. The theory of near-decomposability has been independently discovered several times and is now widely used in engineering and science to facilitate the solution of large systems of equations, especially those involving a wide range of temporal frequencies: for example, it is used to analyze large electrical power grids and in so-called "renormalization" in quantum physics. Nearly decomposable systems are close relatives of fractals.

Because near-decomposability is a structural feature, it has relevant implications for issues connected with firm scope. But when combined with the effectuation *process* that creates a structure that is nearly decomposable, the resulting theory has implications for firm performance especially for the creation and sustenance of large and diversified firms such as the DMNCs. Careful inquiry into the reasons for the recurring appearance of near-decomposability as a common property of complex systems traces it (near-decomposability) to the processes of their (complex systems') evolution. If we begin with a population of systems of comparable complexity, some of them nearly decomposable and some not, but all having similar frequencies of mutation, the nearly decomposable systems will increase their fitness through evolutionary processes much faster than the remaining systems, and will soon come to dominate the entire population. The complex systems we see in the world today are the products of such competitive selection, hence are predominately nearly decomposable (Simon, 1996).

The connection between near-decomposability and rapid evolution is simple and direct. In nearly decomposable systems, each component can evolve toward greater fitness with little dependence upon the changes taking place in the details of other components. Simple mathematics shows that, if and only if these conditions hold, natural selection can take advantage of the random alterations of components with little concern for countervailing cross effects between them. Such a system is like a defective safe that clicks whenever one of its dials is set correctly, independently of where the other dials are currently set.

The power of near-decomposability to produce rapid evolution has been demonstrated by an ingenious simulation by Marengo, Frenken, and Valente (1999), who, employing a genetic algorithm proposed by Stuart Kauffman for evolution of mutating systems in a fitness landscape, demonstrated a greatly superior rate of evolution of nearly decomposable systems over systems having the same rates of mutation but lacking near-decomposability.

*Effectuation and the creation of near-decomposable systems.* Empirical evidence from the study cited earlier indicates that the process the expert entrepreneurs use to grow their companies from a single customer to a firm with specific products in explicit markets can best be described through the metaphor of stitching together a patchwork quilt. While each patch used in the quilt is a rather arbitrary piece of fabric, some belonging to the quilter and others brought to them at one time or another by friends, a good quilter manages to construct an aesthetically appealing and even meaningful pattern in the quilt that emerges from the endeavor. The 27 entrepreneurs in the study, starting with exactly the same detailed product description, built completely different firms in 18 disparate industries by adding products and segments to their initial product in a patchwork quilt fashion.

They were able to do this, in part because of the ideas for each component that they were able to evoke based on who they were, what they knew and whom they knew. Their design efforts were greatly facilitated by the fact that, as in the quilting endeavor, each component could be examined and developed in detail with only general reference to the basic requirements and products (inputs and outputs) of the other components. So there was a large element of near-decomposability in the process and its product.

Just as effectuation creates rapidly evolving artifacts that leverage interdependence to exploit locality and contingency, so near-decomposability in the structure of such systems leverages independence to exploit the same locality and contingency. While effectuation stitches together pieces of entrepreneurial fabric into economic quilts that continue to make sense in an interactive and dynamically changing environment, near-decomposability identifies lines of "tearing" so that pieces can be re-worked in synchrony with the overall pattern as the needs imposed by the environment change. Together they provide a convincing explanation, in our opinion, for the creation and growth of large DMNCs in the real world. Investigations into effectuation processes are just beginning. But the admittedly limited evidence examined so far suggests that the theory could hold interesting implications for firm performance, particularly survival and growth over the long run.

## CONCLUSION

To summarize, entrepreneurship offers strategic management a set of relatively new answers to fundamental questions: (1) that firms effectuate; (2) that effectuation, being innately a pluralistic process, explains differentiation even among successful firms; (3) that underlying logic of control in effectuation suggests ways for the headquarters of a large corporation to deal with the inherent tension between creativity and efficiency in their strategy; and, (4) that effectuation combined with the near-decomposable systems it creates can explain firm performance.

The theoretical perspective from entrepreneurship used in this chapter provides several potential avenues for future research in strategic management. In particular, it calls into question the predominant mode of empirical investigations into resource-based theories that seeks to explain firm performance as directly dependent on the resources of the firm. Instead, the ideas presented in this chapter demonstrate the importance of putting Romeo back into the balcony and undertake the more useful approach of connecting particular methods and processes of *resource-use* with firm performance. The dominant implication here is that the mere existence of or access to resources does not by itself explain firm performance. *How* people or firms combine, extrapolate and use those resources matter, and matter greatly. We could speculate, for example, that the strategic history of IBM and Apple with regard to the PC market differed not because they had different resources, but they chose to use them differently – while IBM allowed clones to be manufactured, Apple did not. Similarly, Microsoft and Sun Microsystems use their considerable resources very differently – the former preferring a strictly proprietary and barrier-building approach (the citadel model) to software development as opposed to the latter's open source methods (the bazaar model). Strategic management research should investigate such differential dyadic phenomena at a process level (examining the use of causation versus effectuation, for example) in addition to testing aggregate models of direct relationships between resources and firm performance. Just as, starting with exactly the same set of objects, a Degas and a Dali would create completely different still life paintings, it is conceivable that with the exact same set of resources, different strategic managers might create entirely different strategic universes for their firms.

Strategic management strives to extend economics beyond its preoccupation with the static equilibrium model by injecting time and purposive direction into our understanding of business. Entrepreneurship seeks to enhance strategic management and our larger understanding of business, by turning the spotlight on to the inherent creativity of human action, and by allowing a plurality of human aspirations to emerge as effectual purposes that shape economic endeavors.

## NOTES

1 Weiner took his inspiration from the work of the English writer, Rudyard Kipling.
2 It is worth pointing out when discussing creative processes in the economic domain that for any given new technical invention there are, at least in theory, an infinite number of product possibilities that may flow out of that invention. But, in practice, only a finite sub-set of those possibilities will come into existence. Of those new products that come into existence, only a sub-set is introduced by existing firms. Indeed, a large number of new products are introduced into the economy by new firms. Strategy essentially focuses on existing firms and the activities of existing firms. Entrepreneurship, on the other hand, has been focusing attention on the creative process, particularly of new firms. Where they overlap is at the nexus of the creative process of existing firms. Thus, each field has vast terrains that do not overlap.
3 The choice of the term *firm* and the choice of *focusing on the pre-existing firm* by Rumelt, Schendel, and Teece (1994) only affirm our assertion in the previous footnote.
4 This section summarizes our more detailed exposition titled "Three views of entrepreneurial opportunity."
5 The entrepreneur not only has an idea for a product or firm, but also has some personal aspirations and/or goals in pursuing the opportunity. Goals could be as specific as making an initial public offering (IPO) in five years to creating a legacy for their children. And aspirations could range from making money to enjoying an independent lifestyle to changing the world. Furthermore, these aspirations and goals could change and new ones could emerge over time.
6 We use the terms "rational action" and "creative action" in their precise philosophical/ sociological meanings – such as those used by Parsons (1947) and Joas (1996) respectively. We want to stress that we do not mean creative action to be "irrational," nor do we suggest that rationality cannot lead to creative outcomes in the colloquial sense.
7 In answering these questions posed by Rumelt et al. (1994), we provide a plausible explanation for the survival and growth of *any* large firm, including international firms; rather than focus on the *international* aspects of large firms, we focus on the reasons for their survival and growth.

## REFERENCES

Bar-Hillel, M. (1980). The base-rate fallacy in probability judgments. *Acta Psychologica*, 44: 211–33.

Barney, J. (1991). Firm resources and sustained competitive advantage. *Journal Of Management*, 17(1): 99–121.

Buchanan, J. M. V., and Vanberg, V. J. (1991). The market as a creative process. *Economics and Philosophy*, 7: 167–86.

Chandler, A. D. (1962). *Strategy and structure: Chapters in the History of the Industrial Enterprise.* Cambridge, MA: MIT Press.

Doz, Y. L., and Prahalad, C. K. (1994). Managing DMNCs: A Search for a new Paradigm. In R. Rumelt, D. Schendel, and D. Teece (eds.), *Fundamental Issues in Strategy: A Research Agenda* (495–526). Boston, MA: Harvard Business School Press.

Galambos, L. (1988). What have CEOs been doing? *Journal of Economic History*, 48(2): 242–58.

Gigerenzer, G., Hell, W., and Blank, H. (1988). Presentation and content: The use of base rates as a continuous variable. *Journal of Experimental Psychology: Human Perception and Performance*, 14: 512–25.

Hayek, F. A. (1945). The use of knowledge in society. *The American Economic Review*, 35(4): September, 519–30.

Joas, H. (1996). *The Creativity of Action.* Chicago: University of Chicago Press.

Kirzner, I. (1979). *Perception, Opportunity, and Profit: Studies in the Theory of Entrepreneurship.* Chicago: University of Chicago Press.

Knight, F. H. (1921). *Risk, Uncertainty and Profit.* 1933 edition. New York: Houghton Mifflin.

March, J. G. (1982). The technology of foolishness. In J. G. March and J. P. Olsen (eds.), *Ambiguity and Choice in Organizations.* Bergen: Universitetsforlaget.

March, J. G. (1991). Exploration and exploitation in organizational learning. *Organization Science*, 2(1): 71–87.

Marengo, L., Frenken, K., and Valente, M. (1999). Interdependencies, nearly-decomposability and adaptation. In T. Brenner (ed.), *Computational Techniques for Modelling Learning in Economics.* Kluwer Academic.

McGrath, R. G. (1997). A real options logic for initiating technology positioning investments. *Academy of Management Review*, 22(4): 974–96.

Mintzberg, H. (1978). Patterns in strategy formation. *Management Science*, 24(9): 934–50.

Newman, K. L. (2000). Organizational transformation during institutional upheaval. *Academy of Management Review*, 25(3): 602–19.

Olegario, R. (1997). IBM and the two Thomas J. Watsons. In T. K. McCraw (ed.), *Creating Modern Capitalism.* Cambridge, MA: Harvard University Press.

Parsons, T. (1947). *The Theory of Social and Economic Organizations.* New York: Oxford University Press.

Payne, J. W., Bettman, J. R., and Johnson, E. J. (1993). *The Adaptive Decision Maker.* New York: Cambridge University Press.

Raynor, M. (2000). In R. K. Bresser, M. A. Hitt, R. Nixon, and D. Heuskel (eds). *Winning Strategies in a Deconstructing World*, New York: John Wiley and Sons.

Rumelt, R., Schendel, D., and Teece, D. (1994). Fundamental issues in strategy. In R. Rumelt, D. Schendel and D. Teece (eds.), *Fundamental Issues in Strategy: A Research Agenda:* 9–47. Boston, MA: Harvard Business School Press.

Sarasvathy S. D. (1998). How do firms come to be? Towards a theory of the prefirm. Dissertation. Graduate School of Industrial Administration: Carnegie Mellon University.

Sarasvathy, S. D. (2000). Report on the seminar on research perspectives in entrepreneurship. *Journal of Business Venturing*, 15(1): January, 1–57.

Sarasvathy, S. D. (2001). Causation and Effectuation: Towards a theoretical shift from economic inevitability to entrepreneurial contingency. *Academy of Management Review*, 26, 243–63.

Sarasvathy, S. D., and Simon, H. A. (2000). Effectuation, near decomposability, and the growth of entrepreneurial firms. Paper presented at The First Annual Technology Entrepreneurship Research Policy Conference. University of Maryland, May 2000.

Schumpeter, J. A. (1976). *Capitalism, Socialism, and Democracy.* New York: Harper and Row.

Shane, S., and Venkataraman, S. (2000). The promise of entrepreneurship as a field of research. *Academy of Management Review*, 25(1): 217–27.

Simon, H. A. (1959). Theories of decision making in economics and behavioral science. *American Economic Review*, 49(3): 252–83.

Simon, H. A. (1969). *The Sciences of the Artificial*. Cambridge, MA: MIT Press.

Simon, H. A. (1996). The architecture of complexity. In *The Sciences of the Artificial*, 3rd edn. Cambridge, MA: MIT Press.

Trigeorgis, L. (1993). The nature of option interactions and the valuation of investments with multiple real options. *Journal of Financial and Quantitative Analysis*, 28(1): 1–20.

Tversky, A., and Kahneman, D. (1982). Judgment and uncertainty: Heuristics and biases. In D. Kahneman, P. S. and A. Tversky (eds.), *Judgment and Uncertainty*. (2–20). New York: Cambridge University Press.

Ulrich, D., and Barney, J. B. (1984). Perspectives in organizations: resource dependence, efficiency, and population. *The Academy of Management Review*, 9(3): 471–82.

Venkataraman, S. (1989). *Problems of Small Venture Start-up, Survival, and Growth: A Transaction Set Approach*. Ph.D. Dissertation, University of Minnesota.

Venkataraman, S. (1990). Liabilities of newness, transaction set and new venture development. Working paper No. 104, Department of Management, The Wharton School, University of Pennsylvania.

Venkataraman, S. (1997). The distinctive domain of entrepreneurship research. In *Advances in Entrepreneurship, Firm Emergence and Growth* Vol. 3: 119–38. JAI Press Inc.

Weick, K. E. (1979). *The Social Psychology of Organizing*. Reading, MA: Addison-Wesley.

Wiener, N. (1993). *Invention: The Care and Feeding of Ideas*. Cambridge, MA: MIT Press.

Williamson, O. E. (1975). *Markets and Hierarchies, Analysis and Antitrust Implications: A Study in the Economics of Internal Organization*. New York: Free Press.

# Part V

## TEACHING METHODS

# 25

## The Strategic Management Course: Tools and Techniques for Successful Teaching

### Idalene F. Kesner

As the preceding chapters suggest, the field of strategic management presents many rich and rewarding avenues for conducting research. The same could also be said with regard to teaching in the field. The fact that strategy incorporates many theoretical perspectives and spans many diverse topics allows for tremendous variety in content and teaching methods. In this chapter, these different techniques are reviewed. Prior to this review, however, it is important to note that the emphasis of this chapter is on teaching at the undergraduate and MBA levels. In light of this emphasis, it is useful to begin with a review of the history of the strategy course and its place in the business school curriculum.

### History of the Business Policy/Strategic Management Course

In contrast to accounting and operations, the strategic management discipline and the courses offered in this area have had a relatively short history. Typically labeled as "business policy," early versions of the strategy course were designed as capstone or integrative reviews of the business school curriculum. Indeed, when business schools were first established in the US, they rarely offered separate courses devoted to studying the functions of the general manager. Unterman and Hegarty (1979: 479–80) speculate as to why this might have been the case. According to the authors:

> This may have been because most firms at the time had only one general manager (the president), so that there was little demand for such training; or because the major problems facing businesses at the time were of a financial, manufacturing, or marketing nature; or because no one was available who had the background and skills to teach such a course.

In the late 1950s and early 1960s, however, the environment shifted. Businesses were growing in complexity and size and business school disciplines were being applied to help solve business problems (Unterman and Hegarty, 1979). Moreover, two key 1959 reports (Gordon and Howell, 1959; Pierson, 1959) encouraged the application of academic research to business problems. Speaking directly to the matter of undergraduate business education, Gordon and Howell (1959) recommended that the capstone of the core curriculum be a course in business policy. The objective of this course was to give students an opportunity to combine what they had learned in separate business fields and to utilize this knowledge in analyzing complex business problems. Similarly, on the matter of graduate/masters business education, the authors noted the "obvious" need for an integrating case course in business policy.

Despite the fact that the changing business environment was a key impetus for the inclusion of the policy course in business school curricula in the 1950s and 1960s, the focus of the course during this period was still oriented toward *integration* (of other disciplines) and *culmination* (of a multi-year academic program). The course was rarely seen as having a unique discipline separate and apart from traditional functional areas. Moreover, the faculty who served as the primary instructors were often senior faculty drawn from multiple functional disciplines across the business school. In cases where senior faculty members were not available, outside consultants or senior business executives were often tapped to teach the course.

By the late 1960s, however, things had begun to change. In course syllabi from this period the word "strategy" was pervasive – a stark contrast with the observation in a 1963 Harvard Business School conference, where the use of the word "strategy" appeared in only two syllabi (Hochmuth, 1973). Throughout the 1970s and early 1980s, the field evolved and matured quickly. More and more emphasis was placed on strategy as a differentiated discipline, separate and apart from the other functional areas. This, in turn, led to the emergence of doctoral programs in strategic management – a key step in developing faculty members uniquely trained to teach and conduct research in the area.

Supporting this growth was an emphasis by examining committees of the American Assembly of Collegiate Schools of Business (AACSB). Linked to the accreditation process, *Standard E* called for a course which emphasized the "study of administrative processes under conditions of uncertainty, including integrative analysis and policy determination at the overall management level." Although this standard did not identify a "business policy" or "strategic management" course specifically, it ultimately had the effect of motivating school administrators to include one or more courses in their core curriculum for undergraduate business majors (Unterman, 1979). Indeed, survey results from the early 1980s revealed that 96 percent of 198 schools surveyed required business policy in their AACSB-accredited undergraduate programs (Eldredge and Galloway, 1983).

Despite the convergence of business schools in using the policy course to fulfill AACSB accreditation standards, the proliferation of the course led to a divergence in pedagogical methods and content. Structurally, the courses looked the same, as evidenced by a survey conducted by Eldredge and Galloway (1983).[1] However, the content covered and the teaching methods used varied considerably. In contrast to the early versions of the course in which case teaching was used almost exclusively, other teaching methods such as lectures, simulations, experiential exercises, role-playing, and field projects, were often added to supplement traditional case analysis (Eldredge and Galloway, 1983; Gomolka and Steinhauer, 1977; Unterman, 1979). Content-wise, too, faculty during the early 1980s expanded the topical coverage of the course by including or increasing emphasis in many areas such as international business, non-profit organizations, and small business problems (Eldredge and Galloway, 1983).

Today, the environment has changed dramatically. The strategy course is no longer regarded as the necessary course for meeting AACSB standards. Nevertheless, the course is a well-established part of the core business school curriculum, both at the undergraduate and graduate levels. Moreover, it is common for business schools to offer electives in addition to introductory level strategy courses, and for these courses to be taught by faculty whose educational background and training is in the area of strategic management. The courses taught also use a broad range of pedagogical methods. In the following sections, many of these tools and techniques are explored. The bulk of this chapter is spent discussing the case method because it is the most popular approach for teaching strategy courses. However, in later sections, other methods are explored along with the advantages and disadvantages of each.

## CASE TEACHING

Perhaps the oldest and most popular technique used in the strategy course is the case method (Masoner, 1988). This approach has been used in a variety of disciplines both inside and outside the business school (e.g., law, psychology, public administration, religious studies), but its role in shaping the strategy course cannot be overestimated. Moreover, no school has been more closely associated with this method than the Harvard Business School (Corey, 1980).

When teaching by the case method, an instructor uses a case (or description of a business situation) as a vehicle for students to apply conceptual and decision-making skills. Most cases highlight opportunities or challenges facing an organization and/or its managers. As such, students preparing a case are asked to make decisions about how to address these matters. Case preparation not only requires students to analyze the situation described, but they must also assume the role of decision-maker. Ultimately, what students bring to class discussions is their recommendations as to what actions should be taken. For this reason, cases are a useful pedagogical tool for developing students' creative thinking and problem solving skills.

While there are many differences between case teaching and other methods, what distinguishes this technique most from traditional approaches such as lecture is the active role of students. The cases serve as focal points of the class discussion, and students are encouraged to share their insights throughout the session. While most instructors offer brief formal remarks at the very beginning of a class (to place the case in the context of the overall course) and at the end (to debrief the case analysis process, to summarize lessons learned, and to review how the lessons can be applied in other settings), the bulk of the session is spent discussing the case itself. Consequently, students take the primary responsibility for learning. They help drive the content and direction of that discussion. This spontaneity causes some instructors to feel uncomfortable because they have less control over a case class than a traditional lecture.

Effective case teaching requires that the instructor assume a number of roles and responsibilities (Applegate, 1988; Barnes, Christensen, and Hansen, 1994; Charan, 1975; Corey, 1980; Rangan, 1995; Shapiro, 1984b). Not surprisingly, many of these responsibilities begin even before the actual case class session, and they fall in two main areas: content and process. Content responsibilities include things such as proper selection of cases and readings, while process responsibilities include things such as managing the in-class discussion. Elements of both areas are discussed below.

## Case selection

Case selection is an important first step in the teaching process. There is tremendous variety in the types of cases; therefore matching the case to the class objectives is essential. Case length, style, medium and content are just a few key considerations. In terms of length, strategy cases vary significantly, although most will contain approximately 10–15 pages of text plus another 5–10 pages of exhibits. The length of a case is often a function of the number and complexity of issues addressed. Single-issue cases tend to be shorter and more focused on specific challenges, while multi-issue cases are typically longer and more comprehensive in their coverage. There are also mini-cases, which may be only one or two pages in length. These can be used if instructors want to illustrate specific concepts, and they are short enough to allow multiple cases to be assigned in a single class session. Using two or more mini-cases gives students a chance to compare and contrast industry competitors. Mini-cases are also useful when instructors want to combine case analysis and lecture in a single class session.

In addition to length and complexity, cases also vary significantly in style. Data-rich cases lend themselves to in-depth analyses by students. They are ideal for the latter stages of strategy courses or for strategy courses that are positioned late in a business school's curriculum, because students have had an opportunity to learn various financial analysis tools. In contrast, more qualitative strategy cases can be used effectively to address organizational and cultural matters.

Case length, complexity, and style are important factors to consider when selecting materials for MBA level courses versus undergraduate level courses. MBAs may have an easier time analyzing more complex, lengthy data-rich cases even early in the business school curriculum. This is especially true if a large percentage of students have undergraduate business degrees or extensive managerial work experience. On the other hand, at the undergraduate level, instructors may need to begin with simpler, shorter cases to allow students time to build their case analysis skill. This is especially true if cases are used infrequently in other business courses in the curriculum.

Another stylistic difference is the perspective from which a case is written. Most strategy cases are written from the point of view of the key decision-makers such as the CEO or division president. As such, these cases often end by asking students to compare and contrast alternatives available to the firms' managements, or they invite students to offer their own creative recommendations or "solutions" for the issues facing the subject companies.[2] In still other instances, cases may be written in a manner that reviews a series of past industry or company events. In these instances, the in-class discussion may focus more on lessons learned and only minimally on decision-making and recommendations for the future.

Typically the data and information used in publishing cases has been taken from a variety of different sources. Archival data and materials are often combined with interviews of subject company executives, giving most strategy cases significant depth and breadth of perspective. In most cases, company names and data are real although in some cases certain financial data and/or the names of certain characters may be changed to protect the company and its executives. Using the actual company name is important for a number of reasons. First, it suggests that faculty members can conduct follow-up research to uncover what happened in the events or issues described in the case. Indeed some cases have supplementary materials (e.g., "B" cases), which either reveal outcomes or present the next stages of events described in the primary (or "A") case. Any follow-up research and/or published supplements allow instructors to update students about the industries, the companies, or the managers involved. In fact, some published cases come complete with videotaped Q&A sessions or interviews of company executives. In other instances, instructors may want to take matters one step further by contacting executives from the subject companies and inviting them to participate in the case discussion (either in person or via videoconferencing). While providing updated material and/or executive interactions is not essential to an effective case discussion, it is often well received by students and can add tremendously to the classroom experience.

Perhaps a disadvantage of having undisguised cases is that students can also investigate the subject companies and uncover what happened in the situations described. This is especially easy to accomplish today using the internet. While some instructors see this follow-up research by students as an advantage, it can be a challenge if students are new to case analysis. This is because students often believe that by parroting back what actually happened, they have reached the "correct solution" to the case. This not only runs counter to the notion that there is no single solution, but it can also give a false impression that the actual outcome was the most appropriate. Over time, these disadvantages can be easily handled especially if the actions taken by the actual decision makers proved to be problematic. Instructors can also push students to identify alternative courses of action that would have been equally effective or even more effective for the subject companies.

Today, most cases appear in printed form; however, electronic versions are increasing in popularity. CD-ROM and Web-based cases allow case writers to present information that is not easily covered in hardcopy versions. For example, plant tours, executive interviews, product and/or service demonstrations, and access to the web sites of the company, its competitors and/or suppliers can be integrated into the case text and retrieved on an as needed basis by students. Often, these electronic cases are better able to capture the multidimensional nature of the information available to actual decision-makers.

All of these elements (length, complexity, style, and medium) are important considerations when selecting the ideal cases. For most instructors, the process begins by establishing the objectives for the strategy course overall and for each individual session. This is followed by a search for cases that best fit these needs. Most case collections (e.g., Harvard Business School, Richard Ivey Business School, Darden Business School, and the European Case Clearing House) can be searched online using key words. This produces a list of appropriate abstracts that can be used to further narrow the search process. In some instances, instructors can register in advance with publishers, allowing them to read the full text of the case online. In other instances, instructors must write to publishers for examination copies. Ultimately, however, the process involves reading numerous cases from which only a few may fit an instructor's needs. It is not uncommon, for example, to read three to five cases for each case ultimately selected.

Even after selecting a new case, there is no guarantee it will work well in the classroom setting. Instructors may have to teach a case three or four times before they become familiar with its nuances and can anticipate likely student reactions. Faculty members can enhance this learning process by recording their observations about the case immediately after teaching it. These notes should include information about what worked, what did not work, and new things to try the next time the case is taught. It is important that these notes cover both content and process issues and then to review these notes prior to teaching the case again.

Given the lengthy selection process, instructors will typically use cases for multiple semesters and over multiple years. Nevertheless, it is a good idea to periodically replace cases. One reason is that students may pass down discussion notes or assignments to others from one year to the next. Even in schools where this practice is discouraged, the sharing of material can still occur. Naturally, this can take away from the richness of in-class case discussions, and changing cases periodically can minimize this type of information sharing. Still another reason for periodically changing cases is that new, more recent cases can be added. This process helps ensure that the course and the instructor remain relevant and up-to-date over time.

## *Case preparation*

Although case selection is an important responsibility of the case instructor, it is by no means the only pre-class preparation required. After having selected appropriate cases, an instructor must prepare the materials. This begins by reading the case multiple times to ensure he/she has a command of the basic facts and a thorough understanding of the strategic issues. Indeed, interjecting specific case facts into the in-class discussion is an important way to signal to students that careful and thorough preparation is critical. For this reason, it is not uncommon for top instructors to read the case again prior to each session in which it is used even if they have taught the case many times.

After reading the case, instructors must analyze it. This analysis should be handled using the same strategic tools and frameworks the instructor has introduced to the students. In some instances, case teaching notes are available to help with this analysis. These notes are often written by the author and can enlighten instructors on the author's interpretation and analysis of key issues. While these teaching notes can be helpful, instructors should not rely on them too heavily. First, the issues identified by the author may or may not be the same issues the instructor wants to highlight when teaching the case. Second, the content and process prescribed by the author may not work equally well with all types of students or in all classroom settings or environments. Some teaching notes, for example, may present discussion questions or identify analytical tools that are geared to MBA level courses. Therefore, when using the case in an undergraduate course, instructors may need to change the nature of the discussion questions or simplify the types of analyses conducted. Conversely, other teaching notes may be written in a manner better suited to the undergraduate classroom. In these instances, instructors may need to add questions that will challenge graduate level students. Thus, instructors should be prepared to tailor existing teaching notes or create their own teaching notes depending on the situation.

Most teaching notes include a list of discussion questions. These questions (or customized questions prepared by the instructor) can be distributed in advance to guide students. There are both advantages and disadvantages of providing discussion questions. On the positive side, they tend to increase advanced preparation. This is true regardless of whether students are asked to prepare cases on an individual basis or work in study teams. Discussion questions direct attention toward key issues that the instructor intends to cover during the in-class analysis, and therefore, less time is wasted pursuing unproductive or minor issues when students prepare the case. This type of assistance can also minimize some of the frustrations normally experienced by students, especially undergraduate students or graduate students with non-business backgrounds, who are new to case analysis. Because strategy cases often cover many diverse issues, it can be difficult for students to pinpoint the areas on which to concentrate. Moreover, by increasing advanced preparation, participation in the classroom tends to increase as well.

Despite these advantages, there are also disadvantages of using discussion questions. Importantly, by using this approach, the instructor, not the student, defines the key challenges facing the company and its management. However, an important aspect of strategic thinking is learning how to identify the key issues, and learning how to distinguish relevant information from irrelevant information. If discussion questions provide too much guidance in this area, students may not develop these much needed skills. Furthermore, a list of questions in advance may narrow students' attention too much and limit the instructor's flexibility in the classroom, especially if the expectation is that the in-class analysis will not venture beyond the boundaries set by the discussion questions. Ultimately, the best approach may be one of balance, which can be accomplished in any number of ways. Some instructors may choose to provide discussion questions early in the semester, but eliminate them later to ensure students are able to identify key issues for themselves. Other instructors may alert students in advance that the in-class discussion will go beyond these questions, and therefore, students must extend their preparations as well.

As noted earlier, the ability to update cases is a key advantage when using undisguised companies. Even if an instructor is not interested in presenting this updated information to the students, it is still beneficial to research the company and its situation since the time of the case events. This type of preparation is especially important if students have a tendency to bring current company or industry information into the classroom discussion.

## *Session planning*

When it comes to case teaching, it is important to plan for a session by first thinking about "take-aways" (i.e., themes the instructor wants students to remember as part of the in-class experience). Take-aways can range from defining key strategic concepts to introducing students to essential frameworks or analytical tools. They may even come in the form of general lessons learned. The reason for beginning the planning process this way is that the road map for the session can only be established if the destination is known. An instructor must know where he/she wants to end up before devising the best plan (and timing) for getting there. Moreover, the plan must be flexible. Too much rigidity runs counter to some of the advantages inherent in the case method. On the other hand, teaching a case without any plan can lead to lack of direction and/or incomplete analysis.

For most instructors, the right level of planning begins with establishing several broad themes or topics of discussion and the key questions that will be used to guide that discussion. Next, it is important to consider the weight (in terms of time) to be allocated to each theme. Finally, the instructor must plan any formal remarks (i.e., introductory and concluding remarks), which serve as bookends to the case discussion.

On a related note, some faculty members may take their plans to an even higher level of preparation by doing what is referred to as "planning the boards." Essentially, what this means is the instructor is planning where various points will be placed on the classroom blackboards. This adds a higher level of organization to the case discussion and may even improve student learning. On the downside, not every classroom is properly configured to accommodate this level of planning, and if the boards are planned in too much detail, this can result in an overly structured classroom discussion.

## Room configuration/preparation

Most instructors give little thought to room configuration, but when it comes to case teaching, this is an important consideration. Of course, faculty members may not always have the freedom or flexibility to select the room they want. In these circumstances, an instructor must work with what is available. Ideally, however, in case discussions, it is best to have students facing each other (e.g., in a U-shaped classroom) rather than having them face forward (e.g., in a theater-style classroom). When facing each other, students are more likely to engage classmates in a debate over issues rather than filtering their comments through the instructor, who is positioned in the front of the room. This reinforces the notion that in a case course much of the learning is student-driven. When ideal room configurations are not available, instructors can use a variety of techniques to encourage direct student-to-student interactions. One approach is for the instructor to move throughout the classroom. This invites broad participation and a multidirectional flow of conversation. Another approach is to ask questions in a manner that forces students to respond to each other. For example, once a student has made a comment, the instructor can ask the next student to respond directly to the preceding remark.

There are still other classroom features that should be taken into consideration when planning a case session. Natural breaks or sections in a classroom or moveable chairs can be used to divide the group. Different sides of the room can be asked to assume different roles/perspectives (e.g., executive A versus executive B; country A versus country B; parent company versus subsidiary) or different sides can be asked to defend different options or strategic recommendations (e.g., option A versus option B versus option C).

## Equipment preparation

Unlike other teaching methods such as computer simulation, no special equipment is needed for case discussion. A blackboard, overhead projector, or flipchart can be used to track the discussion as it progresses. A videocassette recorder (VCR) is required if cases include taped interviews and/or executive Q&A sessions. Some instructors find, however, that multiple blackboards and computer projection devices can be very advantageous. The former ensures adequate space to organize the discussion and the latter can be very effective for summarizing various points at the end of the class or for showing back-up financial analyses to support one's recommendations.

## Readings selection and preparation

In addition to the case, many instructors also assign supplemental readings. These may be readings from various practitioner business journals (e.g., *Harvard Business Review*, *California Management Review*, *Sloan Management Review*, *Academy of Management Executive*, *Business Horizons*) or from business newspapers and magazines (e.g., *The Wall Street Journal*, *Business Week*, *Fortune*, *Forbes*, *The Economist*). The key in selecting readings is to make sure that the topic and level are appropriate for the class and course. Readings should reinforce key concepts that will be drawn out in case discussions and/or introduce students to frameworks useful in analyzing cases. Emphasizing readings during the in-class case discussion can help students make the connections between strategic theory and practice. It is also important that instructors assign an appropriate number of readings. Graduate level students can often read two or three supplemental articles in addition to a lengthy strategy case. This is especially true if there is a mixture of longer, journal articles and shorter, magazine or newspaper articles. When teaching an under-graduate strategy course, instructors may need to limit the number of supplemental readings to one or two.

## In-class discussion management

Much like the conductor in an orchestra, the case teacher's main role during the actual discussion is to act as facilitator. As such, he/she must engage as many students as possible in the conversation. The most effective case instructors often use a variety of techniques to promote participation.

The most common format in case teaching is for the instructor to pose questions throughout the session that guide the conversation in certain directions. There is no single best direction; rather progression depends on the case. In some instances it is best to begin the discussion with a review of the facts and a basic description of the situation. From here, the discussion may progress to analysis and recommendations. In other instances, the case discussion is best handled by beginning with recommendations and then moving backwards to identify reasons or justifications for the recommendations offered.

With either of these approaches, it is important to promote student involvement and participation in the discussion. One method for doing this is to use what is referred to as "cold calling." This means calling on students to contribute to the discussion even when they do not volunteer by raising their hands. While cold calling is a more popular technique at the graduate level, some instructors are hesitant to use this in an under-graduate classroom, where students may have less work and academic experience. The successful use of cold calling at either level may also be a function of the school's culture and history with this technique. In schools where cold calling is not commonly used, it is important that instructors using this approach set clear and consistent expectations at the start of the course.

It is also important to note that cold calling may be more challenging in classrooms with a high percentage of international students. Depending on students' language skills and cultural backgrounds, they may feel uncomfortable speaking in classroom settings especially when the class size is large. In other cases, international students may appreciate cold calling because this technique forces a more rapid integration into the classroom environment. Instructors who are worried about using this technique with international students may want to begin with milder versions sometimes referred to as "warm calling." In this instance, an instructor may speak to students prior to the class and alert them to questions that they will be called on to answer. This gives international students a chance to consider questions in advance without the pressure and intensity often associated with cold calling. Over time, as students gain greater comfort with the classroom environment, the instructor can move away from the practice of advanced notification.

Many instructors use a combination of volunteers and cold calls. Mixing classroom management techniques in this way ensures adequate advanced preparation and comprehensive participation. Another method for increasing participation is to invite students to assist with key transition points. This is particularly useful for engaging graduate and undergraduate students who are new to case analysis and, therefore, may be hesitant to share their recommendations about how to resolve case issues. It also sends a strong signal that active listening is an important part of the case process. An example of this may be to ask a student to summarize the main points he/she has heard or to share his/her impressions about the overall class sentiment(s).

A third method for increasing student participation at both the undergraduate and MBA levels is to identify a limited set of options available to the decision-maker, and then ask each student to vote on which course of action he/she would recommend. Having the information in advance of the in-class discussion may be helpful, and therefore, some instructors may ask students to cast their votes electronically. In other cases, instructors can better orchestrate the in-class discussion by having students post their votes in front of them during the class sessions. Simple codes such as arrows ($\uparrow$, $\downarrow$) letters (A, B, C) or numbers (1, 2, 3) can be used to effectively communicate students' recommendations regarding particular courses of action. For example, students posting up arrows ($\uparrow$) may support a particular action by a company, while students posting down arrows ($\downarrow$) may be opposed to the action. When using this method in the classroom, instructors can choose when to bring certain students into the conversation depending on the vote cast. This creates a debate-like atmosphere, which often increases overall participation. Another advantage of this procedure is that students often show greater commitment to or ownership of a particular course of action if they have to visibly display their position.

While faculty-directed discussion is the most popular technique, it is by no means the only method used to teach cases. Some instructors use participant-led discussions (individually-based or team-based) to increase student involvement in both undergraduate and MBA classes. This approach can be useful but often requires meeting with discussion leaders in advance to review their analyses and class plans. Assigning roles to students in advance of class or asking some students to serve as devil's advocates during the in-class discussion are also useful techniques for increasing participation. Individuals and/or teams may be asked to assume unique perspectives and defend those positions. This technique can be especially useful if it is important to surface all sides or positions during the course of the discussion.

Some instructors take this approach one step further by requiring students (or student teams) to prepare formal presentations. Speakers may be asked to assume the role of an outside consultant, an external analyst, a member of management or even a board of directors member. Using this perspective, they are required to present their analysis of the case and/or their recommendations. Audience members may also be asked to assume roles as they listen to the presentations, and in some instances, classmates may be encouraged to participate by asking questions after the presenter concludes his/her formal remarks.

There are both advantages and disadvantages to requiring these types of formal presentations. On the positive side, these presentations allow students to develop their oral communication skills and to practice team skills if the analysis is handled as a group assignment. Development of communication skills is important for both undergraduates and MBAs, but it may be especially important for international students. Moreover, using groups to prepare cases can promote valuable cross-cultural interaction especially between domestic and international students. This approach encourages students to learn from each other (both in terms of content and process issues), and it introduces variety into the classroom format. On the downside, formal presentations are not always the best use of limited class time. Students may not be interested in each other's presentations or interest may wane over time. This is especially true if this approach is overused or if the presentations are of poor quality.

One way to mitigate these limitations may be to set up out-of-class sessions where students make presentations to the instructor rather than the entire class. While this approach offers class members an opportunity to practice communication skills, it can be very time consuming for instructors. It also limits the ability of students to learn by observing each other. Another option is to design a case competition. In this type of exercise, multiple student teams analyze the same case and present to evaluators. In addition to the instructor, other academics and/or business practitioners might be used to judge presentations. If the competition is set up in a tournament format with multiple rounds, final round presentations can be made during actual class sessions. This approach limits the number of overall sessions used for student presentations yet allows for at least some learning by allowing participants to observe finalists. Case competitions can be used at both the graduate and undergraduate level. They can also be used across class sections and even between schools.

## Evaluation techniques

As with any teaching method, instructors using the case method must give ample consideration to feedback and evaluation procedures. There are two categories of feedback – short-term and long-term. Short-term or immediate feedback is information provided to students during or immediately after the in-class case discussion. This includes things such as recognizing students who make key points or aid the discussion by challenging fellow classmates. This feedback, plus recognizing good performance by the class as a whole, reinforces positive behaviors such as insightful observations/questions, thorough analysis, advanced preparation, and active debate. This short-term feedback need not be unidirectional, however. Students can provide feedback to the instructor by summarizing "lessons learned" at the end of the case discussion. If these comments miss the mark, instructors may want to help draw out more relevant observations and make adjustments when teaching this or other cases in the future.

Providing long-term feedback, especially on an individual basis, is more challenging. Because participation is often a significant part of students' grades in case courses, instructors need effective evaluation techniques for tracking participation over time. Many instructors simply take notes after each class session, highlighting the contributions of members. Grading schemes need not be elaborate. Some instructors use three to five point scales ranging from "excellent" to "unsatisfactory/poor." For instructors who want greater accuracy or precision, another option is to record sessions and evaluate participation afterwards by reviewing the audiotapes. Still other instructors use assistants or even students to serve as scribes, recording the contributions of participants. If students are used as scribes, they should be encouraged to record only the content of what is said; they should not assess the value of the contributions. At a later point, when reviewing the scribes' notes, the instructor can evaluate value or quality and assign appropriate grades. Using multiple scribes and comparing their notes can help ensure accuracy. If students are used to assist with recording the case discussions, it may be a good idea to rotate the position so that the scribes are not excluded from future case discussions.

All of the above evaluation techniques can be used to establish participation grades and provide feedback to students. Regardless of the technique used, however, it is important that instructors evaluate more than just the quantity of comments made. Evaluating the quality of students' contributions is essential and signals that effective case discussion means more than controlling "air time." Poor quality remarks are those that demonstrate poor preparation, show lack of thought or logic and/or are inconsistent with case facts/data. In contrast, high quality comments contribute positively either to problem definition or resolution of the case issues. According to Corey (1976), high-quality problem definition means that students have: (a) named immediate issues and defined them in ways that call for action, (b) put these issues in the proper context, and (c) dealt with the problems from the perspective of an individual manager. On the other hand, a high quality response to case issues means that students have: (a) explicitly responded to specific problems and broad issues, (b) supported their recommendations by sound analysis and balanced arguments (including both the pros and cons of a recommended course of action), and (c) included ideas for implementation.

One challenge many instructors face is deciding what percentage of a student's overall course grade should be attributed to in-class participation. For some instructors who rely heavily on the case method, student participation counts for a high percentage of a student's overall course grade (e.g., 50–75 percent). For other instructors, participation may account for a smaller percentage (e.g., 10–25 percent). In general, graduate level courses tend to place greater emphasis on this element than undergraduate courses. Regardless of the course level, however, the decision of how much to emphasize in-class participation in the grading scheme of the course should be based on the instructor's objectives and his/her comfort level with facilitating, measuring and evaluating participation.

If formal presentations are used as part of case analyses in a strategy course, instructors should be prepared to provide feedback on content and process matters. This feedback can be communicated using a structured or unstructured evaluation form. If a structured form is used, instructors are encouraged to distribute the form to students in advance. This step can help improve student performance and enhance learning.

In addition to evaluating in-class participation and presentations, many case instructors also use written assignments to evaluate students. In strategy courses, it is common for instructors to assign "briefs" or short papers. These may be structured using assignment questions provided in advance, or they may be open-ended such that students must identify the key issues and offer their analyses and recommendations. In general, structured briefs may be more effective in undergraduate courses or where students are less familiar with cases analysis. International students, too, may prefer more structured written assignments. Unstructured briefs work well in graduate level courses especially later in the semester once students have developed their skills in the area of case analysis.

Cases can be used for midterm or final exams in courses as well. As with briefs, these exams may or may not involve the use of assignment questions, and they may or may not be handled as in-class assignments. When using case exams, instructors will want to pay particular attention to length and complexity. Shorter, less complex cases may be best suited to undergraduate strategy courses. Longer, more complex cases may be best suited to MBA level courses. Corey (1980) offers suggestions as to the cases best suited for exams. According to the author, an exam case should:

- provide adequate coverage of course material;
- be of reasonable length (i.e., so that the bulk of the exam period may be used for analysis rather than reading and digesting facts);
- require some quantitative analysis;
- contain both explicitly stated problems and broad issues;
- allow for multiple responses (i.e., avoid "one right answer"); and
- offer a wide range of student performance.

Corey also highlights elements an instructor should look for when evaluating case exams such as effective problem definition, adequate coverage of issues, relevant conclusions, supportive quantitative analyses, logical recommendations, and explicit action plans.

## Summary

Overall, there are both advantages and disadvantages of using the case method in strategy courses. On the positive side, cases provide a real world context in which to teach strategy concepts and tools and essential skills (e.g., critical thinking, quantitative and qualitative analysis, communications). Rather than a passive approach to education, case teaching is active. It promotes a dynamic interchange between faculty members and their students as well as among students. Moreover, case teaching reinforces the fact that there is no single right answer and that strategic challenges as well as solutions are multidisciplinary and multidimensional.

On the downside, however, some instructors may feel that they have less control in classes taught using the case method, especially when compared to lecture format. Given the cross-disciplinary nature of strategy cases, this can be particularly challenging if faculty members have limited cross-functional knowledge or experience. Furthermore, if the case class is poorly managed, take-aways may be limited. This, in turn, could lead students to question the value of case discourse. One way to mitigate this problem is for instructors to prepare adequately in advance. This includes thoroughly reviewing the case materials and external resources, planning the session (including timing, board plans, and formal remarks), using techniques to promote active student participation, and facilitating (versus controlling) the in-class discussion. Another way to mitigate the problem is to encourage adequate advanced preparation on the part of students. Instructors should make clear their expectations regarding preparation and participation. Indeed, the earlier these expectations are set, and the more consistently they are applied, the better the experience. For students who are unfamiliar with case analysis, instructors may want to provide reading materials, which inform them about their roles and responsibilities in a case class (e.g., Mauffette-Leenders, Erskine and Leenders, 1997; Corey, 1976; Shapiro, 1984a; Bonoma, 1989; Hammond, 1990).

## OTHER TEACHING METHODS

While the case method is one of the most popular pedagogical techniques used in strategy courses, it is by no means the only approach used. Other methods include lecture, experiential exercises, field projects, computer simulations, problem-based learning, and online distance education. Each is discussed in turn.

### *Lecture*

Some instructors rely heavily on lecture to convey important strategic concepts and to educate students about various strategic analysis tools. Typically, in a lecture format, there is less interaction and discussion between an instructor and class members than in a case discussion format. Indeed, in lecture courses with very large enrollments, the professor may be the only verbal participant. There are both advantages and disadvantages of using a lecture format. On the positive side, lectures can be very efficient for disseminating information. This is especially true if the instructor does a good job of organizing material. From the faculty member's perspective, a lecture format is easier to control and requires less preparation on the part of students.

On the downside, a lecture approach is a more passive teaching method, and if managed poorly, lectures can become monotonous. Students may not retain the bulk of the information disseminated especially if they do not use the material relatively quickly or if they find little direct relevance or value to what is presented. This can be an important issue especially when teaching strategy to undergraduates. Many strategy topics (especially at the corporate strategy level) are aimed at the highest levels of an organization. Therefore, students may not regard the lecture content as directly applicable or immediately useful. The passive nature of lectures may also signal to students that advanced preparation is not required. Like other teaching methods, the effectiveness of the lecture format is heavily dependent on the quality of instruction. Faculty members who are poor presenters and have ineffective oral communication styles tend to be poorly received by students.

Another disadvantage of the lecture method is that it tends to focus on one particular type of student learner – reflective, abstract conceptual learners. These learners tend to perceive information using mental or visual conceptualizations. The lecture method may be less effective with students who learn through concrete experience or active experimentation.

Fortunately, there are many things faculty members can do to mitigate some of these disadvantages. One way to engage students is to intersperse other teaching techniques with the lecture method. Mini-case discussions, small group problem solving, experiential exercise, role play, film clips and other multimedia elements can all be used to add variety to a traditional lecture format and increase student participation and active learning. Some instructors, for example, organize students into small teams during class sessions. This allows students an opportunity to discuss case issues, apply strategy concepts or solve problems using illustrative data. Other instructors manage in-class participation by using some of the techniques identified earlier such as cold calling or calling on student volunteers to answer questions about cases or readings prepared in advance.

If lecture is used exclusively, instructors are advised to be cautious about presenting too many concepts or tools in any one session. When lecturing, it is easy to overwhelm students by covering too much material. Moreover, incorporating ample company and industry examples can reinforce the various concepts discussed. For students who have little prior business experience, instructors may need to begin by highlighting basic strategy concepts in more personal ways. Asking students to think first about their own personal "core competencies," for example, may be a way to introduce students to this complex concept before elevating the discussion to the corporate level.

Effective use of handouts can also help minimize some of the disadvantages of lecture. While students express a preference for complete handouts which contain everything said or displayed by the instructor, successful lecturers often recommend using more of an outline handout where students are forced to fill in information based on material presented in the lecture itself. The belief is that this approach keeps students more actively engaged in the presentation.

When using the lecture method, tracking students' comprehension and understanding can be more challenging than when using more interactive teaching techniques. In case classes, for instance, dialogue can be evaluated continuously and when the instructor hears points that are off-target or in error, he/she can interject with clarifying or corrective comments. In a lecture, problems or confusion on the part of students may be harder to detect because there is less in-class dialogue. To facilitate feedback to the instructor, some faculty members select several students at random after the lecture is complete to summarize in writing the key points learned during the session. This information can be both enlightening and humbling, and it provides a quick snapshot about presentation effectiveness. Instructors can then use this feedback when structuring and revising future lectures.

Instructors who rely heavily on the lecture method typically use supporting materials such as strategy textbooks and/or readings. There are many textbooks from which to choose, and faculty members should request examination copies to review before making their final selection. Some texts are divided into chapters covering both strategy formulation and strategy implementation (e.g., David, 1999; Thompson and Strickland, 1998). These books often include chapters that closely follow the sequence of strategic planning from establishment of mission/vision, analysis of the external and internal environment, identification, evaluation and choice of strategic alternatives, and implementation. There is, however, significant variety from one textbook to the next, and there are several other approaches that are gaining in popularity. The resource-based approach (e.g., Collis and

Montgomery, 1997; Hitt, Ireland, and Hoskisson, 2001) and the decision-making/ learning approach (e.g., Bourgeous, Duhaime, and Stimpert, 1999) are just two examples of the newer frameworks being used. Importantly, each instructor should search for the presentation approach that best matches the framework he/she intends to follow in the course.

Many texts come complete with supplemental materials such as videotapes and CD-ROMs. These tools can be very effective for introducing variety into traditional lectures, and they can help students link theory to practice. Readings can also be used to supplement text material whenever an instructor wants to offer more thorough coverage of a topic or issue. As noted earlier, these readings can be selected from practitioner-oriented business journals and business newspapers and magazines.

Another technique for combining theory and practice is for instructors to blend lecture and case analysis. Many strategy textbooks include cases to facilitate this process. Indeed, most publishers publish strategy texts as whole units (i.e., combining text, cases and/or readings) and as separate pieces. The latter allows instructors to pick-and-choose the items they want to use. Some authors have published smaller texts in order to allow instructors greater flexibility to supplement the material with individually selected cases, readings, simulations, and exercises. There are also several publishing firms which allow instructors to design their own books, combining selected text, readings, and cases from the company's inventory of published materials.

Alternating between lecture and case analysis from one class session to the next can be especially effective in undergraduate strategy courses where students may have had little exposure to strategy concepts and tools in either their previous educational or work experiences. There are several ways to combine case teaching and lecture (Rangan, 1995). "Theorizing a case" is when instructors use cases as the vehicles in their lectures to convey conceptual and theoretical knowledge. "Illustrating a case" is when instructors use cases in their lectures to illustrate certain management ideas. The third approach, "choreographing a case" is the process described earlier in this chapter. According to Rangan (1995), all three methods can be effective but the value of the learning experience may differ depending on student level and instructor skill.

The same equipment required for case teaching works well when using a lecture format, and no special class configuration is needed. Evaluation often occurs in the form of exams and quizzes. The type of exam (e.g., essay, short answer, or multiple choice) varies depending on the course level. In undergraduate courses, instructors may prefer using techniques like short answer and multiple choice exams to ensure students are learning basic strategic concepts and tools. Essay questions can be used too, and they are especially effective if an instructor wants to assess students' abilities to apply concepts and tools. At the graduate level, instructors may want to rely more on essay questions and case analysis in order to assess students' strategic thinking skills.

### Experiential exercises

Another way to add variety to the strategy classroom is to use experiential exercises. Although this method is more commonly used in organizational behavior and human resource courses, some exercises may be very effective when teaching basic strategy concepts. Game theory principles, for example, or merger negotiations can be easily demonstrated using this method and can work well in either undergraduate or MBA classrooms.

Role-play, which was discussed briefly in the section on case analysis, is one type of experiential exercise that can be used in the strategy course. When first introducing role play exercises, students may have a difficult time staying "in character." One technique to overcome this problem is for the instructor to assume one of the roles in the exercise. This works well especially if a student is assigned the role of the chief decision-maker in the case, while the instructor assumes the perspective of someone negatively impacted by the proposed recommendation(s).

One obstacle instructors may face when using this teaching method is finding experiential exercises that are well suited to strategy courses. There are few books written specifically for this area. In some instances, however, instructors can modify exercises used in other areas such as economics, marketing, organizational behavior, and human resource management. Another challenge instructors may face is evaluating students. While it may be difficult to assign a grade on performance in the exercise, some instructors require students to write a summary of lessons learned. This can be a useful tool when assessing the effectiveness of this teaching technique.

## Field projects

There are many types of field projects that can be used in strategy courses. One type is archival in nature. Students conduct research on specific strategy topics or investigate companies under the supervision of an instructor. The topics for these reports can either be generated by the instructor or by the students. Many students like the independence and individuality of field research projects. They value the ability to explore timely strategy issues (or companies) in an in-depth manner. Even so, field research may require instructor involvement outside of class to assist students with their projects, and these projects can be very time consuming to evaluate. Archival projects of this type can be useful in both undergraduate and graduate level courses, where students need to develop their research skills.

Practicums are another type of field project. In this case, students are required to interact with executives from actual companies. These assignments can be very effective tools for linking strategy theory and practice, and students tend to evaluate these projects quite highly because of the hands-on experience involved. Moreover, practicums can help students build skills across a number of areas ranging from critical thinking and analysis to creativity and communications. Practicums are especially effective in MBA level courses where some students can rely on prior business experience.

While practicums are extremely popular in courses such as entrepreneurship and management consulting, they can be somewhat challenging to use in strategy courses for a number of reasons. First, many of the projects that students might be exposed to are functional-level strategy issues rather than corporate-level or business-level. Corporate executives may be hesitant to involve students, especially undergraduates, in high-level strategic matters. Second, arranging sufficient projects can be difficult, particularly when class size is large. In some instances, instructors may choose to assign the same company project to multiple class members or teams; however, this arrangement can place a burden on the company and executives involved. Like field research projects, grading final reports and/or presentations can be difficult. This is especially true given that external cooperation will vary from one firm to the next giving student teams more or less access to relevant information. Because of the interaction with real world companies, practicums often require an even higher level of out-of-class instructor involvement than field research projects.

## Computer simulations

Like practicums, simulations can be another effective means of linking strategic theory and practice. Each participating team competes head-to-head with others in a computer game. There are literally dozens of different simulations available for use in strategy courses, and many of these programs do an excellent job of simulating real world market conditions. They offer students a wide range of strategic decision-making possibilities at both the business-level and functional level, and some even offer students the opportunity to make corporate-level strategic decisions. Simulations can be especially effective at the undergraduate level where students may have limited or no prior work experience.

Simulations are usually centered on a single industry and particular product(s). Some popular examples include the athletic footwear industry, the cereal food industry, and the airline industry. In most simulations, student teams make decisions across all functional areas – marketing, distribution, operations/manufacturing, human resource management, and finance. Today, most games are global in nature and include added features that can be activated (or deactivated) depending on the needs of the instructor and student level (i.e., undergraduate versus MBA). These features can be as simple as unexpected changes in tariffs, interest rates or exchange rates or as complex as product failure crises or labor strikes.

Prior to the start of the game, an instructor must determine the number of industries, the number of companies/teams per industry, and the number of students per team. These decisions are often a function of class size. If the desired team size is three to five members, for example, the instructor can work backwards to determine the number of teams needed. The parameters of the computer simulation will often determine whether these teams can operate in a single industry or whether they need to be divided across multiple industries. A faculty member must also decide how much time to allow between decision periods and how many rounds to play.

There are both advantages and disadvantages to using computer simulations. In general, students tend to rate simulations highly because they are dynamic and provide direct, hands-on experience. However, some students may link their evaluations of the experience to their team's outcome in the game (e.g., if their team won, students may rate the experience highly, while if their team lost, they may give the experience a lower rating). In turn, this suggests that students may not always be able to separate their successes and failures in the game from the lessons learned in the broader strategic environment.

Still another disadvantage is that simulations can be costly and often place a high administrative burden on the instructor. Running the game requires an extensive commitment of time outside of the classroom dealing with questions and problems. One way to mitigate the costs in terms of administration time is to use Web-based interactive simulations. These are relatively new, but offer many benefits including online administration services, which are centrally located. Typically, user fees are charged on a per student basis. Another advantage of Web-based games is that the competition can reach beyond the confines of a single classroom. Many of these games allow students to compete with teams from other schools around the world.

Another drawback of simulations is that some students may spend much of their time trying to figure out the computer model used to build the simulation rather than focusing on the business concepts being emphasized. This naturally detracts from the value of the game as a learning tool for strategy. Related to this is a problem often referred to as "end-gaming." When an instructor announces the number of decision periods in advance, he/she may encourage end-game strategies on the part of students. These strategies might include things such as divesting assets, dumping inventory, and/or eliminating maintenance or capital expenditures, all of which may be considered poor long-term decisions. To avoid these types of end-game actions, instructors may want to keep secret the number of rounds that will be played. If this is not an option, it is important to use multiple performance measures when determining a "winner." By using several measures, including both long-term and short-term indicators, end-game maneuvers can be discouraged.

As pedagogical tools, many instructors feel simulations are uniquely positioned to provide students with a feel for the multi-functional nature of business and a sense of the consequences of their decisions. According to Thompson and Strickland (1998: xii), for example:

> simulations games are *the single best exercise available* for helping students understand how the functional pieces of a business fit together and giving students an integrated, capstone experience . . . [Students] become active strategic thinkers, planners, analysts, and decision-makers. By having to live with the decisions they make, students experience what it means to be accountable for decisions and responsible for achieving satisfactory results. All this serves to drill students in responsible decision-making and improve their business acumen and managerial judgment.

In addition to assisting students in developing business judgment, encouraging students to integrate what they have learned from previous courses, and forcing students to implement their decisions and live with the consequences, simulations also offer students an opportunity to test strategy concepts in an entrepreneurial environment. Few teaching methods engender as much enthusiasm and competitive spirit as computer simulations. Motivation levels tend to be high through the duration of the game, and students often devote incredible amounts of time analyzing computer output.

While simulations inspire students to use the quantitative tools they have learned in their various courses, games can also be a good opportunity to explore qualitative issues. Because most simulations are team-based, students face many of the challenges typically found in group settings. Satisficing behavior, tendency toward individual domination, groupthink, conflicting norms and expectations, and slower decision-making are just a few of the many issues that students must work through to establish an effective team. Thus, participants get hands-on experience in dealing with many of the issues covered in their organizational behavior courses.

Some instructors may wish to add even more depth to the team experience by requiring students to establish an organizational structure and requiring team members to assume specific roles or positions (e.g., CEO/president, vice president, director, supervisor). Using games that permit takeovers, for example, and allowing students to manage the human dynamics of this action is an effective way to teach students about the human side of acquisitions. Establishing external boards of directors adds still another layer of realism to simulations especially if these boards use business practitioners. Involvement of directors can be frequent (e.g., beginning with interviewing candidates for key positions such as CEO and including periodic company updates and final presentations) or infrequent (e.g., evaluating final presentations only). The level of involvement would depend on the amount of time available to run the simulation and the amount of time and energy external participants (and instructors) are willing to devote to the exercise.

Clearly, simulations require specially equipped classrooms if decisions are run during class sessions. If instructors do not have access to computer classrooms, they can require students to input decisions outside of class. However, at a minimum, it is useful to have a computer projection device available when training students on the basic procedures of the simulation.

Evaluating and grading simulations is another key issue that must be considered. Instructors may want to base at least a portion of students' grades on the outcome of the simulation. Requiring students to write (and present) periodic memos and/or final reports, which summarize their firm's strategy and their view of the competitive landscape, are also elements that can be graded. Reports of this type are effective because they require students to reflect on what they have learned throughout the experience. Some instructors may even want to take the next step of requiring students to present a future plan based on circumstances at the end of the game.

## Problem-based learning

While the teaching methods described above are used frequently in strategy courses, a newer technique, known as problem-based learning (PBL), is rapidly making its way into the classroom environment. Simply put, PBL is an instructional approach in which students are asked to find solutions to ill-structured problems. *PBL Insight* (1998: 5), a newsletter devoted to the subject, offers the following description:

> In PBL, the student actively, and often collaboratively, pursues knowledge and gains problem solving and critical thinking skills. Students are self-directed and, therefore, assume greater responsibility for their learning. The instructor acts as facilitator, resource guide, and/or task group consultant, while retaining the role of subject matter expert and carrying out the tasks of determining critical course content and desired learning outcomes ... Problems function to provide a context for the information. They allow students to develop flexible, cognitive strategies, which help them analyze unanticipated situations to produce viable solutions. To that end, PBL emphasizes the importance of interdisciplinary connection and finding and using appropriate learning resources.

Although a couple of schools have used PBL to structure their entire MBA program, in most cases instructors imbed PBL exercises into individual courses at the graduate and undergraduate level. The process often begins in the first few weeks of a course by having an instructor present a complex, ill-structured and open-ended problem to students who are organized into teams. The problem presented should be controversial so that students are quickly drawn into the discussion and so that no single answer or solution exists. Selecting an appropriate problem is critical for success. According to Duch, Allen, and White (1998), a good PBL problem:

- engages students' interests and motivates them to probe for deeper understanding of the concepts;
- relates the subject to the real world so that students have a stake in solving the problem;
- requires students to make decisions based on facts, information, logic and/or rationalization;
- requires students to define what assumptions are needed (and why), what information is relevant, and/or what steps or procedures are required to solve the problem;
- conveys only a portion of the information needed to solve the problem, thereby requiring students to use external resources,
- requires students to work together to solve the problem (versus a "divide and conquer" approach); and
- incorporates the content (and skill-building) objectives of the course.

Full class sessions typically serve as bookends to PBL exercises. A class may meet at the beginning of a PBL exercise as the assignment is made and at the end of the project to allow student teams to present their findings, summarize lessons learned, and debrief the exercise. Periodic meetings of the full class may be called throughout the PBL process to reveal additional information, discuss common issues or concerns across teams, and/or educate students on new tools and concepts useful in completing the assignment. For the most part, however, student teams are required to work independently in order to solve problems. Thus, each team is responsible for all aspects of the solution including selecting appropriate resources, deciding which analyses to perform, and fashioning recommendations for how the problem can be resolved. In essence, PBL requires that students do the following: (a) confront real world problems, (b) assess what is known and unknown, (c) identify, locate and analyze critical information, and (d) formulate and communicate their solutions to others.

For each PBL exercise imbedded in a course, instructors serve as facilitators. Students may consult with faculty members for advice; however, the amount of assistance they receive (and the number of interim full class meetings held) will depend on their experience with PBL and the objectives of the instructor. Students new to the PBL process may be given more assistance in the first PBL assignment, but less assistance in subsequent assignments as they build problem-solving skills. Similarly, students in undergraduate strategy courses may be given more guidance than MBA students, who have more experience in solving complex, ill-structured problems because of prior work and educational experiences. According to Duch, Allen, and White (1998), the faculty member's role in the process is to guide, probe for deeper understanding, and support student initiatives. Faculty members should not offer too much information in the form of lectures. Instead, students should be required to uncover essential problem-related concepts as part of the PBL exercise.

PBL shares many of the advantages found in other teaching methods. For example, because it is team-based, it shares many of the same behavioral benefits as computer simulations. Like case analysis, PBL treats the instructor's role as that of facilitator, and the method places a high degree of emphasis on creative thinking and problem solving. Like field projects, PBL allows students to develop the key skills of retrieving and utilizing external resources.

While PBL has many advantages, there are also some downside issues that faculty members need to consider. First, PBL is a very time-consuming teaching method and often requires strong administrative support. While less in-class time is needed, extensive interaction is often required outside of the classroom. If the method is to be effective, faculty members must be available when students run into major challenges requiring insight and advice. Second, evaluating projects can be challenging. Team reports and presentations are likely to be very unique making comparisons across teams very difficult. Moreover, because PBL works best when the instructor provides relatively little advanced guidance and formal structure to the output, students may not always understand or feel comfortable with the criteria on which they are being evaluated. Third, many students unaccustomed to PBL, may experience high degrees of anxiety and frustration during initial stages. Students may long for traditional teaching approaches where they take notes, go home and memorize them. This reaction is likely to wane over time, however, as students gain a greater level of comfort with PBL. Yet, it is not only the students who may feel unease with this approach. Faculty members, too, may experience some discomfort because of a perceived loss of control. Instructors who are flexible, capable of coping with ambiguity and uncertainty, and reasonably knowledgeable from a cross-disciplinary perspective are best able to handle this teaching method.

### Web-based education

Another new area of teaching is Web-based education. Although still in its infancy, there are already numerous Web-based interfaces, which faculty members can use to build online courses. In some cases, these are customized, exclusive programs produced by universities, while in other instances the programs are produced and maintained by independent organizations but shared by subscribing institutions and/or instructors.

Many strategy instructors, who have created internet-based courses, use the Web to post materials such as syllabi, readings, case resources, and links to company Web sites and reference materials (e.g., business newspapers and magazines). In these instances, use of the internet tends to be unidirectional; students use the course Web site primarily to retrieve information or data. More advanced uses of the internet promote two-way communications by allowing students to complete assignments and conduct research online. They also promote instructor-to-student and student-to-student interactivity via synchronous (e.g., course chatrooms and video-based instruction) and asynchronous (electronic bulletin boards/discussion forums) communications. Some instructors have even extended this use by including student-to-executive communications as a means of supplementing case analyses and strategy concept discussions.

The benefits of online courses are many. First, the technology allows instructors to build a group of interested learners. For example, instructors may use the technology to link current and former students and to link current students with academics and practitioners who have specialized knowledge in key areas. Second, the internet provides instructors a way of easily compiling electronic resources (text material, readings, cases, simulations, exercises, etc.) from a variety of different sources. This means that large amounts of multimedia material can be collected into a single, unified package. Third, materials can be easily added, deleted, or modified in real time. This ensures that courses can be kept current and relevant. Importantly, there are no space or time limitations that characterize other teaching methods. All materials and interactive features are accessible anytime and anyplace with a basic computer and internet connection. Many Web-based course development services even offer electronic testing capabilities so assignments such as case briefs and quizzes can be used to evaluate students. Finally, while access to most Web-based courses is free to students, some shared sites operate by charging students (and/or universities) an access fee (typically on a per course basis). Even when fees are involved, however, the costs are often less than the price of textbooks and other reading materials.

Despite these many advantages, there are also disadvantages when using this approach. In distance education courses, where face-to-face contact is not available, students and faculty may experience a sense of "isolation" or "loss of community." While some instructors have attempted to address this issue by posting students' pictures and encouraging class members to create individual home pages, these measures may provide only a partial solution. While not a viable option yet, in the future real-time video capability may allow students to converse with each other and with course instructors, thereby reducing any sense of isolation or distance. A related issue concerns participation levels. Some distance education instructors complain that students do not avail themselves of the student-to-student interaction mechanisms preferring instead to communicate with the instructor only. This, in turn, can produce heavy demands on faculty members. Another potential disadvantage concerns equipment compatibility. Students with old or outdated hardware may find communications costly and slow.

Ultimately, online delivery of strategy course material is certain to increase in the future either as part of traditional face-to-face courses, as standalone distance education courses, or as hybrids between these two models. Furthermore, as technology improves, the value of this type of teaching methodology will increase as well.

## CONCLUSION

As illustrated from the many teaching methods described in this chapter, strategy instructors use a variety of tools ranging from traditional case method to newer techniques such as problem-based learning.[3] In the future, we are likely to see continued use of these same techniques although with a growing emphasis on leveraging advanced technology. In the area of case teaching, for example, the field is likely to see a steady increase in the use of CD-ROM cases and Web-based materials. The latter, in particular, offers instructors the ability to supplement and update materials frequently and at low costs.

Technology will also play an increasingly important role for other pedagogies. In the area of practicums, for instance, company executives will be able to disseminate more background information electronically, and students will be able to interact with executives more frequently via online conferencing. This is especially important for instructors who want to use these types of projects to expose students to international firms and global strategy issues. Advanced technology will reduce significantly the costs to the participating organizations, which in turn will make this teaching technique more accessible to a larger number of schools.

Another change we are likely to see is the customization of strategy courses. Technology will enable strategy instructors to tailor portions of their courses to individual student needs. For instance, one can envision a strategy course Web site that allows students to select study modules from a menu of different industries or career paths. If a subset of students wants to pursue a career in the healthcare industry, the instructor could provide specialized strategy cases, a practicum or field project, or simulation that is uniquely designed for that industry. Conversely, if another subset of students wants to pursue a career in entrepreneurship, the instructor could provide different cases, projects, or simulations.

Technology will also provide a link to other schools, including schools in international locations. Even today, some instructors participate in competitive simulations across schools and across countries. In the future, not only will we see increased interactions of this type, but we will also see increased leveraging of faculty resources. Faculty members who are experts in a particular area can make their lecture material readily accessible and even be available for a follow-up question and answer session via online conferencing. Instructors will be able to participate in multi-organization consortia in which they share their specialized knowledge as well as tap into the broader base of academic and practitioner talent worldwide. These types of joint programs will improve the quality of strategy education by bringing the most advanced research and thinking into the strategy classroom.

Overall, the variety of pedagogical tools and techniques make teaching strategy a fun and rewarding experience both for the instructor and the students. Ultimately, the aim of the course should be to educate students about the role strategy plays in all organizations and at all levels. To do so, instructors must use the most effective techniques for linking theory and practice – techniques that engage students in the fundamental processes of strategic analysis and decision-making.

## NOTES

1 The survey results indicated the following: (a) 99.1 percent of the responding schools requiring at least 3 credit hours devoted to the subject, (b) 96.5 percent of the business policy courses were offered at the senior level, (c) 67.7 percent of business policy courses were taught by the management department, (d) 70 percent of the respondents reported class sizes of 35 or less.

2 The word "solution" should not be taken to mean that there is a single, right answer in resolving the issues depicted in the case. Many cases reflect the realities of actual business situations. As such, they may be written to accommodate a number of different options.

3 For research articles comparing the effectiveness of these various teaching techniques, consult the *Journal of Management Education*. Other possible resources for studies in this area include the *Journal of Teaching International Business*, which publishes research on teaching methods in international business, and the *Journal of Education for Business* and *Business Education Today*, which publish general articles devoted to the subject of teaching.

# REFERENCES

Applegate, L. M. (1988). Case teaching at Harvard Business School: Some advice for new faculty. *Harvard Business School Note (9-189-062)*. Boston: Harvard Business School Press.

Barnes, L. B., Christensen, C. R., and Hansen, A. J. (1994). *Teaching and the Case Method*. Boston: Harvard Business School Press.

Bonoma, T. V. (1989). Learning with cases. *Harvard Business School Note (9-589-080)*. Boston: Harvard Business School Publishing.

Bourgeois, L. J., Duhaime, I. M., and Stimpert, J. L. (1999). *Strategic Management: A Managerial Perspective*. Fort Worth: Dryden Press.

Charan, R. (1975). Classroom techniques in teaching by the case method. *Academy of Management Proceedings*, 55–7.

Collis, D. J., and Montgomery, C. A. (1997). *Corporate Strategy: Resources and the Scope of the Firm*, 2nd edn. Chicago: Irwin.

Corey, E. R. (1976). The use of cases in management education. *Harvard Business School Note (9–376–240)*, Boston: Harvard Business School Publishing.

Corey, E. R. (1980). Case method teaching. *Harvard Business School Note (9-581-058)*. Boston: Harvard Business School Publishing.

David, F. (1999). *Strategic Management*, 7th edn. Upper Saddle River, NJ: Prentice-Hall.

Duch, B. J., Allen, D. E., and White, H. B. (1998). PBL: Preparing students to succeed in the 21st century. *PBL Insight*, 1(2): 3–4.

Eldredge, D. L., and Galloway, R. F. (1983). Study of the undergraduate business policy course at AACSB-accredited universities. *Strategic Management Journal*, 4: 85–90.

Gomolka, E. G., and Steinhauer, R. F. (1977). The frequency and perceived effectiveness of various methods for teaching undergraduate and graduate business policy. *Academy of Management Proceedings*, 104–8.

Gordon, R. A., and Howell, J. E. (1959). *Higher Education for Business*. New York: Columbia University Press.

Hammond, J. S. (1990). Learning by the case method. *Harvard Business School Note (9-376-241)*. Boston: Harvard Business School Publishing.

Hitt, M. A., Ireland, R. D., and Hoskisson, R. E. (2001). *Strategic Management: Competitiveness and Globalization*, 4th edn. Cincinnati: South-Western College Publishing.

Hochmuth, M. S. (1973). Thinking and teaching business policy – eight years later. In B. Taylor and K. MacMillan (eds.), *Business Policy: Teaching and Research*, 95–134. London: Bradford University Press.

Masoner, M. (1988). *An Audit of the Case Study Method*. New York: Praeger.

Mauffette-Leenders, L. A., Erskine, J. A., and Leenders, M. R. (1997). *Learning with Cases*. London: Ontario, Canada: Ivey Publishing.

*PBL Insight* (1998). What is problem-based learning. *PBL Insight*, 1(1): 5.

Pierson, F. C. (1959). *The Education of American Businessmen: A Study of University-College Programs in Business Administration*. New York: McGraw-Hill.

Rangan, V. K. (1995). Choreographing a case class. *Harvard Business School Note (9-595-074)*. Boston: Harvard Business School Publishing.

Shapiro, B. P. (1984a). An introduction to cases. *Harvard Business School Note (9-584-097)*. Boston: Harvard Business School Publishing.

Shapiro, B. P. (1984b). Hints for case teaching. *Harvard Business School Note (9-585-012)*. Boston: Harvard Business School Publishing.

Thompson, A. A., Jr., and Strickland, A. J., III (1998). *Crafting and Implementing Strategy: Text and Readings* (10th Edition). Boston: Irwin McGraw-Hill:

Unterman, I. (1979). The teaching implications of the research in policy and planning: An overview. In D. E. Schendel, and C. W. Hofer (eds.), *Strategic Management: A New View of Business Policy and Planning*, 484–92. Boston: Little, Brown and Company.

Unterman, I., and Hegarty, W. H. (1979). Teaching implications of policy and planning research. In D. E. Schendel and C. W. Hofer (eds.), *Strategic Management: A New View of Business Policy and Planning*, 479–83. Boston: Little, Brown and Company.

# Index